What's New in This Edition

The first edition of this book was a rousing success, and I received lots of kudos from readers and reviewers. I thank all of you for your kind and often too-generous comments.

Windows 95 is a moving target, however, what with the service packs, driver and software updates, service releases, and so on. To keep this book current, this special Professional Reference Edition boasts an array of changes and additions. Here's a summary of what to expect:

Better organization: I revamped the book's outline to make things easier to find, and I grouped topics in a more logical manner. For example, there is now a separate architecture chapter and a separate network administration and security chapter.

New tips and notes: I've discovered (or, more often, stumbled upon) a boatload of interesting Windows 95 tips and ideas in the year or so since I completed the first edition. I've incorporated many of these gems throughout the book.

OSR2 coverage: Microsoft's release of the OEM Service Release 2 (OSR2) represents an important step in the continuing evolution of Windows 95. I cover all of the new OSR2 features and updates, and I tell you how to get OSR2 components if you're not lucky enough to have an OSR2 machine.

Improved networking coverage: Windows 95 networking is a crucial yet confusing topic. To help you get over this often formidable hurdle, I expanded the networking coverage from two chapters to four, and I included an entirely new chapter on troubleshooting Windows 95 networking.

Expanded Internet material: The Internet seems to be where all the action is these days, and Windows 95 is a big part of that. So it made sense to beef up the Internet coverage considerably. To that end, I've updated all the existing material and added four new chapters that cover NetMeeting, Internet Mail, Internet News, and Personal Web Server.

More appendixes: This edition has several new appendixes. The extra material covers how to perform custom and server-based Windows 95 installations, the Windows ANSI character set, and primers on both HTML and batch files.

Overview

Contents

Part II Unleashing Windows Customization and Optimization

7 Customizing Windows 95   211

Part III   Unleashing Files, Folders, and Disks

13   Working with Files and Folders   413

Acknowledgments: Kudos, Plaudits, and Assorted Pats on the Back

Being an author is the most wonderful vocation (I don't think of it as a job) I can imagine. I get to play with words, I get to talk about things I'm intensely interested in, and I get some big-time warm, fuzzy feelings when people write to me to tell me that, in some small way, something I've written has helped them.

However, just because my name is the only one that appears on the cover, don't think that this book is solely my creation. Any book, but especially a project as massive as this one, is the end result of the efforts of many hard-working people. The Sams editorial staff, in particular, never fails to impress me with their dedication, work ethic, and commitment to quality. You'll find a list of all the people who worked on this book on the second page, but there are a few I'd like to thank personally:

Kim Spilker: Kim is the Acquisitions Editor for this book, which means that she "acquired" me to write it. I'm honored that she would choose me for such an important project, and I thank her for the confidence she has shown in my abilities.

Brian-Kent Proffitt: As Development Editor, it was Brian's job to work with me in determining the overall structure of the book and to make sure that all the relevant topics were covered in an order that made sense. If we succeeded in this (and I think we did), it's due in no small part to Brian's experience, knowledge, and unmatched judgment. Thanks, Brian, for your hard work and dedication, even while in the throes of fatherhood.

Gayle Johnson: Gayle is the book's Production Editor, which means she works long hours making sure the manuscript is ready for the page layout and proofreading process. We've collaborated on several projects over the years, and I never cease to be amazed at Gayle's professionalism, competence, and good humor. (Gayle has distinguished herself by being the only person in publishing I know who is, like me, a fan of *The Kids In the Hall.*) Thanks, Gayle, for yet another outstanding effort.

Patty Brooks: I like to think my books are worth the price of admission all by themselves, but these days you have to give people a few extra goodies. The CD-ROM material that comes with this book is chock-full of such goodies, and it was Patty's job as Software Development Specialist to pull everything together. That's no easy task, because it involves negotiating with software developers, keeping track of updates, planning the structure of the disc, coordinating with authors and editors, and getting everything to production on time. Thanks, Patty, for all your hard work.

Cheri Clark and Heather Urschel: As Copy Editors, Cheri and Heather have the often thankless task of cleaning up authors' slapdash punctuation, rearranging their slipshod sentence structure, and just generally dotting their i's and crossing their t's. This requires an unerring eye for detail and the patience of a saint, so I extend a big thank-you to Cheri and Heather: Once again, you've made me look good.

Peter Kuo: Peter is a NetWare guru who wrote all the NetWare material in Chapters 30, 31, and 32 . Thanks, Peter, for a job well done.

Jeff Perkins: Jeff was the book's Technical Editor. This means that he verified all my facts and tried out all my techniques to make sure I didn't steer you in the wrong direction.

About the Author

Paul McFedries is a computer consultant, programmer, and freelance writer. He has worked with computers in one form or another since 1975, he has a degree in mathematics, and he can swap out a hard drive in seconds flat, yet still, inexplicably, he has a life. He is the author or coauthor of more than two dozen computer books that have sold over one million copies worldwide. His titles include the Sams Publishing books *Microsoft Office 97 Unleashed* and *Visual Basic for Applications Unleashed* and the Que book *The Complete Idiot's Guide to Windows 95*.

Other hats worn by McFedries on occasion include video editor, breadmaker, Webmaster, brewmaster, cruciverbalist, and neologist. He has no cats, and his favorite hobbies are shooting pool, taking naps, and talking about himself in the third person.

Tell Us What You Think

As a reader, you are the most important critic of and commentator on our books. We value your opinion, and we want to know what we're doing right, what we could do better, what areas you'd like to see us publish in, and any other words of wisdom you're willing to pass our way. You can help us make strong books that meet your needs and give you the computer guidance you require.

Do you have access to CompuServe or the World Wide Web? Then check out our CompuServe forum by typing GO SAMS at any prompt. If you prefer the World Wide Web, check out our site at http://www.mcp.com.

> **NOTE**
>
> If you have a technical question about this book, call the technical support line at (317) 581-4669.

As the team leader of the group that created this book, I welcome your comments. You can fax, e-mail, or write me directly to let me know what you did or didn't like about this book—as well as what we can do to make our books stronger. Here's the information:

Fax: (317) 581-4669

E-mail: opsys_mgr@sams.mcp.com

Mail: Dean Miller
          Comments Department
          Sams Publishing
          201 W. 103rd Street
          Indianapolis, IN 46290

Introduction

We shall not cease from exploration
And the end of all our exploring
Will be to arrive where we started
And know the place for the first time.

—*T. S. Eliot*

My trusty *Webster's Third New International Dictionary* was published in 1986, so when I look up the word *hyperbole,* it only tells me the following: "extravagant exaggeration that represents something as much greater or less, better or worse, or more intense than it really is or that depicts the impossible as actual." I expect that future editions will also display in the margin a small picture of the Windows 95 box as an illustrative example.

I'm kidding, of course (in fact, I may be accused of indulging in a bit of overstatement myself), but hyperbole is the first word that comes to mind when thinking about the lead-up to and launch of Windows 95. All that anticipation, all those greatest-thing-since-sliced-bread promises, all the sheer *ballyhoo* that preceded the release date.

Then, on launch day, there were those indelible images: the oh-so-odd couple of Bill Gates and Jay Leno mugging on stage; people lined up around the block in cities all over the world; the mountaineer rappelling halfway down the CN Tower in Toronto, pulling out a notebook computer, and then demonstrating Windows 95 remote computing features 800 feet above the ground. (No, I'm not making up that last one.)

Welcome to Windows 95

The big problem with all that hype and puffery is that it turned off a lot of people and prevented many folks from seeing an important fact: Windows 95 really *is* a good operating system, and it represents a *huge* improvement over both Windows 3.1 and Windows for Workgroups. However, truckloads of people *did* figure this out eventually, and Windows 95 has been a rousing success by any yardstick, selling over 40 million copies in the first year.

So what have these brave pioneers got themselves into? Nothing less than an operating system that's more robust and faster than its predecessors, that multitasks willingly, makes it easier than ever to add new hardware, and supports 32-bit applications, yet will still run most older applications without a complaint. They've also got themselves quite a few new toys to play with:

The desktop: All the Windows 95 action occurs on the *desktop,* the teal expanse shown in Figure I.1. The programs you launch (either by double-clicking the desktop icons or by clicking the Start button in the lower-left corner) sit on this desktop. You can also use the desktop as a storage area for files or *shortcuts* (files that point to other files).

FIGURE I.1.

The Windows 95 desktop.

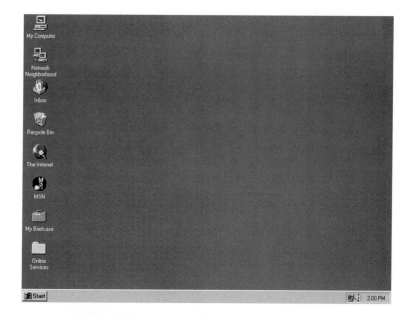

The taskbar: The horizontal strip along the bottom of the Windows 95 screen is the *taskbar.* It includes the Start button on the left (which displays various menus from which you launch programs) and the system tray on the right (icons that give you information about launched programs). In between, each running application has its own button that you can click for easy navigation.

Long filenames: Windows 95 does away with the restrictive "8.3" filenames of the DOS regime and ushers in a new era in which files (and *folders,* which is what directories are now called) can boast names of up to about 250 characters, and that can even include spaces.

Context menus: Much of the Windows 95 interface consists of various *objects* that have certain properties and that can perform certain actions. To give you access to these properties and actions, Windows 95 uses context menus, which appear when you right-click an object, as shown in Figure I.2.

FIGURE I.2.

Right-click on the desktop to display this example of a context menu.

Plug and Play support: Windows 95 offers full support of the Plug and Play initiative, which means that it can query your hardware for information and set up these devices automatically—theoretically, anyway. In practice, Windows 95's success at recognizing legacy hardware is limited. However, if your system has a Plug and Play BIOS and you use Plug and Play devices, this process works quite well.

Improved performance and memory management: Windows 95's mostly 32-bit architecture makes it generally faster than Windows 3.x in most tasks. For 32-bit applications, the old 640 KB barrier is effectively gone, because Windows 95's Virtual Machine Manager now supplies these programs with 4 GB of virtual memory. Also, the allocation and management of system resources have been greatly improved, allowing you to open more programs than ever while maintaining acceptable performance.

Explorer: Windows 95's replacement for File Manager is called Explorer (see Figure I.3). This utility gives you integrated access to all your system's drives, folders, and files. It also includes many powerful features that File Manager lacked, including a slick search engine and the ability to edit filenames in place.

FIGURE I.3.

Explorer: Windows 95's file management utility.

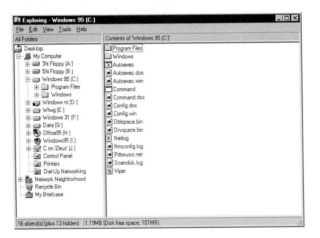

The Microsoft Network: This is Microsoft's new online service. Its content has improved tremendously since its inception, to the point where it's now an interesting place to hang out online. You can even use The Microsoft Network as your Internet service provider.

Microsoft Exchange: Windows 95 includes an e-mail client called Microsoft Exchange that can handle various types of messages, including e-mail through Microsoft Mail, The Microsoft Network, CompuServe, and the Internet, as well as faxes.

Notebook features: Notebook users get a number of presents in their Windows 95 stockings. These include support for Advanced Power Management, hot-docking, and PC Card (PCMCIA) devices. Also, a utility called Briefcase makes it easy to coordinate files shared between a desktop and a notebook. Finally, the Direct Cable Con-nection applet lets you set up a mini-network between two computers using a null-modem cable.

New applets: Many of the applets found in Windows 3.x have been either revamped or replaced entirely. Newcomers to the Windows 95 line-up include HyperTerminal (for modem communications), Paint (an update of Paintbrush), WordPad (a much-improved version of Write), Phone Dialer (which dials your phone automatically), CD Player (which plays audio CDs in a CD-ROM drive), and FreeCell (a variation on the Solitaire theme). Windows 95 also comes with a full collection of powerful system utilities, including a backup program, a disk defragmenter, a disk compression utility, and a disk repair program.

Networking: Windows 95 is ready to network right out of the box. It includes support for multiple protocols, including NetBEUI, IPX/SPX, and TCP/IP. The Network Neighborhood is a folder that gives you easy access to other workgroups and computers on the network, and to the resources shared by these machines.

The Internet: Windows 95 was built with the Internet in mind. Not only does it come with its own TCP/IP stack, but the Dial-Up Networking utility makes it easy to create connections for your Internet service provider.

What You Should Know Before Reading This Book

My goal in writing *Paul McFedries' Windows 95 Unleashed* was to give you complete coverage of the intermediate-to-advanced features of Windows 95. This means that I bypass basic top-ics such as wielding the mouse in favor of more complex operations such as working with the Registry, setting up hardware profiles, networking, and getting connected to the Internet.

I've tried to keep the chapters focused on the topic at hand and unburdened with long-winded theoretical discussions. However, there are plenty of situations in which you won't be able to unleash the full power of Windows 95 and truly understand what's going on unless you have a solid base on which to stand. In these cases, I'll give you whatever theory and background you need to get up to speed. From there, I'll get right down to brass tacks without any further fuss and bother. To keep the chapters uncluttered, I've made a few assumptions about what you know and what you don't know:

- I assume that you have knowledge of rudimentary computer concepts such as files and folders.

- I assume that you're familiar with the basic Windows skills: mouse maneuvering, dialog box negotiation, pull-down menus, and so on.

- I assume that you can operate peripherals attached to your computer, such as the keyboard and printer.

■ I assume that you've used Windows for a while and are comfortable with concepts such as toolbars, scroll bars, and, of course, windows.

■ I assume that you have a brain that you're willing to use and a good supply of innate curiosity.

How This Book Is Organized

To help you find the information you need, this book is divided into eight parts that group related tasks. The next few sections offer a summary of each part.

Part I: Unleashing Windows 95 Installation and Optimization

The six chapters in Part I get your advanced Windows 95 education off to a flying start by covering the ins and outs of the installation process, including an extensive troubleshooting chapter in case things go awry. From there, you'll learn a myriad of ways to get Windows 95 off the ground. Once you do, I'll give you a tour of the landscape, including an in-depth look at the Windows 95 architecture.

Part II: Unleashing Windows Customization and Optimization

With this introduction out of the way, in Part II you'll dive into the deep end of advanced Windows work: customizing, performance tuning, optimization, and hardware considerations. I've also included a couple of chapters (11 and 12) that show you how to work with that most important of Windows 95 features: the Registry.

Part III: Unleashing Files, Folders, and Disks

Part III takes a hard look at how to use Windows 95 to work with files and folders (Chapter 13) and disks (Chapter 14). You'll also learn some invaluable techniques for protecting your data (Chapter 15), including backing up data and checking for disk problems and viruses.

Part IV: Unleashing Day-to-Day Windows 95

Part IV takes your basic, workaday Windows chores and reveals their inner mysteries, allowing you to become more productive. Topics include installing applications (Chapter 16), sharing data (Chapter 17), fonts and printing (Chapters 18 and 19), notebook computers (Chapter 20), and the Windows 95 DOS prompt (Chapter 21).

Part V: Unleashing Multimedia: The Sights and Sounds of Windows 95

Windows 95 is rich in multimedia goodies, and Part V shows you how to work with them to your best advantage. Chapter 22 kicks things off with a general look at these multimedia features, including Windows 95's multimedia architecture, what hardware you need, getting great graphics, CD-ROMs, and the Media Player. From there, Chapter 23 gives you a frame-by-frame look at Windows 95 video, and Chapter 24 gives you the nitty-gritty of audio in Windows 95.

Part VI: Unleashing Windows 95 Communications

Compared to Windows 3.x, the communications tools that come with Windows 95 are first-rate. I'll show you how to take full advantage of all they have to offer in Part VI. For starters, Chapter 25 gives you the full scoop on modem communications and how to configure your modem in Windows 95. Once that's done, I'll show you how to work with two communications applets: Phone Dialer and HyperTerminal. Subsequent chapters get you connected to The Microsoft Network, show you how to configure and work with Microsoft Exchange for e-mail, and show you how to get Microsoft Fax to send faxes right from your PC.

Part VII: Unleashing Windows 95 Networking and Internet Connectivity

To close out the main part of this book, Part VII provides 13 chapters that cover two of today's hottest topics: networking and the Internet. Chapters 30 through 33 give you all the background and know-how you need to get a network up and running. I'll then show you how to use Direct Cable Connection (Chapter 34) and Dial-Up Networking (Chapter 35). From there, the focus turns to the Internet as I give you the details behind TCP/IP (Chapter 36) and the specifics of how to get an Internet connection up and running in Windows 95 (Chapter 37). Finally, the last five chapters show you how to wield the following Internet programs: Internet Explorer, NetMeeting, Internet Mail, Internet News, and Personal Web Server.

Part VIII: Appendixes

To round out your Windows 95 education, Part VIII presents a few appendixes that contain extra goodies. You'll find, among other things, a summary of online Windows 95 resources (Appendix A), a glossary of terms (Appendix B), how to perform custom and server-based setups (Appendix C), the Windows ANSI character set (Appendix D), primers on HTML and batch files (Appendixes E and F), a list of dirty and deadly TSRs (Appendix G), and a list of what's on the CD-ROM that comes with this book (Appendix H).

This Book's Special Features

To make your life easier, this book includes various features and conventions that help you get the most out of this book and Windows 95 itself.

Steps: Throughout the book, I've broken many Windows 95 tasks into easy-to-follow step-by-step procedures.

Things you type: Whenever I suggest that you type something, what you type appears in a monospace font.

Filenames, folder names, and dialog box controls: These things also appear in `monospace`.

DOS commands: DOS commands and their syntax use the `monospace` font as well. Command placeholders (which stand for what you actually type) appear in an *`italic monospace`* font.

Menu commands: I use the following style for all application menu commands: File | Open. This means that you pull down the File menu and select the Open command.

The Microsoft Plus! icon: Windows 95 programs and files that are part of the Microsoft Plus! add-on are marked with the Microsoft Plus! icon.

The Windows 95 Service Pack icon: Programs and files that are part of the Windows 95 Service Pack 1 are marked with the Service Pack icon.

The OSR2 icon: Updates, programs, and files associated with OEM Service Release 2 (OSR2) are marked with the OSR2 icon.

Code continuation character: When a line of code is too long to fit on only one line of this book, it is broken at a convenient place and continued to the next line. The continuation of the line is preceded by a code continuation character (➡). You should type a line of code that has this character as one long line without breaking it.

This book also uses the following boxes to draw your attention to important (or merely interesting) information:

NOTE

The Note box presents asides that give you more information about the current topic. These tidbits provide extra insights that give you a better understanding of the task at hand. In many cases, they refer you to other sections of the book for more information.

TROUBLESHOOTING

Troubleshooting boxes point out common Windows 95 problems and tell you how to solve them.

TIP

The Tip box tells you about Windows 95 methods that are easier, faster, or more efficient than the standard methods.

CAUTION

The all-important Caution box tells you about potential accidents waiting to happen. There are always ways to mess things up when you're working with computers. These boxes help you avoid at least some of the pitfalls.

How to Contact the Author

If you have any comments about this book, or if you wish to register a complaint or a compliment (I prefer the latter), please don't hesitate to send a missive my way. If you're still into the snail mail thing, just address your note to Sams Publishing, and I'll be sure to get it. If you're online, however, please drop me a line at the following e-mail address:

`paul@mcfedries.com`

Better yet, feel free to drop by my Web site, have a look around, and sign the Guest Book:

`http://www.mcfedries.com/`

Note that I have a home page for *Paul McFedries' Windows 95 Unleashed* at this site. Here you'll find book excerpts and info, links to Windows 95 information online, and lots more. To go straight there, dial the following address into your Web browser:

`http://www.mcfedries.com/Books/Win95Unleashed/`

IN THIS PART

I

PART

Unleashing Windows 95 Installation

Understanding the Windows 95 Installation

CHAPTER 1

In preparing for battle I have always found that plans are useless, but planning is indispensable.

—Dwight D. Eisenhower

Before you can unleash the power of Windows 95, you need to unleash Windows 95 on your system (or on your users' systems). Still, that's no big deal, right? Don't you just slip the CD-ROM into the drive, run some kind of setup program, and then kick back while Windows handles all the dirty work for you? Well, that might be true if you were installing just another run-of-the-mill application, but you're dealing with your computer's operating system (OS) here. This isn't some dinky little utility you can toss willy-nilly onto your hard drive to check out. Windows 95 is a demanding program that will take over your whole system, so you need to be prepared for the ordeal to come.

Before diving into the deep end of the Windows 95 installation, you should dip a toe or two into the waters to make sure that you know what's in store. That's just what you'll do in this chapter as you explore the setup process in depth, and as you get yourself and your computer ready for the installation. Then, in Chapter 2, I'll take you through the entire setup procedure, whether you're installing Windows 95 "clean" or upgrading from another operating system.

How the Setup Process Works

As you'll soon see, the Windows 95 installation process is a relatively painless affair that, in most cases, requires only a minimum of intervention on your part. These still setup waters run deep, however, and plenty of things are going on below the surface. Understanding what machinations the setup program has in store for your computer will help you understand the best way to install Windows 95 and will help you recover gracefully from any errors or problems that might crop up.

We can divide the setup process into five discrete steps:

1. Startup and system check
2. Information collection
3. Hardware detection
4. Startup disk creation and file installation
5. Windows 95 configuration

The next few sections explore each of these steps in detail.

Startup and System Check

The Windows 95 CD-ROM contains a file named SETUP.EXE that starts the installation procedure. If you're installing Windows 95 from floppy disks, SETUP.EXE is on Disk 1. You can run this file either from an existing Windows installation, provided that you have Windows 3.1 or Windows for Workgroups 3.1x, or from the DOS prompt. (See the section "Getting Started" in Chapter 2 for more information on starting Setup.) After Setup is on its way, it performs no fewer than nine different system checks to make sure that your computer is ready to receive Windows 95:

1. If you ran SETUP.EXE from the DOS prompt, Setup scours your hard disk looking for a previous installation of Windows. If it finds one, Setup suggests that you bail out and run SETUP.EXE from within Windows. At this point, you can just press Esc to continue with Setup. If, however, you have Windows installed, you should probably start Setup from within Windows anyway. You'll have fewer prompts to respond to, and Setup can skip several of the following steps (specifically, steps 4, 6, and 7).

2. Setup runs the ScanDisk program to look for errors (such as lost clusters and cross-linked files; see Chapter 9, "Windows 95 Performance Tuning and Optimization," to learn about these and other ScanDisk errors). If ScanDisk finds a problem, it displays a message explaining what's wrong and usually gives you several options for correcting the error.

3. Setup confirms that your system is ready, willing, and able to accept Windows 95 as its new OS. Not all systems are capable of meeting the onerous demands Windows 95 makes, so this is an important step. Setup checks the system's CPU, installed memory, available hard disk space, DOS version, and more. If anything isn't up to snuff, Setup will let you know the problem. (For example, if your system doesn't have enough disk space, you'll see the Low Disk Space dialog box that gives you several options.) See the later section titled "Windows 95 System Requirements" to learn what Windows 95 expects from a computer.

4. To get through the installation, Setup needs both an extended memory manager (such as HIMEM.SYS) and a disk cache (such as SMARTDrive) to be loaded. These might not be present if you started Setup from DOS, so the program checks for them automatically. If no extended memory provider is present, Setup installs XMSMMGR.EXE; if no disk cache is present, Setup loads SMARTDrive. (I give in-depth coverage of extended memory, disk caches, and other memory concerns in Chapter 9.)

5. Setup checks for certain terminate-and-stay-resident (TSR) programs and device drivers known to wreak havoc with Windows 95 Setup. These are classified as *dirty* or *deadly* TSRs:

   ■ A dirty TSR (or device driver) is one that might cause problems with Setup, but it doesn't cause Setup to hang. If Setup finds a dirty TSR, it recommends that you disable it before continuing with the installation. In most cases, you can ignore this warning and proceed with Setup.

   ■ A deadly TSR (or device driver) is one that is known to hang Setup. If Setup finds one of these rogue TSRs, it won't let you continue with the installation. You'll have to exit Setup, unload the TSR, restart your machine, and start Setup again.

CAUTION: SOME DIRTY/DEADLY TSRS ARE QUITE COMMON

Although you might expect dirty and deadly TSRs to be obscure, older programs and drivers, some of them are quite common. For example, some known dirty TSRs are the DOS utilities ASSIGN, SUBST, JOIN, and PRINT, as well as Sidekick Plus and the Norton Disk Monitor. Examples of deadly TSRs are the Norton Anti-Virus Software and the PC Tools Disk Cache Utility. For a complete list of these TSRs and device drivers, see Appendix G, "Known Dirty and Deadly TSRs and Device Drivers."

6. If you used DOS to start SETUP.EXE, the program copies the basic Windows 3.1 (yes, Windows *3.1*) files to your hard disk (in a temporary directory named WININST0.400) and then starts Windows 3.1. Setup uses the Windows 3.1 graphical user interface (GUI) for the bulk of the installation process. The Windows 95 GUI doesn't show up until Setup reboots your system.

7. If you launched Setup from DOS, the program switches from real mode to standard mode and starts using your computer's extended memory.

NOTE: REAL MODE VERSUS STANDARD MODE

Real mode (also called *MS-DOS mode*) is the operating mode of early Intel microprocessors (the 8088 and 8086). It's a single-tasking mode in which the running program has full access to the computer's memory and peripherals. *Standard mode* is a Windows 3.x operating mode that takes advantage of the extended memory available through 80286 and higher processors. Standard mode lets Windows programs multitask, but DOS apps take over the system. Except for the Setup program, Windows 95 doesn't use either of these modes. Instead, it uses 386 *enhanced mode*. This mode utilizes the virtual memory features (which I discuss in Chapter 9) of Intel's 80386 and higher processors and lets DOS programs multitask and run inside windows.

8. Setup looks for a directory named OLD_DOS.*x* (for example, OLD_DOS.1). If it finds one, it asks whether you want to remove this "Uninstall information" to free up some hard disk space. (You'll have an OLD_DOS.*x* directory if you installed DOS 6 over an existing version of DOS; it's used to restore the previous DOS version.) Windows 95 doesn't need these files, so Setup rightly asks whether you want to delete them.

9. Setup adds the following lines to your AUTOEXEC.BAT file:

```
@if exist c:\wininst0.400\suwarn.bat call c:\wininst0.400\suwarn.bat
@if exist c:\wininst0.400\suwarn.bat del c:\wininst0.400\suwarn.bat
```

If Setup hangs or if the installation process aborts for any reason, the SUWARN.BAT file displays a warning that Windows 95 was not installed completely and that you need to rerun Setup and choose the Safe Recovery option. I talk more about Safe Recovery in Chapter 3, "Troubleshooting Setup Woes."

Information Collection

After all those checks are complete, Setup is ready to start gathering information by pestering you with questions. This interrogation is handled by the Windows 95 Setup Wizard (which is much like the Wizards used in Microsoft's Office suite of applications). A Wizard is an application that takes you through a task step-by-step by displaying a series of dialog boxes. These dialog boxes ask questions and provide you with various dialog box controls (such as text boxes, check boxes, and option buttons) in which you can enter your replies. In Chapter 2, I'll take you through the dialog boxes you're likely to see, in the section "Supplying the Setup Wizard with Information," but for now, here's a sample of the kinds of data the Setup Wizard will ask you for:

- The directory in which you want to install Windows 95
- The Windows 95 components you want to install
- Your name and company name
- Your network configuration

Setup creates a text file named SETUPLOG.TXT in the root directory of your hard drive and then uses SETUPLOG.TXT to store your responses to each of these queries.

Hardware Detection

Before Setup gets too far into the installation, it needs to perform a separate interrogation of your computer's hardware. In this *hardware detection* phase, Setup attempts to automatically detect your computer's hardware: the system's components, installed hardware devices, and attached peripherals. It also tries to detect the resources used by each piece of hardware—including IRQ (Interrupt Request) lines, DMA (Direct Memory Access) channels, I/O (Input/Output) addresses, and other acronymic hardware flora and fauna. (All this hardware rigmarole is covered in depth in Chapter 10, "How Windows 95 Handles Hardware.")

Setup takes advantage of the Windows 95 Detection Manager's (SYSDETMG.DLL) *hardware detection modules* to scope out the devices on your system. Depending on the computer, Detection Manager takes either the "high road" or the "low road" to query your system.

Detection Manager takes the high road on computers that have a Plug and Play (PnP) BIOS installed. PnP is a hardware standard that allows for automatic installation, configuration, and detection of PnP-compatible devices. (You'll read more about this topic in Chapter 10.) If your system has a Plug and Play BIOS, Detection Manager simply queries the BIOS to identify the attached components and get their current configuration.

Detection Manager takes the low road on so-called legacy machines that don't use the PnP BIOS. In this case, the various hardware detection modules must methodically check all the computer's slots, I/O ports, and memory addresses to see which legacy devices reside in which locations. (If you have a PnP-compatible device attached to a legacy computer, the device automatically supplies Setup with a *device identification code* that describes the hardware and its configuration.) These modules get their cues from a file named MSDET.INF. This file includes information on all the devices known to Windows 95.

This low-level checking can be dangerous (for example, polling a sound card's I/O port might cause its device driver to go haywire and hang the system), so Detection Manager performs some true detective work to avoid trouble. This process, called *safe detection*, involves looking for "hints" about which devices and drivers are present. Safe detection is used on four classes of hardware: sound cards, SCSI controllers, network adapters, and proprietary CD-ROM adapters. Here are some of the hints that the safe detection method looks for:

- DEVICE= lines in CONFIG.SYS.
- Device drivers residing in memory.
- Specific files residing on the hard drive. For example, Detection Manager tries to detect the installed network adapter by scanning the PROTOCOL.INI file in the current Windows for Workgroups directory.
- Read-only memory (ROM) strings.
- Warnings in MSDET.INF that spell out proscribed actions. A sound card's entry, for example, might include RISK_IOWR, which tells setup not to try to detect the card by sending (writing) a signal to the I/O port.

If Detection Manager reports that it can find no such hints for a class of hardware, Setup skips the class altogether. Setup might, however, also ask you to confirm that certain classes should be skipped. It does this by presenting you with a list of the classes with check boxes beside them, as shown in Figure 1.1. If you know you have such a device (or devices) installed, you can force Setup to detect it by activating the appropriate check box.

FIGURE 1.1.

Setup might ask you to confirm that you have certain devices installed on your system.

When Setup has gathered all this hardware information, it checks for resource conflicts (such as two devices sharing the same IRQ line) and tries to resolve them. Each entry in MSDET.INF points to another INF file that contains specific information on the particular hardware class, including possible configuration choices for the device. For example, SCSI device information is located in the SCSI.INF file. Setup uses these configuration options only to try to resolve any conflicts. Also note that these hardware class-specific INF files also contain the Windows 95 Registry entries needed for each device (see Chapter 11, "Introducing the Windows 95 Registry").

NOTE: CHECKING OUT INF FILES

You can examine any of these INF files after Windows 95 is installed. You'll find them in the hidden Inf subdirectory of your main Windows 95 directory. (To view hidden files and directories, select Explorer's View | Options command, activate the Show all files option, and click OK.) Be warned, however: There are more than 150 of these INF files (and the programs you've installed might have added even more).

Setup then creates the Windows 95 Registry and uses it to store all this hardware data. Setup will later use these Registry settings to determine the correct device drivers to install. When the hardware detection is complete, Setup stores all of its findings in a file named DETLOG.TXT and copies this file to your computer's root directory. (This file remains in place after Setup is complete, so you're free to examine it, if you're interested.)

Note that the hardware detection phase can take quite a while on some systems (a few minutes, at least), so it's a good time to grab a coffee or hang out at the water cooler for a while. If, however, the progress bar stops and there's no hard disk activity for three minutes or more, Setup has choked on some aspect of the hardware detection. In this case, turn your computer off and then back on (to ensure that any stuck devices become unstuck), rerun Setup, and choose Safe Recovery. (For more hints on troubleshooting installation hardware problems, see Chapter 3.)

Startup Disk Creation and File Installation

At this point, Setup is almost ready to start foisting the Windows 95 files on your computer. Only two chores remain: to ask whether you want to create a startup disk (and, if you do, to create it), and to build the list of Windows 95 files to install on your machine.

The startup disk is a bootable floppy disk that contains various files and utilities (such as ScanDisk) you can use to troubleshoot a system that's on the fritz. For example, if Windows 95 won't load, or if your hard disk won't boot, you can restart your computer with the startup disk in drive A and regain control of the system. From there, you can use the startup disk's utilities to investigate (and hopefully fix) the problem.

If you elect to create a startup disk (which I highly recommend you do), Setup formats the disk and then copies several files to the disk. See Chapter 15, "Protecting Your Windows 95 Investment," for more details.

After the startup disk is complete, Setup begins building the list of files it needs to copy onto your hard drive. (This is what's happening while you see the little drum-roll animation and the message Preparing to copy files.) This is a four-step process:

1. Setup checks the SETUPLOG.TXT file to see which components you chose to install.

2. For hardware, Setup cross-references the SETUPLOG.TXT entries with the appropriate INF files, which specify the files that need installing.

3. Setup looks up the filenames in LAYOUT.INF to determine where the files are located on the installation CD-ROM (or floppy disks, if you're installing the old-fashioned way), what the file size is, and so on.

4. A file named SETUPX.DLL builds the list of files.

With the file list ready to go, Setup creates the necessary Windows directories and then starts copying the files to your hard drive.

Windows 95 Configuration

When Setup has safely stowed the files on your hard disk, it's now ready to start Windows 95 for the first time. You'll see the Setup Wizard's Finishing Setup dialog box, which explains what's about to happen. Click the Finish button to continue.

Setup then busies itself preparing your hard disk so that Windows 95 can take over the operating system duties of your computer. To do this, Setup first finds the existing master boot record (MBR) of whatever drive you boot from and replaces it with the Windows 95 version. Then Setup renames the existing operating system files (IO.SYS becomes IO.DOS, MSDOS.SYS becomes MSDOS.DOS, and COMMAND.COM becomes COMMAND.DOS) and copies its own operating system files to the root directory. (Note that Windows 95 replaces the old IO.SYS and MSDOS.SYS system files with a single file: IO.SYS. The old MSDOS.SYS still exists, but it's used for a different purpose in Windows 95, as you'll see in Chapter 4, "Start It Your Way: Understanding Windows 95 Startup.") With that chore complete, Setup reboots and Windows 95 runs for the first time.

NOTE: THE MASTER BOOT RECORD

The MBR is the first 512-byte sector on your system's active partition (the partition your system boots from). Most of the MBR consists of a small program that locates and runs the core operating system files (IO.SYS and MSDOS.SYS). I talk more about the MBR and the boot process when I discuss viruses in Chapter 15.

When your machine reboots, Setup trudges through a large checklist of items that perform the final configuration steps for Windows 95. Here's a list of some of the things that happen:

■ A program named WININIT.EXE combines all the virtual device drivers (VxDs) into a single file named VMM32.VXD and renames files that Setup used but that are no longer needed. (For example, the original Registry file was created as SYSTEM.NEW, and it now gets renamed to SYSTEM.DAT.)

- A version of Windows 95 called the *Run-Once* module is loaded. This Run-Once module is used to set up the remaining configuration options.

- Run-Once configures Windows 95 for your computer's hardware.

- If you're installing Windows 95 on a networked machine, Run-Once asks you to supply the network data (computer name, workgroup, and so on).

- If you installed Windows 95 over an existing version of Windows 3.x, the utility GRPCONV.EXE (Program Group Converter) is run to convert your program groups (.GRP files) into Windows 95 shortcuts (which will appear on the Start menu). Also, settings in your existing WIN.INI and SYSTEM.INI files are converted into Registry entries.

- Wizards are activated to take you through the setup and configuration of your printer, Microsoft Exchange (if you installed it), and any other custom hardware setup programs.

- The Windows 95 Help system is initialized.

- MS-DOS program settings are set up.

- The Date/Time Properties dialog box appears so you can set your system's current date and time, if necessary, and choose your time zone.

When all these items are checked off its list, Setup might then need to reboot your computer to finalize a few more hardware settings. In this case, Setup is looking for devices it couldn't detect in the initial hardware detection phase. For example, if you have a SCSI controller in your computer, rebooting lets Windows 95 load the SCSI driver and then detect which devices are attached to the controller (such as a CD-ROM or scanner). Setup finalizes its settings and then runs the full Windows 95 GUI for the first time.

Root Directory Files Created by Setup

It used to be that the sign of a true computer wizard was a clean, uncluttered root directory. Windows 95 changes all that by tossing umpteen different files into the root directory. In case you're wondering what all those files are for, Table 1.1 describes each file.

Table 1.1. Root directory files created by Windows 95 Setup.

File	Description
AUTOEXEC.BAT	A Windows 95-updated version of your old AUTOEXEC.BAT file.
COMMAND.COM	The real-mode command interpreter.
CONFIG.SYS	A Windows 95-updated version of your old CONFIG.SYS file.
DETLOG.TXT	A text file containing the log of the hardware detection phase.
IO.SYS	The Windows 95 system file.
MSDOS.SYS	A text file containing various startup options (see Chapter 4).

continues

Table 1.1. continued

File	Description
NETLOG.TXT	A text file containing the log of the network setup.
SETUPLOG.TXT	A text file containing the log of the Windows 95 options and components you selected during Setup.
SUHDLOG.DAT	Contains a copy of all Master Boot Records and Partition Boot Records on the system both before and after the upgrade to Windows 95. It's used to restore the original boot sectors if you uninstall Windows 95.
SYSTEM.1ST	A copy of the Registry file (SYSTEM.DAT) that was created after Setup.
W95UNDO.DAT	A compressed backup copy of your old Windows 3.x directory. It's used for uninstalling Windows 95.
W95UNDO.INI	A listing of files backed up in the W95UNDO.DAT file, as well as the new Windows 95 files installed by Setup.

What Happens to Existing DOS Files?

Early reports about Windows 95 (or "Chicago," as it was nicknamed at the time) indicated that this would be the first version of Windows that didn't use DOS. That proved to be more or less true, but there *is* a DOS component to Windows 95 (call it DOS 7, if you will). Windows 95 stores all its DOS files in a separate COMMAND subdirectory. (I discuss Windows 95's DOS details in Chapter 21, "DOS Isn't Dead: Optimizing DOS Applications Under Windows 95.")

So what happens to your existing DOS version after Windows 95 is installed? Well, that depends on whether you upgrade from an existing version of Windows:

- If you don't upgrade, Setup leaves your DOS directory intact, except that it deletes the files DEFRAG.EXE and SCANDISK.EXE. These utilities can play havoc with Windows 95's long filenames, so they shouldn't be used under any circumstances. They're replaced by batch files named DEFRAG.BAT and SCANDISK.BAT, which remind you to use the Windows 95 versions of these programs. Otherwise, DOS is kept as is, so you have full functionality whenever you boot to the previous DOS version. (I show you how to do this in Chapter 4.)

- If you upgrade, Setup deletes almost 40 files from the DOS directory (saving you a little over 1 MB of disk space in the process). These are files that either are dangerous to use under Windows 95 (such as DEFRAG.EXE and SCANDISK.EXE) or are duplicated by new versions of the same files in Windows 95's COMMAND directory. Again, DEFRAG.EXE is replaced by DEFRAG.BAT, and SCANDISK.EXE is replaced by SCANDISK.BAT.

Windows 95 System Requirements

Personal computing is governed by two inexorable, and not unrelated, "laws":

Moore's Law: Processing power doubles every 18 months (from Gordon Moore, cofounder of Intel).

Parkinson's Law of Data: Data expands to fill the space available for storage (from the original Parkinson's Law: Work expands to fill the time available).

These two observations help explain why, when the computers we use are becoming increasingly powerful, our day-to-day tasks never really seem all that much faster. The leaps in processing power and memory are being matched by the increasing complexity and resource requirements of the latest programs. So the computer you're using today might be twice as muscular as the one you were using a year and a half ago, but the applications you're using are twice the size and require twice as many resources.

Windows fits neatly into this scenario. With each new release of Microsoft's flagship operating system, the hardware requirements become more stringent, and our computers' processing power is taxed a little more. Windows 95 is no exception. Even though Microsoft spent an enormous amount of time and effort trying to shoehorn Windows 95 into a minimal system configuration, you need a reasonably powerful computer if you don't want to spend most of your day cursing the dreaded hourglass icon. (Windows changes your mouse pointer into an hourglass when it's performing a lengthy task that prevents you from using your computer.) Table 1.2 presents a rundown of the minimal and reasonable system requirements you'll need to install and work with Windows 95.

Table 1.2. System requirements for Windows 95.

System Component	What You Need
DOS version	**Minimum:** DOS 3.2. **Reasonable:** DOS 5.0 or higher. Windows 95 might not install on some DOS 3.2 systems because not all flavors of 3.2 support partitions greater than 32 MB (and Windows 95 usually requires more than 32 MB of disk space). And DOS 4.0 was so buggy that you're really taking a chance installing Windows 95 over it.
Processor	**Minimum:** 386DX (although Windows 95 won't install on a 386 with a B-step processor—ID 0303). Yes, you can run Windows 95 on a 386SX system, but it isn't pretty. The 386SX has a 16-bit data path that creates a serious bottleneck for Windows 95's 32-bit program code.

continues

Table 1.2. continued

System Component	What You Need
	Reasonable: 486 or better. Note, however, that the new Pentium Pro systems do *not* run Windows 95 noticeably faster than regular Pentiums running at the same clock speed. The Pentium Pros are optimized for pure 32-bit code (such as you find in Windows NT), and Windows 95 contains enough 16-bit code to prevent any significant speed increases.
Memory	**Minimum:** 4 MB, although Microsoft recommends 8 MB. 8 MB is required if you plan on using Microsoft Exchange or The Microsoft Network. Also note that many Windows 95 applications require at least 8 MB. **Reasonable:** Windows 95 runs much better with 12 MB of RAM, and performance is almost snappy with 16 MB, which is what I recommend.
Hard disk free space	**Minimum:** If you're upgrading from Windows 3.x, Setup will need about 40 to 45 MB of free disk space. For a clean installation, you'll need 50 to 55 MB. **Reasonable:** If you're upgrading, you'll need about 85 MB, including room for Windows 95's dynamic swap file. A clean installation requires about 100 MB free. (See the following Note box.)
Video	**Minimum:** VGA, 14-inch monitor. **Reasonable:** Super VGA, 17-inch monitor. Windows 95 lets you open and work with many more applications at once than did Windows 3.x. So to maximize screen space, your video card and monitor should be capable of displaying 256 colors at 1,024×768 resolution. If you plan on using Windows 95's multimedia features (such as video), a video card that can handle true color (16 million colors) is a must.
Peripherals	**Minimum:** 3½-inch high-density floppy drive. **Reasonable:** A mouse (Microsoft or compatible) is really a must for getting the most out of Windows 95. If you plan on using The Microsoft Network, Microsoft Fax, HyperTerminal, or any other communications packages, you'll need a modem or a fax/modem. A CD-ROM drive is almost more important than a floppy drive these days, especially because you can install many programs (including Windows 95 itself) from CD-ROM. To take advantage of Windows 95's built-in sound support, you'll

System Component	*What You Need*

need a sound card and speakers. If you plan on using Windows 95's networking features, your system must have a network interface card installed.

NOTE: SOME NOTES ABOUT THE HARD DISK SPACE REQUIREMENTS

Here are a few things to keep in mind when thinking about Windows 95's hard disk requirements:

- These recommendations for hard disk free space are a bit higher than what Windows 95 actually usurps. The extra few megabytes are used by Setup for temporary files that it creates during the installation process (and deletes when it's done).

- The actual number of megabytes Windows 95 requires depends on the installation options you select. For more information on these options, see the section in Chapter 2 titled "Setup Options."

- You don't have to install Windows 95 on your system's boot drive (usually drive C). If you have a hard disk partitioned into multiple drives, or if you have multiple physical disk drives, you can install Windows 95 on any drive. Note, however, that Setup will install a bit less than a megabyte's worth of files on the boot drive. (Don't assume, however, that you can therefore partition your boot drive down to 1 MB. Setup insists on using the boot drive to install its temporary files, so you really need your boot drive to be at least 4 or 5 MB.)

- Most Windows applications like to add optional components (such as DLL files, fonts, and Help files) to either the main Windows directory or Windows's SYSTEM subdirectory. So even if you install these programs on a different drive, this extra clutter will still add to the disk space needs of whatever drive you use to install Windows.

In addition to these requirements, your system must also meet the following guidelines:

- Your system's BIOS shouldn't be any older than January 1994. Windows 95 often seems to have trouble with any BIOS older than that.

- Your hard disk must have a DOS FAT (File Allocation Table) partition. Windows 95 doesn't recognize, and therefore can't be installed onto, drives partitioned as NTFS (Windows NT File System) or HPFS (OS/2's High Performance File System).

- If your computer's boot drive is compressed, it must have at least 3 MB of uncompressed space available. Windows 95 works with disks that have been compressed with DoubleSpace, DriveSpace, Stacker 3.0 and 4.x, and SuperStor compression schemes.

■ If you have the Windows 95 upgrade package, you must either have Windows 3.x installed on your system or have the original installation disks. If you have the full Windows 95 package, your system doesn't need to have an existing operating system.

> **NOTE: THE WINDOWS 95 SYSTEM CHECK UTILITY**
>
> Microsoft has a utility called Windows 95 System Check that looks at your system's processor, memory, hard disk space, and more to see if your machine passes the Windows 95 muster. This utility is available from the usual Microsoft download sites (which I'll outline in the next chapter; in this case, look for SYSCHECK.EXE), including the following Web address:
>
> `http://www.microsoft.com/windows/download/syscheck.exe`

Preparing Your System: A Checklist

Installing a new operating system—especially one that makes relatively radical changes to your system, as Windows 95 does—is definitely a "look before you leap" operation. Your computer's operating system is just too important to dive blindly into the installation process. To make sure that things go well, and to prevent any permanent damage just in case disaster strikes, you need to practice "safe" installing. This means taking a few minutes beforehand to run through a few precautionary measures and to make sure that your system is ready to welcome Windows 95. To that end, the next few sections run through a checklist of items you should take care of before firing up the Setup program.

Check Your System Requirements

Before getting too involved in the Setup process, you need to make sure that your computer is capable of supporting Windows 95. Go back over the system requirements I outlined earlier to make sure that your machine is Windows 95–ready.

Back Up Your Files

Although the vast majority of Windows 95 installations make it through without a hitch, there's another law that software (particularly complex operating system software) always seems to follow: Murphy's Law (that is, if anything can go wrong, it will). Windows 95 Setup has a Smart Recovery option that should get you out of most jams, but you should still make backup copies of important files, just in case Smart Recovery is, for once, just not smart enough. Here are some suggestions for files to archive:

■ All your data files. (If you're reinstalling Windows 95, be sure to back up your Exchange personal folder file (usually named Exchange.pst) and your personal address book (usually named Exchange.pab).)

■ Important configuration files, such as AUTOEXEC.BAT and CONFIG.SYS (in your hard drive's root directory), WIN.INI, SYSTEM.INI, all your password list files (*.PWL), and all your .GRP files (in your main Windows directory).

■ Configuration files used by your applications. Windows applications usually store their configuration data in INI files in your main Windows directory.

If you use backup software to archive your files, make sure that when you move to Windows 95 you keep not only the backup program, but also any "catalog" files that the program needs in order to restore the files. These catalogs spell out which files you backed up, their original locations, and where the files were backed up.

Clean Up Your Hard Disk

To maximize the amount of free space on your hard disk (and just for the sake of doing some spring cleaning), you should go through your hard disk with a fine-toothed comb, looking for unnecessary files you can delete. Here are some candidates:

Old DOS uninstall files: As I mentioned earlier, if you installed DOS 6 on your system, the program backs up your existing DOS files in a directory called OLD_DOS.1. (If you've upgraded more than once, you might also have an OLD_DOS.2 directory.) Setup will detect and offer to delete these files for you, but it's perfectly safe to delete them by hand in advance. In fact, it's better to do it in advance if you plan on defragmenting your hard drive (as I'll suggest shortly).

Stray TMP files that Windows 3.x hasn't deleted: Windows 3.x stores temporary files in a directory named TEMP. (This is usually C:\WINDOWS\TEMP. To find out for sure, examine the SET TEMP= line in your AUTOEXEC.BAT file.) These files have a TMP extension, and Windows normally deletes them when you exit the program. (Other programs might also store temporary files in this directory.) If, however, your system crashes, or if a power failure shuts down your system before you get a chance to exit Windows, you might end up with a few TMP stragglers clinging to the TEMP directory. Exit Windows and then clean out the TEMP directory.

CAUTION: EXIT WINDOWS BEFORE DELETING TMP FILES

It's very important that you exit Windows completely before deleting *anything* from the TEMP directory. If you do this while Windows is running—even if you do it from a Windows DOS session—you run the risk of losing data or having Windows lock up on you.

Unneeded backup files created by applications: Many programs create backup files as you work. It's likely you don't need these backups, so you can delete them. Most backups have the extension BAK, although you'll also see some with the extensions TMP and $$$. To make this chore easier, use File Manager's Search feature to scope out the *.BAK files on your hard drive. In File Manager, select the root directory, and then select File | Search. Type `*.bak` in the Search dialog box and click OK. A new window appears, showing all the BAK files on your system. You can delete the files from there. If you don't have Windows 3.x, run the following DOS command from the root directory: `dir *.bak /s`.

Unused programs and data files: Most people have hard disks that are littered with the rusting hulks of programs they tried a few times and then gave up on. Now is as good a time as any to remove this detritus from your system once and for all.

If You're Upgrading, Prepare Windows

If you're upgrading to Windows 95 from an existing version of Windows 3.x, here are a few chores to run through to make sure that the upgrade is a smooth one:

- You can free up a large chunk of disk territory by getting rid of your Windows 3.x permanent swap file (assuming that you have one). In Windows 3.x, open the Control Panel, open the 386 Enhanced icon, and click the Virtual Memory button. If you see Permanent in the `Type` field, click the Change>> button. If you don't plan on dual-booting between Windows 95 and Windows 3.x, select `None` from the `Type` drop-down list (the one in the New Settings box); otherwise, select `Temporary` (in this case, the swap file will exist only while Windows 3.x is active).

- If you'll be starting Windows 95 Setup from within Windows 3.x, shut down all programs except Program Manager. If you have any other files open, Setup might not be able to install some of the new Windows 95 files properly. (And besides, having other programs open just slows the whole installation process.)

- If you have programs in your Startup group, Setup will add them automatically to the new `Startup` folder in Windows 95. However, some of your existing programs might not work with Windows 95, so you should clean out your existing `Startup` folder to prevent problems when Windows 95 starts.

- If you're running Microsoft Mail (on a LAN or remotely) and you want to upgrade to Windows 95's new e-mail client, Microsoft Exchange, back up all your mail files (the ones with the MMF extension), and uninstall Microsoft Mail.

- If you're using a replacement shell (such as the Norton Desktop), disable it before starting Setup. You do this by opening `SYSTEM.INI` (it's in your main Windows folder), finding the `[Boot]` section, and editing the `shell=` line so that it reads as follows:

  ```
  shell=progman.exe
  ```

- Setup deletes Write, the little word processor that came with Windows 3.x. If you've grown accustomed to Write and want to preserve it, you'll need to store `WRITE.EXE` (and, if necessary, Write's Help file, `WRITE.HLP`) in a separate directory. After installation is complete, you can restore these files to their Write-ful place. (Note that you'll find a file named WRITE.EXE already in your Windows folder. That's just a stub that loads WordPad, the new Windows 95 word processor. Don't worry, though: Overwriting or renaming this file has no effect on WordPad.)

■ Similarly, Setup also deletes Paintbrush and replaces it with the new Paint program. Although Paint is generally an improvement over Paintbrush, it's disappointing that Paint can't save files in the .PCX graphics format. (It can read .PCX files, but it can save files only in Windows' native .BMP format.) If you'd like to preserve the ability to write .PCX files, you'll need to save the following Paintbrush files in a separate directory: PBRUSH.EXE, PBRUSH.DLL, and PBRUSH.HLP. Once the installation is complete, copy these files to your main Windows 95 folder. (Again, note that Windows 95 already has a PBRUSH.EXE file, which is a stub that loads Paint. You'll need to overwrite or rename this file.)

Check and Defragment Your Hard Disk

As you learned earlier, Setup uses ScanDisk to give your hard disk a quick once-over before settling down to the serious business of installation. Sure, a "quick once-over" is better than nothing, but *you* should be more thorough. Specifically, use the DOS 6.2x ScanDisk utility (or some other disk-checking utility, such as Norton Disk Doctor) to give your hard disk a "surface" scan. The surface scan (it's called a *Thorough* scan in ScanDisk) checks your hard disk for physical imperfections that could lead to trouble down the road. (I discuss the Windows 95 version of ScanDisk in Chapter 15.)

Also, don't forget to do a virus check if you have anti-virus software. Viruses have been known to wreak havoc on the Windows 95 Setup program (in addition to their other less-endearing qualities, such as locking up your system and trashing your hard drive).

NOTE: THE FAMOUS "DISK 2" VIRUS PROBLEM

When Windows 95 was first released, several customers installing via floppy disk reported that Setup complained about a bad Disk 2. Subsequent investigation turned up preexisting viruses on each of these systems that had infected the second disk. Why just disk 2? That's the disk that Setup uses to record your registration information, and these viruses (there were several) were designed to infect floppies during write operations. Although normally these viruses infect disks undetected, the unique high-density format used by the Windows 95 disks exposed the virus.

When that's done, you should next defragment the files on your hard drive. This action ensures that Setup will store the Windows 95 files with optimal efficiency, which will improve performance and lessen the risk of corrupted data. (I explain file fragmentation in all its glorious detail, as well as how to use the Windows 95 Disk Defragmenter utility, in Chapter 9.)

Create a Bootable Floppy Disk

If you don't have one already, you should make a bootable floppy disk. That way, if Setup makes a complete mess of your boot drive (which is entirely possible, because Setup does tamper with the master boot record), you'll still be able to boot your system and make repairs.

Insert a disk in drive A, and then use either of the following methods to make the disk bootable:

- In File Manager, select Disk | Make System Disk. Insert a disk in drive A and click OK in the Make System Disk dialog box.

- At the DOS prompt, enter the following command:

  `FORMAT A: /S`

(Although DOS has a SYS command that will make an already-formatted disk bootable, you're better off using FORMAT. By formatting the disk, you can be sure that you're starting with a "fresh" disk that isn't cluttered with other files or, more important, doesn't have any viruses lurking in the weeds.)

After you've created a system disk, you need to copy a few more files in order to create a true "emergency disk" you can use to investigate and troubleshoot problems. The number of files you copy depends on the capacity of the disk and what you have in the way of recovery software. Here are some suggestions:

A text editor: This lets you make changes to your configuration files. If you have at least DOS 5, use the Edit program (copy both EDIT.COM and QBASIC.EXE from your DOS directory).

Your computer's setup program: Some computers come with a setup program on a separate disk (it might be called something like SETUP.EXE). In many cases, you just need to rerun this program to get your hard disk back up and running.

Recovery utilities: If you've accidentally deleted one or more of the system files, or if you've accidentally formatted your hard disk, you can recover with special software. If you have DOS 5 or 6, copy UNDELETE.EXE and UNFORMAT.COM from your DOS directory. You should also include FDISK.EXE, the DOS partitioning utility, just in case you end up with a corrupted partition table. ATTRIB.EXE is useful if you have to adjust the attributes of a file. I'd also recommend SYS.COM, the DOS utility that makes a drive bootable by copying the system files. If you have any other utility programs you like to use, copy the appropriate files.

Startup files: Copy your current AUTOEXEC.BAT and CONFIG.SYS files from your root directory. To make sure that DOS doesn't try to execute these files at startup, however, you should rename them (because I boot from drive C, I call mine AUTOEXEC.C and CONFIG.C).

Disk diagnostics: If you have DOS 6 or Windows 3.1, copy MSD.EXE, the Microsoft diagnostics program.

Virus checker: Just in case your hard disk goes down for the count because of a virus, you should include an anti-virus program on your emergency disk. Make sure that the program can "disinfect" (and not just detect) viruses.

Hardware drivers: Include any drivers you need for devices such as a CD-ROM drive, removable hard disk, SCSI controller, disk compression (such as DBLSPACE.BIN), and so on.

Ideally, you should create new AUTOEXEC.BAT and CONFIG.SYS files for the bootable disk. One easy way to do this is to use your existing AUTOEXEC.BAT and CONFIG.SYS files as starting points. Edit them to change hard drive references to drive A. For example, if you have the line C:\SCSI\ASPI2DOS.SYS in your regular CONFIG.SYS, change it to read just A:\ASPI2DOS.SYS in the bootable disk version (assuming, of course, that you've copied the file ASPI2DOS.SYS to the bootable disk). You might need to try a few reboots with the bootable disk in drive A to get things working right.

Shut Down Any Unnecessary TSRs

As I mentioned earlier, TSRs and device drivers can cause Setup to choke, so you should remove all unnecessary memory-resident programs before starting Setup. This is particularly true of virus detection software. Because Setup alters your system's master boot record, any virus scanner in memory will assume that a virus attack is under way. The battle between Setup and the anti-virus program will most likely cause your system to hang, and you might not be able to reboot.

The only TSRs and device drivers you need are these: drivers for disk partitions, hard disks, networking, video, CD-ROMs, SCSI controllers, and whatever other devices are crucial to the operation of your system.

To remove TSRs, you can either run a command at the DOS prompt (some TSR commands have switches that remove them from memory) or disable the appropriate lines in CONFIG.SYS and AUTOEXEC.BAT. You do this by appending REM and a space to the beginning of the line so that DOS will ignore the line at startup. You'll need to reboot your machine to put these changes into effect.

Use MSD to Print a System Report

It's a good idea to take a "snapshot" of your current system configuration before running Setup. If you have Windows 3.1 or higher on your system, you'll have a handy utility in your main Windows directory called MSD (Microsoft Diagnostics). You can use MSD to print a report showing all your major system parameters, including important hardware configuration values such as IRQ settings and memory addresses. Here are the steps to follow to print this report:

1. Exit Windows. You can run MSD from within Windows, but you need to run it outside of Windows to get the most accurate picture of your system.

2. Type msd and press Enter. You'll see the MSD window, shown in Figure 1.2.

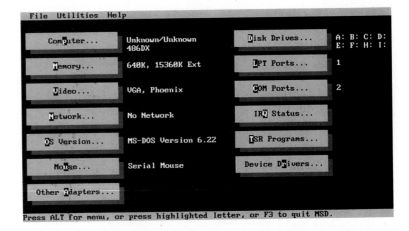

3. Select File | Print Report.

4. In the Report Information section, activate the Report All check box.

5. In the Print to section, select the port to which your printer is attached.

6. Make sure that your printer is turned on, and then click OK.

7. Fill out the Customer Information dialog box, if desired, and click OK. MSD prints
   the report.

8. Select File | Exit or press F3 to exit MSD.

CAUTION: UNZIP YOUR ZIP DRIVE!

Are you using an Iomega ZIP drive with a printer attached to its pass-through port? If so,
disconnect the ZIP drive before running Setup. Otherwise, Windows 95 won't be able to
print to the printer. After Setup is complete, reconnect the ZIP drive and install the 32-bit ZIP
drive drivers (see Chapter 10 to learn about installing hardware drivers). You'll find these
drivers on the Windows 95 CD-ROM, in the \DRIVERS\STORAGE\IOMEGA directory.

OSR2 Installing OSR2

The OEM Service Release 2 for Windows 95 began shipping exclusively in new PCs in the fall
of 1996. (I discuss the new features available in OSR2 in Chapter 5, "Windows 95: the 50¢
Tour.") Because Microsoft made this Windows 95 update available only to OEMs (original
equipment manufacturers), most people will receive OSR2 preinstalled. However, most new
PCs come with a CD-ROM that contains OSR2, so you might want to install this version on
another PC that doesn't have OSR2. (OSR2 is also available as part of the Microsoft Developer Network Professional level or above. You might also receive a copy of the OSR2 disc if

you purchase a new hard drive or motherboard.) This section presents some notes to bear in mind when doing this.

Upgrading to OSR2

Officially, OSR2 will install only on a system that has either a fresh hard disk (that is, a hard disk that currently has no operating system installed) or just DOS. Unofficially, however, you can upgrade to OSR2 from an existing version of Windows 95 by following these steps:

1. To avoid running programs when Setup boots Windows 95, clear out your `Startup` folder. If you installed Windows 95 in `C:\Windows`, you'll find the `Startup` folder in the following location:

   `C:\Windows\Start Menu\Programs\Startup`

2. You'll be performing the upgrade from the DOS prompt, so make sure you have real-mode CD-ROM drivers installed in `CONFIG.SYS` and `AUTOEXEC.BAT`.

3. Restart your computer and, when you see the `Starting Windows 95...` message, press F8 to display the Startup menu.

4. Choose the `Command prompt only` option. This will process `CONFIG.SYS` and `AUTOEXEC.BAT` and leave you at the DOS prompt.

5. Use the DOS `REN` (rename) command to rename every instance of `WIN.COM` on your system, including those associated with previous versions of Windows. For example, to rename the Windows 95 version of `WIN.COM` `WIN.95`, you would enter the following commands (assuming that `C:\Windows` is your main Windows 95 folder):

   ```
   cd\windows
   ren win.com win.95
   ```

6. Insert the OSR2 CD-ROM and run the Setup program. When you get to the part where Setup asks for the folder in which to install OSR2, make sure that you specify the same folder used by your existing Windows 95 installation.

Note that if you're currently dual-booting between Windows 95 and an older version of Windows, you'll lose this ability when you install OSR2. If you still want to dual-boot, you'll need to use a third-party utility (I mention a few of them near the end of this chapter).

Converting Your Hard Disk to FAT32

There is no utility in OSR2 that will convert a hard disk to the new FAT32 format. The only way to get a FAT32 drive is to format the disk using the OSR2 `FORMAT` command.

If you're installing OSR2 and you want the benefits of FAT32, there is a way to avoid having to install OSR2 twice:

1. Back up your data and initialization files, as described earlier.

2. Run OSR2 Setup until you've created a startup disk, and then cancel the installation.

3. Test the startup disk to make sure it works correctly.

4. Use the FORMAT command on the startup disk to format your hard drive. Since this is an OSR2 DOS utility, the drive will be formatted as FAT32.

5. Run the full installation of OSR2.

TIP: PARTITION MAGIC DOES FAT32

An easier way to get the benefits of FAT32 is to use a program called Partition Magic. Version 3.0 is compatible with FAT32 and will partition a hard drive *without* trashing the drive's files. This is a must-have utility for any Windows 95 power user. Partition Magic is available from PowerQuest Corporation ((800) 379-2566; www.powerquest.com).

CAUTION: AVOID PRE-FAT32 DISK UTILITIES

After you've converted your drive to FAT32, don't use any disk utilities (such as compression or defragmentation programs) that were designed for pre-FAT32 partitions. Only use either the disk utilities that come on the OSR2 disc or those that have been updated to work with FAT32 drives.

Some Notes About Dual- (and Multi-) Booting

The last thing you need to mull over before getting down to the nitty-gritty of the Setup program is whether you want to run Windows 95 exclusively or "dual-boot" with another operating system. *Dual-booting* means that when you start your computer, you have the option of running Windows 95 or some other operating system, such as Windows 3.x. It's even possible to *multi-boot*, which means having the choice of three or more operating systems at startup. The next few sections show you how to dual-boot Windows 95 with various other systems.

Dual-Booting with Windows 3.x

If you've been using Windows 3.x (including Windows for Workgroups), setting up your system to dual-boot with Windows 95 has its advantages. For one thing, you get to start Windows 95 with a clean slate and without any of the DLL and INI file baggage that your Windows 3.x installation might have accumulated over the years. For another, it's handy to be able to return to Windows 3.x at any time just in case you have a program that Windows 95 doesn't like.

On the down side, dual-booting with Windows 95 means your program and configuration settings won't migrate over to Windows 95. You'll have to reinstall most of your applications, reconfigure your network, and so on.

TIP: RUN WINDOWS 3.X PROGRAMS WITHOUT REINSTALLING

Actually, you might be able to get away with not having to reinstall many of your applications in Windows 95. Some enlightened programs store all the files they need (including DLLs and INI files) in their own directory. These all-too-rare applications should run fine under Windows 95. Most other applications store files in the Windows 3.x main directories: `\WINDOWS` and `\WINDOWS\SYSTEM`. If you try to run these programs from Windows 95, they'll fail because they can't find these files. The solution? Add the Windows 3.x directories to your Windows 95 path. In `AUTOEXEC.BAT`, look for the `PATH` statement. If you installed Windows 95 in a directory named `WIN95`, it should look like this:

```
PATH C:\WIN95;C:\WIN95\COMMAND;C:\DOS
```

If Windows 3.x is in `C:\WINDOWS`, edit this statement so that it reads as follows:

```
PATH C:\WIN95;C:\WIN95\COMMAND;C:\DOS;C:\WINDOWS;C:\WINDOWS\SYSTEM
```

TIP: CONVERTING PROGRAM GROUPS IN WINDOWS 95

If you have some carefully constructed program groups in Windows 3.x, you might not like the idea of losing them if you install Windows 95 in a separate directory. Well, you don't have to because Windows 95 has a utility called Program Group Converter (`GRPCONV.EXE`) that can convert existing Program Manager groups into Windows 95 Start menu folders. First, for each program group you want to convert, copy the appropriate GRP file from your main Windows 3.x directory over to your main Windows 95 directory. Open the Windows 95 Start menu, select Run, type grpconv /m, and click OK. In the Select a Group to Convert dialog box, highlight one of the program group files and click Open. When you're asked whether you're sure you want to convert the group, click Yes. The group is converted into a Start menu folder, and the Select a Group to Convert dialog box is redisplayed. Repeat the process for any other groups you want to convert.

Installing Windows 95 if Windows 3.x Is Already Installed

As long as your system is running DOS 5.x or 6.x, dual-booting with an existing version of Windows 3.x is a no-brainer. When Setup asks you to specify the directory to use for Windows 95, be sure to choose a *different* directory than the one you're currently using for Windows 3.x. Setup will leave your existing version of Windows (and DOS) intact, and you'll be able to run them normally any time you like.

You do this by first rebooting your computer. When you see the `Starting Windows 95...` message, press F8. You'll see the following menu:

```
Microsoft Windows 95 Startup Menu
=================================
   1. Normal
   2. Logged (\BOOTLOG.TXT)
```

```
      3. Safe mode
      4. Step-by-step confirmation
      5. Command prompt only
      6. Safe mode command prompt only
      7. Previous version of MS-DOS
Enter a choice: 1
```

(If you're running Windows 95 on a network, you'll see a total of eight choices.) Highlight the Previous version of MS-DOS item and press Enter to load your old DOS version. (You can also start Windows 3.x directly from Windows 95. I'll show you how this trick works in Chapter 21.) Windows 95 uses your old system and configuration files (IO.DOS, MSDOS.DOS, COMMAND.DOS, CONFIG.DOS, and AUTOEXEC.DOS) to load your previous DOS version.

TIP: BYPASSING THE STARTUP MENU

For faster service, you can load the previous version of DOS without using the Windows 95 Startup menu. When you see the Starting Windows 95... message, press F4.

Installing Windows 3.x if Windows 95 Is Already Installed

In Chapter 2, I'll show you how to install Windows 95 on a clean system (that is, a system with a freshly formatted boot drive). But what happens if, after you've installed Windows 95, you find you need to reinstall Windows 3.x (say, to run a program that Windows 95 doesn't get along with)? It's still possible to dual-boot between the two systems, but it takes a bit more work. Here are the steps to follow:

1. Using the bootable disk you created before installing Windows 95, copy IO.SYS to IO.DOS in your root directory of your boot drive. You can use one of two methods:

   ■ In Windows 95, open Explorer, select View | Options, activate the Show all files option, deactivate the Hide MS-DOS file extensions for file types that are registered option, and click OK. Select drive A and copy IO.SYS to a separate directory (*not* your root directory). Rename IO.SYS to IO.DOS, and then move it into the root directory. (If Windows 95 asks whether you're sure you want to rename the file, click Yes.)

   ■ At the DOS prompt, run the following two commands to remove any attributes from IO.SYS and copy it to IO.DOS in the root directory:

   ```
   attrib -h -r -s a:\io.sys
   copy a:\io.sys c:\io.dos
   ```

2. Repeat step 2 for MSDOS.SYS (in other words, copy it to MSDOS.DOS in the root directory).

3. Copy COMMAND.COM to COMMAND.DOS, AUTOEXEC.BAT to AUTOEXEC.DOS, and CONFIG.SYS to CONFIG.DOS (again, your destination in each case is the root directory).

4. Copy any device drivers your system needs to the hard drive. You might want to create a separate directory to hold these files and avoid cluttering the root directory.

5. Adjust CONFIG.DOS and AUTOEXEC.DOS so that the device driver lines point to the appropriate files on the hard drive.

6. Open the file MSDOS.SYS (it's in the root directory) in your favorite text editor, find the [Options] section, and add the line BootMulti=1. The file should now look something like this:

```
[Options]
BootGUI=1
BootMulti=1
```

7. Save the file.

At this point, you should be able to load the version of DOS you used for your bootable disk. Make sure that the disk is removed from the drive, and then restart Windows 95. When you see the Starting Windows 95... message, press F4 to load the previous version of MS-DOS. You can now reinstall Windows 3.x. Make sure, of course, that you install into a different directory than the one you used for Windows 95. When Windows 3.x asks about modifying your CONFIG.SYS and AUTOEXEC.BAT files, go ahead and let it do so. This might seem counterintuitive because the files used by your previous version of DOS are CONFIG.DOS and AUTOEXEC.DOS. But when Windows 95 loads the previous DOS version, it does two things:

■ It temporarily renames CONFIG.SYS to CONFIG.W40 and AUTOEXEC.BAT to AUTOEXEC.W40 (it also renames COMMAND.COM to COMMAND.W40).

■ It restores CONFIG.DOS to CONFIG.SYS and AUTOEXEC.DOS to AUTOEXEC.BAT (and COMMAND.DOS to COMMAND.COM).

The upshot of all this is that you can let Windows 3.x modify CONFIG.SYS and AUTOEXEC.BAT without fear of crippling your Windows 95 setup.

Dual-Booting with Windows NT

Windows 95 and Windows NT are happy to share the same machine, so dual-booting between the two is no problem. You do, however, need to watch out for a few things:

■ Your hard disk must have a FAT partition into which you can install Windows 95. If your hard disk uses only an NTFS (NT File System) partition, you won't be able to install Windows 95.

■ Windows 95 doesn't understand NTFS, so even if you install Windows 95 into a separate FAT partition, you won't be able to read NTFS partitions from within Windows 95.

■ The Windows 95 compression scheme (DriveSpace) is different from the one used by Windows NT 3.51, and more important, the two are incompatible. So even if both Windows 95 and Windows NT are installed on a FAT partition, they won't be able to read each other's compressed files.

TIP: HOW TO AVOID REINSTALLING APPS IN NT

To avoid reinstalling all your Windows 95 applications in Windows NT, there's a way to make NT recognize and run your existing applications. In NT's Control Panel, open the System icon. In the System dialog box that appears, highlight the Path line in the System Environment Variables section. Move down to the Value text box, and then add the following string to the end of the existing value:

`;C:\WINDOWS;C:\WINDOWS\SYSTEM`

Yes, that's a semicolon at the beginning. If you installed Windows 95 in a directory other than `C:\WINDOWS`, make the appropriate change to the string. Click the Set button and then click OK to put the change into effect.

Installing Windows NT After Installing Windows 95

There's no problem loading Windows NT on your system after Windows 95 is already installed. In fact, if you can manage it, it's always best to install Windows 95 first and *then* install Windows NT. (If NT is already on your system, though, I'll show you how to install Windows 95 alongside it in the next section.) To ensure a hassle-free setup, you need do only two things:

■ In Windows 95, open the DOS command prompt, change to the directory where the Windows NT source files are stored, and enter the command winnt /w. The /w switch lets the Windows NT Setup program operate under Windows 95.

■ When Setup asks which directory you want to use to install Windows NT, be sure to specify a different directory than the one you used for Windows 95.

After Windows NT is ensconced on your system, rebooting will display NT's OS Loader menu:

```
OS Loader V3.51
Please select the operating system to start:
    Windows NT Workstation Version 4.00
    Windows NT Workstation Version 4.00 (VGA mode)
    Microsoft Windows
Use ↑ and ↓ to move the highlight to your choice.
Press Enter to Choose.
```

Highlight the operating system you want to work with, and then press Enter.

Installing Windows 95 After Installing Windows NT

If Windows NT is already installed on your system, setting up a dual-boot system with Windows 95 requires a few extra steps. How you run the Windows 95 Setup program depends on how Windows NT is configured:

■ If you installed NT over DOS or alongside Windows 3.x, you should see the OS Loader menu at startup (as described in the preceding section). In this case, select either DOS or Windows from the menu, and then run Windows 95 Setup.

- If you have no other operating system to work with, boot from a floppy disk that has a previous version of MS-DOS. When you run Windows 95 Setup, it will trash NT's master boot record. To fix this, insert your NT boot floppy, reboot, and follow the on-screen instructions. When you get to the Welcome to Setup screen, select the Repair option by pressing R. This will restore the boot sector and give you a choice of operating systems in the OS Loader menu.

Dual-Booting with OS/2 Warp

These days, many people are wondering which of the three major operating systems—Windows 95, Windows NT, and OS/2 Warp—is best suited to their needs. Each system boasts certain advantages over the other, and to be sure, each has its pitfalls. The best way to compare one OS against another is to load a couple of them onto your system and dual-boot between them. If you're looking to compare Windows 95 and OS/2, here are some notes to think about beforehand:

- Your hard disk must have a FAT partition into which you can install Windows 95. You can't install Windows 95 into an OS/2 HPFS partition.

- Windows 95 won't work with HPFS, so even if you install Windows 95 into a separate FAT partition, you won't be able to read HPFS partitions from within Windows 95.

- Windows 95 won't migrate any existing OS/2 settings.

- If you were running Windows 3.x applications under OS/2, you might have to reinstall them under Windows 95.

Ideally, you should install OS/2 first and then install Windows 95. When installing OS/2, be sure to create a "startable" Boot Manager partition and a separate "bootable" FAT partition for Windows 95 (you do all this inside OS/2's FDISK utility). If OS/2 is already installed, run the FDISK utility from within OS/2 to create the Boot Manager and FAT partitions.

Use a bootable floppy to boot your computer to DOS, and then run the Windows 95 Setup program. Boot Manager will display a message warning you that continuing with Setup will disable Boot Manager. Why does Setup disable Boot Manager? Well, Setup needs to reboot your system a couple of times during the installation process. If Boot Manager is active, Setup has no way of knowing which operating system will be used to boot the computer. To make sure that Windows 95 is booted during Setup's restarts, Boot Manager's partition information is removed. That's OK, though, because you'll restore Boot Manager later.

After Windows 95 is safely installed, insert your OS/2 boot disk and restart the system. Now run OS/2's FDISK utility to restore the Boot Manager partition. With Boot Manager back up and running, the Boot Manager menu will give you a choice of either OS/2 or Windows 95 each time you restart your computer.

Multi-Booting with Three or More Operating Systems

For maximum OS flexibility, you'll want to have three or more systems available on your machine so that you can multi-boot among them. Depending on the operating systems you want to use, this isn't all that much more work than setting up a dual-boot system.

If you want to use Windows 3.x, Windows 95, and Windows NT, go ahead and install all three operating systems, in separate directories, using the dual-boot guidelines outlined earlier. The best installation sequence is to install Windows 3.x first, then Windows 95, then Windows NT. As explained earlier, each time you start your machine, you'll see the Windows NT Boot Loader menu. Here's how to boot each operating system:

- To boot Windows NT, select the `Windows NT Workstation` option.
- To boot to Windows 95, select the `Windows` option.
- To boot to Windows 3.x, select the `Windows` option. Then, when you see the `Starting Windows 95...` message, press F4 to load the previous version of DOS.

If you want to multi-boot with OS/2, Windows 95, and some other operating system, install OS/2 first and use Boot Manager to set up bootable partitions for the other operating systems. Install the other operating systems into these partitions, use OS/2's FDISK utility to repair the Boot Manager partition (if necessary), and use the Boot Manager menu to select the operating system you want to use.

If you don't have OS/2, you can use one of the other multi-boot programs that are around. You might want to check out any of the following:

- System Commander
  $99.95 from V Communications
  (408) 296-4224
  `http://www.v-com.com/`

- Partition Magic
  $69.95 from PowerQuest Corporation
  (800) 379-2566
  `http://www.powerquest.com/`

- Wizard of OS
  $99 from Modular Software Systems
  (360) 886-8882
  `http://www.netusa.com/pcsoft/library/p_960.htm`

Summary

This chapter explained the Windows 95 installation process in depth. As you saw, even though Windows 95 Setup is the friendliest and most intelligent of the Windows install programs we've seen to date, the installation process is far from trivial. You have upgrade issues to consider and preparatory chores to perform. Still, thanks to innovations such as the CD-ROM-based installation and the Hardware Detection Manager, Windows 95 Setup is a relatively painless affair.

Here's a list of chapters where you'll find related information:

- If you're having problems with Windows 95 Setup, head for Chapter 3, "Troubleshooting Setup Woes."

- For more information about the Windows 95 Startup menu and MSDOS.SYS, check out Chapter 4, "Start It Your Way: Understanding Windows 95 Startup."

- To get your feet wet with the new Windows 95 interface and tools, read Chapter 5, "Windows 95: The 50¢ Tour."

- Plug and Play and other hardware-related issues are covered in Chapter 10, "How Windows 95 Handles Hardware."

- I offer extended coverage of ScanDisk in Chapter 15, "Protecting Your Windows 95 Investment."

- Printer installation is covered in Chapter 19, "Prescriptions for Perfect Printing."

- For an in-depth discussion of Microsoft Exchange setup and configuration, see Chapter 27, "Setting Up Microsoft Exchange."

- For network installations, try Chapter 31, "Windows 95 Networking."

- I show you how to perform network and custom setups in Appendix C, "A Setup Smorgasbord: Server-Based and Custom Setups."

Running the Windows 95 Setup

CHAPTER 2

Would not this be that best beginning which would naturally and proverbially lead to the best end?

—Plato

This chapter takes you through the entire setup procedure, whether you're installing Windows 95 "clean" or upgrading from another operating system. For good measure, I'll also take you through the installation of individual Windows 95 components, Microsoft Plus!, and the Windows 95 Service Pack. I'll even show you how to uninstall Windows 95.

Getting Setup Started

At long last, we get down to brass tacks and run the Windows 95 Setup program. This section takes you through the specifics of the procedure, including the various prompts and dialog boxes you can expect.

How you start Setup depends on how you want to install Windows 95, which version you're using, and which operating system (if any) is currently installed on your machine. The next couple of sections run through the various possibilities.

Performing a Clean Installation

In many ways, the best Windows 95 installation method is to start with a clean slate. In other words, you wipe everything off your hard drive (after first backing up your data, of course) and install Windows 95 on the freshly formatted disk. This is called a *clean* installation. Its chief advantage is that you can be sure that you're not saddling Windows 95 with any excess (and potentially troublesome) baggage from an earlier operating system. It also serves to rid your system of excess files that might be hanging around, it freshens the hard disk sectors, and it puts the boot to any viruses that might be hiding out. The disadvantage, of course, is that you'll need to reinstall all your programs.

Here's how to get started with a clean Windows 95 installation:

1. Back up all your important data, including the configuration files used by your programs.

2. If you haven't done so already, create a bootable disk as described in the preceding chapter. Make sure that the disk has the FORMAT.COM and FDISK.EXE programs on it.

3. Insert the bootable disk and restart your computer. Watch the startup routine carefully, looking for any error messages that might crop up. When you get to the DOS prompt, check to make sure that all the devices you need (CD-ROM, SCSI controller, and so on) are functioning properly.

4. At this point, you might want to consider using FDISK to repartition your hard drive. At the very least, you should have one partition for your operating system files and

another for your program and data files. This way, if you ever have to attempt a clean installation again, you need only reformat the drive that contains the operating system; you can leave the data drive intact. If you want to load multiple operating systems on the computer, consider creating a partition for each operating system.

CAUTION: FDISK IS DESTRUCTIVE!

Note that, when you partition a disk, FDISK destroys all the disk's data. So after you've changed your partitions, there's no going back!

5. Enter the command `format c: /s` to format drive C and install the DOS system files. DOS displays the following message:

```
WARNING: ALL DATA ON NON_REMOVABLE DISK
DRIVE C: WILL BE LOST!
Proceed with Format (Y/N)?
```

6. Press Y and then press Enter to start the format. When DOS is done, it will prompt you for a volume label. If you like, you can type a label of 11 or fewer characters and then press Enter (don't use a space or any of the following characters in your label: + = \ ¦ [ ] ; : , . < > ? /). If you don't want to include a label now, just press Enter; you can use Windows 95 to label your disk, as described in Chapter 13, "Working with Files and Folders."

7. If you used FDISK to create any other drives, format them (but don't add the /s switch).

Now that your hard disk is scrubbed clean, it's time to install Windows 95. If you're installing the full version of Windows 95 from floppy disks, insert the Windows 95 Boot Disk in drive A, and then reboot your computer.

If you're installing Windows 95 from CD-ROM, follow these steps:

1. Copy the hard disk versions of AUTOEXEC.BAT and CONFIG.SYS from the boot disk to the hard drive's root directory. Earlier, I suggested that you name these files AUTOEXEC.C and CONFIG.C, so you'll also need to rename the copied versions.

2. Copy your system's device drivers from the boot disk to the hard disk.

3. Remove the boot disk and restart your computer.

If all went well, your system should boot to the C:\ prompt, and your CD-ROM drive will be available. (If it's not, make sure that the DEVICE= line in CONFIG.SYS points to the location of your CD-ROM driver. Also, make sure that the MSCDEX.EXE line in AUTOEXEC.BAT points to the correct location of MSCDEX.EXE.) Switch to the CD-ROM drive, type setup, and press Enter to start Windows 95 Setup.

2

RUNNING THE
WINDOWS 95
SETUP

Options for Starting Setup

Here's a list of the options you have for starting Setup, depending on which operating system you have installed:

Upgrading from Windows 3.1 or Windows for Workgroups: First, insert the Windows 95 CD-ROM or Disk 1 in the appropriate drive. In Program Manager, select File | Run, enter *drive*:\setup.exe (where *drive* is the letter of the drive containing the Setup disk) in the Run dialog box, and click OK. (Alternatively, you can run Setup from the DOS prompt, as described next.)

Upgrading from DOS or Windows 3.0: In either case, you must run Setup from the DOS prompt. First, insert the Windows 95 CD-ROM or Disk 1 in the appropriate drive. Type *drive*: (where *drive* is the letter of the drive containing the Setup disk), and press Enter. Type setup and press Enter.

Installing Windows 95 on a computer that doesn't have DOS: If you're installing from floppy disks, insert the Boot Disk in drive A, and restart your computer. If you're installing from CD-ROM, follow the instructions in the preceding section for performing a clean install.

Moving to Windows 95 from other operating systems: For all other operating systems—including Windows NT and OS/2—you need to get to a DOS prompt—either by dual-booting or by restarting your system with a bootable DOS floppy in drive A. Insert the Setup floppy disk or CD-ROM, change to the appropriate drive, type setup, and press Enter.

Running Setup from Your Hard Disk

Compared to floppy disks, it's a true pleasure installing Windows 95 from CD-ROM. However, Setup can still take quite a while if you have a slow CD-ROM drive. You can speed up the Windows 95 installation considerably by copying all the source files to your hard drive. Use File Manager (or the DOS XCOPY command) to copy the CD-ROM's \WIN95 directory to your hard drive. (Don't copy any of the other directories on the CD-ROM!) Note that these files will consume a little over 33 MB of hard disk acreage.

To start the installation, run the SETUP.EXE program in the WIN95 directory on your hard disk.

Setup's Command-Line Options

Setup boasts quite a number of command-line switches you can use to control the way Setup operates. A *switch* is an extra parameter you tack on to the end of the setup command. Each switch consists of a slash (/) followed by one or more characters. For example, the /? switch doesn't start Setup at all. Rather, it displays a list of all the available switches. Note that you must include a space between the setup command and the switch, like so:

```
setup /?
```

Table 2.1 details some of the more important Setup switches.

Table 2.1. Setup's command-line switches.

Switch	Description
/?	Provides a brief summary of the available Setup switches.
/C	Tells Setup not to run SMARTDrive.
/d	Tells Setup not to use your existing copy of Windows.
/id	Tells Setup not to check for the minimum disk space required to install Windows 95.
/iL	Tells Setup to load the Logitech mouse driver rather than the Microsoft mouse driver.
/in	Tells Setup not to run the Network Setup module.
/it	Tells Setup not to check for the presence of dirty or deadly TSRs.
/ih	Tells Setup to run ScanDisk in the foreground (if you start Setup from within Windows 3.x).
/iq	Tells Setup not to check your drive for cross-linked files. This switch is valid only if you use the /is switch to bypass ScanDisk or if ScanDisk fails.
/is	Tells Setup not to run ScanDisk.
/T:*dir*	Specifies an alternative directory in which Setup should store its temporary files. (Note that Setup will delete all the files in this directory when it's done!)

After Setup Is Under Way

With Setup off the launch pad, you receive several prompts before the installation process begins in earnest:

1. If you started Setup from DOS, you see the following prompt:

   ```
   Setup is now going to perform a routine check on your system.

   To continue, Press Enter. To quit Setup, press Esc.
   ```
   If you started Setup from Windows 3.x, you see the Windows 95 Setup dialog box, shown in Figure 2.1.

2. Setup performs the ScanDisk check you learned about earlier. To start the check, click Continue or press Enter. If ScanDisk finds any problems, it lets you know and gives you various options on how to proceed. (I discuss ScanDisk in detail in Chapter 6, "Under the Hood: Understanding the Windows 95 Architecture.") When ScanDisk has completed its labors, click the Exit button (which appears only if you started Setup from DOS) to continue with Setup.

FIGURE 2.1.

The Windows 95 Setup dialog box appears when you start the Windows 95 Setup program from within Windows 3.x.

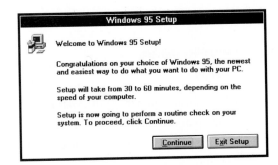

3. If you started Setup from DOS but you have an existing version of Windows on your system, Setup recommends that you run Setup from within Windows. If you want to start over from Windows, press Enter to exit Setup; otherwise, press Esc to continue the installation.

4. At this point, the DOS version of Setup switches to Windows mode, and you see the Welcome to Windows 95 Setup! dialog box. Click Continue to proceed with the installation.

5. If Setup finds an OLD_DOS.X directory (which contains uninstall data for a previous version of DOS), it asks whether you want to delete these files. Because you don't need them any more, you should probably select Yes to free up the disk space. Otherwise, just click No to leave them alone.

6. Setup might display a warning about low disk space or some other condition that could prevent Windows 95 from installing. You might have no choice but to quit Setup, but in some cases you can click OK to proceed.

7. The program initializes the Setup Wizard. This Wizard is a series of dialog boxes that take you through the entire installation procedure. When the Wizard is ready, Setup displays the Windows 95 software license agreement. Read the license agreement (if you dare!) and then click Yes to indicate acceptance of the agreement.

8. If you have any other programs running, Setup displays a dialog box recommending that you shut them down. To close any running programs, press Alt-Tab to switch to each program, and close them. When you're finished, click OK to continue with the installation.

9. If you're installing the Windows 95 Upgrade and Setup doesn't automatically detect an existing version of Windows, you see the Windows - Upgrade Check dialog box. When you click Continue, Setup scours your drive for an existing version of Windows. If it doesn't find one, you see the Upgrade Check - Hard Disk Search Failed dialog box. In this case, place Disk 1 of your Windows 3.x system disks in the appropriate drive, and click the Locate button. In the Locate Directory dialog box, use the Drives list to select the drive containing the disk and click OK.

10. The Windows Setup Wizard starts and displays the first of its dialog boxes, shown in Figure 2.2. The next section describes each of the Setup Wizard's dialog boxes.

FIGURE 2.2.

The first of the Setup Wizard's dialog boxes.

Supplying the Setup Wizard with Information

As I mentioned earlier, the Setup Wizard's job is to display a series of dialog boxes that ask you for various tidbits of information Setup needs in order to install Windows 95 to your liking. So that you know what to expect, this section explains each dialog box and what Setup expects from you.

Each Setup Wizard dialog box contains various buttons at the bottom. You can use these buttons to move forward and backward through the installation process. Table 2.2 outlines the function of each button.

Table 2.2. The Setup Wizard's command buttons.

Button	Description
< Back	Takes you back to the previous Setup Wizard dialog box.
Next >	Accepts the data in the current dialog box and moves ahead to the next dialog box.
Cancel	Quits the installation process.
Finish	Finishes the information-gathering stage. This button appears in only the last of the Setup Wizard's dialog boxes.

The first dialog box (titled Windows 95 Setup Wizard) just gives you an overview of the installation process, so click Next > to continue. The next few sections give you a rundown of the rest of the dialog boxes.

Choose Directory

The Choose Directory dialog box gives you two options: You can install Windows 95 in your current Windows directory (usually C:\WINDOWS), or you can use a different directory. For the former choice, just click the Next > button. For the latter, activate the Other Directory option, and click Next >.

Change Directory

The Change Directory dialog box appears if you selected the Other Directory option in the Choose Directory dialog box. Enter the new directory in the dialog box and click Next >. Setup then warns you that installing Windows 95 in a new directory means you will have to reinstall your programs, and it asks whether you want to continue. Click Yes.

Save System Files

If you're installing Windows 95 over an existing version of Windows, the Save System Files dialog box asks whether you want to save your system files. Saving them lets you uninstall Windows 95, so it's a good idea. Here's how you do it:

1. Make sure that the Yes option is activated.
2. Click Next >. Windows gathers the system files and then prompts you for the disk drive to use to store them.
3. Use the Hard disk drop-down list to select the drive you want to use.

NOTE: DISK SPACE REQUIREMENTS FOR SAVED SYSTEM FILES

Saving your system files uses up another 4 to 6 MB or so of hard disk space (depending on the size of your Windows 3.x directory).

---

4. Click OK. Setup stows the system files on the drive you selected.

Setup Options

You use the Setup Options dialog box, shown in Figure 2.3, to specify the Windows 95 components you want installed. Select the option you want and click Next >.

Which Setup option should you choose? That depends on two factors: the amount of hard disk space you have available and the optional Windows 95 components you need. Here's a summary of what you get with each option (I'll discuss each option in more detail a little later):

Typical: Installs the Windows 95 components that will be needed (in Microsoft's estimation, anyway) by most Windows 95 users.

Portable: Uses less disk space than the Typical option, but focuses on components suited to portable computers.

Compact: Bypasses all the optional Windows 95 components to save disk space.

Custom: Lets you pick and choose specific Windows 95 components (although, as you'll see, you can "customize" any of the Setup options).

FIGURE 2.3.

Use the Setup Options dialog box to choose the type of installation you want.

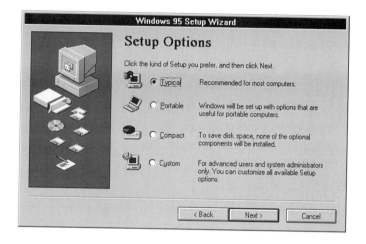

To help you make this decision, I've put together a couple of tables that spell out not only how much disk space each option uses, but also which components are included in each option.

NOTE: YOU CAN INSTALL AND REMOVE COMPONENTS LATER

Don't worry if you're not sure which components you need. You can always add and remove components from within Windows 95. See the section titled "Adding and Removing Windows 95 Components" later in this chapter.

For starters, Table 2.3 presents approximate hard disk space requirements for each Setup option (including the extra disk space that Setup needs for its temporary files). These are only approximate because the actual number depends on the hardware you have in your system (Setup installs different device drivers depending on the hardware it detects) and whether you're installing Windows 95 on a network (Setup installs extra networking software). Also, the Custom option assumes that you're selecting *all* the Windows 95 components.

Table 2.3. Disk space used by each Setup option.

Install Option	Upgrade	Clean Install
Compact	40.0 MB	50.1 MB
Portable	43.3 MB	50.8 MB
Typical	44.2 MB	53.4 MB
Custom (All)	71.6 MB	83.9 MB

2

RUNNING THE
WINDOWS 95
SETUP

Table 2.4 details which Windows 95 components Setup installs for each option. Here are some notes about this table:

- There is no column for Custom because you use the Custom option to hand-pick the components you want.
- The Component column groups the Windows 95 components according to how they appear in the Select Components Setup Wizard dialog box (which you'll get to later in the installation process). For example, the Select Components dialog box has an Accessories component, which has several "subcomponents," such as Briefcase and Calculator.
- The CD-ROM Only column tells you which components are available only on the Windows 95 CD-ROM. Note that if you want to install any components that are "CD-ROM only," you must select the Custom option and choose the components by hand.

Table 2.4. Windows 95 components associated with each Setup option.

Component	Typical	Portable	Compact	CD-ROM Only
Accessibility Options	■	■		
Accessories:				
Briefcase		■		
Calculator	■			
Character Map				■
Clipboard Viewer[1]				
Desktop Wallpaper				
Document Templates	■			
Games:				
FreeCell				
Hearts				
Minesweeper				
Solitaire				
Imaging[6]	■			
Mouse Pointers				■
Net Watcher				■
Online User's Guide				■
Paint	■			
Quick View				■

Component	Typical	Portable	Compact	CD-ROM Only
Screen Savers:				
Blank Screen				
Curves and Colors				
Flying Through Space				
Flying Windows	■			
Mystify Your Mind				
Scrolling Marquee				
System Monitor				■
System Resource Meter				
Windows 95 Tour				■
WinPopup[2]	■	■	■	
WordPad	■			
Communications:				
Dial-Up Networking		■		
Direct Cable Connection		■		
HyperTerminal	■	■		
Microsoft NetMeeting[6]	■			
Phone Dialer	■	■		
Disk Tools:				
Backup				
Defrag	■	■	■	
Disk compression tools[3]		■		
Microsoft Exchange:				
Microsoft Exchange				
Microsoft Mail Services				
Microsoft Fax:				
Microsoft Fax Services				
Microsoft Fax Viewer				
Multimedia:				
Audio Compression[4]				
CD Player[5]				■
Jungle Sound Scheme				■

2

continues

Table 2.4. continued

Component	Typical	Portable	Compact	CD-ROM Only
Media Player	■	■		
Multimedia Sound Scheme[6]				■
Musica Sound Scheme				■
Robotz Sound Scheme				■
Sample Sounds				■
Sound Recorder[4]				
Utopia Sound Scheme				■
Video Compression	■	■		
Volume Control[4]		■		
The Microsoft Network				

[1]Setup installs this component automatically if you upgrade over Windows 3.x (not Windows for Workgroups).

[2]Setup installs this component automatically if it detects an installed Microsoft or NetWare network client.

[3]Setup installs this component automatically if it detects DoubleSpace or DriveSpace.

[4]Setup installs these components automatically if you specified that you have a sound card in your system.

[5]Setup installs this component automatically if it detects a CD-ROM drive.

[6]Available only in OSR2.

NOTE: CD-ROM EXTRAS

The Windows 95 CD-ROM also comes loaded with many other programs, files, and utilities. Some of these knickknacks are quite useful, so I'll be discussing some of them as we progress through this book.

If you don't have the Windows 95 CD-ROM, you can still get your hands on any of the CD-ROM extras. At the back of your *Introducing Microsoft Windows 95* manual, you'll find an order form you can send in to Microsoft. Alternatively, you can get the extras online at the following sites:

- On the Internet: The files are available via anonymous FTP at `ftp.microsoft.com/Softlib/Mslfiles`, or via the World Wide Web at `http://www.windows.com/windows/common/aa2724.htm`.
- On the Microsoft Network: Select Edit | Go To | Other Location. Type `mssupport` and double-click the MS Software Library icon.

- On CompuServe: Enter GO MSL.
- At the Microsoft Download Service bulletin board: Call (206) 936-6735.

FIGURE 2.4.
Use this dialog box to enter your name and, optionally, your company name.

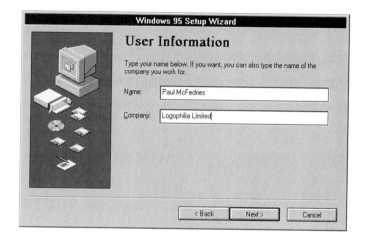

User Information

The User Information dialog box, shown in Figure 2.4, asks you for your name and, optionally, your company name. Fill in the appropriate values and click Next >.

Key Identification or Product Identification

The next dialog box you see depends on the version of Windows 95 you're installing. If you're installing the full retail version, you see the Key Identification dialog box; if you're upgrading or installing (or reinstalling) the version of Windows that came with your machine, you see the Product Identification dialog box. (If you're running Setup from a network, you might not see either dialog box.) Dig out the Certificate of Authenticity that came with your Windows 95 package, enter either the 10-digit Key value or the 20-digit Product Identification Number, and click Next >.

Product Identification

The Product Identification dialog box appears if you're installing the full retail version. It shows your Product Identification Number. You'll be asked for this number if you ever contact Microsoft technical support, so you'll want to make a note of it.

NOTE: WINDOWS 95 KNOWS YOUR PIN

If you don't jot down your Product Identification Number, or if you lose it, you can always find out what it is from within Windows 95. Right-click the My Computer icon on the Windows 95 desktop and select Properties. The dialog box that appears displays your PIN.

Analyzing Your Computer: The Typical, Portable, and Compact Options

If you selected the Typical, Portable, or Compact Setup option, you see the Analyzing Your Computer dialog box shown in Figure 2.5. This dialog box lets you know that Setup is about to enter the hardware detection phase. You can also see a list of devices on which Setup normally uses Safe Detection. If your system contains any of the displayed hardware, you can help out the Detection Manager by activating the appropriate check boxes. When that's done, click Next > to continue.

Figure 2.5.

Setup might present you with a list of hardware devices. Check all that apply to your system.

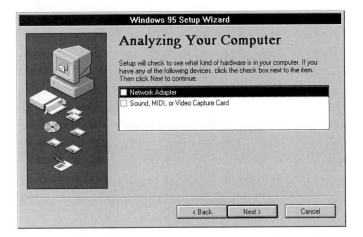

Setup runs through the hardware detection phase, as described earlier in this chapter. This process usually takes a few minutes (and always seems to slow down at the end), so some patience is in order. If you find that the Progress meter stops and there's no hard disk activity for a long time, the Detection Manager is likely hung. Turn off your computer (don't just press Ctrl-Alt-Delete or the Reset button), turn it back on, and then run through the Safe Recovery option (which I describe in the next chapter).

Analyzing Your Computer: The Custom Option

If you chose the Custom Setup option, you see the version of the Analyzing Your Computer dialog box shown in Figure 2.6. You have two choices:

Yes (recommended): Select this option to let Setup examine your computer for hardware. For most people, this is the safest and easiest road to take.

No, I want to modify the hardware list: Select this option if you want to specify the hardware on your system. Select this option only if you're sure you know which devices are installed on your system, or if you've run into problems during the hardware detection phase in a previous installation attempt.

FIGURE 2.6.

If you're running a Custom install, you can either let Setup detect your hardware or specify devices yourself.

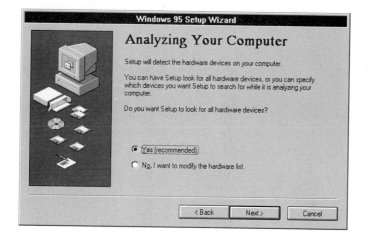

Make your choice and click Next >. If you elected to specify hardware yourself, you see the new version of the Analyzing Your Computer dialog box shown in Figure 2.7. The box on the left lists the various hardware classes. When you highlight a class, a list of devices appears in the box on the right. Activate and deactivate check boxes as needed, click Next >, and then click Next > again.

Get Connected

The Get Connected dialog box presents you with a selection of Windows 95's e-mail and fax tools, as you can see in Figure 2.8. Activate the check boxes for the options you want to install, and then click Next >.

FIGURE 2.7.

Use this dialog box to specify the hardware devices on your system.

FIGURE 2.8.

Use the Get Connected dialog box to select the e-mail and fax tools you want to use.

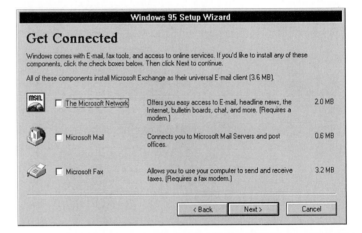

CAUTION: DON'T EXCHANGE MAIL WITH EXCHANGE!

If you activate any of the options in the Get Connected dialog box, Setup also installs Microsoft Exchange. If you're using Microsoft Mail 3.x, this can cause two problems:

■ If you're using Microsoft Mail Remote to get your mail from a Microsoft Remote Mail server, some of your files will get overwritten in the upgrade to Exchange. This will prevent you from connecting to the remote server.

■ There's no way to uninstall Exchange and get back your original Microsoft Mail setup.

If you really want to upgrade to Exchange, back up all your mail files (they use the MMF extension), and uninstall Mail.

Windows Components

If you chose the Typical, Portable, or Compact Setup option, you next see the Windows Components dialog box, shown in Figure 2.9. This dialog box presents you with two options:

> **Install the most common components (recommended):** If you activate this option, Setup installs the default components for the Setup option you selected earlier (as listed in Table 2.4).

> **Show me the list of components so I can choose:** If you activate this option, Setup displays the Select Components dialog box (discussed in the next section) so that you can customize the component selection.

Make your choice and click Next >.

FIGURE 2.9.

You can either let Setup install the default components or select the specific components you need.

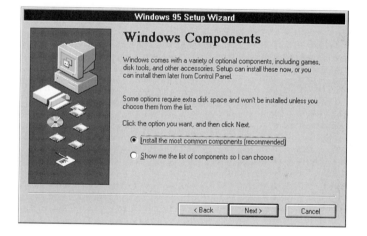

Select Components

The Select Components dialog box, shown in Figure 2.10, appears either if you chose the Custom Setup option or if you activated the Show me the list of components so I can choose option in the Windows Components dialog box. Here's how you use this dialog box to select components:

- To install a component, activate its check box.
- To bypass a component, deactivate its check box.
- Some options (such as Accessories and Communications) consist of multiple components. To choose specific components for any of these options, highlight the option and click the Details button. In the dialog box that appears (Figure 2.11 shows the dialog box for the Accessories components), choose the components you want to install and click OK.

When you've completed your choices, click Next >.

FIGURE 2.10.

Use the Select Components dialog box to pick and choose the specific Windows 95 components you want to install.

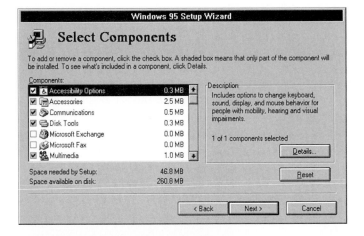

FIGURE 2.11.

For options with multiple components, clicking the Details button brings up a dialog box that lists the available components.

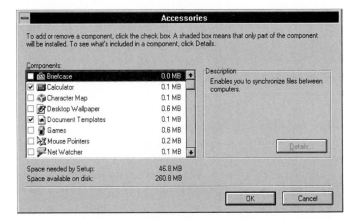

NOTE: NETWORK INSTALLATION INSTRUCTIONS

At this point in the installation, Setup might ask you to enter network information. I'm going to put off a discussion of network installation issues until later in this book. See Chapter 31, "Windows 95 Networking."

Computer Settings

If you selected the Custom Setup option, Setup displays the Computer Settings dialog box, shown in Figure 2.12. This dialog box displays a list of the hardware that the Detection Manager detected. (It also sports a few other settings, such as the Windows 95 language support and the user interface you want to use.)

FIGURE 2.12.

The Computer Settings dialog box summarizes the hardware that Setup found on your system.

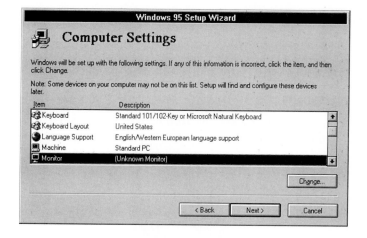

After reviewing the settings, you might find you need to make some changes. If so, here are the steps to follow:

1. Highlight the hardware item you want to modify.
2. Click the Change button. Setup displays a dialog box of hardware options. For example, Figure 2.13 shows the available monitor options.

FIGURE 2.13.

Clicking the Change button brings up a list of the available hardware options for the highlighted hardware item.

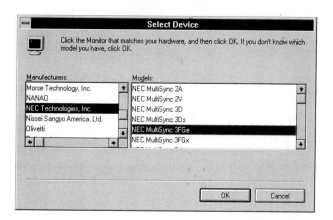

3. Use the Manufacturers list to highlight the manufacturer of the device.
4. Use the Models list to highlight the hardware model.
5. Click OK to return to the Change Settings dialog box.
6. Repeat steps 1 through 5 to adjust other settings.
7. When you're done, click Next >.

Startup Disk

The Setup Wizard now asks whether you want to create a startup disk (see Figure 2.14), as described earlier. You have two choices:

Yes, I want a startup disk (recommended): Activate this option if you want to create a startup disk.

No, I do not want a startup disk: Activate this option to bypass the startup disk. (This option is useful if you created a startup disk during a previous install.)

Make your selection and click Next >.

FIGURE 2.14.

Use the Startup Disk dialog box to choose whether you want Setup to create a startup disk.

Start Copying Files

Setup is now ready to start installing the Windows 95 files on your computer. When you see the Start Copying Files dialog box, click Next > to crank up the copying process. If you elected to create a startup disk, Setup prompts you to insert a disk in drive A. Insert the disk and click OK. Another dialog box appears when the disk is complete. Remove the disk and click OK to resume copying files.

Finishing Setup

After Setup has finished copying all the Windows 95 files, you see the Finishing Setup dialog box, shown in Figure 2.15. Click the Finish button. Setup now reboots your computer and attempts to start Windows 95 for the first time.

Figure 2.15.

This dialog box appears after Setup has completed its copying chores.

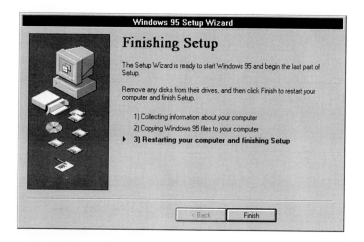

Finishing the Installation

For the final phase of the installation, Setup takes you through a few tasks designed to configure Windows 95 the way you want. The next few sections run through each of these tasks.

Entering a Windows Password

Your first task during this final Setup phase is to enter a user name and password. You have several ways to proceed, depending on whether your computer is (or will be) connected to a network.

For a standalone machine (you'll see the Enter Windows Password dialog box), you can leave the user name and password fields blank and click OK. A password is optional on a standalone computer, so Windows 95 won't bother you with this dialog box again in future startups.

For a networked machine (you'll see the Enter Network Password dialog box), you can't bypass the password dialog box, but you do have two ways to handle it:

- Enter a user name and password. You'll be required to enter these values each time you log on to Windows.
- Enter a user name and leave the password field blank. This way, each time Windows prompts you for a password, you can just press Enter to dismiss the dialog box.

If you do enter a password, Setup asks you to confirm it by displaying the Set Windows Password dialog box. Reenter your password and click OK.

Setting the Time Zone

Setup next displays the Date/Time Properties dialog box, shown in Figure 2.16. You use this dialog box to specify your time zone. This is important for networked computers that need to keep file time stamps synchronized. Also, Windows 95 understands daylight savings time and adjusts for it automatically if you specify your correct time zone. This dialog box defaults to the Pacific time zone. If you live in a different time zone, you can either select it from the drop-down list or use the left- and right-arrow keys to select it visually on the map. Click Close when you're done. (I talk about adjusting your system's date and time in Chapter 7, "Customizing Windows 95.")

FIGURE 2.16.

Use this dialog box to tell Windows 95 which time zone you live in.

Configuring Microsoft Exchange

If you installed Microsoft Exchange (or Windows Messaging, as it's called in OSR2), the Inbox Setup Wizard appears. If you want to configure Exchange now, click Next > and head for Chapter 27, "Setting Up Microsoft Exchange," to learn how it's done. If you'd prefer to leave this task until later, click Cancel, and then click Yes when Setup asks if you're sure.

Configuring a Printer

Next, Setup displays the Add Printer Wizard, shown in Figure 2.17. If you have a printer attached to your computer, you can install the appropriate drivers and configure the printer by clicking Next >. I take you through the steps for installing and configuring a printer in Chapter 19, "Prescriptions for Perfect Printing." To bypass this step, click Cancel.

FIGURE 2.17.

Use the Add Printer Wizard to install and configure a printer.

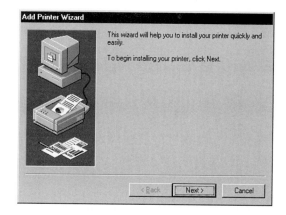

2

RUNNING THE WINDOWS 95 SETUP

The Home Stretch

Setup is just about done at this point. All that remains is (in most cases) to restart the computer one more time so that these new settings can take effect. Setup displays a dialog box telling you that it has finished configuring your system. Click OK to restart your system one last time. You'll eventually see the Welcome to Windows 95 dialog box, shown in Figure 2.18.

FIGURE 2.18.

The sign of a successful setup: the Welcome to Windows 95 dialog box.

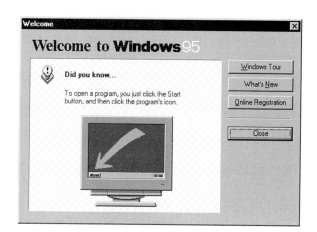

Do You Need AUTOEXEC.BAT and CONFIG.SYS?

As I mentioned earlier in this chapter, Setup creates its own AUTOEXEC.BAT and CONFIG.SYS files, based on your existing files, and renames the existing files with .DOS extensions. The only reason you need these files in Windows 95 is to load real-mode drivers for devices such as sound cards and CD-ROM drives. However, Windows 95 comes with protected-mode drivers for just about any kind of hardware you can throw at it. This means you might not need your real-mode drivers, so you might not need AUTOEXEC.BAT and CONFIG.SYS.

To test whether you need them, rename your AUTOEXEC.BAT and CONFIG.SYS files (to, say, AUTOEXEC.95 and CONFIG.95). Restart your system and see whether Windows 95 loads properly. If it does, you're in luck: You don't have to bother with AUTOEXEC.BAT and CONFIG.SYS at all! The advantages of this are quicker load times and increased conventional memory.

On the other hand, you might not be using your startup files to load any device drivers. Many people keep AUTOEXEC.BAT on hand only to set a few DOS environment variables (for, say, a Sound Blaster card). In this case, you can still eliminate your AUTOEXEC.BAT file by using a Windows 95 utility called WINSET. This utility works like the DOS SET command, except that it modifies environment variables for Windows 95's global DOS environment. (In contrast, if you run the SET command within a DOS session, the change applies only to that session.) By including the appropriate WINSET commands in a batch file and then including that batch file in your Windows 95 Startup folder, you eliminate the need for an AUTOEXEC.BAT file.

WINSET is available on the Windows 95 CD-ROM in the \Admin\Apptools\Envars folder. Copy the WINSET.EXE file to your main Windows 95 folder and then use the following syntax:

```
WINSET variable=string
```

> variable   The name of the environment variable.
>
> string   The value you want to assign to the variable.

For example, suppose you use the following command in AUTOEXEC.BAT to set the default parameters for the DIR command:

```
SET DIRCMD=/OGN /P
```

To do the same thing with WINSET, you'd use the following command:

```
WINSET DIRCMD=/OGN /P
```

Adding and Removing Windows 95 Components

The Windows 95 components you installed during Setup are by no means set in stone. You're free at any time to add new components and to remove components you don't need. The good news is that, thanks to its new Add/Remove Programs feature, Windows 95 makes it a breeze to install and uninstall chunks of the system. (If you want to delete Windows entirely, head for the section titled "Uninstalling Windows 95" later in this chapter.)

For starters, you need to get to the Windows Setup tab of the Add/Remove Programs Properties dialog box:

1. Click the Start button, open the Settings folder, and select Control Panel.
2. In the Control Panel window, open the Add/Remove Programs icon to display the Add/Remove Programs Properties dialog box.
3. Select the Windows Setup tab, shown in Figure 2.19.

FIGURE 2.19.

Use the Windows Setup tab to add or remove pieces of Windows 95.

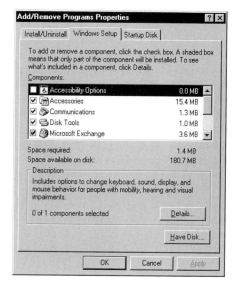

As you can see, this dialog box is reminiscent of the Setup Wizard's Select Components dialog box. In this case, though, you interpret the component check boxes as explained here:

- If a component's check box is activated, the component is already installed.
- If a component's check box is deactivated, the component isn't currently installed.
- If a component's check box has a gray background, the item contains multiple components, and only some of them are installed. (To find out how many of the item's components are installed, highlight the item and look inside the Description box. You'll see something like 3 of 4 components selected.

Adding Windows 95 Components

Adding components is a simple matter of activating the appropriate check boxes. If an item contains multiple components, highlight it and click the Details button to see the list of components. Activate the check boxes for the components you want to install, and then click OK to get back to the Windows Setup tab.

When you're done, click OK. Windows 95 will likely ask you to insert one or more of your original Windows 95 disks (or your Windows 95 CD-ROM). Insert the disk and click OK to continue. Depending on the components you're adding, Windows 95 might ask you to restart your computer. If it does, click Yes to let Windows 95 handle this job for you. When the restart is complete, the new programs are ready for action.

Adding Components from the Windows 95 CD-ROM

The Windows 95 CD-ROM contains not only the basic Windows 95 files, but also a truckload of other programs and files, including extra device drivers, handy utilities, multimedia files, and even a game. I'll be talking about many of these files as you trudge through this book, but here's the general procedure for installing files from the CD-ROM:

1. In the Windows Setup tab, click the Have Disk button. The Install From Disk dialog box appears.
2. Use the `Copy manufacturer's files from` box to enter the drive letter containing the Windows 95 CD-ROM and the full path of the folder containing the files you want to install. If you're not sure of the path, click the Browse button, use the Open dialog box to highlight the drive and path, and click OK to return to the Install From Disk dialog box.
3. Click OK. Windows 95 displays the Have Disk dialog box with a list of components to install.
4. Activate the check boxes for the components you want to install.
5. Click Install. Windows 95 installs the components and returns you to the Windows Setup tab. (In some cases, Windows 95 might need to restart your computer.)

Removing Windows 95 Components

If you've installed a Windows 95 component that you know you won't need in the future, you should delete it. This frees up disk space and reduces the clutter in the Start menu's folders.

In the Windows Setup tab, deactivate the check boxes for the components you want to expunge. Again, if an item has multiple components, highlight it, click Details, deactivate the appropriate check boxes, and click OK.

When you've finished deactivating check boxes, click OK. Windows 95 removes the components and might ask you to restart your computer.

Installing Microsoft Plus!

Windows 95 is a decent operating system right out of the box, but Microsoft left out a few goodies in the push to get the program out the door on time. Microsoft then gathered these knickknacks, tossed them onto a CD-ROM, called it Microsoft Plus!, and slapped a price tag on it. Is it worth the extra bucks? Well, if you can get past the fact that all of this stuff *should* have shipped with Windows 95, then, yes, it's definitely worth the cost. Here's what you get:

3D Pinball: This is a very slick arcade game that does an amazing job of mimicking an actual pinball machine, with great graphics, realistic sound, and even a "tilt" feature.

Desktop Themes: This is a collection of "themes" that alter the look of your desktop. Each theme includes wallpaper, icons, mouse pointers, sounds, and animation to dress up that drab desktop. Themes include Nature, Science, Sports, and The 60's USA.

Dial-Up Networking Server: This option configures your computer so that you can connect to it via modem from a remote location by using the Windows 95 Dial-Up Networking feature.

DriveSpace 3: This is a new-and-improved version of the DriveSpace disk compression that ships with Windows 95. It also includes the handy Compression Agent, which can compress your files automatically.

Internet Explorer: This is the original version of Microsoft's World Wide Web browser. Although a newer (and better) version of Internet Explorer is available on the Web, this option is still worth installing, thanks to the Internet Setup Wizard, which makes it easy to get your Internet connections up and running. (You can also get Internet Explorer 2.0 in the Windows 95 Service Pack; see the next section, "Installing the Windows 95 Service Pack.")

System Agent: This program lets you schedule certain system maintenance chores (such as backing up your data or checking your hard disk with ScanDisk) at regular intervals.

Visual Enhancements: This is a series of enhancements that improve the Windows 95 display. The best of them is "full window drag," which displays the full contents of a window as you drag it from one place to another. Other enhancements include font smoothing and wallpaper stretching.

NOTE: WATCH FOR THE MICROSOFT PLUS! ICON

I'll be explaining how to use these Microsoft Plus! features in the appropriate sections of this book. (For example, I talk about the Dial-Up Networking Server in Chapter 35, "Remote Computing with Dial-Up Networking.") So that you know when we're dealing with a Microsoft Plus! feature and not a Windows 95 feature, I'll mark the Microsoft Plus! information with the icon shown on the right.

To install Microsoft Plus!, your system must meet the following hardware requirements:

- 486 or higher processor
- 8 MB or more of RAM
- Up to 37 MB of free hard disk space (depending on the components you install)
- A monitor and video card capable of displaying at least 256 colors
- A modem (for the Dial-Up Networking Server and the Internet features)
- A sound card (for the sound features in the Desktop Themes)

If your machine is up to snuff, here's how to install Microsoft Plus!:

1. Insert the Microsoft Plus! CD in your CD-ROM drive. You should automatically see the Microsoft Plus! for Windows 95 window, shown in Figure 2.20. If you don't see

this window, open the Start menu, select Run, type *drive*:\setup.exe (where *drive* is the letter of your CD-ROM drive), click OK, and skip to step 3.

FIGURE 2.20.

*This window appears
after you insert the
Microsoft Plus! CD.*

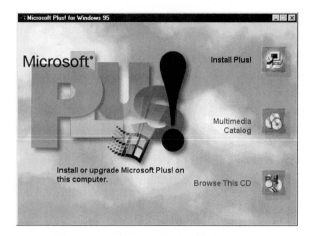

2. Open the Install Plus! icon. A Welcome dialog box appears.

3. Click Continue. Microsoft Plus! Setup prompts you for your name and company name.

4. Fill in the text boxes if necessary (the data should be the same as what you specified during the Windows 95 installation) and click OK. Setup asks you to confirm the entries.

5. Click OK. Setup prompts you for your 10-digit "CD Key" (which you can find either on the back of the Microsoft Plus! CD sleeve or with the CD liner notes).

6. Enter the Key and click OK. Setup displays your Product ID. (You should record this number just in case you need to contact Microsoft Technical Support. If you lose the number, you can retrieve it by right-clicking the My Computer icon and selecting Properties.)

7. Click OK. Setup prompts you for the folder in which you want to install Microsoft Plus!.

NOTE: DIRECTORIES ARE NOW CALLED "FOLDERS"

This is your first look at the word *folder*, which is the Windows 95 term for a directory. Although I use both terms interchangeably throughout this book, I put the emphasis on *folder* because that is Microsoft's preferred word.

8. If you don't want to accept the default folder (usually `C:\Program Files\Plus!`), click Change Folder, highlight the folder you want to use in the Change Folder dialog box, and click OK. (If Setup asks whether it's OK to create the folder, click Yes.)

9. Click OK. Setup prompts you to select a `Typical` or `Custom` installation. Make your choice and click OK.

10. If you selected the `Custom` option, the dialog box shown in Figure 2.21 appears. Use the check boxes to choose which options you want to install. For items that have multiple components (such as Desktop Themes), highlight the item, click Change Option, make your choices, and click OK. When you're done, click OK.

FIGURE 2.21.

This dialog box appears if you selected the `Custom` *option.*

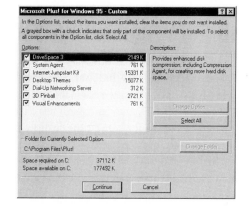

11. Setup asks whether you want to run System Agent at night. If you normally leave your machine on all night, click Yes; otherwise, click No.

12. At long last, Setup starts copying the Microsoft Plus! files to your hard disk. When it's done, the Internet Setup Wizard appears (assuming that you chose to install the Internet Jumpstart Kit). I cover Internet setup in Chapter 37, "Windows 95 and the Internet," so you can either head to that chapter now or click Cancel (and click Yes when Setup asks whether you're sure you want to cancel).

13. Setup now warns you that it will display the Desktop Themes window. Click OK. Sure enough, the Desktop Themes window appears.

14. I cover desktop themes in Chapter 5, "Windows 95: The 50¢ Tour," so you can either continue from that chapter or click Cancel.

15. A final dialog box appears to let you know that you have to restart Windows 95. Click the Restart Windows button to let Setup handle this task for you.

> ### CAUTION: UPDATE YOUR STARTUP DISK!
>
> If you plan on using the slick DriveSpace 3 compression utility that comes with Microsoft Plus!, you must update your Windows 95 Startup disk. After Plus! is installed, open the Start menu and select Settings | Control Panel. Open the Add/Remove Programs icon and select the Startup Disk tab in the Add/Remove Programs Properties dialog box. Click the Create Disk button and follow the instructions.
>
> If you can't start Windows 95, you need to modify the Startup disk manually. I show you how to do this in Chapter 3, "Troubleshooting Setup Woes," in the section "Startup Disk Problems."

Installing the Windows 95 Service Pack 1

In the past, Microsoft usually waited quite a while before releasing an upgrade to its mainstream operating systems (DOS and Windows). Sure, it often would make updated device drivers and files available on its BBS, but any reasonably major changes had to wait until the next upgrade. With Windows 95, however, Microsoft has changed its policy. As it has done with its high-end NT operating system for some time, it now intends to release interim updates to Windows 95 in the form of "service packs." These will be collections of drivers, utilities, and program updates that extend the functionality of Windows 95 and ensure that core technologies (such as NetWare Directory Services and IrDA) are implemented sooner rather than later.

The first of these service packs shipped in February 1996. It included, among other things, the following goodies:

- Fixes and patches to bugs reported since Windows 95's initial launch
- Internet Explorer 2.0
- A shell update that supports the NetWare Directory Services (NDS) client and fixes a file-copy problem
- Infrared Data Association (IrDA) drivers
- 32-bit Data Link Control protocol stacks for IBM Token Ring networks
- The OLE 32 update to fix file management problems
- A stronger password cache
- An updated common dialog box that supports Windows 3.1 printer drivers
- Updated file- and print-sharing drivers
- A complete Dial-Up Networking scripting tool and support for SLIP connections
- A library of drivers for printers, video cards, sound cards, and network adapters that weren't supported in the original Windows 95 release
- Microsoft Word Viewer, a utility that lets you view Microsoft Word for Windows files even if you don't have Word for Windows
- Shared-folder support in the Microsoft Exchange Inbox

You can buy Service Pack 1 from your local reseller, or you can download it from the Internet at the following site:

`http://www.microsoft.com/windows/windows95/info/service-packs.htm`

If you download the Service Pack 1 file (`SETUP.EXE`) from the Internet, make sure that you store it in an empty folder.

NOTE: NEW WINDOWS VERSION NUMBER

After you install Service Pack 1, your Windows 95 version number changes from 4.00.950 to 4.00.950A. Hence, the combination of Windows 95 and Service Pack 1 is often referred to as Windows 95A.

CAUTION: SERVICE PACK 1 AND OSR2 DON'T MIX!

If your system is running OSR2, Microsoft strongly recommends that you not install Service Pack 1, because some of the latter's utilities aren't compatible with OSR2.

To install the Windows 95 Service Pack 1, follow these steps:

1. If you're using System Agent from Microsoft Plus!, right-click the System Agent icon in the taskbar and then select Suspend System Agent.
2. If you downloaded Service Pack 1 from the Internet, run `SETUP.EXE`. If you have the Service Pack 1 CD-ROM, run `SETUP.EXE` in the CD-ROM root folder.
3. When the program asks if you want to continue, click Yes.
4. Click Yes when the Service Pack license agreement appears.
5. When the Setup program is complete, click OK.
6. Shut down all your running programs, select Start | Shut Down, activate the `Restart the computer` option, and click Yes.

Removing Your Old Windows 3.x and DOS Files

After you have used Windows 95 for a while, have weaned yourself off the Windows 3.x way of doing things, and are sure you want to stick with Windows 95 for the duration, you'll likely want to get rid of your old Windows 3.x and DOS files. Windows 95 can handle this for you automatically. Just follow these steps:

1. Click the Start button, open the Settings folder, and select Control Panel.
2. In the Control Panel window, open the Add/Remove Programs icon to display the Add/Remove Programs Properties dialog box, shown in Figure 2.22.

OSR2

FIGURE 2.22.

*Use the Install/
Uninstall tab to remove
your old Windows 3.x
and DOS files.*

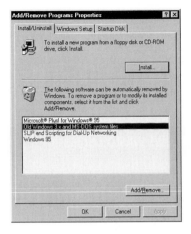

3. In the list box, highlight Old Windows 3.x and MS-DOS system files.

4. Click the Add/Remove button. If you saved your old system files during Setup, Windows 95 uses the dialog box shown in Figure 2.23 to warn you that this uninstall information will be deleted.

FIGURE 2.23.

*Windows 95 warns you
that your uninstall
information will be
deleted.*

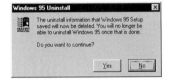

5. Click Yes. Windows 95 deletes the Windows 3.x uninstall files and lets you know that you can no longer uninstall Windows 95.

6. Click OK.

Reinstalling Windows 95

If you find that Windows 95 acts strangely, crashes regularly, or just won't load, some crucial Windows 95 files might have become corrupted. This could happen if you turned off your computer before shutting down Windows 95, if a power failure forced your system off, or if a power surge wreaked havoc on your machine's delicate innards. In most cases, you can set Windows 95 back on its feet by running the Setup program again. Setup gives you the option of restoring just those files that are corrupted or of copying everything all over again. Here's how it works:

1. Start the Windows 95 Setup program, and follow the prompts on-screen until the Setup Wizard loads. You'll eventually see the Run Setup Again? dialog box, shown in Figure 2.24.

FIGURE 2.24.

Setup can replace changed or corrupted Windows 95 files.

2. This dialog box gives you two choices:

   Restore Windows files that are changed or corrupted: Select this option if you suspect that one or more Windows 95 files have become damaged.

   Copy all Windows files again: Select this option to repeat the entire Setup procedure.

3. Click Next >.

4. Follow the rest of the Setup Wizard's prompts to reinstall your files.

Uninstalling Windows 95

If for some reason you and Windows 95 just aren't getting along, you can always get a divorce. In other words, you can always uninstall Windows 95 and put that part of your life behind you. Uninstalling Windows 95 can be easy or hard, depending on how you installed it in the first place:

The easy method: If you upgraded over Windows 3.x, told Setup to save backup copies of your system files, and haven't compressed your hard drive with DriveSpace, you can use Windows 95's Uninstall feature to remove Windows 95.

The hard method: If you installed Windows 95 in a separate directory, or if you've already deleted your old Windows 3.x files, you need to uninstall Widows 95 by hand.

Using the Windows 95 Uninstall Feature

If Setup saved your Windows 3.x files during an upgrade (and if you haven't deleted your old Windows 3.x files), kicking Windows 95 off your system is easy. In this case, Windows 95 has all the information it needs to remove itself, and the job is all automated by the new Uninstall feature. Table 2.5 lists the various files that Uninstall uses.

Table 2.5. Files used by the Windows 95 Uninstall feature.

Filename	Purpose
MSDOS.SYS	Contains an entry pointing to the location of the W95UNDO.DAT and W95UNDO.INI files.
SUHDLOG.DAT	Contains a copy of all master boot records and partition boot records on the system both before and after the upgrade to Windows 95. Is used to restore the original boot sectors.
W95UNDO.DAT	Contains a compressed backup of the Windows 3.x directory.
W95UNDO.INI	Contains a listing of files backed up in the W95UNDO.DAT file, as well as the new Windows 95 files installed by Setup.

Uninstall also restores the saved system files (IO.DOS, MSDOS.DOS, COMMAND.DOS, CONFIG.DOS, and AUTOEXEC.DOS) to their original names (IO.SYS, MSDOS.SYS, COMMAND.COM, CONFIG.SYS, and AUTOEXEC.BAT).

Here are the steps to follow to uninstall Windows 95:

1. Click the Start button, open the Settings folder, and select Control Panel.
2. In the Control Panel window, open the Add/Remove Programs icon to display the Add/Remove Programs Properties dialog box, shown in Figure 2.25.

FIGURE 2.25.

Use Windows 95's Uninstall feature to remove Windows 95 from your system.

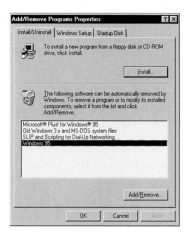

3. In the list box, highlight Windows 95.

4. Click the Add/Remove button. Windows 95 displays a dialog box with several warnings, as shown in Figure 2.26.

FIGURE 2.26.

Windows 95 displays this dialog box when you begin the uninstall procedure.

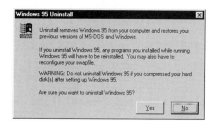

5. Click Yes. Another dialog box appears to let you know that Uninstall is about to check for disk errors and remove all the long filename information created by Windows 95.

6. Click Yes. Uninstall runs ScanDisk to check your hard disk for problems. When ScanDisk is done, another dialog box appears to let you know that Uninstall is ready to do its thing.

7. Click OK. Uninstall shuts down your computer, removes the Windows 95 files, and restores your previous configuration (this process takes several minutes).

8. When Uninstall is finished, remove any floppy disks you might have in your computer, and then press Enter to restart your machine. Your old version of DOS will load.

NOTE: ALTERNATIVE UNINSTALL STARTUPS

If you can't load Windows 95 (which would be a good reason for uninstalling it!), you can still run the Uninstall program. You have two choices:

■ If you have a Windows 95 startup disk, reboot your system with the disk in drive A, and when you get to the A:\ prompt, type uninstall, press Enter, and follow the on-screen instructions.

■ If you have a disk that boots to your previous operating system, reboot your system with the disk in drive A, and when you get to the A:\ prompt, type c:\windows\command\uninstall (assuming that you installed Windows 95 in the C:\WINDOWS directory), press Enter, and follow the on-screen instructions.

Uninstalling Windows 95 by Hand

If you installed Windows 95 in a separate directory, or if you've already removed your old Windows 3.x files, it takes quite a bit more work to uninstall Windows 95. Note that you must have a bootable disk that boots your system to a previous version of DOS, and that this disk must have the SYS.COM utility on it.

For starters, you need to make a slight adjustment to the ScanDisk initialization file. Using Notepad or some other text editor, open SCANDISK.INI and look for the [ENVIRONMENT] section. You need to make two adjustments:

LabelCheck=On: This tells ScanDisk to check disk volume labels for invalid characters.

SpaceCheck=On: This tells ScanDisk to check for invalid spaces in filenames.

When you're done, save the file and exit the text editor. Now follow these steps:

1. Restart your system, and when you see the Starting Windows 95... message, press F8 to display the Windows 95 Startup menu. Then select the Command prompt only option. When you get to DOS, make sure that you're in the root directory (if you're not sure, type cd\ and press Enter).

2. Use the following two commands to copy the files DELTREE.EXE, SCANDISK.EXE, and SCANDISK.INI from \WINDOWS\COMMAND to the root directory (if you installed Windows 95 in a directory other than C:\WINDOWS, substitute the appropriate directory in the following commands):

   ```
   copy c:\windows\command\deltree.exe
   copy c:\windows\command\scandisk.*
   ```

3. Run ScanDisk to remove all volume labels and filenames that your previous version of DOS will consider invalid. Type scandisk *drive*: (where *drive* is the drive on which Windows is installed), and press Enter. If you have other drives, run ScanDisk on them as well.

4. Use the DELTREE utility to delete all the Windows 95 files on your system. Here are the commands to run (note that the /y switch suppresses the DELTREE confirmation prompt; if you want to be prompted, remove /y from each command; also, in the first command, replace windows with the name of your main Windows 95 directory, if it's different):

   ```
   deltree /y windows
   deltree /y recycled
   deltree /y winboot.*
   deltree /y io.sys
   deltree /y msdos.sys
   deltree /y commmand.com
   deltree /y config.sys
   deltree /y autoexec.bat
   deltree /y detlog.txt
   deltree /y netlog.txt
   deltree /y setuplog.txt
   deltree /y suhdlog.dat
   deltree /y system.1st
   deltree /y d??space.bin
   ```

5. Rename `CONFIG.DOS` to `CONFIG.SYS` and `AUTOEXEC.DOS` to `AUTOEXEC.BAT` using the following commands:

   ```
   ren config.dos config.sys
   ren autoexec.dos autoexec.bat
   ```

6. Insert the bootable disk containing your previous version of DOS in drive A, and restart your computer.

7. Type `sys c:` (assuming that drive C is your boot drive; if drive C is compressed, substitute the letter of the host drive—such as H—for drive C), and press Enter. This command transfers the system files for the previous DOS version and overwrites the Windows 95 master boot record.

8. Remove the disk and restart your computer to boot to the previous version of DOS. Note that if you replaced your existing version of Windows with Windows 3.x and did *not* save the old system files, you'll have to reinstall Windows 3.x.

Summary

This chapter showed you how to use Setup to install Windows 95 on your system. You also learned how to install Windows 95 components, Microsoft Plus!, and Service Pack 1, as well as how to reinstall and uninstall Windows 95.

Here's a list of chapters where you'll find related information:

- I explained the theory behind the Setup program in Chapter 1, "Understanding the Windows 95 Installation."

- If you're having problems with Windows 95 Setup, head for Chapter 3, "Troubleshooting Setup Woes."

- For more information about the Windows 95 Startup menu and `MSDOS.SYS`, check out Chapter 4, "Start It Your Way: Understanding Windows 95 Startup."

- To get your feet wet with the new Windows 95 interface and tools, read Chapter 5, "Windows 95: The 50¢ Tour."

- Plug and Play and other hardware-related issues are covered in Chapter 10, "How Windows 95 Handles Hardware."

- I give extended coverage of ScanDisk in Chapter 15, "Protecting Your Windows 95 Investment."

- Printer installation is covered in Chapter 19, "Prescriptions for Perfect Printing."

- For an in-depth discussion of Microsoft Exchange setup and configuration, see Chapter 27, "Setting Up Microsoft Exchange."

- For network installations, try Chapter 31, "Windows 95 Networking."

- I show you how to perform network and custom setups in Appendix C, "A Setup Smorgasbord: Custom and Server-Based Setups."

2

RUNNING THE
WINDOWS 95
SETUP

Troubleshooting Setup Woes

IN THIS CHAPTER

CHAPTER 3

One woe doth tread upon another's heel,
So fast they follow.

—Shakespeare

Microsoft strove hard to make Windows 95 Setup as bulletproof as possible. From its extensive testing in all kinds of environments, to its mammoth database of hardware drivers, to its sophisticated Detection Manager and Safe Detection features, Setup is as robust a program as you can get. However, it just isn't feasible (or realistic) for Windows 95 to account for all potential hardware and software combinations. The number of possible permutations is just this side of infinite, so there's no way to ensure that Setup can handle everything you throw at it. Sooner or later, Setup will trip over some obscure combination of system resources and won't be able to install Windows 95. If this happens to you, various troubleshooting techniques are at your disposal to help you over whatever hump is impeding the installation. This chapter takes you through these techniques and examines a large number of specific installation problems.

Understanding Safe Recovery

The Windows 95 Setup program, like all good high-wire artists, works with a net. In this case, the "net" is a feature called Safe Recovery. It helps Setup diagnose—and usually avoid—problems during the installation process.

When you first start Setup, one of the items on its internal to-do list is to copy a batch file called SUWARN.BAT into the WININST0.400 directory. (Recall from Chapter 1, "Understanding the Windows 95 Installation," that Setup creates the WININST0.400 directory and uses it to store the temporary files that Setup needs during the installation.) If all goes well during the install, Setup deletes SUWARN.BAT along with all the other files in WININST0.400 (including the directory itself).

If, on the other hand, Setup can't complete the installation, the WININST0.400 directory remains in place, and so does SUWARN.BAT. What good is that? Well, Setup also installs a "marker" that will warn you if something went awry during a previous Setup operation. Setup does this by adding the following lines to your AUTOEXEC.BAT file:

```
@if exist c:\wininst0.400\suwarn.bat call c:\wininst0.400\suwarn.bat
@if exist c:\wininst0.400\suwarn.bat del c:\wininst0.400\suwarn.bat
```

The first line checks for the existence of SUWARN.BAT. If it exists (this implies that Setup failed), SUWARN.BAT is called. This batch file displays the following message:

```
Windows Setup Safe Recovery
Windows Setup could not completely install Windows. You need to
run Setup again, and choose Safe Recovery when prompted.
If you started Setup from Windows, type WIN to restart Windows, and
then run Setup again.
```

```
Note: Do not delete any files or reconfigure your system.
      If Setup had started copying files, your previous version
      of Windows may not run properly. If you have problems
      running your previous version of Windows, you will need
      to run Setup from MS-DOS.
Press any key to continue . . .
```

Press a key to continue the boot process. Note that the second of the two lines added to AUTOEXEC.BAT deletes SUWARN.BAT, so you'll see the preceding message only once.

When you run Setup again, the first Setup Wizard dialog box you'll see is called Safe Recovery; it's shown in Figure 3.1. Make sure that the Use Safe Recovery (recommended) option is activated, and then click Next >.

FIGURE 3.1.

If Setup detects a failed installation, it displays the Safe Recovery dialog box.

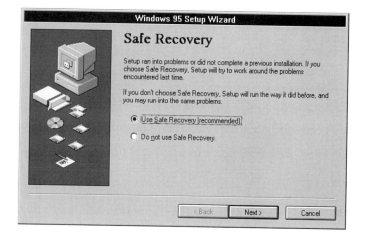

The Safe Recovery feature recognizes that there was a problem and either tries to fix it or, more likely, tries to steer around it. Safe Recovery performs this magic by looking for clues that might indicate where and when the problem occurred. There are three possibilities:

- Setup failed before the hardware detection phase.
- Setup failed during the hardware detection phase.
- Setup failed after the hardware detection phase.

Safe Recovery if Setup Failed Before Hardware Detection

I mentioned in Chapter 1 that Setup records information about the installation in a hidden text file called SETUPLOG.TXT (it's stored in the root directory of your boot drive). If the installation fails before the hardware detection phase, Setup recovers by examining SETUPLOG.TXT to see where things went wrong. SETUPLOG.TXT not only stores the data you supply to Setup (such as your name), but also records the progress of the installation, which processes were started, which ones finished successfully, and, most important, which ones failed. If Setup notices that a particular operation failed, it bypasses the operation in the hope that this will allow the installation to proceed without further incident. Of course, it also means that some aspect of the installation gets missed. The idea, though, is that if you can at least get a basic installation in place, you can always correct the problem by hand from within Windows 95.

How do you know where the problem occurred and what caused it? Unfortunately, Setup is less than forthcoming with this information; if it knows the answer, it keeps that answer to itself. So, unless the problem is obvious (such as a CD-ROM drive that doesn't appear in Explorer), you might have to resort to some detective work. This means examining the SETUPLOG.TXT file yourself and looking for clues. To help in this quest, I'll lead you as you examine SETUPLOG.TXT and try to decipher its contents.

On a general level, the contents of SETUPLOG.TXT can be divided into six categories:

- Information you supplied to the Setup Wizard (your name and company name, the components you selected, and so on)
- System startup parameters
- The directory into which you installed Windows 95
- Information gleaned from the beginning of the installation process
- The list of Windows 95 files copied to your system
- Tasks performed after restarting the system

Table 3.1 details some of the sections (the items surrounded by square brackets, such as [System]) and entries you'll find in a typical SETUPLOG.TXT file. Note that these lines are entered more or less in the order in which Setup progresses through the installation, so you're more likely to find problems toward the end of the file.

Table 3.1. Sections and entries in a typical SETUPLOG.TXT file.

SETUPLOG.TXT *Entry*	*Description*
[OptionalComponents]	A list of the Windows 95 components. Items with a 1 were selected for installation; items with a 0 weren't selected.
[System]	The results of the hardware detection phase. This section shows the devices found by the Detection Manager.
[NameAndOrg]	The name and company name you supplied to Setup.
[Destination]	Various paths that Setup used to read and install files.
[Setup]	Various Setup options, including the installation directory.
[Started]	Parameters generated by Setup during the initial phase of the installation.

SETUPLOG.TXT *Entry*	*Description*
[Detection]	Information about, and the progress of, the startup of the hardware detection phase.
[FileCopy]	A (long) list of the files Setup installed on your system.
[Restart]	A list of issues and processes Setup dealt with after restarting your system.

Safe Recovery if Setup Failed During Hardware Detection

If Setup makes it as far as the hardware detection phase, a different logging scheme takes over. In this case, Setup logs the progress of the detection procedure in another hidden root directory file: DETLOG.TXT. If Setup goes up in flames during hardware detection, it uses the information from this log to recover. Actually, Setup creates a binary file named DETCRASH.LOG, which details which detection module was running at the time of the crash and which resources (memory addresses, I/O ports, and so on) it was accessing. If Setup detects the DETCRASH.LOG file, it runs Safe Recovery mode automatically and uses this information to bypass the problem area.

Again, avoiding the source of the problem might get Windows 95 installed, but it still means that a device might not have been set up properly. You might need to examine DETLOG.TXT to see where Setup stumbled. To that end, take a closer look at the contents of DETLOG.TXT.

For starters, DETLOG.TXT begins with a few lines that control how the Detection Manager performs its duties. Table 3.2 outlines a few of these entries.

Table 3.2. Entries at the beginning of a typical DETLOG.TXT file.

DETLOG.TXT *Entry*	*Description*
Parameters	Switches specified with the setup command.
SDMVer	The version number of the Detection Manager.
WinVer	A number that combines the DOS and Windows version detected by Setup.
AvoidMem	Specifies upper memory blocks that Setup avoided during hardware detection.
LogCrash	Specifies whether Setup detected DETCRASH.LOG.
DetectClass: skip	Specifies the hardware classes for which Safe Detection found no hints. For example, DetectClass: skip class MEDIA tells you that Setup found no hints for sound cards in your configuration files. The Detection Manager will skip these hardware classes.

continues

3

TROUBLESHOOTING SETUP WOES

Table 3.2. continued

DETLOG.TXT Entry	Description
UserOverride	If Setup finds any DetectClass entries, it adds them to the Analyzing Your Computer dialog box (shown in Figure 2.5 in Chapter 2). If you activate any of these check boxes, you're overriding the DetectClass entry, and Setup makes a note of this with a UserOverride entry. For example, if you activate the Sound Card check box, Setup records a UserOverride: MEDIA=1 entry.
Devices verified	The number of devices Setup verified using an existing version of the Registry. If this number is 0, there was no existing Registry.

The rest of DETLOG.TXT documents the progress of the various detection modules. Here's a typical sequence:

```
Checking for: Standard IDE/ESDI Hard Disk Controller
QueryIOMem: Caller=DETECTESDI, rcQuery=0
     IO=1f0-1f7
QueryIOMem: Caller=DETECTESDI, rcQuery=0
     IO=3f6-3f6
Detected: *PNP0600\0000 = [16] Standard IDE/ESDI hard Disk Controller
     IO=1f0-1f7,3f6-3f6
     IRQ=14
```

Here, the detection module is checking the system for a standard IDE or ESDI hard disk controller. The two QueryIOMem lines tell you the memory addresses that the module used to check for the controller. The Detected line indicates that the device was found successfully, and it shows the resources used by the device.

If your system locks up during hardware detection, you can usually figure out the problem by opening DETLOG.TXT and heading to the end of the file. Look for an incomplete Checking sequence or a specific error message.

Safe Recovery if Setup Failed After Hardware Detection

Even if you get through the hardware detection phase without a scratch, the detection process might cause one or more devices to stop working. For example, your CD-ROM might lock up or become otherwise unusable, and you'll have no way to continue with Setup. When you start Setup again after rebooting, Safe Recovery sees that the hardware detection was already completed. So, smartly, it avoids the detection phase this time around, thus (you hope) bypassing whatever caused your device to stall.

Setup Won't Start

If Setup refuses to even start, the most likely culprit is low memory. Setup requires 420 KB of free conventional memory before it will grace your screen. To see how much memory you have available, head for the DOS prompt, type mem, and press Enter. In the report that appears, look for the Conventional line, and note the number in the Free column. If it indicates that your system has less than 420 KB free, you'll need to adjust your memory configuration before you can coax Setup into starting. Here are some things to try:

■ Make sure that CONFIG.SYS is loading an extended memory manager (such as HIMEM.SYS) and that DOS is being loaded into the high memory area. Here are the lines to look for:

```
DEVICE=C:\WINDOWS\HIMEM.SYS
DOS=HIGH
```

■ Make sure that your system has at least 3 MB of extended memory (4 MB total). If you're not sure, run the MEM utility again, and examine the Extended (XMS) line to see the total extended memory available.

■ Remove or comment out any lines in CONFIG.SYS or AUTOEXEC.BAT that load device drivers or TSRs you don't need. (You comment out a line by preceding it with REM and a space.)

■ Run the DOS MemMaker program to optimize conventional memory.

If you have plenty of free conventional memory, a virus might be preventing Setup from starting. Use a virus checker to see whether your system has been infected.

Setup Hangs During Installation

Although Setup's Safe Recovery feature can usually work around a problem and get at least a bare-bones or incomplete version of Windows 95 installed, there are still other problems that Safe Recovery can't help you with. This section looks at a few causes and solutions if Setup repeatedly hangs at specific phases of the installation.

The Clean Boot

The typical PC setup is a complex affair with all kinds of TSRs and device drivers crammed into memory. If you're having problems with your Windows 95 installation, it might be caused by Setup butting heads with one of these memory-resident programs.

The solution, typically, is to do a *clean boot*—to restart your system without loading any TSRs or device drivers. This means you either bypass your CONFIG.SYS and AUTOEXEC.BAT files at startup or create replacements for these files that don't reference any unnecessary TSRs.

Bypassing `CONFIG.SYS` and `AUTOEXEC.BAT`

If you don't use `CONFIG.SYS` or `AUTOEXEC.BAT` to load device drivers that are crucial to the operation of your computer (such as drivers for a SCSI controller or disk compression), you can get an easy clean boot by bypassing `CONFIG.SYS` and `AUTOEXEC.BAT` altogether. You can use either of two possible methods to go about this:

■ If you have DOS 6.x, reboot and watch for the `Starting MS-DOS...` message. When you see it, press F5.

■ For earlier DOS versions, rename `CONFIG.SYS` and `AUTOEXEC.BAT` (to, say, `CONFIG.NOT` and `AUTOEXEC.NOT`), and then reboot.

Creating Clean `AUTOEXEC.BAT` and `CONFIG.SYS` Files

If you can't skip `CONFIG.SYS` and `AUTOEXEC.BAT` because they contain device drivers needed by your system, you'll need to create "clean" versions of these files (named, for example, `CONFIG.CLN` and `AUTOEXEC.CLN`). The exact composition of these files depends on the drivers you need and whether you're running Setup from DOS or from an existing version of Windows.

If You're Running Setup from DOS

If you'll be running Setup from the DOS prompt, here's a typical clean `CONFIG.SYS` file (assuming that DOS is installed in `C:\DOS`):

```
FILES=45
BUFFERS=20
<SCSI controller driver>
<SCSI CD-ROM driver>
<Disk compression driver>
<Other required third-party drivers>
SHELL=C:\DOS\COMMAND.COM  /E:1024 /P
```

Here's the clean version of `AUTOEXEC.BAT` (again, assuming that DOS is in `C:\DOS`):

```
PROMPT $P$G
PATH=C:\DOS;C:\
<Necessary TSRs, such as MSCDEX.EXE>
```

If You're Running Setup from Windows 3.x

If you intend to run Setup from within an existing version of Windows 3.x or Windows for Workgroups, here's the clean version of `CONFIG.SYS` (assuming that Windows is installed in `C:\WINDOWS` and DOS is installed in `C:\DOS`):

```
DEVICE=C:\WINDOWS\HIMEM.SYS
FILES=45
BUFFERS=20
STACKS=9,256
<SCSI controller driver>
<SCSI CD-ROM driver>
<Disk compression driver>
<Other required third-party drivers>
SHELL=C:\DOS\COMMAND.COM  /E:1024 /P
```

Here's the clean `AUTOEXEC.BAT`:

```
PROMPT $P$G
PATH=C:\DOS;C:\
SET TEMP=C:\WINDOWS\TEMP
<Necessary TSRs, such as MSCDEX.EXE>
```

When you need to do a clean boot, rename your regular versions of `CONFIG.SYS` and `AUTOEXEC.BAT`, and then copy the clean versions to the root directory as `AUTOEXEC.BAT` and `CONFIG.SYS`.

Setup Hangs During the ScanDisk Check

If Setup locks up while it's using ScanDisk to perform the "routine" check of your system, something is likely going on that's not at all routine! Setup should recognize if ScanDisk gets stuck, and it should return control of the system to you after about three minutes of inactivity. If, after the allotted time, ScanDisk is still refusing to let go of your system, reboot, get to the DOS prompt, and run ScanDisk manually from there. If ScanDisk hangs, you have a serious problem with your hard disk.

If the manual ScanDisk check goes well (in other words, if it completes normally, even if there were problems that needed fixing), try running Setup again. If Setup still freezes, try again, but this time use the command `setup /is`, which tells Setup not to bother with the ScanDisk check. (Instead, Setup runs the DOS CHKDSK utility to check for cross-linked files. To bypass this check as well, add the `/iq` switch to the `setup` command.)

Setup Hangs on Disk 2 or Later

If you're installing Windows 95 from floppy disks, Setup might hang while trying to access one of the disks. If this always occurs on the same disk, either of two problems might be occurring:

- A virus program might be trying to infect Disk 2.
- The disk might be corrupted.

Setup writes information to Disk 2, and many viruses infect disks during write operations. The conflict could therefore cause the system to hang. (More likely, Setup will complain about Disk 2 being "bad.") You'll need to run a virus checker to rid your system of the invader, and you'll likely need to order a replacement Disk 2 from Microsoft.

Here's one way you can check to see whether a disk is corrupted:

1. Insert Disk 1 and copy the Extract utility (`EXTRACT.EXE`) to the root directory of drive C.
2. Create a temporary directory on your hard disk (called, for example, `W95TEMP`).
3. Insert the disk you're having trouble with.

4. Use the Extract utility to extract each of the files on the disk to drive C. (Use the DOS DIR command to get a list of files on the disk.) For example, if you're using Disk 2, you can extract the PRECOPY2.CAB and WIN95_02.CAB files with the following commands:

```
extract /e a:\precopy2.cab /l c:\w95temp
extract /e a:\win95_02.cab /l c:\w95temp
```

If the extract procedure fails for one of the disk's files, you need a replacement disk.

Setup Hangs During Hardware Detection

If Setup goes to the Bahamas during the hardware detection phase, you can use the DETLOG.TXT file to try to diagnose the problem as discussed earlier. If that doesn't get you anywhere, try these steps:

1. Shut down your system, wait a few seconds (to give any stuck devices time to get unstuck), and then restart it. (Note that pressing Ctrl-Alt-Delete or even pressing your machine's Reset button isn't good enough.)

2. Start Setup again and make sure that you select Safe Recovery.

3. In the Setup Options dialog box, activate the Custom option.

4. In the Analyzing Your Computer dialog box, activate the No, I want to modify the hardware list option and click Next >.

5. When the Setup Wizard displays the list of hardware classes (see Figure 2.7 in Chapter 2), activate only the following types in the Hardware types list:

> Display
> Floppy Disk Controllers
> Hard Disk Controllers
> Keyboard
> Mouse

Setup Hangs After the First Reboot

If your system doesn't respond for a long time after Setup tries to restart your system for the first time, turn off your computer, wait a few seconds, and then turn it back on. (Don't use Ctrl-Alt-Delete or the Reset button to restart your computer.) Let the computer boot normally, and Setup should pick up where it left off automatically.

If your system still won't restart, the next few sections take you through some possible solutions.

Disable Anti-Virus Software

A conflict might exist between an anti-virus TSR and Setup. As you learned in Chapter 1, just before Setup reboots, it replaces your system's master boot record with a new Windows 95 version. Because replacing the master boot record is the modus operandi of many viruses, any anti-virus program worth its salt will assume that Setup is trying to infect your system. The resulting collision will lock up your machine tighter than a drum. You'll need to disable the anti-virus software and run Setup again.

Also, check to see whether your computer's CMOS setup program has a feature that disables writes to the boot sector. (You can usually get into the CMOS setup program at startup. On many machines, you press F2 or Ctrl-Alt-Esc to load the setup utility.) If so, you need to enable boot sector writes before starting Windows 95 Setup again.

NOTE: SETUP DOESN'T LIKE COMPAQ'S SAFESTART FEATURE

If you have a Compaq Deskpro XL computer, you must disable the SafeStart feature before installing Windows 95.

Check for Viruses

A virus that has already taken up residence in your computer's boot sector might be what's causing setup to hang. Use an anti-virus program to scour your computer for any existing viruses.

Resolve a Video Driver Conflict

A common cause of lockups is a conflict with the video driver. In other words, Setup chooses the wrong type of video driver, so your system stalls when Setup tries to load the driver. You can combat this problem in two ways:

- Try restarting Windows 95 in Safe mode. Safe mode is a diagnostic mode that loads only a basic configuration in an effort to minimize conflicts. (It's the Windows 95 equivalent of a clean boot. I discuss Safe mode in more detail when I talk about custom startups in Chapter 4, "Start It Your Way: Understanding Windows 95 Startup.") Restart the computer, and when you see the Starting Windows 95... message, press F8 to invoke the Windows 95 Startup menu. Select the Safe Mode option to start Windows 95 in Safe mode. If Windows 95 loads properly, select the Standard VGA Display Adapter. (See Chapter 23, "Windows 95 Video: The Big Picture," to learn how to select a different display adapter in Windows 95.)

- Rerun the Setup program, and in the Setup Options dialog box, activate the Custom option. In the Analyzing Your Computer dialog box, activate the No, I want to modify the hardware list option and click Next >. When the Setup Wizard displays the list of hardware classes, highlight Display and select the correct video card from the list. If you don't see your card listed, choose Standard VGA Display Adapter.

Convert Windows 3.x Program Groups by Hand

If you're upgrading from Windows 3.x, one of the tasks Setup must perform when it reboots your computer is to convert existing Windows 3.x program groups into Windows 95 Start menu folders. However, Setup might hang if it comes across a corrupted Windows 3.x program group file. To get past this problem, use the Program Group Converter utility (`GRPCONV.EXE`) to convert the program groups to folders by hand. (I explained how this utility works in Chapter 1; see the section titled "Some Notes About Dual- (and Multi-) Booting.")

If the Program Group Converter stumbles on one of these files, you know you've found the culprit. Delete the GRP file and restart your system.

Reinstall INF Files

If Setup hangs while the `Windows 95 is now setting up your hardware and any Plug and Play devices you may have` message is displayed, it likely means that one of the INF files is damaged. Setup hangs when it tries to index the contents of the INF files. You'll know this is the problem if you examine `SETUPLOG.TXT` and the last three lines are as shown here:

```
[First Process Tree]
[Build Driver Index File]
Start
```

You need to get rid of all the INF files and then rerun Setup. Here are the steps:

1. At the DOS prompt, remove the `INF` directory's hidden attribute by entering the following command (assuming that Windows 95 is installed in the `C:\WINDOWS` directory):

   ```
   attrib -h c:\windows\inf
   ```

2. Delete all the INF files by entering the following command:

   ```
   del c:\windows\inf\*.*
   ```

3. Rerun Setup, and when you get to the Run Setup Again? dialog box, activate the `Restore Windows files that are changed or corrupted` option.

Install the Windows 95 System Files Manually

If Setup doesn't correctly transfer the new Windows 95 system files to your boot drive, you'll likely get an `Incorrect System Disk` or `Invalid System Disk` error message. If this happens and you created a Windows 95 Startup disk, you can install the system files by hand. Here are the steps to follow:

1. Place the Windows 95 Startup disk in drive A, and restart your computer.

2. When you get to the `A:\` prompt, make a backup copy of the current `MSDOS.SYS` file by entering the following commands (these commands assume that your boot drive is C and that Windows 95 is installed in `C:\WINDOWS`):

   ```
   c:
   cd\windows\command
   attrib c:\msdos.sys -r -s -h
   ren c:\msdos.sys msdos.ok
   ```

3. Transfer the system files from the Startup disk to the hard disk by entering the following commands:

   ```
   a:
   sys c:
   ```

4. Replace the MSDOS.SYS file that SYS.COM created with the copy you renamed in Step 2 by entering the following commands:

```
c:
cd\windows\command
attrib c:\msdos.sys -r -s -h
del c:\msdos.sys
ren c:\msdos.ok msdos.sys
attrib c:\msdos.sys +r +s +h
```

NOTE: SETUP HANGS WITH ADAPTEC AIC-6360 SCSI CONTROLLER

Many computers use the Adaptec AIC-6360 SCSI controller chip. If the chip has been disabled in your computer's CMOS settings, Setup still detects it but can't detect that it has been disabled. So when Setup attempts to load the drivers after restarting, your system will hang. To fix this problem, start Windows 95 in Safe mode (as described earlier), right-click the My Computer icon, and select Properties. In the System Properties dialog box, activate the Device Manager tab, double-click the SCSI Controller item, highlight the SCSI adapter, and click Properties. Deactivate the Original Configuration check box and click OK. Click OK to close the System Properties dialog box, and then restart your computer.

Hardware Problems

Besides hanging during the hardware detection phase (discussed earlier in this chapter), other issues might arise during Setup. This section looks at various hardware-related problems you might come across while attempting to install Windows 95.

During the hardware detection phase, Setup displays the following error message:

SDMErr(80000003): Registry access failed.

This error message tells you that the Registry is damaged. To fix this problem, follow these steps:

1. Restart your computer, and when you see the Starting Windows 95... message, press F8 to display the Windows 95 Startup menu.

2. Select the Safe Mode Command Prompt Only option.

3. When you get to the DOS prompt, enter the following command (if REGEDIT complains about missing data, just ignore it):

   regedit /e reg.txt

4. Enter the following command to regenerate the Registry's internal data structures:

   regedit /c reg.txt

5. Restart your computer and try Setup again.

Setup can't locate a valid boot partition.

As mentioned in Chapter 1, Setup needs a DOS FAT partition to use for the Windows 95 installation. If Setup can't find such a partition, it will generate an error and you'll be unable to continue the installation.

The most obvious problem is that your system has no valid DOS boot partition. You might be using an NTFS or HPFS partition, for example. You'll need to repartition the drive to create a FAT partition for Windows 95.

If you have no other operating system on your computer, check to see whether you can boot from your hard drive. If you can't, there is no valid DOS boot partition. In this case, you should run the DOS FDISK utility to make your primary partition active.

Otherwise, Setup might just be having trouble finding the boot partition. One possible cause is that you've mapped a network drive to the hidden host drive of a compressed disk. For example, the host drive of your compressed disk might be drive H, but you could have accidentally mapped a network drive to drive H as well.

After you set up Windows 95 on your computer, you can no longer boot from a different physical hard disk.

Setup examines all the hard disks in your system and makes sure that only one is the primary active partition (that is, the boot disk). If Setup finds other hard disks that are bootable, the program modifies the boot sector of the disks so that only drive C is bootable. This way, Setup ensures that it can find the boot disk when it restarts the system. If you'd prefer to use a different boot disk, you'll need to use the DOS FDISK utility to set the appropriate drive to be the active primary partition.

Your system has two CD-ROM drives, but Setup doesn't detect one of them.

This problem occurs when Setup installs protected-mode drivers for one of the CD-ROM drives and the second CD-ROM drive is running with real-mode drivers loaded from CONFIG.SYS and AUTOEXEC.BAT. Windows 95 assumes that the real-mode and protected-mode drivers reference the same drive, so no drive letter is assigned to the real-mode driver.

You can force Windows 95 to assign a drive letter to the real-mode driver by adding the /L switch to MSCDEX.EXE in AUTOEXEC.BAT. For example, to assign drive E to the CD-ROM, you'd use the following line in AUTOEXEC.BAT:

```
c:\windows\command\mscdex.exe /l:e
```

When you install Windows 95 on a computer with a Plug and Play system ROM BIOS, system performance is unusually slow after Windows 95 starts for the first time.

When configuring Plug and Play hard disk controllers, Windows 95 must first access the devices in real mode. After the devices have been fully configured after Windows 95 starts for the first time, protected-mode drivers are loaded for compatible hard disk controllers, and performance returns to normal.

To check whether a drive is using MS-DOS compatibility mode, right-click the My Computer icon and select Properties from the context menu that appears. In the System Properties dialog box, shown in Figure 3.2, select the Performance tab, and examine the contents of the Performance group. If any drives are using MS-DOS compatibility mode, the `File System` line will say so, and the specific drives will appear in the `Select an item and then click Details for more information` list box.

FIGURE 3.2.

The Performance tab lets you know whether any drives are using MS-DOS compatibility mode.

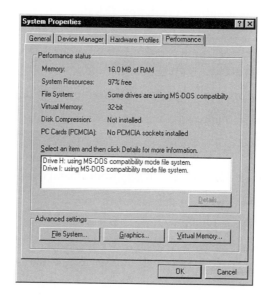

If Setup doesn't prompt you to restart your computer after Windows 95 starts for the first time and Setup finishes the configuration process, restart your computer to ensure that all appropriate protected-mode disk drivers are loaded.

NOTE: MS-DOS COMPATIBILITY MODE INFORMATION

See Chapter 10, "How Windows 95 Handles Hardware," to learn all you need to know about MS-DOS compatibility mode, and about real-mode drivers versus protected-mode drivers.

Setup gives you a "B1" error during installation.

As I mentioned in Chapter 1, you won't be able to install Windows 95 if your computer is a 386 that uses the B1 stepping processor. (Intel manufactured these chips prior to April 1987; many of them also sport a label that says "For 16-bit operations only.") It turns out that the B1 stepping chip, like many people, isn't very good at math. In particular, it has a bug that returns random, erroneous results in 32-bit math operations, which are crucial in Windows 95. You'll need to upgrade your CPU before you can install Windows 95.

Startup Disk Problems

The Windows 95 Startup disk is a crucial troubleshooting tool, and creating one during Setup should be automatic. But what if something goes wrong with the Startup disk? How do you troubleshoot a troubleshooting tool? This section presents a few common Startup disk woes and offers up some easy solutions.

Setup is unable to format the floppy disk that you want to use as your Startup disk (or you see a `device not ready` error).

This problem can occur if you insert a 2.0 MB or 2.88 MB floppy disk in the drive. Windows 95 doesn't support floppy disks with a capacity greater than 1.44 MB.

Setup doesn't prompt you to create a Startup Disk.

If Setup doesn't prompt you to create a Startup disk, a mounted DoubleSpace (or DriveSpace) compressed floppy disk is in drive A, and Setup has incorrectly identified drive A as a local fixed disk. This is a bug in Windows 95.

Use either of the following methods to work around this problem:

- Remove the compressed floppy disk from drive A before starting Windows 95 Setup.
- Create the Startup disk after Setup is finished.

If you don't update your Startup disk either when you install Microsoft Plus! or when you run DriveSpace 3, you might not be able to boot your system by using the Startup disk.

One of the tidbits you get with Microsoft Plus! is DriveSpace 3, an enhanced version of the Windows 95 compression utility. If the Startup disk hasn't been updated for DriveSpace 3, it won't be able to mount a DriveSpace 3 compressed volume file (CVF) or repair a damaged DriveSpace 3 CVF.

If Windows 95 starts normally, you can create a new Startup disk with updated files from within Windows 95. This action is covered in Chapter 15, "Protecting Your Windows 95 Investment."

If you can't start Windows 95 normally, you have to replace the `SCANDISK.EXE` and `DRVSPACE.BIN` files on the Startup disk with updated versions compatible with DriveSpace 3. You'll find these files on the Microsoft Plus! CD-ROM, in the `\WIN95` folder.

To update the Startup disk, follow these steps:

1. Boot your computer to a command prompt, and then insert the Startup disk in drive A.
2. Insert the Microsoft Plus! CD-ROM in the CD-ROM drive.
3. Copy the updated files from the Microsoft Plus! CD-ROM to your hard drive by entering the following command (replace *drive* with the letter of your CD-ROM drive):

```
copy drive:\win95
```

4. Copy SCANPLUS.EXE to A:\SCANDISK.EXE and DRVPLUS.BIN to A:\DRVSPACE.BIN by entering the following two commands:

```
copy scanplus.exe a:\scandisk.exe /y
copy drvplus.bin a:\drvspace.bin /y
```

5. Restart your computer with the Startup disk in the drive.

Setup Error Messages

Unless Setup hangs or if it comes across a particularly head-scratching problem, it's pretty good about spitting out error messages to help fill you in on what's happening (or not happening, as the case may be). Some of these messages, however, are cryptic, to say the least. This section looks at a few common error messages, deciphers them for the benefit of mere mortals like us, and offers solutions to the underlying problems.

Setup reports the following error message:

```
Incorrect DOS version
```

This error usually appears if you're using DOS 3.1 or earlier. You need to upgrade to a later version of DOS before you can install Windows 95.

This error might also occur if you're using the 386MAX memory manager. Disable the 386MAX commands in CONFIG.SYS and AUTOEXEC.BAT, reboot, and run Setup again.

When running Setup from the DOS prompt, you receive the following error message:

```
Standard Mode: Fault in MS-DOS Extender
```

This error probably means there's a device conflict in the upper memory region (the area between 640 KB and 1 MB). There are two ways around this problem:

- Disable EMM386 (the program that gives drivers access to upper memory blocks) in CONFIG.SYS by appending REM and a space to the left of the DEVICE= line that loads EMM386.EXE.

- Run Setup from Windows 3.x.

During the installation of Windows 95, you receive the following error message:

```
Setup Detection Warning
Warning SU-0014
Setup has found a hardware device on your computer that is not responding.
Click Continue to try this device again. If problems persist, click Exit
Setup, quit all programs, remove floppy disks from their drives, and turn
your computer off. Then, turn your computer on and run Setup again
(choose Safe Recovery when prompted).
```

This error message can be caused by any of the following conditions:

- The network has stopped responding.
- The CD-ROM has stopped responding.

■ The floppy disk drive has stopped responding.

■ You no longer have access to the hard disk to complete the installation process.

■ An unsupported device has been detected.

Following the recommendation in the error message (that is, turning your computer off and then back on, and then running Setup again and choosing Safe Recovery) might correct this problem. If it doesn't, you'll have to figure out which of the previously listed conditions exists and then correct the problem (or problems).

When you're reinstalling Windows 95, the following error message appears when you try to start Setup:

```
This program cannot be run due to restrictions in effect on this computer.
Please contact your system administrator.
```

When you click OK, Setup continues normally.

This error message occurs when you're reinstalling Windows 95 on a system on which System Policies have been used to disable the DOS command prompt. (I'll show you how to customize your system with the System Policy Editor in Chapter 31, "Windows 95 Networking.") When Setup tries to run the real-mode version of ScanDisk, it fails because the DOS prompt is unavailable.

To work around this problem, use either of the following methods:

■ Contact your system administrator to have the DOS prompt enabled again.

■ Run Setup with the /IS switch to prevent Setup from running ScanDisk.

When you try to set up Windows 95, you receive the following error message (where *x* is the directory where you told Setup to install Windows 95—for example, C:\WINDOWS):

```
The path x is invalid
```

You'll receive this error message only if the drive you specified has exactly zero bytes available. If more than zero bytes of hard disk space are available, but not enough for Windows 95 to be successfully installed, you receive the error message `Insufficient disk space` or `Not enough disk space`.

To resolve this problem, either install Windows 95 to a different drive or make additional hard disk drive space available.

While upgrading from within Windows 3.x, Setup displays the Active MS-DOS Session Detected dialog box with error SU0358, shown in Figure 3.3.

Setup refuses to continue if it detects a DOS program running on your system. You'll need to shut down the program (by pressing Alt-Tab until its window is activated and then exiting the program).

FIGURE 3.3.

Setup displays this error message if you have a DOS program running.

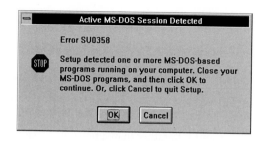

Some DOS-based programs, however, run in the background and so aren't visible when you press Alt-Tab to cycle through the open programs. They don't even show up if you press Ctrl-Esc to open the Task List. (The WinPrinter driver by LaserMaster is an example of a DOS-based program that runs in the background.) You'll need to quit Setup (by clicking Cancel) and then disable such programs by trying either of the following methods:

- Look inside your Startup group to see whether DOS programs are being loaded from there. If so, delete their icons.

- Edit WIN.INI and remove the startup commands for such programs from the Load= or Run= lines.

Restart Windows and then try Setup again.

When you're installing Windows 95, you receive the following error message:

```
Generic install error
Invalid GenInstall INF file. -[Exiting with error code = 402(0x192).]
```

When you click OK, the Setup program exits.

This error occurs if the Windows 3.x WIN.INI file contains a Load line that's missing the equal sign (=). During Setup, SETUPX.DLL parses the WIN.INI file, and MBASE.INF searches for the Load= entry. (MBASE.INF exists only while Setup is running. When Setup is finished, this file is deleted. You won't find this file in the Windows\INF subdirectory.) If the entry doesn't have an equal sign, Setup bails out.

Edit the WIN.INI file and either remove the Load line or add an equal sign to it (so that it reads Load=), and then run the Windows 95 Setup program again.

When Windows 95 restarts after you run Setup, you receive the following error message, and your system hangs:

```
Please wait while Setup updates your Configuration files.
This may take a few seconds...
Windows could not combine VxDs into a monolithic file before starting.
Windows may not start or run properly.
If Windows fails to start, run SETUP again.
Press any key to continue...
```

If this error occurs, it probably means that either you don't have at least 3 MB of free space after installing Windows 95 or your hard disk contains bad sectors.

To correct this problem, try any of the following fixes:

- Increase the hard disk space available by rebooting your computer and pressing the F5 key when you see the `Starting Windows 95...` message. Use the DOS `DEL` command to delete unnecessary files and make additional hard disk space available.
- Use a hard disk utility, such as ScanDisk, to correct the bad sectors or mark them as being bad.
- Run Setup from DOS rather than a previous version of Windows.

After you install Windows 95 and restart the system, Setup dumps you at the DOS prompt with the following error message:

```
Incorrect MS-DOS version
Enter the name of Command Interpreter (e.g., C:\WINDOWS\COMMAND.COM)
```

This problem can occur if `SETVER.EXE` is being loaded in `CONFIG.SYS` and has a setting indicating that `COMMAND.COM` should look for a version of MS-DOS earlier than 7.0. When Windows 95 is installed, the new `SETVER.EXE` assumes the settings of the currently loaded `SETVER.EXE` in an effort to maintain compatibility with existing DOS-based applications.

Reboot, and when you see the `Starting Windows 95...` message, press F5 to bypass the startup files. Here are the steps to follow to fix this problem:

1. Change to the main Windows directory by entering the following command (assuming that Windows is installed in the `\Windows` folder):

   `cd\windows`

2. Rename the `SETVER.EXE` file by entering the following command:

   `ren setver.exe setver.old`

3. Restart your system (Windows 95 loads at this point).

4. Open the Start menu and select Programs | MS-DOS Prompt.

5. Change to the main Windows directory using the same command you used in step 1.

6. Rename the `SETVER.EXE` file again by entering the following command:

   `ren setver.old setver.exe`

7. Remove the `COMMAND.COM` entry by entering the following command:

   `setver command.com /d`

8. Restart the computer to put the SETVER changes into effect.

Uninstall Problems

This section takes you through a few difficulties you might encounter while trying to uninstall Windows 95.

When you try to uninstall Windows 95, you receive the following error message when your computer restarts:

```
Uninstall is unable to write to the MBR
```

When this problem occurs, the uninstall procedure can't be completed, and you might not be able to boot the computer from the hard disk. This problem can occur when any of the following conditions exists:

- The hard disk's master boot record (MBR) is damaged.
- A software or hardware-level virus scanning program is protecting the MBR.
- You're using third-party disk partitioning software.
- Your computer has been infected with a boot-sector virus.

Use the following solutions to try to resolve the problem. If you can't boot your computer from the hard disk, use your Windows 95 Start disk instead.

If the MBR is protected by virus scanning software: If you suspect that a virus scanning program is preventing Uninstall from writing to the MBR, disable the virus scanning program by editing the CONFIG.SYS or AUTOEXEC.BAT file to disable the program temporarily. Place the word REM (followed by a space) at the beginning of the line or lines used to load the virus scanning program. After you make this change, restart the computer.

If the MBR is protected by a hardware-level virus scanning program: To disable hardware-level virus detection, run your computer's CMOS configuration utility, and disable the virus detection.

If your system uses third-party partitioning software: If third-party partitioning software is preventing Uninstall from writing to the MBR, refer to the software's documentation for information about restoring the previous MBR or modifying the current MBR.

If you suspect that your system is infected with a boot-sector virus: If you suspect that your computer has been infected with a boot-sector virus, use an anti-virus program to detect and remove the virus.

After you resolve the problem, start your computer with your Windows 95 Startup disk, and then run the uninstall command.

When you try to uninstall Windows 95, you receive one of the following error messages:

```
The file C:\W95undo.dat cannot be read.
Error Code -6: Unexpected end of file.
The file C:\W95undo.dat is invalid or incomplete.
Error code -4: Invalid signature.
```

As you learned in Chapter 2, when you install Windows 95, you're prompted to back up the current system files. If you choose to do so, the Windows folder and all its contents are backed up to a hidden, compressed file called `W95UNDO.DAT`. This file is used to restore the previous version of Windows. The preceding error messages indicate that `W95UNDO.DAT` is missing or damaged, which means you can't uninstall Windows 95. Use the procedure outlined in Chapter 2, in the section titled "Uninstalling Windows 95 by Hand," to remove Windows 95.

After you uninstall Windows 95, Windows 3.x reports a `Corrupt Swapfile` error.

This error is quite common after uninstalling Window 95. All you have to do is click OK when Windows 3.x asks whether you want to delete the current swap file. When Windows 3.x loads, start the Control Panel, open the 386 Enhanced icon, click Virtual Memory, click Change>>, and select None from the Type drop-down list. Exit the dialog boxes and restart Windows when prompted. After you're back in Windows, open Control Panel's 386 Enhanced icon again to set up a permanent swap file.

You have video problems in Windows 3.x after uninstalling Windows 95.

Windows 95 doesn't always do a good job of resetting your old Windows 3.x video driver. Check the driver in Windows 3.x, and reinstall if necessary.

Miscellaneous Problems

After you install Windows 95 in a directory other than the current Windows directory, Windows 95 doesn't start; instead, the boot process invokes the previous version of Windows, or the system hangs after the Windows logo screen is displayed.

This problem occurs when the previous version of Windows is automatically loaded at startup using the following commands in the `AUTOEXEC.BAT` file (assuming that the previous version of Windows is installed in the `WIN31` directory):

```
cd\win31
win
```

When you're installing Windows 95, Setup creates the `AUTOEXEC.W40` file based on the existing `AUTOEXEC.BAT` file. Windows 95 removes the command to load the previous version of Windows (that is, `WIN`) but fails to remove the change directory command. In this configuration, Windows 95 executes the `WIN` command from the `C:\WIN31` folder and starts the previous version of Windows.

Follow these steps to correct this problem:

1. Perform an interactive boot by restarting the computer and pressing the F8 key when the `Starting Windows 95...` prompt appears.
2. Answer Yes to all prompts except the `cd\win31` (or whatever) prompt; answer No to this prompt. This avoids the change into the Windows 3.x directory and allows Windows 95 to start.
3. In Windows 95, use Notepad or another text editor to open `AUTOEXEC.BAT`.
4. Remove the `cd\win31` line, save the file, and exit.

The next time you start your system. Windows 95 will load normally.

Setup displays the following error message:

```
Cannot Write to Disk
Setup cannot write to the Windows 95 Setup disk.
Make sure that the disk is not write-protected and is properly
inserted in the drive. Then click Retry.
```

When you install Windows 95 from floppy disks for the first time, the Setup program writes the name and company you enter in the Setup Wizard's User Information dialog box to Disk 2. If the disk is write-protected, the error message just shown is displayed when Setup tries to write to the disk. You won't be able to proceed until you remove the write protection on Disk 2. Remove the disk and find the small, movable plastic tab on the back of the disk. Slide the tab so that it covers the hole and clicks into place, and then reinsert the disk in the drive. Click Retry to continue with Setup.

When you install Windows 95, Setup comments out some of the commands—REN, COPY, MOVE, and DEL—in the AUTOEXEC.BAT file.

This behavior is by design. Setup disables these lines to prevent changes from being made to files that might be required for Setup to finish successfully.

After Windows 95 is installed and working correctly, use any text editor (such as Notepad) to edit the AUTOEXEC.BAT file and remove the REM command from the beginning of lines that you want to re-enable.

When you upgrade Windows 3.1 to Windows 95, you find duplicate FON (font) files in the Fonts and System folders of your main Windows folder.

Setup does a lot of things, but one of the things it *doesn't* do is delete the font files (those with the FON extension) in the System folder. Why? Because these files are in use (by Windows 3.x) when you upgrade to Windows 95. After Windows 95 is installed, however, these files are no longer needed because Windows 95 has its own font files safely tucked away in the Fonts folder.

To delete the FON files in the System folder, follow these steps:

1. Restart your computer. When you see the Starting Windows 95... message, press F8, and choose Safe Mode Command Prompt Only from the Startup menu.

2. Change to the System folder by entering the following command (assuming that Windows 95 is installed in the \Windows folder):

   ```
   cd windows\system
   ```

3. Delete the FON files by entering the following command:

   ```
   del *.fon
   ```

4. Restart your computer normally.

3

TROUBLESHOOTING
SETUP WOES

While you're reinstalling Windows 95, Setup asks for the original installation disks or the Windows 95 CD-ROM in order to copy files that are already present on the hard disk.

During a reinstall, Setup deletes a Registry key that contains the list of Plug and Play–related files that have been installed. Because the list is empty, Setup doesn't know that the driver files are present and copies them again.

There's no real solution to this one. You just have to provide Setup with the requested disks or CD-ROM, or choose to skip the requested files.

When you start your computer, you see the `Starting Windows 95...` message, followed by the `It is now safe to turn off your computer` message.

This behavior can occur if the `VMM32.VXD` file is missing or damaged. There *is* a version of `VMM32.VXD` on the Windows 95 disks and CD-ROM. Extracting this version of the file won't solve the problem, however, because it's an incomplete version of the file. You'll have to run Setup again to re-create a system-specific `VMM32.VXD` file. Here are the steps to follow:

1. Restart your computer. When you see the `Starting Windows 95...` message, press the F8 key and choose Command Prompt Only from the Startup menu.

2. Enter the following command to change to the `System` folder (assuming that Windows 95 is installed in the `\Windows` folder):

   ```
   cd \windows\system
   ```

3. Enter the following command:

   ```
   ren vmm32.vxd vmm32.old
   ```

4. Repeat step 1.

5. Reinstall Windows 95.

When you reinstall Windows 95, Setup creates a folder named `!$!$!$!$.$!$` instead of a folder named `Program Files`.

This behavior can occur if you change the DOS name of the `Program Files` folder from `PROGRA~1` to something else. Setup can't install files to the `Program Files` folder because it tracks the folder's DOS name as `PROGRA~1`.

To restore the MS-DOS name for the `Program Files` folder and verify that the programs function correctly, follow these steps:

1. In Explorer, right-click the `Program Files` folder, and then click Properties on the menu that appears. Verify that the folder's DOS name isn't `PROGRA~1`.

2. Remove the `!$!$!$!$.$!$!` folder and all its contents.

3. Rename the `Program Files` folder to `Test`. Acknowledge the error messages that occur.

4. Rename the `Test` folder to `Program Files`. Acknowledge the error messages that occur.

5. Reinstall any of the following programs you want to use:

> WordPad
> Paint
> Backup
> HyperTerminal
> The Microsoft Network
> Microsoft Exchange

6. Verify that you can still use the Start button to start any other programs you manually installed in the `Program Files` folder.

When you start Windows or Windows for Workgroups versions 3.1 or 3.11 on a computer that has Windows 95 and dual boot installed, you receive a warning about a corrupt swap file. This occurs only after you run Windows 95 and then boot the previous version of Windows.

When Windows 95 is installed to a clean directory on a computer that also has Windows 3.x or Windows for Workgroups installed, Windows 95 attempts to share a swap file with the existing Windows installation. It does so to save disk space. In most cases, this activity causes no conflict. If, however, you change the virtual memory setting from within the previous version of Windows, or if you reinstall Windows 95 over the existing Windows 95 directory, when you run Windows 95 again, it might change the swap file in such a way that Windows 3.1 displays the `Corrupt Swapfile` message.

To work around this behavior, delete the `PagingFile` and `MinPagingFileSize` lines from the `SYSTEM.INI` file so that Windows 95 has its own swap file.

To save disk space, you can change the Windows 3.x virtual memory settings to use a temporary swap file (as described in Chapter 1). If you want Windows 3.x to use a permanent swap file, run its Virtual Memory applet to reconstruct the swap file.

You want to change the path from which Windows 95 Setup obtains source files.

If, for example, you originally installed Windows 95 from floppy disks, but later obtained a Windows 95 CD-ROM, you might want to change the Setup source path to retrieve files from the CD-ROM rather than from the floppy disks. This task involves editing the Windows 95 Registry, so I'll leave this solution until you've examined the Registry in Part II, "Unleashing Windows Customization and Optimization." You'll get an initial look at the Registry in Chapter 11, "Introducing the Windows 95 Registry." The solution appears in Chapter 12, "Hacking the Registry."

You want to extract a file from one of Windows 95's cabinet (.CAB) files, but you're not sure which cabinet file to use.

You can find out the contents of any .CAB file by running the Windows 95 EXTRACT utility with the /D parameter:

```
EXTRACT /D d:\Win95\filename.CAB
```

d   The letter of the CD-ROM drive that contains the Windows 95 install disk.

filename.CAB   The name of the .CAB file.

Running EXTRACT with /D prints a listing of the .CAB file's contents.

However, because there are 20 separate .CAB files, running EXTRACT on all of them would get tedious in a hurry. Instead, here's a small batch file that writes the contents of every .CAB file to a text file:

```
@ECHO OFF
ECHO Writing CAB file contents...
FOR %%f In (D:\WIN95\*.CAB) DO EXTRACT /D %%f >> C:\CABFILES.TXT
ECHO.
ECHO CAB file contents now stored in C:\CABFILES.TXT
```

This batch file uses the FOR command to run EXTRACT /D on every .CAB file. (See Appendix F, "A Batch File Primer," for information on FOR and other batch file commands.) Note that the batch file assumes your CD-ROM is drive D; you'll need to modify this as necessary. In each case, the listing is redirected into a text file named CABFILES.TXT.

To find the file you want to extract, load this text file into WordPad (it's too big for Notepad to handle), and do a search for the filename.

Summary

This chapter rounded out your Setup education by examining a few troubleshooting issues related to Windows 95 installation. You learned how Setup's Safe Recovery mode operates, you learned what to do if Setup won't start or if it hangs, and you saw a number of solutions to common installation problems.

Here's a list of chapters where you'll find related information:

- For the full nitty-gritty about the installation procedure, see Chapter 1, "Understanding the Windows 95 Installation," and Chapter 2, "Running the Windows 95 Setup."

- For more information on the various options in the Windows 95 Startup menu, see Chapter 4, "Start It Your Way: Understanding Windows 95 Setup."

- You can find hardware concerns, including how to install new hardware devices and drivers, in Chapter 10, "How Windows 95 Handles Hardware."

- The Registry is a major weapon for unleashing Windows 95, so I cover it Chapter 11, "Introducing the Windows 95 Registry," and Chapter 12, "Hacking the Registry."

- To learn more about viruses, see Chapter 15, "Protecting Your Windows 95 Investment."

- I'll give you the lowdown on batch files in Appendix F, "A Batch File Primer."

Start It Your Way: Understanding Windows 95 Startup

CHAPTER 4

IN THIS CHAPTER

> *The White Rabbit put on his spectacles. "Where shall I begin, your Majesty?" he asked.*
>
> *"Begin at the beginning," the King said, very gravely, "and go on till you come to the end: then stop."*
>
> *—Lewis Carroll,* Alice's Adventures in Wonderland

Assuming that Windows 95 is now safely installed, we can now begin our journey, appropriately enough, at the beginning: the startup process. At first blush, this might seem like a surprising topic for an entire chapter. After all, the Windows 95 startup procedure gives new meaning to the term *no-brainer:* You turn on your system, and a few seconds later, Windows 95 reports for duty. What's to write about?

You'd be surprised. The progress of a typical boot appears uneventful only because Windows 95 uses a whole host of default options for startup. By changing these defaults, you can take control of the startup process and make Windows 95 start *your* way. This chapter takes you through the entire startup process, from go to whoa, and shows you the options you can use to customize it.

The Boot Process, from Powerup to Startup

To better help you understand your Windows 95 startup options, let's take a closer look at what happens each time you fire up your machine. Although a computer performs dozens of actions during the boot process, most of them appeal to wireheads and other hardware hackers. (A *wirehead* is, broadly speaking, an expert in the hardware aspects of PCs.) For our purposes, we can reduce the entire journey down to the following 12-step program:

1. When you flip the switch on your computer (or press the Restart button, if the machine is already running), the system performs various hardware checks. The system's microprocessor executes the ROM BIOS code, which, among other things, performs the Power-On Self Test (POST). The POST detects and tests memory, ports, and basic devices such as the video adapter, keyboard, and disk drives. (You hear your floppy disk motors kick in briefly and the drive lights come on.) If the system has a Plug and Play BIOS, the BIOS also enumerates and tests the PnP-compliant devices in the system. If the POST goes well, you hear a single beep.

2. Now the BIOS code looks for a boot sector on drive A (the drive light illuminates once more). If no disk is in the drive, the BIOS turns its attention to the hard disk and looks for the active (that is, bootable) partition and its boot sector.

NOTE: THE STARTUP DISK SECRET

This explains why the Windows 95 Startup disk (see Chapter 1, "Understanding the Windows 95 Installation") lets you regain control of your system in the event of a hard drive crash. The BIOS first looks for a bootable disk in drive A. If it finds one, it bypasses the hard drive altogether. This is also why your Startup disk must be readable by drive A: The BIOS normally doesn't attempt to boot from drive B (although some system have CMOS settings that let you reverse drives A and B).

3. With the boot sector located, the BIOS program runs the boot sector as a program. The Windows 95 boot sector runs IO.SYS, which is basically just DOS. IO.SYS (which combines the functionality of both IO.SYS and MSDOS.SYS from previous DOS versions), initializes some device drivers and performs a few real-mode chores.

4. IO.SYS reads MSDOS.SYS. Note that MSDOS.SYS does *not* have the same functionality as MSDOS.SYS in previous DOS versions. The Windows 95 MSDOS.SYS is a text file that controls various startup options. (See "Custom Startups with MSDOS.SYS" later in this chapter.) Note too that you'll see the Starting Windows 95... message after IO.SYS has finished with MSDOS.SYS.

5. IO.SYS reads CONFIG.SYS, if it exists, and processes its statements (real-mode device drivers, and so forth).

6. IO.SYS reads AUTOEXEC.BAT, if it exists, and processes its commands.

7. IO.SYS reads the Registry and loads a number of drivers and settings. Here's a partial list:

> **DBLSPACE.BIN or DRVSPACE.BIN:** The disk compression driver.
>
> **HIMEM.SYS:** The real-mode extended memory manager. Note that IO.SYS doesn't load this driver if a HIMEM.SYS line already exists in CONFIG.SYS.
>
> **IFSHLP.SYS:** The Installable File System Helper, which helps load VFAT and other Windows 95 installable file systems.
>
> **SETVER.EXE:** A program that handles operating system version number requests from legacy applications. If an application requires a particular version of DOS, SETVER can "lie" to the application and thus fool the program into running properly.
>
> **DOS=HIGH:** Loads DOS into the high memory area (HMA). If you load EMM386.EXE in CONFIG.SYS, IO.SYS also includes the UMB parameter, which enables memory management using upper memory blocks. Note, however, that IO.SYS doesn't load EMM386; if you need to use it, include the appropriate DEVICE line in CONFIG.SYS.
>
> **FILES=30:** Determines the number of file handles to create. Windows 95 doesn't use this setting, and it's included only for backward compatibility with legacy programs. If you have DOS programs that require a higher value, include a FILES setting in CONFIG.SYS.

4

UNDERSTANDING WINDOWS 95 STARTUP

LASTRIVE=Z: Determines the last drive letter that can be assigned to a disk drive. This is another setting that's needed only for backward compatibility; Windows 95 doesn't use this setting.

BUFFERS=30: Determines the number of file buffers to create for applications using file I/O calls to IO.SYS; it's not required by Windows 95. To specify a different value, include a BUFFERS line in CONFIG.SYS.

STACKS=9,256: Determines the number of stack frames and the size of each frame. For backward compatibility only. To specify different values, add a STACKS line to CONFIG.SYS.

SHELL=COMMAND.COM /P: Determines the name of the command-line interpreter.

FCBS=4: Determines the number of file control blocks that can be open at any one time. For backward compatibility only.

CAUTION: DON'T USE VALUES LOWER THAN THE DEFAULTS

If you plan on adding (or modifying) FILES, BUFFERS, or STACKS in CONFIG.SYS, make sure that the values you use are greater than or equal to those used in IO.SYS.

---

8. IO.SYS switches the processor into protected mode and then calls on VMM32.VXD to load the Windows 95 protected-mode drivers.

9. Plug and Play information— new devices detected during the initial boot phase, removed devices, hardware conflicts, and so on—is processed. Windows 95 might ask you to insert a source disk to load new drivers.

10. Windows 95 is started and the Windows 95 GUI and other core subsystems are loaded.

11. Windows 95 prompts you for a password if you're logging onto a network or if you specified a password for the Windows logon.

12. The contents of the Startup folder are processed.

The three most obvious ways to customize this startup procedure would be to insert a bootable disk (such as the Windows 95 Startup disk) before the POST is done, modify CONFIG.SYS, and modify AUTOEXEC.BAT. However, Windows 95 also provides some less obvious routes for personalizing your startup:

■ Invoke the Windows 95 Startup menu while the message Starting Windows 95... is displayed.

■ Edit the MSDOS.SYS file to change the default startup options.

■ Use one of the first two methods to boot to the DOS prompt, and then run Windows from there with command-line switches.

■ Add programs or documents to the Windows 95 Startup folder.

The next three sections cover the first three of these techniques. To learn how to add applications and documents to the Startup folder, see Chapter 13, "Working with Files and Folders."

Custom Startups with the Windows 95 Startup Menu

In previous versions of Windows, you had to run the win command (the WIN.COM file) to start Windows. This was handy because if you were having trouble with Windows (a garbled display, for example), you could always boot to the DOS prompt, fix the problem (by editing an .INI file, for example), and then restart. Even if you had the win command in AUTOEXEC.BAT, you could always bypass it by commenting it out.

Although Windows 95 still has WIN.COM, you never really use it because, as you've seen, Windows 95 loads automatically. So what do you do if you need to bypass Windows 95? You could put a bootable disk in drive A, but that's not always convenient. Instead, Windows 95 comes with a Startup menu that gives you various options for loading Windows 95, booting to the DOS prompt, or even loading your old DOS version.

To see the menu, press F8 at any time after the POST is complete and before the Starting Windows 95... message disappears. Here's an example of the Startup menu:

```
Microsoft Windows 95 Startup Menu
=====================================
    1. Normal
    2. Logged (\BOOTLOG.TXT)
    3. Safe mode
    4. Safe mode without compression
    5. Safe mode with network support
    6. Step-by-step confirmation
    7. Command prompt only
    8. Safe mode command prompt only
    9. Previous version of MS-DOS
Enter a choice: 1
```

The layout of the Startup menu depends on your Windows 95 configuration, as explained here:

- You'll see only the Safe mode with network support option if you installed network support with Windows 95.

- You'll see only the Safe mode without compression option if you have a drive that has been compressed.

- You'll see only the Previous version of MS-DOS option if you installed Windows 95 on a machine that had an existing version of DOS. (You also need the line BootMulti=1 in MSDOS.SYS, as described later in this chapter.)

The Normal option just loads Windows 95 in the usual fashion. You can use the other options to control the rest of the startup procedure.

4

UNDERSTANDING
WINDOWS 95
STARTUP

Logged (\BOOTLOG.TXT)

This option is the same as the Normal option, except that Windows 95 logs the boot process in a text file named BOOTLOG.TXT, which you'll find in the boot drive's root folder. BOOTLOG.TXT is useful as a troubleshooting tool, especially if Windows 95 is hanging during startup. (See "Troubleshooting Windows 95 Startup" later in this chapter.)

Safe mode

If you're having trouble with Windows 95—for example, if a corrupt or incorrect video driver is mangling your display, or if Windows 95 won't start—you can use the Safe mode option to run a stripped-down version of Windows 95. Note that if Windows 95 failed to start properly, rebooting will display the Windows 95 Startup menu automatically, with the Safe mode option highlighted. You'll also see the following message:

```
Warning: Windows did not finish loading on the previous attempt.
Choose Safe mode, to start Windows with a minimal set of drivers.
```

Here's what happens when Windows 95 boots in Safe mode:

1. Windows 95 bypasses CONFIG.SYS, AUTOEXEC.BAT, and the Registry.

2. HIMEM.SYS is loaded. Note that Safe mode does *not* process any command-line switches for HIMEM.SYS. If your system requires switches (such as /M, the machine switch), you won't be able to run Safe mode. For an alternative, see "Troubleshooting Windows 95 Startup" later in this chapter.

3. IFSHLP.SYS, a real-mode file that helps install the Windows 95 Installable File System (IFS), is loaded. The IFS adds support for VFAT, CDFS (CD-ROM file system), and other Windows 95 file systems.

4. The MSDOS.SYS file is checked for the location of the Windows 95 files. (I'll talk more about MSDOS.SYS later.)

5. If the Windows 95 files are found, the command win /d:m (which enables a Safe-mode boot) is executed, and COMMAND.COM is skipped. If the Windows 95 files aren't found, COMMAND.COM is executed instead. (For more info on command-line switches for starting Windows 95, see "Command-Line Switches for Starting Windows 95" later in this chapter.)

6. Windows 95 loads only the virtual device drivers (VxDs) for the keyboard, mouse, and standard VGA display.

7. Windows 95 processes SYSTEM.INI and WIN.INI as detailed here:

   - The [Boot] and [386Enh] sections of the SYSTEM.INI file are bypassed.

   - However, Windows 95 *does* run the shell= and drivers= lines from SYSTEM.INI's [Boot] section.

   - The Load= and Run= lines in the [Windows] section of WIN.INI are bypassed.

8. Windows 95 resizes the desktop to a resolution of 640×480 using the Standard VGA display driver.

9. The dialog box shown in Figure 4.1 appears to remind you that Windows 95 is running in Safe mode. Click OK to finish loading Windows 95.

FIGURE 4.1.

This dialog box appears each time you start Windows 95 in Safe mode.

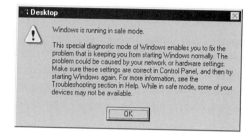

When Windows 95 finally loads, the desktop reminds you that you're in Safe mode by displaying Safe mode in each corner, as shown in Figure 4.2.

FIGURE 4.2.

Windows 95 running in Safe mode.

Safe mode without compression

If you select this Startup menu item, Windows 95 boots in Safe mode, but it doesn't load the drivers necessary for accessing a compressed disk drive. Use this option if you suspect that your system problems are being caused by either a wacky compressed drive or a corrupted compression driver.

Safe mode with network support

This option is similar to Safe mode, except that Windows 95 also loads real-mode device drivers for network support. This is handy if you need to access a network resource to, say, download an updated device driver.

Step-by-step confirmation

This option lets you step through each command in IO.SYS, CONFIG.SYS, and AUTOEXEC.BAT and confirm whether you want Windows 95 to run the command. This technique is invaluable for isolating problems. By stepping though the commands, you can watch your screen for error messages and try to narrow the problem to a specific command or driver. (For more details, see the section "A Step-by-Step Strategy" later in this chapter.)

When you select this option, Windows 95 prompts you like this:

```
Load DoubleSpace driver [Enter=Y,Esc=N]?
```

To load the driver or run the command, press Enter or Y; to bypass the command or driver, press Esc or N.

Command prompt only

This option boots you to DOS; it doesn't load the Windows 95 GUI, and it doesn't process Windows 95's protected-mode drivers. This option does, however, process CONFIG.SYS and AUTOEXEC.BAT, if you have them.

This option boots quickly to the DOS prompt, so it's useful for running DOS programs or performing quick file maintenance chores. When you're at the prompt, you can start Windows 95 by typing win and pressing Enter. You'll want to use this option each time you need to start Windows 95 with command-line switches.

Safe mode command prompt only

This option runs Safe mode, but it boots you to DOS without loading the Windows 95 GUI or any protected-mode drivers. CONFIG.SYS and AUTOEXEC.BAT are also bypassed.

Previous version of MS-DOS

If your system had an existing version of DOS when you installed Windows 95, Setup renames your old startup files and saves them in the root directory as IO.DOS, MSDOS.DOS, COMMAND.DOS, CONFIG.DOS, and AUTOEXEC.DOS. When you select the Previous version of MS-DOS option, Windows 95 takes the following actions:

- Renames IO.SYS to WINBOOT.SYS, MSDOS.SYS to MSDOS.W40, COMMAND.COM to COMMAND.W40, CONFIG.SYS to CONFIG.W40, and AUTOEXEC.BAT to AUTOEXEC.W40.

- Renames IO.DOS to IO.SYS, MSDOS.DOS to MSDOS.SYS, COMMAND.DOS to COMMAND.COM, CONFIG.DOS to CONFIG.SYS, and AUTOEXEC.DOS to AUTOEXEC.BAT.

Windows 95 then boots your system, and your previous version of DOS loads.

Shortcut Keys for Startup Menu Options

To save a bit of time, Windows 95 recognizes several shortcut keys for some of the Startup menu options. These are called *BootKeys*. I've spelled out the available keys and key combinations in Table 4.1. As before, you can press the key or key combination any time after the POST ends and before the `Starting Windows 95...` message disappears.

Table 4.1. BootKeys for Windows 95 Startup options.

BootKey	*Startup Menu Equivalent*
F4	`Previous version of MS-DOS`
F5	`Safe mode`
Shift-F5	`Safe mode command prompt only`
Ctrl-F5	`Safe mode without compression`
F6	`Safe mode with network support`
Shift-F8	`Step-by-step confirmation`

Custom Startups with MSDOS.SYS

In days of yore, before "Windows 95" and "hype" were synonyms, DOS used two system files to pull itself up by its own bootstraps. Those system files were IO.SYS, which provided the system initialization code, and MSDOS.SYS, which was called by IO.SYS and which served to load the basic system drivers, determine equipment status, and perform a few other first-thing-in-the-morning routines.

In the Windows 95 scheme of things, however, these MSDOS.SYS functions have been rolled into IO.SYS, and the new MSDOS.SYS is a text file that controls certain Windows 95 startup parameters. This section shows you how to edit MSDOS.SYS and explains all the options you can use to customize your startup.

Opening MSDOS.SYS

MSDOS.SYS is a read-only, hidden system file that resides in the root folder of your boot drive (usually drive C). To view and edit this file, you need to make a few adjustments, as described in the following steps:

1. In Explorer, select View | Options to display the Options dialog box.
2. Activate the `Show all files` option and click OK.
3. In the Folders pane, highlight the root folder of your boot drive.

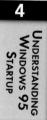

4

UNDERSTANDING
WINDOWS 95
STARTUP

4. Find `Msdos.sys` in the contents pane, right-click it, and select Properties from the context menu. The Msdos.sys Properties dialog box, shown in Figure 4.3, appears.

FIGURE 4.3.

Use this dialog box to adjust the read-only attribute of `MSDOS.SYS`.

5. Deactivate the `Read-only` check box and click OK.

NOTE: EDITING MSDOS.SYS FROM THE COMMAND LINE

If you need to edit `MSDOS.SYS` from the command line (by using `EDIT.COM`), enter the following command to change the file's attributes:

```
attrib -r -h -s c:\msdos.sys
```

(Note that this command assumes drive C: is your boot drive. If that isn't the case, you'll need to edit the command accordingly.) After you've finished editing the file, run the following command to reset the attributes:

```
attrib +r +h +s c:\msdos.sys
```

You can now use Notepad or some other text editor to open the file. When you do, you'll see a file similar to the one shown in Figure 4.4. Note that `MSDOS.SYS` is divided into two sections—[Paths] and [Options]—which I'll discuss next. When you've finished editing the file, save it, and then return to Explorer to reset the file's read-only attribute.

NOTE: WHAT'S WITH ALL THE X'S?

`MSDOS.SYS`, you no doubt have noticed, contains 19 lines that consist mostly of the letter x. The note above these lines says that they "are required for compatibility with other programs." What does this mean? It seems that some older programs—especially virus protection utilities—expect MSDOS.SYS to be larger than 1,024 bytes. If a virus checker sees that MSDOS.SYS is less than 1,024 bytes, it might assume that your system has been infected with a virus. These extra lines push the MSDOS.SYS file size beyond 1,024 bytes.

FIGURE 4.4.

A typical MSDOS.SYS *file.*

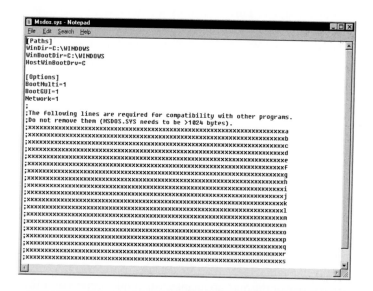

CAUTION: MSDOS.SYS MIGHT BE TOO SMALL

The Windows 95 Startup disk has a SYS utility that transfers the system files (including MSDOS.SYS) to your boot drive. Note, however, that the MSDOS.SYS file that gets transferred is *less than* 1,024 bytes. To be safe, you should add the dummy lines shown in Figure 4.4 to make sure that MSDOS.SYS meets the minimum size requirements.

The [Paths] Section

The first section in MSDOS.SYS is called [Paths]. It includes information that lets IO.SYS locate the Windows 95 files, including the Registry. This section includes three settings:

WinDir: This is the path you specified for the Windows installation during Setup. This is your main Windows 95 folder.

WinBootDir: This path specifies the location of the files needed to boot Windows 95. By default, WinBootDir is the same as WinDir.

HostWinBootDrv: This is the drive letter of your system's boot drive.

The [Options] Section

The [Options] section contains the settings you can use to customize various aspects of the Windows 95 startup. Although the default [Options] section contains only two or three entries, there are actually at least 16 you can add and edit. Here's the rundown:

OSR2

AutoScan=0¦1¦2: This is a new option in OSR2. It determines whether Windows 95 runs ScanDisk after a bad shutdown (for example, if the system power is switched off before you exit Windows 95). When AutoScan is set to 1 (the default), Windows 95 warns you that your system was shut down improperly and then runs the real-mode version of ScanDisk. If you set AutoScan to 2, Windows 95 bypasses the prompt and runs ScanDisk automatically. If AutoScan is 0, Windows 95 doesn't run ScanDisk. (See Chapter 15, "Protecting Your Windows 95 Investment," for a more detailed explanation of this feature.)

BootDelay=*seconds*: Determines the number of seconds that the Starting Windows 95... message appears during startup. The default is 2 seconds. If you want more time to invoke the Windows 95 Startup menu or press one of the other BootKeys (see Table 4.1), you can increase this setting. If you set BootDelay to 0, the Starting Windows 95... message doesn't appear. Note that this setting is meaningless if the BootKeys setting is 0.

BootFailSafe=0¦1: Determines whether Windows 95 boots in Safe mode automatically. If BootFailSafe is 0 (the default), Windows 95 boots in Safe mode only if you select one of the Startup menu's Safe-mode options or if the system failed to start properly on the preceding boot. If BootFailSafe is 1, your computer boots in Safe mode automatically.

BootGUI=1¦0: Determines whether IO.SYS loads the Windows 95 GUI. If BootGUI is 1 (the default), the GUI is loaded; if BootGUI is 0, your system boots to the command line (this is the same as selecting Command prompt only from the Windows 95 Startup menu).

BootKeys=1¦0: Determines whether the BootKeys are enabled. If BootKeys is 1 (the default), you can use the BootKeys to invoke, or choose an item from, the Windows 95 Startup menu; if BootKeys is 0, the BootKeys are disabled.

BootMenu=0¦1: Determines whether the Windows 95 Startup menu appears automatically. If BootMenu is 0 (the default), you have to press F8 before the Starting Windows 95... message disappears to get the Startup menu; if BootMenu is 1, the Startup menu appears without user intervention. Note that when this setting is 1, the Startup menu runs a countdown, after which it selects the default option automatically. (See BootMenuDefault to set the default option; see BootMenuDelay to set the length of the countdown.)

BootMenuDefault=*value*: Determines which of the Startup menu options is highlighted automatically when you invoke the menu. Here, *value* is the number of the option you want to highlight. The default value is 1 (the `Normal` option) if the system started normally on the previous boot; the default value is 4 (Safe mode) if the system encountered problems on the previous boot.

BootMenuDelay=*seconds*: Determines the length of the countdown that appears with the Startup menu if `BootMenu` is 1.

BootMulti=1¦0: Determines whether the system supports a dual-boot with your previous version of DOS. If `BootMulti` is 1, the `Previous version of MS-DOS` command appears on the Startup menu; if `BootMulti` is 0, this command doesn't appear.

BootWarn=1¦0: Determines whether `IO.SYS` runs Safe mode automatically if it encountered problems on the previous boot. If `BootWarn` is 1 (the default) and the previous boot was incomplete, `IO.SYS` invokes the Startup menu, sets the `Safe mode` option as the default, and displays a warning message; if `BootWarn` is 0 and the previous boot was incomplete, `IO.SYS` loads Windows 95 normally.

BootWin=1¦0: Determines whether `IO.SYS` runs Windows 95 or your previous version of DOS. If `BootWin` is 1 (the default), `IO.SYS` loads Windows 95; if `BootWin` is 0, IO.SYS loads your previous version of DOS (equivalent to selecting the `Previous version of MS-DOS` command on the Startup menu).

DoubleBuffer=0¦1¦2: Determines whether `IO.SYS` loads double buffering for SCSI drive memory caching. If `DoubleBuffer` is 0 (the default), double buffering is disabled; if `DoubleBuffer` is 1, `IO.SYS` enables double buffering only for controllers that require it; if `DoubleBuffer` is 2, `IO.SYS` enables double buffering whether the controller needs it or not.

DBLSpace=1¦0: Determines whether `IO.SYS` loads `DBLSPACE.BIN` (the DOS 6.x disk compression driver) automatically. If `DBLSpace` is 1 (the default), `DBLSPACE.BIN` is loaded automatically; if `DBLSpace` is 0, `DBLSPACE.BIN` isn't loaded.

DRVSpace=1¦0: Determines whether `IO.SYS` loads `DRVSPACE.BIN` (the Windows 95 disk compression driver) automatically. If `DRVSpace` is 1 (the default), `DRVSPACE.BIN` is loaded automatically; if `DRVSpace` is 0, `DRVSPACE.BIN` isn't loaded.

LoadTop=1¦0: Determines whether `COMMAND.COM` and `DRVSPACE.BIN` are loaded into the Upper Memory Area (UMA). If `LoadTop` is 1 (the default), `IO.SYS` loads `COMMAND.COM` and `DRVSPACE.BIN` into the UMA and increases the amount of free conventional memory; if `LoadTop` is 0, `IO.SYS` loads `COMMAND.COM` and `DRVSPACE.BIN` into conventional memory. This might eliminate conflicts with NetWare or any other programs or drivers that load into specific addresses of the UMA and might therefore butt heads with `COMMAND.COM` or `DRVSPACE.BIN`.

Logo=1¦0: Determines whether `IO.SYS` displays the animated Windows 95 logo at startup. If `Logo` is 1 (the default), the logo is displayed; if `Logo` is 0, the logo isn't displayed. The latter setting might also help to avoid conflicts with some third-party memory management utilities. (If you want to try your hand at creating a custom startup logo, check out the next section.)

TIP: BYPASSING THE WINDOWS 95 LOGO AD HOC

You can also bypass the animated Windows 95 startup logo by pressing Esc when you see the `Starting Windows 95...` message. Note as well that this also lets you see the progress of the commands in your `CONFIG.SYS` and `AUTOEXEC.BAT` files. Bear in mind, however, that some video cards can't handle the mode switch that occurs when you press Esc. You'll know this is the case on your system if you see a garbled display after you press Esc.

`Network=1¦0:` Determines whether the `Safe mode with network support` option appears on the Startup menu. If `Network` is 1 (the default), the option is enabled; if `Network` is 0, the option is disabled.

Creating Your Own Startup Logo

The Windows 95 startup logo, with its relaxing blue-sky-and-clouds background and interesting animation effects, is nice, but you might prefer to see your own custom screen. For example, you might want to display your company logo or some artwork from one of the kids. Impossible? Not at all, as you'll see in this section.

The Windows 95 startup logo normally resides on your system as a bitmap embedded within the Windows 95 system files. If you install Microsoft Plus!, however, you'll notice that the startup logo changes to include the Microsoft Plus! logo. This doesn't mean that Microsoft Plus! strategically altered the appropriate system file. Instead, it copied a hidden bitmap file to your boot drive's root folder. Don't go looking for a .BMP file, however. The file is named LOGO.SYS. But believe me, it's a .BMP file in disguise—as you can see in Figure 4.5. (Note, too, that you also get LOGO.SYS if you install Internet Explorer 3.0.)

FIGURE 4.5.

The Windows 95 startup logo is housed in LOGO.SYS.

So the secret to creating your own startup logo is to do either of the following:

- Create a bitmap from scratch, name it LOGO.SYS, and save it in the root folder of your boot drive.
- Alter the existing LOGO.SYS if you have one.

Assuming that you have LOGO.SYS on your system, the first step is to rename this file. This prevents you from overwriting the default LOGO.SYS file, so you can always reinstate it as the startup logo down the road. In Explorer, highlight the LOGO.SYS file in your boot drive's root folder. (If you haven't already done so, you need to turn on the Show all files option, as described earlier.) Now select File | Rename, type logo.sav (or whatever), and press Enter.

Now open Paint by selecting Start | Programs | Accessories | Paint. LOGO.SYS uses a 320×400 bitmap, and the image you use must be the same size. (This is despite the fact that IO.SYS displays LOGO.SYS at 640×480. Go figure.) How you proceed from here depends on whether you want to create a new image or use an existing image.

If you're creating a new image, follow these steps:

1. Select Image | Attributes (or press Ctrl-E) to display the Attributes dialog box, shown in Figure 4.6.

FIGURE 4.6.

Use the Attributes dialog box to set the size of the new image.

2. Enter 320 in the Width text box and 400 in the Height text box.
3. Click OK to return to the image.
4. Create your image.
5. Select File | Save (or press Ctrl-S), and save the bitmap as LOGO.SYS in the boot drive's root folder.

If you want to use an existing image, follow these steps:

1. Select File | Open (or press Ctrl-O) to display the Open dialog box.
2. Highlight the file you want to use, and click Open.
3. If the file is 320×400, skip to step 5. Otherwise, you need to resize the bitmap. First, resize the horizontal dimension to 320 pixels by selecting Image | Stretch/Skew (or pressing Ctrl-W), entering an appropriate percentage in the Horizontal text box (the one in the Stretch group), and clicking OK. For example, if your bitmap is 640 pixels wide, you'd enter 50, as shown in Figure 4.7.

4

UNDERSTANDING
WINDOWS 95
STARTUP

FIGURE 4.7.

Use the Stretch and Skew dialog box to size your image to 320×400.

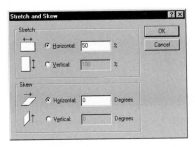

4. Resize the vertical dimension to 400 pixels by selecting Image | Stretch/Skew again, entering an appropriate percentage in the Vertical text box (again, the one in the Stretch group), and clicking OK. For example, if your bitmap is 500 pixels wide, you'd enter 80. Your image should now be 320×400, as shown in Figure 4.8.

FIGURE 4.8.

A 320×400 image ready to use as a startup logo.

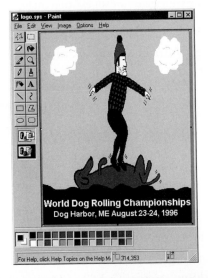

NOTE: ADJUSTING THE STRETCH

These stretch percentages might not give you an image that's exactly 320×400. For example, if your image is 480 pixels vertically, an 83 percent stretch would bring the image down to 399 pixels. In this case, use the Image Attributes dialog box to enter the exact dimension.

5. Modify the image, if necessary. (For example, stretching the image might mess up some of the colors, so you might need to make some adjustments.)
6. Select File | Save As and save the bitmap as LOGO.SYS in the boot drive's root folder.

The next time you start Windows 95, your image will appear as the startup logo.

TIP: REANIMATING THE STARTUP LOGO

If you edit LOGO.SYS, you'll find that the color bar at the bottom of the image is no longer animated. To fix this, start a DOS session and run the following commands:

```
DEBUG C:\MSDOS.SYS
E CS:132 EC
W
Q
```

Command-Line Switches for Starting Windows 95

If you boot to the command line, you can load the Windows 95 GUI and the protected-mode drivers by typing win and pressing Enter to run WIN.COM. You can also modify the startup by specifying switches with WIN.COM according to the following syntax:

```
WIN [/?] [/B] [/W] /WX [/D:[F] [M] [N] [S] [T] [V] [X]]
```

Table 4.2 describes these switches and how they modify the startup.

Table 4.2. WIN.COM switches.

Switch	Description
/?	Displays a partial list of the available WIN.COM switches.
/B	Logs the startup progress to a BOOTLOG.TXT in the boot drive's root directory. This is the same as selecting the Logged (\BOOTLOG.TXT) option in the Windows 95 Startup menu.
/W	Restores CONFIG.SYS from CONFIG.WOS and AUTOEXEC.BAT from AUTOEXEC.WOS, and then prompts you to press any key to start Windows 95.
/WX	Restores CONFIG.SYS from CONFIG.WOS and AUTOEXEC.BAT from AUTOEXEC.WOS, and then starts Windows 95.
/D:	Used for troubleshooting the Windows 95 startup. It's used in conjunction with other switches, as described in the following entries.
/D:F	Disables 32-bit disk access and forces all drive access to go through the real-mode mapper (RMM). Normally, the RMM provides compatibility with real-mode device drivers that have no protected-mode counterparts. This switch is equivalent to setting 32BitDiskAccess=FALSE in SYSTEM.INI.
/D:M	Starts Windows 95 in Safe mode. This is equivalent to selecting the Safe mode option on the Windows 95 Startup menu.

Table 4.2. continued

Switch	Description
/D:N	Starts Windows 95 in Safe mode, but also enables networking support. This is equivalent to selecting the Safe mode with networking option on the Windows 95 Startup menu.
/D:S	Tells Windows 95 not to use the ROM address space between F000:0000 and 1 MB for a break point. This switch is equivalent to setting SystemROMBreakPoint=FALSE in SYSTEM.INI.
/D:T	Starts Windows 95 in a mode similar to that used by Setup. Internal and external VxDs aren't loaded, no EMS page frame is set up, and FastDisk isn't enabled.
/D:V	Tells Windows 95 that the ROM routine will handle interrupts from the hard disk controller. This is equivalent to setting VirtualHDIRQ=FALSE in SYSTEM.INI.
/D:X	Excludes the entire adapter range of the UMA from memory addresses that Windows 95 scans to find unused upper memory blocks. This is equivalent to setting EMMExclude=A000-FFFF in SYSTEM.INI.

NOTE: WHAT ARE WOS FILES?

As you'll learn in Chapter 21, "DOS Isn't Dead: Optimizing DOS Applications Under Windows 95," you can set up a program to run in MS-DOS mode and specify custom CONFIG.SYS and AUTOEXEC.BAT files for the program. When you then run the program, Windows 95 renames the existing CONFIG.SYS file to CONFIG.WOS and renames AUTOEXEC.BAT to AUTOEXEC.WOS.

Troubleshooting Windows 95 Startup

Computers are often frustrating beasts, but few things in computerdom are as hair-pullingly, teeth-gnashingly frustrating as an operating system that won't operate. To help save some wear and tear on your hair and teeth, this section outlines a few common startup difficulties and their solutions.

When to Use the Various Startup Menu Options

You saw earlier that Windows 95 has some useful options on its Startup menu. But under what circumstances should you use each option? Well, because there is some overlap in what each option brings to the table, there are no hard and fast rules. It is possible, however, to lay down some general guidelines.

You should use the Safe mode option if one of the following conditions occurs:

- Windows 95 doesn't start after the Starting Windows 95... message appears.
- Windows 95 seems to stall for an extended period.
- Windows 95 doesn't work correctly or produces unexpected results.
- You can't print to a local printer (although you can try some other troubleshooting steps for printing problems; see Chapter 19, "Prescriptions for Perfect Printing").
- Your video display is distorted and, possibly, unreadable.
- Your computer stalls repeatedly.
- Your computer suddenly slows down.
- You need to test an intermittent error condition.

You should use the Logged (\BOOTLOG.TXT) option in the following situations:

- The Windows 95 startup hangs after switching to protected mode.
- You need a detailed record of the startup process.
- You suspect (after using one of the other Startup menu options) that a protected-mode driver is causing Windows 95 startup to fail.

After starting (or attempting to start) Windows 95 with this option, you'll end up with a file named BOOTLOG.TXT in your boot drive's root folder. This is a text file, so you can examine it with any text editor. For example, you could boot to the DOS prompt (using the Command prompt only or Safe mode command prompt only option) and then use EDIT.COM to examine the file.

Scour the file for a couple of lines that look like this:

```
[0016586B] Loading Vxd = vmouse
[0016586B] LoadFailed  = vmouse
```

These lines tell you which driver Windows 95 choked on during the startup. You'll probably need to reinstall the driver, as described in Chapter 10, "How Windows 95 Handles Hardware." Note, however, that there are a few cases in which a LoadFailed message doesn't necessarily indicate a problem. Here's a summary of these exceptions:

```
LoadFailed = dsound.vxd
```

DSOUND.VXD is the library of DirectSound routines. (See Chapter 22, "Miscellaneous Multimedia: Graphics, CD-ROMs, and More," for explanations of the various DirectX components.) The failure of this driver to load properly might only mean that you have no DirectSound-enabled games on your system.

```
LoadFailed = ebios
```

You'll see this message if the extended BIOS driver didn't find an extended BIOS on your system.

```
LoadFailed = ndis2sup.vxd
```

4

UNDERSTANDING WINDOWS 95 STARTUP

This message might only mean that the NDIS 2 support driver didn't locate any NDIS 2 drivers to support.

```
LoadFailed = vpowerd
```

VPOWERD is the Advanced Power Management (APM) driver. If your system doesn't support APM, this driver will fail to load.

```
LoadFailed = vserver.vxd
```

VSERVER.VXD attempts to saves memory by loading later in the boot process only if it's needed.

```
LoadFailed = vshare
```

It's likely that VSHARE loaded successfully earlier in the boot process. This second copy of VSHARE realizes that VSHARE is already loaded, so it fails.

```
InitCompleteFailed=SDVXD
```

This line indicates that a temporary disk cache used by Windows 95 to speed the boot process has been unloaded from memory.

You should use the Safe mode command prompt only option if you're facing one of the following situations:

- Windows 95 won't start, even with the Safe mode option.
- You want to use WIN.COM's command-line switches (see Table 4.2).
- You want to run a program from the command line (such as EDIT.COM to edit a startup file).
- You want to avoid loading HIMEM.SYS or IFSHLP.SYS.

You should use the Safe mode without compression option in the following situations:

- Your computer hangs each time it tries to access a compressed drive.
- A Corrupt CVF error occurs during the startup process.
- Windows 95 fails to start, and it won't start if you use either the Safe mode or the Safe mode command prompt only option.
- You want to prevent IO.SYS from loading the compression driver (DBLSPACE.BIN or DRVSPACE.BIN).

You should use the Safe mode with network support option if one of the following situations occurs:

- Windows 95 fails to start using any of the other Safe mode options.
- The drivers or programs you need in order to repair a problem exist on a shared network resource.

■ You need access to e-mail or other network-based communications for technical support.

■ Your computer is running a shared Windows 95 installation.

You should use the `Step-by-step confirmation` option if one of the following conditions is true:

■ The Windows 95 startup fails while processing any of the startup files.

■ You need to check for failure messages related to real-mode drivers while processing `CONFIG.SYS` and `AUTOEXEC.BAT`.

■ You need to check for failure messages related to the `IO.SYS` commands.

■ You need to check for failure messages related to the Registry.

■ You need to verify that the expected drivers are being loaded.

■ You need to bypass a specific driver or a set of drivers.

A Step-by-Step Strategy

If Windows 95 starts in Safe mode, your next move should be to try the `Step-by-step confirmation` option in the Startup menu. Rather than just guessing at which options you should load and which you should avoid, let's put together a strategy. Table 4.3 lists the various prompts you see during a step-by-step boot. Columns A, B, C, and D list various response combinations you should try.

Table 4.3. Response combinations for a step-by-step boot.

Step-by-Step Prompt	A	B	C	D
Load DoubleSpace Driver?	Yes	Yes	Yes	Yes
Process the system registry?	Yes	Yes	Yes	No
Create a startup log file (`BOOTLOG.TXT`)?	Yes	Yes	Yes	Yes
Process your startup device drivers (`CONFIG.SYS`)?	No	No	Yes	Yes
DEVICE=*PATH*\HIMEM.SYS?	Yes	Yes	Yes	Yes
DEVICE=*PATH*\IFSHLP.SYS?	Yes	Yes	Yes	Yes
DEVICE=*PATH*\SETVER.EXE?	Yes	Yes	Yes	Yes
Process your startup command file (`AUTOEXEC.BAT`)?	No	No	Yes	Yes
Load the Windows graphical user interface?	Yes	Yes	Yes	Yes
Load all Windows drivers?	No	Yes	No	Yes

Option A: If Windows 95 starts properly when you use the responses in option A, you know you have a problem with a device driver or TSR. Use options B and C (see the following paragraphs) to narrow down the problem. If Windows fails to start when you use the responses in option A, try option D.

Option B: If Windows 95 starts properly when you use the responses in option B, you know you have a problem with a real-mode device driver or TSR in `CONFIG.SYS` or `AUTOEXEC.BAT`. You can pinpoint the problem by stepping through these files. If Windows 95 fails to start when you use the responses in option B, try option C.

Option C: If Windows 95 starts properly when you use the responses in option C, you know you have a problem with a protected-mode device driver. You have two choices: Run the Startup menu's `Logged (\BOOTLOG.TXT)` option to see which driver is causing the problem, or turn to Chapter 10 and read the section titled "Troubleshooting Protected-Mode Driver Problems." If Windows fails to start when you use the responses in option C, try option D.

Option D: If Windows 95 starts properly when you use the responses in option D, you know you have a problem with the Registry. See Chapter 12, "Hacking the Registry." If Windows fails to start when you use the responses in option D, `SYSTEM.INI` or `WIN.INI` likely has a problem. Rename these two files (to, say, `SYSTEM.SAV` and `WIN.SAV`), rename `SYSTEM.CB` to `SYSTEM.INI`, and reboot normally. If Windows 95 loads successfully, you need to examine the original `SYSTEM.INI` and `WIN.INI` files for problems (such as attempting to load a device driver that no longer exists on your system).

NOTE: RECOVERING YOUR MOUSE

When you reboot with `SYSTEM.CB` saved as `SYSTEM.INI`, your mouse probably won't work. To fix this problem, first add the following line to the `[boot]` section of the new `SYSTEM.INI` file:

```
mouse.drv=mouse.drv
```

Now add the following line to the `[386Enh]` section:

```
mouse=*vmouse, msmouse.vxd
```

Windows 95 Won't Start in Safe Mode

If Windows 95 is so intractable that it won't even start in Safe mode, your system is likely afflicted with one of the following problems:

■ Your system is infected with a virus. See Chapter 15, "Protecting Your Windows 95 Investment," for more information on viruses and how to get rid of them.

- Your system has incorrect CMOS settings. Run the machine's CMOS setup program to see whether any of these settings needs to be changed or whether the CMOS battery needs to be replaced.

- Your system has a hardware conflict. See Chapter 10 for hardware troubleshooting procedures.

- You need to make an adjustment to MSDOS.SYS. For example, I mentioned earlier that some third-party memory managers don't like LOGO.SYS, so you might need to change the Logo setting to 0.

- If your system uses an Intel Triton PCI controller or a PCI-based display adapter, you might need to use the special VGA.DRV or VGA.VXD video drivers from the Windows 95 CD-ROM. See Chapter 22, for more information.

Another possibility is that your system needs to run HIMEM.SYS with a machine switch, such as the following one:

```
c:\windows\himem.sys /machine:1
```

Windows 95 normally runs HIMEM.SYS from IO.SYS. If, however, you need a machine switch, you must add it to the HIMEM.SYS line in CONFIG.SYS because you can't edit IO.SYS. The problem is that a Safe-mode boot doesn't process CONFIG.SYS; therefore, the machine switch doesn't get processed and your system might hang. Here's how to get a Safe-mode boot *and* process HIMEM.SYS with the machine switch:

1. Reboot, display the Windows 95 Startup menu, and select the Step-by-step confirmation option.

2. Respond to the prompts as follows:

Load DoubleSpace Driver?	Yes
Process the system registry?	No
Create a startup log file (BOOTLOG.TXT)?	Yes
Process your startup device drivers (CONFIG.SYS)?	Yes
DEVICE=*PATH*\HIMEM.SYS?	Yes
DEVICE=*PATH*\IFSHLP.SYS?	Yes
DEVICE=*PATH*\SETVER.EXE?	Yes
Process your startup command file (AUTOEXEC.BAT)?	No
Load the Windows graphical user interface?	No
Load all Windows drivers?	No

3. At the DOS prompt, type win /d:m and press Enter to start Windows 95 in Safe mode.

4

Miscellaneous Startup Snags

This section runs through a few more common startup complaints.

When you start your computer, the Windows 95 Startup menu is displayed automatically, and the following message appears:

```
Warning: Windows has detected a registry/configuration error.
Choose Safe mode, to start Windows with a minimal set of drivers.
```

This error indicates that the Registry files (they're hidden files named SYSTEM.DAT and USER.DAT in your main Windows directory) are either missing or corrupted. You need to boot Windows 95 in Safe mode.

Windows 95 first tries to restore the Registry from its backup copies. (Each time the Registry is modified, Windows 95 saves a backup of the current Registry files in SYSTEM.DA0 and USER.DA0.) You'll see the Registry Problem dialog box with an explanation of the problem. Click the Restore From Backup and Restart button.

If it restores the backups, Windows 95 will prompt you to restart your computer. Click Yes to reboot.

If it can't restore the backups, Windows 95 suggests that you shut down your system and reinstall Windows 95. Although you might have to reinstall Windows 95 as a last resort, you can still try two other things:

- If you have your own backup copies of the Registry files on floppy disk (this is always a good idea), you can restore those files from there.

- Reboot to the command prompt and check MSDOS.SYS. Make sure that the WinDir and WinBootDir settings point to the correct folder (that is, your main Windows 95 folder, which is where the Registry files are stored).

When you start your computer, you see the Starting Windows 95... message, followed by the It is now safe to turn off your computer message.

This behavior can occur if the VMM32.VXD file is missing or damaged. The Windows 95 disks and CD-ROM do include a version of VMM32.VXD. Extracting this version of the file won't solve the problem, however, because it's an incomplete version of the file. You'll have to run Setup again to re-create a system-specific VMM32.VXD file. Here are the steps to follow:

1. Restart your computer. When you see the Starting Windows 95... message, press the F8 key, and then choose Command prompt only from the Startup menu.

2. Enter the following command to change to the System folder (assuming that Windows 95 is installed in \WINDOWS):

   ```
   cd \windows\system
   ```

3. Enter the following command:

   ```
   ren vmm32.vxd vmm32.old
   ```

4. Repeat step 1.

5. Reinstall Windows 95.

A DOS program you were running in MS-DOS mode starts every time you restart your computer.

As you'll learn in Chapter 21, it's possible to create custom CONFIG.SYS and AUTOEXEC.BAT files for each of your DOS applications. In this case, Windows 95 uses these new startup files to replace the current CONFIG.SYS and AUTOEXEC.BAT files (which are renamed to CONFIG.WOS and AUTOEXEC.WOS).

If you restart or turn off your computer while running the DOS program, Windows 95 doesn't get a chance to restore the correct CONFIG.SYS and AUTOEXEC.BAT files. Instead, the program-specific startup files are executed, and you end up back in the DOS program. The solution is to exit the program normally to allow Windows 95 to restore the correct startup files.

When you start Windows 95, you receive one of the following error messages and are then dumped at the DOS prompt:

```
The following file is missing or corrupted: WIN.COM
Program too big to fit in memory
Cannot find WIN.COM, unable to continue loading Windows
```

These errors imply that WIN.COM either is missing or has been damaged. Windows 95 expects WIN.COM to be 22,679 bytes. If WIN.COM weighs in less than that, you'll see the first error message; if WIN.COM is larger, you'll see the second error message; if WIN.COM is missing in action, you see the third error. The solution in all cases is to re-create WIN.COM from your Windows 95 CD-ROM or installation disks.

If you have the Windows 95 CD-ROM, follow these steps:

1. If your CD-ROM drive uses protected-mode drivers, insert your Windows 95 Startup disk in drive A, and reboot. (I'm assuming here that you have access to real-mode drivers for your CD-ROM on the Startup disk.) If your CD-ROM uses real-mode drivers, reboot your computer, display the Windows 95 Startup menu, and select the Command prompt only option.

2. Insert the Windows 95 CD-ROM.

3. Enter the following command (where *drive* is the letter of your CD-ROM drive; this command assumes that your main Windows folder is C:\WINDOWS):

```
extract drive:\win95\win95_03.cab win.cnf /L c:\windows win.cnf
```

If you have the Windows source files on floppy disks, follow these steps:

1. Reboot your computer, display the Windows 95 Startup menu, and select the Command prompt only option.

2. Insert Disk 3 of the Windows 95 source disks.

4

UNDERSTANDING
WINDOWS 95
STARTUP

3. Enter the following command (where *drive* is the letter of your floppy drive; this command assumes that your main Windows folder is C:\WINDOWS):

```
extract drive:\win95_03.cab win.cnf /L c:\windows win.cnf
```

WIN.CNF is actually WIN.COM, so you need to rename it. The following commands change to the main Windows folder (you must change the first command if your Windows folder is different from C:\WINDOWS), delete the existing (and presumably corrupted) WIN.COM file, and rename WIN.CNF to WIN.COM:

```
c:
cd\windows
del win.com
ren win.cnf win.com
```

When you're done, restart your computer, and Windows 95 should load properly.

When you start Windows 95, you receive the following error message:

```
VFAT Device Initialization Failed
A device or resource required by VFAT is not present
or is unavailable. VFAT cannot continue loading.
System halted.
```

This error message suggests one of the following problems:

CONFIG.SYS contains a line pointing to a previous version of IFSHLP.SYS. Windows 95 has a protected-mode version of the IFSHLP.SYS driver, so CONFIG.SYS shouldn't be loading it. In this case, reboot, invoke the Windows 95 Startup menu, and select the Safe mode command prompt only option. When you get to the DOS prompt, open CONFIG.SYS in a text editor, and remove the DEVICE line that loads IFSHLP.SYS.

IFSHLP.SYS is missing from the Windows folder. In this case, you'll need to extract IFSHLP.SYS from the Windows 95 CD-ROM or from Disk 12 of the source floppy disks. Follow the steps outlined in the preceding solution. For the CD-ROM, use the following EXTRACT command:

```
extract drive:\win95\win95_12.cab ifshlp.sys /L c:\windows ifshlp.sys
```

Here's the command to use for the floppy disk:

```
extract drive:\win95_12.cab ifshlp.sys /L c:\windows ifshlp.sys
```

The [Paths] section in MSDOS.SYS is incorrect. Reboot to the command prompt, and check MSDOS.SYS. Make sure that the WinDir and WinBootDir settings point to your main Windows folder.

A file named WINBOOT.INI still exists in the root folder of the boot drive. Windows 95 creates WINBOOT.INI in the root folder if it detects that the previous startup was incomplete. It normally deletes this file after you run a successful boot. If Windows 95 doesn't do this for some reason, reboot, display the Windows 95 Startup menu, and select the Safe mode command prompt only option. At the DOS prompt, delete WINBOOT.INI and restart your computer.

You want the ability to toggle the Num Lock and Caps Lock keys at startup.

Unfortunately, Windows 95 doesn't have a built-in mechanism for toggling Num Lock and Caps Lock. You *can* do this if you have Microsoft's IntelliType software installed on your system (I'll show you how it's done in Chapter 8, "Personalizing the Mouse, Keyboard, and Joystick"). Otherwise, you'll need to use the DOS DEBUG program to create your own utilities for toggling these keys.

Let's begin with Num Lock. If you want to create a program that turns Num Lock off, create a new text file, name it NUMOFF.SCR, and enter the code shown in Listing 4.1.

Listing 4.1. A DEBUG script that turns Num Lock off.

```
a 100
mov ax,0040
mov ds,ax
and byte ptr [0017],df
mov ax,4c00
int 21
r cx
000f
n NUMOFF.COM
w
q
```

At the DOS prompt, enter the following command:

```
DEBUG < NUMOFF.SCR
```

This creates a program named NUMOFF.COM, which will turn Num Lock off.

If you want to turn Num Lock back on, create a text file named NUMON.SCR, and enter the code shown in Listing 4.2.

Listing 4.2. A DEBUG script that turns Num Lock on.

```
a 100
mov ax,0040
mov ds,ax
or byte ptr [0017],20
mov ax,4c00
int 21
r cx
000f
n NUMON.COM
w
q
```

At the DOS prompt, enter the following command:

```
DEBUG < NUMON.SCR
```

4

UNDERSTANDING
WINDOWS 95
STARTUP

This creates a program named NUMON.COM, which turns Num Lock on.

You can create similar DEBUG scripts for toggling Caps Lock. To turn Caps Lock off, create a text file named CAPSOFF.SCR, and enter the code shown in Listing 4.3.

Listing 4.3. A DEBUG script that turns Caps Lock off.

```
a 100
mov ax,0040
mov ds,ax
and byte ptr [0017],bf
mov ax,4c00
int 21
r cx
000f
n CAPSOFF.COM
w
q
```

At the DOS prompt, enter the following command:

```
DEBUG < CAPSOFF.SCR
```

This creates a program named CAPSOFF.COM, which turns Caps Lock off.

Finally, to turn Caps Lock on, create a text file named CAPSON.SCR, and enter the code shown in Listing 4.4.

Listing 4.4. A DEBUG script that turns Caps Lock on.

```
a 100
mov ax,0040
mov ds,ax
or byte ptr [0017],40
mov ax,4c00
int 21
r cx
000f
n CAPSON.COM
w
q
```

At the DOS prompt, enter the following command:

```
DEBUG < CAPSON.SCR
```

You now have a program named CAPSON.COM, which turns Caps Lock on.

Understanding the Windows 95 Shutdown Process

We began at the beginning by looking at how Windows 95 starts up. Now we'll end at the ending by examining the Windows 95 shutdown process.

The Shut Down Command

One of the cardinal rules when working with Windows 3.x was that you should always exit Windows and wait until you got to the DOS prompt before turning off your computer. This gave the Windows cache a chance to flush, and it prevented damage to Program Manager's groups and icons.

This rule still applies to Windows 95 and is, in fact, even more important, for the following reasons:

- Windows 95's write-behind cache waits for idle CPU time before it writes data from the cache to the hard disk. If you turn off your machine willy-nilly, you could lose valuable data that Windows 95 hadn't yet saved to disk. (I discuss write-behind caching in more detail in Chapter 9, "Windows 95 Performance Tuning and Optimization.")

- Windows 95 waits until shutdown to update any Registry settings that have changed. Turning off your system prematurely causes you to lose unsaved configuration data, and your system might not work properly.

- At shutdown, Windows 95 warns you if any network users are connected to any of your shared resources. Turning off your machine without going through the proper channels disconnects those users and interrupts their current operation (such as a file download or a print job).

To avoid all of these problems (and the ulcers that go with them), always run through the Windows 95 shutdown procedure before shutting off your machine for the night. You begin by selecting Start | Shut Down. Windows 95 displays the Shut Down Windows dialog box, shown in Figure 4.9.

FIGURE 4.9.

The Shut Down Windows dialog box: a requisite part of any system shutdown.

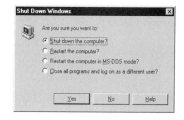

NOTE: CLICK START TO STOP? WHO CARES?

Some people have conniption fits over the fact that when you want to *stop* Windows 95, you have to first click the *Start* button. I think these people need to get out more.

If it bothers you, though, think of it this way: Selecting the Shut Down command doesn't actually exit Windows 95; it just *starts* the exiting process by displaying the Shut Down Windows dialog box. There—isn't that better?

Use the Shut Down Windows dialog box to select one of the following options and click Yes:

Shut down the computer? Select this option if you'll be turning off your machine. After you hear a flourish of trumpets (the Windows 95 closing WAV file) and after Windows 95 has completed its shutdown duties, you'll see a screen that says It's now safe to turn off your computer. This is your go-ahead to turn off the computer. If you change your mind and decide to restart Windows 95, just press Ctrl-Alt-Delete.

Restart the computer? Select this option to give Windows 95 a fresh start. In this case, Windows 95 performs the equivalent of a cold reboot: The POST is run all over again, and you have a chance to invoke the Windows 95 Startup menu.

TIP: A FASTER RESTART

If you just need a quick restart to update a Registry setting or some other small change, the Restart the computer option is overkill (not to mention that it's time-consuming). Luckily, there *is* a quicker way. After selecting the Restart the computer option, hold down Shift and click Yes. This tells Windows 95 to bypass the cold reboot. Instead, you see a Windows is now restarting message (at which point it's OK to release the Shift key), and Windows 95 restarts almost immediately.

TIP: A FASTER REBOOT

If you *do* want to perform a cold reboot, you can do so without having to display the Shut Down Windows dialog box. First, create a new batch file (named, say, REBOOT.BAT), and include only the following command in it:

@EXIT

Right-click the batch file and select Properties from the context menu. In the Program tab, activate the Close on exit check box, and then click the Advanced button. In the Advanced Program Settings dialog box, activate the MS-DOS mode check box and deactivate the Warn before entering MS-DOS mode check box. Click OK, and then click OK again to create a DOS mode shortcut for the batch file. Copy this shortcut to the desktop, and then double-click the shortcut whenever you want to reboot your system. (See Chapter 21 to learn more about MS-DOS mode.)

Restart the computer in MS-DOS mode? Select this option to exit the Windows 95 GUI and get to the DOS prompt. Note that this option has nothing whatsoever to do with restarting your computer. Nothing is rebooted and no initialization files are run; you're simply exiting to DOS the way you used to with Windows 3.x. To get back to Windows 95, type win or exit, and press Enter.

Close all programs and log on as a different user? This option appears only if Windows 95 networking is enabled, or if you've set up different user profiles (which I'll show you how to do in Chapter 7, "Customizing Windows 95"). It shuts down all your programs and then redisplays the Enter Network Password dialog box so that you can enter a different user name and password. Note that this option is *not* the same as Restart the computer, because Windows 95 doesn't perform its shutdown chores.

TIP: ANOTHER WAY TO RESET WINDOWS 95

The Close all programs and log on as a different user option is a useful way to reset Windows 95 and get a fresh batch of system resources. You just log on with the same user name. What do you do, though, if you want to reset Windows 95 but your system doesn't have the Close all programs and log on as a different user option? No sweat. Press Ctrl-Alt-Delete to display the Close Program dialog box, highlight Explorer, and click End Task. Because Explorer is the Windows 95 shell, the Shut Down Windows dialog box appears. Click No. The Explorer dialog box appears a few seconds later, complaining that the "program is not responding." Don't worry about that; just click End Task. This shuts down the shell, but Windows 95 restarts it right away.

Customizing the Windows 95 Shutdown Screens

You saw earlier how the Windows 95 startup logo was a bitmap file named LOGO.SYS (see the section "Creating Your Own Startup Logo"). Well, as you might imagine, the two Windows 95 shutdown screens are also bitmaps, and they also have the unintuitive SYS extension.

The Please wait while your computer shuts down screen is actually a bitmap file named LOGOW.SYS (LOGO Wait), shown in Figure 4.10. The It's now safe to turn off your computer screen is the bitmap file LOGOS.SYS (LOGO Shutdown), shown in Figure 4.11. You'll find both files in your main Windows 95 folder.

As before, you can rename these files, create your own, and name them LOGOW.SYS and LOGOS.SYS. (Make sure that each bitmap is 320×400.) For the LOGOS.SYS file, you could create a message saying that you've gone to lunch or that you're at a meeting. Paint's Text tool is perfect for these applications.

FIGURE 4.10.

The LOGOW.SYS *bitmap.*

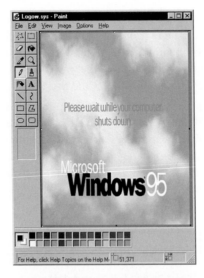

FIGURE 4.11.

The LOGOS.SYS *bitmap.*

Summary

This chapter got your Windows 95 education off to a rousing start with a close look at the Windows 95 startup process. I took you through the full startup procedure; showed you how to customize the startup by using the Startup menu, MSDOS.SYS, and WIN.COM's command-line switches; solved some common startup problems; and examined the shutdown process. You even learned how to create your own startup and shutdown logos.

Here's a list of chapters where you'll find related information:

- For other Windows 95 customization techniques, see Chapter 7, "Customizing Windows 95."

- The various memory-related concepts that I glossed over in this chapter—upper memory, high memory, conventional memory, caching, and resources—are explained in detail in Chapter 9, "Windows 95 Performance Tuning and Optimization."

- To learn more about device drivers—especially the difference between real-mode drivers and protected-mode drivers—head for Chapter 10, "How Windows 95 Handles Hardware."

- To learn how to add applications and documents to the Startup folder, see Chapter 13, "Working with Files and Folders."

- You'll find lots of background information about the Registry in Chapter 11, "Introducing the Windows 95 Registry."

- To learn about MS-DOS mode, see Chapter 21, "DOS Isn't Dead: Optimizing DOS Applications Under Windows 95."

- You can get the full batch file nitty-gritty in Appendix F, "A Batch File Primer."

4

UNDERSTANDING
WINDOWS 95
STARTUP

Windows 95:
The 50¢ Tour

The world can doubtless never be well known by theory: practice is absolutely necessary; but surely it is of great use to a young man, before he sets out for that country, full of mazes, windings, and turnings, to have at least a general map of it, made by some experienced traveler.

—*Lord Chesterfield*

The whole point of this book is to traverse the seldom-seen nooks and crannies of Microsoft's most popular operating system. My goal is to shepherd you through the thickets and thatches of the Windows 95 landscape in an effort to discover new and useful information and uncover hidden techniques. These newfound treasures will let you squeeze the most out of your Windows 95 investment, whether you're a single-copy user or a 10,000-copy administrator.

Before setting out on your travels, however, you need to take a moment to get your bearings and scope out the lay of the Windows 95 land. In other words, before lighting out for the hinterland, it helps if you first get to know the heartland. That's the job of this chapter. Here you'll check out the forest of Windows 95 as a whole, which will stand you in good stead when you start examining specific Windows 95 trees in subsequent chapters.

The Desktop: Your New Windows Home

Assuming that Windows 95 is safely ensconced on your system, each time you boot your machine, you'll be whisked (or walked, depending on how powerful your computer is) right into Windows 95. Along the way, you might have to pass through a checkpoint or two—such as a network login or the Welcome to Windows 95 dialog box—but you'll eventually end up at the *desktop,* shown in Figure 5.1. (By the way, if you don't want to be bothered by the Welcome to Windows 95 dialog box each time, deactivate the Show this Welcome Screen next time you start Windows check box and click Close.)

If you're a former Windows 3.x user, the first thing you'll notice is that Program Manager is nowhere in sight. In its stead, you're presented with a vast, green sward studded with a few icons. This rather Spartan expanse is the *desktop,* and it's where most of the Windows 95 action occurs. The Windows 95 designers have consigned Program Manager—with its untidy collection of program groups and program items—to the dustbin of operating system history.

NOTE: PROGRAM MANAGER RIDES THE PINE

Actually, Program Manager is only in semi-retirement, occupying a spot on the bench while the Windows 95 upstarts hog the spotlight. If you find that you miss Program Manager, or if you want to crank it up for old time's sake, select Start | Run, type progman in the Run dialog box, and click OK. Believe me, though, spending only a few hours with the new Windows 95 interface will be enough to make you forget that Program Manager ever existed.

FIGURE 5.1.

The Windows 95 desktop.

Icons

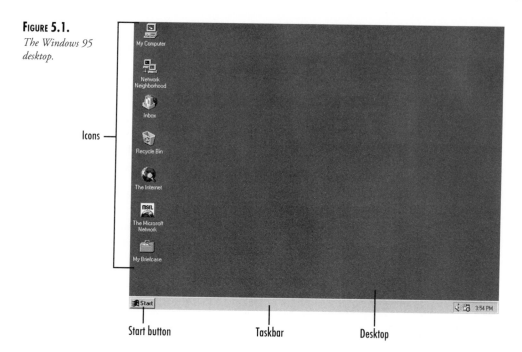

Start button   Taskbar   Desktop

Although Windows 3.x had a "desktop," the Windows 95 desktop is a more accurate representation of the metaphor because it behaves more like the top of a desk. So, yes, your application windows still appear on the desktop as they did in Windows 3.x, but the Windows 95 desktop can handle many more items:

- **Icons that take you to specific Windows 95 features.** For example, the Inbox icon opens Microsoft Exchange, Windows 95's all-in-one e-mail and fax client.

- **Pointers to applications.** These pointers, called *shortcuts*, let you launch an application simply by double-clicking the shortcut's icon.

- **Shortcuts to files, folders, and drives.** As you'll see a bit later, shortcuts can point to much more than just programs.

- **Data snippets.** You can store text, graphics, and other data right on the desktop for handy reuse.

Overall, the Windows 95 desktop is a much more versatile and powerful way to work than anything you saw in Windows 3.x.

Some New Windows 95 Concepts You Should Know

Before we start poking and prodding Windows 95's new interface and tools, we need to take a second to nail down a few concepts and ideas that Microsoft introduced in its bouncing baby operating system. Of course, Windows 95 is such a radical departure from previous versions of

5

WINDOWS 95:
THE 50¢ TOUR

Windows that I could spend a hundred pages going over its many theoretical and architectural innovations. Instead, the next few sections target just those concepts that form a ubiquitous part of the Windows 95 topography.

Understanding Windows 95 Objects

One of the major differences between Windows 95 and Windows 3.x—and one of the keys to using Windows 95 powerfully and efficiently—is the idea of the object-oriented user interface. This means that Windows 95 views most of what you see, such as the desktop, the icons, and the taskbar, as objects: separate entities with their own properties and actions.

What does this mean in the real world? Well, let's consider a real-world analogy: a car. A car is an object, to be sure, but what does it mean to say that it has its own "properties and actions"? The car's properties are simply its physical characteristics: its model, color, engine size, and so on. The car's actions define what you can *do* with the car: accelerate, brake, and so on.

The Windows 95 interface is populated with all kinds of objects, each of which has its own properties and actions. This means that you have unprecedented control over the appearance and operation of most of the basic building blocks of the interface.

Object Context Menus

To show you the power of Windows 95 objects, let's examine one of the interface's most useful features: context menus. Move the mouse pointer so that it rests anywhere on the desktop—but not over an icon—and then right-click. You'll immediately see a small menu, as shown in Figure 5.2. This is called a *context menu*. As you'll see, these context menus are a pervasive feature of the Windows 95 terrain.

FIGURE 5.2.

Right-click the desktop to display this example of a context menu.

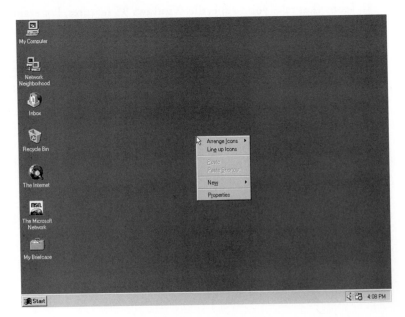

Why are they called *context* menus? Well, the purpose of the menu is to give you easy access to some of the object's properties and actions. But each type of object has a unique collection of properties and actions, so each object type needs a different menu. Which menu appears depends on which object you right-click. In other words, it depends on the *context* of the right-click.

After you have the context menu displayed, you can click one of its commands to either modify the object's properties or run one of the object's actions. If you decide you don't want to do anything with the context menu, you can close it by pressing Esc or by left-clicking elsewhere.

NOTE: WINDOWS 95'S FLEXIBLE FEATURES

The Windows 95 interface is extremely flexible in that it rarely gives you only one means to a particular end. When you need to work with an object's properties or actions, for example, the context menu is only one way to go about your work. Depending on the object in question, you might also have the choice of using menu commands, toolbar buttons, Control Panel icons, or the Windows 95 Registry. If anything, the interface might be *too* flexible because it's often not clear which approach is the best way to reach the goal.

Object Properties

An object's properties govern, for the most part, the look and feel of the object. For example, right-click the desktop to display the context menu shown in Figure 5.2 (if it isn't displayed already) and select the Properties command. Many of the Windows 95 context menus you'll deal with will have a Properties command, and it almost always displays a Properties dialog box (also called a *properties sheet*) specific to the underlying object. In this case, the Display Properties dialog box, shown in Figure 5.3, appears. (Note that the Display Properties dialog box shows the Plus! tab only if you've installed the Microsoft Plus! add-on.)

FIGURE 5.3.

The properties sheet for the desktop object.

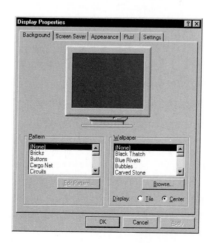

NOTE: WINDOWS 95'S DIALOG BOXES

Windows 95 makes extensive use of so-called *tabbed* dialog boxes like the one shown in Figure 5.3. The "tabs" are the headings that run across the top of the dialog box, just below the title bar (in Figure 5.3, they're Background, Screen Saver, and so on). When you activate a tab, a new set of controls appears. You navigate the tabs either by clicking them or by using the Ctrl-Tab and Ctrl-Shift-Tab key combinations.

Also, you'll notice that the dialog boxes in Windows 95 have a couple of buttons in the upper-right corner. The button with the × is the Close button; it's equivalent to clicking the Cancel command button. The button with the question mark (?) is part of the Windows 95 Help system. If you click this button and then click a control, a message appears that gives you a brief description of the control. (This button doesn't appear on all dialog boxes.)

I won't cover the options in this dialog box in depth here (see Chapter 7, "Customizing Windows 95"), but you might want to poke around the tabs to get an idea of the kinds of properties you can work with. Remember, this is the properties sheet for the *desktop*, so the options control the look of the desktop and the look of any objects displayed on the desktop. For example, the Background tab lets you specify a pattern or a wallpaper to cover the desktop with. Similarly, the Appearance tab lets you set the color of the desktop (as well as other objects that appear on the desktop, such as menus and window title bars).

When you're finished with the dialog box, you can close it by clicking Cancel, clicking the Close button, or pressing Esc.

Object Actions

An object's actions define the kinds of actions you can take with the object. For example, try this little experiment:

1. Move the mouse pointer over one of the desktop icons.
2. Hold down the left mouse button, and move the mouse pointer slightly to the left. This causes the icon to move to the left as well.
3. Release the mouse button.
4. Right-click the desktop to display its context menu (shown in Figure 5.2).
5. Select the Line up Icons command. Windows 95 moves the icon back to its original position.

In this simple example, you see that one of the desktop object's "actions" is to line up the icons in apple-pie order. Similarly, you can use the Arrange Icons command to display a cascade menu of commands that sort the icons in various ways, and you can use the New command to create new desktop objects, such as folders and documents. (Again, I cover all of this ground in later chapters.)

Folders: Directories and Then Some

I mentioned in Chapter 1, "Understanding the Windows 95 Installation," that Windows 95 has tossed out the word *directory* and replaced it with *folder*. This is in keeping with the re-vamped desktop metaphor in Windows 95. After all, the real world's filing cabinets don't use "directories" to store their memos, forms, contracts, and other paperish bric-a-brac; they use file folders. So it makes sense that our electronic filing cabinets (hard disks, floppy disks, and CD-ROMs) should store their documents in folders as well.

However, if Microsoft had introduced the term "folder" merely as a replacement and an up-date for "directory," we could all yawn a couple of times and go back to what we were doing. But Windows 95's folders go beyond just disk directories, to the point where they are truly universal storage areas. So, yes, your hard disk is filled with folders that contain programs and data, but plenty of other folders also contain other, less obvious, objects:

- The desktop itself is a folder. This is the Big Kahuna, the Top Dog, the Numero Uno of folderdom; it serves as a container for all the other folders associated with your system. (This concept will become clearer later when you work with the Windows Explorer.)

- Disks (hard, floppy, and CD-ROM) are folders containing not only the files in their root, but also other garden-variety folders used to store programs and data.

- The Start menu's submenus are all folders containing shortcuts to programs and documents.

- Control Panel is a folder containing icons that let you customize various aspects of Windows 95.

- The `Printers` folder contains icons for all the printers you've installed in Windows 95.

- The Recycle Bin is a folder that contains files you've deleted.

- The Network Neighborhood is a folder that contains computers, workgroups, and domains associated with your network.

This folder-happy nature might sound like a lot of foolishness (*folderol,* if you will), but it has important ramifications for people looking to unleash Windows 95's full potential. In other words, because you can view the contents of any folder by using Explorer (as you'll see a bit later), you have full access to all of Windows 95's folders. This makes it blindingly simple to customize these folders: You can add new objects, rename or delete existing objects, and work with the properties and actions of objects. As you work through this book, you'll see that I return to this basic concept again and again.

Long Filenames (Finally!)

Ask DOS or Windows 3.x users to catalog their operating system pet peeves, and it will be a rare list that doesn't include "8.3 filename format." They're referring, of course, to the procrustean filename restrictions foisted on us by DOS: a primary name with an eight-character maximum, followed by a period (.), followed by an extension with a three-character maximum.

This constraint has led to hard disks all over the world being littered with filenames like 1STQTR96.XLS and LTR2MOM.DOC. While trying in vain to decipher these filename hieroglyphics, DOS and Windows users would look on in envy at Macintosh, UNIX, and Windows NT mavens with their longer filenames and wonder, "Why not us?"

The problem was that the entire DOS (and Windows 3.x) world was built on the creaky foundations of the file allocation table (FAT) file system. The FAT file structure carved the 8.3 filename format in stone, and any attempt to change this would result in that hobgoblin of DOS functionality: complete incompatibility with all existing applications!

Not to be dissuaded by the impossible, the wizards at Microsoft were determined to build long filename support into Windows 95 *and* maintain compatibility with existing files. So, using an obscure loophole in the FAT file structure, they set up a new file system called the virtual file allocation table (VFAT), which broke through the 8.3 barrier. VFAT now lets you use filenames (and folder names) of up to about 250 characters. As a bonus, for an extra level of readability, you can even use spaces, multiple periods, and the following characters:

~ ' ! @ # $ % ^ & ( ) _ - + = [ ] ; ' ,

Not only that, but, yes, Microsoft *was* able to maintain compatibility with existing 8.3 filenames and the 16-bit applications that require them. The key is that Windows 95 keeps track of *two* names for each file: the long filename and an 8.3 equivalent that's generated from the long name. I explain how this is done when I talk about Windows 95's file system architecture in Chapter 6, "Under the Hood: Understanding the Windows 95 Architecture."

Shortcuts (Or, Can I Get There from Here?)

When I introduced you to your new desktop abode earlier, I mentioned that one thing you can place on the desktop is the *shortcut*. In a way, a shortcut is similar to a program item in the old Windows 3.x Program Manager. For example, you can set up a shortcut or a program item for an application, and double-clicking the new object then launches the application. In both cases, the object is *not* the application itself; instead, it merely points to the file that runs the application, and if you delete the pointer, it has no effect on the application.

But shortcuts go far beyond the capabilities of program items. For one thing, you can create them anywhere you please. Unlike a program item, a shortcut is a separate file (they use the LNK extension), so you can store a shortcut inside any folder, including the desktop. Not only that, but shortcuts can point to many kinds of Windows 95 objects: programs, documents, disk drives, folders—even printers. As you'll see throughout this book, this functionality gives you tremendous flexibility when you're customizing your system to suit the way you work.

To give you an example of how shortcuts work, consider the shortcut I've created on my desktop in Figure 5.4 (the icon to the right of My Computer). Notice three things about this icon:

■ The small arrow in the lower-left corner of the icon identifies this as a shortcut.

■ The icon itself is a folder, which tells you that the shortcut points to a folder.

■ The name of the shortcut is "Shortcut to Windows," so you know that this shortcut takes you to the Windows folder.

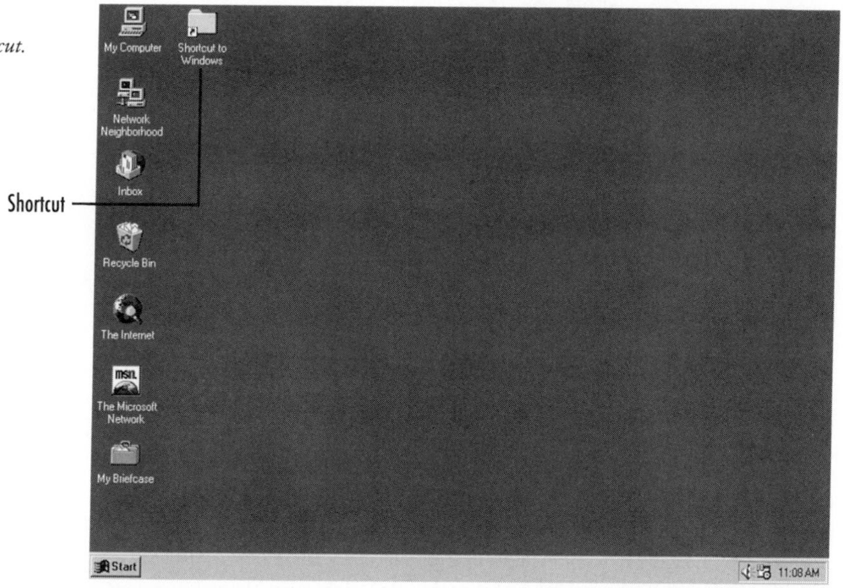

FIGURE 5.4.

A desktop shortcut.

NOTE: SHORTCUT HOW-TO

I show you how to create shortcuts for folders (as well as files) in Chapter 13, "Working with Files and Folders."

Normally you'd have to use either My Computer or Explorer to view the contents of any folder. Double-clicking the shortcut, however, takes you directly to the Windows folder, as shown in Figure 5.5.

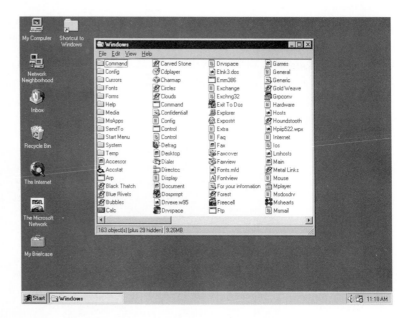

The Desktop Redux

OK, now that you're up to speed on some crucial Windows 95 concepts, we can return to our tour. We'll begin by revisiting the desktop.

For the most part, you need to "place" things on the desktop to work with them. As you saw in Figure 5.1, however, the desktop comes loaded with a few default icons. The number of icons you see on your desktop depends on which Windows 95 components you installed. The next few sections take a quick look at these default icons.

My Computer: A Version of Your Stuff

Windows 95 replaces the venerable Windows 3.x File Manager with not one but two utilities: My Computer and Explorer (discussed later). My Computer is the simpler and less powerful of the two because it shows only the resources available to your computer (hence the name). To open My Computer (and any desktop-bound icon), you can use any of the following methods:

■ Double-click the icon with the mouse.

■ Right-click the icon and select Open from the context menu that appears.

■ From the keyboard, press Ctrl-Esc, then Esc by itself, then Shift-Tab. Use the up- and down-arrow keys to highlight the icon, and then press Enter. (Do you get the idea that Windows 95 was designed with a mouse in mind?)

NOTE: FIRING UP FILE MANAGER

Yes, File Manager, like its antiquated cousin, Program Manager, is still available in Windows 95. My guess is that you'll wonder how you ever performed Windows-based file management chores without Explorer, but there is a way to run File Manager if you really have to. Select Start | Run, type `winfile` in the Run dialog box, and click OK.

When you open the My Computer folder, you'll see a window similar to (but almost certainly different from) the one shown in Figure 5.6.

FIGURE 5.6.

A typical My Computer window.

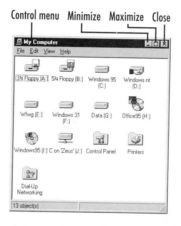

Control menu   Minimize   Maximize   Close

NOTE: A WORD ABOUT WINDOWS 95'S WINDOWS

As you can see in Figure 5.6, the windows in Windows 95 look slightly different from the ones you might be used to in Windows 3.x. For starters, the old control menu box in the upper-left corner has been replaced by an icon. (The icon you see depends on the window.) Also, the Minimize and Maximize buttons are different, and a third button—Close—has been added to the upper-right corner. As you might expect, clicking the Close button closes the window. (Yes, having the Maximize and Close buttons side-by-side *is* a bit uncomfortable at first. Like me, you'll probably shut down a few windows that you were trying to maximize before you get used to the new layout.)

The My Computer window plays host to various icons representing all the disk drives attached to your computer:

- Floppy disk drives (drives A and B in Figure 5.6).
- Hard disk drives (drives C through G in Figure 5.6). Note that drives you're sharing on a network are marked by a hand underneath their icon (see drive D in the figure).

- CD-ROM drives (drives H and I in Figure 5.6).
- Mapped network drives (drive J in Figure 5.6).

For good measure, My Computer also has icons for Control Panel (similar to the Windows 3.x Control Panel applet; see the later discussion), Printers (for the printers you've installed), and Dial-Up Networking (assuming that you installed Dial-Up Networking, that is). Notice that these are all folder icons.

You'd normally use My Computer to display the contents of a disk drive. You do that by double-clicking a drive icon (or by using the arrow keys to highlight an icon and then pressing Enter). For example, opening drive C displays the window shown in Figure 5.7. In this case, drive C contains two folders and 10 files. (The status bar also indicates that 13 hidden files are also on drive C.) From here, you can open a folder to see its contents, and so on.

FIGURE 5.7.

You can use My Computer to display the contents of disk drives.

My Computer is OK, but I'll bet dollars to doughnuts that you'll use Explorer—Windows 95's more muscular file management tool—exclusively and leave the My Computer icon relatively untouched.

Network Neighborhood: Your Network Community

Like Windows for Workgroups, Windows 95 comes with local area network (LAN) support right out of the box. However, besides far superior support for network interface cards and protocols, Windows 95 beats Windows for Workgroups hands-down when it comes to network management. The Network Neighborhood is a good example. Whereas with Windows for Workgroups you couldn't view shared network resources without mapping, say, a network drive to your computer, Windows 95's Network Neighborhood gives you the big picture of everything that's attached to your LAN. (Note that you'll see the Network Neighborhood icon on your desktop only if you have a network interface card installed in your computer and if you've installed a networking client.)

Opening the Network Neighborhood folder displays a window similar to the one shown in Figure 5.8. Selecting the first object—Entire Network—displays a new window that lists all the workgroups and domains on your LAN. The other objects in the Network Neighborhood window (Apollo, Dionysus, Hermes, and Zeus in Figure 5.8) show the computers associated with your own workgroup or domain. Selecting one of these objects opens a window that shows you the resources which that computer is sharing with the network. For example, Figure 5.9 shows the resources being shared by the Apollo computer (in this case, three disk drives and a printer).

FIGURE 5.8.

The Network Neighborhood *folder lets you view the computers and resources attached to your LAN.*

FIGURE 5.9.

Opening a network computer's folder displays the resources which that computer is sharing with the rest of the LAN.

A corollary to this Network Neighborhood approach is that Windows 95 now supports the Universal Naming Convention (UNC) for shared network resources. So instead of mapping a network drive to your machine or even searching for a shared resource in the Network Neighborhood, you can just specify the resource by name (for example, \\SERVER\COMMON).

Here's a summary of a few of the other networking enhancements introduced in Windows 95:

TCP/IP support: The TCP/IP protocol—the *lingua franca* of the Internet—is now built into Windows 95.

Multiple network support: You can install multiple protocols in Windows 95 and thus access resources from different networks (for example, Windows NT and NetWare) at the same time.

User-level profiles and security: You can define multiple users on one computer, each with his own system configuration, including user-level passwords authenticated by a Windows NT or NetWare server.

NetWare client: Windows 95 comes with a client for NetWare that gives you full NetWare support from within Windows 95.

NOTE: NETWORK KNOW-HOW

To learn about Windows 95 networking in detail, turn to Part VII, "Unleashing Windows 95 Networking and Internet Connectivity."

Inbox: The (Almost) Universal Messaging Client

It used to be that the only way to "reach out and touch someone" was via the telephone. Nowadays, however, you can make contact via umpteen different e-mail systems, fax, pager, voice mail, and who knows what else. Managing all this communication is one of the prime skills for the wired worker of the 90s. The Promised Land of communications management is the "universal in-box" that stores all these kinds of messages in one easily accessible location. We're not there yet, but Windows 95 brings us one step closer with Microsoft Exchange (called Windows Messaging in OSR2), a messaging client that can handle not only e-mail via LAN-based Microsoft Mail systems, the Internet, the Microsoft Network, and CompuServe, but also faxes.

The desktop's Inbox icon starts Exchange and displays a window similar to the one shown in Figure 5.10. (If you haven't yet set up Exchange, double-clicking the Inbox icon displays the Inbox Setup Wizard.) The pane on the left consists of various folders you can use to store messages for posterity (you can create your own folders if you like). The pane on the right shows the available messages. You can use this window to read and compose messages, configure Exchange, and more.

Figure 5.10.

Microsoft Exchange can accept e-mail messages from multiple systems as well as faxes.

NOTE: EXCHANGE DETAILS

I cover Exchange in Part VI, "Unleashing Windows 95 Communications." See Chapter 27, "Setting Up Microsoft Exchange," Chapter 28, "Exchanging E-Mail with Microsoft Exchange," and Chapter 29, "Using Microsoft Fax to Send and Receive Faxes."

The Recycle Bin: Your Windows 95 Trash Can

Accidentally deleting important files has long been the bugbear of personal computing. So, over the years, various programming wizards have come up with solutions that allow the butterfingered to recover from slips of the keyboard.

The scheme that Windows 95 uses is simple, and not at all new: When the user deletes a file, instead of sending the unfortunate creature into some never-never land of nuked data, the operating system moves it into a separate directory. The file remains intact, and Windows 95 keeps track of where it came from. Undeleting the file is then a simple matter of moving it back to its original location. The hidden folder that Windows 95 uses for this job is called `Recycled`, and the mechanism by which you recover files is called the Recycle Bin.

Double-clicking the Recycle Bin icon opens the `Recycle Bin` folder, as shown in Figure 5.11. The Recycle Bin lists each recently deleted file, its original location, the date it was deleted, and so on. To recover a file, highlight it and select File | Restore.

FIGURE 5.11.

You can use the Recycle Bin to restore accidentally deleted files.

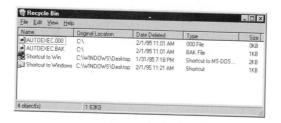

NOTE: LEARNING ABOUT THE RECYCLE BIN

Head for Chapter 13 to get the full scoop on using the Recycle Bin.

The Internet: Surfing the Web

This icon launches Internet Explorer, as shown in Figure 5.12. Internet Explorer is Microsoft's entry in the World Wide Web browser sweepstakes. This icon appears only if you installed Microsoft Plus!, the Windows 95 Service Pack, or OSR2, or if you've downloaded (and installed) Internet Explorer from the Internet. (If you installed Internet Explorer from Microsoft Plus! or the Service Pack, or if you have OSR2, and you didn't configure your Internet connection during Setup, opening the Internet icon launches the Internet Setup Wizard.)

NOTE: EXPLORING THE NET

I talk about Internet Explorer in depth in Chapter 38, "Exploring the Web with Internet Explorer." To get your Internet connection established, check out Chapter 36, "Implementing TCP/IP for Internet and Network Connections," and Chapter 37, "Windows 95 and the Internet."

FIGURE 5.12.

FIGURE 5.12.

If you've installed Microsoft Plus!, the Windows 95 Service Pack, or OSR2, you have access to the Internet Explorer Web browser.

The Microsoft Network

The release of Windows 95 also marked the official debut of The Microsoft Network (MSN), Microsoft's online service. Although initially it wasn't particularly remarkable as far as online services go, the real "hook" for MSN (and the source of most of its pre-launch controversy) was its seamless integration with Windows 95. MSN uses the same folder/shortcut metaphor and navigation techniques as Windows 95 (Explorer, in particular), and it's a relatively easy matter to drag data from MSN and drop it inside running applications. Not only that, but MSN e-mail is a no-brainer thanks to Microsoft Exchange. And, lastly, starting MSN is the easiest operation of all: Just double-click The Microsoft Network desktop icon to display the Sign In screen, and click Connect. A few seconds later, you're inside MSN and you can start exploring items such as MSNBC, as shown in Figure 5.13. (If you haven't yet configured MSN, double-clicking its desktop icon launches the setup process.)

NOTE: WHERE TO FIND MSN INFO

I'll take you through the full MSN story—from configuration to connection—in Chapter 26, "Getting Online with The Microsoft Network."

FIGURE 5.13.

MSN includes goodies such as MSNBC.

My Briefcase: Coordinating Desktop and Laptop

Windows 95, unlike any of its predecessors, recognizes an important fact of notebook computing life: Your notebook often has to use documents from your desktop machine, and vice versa. Windows 95's Briefcase feature makes it a breeze to swap documents between a desktop and a notebook (provided, of course, that both machines are running Windows 95) because it keeps track of which files are changed. Updating one system or the other takes only a couple of mouse clicks or keystrokes.

The desktop's My Briefcase icon opens the `Briefcase` folder, which you can use to hold the documents you transfer between your desktop and notebook computers. Instead of always copying individual documents back and forth, you usually just work with the `Briefcase` folder. The real advantage of using Briefcase, however, is that it synchronizes the documents on both machines automatically. If you work on a few documents on your notebook, for example, Windows 95 can figure out which ones have been modified and then lets you update the desktop machine by running a simple command. There's no guesswork and no chance of copying a file to the wrong folder.

Briefcase isn't the only Windows 95 tool for folks who lug their computers around. Here are a few more of these handy tools:

Dial-Up networking: Lets you connect to a network (or another computer) via modem and use the shared network resources remotely.

Direct cable connection: Lets you connect two computers (such as a desktop and a portable) via cable and transfer files between them.

Hot docking support: Windows 95's Plug and Play architecture lets you "hot dock" your portable. When you attach the machine to, or remove it from, its docking station, Windows 95 automatically reconfigures the hardware configuration.

Power management support: Windows 95 can work with the power management features of most modern notebooks.

NOTE: PORTABLE PARTICULARS

Briefcase and other notebook notions are covered in depth in Chapter 20, "Windows 95 on the Road: Notebook Computers and the Briefcase."

A Tour of the Taskbar

One of the reasons a world in love with the DOS command line was dragged (kicking and screaming, in some cases) into the Windows way of doing things a few years back was that Windows made it so much easier to do two things: launch applications and navigate among multiple open applications. After all, what could be easier than double-clicking an icon to fire up a program, or pressing Alt-Tab to cycle through several running apps?

However, after we got used to doing things this way and started pushing its limits, cracks started to form:

- The more applications we installed, the more crowded and cumbersome Program Manager became. It seemed that every install program around liked to create its own program group and populate it with not only the icon that started the installed application, but also "Read Me" files, Help files, and so on. So, yes, double-clicking an icon was an easy way to start a program, but *finding* the icon became a real needle-in-a-haystack exercise.

- Windows 3.x, although by no means the best multitasking operating system around, still let us open lots of small- to medium-sized applications. Pressing Alt-Tab is a reasonable way to navigate two or three open programs, but it gets tiresome cycling through six or seven.

- Windows offered no easy way to know which programs were running, which was a real problem considering that it was possible to open multiple copies of accessories such as Write and Notepad. You could minimize all your windows and adjust the active window so that it didn't cover the bottom of the screen, but that was a pain. You could use the Task List, but that was an awkward tool at best.

The Windows 95 solution to all of these problems (although it's an imperfect solution, as you'll see) is the *taskbar*: the gray strip that runs across the bottom of the screen, as shown in Figure 5.14. The next few sections describe the taskbar and show you how it improves on the Windows 3.x tools.

FIGURE 5.14.
The Windows 95 taskbar.

 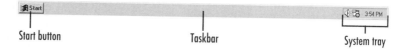

Start button   Taskbar   System tray

The Start Button: The Windows 95 Launch Pad

Perhaps the most recognized feature of Windows 95 is the Start button in the lower-left corner. (This isn't even remotely surprising considering that most of Microsoft's marketing—both pre- and post-launch—featured the Start button in some way, and there was, of course, the famous multimillion-dollar license to use the Rolling Stones song "Start Me Up.") This is as it should be because the Start button is the doorway into most of Windows 95's features.

Several methods are available for accessing the Start button:

- Click it with the mouse.
- Press Ctrl-Esc.
- If you have the Microsoft Natural Keyboard or some other Windows 95-ready keyboard, press the Windows logo key (⊞).

In each case, the Start menu appears, as shown in Figure 5.15.

FIGURE 5.15.
Clicking the Start button opens the Start menu.

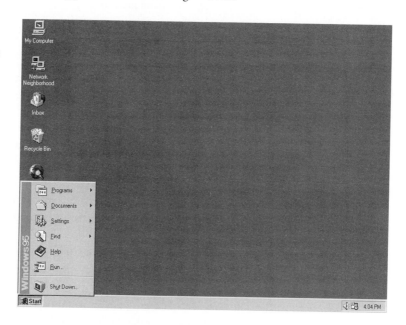

Here's a summary of the commands that appear on the Start menu:

Shut Down: You select this command when you want to either restart Windows 95 or shut down your computer. It displays the Shut Down Windows dialog box, which gives you various options (I discussed them in Chapter 4, "Start It Your Way: Understanding Windows 95 Startup").

Eject PC: This command appears only on some notebook docking stations. You use this command to separate the notebook from the docking station.

Suspend: This command appears only if you have a monitor or a portable computer that supports Advanced Power Management. This command shuts off the power to the monitor or portable without exiting Windows 95.

Run: This command displays the Run dialog box, which lets you run programs by entering the name of the file that starts the application (you'll often need to include the appropriate drive and folder as well). It's handy if the program you want to run doesn't appear on any of the Start menu's other folders, or if you need to specify command-line parameters.

CAUTION: USING LONG FILENAMES IN THE RUN DIALOG BOX

In the Run dialog box, if you enter a filename that includes a space, Windows 95 generates an error. To avoid this problem, enclose the filename in quotation marks. For example, suppose that you want to run WordPad with the following command:

```
c:\program files\accessories\wordpad.exe
```

In the Run dialog box, you must enter this command like so:

```
"c:\program files\accessories\wordpad.exe"
```

Alternatively, you can use the DOS 8.3 filename without quotes:

```
c:\progra~1\access~1\wordpad.exe
```

Help: This command loads the Windows 95 Help system, which I'll talk about later in this chapter.

Find: This command displays a folder that contains several tools for finding files, folders, network computers, or information in The Microsoft Network. I give you the details in Chapter 13.

Settings: Selecting this command displays a folder with three items: Control Panel (which opens the Control Panel folder; discussed later in this chapter), Printers (which opens the Printers folder; see Chapter 19, "Prescriptions for Perfect Printing"), and Taskbar (which displays the Taskbar Properties dialog box, discussed in Chapter 7).

Documents: This command displays the Documents folder, which contains a list of the last 15 documents you worked with in any of your applications. (In this sense, a *document* is any file you work with in a program. It could be a spreadsheet, a drawing, a letter, or whatever.) When you select a document from this folder, Windows launches the appropriate program and loads the document automatically.

Programs: This command opens the Programs folder, which contains shortcuts to various applications as well as other folders. Note that, if you upgraded over Windows 3.x, you'll find your old program groups in the Programs folder. To launch a program, just select its Start menu shortcut. (I'll show you how to add more folders and shortcuts to the Start menu in Chapter 7.)

TIP: CLICKLESS FOLDER OPENING

Normally, you open a Start menu folder by clicking an item. (You can also highlight an item and press either Enter or the left-arrow key.) If you're feeling lazy, or if your clicking finger is out of commission, you can still open the folder by hovering the mouse pointer over the item for a second or two.

The Start menu's folder-within-a-folder concept is, to my mind, one of the least attractive facets of the Windows 95 interface. The problem is that you often have to drill down several folders to get to the shortcut you need. For example, if I want to run ScanDisk, I have to open the Programs folder, open the Accessories folder, open the System Tools folder, and select ScanDisk, as shown in Figure 5.16. It's still better than opening and closing program groups, but it's far from ideal. I'll show you a few pointers for streamlining program startups in Chapters 7 and 13.

FIGURE 5.16.

Windows 95 often makes you jump through quite a few Start menu hoops to find the shortcut you need.

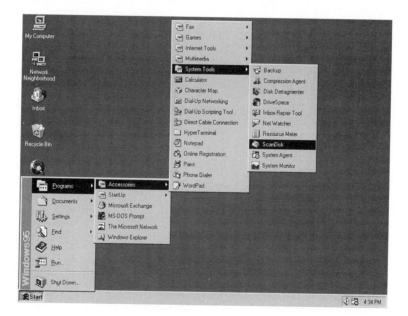

Navigating Applications with the Taskbar

After you've opened some programs or windows from the Start menu (or the desktop icons), the taskbar really comes into its own. To see why, look at Figure 5.17. Here I have three application windows open: FreeCell, WordPad, and Calculator.

FIGURE 5.17.

Each running program has its own taskbar icon.

Running programs   Active program

Notice how the taskbar sports an icon for each running program. The taskbar tells you two things: which programs are running and which of those programs has the focus (is the active program). On the taskbar, the program with the focus is shown with a "pressed" button (Calculator in Figure 5.17). That's a nice improvement over Windows 3.x, because now you can tell at a glance exactly which programs and folders are open.

But there's more to the taskbar than that. You can also use it to navigate among running programs. To activate a window, simply click its taskbar icon, and Windows 95 immediately brings the window to the foreground and gives it the focus. This feature is particularly handy when you're working with maximized windows where you can't see any piece of the other open windows. Even when you maximize a window, *the taskbar stays visible on-screen,* so other windows remain only a mouse-click away.

TIP: GETTING THE PROGRAM NAME

One of the problems you'll run into is that after you've opened a few programs, Windows 95 shrinks the buttons so that they can all fit on the taskbar. As a result, some buttons are bound to show only part of the program name. To see the entire name, point the mouse at the button and leave it there for a couple of seconds. Windows 95 then displays a small banner above the button that spells out the entire program name.

TIP: MORE METHODS FOR SWITCHING BETWEEN PROGRAMS

The taskbar isn't the only program navigation game in town. Windows 95 also lets you navigate open programs by using old-fashioned Windows 3.1 methods:

■ You can cycle through the icons of the programs by pressing Alt-Tab (or Alt-Shift-Tab to cycle backward).

■ If you'd prefer to see the entire application window as you cycle, try Alt-Esc (or Alt-Shift-Esc).

■ If you liked the Task Manager in Windows 3.1, you can still use it in Windows 95. Unfortunately, you can't display it by double-clicking the desktop, as before. Instead, select Start | Run, type `taskman.exe` in the Run dialog box, and click OK.

The System Tray

The right side of the taskbar is devoted to the *system tray*. Here, Windows 95 displays icons that provide you with information and let you know when certain background processes are active. Table 5.1 lists a few of the icons you're likely to see.

Table 5.1. Some icons that Windows 95 displays in the system tray.

Icon	Description
	Volume control icon (appears only if you have a sound card in your system). Double-click this icon to display the Volume Control applet.
	System Agent icon (appears only if you've installed Microsoft Plus!). Double-click this icon to display the System Agent window (see Chapter 15, "Protecting Your Windows 95 Investment").
	Resource meter icon. Displays a graphical view of the available system resources (as explained in Chapter 9, "Windows 95 Performance Tuning and Optimization"). If you hover the mouse pointer over this icon for a second or two, Windows 95 displays the exact state of the system resources. Alternatively, you can double-click the icon to see the resources displayed in a dialog box.
	Modem status icon. This icon appears when you've established a modem connection with another site. Double-click this icon to see the number of bytes sent and received during the session and the total connect time.
	Microsoft Network icon. This icon appears while you're connected to The Microsoft Network. Double-click this icon to disconnect.

Microsoft PLUS

5

WINDOWS 95:
THE 50¢ TOUR

continues

Table 5.1. continued

Icon	Description
	Microsoft Fax icon. This icon indicates that Microsoft Fax is running in the background. Double-click the icon to see the Microsoft Fax Status dialog box (explained in Chapter 29).
	New mail icon. This icon appears when you receive new mail in Microsoft Exchange.
	Printing icon. This icon appears while Windows 95 is processing a print job. Double-click this icon to open the printer (see Chapter 19).
	AC power icon. This icon appears on a portable computer that is connected to its AC power supply.
	Battery meter icon. This icon appears on a portable computer that is running on its battery.
En	The current keyboard language. See Chapter 7 to learn how to add different keyboard languages to Windows 95.
12:23 PM	The current time. Hold the mouse pointer over this icon for a second or two to see the current date. Double-click this icon to display the Date/Time Properties dialog box.

Besides the icons listed in Table 5.1, some applications display their own icons in this area.

Explorer: File Manager on Steroids

You saw earlier that you can use My Computer to examine the contents of the disk drives attached to your system. And as you'll see later in this book (Chapter 13, to be exact), you can also use My Computer to perform basic file management duties, such as copying and renaming files.

But Windows 95's toolbox comes equipped with a second file management utility: Windows Explorer. Although I'll compare the features of these two programs in more depth a bit later (see the section "Explorer Versus My Computer"), I can tell you now that Explorer is the more advanced of the two. (Which is why the people at Microsoft decided to make My Computer, with its easily accessible desktop icon, the more obvious tool; they assumed, rightly, that in the end most Windows 95 users would be new or inexperienced. In fact, as you'll soon see, My Computer is actually a subset of Explorer.) Explorer's extra bells and whistles make it a worthy successor to File Manager, the much-maligned file management program from Windows 3.x. This section introduces you to Explorer by starting it and checking out how things are arranged in the Explorer universe.

NOTE: THE REAL EXPLORER DEAL

You'll just kick a few of Explorer's tires in this section. If you want to get behind the wheel and take it for a spin, Chapter 13 is the place to be. I'll present lots of tricks and advanced techniques for taking full advantage of Explorer's power.

Taking a Look Around

To start Explorer, select Start | Programs | Windows Explorer. Windows 95 displays the Explorer window, shown in Figure 5.18. (Because your computer almost certainly has a different configuration than mine, your Explorer window won't appear exactly as shown in the figure.)

FIGURE 5.18.

The Explorer window.

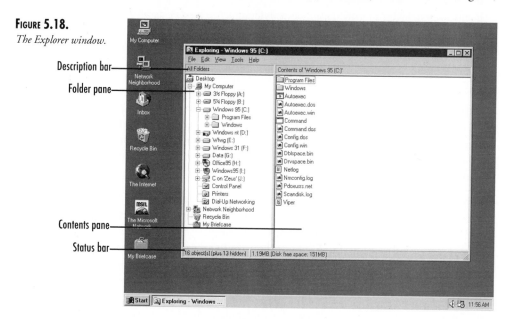

On the surface, Explorer's layout is reminiscent of File Manager. The window is split in two: On the left, File Manager's directory tree has been replaced by Explorer's *Folder pane,* and on the right, File Manager's contents list has been replaced by Explorer's *Contents pane.* There are, however, two significant differences between the two:

- File Manager's drive icons are gone. Instead, the Folder pane in Explorer includes disk drives (as well as a few other goodies, such as the Network Neighborhood).

- Explorer isn't a Multiple Document Interface (MDI) application. So, unlike with File Manager, you can't open multiple windows for different drives or folders. This sounds like a drawback, and it feels like one at first if you're used to the File Manager's way of doing things. But Explorer's Folder pane has some slick navigation options that render the lack of multiple window support moot. And, besides, if you *really* need to open a second window, you can always start a second copy of Explorer.

Navigating the Folder Pane

The Folder pane's job is to display (and let you work with) all the folders to which your system has access. Remember that the desktop is the main folder for your system. If you think of the desktop as a sort of "root" folder, it makes sense that Explorer shows a "Desktop" folder at the top of the Folder pane. From there, the Desktop folder's subfolders branch out in that multi-level, "upside-down tree" layout that you might be used to from File Manager.

> ### NOTE: THE DESKTOP DIFFERENCE
>
> In this section, I want to distinguish between the desktop proper and the desktop's folder in Explorer. To do this, I use "desktop" when I'm speaking of the actual desktop (as I've done throughout this chapter), and I use "Desktop" when I'm speaking of the folder.

The first "branch" is the My Computer folder. It shows, among a few other things, the various disk drives attached directly to your machine (either attached physically or attached via a network connection). Yes, this is the same My Computer folder you saw earlier, but in a slightly different guise. Below My Computer, the Desktop folder's other first-level branches include a few more folders, depending on what's installed on your system. (At the very least, you'll see the Recycle Bin folder.)

You might be wondering why the Desktop folder's first-level folders don't correspond to the icons displayed on the desktop itself. In Figure 5.18, for example, seven desktop icons are shown (My Computer, Network Neighborhood, Inbox, Recycle Bin, The Internet, The Microsoft Network, and My Briefcase), but Explorer shows only four first-level branches for the Desktop folder (My Computer, Network Neighborhood, Recycle Bin, and My Briefcase). The answer is that three of the icons—Inbox, The Internet, and The Microsoft Network—aren't folders. They start programs, which makes them files, really, so they appear in the Contents pane. Figure 5.19 shows the Explorer with the Desktop folder highlighted. As you can see, all seven desktop icons appear in the Contents pane.

Navigating among the visible folders is straightforward: Either click a folder or use the up- and down-arrow keys to move through the folders. Whenever you highlight a folder, its contents (subfolders and files) appear automatically in the Contents pane.

Explorer's default Folder pane displays the subfolders for both My Computer and drive C. To open any other folders, either click the plus sign (+) to the left of the folder name, or highlight the folder and press the plus sign on the keyboard's numeric keypad. The plus sign then changes to a minus sign (–) to indicate an open branch. Closing a folder is just as easy: Either click the minus sign, or highlight the folder and press the minus sign key on the numeric keypad.

Figure 5.19.

When you select the Desktop *folder, all the desktop icons appear in the Contents pane.*

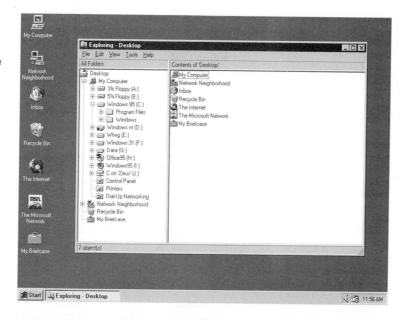

NOTE: EXPLORER'S PLUS SIGNS CAN BE DECEIVING

Explorer is a bit lazy in that it doesn't check all the folders associated with disk drives to see whether they have subfolders. (Actually, this is to save time when Explorer starts.) This means that it places a plus sign beside every folder (except the ones that are open, of course). If you click a plus sign for a drive or folder that doesn't have any subfolders, Explorer clues in and simply removes the plus sign.

CAUTION: DON'T FORGET TO INSERT A FLOPPY DISK

To avoid an error message, before highlighting a floppy disk folder, make sure that you have a disk in the drive.

Working with the Contents Pane

The job of the Contents pane is to show you what's inside whatever folder is currently highlighted in the Folders pane. This means you'll see not only the files that the folder contains, but all of its subfolders as well. The Description bar above the Contents pane tells you the name of the current folder. When you first open Explorer, the Contents pane shows the contents of drive C. (Somewhat confusingly, Explorer doesn't actually highlight drive C in the Folder pane. Fortunately, the Description bar tells you what you're viewing.)

For example, Figure 5.20 shows the Contents pane with the Windows folder highlighted. The first dozen items are subfolders (as evidenced by their folder icons), and the rest of the entries are files (the icon that Explorer displays depends on the file and, in the case of documents, the program used to create the file). Notice too that the status bar supplies you with a few tidbits of information:

■ The number of objects (subfolders and files) in the folder

■ The number of hidden objects

■ The number of megabytes used by the files (this value doesn't count the files in the subfolders)

■ The amount of free space left on the drive

FIGURE 5.20.

The contents of the Windows *folder.*

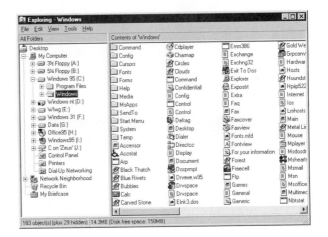

Are you wondering why most of the files in Figure 5.20 don't have an extension? That's because, by default, Explorer hides the extensions for file types that are "registered" with Windows 95 (which is similar to the file associations you might have worked with in File Manager). For example, BMP files are registered (associated) with the Paint accessory. So instead of showing the BMP extension, Explorer displays each BMP file with the Paint program's icon. In Figure 5.20, take a look at the files named Black Thatch, Blue Rivets, and Bubbles (BMP files all) to see what I mean.

The Contents pane layout you see in Figure 5.20 is called the *List view* because it shows a simple columnar list of the folder's contents. You can also try three other views: *Large Icons, Small Icons,* and *Details*.

To check out the Large Icons view, select View | Large Icons. As you can see in Figure 5.21, this view increases the size of the folder and file icons to make them easier to see and displays them across the pane. This view is similar to the default view of My Computer (shown earlier in Figure 5.6).

FIGURE 5.21.

The Contents pane using the Large Icons view.

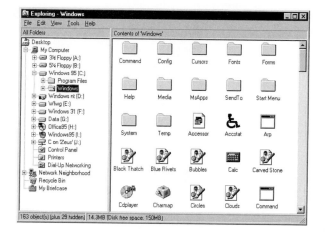

For the Small Icons view, shown in Figure 5.22, select View | Small Icons. In this view, Explorer also displays the objects across the Contents pane, but it uses much smaller icons to fit more into the pane.

FIGURE 5.22.

The Contents pane using the Small Icons view.

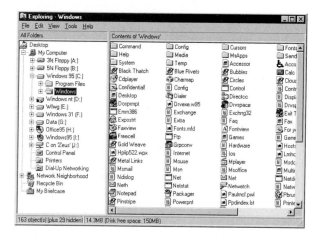

Finally, for the Details view, select View | Details. As shown in Figure 5.23, the Details view displays the folder's objects in a single column, and for each item, Explorer shows you the size, type, and date and time the object was created or last modified.

Using Explorer's Toolbar

Explorer, like quite a few of the Windows 95 accessories, comes with its own toolbar for single-click access to many Explorer features. To display the toolbar, select View | Toolbar. As you can see in Figure 5.24, the toolbar appears just below the menu bar.

5

WINDOWS 95:
THE 50¢ TOUR

FIGURE 5.23.

The Contents pane using the Details view.

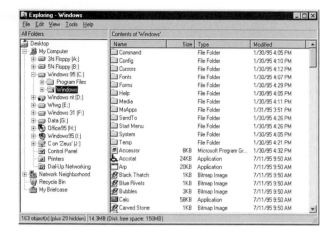

FIGURE 5.24.

Display the Explorer toolbar to give yourself easier access to several Explorer commands.

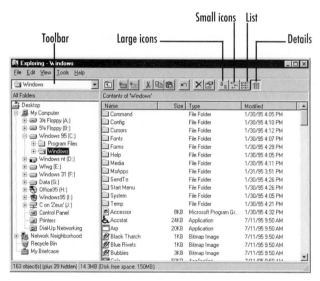

I'll hold off on discussing many of these buttons until Chapter 13, but note that the last four (as shown in Figure 5.24) let you switch quickly among the four Content pane views.

TIP: TOOLBAR BUTTON HINTS

If you're not sure which toolbar button does what, you can get a hint by placing the mouse pointer over a button. After a couple of seconds, a banner (or *tooltip*, as it's called) appears that tells you the button's name.

Basic File and Folder Operations

You'll be learning many advanced techniques for dealing with files and folders in Chapter 13, but let's take a few minutes now to run through a few fundamentals.

Selecting Multiple Files and Folders

If you need to work with multiple files or folders (which, to save some verbiage, I'll just call *objects* in the next few sections), Explorer has various techniques you can exploit.

With the mouse, you can use three methods to select multiple objects (note that all of these techniques apply to the Contents pane only):

■ To select noncontiguous objects, hold down the Ctrl key and click each object.

■ To select contiguous objects, click the first object, hold down the Shift key, and click the last object.

■ You can also select a group of objects by "boxing" them with the mouse. Move the mouse pointer to the right of the first object's name (make sure that it's not over the object's name or icon), and then drag the mouse down and to the left. As you're dragging, Explorer displays a dotted-line box, and every object that falls at least partially within that box gets highlighted. When all the objects you need are highlighted, release the mouse button.

Here's how to select multiple objects from the keyboard:

■ To select every object in the current folder, press Ctrl-A.

■ To select noncontiguous objects, use the arrow keys to highlight the first object, and then hold down Ctrl. For each of the other objects you want to select, use the arrow keys to highlight the object (actually, it's not a true highlight; just a dotted-line box), and then press the Spacebar. When you're done, release Ctrl.

■ To select contiguous objects, highlight the first object, hold down Shift, and use the arrow keys to highlight the other objects.

Copying Files and Folders

One of the things that often has people scratching their heads when they start using Explorer is that the File menu has no Copy command (as it did in File Manager). Instead, in keeping with Windows 95's OLE-centric architecture (which I'll explain in Chapter 17, "Sharing Data in Windows 95: The Clipboard and OLE"), you copy files and folders by using a copy-and-paste technique, as though the object were a chunk of data (which is exactly how OLE views a file). That is, you make a copy of an object by copying it to the Clipboard, selecting the destination, and pasting the object from the Clipboard.

Given this background, it makes more sense then that the Copy command is on Explorer's *Edit* menu. Here's how to copy an object:

1. Select the object or objects you want to copy.
2. Select Edit | Copy.

TIP: FASTER COPYING

You can also send the selected objects to the Clipboard by pressing Ctrl-C, by clicking the Copy button in the toolbar, or by right-clicking any selected object and choosing Copy from the context menu.

---

3. Move to the destination folder.
4. Select Edit | Paste.

TIP: FASTER PASTING

You can also paste the copied objects from the Clipboard by pressing Ctrl-V, by clicking the Paste button in the toolbar, or by right-clicking inside the destination folder and choosing Paste from the context menu.

Moving Files and Folders

Moving an object is similar to copying it. In this case, though, you "cut" the object to the Clipboard and paste it to the destination folder:

1. Select the object or objects you want to move.
2. Select Edit | Cut.

TIP: FASTER CUTTING

You can also cut the selected objects by pressing Ctrl-X, by clicking the Cut button in the toolbar, or by right-clicking any selected object and choosing Cut from the context menu.

---

3. Move to the destination folder.
4. Select Edit | Paste.

Copying and Moving with Drag-and-Drop

For most copy and move operations, you might find that using the mouse to drag the selected objects to their destination folder is much easier. First make sure that the destination folder is available in Explorer's Folders pane. (In other words, if the destination folder is a subfolder, open its parent folder so that the destination is visible.) Select the objects you want to copy or move, and then use the Folders pane to bring the destination folder into view. (Be sure to use the Folders pane's scrollbars to do this; otherwise, your objects will no longer be selected.)

Depending on whether you want to copy or move the objects, you might need to hold down a key before you start dragging:

■ If you're dragging the objects to a folder on the *same* drive, Explorer assumes that you're moving the objects. To make Explorer copy the objects, hold down Ctrl while dragging. (When you're copying an object, Explorer appends a small plus sign (+) to the mouse pointer.)

■ If you're dragging the objects to a folder on a *different* drive, Explorer assumes that you're copying the objects. To make Explorer move the objects, hold down Shift while dragging.

■ If you're dragging an executable file, Explorer assumes that you want to create a shortcut. To copy the file, hold down Ctrl; to move the file, hold down Shift. (Explorer signifies that it will create a shortcut by appending a small box with an arrow inside it to the mouse pointer.)

Hold down the appropriate key (if any), drag the objects to the destination folder, and drop them.

Renaming Files and Folders

One of Windows 95's nice features is that you can rename objects "in place." In other words, instead of using some sort of "Rename" dialog box (à la File Manager), you just edit the file or folder name directly. To try this, use one of the following techniques:

■ Highlight the object and then select File | Rename.

■ Click the object's name, wait for a couple of beats, and click the name again. (You wait in between clicks to avoid a double-click.)

Explorer creates a text box around the object's name, complete with insertion-point cursor. You can then use the standard text box techniques (arrow keys, Backspace, Delete, and so on) to edit the name. When you're done, press Enter.

TIP: FASTER RENAMING

You can also rename an object by highlighting it and pressing F2, or by right-clicking the object and choosing Rename from the context menu.

Creating New Files and Folders

You can use Explorer to create new folders *and* new files. It's not surprising that you can create new folders in Explorer—this is, after all, a common task in any file management system—but it's certainly unusual that you can create new files. However, this is in keeping with Windows 95 "think documents, not applications" approach. Explorer "understands" certain file types (and can be taught new file types, as you'll see in Chapter 13), so it's easy for it to create new, empty files.

To create a new object, first highlight the folder in which you want the new object stored. Now select File | New. The cascade menu that appears contains the following commands:

Folder: Creates a new folder.

Shortcut: Creates a new shortcut and displays the Create Shortcut dialog box. See Chapter 13 to learn how to create shortcuts.

Text Document: Creates a new document in text (TXT) format.

WordPad Document: Creates a new document in WordPad (DOC) format.

Bitmap Image: Creates a new document in bitmap (BMP) format.

Wave Sound: Creates a new document in wave (WAV) format.

Briefcase: Creates a new Briefcase container.

In most cases, you'll need to rename the new object and then (in the case of a document) open it in its native application.

TIP: RIGHT-CLICKING TO THE NEW MENU

You can also display the New menu by highlighting the parent folder in the Folders pane, right-clicking an empty part of the Contents pane, and selecting New from the context menu that appears.

Deleting Files and Folders

Deleting objects you no longer need is easy: Just highlight the objects and then select File | Delete. When Windows 95 asks you to confirm the deletion, click Yes.

TIP: FASTER DELETING

You can also delete the selected objects by pressing Delete, by clicking the Delete button in the toolbar, or by right-clicking any selected object and choosing Delete from the context menu. Another handy technique is to drag the object from Explorer and drop it on the Recycle Bin icon.

TIP: USE NEW DIALOG BOXES FOR FILE CHORES

If you're using 32-bit applications designed for Windows 95, these programs come with powerful new Open and Save As dialog boxes. These dialog boxes are like scaled-down versions of Explorer. For example, you can use them to rename files by pressing F2 when a file is highlighted. Also, you can right-click a file and use the context menu to copy, cut, and delete files.

Explorer Versus My Computer

Few experienced computer users are dispassionate about file management software. The more time you spend on a PC, it seems, the more you fiddle with files, folders, and floppy disks. So the software you use to perform that fiddling becomes crucial. On the other hand, few inexperienced computer users are comfortable with file management software. They spend comparatively less time on their machines, so basic file legwork becomes more like forced file labor.

With these opposing viewpoints in mind, one of Microsoft's main design goals in Windows 95 was to come up with a system to manage files and folders that would appeal to both experienced and inexperienced users alike. In the end, they couldn't come up with one, so they created two: Explorer and My Computer. Although there are no absolutes here, you can say that Explorer was basically designed with the more advanced user in mind, whereas My Computer should appeal more to Windows neophytes.

To decide which system is right for you or for your users (or, more accurately, which one is right in which circumstances), you need to examine the three main ways that My Computer differs from Explorer, which is what you'll do in the next few sections.

My Computer Doesn't Have a Folders Pane

The entire My Computer window is taken up by the current folder's contents, which gives My Computer a simpler, less cluttered layout. This means that if you need quick access to a disk drive or top-level folder, My Computer is often a faster way to get there. If, however, you need to drill down a few layers into a lower-level folder, Explorer is your best bet.

If you do a lot of file copying or moving, you'll almost certainly prefer Explorer. As you'll see in Chapter 13, the easiest way to copy (or move) a file is to drag it from its current folder and drop it on the destination folder. To do this successfully in My Computer requires two open windows: one for the source folder and one for the destination folder. In Explorer, however, you need only make sure that the destination folder is visible in the Folders pane.

NOTE: DRAG-AND-DROP: A PRIMER

Windows 95 provides extensive support for drag-and-drop operations, and you'll be using this technique throughout this book to simplify many day-to-day tasks. So to be on the safe side, let me make it clear what I mean by drag-and-drop. *Dragging* an object with the mouse means that you move the mouse pointer over the object, press and hold down the left mouse button, and move the mouse. The result is that the object moves along with the pointer. When you get to your destination, you *drop* the object by releasing the mouse button.

My Computer Doesn't Have a Tools Menu

Explorer's Tools menu has several highly useful commands, including a Find command (to search for files or folders), a Map Network Drive command (to map a network drive to your computer), and a Go To command (to head directly to a specific folder). I'll discuss each of these in more detail in Chapter 13.

My Computer doesn't have the Tools menu, so you don't have access to these commands. (Although you can right-click a drive or folder in My Computer and then click Find in the context menu that appears.) Other methods are available for executing these features, but they're not as convenient.

Each Time You Open a Folder, My Computer Opens a New Window

This is one of My Computer's less endearing features. It's OK if you don't have far to go, but heading down a few folder levels results in a confusing mess of windows on-screen. Fortunately, you can turn off this feature by selecting View | Options from My Computer. In the Options dialog box, shown in Figure 5.25, activate the Browse folders by using a single window that changes as you open each folder option, and click OK.

FIGURE 5.25.

Use the Options dialog box to stop My Computer from opening all those windows.

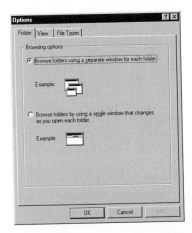

`folder` option is selected in the Options dialog box. Next, as you select folders in My Computer, hold down the Ctrl key. This bypasses the options just discussed and tells My Computer to open each folder in the same window. Then, when you're about to open the folder you want, release Ctrl to open the folder in a separate window. You can then return to the original window and use the same technique to open another folder.

TIP: CLOSING MY COMPUTER WINDOWS QUICKLY

Not only are all those My Computer windows confusing, but it's a pain to have to close each one in turn. To relieve yourself of this drudgery, here's a tip: Hold down the Shift key and close the lowest-level folder. Windows 95 closes all the parent folders automatically, including My Computer itself.

Control Panel: The Windows 95 Customization Center

If you were a Windows 3.x user, you'll no doubt be intimately familiar with the Control Panel, that motley collection of icons that allowed you to customize your system to suit your tastes. You'll be happy to know that the Control Panel still exists in Windows 95 and that it has been beefed up to give you even greater customization options.

To display the `Control Panel` folder, select Start | Settings | Control Panel. You can also get to the `Control Panel` folder by highlighting Control Panel in Explorer's Folders pane or by double-clicking the Control Panel icon in My Computer. Figure 5.26 shows the `Control Panel` folder that appears.

I'll be taking you through each of these icons in later chapters, but Table 5.2 summarizes the available icons and describes each one's role in the Windows 95 world.

FIGURE 5.26.

As it did in Windows 3.x, Control Panel still gives you lots of customization options.

5

WINDOWS 95: THE 50¢ TOUR

Table 5.2. Control Panel icons.

Icon	Chapter(s) Where It's Covered	Description
	7	Lets you customize Windows 95 to give the disabled easier access.
	10	Runs the Add New Hardware Wizard to let Windows 95 detect new hardware devices on your system. You can also specify new devices manually.
	2 and 16	Used for installing and uninstalling applications and Windows 95 components. Also has an option for creating a Windows 95 Startup disk.
	7	Lets you set the current date and time as well as specify your time zone.
Microsoft PLUS	7	Lets you specify a desktop theme (wallpaper, icons, mouse pointers, and so on). This icon appears only if you've installed Microsoft Plus!.
	7	Opens the Display Properties dialog box (shown in Figure 5.3).
	18	Lets you view and install fonts on your system.
Windows 95 SERVICE PACK	10	Lets you set options for infrared devices on your system. This icon appears only if you've installed the Windows 95 Service Pack.
Microsoft PLUS	37	Lets you modify your system's Internet configuration. This icon is available only if you've installed Microsoft Plus!.
	8	Displays the Joystick Properties dialog box, which lets you modify various joystick attributes.
	8	Displays the Keyboard Properties dialog box, which lets you modify various keyboard attributes.
	27	Lets you make adjustments to your Microsoft Exchange settings.

Icon	Chapter(s) Where It's Covered	Description
	27	Starts the Workgroup Postoffice Admin utility, with which you can administer and create Microsoft Mail postoffices.
	25	Used for installing and configuring modems.
	8	Displays the Mouse Properties dialog box, which lets you modify various attributes for the mouse and the mouse pointer.
	22, 23, and 24	Contains options for configuring multimedia properties for sound, video, MIDI, and more.
	31	Lets you install network devices and protocols and adjust their properties.
	7, 31, and 34	Lets you change your Windows password and set up user profiles.
	20	Used to enable PC Card sockets and modify PC Card settings.
	20	Sets various Advanced Power Management properties for portable computers.
	19	Used for installing and configuring printers.
	7	Specifies various default international settings, such as the currency symbol and date format.
	24	Lets you map sounds to various Windows 95 events.
	10	Gives you access to the Device Manager and lets you establish hardware profiles.

A Quick Look at the Windows 95 Accessories

The economists say that there's no such thing as a free lunch, but apparently they don't use Windows. That's because Windows 3.x came loaded for bear with lots of little—and free—

programs called *accessories* (they're also known as *applets*, in some necks of the Windows woods). Well, Windows 95 continues that tradition, but in a greatly expanded form. Many of the existing Windows 3.x accessories have been updated for the Windows 95 interface (and some have been bounced from the lineup), and there's no shortage of brand-new accessories to keep you busy. This section gives you a quick run-through of most of the Windows 95 accessories.

Calculator

Calculator is unchanged from its Windows 3.x ancestor. This means, unfortunately, that the Scientific view, shown in Figure 5.27, *still* doesn't have a square root key! Oh well. To open Calculator, select Start | Programs | Accessories | Calculator.

CAUTION: A BUG IN CALCULATOR'S PERCENT KEY

Use the Percent (%) key in Calculator's Standard view with caution. Thanks to a bug in the program, whenever you use the Percent key followed by an operator, Calculator performs a multiplication operation regardless of which operator you select.

FIGURE 5.27.

The Windows 95 Calculator applet.

Character Map

If you have a document that needs foreign characters (such as ñ or ö), common symbols (such as ¢ or ½), or any number of other characters that don't come on the ordinary keyboard, check out Character Map, shown in Figure 5.28. Again, this program wasn't changed in the transition to Windows 95. To run Character Map, select Start | Programs | Accessories | Character Map.

Dial-Up Networking

New to Windows 95, the Dial-Up Networking accessory (Start | Programs | Accessories | Dial-Up Networking) lets you connect to another computer via modem and to use that computer's shared resources. You can also use Dial-Up Networking to dial in to your network and access its resources remotely. I cover Dial-Up Networking in Chapter 35, "Remote Computing with Dial-Up Networking."

FIGURE 5.28.

Use the Character Map accessory to add symbols to your documents that you won't find on the keyboard.

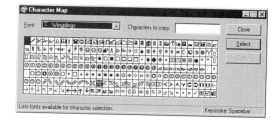

Direct Cable Connection

What do you do if you have a couple of non-networked computers—such as a desktop and a notebook—and you need to share files between them? Well, there's the old "sneakernet" solution: Copy the files back and forth using floppy disks. If, however, you have a special cable (called a *null modem cable*), you can connect the two machines' serial ports and then use Windows 95's Direct Cable Connection (Start | Programs | Accessories | Direct Cable Connection) accessory to send the files via the cable. Add the Briefcase folder to the mix (as described earlier), and you have an easy way to share data and keep files synchronized. I show you how to set up and use Direct Cable Connection in Chapter 34, "From Laptop to Desktop and Back: Direct Cable Connection."

Games

In the all-work-and-no-play-makes-Jack-a-dull-boy category, Windows 95 provides a few games that just might turn that old saw on its head. Select Start | Programs | Accessories | Games to see the menu of Windows 95 games. They include the Windows 3.x holdovers Solitaire and Minesweeper, as well as two new games: Hearts (for network play) and FreeCell, an interesting solitaire variation, shown in Figure 5.29.

FIGURE 5.29.

Windows 95 comes with FreeCell and several other stress busters.

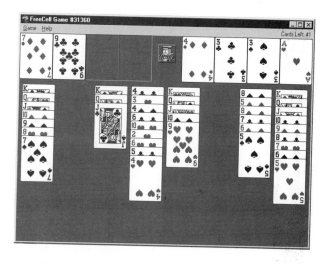

HyperTerminal

One of the worst of Windows 3.x's accessories was the brain-dead Terminal program. Sure, it let you set up basic connections to bulletin boards and online services, but it was sadly lacking in features. In today's wired world, a bad communications program is a millstone around the neck of your online persona. Happily, Windows 95 corrects this problem by offering HyperTerminal, shown in Figure 5.30, a much nicer communications program (select Start | Programs | Accessories | HyperTerminal). To see what makes HyperTerminal vastly superior to Terminal, head for Chapter 25, "Maximizing Modem Communications."

FIGURE 5.30.

You can use Hyper-Terminal to connect to online services and bulletin boards.

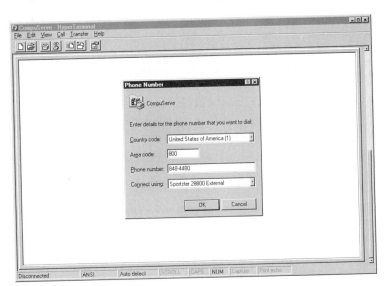

Multimedia

No self-respecting computer heads out the factory door these days unless it's "multimedia-ready" (whatever that means). Windows 95 is also ready for multimedia, and it comes with a few accessories to prove it. Select Start | Programs | Accessories | Multimedia to display a menu of multimedia goodies. These include CD Player (a program that plays audio CDs in your CD-ROM drive; see Figure 5.31), Media Player (for playing sound files, video clips, and more), Sound Recorder (for playing, recording, and manipulating sound files), and Volume Control.

FIGURE 5.31.

The CD Player applet lets you play audio CDs in your CD-ROM drive.

I discuss all of these programs in Part V, "Unleashing Multimedia: The Sights and Sounds of Windows 95."

Notepad

If you need to edit a text file (such as CONFIG.SYS) or if you need to view a text file (such as the README files that come with many applications), you can count on Notepad (select Start | Programs | Accessories | Notepad) to handle most of those tasks. The Windows 95 version of Notepad is the same as the Windows 3.x version. Unfortunately, this also means that the new version still can't handle text files larger than about 50 KB or so. If you try to open a larger file, you see the error message shown in Figure 5.32.

FIGURE 5.32.

Notepad still can't handle large text files.

Paint

The Windows 3.x Paintbrush accessory has been replaced by a new and ever-so-slightly improved program: Paint. To check this out, select Start | Programs | Accessories | Paint. You'll see the window shown in Figure 5.33. Here's a list of the improvements Paint brings to the canvas:

- Paint's tools are the same as those found in Paintbrush, but most of them have a few extra options.

- The Zoom feature gives you greater flexibility by letting you set a custom zoom percentage.

- Paint offers Windows 95 interface support, including long filenames and the Windows 95 common dialog boxes.

- If you like to use Paint to create wallpaper bitmaps, the File menu has two handy new commands: Set As Wallpaper (Tiled) and Set As Wallpaper (Centered).

Phone Dialer

As you might know, Windows 3.x's Cardfile accessory had an AutoDial feature that dialed your phone for you automatically (as long as you had a modem attached to your computer). Cardfile didn't make the cut for Windows 95 (although if you upgraded over Windows 3.x, Cardfile remains in place), but you can still get your computer to dial your phone for you. The tool that does this is called Phone Dialer. You can open Phone Dialer, shown in Figure 5.34, by selecting Start | Programs | Accessories | Phone Dialer. I'll show you how to use Phone Dialer in Chapter 25.

FIGURE 5.33.

Paint is a marginally improved update to Paintbrush.

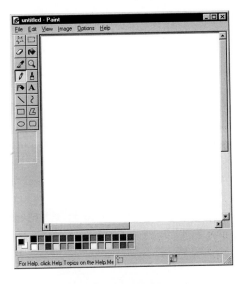

FIGURE 5.34.

If you have a modem, the Phone Dialer accessory is only too happy to dial your phone for you.

System Tools

Windows 95 is only as reliable and efficient as the system it runs on. So to help keep things in fighting trim, Windows 95 comes with a whole host of maintenance and diagnostic utilities. You can find them by selecting Start | Programs | Accessories | System Tools. The menu that's displayed includes Backup (for backing up your files; see Chapter 15), Disk Defragmenter (for defragmenting files; see Chapter 9), DriveSpace (for decompressing disks; see Chapter 14), Resource Meter (for keeping an eye on Windows 95's system resources; see Chapter 9), and ScanDisk (for diagnosing and repairing disks; see Chapter 15).

WordPad

WordPad (select Start | Programs | Accessories | WordPad) is the Windows 95 word processing replacement for Write. WordPad, shown in Figure 5.35, is a much slicker package, and it boasts numerous improvements over Write:

- A toolbar and format bar for easy access to common features
- Support for multiple file types, including text (read and write), Word for Windows 6.0 (read and write), RTF (read and write), and Write (read only)
- Windows 95 interface support, including long filenames and the Windows 95 common dialog boxes
- Improved paragraph formatting options
- The capability to preview documents before printing them

FIGURE 5.35.

WordPad is a definite improvement over Write.

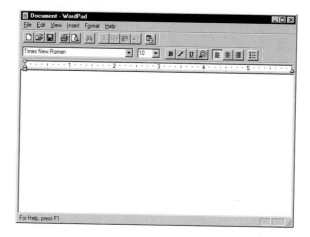

The one thing WordPad can't do is open binary files. Write was happy to do this, and it let you edit programs (carefully!) to customize certain (very limited) aspects of the program.

Windows 95's Powerful New Help System

If you run into a problem with Windows 95, or if you simply find yourself in an unexpected spot, the Help system is always on standby to bail you out. The good news is that Windows 95's Help system is a decided improvement over the one used in Windows 3.x. The topics are easier to navigate, the topic search is more complete, and you can even search for specific keywords. The next few sections introduce you to these welcome improvements.

Invoking the Help System

Windows 95 has more ways than ever to access the Help system. In fact, four basic methods are now available to you:

- Select Start | Help to get help on Windows 95 itself. In this case, you'll see the Windows Help dialog box shown in Figure 5.36.

FIGURE 5.36.

*This dialog box appears
when you select Start |
Help.*

- Press F1 to get help that is *context-sensitive.* This means that the Help screen that appears is related to the Windows area you're in when you press F1. For example, when you're in WordPad, pressing F1 displays the Help Topics: WordPad Help dialog box with WordPad-specific Help topics.

- Most Windows applications have a Help menu that has one or more commands for accessing different parts of the program's own Help system.

- Some dialog boxes have a question mark (?) button in the upper-right corner. If you click this button and then click a dialog box control, a pop-up box appears that tells you a bit about the control. This is called, appropriately enough, *What's This?* Help. In the Windows Help dialog box, for example, clicking ? and then clicking a topic displays the pop-up box shown in Figure 5.37.

FIGURE 5.37.

*Click the ? button in a
dialog box and then
click a control to display
the What's This? Help
pop-up box.*

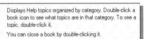

TIP: SOME WHAT'S THIS? HELP TIPS

Another way to invoke What's This? Help is to right-click a control and then select What's This? from the context menu that appears.

Also, you can copy the pop-up box text to the Clipboard or print it. While the pop-up box is displayed, right-click it and then select either Copy or Print Topic from the context menu.

Navigating Help Topics

The Help system dialog boxes give you a list of items, and the icons to the left of these items tell you what you're dealing with:

- ■ If the item has a question mark icon, it's a Help topic.
- ■ If the item has a book icon, it's a Help category (called a *book* in Help system parlance) that contains either Help topics or more books.

To get to the topic you want, open the appropriate book either by double-clicking it or by highlighting it and clicking the Open button. If the book displays more books, keep opening them until you get to the subject area you need. When you've found your topic, display it either by double-clicking it or by highlighting it and clicking the Display button.

TIP: CUSTOMIZING THE TOPICS OUTLINE

The outline of the books and topics in a Help Topics dialog box is controlled by a text file. These text files have the same name as the Help file, but with a CNT extension. (For example, the Windows Help file is WINDOWS.HLP, and its topics outline is in WINDOWS.CNT.) You'll find all these files in the \Windows\Help folder. If you want to rearrange the order of the topics, it's a simple matter of rearranging the lines in the CNT file (by using Notepad or some other text editor). Top-level entries have a 1 beside them, second-level entries have a 2, and so on. (As a precaution, you should make a backup copy of the original CNT file before making any changes.)

After you've chosen a topic, Windows 95 opens a new window and displays the topic text. For example, opening the How To book, then opening the Run Programs book, and then choosing the Starting a program topic displays the Help window shown in Figure 5.38. Besides reading the displayed text to get the info you need, you can also perform any of the following actions:

- ■ If you see a word in green text with a dashed underline, you can click that word to display a pop-up box containing the word's definition. When you've read the definition, press Esc to close the pop-up box.
- ■ Click Related Topics at the bottom of the window to see a new Help window with info related to the current topic. This is an example of a Help system *hyperlink:* a button or piece of text that takes you to another topic (they're also known as *jumps*).
- ■ Click the Back button to see the previous Help topic.
- ■ Click the Help Topics button to return to the topics window.
- ■ Click the Options button to set various Help system options. The Annotate command lets you add your own notes to a topic; the Copy command copies the entire topic to the Clipboard; the Print Topic command prints the topic; the Font command lets you change the topic's font size (Small, Normal, or Large); the Keep Help on Top

command determines whether the topic window remains on top of other windows; and the Use System Colors command tells Windows 95 to use the system's currently defined background and text colors for the topic window.

TIP: MORE TOPIC TIPS

Another way to access the various Help topic options is to right-click anywhere inside the topic and select a command from the context menu that appears.

The Copy command copies the entire topic, but what if you want to copy just part of the topic? Easy: Use the mouse to highlight the text you want to copy, and then press Ctrl-C.

■ Click the Close (×) button to close Help.

FIGURE 5.38.

A typical Help topic window.

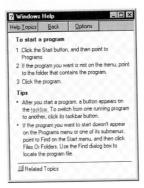

One of the slick new features in the Windows 95 Help system is that it can run programs and display dialog boxes for you. For example, return to the Help Topics: Windows Help dialog box, and open the following books: `Introducing Windows`, `Using Windows Accessories`, and `For Writing and Drawing`. Now display the `Paint: for creating a picture` topic. Notice that the Help window that appears includes a hyperlink named `To start Paint, click here`, as shown in Figure 5.39. Clicking the button with the arrow loads the Paint program.

FIGURE 5.39.

Some Help windows include hyperlinks that start programs for you.

Searching for Help Topics in the Index Tab

As handy as the Help system is, it can become a bit of a maze when you start jumping from topic to topic. To make it easier to find what you want, the Help system includes an Index feature that lets you either search for a Help topic in an alphabetical list of topics or simply type a keyword. Here's how it works:

1. In a Help Topics window, select the Index tab.
2. Type the first few letters of the topic you want. For example, if you type hyper, the Index list highlights the HyperTerminal topic, as shown in Figure 5.40.

FIGURE 5.40.

In the Index tab, enter the first few letters of the topic you want to find.

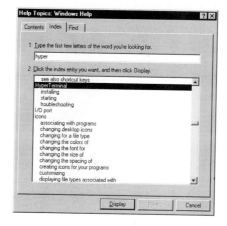

3. Either double-click the topic you want, or highlight it and click the Display button. The Help system displays the topic.

Searching for Help Topics in the Find Tab

The Index tab is well constructed, so it should suffice for finding most topics. But what if your keyword doesn't correspond to an appropriate topic? Or what if you want to find a topic that satisfies multiple keywords (a *keyphrase*)? Or what if you want to see a list of *all* the Help topics that contain a keyword or a keyphrase?

For these situations, Windows 95 has an excellent Help system search engine. This engine works by building a database of words from the Help topics and cross-referencing each word with the particular topic (or topics) from which it came. If you enter a word, Help checks the database and displays every Help topic that contains the word. If you enter multiple words, Help finds either all the topics that contain each word, or all the topics that contain at least one of the words (this is your choice).

To try this, select the Find tab in a Help Topics dialog box. The first time you select this tab, the Find Setup Wizard appears, as shown in Figure 5.41. This dialog box gives you three options:

Minimize database size (recommended): This option leaves out certain parts of the Help system (such as the text from definition pop-ups) and reduces some of Find's capabilities. (I'll explain what happens later, in the "Find Options" section.) Still, Find remains a powerful search tool, so this option will suit most people.

Maximize search capabilities: This option indexes every Help system word and includes every possible Find option. If you have sophisticated search needs and lots of free hard disk space, select this option.

Customize search capabilities: Select this option to tailor Find to suit your needs. This option provides Find capabilities somewhere in between the first two options.

FIGURE 5.41.

Use the Find Setup Wizard dialog box to choose the Find option you want to use.

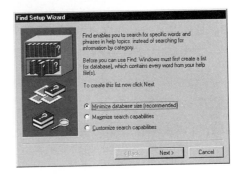

When you've made your selection, click Next >. If you chose either Minimize database size or Maximize search capabilities, click Finish in the next Find Setup Wizard dialog box that appears. If you chose Customize search capabilities, the Find Setup Wizard takes you through a series of dialog boxes. (Note that the options in these dialog boxes might make more sense after you've read the next couple of sections.)

NOTE: CHANGING THE DATABASE OPTION

If you want to redo the database of Help words, you can click the Rebuild button when you get to the Find tab (shown in Figure 5.42). This action displays the Find Setup Wizard again so that you can select a different option.

Searching with Find

After Find has built its database of Help words (which might take a minute or two, depending on the option you selected and the speed of your computer), you'll see the Find tab, shown in Figure 5.42. Here's how to search for a topic using this dialog box:

1. In the Type the word(s) you want to find text box, enter the word or words you want to locate. If you like, you can enter just the first few letters of the word. As you type, Find displays a list of words that match.

2. To fine-tune the search, use the Select some matching words to narrow your search list to highlight the word or words you want to find.

3. Use the Click a topic, then click Display list to highlight the topic you want to see.

4. Click the Display button to open the topic.

FIGURE 5.42.

Use the Find tab to search for specific words in the Help system.

Find Options

Find boasts various options you can take advantage of for more sophisticated searching. To see these options, click the Find tab's Options button. You'll see the Find Options dialog box, shown in Figure 5.43.

FIGURE 5.43.

Use the Find Options dialog box to specify how you want Find to interpret the words you enter.

The `Search for topics containing` group has three options:

`All the words you typed in any order:` Selects topics that contain every word you enter, regardless of the order in which you enter them. For example, if you enter `cable connect`, Find selects only the topics that contain both the words "cable" *and* "connect."

`At least one of the words you typed:` Selects topics that contain one or more of the words you enter. For example, if you enter `cable connect`, Find selects only the topics that contain either the word "cable" *or* "connect" (or both).

`The words you typed in exact order:` Selects topics that contain every word you enter, in the same order in which you enter them. For example, if you enter `connect cable`, Find selects only the topics that contain the phrase "connect cable." (So it wouldn't, for example, find topics about the Direct Cable Connection accessory.) Note that this option isn't available if you chose the `Minimize database size` option.

The `Show words that` drop-down list contains the following items:

`Begin with the characters you type:` Selects topics that contain words that start with the characters you enter. For example, if you type `inter`, Find selects topics with words that begin with "inter," such as *Internet, internal,* and *international.*

`Contain:` Selects topics for which the characters you enter are included anywhere in a word. For example, if you type `inter`, Find selects topics with words that contain "inter," such as *Internet, pointers,* and *printers.*

`End with:` Selects topics that contain words that finish with the characters you enter. For example, if you type `inter`, Find selects topics with words that end with "inter," such as *pointer* and *printer.*

`Match:` Selects topics that contain words that exactly match what you enter. For example, if you type `mode`, Find selects topics that contain the word "mode," but not *modes* or *modem.*

`Have the same root:` Selects topics that have the same linguistic root as the word you enter. For example, if you enter `type`, Find selects topics that contain the words *type, types, typing, typed, typist,* and so on. Note that this option isn't available if you chose the `Minimize database size` option.

The `Begin searching` group contains options that specify when you want Find to begin searching the database:

`After you click the Find Now button:` If you activate this option, Find doesn't search the database until you click Find Now.

`Immediately after each keystroke:` If you activate this option, Find begins searching the database as soon as you enter a character and revises its search criteria with each new keystroke. To avoid getting bogged down, you should make sure that the `Wait for a pause before searching` check box is activated. This tells Find to wait until you stop typing before starting the search.

Find Options also has a Files button that you can use to specify which Help files are included in the database. When you click Files, a list of the Help files appears. Highlight the files you want to use and click OK.

When you've selected all your options, click OK to return to the Find tab.

Updates to Windows 95

Since the launch of Windows 95 in August 1995, Microsoft has been busy with bug fixes, driver patches, program upgrades, and new enhancements to the core operating system. Rather than waiting for Windows 97 (or whatever) to incorporate these updates, Microsoft has made some or all of them available through retail channels, OEMs, and online sources. Just so you know which version of Windows 95 you're dealing with, Table 5.3 presents a summary of the operating system updates, their official version numbers, and their file dates.

Table 5.3. Windows 95 version numbers and file dates.

Release	Version Number	File Dates
Windows 95 retail	4.00.950	7/11/95
OEM Service Release 1	4.00.950	12/31/95
Service Pack 1	4.00.950 A	12/31/95
OEM Service Release 2	4.00.1111 B	8/24/96

To check your version number and see which updates have been installed on your system, run the Update Information Tool by launching QFECHECK.EXE from your main Windows 95 folder. The properties sheet that appears, shown in Figure 5.44, lists your Windows 95 version number and the updates that are registered on your system. You can also use the Updated Files Found tab to get a complete list of the updated Windows system files and their version numbers.

FIGURE 5.44.

The Update Information Tool (QFECHECK.EXE) tells you which Windows 95 components have been updated on your system.

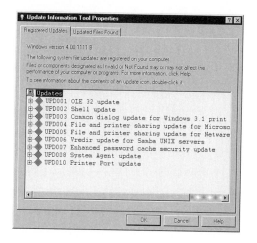

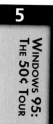

NOTE: FILE VERSION NUMBERS

You can see the version number of any file on your system by right-clicking the file in Explorer or My Computer, choosing Properties from the context menu, and then activating the Version tab in the properties sheet that appears.

OSR2 What's New in OSR2?

If you purchased a new PC from a major manufacturer, and you made that purchase in late 1996 or later, chances are that your machine came with a new version of Windows 95, called the Original Equipment Manufacturers Service Release 2 (or OSR2 for short). This Windows 95 update—which isn't available as a retail package, although you can also get a copy by purchasing a new motherboard or hard drive—fixes a few bugs from the Windows 95 retail product and implements several new technologies.

How to Tell if OSR2 Is Installed

How do you know whether you have OSR2? The easiest way to tell is to right-click the My Computer icon and then select Properties from the context menu. The System Properties dialog box that appears tells you your Windows 95 version number. As you can see in Figure 5.45, an OSR2 system sports a version number of 4.00.950 B (which is why OSR2 is often called Windows 95 B).

FIGURE 5.45.

You know you're running OSR2 if the System Properties dialog box tells you that your Windows 95 version number is 4.00.950 B.

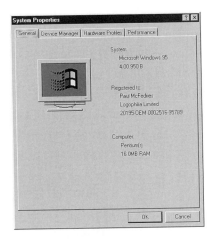

New OSR2 Goodies (and How to Get Them if You Don't Have OSR2)

I mentioned earlier that Microsoft will sell OSR2 only to system vendors. If you want to get the new version's enhancements in a retail product, you'll have to wait for the next major Windows release. However, that's not to say that you can't build yourself a near-OSR2 system. As long as you have a connection to the Internet, you can download many OSR2 components for free and upgrade your system in the process. This section tells you what's new in OSR2 and tells you (where applicable) how to find these components online.

Internet and Networking Enhancements

In continuing Microsoft's "hardcore" approach to the Internet, OSR2 contains quite a few Net-related enhancements, as well as enhancements to the networking subsystem. Table 5.4 provides a summary.

Table 5.4. Internet and networking enhancements in OSR2.

Enhancement	*Online Location* (http://www.microsoft.com)	*Description*
Internet Explorer 3.0	/ie/	Version 3.0 of Microsoft's popular World Wide Web browser. Note that this version of IE contains serious security flaws. To be safe, you should be running at least version 3.02. See Chapter 38 for details.
Internet Connection Wizard	/ie/download/	A step-by-step method for setting up a Windows 95 Internet connection (see Chapter 37).
Internet Mail and News	/ie/download/	Internet Mail is a simplified e-mail client for SMTP and POP3 connections; Internet News is Microsoft's Usenet newsreader. I describe these products in Chapters 40 and 41.
Personal Web Server	/ie/download/	A scaled-down Web server that gives you an easy way to host Web pages. I describe this program in Chapter 42.

continues

5

WINDOWS 95:
THE 50¢ TOUR

Table 5.4. continued

Enhancement	Online Location (`http://www.microsoft.com`)	Description
NetMeeting	`/ie/download/`	This application lets you make Net-based phone calls as well as collaborate remotely via phone, chat, or whiteboard (see Chapter 39).
Online Services	None	Client programs for America Online, CompuServe, and AT&T (see Chapter 25).
MSN 1.3	See MSN	The latest version of the MSN client.
Windows Messaging	None	This is the new name for Microsoft Exchange. It includes a few minor enhancements (such as support for MAPI 1.0b). See Chapters 27 through 29.
Dial-Up Networking	`/windows/software.htm`	An improved user interface for connectoids, built-in scripting support, and hands-free dial-up. I describe all of these enhancements in Chapter 35.
Voice Modem support	`/windowssupport/default-sl.htm`	Support for VoiceView and AT+V modems.
Novell NetWare 4.x	None	Full client for NetWare 4.x, including NetWare Directory Services.
NDIS 4.0	None	Support for NDIS 4.0 network adapters.
32-Bit DLC	`/windows/software.htm`	32-bit support for the Data Link Control protocol.

File System Enhancements

The star attraction in OSR2 is probably the new FAT32 file system. I'll describe this update to the FAT system in detail in Chapter 6. For now, Table 5.5 lists FAT32 and the other file system enhancements that come with the OSR2 package.

Table 5.5. File system enhancements in OSR2.

Enhancement	Online Location (http://www.microsoft.com)	Description
FAT32	None	Enhanced FAT file system featuring more efficient storage and support for large (over 2 GB) drives. See Chapter 6 for a complete description.
FAT32 utilities	None	New utilities designed to work with FAT32: FDISK, FORMAT, ScanDisk, and DEFRAG. See Chapters 14 and 15.
Boot ScanDisk check	None	ScanDisk runs automatically at boot time if system was shut down improperly (see Chapter 15).
DriveSpace 3	None	Now supports compressed volume files up to 2 GB in size. Also includes Compression Agent. See Chapter 14.
CDFS enhancements	None	CD-ROM File System improvements include support for CD-I discs and for ISO 9660 disks up to 4 GB in size.

Multimedia Enhancements

Table 5.6 summarizes the various multimedia enhancements that you'll find in OSR2.

Table 5.6. Multimedia enhancements in OSR2.

Enhancement	Online Location (http://www.microsoft.com)	Description
DirectX 2.0	/ie/download/	The DirectX family of APIs (see Chapter 22).
ActiveMovie	/ie/download/	Microsoft's next-generation streaming digital video technology (see Chapter 23).

continues

Table 5.6. continued

Enhancement	Online Location (http://www.microsoft.com)	Description
MMX support	None	Support for third-party programs that take advantage of Intel's Pentium Multimedia Extensions (MMX).
Color depth changes	/windows/download/ quik_res.exe	Allows color depth changes on-the-fly.
Wang Imaging	/windows/software/ img_us.htm	Image viewer that supports a number of graphics formats; integrates with Microsoft Fax and support scanning.
OpenGL	None	Support for OpenGL graphics libraries (includes 3D screen savers).

Hardware Enhancements

OSR2 comes with a whole slew of enhancements that give Windows 95 better hardware support. Table 5.7 summarizes these improvements.

Table 5.7. Hardware enhancements in OSR2.

Enhancement	Online Location (http://www.microsoft.com)	Description
APM 1.2	None	Support for APM 1.2, including modem wake-on-ring, a Control Panel Power icon, and support for multiple batteries.
Drive spin down	None	Allows machines to place the hard disk in low power mode when not in use.
IRQ routing	None	Support for the new PCI interrupt routers.
PC Card	None	Support for PC Card 32, 3.3 volt PC Card devices, and Global Positioning Satellite devices.

Enhancement	Online Location (http://www.microsoft.com)	Description
IrDA 2.0	/windows/software/irda.htm	Support for IrDA 2.0-compliant devices and Infrared LAN connectivity.
Hardware profiles	None	User interface enhancements (see Chapter 10).
Storage devices	None	Support for IDE Bus Mastering, 120 MB Floptical drives, removable IDE media, CD changers, Zip drives.

The Registry: Say Good-Bye to INIs (Sort Of)

In the Windows 3.x world, applications stored program settings, user preferences, and other options in initialization files, or INI files, as they were usually called. (That's because these files used the INI extension.) Windows, too, used INI files (such as WIN.INI and SYSTEM.INI) to store its data. The result of all this INI madness was usually a WINDOWS directory littered with INI files from disparate applications.

In an effort to reign in this plethora of INI files, Windows 95 changes things drastically. There's now a central repository for all program settings and options: the Registry. This database contains not only entries for application settings, but also all of Windows 95's settings and preferences. Many of these values are generated by selecting customization options in, say, the Control Panel. But a sizable number are controlled internally by Windows 95. Fortunately, Windows 95 comes with a tool—called the Registry Editor—that lets you view and, more important, *change* these values. This lets you perform highly sophisticated (and, in some cases, just plain cool) customizations of the Windows 95 interface. Sound interesting? It *is*, and it's the royal road to truly unleashing Windows 95. Because of that, I've devoted two full chapters to unlocking the Registry's secrets: Chapter 11, "Introducing the Windows 95 Registry," and Chapter 12, "Hacking the Registry."

Is Windows 95 an Honest-to-Goodness Operating System?

Unlike previous versions of Windows, the answer to that question is a resounding "Yes!" Windows 3.x and its predecessors were often called "operating systems," but only by the most charitable among us. Those versions were supported by the spindly legs of the real operating system: DOS. Windows 3.x was more accurately called an "operating environment," because all it really did was provide a user interface that put a pretty face on DOS. Although there were attempts to remake Windows as more of a true OS—Windows for Workgroups' 32-bit file access, for example—in the end, DOS was still boss.

Not so with Windows 95. It now takes over full responsibility for all your system's hardware and software operations, including disk reads and writes, input/output, device management, and more. Yes, there is a DOS component to Windows 95, but the tables have been turned: The DOS command line is now an adjunct to the main operating system, Windows 95.

All this means that Windows 95 gives you unprecedented (for Windows, anyway) new functionality, including such boons as long filenames, Plug and Play hardware support, preemptive multitasking, and multithreading.

A Final Treat: A Couple of Windows 95 Easter Eggs

As you might know, many applications (whose programmers apparently have *way* too much time on their hands) include small multimedia files inside their code that list the names of all the people involved in the project. These exercises in self-indulgence are called *Easter eggs* (because, presumably, they're usually hard to find) or *gang screens*.

Windows 95 has a couple of its own Easter eggs. They're a bit lame as far as these things go, and they won't appear on all systems, but you might want to check them out anyway.

Here are the instructions for the first Easter egg:

1. Right-click the desktop and select New | Folder.
2. In the new folder that appears, type the following line (actually, you can change the "EasterEgg" part to whatever you like):

   `EasterEgg.{869DADA0-42A0-1069-A2E7-08002B30309D}`

3. Press Enter.
4. Double-click the folder. The Easter egg starts playing inside the folder window, as shown in Figure 5.46.

To get to the second Easter egg, follow these admittedly convoluted steps:

1. Select Start | Help.
2. Activate the Find tab. (If the Find Setup Wizard appears, go through the steps to set up the Find feature.)
3. Click Options to display the Find Options dialog box. Select the following options and then click OK:

   Search for topics containing: Select All the words you typed in any order.

   Show words that: Select Begin with the characters you type.

4. In the Type the words you want to find text box, enter Who knows who built this tool? (be sure to match the capitalization).

5. Hold down Ctrl and Shift and click Clear.

6. Click Options to display the Find Options dialog box again. Select the following options and then click OK:

> **Search for topics containing:** Select At least one of the words you typed.

> **Show words that:** Select contain the characters you type.

7. In the Type the words you want to find text box, enter The Shadow knows! (again, be sure to match the capitalization).

8. Hold down Ctrl and Shift and click Clear. The Easter egg commences, as shown in Figure 5.47.

FIGURE 5.46.

One of Windows 95's Easter eggs.

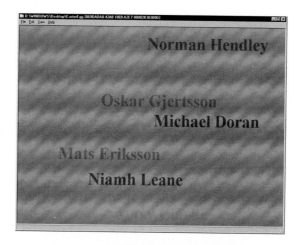

FIGURE 5.47.

The other Windows 95 Easter egg.

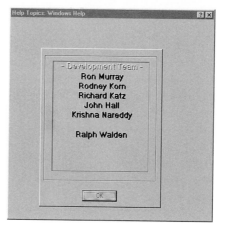

Summary

This chapter took you on a tour of Windows 95. You saw many new sights along the way, and some of what you saw went by rather quickly. Not to worry, though. I'll return to many of these topics and discuss them in greater detail later in this book.

To complete your look at the Windows 95 big picture, Chapter 6 takes you on a tour of the guts of the operating system as we turn our attention to the design of the Windows 95 architecture.

Under the Hood: Understanding the Windows 95 Architecture

CHAPTER 6

IN THIS CHAPTER

> *The job of buildings is to improve human relations: architecture must ease them, not make them worse.*

> —*Ralph Erskine*

You don't have to be a full-fledged auto mechanic to give your car a tune-up or change the oil. On the other hand, you can't perform these tasks unless you know a little bit about what happens under the hood. Windows 95 is the same way: You don't have to become a Microsoft Certified Professional Systems Engineer to optimize Windows 95, but it really helps to know something about how the operating system works.

To that end, this chapter cracks the hood and takes a look at the various software equivalents of cylinders, spark plugs, carburetors, and other components that make your Windows 95 vehicle run.

The Windows 95 Architecture: A Modular Approach

The Windows 95 architecture is modular in design, with separate subsystems arranged in layers, from the lowest-level modules, which deal directly with hardware, to the highest-level modules, which provide application support. Figure 6.1 illustrates, in broad strokes, this modular, multilayered approach. The next few sections take a closer look at these components.

Device Drivers

Device drivers are small software programs that serve as intermediaries between hardware devices and the operating system. Device drivers encode software instructions into signals that the device understands, and, conversely, they interpret device signals and report them to the operating system. Although Windows 95 still supports real-mode device drivers for compatibility reasons, most device issues are now handled by *virtual device drivers* (VxDs), which are 32-bit protected-mode drivers. I'll explain the architecture of the device driver layer in more detail in Chapter 10, "How Windows 95 Handles Hardware."

Configuration Manager

With tens of millions of legacy systems—and all their myriad combinations of bus types, devices, and protocols—still being put to good use, and with all the new Plug and Play (PnP) functionality being added to new machines, the number of potential hardware configurations is astronomical. To help sort all this out, Windows 95 includes a component called the Configuration Manager. It's the Configuration Manager's job to enumerate the various Plug and Play devices on your system, identify the resources used by each device, resolve resource conflicts, monitor the system for hardware changes, and ensure that the proper device drivers are loaded. Again, turn to Chapter 10 for more detailed information on this crucial component.

Under the Hood: Understanding the Windows 95 Architecture

CHAPTER 6

195

6

UNDERSTANDING
THE WINDOWS
95 ARCHITECTURE

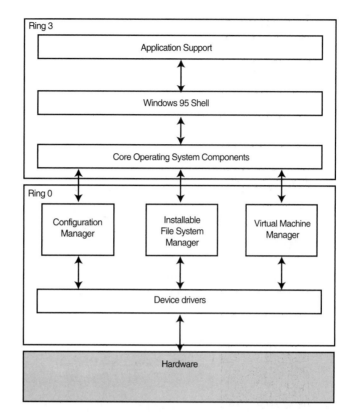

The Installable File System Manager

In Chapter 5, "Windows 95: The 50¢ Tour," I told you about VFAT (Virtual File Allocation Table), the new Windows 95 file system that supports long filenames. In fact, Windows 95 supports several file systems besides VFAT, including CDFS (CD-ROM File System) and network redirectors for connectivity to network servers. All this is handled by the Installable File System Manager, which not only includes access to the various file systems, but also handles the file system drivers and the block I/O subsystem, which interacts directly with your system's physical disks. You'll get more information about the Installable File System Manager in Chapter 13, "Working with Files and Folders."

Virtual Machine Manager

If Windows 95 has an "engine," it's probably the Virtual Machine Manager. In the same way that the Configuration Manager allocates and manages the resources needed by your system's hardware, the Virtual Machine Manager allocates and manages the resources needed by your system's software—your applications and the various operating system processes. If a program or the operating system needs a resource—whether it's a chunk of memory or access to an I/O port—the Virtual Machine Manager handles the request and allocates the resource appropriately. The Virtual Machine Manager does this by taking advantage of two advanced features of Intel's microprocessors: *protected mode* and *virtual machines.*

Protected mode is an operating mode that was introduced with the 80286 microprocessor. *Real mode* can address only up to 640 KB of memory and gives a running program direct access to hardware. Protected mode, on the other hand, lets software use memory beyond 640 KB, and it sets up a protection scheme so that multiple programs can share the same computer resources without stepping on each other's toes (and, usually, crashing the system).

Virtual machines were born with the release of Intel's 80386 microprocessor. Thanks to protected mode, the 80386 circuitry could address up to 4 GB of memory. Using this potentially huge address space, the 80386 let software carve out separate chunks of memory and use these areas to emulate the full operation of a computer. This emulation is so complete and effective that a program running in a virtual machine thinks it's dealing with a real computer. Combined with the resource-sharing features of protected mode, virtual machines can run their programs simultaneously without bumping into each other.

In Windows 3.x, you had one virtual machine for Windows itself (including all running Windows applications) and separate virtual machines for each DOS session. In Windows 95, the Virtual Machine Manager creates a System Virtual Machine for Windows applications and operating system resources, and DOS virtual machines for each DOS session. I'll discus this topic in greater depth later (see the section "Application Support").

The Virtual Machine Manager's responsibilities fall into three categories:

- Process scheduling and multitasking
- Memory paging
- Support for MS-DOS mode

Process Scheduling and Multitasking

There's certainly no shortage of reasons to leave DOS in the dust, but one of the biggest is its lack of a multitasking feature. DOS, with its real-mode–only support, exists in can't-walk-and-chew-gum-at-the-same-time territory. And that's despite the fact that multitasking has been available, at least theoretically, since virtual machines were introduced with the 80386.

Windows 3.x changed that by bringing true multitasking (and not just mere task switching, which is all that DOS is capable of) to the masses. Windows 95 ups the multitasking ante even further. The Virtual Machine Manager has a component called the Process Scheduler that doles out resources to applications and operating system processes. In particular, the Process Scheduler organizes running applications so that they take advantage of *preemptive multitasking* and *multithreading.* The next two sections discuss these powerful operating modes.

Understanding Preemptive Multitasking

Although Windows 3.x supported true multitasking, it wasn't implemented optimally. That's because Windows 3.x used *cooperative multitasking*. This meant that you could have several applications running, but it was up to the individual applications to decide when they relinquished control of the system. It wasn't unusual for an ill-behaved application to start an operation and then refuse to hand over control until it was good and ready. You had no choice but to fume at the hourglass icon and wait until the program had completed its labors. In other words, cooperative multitasking was often very *uncooperative*.

Windows 95 abandons cooperative multitasking, for the most part, and replaces it with something much better: *preemptive multitasking*. In this model, the Process Scheduler uses a sophisticated algorithm to monitor all running processes, assign each a priority level, and allocate CPU resources according to the relative priority of each process. So if a particular process—such as a print job—is running, and a process with a higher priority—such as a spreadsheet recalculation—comes along, the Process Scheduler preempts the print job (hence the name *preemptive* multitasking) and allocates CPU cycles to the recalculation process. (All of this is measured in milliseconds, however, so everything seems totally seamless to you and me.) The result is extremely smooth multitasking, and interruptions to wait for a process to finish are rare, if not nonexistent, under Windows 95.

Note, however, that Windows 95 applies preemptive multitasking only to 32-bit applications. Any 16-bit applications are still multitasked cooperatively within their virtual machine.

Understanding Multithreading

Preemptive multitasking is a great leap forward in multiple application support, but there is one fly in the ointment: For all this high-tech talk of schedulers and CPU cycles, there is still only *one* process happening at a time. The switching occurs so quickly that it only *seems* as though multiple things are happening at once. To see what I mean, imagine a film of a busy intersection. In regular motion, you see that the traffic light lets some cars through while others have to wait their turn. If you speed up the film, however, it looks as though a steady stream of cars is passing through in all directions.

If you want processes to occur simultaneously, you need to look at *multithreading*. A *thread* is a small chunk of executable code with a very narrow focus. In a spreadsheet, for example, you might have one thread for recalculating, another for printing, and a third for accepting keyboard input. You can set all these threads in motion and they'll run concurrently, without interfering with each other. Windows 95 supports multithreading in those (still relatively rare) 32-bit programs that implement it. (Windows 95 even uses multithreading in some of its accessories, such as WordPad.)

Memory Paging

The Virtual Machine Manager includes a second component called the Memory Pager. Its job is to move data back and forth between the hard disk and the system's physical memory and to allocate hard disk space as virtual memory addresses. This is called *paging*. I'll explain everything in detail when I discuss virtual memory in Chapter 9, "Windows 95 Performance Tuning and Optimization" (see the section titled "Windows 95 and Memory: A Primer").

Support for MS-DOS Mode

Nearly all DOS programs are perfectly content to run inside an MS-DOS virtual machine. DOS programs expect to have full run of the computer, and the Virtual Machine Manager fools them into thinking that's exactly what they have. However, a few (thankfully rare) DOS applications really do need direct control over the computer. For these programs, Windows 95 can run in *MS-DOS mode*, which gives the program exclusive access to the computer. When you run such a program, the Virtual Machine Manager takes care of the behind-the-scenes prep work, including shutting down any running programs and "rebooting" the system into a pure DOS environment.

Core Operating System Components

The next layer in the Windows 95 hierarchy consists of the core operating system components: the User, the Graphical Device Interface (GDI), and the Kernel. Actually, each of these components comes in two flavors: 16-bit and 32-bit. The 16-bit versions handle services that are needed to maintain compatibility with 16-bit applications; the 32-bit versions are used to improve the performance of Windows 95 in areas where compatibility isn't an issue.

The User Component

The User component handles all user-related I/O tasks. On the input side, User manages incoming data from the keyboard, mouse, joystick, and any other input devices that might be attached to your computer. For "output," User sends data to windows, icons, menus, and other components of the Windows 95 user interface. User also handles the sound driver, the system timer, and the communications ports. For compatibility, most of the User component is implemented as 16-bit code.

The GDI Component

The GDI manages Windows 95's graphical interface. It contains routines that draw graphics primitives (such as lines), manage colors, display fonts, manipulate bitmap images, and interact with graphics drivers. The GDI uses a mix of 16-bit and 32-bit code.

The Kernel Component

As its name implies, the Kernel makes up the heart of Windows 95. The Kernel loads applications (including any DLLs needed by the program), handles all aspects of file I/O, allocates virtual memory and works with the Memory Pager, and schedules and runs threads started by applications. The Kernel is mostly 32-bit for maximum performance.

The Windows 95 Shell

The next layer in the Windows 95 architecture is the shell. (Note that the shell is called Explorer, which isn't to be confused with the Windows Explorer file management accessory.) The shell provides the user interface and supplies applications with various common controls, including common dialog boxes (such as Open and Save As), tree views, list views, and so on.

Application Support

The top layer of the Windows 95 architecture consists of the applications, including the Windows 95 accessories. Windows 95 can run three types of applications:

Win32: These are 32-bit applications built using the Win32 application programming interface (API). The Virtual Machine Manager creates a separate virtual machine (within the System Virtual Machine) for each running Win32 application, so these programs always have their own private address space. In addition, Win32 applications take full advantage of the Windows 95 environment, including preemptive multitasking, long filenames, and so on.

Win16: These are 16-bit applications built using the Win16 API. Although most Win16 programs run fine under Windows 95, you should know that the Virtual Machine Manager doesn't create a separate virtual machine for each running Win16 application. Instead, all Win16 applications run inside the *same* virtual machine, as they did with Windows 3.x. (These applications are cooperatively multitasked within this virtual machine.) Thus, using Win16 programs with Windows 95 leaves you open to the same vulnerabilities associated with Windows 3.x.

DOS: These are programs designed to be run in a DOS environment. The Virtual Machine Manager creates a separate DOS virtual machine (with 1 MB of virtual memory) for each running DOS program. The environment that the Virtual Machine Manager uses for each DOS virtual machine is determined at startup. Based on the entries in CONFIG.SYS and AUTOEXEC.BAT, Windows 95 established an "invisible" virtual DOS machine that acts as a sort of template. Each time a DOS program is run, the Virtual Machine Manager uses this template to create the DOS environment for the new virtual machine. As you'll see in Chapter 21, "DOS Isn't Dead: Optimizing DOS Applications Under Windows 95," it's possible to customize this environment for individual DOS programs.

The Windows 95 Registry

As I mentioned in Chapter 5, the Registry is Windows 95's central database for configuration data, options, and any information that affects the operation of Windows 95 itself, your system's devices, or your applications. In that sense, the Registry is used by each layer of the Windows 95 architecture to read the current settings for your system and to store any new values that get set during a session. See Chapter 11, "Introducing the Windows 95 Registry," for more information.

Intel's Protection Ring Architecture

Another way to look at the Windows 95 architecture is in terms of Intel's *protection ring architecture*. Beginning with the 80386 processor, Intel implemented a system of *privilege levels* for all running applications and system processes. These levels determine how much freedom the code has to perform certain operations. For example, code running on a level of lesser privilege won't be able to access certain memory regions.

These levels, called *rings,* range from ring 0, the highest privilege level, to ring 3, the lowest level. Unlike Windows NT, which uses all four levels, Windows 95 uses only two levels:

Ring 0: Windows 95 uses the highest privilege level for its most fundamental services: Configuration Manager, Virtual Machine Manager, and Installable File System Manager. This ensures that these key components can't be compromised by running applications (which run in ring 3). However, Windows 95 also allows virtual device drivers to run in ring 0, thus opening the system to potential problems caused by misbehaving or poorly written drivers.

Ring 3: Windows 95 uses the lowest privilege level for the core operating system components (User, GDI, and Kernel) and applications. This prevents applications from executing instructions or functions that are the responsibility of the operating system, and it prevents applications from overwriting memory areas that contain key operating system components.

Improvements in the Windows 95 File System

Microsoft put a great deal of time and effort into making the Windows 95 file system better and faster than the one that powered Windows 3.x (even the one in Windows for Workgroups). Here's a summary of just some of the changes you can expect:

32-bit VFAT: Disk access is provided by the 32-bit VFAT (virtual file allocation table). Unlike the 16-bit FAT (file allocation table) used in Windows 3.1, VFAT is a virtual device driver that operates in protected mode, so there are no time-consuming mode switches to real mode every time an application needs to write to the disk. Windows for Workgroups used an early version of VFAT (called *32-bit file access*), but the Windows 95 version is more reliable and operates with a greater variety of hardware. (Note that OSR2 replaces VFAT with the more efficient FAT32. See "What's New with Fat32?" later in this chapter.)

Long filenames: You can create files that use names that have up to 255 characters (including the path). Windows 95 implements long filenames without creating incompatibilities with 16-bit applications that don't recognize long filenames.

Demand paging: This is an advanced algorithm for paging memory to the swap file. Not only is it faster than even the permanent swap file used in Windows 3.x, but it also is *dynamic:* The swap file's size is adjusted according to the load on the system.

VCACHE: This is the Windows 95 32-bit disk cache driver. It replaced SMARTDrive, the 16-bit real-mode driver used in Windows 3.x. Like the swap file, VCACHE is dynamic, which means that it tailors the size of the cache based on how much memory is available and the intensity of disk paging.

Built-in CD-ROM support: Windows 3.x relied on real-mode drivers to work with CD-ROM drives. In Windows 95, CD-ROMs get their own 32-bit file system (CDFS).

Built-in EIDE and SCSI support: Windows 3.x didn't support either EIDE or SCSI and relied on third-party manufacturers to supply drivers for these devices. Windows 95 supports both EIDE and SCSI right out of the box.

Port drivers: These are 32-bit drivers that communicate with specific disk devices. For example, the port driver that manages the floppy disk controller lets you format a floppy disk in the background while you continue working on other tasks.

The Windows 95 File System Architecture

To implement all the new features discussed in the preceding section, the Windows 95 development team revamped the file system architecture into a layered model that makes extensive use of 32-bit protected-mode drivers for increased performance and reliability. Figure 6.2 shows the various components of this new architecture, and the next few sections explain each component.

More About the Installable File System Manager

An *installable file system* is a file system that can be loaded into the operating system dynamically. FAT is built right in at the hardware level, so to speak, when you format a disk. Any other file system you want to use either must come from a low-level format or must be *installed* on top of the existing file system. The advantage of the latter situation is that your operating system can then work with multiple file systems at once, which is what Windows 95 does.

The software that manages file systems in Windows 95 is called, appropriately enough, the Installable File System (IFS) Manager. It's a 32-bit protected-mode device driver that's loaded at startup (along with the other device drivers that make up VMM32.VXD). The IFS Manager installs the file systems (see the next section) and arbitrates access to these systems. IFS Manager automatically determines the format of a storage medium and reads and writes files in the correct format.

Figure 6.2.
The Windows 95 file system architecture.

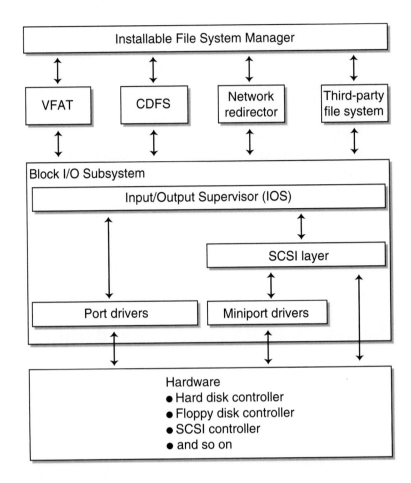

Note that IFS Manager is designed as an open system, meaning that third-party developers can use it to install extra file systems. (For example, you might see third-party file systems that give you access to the Windows NT file system (NTFS) on a local hard disk partition—which would be a real boon to those running both Windows 95 and Windows NT on one system.)

File System Device Drivers

In its default incarnation, the IFS Manager loads three file system drivers: VFAT, CDFS, and one or more network redirectors.

The Virtual File Allocation Table (VFAT)

VFAT is the file system driver that works with the block I/O subsystem (described later) to access disk services. Because it's a 32-bit protected-mode VxD and is multithreaded, VFAT provides superior performance (especially compared to the 16-bit real-mode disk access found in Windows 3.1), enhanced reliability, and easier multitasking. In particular, VFAT avoids the slow processor mode switches between protected mode and real mode that plagued Windows 3.1.

VFAT also supports many more drive and controller types than did Windows 3.x. For disk drives, VFAT has drivers that can work with the types IDE, EIDE, ESDI, and Hardcard. For disk drive controllers, VFAT has drivers for the types MFM, RLL, PCI, PCMCIA, SCSI, and SCSI 2.

VFAT is far from perfect, however. It still uses the 16-bit FAT for physical storage of files and folders, so it inherits FAT's legendary fragility. (For example, you're just asking for trouble if you shut down your computer while Windows 95 is still running.)

Using a mechanism called the Real Mode Mapper (RMM), VFAT can also work with any real-mode disk drivers you might still be using (such as DBLSPACE.BIN or a third-party disk not supported by Windows 95). The RMM makes the real-mode driver appear as though it's operating in protected mode.

Besides enhanced speed and multitasking, perhaps the greatest advantage VFAT brings to the file system table is long filenames. I introduced long filenames in Chapter 5, and I'll discuss them in greater depth later in this chapter.

The CD-ROM File System (CDFS)

Like Windows NT, Windows 95 now implements a separate installable file system for CD-ROM drives: CDFS. CDFS uses a 32-bit protected-mode VxD (VCDFSD.VXD) that replaces MSCDEX.EXE, the 16-bit real-mode driver used in previous versions of Windows. The new driver provides many of the same benefits you saw with VFAT, including improved performance and better multitasking. CDFS also supports a separate, dynamic pool of cache memory to further enhance CD-ROM performance.

Network Redirectors

A network redirector is a virtual device driver that lets applications find, open, read, write, and delete files on a remote drive. Windows 95 comes with network redirectors for Microsoft network clients (VREDIR.VXD) and NetWare network clients (NWREDIR.VXD). I'll talk more about this topic when I discuss networking architecture in Chapter 30, "A Networking Primer."

The Block I/O Subsystem

The block I/O subsystem is the Windows 95 mechanism that talks directly to disk hardware. It's the replacement for the FastDisk feature used in pervious versions of Windows. The next few sections discuss the various parts of the block I/O subsystem.

The I/O Supervisor

The I/O Supervisor acts as an intermediary between the disk drivers and the file systems. Besides loading the appropriate drivers for accessing disk controllers and disk drives, the I/O Supervisor arbitrates all I/O operations, including the queuing and routing of file service requests. It also assumes control of any real-mode drivers that have been loaded. The Real Mode Mapper is part of the I/O Supervisor, and it translates file I/O requests from protected mode to real mode so that the real-mode driver can complete its work. Note that drivers designed to work specifically with the I/O Supervisor are stored in the \WINDOWS\SYSTEM\IOSUBSYS folder.

The Port Drivers

This is one of the few examples in which old-style monolithic drivers are used in Windows 95. *Port drivers* are 32-bit protected-mode drivers that provide complete functionality for working with devices such as hard disk controllers or floppy disk controllers.

SCSI Support

Windows 95 uses the universal driver/minidriver model for SCSI device support. A 32-bit protected-mode driver called the *SCSI layer* provides the basic high-level functionality common to all SCSI devices and then relies on manufacturers to provide minidrivers (called *miniport drivers*) for device-specific I/O requests.

A separate component called the *SCSI Manager* (SCSIPORT.PDR) ensures compatibility between the SCSI layer and Windows NT miniport drivers.

More About Long Filenames

I mentioned in Chapter 5 that Windows 95 stomps all over the old 8.3 filename limitation that people had to suffer with for so many years. Now you can create long, sentence-like names that actually describe what's in a particular file.

So just how long can your filenames be? Well, according to Microsoft, the limit is 255 characters, but that's not right. Here's the correct rule: The total number of characters in the pathname—that's the filename *plus* the file's path information (drive and folder)—cannot exceed 253.

For example, if you create a file in the root folder of drive C, your path is three characters long (C:\), so the maximum length of the filename is 250 characters. If you create a verbosely named file and then try to copy it into, say, the C:\WINDOWS folder, you get an error message because the new pathname is actually 260 characters (250 for the filename plus 10 for the path).

One of the keys to understanding how Windows 95 works is understanding how it converts long filenames into 8.3 filenames, so let's take a closer look. When converting a long filename to an 8.3 filename, VFAT goes through no fewer than seven steps:

1. All spaces are removed from the long filename.

2. All characters that are illegal under DOS (such as ; and =) are replaced by the underscore character (_).

3. The resulting primary name is truncated at six characters.

4. The first three characters in the extension are kept.

5. A tilde (~) and a 1 are appended to the six-character primary name.

6. All letters in the filename are converted to uppercase.

7. VFAT checks to see whether the resulting 8.3 filename is unique in the folder. If it's not, the 1 at the end of the primary name is changed to 2. If it's still not unique, the number is incremented until a unique filename is found.

For example, consider the following 10 long filenames:

```
Testing, testing, one.txt
Testing, testing, two.txt
Testing, testing, three.txt
Testing, testing, four.txt
Testing, testing, five.txt
Testing, testing, six.txt
Testing, testing, seven.txt
Testing, testing, eight.txt
Testing, testing, nine.txt
Testing, testing, ten.txt
```

The VFAT system converts these files to the following in 8.3 format:

```
TESTIN~1.TXT
TESTIN~2.TXT
TESTIN~3.TXT
TESTIN~4.TXT
TESTIN~5.TXT
TESTIN~6.TXT
TESTIN~7.TXT
TESTIN~8.TXT
TESTIN~9.TXT
TESTI~10.TXT
```

Notice that in the last filename, VFAT truncates the primary name to five characters because the trailing number is now in double digits.

Although this conversion is an admirable attempt to maintain compatibility with older systems, the addition of two (and sometimes three) superfluous characters (the tilde and the number) at the end of the primary name isn't a great solution. The problem is that you're now down to just six (or even five) characters in the primary name, which gives you even *less* flexibility with respect to naming files. This is of little importance if you'll be using your files only on a Windows 95 (or Windows NT) system, but it can make a big difference if you'll be distributing your files to people still using DOS or Windows 3.x. Happily, there's a way to tell Windows 95 not to append the tilde/number combination (known as the *numeric tail*) to 8.3 names. I explain how in Chapter 12, "Hacking the Registry."

How Did They Do It?

So just how did Microsoft perform the seemingly impossible task of giving us long filenames *and* backward compatibility? Well, they did it by keeping track of *two* names for every file and directory: a regular 8.3 name and a long name. When you create a file with a long name, VFAT creates a regular FAT-compatible directory entry as well as a *secondary* directory entry. This new entry stores the first 26 bytes of the long filename. If the name is longer than that, VFAT just keeps adding secondary directory entries until the entire name is concatenated. The 8.3 name is stored in the initial directory entry, so complete compatibility is maintained.

Why don't older programs get confused by all these extra directory entries? Cleverly, Microsoft took advantage of an obscure property of the FAT system. In the FAT file structure, each file has a 32-byte directory entry that specifies, among other things, the file's name, its extension, the date and time it was created, and the file's attributes: read-only, hidden, and so on.

The obscurity is that, under DOS, it isn't logical for a file to have the following four attributes set: read-only, hidden, system, and volume label. In fact, DOS will just ignore any directory entry that has these four attributes set. So that's what VFAT does: It sets these four attributes on all the secondary directory entries so that they'll be ignored by all older programs.

This works for older programs because they use the built-in DOS enumeration functions to work with filenames. However, many older disk utilities (such as Norton Disk Doctor) bypass DOS and work with directory entries directly. Such utilities see VFAT's secondary directory entries as corrupted entries that aren't associated with any file. When they "fix" them, you lose your long filenames.

To avoid this problem, use only disk utilities that were made to run under VFAT. (If you don't have any VFAT-compatible utilities, you can use Microsoft's LFNBK utility to avoid problems with older disk utilities. See Chapter 15, "Protecting Your Windows 95 Investment," for details.)

OSR2 ## What's New with Fat32?

Back in 1981, when Bill Gates was asked about the 640 KB memory constraint in the original IBM PC architecture, he said, "640K ought to be enough for anybody." In fact, a case could be made that the entire history of the PC involves someone saying that "*x* ought to be enough for anybody" and then a few years later saying "*x* just doesn't cut it anymore." Hard disk size is a good example. When the FAT file system was modified a few years ago to accommodate disks with up to 2 GB capacity, such a vast number seemed laughably large at the time. (After all, it wasn't that long before that DOS 4.0 had finally broken the 32 MB barrier!) Now, however, 2 GB disks are *de rigueur* on even modest systems and notebooks (and can be purchased for less than 10 cents a megabyte), and disks with 4 GB and even 9 GB capacities aren't all that unusual.

Under the Hood: Understanding the Windows 95 Architecture

CHAPTER 6

207

6

UNDERSTANDING
THE WINDOWS
95 ARCHITECTURE

So, once again, we're at an architectural crossroads in the PC industry:

- Until now, manufacturers had been handling large (over 2 GB) hard disks by splitting them into multiple partitions.

- The FAT system is extremely wasteful at large partition sizes. As I'll explain in detail in Chapter 9, on partitions that are between 1 GB and 2 GB in size, FAT allocates a full 32 KB to even the tiniest file. The result is as much as 30 percent wasted hard disk space.

FAT32 to the Rescue

To get us through this crossroads and into the next era, Microsoft has updated the FAT portion of the file system to the new FAT32 architecture. This is one of the key new features found in OSR2, and Microsoft promises it will be a feature in the next major release of Windows. How does FAT32 help? Here's a summary:

Support for larger hard disks: FAT32 can handle hard disks that have a capacity of up to 2 terabytes (2,024 GB). The "32" in FAT32 means that the sector numbers used in directory entries are now 32-bit values. This means that the file system can track 4,294,967,296 (2 to the power of 32) distinct values, which, at 512 bytes per sector, yields the 2-terabyte limit.

Smaller cluster sizes: Instead of the massive 32 KB clusters used in large FAT16 partitions, FAT32 uses only 4 KB clusters in partitions up to 8 GB. This will improve storage efficiency on the vast majority of systems and should free up large amounts of disk space automatically.

Improved robustness: FAT32 implements three new features that should improve the reliability of the file system: a moveable root directory (useful for avoiding corrupt disk areas), the ability to use the backup copy of the FAT (FAT16 maintained two copies of the FAT but could use only one of them), and an internal backup copy of some critical FAT data structures.

Flexible partitioning: Unlike FAT16, FAT32 imposes no restrictions on the number of directory entries in a partition's root folder, and it allows the root to be located anywhere on the hard drive. These features mean, at least theoretically, that it's possible to dynamically resize a FAT32 partition without losing data (in other words, good riddance to the wretched FDISK utility!). At the time this chapter was written, however, no partitioning utilities that take advantage of this had been released.

Working with FAT32

Although Microsoft took great pains to avoid upsetting the file system apple cart with FAT32, any major change in this critical area is going to break a few applications and be cause for a few caveats. Here are a few notes to bear in mind when working with FAT32:

- The change from a 16-bit to a 32-bit cluster numbering scheme should have no effect on mainstream applications. Disk utilities are another story, however. Because these programs expect a 2-byte cluster value, they won't work with FAT32. You'll need to get updated versions of your favorite utilities before you use them on your FAT32 drives.

■ FAT32 comes with updated versions of its disk utilities, including the real-mode FDISK, FORMAT, SCANDISK, and DEFRAG commands, and the protected-mode Format, ScanDisk, and Disk Defragmenter applets.

■ DriveSpace 3 does *not* work on FAT32 partitions.

■ Existing file systems, including FAT16 and the NTFS used in Windows NT, aren't compatible with FAT32, so FAT32 drives won't be visible locally. (You'll be able to see them across network connections, however.) This also means that you can't dual-boot on a FAT32 partition.

■ Don't expect large changes in file system performance under FAT32. Although an improved caching system helps performance, this benefit is offset by the larger number of clusters that the system must deal with.

Summary

This chapter ends your preparatory work in Windows 95. Now that the new operating system is installed and you're comfortable with the lay of the Windows land, it's time to move on to more practical matters. You'll do just that in the next chapter, as I show you how to customize Windows 95 to suit your style.

Here's a list of chapters where you'll find related information:

■ To learn how Windows 95 handles memory, and to get the full scoop on clusters and partitioning, see Chapter 9, "Windows 95 Performance Tuning and Optimization."

■ You'll find information on device drivers and Plug and Play in Chapter 10, "How Windows 95 Handles Hardware."

■ I explain the Registry in detail in Chapter 11, "Introducing the Windows 95 Registry."

II

PART

Unleashing Windows Customization and Optimization

Customizing
Windows 95

IN THIS CHAPTER

CHAPTER 7

Whoso would be a man, must be a nonconformist.

—*Ralph Waldo Emerson*

Microsoft spent countless hours and untold millions testing and retesting the Windows 95 interface in its usability labs. A person—usually an ordinary computer-using Joe or Josephine— would sit at a computer while researchers shod in white coats (at least that's how I imagine them) would watch how the person worked. Tendencies were tracked, inefficiencies were noted, and questions were asked. All this data—suitably normalized, bell-curved, and otherwise statisticized—was studied and converted into ideas for the Windows 95 user interface (UI). Programmers would then implement these ideas, more subjects would be brought in to give them a whirl, and the whole process would be repeated.

The result, as you've seen, is a UI that is radically different from any previous system that bore the Windows moniker. It's friendlier, more sensible, and more Mac-like. (The Mac resemblance seems to be the inevitable—and defining—trend of Windows interface design; this has led more than one Mac wag to say that Windows 95 is more like "Macintosh 88." Of course, a typical Mac in those days didn't have color, and it had a screen the size of a postage stamp, and it couldn't multitask its way out of a paper bag, and...well, you get the idea.)

It's important, however, to remember that Windows 95 is Microsoft's operating system for the masses. With an expected installed base running in the tens of millions, it's only natural that the Windows UI would incorporate lots of "lowest common denominator" thinking. So, in the end, you have an interface that most people find easy to use most of the time; an interface that's skewed toward accommodating neophytes and the newly digital; an interface designed for a "typical" computer user, whoever the heck she is.

In other words, unless you consider yourself a typical user (and your purchase of this book proves otherwise), Windows 95 in its right-out-of-the-box getup won't be right for you. Fortunately, you'll find no shortage of options and programs that will help you remake Windows 95 in your own image, and that's just what this chapter shows you how to do. After all, you weren't produced by a cookie cutter, so why should your operating system look like it was?

Customizing the Taskbar

The taskbar is so convenient and such an elegantly simple idea that it might be worth the price of Windows 95 admission all by itself. Sure, if I'm switching constantly back and forth between a couple of applications, nothing's faster than a quick slam of the Alt-Tab "cool switch." But when it comes to navigating several open programs, or just knowing what's up and running, the taskbar can't be beat.

That's not to say it's perfect, however. For example, if you have too many windows open, the taskbar buttons become too small, and you can't make out the window titles; and folks with small screens or video cards that have limited resolution might resent giving up a strip of screen real estate.

Fortunately, these quibbles are easily dealt with because the taskbar is quite flexible. Let's look at some of the features that make the taskbar such a tractable tool.

Sizing the Taskbar

If you don't mind giving up even more screen acreage, there's a sure cure for taskbar button crunch: Make the taskbar bigger. For example, take a look at the taskbar shown in Figure 7.1. With 10 windows open (not an outrageous number), the taskbar buttons become too small to read, so the taskbar itself loses much of its convenience.

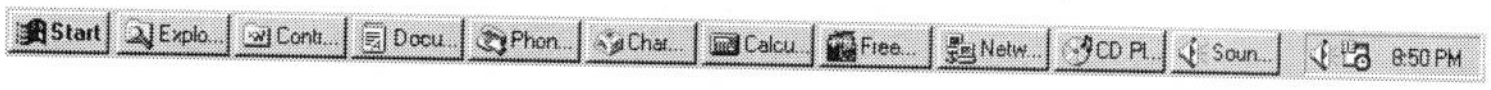
Start
Explo...
Conti...
Docu...
Phon...
Char...
Calcu...
Free...
Netw...
CD Pl...
Soun...
8:50 PM

FIGURE 7.1.
Taskbar overpopulation: too many windows and too little space.

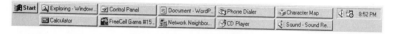

Surprisingly, however, the taskbar's height isn't fixed at a single row of icons. You can, if you like, expand the taskbar to show anywhere from 2 to 10 (yes, 10!) rows. To try this, move the mouse pointer to the top edge of the taskbar; the pointer turns into a two-headed arrow. Now simply drag the edge of the taskbar up until the second row appears. Figure 7.2 shows the same taskbar displayed with two rows. As you can see, the individual buttons are much easier to read.

Start
Exploring - Window...
Control Panel
Document - WordP...
Phone Dialer
Character Map
8:52 PM
Calculator
FreeCell Game #15...
Network Neighbor...
CD Player
Sound - Sound Re...

FIGURE 7.2.
The taskbar displayed with two rows of icons.

TIP: VIEWING TASKBAR BUTTON TEXT

Not interested in making the desktop any smaller than it actually is? You can still figure out the full window title that appears on any taskbar button. Just let the mouse pointer linger over a button. After a second or two, a small banner appears that spells out the entire window title.

Moving the Taskbar

The position of the taskbar isn't set in stone either. Although its default position is the bottom edge of the screen, you can move it to the top edge, the left edge, or the right edge. For example, when I'm writing, I like to maximize the vertical area of my word processor's window so that I can see as much text as possible at a glance. One easy way to gain more vertical space is to move the taskbar to one of the side edges.

To move the taskbar, position the mouse pointer over an empty part of the taskbar. Now drag the pointer to the edge of the screen where you want to position the taskbar. As you approach the edge, the taskbar leaps into place. Also note that you can size the taskbar from any edge.

Figure 7.3 shows the taskbar on the left edge of the screen. Notice how the desktop icons are shifted to the right to remain visible.

Figure 7.3.

You can move the taskbar to any edge of the screen.

Taskbar Properties

The taskbar is a Windows 95 object, so it has various properties you can set for some extra customization fun. To check out these properties, try either of the following methods:

- Select Start | Settings | Taskbar.
- Right-click an empty part of the taskbar, and select Properties from the context menu.

Windows 95 displays the Taskbar Properties dialog box, shown in Figure 7.4.

The Taskbar Options tab presents several check boxes that control the behavior of the taskbar. After you've made your selections, you can put them into effect either by clicking the Apply button (to see the effect of the selected options without dismissing the dialog box) or by clicking OK. Here are the options that affect the taskbar:

Always on top: In Windows 3.x, a maximized window took up the entire screen, lock, stock, and barrel. In Windows 95, however, a maximized window consumes only the entire desktop; the taskbar remains visible. If you'd prefer to hand over *all* the screen to your applications, deactivate the Always on top check box.

FIGURE 7.4.

Use the Taskbar Properties dialog box to set a few taskbar options.

TIP: DISPLAYING THE TASKBAR

With `Always on top` deactivated, a maximized window will cover the taskbar. To display the taskbar again, press Ctrl-Esc to display both the taskbar and the Start menu, and press Esc by itself to close the Start menu.

Auto hide: This option provides an alternative method for giving your windows extra room on the desktop. When you activate the `Auto hide` check box, the taskbar sinks below the bottom edge of the screen (assuming, of course, that the taskbar is still situated on the bottom edge). All that remains is a thin gray line. Move the mouse pointer over this line, however, and the taskbar slides back into view; move the pointer off the taskbar, and the taskbar resumes its position below the screen's horizon. In other words, the taskbar appears on-screen only when you need it.

TIP: ADJUSTING THE WIDTH OF THE TASKBAR'S GRAY LINE

The width of the gray line that the taskbar leaves behind when `Auto hide` is activated is the same as the width of the window borders. I'll show you how to adjust this width later (see the later section "A Desktop to Call Your Own").

Show small icons in Start menu: If you activate this check box, Windows 95 displays the Start menu and its folders with smaller icons. This reduces the overall size of each menu and makes the menus marginally easier to navigate. The trade-off is that the icons are a bit harder to see, and the individual items are closer together, making them a slightly harder target to hit with the mouse.

Show Clock: This check box toggles the Clock in the lower-right corner on and off.

NOTE: THE TASKBAR'S ACTIONS

If the taskbar is an object, what are its actions? To find out, right-click an empty part of the taskbar. The context menu that appears gives you four taskbar actions:

Cascade: This command arranges all the nonminimized windows in an overlapping, diagonal pattern. When you select this command, the taskbar's context menu gains an Undo Cascade command that you can use to undo the arrangement.

Tile Horizontally: This command arranges the nonminimized windows into evenly sized horizontal strips that cover the desktop. To reverse this procedure, select Undo Tile from the taskbar's context menu.

Tile Vertically: This command arranges the nonminimized windows into evenly sized vertical strips that cover the desktop. To reverse this procedure, select Undo Tile from the taskbar's context menu.

Minimize All Windows: Clears the desktop by minimizing each open window to its taskbar icon. To restore the windows, select Undo Minimize All from the taskbar's context menu.

Customizing the Start Menu

I mentioned in Chapter 5, "Windows 95: The 50¢ Tour," that even though the Start menu is leaps and bounds ahead of Program Manager, it's still not a particularly satisfying application launcher. It's not so bad if the item you need is on the Start menu itself, or on one of its immediate submenus (such as Programs or Settings). But if you find yourself constantly opening three or even four menus, the whole thing loses its appeal very quickly. When you think about it, though, the problem isn't so much that the Start menu itself is a bad idea; it's just that, in its default incarnation, the Start menu is organized poorly.

For example, Windows 95 comes with an Inbox Repair Tool accessory for fixing an Exchange Inbox that's gone south. To run it, you select Start | Programs | Accessories | System Tools | Inbox Repair Tool. That's five clicks in all, which isn't outrageous considering that this is an obscure program you'll use rarely (hopefully never).

On the other hand, the CD Player applet is an essential tool for those who enjoy listening to music while they slave away. Unfortunately, you have to expend the same amount of energy to run CD Player (Start | Programs | Accessories | Multimedia | CD Player) as you do to run Inbox Repair Tool.

In other words, although the Start menu has a hierarchical structure, its layout is only semi-hierarchical: Some popular programs are easily accessible (such as Explorer on the Program menu), whereas others are tucked away in obscure nooks (such as CD Player on the Multimedia menu).

NOTE: INSTALL PROGRAMS JUST MAKE THINGS WORSE

Just to add to the confusion, the install programs for most Windows applications add a folder and a few shortcuts to the Programs menu. Some (such as Microsoft Office 95) are even rude enough to toss a few shortcuts onto the Start menu itself.

The solution? Scrap Microsoft's dumb Start menu layout, and customize the menus to create a hierarchy of programs that suits the way you work, like this:

- Move the programs, accessories, and documents you use most often into higher layers of the Start menu tree.

- Move the items you use less often into lower layers of the Start menu.

Windows 95 gives you two ways to customize your Start menu in this manner: Use the Taskbar Properties dialog box to add and remove Start menu shortcuts, or work with the Start Menu folder directly.

Adding and Removing Start Menu Shortcuts

For simple Start menu customization needs, the Taskbar Properties dialog box offers a couple of simple tools that let you add and remove Start menu shortcuts. First, display the Taskbar Properties dialog box by right-clicking an empty part of the Taskbar and selecting Properties from the context menu, or by selecting Start | Settings | Taskbar. Now select the Start Menu Programs tab, shown in Figure 7.5.

FIGURE 7.5.

Use the Start Menu Programs tab to customize your Start menu.

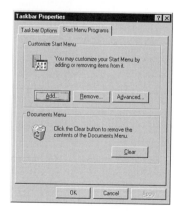

Adding a Shortcut

If the Start menu doesn't contain an item for a program or document you use regularly, you can easily add a shortcut to whichever menu you like. Even if a Start menu already has an item for a program or document, you might want to create a second shortcut in a different folder.

7

CUSTOMIZING
WINDOWS 95

(I'll show you how to delete the old shortcut in the next section.) To add a new shortcut to one of the Start menus, follow these steps:

1. Click the Add button. Windows 95 displays the Create Shortcut dialog box, shown in Figure 7.6.

FIGURE 7.6.

Use the Create Shortcut dialog box to specify the shortcut you want to add.

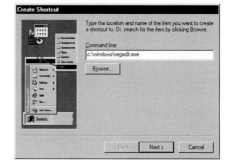

2. If you know the full path (drive, folder, and filename) of the program, accessory, or document you want to add to the Start menu, enter it in the Command line text box.

    If you're not sure of the correct path, click Browse, use the Browse dialog box to highlight the appropriate file, and click Open.

3. Click Next >. The Select Program Folder dialog box, shown in Figure 7.7, appears.

FIGURE 7.7.

Your next step is to use this dialog box to choose a Start menu home for the new shortcut.

4. If you want to create a new folder for the shortcut, first highlight the folder you want to use as the parent. (For example, if you want to create a new folder off the Start menu, highlight Start Menu.) Now click the New Folder button and type the folder name.

    If you'd prefer to use an existing folder, highlight the folder name.

5. Click Next >. The Select a Title for the Program dialog box appears. This is the text that will appear on the menu.

6. Enter a title and then click Finish. Windows 95 adds the new shortcut (and the new folder, if you created one) to the Start menu tree.

Removing a Shortcut

If there is a Start menu shortcut you'll never use, or if you've added an existing shortcut to a different folder, you can delete the unneeded shortcut to make the menus easier to navigate. (Note that deleting a shortcut has absolutely no effect on the underlying program or document; all you're removing is a file that *points to* the real McCoy.) Here's the procedure:

1. In the Start Menu Programs tab, click the Remove button. Windows 95 displays the Remove Shortcuts/Folders dialog box, shown in Figure 7.8.

FIGURE 7.8.

Use this dialog box to select the shortcut or folder you want to delete.

2. Highlight the shortcut or folder you want to delete.
3. Click the Remove button. If you delete a folder, Windows 95 asks whether you're sure you want to go through with the deletion.
4. Click Yes.
5. Repeat steps 2 through 4 to delete any other shortcuts or folders.
6. When you're done, click Close.

Dealing with the Documents Menu

You'll notice in Figure 7.5 that the Start Menu Programs tab has a Documents Menu group. Clicking the Clear button in this group removes all the items from the Start menu's Documents menu (which, you'll recall, stores shortcuts to the last 15 documents you worked on).

Windows 95 stores the shortcuts for the Documents menu in the Recent folder (which is a subfolder of your main Windows 95 folder). So instead of clearing the Documents menu via the Start Menu Programs tab, you can simply delete the shortcuts that appear in the Recent folder.

For faster service, you can also use the following DOS command to clear the Documents menu (I'm assuming here that your main Windows 95 folder is C:\Windows):

```
DEL c:\windows\recent\*.lnk
```

You can run this command from a DOS session or the Run dialog box, place this command within your AUTOEXEC.BAT file (before the WIN command), or create a separate batch file that runs only this command. For the latter, you could create a shortcut for the batch file and place this shortcut either on your desktop or inside the Startup folder.

TIP: USE A BATCH FILE TO ADD DOCUMENTS TO THE RECENT FOLDER

Besides clearing the Recent folder, you can also use batch file commands to add shortcuts for oft-used documents to the Recent folder. First, create shortcuts for your documents in a separate folder (this folder should contain no other shortcut files). Then create a batch file command that copies these shortcuts into the Recent folder. For example, if the shortcuts are stored in the C:\Windows\MyDocs folder, the following command will copy them to the Recent folder:

```
COPY c:\windows\mydocs\*.lnk c:\windows\recent
```

NOTE: THE RECENT FOLDER AND USER PROFILES

If you've implemented user profiles on your system (as described later in this chapter in the section "Working with User Profiles"), note that each user will have his or her own Recent folder that will appear in the following Windows 95 subfolder (where *User* is the name of the user):

```
\Profiles\User\Recent
```

Working with the Start Menu Folder Directly

All this adding and removing of shortcuts works fine, but if you truly want to unleash the program-launching prowess of the Start menu, you need a less cumbersome approach. The key to this new approach is that the Start menu is really just a folder that branches off from your main Windows folder. If Windows 95 is installed in C:\Windows, for example, the Start Menu folder is C:\Windows\Start Menu. This allows you to work with the contents of the Start menu within Explorer (or even My Computer, if you like).

To display the Start Menu folder, use either of the following techniques:

- In Explorer, open your main Windows 95 folder, and then highlight the Start Menu folder.
- Right-click the Start button and select Explore from the context menu.

Figure 7.9 shows the Explorer window with the Start Menu folder highlighted.

FIGURE 7.9.

You can use Explorer to customize the Start Menu *folder directly.*

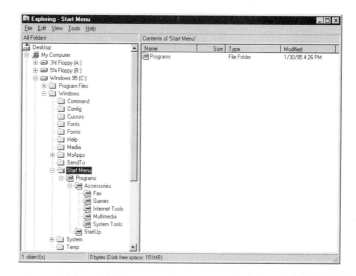

NOTE: THE START MENU FOLDER AND USER PROFILES

As with the Recent folder, if you're working with user profiles, each user will have his or her own Start Menu folder, which will appear in the following Windows 95 subfolder (where *user* is the name of the user):

\Profiles*user*\Start Menu

NOTE: AVOID THE ADVANCED BUTTON

Another way to open an Explorer window on the Start Menu folder is to click the Advanced button in the Start Menu Programs tab of the Taskbar Properties dialog box. Unfortunately, the window that appears gives you access to only the Start Menu folder; the rest of your folders and drives are off-limits. That makes this technique less attractive, so I'd suggest avoiding it.

The first thing you'll notice is that the Start Menu folder doesn't display all the items in the Start menu. In fact, it shows only one: Programs. Unfortunately, the items that appear below the Programs command in the Start menu are part of the Windows 95 interface, so you can't change them. That's not a big deal, though, because you still have lots of customization possibilities.

As you can see in Figure 7.9, the Start Menu folder contains subfolders that correspond to each submenu. For example, the Programs folder has a subfolder named Accessories; and the Accessories folder has subfolders named Multimedia, System Tools, and so on.

Taken together, the Start Menu folder and all of its subfolders constitute what I'll call the *Start Menu hierarchy*. How you work with the Start menu's contents—the folders and shortcuts—depends on whether you're working inside this hierarchy or outside it.

Working Within the Start Menu Hierarchy

Working within the Start Menu hierarchy means you're moving or copying existing shortcuts or Start Menu subfolders, or creating new subfolders below Start Menu. This is all straightforward, and you can use any of the techniques for copying, moving, renaming, and deleting objects that I outlined in the preceding chapter. Here are a few notes to bear in mind:

■ Feel free to move any of the Start Menu subfolders to a different parent. For example, if you find that you constantly use the programs in the System Tools folder, you can put it within closer reach by moving it to, say, the Programs folder or even the Start Menu folder itself.

■ You can create new folders, and they'll appear as new menus off the Start menu (depending on which folder you use for the parent).

■ If you move or copy an object to the Start Menu folder, it appears above the Programs command at the top of the Start menu. In Figure 7.10, for example, I've moved three objects into the Start Menu folder: the Games folder, and the shortcuts for Backup and CD Player.

FIGURE 7.10.

Objects copied to the Start Menu *folder appear at the top of the Start menu.*

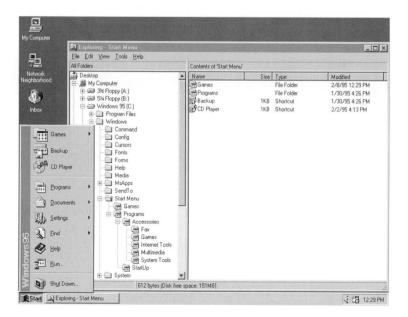

Working Outside the Start Menu Hierarchy

If you want to work with objects that exist outside the Start Menu hierarchy, you need to be a little more careful. That's because when you perform a copy or move operation in Explorer, you're copying or moving the *object* itself. And moving, for example, an executable file into a Start Menu folder can cause all kinds of problems because the program (and Windows 95) probably expects the file to reside in a certain locale.

To avoid these kinds of snafus, always paste a copied or cut file or folder as a *shortcut.* Here's how:

- Copy or cut the object normally, highlight the Start Menu folder you want to use as the destination, and select Edit | Paste Shortcut. (You can also right-click inside the destination folder's Contents pane and select Paste Shortcut from the context menu.)

- If you're dragging an executable file, Explorer assumes that you want to create a shortcut, so you can just drop the file on the destination folder.

- If you want to drag any other type of object (that is, a document or a folder), you can't use the traditional drag-and-drop technique. Instead, you need to right-drag the object (hold down the *right* mouse button and drag the object) and then drop it on the destination folder. In the context menu that appears, select Create Shortcut(s) Here, as shown in Figure 7.11.

FIGURE 7.11.

To create shortcuts for documents and folders, right-drag the object and select Create Shortcut(s) Here from the context menu.

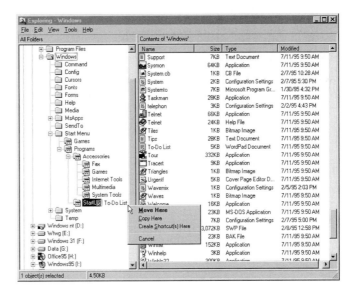

7

CUSTOMIZING
WINDOWS 95

> **NOTE: CREATING DESKTOP SHORTCUTS**
>
> As I mentioned in the preceding chapter, the desktop is also a folder. So you can use any of the techniques outlined in this section to create shortcuts right on the desktop. Just drag (or right-drag, as the case may be) the appropriate file from Explorer, and drop it anywhere on the desktop. (If you can't see the desktop, you can also drop the file on the Desktop folder at the top of Explorer's Folders pane.)

Start Menu Tricks

Let's finish our look at customizing the Start menu with a few interesting tricks and techniques.

Easier Start Menu Shortcuts

For easy access, you should populate the main Start menu with those programs and documents you use every day. This puts these important objects just a couple of mouse clicks away.

Here's an easy way to create shortcuts that appear at the top of the Start menu: Drag the appropriate file from Explorer or My Computer, and drop it on the Start button. Windows 95 adds a shortcut for the file at the top of the Start menu. Note that Windows 95 automatically creates a shortcut for any type of file; there's no need to right-drag documents (or even folders, for that matter).

Accelerator Keys for Start Menu Items

When you display the Start menu, you can select an item quickly by pressing the first letter of the item's name. If you add several shortcuts to the top of the Start menu, however, you might end up with more than one item that begins with the same letter. To avoid conflicts, rename each of these items so that they begin with a number. For example, renaming "Backup" to "1 Backup" means you can select this item by pressing 1. Figure 7.12 shows a sample Start menu that uses this technique.

Adding Control Panel Icons to the Start Menu

The eagle-eyed in the crowd will have noticed that the Start menu shown in Figure 7.12 has two Control Panel icons: Display Properties and Network Properties. How did I get them there? Easy: I just highlighted the Control Panel folder in Explorer and then dragged the icons onto the Start button. You can do the same thing with items in the Printers folder and the Dial-Up Networking folder.

FIGURE 7.12.

Prefacing Start menu names with a number prevents accelerator key conflicts.

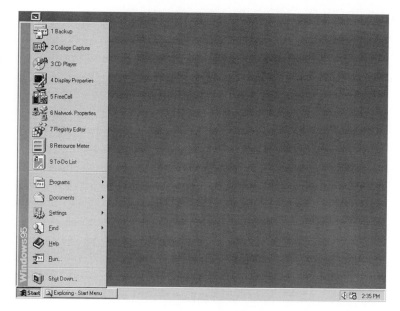

You might think that you could just drag the Control Panel folder and drop it on the Start button to create a new menu that displays each Control Panel icon. Unfortunately, the short-cut created just opens the Control Panel window. Alternatively, you could create a new folder off the Start Menu folder—called, say, Control Panel—and then drag all the Control Panel icons into this new folder.

This technique works, but it means that every time an application adds an icon to the Control Panel (and there's no shortage of programs that do this), you have to remember to update your Start Menu folder. To avoid this chore, create a new folder off the Start Menu folder, and give it the following name:

```
Control Panel.{21EC2020-3AEA-1069-A2DD-08002B30309D}
```

Actually, the text to the left of the period can be any string you like; it's just the name that appears on the Start menu. The long value to the right of the period is Control Panel's re-source identifier. As you can see in Figure 7.13, the menu it creates contains all the Control Panel icons. The advantage of this technique is that Windows 95 updates the menu automati-cally whenever Control Panel icons are added or removed.

FIGURE 7.13.

A menu of Control Panel icons.

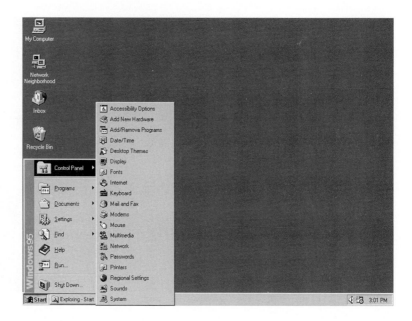

You can also achieve the same effect with the Printers and Dial-Up Networking folders. For the Printers folder, create a new folder with the following name:

```
Printers.{2227A280-3AEA-1069-A2DE-08002B30309D}
```

For the Dial-Up Networking folder, create a new folder with this name:

```
Dial-Up Networking.{992CFFA0-F557-101A-88EC-00DD010CCC48}
```

In both cases, the string to the left of the period is what appears on the menu, so it can be whatever you like.

There's even another method you can use to create shortcuts for Control Panel icons. It's not nearly as efficient as the methods we've examined so far, but it demonstrates some interesting facts about how Control Panel works.

The idea is that, for each Control Panel icon you want to use, you create a new shortcut in the appropriate folder. When the Create Shortcut dialog box appears, use the Command line text box to enter a command with the following syntax:

```
C:\WINDOWS\CONTROL.EXE CPL_NAME.CPL [MODULE]
```

If you installed Windows 95 in a folder other than `C:\WINDOWS`, make the appropriate substitution. Here, `CPL_NAME.CPL` is the name of the CPL (Control Panel) file that corresponds to the icon, and `MODULE` is an optional parameter used with `MAIN.CPL`. Table 7.1 lists the command lines to use with various Control Panel icons. (The Control Panel icons that are missing—such as Add New Hardware and Sounds—can't be accessed with this technique.)

Table 7.1. Shortcut parameters for Control Panel icons.

Control Panel Icon	Command Line
Accessibility Options	`C:\WINDOWS\CONTROL.EXE ACCESS.CPL`
Add/Remove Programs	`C:\WINDOWS\CONTROL.EXE APPWIZ.CPL`
Date/Time	`C:\WINDOWS\CONTROL.EXE TIMEDATE.CPL`
Desktop Themes	`C:\WINDOWS\CONTROL.EXE THEMES.CPL`
Display	`C:\WINDOWS\CONTROL.EXE DESK.CPL`
Fonts	`C:\WINDOWS\CONTROL.EXE MAIN.CPL FONTS`
Internet	`C:\WINDOWS\CONTROL.EXE INETCPL.CPL`
Joystick	`C:\WINDOWS\CONTROL.EXE JOY.CPL`
Keyboard	`C:\WINDOWS\CONTROL.EXE MAIN.CPL KEYBOARD`
Mail and Fax	`C:\WINDOWS\CONTROL.EXE MLCFG32.CPL`
Microsoft Mail Postoffice	`C:\WINDOWS\CONTROL.EXE WGPOCPL.CPL`
Modems	`C:\WINDOWS\CONTROL.EXE MODEM.CPL`
Mouse	`C:\WINDOWS\CONTROL.EXE MAIN.CPL MOUSE`
Multimedia	`C:\WINDOWS\CONTROL.EXE MMSYS.CPL`
Network	`C:\WINDOWS\CONTROL.EXE NETCPL.CPL`
Passwords	`C:\WINDOWS\CONTROL.EXE PASSWORD.CPL`
Printers	`C:\WINDOWS\CONTROL.EXE MAIN.CPL PRINTERS`
Regional Settings	`C:\WINDOWS\CONTROL.EXE INTL.CPL`
System	`C:\WINDOWS\CONTROL.EXE SYSDM.CPL`

7

CUSTOMIZING WINDOWS 95

NOTE: WHAT IS `TELEPHON.CP$`?

If you examine your Windows 95 `System` subfolder, you'll see a file named `Telephon.cp$`. This is actually a Control Panel file that's designed for telephony-related settings. Because no telephony applications are built into Windows 95 (except those connected to your modem), Microsoft disabled this file by replacing the last letter in the extension with a dollar sign ($). Future telephony applications will make use of this file.

TIP: HIDING CONTROL PANEL ICONS

Depending on your system's configuration, you might have a couple dozen or more Control Panel icons to deal with. If there are any icons you never use, it's possible to hide them and thus reduce Control Panel clutter. This is also handy for system administrators who want to keep certain icons out of reach of their users.

To see how this works, first open CONTROL.INI (which you'll find in your main Windows 95 folder). In the section labeled [don't load], enter the name of the CPL file that corresponds to the Control Panel icon you want to hide, followed by =yes. For example, to hide the Passwords (PASSWORD.CPL) icon, you would set up CONTROL.INI as follows:

```
[don't load]
password.cpl=yes
```

Exit and save your work to put the new settings into effect.

Moving the Start Button

The Start button is really a miniwindow within the taskbar. It doesn't act much like a typical window, except for one thing: You can move it using the same keyboard techniques you would use to move a regular window. Here's how it works:

1. Activate the Start button by pressing Ctrl-Esc, and then press Esc.
2. Press Alt-hyphen to display the Start button's Control menu.
3. Select the Move command.
4. Use the left and right arrow keys to move the button within the taskbar. (If you're using a multiline taskbar, you can also use the up and down arrow keys.)
5. When the button is positioned where you want it, press Enter.

One of the advantages of moving the Start button is that you can force Windows 95 to cascade the Start menu on the left instead of on the right (which is inconvenient for many left-handed users). All you have to do is move the Start button to the right side of the taskbar (just to the left of the system tray).

A Desktop to Call Your Own

Windows 95's default desktop is pleasant enough to look at, I suppose, but *exciting* isn't an adjective that springs to my mind when describing it. That's OK, though, because (as far as I know) the tops of desks aren't supposed to be exciting. Still, that doesn't mean you have to settle for Microsoft's focus-group–inspired decorating job. For something a little more personal, the desktop has all kinds of properties you can fiddle with.

To get to these properties, use either of the following techniques:

- Right-click an empty area of the desktop and click Properties in the context menu.
- Select Start | Settings | Control Panel and open the Display icon in the `Control Panel` folder.

Whichever method you choose, the Display Properties dialog box, shown in Figure 7.14, is displayed. The next few sections take you through each of the tabs in this dialog box. (Note that while you're working in this dialog box, you can click the Apply button at any time to see what effect the choices you've made will have on your desktop. When you're done, click OK— or possibly Close, depending on the options you chose—to put your changes into effect.)

FIGURE 7.14.

Use this dialog box to alter your desktop's properties.

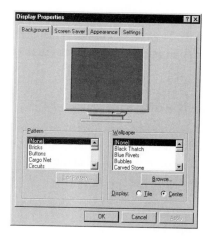

Working with Desktop Patterns

The Windows 95 desktop is normally a large, unbroken expanse of unremitting teal. To break up the monotony, you can define a *desktop pattern* that sits on top of the desktop.

Choosing a Predefined Pattern

To choose one of these patterns, first make sure that the Background tab is activated. Then use the `Pattern` list box to select a pattern. The sample computer screen above the list shows you what each pattern looks like.

Creating Your Own Pattern

Some of the predefined patterns are just plain hard on the eyes, but a few are quite creative. If you want to try your hand at creating a pattern, follow these steps:

1. In the `Pattern` list, select a pattern to work with.
2. Click the Edit Pattern button. The Pattern Editor dialog box, shown in Figure 7.15, appears.

FIGURE 7.15.

*Use the Pattern Editor
to create your own
desktop pattern.*

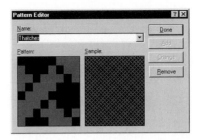

3. Create a pattern by clicking inside the `Pattern` box. Each click toggles a pixel between the desktop color and black. As you click, the `Sample` box shows you what the pattern will look like.

4. When you're done, use the `Name` text box to enter a name for the pattern.

5. Click the Add button to add the pattern to the list.

6. Click Done to return to the Display Properties dialog box.

Wallpapering the Desktop?

Windows 95's desktop metaphor is implemented in a fairly consistent manner through the interface, but it hits a bit of a snag when it comes to wallpaper. The problem is that *wallpaper* is a bitmap image that covers some or all of the desktop. Of course, in the real world, wallpaper covers walls, not the tops of desks, so someone on the Windows design team is guilty of mixing his metaphors.

Choosing a Wallpaper

This semantic quibble aside, wallpaper is an easy way to spruce up an otherwise drab desktop. To try it, select a file from the `Wallpaper` list in the Background tab. Activating the `Center` option places the image in the center of the screen; if the image is smaller than the desktop, activating the `Tile` option displays multiple copies of the image so that it covers the entire desktop. (Most of the bitmaps in the `Wallpaper` list are tiny, so you'll have to select `Tile` to get the full effect.)

Note that the files listed here are all bitmaps (BMP files) that reside in the main Windows folder. If you have a bitmap (either a BMP file or a DIB—Device-Independent Bitmap—file) in another folder, click the Browse button, highlight the file in the Browsing for wallpaper dialog box, and click OK.

Creating a Custom Wallpaper

Because the wallpapers are just bitmaps, you don't need to do anything special to create your own images to use as wallpaper. By using Paint or any other graphics program that can work with files in BMP or DIB format, create your image (or convert it to BMP or DIB), and save it in your main Windows 95 folder. Alternatively, you can scan an image and save the scan in the Windows folder as a BMP or DIB file.

If you have an image you'd like to use as a wallpaper but you can't move it into the Windows folder, Paint has a couple of commands that can help. Open the image in Paint, and then select one of the following File menu commands:

Set As Wallpaper (Tiled): This command sets the current image as the desktop wallpaper and displays the image tiled.

Set As Wallpaper (Centered): This command sets the current image as the desktop wallpaper and displays the image centered.

Setting Screen Saver and Energy-Saving Features

Back when most people worked in character-mode applications, monitors weren't as advanced as those used today. One of the problems people faced was leaving their monitors turned on and idle for extended periods and ending up with characters burned permanently into the screen. Screen savers were invented to help prevent this from happening. The screen saver resided in memory and kicked in only after the computer had been idle for some predetermined length of time. The screen saver would display some kind of moving pattern, so burn-in could never occur.

Nowadays, though, it's pretty tough to burn an image into your screen. Improvements in monitor quality and the graphical nature of Windows 95 have made such a fate virtually impossible. Curiously, though, screen savers are still around and are, in fact, flourishing. The reason: Modern screen savers, with their flying toasters and psychedelic patterns, are a lot of fun!

Of more importance than burn-in these days is energy savings. Although improvements have been made in monitor power consumption, most displays are still the energy hogs of your system. As an aid to reducing monitor power appetites, many displays now support energy-saving features that can reduce monitor power, or even turn off the monitor completely, after a predetermined period.

Windows 95 supports these monitor energy-saving features, and it even comes with a few screen savers for good measure. To try them, select the Screen Saver tab in the Display Properties dialog box, as shown in Figure 7.16. Note that the controls for energy saving appear only if your monitor supports these features.

Selecting a Screen Saver

The various screen savers that ship with Windows 95 are shown in the Screen Saver drop-down list. After you've chosen a screen saver, you can use the following controls to set it up:

Wait: This spinner controls the amount of time your computer must be inactive before the screen saver goes to work. You can enter a number between 1 and 60 minutes.

Preview: Click this button to give the screen saver a trial run. To return to the dialog box, move the mouse or press any key.

FIGURE 7.16.

Use this dialog box to set up a screen saver and your monitor's energy-saving features.

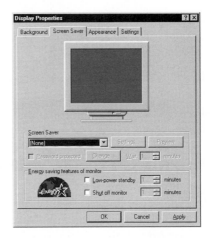

Password protected: If you activate this check box, Windows 95 requires you to enter a password before it shuts down the screen saver and returns the normal screen. To set the password, click the Change button, enter the password in the Change Password dialog box (note that you must enter it twice), and click OK. When Windows 95 tells you that the password has been changed, click OK.

CAUTION: PASSWORD PROTECTION? NOT!

If you think entering a password for the screen saver will protect your system from snoops, think again. All someone has to do is turn off and restart your computer, open the Display Properties dialog box, and clear the `Password protected` check box! Windows 95 doesn't bat an eye. (If you do use a password, though, this is a handy technique to know just in case you forget your password.)

Settings: Click this button to set various options for the screen saver. The Options dialog box that appears depends on which screen saver you chose. For example, Figure 7.17 shows the dialog box that appears for the Mystify Your Mind screen saver. Make your choices, and then click OK to return to the Display Properties dialog box.

FIGURE 7.17.

Each screen saver comes with a few customization options.

Creating an Instant Screen Saver

If you deal with sensitive data, you'll probably want to guard against visitors accidentally seeing what's on your screen. Short of always locking your door, an easy way to do this is to create an "instant" screen saver that can be activated using a quick key combination. To try this out, follow these steps:

1. Find your favorite screen saver file (it will have an .SCR extension) in the Windows 95 System folder.
2. Right-drag the file from Explorer, drop it on the desktop, and click Create Shortcut(s) Here. Windows 95 creates a desktop shortcut for the file.
3. Right-click the shortcut, and then choose Properties from the context menu.
4. In the properties sheet that appears, activate the Shortcut tab, click inside the Shortcut key box, and press the key you want to use as part of the Ctrl-Alt key combination. (For example, if you press Z, Windows 95 sets the key combination to Ctrl-Alt-Z.)
5. Click OK.

Now, no matter which application you're working in, you can activate your screen saver immediately simply by pressing the key combination you defined in step 4.

Activating Your Monitor's Energy-Saving Features

If you're more interested in reducing your energy costs than watching toasters fly across the screen, you'll prefer to activate your monitor's energy-saving features. Many newer monitors support the VESA Display Power Management Signaling (DPMS) specification. Using the video adapter, a software driver sends a signal to the monitor that can either blank the screen (standby mode) or turn off the monitor.

I'm assuming, of course, that your system supports power management. Specifically, you need two things:

■ An Energy Star–compliant monitor that supports the VESA DPMS specification.

■ A video driver that uses either the Advanced Power Management (APM) 1.1 BIOS interface with support for device "01FF" (which isn't supported by every APM 1.1 BIOS), or the VESA BIOS Extensions for Power Management (VBE/PM). (If you have OSR2, Windows 95 supports the APM 1.2 BIOS.)

If your system meets these criteria, you'll see two options in the Energy saving features of monitor group:

Low-power standby: If you activate this check box, Windows 95 blanks the screen and puts your monitor in standby mode. Windows 95 waits for a period of inactivity equal to the number of minutes specified in the minutes spinner. To reactivate the screen, jiggle the mouse or press any key (although, to be safe, you should just press a do-nothing key such as Shift).

Shut off monitor: If you activate this check box, Windows 95 turns off the monitor to save even more energy. Windows 95 waits for a period of inactivity equal to the number of minutes specified in the `minutes` spinner.

NOTE: ENABLING THE ENERGY-SAVING FEATURES

What do you do if you know that your system supports either APM or VBE/PM, but the Screen Saver tab doesn't show the energy-saving features check boxes? Activate the Settings tab, click the Change Display Type button, and activate the `Monitor is Energy Star compliant` check box.

TIP: COMBINING MONITOR-SAVING FEATURES

For optimum flexibility, you can combine these three options. For example, you could set your screen saver to kick in after 10 minutes of inactivity, set the low-power standby to take over after 20 minutes, and set your monitor to shut down after 30 minutes.

Renovating the Desktop: Colors, Fonts, and Sizes

If you're truly determined to put your personal stamp on the Windows 95 interface, the Appearance tab in the Display Properties dialog box is a great place to start. This tab, shown Figure 7.18, is brim full to bursting with controls and options that let you specify the colors, fonts, and sizes that Windows 95 uses to display objects on the desktop.

Figure 7.18.

Use the Appearance tab to give the desktop and its objects a makeover.

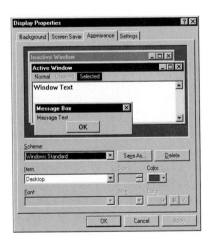

The Appearance tab is divided into two sections. The top half shows a fake desktop displaying a few objects; the bottom half contains the various controls you'll use to alter the appearance. The idea is that as you work with the controls, the fake objects reflect how your new desktop will look.

Selecting a Scheme

The easiest way to alter the appearance of the Windows 95 desktop is to select one of the 27 predefined *schemes*. A scheme is a collection of desktop attributes that includes the color of the desktop and window title bars, the fonts used in dialog boxes and pull-down menus, the size of window borders and desktop icons, and much more.

Use the Scheme list to choose a scheme name that sounds interesting, and then check out the fake desktop to see how things look. Note that, if your eyesight isn't what it used to be (and some of these schemes—such as the Pumpkin and Wheat eyesores—might make your eyesight worse!), several of the schemes use larger fonts. Look for the scheme names that end with either (large) or (extra large).

Creating a Custom Scheme

Some of the schemes look as though they were created in the Phyllis Diller House of Design. If you think you can do better, it's easy enough to create your own scheme. The basic procedure is to select an object from the Item drop-down list and then use the other controls—such as Size, Color, and Font—to customize the item. Note that not all the controls are available for each option. (For example, it doesn't make sense to specify a font for the scrollbars.)

> **TIP: A QUICK WAY TO SELECT ITEMS**
>
> Another way to select some of objects in the Item list is to click the appropriate part of the fake desktop. For example, clicking the title bar of the active window selects the Active Title Bar item.

Here's a rundown of the various objects available in the Item list:

3D Objects: Dialog box command buttons and tabs, caption buttons (see the "Caption Buttons" entry), scrollbars, status bars, taskbar, and window borders. You can set the background color and font color for these objects.

Active Title Bar: The title bar of the window that has the focus. You can set the size (height) and background color of the bar, as well as the font, font size, font color, and font style of the title bar text.

Active Window Border: The border surrounding the window that has the focus. You can set the border's width and color. Note that the width setting also controls the width of the taskbar when the Auto hide option is activated (as described earlier).

Application Background: The background on which windows are displayed in applications that support the Multiple Document Interface (MDI). You can set the color of the background.

Caption Buttons: The buttons that appear in the upper-right corner of windows and dialog boxes. You can set the size of these buttons.

Desktop: The desktop color. Note that this setting also controls the color of the backgrounds used with the desktop icons. You see this background color only if your desktop is covered with either a pattern or wallpaper.

Icon: The icons that appear on the desktop. You can set the icon size as well as the font attributes of the icon titles. Note that this font setting also controls the fonts displayed in Explorer and all open folders (such as `Control Panel` and `My Computer`).

Icon Spacing (Horizontal): The distance allotted (in pixels) between desktop and folder icons on the left and right.

Icon Spacing (Vertical): The distance allotted (in pixels) between desktop and folder icons on the top and bottom.

Inactive Title Bar: The title bars of the open windows that don't have the focus. You can set the size (height) and background color of the bar, as well as the font, font size, and font color of the title bar text.

Inactive Window Border: The borders surrounding the open windows that don't have the focus. You can set the border's width and color.

Menu: The window menu bar. You can set the size (height) and background color of the menu bar, as well as the font attributes of the menu bar text.

Message Box: Message boxes, such as error messages and information prompts. (Note that this setting doesn't apply to regular dialog boxes.) You can set the font attributes of the message text.

Palette Title: The application of this item is unknown.

Scrollbar: The scrollbars that appear in windows and list boxes. You can set the width (or height, depending on the orientation) of the scrollbars.

Selected Items: The currently selected menu in a menu bar and the currently selected command in a menu. You can set the height and background color of the selection bar, as well as the font attributes of the item text.

ToolTip: The small banners that appear if you hover the mouse pointer over a toolbar for a couple of seconds. You can set the background color and the font attributes of the ToolTip text. Note that the ToolTip font size also controls the size of a window's status bar text.

Window: The window background and text. You can set the color of these items.

When you're done, click the Save As button. In the Save Scheme dialog box that appears, enter a name for the scheme in the text box provided and click OK. Your newly created color scheme appears in the Scheme list.

If you've created some schemes you no longer need, you should delete them to make the Scheme list easier to navigate. To delete a scheme, highlight it in the Scheme list and click the Delete button.

Creating Your Own Colors

You might have noticed that the Appearance tab's Color lists have an Other button. You can use this option to pick a different color from Windows 95's color palette, or you can create your own color. When you click the Other button, you see the Color dialog box, shown in Figure 7.19.

FIGURE 7.19.

Use this dialog box to choose or create a different color.

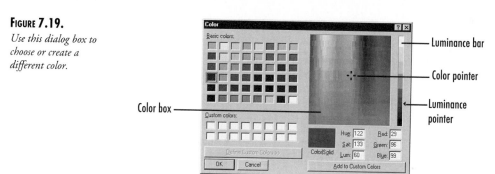

If you want to use one of the colors displayed in the Basic colors area, click it and then click OK.

To create your own color, you can use one of two methods. The first method utilizes the fact that you can create any color in the spectrum by mixing the three primary colors: red, green, and blue. The Color dialog box lets you enter specific numbers between 0 and 255 for each of these colors, by using the Red, Green, and Blue text boxes. A lower number means the color is less intense, and a higher number means the color is more intense.

To give you some idea of how this works, Table 7.2 lists eight common colors and their respective red, green, and blue numbers.

Table 7.2. The red, green, and blue numbers for eight common colors.

Color	Red	Green	Blue
Black	0	0	0
White	255	255	255

continues

Table 7.2. continued

Color	Red	Green	Blue
Red	255	0	0
Green	0	255	0
Blue	0	0	255
Yellow	255	255	0
Magenta	255	0	255
Cyan	0	255	255

NOTE: GRAY-SCALE COLORS

Whenever the Red, Green, and Blue values are equal, you get a gray-scale color. Lower numbers produce darker grays, and higher numbers produce lighter grays.

The second method for selecting colors involves setting three different attributes: hue, saturation, and luminance.

> **Hue:** This number (which is more or less equivalent to the term *color*) measures the position on the color spectrum. Lower numbers indicate a position near the red end, and higher numbers move through the yellow, green, blue, and violet parts of the spectrum. As you increase the hue, the color pointer moves from left to right.

> **Sat:** This number is a measure of the purity of a given hue. A saturation setting of 240 means that the hue is a pure color. Lower numbers indicate that more gray is mixed with the hue until, at 0, the color becomes part of the gray-scale. As you increase the saturation, the color pointer moves toward the top of the color box.

> **Lum:** This number is a measure of the brightness of a color. Lower numbers are darker, and higher numbers are brighter. The luminance bar to the right of the color box shows the luminance scale for the selected color. As you increase the luminance, the slider moves toward the top of the bar.

To create a custom color, you can either enter values in the text boxes, as just described, or you can use the mouse to click inside the color box and luminance bar. The Color¦Solid box shows the selected color on the left and the nearest solid color on the right (if you're using a 16-color video driver). If you think you'll want to reuse the color down the road, click the Add to Custom Colors button to place the color in one of the boxes in the Custom colors area. When you're done, click OK.

Changing the Display Settings

The Settings tab of the Display Properties dialog box, shown in Figure 7.20, controls various properties of your video display. These properties include the color depth, the resolution, and the default font size. The options available for each property depend on the type of video card and monitor you have and are limited by the capabilities of this hardware. Because of that, you can also use this tab to change your video driver or monitor type (although I won't cover how you do this until Chapter 22, "Miscellaneous Multimedia: Graphics, CD-ROMs, and More").

Figure 7.20.

Use the Settings tab to customize your video display.

The `Color palette` drop-down list contains the four basic color palettes: `16 color`, `256 color`, `High Color (16 bit)`, and `True Color (32 bit)`. The latter two depths give you 65,536 colors and 16,777,216 colors, respectively. When you apply a different palette, you'll be prompted to restart Windows 95 (unless you have OSR2; in that case, see the next section).

In general, fewer colors speed up your display, but you'll need higher color depths to display complex graphics. Note, too, that the number of colors available at a given resolution is limited by your video adapter. If you select a higher color depth, Windows 95 might have to reduce the resolution.

The `Desktop area` slider controls the screen resolution. Move the slider to the left to get a lower resolution; move the slider to the right to get a higher resolution. Again, the maximum available resolution depends on your video hardware and on the current color palette.

Changing resolutions in Windows 3.x meant having to restart Windows to put the new setting into effect. One of the major improvements that Windows 95 brings to the table is the capability to change the resolution on-the-fly. If you change the resolution and then click OK (or Apply), Windows 95 displays the dialog box shown in Figure 7.21. Click OK, and your display resolution is changed automatically. A new dialog box appears to ask whether you want to keep the new settings. Click Yes if you want to keep the new resolution. To return to the original resolution, either click No or wait 15 seconds, and Windows 95 will restore the resolution automatically.

FIGURE 7.21.

*Windows 95 can
change display
resolutions on-the-fly.*

The Font size drop-down list contains two options that control the size of the Windows 95 *system font* (the font Windows 95 uses for objects such as desktop icons, taskbar text, dialog boxes, menus, and windows). If this option isn't available, your video hardware doesn't support custom font sizes.

Actually, the name "Font size" is a bit of a misnomer because it might lead you to expect that it lets you specify a particular point size. That's not the case, however. Instead, Font size serves to *scale* the existing fonts so that they consume a larger or smaller amount of screen real estate. For example, suppose that a standard 10-point font uses up 100 pixels per inch; increasing this value to, say, 125 pixels per inch makes the font appear 25 percent larger. For this reason, a name such as "Font scale" would probably have made more sense.

The default value is Small Fonts, which displays the standard 10-point Arial font at 96 pixels per inch; alternatively, you can select Large Fonts, which displays the standard 10-point Arial font at 120 pixels per inch (a 25 percent increase).

If you'd prefer to customize the font size, click the Custom button to display the Custom Font Size dialog box, shown in Figure 7.22. Either select one of the five percentages in the drop-down list (75%, 100%, 125%, 150%, or 200%) or drag the mouse pointer along the ruler to set a specific percentage. The available values are between 20 percent and 500 percent. When you're done, click OK to return to the Settings tab. When you apply the new font scale, Windows 95 prompts you to restart your computer.

FIGURE 7.22.

*Use this dialog box to
set the font size
manually.*

Display Settings in OSR2

As you can see in Figure 7.23, the Settings tab in OSR2 boasts a few small changes. For one, the `Font size` group shows you some extra information about the current font, such as `Normal size (96 dpi)`. For another, there is also a `Show settings icon on task bar` check box. When this check box is activated, Windows 95 adds a display icon to the system tray. As shown in Figure 7.24, clicking this icon produces a list of all the resolutions and color depths that your video card supports. Click one of these values to change your display settings.

OSR2

FIGURE 7.23.

The Settings tab in OSR2.

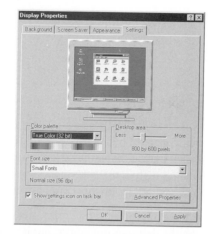

FIGURE 7.24.

Click the display icon in the system tray to see a list of supported resolutions and color depths.

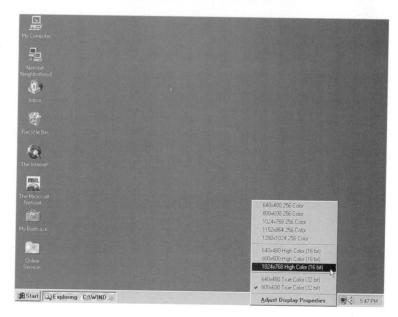

7

CUSTOMIZING
WINDOWS 95

Unlike the retail version of Windows 95, OSR2 implements on-the-fly color depth changes. When you change the color depth, you see the dialog box shown in Figure 7.25. You can either apply the change without rebooting, or you can reboot to ensure compatibility. (The latter should be an issue only if you're dropping to a lower color depth. In other words, if you're using an application that expects, say, 32-bit color, you could have problems if you drop down to 16-bit color or lower.)

FIGURE 7.25.

OSR2 displays this warning when you change color depths.

Easy Access to the Desktop

The desktop is a handy place to put shortcuts to folders, documents, and applications, and as you've just seen, a quick right-click on the desktop can get you to the Display Properties dialog box fast. The problem, though, is that you might not always have access to the desktop because one or more maximized windows might stand in your way.

One solution would be to right-click an empty area of the taskbar and select Minimize All Windows to clear off the desktop; this works, but it's a bit of a pain.

Another solution would be to max out the total desktop area by using the highest display resolution your video hardware can handle. Then, instead of maximizing windows, you can adjust them so that you're left with a strip of the desktop still visible on the left side of the screen. For example, Figure 7.26 shows a screen running at 1024×768. There's plenty of room to create a large Explorer window *and* leave part of the desktop visible. Unfortunately, this solution really works only at resolutions of 1024×768 and higher, and not all video hardware can handle this.

If you must run your applications maximized, there's still a way to get easy access to the desktop:

1. Open the My Computer folder.
2. If the toolbar isn't displayed, select View | Toolbar to activate it.
3. Open the toolbar's Go to a different folder drop-down list and select Desktop at the top of the list. The desktop's icons appear in the window.
4. Minimize the window. This leaves you with a Desktop button on the taskbar that you can access at any time.

Figure 7.26.

Running at high display resolutions gives you enough room on-screen to leave part of the desktop visible at all times.

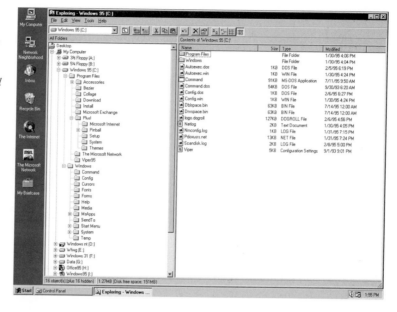

Setting the Date and Time

As you know, the taskbar displays the current time in the lower-right corner. As I've mentioned before, you can display the date by letting the mouse pointer linger over the time for a second or two. If you need to change the time or the date, however, you must use the Date/Time Properties dialog box shown in Figure 7.27. To display this dialog box, use any of the following methods:

- ■ Double-click the time.
- ■ Right-click the time and select Adjust Date/Time from the context menu.
- ■ Select Start | Settings | Control Panel, and open the Date/Time icon.

Figure 7.27.

Use the Date/Time dialog box to adjust the current date and time.

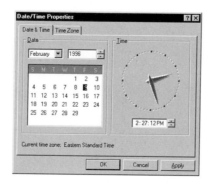

To work with this dialog box, use the following techniques:

- To select a different day in the current month, click the date in the calendar.
- To display a different month, select it from the Date drop-down list.
- To work with a different year, use the Date spinner to choose the year.
- To adjust the time, use the Time text box/spinner combination to enter the new time. You can type the correct values, or you can place the cursor inside a field (hour, minute, second, AM/PM) and use the spinner.
- To adjust the time zone, first select the Time Zone tab. Then either use the drop-down list to select your time zone or use the map to click on your locale.
- If your time zone doesn't bother with daylight savings time, deactivate the Automatically adjust clock for daylight saving changes check box.

When you're done, click OK to put the new settings into effect.

Worldwide Windows: Customizing the Regional Settings

If you'll be writing documents to send to foreign countries, you'll need to tailor certain aspects of your writing for your readership. For example, if you'll be using foreign currency amounts, not only will you need to use the appropriate currency symbol, but you also will want to place the symbol in the correct position relative to the amount. In Germany, for example, the deutsche mark symbol (DM) is placed *after* the amount (for example, 5,000 DM). Similarly, date formats are different around the world. In the United States, for example, 12/11/96 means December 11, 1996; in Great Britain, however, 12/11/96 is interpreted as the 12th of November, 1996.

To make your documents easier for foreign readers (and to avoid being embarrassingly late for some appointments!), Windows 95 supports different regional settings for various countries. These settings apply to all Windows applications, and they set the defaults for such things as number formats, currency symbols, and date and time formats.

 To view these settings, select Start | Settings | Control Panel, and then open the Regional Settings icon from the Control Panel folder. Windows 95 displays the Regional Settings Properties dialog box, shown in Figure 7.28. Use the drop-down list to select the country whose settings you want to work with, and click OK. Windows 95 then prompts you to restart the computer.

FIGURE 7.28.

Use this dialog box to set the default values for various regional settings used by your Windows applications.

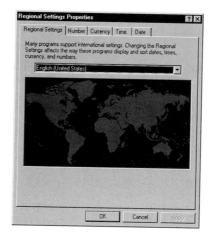

7

If you need to change only a few settings, use the following tabs:

Number: The controls on this tab determine the default format for numeric values, including the number of decimal places, the negative number format, and the measurement system (Metric or U.S.).

Currency: The controls on this tab determine the default format for currency values, including the currency symbol and its position.

Time: The controls on this tab determine the default format for time values, including the time style and the time separator.

Date: The controls on this tab determine the default format for date values, including the short date style and separator, and the long date style.

When you've made your selections, click OK.

Working with the Accessibility Options

Although the rest of the world has, over the past few years, striven to increase access for the disabled (in the form of Braille elevator buttons, wheelchair ramps, and handicapped parking spaces, to name a few changes), the computer industry has lagged sadly behind. Most disabled people either had to somehow adapt to the existing systems or use expensive add-ons and software to meet their particular needs.

Now, however, Windows 95 offers accessibility options that let disabled persons customize their systems themselves. You'll find these options in the Accessibility Properties dialog box, shown in Figure 7.29. To display this properties sheet, select Start | Settings | Control Panel and open the Accessibility Options icon. You can activate your selected options by clicking Apply or OK.

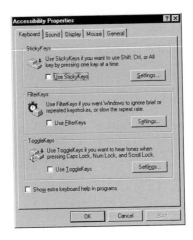

Keyboard Options

The Keyboard tab offers several options that make it easier for you to work with your keyboard:

StickyKeys: If you have trouble with certain key combinations (such as combining Ctrl and Alt with the function keys—a tough stretch even for people with full mobility in their hands), activate the Use StickyKeys check box to enable the StickyKeys feature. When StickyKeys is on, you can press a modifier key (such as Ctrl, Alt, Shift, or any combination of these), and the key remains active until you press another key. For example, to use the Ctrl-S key combination, you'd press Ctrl and then you'd press S. The Settings button lets you set various StickyKeys options.

FilterKeys: If you tend to hold keys down too long or press keys multiple times, the FilterKeys feature lets you filter out the extra characters that appear in these situations. Activate the Use FilterKeys check box to enable this feature. Windows 95 lets you know that the FilterKeys feature is active by displaying a stopwatch icon in the taskbar's information area. Again, click the Settings button to customize FilterKeys.

ToggleKeys: Enabling the ToggleKeys feature (by activating the Use ToggleKeys check box) tells Windows 95 to beep the speaker whenever you press Caps Lock, Num Lock, and Scroll Lock. Click the Settings button to enable the shortcut for ToggleKeys.

Sound Options

The Sound tab, shown in Figure 7.30, contains a couple of options to assist those who are hearing-impaired:

SoundSentry: The SoundSentry feature displays a visual indicator each time your system makes a sound. By default, SoundSentry flashes the caption bar of the active window (although you can change this default by clicking the Settings button). To enable SoundSentry, activate the `Use SoundSentry` check box.

ShowSounds: The ShowSounds feature displays a visual equivalent for sounds generated by your programs. To enable ShowSounds, activate the `Use ShowSounds` check box.

Figure 7.30.

Use the Sound tab to generate visual cues for audible Windows 95 events.

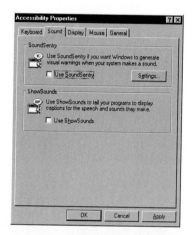

NOTE: A USEFUL TOOL FOR THOSE WHO ARE HEARING IMPAIRED

Another useful tool for those who are hearing impaired is the WinChat utility. This program lets users converse in real time, via typed messages, with other people on the network. WinChat is available only on the Windows 95 CD-ROM, in the `\Other\Chat\` folder.

Display Options

Windows 95 has no shortage of options for those who are visually impaired. Here's a recap of some of the customization options you've seen so far in this chapter that can improve the visibility of Windows 95 objects:

- In the Appearance tab of the Display Properties dialog box, you can select any of the "large" or "extra large" schemes. You can also increase the size of fonts and objects by using the other controls on this tab.

- In the Settings tab of the Display Properties dialog box, you can use the `Font size` feature to scale fonts to a larger size.

- In the Pointer tab of the Mouse Properties dialog box, you can select one of the schemes that produces larger pointer sizes.

- In the Motion tab of the Mouse Properties dialog box, you can activate the `Pointer trail` feature to display trails as you move the mouse.

The Display tab of the Accessibility Properties dialog box offers yet another feature for increasing the visibility of screen components: High Contrast. If you activate the `Use High Contrast` check box and apply this setting, Windows 95 changes the desktop's colors and fonts to make the screen easier to read, as shown in Figure 7.31.

FIGURE 7.31.

The High Contrast feature makes it easier to view the desktop's components.

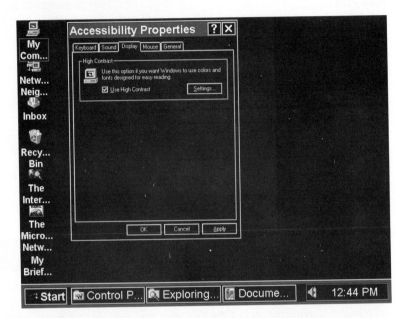

TIP: INCREASE THE ICON SIZE IN HIGH CONTRAST MODE

One of the problems with High Contrast mode is that the desktop icon text doesn't fit inside the standard icon size. To fix this problem, open the Display Properties dialog box, select the Appearance tab, select `Icon` in the `Item` drop-down list, crank up the `Size` spinner to 72, and click OK. Now right-click the desktop, select Arrange Icons from the context menu, and select by Name.

Mouse Options

The Mouse tab of the Accessibility Options dialog box, shown in Figure 7.32, controls the MouseKeys feature. If you activate the `Use MouseKeys` check box, Windows 95 lets you move the mouse pointer by using the arrow keys on the keyboard's numeric keypad. (Make sure that you have Num Lock turned on, however. Note too that MouseKeys doesn't work with the separate arrow-key keypads found on most modern keyboards.) Click the Settings button to customize MouseKeys options such as the speed of the pointer.

FIGURE 7.32.

Use the Mouse tab to activate the MouseKeys feature.

Besides the basic arrow movements, you can also use the numeric keypad keys outlined in Table 7.3.

Table 7.3. Numeric keypad keys to use with the MouseKeys feature.

Key	Equivalent Mouse Action
5	Click
+	Double-click
/	Select the left mouse button
*	Select both mouse buttons
–	Select the right mouse button
Insert	Lock the selected button
Delete	Release the selected button

Here's how you use these keys:

■ To click an object, use the arrow keys to move the pointer over the object, press / to select the left mouse button (if it isn't selected already), and press 5 to click.

> **TIP: DETERMINING THE SELECTED MOUSE BUTTON**
>
> How do you know which mouse button is currently selected? When you activate Mouse-Keys, Windows 95 adds a mouse icon to the information area. It indicates the currently selected button by shading the equivalent button on the mouse icon.

- To double-click an object, use the arrow keys to move the pointer over the object, press / to select the left mouse button, and press + to double-click.
- To right-click an object, use the arrow keys to move the pointer over the object, press − to select the right mouse button, and press 5.
- To drag-and-drop an object, use the arrow keys to move the pointer over the object, press / to select the left mouse button, press Insert to lock the button, use the arrow keys to move the object to its destination, and press Delete to release the button and drop the object.
- To right-drag-and-drop an object, use the arrow keys to move the pointer over the object; press − to select the right mouse button; press Insert to lock the button; use the arrow keys to move the object to its destination; and then press Delete to release the button, drop the object, and display the context menu.

General Options

The General tab of the Accessibility Properties dialog box, shown in Figure 7.33, contains the following options that apply to all the accessibility features:

Turn off accessibility features after idle for: If you want to leave the accessibility options turned on all the time, deactivate this check box. Otherwise, activate the check box to put a time limit on the accessibility options. Also, enter the number of minutes after which all the options are turned off.

Notification: Activate the Give warning message when turning a feature on check box to tell Windows 95 to display a message whenever a feature is activated. Activate the Make a sound when turning a feature on or off check box to tell Windows 95 to beep the speaker each time a feature is turned on or off.

SerialKey devices: A SerialKey device is an alternative input device (also known as an augmentative communications device) attached to the system's serial port. These devices let the user send equivalent mouse or keyboard commands via the serial port. To enable support for SerialKey devices, activate the Support SerialKey devices check box. Click the Settings button to specify a serial port and baud rate.

7

CUSTOMIZING
WINDOWS 95

FIGURE 7.33.

Use the General tab to set various options that apply to all the accessibility features.

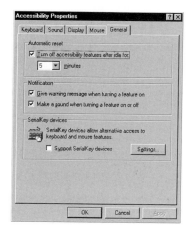

Working with User Profiles

Do you share your computer with other people either at work or at home? Then you're no doubt all too aware of one undeniable fact of human psychology: People are individuals with minds of their own! One person prefers Windows in a black-and-purple color scheme; another person just loves that annoying "Pinstripe" wallpaper; yet another person prefers to have a zillion shortcuts on the Windows 95 desktop; and, of course, *everybody* uses a different mix of applications. How can you possibly satisfy all these diverse tastes and prevent people from coming to blows?

It's a lot easier than you might think. Windows 95 lets you set up a different *user profile* for each person who uses the computer. Each profile includes all the customization options we've covered in this chapter, such as colors, patterns, wallpapers, shortcut icons, the screen saver, and the programs that appear on the Start menu.

This means that each person can customize Windows 95 to his heart's content without foisting his tastes on anyone else. To set up a user profile, follow these steps:

1. Select Start | Settings | Control Panel, and the open the Passwords icon. Windows 95 displays the Passwords Properties dialog box.
2. Select the User Profiles tab, as shown in Figure 7.34.
3. Activate the Users can customize their preferences and desktop settings option button. Windows 95 enables the check boxes in the User Profile Settings group.
4. If you want each user to be able to customize the desktop icons and Network Neighborhood, activate the Include desktop icons and Network Neighborhood contents in user settings check box.

FIGURE 7.34.

The User Profiles tab lets you activate multiple profiles on your computer.

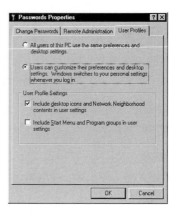

5. If you want each user to be able to customize the Start menu, activate the Include Start Menu and Program groups in user settings check box.

6. Click OK. Windows 95 asks whether you want to restart your computer.

7. Click Yes.

When Windows 95 reloads (and each subsequent time you restart Windows 95), you'll see the Welcome to Windows dialog box. The idea here is that each person who uses the computer will have her own user name, which Windows will use to save her settings. So when you log on, you type your user name in the User name field, type an optional password in the Password field, and click OK.

If this is the first time you've entered your password (even if you leave it blank), the Set Windows Password dialog box appears. In the Confirm new password text box, reenter the password and click OK.

If this is the first time you've logged on, the Windows Networking dialog box appears to ask whether you want Windows 95 to save your settings. Click Yes. Windows 95 loads normally, and you can start customizing.

Note that, for each user, Windows 95 creates a new subfolder in the Profiles folder. For example, if you create a profile for a user named Biff, you'll end up with the following new folder (assuming that your main Windows 95 folder is C:\Windows):

```
C:\Windows\Profiles\Biff
```

This new folder contains several subfolders that you can use to store various shortcuts for the user. These subfolders include Desktop, Recent, SendTo, and Start Menu.

> ### TIP: FASTER LOGONS
>
> Don't forget that if someone else is logged on to Windows 95 and you prefer to use your settings, you don't have to restart Windows 95. Instead, select Start | Shut Down. In the Shut Down Windows dialog box that appears, activate the Close all programs and log on as a different user? option, and click Yes.

> ### NOTE: ACCESSING THE ORIGINAL DESKTOP
>
> The settings for each new user are based on the original desktop configuration that existed when you enabled user profiles. If you want to change this configuration, restart Windows and, when you get to the logon dialog box, click Cancel. This will force Windows 95 to load the original desktop.

7

CUSTOMIZING WINDOWS 95

Microsoft Plus! Customization Options

If you've installed the Microsoft Plus! add-on, you have a few more customization options at your disposal. The next two sections finish or look at customizing Windows 95 by taking you through these extra features.

Microsoft Plus

Microsoft Plus! Display Properties

Microsoft Plus! takes the liberty of adding a fifth tab—called Plus!—to the Display Properties dialog box, shown in Figure 7.35. Here's a rundown of the extra goodies you get on this tab:

Microsoft Plus

Desktop icons: This group lets you modify the icon for the three basic desktop folders: My Computer, Network Neighborhood, and Recycle Bin (both the full and the empty icons). Highlight the icon you want to change, click the Change Icon button, choose the new icon from the Change Icon dialog box, and click OK. To change an icon back to its original, highlight it and click the Default Icon button.

Use large icons: Activating this check box increases the size of the desktop icons (and any other folder) from the default value of 32 pixels on each side, to 48 pixels.

Show window contents while dragging: This check box toggles *full-window drag* on and off. When it's deactivated, Windows 95 shows only the outline of any window you drag with the mouse (by dragging the title bar); if you activate full-window drag, however, Windows 95 displays the window's contents while you're dragging. You need a fast video card to make the full-window drag feature worthwhile.

Smooth edges of screen fonts: If you activate this check box, Windows 95 smoothes the jagged edges of large fonts, which makes them more readable. You need to have your display set up with a color depth of at least high color (16 bits) to use this feature.

Show icons using all possible colors: When activated, this check box tells Windows 95 to use all the available colors to display the desktop icons. If you have a slower computer or video card and you find that Windows 95 takes a long time to refresh your desktop, deactivate this option.

Stretch desktop wallpaper to fit the screen: If the bitmap file you're using for wallpaper isn't as large as the desktop, you might not see some or all of the bitmap while you have windows open. You could tile the bitmap, but the result is usually unattractive for large images. If you activate this check box, however, Windows 95 expands the image so that it takes up the entire desktop. Again, this option is a real performance hog on slower machines.

Figure 7.35.

Microsoft Plus! adds an extra tab to the Display Properties dialog box.

Selecting a Desktop Theme

You saw earlier how Windows 95 lets you select desktop schemes that govern the look of various objects, including menu bars, window borders and title bars, icons, and more. Microsoft Plus! takes this idea a step further with desktop *themes*. A theme is also a collection of object properties, but it covers more ground than a simple scheme. Each theme specifies various settings for not only windows and message boxes, but also a screen saver, a wallpaper, mouse pointers, sounds, desktop icons, and more.

To try out some of these Microsoft Plus! desktop themes, select Start | Settings | Control Panel, and then open the Desktop Themes icon in the Control Panel folder. In the Desktop Themes dialog box that appears, use the Theme drop-down list to choose the theme you want to use and click OK. Figure 7.36 shows the Desktop Themes dialog box with the Dangerous Creatures theme selected.

FIGURE 7.36.

Use the Desktop Themes dialog box to choose one of the wild desktop themes that come with Microsoft Plus!.

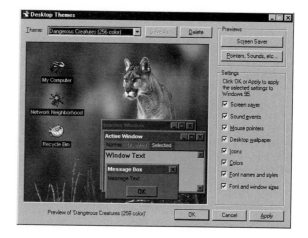

The window that takes up the bulk of the dialog box shows you a preview of the theme. You see not only how the theme will affect the various window objects, but also the wallpaper and desktop icons the theme uses. To preview the screen saver associated with the theme, click the Screen Saver button. To preview the mouse pointers and sounds associated with the theme, click the Pointers, Sounds, etc button. Note too that you can control which objects are affected by the theme. The Settings group contains check boxes for each object contained in the theme. To remove an object, simply deactivate its check box.

NOTE: WATCH YOUR COLOR DEPTH

Many of the desktop themes require a color depth of 16 bits (high color) or more. Each theme shows the color requirements beside its name (for example, 256 color, high color) in the Theme drop-down list.

Microsoft's Power Toys

A few Microsoft programmers have put together some small programs that extend the functionality of Windows 95. These utilities are called *Power Toys*, and some of them are quite handy. On the customization front, you might want to check out two of them:

QuickRes: This program lets you change both display resolution *and* color depth on-the-fly.

TweakUI: This program lets you modify many aspects of the Windows 95 interface, including mouse sensitivity, window animation, shortcut appearance, and more.

You'll find all the Power Toys on the following Web page:

`http://www.microsoft.com/windows95/info/powertoys.htm`

Summary

This chapter showed you how to remake Windows 95 in your own image. I showed you how to customize the taskbar and Start menu, how to modify the desktop's appearance, how to work with Windows 95's regional settings, and lots more.

Here's a list of chapters where you'll find related information:

- I showed you how to customize your Windows 95 startup in Chapter 4, "Start It Your Way: Understanding Windows 95 Startup."
- I cover adding and changing device drivers in Chapter 10, "How Windows 95 Handles Hardware."
- The Registry gives you tremendous power to customize Windows 95. I take you through lots of examples in Chapter 12, "Hacking the Registry."
- To learn how to customize the `Startup` folder, see Chapter 13, "Working with Files and Folders."
- Windows 95 video basics are covered in Chapter 23, "Windows 95 Video: The Big Picture."
- I show you how to associate sounds with various Windows 95 events in Chapter 24, "Getting the Most Out of Windows 95 Sound."
- The System Policy Editor lets system administrators set up access restrictions to things like the Control Panel icons and programs. I cover this handy tool in Chapter 31, "Windows 95 Networking."

Personalizing the Mouse, Keyboard, and Joystick

CHAPTER 8

> *The mark of our time is its revulsion against imposed patterns.*
>
> —*Marshall McLuhan*

Windows 95's new look is certainly slick, and it's infinitely more attractive than the ugly mug we had to look at every day with Windows 3.x. But Windows 95 would be just another pretty interface if it didn't afford us some flexibility in terms of how we interact with that interface. In other words, under different circumstances we demand different input devices—whether a mouse, keyboard, or joystick—and we demand a certain level of customization so that these input devices operate the way we want them to. To that end, this chapter looks at the various customization options Windows 95 makes available to mouse, keyboard, and joystick users.

Customizing the Mouse

Much of Windows 95 was made with the mouse in mind, so it's important that you're comfortable handling the little rodent. To help out, Windows 95 offers the Mouse Properties dialog box, shown in Figure 8.1. To display this dialog box, select Start | Settings | Control Panel, and then select the Mouse icon from the `Control Panel` folder. As usual, you can put your new settings into effect at any time by clicking the Apply button. When you're done, click OK to vacate the dialog box.

FIGURE 8.1.

Use the Mouse Properties dialog box to customize your mouse.

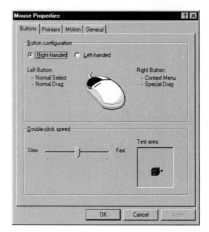

Setting Up the Mouse for Southpaws

In Windows 95, you click the left mouse button to select an object, and you drag with the left mouse button held down to copy or move an object. Similarly, you click the right mouse button to display the context menu for the current object, and you drag with the right mouse button held down to display the "special drag" context menu when you drop the object.

If you're a left-hander and this "rightist" orientation bothers you, it's easy enough to reverse things: Just activate the Left-handed option in the Buttons tab of the Mouse Properties dialog box. After you've applied this new setting, here's how it affects your mouse movements:

- ■ You now click and double-click with the right mouse button.
- ■ To drag something, you now press and hold down the right button.
- ■ To display a context menu, you now left-click an object.
- ■ To perform the "special drag" in Explorer, you now hold down the left mouse button.

Setting the Double-Click Speed

One of the things a mouse-aware program must do is distinguish between two consecutive single-clicks and a double-click. For example, if you click once, wait five seconds, and then click again, that would qualify as two single-clicks in most people's books. But what if there's only a second between clicks? Or half a second? This threshold is called the *double-click speed:* Anything faster is handled as a double-click; anything slower is handled as two single clicks.

You can adjust this threshold by using the Double-click speed slider in the Buttons tab of the Mouse Properties dialog box. You have two options:

- ■ If you find that Windows 95 doesn't always recognize your double-clicks, set up a slower double-click speed by moving the slider bar to the left.
- ■ If you find that Windows 95 is sometimes interpreting two consecutive single clicks as a double-click, set up a faster double-click speed by moving the slider bar to the right.

To test the new speed, double-click the Test area. If Windows 95 recognizes your double-click, a Jack-in-the-box pops up.

Trying Different Pointers on for Size

As you trudge through Windows 95, you'll notice that the mouse pointer busies itself by changing into different icons depending on what you're doing. There's the standard arrow for selecting everything from check boxes to files and folders, there's the two-headed arrow for sizing window borders, and, of course, there's the dreaded hourglass icon that appears whenever a program or Windows 95 is too busy to bother with you right now. (However, as you'll see in Chapter 9, "Windows 95 Performance Tuning and Optimization," the preemptive multitasking used with 32-bit applications means that seeing an hourglass icon in one program usually doesn't prevent you from working in a different program.)

Surprisingly, the pointers used by Windows 95 in these and other situations aren't set in stone. You can specify pointers of different shapes and sizes. Also, Microsoft Plus! comes with a few theme-related pointers, and Windows 95 even supports animated pointers (such as an hourglass with falling sand). To see how you can specify different pointers, in the Mouse Properties dialog box, select the Pointers tab, shown in Figure 8.2.

8

THE MOUSE, KEYBOARD, AND JOYSTICK

FIGURE 8.2.

Use the Pointers tab to select a different set of mouse pointers.

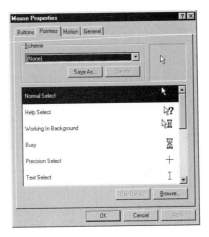

The easiest way to try out different pointers is to choose one of the pointer schemes that come with Windows 95. To select a scheme, use the Scheme drop-down list, and then take a look at the sample pointers in the box below the list to see what they look like.

TIP: TRY THE LARGER POINTERS FOR EASIER VISIBILITY

The Scheme list has two items—Windows standard (large) and Windows Standard (extra large)—that produce much bigger pointers. These mutant pointers are handy if you're having trouble picking up the regular pointers in a sea of windows (especially on some cramped notebook screens).

If you feel like creating a scheme of your own, here are the steps to follow:

1. Highlight the type of pointer you want to change.
2. Click the Browse button. Windows 95 displays the Browse dialog box.
3. Choose the pointer you want to use and click Open.
4. Repeat steps 1 through 3 to customize any other pointers.
5. To save your scheme, click the Save As button, enter a name in the Save Scheme dialog box, and click OK.

NOTE: RESETTING THE POINTERS

If you'd prefer to return your mouse pointers to their natural state, click the Use Default button.

Controlling the Tracking Speed

When you move the mouse, Windows 95 translates this movement and tracks the mouse pointer on-screen accordingly. How quickly the mouse moves across the screen is called the *tracking speed.* If this speed is out of whack (for example, if you move the mouse furiously but the pointer just creeps along, or, conversely, if the slightest hand tremor causes the pointer to go racing across the screen), your mouse is likely to end up in the nearest garbage can.

The good news is that adjusting the tracking speed is a snap. In the Mouse Properties dialog box, select the Motion tab, shown in Figure 8.3. Then take a look at the Pointer speed slider. You can do two things with this control:

- If the mouse pointer is flying around the screen, slow it down by dragging the slider bar to the left.
- If the pointer is too slow, drag the slider bar to the right.

If you'd like to test the new setting, click the Apply button and then try moving the mouse around.

FIGURE 8.3.

The Motion tab controls the mouse tracking speed and mouse trails (see the next section).

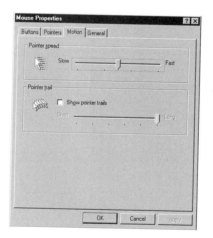

Activating Pointer Trails

Many people with notebook computers or eyesight that isn't quite what it used to be complained they had trouble finding the little mouse pointer on their screen. So Microsoft, ever sensitive, included a Pointer trail feature in Windows 95. (Not all video displays support this feature, however.) When you activate the Show pointer trails check box and move the mouse, you'll see a trail of pointers following behind the main pointer. You can also use the slider bar to make the trail longer or shorter.

> **NOTE: CHANGING THE MOUSE DRIVER**
>
> The General tab on the Mouse Properties dialog box lets you change your mouse driver. I cover the general steps for changing hardware drivers in Chapter 10, "How Windows 95 Handles Hardware."

IntelliPoint Options

When Microsoft introduced version 2.0 of its mouse back in 1993, it also updated the mouse utilities with a few extra options. The latest iteration of this software is IntelliPoint 1.1, and it comes with a fistful of controls for tailoring your mouse to suit your style. This section reviews the new tidbits that come with IntelliPoint 1.1.

When you launch the Control Panel's Mouse icon (or if you select Start | Programs | Microsoft Input Devices | IntelliPoint Tools and Controls), you'll see the dialog box shown in Figure 8.4. This dialog box incorporates all the options found in the standard Mouse properties sheet, and adds quite a few more. The Pointers and General tabs are identical, but the rest have new tools that are explained in the next few sections.

FIGURE 8.4.

The revised Mouse Properties dialog box that comes with IntelliPoint 1.1.

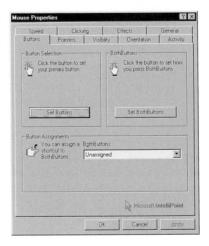

The Buttons Tab

The new Buttons tab controls the mouse button orientation using the following options:

> **Button Selection:** Use this group to select your primary mouse button (that is, the "click" button). To do so, click Set Buttons using the mouse button that you want to use as your primary button.

BothButtons: IntelliPoint supports a "third" mouse button that is really both buttons pressed simultaneously. To train IntelliPoint to recognize when you press both buttons (some people press one button slightly before the other), point at Set BothButtons and then click both mouse buttons.

Button Assignments: If you want to use the BothButtons feature, use this drop-down list to choose the action that will occur when you press both mouse buttons.

The Visibility Tab

The Visibility tab, shown in Figure 8.5, contains various options that control the visibility of the mouse pointer in different circumstances:

Sonar: This is a handy option if you find yourself losing the mouse pointer in a sea of windows, text, and toolbars. When you activate this check box, pressing Ctrl displays a series of concentric circles that zero in on the mouse pointer.

Trails: This is the same mouse trails option that I discussed earlier.

Vanish: Activate this check box to make the mouse pointer disappear whenever you begin typing. The pointer will reappear as soon as you move the mouse.

FIGURE 8.5.

The Visibility tab controls the appearance of the pointer.

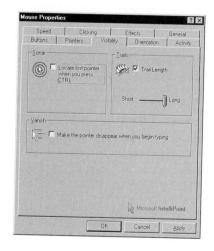

The Orientation Tab

If you have a unique way of holding the mouse, or if the ergonomics of your workspace dictate that you can't use the standard mouse movements, the Orientation tab, shown in Figure 8.6, may be able to help.

The idea here is that you tell IntelliPoint which mouse direction is "up" for you. Normally, "up" means moving the mouse forward (that is, toward the cable). To define a different direction, click Set Orientation and then carefully move the mouse in the new direction. (To return the mouse to its standard behavior, click Use Defaults.)

FIGURE 8.6.

Use the Orientation tab to tell Windows 95 which way is "up" for you.

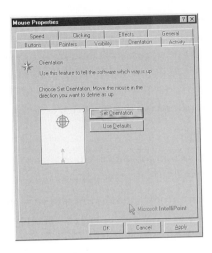

The Activity Tab

The Activity tab, shown in Figure 8.7, contains three options related to mouse movements:

SnapTo: This is a handy feature that can make it easier to navigate dialog boxes. Most dialog boxes have a default command button (usually the OK button, but not always) that you can select by pressing Enter. When you activate the SnapTo check box, Windows 95 automatically places the mouse pointer over the default button. So, to select this button, you just have to click.

Focus: When you enable this check box, you can activate any open window by hovering the mouse pointer over the window's title bar.

PointerWrap: This is one of my favorite features of the new mouse. If you activate this button and then, say, move the mouse pointer off the left edge of the screen, it reappears on the right side. It's not for everyone, and it does take some getting used to, but it can make mousing around remarkably easier.

The Speed Tab

Earlier you saw how the standard mouse's Pointer speed slider controlled the rate at which the mouse tracks across the screen. The new Speed tab is similar (see Figure 8.8), but it comes with a few more advanced options:

Pointer Speed: This is basically the same as the standard Pointer speed slider, except that you have two sliders: one to control the vertical speed, and one to control the horizontal speed.

Acceleration: If you activate this check box, Windows 95 changes the speed of the pointer in relation to the speed at which you move the mouse. In other words, the faster you move the mouse, the faster the pointer tracks.

SmartSpeed: Most mouse movements involve tracking across the screen to a specific element, such as a title bar, scroll bar, window border, dialog box button, toolbar icon, and so on. When you activate this check box, Windows 95 slows down the mouse pointer when it tracks over one of these elements.

FIGURE 8.7.

The Activity tab controls options related to mouse movements.

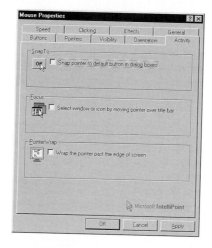

FIGURE 8.8.

The Speed tab governs several factors related to pointer speed.

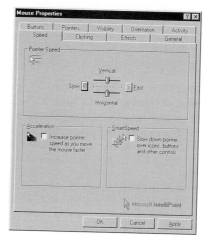

The Clicking Tab

As you might expect, mouse clicks are the theme of the Clicking tab, shown in Figure 8.9:

Double-Click Speed: This group lets you set your optimal double-click speed. To do so, first double-click the Set Double-Click button, and then double-click the clapper to see the effect of the new setting. (If the clapper opens, Windows 95 recognized your double-click.)

ClickSaver: If you activate this option, you can use a single click in place of a double-click. For example, you can launch a desktop icon by clicking it. (To select something, hold down Shift and click the item.)

CAUTION: CLICKSAVER CAN BE DANGEROUS

The ClickSaver feature sounds like a good idea, and it certainly saves wear and tear on your clicking finger. However, you need to be cautious until you get used to it. I once had this feature activated and then clicked a .REG file that included all the Registry information from another computer (see Chapter 11, "Introducing the Windows 95 Registry," for details). This caused the .REG file to run, which meant that it imported all the other computer's Registry settings into my computer's Registry, a nightmare from which it took me days to recover.

FIGURE 8.9.

The Clicking tab controls various mouse-clicking options.

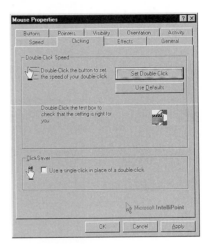

The Effects Tab

The options in the Effects tab, shown in Figure 8.10, let you assign animation effects to clicks, double-clicks, and both-button clicks. The easiest way to use this tab is to select one of the predefined animation schemes from the Schemes drop-down list. To create a custom scheme, click the action you want to work with, and then click Browse Animation to choose an effect. When you're done, click Save Scheme to add your selections to the Schemes list.

FIGURE 8.10.

Use the Effects tab to customize your pointer with animation effects.

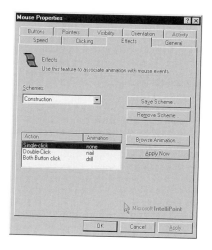

Customizing the Keyboard

Although a mouse makes many everyday Windows 95 tasks easier, we're still a long way from having to ditch our trusty keyboards. In fact, after you get used to a few Windows 95 keyboard shortcuts, you'll find yourself reaching for the mouse less and less. This section shows you a few techniques for customizing your keyboard.

Setting the Delay and Repeat Rate

When you press and hold down a key on the keyboard, you notice two things: First, when you press the key, there is a slight *delay* before the second letter appears; second, the subsequent characters appear at a constant rate (called the *repeat rate*). Beginning keyboardists are usually better off with a longer delay and a slower repeat rate. More experienced typists, on the other hand, would probably prefer a short delay combined with a fast repeat rate.

Happily, Windows 95 lets you change both of these values. To see how, select Start | Settings | Control Panel, and then open the Control Panel's Keyboard icon. Windows 95 displays the Keyboard Properties dialog box, shown in Figure 8.11.

You control the delay by using the `Repeat delay` slider. Move the slider bar (by dragging it with the mouse or by using the left- and right-arrow keys) to the left for a longer delay or to the right for a shorter delay.

As you've no doubt guessed by now, the `Repeat rate` slider controls the repeat rate. Move the slider bar to the left for a slower rate or to the right for a faster one.

To try out the new settings, head for the `Click here and hold down a key to test repeat rate` text box. Press and hold down any key, and check out the delay and the repeat rate.

FIGURE 8.11.

Use the Keyboard
Properties dialog box to
adjust your keyboard's
delay and repeat rate.

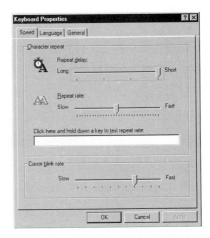

Typing with the United States-International Keyboard Layout

The Windows 95 character set consists of many more characters than those you can peck out on the keyboard. Symbols such as £ and ¢, and foreign letters such as ä and ç are all part of the Windows ANSI character set. If you need to access these characters only occasionally, it's best to use the Character Map accessory (Start | Programs | Accessories | Character Map). For those who use these symbols regularly, however, Windows 95 provides a way to type them directly on the keyboard.

The trick is that Windows 95 supports various keyboard layouts. In particular, it supports a layout called United States-International that augments the normal keys with many new symbols. To switch to this layout, follow these steps:

1. In the Keyboard Properties dialog box, select the Language tab.
2. In the Language list, highlight the English (United States) item.
3. Click the Properties button. Windows 95 displays the Language Properties dialog box, shown in Figure 8.12.

FIGURE 8.12.

Use the Language
Properties dialog box to
choose the United
States-International
keyboard layout.

4. In the Keyboard layout drop-down list, select United States-International.
5. Click OK to return to the Keyboard Properties dialog box.
6. Click OK or Apply.

7. Follow the prompts on-screen when Windows 95 asks you for your source CD-ROM or disks.

Table 8.1 outlines the changes this new layout makes to your keyboard. The Ctrl-Alt column means that you hold down Ctrl and Alt and press the key; the Ctrl-Alt-Shift column means that you hold down Ctrl, Alt, and Shift and press the key.

Table 8.1. Keyboard changes with the United States-International layout.

Key	Ctrl-Alt	Ctrl-Alt-Shift	Key	Ctrl-Alt	Ctrl-Alt-Shift
1	¡	¹	I	í	Í
2	²	N/A	O	ó	Ó
3	³	N/A	P	ö	Ö
4	¤	£	[	«	N/A
6	¼	N/A	]	»	N/A
7	½	N/A	\	¬	¦
8	¾	N/A	A	á	Á
9	`	N/A	S	ß	§
0	´	N/A	D	ð	Đ
-	¥	N/A	L	ø	Ø
=	×	÷	;	¶	°
Q	ä	Ä	Z	æ	Æ
W	å	Å	C	©	¢
E	é	É	N	ñ	Ñ
R	®	N/A	M	µ	N/A
T	þ	Þ	<	ç	Ç
Y	ü	Ü	?	¿	N/A
U	ú	Ú			

8
THE MOUSE,
KEYBOARD, AND
JOYSTICK

TIP: RIGHT ALT EQUALS CTRL-ALT

Instead of holding down both Ctrl and Alt, you can also use just the *right* Alt key by itself.

Besides the layout changes shown in Table 8.1, Windows 95 also sets up several so-called *dead keys*. These are keys that do nothing until you press another key. When you do, Windows 95 inserts the second key with an accent. Table 8.2 lists the dead keys. Note that, in each case, you press and release the dead key (such as ~) and then press and release the other key (such as N). If you want to type a particular dead key itself, press the key and then press the Spacebar.

Table 8.2. Dead keys used with the United States-International layout.

Dead Key	Accent Created	Example
~ (tilde)	Tilde	Press ~ and then N to get ñ.
` (back quote)	Grave accent	Press ` and then A to get à.
^ (caret)	Circumflex	Press ^ and then E to get ê.
" (quotation mark)	Diaeresis	Press " and then I to get ï.
' (apostrophe)	Acute accent	Press ' and then E to get é.

Working with Keyboard Languages

If you need to write documents in different languages, or even if you need to use multiple languages in a single document, Windows 95 can make your life a lot easier. That's because no matter what kind of keyboard you have, Windows 95 supports keyboard layouts for various languages.

To add another keyboard language to Windows 95, follow these steps:

1. Display the Language tab in the Keyboard Properties dialog box.
2. Click the Add button. The Add Language dialog box, shown in Figure 8.13, is displayed.

Figure 8.13.

Use the Add Language dialog box to select the keyboard language you want to add.

3. Use the Language drop-down list to select the language you want to work with.
4. Click OK to return to the Keyboard Properties dialog box.
5. Click OK or Apply.
6. Follow the prompts on-screen when Windows 95 asks you for your source CD-ROM or disks.

After you add a second keyboard language, Windows 95 displays a language indicator in the taskbar's information area. Clicking this indicator displays a pop-up list of the available languages, as shown in Figure 8.14. Click the language you want to use. (You can also cycle between languages by pressing Left Alt-Shift.)

FIGURE 8.14.

Use the taskbar's language indicator to choose the language in which you want to type.

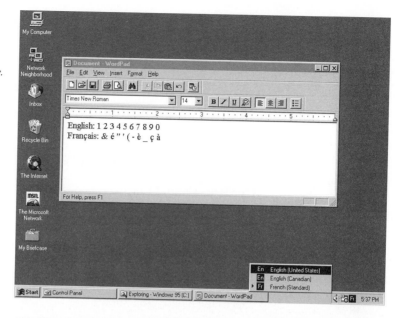

NOTE: MULTILANGUAGE SUPPORT

If you installed the Multilanguage Support component when you installed Windows 95 (or by using the Add/Remove Programs Wizard), you can use WordPad to write documents in the Baltic, Cyrillic (Bulgarian, Belarusian, and Russian), Greek, Turkish, and Central European (Czech, Hungarian, Polish, and Slovenian) languages. You'll also need to add the appropriate keyboard language. Use the taskbar to switch to the keyboard language you want to use; then open WordPad's Font dialog box and choose the language (or language group) from the Script drop-down list.

NOTE: CHANGING THE KEYBOARD DRIVER

The General tab on the Keyboard Properties dialog box lets you change your keyboard driver. I provide the general steps for changing hardware drivers in Chapter 10.

Using the Microsoft Natural Keyboard

If you have the Microsoft Natural Keyboard (or a compatible keyboard), you have access to a wealth of Windows 95 shortcuts. In particular, the ⌨ key saves lots of wear and tear on your wrists and fingers. Used by itself, this key opens the Start menu, which is a lot easier than pressing the tough-to-reach Ctrl-Esc key combination. But you also can use it in various key combinations to gain quick access to many Windows 95 features. Table 8.3 summarizes these key combinations.

Table 8.3. The Microsoft Natural Keyboard—the ⊞ key.

Key	Action
⊞	Opens the Start menu.
⊞-A	Opens the Accessibility Options (if installed).
⊞-C	Opens the Control Panel.
⊞-E	Opens the Explorer.
⊞-F	Finds a file or folder.
Ctrl-⊞-F	Finds a computer.
⊞-I	Opens the mouse properties.
⊞-K	Opens the keyboard properties.
⊞-L	Logs on and off Windows.
⊞-M	Minimizes all.
Shift-⊞-M	Undoes minimize all.
⊞-P	Opens the Print Manager.
⊞-R	Displays the Run dialog box.
⊞-S	Enables or disables the Caps Lock key.
⊞-V	Views the Clipboard.
⊞-F1	Displays Windows Help.
⊞-Break	Displays the system properties.
⊞-Spacebar	Displays this list of shortcuts.
⊞-Tab	Activates open programs in order.

For good measure, the Microsoft Natural Keyboard also includes an Application key. It has a picture of a little pulled-down menu. Pressing this key activates the context menu for the current object.

IntelliType Options

The Microsoft Natural Keyboard also comes with version 1.1 of Microsoft's IntelliType software. Installing IntelliType adds an extra Options tab to the Keyboard Properties dialog box, as shown in Figure 8.15. (You also get the Pointer Activity tab, which contains the Sonar, PointerWrap, SnapTo, and Vanish options discussed earlier.) Here's a review of the new options found on this tab:

Windows Logon/Logoff: When activated, this options lets you display the Windows Logon dialog box by pressing both ⊞ keys on your keyboard. Note, however, that this option is available only in Windows NT and Windows for Workgroups.

Key Locks: These check boxes specify the state of the Num Lock, Caps Lock, and Scroll Lock keys at system startup. Activating a check box tells Windows 95 to activate the corresponding key at boot time.

Sounds: This drop-down list lets you assign sounds to keyboard events. A number of sound schemes are available.

Disable CAPS LOCK while in Windows: If you activate this check box, Windows 95 ignores the Caps Lock key while you're working in Windows. This is an excellent idea, because it prevents accidental activation of Caps Lock and long runs of all-uppercase letters. If you find that you *do* need Caps Lock turned on, press the key three times in succession.

FIGURE 8.15.

The IntelliType keyboard software adds an extra Options tab to the Keyboard Properties dialog box.

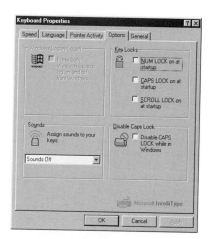

8

THE MOUSE, KEYBOARD, AND JOYSTICK

Calibrating Your Joystick

Nothing takes the joy out of playing certain kinds of games more than a joystick that's out of whack. If you use a joystick for your Windows 95–based games, you'll want to calibrate it so that Windows 95 understands its features (range of motion, throttle, rudder, and so on). Here are the steps to follow to calibrate your joystick:

1. Select Start | Settings | Control Panel and select the Joystick icon. Windows 95 displays the Joystick Properties dialog box, shown in Figure 8.16.

FIGURE 8.16.

Use the Joystick Properties dialog box to customize your joystick.

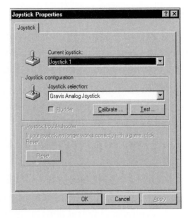

2. If you have multiple joysticks, select the one you want to calibrate from the Current joystick drop-down list.
3. Highlight the type of joystick you have in the Joystick selection drop-down list.

NOTE: CUSTOM JOYSTICK

If your joystick doesn't show up on the Joystick selection list, select the Custom item to display the Custom Joystick dialog box. Enter the number of axes, the number of buttons, special features (flight yoke, game pod, or race car controller), and whether or not the stick has a point of view (POV) hat. Click OK to return to the Joystick Properties dialog box.

---

4. If your joystick has a rudder, activate the Rudder check box.
5. Click the Calibrate button. The Calibration dialog box for the selected joystick appears.
6. You'll now work through a series of dialog boxes that set various properties of the joystick (such as its center position, as shown in Figure 8.17, and its range of motion). In each, perform the requested action, press a joystick button, and click Next >.

FIGURE 8.17.

To calibrate your joystick, you'll run through a series of dialog boxes like this one.

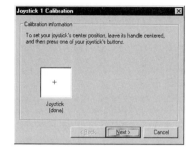

7. When the calibration is complete, click Finish to return to the Joystick Properties dialog box.

8. To test your calibration, click the Test button to display the Test dialog box, shown in Figure 8.18.

FIGURE 8.18.

Use this dialog box to test your calibration.

9. Move the joystick and press its buttons to test the calibration; then click OK.

Summary

This chapter took you through various options for customizing your input devices in Windows 95. For the mouse, you learned how to set options such as the double-click speed, pointers, and tracking speed. You also learned about the new options found in IntelliPoint 1.1. For the keyboard, I showed you how to set the delay and repeat rate, how to use the United States-International keyboard layout and keyboard languages, and how to use the Microsoft Natural Keyboard. You also learned how to calibrate a joystick in Windows 95.

Here's a list of chapters where you'll find related information:

■ Windows 95's Accessibility Options contains a number of mouse- and keyboard-related tools. I told you about them in Chapter 7, "Customizing Windows 95."

■ To learn how to install device drivers, see Chapter 10, "How Windows 95 Handles Hardware."

Windows 95 Performance Tuning and Optimization

CHAPTER 9

Speed, it seems to me, provides the one genuinely modern pleasure.

—*Aldous Huxley*

In Chapter 1, "Understanding the Windows 95 Installation," I spent some time musing about why our workaday computer chores seem to take just as long as they ever did, despite the fact that our hardware is, generally speaking, bigger, better, and faster than ever. The answer to this apparent riddle is related to Parkinson's Law of Data: Data expands to fill the space available for storage. On a more general level, Parkinson's Law could be restated as follows: The increase in software system requirements is directly proportional to the increase in hardware system capabilities. A slick new chip is released that promises a 30 percent speed boost; software designers, seeing the new chip gain wide acceptance, add extra features to their already bloated code to take advantage of the higher performance level; then another new chip is released, followed by another software upgrade—and the cycle continues *ad nauseum* as these twin engines of computer progress lurch codependently into the future.

So how do you break out of the performance deadlock created by the immovable object of software code bloat meeting the irresistible force of hardware advancement? By optimizing your system to minimize the effects of overgrown applications and to maximize the native capabilities of your hardware. Learning how to optimize memory, hard disks, and devices is the key to unleashing your system's performance potential, and that's exactly what I'll show you how to do in this chapter.

Windows 95 and Memory: A Primer

Entire books can be (and, indeed, have been) written about the relationship between Windows and memory. What it all boils down to, though, is quite simple: The more memory you have, the happier Windows (and most of your programs) will be. However, not everyone can afford to throw 64 megabytes of memory at their problems. We have to make do with less, and that, in essence, is what this chapter is all about. Later, I'll show you some ways to fight back if a lack of memory is slowing Windows 95 to a crawl.

Your computer's *random access memory* (RAM) is just an innocuous collection of chips on the system's main circuit board. But although these chips might not look like much, they perform some pretty important tasks.

Their basic purpose in life is to be used as a work area for your programs and your data. These things normally slumber peacefully on your hard disk, but when you need them, Windows 95 rouses everyone from their spacious beds and herds the program code and data into the cramped confines of memory. From there, different bits of code and data are swapped in and out of memory, as needed. Why not just work with everything from the hard disk itself? One word: *speed.* Even the highest of high-tech hard drives is a tortoise compared to the blazing memory chips.

Memory in the Pre-Windows 95 World

This all sounds well and good, but a fundamental problem underlies everything. Most hard disks can store dozens or even hundreds of megabytes of data, but the memory capacity of a typical computer is limited to a measly few megabytes or so.

Picture it this way: Think of your computer as, say, a carpenter's workshop divided into two areas: a storage space for your tools and materials (the hard disk) and a work area where you actually use these things (memory). The problem is that your computer's "work space" is much smaller than its "storage space." For a carpenter, a small work space limits the number of tools and the amount of wood that can be used at any one time. For a computer, it limits the number of programs and data files you can load.

Conventional Memory

In the DOS world, the basic restriction placed on your computer's work space is the so-called "640 KB barrier." This means that the maximum amount of memory DOS can use to run your programs and data files is 640 KB. This first 640 KB is called *conventional memory*.

Why 640 KB? Why not 650 KB or 6,400 KB? Well, 640 KB was the maximum amount of memory available to programs on the original IBM PC. To see how that number was arrived at, you need to look at two things: the physical characteristics of the IBM PC's microprocessor, and a decision made by its engineers.

First off, microprocessors work with memory chips via *address lines*, which are (more or less) physical connections between the processor and the individual memory locations (each of which stores a single byte of data). Each address line carries a single bit of a memory address, so the total amount of memory—the *address space*—any microprocessor can work with is limited by the number of address lines. If you had only a single address line, for example, you could address only two memory locations (addresses 1 and 0; see the following sidebar for details), two lines could address four locations, and so on.

> **NOTE: UNDERSTANDING ADDRESS-LINE STATES**
>
> Each address line can take on only one of two states: high current or low current (on or off). These two states are represented inside the processor by 1 and 0, respectively. Computers have to store all their data using this binary number system. In the simplest case (one address line), you have two memory locations. If you send a low current through the line, you get the byte stored at location 0. A high current refers to memory location 1. In a two-line situation (call them lines A and B), you have four possibilities: both lines low (memory location 00), line A low and line B high (01), line A high and line B low (10), and both lines high (11).

The IBM PC used Intel's 8088 microprocessor, which has 20 address lines. This might seem like a lot (it sure did back then), but it gives you an address space of only 1,048,576 bytes (2 to the power of 20), or a mere 1 MB. By contrast, the 80286 with its 24 address lines can access up to 16 MB, and the 80386 (and later) has an address space of 4 GB, thanks to its 32 address lines.

So if the 8088 could address 1 MB, why was DOS restricted to 640 KB? Well, the IBM PC engineers, in their not-so-infinite wisdom, decided to reserve the last 384 KB of the address space for hardware uses (video buffers, ROM BIOS, and so on). This is called the *upper memory area*. Subtracting 384 KB from 1 MB (1,024 KB) leaves 640 KB.

Clearly, with so much addressable memory available with the more advanced processors, especially the 80386 and higher, something had to be done about the 640 KB barrier. In fact, before Windows 95 came along, four solutions were offered: *expanded memory, extended memory, upper memory blocks,* and the *high memory area*.

Expanded Versus Extended Memory

Let's return for a moment to the idea of a computer as a workshop. As a carpenter, you can increase your work space in two ways: You can *expand* the total area by erecting a separate building, or you can *extend* the existing work space itself with an addition.

This is the principal difference between expanded memory and extended memory. Expanded memory usually comes in the form of a separate piece of equipment (called a *memory board*) you must install. You get extended memory, on the other hand, just by plugging memory chips directly into your computer's main circuit board (provided that you have an 80286 or better computer).

How does this extra memory help? Well, applications still had to stay within the 640 KB region, but small programs (called *memory managers*) shuffled bits of program code and data files between the conventional memory area and the expanded or extended memory.

For example, suppose that you're in your workshop and you need to use a lathe, but you haven't got the room. No problem. Your assistant (the memory manager) knows that the lathe is either outside in a separate building (expanded memory) or in an adjacent area (extended memory). He grabs something you don't need for now (a band saw, for instance), takes it to the expanded or extended memory area, exchanges it for the lathe, and brings the lathe to your workshop.

NOTE: HOW EXPANDED MEMORY WORKS

An expanded memory manager operates by establishing a 64 KB chunk of upper memory called a *page frame*. For programs that can use expanded memory, it swaps data from the expanded memory board into the page frame one 16 KB page at a time and then makes this data available to the program. This technique is called *bank switching*.

The Upper Memory Area

The upper memory area (the memory between the first 640 KB area and 1 MB) is never completely filled in. It always contains gaps not used by the BIOS or video buffers. These gaps are called *upper memory blocks* (UMBs). If you have an 80386 or higher computer, you can use a program called a *386 memory manager* to send TSRs and device drivers over the 640 KB barrier so that they reside not in conventional memory, but in the UMBs.

The High Memory Area

The high memory area (HMA) is a 64 KB segment of extended memory on 80286 or better computers (provided that they have more than 1 MB of total memory). Recent versions of DOS and Windows created more room in conventional memory by loading parts of the operating system into the HMA.

Another Problem: 16-Bit Memory

The 640 KB barrier and the 1 MB addressing limit were serious bumps on the road to modern, high-powered applications. However, programmers faced another, even greater, challenge in their day-to-day coding: 16-bit memory. The original 8086 processor (and its cousin the 8088, which was used in the original IBM PC) processed data in 16-bit chunks. Now, 16 bits can be arranged in 2^{16}, or 65,536, different ways. This meant that a programmer could work directly with numbers only as high as 65,536. So, for example, when referring to an address in memory, the programmer could directly reference only addresses from 0 to 65,536, or 64 KB.

The problem, of course, was that the total address space was 1 MB. If programmers could work with only 64 KB at a time, how did they access the rest of the address space? The solution was to divide the full 1 MB address space into 16 *segments,* each with 64 KB. In this *segmented memory model,* the programmer used two values to refer to any memory location: the segment in which the address resided, and an *offset* from the beginning of the segment that pointed to the exact memory address needed. This memory model has two major drawbacks:

- Programming is inherently more complex because you always need two values to refer to a memory address.

- Data is also restricted to 64 KB. This means that there is much more overhead when a program has to work with data larger than 64 KB (which isn't at all uncommon) because several calls to memory need to be made, depending on the size of the data.

DOS used this segmented memory model, so these restrictions were part of Windows 3.x as well.

The Move to 32 Bits

Windows 95 simplifies things (relatively speaking) by moving from the 16-bit segmented memory addressing that shackled DOS for so many years to the full 32-bit addressing associated with 80386 and higher processors. As you saw earlier, 32 bits can be arranged in 2^{32}, or 4,294,967,296, different ways, which gives programs an address space of 4 GB. Not only that, but the 80386 and higher processors handle data in 32-bit pieces. This means that programmers no longer have the 64 KB segment restrictions. Instead, they're free to reference any memory location in the full 4 GB address space directly (with certain restrictions, as you'll see later). This is called a *flat memory space*. (Technically, they still use the segment/offset model; however, the segment register always points to the beginning of the address space.) Data is also no longer restricted to 64 KB, but can be as large as 4 GB. This new memory model is called a *flat memory model*, or sometimes a *linear addressing model*.

NOTE: 32-BIT APPLICATIONS

To take full advantage of Windows 95's "32-bitness," however, you need to use 32-bit applications. Sixteen-bit programs still must use the old segmented memory model, so they remain inherently inefficient. That's not to say, though, that the move to 32-bit programs will result in instant speed increases. If the program always works with small data (less than 64 KB), a 32-bit program won't process this data any faster. However, 32-bit programs will likely be better bets in the long run because of the Win32 advantages we looked at earlier (such as preemptive multitasking and multithreading).

How Windows 95 Handles Memory

One of the big breakthroughs with Windows 95 is that it uses this flat memory model. So all that messing about with extended, expanded, upper, and high memory is, more or less, a thing of the past.

A 4 GB address space is, obviously, a huge amount of memory, and few systems will be stocked with anything approaching that figure. Machines with 8 MB and 16 MB are currently the norm, so how do we reconcile the massive difference between the size of the address space and the size of physical RAM? The Windows 95 solution to this disparity is called *virtual memory management*.

Understanding Windows 95's Virtual Memory Management

To overcome the discrepancy between addressable memory and physical memory, Windows 95 uses a concept called *virtual memory*. Regardless of how much RAM is actually installed on your system, Windows 95 lets each application think it has the entire 4 GB address space to deal with. In reality, Windows 95 uses up the physical RAM first, and then, if more memory is needed, it uses hard disk locations as though they were memory locations.

To understand how this process works, you need to know a bit more about the 80386 (and higher) processors. The 80386 looks at memory in 4 KB chunks called *pages*. The processor divides the entire address space into the 4 KB pages and assigns pages as needed. When you begin running programs and opening documents, the processor assigns pages that correspond to physical RAM. The processor uses a *page table* to keep track of which piece of data is in which page, which process the page belongs to, whether or not the data has changed, and so on.

The key is that the pages can be moved to a different location simply by changing the appropriate entry in the page table. In particular, pages can be moved *outside* of physical memory and stored temporarily in a special file on the hard disk. This file—it's called a *swap file* or a *paging file*—is set up to emulate physical memory. If you open enough programs or data files so that physical memory is exhausted, the swap file is brought into play to augment memory storage.

In the carpenter analogy, the swap file would be like a nearby tool shed that holds tools and materials the carpenter might need soon. This method is faster than returning these items to the main storage area.

Demand Paging and the Virtual Memory Manager

Windows 3.x also used a swap file to "extend" physical RAM, so the idea of virtual memory is nothing new. Windows 95, however, has vastly improved its virtual memory management by implementing a *demand-paged* virtual memory model similar to the one used by Windows NT.

Demand paging is an efficient algorithm for swapping program code and data between physical RAM and the paging file. After physical RAM has been used up, the Virtual Memory Manager (part of the Windows 95 Kernel) begins to manage the paging file. Here's how the entire process works:

1. At first, the Virtual Memory Manager loads code and data into physical RAM. (The mapping of virtual addresses from the program's address space to the physical pages in the computer's memory is handled by the Memory Pager.)

2. A program requests code or data that can't fit inside physical RAM.

3. The Virtual Memory Manager uses the processor's built-in least-recently used (LRU) routine to determine which memory pages haven't been used for the longest time.

4. These pages are checked to see whether the data they contain has changed. (Changed pages are often called *dirty* pages.)

5. If the data has changed, the Virtual Memory Manager swaps these LRU pages out to disk and increases the size of the paging file to compensate. If the data hasn't changed, the pages are made available without being swapped to disk.

6. The freed-up pages are used for the new code or data.

7. Steps 2 through 6 are repeated, as necessary, while you work with the program.

8. When you close a program or document, the Virtual Memory Manager removes related code and data from both physical RAM and the paging file. It also fills in freed-up physical RAM pages with pages from the paging file.

In Windows 3.x, you had two swap file choices: You could either use a permanent swap file that remained on your hard drive whether or not Windows was running, or you could create a temporary swap file that was deleted each time you exited Windows. In both cases, however, the swap file was static: Its size remained constant no matter which operations the system was running.

Windows 95 improves this situation by using a dynamic swap file. As you saw in the preceding steps, the Virtual Memory Manager grows the paging file as you work with applications and data, and it shrinks the paging file as you shut down your programs and close documents. This technique makes the most efficient use of your hard disk, and it eliminates the guesswork involved in deciding how big to make the paging file. (As you'll soon see, though, you can still set maximum and minimum sizes.)

The Windows 95 Memory Map

The 4 GB virtual address space isn't made available in its entirety to your applications. For example, certain areas are reserved for system processes, and other areas are used as private address space for Win32 applications. Figure 9.1 shows how the virtual address space looks from an application's point of view. Here are some notes about this diagram:

■ The area from 0 to 1 MB is used for virtual DOS machines (VDMs) and real-mode device drivers.

■ The area between 1 MB and 4 MB is rarely used.

■ Memory locations from 4 MB to 2 GB are mapped to the private address space of Win32 applications. Each running 32-bit program thinks that it has the entire 2 GB space available, and it can't see any other running 32-bit application. This prevents Win32 programs from compromising each other's memory locations.

■ Between 2 GB and 3 GB, Windows 95 runs the core system components (User, GDI, and Kernel), DLLs and OLE objects shared by multiple applications, and the virtual machine that houses all running Win16 applications.

■ Addresses between 3 GB and 4 GB are reserved for all the ring 0 components: Configuration Manager, Installable File System Manager, Virtual Machine Manager, and the virtual device drivers.

FIGURE 9.1.

Windows 95's memory map.

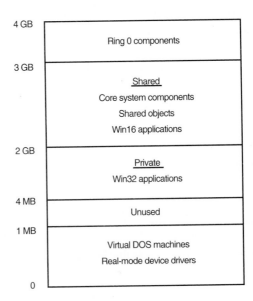

VCACHE: The Protected-Mode Disk Cache

In Windows 3.x, you probably used a 16-bit real-mode driver named SMARTDrive as a disk cache. Windows uses the cache—an area of memory the size of which is user-selected (and fixed) via the command that loads SMARTDrive—to store frequently used bits of program code and data. This technique improves performance because Windows can often load code and data directly from the cache rather than the much slower hard disk.

In Windows 95, the VFAT file system now works with a new disk cache: VCACHE. The VCACHE driver offers the following improvements over SMARTDrive:

- VCACHE is a 32-bit protected-mode virtual device driver (VCACHE.VXD), so it's faster and uses no conventional memory.

- The VCACHE driver uses an improved algorithm that makes caching faster and more intelligent, resulting in greater "hits" (a hit is when the driver requests a piece of data that already exists in the cache).

- VCACHE works with CD-ROMs and network redirectors as well as regular disks.

- The memory pool used by VCACHE is dynamic and adjusts itself according to the total memory available and the processes that are running.

System Resources in Windows 95

One of the biggest frustrations with Windows 3.x was its inefficient use of system resources. You could have megabytes of free memory, but you'd still get Out of memory errors because Windows had run out of system resources. These resources are memory areas—called *heaps*—devoted to the User and GDI components. They hold the data structures used for windows and menus (for User), brushes, pens, and fonts (for GDI), and other resources created by applications (such as toolbars).

The resource data structures are stored in these segments as they're needed, so the percentage of free system resources was just the percentage of free memory available on the heap. (Actually, the percentage of free system resources reported in Program Manager's About dialog box was the *lower* of the values for the User and GDI heaps.)

The problem was that Windows 3.x used 16-bit heaps, so their size was restricted to a single 64 KB segment. This is quite small, so it wasn't hard to run out of resources and receive an Out of memory complaint.

Windows 95 provides greatly improved resource management. The major change was in moving all the User component's system resources into a 32-bit heap, where storage area is now measured in gigabytes instead of kilobytes. As well, some of the GDI's data structures have been moved into a 32-bit heap, although, for compatibility reasons, about half the data structures remain in the 16-bit heap. To give you an idea of the improvement, Table 9.1 compares the resource limits in Windows 3.1 to those now available in Windows 95. (The note "All in a 64 KB segment" means that the resource must fit within the 64 KB segment allotted to the appropriate component—User or GDI. Since the segment also contains other resources, there is no way to specify an exact limit for these resources.)

Table 9.1. System resource limits in Windows 3.1 versus Windows 95.

Resource	Windows 3.1	Windows 95
Windows menu handles	About 299	32 KB
Timers	32	Unlimited
COM and LPT ports	4 per type	Unlimited
Items per list box	8 KB	32 KB
Data per list box	64 KB	Unlimited
Data per edit control	64 KB	Unlimited
Regions	All in a 64 KB segment	Unlimited
Physical pens and brushes	All in a 64 KB segment	Unlimited
Logical pens and brushes	All in a 64 KB segment	All in a 64 KB segment
Logical fonts	All in 64 KB segment	750 to 800
Installed fonts	250 to 300	1,000
Device contexts	200	16 KB

Besides providing larger heaps to store the system resources, Windows 95 is also much better at freeing up system resources for programs that forget (or refuse) to clean up after themselves. When Windows 95 sees that a particular Win32-based process has ended, it automatically checks for resources that remain allocated and removes them from the heap. Win16 applications are a slightly different story, however. Some Win16 programs *intentionally* leave their system resources allocated so that they can be used by shared DLLs, or even other programs. In this case, Windows 95 waits until you exit *all* your Win16 applications before it frees up the resources.

Performance Tuning: General Considerations

Now that you've seen some of the nuts and bolts of Windows 95, it's time to put all this information to good use and tune Windows 95 for optimal performance. Of course, you've just seen that Windows 95 has plenty of built-in features that offer superior performance over Windows 3.x right out of the box. These include the 32-bit Kernel, the flat memory model, preemptive multitasking and multithreading for Win32 applications, a 32-bit disk cache and file system, and improved handling of system resources.

Besides these improvements, Windows 95 also has a number of *self-tuning* features which ensure that a reasonable level of performance is maintained at all times:

- The virtual memory paging file is expanded or contracted dynamically.
- The memory footprint of the disk cache is changed dynamically.
- Setup examines your system and (hopefully) adjusts the Windows 95 configuration to best suit your system.
- Plug and Play ensures that Windows 95 always knows your current configuration and can easily adjust to device changes (assuming that these devices are Plug and Play-compatible, that is).

Windows 95 also includes several tools you can use to monitor and optimize various settings. These tools include System Monitor (discussed next), Resource Monitor (see the later section "Optimizing Memory"), and Disk Defragmenter (see the later section "Optimizing Disk Access"). And if you've installed Microsoft Plus!, you can use the System Agent utility (see Chapter 15, "Protecting Your Windows 95 Investment") to perform many optimization tasks automatically.

Using System Monitor

Before you get too involved with optimizing your system, it will help to have some way of monitoring your progress (and seeing whether your system needs any tuning in the first place). One of the best (albeit advanced) tools for this is System Monitor. Assuming that System Monitor is installed, select Start | Programs | Accessories | System Tools | System Monitor. You'll see the System Monitor window, shown in Figure 9.2.

FIGURE 9.2.

Use the System Monitor to keep an eye on various system processes.

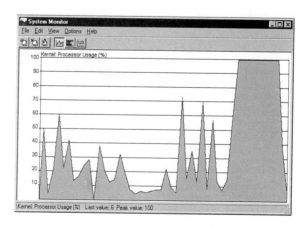

9

PERFORMANCE
TUNING AND
OPTIMIZATION

System Monitor's job is to provide you with real-time reports on how various system processes are performing. The idea is that you should configure System Monitor to show the processes you're interested in (swap file size, free memory, and so on) and then keep System Monitor running while you perform your normal chores. By examining the System Monitor readouts from time to time, you gain an appreciation of what is "typical" on your system. Then, if you run into performance problems, you can check System Monitor to see whether you've run into any bottlenecks or anomalies.

Setting Up System Monitor

By default, System Monitor shows only the Kernel Processor Usage setting, which tells you the percentage of time the processor is busy. To add another setting to the System Monitor window, follow these steps:

1. Select Edit | Add Item or click the Add Item button in the toolbar. The Add Item dialog box, shown in Figure 9.3, appears.

FIGURE 9.3.

Use this dialog box to choose the settings you want to track with System Monitor.

2. Use the Category list to highlight one of the following categories:

> **File System:** Tracks file system performance (reads and writes).
>
> **IPX/SPX compatible protocol:** Tracks packet performance using NetWare's IPX/SPX protocol.
>
> **Kernel:** Tracks Kernel performance, including processor usage, the number of active threads, and the number of active virtual machines.
>
> **Memory Manager:** Tracks a large number of memory-related settings, including allocated memory, cache size, and swap file size.
>
> **Microsoft Client for NetWare Networks:** Tracks network performance via Microsoft's NetWare client.
>
> **Microsoft Network Client:** Tracks network performance via the Microsoft network client.
>
> **Microsoft Network Server:** Tracks network server performance.

NOTE: SYSTEM MONITOR'S SETTINGS

I'll discuss the individual items in the File System and Memory Manager categories later in this chapter.

3. Use the Item list to highlight the setting you want to monitor. (If you need more information about the item, click the Explain button.)
4. Click OK.

System Monitor also gives you several customization options:

■ You can change how you view the data. The default view is a line chart that shows the progress of each setting over time. If you're more interested in the current value, you might prefer either the bar chart view (select View | Bar Charts or click the Bar Charts toolbar button) or the numeric view (select View | Numeric Charts or click the Numeric Charts toolbar button).

■ To adjust the frequency with which System Monitor updates its charts, select Options | Chart, select an update interval in the Options dialog box, and click OK.

■ To adjust the color and scale of a particular chart, select Edit | Edit Item or click the Edit button in the toolbar. Highlight the item you want to edit, and click OK. Use the Chart Options dialog box to select a different color and enter a new scale, and then click OK.

To remove settings from the System Monitor window, select Edit | Remove Item or click the Remove Item button in the toolbar. In the Remove Item dialog box, highlight the item you want to remove, and click OK.

Examining Performance Properties

Another tool you can use to monitor and improve performance is the Performance tab in the System Properties dialog box. To check it out, use either of the following techniques:

■ Right-click My Computer (either on the desktop or in Explorer), and click Properties.
■ Select Start | Settings | Control Panel, and open the System icon in the Control Panel folder.

In the System Properties dialog box that appears, select the Performance tab, shown in Figure 9.4. The Performance status group shows the current status of several crucial settings, including physical memory, free system resources, file system, virtual memory, and disk compression. If the last three are all 32-bit, Windows 95 declares your system to be configured for optimal performance, as shown in Figure 9.4. Otherwise, the Performance tab shows which elements of your system aren't configured optimally. For example, Figure 9.5 shows the Performance tab when real-mode drivers are being used for two CD-ROM drives. (I'll explain MS-DOS compatibility mode in the next chapter.) You can use the buttons in the Performance tab (File System, Graphics, and Virtual Memory) to control various performance-related settings, as I'll show you later in this chapter.

FIGURE 9.4.

The Performance tab summarizes the current performance settings of your computer and offers tools for changing these settings.

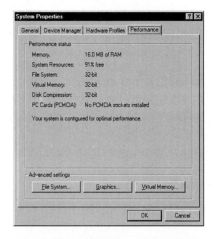

FIGURE 9.5.

This is the version of the Performance tab you'll see when your system isn't configured optimally.

General Performance Tuning Suggestions

Before we get to some specific optimization techniques for memory and disk access, let's look at a few issues that affect performance in more general ways:

Processor: Although Windows 95 will run on machines equipped with an Intel (or compatible) processor from the 80386SX to the Pentium Pro, the performance you get depends greatly on the processor. The 80386SX, for example, runs Windows 95 pathetically slow due to its 16-bit internal data registers. The 80386DX is better, but because it was optimized for 16-bit code, Windows 95 is no speed demon. Windows 95 comes into its own only with the 80486 processor, thanks to the 486's 32-bit optimization. In fact, everything else being equal (memory, clock speed, and so on), the 80486 delivers performance close to that of a Pentium. The Pentium's real advantage over the 486 is that it's available in much higher clock speeds (150 MHz, with faster processors planned in the near future). The Pentium Pro won't run Windows 95 much faster than a garden variety Pentium (given the same clock speed). That's because the Pentium Pro chokes on Windows 95's 16-bit code.

Data bus: The right data bus can make a tremendous difference in performance under Windows 95. Older ISA and VL bus machines cause CPU bottlenecks due to their typically poor throughput. The PCI bus, however, when combined with Windows 95's miniport drivers (explained in the next chapter) handles data at maximum speed with no CPU bottlenecks. PCI buses are also Plug and Play-compliant, which is another big advantage under Windows 95.

Hard disk access time: Unless you have scads of physical RAM in your machine, or just play FreeCell all day long, Windows 95 will spend a good chunk of its time paging code and data to and from the swap file. Although no hard disk even remotely approaches the speed of RAM, having the fastest hard disk you can afford will greatly improve paging performance. Note too that Windows 95 loves a large hard disk because it poses no restrictions on the size of the swap file.

Video hardware and drivers: Windows 95 is a *graphical* user interface, so its performance is in large measure dictated by your graphics hardware. Video accelerator cards can make a huge difference in display performance by removing some of the graphics burden from the shoulders of the CPU. Also, be sure to use the appropriate Windows 95 mini-driver for your video adapter. The new drivers offer much faster performance than their Windows 3.x ancestors.

Protected-mode drivers: For maximum device performance, you should use protected-mode drivers wherever possible. With real-mode drivers, Windows 95 must switch out of its native protected mode and operate in virtual 8088 mode (sometimes several times in a single operation), which is very time-consuming from the processor's point of view.

Optimizing Memory

Memory is the lifeblood of your PC, and it is, by far, the single most important factor affecting your computer's performance. Microsoft claims, *very* optimistically, that Windows 95 will run on systems equipped with only 4 MB of RAM. Whether you believe that claim depends on how you define "run." If by that you mean that Windows 95 will load (eventually) and that you'll be able to work with one or two small applications, then, yes, Windows 95 runs in 4 MB. If what you're really after, however, is a system that will let you work in a high-end word processor, handle large spreadsheet files, send and receive e-mail, access material on a CD-ROM, and surf the Internet, 4 MB just won't cut the electronic mustard. A more realistic minimum would be 8 MB, and 16 MB is required if you want to squeeze any kind of performance out of Windows 95. And if your needs are more high-end—manipulating large graphics files, working with video, heavy database querying—you should be thinking 32 MB.

Whatever amount of RAM you have crammed into your system, though, you can use some techniques to optimize that memory for top performance. The next few sections take you through these techniques.

Using System Monitor to Track Memory Settings

System Monitor is a great tool for tracking memory usage and identifying where memory problems might be occurring. This section takes a closer look at the various memory-related settings you can track with System Monitor.

System Monitor's Memory Manager Settings

System Monitor's Memory Manager category is chock-full of important settings that track various memory processes. Table 9.2 provides a summary of these settings to help you decide which ones to monitor.

Table 9.2. System Monitor's Memory Manager settings.

Setting	Description
Allocated Memory	The total number of bytes allocated to applications and system processes. This is the sum of the Other Memory and Swappable Memory settings.
Discards	The number of pages discarded per second from memory. (These are pages where the data hasn't changed. They're discarded rather than swapped because the data already exists on the hard disk.)
Disk Cache Size	The current size, in bytes, of the disk cache.
Free Memory	The total amount of free physical RAM, in bytes.
Instance Faults	The number of instance faults per second.
Locked Memory	The amount of allocated memory, in bytes, that is locked (that can't be swapped out to disk) by applications or the operating system.
Maximum Disk Cache Size	The largest size possible for the disk cache, in bytes.
Minimum Disk Cache Size	The smallest size possible for the disk cache, in bytes.
Other Memory	The amount of allocated memory, in bytes, that can't be stored in the swap file. This includes code from Win32 DLLs and executable files, memory-mapped files, non-pageable memory, and disk cache pages.

Setting	Description
Page Faults	The number of page faults per second.
Page-ins	The number of pages swapped from the page file to physical RAM per second.
Page-outs	The number of pages swapped from physical RAM to the page file per second.
Swapfile Defective	The number of defective bytes in the swap file. These defective bytes are caused by bad sectors on the hard drive.
Swapfile In Use	The number of bytes currently being used in the swap file.
Swapfile Size	The current size, in bytes, of the swap file.
Swappable Memory	The number of bytes allocated from the swap file. This value includes locked pages.

Using System Monitor to Troubleshoot Memory Issues

Here are a few ideas on how to use System Monitor to investigate and narrow down particular memory-related performance problems:

- If you're monitoring the Kernel: Threads setting, watch for applications that create new threads and then don't release them. Although Windows 95 does a good job of reclaiming these "memory leaks" after you exit the application, the threads remain lost while the program is running. You can free up memory by stopping and restarting the program occasionally.

- If your system seems slow, keep an eye on the Discards and Page-outs settings. High values for these items might mean that system memory is having trouble handling the load and that you might have to add more physical memory.

- If your system feels slow, watch the Page Faults setting. A high value might mean that you're using an application that requires more memory than your system can deliver.

- Locked memory can't be paged to the swap file. If you find that the Locked Memory value is always a large percentage of the Allocated Memory setting, inadequate free memory might be affecting performance. Also, you might be running an application that locks memory unnecessarily.

Managing the Swap File

The less RAM you have in your system, the more important Windows 95's virtual memory features become. That's because if you're dealing with a relatively small amount of physical RAM, Windows 95 can still create a swap file and therefore let you open many more programs than you could otherwise. No matter how much RAM you have, however, Windows 95 will still create a swap file and will still use it for paging data blocks. To make this process as efficient as possible, you need to optimize your swap file. The next couple of sections show you how to do just that.

Some Swap File Notes

Here are some ideas to bear in mind for maximum swap file performance:

Use the hard disk with the most free space. The best way to ensure top swap file performance is to make sure that the hard disk containing the swap file has lots of free space. This extra space gives the swap file enough room to expand and contract as needed. (If you want to use a different hard disk for your swap file, I'll show you how to do this in the next section.)

Use the hard disk with the fastest access time. If you have multiple physical hard disks on your system, make sure that the swap file is using the disk that has the fastest access time.

Don't use an old Windows 3.x permanent swap file. If you haven't yet installed Windows 95 and are planning to upgrade from Windows 3.x, turn off your permanent swap file before running Setup (I showed you how to do this in Chapter 1). Windows 95 can use a Windows 3.x permanent swap file, but the existing swap file's size becomes the *minimum* size of the Windows 95 swap file.

TIP: GETTING RID OF THE WINDOWS 3.X SWAP FILE

What do you do if you've already upgraded and Windows 95 is using the old Windows 3.x swap file? (You'll know this is the case if you see a file named 386SPART.PAR in your boot drive's root folder.) Here's how to force Windows 95 to use its own swap file (WIN386.SWP):

1. Select Start | Shut Down, activate the Restart the computer in MS-DOS mode option, and then click Yes.

2. When you get to the DOS prompt, make sure you're in your main Windows 95 folder, and then enter the following command:

   ```
   edit system.ini
   ```

3. Find the [386Enh] section and look for the pagingfile= entry. Change this entry to read as follows (assuming that C:\Windows is your main Windows 95 folder):

   ```
   pagingfile=c:\windows\win386.swp
   ```

4. Save the changes and exit to the DOS prompt.

5. Enter the following commands to delete the old Windows 3.x swap file:

   ```
   deltree spart.par
   deltree 386spart.par
   ```

6. Restart Windows 95.

Use System Monitor to track your swap file. The System Monitor's Memory Manager: Swap file size setting shows you the current size of the swap file. If you see that this size is approaching the amount of free space left on the disk, you should free up some disk space to ensure that the swap file has complete flexibility.

Defragment the swap file's hard drive. Unlike the Windows 3.x swap file, the Windows 95 swap file can occupy noncontiguous clusters. However, this fragmentation slows down the swap file operation (not substantially, but a little). For best results, keep the disk drive containing the swap file defragmented (as described later in this chapter).

Use an uncompressed hard disk. If you're using a protected-mode driver for a compressed disk, Windows 95 can store the swap file on the compressed drive (again, unlike Windows 3.x). You'll see a small performance degradation if you do this, however, so it's best to use an uncompressed drive for the swap file.

Compacting the swap file. Have you ever heard hard drive activity when you're not using your computer? It might seem like your system is possessed, but it's really just Windows 95 performing some housekeeping chores. In particular, Windows 95 begins compacting your swap file as soon as you haven't used your computer for a minute.

Don't use a network drive. Avoid placing your swap file on a network drive. Access to these drives is usually slow, so your swap file's performance will suffer correspondingly.

Changing Swap File Settings

As I mentioned earlier, virtual memory is one of Windows 95's self-tuning features. The system uses a highly sophisticated algorithm to determine the optimum parameters for the swap file, so in nearly all cases you won't have to change a thing. (This is a welcome relief from the constant swap file fiddling we had to perform in Windows 3.x.)

At times, however, you might need to adjust some swap file settings. For example, you might want to change the hard disk used by the swap file. Here are the steps to follow to make adjustments to the swap file:

1. Open the System Properties dialog box, and select the Performance tab, as described earlier.

2. Click the Virtual Memory button. Windows 95 displays the Virtual Memory dialog box, shown in Figure 9.6.

3. Activate the Let me specify my own virtual memory settings option. The controls below this option become available.

4. Use the Hard disk drop-down list to specify a different hard disk.

5. Use the Minimum spinner to set the smallest possible size, in megabytes, for the swap file.

9

PERFORMANCE
TUNING AND
OPTIMIZATION

FIGURE 9.6.

*Use the Virtual
Memory dialog box
to adjust the swap file
settings.*

6. Use the Maximum spinner to set the largest possible size, in megabytes, for the swap file.

NOTE: WATCH YOUR MAXIMUM

If you set the Maximum value equal to the amount of free space on the hard disk, Windows 95 assumes that it can always use all the available free space. So if you free up space on the disk down the road, Windows 95 will increase the maximum swap file size accordingly. If this isn't what you want, be sure to set the Maximum to a value that's less than the current free space on the disk.

7. If you'd prefer to disable the swap file, activate the Disable virtual memory (not recommended) check box.

CAUTION: DON'T DISABLE VIRTUAL MEMORY

Disabling virtual memory is a sure way to send Windows 95's performance down the tubes. If you're running out of disk space, you're better off deleting files or compressing the hard disk to create more room.

8. Click OK. Windows 95 prompts you to restart your system.

Optimizing System Resources

The changes made to the system resources in Windows 95—especially moving the User resources to a 32-bit heap—have resulted in dramatically better resource management. You start with a higher percentage of resources free (typically over 90 percent, as compared to about 80 percent in Windows 3.x), and you can open many more applications and document windows before the resources start to hit stress levels. Still, Windows 95's resources aren't infinite, so there *are* limits to what you can do. It still pays to monitor your resources and take steps to conserve resources wherever possible.

Using the Resource Meter

In Windows 3.x, you could keep an eye on your free system resources by displaying Program Manager's About dialog box (Help | About Program Manager). Also, there was no shortage of utilities that would display the current health of your system's resources and warn you when they were getting low.

Windows 95 has improved resource monitoring in two ways:

- Windows 95 now warns you when your system resources get too low.
- Windows 95 includes a Resource Meter utility that gives you a visual readout of the current state of the system resources.

To try out Resource Meter, select Start | Programs | Accessories | System Tools | Resource Meter. If this is the first time you're starting Resource Meter, you'll see the dialog box shown in Figure 9.7. This dialog box just states the obvious: that Resource Meter itself will use up a few system resources. To avoid this dialog box in the future, activate the Don't display this message again check box, and then click OK.

FIGURE 9.7.

This dialog box appears when you start Resource Meter for the first time.

When the Resource Meter loads, it adds an icon to the taskbar's information area that gives you a visual representation of the system resource status. The green bars indicate free system resources, and the "level" goes up and down as you open and close applications, windows, and objects. You can get an exact figure for User resources, GDI resources, and System resources (the lower of the User and GDI values) by using either of the following techniques:

- Hover the mouse pointer over the Resource Meter icon for a second or two to display a banner showing the individual resource percentages.
- Double-click the Resource Meter icon to display the Resource Meter dialog box that shows a bar chart for each resource percentage.

Figure 9.8 shows the results of both techniques.

So what do these numbers mean in the real world? Well, as long as the bars in the Resource Meter icon are green, you're fine: This means that Windows 95 has plenty of resources available. As the bar inches downward, however, keep an eye out for a color change:

- When the bars change to yellow, the free resources have dropped below 30 percent. You should exercise caution at this point and avoid opening more applications or windows. Run through some of the techniques discussed in the next section for saving system resources.

9

PERFORMANCE TUNING AND OPTIMIZATION

■ When the bars change to red, the free resources have dropped to 15 percent or less. This is very dangerous territory, and you should immediately start shutting down applications.

FIGURE 9.8.

Double-click the Resource Meter icon in the toolbar to display a graphical representation of your free system resources.

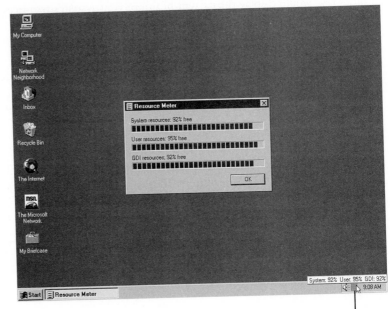

The Resource Meter Icon

When the free resources drop to 10 percent or less, you'll see the dialog box shown in Figure 9.9. Your system is in imminent danger of hanging, so you must start closing applications to avoid losing data. It's interesting to note just how many applications and windows are running in Figure 9.9. Twenty-five windows are open, including such "large" applications as Excel, Access, PowerPoint, Exchange, The Microsoft Network, and Internet Explorer. Clearly, this is vastly superior to what we could accomplish in Windows 3.x. (Note, however, that your mileage may vary. Figure 9.9 was produced on a machine with 32 MB of memory, which is certainly not your ordinary Windows 95 machine.)

Saving System Resources

If you find that your system resources are getting low, here are some ideas that will send the Resource Meter bar up:

■ Close any applications you won't be using for a while.

■ If your applications support multiple open documents, close files you aren't using.

■ Run DOS applications full screen rather than in a window.

■ Turn off application objects you don't use, such as toolbars, rulers, and status bars.

- Minimize any running applications you aren't using.

- Turn off desktop wallpaper and animated cursors. You should especially avoid the Microsoft Plus! desktop themes, which are real resource hogs.

FIGURE 9.9.

Windows 95 warns you when your free system resources drop to 10 percent or less.

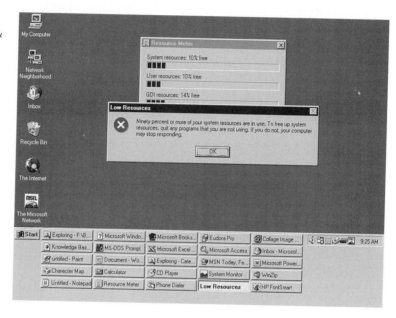

Miscellaneous Ideas for Optimizing Memory

To finish our look at optimizing memory, here are a few random ideas that create more memory and give your programs more room to roam:

Run only the programs you need. Each running program usurps some physical RAM, so the more programs you have open, the more paging Windows 95 will have to do.

Minimize your network services. Network services—clients and protocols—use up memory even when you're not logged on to your network. To minimize this footprint, run only one network client, and use only those protocols you really need.

Use system resources wisely. Remember that system resource heaps exist in memory, so saving resources saves overall memory. Follow the guidelines from the preceding section to keep your resource use in check.

Make sure that your system's RAM cache is enabled. RAM caches are small processor-based memory areas that store frequently used processor instructions, and they can increase performance tremendously. If your system feels slow, enter your BIOS setup program the next time you reboot, and make sure that its RAM cache

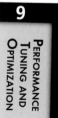

isn't disabled. Depending on your BIOS, the RAM cache might be called an "L1 cache," an "internal cache," or a "system memory cache."

Delete the contents of the Clipboard. When you cut or copy a selection in a Windows application, the program stores the data in an area of memory called the Clipboard. If you're working with only a few lines of text, this area remains fairly small. Cutting or copying a graphics image, however, can increase the size of the Clipboard to several hundred kilobytes or more. If you've run out of memory, a large Clipboard might be the problem. To release this memory, try one of the following methods:

■ If you have an application running, highlight a small section of text (a single character will do) and select Edit | Copy. This action replaces the current Clipboard with a much smaller one.

■ Select Start | Programs | Accessories | Clipboard Viewer. When the Clipboard Viewer window appears, select Edit | Delete to clear the contents of the Clipboard.

Buy more memory. The ultimate way to beat the low-memory blues, of course, is simply to add more memory to your system. Unlike Windows 3.x, which couldn't care less if your system had more than 16 MB of RAM, Windows 95 can take advantage of every last megabyte in your system. I've run Windows 95 on a machine with 64 MB, and it absolutely soars. Unfortunately, memory prices have risen over the past couple of years, so it might not be possible to add more than a few megabytes without breaking your budget. Contact your computer manufacturer to find out the best kind of memory to add to your system.

Optimizing Disk Access

Memory and hard disk access are the "Twin Towers" of Windows 95 performance. Memory, as you've just seen, is where you spend most of your productive computer life. In the carpenter analogy I introduced earlier, memory is the work area where you perform the digital equivalents of sawing, planing, and sanding. Your hard disk, though, is the storage area where you keep all your tools (applications) and raw materials (data). Keeping your hard disk tuned and optimized benefits three areas:

Storage: Given a finite amount of hard disk space, you want to optimize not only the amount of data that can be stored, but also how the data is stored.

Program loading: Your applications are started from the hard disk, so a fast, efficient disk will load programs more quickly.

Paging and caching: Windows 95 uses dynamic paging files and caching, so a well-tuned disk will increase performance in these crucial areas.

The next few sections take you through various techniques for optimizing hard disk access.

Using System Monitor to Track File System Settings

You can use the System Monitor utility (discussed earlier) to keep an eye on your hard disk's performance. Besides monitoring the swap file settings, System Monitor also tracks various settings related to disk reads and writes in the File System category. I've summarized these settings in Table 9.3.

Table 9.3. System Monitor's File System settings.

Setting	Description
Bytes Read/Second	The number of bytes read from the file system per second.
Bytes Written/Second	The number of bytes written to the file system per second.
Dirty Data	The total number of bytes in changed memory pages ("dirty" pages) waiting to be written to the disk. (Because a page is 4 KB and not all the data on the page might have changed, the actual number of dirty bytes might be less than the number shown.)
Reads/Second	The number of read operations delivered from the file system per second.
Writes/Second	The number of write operations delivered to the file system per second.

If you notice these numbers dropping off over time, your hard disk is probably slowing down and becoming less efficient.

Optimizing Cluster Size

When it comes to hard disk inefficiency, one of the biggest culprits is the capacity of the disk. That might sound strange, but it's true: The bigger the hard disk, the greater the waste. This section explains what I mean and shows you how to reduce this inefficiency.

VFAT and Clusters

To see why large hard disks are inherently inefficient, you need to understand how VFAT, Windows 95's file system, stores files. When you format a disk, the disk's magnetic medium is divided into small storage areas called *sectors*, which usually hold up to 512 bytes of data. Hard disks typically contain hundreds of thousands of sectors, so it would be just too inefficient for Windows 95 to deal with individual sectors. Instead, Windows 95 groups sectors into *clusters*, the size of which, as you'll see, depends on the size of the disk.

Still, each hard disk has tens of thousands of clusters (up to 65,536), so some sort of "file filing system" is necessary to keep track of everything. Every formatted disk comes with its own built-in filing system called the File Allocation Table, or FAT for short. The FAT contains a 16-bit entry for every cluster on the disk, and these entries can assume any of the values shown in Table 9.4.

Table 9.4. Values for each FAT entry.

Entry	Description
0	The cluster is available to store data.
nnn	This value indicates the cluster number that contains the next part of the file.
BAD	The cluster contains one or more bad sectors. The file system won't use this cluster for storage.
EOF	The cluster represents the end of the file.
Reserved	The cluster is to be used only by Windows 95.

But how does the FAT know where the file begins? For each file on the disk, the FAT maintains an entry in a *file directory*, a sort of table of contents for your files. Table 9.5 lists the contents of each entry in the file directory. (Note that this is the VFAT—Virtual File Allocation Table—version of the file directory, which is slightly different from the one used by DOS and Windows 3.x. VFAT serves as a protected-mode go-between for applications and the disk's FAT.)

Table 9.5. The structure of each file directory entry in Windows 95.

Field	Size
Filename	8 bytes
Extension	3 bytes
Attributes (archive, hidden, and so on)	1 byte
Reserved (these bytes aren't used)	6 bytes
Date the file was last modified	2 bytes
Exclusive access handle	2 bytes
Time the file was created	2 bytes
Date the file was created	2 bytes
Starting cluster number in the FAT	2 bytes
File size in bytes	4 bytes

NOTE: WHERE ARE THE LONG FILENAMES?

You might be wondering how Windows 95 implements long filenames if the directory entry for each file has room for only the traditional 8.3 name. The answer is that in Windows 95, the directory structure shown in Table 9.4 is only for each file's *initial* directory entry. VFAT also keeps track of several other directory entries for each file, and it's in these secondary entries that the long filenames are stored.

For our purposes, the key item is the starting cluster number. This 16-bit value tells VFAT the number of the cluster where the file begins. When VFAT needs to open a file, it follows these steps:

1. It looks up the file in the file directory.
2. It uses the file's directory entry to get the starting cluster number.
3. It looks up the cluster number in the FAT.
4. If the cluster entry points to another cluster number, there is still more of the file to read, so VFAT repeats step 3.

   If the cluster entry is EOF, the entire file has been read, so VFAT is done.

For example, Figure 9.10 shows a simplified version of the file directory and FAT. The file LETTER.DOC, for instance, has a starting cluster number of 100. When VFAT checks the FAT entry for cluster 100, it sees that the entry contains the value 101. This tells VFAT that it will find the next portion of the file in cluster 101. So now it moves to the entry for cluster 101 and finds that the entry contains EOF. This tells VFAT that the file ends within this cluster, so it knows that clusters 100 and 101 contain the entire file (this is called a *cluster chain*).

FIGURE 9.10.

The relationship between the file directory and the FAT.

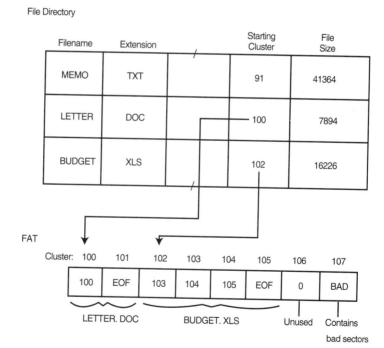

9

PERFORMANCE
TUNING AND
OPTIMIZATION

The Relationship Between Disk Size and Cluster Size

One of the hard disk facts of life is that every formatted disk, from 40 MB pip-squeaks to 4 GB behemoths can't have any more than 65,536 clusters. Why? Recall that the FAT entries for each cluster are 16 bits long. This means that the largest possible cluster number is 65,536, so that's the maximum number of clusters on any hard disk. (Note that non-FAT partitions such as NTFS and HPFS don't have this restriction.) This means that the larger the hard disk, the larger the cluster size, as shown in Table 9.6.

Table 9.6. The relationship between disk size and cluster size.

Disk Size	Cluster Size
16 to 127 MB	2,048 bytes
128 to 255 MB	4,096 bytes
256 to 511 MB	8,192 bytes
512 MB to 1,023 MB	16,384 bytes
1,024 MB to 2,047 MB	32,768 bytes
2,048 MB to 4,191 MB	65,536 bytes

NOTE: HARD DISKS UNDER 16 MB

Hard disks with capacities less than 16 MB are anomalies and don't quite fit this pattern. These disks use a 12-bit FAT, so they have cluster sizes of 4,096 bytes.

The key point is that VFAT always allocates entire clusters when storing files. For example, assume that the files shown in Figure 9.10 exist on a 200 MB hard drive that therefore uses a cluster size of 4,096 bytes. The file size of LETTER.DOC is 7,894 bytes, but it takes up two whole clusters, or 8,192 bytes. This means that the second cluster has an extra 298 bytes of wasted space. This wasted space is called *cluster overhang*. 298 bytes isn't anything to worry about, but suppose that LETTER.DOC was stored on a 550 MB disk. This disk uses 16,384-byte clusters, which means LETTER.DOC could be housed in a single cluster. However, the cluster overhang jumps to a whopping 5,490 bytes. Put LETTER.DOC on a 1 GB drive, and the overhang leaps to a little over 24 KB, over three times the size of the actual file!

Think this is a bad example because LETTER.DOC is such a small file? Think again. Suppose you store a 100 KB file on a 1 GB drive that uses 32 KB clusters. The file's first three clusters hold 96 KB, but the remaining 4 KB sits in the last cluster, wasting 28 KB in cluster overhang.

Checking Cluster Overhang

If you're wondering how much space is being wasted on your hard disk due to cluster overhang, there's an easy way to figure it out. In a DOS session, change to the root folder of the
drive you want to check, and then enter the following DOS command:

```
dir /s/a/v
```

The /A parameter tells DIR to find hidden and system files, and the /S parameter tells DIR to run
through the drive's subfolders. However, it's the /V parameter that helps you with cluster overhang. This switch tells DIR to display a few extra numbers: the size of each file, the amount of
space allocated to each file, the total size of all the files, and the total amount allocated to all the
files. Here's an example of such a listing:

```
C:\dir /s/a/v
 Volume in drive C is HARD DRIVE
 Volume Serial Number is 3441-1201
Directory of C:\
File Name    Size   Allocated  Modified           Accessed   Attrib
SUHDLOG  DAT   5,166   32,768   12-18-96 12:13p   12-18-96   RH        SUHDLOG.DAT
BOOTLOG  TXT  26,942   32,768   03-04-97  3:37p   03-04-97   H    A    BOOTLOG.TXT
COMMAND  COM  93,812   98,304   08-24-96 11:11a   03-28-97        A    COMMAND.COM
BOOTLOG  PRV  26,942   32,768   02-08-97  6:10p   02-08-97   H    A    BOOTLOG.PRV
CONFIG   SYS     823   32,768   03-08-97  5:55p   03-28-97        A    CONFIG.SYS
MSDOS    SYS   1,653   32,768   03-20-97  1:43p   03-25-97        A    MSDOS.SYS
CONFIG   DOS     845   32,768   12-18-96 11:41a   12-18-96        A    CONFIG.DOS
AUTOEXEC DOS     429   32,768   12-18-96 11:23a   12-18-96        A    AUTOEXEC.DOS
etc.
Total files listed:
   3,017 file(s)     326,412,057 bytes
     481 dir(s)      388,005,888 bytes allocated
                     844,464,128 bytes free
                   1,259,044,864 bytes total disk space,  32% in use
```

With this data in hand, calculating cluster overhang becomes a simple two-step procedure:

1. Subtract the bytes value from the bytes allocated value.
2. Divide the difference calculated in step 1 by the bytes allocated value.

In the preceding example, the difference between the bytes value and the bytes allocated value
is 61,593,831 (388,005,888 minus 326,412,057), and dividing 61,593,831 by 388,005,888
gives a cluster overhang of just under 16 percent.

Partitioning for More Efficient Disks

The massive amounts of cluster overhang in large hard disks is clearly inefficient, but what can
be done? Well, it turns out that cluster size is determined not by the overall capacity of the
hard disk, but by the size of each *partition* on the hard disk. So if you create a 200 MB partition
on a 1 GB disk, the partition will use cluster sizes of 4,096 bytes. So the secret to increase

storage efficiency is to chop up your hard disk into smaller partitions. How small? That depends on how you use your computer:

- If your data consists mostly of small files, use small partitions (127 MB or less).
- If you work with very large files (such as graphics, video, or music files), use big partitions to give yourself room to store these files. Cluster overhang is less of an issue on massive data files (say, greater than 1 MB).
- Remember that many applications usurp huge amounts of disk real estate, so you'll need partitions big enough to hold them. A 127 MB partition, for example, isn't large enough to store a complete installation of Microsoft Office.
- Make sure that the partitions you use are a bit less than the changeover point for cluster sizes. Partitioning a disk to 127 MB gives you 2 KB clusters, but adding a mere megabyte to the partition bumps the drive up to 4 KB clusters.
- Ideally, you should have separate partitions for programs and data, using a larger partition for the programs and a smaller partition for the data. An added advantage of this technique is that backing up your data is easier.
- Remember that each partition creates a new drive letter. Dividing a 1 GB disk into a dozen small partitions might make for efficient storage, but finding what you want in all those drives can be difficult. ("Let's see...did I store that budget file on drive F or drive N?")

After you've decided on the partition sizes you need, you use Windows 95's FDISK program to repartition a hard disk. I show you how to wield FDISK in Chapter 14, "Disk Driving: Dealing with Disks."

OSR2 Cluster Sizes in OSR2

As I mentioned in Chapter 6, "Under the Hood: Understanding the Windows 95 Architecture," the FAT32 file system used in OSR2 is designed to help alleviate the cluster overhang problems that plagued FAT16. To do that, FAT32 sets up a new (and more efficient) relationship between disk size and cluster size, as shown in Table 9.7.

Table 9.7. The relationship between disk size and cluster size in FAT32.

Disk Size	Cluster Size
512 MB to 8 GB	4,096 bytes
8 GB to 16 GB	8,192 bytes
16 GB to 32 GB	16,384 bytes
Over 32 GB	32,768 bytes

Note that the minimum FAT32 partition size that you can create using FDISK is 512 MB. (Third-party partitioning utilities such as Partition Magic *will* create FAT32 partitions smaller than 512 MB.)

Using Protected-Mode Drivers

In Windows 3.x (except Windows 3.0), there was an obscure, hard-to-find option called FastDisk that enabled a 32-bit disk driver and greatly improved hard disk performance. Windows 95 brings 32-bit disk performance out of the shadows and into the light by defaulting to a 32-bit protected-mode driver for most hard disks. However, Windows 95 might be using a 16-bit real-mode driver for your hard disk if you're using Stacker or if Setup didn't have a replacement for your existing driver when you upgraded.

To find out, examine the Performance tab in the System Properties dialog box. In the Performance status group, check the File System line:

- If it says 32-bit, Windows 95 is using the 32-bit driver.
- If it says Some drives are using MS-DOS compatibility mode, Windows 95 is using a real-mode driver for one of your disks.

In the latter case, the Performance tab also shows a list of disks that are using the real-mode drivers, as shown earlier in Figure 9.9. If your system feels sluggish, this is probably the reason. When Windows 95 accesses data on a disk that's using a real-mode driver, Windows 95 must switch out of protected mode, access the data in real mode, and switch back into protected mode. All this mode switching exacts a heavy price in terms of hard disk performance. There are two solutions:

- Check to see whether you're loading the real-mode driver at startup in either CONFIG.SYS or (less likely) AUTOEXEC.BAT. If so, try commenting out the lines that load the drivers (by adding REM and a space to the left of the lines). Restart Windows 95 and check the Performance tab to see whether a protected-mode driver is being used.
- If Windows 95 doesn't have the correct protected-mode driver, contact the manufacturer of the hard disk or the company that made your system to see whether it has a Windows 95 driver available.

Enabling Hard Drive DMA Support in OSR2

One of the new features in OSR2 is support for hard drive Direct Memory Access (DMA) for IDE drives. If your system can take advantage of this feature (you must be using the default OSR2 bus mastering IDE controller drivers), this allows the system to access the hard drive directly, without having to use up processor cycles. Depending on your system, this can result in a slight performance improvement (as well as reduced overhead for the processor, of course).

Note, however, that hard drive DMA is *disabled* by default in OSR2. To activate this feature, follow these steps:

1. Right-click My Computer and then choose Properties to display the System Properties dialog box.
2. Activate the Device Manager tab.
3. Open the Disk drives branch, highlight your IDE hard drive, and click Properties.
4. In the properties sheet that appears, select the Settings tab and then activate the DMA check box, as shown in Figure 9.11.

Figure 9.11.

Hard drive DMA is deactivated by default in OSR2.

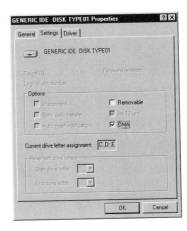

5. Click OK to return to the System Properties dialog box, and then click OK again.
6. When Windows 95 asks if you want to restart your computer, click Yes.

TIP: OSR2 ALSO SUPPORTS CD-ROM DMA

OSR2 can also implement DMA on CD-ROM drives. To activate DMA for your CD-ROM, follow the steps outlined in this section (except that you need to open the CDROM branch in Device Manager).

Making Cache Adjustments

Disk caches are memory areas (*buffers*) that store recently used or frequently used bits of program code and data. If a program requests some data, Windows 95 checks the cache to see whether the data is in the cache. If it is, it's moved into main memory extremely quickly, thus improving performance.

Our carpenter analogy is perfect for explaining how a cache works. So far, we've seen three areas that the carpenter uses:

■ A main storage warehouse (the hard disk)

■ A main workshop area (memory)

■ A tool shed close to the workshop (the swap file)

A "carpenter's cache" would be an area inside the main workshop that holds tools that are used often, tools that will soon be needed, and finished work that will be put into main storage later.

A disk cache works the same way. Not only does it hold in memory code and data that's used frequently, but it also "reads ahead" to get the clusters that are next to the ones just read, and it "writes behind" by holding changed data in the buffer until the system is idle and then writing the data to disk.

VCACHE is the Windows 95 disk caching replacement for SMARTDrive (although SMARTDrive still exists and can be used to optimize DOS application performance; see Chapter 21, "DOS Isn't Dead: Optimizing DOS Applications Under Windows 95"). VCACHE is dynamic, which means that Windows 95 tailors the cache size to suit the current system load. (VCACHE and the dynamic swap file work together on this project.) This dynamic behavior is the best way to manage the cache optimally, so there's no need—and no way—to mess around with different cache sizes, as you could do with SMARTDrive. That's not to say, however, that VCACHE isn't configurable. It is, and the next two sections show you how to configure it.

Adjusting the Hard Disk Cache

To make some adjustments to the hard disk cache, follow these steps:

1. In the Performance tab, select `File System` to display the File System Properties dialog box.

2. Make sure that the Hard Disk tab is selected, as shown in Figure 9.12.

FIGURE 9.12.

Use the Hard Disk tab to adjust some hard disk cache parameters.

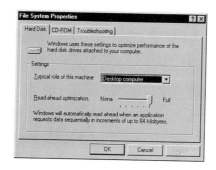

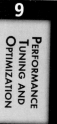

3. In the `Typical role of this machine` drop-down list, select one of the following options:

   Desktop computer: This option is for standalone machines, network clients, and notebook computers running on AC power. In each case, the computer should have at least 8 MB of RAM. Windows 95 uses moderate settings for the cache size and write behind operations. Specifically, VFAT tracks the 32 most recently used folders and the 677 most recently used files. This setting consumes about 10 KB of memory.

Mobile or docking system: This option is for notebook computers running on batteries, docking stations, and desktop machines that use less than 8 MB of RAM. Windows 95 uses conservative settings for the cache size and write behind operations. This ensures that the disk cache is cleaned out regularly. In this case, VFAT tracks the 16 most recently used folders and the 337 most recently used files. This setting usurps only about 5 KB of memory.

Network server: This option is for network servers with plenty of RAM that spend most of their time accessing the disk. Windows 95 assumes that the computer uses an uninterruptible power supply (UPS). Windows 95 uses aggressive settings for the cache size and write behind operations. For this setting, VFAT tracks the 64 most recently used folders and the 2,729 most recently used files (using about 40 KB of memory in the process). This greatly increases performance, but with added risk: If a power failure shuts down the machine, data could easily be lost (hence the need for a UPS).

4. Use the `Read-ahead optimization` slider to specify the maximum size of VCACHE's read-ahead buffer. In most cases, you'll get the best performance with this option set to `Full`.

5. Click OK to return to the System Properties dialog box.

6. Click Close. Windows 95 prompts you to restart your computer.

7. Click Yes.

Adjusting the CD-ROM Cache

VCACHE also maintains a separate cache that works with CD-ROM drives to improve performance. Again, you can configure some parameters for the CD-ROM cache, as described in the following steps:

1. In the Performance tab, select `File System` to display the File System Properties dialog box.

2. Select the CD-ROM tab, shown in Figure 9.13.

FIGURE 9.13.

Use the CD-ROM tab to adjust parameters for the CD-ROM cache.

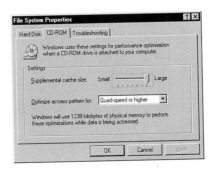

3. Use the `Supplemental cache size` slider to set the size of the CD-ROM cache. Note that this cache is used only while you're working with your CD-ROM applications, so it shouldn't affect how much memory is available to your other programs.

4. The `Optimize access pattern for` drop-down list sets the optimal cache size based on the speed of your CD-ROM and the amount of physical RAM in your system. On the low end, for example, if you have a single-speed drive and less than 8 MB of RAM, the cache is set to 64 KB; on the high end, if you have a quad-speed or higher drive and 12 MB or more of RAM, the cache size is set to 1,238 KB.

5. Click OK to return to the System Properties dialog box.

6. Click Close. Windows 95 prompts you to restart your system.

7. Click Yes.

Overcoming File Fragmentation

Windows 95 comes with a utility called Disk Defragmenter that's an essential tool for tuning your hard disk. Disk Defragmenter's job is to eliminate *file fragmentation* from your hard disk.

File fragmentation is one of those terms that sounds scarier than it actually is. It simply means that a file is stored on your hard disk in scattered, noncontiguous bits. This is a performance drag because it means that Windows 95, when it tries to open such a file, must make several stops to collect the various pieces. If a lot of files are fragmented, it can slow even the fastest hard disk to a crawl.

Why doesn't Windows 95 just store files contiguously? Recall that Windows 95 stores files on disk in clusters, and that these clusters have a fixed size, depending on the disk's capacity. Recall too that Windows 95 uses the FAT to keep track of each file's whereabouts. When you delete a file, Windows 95 doesn't actually clean out the clusters associated with the file. Instead, it just places a 0 in the appropriate FAT cluster entries to reflect that the file's clusters are now available.

To see how fragmentation occurs, let's look at an example. Suppose that three files are stored on a disk—FIRST.TXT, SECOND.TXT, and THIRD.TXT—and that they use up four, three, and five clusters, respectively. Figure 9.14 shows how they might look on the disk.

FIGURE 9.14.

Three files before fragmentation.

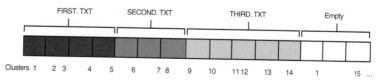

If you now delete SECOND.TXT, clusters 5, 6, and 7 become available. But suppose that the next file you save—call it FOURTH.TXT—takes up five clusters. What happens? Well, Windows 95 starts at the beginning of the FAT and looks for the first available clusters. It finds that 5, 6, and 7 are free, so it uses them for the first three clusters of FOURTH.TXT. Windows continues and finds that clusters 13 and 14 are free, so it uses them for the final two clusters of FOURTH.TXT. Figure 9.15 shows how things look now.

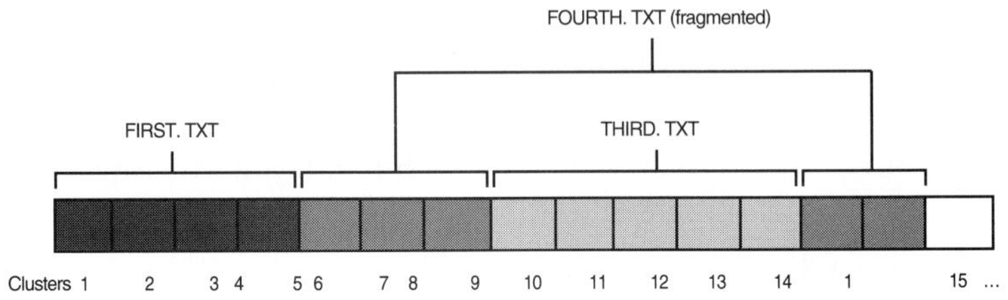

Figure 9.15.
A fragmented file.

As you can see, FOURTH.TXT is stored noncontiguously—in other words, it's fragmented. Although a file fragmented into two pieces isn't that bad, it's possible for large files to get split into dozens of blocks.

NOTE: FRAGMENTATION FOILS THE CACHE

Fragmented files not only take longer to open, but they also defeat the operation of the read-ahead portion of the cache. That's because the cache assumes that the next cluster in the chain is the one most likely to be accessed next. If the file is badly fragmented, chances are the next cluster won't belong to the file.

Using Disk Defragmenter

The Disk Defragmenter accessory works by physically rearranging the files on your hard disk so that each file has its clusters stored contiguously. Before using Disk Defragmenter, you should perform a couple of housekeeping chores:

- Delete any files from your hard disk that you don't need. Defragmenting junk files only slows down the whole process.

- Check for file allocation errors and other disk problems by running ScanDisk (as described in Chapter 15).

CAUTION: DEFRAGMENTATION CAVEATS

Don't use the DEFRAG utility that shipped with DOS 6.x because it doesn't understand long filenames. Also, don't use Disk Defragmenter on drives compressed with Stacker or SuperStor, network drives, CD-ROM drives, or drives created with the DOS commands ASSIGN, JOIN, and SUBST.

Here are the steps to follow to run Disk Defragmenter:

1. Select Start | Programs | Accessories | System Tools | Disk Defragmenter. The Select Drive dialog box, shown in Figure 9.16, appears.

FIGURE 9.16.

Use this dialog box to select the drive you want to defragment.

2. Use the Which drive do you want to defragment? drop-down list to choose a drive, and click OK. Disk Defragmenter analyzes the fragmentation of your files and, if it's not too bad, displays the dialog box shown in Figure 9.17.

FIGURE 9.17.

Disk Defragmenter lets you know if your hard disk isn't too messy.

3. To change the defragmenting options, select Advanced to display the Advanced Options dialog box, shown in Figure 9.18. It has the following controls:

   Full defragmentation (both files and free space): This option takes longer, but it ensures optimum performance.

   Defragment files only: This option rearranges the file clusters so that each file is stored contiguously. It takes less time, but because no attempt is made to fill in any empty clusters between files, subsequent files saved are more likely to be fragmented.

   Consolidate free space only: This option doesn't defragment the existing files. Instead, it rearranges their clusters so that there are no empty clusters between them. This makes it more likely that subsequent files saved won't be fragmented.

   Check drive for errors: When this check box is activated, Windows 95 checks for file and folder errors before starting the defragmentation. If you've already run ScanDisk, you should deactivate this check box to save time.

   When do you want to use these options?: If you want to use the options you've chosen each time you run Disk Defragmenter, select Save these options and use them every time. To use the selected options now but return to the default options the next time you run Disk Defragmenter, select This time only.

FIGURE 9.18.

Use this dialog box to set some advanced Disk Defragmenter options.

4. Click OK to return to the Disk Defragmenter dialog box.

5. If you want to go ahead with the defragment, click Start. Disk Defragmenter starts tidying up your hard disk and displays the dialog box shown in Figure 9.19 to keep you apprised of its progress.

FIGURE 9.19.

Disk Defragmenter displays this dialog box to show you the progress of the defragmentation.

6. If you'd like to see a visual representation of the Disk Defragmenter's labors, click the Show Details button. The window that appears looks something like the one shown in Figure 9.20. To display the Defrag Legend dialog box, click the Legend button.

FIGURE 9.20.

Click the Show Details button to watch Disk Defragmenter do its thing.

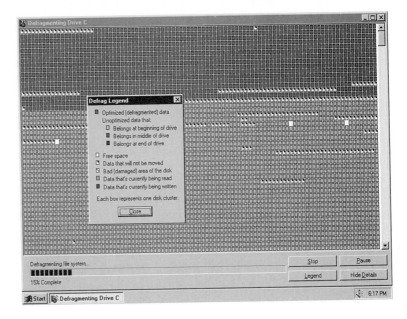

7. When Disk Defragmenter finally finishes its chores (it might take 10 or 15 minutes, depending on the size of your disk, how cluttered it is, and how fast your computer is), your computer beeps, and a dialog box appears to tell you that the defragmentation is complete and ask whether you want to quit Disk Defragmenter. If you do, click Yes; otherwise, click No to return to the Select Drive dialog box.

NOTE: HOW OFTEN SHOULD YOU DEFRAGMENT?

How often you defragment your hard disk depends on how often you use your computer. If you use it every day, you should run Disk Defragmenter about once a week. If your computer doesn't get heavy use, you probably need to run Disk Defragmenter only once a month or so.

Using Disk Defragmenter from the Command Line

For an extra level of control over how Disk Defragmenter performs its duties, you can start the program either by using the Run dialog box or by using the DOS prompt and including one or more command-line parameters. The command that starts Disk Defragmenter is `defrag`. It uses the following syntax:

```
defrag [d: ¦ /all] [/f ¦ /q ¦ /u] [/noprompt] [/concise ¦ /detailed]
```

Here's an explanation of each parameter:

`d:`	The drive letter of the disk you want to defragment.
`/all`	Defragment all (local) hard disk drives.
`/f`	Defragment files and consolidate free space.
`/q`	Consolidate free space only.
`/u`	Defragment files only.
`/noprompt`	Bypass confirmation dialog boxes.
`/concise`	Show the defragmentation progress only (no details; see Figure 9.19). This is the default.
`/detailed`	Display the Show Details view (see Figure 9.20).

Summary

This chapter showed you how to give Windows 95 a tune-up by optimizing memory, hard disk access, the CD-ROM cache, and more. In preparation for these tuning tasks, I also took you "under the hood" to learn about Windows 95 architecture. You'll find more information on performance tuning and architecture in the following chapters:

■ For hardware-related performance issues, see Chapter 10, "How Windows 95 Handles Hardware."

■ You can use the Registry for some performance tuning. I show you how in Chapter 12, "Hacking the Registry."

■ For more data on the Windows 95 file system, including instructions on how to compress disks to get more space, see Chapter 14, "Disk Driving: Dealing with Disks."

■ To learn about backing up files and ScanDisk, see Chapter 15, "Protecting Your Windows 95 Investment."

■ I talk a bit about optimizing printing in Chapter 19, "Prescriptions for Perfect Printing."

■ To get the best performance out of your DOS programs, see Chapter 21, "DOS Isn't Dead: Optimizing DOS Applications Under Windows 95."

■ The three chapters in Part V, "Unleashing Multimedia: The Sights and Sounds of Windows 95," contain tips and techniques for optimizing multimedia.

■ Network optimization and architecture are covered in Chapter 30, "A Networking Primer," and Chapter 31, "Windows 95 Networking."

How Windows 95
Handles Hardware

CHAPTER 10

> *Man is a shrewd inventor, and is ever taking the hint of a new machine from his own structure, adapting some secret of his own anatomy in iron, wood, and leather, to some required function in the work of the world.*
>
> —*Ralph Waldo Emerson*

Emerson's concept of a "machine" was decidedly low-tech ("iron, wood, and leather"), but his basic idea is still apt in these high-tech times. Man has taken yet another "secret of his own anatomy"—the brain—and used it as the "hint of a new machine"—the computer. And although even the most advanced computer is still a mere toy compared to the breathtaking complexity of the human brain, some spectacular advancements have been made in the art of hardware in recent years.

One of the hats an operating system must wear is that of an intermediary between you and your hardware. Any OS worth its salt has to translate incomprehensible "devicespeak" into something you can make sense out of, and it must ensure that devices are ready, willing, and able to carry out your commands. Given the sophistication and diversity of today's hardware market, however, that's no easy task. The good news is that Windows 95 brings to the PC world an unprecedented level of interaction with hardware. From its basic architecture to the advanced device management tools it provides, Windows 95 is built from the ground up to make your hardware travails trivial. Did Microsoft achieve this laudable goal? Not really, no. But it's a huge improvement over the primitive tools that existed in previous versions of Windows, so, if nothing else, it will make your hardware chores easier. This chapter shows you how Windows 95 works with your system's hardware and also shows you how to use Windows 95's device management tools.

Windows 95's Hardware Innovations

We'll begin our examination of Windows 95 hardware issues by looking at a few of the innovations Windows 95 brings to device management. But first, let's recap how people dealt with devices before Windows 95 came along.

The Situation Before Windows 95

Installing and configuring hardware has always been the bête noire of PC owners. Sure, getting cards and drives into their particular slots or bays wasn't a big deal, as long as you were at least minimally dexterous (and could stomach the idea of dealing with your computer's innards). It was the "before" and "after" phases that gave most people ulcers and prematurely gray hair. The before phase usually consisted of adjusting jumpers and setting DIP (dual in-line package) switches; the after phase involved configuring a few more device parameters by using some kind of setup program.

What was the purpose of all this adjusting, setting, and configuring? To coax the device into working with our hardware and to avoid conflicts with other devices. For most devices, this required configuring three resources: the Interrupt Request Line (IRQ), the Input/Output (I/O) port address, and the Direct Memory Access (DMA) channel.

The IRQ

The IRQ is a hardware line over which a device (such as a keyboard or a sound card) can send signals (called *interrupts*) to get the attention of the processor when the device is ready to accept or send data. The basic problem is that although you need a separate IRQ for each device that needs one, only 16 IRQs are available to go around. That might sound like plenty, but many of these IRQs are used by system devices. Table 10.1 lists the IRQ distribution in a typical PC.

Table 10.1. IRQ distribution in a typical computer.

IRQ	Device
0	System timer
1	Keyboard
2	Programmable interrupt controller
3	Serial port 2 (COM2)
4	Serial port 1 (COM1)
5	Available, or parallel port 2 (LPT2)
6	Floppy disk controller
7	Parallel port 1 (LPT1)
8	Real-time clock
9	Same as IRQ2
10	Available
11	Available
12	Available
13	Math coprocessor
14	Hard disk controller
15	Available

This only leaves four or five IRQs for your sound card, network card, SCSI controller, motherboard mouse port, video adapter, and whatever other devices you've stuffed inside your machine. An IRQ conflict—either two devices trying to use the same IRQ, or software that thinks a device is using one IRQ when in fact it's using another—is the cause of many hardware problems. Note that some newer buses, most notably PCI and EISA, let devices share IRQs, but few software programs are set up to support interrupt sharing.

The I/O Port Address

An I/O port is a memory address that the processor uses to communicate with a device directly. After a device has used its IRQ to catch the attention of the processor, the actual exchange of data or commands takes place through the device's I/O port address. An I/O port address is expressed as a hexadecimal (base 16) number.

There are 1,024 I/O ports available—more than enough to satisfy all your device needs. As with IRQs, however, no two devices can share an I/O port, so conflicts can lead to problems. Note also that many devices use multiple I/O port addresses. In this case, the I/O port is expressed as a range of hexadecimal numbers.

The DMA Channel

A DMA channel is a connection that lets a device transfer data to and from memory without going through the processor. The transfer is coordinated by a DMA controller chip. Modern computers support eight DMA channels, as shown in Table 10.2.

Table 10.2. IRQ distribution in a typical computer.

DMA Channel	Device
0	Available
1	Available
2	Floppy disk controller
3	Available
4	DMA controller
5	Available
6	Available
7	Available

As with the other resources, problems can arise when two devices attempt to use the same DMA channel. This is a rarer problem, however, because few devices use DMA and most of the DMA channels are available.

More Device Woes

It's bad enough just trying to make sense of all these acronyms and abbreviations, but installing hardware devices is a lonely business because you're on your own. The situation has improved somewhat, because some device setup programs have improved in recent years, and the resources for many recent devices are software selectable. However, we're still left with lots of troubling questions:

- How do you know which resources a device is currently using?
- If a device isn't working properly, which resource—IRQ, I/O port, or DMA channel—is causing the problem?
- Is the problem a conflict with an existing device, or is it that the software trying to access the device is referencing the wrong resource?

■ How do you handle computers that use multiple configurations, such as a notebook computer that has a docking station?

■ How do you handle all the different PC Card (PCMCIA) configurations and standards?

■ What if you change your hardware? Do you have to constantly adjust the resources for your devices?

What the PC world needed badly was a way to manage devices easily. In other words, some kind of new approach to device management was needed that would provide two things:

■ A central repository for hardware information that showed us not only the peripherals attached to our systems, but also which resources they were using and whether any devices were in conflict with each other.

■ "Smart" devices and software that could examine the resources currently being used and that configured the devices accordingly.

Device Support in Windows 95

Windows 95 is the boldest and most ambitious attempt yet by the PC community to solve the thorny problem of device management. From day one, Microsoft designed its new operating system to offer greatly improved support for all kinds of peripherals, including CD-ROMs, printers, SCSI controllers, modems, PCMCIA devices, and video adapters. To that end, Windows 95 comes loaded with new device management features, including the following:

Universal driver/mini-driver architecture: For each hardware class, Windows 95 has a *universal driver* that incorporates the code necessary for the devices in that class to work with the appropriate operating system component (such as the printing subsystem). This universal driver is then augmented with smaller, simpler *mini-drivers* that provide the commands and routines necessary to operate a specific device. (See the later section "Device Driver Architecture" for more information.)

Virtual device drivers: These are drivers that Windows 95 uses to replace the real-mode device drivers used by DOS. They're 32-bit protected-mode drivers that reside in extended memory and that let multiple applications use the device simultaneously. Virtual device driver files use the VXD extension, so they're often referred to as *VxDs*, in which the *x* depends on the device. For example, the virtual device driver for a printer is a VPD, and the virtual device driver for a display is a VDD. Although Windows 3.x also had virtual device drivers (they used the extension 386), they were static: After they were loaded into memory, they stayed there. Windows 95 VxDs, however, are dynamic: They remain in memory only as long as they're needed. Note too that VxDs are used to manage not only devices, but software as well. For example, Windows 95 might load a VxD to emulate, or just keep tabs on, a real-mode driver that was loaded via CONFIG.SYS. (You can get more info on VxDs later, in the section titled "Virtual Device Drivers Versus Real-Mode Drivers.")

10

HOW WINDOWS
95 HANDLES
HARDWARE

Plug and Play support: This is the big news for people who are sick of wrestling with IRQs and other hardware mysteries. The theory behind Plug and Play (PnP) is simple: PnP-compliant hardware can report its current configuration and adjust itself automatically to a new configuration to avoid conflicts with other devices. Windows 95 supports PnP, which means it can work with the reports given by these devices and automatically load or unload the appropriate device drivers. (For a more detailed treatment of Plug and Play, see the section titled "Understanding Plug and Play" later in this chapter.)

Device Manager and the Registry: To satisfy the need for a central repository of device information, Windows 95 serves up two related features: the Device Manager and the Registry. The Device Manager provides a graphical outline of all the devices on your system. It can show you the current configuration of each device (including the IRQ, I/O ports, and DMA channel used by each device). And it even lets you adjust a device's configuration (assuming that the device doesn't require you to make physical adjustments to, say, a DIP switch or jumper). The Device Manager actually gets its data from, and stores modified data in, the Registry. (I'll show you how to use the Device Manager later in this chapter; see the later section "Working with the Device Manager." For the Registry, see Chapter 11, "Introducing the Windows 95 Registry.")

Add New Hardware Wizard: You saw in Chapter 2, "Running the Windows 95 Setup," that the Windows 95 Setup program uses the Detection Manager to automatically detect the devices in your system and the resources used by each device. The Detection Manager is also available after you've installed Windows 95, in the form of the Add New Hardware Wizard. You can use this Wizard to have Windows 95 check your system for new hardware, or you can use it to specify new devices by hand. (I'll take you through the Add New Hardware Wizard in the "Adding New Hardware" section later in this chapter.)

Hardware profiles: Many computers perform double (or even triple) duty. A portable computer, for example, can be used as a simple notebook machine on the road, and it can reside in a docking station at home or at work. It's likely that in each case, the hardware configuration is completely different. To allow for this situation, Windows 95 supports multiple *hardware profiles* for a given machine. In the portable computer example, you could set up one profile to use on the road and another profile to use while the machine is docked. Windows 95 detects the new configuration automatically and switches profiles seamlessly. (See "Setting Up Hardware Profiles" later in this chapter for more information.)

OSR2

IRQ steering: The OSR2 version of Windows 95 supports a relatively new PCI hardware feature called *IRQ steering* (sometimes called *IRQ routing*). This means that the system is capable of intercepting interrupt requests and then "steering" them to the next available IRQ line. This is particularly useful on notebook computers with docking stations, where the hardware configuration can change frequently and drastically.

Understanding Device Drivers

For most users, device drivers exist in the nether regions of the PC world, shrouded in obscurity and the mysteries of assembly language programming. As the middlemen brokering the dialogue between Windows 95 and our hardware, however, these complex chunks of code perform a crucial task. After all, it's just not possible to unleash the full potential of your system unless the hardware and the operating system coexist harmoniously and optimally. To help ensure that this is the case, let's take a closer look at the relationship between Windows 95 and the device drivers it uses to converse with your hardware.

Device Driver Architecture

In Windows 3.x, most device drivers were said to be *monolithic;* that is, each driver included not only the code needed to work with the appropriate operating system component (such as the communications subsystem), but also the specific commands needed for the device. These drivers were large, exceedingly complex, and prone to problems.

Printer drivers were the exception, however. In this case, Windows created a universal printer driver that included all the basic functionality for any printer to work with the Windows printing subsystem. So all that printer manufacturers (or Microsoft itself) had to do was create an extra driver that supplemented the universal driver with the specific commands needed to operate a particular printer. These "mini-drivers" were generally small and simple and much easier to construct than a full-blown piece of monolithic driver code. The result? Printer support in Windows 3.x was, for the most part, seamless (although far from perfect).

In Windows 95, Microsoft decided to take the universal driver/mini-driver model it used for printing in Windows 3.x and apply it to *all* devices. The intent of the Microsoft design team was to make monolithic drivers a thing of the past, so they've been urging developers to write drivers using the new universal driver/mini-driver architecture.

Note that these drivers are all virtual device drivers, so they're fast (because they're 32-bit) and reliable (because they operate in protected mode). Also, many of the universal drivers are robust enough to provide full functionality for standard devices in their class. In these cases, no mini-driver is needed. The universal modem driver (UNIMODEM.VXD), for example, provides complete support for the standard AT command set.

Virtual Device Drivers Versus Real-Mode Drivers

One of the main design goals in Windows 95 was to eliminate, wherever possible, real-mode drivers. Here are a few reasons why real-mode drivers should be *persona non grata* on your system:

■ Real-mode drivers are 16-bit, which means that in some cases, they'll operate slower than the same driver rewritten in 32-bit code. This is *not* universally true, however. A well-written, highly tuned, 16-bit driver can be just as fast as a 32-bit driver that does the same thing.

- Windows 95 operates in protected mode, so when it has to access a real-mode driver, it must perform a time-wasting context switch from protected mode to real mode.

- Real-mode drivers reside either in conventional memory or in upper memory blocks, thus either reducing the pool of available conventional memory (which can slow down DOS programs or cause them to not run at all) or opening the possibility of memory conflicts in upper memory regions.

- The processor provides no built-in protection for real-mode operations, so real-mode drivers are inherently unstable.

All of these problems are fixed by protected-mode drivers: They offer 32-bit performance, Windows 95 doesn't have to waste CPU cycles performing a context switch to use them, they reside in extended memory, and they have the built-in robustness of the processor's protected-mode security.

To help wean users from real-mode drivers, Windows 95 includes VxDs to replace the following Windows 3.x real-mode components:

- The FAT file system (replacement driver: VFAT.VXD)
- The CD-ROM file system (replacement driver: CDFS.VXD)
- SMARTDrive disk cache (replacement driver: VCACHE.VXD)
- Mouse driver (replacement driver: VMOUSE.VXD)
- Network drivers and protocols
- Network client and peer resource sharing server
- SHARE.EXE, the driver for DOS file sharing and locking support (replacement driver: VSHARE.VXD)
- Disk device drivers, including SCSI devices
- DriveSpace (and DoubleSpace) disk compression (replacement driver: DRVSPACX.VXD)

Windows 95 also ships with hundreds of VxDs for specific devices. This means that, in most cases, you can get rid of all the real-mode drivers that you used to load in either CONFIG.SYS or AUTOEXEC.BAT and use the corresponding VxDs in Windows 95. In most cases, this is a simple matter of renaming your CONFIG.SYS and AUTOEXEC.BAT files (to, say, CONFIG.WIN and AUTOEXEC.WIN) and then rebooting. Because Windows 95's Setup program made a note of all the devices in your startup files, it should automatically pick up the slack for each device by loading the appropriate protected-mode driver.

If, after trying this technique, you find that one of your devices isn't working properly, Windows 95 probably doesn't have the correct protected-mode driver. In this case, you need to make two adjustments:

- Restore CONFIG.SYS or AUTOEXEC.BAT (whichever one loads the necessary real-mode driver).

- Edit CONFIG.SYS or AUTOEXEC.BAT to comment out the lines that load real-mode drivers that *do* have a protected-mode counterpart in Windows 95. (Recall that you comment out a line by adding REM and a space to the beginning of the line.)

Reboot your machine when you're done. You should then contact the manufacturer of the device to obtain an updated protected-mode driver. When you get it, follow the instructions given in either the "Drivers for Specific Devices" section or the "Adding New Hardware" section.

Device Driver Loading at Startup

As you learned in Chapter 4, "Start It Your Way: Understanding Windows 95 Startup," when you start or reboot your computer, IO.SYS is called on to perform various jobs. One of those jobs involves processing your startup files and loading any real-mode drivers from the DEVICE lines mentioned in these files.

After IO.SYS has finished dealing with the startup files, it then loads the following components of Windows 95:

- WIN.COM, which starts Windows 95 and controls the loading of the core Windows 95 components

- VMM32.VXD —the Virtual Memory Manager—which creates the virtual machines and initiates the loading of the VxDs

- SYSTEM.INI, which is read for entries that differ from those stored in the Registry

(This process is also followed when you restart Windows 95.) The Virtual Memory Manager then switches the processor into protected-mode and begins loading the protected-mode drivers. Table 10.3 lists just some of the drivers that are loaded via the Virtual Memory Manager.

Table 10.3. A partial list of device drivers loaded from VMM32.VXD.

Driver	Description
BIOS	BIOS Plug and Play Enumerator
BIOSXLAT	BIOS Translation Device Driver
CONFIGMG	Plug and Play Configuration Manager
DOSMGR	MS-DOS Device Driver
EBIOS	PS/2 Extended BIOS Device Driver
IFSMGR	Installable File System Manager
INT13	Fixed Disk Interrupt Driver
IOS	Input/Output Supervisor
PAGEFILE	Paging File Device
PAGESWAP	Demand Paging Swap Device

10

HOW WINDOWS 95 HANDLES HARDWARE

continues

Table 10.3. continued

Driver	Description
PARITY	Parity-checking Device
REBOOT	System Reboot Device
SHELL	Shell Interface Device
SPOOLER	Print Spooler
V86MMGR	Virtual 8086-mode Memory Manager
VCACHE	Virtual Cache Manager
VCD	Virtual Communications Device
VCDFSD	CD-ROM File System Driver
VCOMM	Windows 95 Communications Device Driver
VCOND	Virtual Console Device for WIN32 Console Subsystem
VDD	Virtual Display Device
VDMAD	Virtual Direct Memory Access Device
VFAT	32-bit File System Driver
VFBACKUP	Helper Driver for Backup Applications
VFD	Virtual Floppy Device
VKD	Virtual Keyboard Device
VMCPD	Virtual Math Coprocessor Device
VMD	Virtual Mouse Device
VMM	Virtual Machine Manager
VMPOLL	Virtual Machine Polling Detection Device
VPD	Virtual Printer Device
VPICD	Virtual Programmable Interrupt Controller Device
VPOWERD	Virtual Advanced Power Management Device
VSD	Virtual Sound Device
VSHARE	File Sharing Support Driver
VTD	Virtual Timer Device
VTDAPI	Multimedia Timer Services Driver
VWIN32	Windows 95 Win32 Support Driver
VXDLDR	VxD Loader device

You'll notice in Table 10.3 that one of the devices that's called is CONFIGMG, the Configuration Manager. This driver polls the computer's Plug and Play BIOS (if it has one) for device configuration. If the computer doesn't have a PnP BIOS, Configuration Manager polls the various PnP-compliant devices for their configuration information. The necessary device drivers are loaded for these peripherals, and then Configuration Manager checks for resource conflicts. If it finds any, it resolves them and then sends the new configuration information to the various devices. At this point, Windows 95 is ready to roll. (I'll discuss Configuration Manager in more detail when I talk about Plug and Play later in the next section.)

Understanding Plug and Play

The Holy Grail of device configuration is a setup in which you need only to insert or plug in a peripheral and turn it on (if necessary), and your system configures the device automatically. In other words, the system not only recognizes that a new device is attached to the machine, but it also gleans the device's default resource configuration and, if required, resolves any conflicts that might have arisen with existing devices. And, of course, it should be able to perform all this magic without your ever having to flip a DIP switch, fiddle with a jumper, or fuss with various IRQ, I/O port, and DMA combinations.

Plug and Play, at least as far as the theory goes, is an attempt by members of the PC community to reach this Zen-like state. Did they succeed? Yes and no. Yes, Plug and Play works like a charm, but only if your system meets the following criteria:

- It has a Plug and Play BIOS
- It uses Plug and Play devices
- It uses Windows 95 (or some other Plug and Play operating system)

If you don't have all three components, Plug and Play might or might not work, depending on your configuration. The next few sections take a closer look at each part of the Plug and Play equation.

The Plug and Play BIOS

As I mentioned in Chapter 4, one of the first things that happens inside your computer when you turn it on (or do a hardware reboot) is the ROM BIOS (basic input/output system) code performs a Power-On Self Test to check the system hardware. If you have a system with a Plug and Play BIOS, the initial code also enumerates and tests all the Plug and Play–compliant devices on the system. For each device, the BIOS not only activates the device, but also gathers the device's resource configuration (IRQ, I/O ports, and so forth). When all the Plug and Play devices have been isolated, the BIOS then checks for resource conflicts and, if there are any, takes steps to resolve them.

Most computers sold today have a Plug and Play BIOS. If you're thinking of investing in a new system, be sure to put this type of BIOS on your "must have" list. If your existing system doesn't have a Plug and Play BIOS, contact your computer manufacturer to see whether an upgrade BIOS chip is available. As you'll see, though, as long as you have Windows 95, you can still reap some of the benefits of Plug and Play even if you don't have a Plug and Play BIOS.

10

How Windows 95 Handles Hardware

Plug and Play Devices

Plug and Play devices are the *sine qua non* of the Plug and Play movement, and it's on the device level that Plug and Play will succeed or fail. That's because a Plug and Play BIOS or operating system isn't worth a hill of beans if it has no Plug and Play–compliant devices to enumerate and work with. Sure, Windows 95 does a good job of recognizing legacy devices (as pre–Plug and Play devices are usually called), but any kind of automatic configuration and detection of legacy hardware is highly unlikely.

The secret of Plug and Play devices is that these peripherals are the extroverts of the hardware world. They're only too happy to chat with any old Plug and Play BIOS or operating system that happens along. What do they chat about? The device essentially identifies itself to the BIOS (or the operating system if the BIOS isn't Plug and Play–compliant) by sending its *configuration ID*, which tells the BIOS what the device is and which resources it uses. The BIOS then configures the system's resources accordingly. One of the early hairs found in the Plug and Play soup is that some devices report the same configuration ID! Over time, however, these kinds of problems will sort themselves out as Plug and Play becomes the standard (if it isn't already).

Plug and Play in Windows 95: The Configuration Manager

Windows 95 gathers the information on the system's Plug and Play devices—either by grabbing the data collected by the Plug and Play BIOS at startup (via the BIOS.VXD virtual device driver) or by enumerating the devices directly—and stores everything in the Registry. The component that performs this bit of hardware dirty work is called Configuration Manager. Recall from our look at the Windows 95 architecture in Chapter 9, "Windows 95 Performance Tuning and Optimization," that Configuration Manager sits just above the device driver level, as illustrated in Figure 6.1 in the preceding chapter. It's a virtual device driver (CONFIGMG.VXD) that's loaded at startup as part of the Virtual Memory Manager (VMM32.VXD). Not only can Configuration Manager enumerate all the Plug and Play devices on a system, but it also can check the device resources for conflicts, reconfigure the devices to resolve conflicts, and detect when the system's hardware setup changes.

Here's how Configuration Manager goes about isolating and configuring the system's Plug and Play devices:

1. Configuration Manager calls various *bus enumerators* to identify the devices running off each system bus. (A *bus* is a pathway along which signals are sent between components.) A bus enumerator is a driver that is specific to a particular type of bus (such as the keyboard controller bus or the SCSI bus).

2. Each bus enumerator gathers information on the resources used by each device on the bus, either by using the BIOS or by polling the appropriate device driver (if one is even loaded yet).

3. When the devices have been identified, Configuration Manager loads a driver for each device.

4. Configuration Manager calls various *resource arbitrators* to check the reported device resources for conflicts and, if any are found, to resolve them. Windows 95 has resource arbitrators for IRQs, I/O port addresses, and DMA channels.

5. Configuration Manager assigns resources to each device via the appropriate device driver.

If the system's hardware setup changes while Windows 95 is running (if you insert a PC Card device, for example), either the BIOS or a bus enumerator informs Configuration Manager of the change and the process just described is repeated to keep the current hardware configuration up-to-date.

Working with the Device Manager

As I mentioned earlier, Windows 95 stores all of its hardware data in the Registry, but it provides the Device Manager to give you a graphical view of the devices on your system. To display the Device Manager, use either of the following techniques:

■ Select Start | Settings | Control Panel, and open the System icon in the Control Panel window.

■ Right-click My Computer and select Properties from the context menu.

In the System Properties dialog box that appears, select the Device Manager tab, as shown in Figure 10.1. Device Manager's default display is a treelike outline that lists various hardware classes (CD-ROM, disk drives, and so on).

FIGURE 10.1.

The Device Manager shows you a visual representation of all the devices on your system.

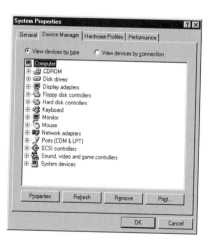

To see the specific devices, click the plus sign (+) to the left of a device class, or highlight the class and press the + key on the keyboard's numeric keypad. For example, opening the Disk drives class displays all the disk drives attached to your computer, as shown in Figure 10.2.

FIGURE 10.2.

Opening a hardware class shows you the specific devices within that class that are attached to your computer.

If you like, you can also view the devices according to the component to which they're connected by activating the View devices by connection option button. This is handy, for example, if you want to see the devices attached to your SCSI controller.

Viewing Devices by IRQ, I/O Port, and DMA Channel

I mentioned earlier that one of the major problems associated with device management was knowing which of your system's hardware resources were being used, and by which device. This is particularly true of limited resources such as IRQs and DMA channels. One of Device Manager's most powerful features is its capability to show you a list of your devices according to the hardware resources they use. To try this, highlight the Computer item at the top of the list and then click the Properties button. You'll see the Computer Properties dialog box, shown in Figure 10.3. Use the option buttons at the top of the dialog box to select the type of resource you want to view. (The Memory option shows you which areas of upper memory are being used by your devices.)

FIGURE 10.3.

Use the Computer Properties dialog box to view your devices by specific resources.

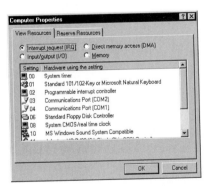

NOTE: RESERVING RESOURCES

If your system has legacy devices and you plan to install a Plug and Play device, there's a chance the Plug and Play device will end up using a resource that belongs to one of the legacy peripherals. To prevent this from happening, Device Manager lets you reserve the resources used by your legacy devices so that they can't be assigned to a different device. In the Computer Properties dialog box, select the Reserve Resources tab. For each resource you want to reserve, use the option buttons to activate the appropriate resource type, click Add, enter the resource value, and click OK.

Printing a System Report

Device Manager's hardware listing and the capability to view devices by resource are among the highlights of the Windows 95 package. However, Device Manager won't do you a lick of good if you're having some kind of hardware problem that prevents you from starting Windows 95. That might never happen, but just in case it does, you should print a hard copy of the device data. Here's how you do so:

1. If you want a printout of only a specific hardware class or device, use the Device Manager list to highlight the class or device.
2. Click the Print button to display the Print dialog box, shown in Figure 10.4.

FIGURE 10.4.

You can get a printout of your system's device information.

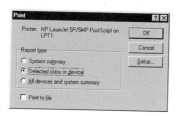

3. In the Report type group, select one of the following report options:

   System summary: A summary of resource usage on your system: IRQs, I/O ports, DMA channels, and upper memory.

   Selected class or device: The driver and resource data for the highlighted hardware class or device.

   All devices and system summary: Both the summary of resource usage on your system, and the driver and resource data for every device.

4. To make printer adjustments, click Setup, select the options you want from the Print Setup dialog box, and click OK.
5. Click OK to print the report.

10

How Windows 95 Handles Hardware

Removing a Device

If your computer has a Plug and Play BIOS and you remove a device, the BIOS informs Windows 95 that the device is no longer present. Windows 95, in turn, updates its device list in the Registry, and the peripheral no longer appears in the Device Manager tab.

If you don't have a Plug and Play BIOS, but the device you're removing is Plug and Play–compliant, Configuration Manager figures out that the device is missing and updates Windows 95 accordingly.

If you're removing a legacy device, however, you need to tell Device Manager that the device no longer exists. To do that, highlight the device in the Device Manager tab and click the Remove button. If you've defined multiple hardware profiles (as described later, in the "Setting Up Hardware Profiles" section), Windows 95 will ask if you want to remove the device from all the profiles or just from a specific profile. Select the appropriate option. When Windows 95 warns you that you're about to remove the device, click OK.

CAUTION: DON'T FORGET TO REMOVE THE DEVICE

If you remove a device from the Device Manager, you must also remove the physical device from your system. Otherwise, either the BIOS or Windows 95 will just detect the device all over again, or the device's resources won't be freed for other devices to use.

Viewing Device Properties

Each device listed in the Device Manager has its own properties sheet. You can use these properties sheets not only to learn more about the device (such as the resources it's currently using), but also to make adjustments to the device's resources, change the device driver, alter the device's settings (if it has any), and make other changes.

To display the properties sheet for a device, display the device in the Device Manager tab, and then either double-click the device or highlight the device and click Properties. Figure 10.5 shows the properties sheet for a SCSI controller. The General tab tells you the name of the device and its hardware class, the manufacturer's name, and the hardware version (if known). The Device status group lets you know whether the device is working properly. You use the Device usage group to add and remove devices from *hardware profiles* (see "Setting Up Hardware Profiles" later in this chapter).

Besides this general information, a device's properties sheet includes a wealth of other useful data. Depending on the device, the properties sheet can also tell you the resources used by the device, the device driver, and miscellaneous settings specific to the device. I cover each of these items in the next few sections.

FIGURE 10.5.

The properties sheet for a SCSI controller.

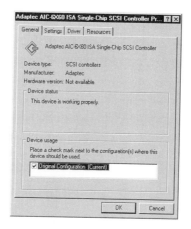

Viewing and Adjusting a Device's Resources

To view the resources being used by the device (if any), select the Resources tab, shown in Figure 10.6. `Resource settings` is a two-column list that shows you the resource type on the left and the resource setting on the right. If you suspect that the device has a resource conflict, check the `Conflicting devices list` to see whether any devices are listed. If the list displays only `No conflicts`, the device's resources aren't conflicting with another device.

FIGURE 10.6.

The Resources tab outlines the resources used by the device.

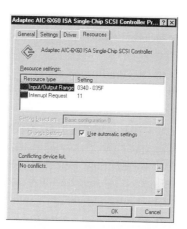

If, however, you do have a conflict, you'll need to change the appropriate resource. Some devices have multiple configurations, so one easy way to change resources is to select a different configuration. To try this, use the `Setting based on` drop-down list to select a different configuration.

Otherwise, you'll need to play around with the resource settings by hand. Here are the steps to follow to change a resource setting:

1. In the Resource settings list, highlight the resource you want to change.

2. Deactivate the Use automatic settings check box, if it's activated.

3. For the setting you want to change, either double-click it or highlight it and click the Change Setting button. You'll see an Edit dialog box similar to the one shown in Figure 10.7.

FIGURE 10.7.

Use this dialog box to change an IRQ. Other resources display similar dialog boxes.

4. Use the Value spinner to select a different resource. Watch the Conflict information group to make sure that your new setting doesn't step on the toes of an existing setting.

5. Click OK to return to the Resources tab.

6. Click OK. If Windows 95 asks whether you want to restart your computer, click Yes.

Changing Drivers via the Device Manager

In a device's properties sheet, the Driver tab tells you the current driver associated with the device. In Figure 10.8, for example, you can see that the driver for this SCSI controller is SPARROW.MPD, and it's located in the C:\WINDOWS\SYSTEM\IOSUBSYS\ folder. The File details group also provides information about the driver's manufacturer and version number.

NOTE: MINIPORT DRIVERS

Why does the driver shown in Figure 10.8 have an MPD extension? This is an example of a mini-driver I told you about earlier. Windows 95 has a universal SCSI driver, so SCSI controller manufacturers need only create mini-drivers for their devices. In this case, these drivers are called *miniport drivers*—hence the MPD extension. I'll fill you in on the details of the Windows 95 file system architecture in Chapter 13, "Working with Files and Folders."

FIGURE 10.8.

Use the Driver tab to get information about the device's driver and to change the driver.

If you need to change the driver (for example, if you've obtained an updated driver from the manufacturer), here are the steps to plow through:

1. Click the Change Driver button to display the Select Device dialog box, shown in Figure 10.9.

FIGURE 10.9.

Use the Select Device dialog box to change the driver.

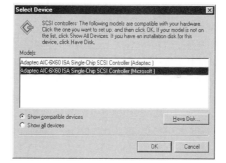

2. If the driver you want to use is shown in the Models list, highlight it and skip to step 8.

3. Activate the Show all devices option to display the full list of available drivers, as shown in Figure 10.10.

FIGURE 10.10.

Activating Show all devices displays Windows 95's complete list of drivers for this hardware class.

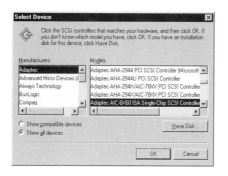

4. If, after you highlight the appropriate device manufacturer in the Manufacturers list, the driver you want appears in the Models list, highlight it and skip to step 8.

5. If you have a disk from the manufacturer, insert the disk and then click the Have Disk button.

6. In the Install from Disk dialog box, enter the appropriate drive and folder in the Copy manufacturer's files from box, and click OK. Windows 95 displays a list of possible device drivers in the Select Device dialog box.

7. Highlight the driver you want to install.

8. Click OK to return to the properties sheet.

9. Click OK. Windows 95 asks whether you want to restart your computer.

10. Click Yes to reboot and put the new driver into effect.

Adjusting Device Settings

Some devices have a Settings tab in their properties sheet that lets you set various options specific to the device. For a CD-ROM drive, for example, you can specify the drive letter to use and whether the drive runs the Windows 95 AutoPlay feature. For a SCSI controller, you can add any command-line parameters or switches the driver might need.

If you have an older Pentium, one of the most useful of the Settings tabs is the one for the numeric data processor. You might recall the big Pentium scandal of late 1994, when it was discovered that the Pentium chip had a bug that produced arithmetic errors in certain (rare) conditions. Windows 95 can check for these faulty Pentium CPUs and optionally disable the numeric data processor until you can get an upgraded chip. To see whether your CPU has this bug, open Device Manager's System devices tree, display the properties sheet for the Numeric data processor, and select the Settings tab. If your CPU is flawed, you'll see the dialog box shown in Figure 10.11. To disable the coprocessor, activate the Never use the numeric data processor option.

FIGURE 10.11.

You'll see this Settings tab if your machine has one of the faulty Pentium processors.

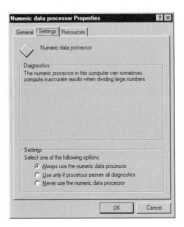

Enabling IRQ Steering in OSR2

Earlier I told you that OSR2 supports IRQ steering on PCI machines. To make sure that this support is enabled on your machine, follow these steps:

1. In Device Manager, open the System devices branch.

2. Highlight PCI bus and then click Properties.

3. In the properties sheet that appears, activate the IRQ Steering tab, shown in Figure 10.12.

FIGURE 10.12.

Use the IRQ Steering tab to activate IRQ steering on your OSR2 machine.

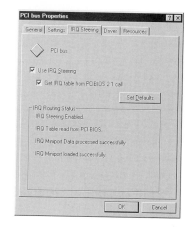

4. Activate the Use IRQ Steering check box.

5. To allow the PCI bus to get the IRQ table directly from the PCI BIOS (that is, without using Windows 95 as an intermediary), activate the Get IRQ table from PCIBIOS 2.1 call check box.

6. Click OK to return to the System Properties dialog box.

7. Click OK.

8. When Windows 95 asks if you want to restart your computer, click Yes.

Adding New Hardware

You've seen how the Windows 95 Setup program made hardware installation a breeze by detecting your devices automatically. You can get the same level of convenience after Windows 95 is installed by cranking up the Add New Hardware Wizard. This Wizard essentially just runs the Detection Manager all over again with a few extra bells and whistles thrown in (I explained in Chapter 1 how the Detection Manager works). If you'd prefer to specify the new device, or if you have a disk from the manufacturer, the Add New Hardware Wizard also lets you install individual devices by hand.

10

HOW WINDOWS 95 HANDLES HARDWARE

In either case, though, you need to display the Add New Hardware Wizard. To do that, select Start | Settings | Control Panel, and then open the Add New Hardware icon in the `Control Panel` folder. Windows 95 displays the first of the Add New Hardware Wizard's dialog boxes. Click Next > to continue and you'll see the dialog box shown in Figure 10.13. You use this dialog box to choose the Add New Hardware Wizard method you want to use. Select `Yes (Recommended)` to have the Wizard detect your hardware automatically; select `No` to specify the device manually. Click Next > to continue. The next two sections take you through both methods.

FIGURE 10.13.

Use this dialog box to decide how you want to work with the Add New Hardware Wizard.

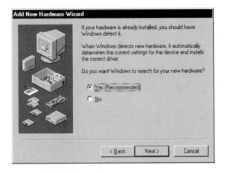

Automatically Detecting New Devices

If you elected to have the Add New Hardware Wizard detect your devices automatically, the next dialog box that appears just warns you that your computer might stop responding. Click Next > to begin the detection progress. Note that the Wizard checks *all* your hardware, so this process will take a few minutes.

When the Wizard has completed its labors, it lets you know whether it found any new devices. (It also lets you know if a device has been removed.) If the Wizard did find new hardware, click the Details button to display a list of the devices, as shown in Figure 10.14. Click Finish. Depending on the device, you might need to run through a configuration process. Follow the instructions on-screen, and reboot when prompted.

FIGURE 10.14.

If the Wizard finds new hardware, click `Details` *to see a list of the devices.*

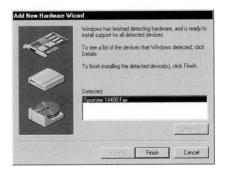

Specifying New Devices Manually

Rather than going through the lengthy detection process, you might prefer just to specify your new hardware manually. This is particularly true if you have a disk from the manufacturer that contains the drivers for the device. If you selected No in the second Add New Hardware Wizard dialog box, clicking Next > displays a list of hardware classes, as shown in Figure 10.15.

FIGURE 10.15.

If you elected to specify a device manually, the Wizard displays this list of hardware classes.

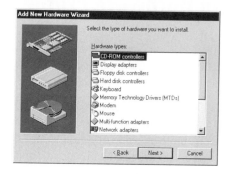

Here are the steps to follow to specify a device manually:

1. In the Hardware types list, highlight the hardware class for your device and click Next >. The Wizard displays the Select Device dialog box with a list of the manufacturers and models that Windows 95 knows about for the hardware class. For example, Figure 10.16 shows the dialog box that appears for the Network adapters class.

FIGURE 10.16.

The device list for the Network adapters class. Other hardware classes display similar lists.

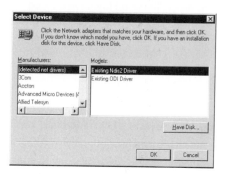

2. If, after you highlight the appropriate device manufacturer the Manufacturers list, the driver you want appears in the Models list, highlight it and skip to step 6.

3. If you have a disk from the manufacturer, insert the disk and then click the Have Disk button.

4. In the Install from Disk dialog box, enter the appropriate drive and folder in the Copy manufacturer's files from box, and then click OK. Windows 95 displays a list of possible device drivers in the Select Device dialog box.

5. Highlight the driver you want to install.

6. Click OK to return to the properties sheet.

7. Click OK. Windows 95 asks whether you want to restart your computer.

8. Click Yes to reboot and put the new driver into effect.

Setting Up Hardware Profiles

In most cases, your hardware configuration will remain relatively static. You might add the odd new device (see "Adding New Hardware" earlier in this chapter) or remove a device (see "Removing a Device" earlier in this chapter), but these are permanent changes. Windows 95 merely updates its current hardware configuration to compensate.

In some situations, however, you might need to switch between hardware configurations regularly. A good example is a notebook computer with a docking station. When the computer is undocked, it uses its built-in keyboard, mouse, and display; when the computer is docked, however, it uses a separate keyboard, mouse, and display. To make it easier to switch between these different configurations, Windows 95 lets you set up a *hardware profile* for each setup. It then becomes a simple matter of your selecting the profile you want to use at startup; Windows 95 handles the hard part of loading the appropriate drivers.

NOTE: YOU DON'T NEED PROFILES WITH PLUG AND PLAY

You don't need to bother with hardware profiles if your computer has a Plug and Play BIOS and you're using Plug and Play devices. Plug and Play detects any new hardware configuration automatically and adjusts accordingly. For example, Plug and Play supports *hot docking* of a notebook computer: While the machine is running, you can insert it into, or remove it from, the docking station, and Plug and Play handles the switch without breaking a sweat.

Creating a New Hardware Profile

Before creating a new hardware profile, run the Add New Hardware Wizard to install the drivers you need for all the hardware you'll be using. If the hardware isn't currently installed, that's OK; just be sure to specify the appropriate devices by hand in the Add New Hardware Wizard. The important thing is to make sure that all the drivers you'll need are installed.

After that's done (and you've rebooted to put the changes into effect), display the System Properties dialog box, and select the Hardware Profiles tab. On most systems, you'll see a single profile named Original Configuration, as shown in Figure 10.17. This profile includes all the installed device drivers. The idea is that you create a new profile by making a copy of this configuration, and then you tell Windows 95 which devices to include in each profile.

FIGURE 10.17.

The Hardware Profiles tab lists the currently defined profiles.

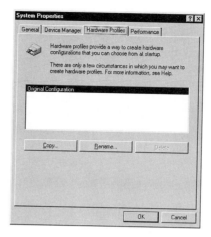

To make a copy of the profile, click the Copy button, enter a name for the new profile in the Copy Profile dialog box, and click OK.

If you want to rename a profile, highlight the profile, click Rename, enter the new name in the Rename Profile dialog box, and click OK. For example, on my notebook machine I renamed `Original Configuration` to `Undocked` to go along with the new `Docked` profile I created, as shown in Figure 10.18.

FIGURE 10.18.

Here, I've added a new profile and renamed the original profile.

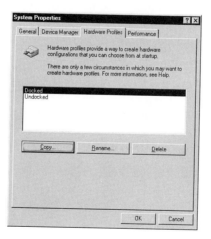

Adding and Removing Devices in a Hardware Profile

Now that you have multiple profiles in place, you need to tell Windows 95 which devices go with which profile. Return to the Device Manager tab, and open the properties sheet for a device you need to adjust. The `Device usage` group lists the names of your profiles with check boxes beside them, as shown in Figure 10.19. If you want to exclude the device from a particular profile, deactivate that profile's check box, and then click OK to return to the Device Manager tab. Repeat this procedure for each device that needs adjusting.

FIGURE 10.19.

The properties sheet for each device lets you include or exclude the device from each profile.

NOTE: DEVICE USAGE IN OSR2

The `Device usage` group is slightly different in OSR2. To remove a device from the current hardware profile, deactivate its `Disable in this hardware profile` check box. There is also an `Exists in all hardware profiles` check box that gives you an easy way to add or remove a device from all your profiles—even new ones that you create.

Dealing with Ambiguous Profiles

How does Windows 95 know which profile to use? Generally, it goes by the current hardware configuration. For example, if you have a Docked hardware profile that uses an external keyboard, Windows 95 will use this profile at startup if it detects an attached keyboard.

Note, however, that *all* of the devices in a profile must match the physical devices present in the system before Windows 95 will use a profile automatically. If there is some ambiguity (that is, the physical devices don't match the devices specified in the profile), Windows 95 will display a menu of hardware profiles at startup. This menu will be similar to the following example:

```
Windows cannot determine what configuration your computer is in.
Select one of the following:
  1. Docked
  2. Undocked
  3. None of the above
Enter your choice:
```

In this case, you need to select the hardware profile you want Windows 95 to use.

Drivers for Specific Devices

Windows 95's device driver list is truly impressive. It includes protected-mode drivers for just about any class of hardware you can think of. The next few sections discuss Windows 95's driver support for specific device classes and show you the basic steps for updating or installing new drivers in each class.

CD-ROM Device Drivers

To support CD-ROM drives, Windows 95 uses a 32-bit protected-mode driver named VCDFSD.VXD (the CDFS stands for CD-ROM File System). This driver replaces MSCDEX.EXE, the real-mode driver used in previous versions of DOS and Windows. If a line loading MSCDEX.EXE already existed in AUTOEXEC.BAT when you installed Windows 95, the Setup program comments out the line and adds VCDFSD.VXD to its list of protected-mode drivers to load at startup. If you've added a CD-ROM drive since installing Windows 95, you need to run the Add New Hardware Wizard (in automatic mode) to detect the drive and load VCDFSD.VXD. (The exception to this rule is if your CD-ROM drive is attached to a SCSI controller. In this case, Windows 95 will detect the drive automatically at startup.)

With CDFS, you should notice improved performance from your CD-ROM drive. Not only is CDFS faster than the old real-mode driver, but it also boasts improved multitasking capabilities, and it works with VCACHE (the protected-mode cache driver) to create a separate (and dynamic) pool of cache memory to help optimize CD-ROM performance. I showed you how to make adjustments to the CD-ROM cache in the preceding chapter.

Communications Device Drivers

The monolithic communications driver from Windows 3.x—COMM.DRV—has been replaced by a new driver in Windows 95: VCOMM. (Actually, Windows replaced COMM.DRV with an entirely new communications architecture, of which VCOMM is a major part.) The VCOMM driver, which loads as part of VMM32.VXD, gives applications a protected-mode interface for accessing communications ports and modems, as detailed here:

Communications port drivers: VCOMM isn't a driver for communications ports (serial and parallel ports) per se, but rather it calls specific *port drivers* that then access the I/O ports directly. For serial ports, VCOMM calls SERIAL.VXD; for parallel ports, VCOMM calls LPT.VXD; for third-party communications products, manufacturers can write mini-drivers that VCOMM can call to access the ports. (In Windows 3.x, the manufacturer would have to write a monolithic driver that covered the entire communications subsystem.)

Modem drivers: VCOMM uses a universal modem driver (UNIMODEM.VXD) that covers the entire AT command set. Applications can then use this driver (via VCOMM) to dial, answer, and configure modems without using AT commands directly. All that each modem manufacturer must supply is a mini-driver that specifies the modem's AT command set variations and enhancements.

To install a modem in Windows 95, select Start | Settings | Control Panel, and then open the Modems icon in the `Control Panel` folder. If this is the first time you've selected this icon, Windows 95 runs the Install New Modem Wizard, as shown in Figure 10.20, which takes you through the installation procedure. Otherwise, the Modems Properties dialog box appears, from which you can add or remove modems. Both procedures are covered in full in Chapter 25, "Maximizing Modem Communications."

FIGURE 10.20.

You use the Install New Modem Wizard to install your first modem.

Graphics Adapter Device Drivers

You'll find that graphics adapters—even if you're still using an older, unaccelerated card—perform much faster under Windows 95 than they did under Windows 3.x. That's because Windows 95 uses a fast 32-bit driver called the *device-independent bitmap* (DIB) engine. The DIB engine uses the 32-bit features found in 386 and higher processors to optimize calls to the GDI and so speed up display operations. Mini-drivers written by graphics adapter manufacturers need only provide routines for managing low-level adapter functions.

The device driver for the graphics adapter is controlled via the Display Properties dialog box (right-click the desktop and select Properties, or open the Display icon in Control Panel). Activate the Settings tab and then click the Change Display Type button. The Change Display Type dialog box that appears, shown in Figure 10.21, lets you change the adapter driver and the monitor type. I run through these and other display issues in Chapter 22, "Miscellaneous Multimedia: Graphics, CD-ROMs, and More."

FIGURE 10.21.

Use the Change Display Type dialog box to change your adapter driver and your monitor type.

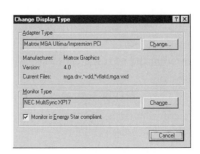

Infrared Device Drivers

For many years, computer gurus touted the "paperless office" as the ultimate goal for the technological revolution. That proved to be a miserable failure (we're all still drowning in paper), so now the gurus have switches horses. Their latest battle cry is for the "cableless office" that uses infrared (IR) ports to exchange data between machines.

We're a long way from the ideal, but inroads are being made. Many of the latest notebook computers and printers have built-in IR ports, and there are even IR devices you can attach to an older computer's serial or parallel ports.

At first, Windows 95 had to rely on third-party drivers to support notebooks and printers with IR ports. However, Microsoft released its own Infrared Data Association (IrDA) communications driver at the end of 1995, and it's included in the Windows 95 Service Pack. If you don't have the Service Pack, you can get the driver from the Microsoft FTP site (the filename is W95IR.EXE) or from the following Web site:

```
http://www.microsoft.com/windows/software/irda.htm
```

I show you how to use notebook IR ports with Windows 95 in Chapter 20, "Windows 95 on the Road: Notebook Computers and the Briefcase," and I show you how to use printer IR ports in Chapter 19, "Prescriptions for Perfect Printing."

Keyboard Device Drivers

Windows 95 replaced the Windows 3.x keyboard driver—KEYBOARD.DRV—with a virtual keyboard driver—VKD.VXD—that loads as part of VMM32.VXD. To specify a different keyboard device, use either of the following techniques:

■ Select Start | Settings | Control Panel, and then open the Keyboard icon in the Control Panel folder. In the Keyboard Properties dialog box, select the General tab, and click the Change button.

■ In Device Manager, open the properties sheet for the keyboard, select the Driver tab, and click Change Driver.

Mouse Device Drivers

In Windows 3.x, mouse support was provided by two different drivers: a driver for Windows-based applications, and a separate driver for DOS-based applications. Both were real-mode drivers. Windows 95 uses a virtual mouse driver called VMOUSE.VXD to provide mouse support for both Windows and DOS programs. VMOUSE is a universal driver, and Windows 95 uses mini-drivers to implement functionality for specific mouse devices. For example, if you have a Microsoft mouse (or one that's compatible), the mini-driver is MSMOUSE.VXD; for a Logitech mouse, Windows 95 uses LMOUSE.VXD.

10

HOW WINDOWS
95 HANDLES
HARDWARE

If you need to change your mouse driver, use either of the following techniques:

■ Select Start | Settings | Control Panel, and open the Mouse icon in the Control Panel folder. In the Mouse Properties dialog box, select the General tab and click the Change button.

■ In Device Manager, open the properties sheet for the mouse, select the Driver tab, and click Change Driver.

PCMCIA (PC Card) Device Drivers

Windows 95 ships with protected-mode drivers for PCMCIA (Personal Computer Memory Card International Association; now called PC Card) sockets and includes protected-mode drivers for PCMCIA devices. If Setup detects any real-mode PCMCIA drivers in CONFIG.SYS, it comments them out. These 32-bit drivers support Plug and Play, so PCMCIA devices are *hot-swappable* in Windows 95 (that is, you can insert and remove a device while Windows 95 is running).

To specify a different PCMCIA driver, use Device Manager to open the properties sheet for the PCMCIA controller, select the Driver tab, and click Change Driver. I discuss Windows 95's support for PCMCIA devices in full when I discuss notebook computers in Chapter 20.

Printer Device Drivers

I mentioned earlier that Windows 95's universal driver/mini-driver architecture was based on the driver model used for printers in Windows 3.x. So it should come as no surprise that this printing model was maintained in Windows 95 and upgraded to an enhanced protected-mode version. The drivers in the new printing subsystem have many new features, including these:

■ Bidirectional communications with printers

■ Improved background spooling and the use of enhanced metafile (EMF) spooling for non-PostScript documents, which reduces the time between sending the data to the printer and returning to your application

■ Improved conflict resolution when DOS and Windows applications attempt to print simultaneously

■ Deferred printing support that lets notebook users send print jobs to the queue and then print them later (for example, when they arrive at the office)

■ Point and Print support that lets network users install printer drivers simply by accessing shared network printers

These and many other Windows printing features are covered in Chapter 19.

To add a printer driver, select Start | Settings | Printers, and then open the Add Printer icon in the Printers folder. The Add Printer Wizard that appears, shown in Figure 10.22, guides you through the steps (as explained in Chapter 19).

FIGURE 10.22.
Use the Add Printer Wizard to set up a printer on your system.

SCSI Controller Device Drivers

Unlike Windows 3.x, Windows 95 comes with SCSI controller support built right into the operating system. A protected-mode driver (called the *SCSI layer*) provides the universal driver support, and then each manufacturer writes mini-drivers (called *miniport drivers*) for its specific devices. I discuss this SCSI support in more detail when I talk about Windows 95's file system architecture in the next chapter.

You work with SCSI controller device drivers (that is, the miniport drivers) via the Device Manager. Under the SCSI controller hardware class, highlight the controller, open its properties sheet, select the Driver tab, and click the Change Driver button.

Troubleshooting Hardware Headaches

As you've seen, Windows 95's support for hardware of all stripes is vastly improved over what was found in Windows 3.x. From Plug and Play to the universal driver/mini-driver architecture, hardware has never been so easy for non-Mac users. Still, that doesn't mean hardware is foolproof; far from it. Things still can, and will, go wrong, so you'll need to perform some kind of troubleshooting. (Assuming, that is, that you're not just dealing with a part that has kicked the electronic bucket.) Fortunately, Windows 95 also has some handy tools to help you both identify and rectify hardware ills.

Troubleshooting with the Performance Tab

If your system feels sluggish, it might be because Windows 95 is being dragged down by 16-bit real-mode drivers. Windows 95 can often recognize this and will warn you. For example, you might see a dialog box like the one shown in Figure 10.23. To find out more about the problem, click Yes. Windows 95 displays the System Properties dialog box and selects the Performance tab. As you can see in Figure 10.24, the performance tab shows the problem: The FLASHPT driver (a SCSI controller driver loaded in CONFIG.SYS) is forcing Windows 95 to operate all disk drives in MS-DOS compatibility mode, which causes a sizable performance hit. The solution here is to remove the driver from CONFIG.SYS and let Windows 95 use its

32-bit SCSI driver. (Note too that an updated, 32-bit miniport driver for the SCSI controller will also likely need to be installed.)

FIGURE 10.23.

Windows 95 often warns you if the system is using a real-mode driver that might adversely affect performance.

FIGURE 10.24.

Use the Performance tab in the System Properties dialog box to investigate the problem.

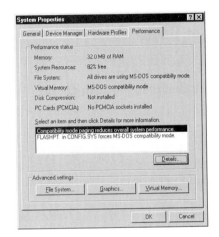

Device Manager as a Troubleshooting Tool

Device Manager's capability to list devices and let you change their resources is impressive enough. But this handy utility is also a powerful troubleshooting tool. To see what I mean, check out the Device Manager tab, shown in Figure 10.25. See how the icon for the MS Windows Sound System Compatible device has an exclamation mark (!) icon superimposed on it? This tells you that there's a problem with the device. If you examine the device's properties, as shown in Figure 10.26, the Device status area tells you a bit more about what's wrong. As you can see in Figure 10.26, though, Windows 95's status messages can be a bit vague. (I'll discuss the various error codes produced by Device Manager later in this section.) To narrow down the problem even further, try the Resources tab. If there's a resource conflict, the Conflicting device list tells you which resource is causing the problem and which device is conflicting, as shown in Figure 10.27. In this case, you'd change the resource setting for one of the devices to resolve the conflict.

FIGURE 10.25.

The Device Manager uses icons to warn you if there's a problem with a device.

FIGURE 10.26.

The Device status *area tells you if the device isn't working properly.*

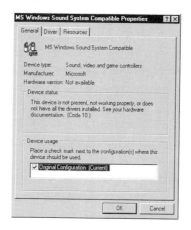

FIGURE 10.27.

If there's a resource conflict, Device Manager supplies the details in the Conflicting device list.

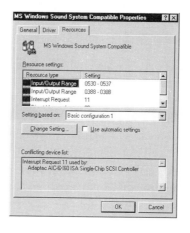

10

HOW WINDOWS 95 HANDLES HARDWARE

In all, Device Manager uses three different icons to give you an indication of the device's current status:

- A black exclamation mark (!) on a yellow field tells you that there's a problem with the device.

- A red X tells you that the device is disabled or missing.

- A blue i on a white field tells you that the device's Use automatic settings check box (on the Resources tab) is deactivated and that at least one of the device's resources was selected manually. Note that the device might be working just fine, so this icon doesn't indicate a problem. If the device *isn't* working properly, however, the manual setting might be the cause. (For example, the device might have a DIP switch or jumper set to a different resource.)

Using the Hardware Conflict Troubleshooter

Instead of your having to use Device Manager to resolve hardware conflicts by hand, Windows 95 has a Hardware Conflict Troubleshooter that can help you through the process. To try this, select Start | Help to activate the Windows 95 Help system, activate the Contents tab, and open the Troubleshooting book. When you display the If you have a hardware conflict topic, you'll see the Help window shown in Figure 10.28.

FIGURE 10.28.

The start of the hardware conflict troubleshooting topic.

Now select the Start the Hardware Conflict Troubleshooter hyperlink. The next window that appears contains a hyperlink button that starts Device Manager. Click that button and then click the Click here to continue hyperlink. From here, the Hardware Conflict Troubleshooter asks you a series of questions, as shown in Figure 10.29, and you select hyperlinks accordingly.

Troubleshooting Protected-Mode Driver Problems

In Chapter 4, I showed you a general procedure for troubleshooting Windows 95 startup. In one of the scenarios, I told you to boot Windows 95 in step-by-step mode and then to click No when you got to the Load all windows drivers? prompt. If Windows 95 started properly, that meant you have a problem with a protected-mode driver.

FIGURE 10.29.

The Hardware Conflict Troubleshooter steps you through a problem by asking you a series of questions.

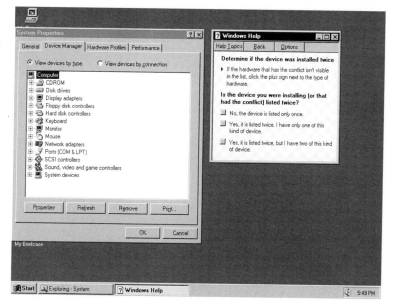

To resolve this problem, restart Windows 95 in Safe mode, display the System Properties dialog box, and select the Device Manager tab. For all the hardware classes shown here, disable each device listed under each class:

Display adapters

Floppy disk controllers

Hard disk controllers

Keyboard

Mouse

Network adapters

PCMCIA socket

Ports

SCSI controllers

Sound, video, and game controllers

You disable a device by displaying its properties sheet, deactivating the `Original Configuration (Current)` check box, and clicking OK. Note that Windows 95 asks whether you want to restart the computer. Don't click Yes until you've deactivated the last device.

When you're done, restart your computer. Now use Device Manager to reenable the devices you disabled earlier one at a time, in the following order:

COM ports

Hard disk controllers

Floppy disk controllers

Other devices

For each device, display its properties sheet, activate the `Original Configuration (Current)` check box, click OK, and click Yes when Windows 95 asks whether you want to shut down your computer.

Restart your computer. If Windows 95 won't start, you've found the culprit. You'll need to remove the device, reinstall the driver, or install an updated driver.

Summary

This chapter showed you how Windows 95 handles hardware. I first reviewed what a mess things were in the not-so-old days of fumbling with IRQs and I/O ports, and then I showed how Windows 95 makes these things easier to deal with. I also explained the major Windows 95 hardware innovations: protected-mode device driver architecture, Plug and Play support, Device Manager, and the Add New Hardware Wizard. I finished by taking you through the Windows 95 hardware troubleshooting features.

I deal with hardware issues in plenty of other locations in this book. Here's a list of those places:

- For some background on Windows 95's automatic hardware detection, see Chapter 1, "Understanding the Windows 95 Installation."

- For a general look at Windows 95 architecture, turn to Chapter 6, "Under the Hood: Understanding the Windows 95 Architecture."

- The Device Manager gets all its hardware info from the Registry. To see where this valuable data is stored, see Chapter 11, "Introducing the Windows 95 Registry."

- I cover printers in Chapter 19, "Prescriptions for Perfect Printing."

- PCMCIA sockets and cards, docking stations, and other notebook-related hardware information can be found in Chapter 20, "Windows 95 on the Road: Notebook Computers and the Briefcase."

- Multimedia hardware tidbits are sprinkled throughout Part V, "Unleashing Multimedia: The Sights and Sounds of Windows 95."

- If you're interested in modems and the Windows 95 communications architecture, head for Chapter 25, "Maximizing Modem Communications."

- Need info on network cards and cables? Try Chapter 30, "A Networking Primer."

Introducing the
Windows 95 Registry

CHAPTER

11

It is almost everywhere the case that soon after it is begotten the greater part of human wisdom is laid to rest in repositories.

—*G.C. Lichtenberg*

As you've learned throughout this book, a big part of unleashing Windows 95 involves customizing the interface and the accessories either to suit your personal style or to extract every last ounce of performance from your system. For the most part, these customization options are handled via the following mechanisms:

- Control Panel
- The properties sheets for individual objects
- Program menu commands and dialog boxes
- Command-line switches

But there is another, even more powerful mechanism you can use to customize Windows 95: the Registry. No, it doesn't have a pretty interface like most of the other customization options, and many aspects of the Registry give new meaning to the word *arcane,* but it gives you unparalleled access to facets of Windows 95 that would be otherwise out of reach. This chapter introduces you to the Registry and its structure, and it shows you how to make changes to the Registry by wielding the Registry Editor. With all that behind you, you'll be ready to start customizing Windows 95 at will, which is what you'll do in Chapter 12, "Hacking the Registry."

A Synopsis of the Registry

When you change the desktop wallpaper using Control Panel's Display icon, the next time you start your computer, how does Windows 95 know which wallpaper you selected? If you change your video display driver, how does Windows 95 know to use that driver at startup and not the original driver loaded during Setup? In other words, how does Windows 95 "remember" the various settings and options either that you've selected yourself or that are appropriate for your system?

The secret to Windows 95's prodigious memory is the Registry. The Registry is a central repository Windows 95 uses to store anything and everything that applies to the configuration of your system. This includes hardware settings, object properties, operating system settings, and application options. It's all stored in one central location, and, thanks to a handy tool called the Registry Editor, it's yours to play with (carefully!) as you see fit.

A Brief History of Configuration Files

It wasn't always this way. In the early days of DOS and Windows (version 1!), system data was stored in two humble files: CONFIG.SYS and AUTOEXEC.BAT, those famous (or infamous) Bobbsey twins of configuration files.

When Windows 2.0 was born (to little or no acclaim), so too were born another couple of configuration files: WIN.INI and SYSTEM.INI. These so-called *initialization files* were also simple text files. It was WIN.INI's job to store configuration data about Windows and about Windows applications; for SYSTEM.INI, life consisted of storing data about hardware and system settings. Not to be outdone, applications started creating their own INI files to store user settings and program options. Before long, the Windows directory was festooned with dozens of these INI garlands.

The air became positively thick with INI files when Windows 3.0 rocked the PC world. Not only did Windows use WIN.INI and SYSTEM.INI to store configuration tidbits, but it also created new INIs for Program Manager (PROGMAN.INI), File Manager (WINFILE.INI), Control Panel (CONTROL.INI), and more.

It wasn't until Windows 3.1 hit the shelves that the Registry saw the light of day, albeit in a decidedly different guise from its Windows 95 descendant. The Windows 3.1 Registry was a database used to store registration information related to OLE (object linking and embedding) applications.

Finally, Windows for Workgroups muddied the configuration file waters even further by adding a few new network-related configuration files, including PROTOCOL.INI.

The Registry Puts an End to INI Chaos

This INI inundation led to all kinds of woes for users and system administrators alike. Because they were just text files in the main Windows directory, INIs were accidents waiting for a place to happen. Like sitting ducks, they were ripe for being picked off by an accidental press of the Delete key from a novice's fumbling fingers. There were so many of the darn things than few people could keep straight which INI file contained which settings. There was no mechanism to help you find the setting you needed in a large INI file. And the linear, headings-and-settings structure made it difficult to maintain complex configurations.

To solve all of these problems, the Windows 95 designers decided to give the old Windows 3.1 Registry a promotion, so to speak, and use it as the central database for all system and application settings. Here are some of the advantages the new Registry brings to Windows 95:

■ The Registry files (discussed in the next section) have their hidden, system, and read-only attributes set, so it's much tougher to delete them accidentally. And even if a user somehow managed to blow away these files, Windows 95 maintains backup copies for easy recovery.

■ Not only does the Registry serve as a warehouse for hardware and operating system settings, but applications are free to use the Registry to store their own configuration morsels, instead of using separate INI files.

■ If you need to examine or modify a Registry entry, the Registry Editor utility gives you a hierarchical, treelike view of the entire Registry database (more on this topic later).

■ The Registry comes with tools that let you search for specific settings and to query the Registry data remotely.

That's not to say that the Registry is a perfect solution. Many of its settings are totally obscure, it uses a structure that only a true geek could love, and finding the setting you need is often an exercise in guesswork. Still, most of these problems can be overcome with a bit of practice and familiarity, which is what this chapter is all about.

Your Old Configuration Files Still Work

Although the Registry appropriates the function of all those old initialization and startup files, it doesn't shoulder the entire configuration file burden by itself. Windows 95 still recognizes and works with the settings in WIN.INI and SYSTEM.INI to maintain compatibility with 16-bit applications that are hard-wired to use these files for configuration data. Also, you'll still need CONFIG.SYS and AUTOEXEC.BAT if you have hardware that requires real-mode drivers, or software that requires specific DOS settings (such as an environment variable or the PATH statement). And, of course, 16-bit programs can still use their private INI files.

Understanding the Registry Files

During the Windows 95 installation, Setup creates the Registry and uses it to store the following settings (among others):

- Options you chose in the Setup Wizard's dialog boxes
- Hardware information gleaned by the Detection Manager during the hardware detection phase
- Settings stored in WIN.INI and SYSTEM.INI, if you upgraded from Windows 3.x
- Settings stored in the OLE registration database, if you upgraded from Windows 3.1

To create the Registry, Setup actually creates two files: USER.DAT and SYSTEM.DAT. These are hidden, system, read-only files that sit in your main Windows folder. Each file takes care of different aspects of the Registry, as described in the next couple of sections.

The Registry, Part I: USER.DAT

The USER.DAT file is designed to store user-specific information. It tracks the following data:

- Wallpaper, color scheme, mouse options, accessibility options, and other Control Panel settings
- Desktop icons
- Start menu folders and shortcuts
- Explorer configuration
- Settings for the Windows 95 accessories
- Network connections and passwords

Each time you exit Windows 95, the system makes a backup copy of USER.DAT. This is another hidden, system, read-only file, and it's called USER.DA0. This backup is handy if USER.DAT becomes corrupted.

If you're the sole user of your computer, your system will have only one USER.DAT file. If, however, you enabled user profiles (as discussed in Chapter 7, "Customizing Windows 95"), Windows 95 creates a USER.DAT file in each user subfolder. (You'll find these subfolders in the \WINDOWS\PROFILES\ folder.)

The Registry, Part II: SYSTEM.DAT

The SYSTEM.DAT file is designed to store system-specific information. Among other things, it keeps track of the following settings:

- The various hardware classes that Windows 95 recognizes
- The devices attached to your machine in each hardware class
- Resources (IRQs, I/O ports, DMA channels) used by each device
- Plug and Play information gleaned from the Plug and Play BIOS or Plug and Play devices
- Protected-mode device drivers loaded at startup
- Internal Windows 95 settings
- Settings for specific 32-bit applications

Each time you exit Windows 95, the system makes a backup copy of SYSTEM.DAT. This is another hidden, system, read-only file, and it's called SYSTEM.DA0. This backup is handy if SYSTEM.DAT becomes corrupted. The root folder of your boot driver has yet another version of SYSTEM.DAT: SYSTEM.1ST. This is the original Registry created by Windows 95 Setup. It's useful as a last-resort backup if SYSTEM.DAT and SYSTEM.DA0 are out of commission.

> **NOTE: THE REGISTRY, PART III: CONFIG.POL**
>
> If you're using system policies to configure your machine or a remote machine, the Registry also uses a third file: CONFIG.POL. This file stores the settings that are configured through the System Policy Editor. I demonstrate how to work with system policies in Chapter 32, "Network Administration and Security."

Starting the Registry Editor

Unlike CONFIG.SYS, AUTOEXEC.BAT, and the INI files, the Registry files are binary, so you can't edit the Registry with a regular text editor. That's not a problem, though, because Windows 95 ships with a utility that lets you view, edit, and delete existing Registry values, and even create new Registry values. This utility, called the Registry Editor, is your ticket into the otherwise inaccessible world of the Windows 95 Registry.

As you can imagine, the Registry Editor is a powerful tool, and it's not something to be wielded lightly. For that reason, the Setup program doesn't install a shortcut for the Registry Editor on any of the Start menus. To crank up the Registry Editor, you must use either of the following techniques:

- Select Start | Run, type regedit in the Run dialog box, and click OK.
- In Explorer, highlight your main Windows 95 folder and double-click the file named REGEDIT.EXE.

> **TIP: CREATE A REGISTRY EDITOR SHORTCUT**
>
> If you think you'll be using the Registry Editor regularly, you should consider adding a shortcut for it either on the Start menu or on the desktop.

When the Registry Editor loads, you'll see the window shown in Figure 11.1.

FIGURE 11.1.

Running REGEDIT.EXE *opens the Registry Editor.*

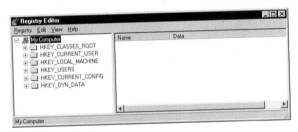

Examining the Structure of the Registry

The Registry Editor window looks a lot like the Explorer window, and it works in basically the same way. The left side of the Registry Editor window is similar to Explorer's Folders pane, except that rather than folders, you see *keys*. For lack of a better phrase, I'll call the left pane the *Keys pane.*

Navigating the Keys Pane

The Keys pane, like Explorer's Folders pane, is organized in a treelike hierarchy. The six keys that are visible when you first open the Registry Editor are special keys called *handles* (which is why their names all begin with HKEY). These keys are referred to collectively as the Registry's *root keys*. I'll tell you what to expect from each of these keys later (see the section called "The Registry's Root Keys").

These keys all contain subkeys, which you can display by clicking the plus sign (+) to the left of each key, or by highlighting a key and pressing the plus-sign key on your keyboard's numeric keypad. When you open a key, the plus sign changes to a minus sign (–). To close a key, click the minus sign, or highlight the key and press the minus-sign key on the numeric keypad. (Again, this is just like navigating folders in Explorer.)

You'll often have to drill down several levels to get to the key you want. For example, Figure 11.2 shows the Registry Editor after I've opened the HKEY_LOCAL_MACHINE key and then opened five more subkeys to get to the WinbootDir key. Notice how the status bar tells you the exact path to the current key, and that this path is structured just like a folder path.

FIGURE 11.2.
You'll often have to dig deep to get to the keys you want to work with.

Keys pane

Settings pane

Current key

The status bar shows the full path to the key

Adjusting the Size of the Registry Editor Panes

To see all the keys properly, you'll likely have to increase the size of the Key pane (and, probably, the Registry Editor window as a whole). To adjust the size of the panes, use either of the following techniques:

- ■ Drag the split bar that separates the panes to the right or left.
- ■ Select View | Split, use the left- and right-arrow keys to adjust the split bar's position, and press Enter.

Registry Settings

If the left side of the Registry Editor window is analogous to Explorer's Folder pane, the right side is analogous to Explorer's Contents pane. In this case, the right side of the Registry Editor window displays the settings contained in each key (so I'll call it the *Settings pane*). The Settings pane is divided into two columns: The Name column tells you the name of each setting in the currently selected key (analogous to a filename in Explorer), and the Data column tells you the value of each setting (you can think of this as analogous to the contents of a file).

In Figure 11.2, for example, the `WinbootDir` key has two settings: `Default` (which isn't set) and `devdir`. The value of the latter is `C:\WINDOWS`. (This setting tells you the name of the main Windows 95 folder.)

Registry key settings can be either of the following types:

Strings: In this case, the value is always surrounded by quotation marks (as in the `devdir` example).

Binary numbers: In this case, the value is a set of hexadecimal digits.

The Registry Editor differentiates between these two types by displaying a different icon to the left of the setting name. For example, take a look at Figure 11.3. This key shows various settings for the SCSI adapter in my computer. As you can see, some of the settings are strings (for example, `Class`) and some are binary (for example, `BootConfig`).

FIGURE 11.3.

Registry Editor displays a different icon for strings and binary values.

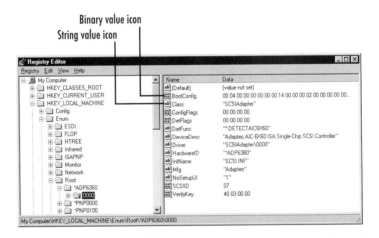

NOTE: DWORD VALUES

A special class of binary values—called DWORD (double word) values—are 32-bit hexadecimal values arranged as eight digits. For example, 11 hex is 17 decimal, so this number would be represented in DWORD form as 0x00000011 (17). This value represents 4 bytes of data; because a "word" in programming circles is 2 bytes, these are "double word" values.

The Registry's Root Keys

The root keys are your Registry starting points, so you'll need to become familiar with what kinds of data each key holds. The next few sections summarize the contents of each key.

The HKEY_CLASSES_ROOT Key

The HKEY_CLASSES_ROOT key contains the same data that the Windows 3.1 Registry showed: file extensions and their associations, as well as applications and their OLE and DDE (Dynamic Data Exchange) information. There are also keys related to shortcuts and other interface features.

The top part of this key contains subkeys for various file extensions. You'll see .bmp for BMP (Paint) files, .doc for DOC (WordPad) files, and so on. In each of these subkeys, the Default setting tells you the name of the registered file type associated with the extension. (I'll discuss registered file types in Chapter 13, "Working with Files and Folders.") For example, in Figure 11.4 I've highlighted the .txt subkey, which, as you can see, is associated with the txtfile file type.

FIGURE 11.4.

The extension subkeys in HKEY_CLASSES_ROOT *tell you the file type associated with the extension.*

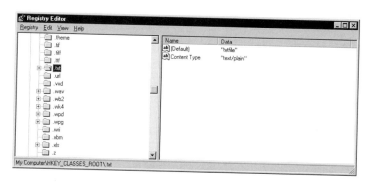

These registered file types appear as subkeys later in the HKEY_CLASSES_ROOT branch. If you scroll down, you'll eventually come across the txtfile subkey, as shown in Figure 11.5. The Registry keeps track of various settings for each registered file type. In particular, the shell subkey tells you the actions associated with this file type. (I added the Open_with_WordPad action by hand; check out the preceding chapter for details.)

FIGURE 11.5.

The registered file type subkeys specify various settings associated with each file type, including its defined actions.

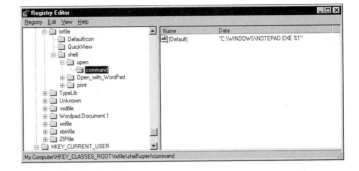

NOTE: CLSID SETTINGS

You'll notice that some registered file type subkeys have CLSID subkeys (check out the Wordpad.Document.1 file type for an example). These are OLE *class IDs,* and they're 32-character strings. Each of these strings points to a subkey of the HKEY_CLASSES_ROOT\CLSID key, which tells you the OLE implementation for that class. I'll talk more about class IDs when I talk about OLE in Chapter 17, "Sharing Data in Windows 95: The Clipboard and OLE."

The HKEY_CLASSES_ROOT key is actually a copy (or an *alias,* as these copied keys are called) of the following HKEY_LOCAL_MACHINE key:

HKEY_LOCAL_MACHINE\SOFTWARE\Classes

The Registry creates an alias for HKEY_CLASSES_ROOT to make these keys easier for applications to access, and to improve compatibility with Windows 3.1 programs.

The HKEY_CURRENT_USER Key

If you've set up multiple user profiles on your computer, the HKEY_CURRENT_USER key contains data that applies to the user that's currently logged on. In other words, it contains the settings from the USER.DAT file in the user's profile folder. (If you don't have multiple user profiles, HKEY_CURRENT_USER is the same as HKEY_USERS.)

HKEY_CURRENT_USER contains user-specific settings for Control Panel options, network connections, applications, and more, as you can see in Figure 11.6. Note that HKEY_CURRENT_USER is an alias for the subkey of HKEY_USERS that corresponds to the current user. For example, if the current user is Biff, HKEY_CURRENT_USER is the same as HKEY_USERS\Biff.

Introducing the Windows 95 Registry

CHAPTER 11

363

11

INTRODUCING THE
WINDOWS 95
REGISTRY

FIGURE 11.6.

The
HKEY_CURRENT_USER *key controls settings for the current user.*

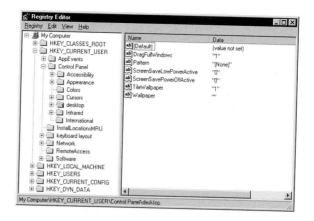

Here's a summary of the settings contained in the various HKEY_CURRENT_USER subkeys:

AppEvents: Sound files that play when particular system events occur (such as maximizing of a window).

Control Panel: Settings related to certain Control Panel icons.

InstallLocationsMRU: A list of the drives and folders that were most recently used (MRU) to install software or drivers.

keyboard layout: The keyboard layout as selected via Control Panel's Keyboard icon.

Network: Settings related to mapped network drives.

RemoteAccess: Settings related to Dial-Up Networking.

Software: User-specific settings related to installed applications. Most 32-bit programs use this key to save their user-specific settings instead of using WIN.INI or private INIs.

The HKEY_LOCAL_MACHINE Key

The HKEY_LOCAL_MACHINE key is SYSTEM.DAT. It contains non-user-specific configuration data for your system's hardware and applications, as you can see in Figure 11.7.

FIGURE 11.7.

The
HKEY_LOCAL_MACHINE
key contains non-user-specific settings for devices and programs.

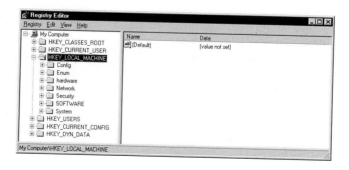

Let's run through the various HKEY_LOCAL_MACHINE subkeys:

Config: Contains subkeys for each hardware profile defined on your system. The subkey name is a unique identifier assigned to each profile (for example, 0001). To find out which profile is current, you have to head to the following subkey:

HKEY_LOCAL_MACHINE\System\CurrentControlSet\control\IDConfigDB

The *Current* setting gives you the identifier of the current profile. The names of each profile are stored in the various "FriendlyName" settings (for example, FriendlyName0001). The current configuration is aliased by the HKEY_CURRENT_CONFIG key (see the section "The HKEY_CURRENT_CONFIG Key" a bit later).

Enum: Contains the data gathered by the Windows 95 bus enumerators. Enum contains subkeys for each hardware class, and each hardware class has subkeys for the installed devices in that class. Each device subkey has various settings related to the device, including its description, its driver, and its hardware ID.

hardware: Contains subkeys related to serial ports and modems (used by HyperTerminal) as well as the floating-point processor.

Network: Contains a Logon subkey with various settings related to the network logon, including the user name and whether or not the logon was validated by a network server.

Security: Contains a Provider subkey that specifies the domain under which network security is administered.

SOFTWARE: Contains computer-specific settings related to installed applications. Most 32-bit programs use this key to save their computer-specific settings instead of using WIN.INI or private INIs. The Classes subkey is aliased by the HKEY_CLASSES_ROOT key. The Microsoft subkey contains settings related to Windows 95 (as well as any other Microsoft products you have installed on your computer).

System: Contains subkeys and settings related to Windows 95 startup, including the following ones in the CurrentControlSet\control subkey: installable file systems (FileSystem subkey), a list of the installed Windows 95 files (InstalledFiles subkey), printers (Print subkey), the time zone (TimeZoneInformation subkey), and a list of the drivers loaded from VMM32.VXD (VMM32Files subkey).

CAUTION: DON'T EDIT THE SERVICES SUBKEY

The HKEY_LOCAL_MACHINE\System\CurrentControlSet\Services subkey contains settings related to the Windows 95 device arbitrators, static descriptions of hardware devices, virtual device drivers, and more. Don't make any changes to these values in the Registry Editor. Only Windows 95 should manage these keys.

The HKEY_USERS Key

The HKEY_USERS key contains settings for Control Panel options, network connections, applications, and more. If you haven't enabled user profiles on your machine, HKEY_USERS has only one subkey, .Default, that contains the same settings as HKEY_CURRENT_USER.

If you have enabled user profiles, HKEY_USERS always has two subkeys: the .Default subkey and a key for the current user, as shown in Figure 11.8. The settings in the .Default subkey are applied to users logging in for the first time, and the subkey for the current user is the same as HKEY_CURRENT_USER. If you want to see a list of all the user profiles, check out the following key:

HKEY_LOCAL_MACHINE\SOFTWARE\Microsoft\Windows\CurrentVersion\ProfileList

FIGURE 11.8.

The HKEY_USERS key contains configuration settings for the current user and a "default" user.

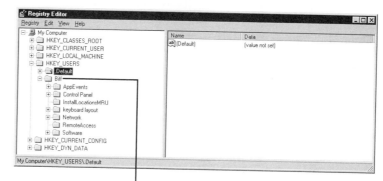

Current user (same as HKEY_CURRENT_USER)

The HKEY_CURRENT_CONFIG Key

The HKEY_CURRENT_CONFIG key contains settings for the current hardware profile, as shown in Figure 11.9. If your machine uses only one hardware profile, HKEY_CURRENT_CONFIG is an alias for HKEY_LOCAL_MACHINE\Config\0001. If your machine uses multiple hardware profiles, HKEY_CURRENT_CONFIG is an alias for HKEY_LOCAL_MACHINE\Config\Current, in which Current is the numeric identifier of the current hardware profile. This identifier is given by the Current setting in the following key:

HKEY_LOCAL_MACHINE\System\CurrentControlSet\control\IDConfigDB

As with HKEY_CLASSES_ROOT, the HKEY_CURRENT_CONFIG alias makes it easier for applications to access the settings in this key.

FIGURE 11.9.

HKEY_CURRENT_CONFIG *is an alias for a subkey of* HKEY_LOCAL_MACHINE\ Config.

The HKEY_DYN_DATA Key

The Registry files (USER.DAT and SYSTEM.DAT) are updated when you shut down Windows 95, when you restart Windows 95, and at regular intervals while you're running Windows 95. (Also, if an application makes a change to the Registry, it can force an update of the Registry files.) This is called *flushing* the Registry data to the hard disk.

However, some data needs to remain in RAM (that is, it must be *dynamic*) at all times for fast access. This data is stored in the HKEY_DYN_DATA key, shown in Figure 11.10. HKEY_DYN_DATA contains two subkeys:

Config Manager: This subkey contains a RAM-based listing of the Windows 95 Plug and Play (PnP) hardware tree. The HKEY_DYN_DATA\ConfigManager\Enum key contains a subkey for each PnP device on the system, and each device has settings for its hardware ID, status, and any problems the device might be having.

PerfStats: This subkey contains performance statistics for the system's network components. You can view these statistics in real time via the System Monitor utility.

FIGURE 11.10.

The HKEY_DYN_DATA *key contains data that must remain in RAM for fast access.*

NOTE: OTHER SYSTEM MONITOR STATISTICS

You'll find the rest of the System Monitor's performance statistics in the following key:

HKEY_LOCAL_MACHINE\System\CurrentControlSet\control\PerfStats\Enum

Introducing the Windows 95 Registry

CHAPTER 11

367

11

INTRODUCING THE
WINDOWS 95
REGISTRY

Summarizing the Structure of the Registry

The various aliases used by the Registry might make it easier for applications to access and write Registry data, but they do little to aid human comprehension. To help you while you navigate the Registry, here's a summary of the various root keys and how they relate to each other:

- HKEY_USERS is USER.DAT.

- HKEY_CURRENT_USER is an alias for either HKEY_USERS\.Default (if user profiles haven't been activated) or HKEY_USERS*UserName* (if user profiles have been activated), in which *UserName* is the user name of the current user.

- HKEY_LOCAL_MACHINE is SYSTEM.DAT.

- HKEY_CLASSES_ROOT is an alias for HKEY_LOCAL_MACHINE\Software\Classes.

- HKEY_CURRENT_CONFIG is an alias for HKEY_LOCAL_MACHINE\Config*Current*, in which *Current* is the numeric identifier for the current hardware profile (0001 if you're using only the original hardware profile).

- HKEY_DYN_DATA holds Registry data that must remain in RAM for fast access.

Figure 11.11 illustrates these relationships.

FIGURE 11.11.

The relationships between the Registry files and the root keys.

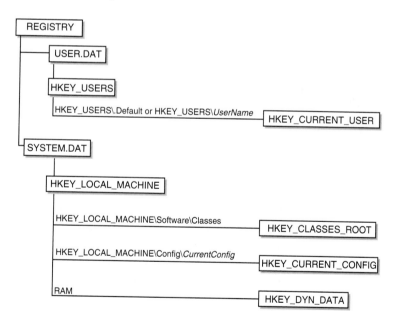

Working with Registry Entries

Now that you've had a look around, you're ready to start working with the Registry's keys and settings. In this section, I'll give you the general procedures for basic tasks such as modifying, adding, renaming, deleting, and searching for entries, and more. These techniques will serve you well in Chapter 12, when I take you through some specific Registry modifications.

Changing the Value of a Registry Entry

Changing the value of a Registry entry is a simple matter of finding the appropriate key, displaying the setting you want to change, and editing the setting's value. Unfortunately, *finding* the key you need isn't always a simple matter. Knowing the root keys and their main subkeys, as described earlier, will certainly help, and the Registry Editor also has a Find feature that's invaluable (I'll show you how to use it later).

To illustrate how this process works, let's work through an example: changing the desktop wallpaper via the Registry. (As you'll see, it's *much* easier to change the wallpaper by using Control Panel. This simple example, however, serves to illustrate the basic technique for altering Registry settings.)

First, use the Keys pane to display the key you want to work with, and then highlight it. The key's settings will appear in the Settings pane. For the example, select the following key:

```
HKEY_CURRENT_USER\Control Panel\desktop
```

Now open the setting (in the example, it's the Wallpaper setting) for editing by using any of the following techniques:

- Highlight the setting name and either select Edit | Modify or press Enter.
- Double-click the setting name.
- Right-click the setting name and select Modify from the context menu.

The dialog box that appears depends on the value type you're dealing with. If the value is a string (as it is in our example), you'll see the Edit String dialog box, shown in Figure 11.12. Use the Value data text box to enter a new string or modify the existing string. For the wallpaper example, enter the full pathname for the bitmap you want to use as the wallpaper (for example, `c:\windows\bubbles.bmp`). When you're done, click OK. (Depending on the bitmap you entered, you might also need to change the value of the `TileWallpaper` setting. Use 1 for tiled or 0 for centered.)

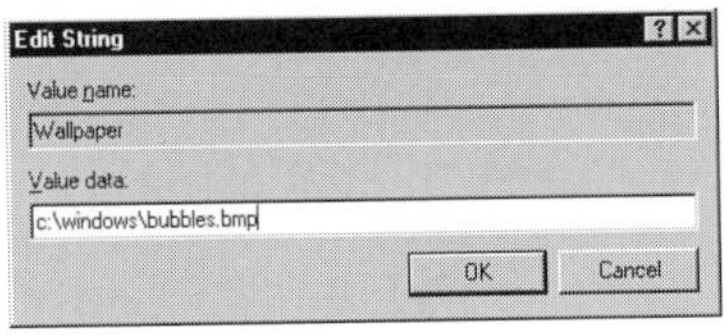

FIGURE 11.12.

You'll see the Edit String dialog box if you're modifying a string value.

Introducing the Windows 95 Registry

CHAPTER 11

369

11

INTRODUCING THE
WINDOWS 95
REGISTRY

If the setting is a binary value, you'll see an Edit Binary Value dialog box like the one shown in Figure 11.13. For binary values, the Value data box is divided into three columns:

Starting byte number: The values in the first column tell you the sequence number of the first byte in each row of hexadecimal numbers. This sequence always begins at 0, so the sequence number of the first byte in the first row is 0. There are 8 bytes in each row, so the sequence number of the first byte in the second row is 8, and so on. These values can't be edited.

Hexadecimal numbers (bytes): The middle column displays the setting's value, arranged in rows of eight hexadecimal numbers, in which each number represents a single byte of information. These values are editable.

ASCII equivalents: The third column shows the ASCII equivalents of the hexadecimal numbers in the middle column. For example, the first byte of the first row is the hexadecimal value 42, which represents the letter B. The values in this column are also editable.

When you're finished editing the value, click OK.

FIGURE 11.13.

You'll see the Edit Binary Value dialog box if you're modifying a binary value.

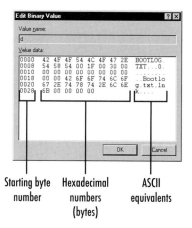

Starting byte number   Hexadecimal numbers (bytes)   ASCII equivalents

Edited settings are written to the Registry right away, but the changes might not go into effect immediately. In most cases, you need to exit the Registry Editor and then restart Windows 95. If you have user profiles activated on your machine, the easiest way to put Registry changes into effect is to select Start | Shut Down, activate the Close all programs and log on as a different user? option, and click Yes.

If you don't have user profiles activated, you'll need to restart Windows 95 by selecting Start | Shut Down and activating the Restart the computer? option. Remember, however, that you can get a faster restart by holding down the Shift key when you click the Yes button. This method bypasses the cold reboot and merely restarts Windows 95.

Other Registry Entry Techniques

Nearly all the modifications you'll make to Registry entries will involve modifying the value of an existing setting. Just so you know, however, you can also rename, add, and delete keys and settings. Here are the basic techniques:

> **Renaming a key or setting:** Highlight the key or setting and select Edit | Rename (or press F2), or right-click and select Rename from the context menu. Make your changes in the text box, and press Enter.

> **Adding a key or setting:** Highlight the key in which you want to add the subkey or setting. Select File | New, or right-click the key and select New from the context menu. In the cascade menu that appears, select Key, String Value, Binary Value, or DWORD Value.

> **Deleting a key or setting:** Highlight the key or setting and select Edit | Delete (or press Delete), or right-click and select Delete from the context menu. When the Registry Editor asks you to confirm the deletion, click Yes.

Finding Registry Entries

The Registry contains only six root keys, but these root keys contain hundreds of subkeys. And the fact that some root keys are aliases for subkeys in a different branch only adds to the confusion. If you know exactly where you're going, the Registry Editor's treelike hierarchy is a reasonable way to get there. If you're not sure where a particular subkey or setting resides, however, you could spend all day poking around in the Registry's labyrinthine nooks and crannies.

To help you get where you want to go, the Registry Editor has a Find feature that lets you search for keys, settings, or values. For example, in Chapter 12 I demonstrate how to change the default icon for the standard desktop icons. The appropriate keys are tough to find, however, because they use those confusing 32-digit class IDs. If you want to change the Recycle Bin icon, for example, there's no "Recycle Bin" key that lets you do it. Let's run through a Find example in which you search for some kind of Recycle Bin–related key that will let you change the icon:

1. In the Keys pane, highlight My Computer at the top of the pane (unless you're certain of which root key contains the value you want to find; in this case, you can highlight the appropriate root key instead).

2. Select Edit | Find or press Ctrl-F. The Registry Editor displays the Find dialog box, shown in Figure 11.14.

Introducing the Windows 95 Registry

CHAPTER 11

371

11

INTRODUCING THE
WINDOWS 95
REGISTRY

FIGURE 11.14.

*The Find feature lets
you search the Registry
for words or phrases.*

3. Use the Find what text box to enter your search string. You can enter partial words or phrases to increase your chances of finding a match.

4. In the Look at group, activate the check boxes for the elements you want to search. For most searches, you'll want to leave all three check boxes activated.

5. If you want find to find only those entries that exactly match your search text, activate the Match whole string only check box.

6. Click the Find Next button.

If the Registry Editor finds a match, it displays the appropriate key or setting, as shown in Figure 11.15. Note that if the matched value is a setting name or data value, Find doesn't highlight the current key (as in Figure 11.15). This is a bit confusing, but just remember that the current key always appears at the *bottom* of the Keys pane.

FIGURE 11.15.

*If Find locates a match,
it displays the key or
setting.*

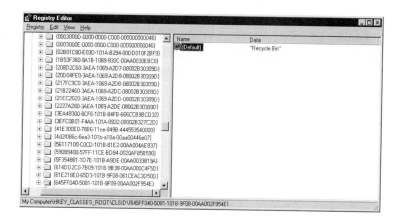

If this isn't the key or setting you want, select Edit | Find Next or press F3 to continue the search.

Importing and Exporting Registry Files

If you'll be making major changes to keys or settings, you should make a backup copy of the Registry. One easy way to do this is to select Registry | Export Registry File to bring up the Export Registry File dialog box, shown in Figure 11.16. Select a location for the exported file, enter a name, and choose whether you want to export all the Registry or just the selected branch. When you're ready, click Save.

FIGURE 11.16.

Use this dialog box to export your Registry to a file.

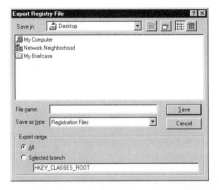

TIP: EXPORT THE ENTIRE REGISTRY FOR GLOBAL CHANGES

You might sometimes need to make changes throughout the Registry. For example, if you want to move an application to a different folder, you would need to update all references to the application's folder. The easiest way to do this is to export the entire Registry, load the resulting REG file into WordPad or some other word processor, and then use the Replace function to make your changes. (For obvious reasons, I highly recommend that you make a backup of the Registry before attempting this procedure.)

NOTE: MORE REGISTRY BACKUP TECHNIQUES

I demonstrate three more methods of backing up your Registry in Chapter 15, "Protecting Your Windows 95 Investment."

The Export Registry File command is also useful if you want to send Registry data to a different machine. In this case, however, you probably don't want to export the entire Registry because the other machine probably won't have the same hardware configuration.

The file created during the export is a Registration file with a REG extension. You can import a REG file into your Registry by selecting File | Import Registry File, highlighting the REG file in the Import Registry File dialog box that appears, and clicking Open.

TIP: FASTER WAYS TO IMPORT REG FILES

You can also import a REG file by double-clicking it, by highlighting it in Explorer and selecting File | Merge, or by right-clicking it and selecting Merge from the context menu.

CAUTION: WATCH FOR APPLICATION REG FILES

Many applications ship with their own REG files for updating the Registry. Unless you're sure that you want to import these files, avoid double-clicking them. They might end up overwriting existing settings and causing problems with your system.

Using REG Files to Modify the Registry

REG files are usually generated by exporting some or all of the Registry from within the Registry Editor. However, the resulting file is a simple text file, so there's nothing to stop you from creating REG files from scratch. Why would you want to do this? Well, suppose you wanted to add or update a Registry setting on a remote user's machine. You could access the computer's Registry Editor directly, or you could use Windows 95's remote Registry feature (discussed in Chapter 32). But what if you need to update a dozen systems, or a hundred? Clearly, in this situation a "hands-on" approach just isn't practical. Instead, you could create the appropriate REG file, e-mail it to the remote users, and instruct them to launch the file and thus update the Registry automatically.

Here's the general structure to use when building your REG files:

```
REGEDIT4
[REGISTRY_KEY]
"SettingName1"="string"
"SettingName2"=hex:value
etc.
```

Here are some notes about this structure:

- The top of the file is always REGEDIT4 followed by a blank line.

- The REGISTRY_KEY is the full path of the Registry key that contains the setting (or settings) you want to modify. You can specify multiple keys if necessary.

- The settings you want to add or modify are listed below the [REGISTRY_KEY] line. In each case, you enter the name of the setting, in double quotation marks, followed by an equals sign (=).

- For string values, enter the value you want to set enclosed in double quotation marks.

- For hexadecimal values, enter hex: followed by the value. If the setting requires multiple hex values, separate them with commas.

Here's an example of a typical REG file:

```
REGEDIT4
[HKEY_LOCAL_MACHINE\SOFTWARE\Microsoft\Windows\CurrentVersion]
"RegisteredOrganization"="Logophilia Limited"
"InstallType"=hex:03,00
```

Printing the Registry

The Registry Editor lets you print either the entire Registry or a selected key. Highlight the key you want to print (if necessary) and select File | Print. In the Print dialog box that appears, select whether you want to print the entire Registry or just the selected key, choose your other print options, and click OK.

CAUTION: AVOID PRINTING THE ENTIRE REGISTRY

You might want to think twice about printing the entire Registry because it consumes more than 100 pages!

Troubleshooting the Registry

The Registry is obviously a crucial component, and you should take no chances with it. Export backup copies of the full Registry regularly, especially if you'll be making significant changes to the Registry's settings, and store a backup copy on a floppy disk just in case your hard disk goes up in flames.

If the Registry itself gets corrupted, however, you might not be able to start Windows 95. This section looks at a few Registry-related problems that can occur and shows you how to fix them.

You made a change to the Registry, and now Windows 95 won't boot.

Because the Registry is such a central part of Windows 95, editing any of the settings isn't a task to be taken lightly. One false move and Windows 95 might refuse to play with you any more. If this happens, you can recover by exporting the Registry to a text file, editing the text file to fix the problem, and importing the changes back into the Registry.

How do you do all this if you can't get into Windows 95, much less run the Registry Editor? You use the real-mode version of the Registry Editor (REGEDIT.EXE). Note that you can start the real-mode version of the Registry Editor only by rebooting to the command prompt (either by selecting Safe mode command prompt only from the Windows 95 Startup menu or by rebooting with the Windows 95 Startup disk in drive A). You'll find REGEDIT.EXE either in your main Windows folder or on your Windows 95 Startup disk.

When you get to the DOS prompt, you first need to run REGEDIT.EXE to export the Registry to a REG text file. Here's the syntax:

```
regedit [/L:system] [/R:user] [/E] filename.reg
```

/L:*system*	Specifies the location of SYSTEM.DAT.
/R:*user*	Specifies the location of USER.DAT.
/E *filename.reg*	Exports the Registry to *filename.reg*.

For example, if you made a change to a key that's part of SYSTEM.DAT, you can export this section of the Registry to a file named SYSTEM.REG with the following command (assuming that C:\WINDOWS is your main Windows 95 folder):

```
regedit /l:c:\windows\system.dat /e c:\system.reg
```

Now use any text editor to load the SYSTEM.REG file, find the change you made that caused Windows 95 to crash, and save the file.

Your next step is to import the REG file back into the Registry by using the following REGEDIT syntax:

```
regedit [/L:system] [/R:user] [/S] filename.reg
```

/L:system	Specifies the location of SYSTEM.DAT.
/R:user	Specifies the location of USER.DAT.
/S	Bypasses the confirmation dialog box.
filename.reg	Specifies the name of the modified REG file.

In our example, you'd enter the following command:

```
regedit /l:c:\windows\system.dat c:\system.reg
```

Restart your computer to put the changes into effect.

Your Registry is corrupted, and your system won't boot.

If your Registry goes down for the count, it might bring your system down along with it. To recover, you need to get rid of the existing Registry files (SYSTEM.DAT and USER.DAT) and use the Registry backups (SYSTEM.DA0 and USER.DA0) in their place.

The first thing you need to do is insert your Windows 95 Startup disk (or any bootable floppy) and reboot. When you get to the A:\ prompt, change to the drive where Windows 95 is installed, and then change to the main Windows 95 folder. For example, if your main Windows 95 folder is C:\WINDOWS, enter the following two commands:

```
c:
cd\windows
```

Both SYSTEM.DAT and SYSTEM.DA0 are hidden, read-only, system files, so you need to turn off these attributes with the following two commands:

```
attrib -h -r -s system.dat
attrib -h -r -s system.da0
```

Now you must delete SYSTEM.DAT and rename SYSTEM.DA0 to SYSTEM.DAT:

```
del system.dat
ren system.da0 system.dat
```

Finally, reset the hidden, read-only, and system attributes for SYSTEM.DAT with the following command:

```
attrib +h +r +s system.dat
```

You need to repeat this procedure for USER.DAT and USER.DA0. When you're done, remove the bootable floppy and restart your system. Your Registry is restored to the state it was in the last time you successfully restarted Windows 95.

Your Registry is corrupted, and you need to restore it from an exported REG file.

If the Registry is corrupted badly enough, you'll need to replace it entirely with an exported REG file. The real-mode version of the Registry Editor can do this for you if you use the following syntax:

```
regedit [/C] filename.reg
```

/C *filename.reg* replaces the entire contents of the existing Registry with *filename.reg*.

If the REG file is named REGBACK.REG, you'd use the following command to do it:

```
regedit /c regback.reg
```

When you start your computer, the Windows 95 Startup menu is displayed automatically, and the following message appears:

```
Warning: Windows has detected a registry/configuration error.
Choose Safe mode, to start Windows with a minimal set of drivers.
```

This error indicates that the Registry files are either missing or corrupted. You need to boot Windows 95 in Safe mode.

Windows 95 first tries to restore the Registry from its backup copies (SYSTEM.DA0 and USER.DA0). You'll see the Registry Problem dialog box with an explanation of the problem. Click the Restore From Backup and Restart button.

If Windows 95 can restore the backups, it prompts you to restart your computer. Click Yes to reboot.

If Windows 95 can't restore the backups, it suggests that you shut down your system and reinstall Windows 95. Although you might have to reinstall Windows 95 as a last resort, you can still try two other things:

- If you have a backup copy of the Registry files on floppy disk in the form of a REG file, you can use it to create a new Registry, as described earlier.

- Delete SYSTEM.DAT (you'll need to remove its hidden, read-only, and system attributes first), and then copy SYSTEM.1ST from your root folder to SYSTEM.DAT in your main Windows 95 folder. (Again, you'll need to adjust the attributes before you can copy SYSTEM.1ST.)

■ Reboot to the command prompt and check `MSDOS.SYS`. Make sure that the `WinDir` and `WinBootDir` settings point to the correct folder (that is, your main Windows 95 folder, which is where the Registry files are stored).

During the hardware detection phase of the Windows 95 installation, Setup displays the following error message:

```
SDMErr(80000003): Registry access failed.
```

This error message tells you that the Registry is damaged. To fix this problem, follow these steps:

1. Restart your computer, and when you see the `Starting Windows 95...` message, press F8 to display the Windows 95 Startup menu.

2. Select the `Safe mode command prompt only` option.

3. When you get to the DOS prompt, enter the following command (if `REGEDIT` complains about missing data, ignore it):

   ```
   regedit /e reg.txt
   ```

4. Enter the following command to regenerate the Registry's internal data structures:

   ```
   regedit /c reg.txt
   ```

5. Restart your computer and then try Setup again.

Summary

This chapter gave you an introduction to one of Windows 95's most important components: the Registry. I gave you a short history of configuration files, from `CONFIG.SYS` and `AUTOEXEC.BAT` to the INI madness that characterized Windows 3.x. I then showed you how Windows 95 improved the situation by consolidating configuration data into a single structure: the Registry. We then took a tour of the Registry structure using the Registry Editor, and I showed you how to use the Registry Editor to work with the Registry entries.

You'll put this newfound knowledge to good use in Chapter 12, as I show you a number of tricks and secrets that take advantage of the Registry to modify Windows 95. Here's a list of a few other chapters that contain related information:

■ You'll find lots more info on Windows 95 startup in Chapter 4, "Start It Your Way: Understanding Windows 95 Startup."

■ Many of the Registry values are generated by Windows 95's customization features. I discuss many of these features in Chapter 7, "Customizing Windows 95."

■ For a broad look at Windows 95 architecture and memory features, as well as how to use the System Monitor, see Chapter 9, "Windows 95 Performance Tuning and Optimization."

■ To better understand the Registry's hardware-related keys, head for Chapter 10, "How Windows 95 Handles Hardware."

■ You'll learn several methods of making backup copies of the Registry's files in Chapter 15, "Protecting Your Windows 95 Investment."

■ In Chapter 17, "Sharing Data in Windows 95: The Clipboard and OLE," I talk about the Registry's OLE-related keys (including the CLSID keys) and settings.

■ I demonstrate how to manage the Registry on a remote computer in Chapter 32, "Network Administration and Security."

Hacking the Registry

A little knowledge that acts is worth infinitely more than much knowledge that is idle.

—Kahlil Gibran

An old Scottish proverb says that "fine words butter no parsnips." Chapter 11, "Introducing the Windows 95 Registry," presented plenty of fine words (if that's not too immodest a thing to say) about the Registry and how you work with it, but now it's time to butter a Registry parsnip or two. In other words, you're well versed in the *theory* of the Registry, so now you need to get up to speed with the *practice*. What kinds of things can you do with the Registry? In particular, what kinds of things can you do with the Registry that *can't* be done via the Control Panel, Explorer, or any of the applets? That's what this chapter is all about. I'll show you a fistful of practical Registry techniques that let you customize Windows 95 in undreamed-of ways.

Working with File Types and Applications

You'll begin your look at Registry tricks by examining a few techniques that will give you more control over file types and applications.

Customizing the New Menu

In Chapter 13, "Working with Files and Folders," I'll show you how to create new file types and modify existing ones. One of Windows 95's handiest features is the New menu, which lets you create a new file without working within an application. In Explorer, just select File | New, or right-click inside the Contents pane and select New, to display the menu shown in Figure 12.1. From there, just select a command to create a new instance of that particular file type.

FIGURE 12.1.

The New menu lets you create new documents without opening an application.

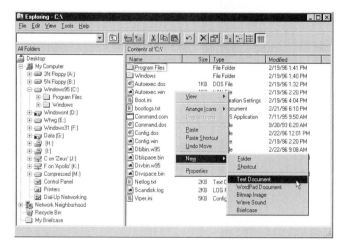

You'll see in Chapter 13 that Windows 95 recognizes more than 50 file types, but the New menu lists only seven. What mechanism determines whether a file type appears on the New menu? The Registry, of course. Start the Registry Editor and open the HKEY_CLASSES_ROOT key. As I mentioned in the preceding chapter, the first 100 or so subkeys of HKEY_CLASSES_ROOT are the extensions that Windows 95 recognizes. Most of these keys contain only a Default setting that takes on either of the following values:

- If the extension is registered with Windows 95, the Default value is a string pointing to the file type associated with the extension. For example, the Default value for .bat is batfile (batch file).

- If the extension isn't registered with Windows 95, the Default value isn't set.

A few of these extension keys, however, also have subkeys. For example, open the .bmp key and you'll see that it has a subkey named ShellNew, as shown in Figure 12.2. This subkey is what determines whether a file type appears on the New menu. Specifically, if the extension is registered with Windows 95 and it has a ShellNew subkey, the New menu sprouts a command for the associated file type.

FIGURE 12.2.

The ShellNew *subkey controls whether a file type appears on the New menu.*

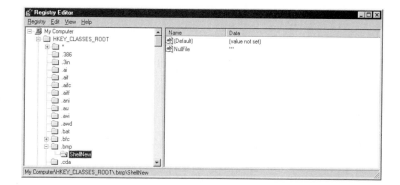

The ShellNew subkey always contains a setting that determines how Windows 95 creates the new file. Four different settings are possible:

NullFile: This setting, the value of which is always set to a null string (""), tells Windows 95 to create an empty file of the associated type. Of the five file types (excluding Folder and Shortcut) that appear on the New menu, three use the NullFile setting: Text Document (.txt), Bitmap Image (.bmp; see Figure 12.2), and Wave Sound (.wav).

FileName: This setting tells Windows 95 to create the new file by making a copy of another file. Windows 95 has a special folder to hold these "template" files. This folder, called ShellNew, is hidden, so you must activate Explorer's Show all files option to view it, as shown in Figure 12.3. On the New menu, only the WordPad

Document (.doc) file type uses the FileName setting, and its value is winword.doc. (Recall that the default file type for WordPad is a Word for Windows 6 document.) To see this value, you need to open the following key:

```
HKEY_CLASSES_ROOT\.doc\Wordpad.Document.1\ShellNew
```

FIGURE 12.3.

The ShellNew *folder holds templates used by the New menu to create new documents.*

NOTE: ABOUT SHELLNEW AND THE FILENAME SETTING

Here are a few notes about the ShellNew key's FileName setting:

- Although the ShellNew menu contains quite a few templates, only the WordPad documents are registered with Windows 95. In other words, the Registry does have a key for, say, .xls (Excel) in HKEY_CLASSES_ROOT, and this key has a ShellNew subkey with a FileName setting that points to Excel.xls; but XLS files aren't registered with Windows 95.

- The FileName setting doesn't have to point to a file in the ShellNew folder. It can point to a file in any folder as long as you include the file's full pathname.

- If you check out the .doc key in HKEY_CLASSES_ROOT, you'll note that it has three subkeys—Word.Document.6, WordDocument, and Wordpad.Document.1—and each has a ShellNew subkey. Why isn't there a New menu command for each document type? Because Windows 95 sets up a New menu command only for registered file types (Wordpad.Document.1, in this case).

Command: This setting tells Windows 95 to create the new file by executing a specific command. This command usually invokes an executable file with a few parameters. The New menu's Briefcase item uses this setting. If you check the ShellNew subkey for .bfc in HKEY_CLASSES_ROOT, you'll see the following value for the Command setting:

```
C:\WINDOWS\rundll32.exe syncui.dll,Briefcase_Create %1!d! %2
```

Data: This setting contains a binary value, and when Windows 95 creates the new file, it copies this binary value into the file.

Adding File Types to the New Menu

To make the New menu even more convenient, you can add new file types for documents you work with regularly. For any file type that's registered with Windows 95, you follow a simple three-step process:

1. Add a `ShellNew` subkey to the appropriate extension key in `HKEY_CLASSES_ROOT`.
2. Add one of the four settings discussed in the preceding list (`NullFile`, `FileName`, `Command`, or `Data`).
3. Enter a value for the setting.

In most cases, the easiest way to go is to use `NullFile` to create an empty file. The `FileName` setting, however, can be quite powerful because you can set up a template file containing text and other data.

Let's try an example. If you've installed Internet Explorer or some other Windows 95–aware browser, `HKEY_CLASSES_ROOT` will have a key for the HTM extension that's registered as an Internet Document (HTML) file type. (There will also be a key for the HTML extension.) These are pages designed to appear on the World Wide Web. If you create your own Web pages, most of them will have the same basic structure. You could set up a template HTM file that uses this basic structure, and you could then assign this template to the New menu.

The first thing you must do is create the template. Using a text editor, word processor, or HTML editor, enter the basic HTML tags and text you want to use for the template, and save the file (using the HTM extension) in the `ShellNew` folder. For example, Figure 12.4 shows a template HTML file (`SKELETON.HTM`) that I use.

FIGURE 12.4.

Create your template and save it in the `ShellNew` *folder.*

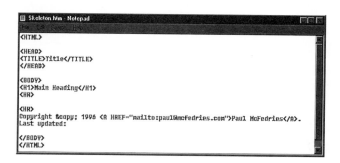

Start the Registry Editor and highlight the `.htm` key in `HKEY_CLASSES_ROOT`. Follow these steps to set up the `ShellNew` subkey:

1. Select Edit | New | Key (or right-click the `.htm` key and select New | Key). The Registry Editor adds a new subkey.

2. Type `ShellNew` and press Enter.

3. Select Edit | New | String Value (or right-click the `ShellNew` subkey and select New | String Value). The Registry Editor adds a new setting.

4. Type `FileName` and press Enter.

5. Press Enter or double-click the `FileName` setting. The Edit String dialog box appears.

6. Type the name of your template file (for the example, type `skeleton.htm`, as shown in Figure 12.5), and click OK.

FIGURE 12.5.

Enter the name of the template file.

7. Exit the Registry editor.

The new setting goes into effect immediately, as you can see in Figure 12.6, so you can try this without having to restart Windows 95.

FIGURE 12.6.

You can try out your new command without having to restart Windows 95.

Using Multiple New Menu Commands for a Single Application

For a given extension, Windows 95 lets you have only one New menu command. But what if you want to use the same application to create multiple kinds of new documents? For example, you might have a WordPad file that you use as a template (such as a daily to-do list). It would be nice to be able to create new WordPad documents that either are empty or use this template.

To accomplish this task, you need to set up a new, registered file type for the template, complete with its own extension, and set up a ShellNew key for this new type. Here are the basic steps to follow:

1. Use Explorer's View | Options command to create a new file type that's associated with the application (see Chapter 13 for details). For a to-do list, you could create a TDL extension associated with WordPad.

2. Copy the template file into the ShellNew folder, and rename it so that it has the extension you just registered. For example, if your WordPad file is named TODOLIST.DOC, rename it TODOLIST.TDL.

3. In the Registry Editor, find the new extension in HKEY_CLASSES_ROOT, and add the ShellNew subkey.

4. Add the FileName setting and use the name of the template file in ShellNew.

Deleting File Types from the New Menu

Many Windows 95 applications like to add their file types to the New menu. (Microsoft Office alone adds five commands to the New menu.) If you find that your New menu is getting overcrowded, you can delete some commands to keep things manageable.

To do this, you need to find the appropriate extension in the Registry and delete the ShellNew subkey. However, it won't work if you delete the ShellNew subkey from HKEY_CLASSES_ROOT. That's because HKEY_CLASSES_ROOT is only an alias for HKEY_LOCAL_MACHINE\Software\Classes. To really get rid of the New menu item, you must delete the appropriate ShellNew subkey from HKEY_LOCAL_MACHINE\Software\Classes.

TIP: DETERMINING THE CORRECT FILE EXTENSION

If you're not sure which extension is associated with the New menu command you want to delete, you could search the Registry all day long looking for it. An easier way is to just use the command to create a new document in any Explorer folder and see the resulting extension. Remember, though, that to see extensions in Explorer you need to select View | Options and deactivate the Hide MS-DOS file extensions for file types that are registered check box.

NOTE: A MORE CAUTIOUS APPROACH

Instead of permanently deleting a ShellNew subkey, you can tread a more cautious path by simply renaming the key (to, say, ShellNewOld). This will still prevent Windows 95 from adding the item to the New menu, but it also means that you can restore the item just by restoring the original key name.

12

Creating Application-Specific Paths

When you install a 32-bit application, it uses the Registry to store the path to its executable file. This means that you can start any 32-bit application simply by entering the name of its executable file either in the Run dialog box or at the prompt in a DOS session. You don't need to spell out the complete pathname. For example, the executable filename for Backup is BACKUP.EXE, so you could type backup and press Enter to start it.

This pathless execution is handy, but in the following two situations it doesn't work:

16-bit applications: These older programs don't store the paths to their executables in the Registry.

Documents: As you'll learn in Chapter 13, you can double-click a document in Explorer, and Windows 95 starts the associated application and loads the document. You can't, however, load a document just by typing its filename in the Run dialog box or at the DOS prompt (unless the document is in the current folder).

To solve both of these problems, you can add a path to an executable file (an *application-specific path*) or to a document (a *document-specific path*) into the Registry by hand.

In the Registry Editor, open the following key:

HKEY_LOCAL_MACHINE\Software\Microsoft\Windows\CurrentVersion\App Paths

As you can see in Figure 12.7, the App Paths key has subkeys for each installed 32-bit application. Each of these subkeys has one or both of the following settings:

Default: This setting spells out the path to the application's executable file. All the App Paths subkeys have this setting.

Path: This setting specifies one or more folders that contain files needed by the application. An application first looks for its files in the same folder as its executable file. If it can't find what it needs there, it checks the folder or folders listed in the Path setting. Not all App Paths subkeys use this setting.

To create an application-specific path, highlight the App Paths key, create a new subkey, and assign it the name of the application's executable file. For example, if the program's executable filename is OLDAPP.EXE, name the new subkey OLDAPP.EXE. For this new subkey, change the Default setting to the full pathname for the executable file.

Actually, you don't have to give the new App Paths subkey the name of the executable file. You can use any name you like as long as it ends with .EXE and doesn't conflict with the name of an existing subkey. Why does it have to end with .EXE? Unless you specify otherwise, Windows 95 assumes that anything you enter into the Run dialog box or at the DOS prompt ends with .EXE. So by ending the subkey with .EXE, you need to type only the subkey's primary name. For example, if you name your new subkey OLDAPP.EXE, you can run the program by typing oldapp.

Figure 12.7.

The App Paths *key contains path information for all installed 32-bit applications.*

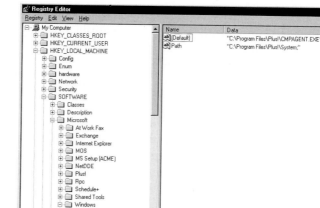

You create document-specific paths the same way. (Note, however, that the document's file type must be registered with Windows 95.) In this case, though, the Default setting takes on the full pathname of the document. Again, if you want to load the document just by typing its primary name, make sure that the new App Paths subkey uses the EXE extension. For example, you can see in Figure 12.8 that I've created a subkey called TODO.EXE that points to G:\Data\Documents\ToDoList.doc. To launch this document, I need only type todo in the Run dialog box or at the DOS prompt.

Figure 12.8.

An example of a document-specific path.

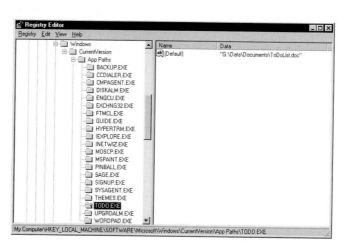

Instead of creating a path for a specific document, you might prefer to set up a path that points to an entire folder of documents. For example, it's usually a good idea to create separate folders for your data files. This technique makes it easier to find your data files and to back them up. Suppose, for example, that you store all your WordPad documents in a folder named `G:\Data\Documents`. Ideally, you'd like to be able to launch any of the documents in this folder just by typing its name in the Run dialog box or at the DOS prompt.

No problem. In the `App Paths` key, highlight the subkey that corresponds to the application you use to work with the documents. Modify the `Path` setting (if it has one; if not, you need to create a `Path` setting) to include the full pathname of the folder that contains the documents. Be sure to end the pathname with a semicolon (;). For example, Figure 12.9 shows a `Path` setting added to the `WORDPAD.EXE` subkey that points to `G:\Data\Documents`.

FIGURE 12.9.

You can add a path that points to a folder full of documents.

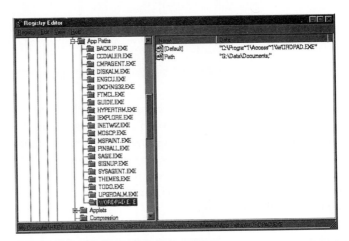

Associating Multiple Extensions with One Application

In Chapter 13, I'll show you how to register new file types with Windows 95. This lets you set up an association between an extension and an application. For example, to handle the `README.1ST` text files that come with some programs, you could associate the 1ST extension with Notepad. This creates a new 1ST file type.

The problem with this approach, however, is that it involves re-creating the wheel by having to set up certain actions—such as Open and Print—for the new file type. In the 1ST file type, for example, the actions you set up are identical to those that are already set up for the Text Document file type. It would be better if you could just augment an existing file type with a new extension, such as adding the 1ST extension to the existing Text Document file type.

You know this is possible because if you look through the list of file types (in Explorer, select View | Options and activate the File Types tab), you'll see that several file types have multiple extensions. The Bitmap Image file type, for example, has two extensions: BMP and PCX. Unfortunately, there's no way you can use the File Types tab to add an extension to an existing file type.

You can, however, do this via the Registry. Here are the steps to follow:

1. In the Registry Editor, open HKEY_CLASSES_ROOT.

2. Find the extension subkey for the file type you want to work with. For the Text Document file type, for example, find the .txt subkey.

3. Make a note of the value of the extension subkey's Default setting. For example, the Default setting for the .txt subkey is txtfile.

4. Highlight HKEY_CLASSES_ROOT and add a key for the new extension. In the 1ST extension example, you'd add a key named .1st.

5. For this new key, change the Default setting to the value you noted in step 3, as shown in Figure 12.10.

FIGURE 12.10.

To associate an extension with an existing file type, you need to add the extension to the Registry.

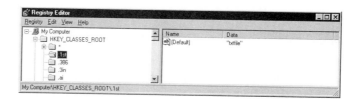

After you've created this new key, it becomes available to Windows 95 immediately. To see for yourself, check out the file type in the File Types tab. You should see the new extension in the File type details group, as shown in Figure 12.11.

FIGURE 12.11.

The new extension shows up in the File Types tab.

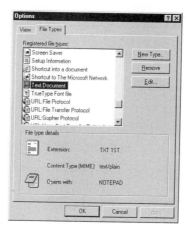

Modifying Windows 95's Desktop Icons

The default icons that populate the Windows 95 desktop are handy, but they can be annoyingly difficult to work with. For example, if you don't use any of the four main desktop icons—

My Computer, Network Neighborhood, Inbox, or Recycle Bin—there's no way to delete them from the desktop. Also, you can rename all the desktop icons except for the Recycle Bin, which stubbornly refuses all renaming attempts.

Fortunately, all of these problems are overcome easily with a few simple tweaks of the Registry. The next few sections show you some tricks for modifying the desktop icons.

Changing the Desktop Icons

If you're getting a bit a tired of seeing the same old icons on your desktop, changing these icons is a nice way to give Windows 95 a quick facelift. If you have Microsoft Plus! installed, changing the icons is easy (I showed you how to do this in Chapter 7, "Customizing Windows 95.") If you don't have Microsoft Plus!, you can still change the icons via the Registry.

Each desktop icon has a subkey in the following key:

```
HKEY_LOCAL_MACHINE\SOFTWARE\Classes\CLSID
```

CLSID is short for *class ID,* and each Windows 95 object has its own unique class ID. These are long, 16-byte values that consist of 32 hexadecimal digits arranged in an 8-4-4-4-12 pattern, surrounded by braces ({}). For example, the CLSID for My Computer is {20D04FE0-3AEA-1069-A2D8-08002B30309D}, so this is My Computer's Registry key:

```
HKEY_LOCAL_MACHINE\SOFTWARE\Classes\CLSID\{20D04FE0-3AEA-1069-A2D8-08002B30309D}
```

Table 12.1 lists the CLSID values for all the desktop icons.

Table 12.1. CLSID values for the desktop icons.

Desktop Icon	CLSID
My Computer	{20D04FE0-3AEA-1069-A2D8-08002B30309D}
Network Neighborhood	{208D2C60-3AEA-1069-A2D7-08002B30309D}
Inbox	{00020D75-0000-0000-C000-000000000046}
Recycle Bin	{645FF040-5081-101B-9F08-00AA002F954E}
The Internet	{FBF23B42-E3F0-101B-8488-00AA003E56F8}
The Microsoft Network	{00028B00-0000-0000-C000-000000000046}
My Briefcase	{85BBD920-42A0-1069-A2E4-08002B30309D}

Each of these desktop icon keys contains various subkeys. In particular, you'll find a subkey named DefaultIcon that determines the icon used by each object. By changing the Default setting in the DefaultIcon subkey, you can define new icons for your desktop.

The DefaultIcon subkey's Default setting always uses the following general value:

```
IconFile,IconNumber
```

Here, `IconFile` is the full pathname of a file that contains one or more icons. Most of the desktop icons use the file `C:\WINDOWS\SYSTEM\SHELL32.DLL` (assuming that Windows 95 is installed in `C:\WINDOWS`). If Microsoft Plus! is installed, however, most of the desktop icons use `C:\WINDOWS\SYSTEM\COOL.DLL` instead. `IconNumber` is an integer that specifies which icon to use in `IconFile`, in which the first icon is 0. For example, the Network Neighborhood's `DefaultIcon` setting is this:

`C:\WINDOWS\SYSTEM\SHELL32.DLL,17`

To change the icon, either specify a different icon number in the existing icon file or use a different icon file altogether.

How do you know which files contain which icons? The best way to browse icon files is to create a shortcut, open its properties sheet, select the Shortcut tab, and click the Change Icon button. In the Change Icon dialog box that appears, shown in Figure 12.12, use the `File Name` text box to enter the name of an icon file (such as a DLL, an EXE, or an ICO file). If you're not sure about which file to try, click the Browse button and choose a file in the dialog box that appears. Here are a few suggestions:

> `C:\WINDOWS\SYSTEM\COOL.DLL` (if Microsoft Plus! is installed)
>
> `C:\WINDOWS\SYSTEM\SHELL32.DLL`
>
> `C:\WINDOWS\SYSTEM\PIFMGR.DLL`
>
> `C:\WINDOWS\SYSTEM\USER.EXE`
>
> `C:\WINDOWS\EXPLORER.EXE`
>
> `C:\WINDOWS\MORICONS.DLL`
>
> `C:\WINDOWS\PROGMAN.EXE`

Figure 12.12.

Use the Change Icon dialog box to browse the available icons in an icon file.

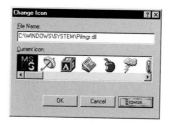

After you've opened a file, use the `Current icon` box to browse the available icons. If you see an icon you want to use, you can get its icon number by counting from the first icon, starting at 0, until you get to the icon.

Deleting Desktop Icons

As I mentioned at the beginning of this section, you can delete only three of the desktop icons: The Internet, The Microsoft Network, and My Briefcase. The rest—My Computer, Network

Neighborhood, Inbox, and Recycle Bin—seem to be permanent fixtures on the desktop. They're not, though. You can use the Registry to delete any of these icons. All you have to do is delete the appropriate subkey in the `CLSID` key:

```
HKEY_LOCAL_MACHINE\SOFTWARE\Classes\CLSID
```

For example, to delete the My Computer icon, you'd delete the following subkey:

```
HKEY_LOCAL_MACHINE\SOFTWARE\Classes\CLSID\{20D04FE0-3AEA-1069-A2D8-08002B30309D}
```

Hiding the Network Neighborhood

Instead of deleting the Network Neighborhood, you can hide it from view by creating a new Registry entry. First, use the Registry Editor to head for the following key:

```
HKEY_CURRENT_USER\.Default\Software\Microsoft\Windows\CurrentVersion\Policies\
➥Explorer
```

Create a new DWORD value named `NoNetHood`. If you assign the value 1 to this setting, Windows 95 hides the Network Neighborhood icon. To display the Network Neighborhood icon again, set `NoNetHood` to 0.

> **NOTE: ANOTHER WAY TO HIDE NETWORK NEIGHBORHOOD**
>
> An easier way to hide the Network Neighborhood icon is to use the System Policy Editor. I explain how this tool works in Chapter 32, "Network Administration and Security."

Renaming the Recycle Bin

Except for the Recycle Bin, you can rename all the desktop icons. If the name "Recycle Bin" just doesn't cut it for you, you can assign this icon a new name—Trash Can, Garbage Pail, Rubbish Heap, Last Stop Before Deletesville, or whatever—via the Registry. First, head for the Recycle Bin's `CLSID` key:

```
HKEY_LOCAL_MACHINE\SOFTWARE\Classes\CLSID\{645FF040-5081-101B-9F08-00AA002F954E}
```

To change the name, edit the `Default` setting for this key. Note, too, that clearing the title from this setting will display the Recycle Bin with no name.

Saving Your Desktop Configuration

Have you ever carefully arranged your desktop icons, only to find that Windows 95 has reverted to its previous state? This is frustrating (and, thanks to its intermittent behavior, puzzling), but there is a work-around.

In the Registry Editor, head for the following key:

`HKEY_CURRENT_USER\Software\Microsoft\Windows\CurrentVersion\Policies\Explorer`

If you don't see a setting named `NoSaveSettings`, go ahead and add it as a binary value. Edit this new setting and enter the following value:

`00 00 00 00`

With this setting in place, Windows 95 will save your current desktop arrangement each time you shut down or reboot. Exit the Registry Editor, adjust your icons as necessary, and then restart Windows 95.

To tell Windows 95 not to save the desktop arrangement at shutdown, return to the Registry Editor, and then change the `NoSaveSettings` value to the following:

`01 00 00 00`

Using the Registry to Fiddle with Files

Let's turn our attention now to some Registry techniques that operate on files. The next five sections introduce you to various Registry keys that change the way you work with files in Windows 95.

Disabling Numeric Tails

As you know, when you create a long filename, Windows 95 also keeps track of a shorter filename in the old 8.3 DOS format. This ensures that any files you create with 32-bit applications can still be read by older 16-bit programs. As you'll see in Chapter 13, however, Windows 95 creates the short primary name by removing spaces and other illegal characters, lopping off all but the first six characters, and adding a *numeric tail:* a tilde (~) followed by a number.

If you or the people you're sharing your files with are still using 16-bit programs, these numeric tails are a hassle because they reduce the number of meaningful characters in the short primary name from eight to six. To regain the use of the full eight-character primary name, you can use the Registry to tell the Windows 95 file system to stop using numeric tails.

Start the Registry Editor and head for the following key:

`HKEY_LOCAL_MACHINE\System\CurrentControlSet\control\FileSystem`

Create a new binary value setting in this key, and call it `NameNumericTail`. Assign this setting the value 0, as shown in Figure 12.13. When you restart Windows 95, the file system will use the first eight legal characters in a long filename to create the primary name. (Note that, because this change affects the file system, you must restart Windows 95. If you just log on again, the change won't go into effect.) For example, if you create a new file named `Long Filename.txt`, the 8.3 filename will be `LONGFILE.TXT`. (The new setting also works on renamed files.)

Figure 12.13.

Create a setting called NameNumericTail, *and assign it the value 0 to disable numeric tails.*

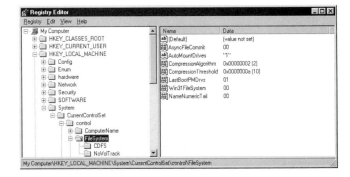

CAUTION: DON'T RENAME THE PROGRAM FILES FOLDER

If you use the Program Files folder to install your programs, you must specify the 8.3 name—PROGRA~1—for 16-bit and DOS applications. You might be tempted to rename this folder to get rid of the annoying numeric tail, but you'll have to resist. The problem is that many Windows 95 accessories (including Paint, WordPad, Microsoft Exchange, and the Microsoft Network) use this folder and expect its short name to be PROGRA~1. Changing this name might break some or all of these applications.

Adjusting Explorer's Refresh Rate

Windows 95 does a pretty good job of updating the Explorer window whenever you use another application to add, delete, or rename files. It sometimes misses some file updates, however, especially if the changes were made at the DOS prompt or with a DOS application. You can always update the Explorer display to show the latest information by selecting View | Refresh or by pressing F5. If, however, you want to make Explorer *really* diligent about keeping its display up-to-date, head for the following Registry key:

```
HKEY_LOCAL_MACHINE\System\CurrentControlSet\control\Update
```

You'll see a setting named UpdateMode, which controls the Explorer refresh rate. To set this rate at its fastest, change the value of UpdateMode to 0.

Removing the Arrows from Shortcut Icons

If you use shortcuts regularly, you know that Windows 95 displays a small arrow in the lower-left corner of the shortcut icon. If you normally leave "Shortcut to" as part of the shortcut's name, you might prefer not to see the arrow. To tell Windows 95 not to add the arrow to your shortcuts, display the following Registry key:

```
HKEY_LOCAL_MACHINE\SOFTWARE\Classes\lnkfile
```

In the Settings pane, find the IsShortcut setting and delete it. Exit the Registry Editor to put this change into effect (you don't need to restart Windows 95).

Customizing the Shortcut Arrow

Instead of deleting the shortcut arrow, you might prefer to customize it by telling Windows 95 to use a different image. The secret to this is that the shortcut arrow is actually a full-fledged icon: The arrow sits in the lower-left corner, and the rest of the icon is "transparent." When you create a shortcut, Windows 95 builds the shortcut icon by taking the regular icon for the target object (say, a folder icon) and superimposing the shortcut arrow icon on it.

To prove this for yourself, open the Change Icon dialog box (as described earlier) and browse through the icons in SHELL32.DLL. The regular shortcut arrow shows up as the 29th icon (counting from 0). As you can see in Figure 12.14, you could use the icons to the left (28) or the right (30) of the regular shortcut arrow as a replacement.

FIGURE 12.14.

The SHELL32.DLL file contains a couple of suitable replacements for the shortcut arrow.

The shortcut arrow icon —

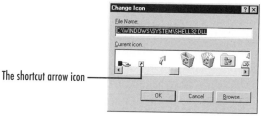

To accomplish this replacement, follow these steps:

1. Use the Registry Editor to display the following key:

   HKEY_LOCAL_MACHINE\SOFTWARE\Microsoft\Windows\CurrentVersion\explorer

2. Add a new subkey named Shell Icons.

NOTE: SHELL ICONS MIGHT ALREADY EXIST

If you've installed Microsoft Plus!, the Shell Icons subkey should already be present. Plus! uses this subkey to remap many of Windows 95's system icons to icons in COOL.DLL.

3. In the Shell Icons subkey, create a new string value setting named 29. This number corresponds to the shortcut arrow's position in SHELL32.DLL.

4. Change the value of the 29 setting to c:\windows\system\shell32.dll,*n*, in which *n* is the number of the replacement icon you want to use. For example, if I wanted to use icon 30 from SHELL32.DLL (the arrow to the right of the regular shortcut arrow in Figure 12.14), I'd change the 29 setting to c:\windows\system\shell32.dll,30, as shown in Figure 12.15.

12

HACKING THE
REGISTRY

FIGURE 12.15.

A setting that customizes the shortcut key arrow.

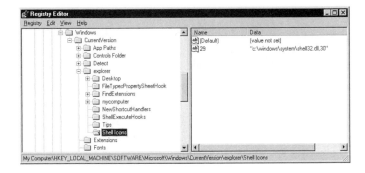

5. Exit the Registry Editor.

Implementing this change isn't as straightforward as logging on again or restarting Windows 95. The problem is that Windows 95 stores all of its system icons in a hidden file named `ShellIconCache` (you'll find it in your main Windows 95 folder). The change you just made to the Registry doesn't update this file, and neither does a restart of Windows 95. To put the change into effect, open the properties sheet for the desktop, select the Appearance tab, and choose `Icon` from the `Item` drop-down list. Modify the `Size` value (it doesn't matter what number you choose), and click Apply. This action refreshes the `ShellIconCache` file and updates the shortcut icons. Return the `Icon` item to its original size (you might also need to select `Windows Standard` from the `Scheme` drop-down list) and click OK to return the icons to their normal size.

TIP: CUSTOMIZING OTHER SYSTEM ICONS

As you might have guessed by now, you can use a similar technique to customize any of Windows 95's system icons. Use the Change Icon dialog box to get the appropriate number for the system icon in `SHELL32.DLL` (remember to start counting at 0), and create a string value setting for that number in the `Shell Icons` key. Change this setting to the icon file and icon number you want to use as a replacement.

To get you started, here are the setting names to use for the icons in the Start menu:

Command	Setting Name
Programs	19
Documents	20
Settings	21
Find	22
Help	23
Run	24
Suspend	25

Command	Setting Name
Eject PC	26
Shut Down	27

Using a Bitmap File's Own Image as Its Icon

Because bitmap files are associated with Paint, they're displayed in Explorer with Paint's icon. Wouldn't it be nice if, rather than the generic Paint icon, each bitmap file used its own image as its icon? With the Registry, all things are possible.

Open the following Registry key:

```
HKEY_CLASSES_ROOT\Paint.Picture\DefaultIcon
```

The `Default` setting for this key should have the following value:

```
C:\Progra~1\Access~1\MSPAINT.EXE,1
```

This is telling Windows 95 to use the generic Paint icon. Change this setting to `%1`. With this value, each BMP file uses its built-in *icon handler* to generate its own icon. This technique is normally used with EXE files that have icons imbedded inside them. Because a BMP file doesn't have an embedded icon, it just uses its own image.

After you've changed the `Default` setting, the new value goes into effect immediately. Switch to Explorer and select View | Refresh to update the display. For each BMP file, the contents of the file are used as the icon, as shown in Figure 12.16.

FIGURE 12.16.

BMP files generating their own icons.

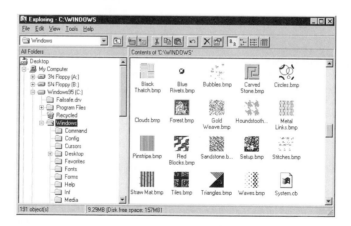

Clearing the MRU List in the Run Dialog Box

One of the features I hated most about Windows 3.x was the inability of the Run commands in Program Manager and File Manager to remember commands you entered previously.

Thankfully, Windows 95 remedied that bit of brain-deadness by building a memory into the Start menu's Run command. This "memory" is actually the following Registry key:

`HKEY_CURRENT_USER\Software\Microsoft\Windows\CurrentVersion\Explorer\RunMRU`

Here, "MRU" stands for Most Recently Used. As you can see in Figure 12.17, this key is just a list of commands that have been entered into the Run dialog box. Notice how each command is assigned a letter. The MRUList setting at the bottom determines the order in which commands appear by arranging these letters in the order you entered each command.

FIGURE 12.17.

The list of commands in the Run dialog box is given by the RunMRU Registry key.

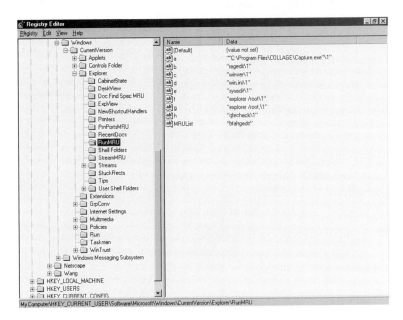

The Run feature will remember up to the last 26 commands you entered (since there are 26 letters in the alphabet). That's a lot of commands to wade through, so you might want to clear the MRU list from time to time and start fresh. To do so, delete every one of the lettered settings in the RunMRU key, as well as the MRUList setting (don't touch the (Default) setting, however).

Customizing the Windows 95 Interface

As you learned in the preceding chapter, Windows 95 uses the Registry to store the current values of the various Control Panel settings. You can, of course, use the Registry Editor to edit these values directly, although you'll usually be better off using the dialog boxes and controls that the Control Panel icons give you.

Plenty of customization keys and settings in the Registry, however, *can't* be modified via the Control Panel. The next few sections show you a few of them.

Creating a Desktop Pattern Without a Mouse

In Chapter 7, I showed you how to create your own desktop pattern. Unfortunately, you have to use a mouse to create a custom pattern in the desktop properties sheet. The Registry, however, lets mouse-averse users create a cool pattern (albeit not quite as intuitively).

The secret to doing this can be found in the following Registry key:

```
HKEY_CURRENT_USER\Control Panel\desktop
```

When you apply a pattern to the desktop, this key contains a `Pattern` setting that's a string value consisting of eight numbers. These digits are a numeric representation of the pattern.

For example, consider the Circuits pattern shown in Figure 12.18. As you can see, the `Pattern` setting represents this pattern with the string "82 41 132 66 148 41 66 132." To see how Windows 95 derives these numbers, recall that each pattern is an 8×8 array of pixels. Each pixel is either "on" (that is, black) or "off" (that is, the desktop color). The following grid shows the On/Off values that make up the Circuits pattern:

Off	On	Off	On	Off	Off	On	Off
Off	Off	On	Off	On	Off	Off	On
On	Off	Off	Off	Off	On	Off	Off
Off	On	Off	Off	Off	Off	On	Off
On	Off	Off	On	Off	On	Off	Off
Off	Off	On	Off	On	Off	Off	On
Off	On	Off	Off	Off	Off	On	Off
On	Off	Off	Off	Off	On	Off	Off

FIGURE 12.18.

Desktop patterns are represented in the Registry as a string of numbers.

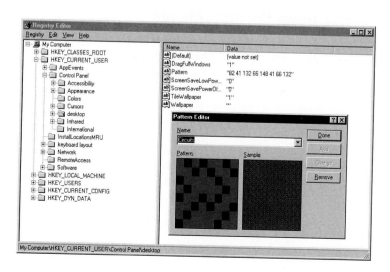

In computing circles, however, "on" is usually represented by a 1, and "off" is usually represented by a 0. So you can rewrite the preceding grid as the following series of 1s and 0s:

```
01010010
00101001
10000100
01000010
10010100
00101001
01000010
10000100
```

Each of these rows, however, can be read as a binary number. Now try this little experiment:

1. Select Start | Programs | Accessories | Calculator.
2. Select View | Scientific to display the Scientific view (if it's not already displayed).
3. Activate the Bin option.
4. Enter the first row—01010010—into the readout.
5. Activate the Dec option. The binary number you entered changes to 82 in decimal format. If you look back at Figure 12.17, you'll see that 82 is the first number of the Pattern setting.

If you repeat steps 3 through 5 for the other rows, you'll see that their decimal equivalents are all in the Pattern setting. In other words, the Pattern setting uses decimal values to represent the binary nature of the pattern.

So to create your own pattern, you need only adjust the Pattern setting. The best way to do this is to create an 8×8 grid, fill it with 1s and 0s in a pattern that looks interesting, and use Calculator to convert the resulting binary numbers in decimal values that you can use with the Pattern setting.

Slowing Down the Start Menus

One of the Windows 95 design goals was to reduce the amount of mouse clicking you had to perform to get anything done. The Start menu is a good example. After you've opened the menu you need, a single click starts the program. Not only that, but the cascade menus are "clickless." In other words, if a particular Start menu item contains a cascade menu, hovering the mouse pointer over that menu item will, after a short delay, display the cascade menu without your having to click the mouse.

By default, that delay is only about a quarter of a second. If you happen to slide the mouse pointer off the menu item for any longer than that, the menu disappears. This can get very frustrating after a while, but there's a way to slow down these cascading menus by using, of course, the Registry.

In the Registry Editor, make a beeline for the following key:

```
HKEY_CURRENT_USER\Control Panel\desktop
```

Create a new string value setting in this key called `MenuShowDelay`. The value you enter for this setting determines how many milliseconds it takes before a cascade menu appears. Internally, Windows 95 uses a value of 250 (a quarter of a second). If you want to bump up the delay to, say, three seconds, change the value of `MenuShowDelay` to 3000. The maximum value you can enter for `MenuShowDelay` is 65534 (a little over 65 seconds). You'll need to log on again or restart Windows 95 to put this change into effect.

Disabling Window Animation

One of the pet peeves many new users had with Windows was that they would click a window's Minimize button (accidentally or otherwise) and the window would "disappear." They didn't realize that it was still there, just minimized as an icon at the bottom of the screen.

To help these users, Microsoft decided to "animate" windows as they were minimized to the taskbar. In other words, when you click the Minimize button in Windows 95, the window's title bar flashes quickly, and then you see the window retreating to the taskbar. (You get the same show when you restore the window from the taskbar.) This is called *window animation,* and it's a real help to novice users because they can follow the window down to the taskbar.

The rest of us, however, *know* where the window goes when we click the Minimize button, so we don't need to bother with the animation. To have your windows snap into place, you can turn off window animation by using the Registry.

The place to be is the following key:

`HKEY_CURRENT_USER\Control Panel\desktop\WindowMetrics`

Create a new string value setting called `MinAnimate`, and then change the value of this setting to 0. Exit the Registry Editor and restart Windows 95 (or log on again) to set up the change.

Playing with Button Shadows

In Chapter 7, I showed you how to use the desktop properties sheet to modify Windows 95's colors. A few objects can't have their colors modified with this method. They're in the Registry, however, so you can work with them there.

Windows 95's 3D objects appear with either a "raised" or a "sunken" effect. Command buttons, for example, appear raised, whereas text boxes appear sunken. These effects are achieved by small strips of color around each object. On the top and left side of a raised object are, for example, a strip of light gray and a strip of white; on the bottom and right side are a strip of dark gray and a strip of black. Sunken objects use an opposite color scheme. These colors are controlled by settings in the following Registry key:

`HKEY_CURRENT_USER\Control Panel\Colors`

NOTE: THE COLORS SUBKEY MIGHT NOT APPEAR

The Colors subkey appears only if you've modified Windows 95's colors via the desktop properties sheet. If you don't see the Colors subkey, open the desktop properties sheet, select the Appearance tab, change the color of any object, and click Apply. Change the color back and click OK. When you're back in the Registry, select View | Refresh to see the Colors subkey.

As you can see in Figure 12.19, this key has many settings that hold the RGB color values of various objects. In particular, four settings control the color of the strips around 3D objects. Table 12.2 lists these settings and shows their default values. For something a bit different, you can reverse the raised and sunken objects by using the values in the Reversed column of the table. Figure 12.20 shows the result (you need to restart Windows 95 to put the new colors into effect).

FIGURE 12.19.

The Colors key uses RGB values to store the color of various Windows 95 objects.

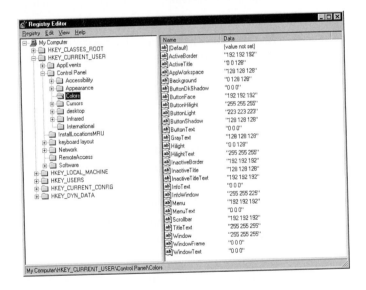

Table 12.2. Color settings for 3D objects.

Setting	Default	Reversed
ButtonDkShadow	0 0 0 (black)	255 255 255
ButtonHiLight	255 255 255 (white)	0 0 0
ButtonLight	223 223 223 (light gray)	128 128 128
ButtonShadow	128 128 128 (dark gray)	223 223 223

FIGURE 12.20.
An interesting effect created by switching the color values for the settings that create 3D objects.

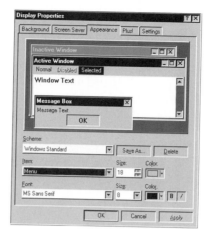

What do you do if you want to try other colors, but you don't know the appropriate RGB values? Windows 95 has a color picker that can help you. Open the desktop properties sheet, select the Appearance tab, drop-down either Color list, and click Other. The Color dialog box shown in Figure 12.21 is displayed. Click a color you like, and then use the Red, Green, and Blue text boxes to make a note of the RGB value.

FIGURE 12.21.
Use the Color dialog box to get the RGB values for any color.

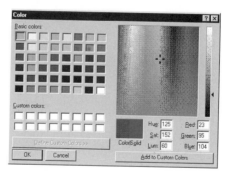

Working with the Welcome Screen

When you first install Windows 95, a Welcome to Windows 95 dialog box appears each time you restart. Besides giving you access to the Windows 95 tour, a product catalog, and online registration, this dialog box also displays a Did you know... Windows 95 tip. If you found yourself constantly restarting Windows 95 early in your career, you might have exhausted the few dozen or so tips that Microsoft assigned to this dialog box.

Creating Your Own Welcome Screen Tips

If you want to give the Welcome dialog box new life, you can use the Registry to create your own tips. This is a handy way to remind yourself of things you've learned in this book, for example, or it's helpful if you're setting up a Windows 95 machine for someone else.

In the Registry Editor, highlight the following key:

`HKEY_LOCAL_MACHINE\SOFTWARE\Microsoft\Windows\CurrentVersion\explorer\Tips`

As you can see in Figure 12.22, this key contains string values for all the tips that appear in the Welcome dialog box. The numbers used for setting names determine the order in which the tips appear. You can either edit the existing tips or create your own (just be sure to preserve the correct number sequence).

FIGURE 12.22.

The `Tips` subkey contains all the tips that are displayed in the Welcome dialog box.

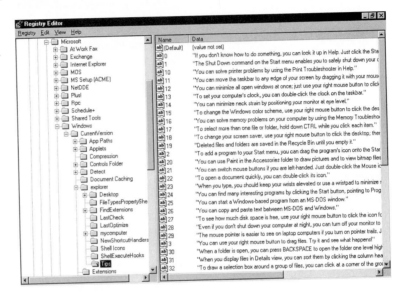

What if you already have a file that contains various tips? Is there any easy way to incorporate them into the `Tips` key? There sure is, and the following steps show you how it's done:

1. With the `Tips` key highlighted, select Registry | Export Registry File. The Export Registry File dialog box appears.
2. Enter a name (for example, `Tips`) in the `File name` text box and click Save. The Registry Editor saves the `Tips` key to a REG file.
3. Make a copy of the REG file, just so you have a backup.
4. Open the REG file in a text editor, as shown in Figure 12.23.

FIGURE 12.23.

You can modify the exported key in a text editor.

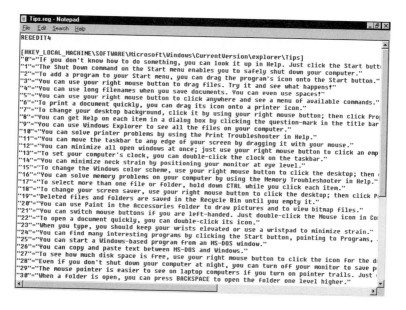

```
Tips.reg - Notepad
File  Edit  Search  Help
REGEDIT4

[HKEY_LOCAL_MACHINE\SOFTWARE\Microsoft\Windows\CurrentVersion\explorer\Tips]
"0"="If you don't know how to do something, you can look it up in Help. Just click the Start butt
"1"="The Shut Down command on the Start menu enables you to safely shut down your computer."
"2"="To add a program to your Start menu, you can drag the program's icon onto the Start button."
"3"="You can use your right mouse button to drag files. Try it and see what happens!"
"4"="You can use long filenames when you save documents. You can even use spaces!"
"5"="You can use your right mouse button to click anywhere and see a menu of available commands."
"6"="To print a document quickly, you can drag its icon onto a printer icon."
"7"="To change your desktop background, click it by using your right mouse button; then click Pro
"8"="You can get Help on each item in a dialog box by clicking the question-mark in the title bar
"9"="You can use Windows Explorer to see all the files on your computer."
"10"="You can solve printer problems by using the Print Troubleshooter in Help."
"11"="You can move the taskbar to any edge of your screen by dragging it with your mouse."
"12"="You can minimize all open windows at once; just use your right mouse button to click an emp
"13"="To set your computer's clock, you can double-click the clock on the taskbar."
"14"="You can minimize neck strain by positioning your monitor at eye level."
"15"="To change the Windows color scheme, use your right mouse button to click the desktop; then
"16"="You can solve memory problems on your computer by using the Memory Troubleshooter in Help."
"17"="To select more than one file or folder, hold down CTRL while you click each item."
"18"="To change your screen saver, use your right mouse button to click the desktop; then click P
"19"="Deleted files and folders are saved in the Recycle Bin until you empty it."
"20"="You can use Paint in the Accessories folder to draw pictures and to view bitmap files."
"21"="You can switch mouse buttons if you are left-handed. Just double-click the Mouse icon in Co
"22"="To open a document quickly, you can double-click its icon."
"23"="When you type, you should keep your wrists elevated or use a wristpad to minimize strain."
"24"="You can find many interesting programs by clicking the Start button, pointing to Programs, 
"25"="You can start a Windows-based program from an MS-DOS window."
"26"="You can copy and paste text between MS-DOS and Windows."
"27"="To see how much disk space is free, use your right mouse button to click the icon for the d
"28"="Even if you don't shut down your computer at night, you can turn off your monitor to save p
"29"="The mouse pointer is easier to see on laptop computers if you turn on pointer trails. Just 
"30"="When a folder is open, you can press BACKSPACE to open the folder one level higher."
```

5. Edit the file by modifying or deleting existing tips, or by adding your own. As you do, keep the following points in mind:

   ■ Don't touch the first three lines of the REG file. Windows 95 will need them when you merge the file back into the Registry later.

   ■ For each line, use the following structure: a number surrounded by quotation marks, followed by an equal sign (=), followed by the tip surrounded by quotation marks.

   ■ Keep the tip numbers in the correct numeric sequence.

6. When you're done, save the file and exit the editor.

7. In Explorer, either highlight the REG file and select File | Merge, or right-click the file and select Merge from the context menu.

8. When Windows 95 reports that the information has been merged successfully, click OK.

Customizing the Display of Welcome Screen Tips

The Registry has another key that contains some useful Welcome screen settings. Point the Registry Editor at the following key:

HKEY_CURRENT_USER\Software\Microsoft\Windows\CurrentVersion\Explorer\Tips

You can customize a couple of settings here. The first is called `Next`. This setting determines the number of the tip that's displayed the next time you start Windows 95. This is a binary setting, so you must enter the value in hexadecimal. If you're not familiar with hex notation, you can use the Calculator to convert decimal values to hexadecimal. (In the Scientific view, activate `Dec`, enter the tip number, and select `Hex`.) This setting has two hexadecimal numbers, but you shouldn't have to worry about the second number; the first number goes up to 255 (FF hex), which should be plenty. Note too that you must enter full bytes (two hexadecimal digits). For example, if you want the next tip to be number 10, be sure to enter 0A 00 (A is 10 in hex notation).

The other setting is called `Show`, and it determines whether the Welcome screen appears each time you start Windows 95. If the value of this setting is 00 00 00 00, the Welcome screen doesn't appear; if the value is 01 00 00 00, the Welcome screen appears.

TIP: WELCOMING BACK THE WELCOME DIALOG BOX

You can display the Welcome screen at any time by selecting File | Run, typing `welcome` in the Run dialog box, and clicking OK.

Getting Better Double-Clicking

In Chapter 7, I showed you how to customize various aspects of your electronic rodent. In particular, I showed you how to modify the double-click speed so that Windows 95 is better able to recognize your double-clicks. If Windows 95 is still balking at some of your double-clicks, or if you're administering novice users who are complaining about this situation, the problem might not be the double-click speed. You see, Windows 95 actually uses *two* criteria to differentiate between a double-click and two single-clicks:

- The time between the two clicks (the double-click speed).
- The *distance* between the two clicks. If you move the mouse more than a few pixels between each click, Windows 95 interprets the action as two single-clicks. I'll call this the *double-click distance*.

The latter criterion is often the real cause of misinterpreted double-clicks for novice users who are still a little unsteady with the mouse. To give them more room to maneuver, you can use the Registry to increase the double-click distance. Begin by highlighting the following key in the Registry Editor:

`HKEY_CURRENT_USER\Control Panel\desktop`

Now create two new string value settings: `DoubleClickHeight` and `DoubleClickWidth`. These settings specify how far the mouse pointer is allowed to travel (in pixels) between each click. I'd suggest starting with values of 10 for each setting and experimenting from there.

Customizing Some Setup Settings

To finish this look at Registry tricks and secrets, I'll close with a couple of techniques for modifying some of the settings you specified during Setup.

Changing Your Registered Name and Company Name

During the Windows 95 installation process, Setup asked you to enter your name and, optionally, your company name. These "registered names" appear in several places as you work with Windows 95:

■ If you right-click My Computer and select Properties (or open the System icon in Control Panel), your registered names appear in the General tab of the System Properties dialog box.

■ If you select Help | About in just about any Windows 95 accessory or folder, your registered names appear in the About dialog box.

■ If you install a 32-bit application, the installation program uses your registered names for its own records (although you usually get a chance to make changes).

With these names appearing in so many places, what do you do if you change one of the names? Why, head for the Registry, of course. In particular, make tracks to the following key:

```
HKEY_LOCAL_MACHINE\SOFTWARE\Microsoft\Windows\CurrentVersion
```

As you can see in Figure 12.24, this key has two settings that store your registered names: `RegisteredOrganization` and `RegisteredOwner`. Use these settings to tell Windows 95 that you want to use different registered names.

FIGURE 12.24.

Your registered names are stored in this Registry key.

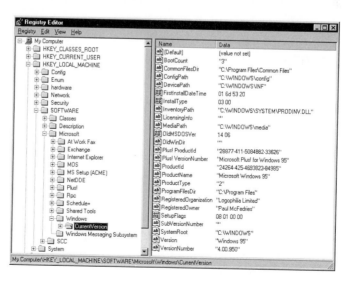

Changing the Windows 95 Source Path

When you install Windows 95, Setup makes a note of the disk drive you used for the source CD-ROM or floppy disks. Later, when you add new Windows 95 applets or adjust your hardware, Windows 95 prompts you to insert a source disk in the same drive. You might, however, need to change this source path:

- You might have used floppies for the original installation and now have the CD-ROM.
- You might have used the CD-ROM originally, but now your CD-ROM is using a different disk drive.
- You might have copied the Windows 95 source files to a hard disk.

For all of these situations, you can let Windows 95 know that the source path has changed. In the Registry Editor, highlight the following key:

```
HKEY_LOCAL_MACHINE\SOFTWARE\Microsoft\Windows\CurrentVersion\Setup
```

Find the `SourcePath` setting and change it to the new path. For example, if you installed Windows 95 originally from floppies in drive A, the `SourcePath` setting will be `A:\`. If you now have the CD-ROM and your CD-ROM drive is drive D, change SourcePath to `D:\WIN95`.

Microsoft Plus

> **TIP: CHANGING THE MICROSOFT PLUS! SOURCE PATH**
>
> You can change the source path for Microsoft Plus! as well. You'll find a `SourcePath` setting for Plus! in the following key:
>
> ```
> HKEY_LOCAL_MACHINE\SOFTWARE\Microsoft\Plus!\Setup
> ```

Summary

This chapter put your hard-won knowledge from Chapter 10 to good use by showing you a few practical tips and tricks for modifying the Registry. I showed you how to customize the New menu, create application-specific paths, modify the desktop icons, change various file settings (such as disabling numeric tails), customize the Windows 95 interface, and make a couple of post-Setup alterations. All in all, not a bad day's work.

I'll be using the Registry throughout the rest of this book, but here are a couple of related chapters you might want to check out:

- To see how the Registry fits into the overall Windows 95 architecture, see Chapter 6, "Under the Hood: Understanding the Windows 95 Architecture."
- For a refresher course in Registry theory and techniques, Chapter 11, "Introducing the Windows 95 Registry," is the place to be.

■ In Chapter 17, "Sharing Data in Windows 95: The Clipboard and OLE," I talk about the Registry's OLE-related keys (including the CLSID keys) and settings.

■ The Windows 95 System Policy Editor is an easy way to change many Registry-based settings. I demonstrate how to use it in Chapter 32, "Network Administration and Security."

12

HACKING THE REGISTRY

PART

III

IN THIS PART

Unleashing Files, Folders, and Disks

Working with Files and Folders

IN THIS CHAPTER

Is not the whole world a vast house of assignation of which the filing system has been lost?
—*Quentin Crisp*

Education might take as its foundation the three Rs (reading, writing, and 'rithmetic), but for Windows 95, it's the three Fs: files, folders, and floppy (or fixed) disks. When you're not slaving away in your applications, you'll spend a good chunk of your Windows 95 life working with at least one of these "f-words."

I introduced you to some Explorer-based file and folder management operations in Chapter 5, "Windows 95: The 50¢ Tour," but those represented only the most basic and rudimentary tasks. Unleashing this area of Windows 95 also requires some background on the Windows 95 file system architecture, and you learned about that in Chapter 6, "Under the Hood: Understanding the Windows 95 Architecture." Now it's time for some unabashed ringing of bells and blowing of whistles in Explorer, and detailed looks at a few other Windows 95 tools. You'll find all that and more in this chapter.

Exploiting Explorer

I introduced you to Explorer—the Windows 95 file management tool—in Chapter 5. I gave you a tour of the Explorer interface, showed you how to get around, and took you through a few basic file chores. These techniques will serve you well in most of your Explorer expeditions, but they represent only the tiniest fraction of what Explorer can do. To help you unleash the true power of Explorer, this section takes a more in-depth look at the program, lets you know what options are available, and runs through some techniques that will let you exploit Explorer's most valuable resources.

The Expedited Explorer

If your job requires working with a computer regularly, chances are you don't make your living performing file maintenance and management tasks. Instead, your computer productivity is more likely measured by how many memos, letters, spreadsheets, databases, presentations, or graphics you crank out in a day. Because unglamorous file chores usually do little to enhance this core productivity, you'll want to get them over with as soon as possible so that you can get back to doing some real work. To that end, the next few sections show you a few tools and techniques that will help put file finagling in the fast lane.

The Economical Explorer Keyboard

If you don't feel like reaching all the way over to your mouse, or if you're just an old keyboard die-hard like me, you'll be happy to know that there's no shortage of keyboard time savers for Explorer. Table 13.1 lists them all.

Table 13.1. Explorer keyboard shortcuts.

Key	*What It Does*
+	Opens the next level of folders below the current folder. Use the + on the numeric keypad.
–	Closes the current folder. Use the – on the numeric keypad.
*	Opens all levels of folders below the current folder. Use the * on the numeric keypad.
Alt-Enter	Displays the properties sheet for the selected objects.
Alt-F4	Closes Explorer.
Backspace	Takes you to the parent folder of the current folder.
Ctrl-A	Selects all the objects in the current folder.
Ctrl-arrow key	Scrolls up, down, left, or right (depending on the arrow key used) without losing the highlight on the currently selected objects.
Ctrl-C	Copies the selected objects to the Clipboard.
Ctrl-G	Opens the Go To Folder dialog box. Enter the name of the folder you want to display (including its drive and full path, if necessary), and click OK.
Ctrl-V	Pastes the most recently cut or copied objects from the Clipboard.
Ctrl-X	Cuts the selected objects to the Clipboard.
Ctrl-Z	Reverses the most recent action.
Delete	Sends the currently selected objects to the Recycle Bin.
F2	Renames the selected object.
F3	Displays the Find dialog box with the current folder as the default.
F4	Opens the toolbar's `Go to a different folder` drop-down list.
F5	Refreshes the Explorer window. This is handy if you've made changes to a folder via the command line or a DOS program and you want to update the Explorer window to display the changes.
F6	Cycles the highlight among the Folder pane, the Contents pane, and the toolbar's `Go to a different folder` drop-down list. Tab does the same thing.
Shift-Delete	Deletes the currently selected objects without sending them to the Recycle Bin.
Shift-F10	Displays the context menu for the selected objects.
Tab	Cycles the highlight among the Folder pane, the Contents pane, and the toolbar's `Go to a different folder` drop-down list. F6 does the same thing.

13

WORKING WITH FILES AND FOLDERS

TIP: MICROSOFT NATURAL KEYBOARD SHORTCUTS

If you have a Microsoft Natural Keyboard (or a compatible keyboard), the Windows logo key (⊞) gives you two Explorer-related shortcuts: Press ⊞-E to start Explorer; press ⊞-F to display the Find dialog box.

The Explorer Toolbar

I'm more of a keyboard connoisseur than a mouse maven, but I appreciate a handy toolbar as much as the next person. In particular, Explorer's toolbar is chock-full of useful buttons. (I'd *really* like the Explorer toolbar, though, if it was customizable, like the one in Windows for Workgroups.) For some reason, Windows 95 hides the Explorer toolbar by default. To display it, select View | Toolbar. Table 13.2 shows each toolbar button and explains what it does. (As in Chapter 5, I use the term *object* to mean either a file or a folder.)

Table 13.2. Explorer's toolbar buttons.

Button	*Name*	*Description*
Windows95 (C:)	Go to a different folder	Displays the name of the current folder. Use the drop-down list to choose a different folder.
	Up One Level	Takes you to the parent folder of the current folder.
	Map Network Drive	Maps a network drive to a drive letter on the local computer.
	Disconnect Net Drive	Disconnects a mapped network drive from its local drive letter.
	Cut	Cuts the currently selected objects to the Clipboard.
	Copy	Copies the currently selected objects to the Clipboard.
	Paste	Pastes the most recently cut or copied objects from the Clipboard.
	Undo	Reverses the most recent action.
	Delete	Sends the selected objects to the Recycle Bin.
	Properties	Displays the properties sheet for the selected objects.

Button	Name	Description
	Large Icons	Displays the Contents pane objects with large icons.
	Small Icons	Displays the Contents pane objects with small icons.
	List	Displays the Contents pane objects in a columnar list.
	Details	Displays the Contents pane objects in a single column that shows each object's name, size, type, and date and time of last modification.

NOTE: DON'T FORGET THE CONTEXT MENUS

Another way to get quick access to many Explorer commands and features is to right-click the selected object (or objects) and select the command you need from the context menu that appears. I'll show you a couple of ways to customize an object's context menus later in this chapter.

Customizing Explorer

Because you and Explorer will be spending a considerable amount of time together, you should be comfortable with Explorer's display. Explorer, unfortunately, isn't quite as customizable as you might like, but a few options can still come in handy. To check them out, select View | Options. You'll see the Options dialog box, shown in Figure 13.1.

FIGURE 13.1.

Use the Options dialog box to set up Explorer to suit your taste.

13

WORKING WITH
FILES AND
FOLDERS

The next few sections give you a rundown of the various controls in this dialog box. Note that you can put the options into effect at any time by clicking the Apply button. When you're done, click OK to return to Explorer.

Hiding and Displaying Files

The two options in the Hidden files group control which files Explorer displays. If you activate Show all files, Explorer's Contents pane displays every file in the currently selected folder. If, however, you activate Hide files of these types (the default), Explorer doesn't display files that have their hidden attribute set or that have one of the following extensions: DLL, SYS, VXD, 386, or DRV. You normally don't need to work with these files directly, so hiding them reduces the clutter in the Contents pane. If you do need to work with one of these files, however (such as CONFIG.SYS, MSDOS.SYS, or BOOTLOG.TXT), you'll need to show all the files.

NOTE: FILES ARE HIDDEN GLOBALLY

The Hidden files options applies not only to Explorer, but to all your Windows applications. In other words, if you activate Hide files of these types, the hidden files won't appear in the Open dialog box of any Windows applications.

NOTE: CHANGING ATTRIBUTES

You might prefer just to change the attributes of individual files. For example, if you like to check out BOOTLOG.TXT regularly, you might want to remove its hidden attribute. To do this, either highlight the file and select File | Properties, or right-click the file and select Properties from the context menu. In the properties sheet that appears, use the various Attributes check boxes to set or remove attributes. For example, to remove the hidden attribute from a file, deactivate the Hidden check box. Click OK when you're done.

Displaying the Folder Path

When the Display the full MS-DOS path in the title bar check box is deactivated (the default), Explorer shows only the name of the current folder in the title bar, as shown in Figure 13.2. Also, Explorer displays only Contents of 'folder' in the description bar above the Contents pane, in which *folder* is the name of the current folder.

If you activate the Display the full MS-DOS path in the title bar check box, Explorer shows the full path for the folder in both the title bar and the description bar, as shown in Figure 13.3. This feature is useful if you can't see one or more of the current folder's parent folders. It's also handy for differentiating folders that have the same name but different parents (especially if you have mapped network drives).

FIGURE 13.2.

By default, Explorer shows only the name of the folder in the title bar.

Title bar   Description bar

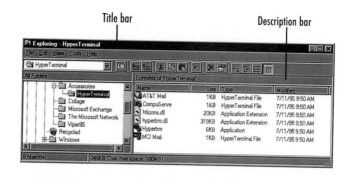

FIGURE 13.3.

For greater clarity, you can tell Explorer to show the full path of each folder.

Displaying File Extensions

By default, the Hide MS-DOS file extensions for file types that are registered check box is activated. To understand what this check box does, you need to know what it means by a *registered* file type. A registered file type is a species of file that Explorer, in a sense, "understands." In other words, Explorer knows what program to use to open the file if you double-click the file. For example, Explorer uses Notepad to open a file if that file's type is text. How does Explorer know what type of file it's dealing with? It's nothing too sophisticated: Explorer just looks at the file's extension. If the extension is TXT, Explorer treats the file as a text file. (I'll discuss all of this in greater detail later in this chapter; see the section "Working with File Types.")

When Explorer sees that a file is one of its registered types, it hides the extension. This is consistent with Windows 95's document focus: Don't worry about the application that creates a document; just worry about the document itself. So all you need to do is double-click a filename, and Explorer handles the dirty work of finding the appropriate application, launching it, and loading the document. The extension is unnecessary, and it makes the Explorer display seem less intimidating for beginners. In the absence of the extension, however, Explorer does give you two hints about the file type:

■ Each file type has its own icon, and Explorer displays the appropriate icon for the file's type to the left of the filename.

■ If you use the Details view, the Type column tells you the file's type.

13

WORKING WITH FILES AND FOLDERS

Hiding the file extensions does, however, have one major drawback: Explorer won't let you change the extension. For example, files ending with DOC are registered with WordPad. Suppose that you have a file named README.TXT that you'd prefer to open in WordPad (for example, because the file is too big for Notepad's britches). All you have to do is rename the file to README.DOC right? Not so fast. If file extensions are hidden, Explorer displays README.TXT as just README. If you change this to README.DOC, Explorer actually renames the file to README.DOC.TXT, and Notepad remains the default application!

If you want to rename a file's extension, you have to deactivate the Hide MS-DOS file extensions for file types that are registered check box to force Explorer to display the extensions. Note, however, that if you change the extension for a registered file type, Explorer displays the warning dialog box shown in Figure 13.4. Click Yes to continue with the rename. (I'll show you how to create new file types later.)

Figure 13.4.

Explorer warns you if you attempt to change the extension of a registered file type.

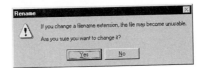

Toggling the Description Bar

The Explorer title bar shows the name of the current folder (and its path if you activated the Display the full MS-DOS path in the title bar check box). This makes the description bar essentially redundant. If you'd like to eke out a bit more room to display files and folders in Explorer, deactivate the Include description bar for right and left panes check box.

Sorting Files and Folders

By default, Explorer arranges the objects in the Contents pane in ascending alphabetical order, with folders first, followed by files. To change this sort order, select View | Arrange Icons, or right-click an empty part of the Contents pane and select Arrange Icons from the context menu. The cascade menu that appears gives you five choices:

by Name: This is the default sort order.

by Type: This option sorts the objects in ascending alphabetical order by file type, with folders first.

by Size: This option sorts the objects in ascending numerical order by file size, with folders first.

by Date: This option sorts the objects in ascending order by the last modified date, with folders first.

AutoArrange: When activated, this command sorts the objects automatically if you move them or add new objects. This command is available only in the Large Icons and Small Icons views.

You'll notice that each of these commands sorts the objects only in ascending order. What if you'd prefer a descending sort? For example, you might want to sort the objects by last modified date in descending order to show the most recently modified files at the top of the list.

To do this, you need to put Explorer in Details view. As shown in Figure 13.5, Details view displays column headings at the top of the Contents pane: Name, Size, Type, and Modified. To sort the objects on a particular column, click the column's heading. For example, clicking the Size heading sorts the objects in ascending order by file size. How do you get a descending sort? Just click the same column heading again.

FIGURE 13.5.

Use the column headings in Details view to sort the Contents pane.

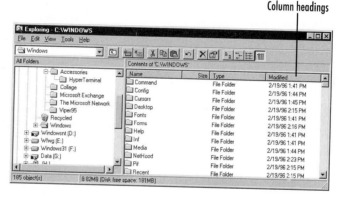

Column headings

Drag-and-Drop Revisited

Explorer's cut-and-paste (or copy-and-paste) file management metaphor takes a bit of getting used to, but it makes sense after a while. Still, in most cases, it's usually faster to drag an object from one location and drop it on another. Explorer's drag-and-drop rules can be confusing, however, so Table 13.3 runs through them one more time for good measure.

Table 13.3. Explorer's default drag-and-drop behavior.

Operation	Mouse Pointer While Dragging	Comments
Copy		If the source and destination folders are on the same disk, Explorer copies the object.
Move		If the source and destination folders are on different disks, Explorer moves the object.
Executable file		If the object is an executable file, Explorer creates a shortcut in the destination folder.

You can also force Explorer to copy or move an object, or to create a shortcut for any object:

■ Hold down Ctrl while you drop the object to force a copy operation.

■ Hold down Shift while you drop the object to force a move operation.

If you don't feel like memorizing any of this information, you can perform a *special drag* instead. In this case, you use the *right* mouse button to drag the object. When you drop it on the destination folder, Explorer displays the context menu shown in Figure 13.6 (the default action is shown in bold). Now just click the action you want.

FIGURE 13.6.

If you right-drag an object, Explorer displays this context menu when you drop the object on its destination.

TIP: HOW TO SPECIAL-DRAG WITH THE LEFT MOUSE BUTTON

If your mouse doesn't have a right mouse button, or if your right mouse button is broken, you can still do the special drag. Just hold down both Ctrl and Shift, and drag the object while holding down the left mouse button. Note that in this case, the default action is always to create a shortcut.

Here are a few drag-and-drop tidbits that should make your object copying and moving a bit easier:

■ Don't forget that you can cancel a drag at any time by pressing Esc.

■ It's possible to drag and scroll at the same time. For example, what do you do if you drag an object into the Folders pane and then realize you can't see the destination folder? Instead of canceling, drag the object to either the top or the bottom of the Folders pane (depending on where the destination folder is). Explorer either scrolls the folders down (if you're at the top of the pane) or scrolls the folders up (if you're at the bottom of the pane).

■ Unlike File Manager, Explorer doesn't let you open two windows and drag between them. The Folders pane is quite flexible, so you shouldn't need to use multiple windows for drag-and-drop. If you feel more comfortable doing it that way, however, feel free to start a second copy of Explorer and arrange them side-by-side.

■ One handy feature that's missing from Windows 95 is the capability to drag an object onto the taskbar. You get the next best thing, however. If you have a folder window minimized on the taskbar, you can drag an object from Explorer and then let the mouse pointer hover over the folder window's taskbar button for couple of seconds. Windows 95 then opens the folder window so that you can drop the object into the folder.

NOTE: HOW DO YOU OPEN A FOLDER WINDOW?

You can use several methods to open a folder in its own window:

- In Explorer, right-click the folder and select Open from the context menu.
- Use My Computer to open the folder.
- Create a desktop shortcut for the folder, and double-click the shortcut. (For more on shortcuts, see "Can I Get There from Here? Working with Shortcuts" later in this chapter.)
- Select Start | Run to display the Run dialog box, type the folder's full pathname in the Open text box, and click OK.

TIP: DRAGGING A FOLDER TO THE RUN DIALOG BOX

If the Run dialog box is open, dragging a folder from Explorer and dropping it anywhere on the Run dialog box pastes the folder's full pathname into the Open text box.

Easier File Finagling with the Send To Command

Copying or moving a file or folder is usually a three-step process: Copy (or cut) the object to the Clipboard, head to the destination folder, and paste the object from the Clipboard. Drag-and-drop is much easier, but it still requires that you have the destination folder in view.

For certain file operations, Explorer offers a method that's much easier than the Clipboard or drag-and-drop: the Send To command. To try this, highlight an object in the Contents pane and select File | Send To. You can also right-click an object in the Contents pane and then select Send To from the context menu. As you can see in Figure 13.7, the cascade menu that appears offers several possible locations. The choices depend on which Windows 95 components you have installed, but you'll at least see commands for your floppy disks. Selecting a floppy disk from this menu sends a copy of the file to that disk. (Of course, you need to make sure that you have a disk in the drive before you try this action.) If you'd prefer to move the file to the floppy disk, hold down Shift while selecting the command from the Send To menu.

What's interesting about the Send To command is that the contents of the Send To cascade menu are shortcut files. For example, if you have a 3½ Floppy (A) command in your Send To menu, this command is just a shortcut to floppy drive A. Selecting this command is identical to dragging the object and dropping it on drive A in the Folders pane.

FIGURE 13.7.

The Send To command offers an easy method of copying files to floppy disks and other locations.

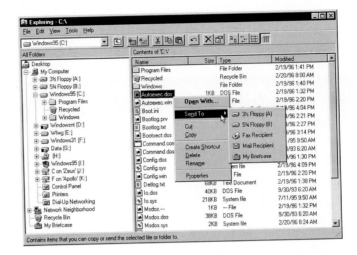

Now here's the real kicker: The contents of the Send To menu—the shortcut files—come from a special `SendTo` folder that runs off your main Windows folder. To see for yourself, open the Windows folder and select the `SendTo` folder, as shown in Figure 13.8. Sure enough, there's a shortcut file for each Send To menu item.

FIGURE 13.8.

The Send To menu items are just shortcut files in the `SendTo` *folder.*

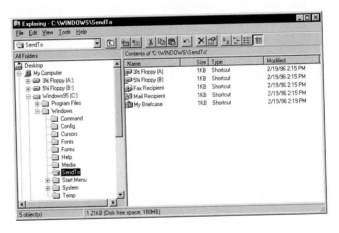

The great thing about this arrangement is that you're free to add your own shortcuts to this folder, and they'll appear on the Send To menu. For example, if you use an `Upload` folder to store files before sending them out via modem, you could create a shortcut to that folder in the `SendTo` folder. Similarly, if you like to include shortcuts to programs in your Start menu folders, include these folders in the Send To menu. You could do the same thing for disk drives, network drives, and any other location you use to store files.

CAUTION: SEND TO USES DRAG-AND-DROP RULES

Bear in mind that Send To uses the same rules for copying and moving objects (including executable files) that drag-and-drop does. For example, if the object and the Send To menu item (or, more specifically, the file or folder *pointed to* by the Send To shortcut) are on the same drive, Send To *moves* the object. Similarly, executable files are always sent to shortcuts. If you want to force a particular operation, use the same Ctrl, Shift, or Ctrl-Shift tricks I showed you for drag-and-drop.

There's no reason why you have to restrict the Send To commands to just folders and disk drives, however. Because you can create shortcuts for just about anything in Windows 95, you can populate the SendTo folder with any number of interesting destinations. I'll talk more about this when I discuss shortcuts in detail later (see "Can I Get There from Here? Working with Shortcuts"), but for now, here are a few examples:

The Desktop: This is handy if you find that you often send documents to the desktop for easy access. To create a Desktop shortcut, make sure that Explorer is showing all files, as described earlier. Now right-drag the \Windows\Desktop folder, drop it on the SendTo folder, and select Create Shortcut(s) Here.

Printers: If you add a printer shortcut to the Send To menu, you can print a document just by sending it to the printer. You'll find your installed printers in the Printers folder.

The Recycle Bin: Adding the Recycle Bin to the Send To menu is handy if you can't see the Recycle Bin icon on your desktop. It also offers one advantage over deleting files in Explorer: You don't have to confirm that you want to send the object to the Recycle Bin.

Executable files: If you create a shortcut to an executable file on the Send To menu, Explorer will open a document that's sent to the underlying application. For example, if you add a shortcut to Notepad, you can send a text file (even one that doesn't have a TXT extension) to the shortcut, and Notepad opens with the document loaded.

Using Explorer from the Command Line

For extra control over how Explorer starts, you can use a few command-line options in the Run dialog box or from the DOS command prompt. Here's the syntax:

```
explorer [/n],[/e],[/root,folder,[subobject]],[/select]
```

Here's a summary of the various switches and parameters:

/n	Opens a new Explorer window.
/e	Starts Explorer in Explorer view (that is, with both the Folders pane and the Contents pane); if you omit /e, Explorer starts in Open view (that is, with only the Contents pane, à la My Computer).

`/root,folder`	Specifies the folder that will be the root of the new Explorer view. (In other words, this folder will appear at the top of the Folders pane.)
`subobject`	Specifies the file or folder (of which `folder` must be the parent) that will be displayed in the Contents pane. Use a path relative to the root. For example, if the root is `C:\WINDOWS` and you want the displayed folder to be `C:\WINDOWS\SYSTEM`, just use `SYSTEM` for `subobject`.
`/select`	Specifies that the `subobject` should be highlighted in the Contents pane.

For example, if you want to open Explorer with `C:\WINDOWS` as the root and you want the `C:\WINDOWS\SYSTEM` folder displayed in the Contents pane, use the following command, the results of which are shown in Figure 13.9:

```
explorer /n,/e,/root,c:\windows,system
```

FIGURE 13.9.

The Explorer window that results when you use the command line `explorer /n,/e,/ root,c:\windows,system`.

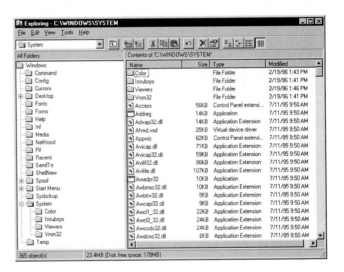

As another example, suppose that you want to open Explorer with `C:\` as the root and you want to highlight the file `BOOTLOG.TXT`. Here's the command that will do it, the results of which are shown in Figure 13.10:

```
explorer /n,/e,/root,c:\,bootlog.txt,/select
```

FIGURE 13.10.

The Explorer window that results when you use the command line explorer /n,/e,/ root,c:\,bootlog.txt,/ select.

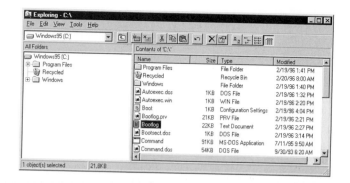

TIP: DISPLAY THE DESKTOP AS THE ROOT

You can open an Explorer window with the desktop as the root by using the following Explorer command (don't miss the comma at the end):

```
explorer /root,
```

Can I Get There from Here? Working with Shortcuts

I've mentioned shortcuts a few times in this book, and you saw earlier how shortcuts are invaluable for enhancing the Send To menu. In your quest to unleash Windows 95, you'll find yourself using shortcuts constantly, so it's time we took a step back and looked a little more closely at these handy files. This section explains shortcuts in more detail, runs through all the possible methods of creating them, and shows umpteen ways to put shortcuts to good use.

What Is a Shortcut?

If you used any flavor of Windows 3.x, shortcuts will already be familiar to you: They're just like program items (icons) in a Program Manager group. In other words, a shortcut is a pointer to an object, such as an executable file or a document. If it points to an executable, double-clicking the shortcut starts the underlying program; if it points to a document, double-clicking the shortcut starts the application associated with the document *and* loads the document. (Assuming, that is, that the document type is registered with Windows 95. See "Working with File Types" later in this chapter for more info.) And, as with a program item, because a shortcut only points to another object (a program or document), you can safely delete a shortcut without affecting the underlying object.

13

WORKING WITH FILES AND FOLDERS

A very important difference exists, however, between a Windows 95 shortcut and a Program Manager icon: The shortcuts themselves are *files*. (They use the LNK—for *link*—extension.) This means you can create shortcuts in any folder, and you're free to move or copy shortcuts anywhere you like, including the desktop. (About the only place that's off-limits is the taskbar.)

Also, shortcuts are much more flexible than program items because shortcuts can point to many more object types. So, yes, they can point to executable files and documents, but they can also point to disk drives, folders, printers, and a whole host of useful objects (I'll show you lots of examples a bit later).

When you create a shortcut, you'll notice that Windows 95 adds an arrow to the lower-left corner of the icon, as shown in Figure 13.11. This is to remind you that the shortcut *points to* another file. Windows 95 also adds the phrase "Shortcut to" to the name of the underlying object. You can delete this extra phrase, if you like. (For desktop shortcuts, click the icon, wait a couple of seconds or press F2, and click the icon again to activate the name text box.)

FIGURE 13.11.

Shortcut icons are marked with an arrow in the lower-left corner.

Shortcut to
Windows

Methods of Creating Shortcuts

Shortcuts are an important part of the Windows 95 interface, so there's no shortage of methods you can use to create them. Here's a summary:

- Unless you hold down Ctrl (for copy) or Shift (for move), dropping a dragged executable file always creates a shortcut that points to the executable. Note that this applies only to executable files that use the EXE and COM extensions; it doesn't work with files with the BAT (batch) extension.

- To create a shortcut for any dragged file, hold down Ctrl and Shift when you drop the file. In the context menu that appears, select Create Shortcut(s) Here.

- Right-drag a file, and after you drop it on its destination, select Create Shortcut(s) Here from the context menu.

- Right-click a file or folder, and select Create Shortcut on the context menu to create a shortcut in the same folder. You can then drag this shortcut to the appropriate destination.

- Copy a file to the Clipboard, highlight the destination, and select Edit | Paste Shortcut.

- In Explorer, highlight a folder and select File | New | Shortcut. (You can also right-click an empty part of the Explorer Contents pane and select New | Shortcut from the context menu.) Explorer displays the Create Shortcut dialog box, shown in Figure 13.12. Enter the command line for the underlying file (or use the Browse button) and click Next >. Enter a name for the shortcut, and click Finish.

FIGURE 13.12.

Use the Create Shortcut Wizard to create a new shortcut.

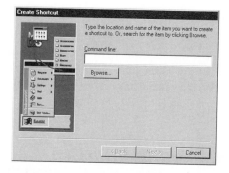

NOTE: NEW DESKTOP SHORTCUTS

To create a new shortcut on the desktop, right-click an empty part of the desktop, and select New | Shortcut from the context menu.

Telling Windows 95 Not to Add "Shortcut To"

One of the many things Microsoft is working on in its research labs is the problem of how to make software adapt automatically to the needs and preferences of individual users. In Office 97, for example, the Office Assistant watches what you do and occasionally offers help based on your actions.

A bit of this behavior also made it into Windows 95. Specifically, if you start deleting the "Shortcut to" prefix in your shortcut names, Windows 95 eventually clues in and stops adding "Shortcut to" for future shortcuts. How does this work? The secret lies inside the Registry at the following key:

```
HKEY_CURRENT_USER\Software\Microsoft\Windows\CurrentVersion\Explorer
```

Here you'll see an item named `link` that is set to the value of 32 (20 hexadecimal) each time you start Windows 95. This value is incremented by 1 each time you create a shortcut, but it's *decremented* by 5 whenever you delete the "Shortcut to" part of a shortcut's name. When this value reaches 0, Windows 95 stops adding the "Shortcut to" prefix.

This is interesting behavior, but it would be truly useful if Windows 95 didn't reset the `link` value with each logon. You might think that you could place a .REG file in your Startup group that would set the Registry's `link` setting to 0 each time you start Windows 95. That's a good idea, but it doesn't work, unfortunately. That's because Windows 95 keeps track of all this by using an internal variable, and the Registry's `link` setting only reflects the current value of the variable, so changing the `link` setting has no effect. (Which means that editing the `link` value to 0 using the Registry Editor won't work either.) No, you can only change the behavior of Windows 95 by deleting the appropriate number of "Shortcut to" snippets.

13

WORKING WITH FILES AND FOLDERS

TIP: THE TWEAKUI POWER TOY CAN DO IT

Actually, there *is* a way to prevent Windows 95 from adding "Shortcut to" to your shortcut names. In the TweakUI utility (part of Microsoft's Power Toys collection; see Chapter 7, "Customizing Windows 95"), display the Explorer tab and then deactivate the `Prefix "Shortcut to" on new shortcuts` check box.

Working with Shortcut Properties

As I mentioned earlier, a shortcut is really a LNK file. This means that, like any file object, a shortcut has properties you can manipulate. To view these properties, highlight the shortcut file in Explorer and select File | Properties. You can also right-click the shortcut icon and select Properties from the context menu. In the properties sheet that appears, the General tab just gives you basic file info: location, name, size, attributes, and so on. The really interesting stuff is in the Shortcut tab, shown in Figure 13.13.

FIGURE 13.13.

Use the Shortcut tab to manipulate various properties for a short-cut file.

Here's an explanation of each control that appears on the Shortcut tab:

Target: This text box gives you the full pathname of the object that's linked to the shortcut. If the shortcut points to a document, you might want to adjust the target so that a different application opens the file. In Figure 13.14, for example, I could force WordPad to open the TODOLIST.TXT file by appending the path to WordPad to the front of the target, like so:

```
"C:\Program Files\Accessories\Wordpad.exe" C:\WINDOWS\ToDoList.txt
```

NOTE: WATCH OUT FOR LONG FILENAMES

Notice that I had to put quotation marks around the WordPad path. That's because the path includes a space and the `Target` box won't accept names that include spaces. You either have to surround the path with quotation marks or use the DOS versions of the name. In the preceding example, the DOS name would look like this:

```
C:\PROGRA~1\ACCESS~1\Wordpad.exe C:\WINDOWS\ToDoList.txt
```

Start in: If your shortcut starts an application, this text box sets the application's default folder.

Shortcut key: Use this text box to assign a key combination to the shortcut. The default key combo is Ctrl-Alt-*character,* in which *character* is any keyboard character key you press while this text box has the focus. If you prefer a key combination that begins with Ctrl-Shift, hold down both Ctrl and Shift, and then press a character; for a Ctrl-Alt-Shift combination, hold down all three keys, and then press a character. To help you remember the key combination, you might want to include it as part of the shortcut's name.

Run: If the shortcut starts an application, this drop-down list determines how the application window appears. Select `Normal window`, `Minimized`, or `Maximized`.

Find Target: This command button opens a folder window and highlights the target file or folder. This provides you with a quick way to get to the target object (for example, to make a copy of it).

Change Icon: Use this command button to assign a different icon to the shortcut. (The little arrow in the lower-left corner remains in place, however.) Clicking this button displays the Change Icon dialog box, shown in Figure 13.14. For other icon collections, try the following files (the first one is a hidden file):

```
C:\WINDOWS\SYSTEM\PIFMGR.DLL
C:\WINDOWS\MORICONS.DLL
C:\WINDOWS\PROGMAN.EXE
```

FIGURE 13.14.

Use the Change Icon dialog box to select a different icon for a shortcut.

13

If You Move, Rename, or Delete the Target

You've just seen that a shortcut points to a specific target. What happens, however, if you move, rename, or delete that target? Let's find out.

If you move or rename the target, Windows 95 tries to find the correct target the next time you invoke the shortcut. Because other files might have the same name as the missing target, Windows 95 doesn't search for the filename. Instead, it uses the original target's size, type, and the date and time it was created, because these attributes are unlikely to be the same for any other file. While it's searching, you'll see the Missing Shortcut dialog box, shown in Figure 13.15.

FIGURE 13.15.

Windows 95 displays this dialog box when searching for a target that you've moved or renamed.

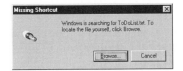

If Windows 95 finds the target, it updates the shortcut and opens the object. If it can't find the target, Windows 95 makes an educated guess and displays a Problem with Shortcut dialog box similar to the one shown in Figure 13.16. If this is the correct target, click Yes; if it's not the correct target, click No, invoke the shortcut again, click the Browse button in the Missing Shortcut dialog box, and use the Open dialog box that appears to select the target.

FIGURE 13.16.

Windows 95 displays this dialog box if it can't find the original target.

NOTE: TARGET TROUBLES

Windows 95 doesn't do a good job of finding targets that have been moved to a different drive. Also, if the target exists on a mapped network drive and the drive's letter changes, Windows 95 won't find the target.

If you delete the target, Windows 95 will, of course, fail to find it. In this case, you should click No in the Problem with Shortcut dialog box and then delete the shortcut.

A Cornucopia of Shortcut Ideas and Techniques

Shortcuts are extremely handy time-savers, and you'll find endless uses for them. To get you started, the next few sections run through a few ideas for using shortcuts.

Folders

If you have a favorite folder you often view or use for file storage, a shortcut to the folder is an easy way to work:

- To view the contents of the folder, double-click the shortcut. Windows 95 displays a folder window (similar to the kind you see in My Computer) showing the objects inside the folder.

- If you want to move or copy objects to the folder, just drag them from Explorer (or My Computer), and drop them on the shortcut icon.

If the folder has subfolders, you might prefer to display the folder in "Explorer" view (that is, with a Folders pane and a Contents pane). To do this, open the properties sheet for the shortcut, select the Shortcut tab, and add `explorer.exe /e,` (include the comma) to the front of the `Target` value. For example, if the current target is `c:\windows`, the new target should be this:

```
explorer.exe /e,c:\windows
```

Of course, you're free to use any of the Explorer command-line switches that we looked at earlier.

The Start Menu

In Chapter 7, I showed you how to customize your Start menu by adding and removing items in the `Start Menu` folder. The Start menu itself is easy to customize: You just drag items onto the Start button. However, to add items to the Start menu's subfolders (Programs, Accessories, and so on), you need to display these folders in Explorer. If you plan on using this technique regularly, you can make your life easier by creating desktop shortcuts for the Start menu's subfolders. This way, you get fast access to these folders, and you can add items to them just by dragging them from Explorer and dropping them on the appropriate shortcut.

> **NOTE: EACH USER HAS A START MENU FOLDER**
>
> If you've set up user profiles on your system (as described in Chapter 7), note that each user gets his own `Start Menu` folder. For example, if you have a user named Biff, you can customize his Start menu by adding shortcuts to the `C:\Windows\Profiles\Biff\Start Menu` folder (assuming that `C:\Windows` is your main Windows 95 folder).
>
> Note that, for each user, the `Profiles` folder also contains `Desktop` and `SendTo` subfolders.

The StartUp Folder

Even if you don't plan on remaking all the Start menu's folders in your own image, there's one folder you'll almost certainly want to customize: the `StartUp` folder. This folder controls the objects that appear on the StartUp menu and that, more importantly, load automatically each time you start Windows 95. The path for the `StartUp` folder is `C:\Windows\Start Menu\Programs\StartUp`.

TIP: BYPASSING STARTUP FILES

To tell Windows 95 not to load your StartUp folder objects at boot time, hold down Shift while Windows 95 starts.

Disk Drives

The Macintosh desktop displays an icon for each disk drive on the computer. To give your system a Mac-like feel, create shortcuts for your disk drives on the desktop. The default drag-and-drop operation for a disk drive is to create a shortcut, so you don't have to hold down any keys or right-drag.

One of the nice things about having this shortcut is that you can work with the shortcut as though it were the actual drive. For example, you can right-click a floppy drive shortcut and use the commands on the context menu to format or copy a disk that's in the drive. (These operations are discussed later, in the section titled "Disk Driving: Dealing with Disks.")

Network Computers

If you're running Windows 95 on a network, you can create shortcuts for those computers that appear in the Network Neighborhood. This applies even to computers you connect to via Dial-Up Networking. In this case, invoking the shortcut dials your modem automatically. The default drag-and-drop operation for a computer is to create a shortcut, so you don't have to hold down any keys or right-drag.

Executable Files

Shortcuts to executable files give you an easy way to launch the application (especially if you create a keyboard shortcut). But there's more to an executable shortcut than that. In particular, you can drag a document from Explorer and drop it on the shortcut. As long as the application knows how to deal with the document, the application starts and it displays the document.

This is a useful technique for those file types that don't have a default application. For example, if you want to open CONFIG.SYS in Notepad, normally you have to start Notepad, select File | Open, display all files, and select CONFIG.SYS. If, however, you have a shortcut to NOTEPAD.EXE on your desktop (or wherever), all you have to do is drag CONFIG.SYS and drop it on the shortcut. Notepad starts and it loads CONFIG.SYS automatically.

Documents

Creating document shortcuts is useful only if the document's file type is registered with Windows 95. In this case, double-clicking the shortcut starts the registered application and loads the document automatically. In Windows 95, this technique works for TXT (text) files, DOC (WordPad document) files, BMP (bitmap) files, HT (HyperTerminal) files, and more. I'll talk about registered file types in detail later, in the section "Working with File Types."

NOTE: THE DOCUMENTS MENU

Another quick way to open a document is to select Start | Documents. The cascade menu that appears contains shortcuts to the last 15 documents you worked with in any of your applications. Selecting one of these shortcuts opens the appropriate applications and loads the document. These shortcuts are stored in the \Windows\Recent folder, so you can always add and remove Document menu shortcuts by hand.

Document Scraps

For applications that support OLE (object linking and embedding), you can create desktop shortcuts to bits of text or part of a graphics image. Just highlight the data you want to use, drag it from the application, and drop it on the desktop. (The default drag-and-drop operation for an OLE object is to create a shortcut, so you don't have to hold down any keys or right-drag.) Windows 95 creates an OLE object—called a document *scrap*—on the desktop. You can then drop this scrap inside another document, or double-click it to start the source application and load the scrap.

Printers

Printers are common shortcuts because they can be quite handy. For one thing, the shortcut gives you easy access to a particular printer so that you can manipulate any pending print jobs (more on this topic in Chapter 19, "Prescriptions for Perfect Printing"). For another, you can drag a document from Explorer and drop it on the printer shortcut, and Windows 95 then prints the document automatically. Use the Printers folder to drag a printer onto the desktop (or wherever). The default drag-and-drop operation for a printer is to create a shortcut, so you don't have to hold down any keys or right-drag.

Control Panel Icons

If you have any Control Panel icons you use regularly, creating a shortcut to the icon is much faster than having to display the Control Panel folder. (I showed you other methods of getting easier access to Control Panel icons in Chapter 7.) To create the shortcuts, drag the icons from the Control Panel folder, and drop them on the desktop. The default drag-and-drop operation for a Control Panel icon is to create a shortcut, so you don't have to hold down any keys or right-drag.

The Microsoft Network

As you'll see in Chapter 26, "Getting Online with The Microsoft Network," MSN has lots of interesting content. The problem, however, is having to navigate endless folders to get to the site you want. MSN has a Favorites folder that you can use to jump immediately to your fave-rave sites, but you can also create shortcuts. Most MSN sites are just folders, so you create short-cuts just like you create a regular folder.

Web Sites

If you have Internet Explorer installed, you can easily create desktop shortcuts to the Web sites you visit most often. Just use Internet Explorer to display the site, and then select File | Create Shortcut (or right-click the page and select Create Shortcut from the context menu). I explain how to use Internet Explorer in Chapter 38, "Exploring the Web with Internet Explorer."

Working with File Types

I've mentioned *file types* a couple of times in this chapter, so perhaps it's time to take a closer look at them. A file is an object, so it has various properties, including its name, its size, and the date and time it was created. The extension part of the filename determines another property: the *file type*. For example, a file with the extension TXT is a text document, and a file with a BMP extension is a bitmap.

The file type, in turn, defines which actions you can use with the file. A text document, for example, has two actions: *Open,* which displays the document in Notepad, and *Print,* which sends the document to the Windows 95 default printer. (Technically, the Print action opens Notepad, loads the document, selects File | Print, and closes Notepad. This all happens in the blink of an eye.) Each file type has a default action that runs when you perform any of the following actions on a document of that file type:

- Double-click the document
- Highlight the document and press Enter
- Pull down the File menu and select the command in bold
- Right-click the document and, in the context menu that appears, select the command in bold

For a text file, the Open action is the default. Any other actions associated with the file type appear below the default action on either the File menu or the context menu. For a text file, you'll see a Print command below the Open command.

File types that have associated actions are said to be *registered* with Windows 95 (because this data is stored in the Registry). If you used Windows 3.x, this whole idea is very similar to File Manager's file associations, but Windows 95's file types are much more powerful.

To see the list of Windows 95's registered file types, in Explorer, select View | Options to display the Options dialog box, and then select the File Types tab. As you can see in Figure 13.17, the Registered file types list contains the icons and names for each registered file type. When you highlight one of these items, the File type details group shows the extensions associated with the file type and the application that opens the file type (if any).

FIGURE 13.17.

The File Types tab displays a list of Windows 95's registered file types.

When working with file types, you can take the following actions:

- Use a different file type to open a document.
- Modify the existing actions for a file type. For example, you could tell Windows 95 to open text files in WordPad rather than Notepad.
- Create new actions for an existing file type. For example, you could define a secondary application to use for displaying a file type (such as WordPad for text files).
- Create new file types and assign actions for the new type. For example, many applications ship with files named README.1ST. You could create a new file type for files that use the 1ST extension and then assign an Open action that uses Notepad to view these files.

Each of these techniques is discussed in the following sections.

Using a Different File Type to Open a Document

Most file types have an Open action that defines the default application that Windows 95 should use to display the file. Sometimes, however, the default application isn't the one you want to use. For example, if you have a text file that you know is too large for Notepad, you'd be better off loading it in WordPad instead. Here are the steps to follow to open a file with a different application:

1. In Explorer, highlight the document you want to open.
2. Hold down Shift and either select File | Open With or right-click the document and select Open With from the context menu. The Open With dialog box, shown in Figure 13.18, appears.

FIGURE 13.18.

Use the Open With dialog box to choose the application you want to use to open the file.

3. In the Choose the program you want to use list, highlight the application you want to use to open the file.

4. If you want to use this application for this file type all the time, activate the Always use this program to open this type of file check box.

5. Click OK. Windows 95 uses the selected program to open the file.

Modifying Actions for an Existing File Type

If an existing file type uses an action you don't like, it's easy enough to change it. For example, if you deal with large text files, Notepad is a pain because it just doesn't have the horsepower to handle anything too large. WordPad can handle such files, however, so you might want to change the Open action for text files to use WordPad instead. Here's how it's done:

1. In the File Types tab, use the Registered file types list to highlight the file type you want to change.

2. Click the Edit button. An Edit File Type dialog box similar to the one shown in Figure 13.19 appears.

FIGURE 13.19.

The Edit File Type dialog box lists the existing actions for the selected file type.

3. The Actions list displays the available actions for this file type. Highlight the action you want to change, and then click Edit. An editing action dialog box similar to the one shown in Figure 13.20 appears.

Figure 13.20.

Use this dialog box to change the selected action.

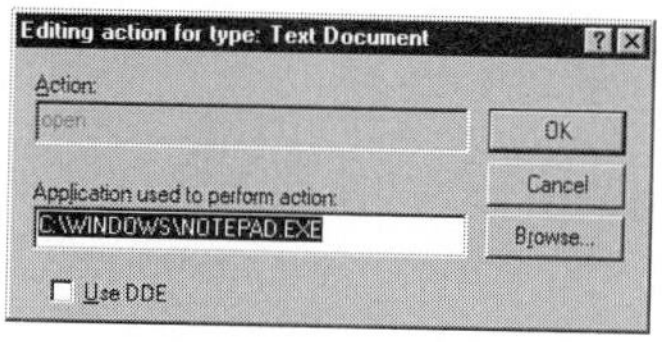

4. In the Application used to perform action text box, enter the full pathname of the application you want to use. If you're not sure, click Browse, highlight the appropriate executable file in the Open With dialog box, and click Open.

CAUTION: USE QUOTATION MARKS ON NAMES WITH SPACES

If the pathname of the executable file contains a space, be sure to enclose the path in quotation marks, like so:

```
"C:\Program Files\Accessories\Wordpad.exe"
```

Also, if you'll be using documents that have spaces in their filenames, add the "%1" parameter after the pathname, like so:

```
"C:\Program Files\Accessories\Wordpad.exe" "%1"
```

The %1 part tells the application to load the specified file (such as a filename you double-click), and the quotation marks ensure that no problems occur with multiple-word filenames.

NOTE: THE PRINT ACTION NEEDS THE PRINT SWITCH

If you're changing the Print action, be sure to include the /P switch after the application's pathname, like this:

```
"C:\Program Files\Accessories\Wordpad.exe" /P
```

---

5. Click OK to return to the Edit File Type dialog box.
6. Click Close to return to the File Types tab.

Creating New Actions for an Existing File Type

Instead of replacing an action's underlying application with a different application, you might prefer to create new actions. In our text file example, you could keep the default Open action as it is and create a new action—called, say, Open with WordPad—that uses WordPad to open a text file. When you highlight a text file and pull down the File menu, or right-click a text file, the menus that appear will show both commands: Open (for Notepad) and Open with WordPad (for WordPad). Follow these steps to create a new action for an existing file type:

1. In the File Types tab, use the `Registered file types` list to highlight the file type you want to change.

2. Click the Edit button to display the Edit File Type dialog box.

3. Click New. The New Action dialog box, shown in Figure 13.21, appears.

Figure 13.21.

Use the New Action dialog box to set up a new action for a file type.

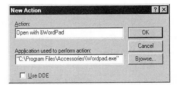

4. Use the `Action` text box to enter a name for the new action.

TIP: ASSIGNING AN ACCELERATOR KEY

In the `Action` text box, if you precede a letter with an ampersand (&), Windows 95 designates that letter as the menu accelerator key. For example, as shown in Figure 13.21, entering `Open with &WordPad` defines W as the accelerator key. You can then press this letter's key to select the command on either the File menu or the context menu (see Figure 13.22).

5. In the `Application used to perform action` text box, enter the full pathname of the application you want to use. If you're not sure, click Browse, highlight the appropriate executable file in the Open With dialog box, and click Open.

6. Click OK to return to the Edit File Type dialog box. The new action appears in the `Actions` list.

7. If you want to make the new action the default, highlight it and click the Set Default button.

8. Click Close to return to the File Types tab.

As I said, the new action appears both in the context menu for the file type and in the File menu when you highlight a document of the file type. For example, Figure 13.22 shows the context menu that appears for a text file after you've added the Open with WordPad action.

TIP: EASIER DISK DEFRAGMENTING

Interestingly, Windows 95 has a file type for disk drives. This lets you set up actions for the drive. In particular, you can create a Defragment action that runs Disk Defragmenter (`C:\WINDOWS\DEFRAG.EXE`) on the drive.

FIGURE 13.22.

New actions appear on the context menu for the file type.

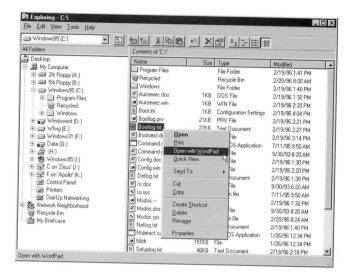

Creating a New File Type

Windows 95 defines about 50 file types, but that isn't nearly enough to cover every possible extension. For example, no actions are defined for files that use the SYS extension, such as CONFIG.SYS or MSDOS.SYS. It would be handy to associate these text files with Notepad. Similarly, you might want to use nonstandard extensions in some of your files. For example, if you use both Word for Windows and Word for DOS, you might want to use the extension WIN for files created with Word for Windows, and the extension DOS for files created with Word for DOS.

To satisfy all of these needs, Windows 95 lets you define new file types and create actions for them. I'll show you two methods: a simple method of creating a new file type with just an Open action, and a more advanced method of creating a new file type with multiple actions.

TIP: CREATE A NEW FILE TYPE FOR WORDPAD

If you use Word for Windows, the DOC extension gets associated with Word rather than WordPad. If you like to create small notes in WordPad, it's a pain to double-click these files and have them open (slowly) in Word. Instead, you should create a new file type for WordPad documents (using an extension of, say, PAD or WPD).

13

WORKING WITH
FILES AND
FOLDERS

TIP: CREATE A TEMPLATE FOR WORDPAD

To create a template file in WordPad, follow these steps:

1. Open a new file in WordPad.
2. Make any changes you want to include in the template, such as font size and style, margin settings, and so on.

   Note that if you want to change the default font, you must type some text into the template and then assign the font.
3. Save the file with a name that will easily identify the template, such as WordPad Courier TEMPLATE.TPL.
4. Double-click My Computer.
5. Select View | Options.
6. On the File Types tab, click the New Type button.
7. Type a description of the template in the Description Of Type box.
8. In the Associated Extension box, type tpl.
9. Click the New button.
10. In the Action box, type open.
11. In the Application Used To Perform Action box, enter the complete path for WordPad.
12. Click OK until the Options dialog box closes.

When you double-click a file that has a .TPL extension, the file will be opened in WordPad.

Creating a Simple File Type

If all you want is to set up an association between a particular file extension and an application, follow these steps:

1. In Explorer, highlight a file that contains the extension you want to use as the new file type.
2. Either select File | Open With or right-click the file and select Open With from the context menu. You then see the Open With dialog box, shown earlier in Figure 13.18.
3. In the Choose the program you want to use list, highlight the application you want to use to open this file type.
4. Activate the Always use this program to open this type of file check box, and click OK.

Windows 95 uses the selected program to open the file, and it also creates a new file type with a single action: Open. The default name for the new file type is *EXT* File, in which *EXT* is the file extension (for example, WIN File). To change this description, display the File Types tab, highlight the file type, click Edit, and enter a new description in the `Description of type` text box.

Creating a More Advanced File Type

If you need to define more than just the Open action (such as the Print action) for a new file type, you need to use the File Types tab. Here are the steps to follow:

1. In the File Types tab, click the New Type button. The Add New File Type dialog box, shown in Figure 13.23, appears. (Note that the Add New File Type dialog box you see might look different than the one shown in Figure 13.23. I'll discuss this difference after these steps.)

Figure 13.23.

Use this dialog box to define your new file type.

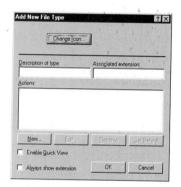

2. Use the `Description of type` text box to enter a description for the new file type. (This is the text that will appear in the `Registered file types` list and in the Type column of Explorer's Details view.)

3. Use the `Associated extension` text box to enter the extension for the file type.

4. Click New. The New Action dialog box appears.

5. Use the `Action` text box to enter a name for the new action.

6. In the `Application used to perform action` text box, enter the full pathname of the application you want to use. If you're not sure, click Browse, highlight the appropriate executable file in the Open With dialog box, and click Open. (Remember to add the `/P` switch for the Print action.)

7. Click OK to return to the Edit File Type dialog box. The new action appears in the `Actions` list.

8. If you want to make the new action the default, highlight it and click the Set Default button.

9. Repeat steps 4 through 8 to define other actions.

10. Click Close to return to the File Types tab.

You might have noticed that the Add New File Type dialog box on your system looks more like the one shown in Figure 13.24 than the one shown in Figure 13.23. That's because this dialog box gets changed when you install Internet Explorer. These changes allow you to work with Internet content. Specifically, three new controls are added:

Content Type (MIME): Use this drop-down to specify the Internet content type. For example, if you're setting up Windows 95 to handle AIFF sound files, you'd select the audio/aiff item.

Default Extension for Content Type: This disabled drop-down list shows you the default extension for the content type you selected.

Confirm Open After Download: When this check box is activated and you choose to open (rather than save) a downloaded file, Windows 95 will ask you to confirm that you want to open the file once the entire file has been received. (See Chapter 38 to learn more about downloading Net files via Internet Explorer.)

Finding File Needles in Hard Disk Haystacks

With multigigabyte hard disks selling for $250 on the street, the days of king-size hard disk storage at a pint-size price are upon us. You'll recall from Chapter 1, "Understanding the Windows 95 Installation and Setup," however, that Parkinson's Law of Data ensures us that data expands to fill the space available. So, yes, our hard disks are massive, but they also contain massive numbers of files. Misplacing a file under these conditions can be a real problem because finding it among thousands of files becomes a chore. To help out, Windows 95 has a Find utility that can search for files (or folders) by name, date, size, or even content. The next few sections describe all of Find's features.

Starting Find

To get the Find utility cranked up, you can use three methods:

- To search in a particular folder or disk drive, highlight the folder or disk drive in Explorer, and then either select Tools | Find | Files or Folders or right-click the folder or disk drive and select Find from the context menu. (You can also press F3.)

- To search the entire Desktop folder, click an empty part of the desktop and press F3.

- To search drive C, select Start | Find | Files or Folders. (If you have a Microsoft Natural Keyboard or a compatible, press ⊞-F.)

In each case, the Find window, shown in Figure 13.24, is displayed.

Searching by Name and Location

The Find window's Name & Location tab lets you search for files or folders by name and specify the drive or folder in which to search.

FIGURE 13.24.

Use the Find window to scope out files or folders on your system.

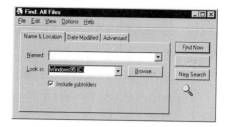

Use the Named combo box to enter a filename specification for the file or files you want to find. (After you've run some searches, you can use the drop-down list to select previous filename specifications.) If you're looking for a specific file, enter the complete name using the following guidelines:

- If the file contains a space, enclose the filename in quotation marks (for example, "Letter To Mom.doc").

- If you want to search for multiple files, separate each name with a space, comma, or semicolon.

- Find's filename searches aren't case-sensitive, so don't worry about whether you use upper- or lowercase.

- Although I keep using the word "file," remember that you can use Find to search for folder names as well.

If you're not sure of the exact filename, or if the name is a long one, Find is happy to accept partial names. For example, an entry of fig will find files named CONFIG.SYS, CHAPTER1_FIGURE57.BMP, and FIG.NEWTON. Notice how Find matches files that contain *fig* anywhere in the name.

To give your searches extra flexibility, the Named combo box also accepts wildcard characters. As with DOS wildcards, you use the question mark (?) to substitute for a single character and the asterisk (*) to substitute for multiple characters. Table 13.4 shows you several examples of these wildcards in action.

Table 13.4. Wildcard character examples.

Named Text	*Which Filenames It Matches*
*.txt	Filenames that have the extension TXT and any primary name (for example, BOOTLOG.TXT, LETTER.TXT).
memo.*	Filenames that have memo as the primary name and any extension (for example, MEMO.TXT, MEMO.DOC).
chapter1*.bmp	Filenames that have a primary name that begins with chapter1 and a BMP extension (for example, CHAPTER1.BMP, CHAPTER1_FIGURE57.BMP, CHAPTER1_NOTES.BMP).

continues

13

WORKING WITH
FILES AND
FOLDERS

Table 13.4. continued

Named Text	Which Filenames It Matches
`*log.txt`	Filenames that have a primary name that ends with `log` and have a TXT extension (for example, `BOOTLOG.TXT`, `SETUPLOG.TXT`, `LOG.TXT`).
`*.*`	Filenames that have any primary name and any extension (that is, all files).
`?o?ato.doc`	Filenames that have the extension DOC and have primary names that are exactly six characters long, in which the first and third letters can be any character, the second character is `o`, and the fourth through sixth characters are `ato` (for example, `POTATO.DOC`, `TOMATO.DOC`, but not `POTATOE.DOC`).
`????.dbf`	Filenames that have a primary name that is exactly four characters long and have the extension DBF (for example, `DATA.DBF`, `BOOT.DBF`).
`?ales*.doc`	Filenames that have the extension DOC and have a primary name that begins with any character followed by `ales` (for example, `SALESMAN.DOC`, `BALES_OF_HAY.DOC`).

After you've filled in the Named box, use the Look in box to enter the drive or folder you want to use for the search. If you want to search multiple drives or folders, separate them with semicolons, like so:

```
c:\windows;d:\data
```

If you want Find to search not only the specified folder, but also all of its subfolders, activate the Include subfolders check box.

TIP: SEARCHING ALL LOCAL DRIVES

If you want Find to search all of your system's local drives (including mapped network folders), don't bother typing each drive letter into the Look in text box. Instead, just enter my computer and make sure that the Include subfolders check box is activated. This tells Find to search My Computer for the files.

Searching by Date

If you know, more or less, when the file was created or when it was last modified, you can narrow your search criteria even further. Select the Date Modified tab to display the controls shown in Figure 13.25. To enter date criteria, select the Find all files created or modified option. The following controls become active:

between: Activate this option to enter a date range in the two text boxes.

during the previous *x* month(s): Activate this option to narrow the search to the previous number of months you enter in the spinner.

during the previous *x* day(s): Activate this option to narrow the search to the previous number of days you enter in the spinner.

FIGURE 13.25.

Use the Date Modified tab to search for files by date.

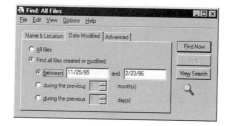

Advanced Searching

Finally, the Advanced tab, shown in Figure 13.26, lets you search for files by type, content, or size. Here are your choices:

Of type: This drop-down box contains a list of all the registered file types.

Containing text: Use this text box to specify a word or phrase that must appear in the file. If you want the search to be case-sensitive, select Options | Case Sensitive.

Size is: Use these controls to specify a file size. In the drop-down list, select either At least or At most; in the spinner, enter a value in kilobytes.

FIGURE 13.26.

Use the Advanced tab to search by file type, file content, or file size.

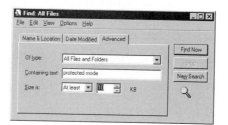

Running the Search

OK, you're ready to go. Click the Find Now button and Find goes to work. As the search progresses, Find displays any matching files at the bottom of the window. When it's done, the status bar shows you the number of files found, as shown in Figure 13.27.

The area where Find displays the matching files is like a scaled-down version of Explorer. You can select files, cut or copy files to the Clipboard, delete or rename files, drag-and-drop files, and do just about anything you can do in Explorer. If you want to open the folder that contains a specific file, highlight the file and select File | Open Containing Folder.

FIGURE 13.27.

Find displays the matching files at the bottom of the window.

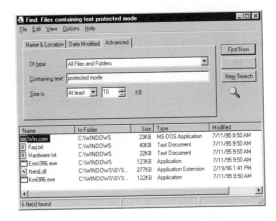

If you think you might want to reuse the search criteria later, select File | Save Search. Find adds a file to your desktop of type Saved Search (with the FND extension). Double-clicking this file redisplays the Find window with your search criteria entered automatically.

Trash Talk: Understanding the Recycle Bin

In the early days of the PC revolution, accidentally deleted files were gone for good, and no amount of cursing, groaning, or bellyaching would get them back.

Then some genius realized that when DOS deleted a file, it didn't actually delete the file's *contents*. Instead, it just changed the file's name so that the first letter began with a lowercase Greek sigma, and it changed all the file's FAT entries to 0 (to indicate that these clusters could be used by another file). Thus was born the "undelete" command, which could restore a deleted file by restoring the FAT entries and the original first character of the filename.

The problem, however, was that if you didn't undelete the file quickly, some other file would come along and use up some of the deleted file's clusters, and the file would be unrecoverable. So the next stage in the evolution of undelete was a separate directory used to hold deleted files. A deleted file was simply moved from its original directory to a hidden directory. Undeleting the file became a trivial matter of moving the file back to its original location.

Which brings us to the state of the art in undeletion technology: the Windows 95 Recycle Bin. The Recycle Bin works by setting up hidden folders named Recycled on each of your disk drives. When you delete a file, the Recycle Bin moves the file to the appropriate Recycled folder. When you restore a file, the Recycle Bin just moves it back to its original folder. The next few sections discuss the Recycle Bin in more detail.

Sending a File or Folder to the Recycle Bin

When you decide to blow away a file or folder, Windows 95 gives you lots of choices on how to proceed. Here's the rundown:

- Highlight the file or folder and select File | Delete.
- Press the Delete key.
- Right-click the file or folder and select Delete from the context menu.
- Highlight the file or folder and click the Delete button in the toolbar.
- Drag the file to the Recycle Bin icon on the desktop or the `Recycle Bin` folder.

For the first four methods, Windows 95 displays a dialog box asking you to confirm that you want to send the file or folder to the Recycle Bin, as shown in Figure 13.28. If you're sure, click Yes; otherwise, you can bail out by clicking No.

FIGURE 13.28.

When you delete a file, Windows 95 displays this dialog box to ask for confirmation.

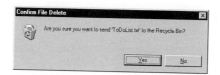

13

CAUTION: FLOPPY AND NETWORK DRIVE DELETIONS ARE PERMANENT

If you delete a file from a floppy disk or a network drive, Windows 95 does *not* send the file to the Recycle Bin (even if you drop the file on the Recycle Bin icon). Instead, Windows 95 deletes the file permanently.

TIP: BYPASSING THE RECYCLE BIN

If you're sure you won't ever need to restore the file, you can delete a file or folder permanently (that is, without placing it in the Recycle Bin) by holding down the Shift key while you delete it. What happens if you use this technique and then decide that you need the file restored? Are you out of luck? Maybe not. You can try using the DOS UNDELETE command to recover the file. I'll show you how this works in Chapter 21, "DOS Isn't Dead: Optimizing DOS Applications Under Windows 95."

Restoring a File from the Recycle Bin

It's axiomatic in computer circles that there are two kinds of users: those who have accidentally deleted the wrong file, and those who will. When this happens to you, it's nice to know that the Recycle Bin is there to bail you out.

Actually, before learning how to restore files from the Recycle Bin, you should know that there's an easier way. If the deletion was the last action you performed, you can reverse it by selecting Edit | Undo Delete, or by right-clicking an empty part of the Contents pane and selecting Undo Delete from the context menu.

The Undo command applies only to the last action you performed, however, so Undo Delete might no longer be available by the time you realize your mistake. No problem, though. You can still recover the file or folder by following these steps:

1. Display the contents of the Recycle Bin either by highlighting the `Recycle Bin` folder in Explorer or by double-clicking the Recycle Bin icon on the desktop.

2. Highlight the file or folder you want to restore.

3. Select File | Restore, or right-click the file or folder and select Restore from the context menu. Windows 95 restores the file or folder to its original location.

NOTE: CLEANING OUT THE RECYCLE BIN

The Recycle Bin contents take up disk space, of course. If you need to free up some disk real estate, you have a couple of choices. If you want to expunge one or more Recycle Bin objects permanently, highlight them and select File | Delete, or right-click them and click Delete. When Windows 95 asks whether you want to delete the objects, click Yes. Alternatively, you can clean out the Recycle Bin entirely either by highlighting the `Recycle Bin` folder and selecting File | Empty Recycle Bin or by right-clicking the Recycle Bin icon and selecting Empty Recycle Bin from the context menu.

Setting Recycle Bin Properties

To give you a measure of control over how the Recycle Bin operates, various properties are available for you to work with. To check out these properties, either highlight the Recycle Bin and select File | Properties, or right-click the Recycle Bin icon and select Properties from the context menu. You'll see a Recycle Bin Properties dialog box similar to the one shown in Figure 13.29.

For starters, you need to decide whether you want to configure the Recycle Bin settings for each drive independently or globally (assuming, of course, that your system has multiple drives). For example, if you have a drive that's perilously low on disk space, you'll probably want to configure the drives independently so that you can tailor the amount of disk space that the Recycle Bin uses.

FIGURE 13.29.

Use this dialog box to set some Recycle Bin properties.

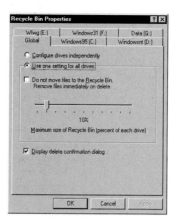

If you want to configure the drives globally, activate the Global tab's Use one setting for all drives option button. You can then manipulate two settings that apply to all your hard disk drives:

> **Do not move files to the Recycle Bin. Remove files immediately on delete:** Activate this option to bypass the Recycle Bin for all deletions.

> **Maximum size of Recycle Bin (percent of each drive):** This slider controls the maximum amount of hard disk acreage that the Recycle Bin usurps on all the drives. The default is 10 percent, which is probably a bit high (100 MB on a 1 GB drive!). Note, however, that the lower the value, the fewer files the Recycle Bin can store.

If you prefer to configure the drives separately, activate the Configure drives independently option button, and then use the various drive tabs to adjust the settings for each drive.

Finally, the Global tab also has a Display delete confirmation dialog check box. If you deactivate this option, Windows 95 doesn't prompt you for confirmation when you select the Delete command or press the Delete key.

When you're done, click OK to put the settings into effect.

Summary

This chapter took a long, hard look at working with files and folders in Windows 95. I began by showing you a number of techniques for unleashing Explorer. From there, you learned about working with shortcuts and file types, finding files and folders, and understanding the Recycle Bin. For related information, here are some chapters to check out:

- ■ For basic file and folder techniques, see Chapter 5, "Windows 95: The 50¢ Tour."
- ■ For the nitty-gritty on Windows 95's file system architecture, see Chapter 6, "Under the Hood: Understanding the Windows 95 Architecture."

13

WORKING WITH FILES AND FOLDERS

■ To see how the file system architecture fits in with the Windows 95 architecture as a whole, head for Chapter 9, "Windows 95 Performance Tuning and Optimization."

■ Various Registry tricks affect files and shortcuts. I showed you a few in Chapter 12, "Hacking the Registry."

■ Disk operations such as formatting, copying, compressing, and partitioning are the subject of Chapter 14, "Disk Driving: Dealing with Disks."

■ To learn how to keep your files safe from harm, check out Chapter 15, "Protecting Your Windows 95 Investment."

■ To learn how to perform file maintenance from the DOS prompt, see Chapter 21, "DOS Isn't Dead: Optimizing DOS Applications Under Windows 95."

■ For network-related file and folder info, see Chapter 31, "Windows 95 Networking."

Disk Driving: Dealing with Disks

IN THIS CHAPTER

CHAPTER 14

Never let a computer know you're in a hurry.

—Anonymous

I concentrated on files and folders in the last chapter, but Windows 95 has plenty of goodies for disk drives as well. This chapter looks at Windows 95's various disk-related commands and utilities.

Formatting a Floppy Disk

Floppy disks come in two standard sizes: 5¼-inch and 3½-inch. The 5¼-inch disks are the veterans of the PC wars. They've been around, in one form or another, since the days of the earliest PCs. They come in two capacities: double-density and high-density. (Actually, the term *double-density* is relatively meaningless in this day and age. It originates from the old days of computers—way back in the 1980s—when there were such things as *single-density* disks. You'll often see double-density disks referred to as *low-density* or *regular-density*.) The 5¼-inch double-density disks have a storage capacity of 360 KB, and the high-density variety can store 1.2 MB.

Although 3½-inch disks are relatively new kids on the floppy drive block, they're now the true "standard" (at least until the next one comes along). They come in three capacities: double-density, high-density, and the new (and still rare) extended-density disks. Double-density disks store up to 720 KB, high-density disks store 1.44 MB, and extended disks can pack a whopping 2.88 MB of data. You can't, of course, just stick any old piece of plastic in a disk drive and expect it to read and write information. Even official I-bought-'em-at-the-local-Radio-Shack floppy disks need to be set up first so that information can be properly stored on the disk.

It's like the difference between a peg board and an ordinary piece of wood. Buying new disks (unless the box says they're "preformatted") is like buying a bunch of flat, featureless pieces of wood. You can try all day to stick pegs in them, but they'll just fall off. What you need to do is "format" the wood so that it has proper holes for the pegs.

This peg-board analogy can also help explain the difference between double-density and high-density disks. Picture two peg-boards: one with large holes and one with smaller holes. The large-holed board can hold a certain number of pegs, but because the holes in the other board are smaller, it can hold even more pegs. So a double-density disk is like the board with large holes: It has fewer "pegs" (fewer *tracks per inch*, technically) on which to place data than a high-density (small-holed) disk. This also helps explain why you can't format double-density disks as high-density. All disks use a magnetic field to hold their data. High-density disks must use a *lower* field strength than double-density because the data, like the holes in the small-holed peg-board, are closer together. If high-density disks didn't use the lower field strength, the various magnetic bits would start moving around because of mutual attraction and repulsion. Not good! This is exactly what happens, though, when you format a double-density disk as high-density. The tracks are placed close together, but the disk's stronger magnetic field eventually trashes the data.

When you need to format a floppy disk, follow these steps:

1. Insert the disk you want to format.

2. In Explorer, right-click the drive containing the disk and select Format. (Don't highlight the drive first, or Windows 95 won't let you format the disk.) Alternatively, you can highlight the drive in My Computer and select File | Format. In either case, the Format dialog box, shown in Figure 14.1, appears.

FIGURE 14.1.

Use the Format dialog box to select your formatting options.

3. Use the `Capacity` drop-down list to select the appropriate capacity for the disk.

4. In the `Format type` group, select one of the following options:

   Quick (erase): This option removes all the files from the disk, but it doesn't check the disk for bad sectors. You can use this option only on disks that have been previously formatted.

   Full: This option removes all the files from the disk and checks the disk for bad sectors. Use this option for new disks and for older disks that you suspect might have bad sectors.

   Copy system files only: This option copies only the Windows 95 system files to the disk: `IO.SYS`, `MSDOS.SYS`, `DRVSPACE.BIN`, and `COMMAND.COM`. The disk then becomes bootable. Any existing files on the disk remain intact.

5. The `Other options` group contains the following controls:

   Label: Use this text box to enter a label for the disk (11 or fewer characters).

   No label: Activate this check box to disable the `Label` check box. Any existing label will be deleted.

   Display summary when finished: If this check box is activated, Windows 95 displays a summary dialog box when the format is complete. This dialog box tells you the total disk space, the total bytes in bad sectors, the size of each cluster, and a few other disk statistics.

   Copy system files: Activate this command to copy the system files to the disk after it has been formatted. This will make the disk bootable.

6. Click Start. Windows 95 formats the disk.

7. If you activated the `Display summary when finished` check box, the Format Results dialog box appears when the format is complete. Click OK to return to the Format dialog box.

8. Click Close.

NOTE: 1.44 MB? NO, NOT REALLY

In the Format Results dialog box, Windows 95 will show that a 1.44 MB floppy has 1,457,664 bytes total disk space. If you divide this value by 1,048,576 (the number of bytes in a megabyte), you end up with 1.39. In other words, the true capacity of a "1.44" MB floppy disk is actually 1.39 MB.

You can also use the Format command to format a hard disk. In this case, though, when you click Start, Windows 95 displays the warning dialog box shown in Figure 14.2. If you're sure you want to continue, click OK.

FIGURE 14.2.

Windows 95 warns you that formatting a hard disk will erase all the data on the disk.

After formatting the hard disk, note that it will no longer be set up to accept long filenames. That's because when you format the drive you wipe out the information cache that Windows 95 stores on each drive. This cache contains data about the drive, including whether or not it supports long filenames. To restore the long filename capability for the drive, you have two choices:

- Restart your computer.
- Highlight the drive in Explorer or My Computer and then select View | Refresh (or press F5).

Copying a Floppy Disk

If you need to make a copy of a floppy disk, Windows 95 is up to the task. Here are the steps you need to follow:

1. Insert the disk you want to copy (this is the *source* disk). If your system has a second drive of the same type, insert the disk you want to use for the copy (this is the *destination* disk) in the other drive.

2. Highlight the source disk drive and select File | Copy Disk, or right-click the source disk drive and select Copy Disk from the context menu. Windows 95 displays the Copy Disk dialog box, shown in Figure 14.3.

FIGURE 14.3.

Use the Copy Disk dialog box to make a copy of a floppy disk.

3. The Copy from box lists the floppy drives on your system. Highlight the drive that contains the source disk.

4. The Copy to box also lists the floppy drives on your system. Highlight the drive you want to use for the destination disk. Make sure that this drive uses disks of the same type as the source disk. If your system has two drives of different types, you can use the same drive for the copy procedure. (For example, suppose that drive A is 3½-inch and drive B is 5¼-inch, and you want to copy a 3½-inch disk. You can select the 3½-inch drive (drive A) in both Copy from and Copy to.)

5. Click Start. Windows 95 reads the data from the source disk. If you're using the same drive for the copy, Windows 95 prompts you to insert the destination disk.

6. Insert the destination disk and click OK. Windows 95 copies the data to the destination disk.

7. When the copy is complete, click Close.

Viewing Disk Properties

Disks are objects in the Windows 95 scheme of things, so they have their own properties and actions. You've just seen a couple of actions—Format and Copy Disk—but what about a disk's properties? To check them out, either highlight a disk and select File | Properties, or right-click a disk and select Properties from the context menu. You'll see a properties sheet similar to the one shown in Figure 14.4. The General tab shows you the disk's label, its type, the amount of used and free space, the total capacity, the drive letter, and a pie chart comparing used and free space.

FIGURE 14.4.

The properties sheet for a disk drive.

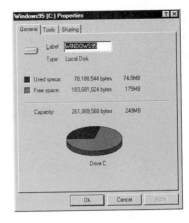

Selecting the Tools tab displays the controls shown in Figure 14.5. This handy tab lets you keep track of when you last performed certain maintenance chores on this disk:

Error-checking status: This group lets you know how long ago you last ran ScanDisk on this disk. If you want to run ScanDisk now, click the Check Now button. (I explain how ScanDisk works in Chapter 15, "Protecting Your Windows 95 Investment.")

Backup status: This group lets you know when you last backed up files from this disk. To perform a backup now, click the Backup Now button. (Again, see Chapter 15 to learn how to use the Backup utility.)

Defragmentation status: This group lets you know when you last defragmented the files on this disk. Click Defragment Now to start Disk Defragmenter for this disk. (I showed you how to use Disk Defragmenter in Chapter 9, "Windows 95 Performance Tuning and Optimization.")

FIGURE 14.5.

Use the Tools tab to monitor when you last performed maintenance on the disk.

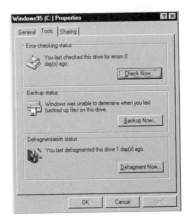

TROUBLESHOOTING: CONSTANT FLOPPY DRIVE ACCESS

If you've performed any floppy disk-based file chores recently, you may have noticed that Windows 95 constantly attempts to access your system's floppy drive whenever you run any kind of file maintenance (saving, renaming, opening, and so on).

This stubborn and annoying behavior is caused by the Documents menu. The problem is that the Documents menu probably still lists the floppy disk file you worked on earlier. Every time you do something to a file, Windows 95 updates the Documents menu, which includes verifying that the floppy disk is still in place.

You can correct this problem by clearing the Documents menu (as described in Chapter 7, "Customizing Windows 95").

Compressing Disks with DriveSpace

Although hard disks have been getting bigger and cheaper over the years, they haven't kept pace with the ever-fatter programs that developers have been throwing at us. As a result, we have a new corollary to Murphy's Law: No matter how huge your hard disk seems today, you'll wish it was twice as big six months from now. Rather than dipping into your savings yet again, you can squeeze more storage space out of your current disk by using DriveSpace, Windows 95's disk compression program.

Disk compression is based on a complex mathematical algorithm (called the Lempel-Ziv algorithm) that searches a file for redundant character strings and replaces them with small tokens. Let's look at a simple example. Consider the following phrase:

```
It was the best of times, it was the worst of times, it was the age of wisdom,
it was the age of foolishness.
```

To compress this quotation, the program starts at the beginning and looks for at least two consecutive characters it has already seen. In this case, the first such match is the *t* and the following space at the end of the word *best*; this matches the *t* and the following space seen earlier at the end of the word *It*. So now the program replaces the match with a token, something like this (I'll just use an asterisk to represent the various tokens):

```
I*was the bes*of times, it was the worst of times, it was the age of wisdom,
it was the age of foolishness.
```

The program chugs along, finding small redundancies (for example, the *es* in *times* matches the *es* seen earlier in *bes**). Then it hits the jackpot: Larger phrases such as *it was the, of times,* and *age of* are repeated, and these can all be replaced by tokens. Finally, you end up with something that looks like this:

14

```
I***b******wors******w*dom******fool*hn*s
```

It looks strange, but the program has reduced the original string from 110 characters to 42. To decompress such data, all the program has to do is translate the tokens back to their original form. It's all handled by a mathematical formula, and it's quite safe.

How DriveSpace Works

DriveSpace can create more room to roam on your hard disk in two ways:

- By compressing both the existing files and the remaining free space on the disk
- By compressing only the remaining free space on the disk

If You Compress Files and Free Space

If you elect to compress the files and free space, DriveSpace works through the following procedure (assuming that you're compressing drive C):

1. The disk's drive letter is changed from C to H (or, if H is already used, the first free drive letter), and the drive is hidden (this is optional). This new drive letter is used as the *host* of the compressed data.

2. DriveSpace compresses the files on drive H and concatenates them into a single file. This is called the *compressed volume file* (CVF). This file is usually named DRVSPACE.000.

3. The CVF's file attributes are set to hidden, read-only, and system.

4. Windows 95 assigns the original disk's drive letter (C) to the CVF.

In other words, your system looks very much the same after compression as it did before: You use the same drive letter to work with your data, and your files and folders are still intact and unchanged. The only difference is that you now have much more free hard disk space on the drive. (You might also notice a very slight decrease in hard disk performance because Windows 95 now must uncompress files as you work with them.)

This method takes quite a while, but you end up with the maximum amount of storage capacity on your disk. For example, suppose that you have a 200 MB hard disk that contains 100 MB of files and, therefore, 100 MB of free space. Assuming an average compression ratio of 2:1, you should be able to fit 200 MB of compressed data into the space formerly used by your 100 MB of uncompressed files, and you should be able to fit 200 MB of new compressed data into the space formerly used by the 100 MB of uncompressed free space. Thus, your total storage capacity for the disk is up to 400 MB.

NOTE: COMPRESSION RATIO

The *compression ratio* of a file is the ratio of the size of the uncompressed file to its compressed size. For example, a file that is 10,000 bytes uncompressed and 5,000 bytes compressed has a compression ratio of 2:1. Some files—especially text, database, and graphics files—achieve high compression ratios because they tend to have many redundant character strings. On the other hand, executable files and Help system files have relatively few redundant character strings, so their compression ratios are usually much lower.

If You Compress Free Space Only

Instead of compressing your existing files, you can elect to compress only the remaining free space on the disk (or part of the free space). In this case, DriveSpace turns the free space into a separate disk drive (say, drive D) with a storage capacity of approximately double the original free space. This new capacity is only a guess on DriveSpace's part, however; it assumes an average compression ratio of 2:1. The real compression ratio (and, so, the actual number of megabytes you'll be able to store on the new drive) depends on the files you place on the drive.

This method is faster, but you end up with less storage capacity than with the other method. For example, consider the 200 MB disk with 100 MB of files and 100 MB of free space. Again, assuming an average compression ratio of 2:1, you end up with two drives: one that has 100 MB of uncompressed files and no free space, and one that has 200 MB of free space. Your total storage capacity, therefore, is 300 MB.

Managing the CVF

After a drive has been compressed, DriveSpace uses a device driver to manage the CVF. When you start your computer, a real-mode driver (DRVSPACE.BIN) is loaded to make the CVF available during the real-mode portion of the startup. When Windows 95 switches to protected mode, DRVSPACE.BIN is unloaded and the protected-mode driver (DRVSPACX.VXD) takes over.

Is it safe to put all your file eggs in one CVF basket? Absolutely. The algorithms used to compress and decompress files are bulletproof, and even in the unlikely event that something does go wrong, DriveSpace has built-in safeguards designed to keeps things in order. The chances of corrupting your data are no different than they are in using uncompressed files.

NOTE: WINDOWS 95 SUPPORTS OTHER COMPRESSION SCHEMES

Windows 95 also supports the DoubleSpace compression that was used in DOS 6.0. In this case, the real-mode driver used at startup is DBLSPACE.BIN (although, in protected mode, DRVSPACX.VXD is used to manage both kinds of compressed drives). Windows 95 also supports (in real mode) the third-party compression schemes Stacker, SuperStor, and AddStor.

14

Compressing Files and Free Space

If you want to compress both the files and the free space on your disk, start DriveSpace by selecting Start | Programs | Accessories | System Tools | DriveSpace. You'll see the DriveSpace window with a list of the disk drives on your system, as shown in Figure 14.6.

FIGURE 14.6.

Use the DriveSpace window to select the drive you want to compress.

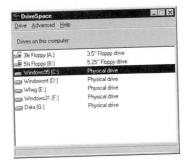

To compress a drive, highlight it in the `Drives on this computer` list, and then select Drive | Compress. At this point, one of three things will happen:

> **If the drive is less than 256 MB:** In this case, you'll see the Compress a Drive dialog box, shown in Figure 14.7. The box on the left shows the current free space and used space; the box on the right shows the free space and used space after compression. (DriveSpace always reports the sizes of compressed files as though they were uncompressed; the extra space created by compressing the existing files is added to the free space number.)

FIGURE 14.7.

You'll see this dialog box if your disk is less than 256 MB.

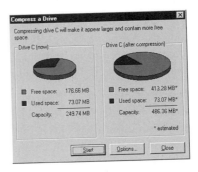

If the drive is greater than 256 MB but has less than 500 MB of files: In this case, you'll see the version of the Compress a Drive dialog box shown in Figure 14.8. DriveSpace can't create a compressed drive that's larger than 512 MB, so it compresses just enough of the drive that the resulting drive has 512 MB of storage. It then creates the remaining (uncompressed) free space on the host drive. You can run DriveSpace again later to compress the remaining free space into a new drive.

FIGURE 14.8.

You'll see this dialog box if your drive is greater than 256 MB but has less than 500 MB of files.

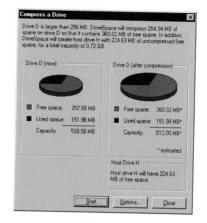

NOTE: FOR LARGER DRIVES, USE DRIVESPACE 3

The version of DriveSpace that comes with Microsoft Plus! (DriveSpace 3) can create compressed drives up to 2 GB. See "Using DriveSpace 3 from Microsoft Plus!" later in this chapter.

If the drive has more than 500 MB of files: In this case, you'll see the error message shown in Figure 14.9. Your only hope is to delete or archive files to get the used space below 500 MB, or to use DriveSpace 3, as described later. (If DriveSpace can work with drives up to 512 MB, why does the error occur at 500 MB? Basically, it's because DriveSpace needs a bit of room to maneuver while compressing the files. For safest operation, Microsoft recommends reducing the total files to 480 MB or so.)

FIGURE 14.9.

You'll see this error message if your drive contains more than 500 MB of files.

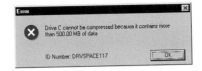

Before starting the compression (assuming that you weren't unlucky enough to get the error message shown in Figure 14.9), you might want to adjust a few compression settings. To view these settings, click the Options button to display the Compression Options dialog box, shown in Figure 14.10. You can work with the following controls:

Drive letter of host drive: Use this drop-down list to change the drive letter that DriveSpace assigns to the host drive. H is usually the default letter, but you can use any unassigned letter for the host drive.

Free space on host drive: This text box specifies the amount of uncompressed free space used on the host drive. Increasing this number reduces the space available for the CVF; decreasing this number (if possible) increases the amount of space available for the CVF. You can't decrease this number below 2 MB, and you can't decrease it if the compressed drive is already at the 512 MB maximum size.

Hide host drive: Activate this check box to set the hidden attribute of the host drive. You'll want to leave this check box deactivated if the host drive has more than the minimum amount of free space (2 MB). This way, you can still see and work with the host drive in Explorer.

When you're done, click OK to return to the Compress a Drive dialog box.

FIGURE 14.10.

Use this dialog box to adjust various compression settings.

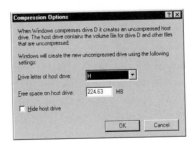

To begin the compression, click the Start button. You might see the Are You Sure? dialog box, which offers to back up your files. If you want to do a backup, click Back Up Files; otherwise, click Compress Now. DriveSpace checks the drive for errors and then starts the compression. Note that DriveSpace might need to restart your computer if you're compressing the drive that contains the Windows 95 system files. In this case, Windows 95 starts with a minimal configuration so that DriveSpace can compress all the files safely. DriveSpace restarts Windows 95 when it's finished.

When DriveSpace has completed its labors, it returns you to the Compress a Drive dialog box and shows the free space now contained in the drive. Click Close. If DriveSpace prompts you to restart your computer, click Yes.

Compressing Free Space Only

If you want to compress only the free space on your drive, follow these steps:

1. Select Start | Programs | Accessories | System Tools | DriveSpace to display the DriveSpace window.
2. Use the `Drives on this computer` list to highlight the drive you want to use.
3. Select Advanced | Create Empty. The Create New Compressed Drive dialog box, shown in Figure 14.11, appears.

FIGURE 14.11.

Use this dialog box to set the parameters for your new compressed drive.

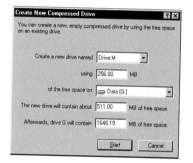

4. You can adjust the following controls:

   Create a new drive named: Use this drop-down list to select an unused drive letter for the new drive.

   using: This text box specifies the amount of uncompressed free space you want to use for the new drive. Because DriveSpace can't work with drives any larger than 512 MB, the maximum value you can enter is 256 MB (DriveSpace assumes a 2:1 compression ratio).

   of the free space on: Use this drop-down list to change the drive you want to use, if necessary.

5. Click Start. DriveSpace checks the drive for errors and then creates the new drive. When it's done, you're returned to the Create New Compressed Drive dialog box.
6. Click Close. When Windows 95 asks whether you want to restart your computer, click Yes.

Modifying the Size of a Compressed Drive

If you want to change the size of a compressed drive, you can do so by following these steps:

1. Select Start | Programs | Accessories | System Tools | DriveSpace to display the DriveSpace window.
2. Use the `Drives on this computer` list to highlight the compressed drive you want to adjust.
3. Select Drive | Adjust Free Space. DriveSpace displays the Adjust Free Space dialog box.
4. Move the slider to the left to create more space on the compressed drive; move the slider to the right to create less space on the compressed drive (that is, more space on the host drive).
5. Click OK. DriveSpace adjusts the free space and displays a dialog box showing you the new size.
6. Click OK. When Windows 95 asks whether you want to restart your computer, click Yes.

Uncompressing a Drive

If you decide you don't want to use compression any longer, it's easy enough to remove it. Here are the steps to follow:

1. Select Start | Programs | Accessories | System Tools | DriveSpace to display the DriveSpace window.
2. Use the `Drives on this computer` list to highlight the compressed drive you want to adjust.
3. Select Drive | Uncompress. DriveSpace displays the Uncompress a Drive dialog box.
4. Click Start. DriveSpace might ask whether you want to back up your files.
5. If you want to do a backup, click Back Up Files.
6. Click Uncompress Now to start uncompressing the files. When the operation is complete, DriveSpace returns you to the Uncompress a Drive dialog box.
7. Click Close. When Windows 95 asks whether you want to restart your computer, click Yes.

Using DriveSpace 3 from Microsoft Plus! and OSR2

If you have OSR2, or if you've installed Microsoft Plus!, you have a more powerful compression engine available: DriveSpace 3. This enhanced version of DriveSpace not only supports compressed drives up to 2 GB (compared to the 512 MB maximum in regular DriveSpace), but it also compresses files about 20 percent faster. In addition, Microsoft Plus! comes with a Compression Agent utility that lets you choose the level of compression you want and even lets you choose specific files or folders for compressing.

When you install Microsoft Plus! (assuming that you chose to install the DriveSpace 3 component), and if you have compressed drives on your system, you'll eventually see the Drive Upgrade Notification dialog box, shown in Figure 14.12. Click OK to upgrade the compressed drive to the DriveSpace 3 format. If you choose one of the other options, you can always upgrade your drive from within DriveSpace 3 (by highlighting the drive and selecting Drive | Upgrade).

FIGURE 14.12.

When you install Microsoft Plus!, you'll see this dialog box if you have compressed drives on your system.

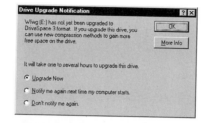

NOTE: UPDATING YOUR STARTUP DISK

When you upgrade a compressed drive for the first time, DriveSpace 3 displays the Create Startup Disk dialog box, which asks whether you want to update your Startup disk. This is a good idea because the real-mode DriveSpace driver on your Startup disk won't work with any compressed drive that you've upgraded to the DriveSpace 3 format. To update the Startup disk, click Yes. (In case you didn't make a Startup disk during the Windows 95 installation, I'll tell you how to do so in Chapter 15.)

You use DriveSpace 3 the same way you use regular DriveSpace. A CVF created with DriveSpace 3, however, compresses files in the CVF on-the-fly as you save them. DriveSpace 3 uses three kinds of compression:

Standard compression: This is the same compression method used with regular DriveSpace.

HiPack compression: This option gives you a higher compression ratio (10 or 20 percent).

UltraPack compression: This option gives you the highest compression ratio possible. This is available only through the Compression Agent.

A few more options are also available for DriveSpace 3. To see them, select Advanced | Settings to display the Disk Compression Settings dialog box, shown in Figure 14.13. These settings control the on-the-fly compression used by DriveSpace 3. You have the following options:

HiPack compression: This option activates on-the-fly HiPack compression.

Standard compression: This option activates on-the-fly standard compression.

No compression, unless drive is at least x % full: This option turns off the on-the-fly compression. If the used space on the disk rises above the percentage entered into the text box, standard compression is activated.

No compression (fastest): This option turns off on-the-fly compression.

When you upgrade a drive for the first time, DriveSpace 3 displays the DriveSpace Performance Tuning dialog box, shown in Figure 14.14. Here are your choices:

FIGURE 14.13.

Use this dialog box to set various options for DriveSpace 3.

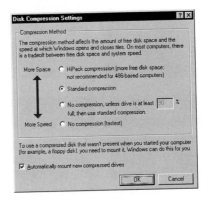

High Performance: If you select this option, the on-the-fly compression is turned off. When you're not using your computer, DriveSpace 3 converts these files into HiPack or UltraPack compression. (The compression scheme used is controlled by the Compression Agent settings, as described in the following steps. The time of day that DriveSpace 3 runs this compression is controlled by the System Agent, which I explain how to use in Chapter 15.)

More Free Disk Space: If you select this option, DriveSpace 3 uses standard compression on-the-fly. When you're not using your computer, DriveSpace 3 converts these files into HiPack or UltraPack compression.

Custom: If you select this option, a Help Wizard appears to lead you through various options for fine-tuning the compression settings.

FIGURE 14.14.

Use this dialog box to select the level of performance you want from DriveSpace.

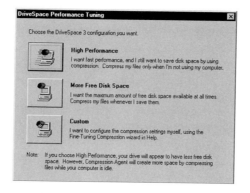

After you've upgraded your compressed drives (or created new compressed drives) with DriveSpace 3, you can start using the Compression Agent:

1. Select Start | Programs | Accessories | System Tools | Compression Agent. The Select Drive dialog box appears.

2. Select the compressed drive you want to recompress and click OK. You'll see the Compression Agent window, shown in Figure 14.15.

FIGURE 14.15.

Use the Compression Agent to fine-tune your DriveSpace 3 compression.

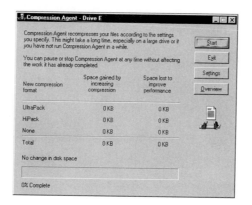

3. Click Settings to display the Compression Agent Settings dialog box.

4. Choose the Compression Agent settings you want to work with (for example, whether or not you want Compression Agent to use UltraPack), and then click OK.

5. Click Start. Compression Agent goes to work recompressing the drive.

6. When it's done, a dialog box is displayed to ask whether you want to recompress another drive. If you do, click Yes and repeat steps 2 through 5; otherwise, click No to return to the Compression Agent dialog box.

7. Click Exit.

Partitioning a Disk

In Chapter 9, I showed you how the size of a hard disk can have a tremendous effect on storage efficiency, thanks to a phenomenon called *cluster overhang*. Generally speaking, the smaller the hard disk, the more efficiently it stores data (provided, that is, that most of your data exists in relatively small files).

Here, "hard disk" size really means *partition* size, a partition being just a subset of the total hard disk storage space. For example, a 1.2 GB (1,200 MB) hard disk could be broken up into four partitions, each one 300 MB in size. This partitioning would reduce the cluster size from 32K for the full disk to 8K for each partition.

When working with partitions, you need to keep the following concepts in mind:

Primary partition: This is the first partition (drive C).

Active partition: This is the bootable partition. Its boot sector tells the ROM BIOS at startup that this partition contains the operating system's bootstrap code. The active partition is usually the same as the primary partition.

Extended partition: This is the hard disk space that isn't allocated to the primary partition. For example, if you have a 1.2 GB disk and you allocate 300 MB to the primary partition, the extended partition is 900 MB. You can then subdivide the extended partition into logical DOS drives (see the next paragraph).

Logical DOS drive: This is a subset of an extended partition. For example, if the extended partition is 900 MB, you could create three logical DOS drives, each with 300 MB, and they would use drive letters D, E, and F. You can assign up to 23 logical DOS drives to an extended partition (letters D through Z).

To adjust partition sizes, you use the FDISK utility from the command line. You can use FDISK in a number of ways, but two scenarios are most common:

- You break up a large partition into two or more smaller partitions.
- You partition a new hard disk.

Here are the general steps to follow if you need to break up an existing partition into smaller partitions (the exact FDISK steps will be explained a bit later):

1. FDISK will destroy all the files on the disk during partitioning, so be sure to back up your important files before beginning.

2. Make sure that you have a bootable floppy disk that contains the FORMAT utility. The Windows 95 Startup disk is ideal.

3. Select Start | Shut Down, activate Restart the computer in MS-DOS mode, and click Yes.

4. At the DOS prompt, type fdisk and press Enter.

5. Delete all your partitions, starting with the extended DOS partition (if you have one).

6. Create a new primary partition, a new extended partition, and new logical drives in the extended partition.

7. Exit FDISK, insert the bootable disk, and reboot the computer.

8. When you get to the A:\ prompt, use the FORMAT utility to format each of the new drives. Be sure to add the /S switch when you format the active partition. This switch adds the system files to the boot drive.

9. Reinstall Windows 95, as described in Chapter 2, "Running the Windows 95 Setup."

10. Restore your backed-up data.

Here are the general steps to follow if you need to set up partitions on a new disk (again, the exact FDISK steps will be explained later):

1. Insert a bootable disk that contains both FDISK.EXE and FORMAT.COM, and reboot the computer.

2. At the A:\ prompt, type fdisk and press Enter.

3. Create a new primary partition, a new extended partition, and new logical drives in the extended partition.

4. Exit FDISK, insert the bootable disk, and reboot the computer.

5. When you get to the A:\ prompt, use the FORMAT utility to format each of the new drives. Be sure to add the /S switch when you format the primary partition. This switch adds the system files to the boot drive.

6. Install Windows 95, as described in Chapter 2.

When you start FDISK, you'll see the FDISK Options screen, which includes the following menu:

```
Current fixed disk drive: 1
Choose one of the following:
1. Create DOS partition of logical DOS Drive
2. Set active partition
3. Delete partition of Logical DOS Drive
4. Display partition information
Enter choice: [1]
```

If you have two or more hard drives, you'll also see the following option:

```
5. Change current fixed disk drive
```

Use this option to change the current fixed disk drive (that is, the drive you'll be working with), if necessary. If you're not sure, use the Display partition information command to display information about the current disk.

When you're done with FDISK, press Esc to get back to the prompt.

Creating a Primary Partition

The following steps show you how to create a primary DOS partition in FDISK:

1. At the FDISK Options screen, press 1 and Enter. FDISK displays the following menu:

    ```
    1. Create Primary DOS Partition
    2. Create Extended DOS Partition
    3. Create Logical DOS Drive(s) in the Extended DOS Partition
    Enter choice: [ ]
    ```

2. Press 1 and Enter. FDISK takes a moment or two to examine the disk and then displays the following prompt:

    ```
    Do you wish to use the maximum available size for a Primary DOS Partition
    and make the partition active (Y/N).....................? [Y]
    ```

3. If you want to use the entire drive as your primary partition, press Y and Enter. FDISK creates the partition and returns you to the DOS prompt.

    If you don't want to use the entire drive as your primary partition, press N and Enter. FDISK prompts you as shown here:

    ```
    Total disk space is 1204 Mbytes (1 Mbyte = 1048576 bytes)
    Maximum space available for partition is 1204 Mbytes (100%)
    Enter partition size in Mbytes or percent of disk space (%) to
    create a Primary DOS Partition...............................: [1204]
    ```

4. Type the number of megabytes you want to use for the primary partition and press Enter. FDISK creates the partition.

5. Press Esc to return to the FDISK Options screen.

6. Press 2 and Enter. FDISK prompts you to enter the number of the partition you want to make active (bootable).

7. Press 1 and Enter (assuming that you want to boot from drive C).

8. Press Esc to return to the FDISK Options screen.

Creating an Extended Partition and Logical DOS Drives

After you've set up the primary partition, you can create an extended partition and divide it into logical DOS drives by following this procedure:

1. At the FDISK Options screen, press 1 and Enter. FDISK displays the following menu:

    ```
    1. Create Primary DOS Partition
    2. Create Extended DOS Partition
    3. Create Logical DOS Drive(s) in the Extended DOS Partition
    Enter choice: [ ]
    ```

2. Press 2 and Enter. FDISK takes a moment or two to examine the disk and then displays the following prompt:

    ```
    Total disk space is 1204 Mbytes (1 Mbyte = 1048576 bytes)
    Maximum space available for partition is  903 Mbytes (75%)
    Enter partition size in Mbytes or percent of disk space (%) to
    create an Extended DOS Partition...............................: [ 903]
    ```

3. If you want to use the rest of the disk as your extended partition, press Enter. Otherwise, type the number of megabytes you want to use for the extended partition, and then press Enter. FDISK creates the partition.

NOTE: USE ALL AVAILABLE SPACE FOR THE EXTENDED PARTITION

You'll probably want to use all the remaining disk space for your extended partition. If you don't, the disk space left out of the extended partition won't be available to DOS (that is, Windows 95). The only time you'll want to use less space for the extended partition is if you plan on using this space for another operating system (such as NT, OS/2, or Linux).

4. Press Esc. FDISK tells you that no logical drives are defined and displays the following prompt:

```
Total Extended DOS Partition size is  903 Mbytes (1 MByte = 1048576 bytes)
Maximum space available for logical drive is  903 Mbytes (100%)
Enter logical drive size in Mbytes or percent of disk space (%)...[ 903]
```

5. Type the number of megabytes you want to use for the logical drive, and press Enter.

6. Repeat step 5 until you've allocated all the available space to logical drives.

7. Press Esc to return to the FDISK Options screen.

Deleting an Extended Partition

Here are the steps to follow to delete an extended partition in FDISK:

1. At the FDISK Options screen, press 3 and Enter. FDISK displays the following menu:

```
1.  Delete Primary DOS Partition
2.  Delete Extended DOS Partition
3.  Delete Logical DOS Drive(s) in the Extended DOS Partition
4.  Delete Non-DOS Partition
Enter choice: [ ]
```

2. Press 3 and Enter. FDISK displays a list of the logical DOS drives—including their drive letters, volume labels, and sizes—and the following prompt:

```
Total Extended DOS Partition size is  253 Mbytes (1 Mbyte = 1048576 bytes)
WARNING! Data in a deleted Logical DOS Drive will be lost.
What drive do you want to delete............................? [ ]
```

3. Type the drive letter and press Enter. FDISK prompts you to enter the volume label for the drive.

4. Type the volume label and press Enter. FDISK, ever cautious, asks whether you're sure.

5. Press Y and Enter.

6. Repeat steps 3 through 5 to delete the other logical DOS drives.

7. Press Esc twice to return to the FDISK Options screen.

8. Press 3 and Enter.

9. Press 2 and Enter. FDISK displays the partition data for the disk and the following prompt:

```
Total disk space is 1204 Mbytes (1 Mbyte = 1048576 bytes)
WARNING! Data in the deleted Extended DOS Partition will be lost.
Do you wish to continue (Y/N).................? [N]
```

10. Press Y and Enter.

11. Press Esc to return to the FDISK Options screen.

Deleting a Primary Partition

Here are the steps to follow to delete a primary partition in FDISK:

1. At the FDISK Options screen, press 3 and Enter to display the following menu:

```
1.  Delete Primary DOS Partition
2.  Delete Extended DOS Partition
3.  Delete Logical DOS Drive(s) in the Extended DOS Partition
4.  Delete Non-DOS Partition
Enter choice: [ ]
```

2. Press 1 and Enter. FDISK displays the disk's partition information and the following prompt:

```
Total disk space is 1204 Mbytes (1 Mbyte = 1048576 bytes)
WARNING! Data in the deleted Primary DOS Partition will be lost.
What primary partition do you want to delete..? [1]
```

3. Press Enter. FDISK prompts you to enter the volume label for the drive.

4. Type the volume label and press Enter. FDISK asks whether you're sure.

5. Press Y and Enter.

6. Press Esc to return to the FDISK Options screen.

Summary

This chapter continued your look at the Windows 95 file system by showing you a few techniques for working with disks. You learned how to format a floppy disk, copy a disk, and view disk properties. I also showed you how to wield Windows 95 disk compression and how to use FDISK to partition a disk. Here are a few chapters that contain related information:

- For basic file and folder techniques, see Chapter 5, "Windows 95: The 50¢ Tour."

- More advanced file and folder data can be found in Chapter 13, "Working with Files and Folders."

- To see how the file system architecture fits in with the Windows 95 architecture as a whole, head for Chapter 6, "Under the Hood: Understanding the Windows 95 Architecture."

- To learn how to perform file maintenance from the DOS prompt, see Chapter 21, "DOS Isn't Dead: Optimizing DOS Applications Under Windows 95."

CHAPTER 15

Protecting Your Windows 95 Investment

IN THIS CHAPTER

He is safe from danger who is on guard even when safe.

—*Publilius Syrus*

Computer problems, like the proverbial death and taxes, seem to be one of those constants in life. Whether it's a hard disk giving up the ghost, a power failure that trashes your files, or a virus that invades your system, the issue isn't *whether* something will go wrong, but rather *when* will it happen.

Instead of dealing with these difficulties only after they occur (what I call *pound-of-cure* mode), you need to get your system prepared in advance (*ounce-of-prevention* mode). This chapter shows you various Windows 95 utilities and techniques that can help you do just that.

Creating an Emergency Boot Disk

When most computers are switched on, the startup BIOS code first runs the Power-On Self Test and then looks for a disk in drive A. If it finds a disk, the BIOS code checks for a boot sector and, if one is present, boots the system via the floppy to get you to the A:\ prompt. If there's no disk in drive A, the system tries to boot via the active hard disk partition. So if your hard disk dies or if Windows 95 refuses to run, you can use a bootable floppy disk to bypass the hard disk and regain control of your system. Windows 95 gives you two methods of creating bootable floppy disks:

- You can use the Format command to either copy the necessary system files to an already formatted disk or format a disk to make it bootable. I showed you how to do this in Chapter 14, "Disk Driving: Dealing with Disks."
- You can create a Windows 95 Startup disk.

When you install Windows 95, the Setup program asks whether you want to create a Startup disk, which is a bootable disk that contains various files you can use to troubleshoot problems. No system should be without a bootable disk of some kind, so if you skipped the Startup disk during setup, you can still create it from within Windows 95.

To do this, open the Control Panel and launch the Add/Remove Programs icon. Activate the Startup Disk tab, shown in Figure 15.1, and then click the Create Disk button. While Windows 95 prepares the startup files, insert a disk in drive A. (Make sure that it's either a new disk or a disk that doesn't contain any files you need.) When you see the Insert Disk dialog box, click OK.

FIGURE 15.1.

*Use the Startup
Disk tab to create
a Windows 95
Startup disk.*

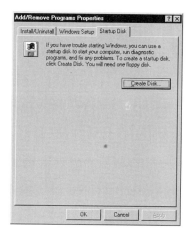

Table 15.1 lists the files Windows 95 adds to the Startup disk.

Table 15.1. Windows 95 startup disk files.

File	*Description*
ATTRIB.EXE	A utility for changing file attributes.
CHKDSK.EXE	A real-mode utility for scanning and repairing a disk.
COMMAND.COM	A real-mode command interpreter.
DEBUG.EXE	A utility for testing and debugging executable files.
DRVSPACE.BIN	A real-mode driver for compressed disks.
EBD.SYS	A utility for the startup disk.
EDIT.COM	A text editor for making changes to configuration files.
FDISK.EXE	A utility for partitioning a disk.
FORMAT.COM	A utility used to format a disk.
IO.SYS	A Windows 95 system file.
MSDOS.SYS	A Windows 95 startup file.
REGEDIT.EXE	A real-mode version of the Registry Editor.
SCANDISK.EXE	A utility for scanning and repairing a disk.
SCANDISK.INI	A configuration file for ScanDisk.
SYS.COM	A utility for transferring Windows 95 system files to a disk.
UNINSTAL.EXE	A utility for uninstalling Windows 95 (if you installed over an existing version of Windows).

15

PROTECTING YOUR
WINDOWS 95
INVESTMENT

You'll probably have a few hundred kilobytes left over on the disk, so to make this a true emergency disk, you should include any other diagnostic or repair utilities you might have. If you want access to your system devices (such as a SCSI controller, CD-ROM drive, or removable hard disk), you should include the necessary device drivers on the disk as well.

TROUBLESHOOTING: YOUR BOOT DISK WON'T BOOT

If your system won't boot from the disk but you're sure that the disk is bootable, check your computer's CMOS settings. Some systems let you bypass the floppy disk boot sector check and boot from the hard drive first. In this case, you'll need to access your computer's setup program and change this setting so that the computer attempts to boot from drive A first.

Protecting Long Filenames

I mentioned in Chapter 14 that you shouldn't use pre–Windows 95 disk utilities on VFAT volumes because they'll destroy your long filenames. If you have a favorite utility you hate to give up, your best bet is to upgrade to the Windows 95 version.

If a 32-bit version of the utility doesn't exist, or you can't upgrade for some reason, there *is* a way to keep using the program, but it's a bit of a pain. You'll need the Windows 95 CD-ROM and the LFNBK.EXE file that you'll find in the \Admin\Apptools\Lfnback\ folder.

LFNBK is the Windows 95 real-mode Long Filename Backup program. The idea behind LFNBK is to back up not your files, but the *names* of your files. In other words, for each file on a disk, LFNBK records both the short 8.3 filename and the long filename in a file named LFNBK.DAT, and it then removes the long filename. This lets you run your old disk utility without mishap. You can then use LFNBK to restore the long filenames. To use LFNBK, copy it from the CD-ROM to your main Windows 95 folder.

Before you can use LFNBK, you must tell Windows 95 to stop *tunneling* long filenames. Tunneling is a process that Windows 95 uses to preserve long filenames when files are used by 16-bit applications. When these programs write a file to disk (during, say, a save), they write only the file's 8.3 filename. Windows 95 recognizes this fact and tacks the file's long filename onto its directory entry.

Unfortunately, tunneling will prevent LFNBK from doing its job, so you must disable tunneling by following these steps:

1. Right-click My Computer, select Properties, and select the Performance tab.

2. Select File System and, in the File System Properties dialog box that appears, select the Troubleshooting tab.

3. Activate the Disable long name preservation for old programs check box, and then click OK.

4. When Windows 95 asks whether you want to restart your computer, click Yes.

5. When you see the `Starting Windows 95...` message, press F8 to get the Startup menu, and select the `Command prompt only` option.

You're now ready to run LFNBK. Here's the syntax:

```
lfnbk [/v] [/b ¦ /r ¦ /pe] [/nt] [/force] [/p] [drive]
```

/v	Reports actions on-screen (verbose mode).
/b	Backs up and removes long filenames on the disk.
/r	Restores previously backed-up long filenames.
/pe	Extracts errors from the backup database.
/nt	Doesn't restore backup dates and times.
/force	Forces LFNBK to run, even in unsafe conditions.
/p	Finds long filenames but doesn't convert them to 8.3 filename aliases. This switch reports the existing long filenames, along with the associated dates for file creation, last access, and last modification of the file.
drive	Indicates the letter of the drive you want to work with.

For example, to back up and remove long filenames on drive D, you enter the following command:

```
lfnbk /b d
```

LFNBK reports the number of directories and files it processed, as well as the number of long filenames it found and removed.

With long filenames removed and safely stowed in `LFNBK.DAT`, you can now run your disk utility. When you're done, run LFNBK with the `/r` switch to restore the long filenames. For drive D, here's the command to run:

```
lfnbk /r d
```

Restart your computer and boot into Windows 95 normally. Use the procedure described earlier to deactivate the `Disable long name preservation for old programs` check box and reenable tunneling.

Backing Up Your Files (the Better-Safe-Than-Sorry Department)

"In theory, theory and practice are the same thing; in practice, they're not." That old saw applies perfectly to data backups. In theory, backing up data is an important part of everyday computing life. After all, we *know* that our data is valuable to the point of irreplaceability, and we *know* that there's no shortage of ways that a hard disk can crash: power surges, rogue applications, virus programs, or just simple wear and tear. In practice, however, backing up our data always seems to be one of those chores we'll get to "tomorrow." After all, that old hard disk seems to be humming along just fine, thank you—and anyway, who has time to work through the couple dozen floppy disks you need for even a small backup?

When it comes to backups, theory and practice don't usually converge until that day you start your system and you get an ugly `Invalid system configuration` or `Hard disk failure` message. Believe me, losing a hard disk that's crammed with unsaved (and now lost) data brings the importance of backing up into focus *real* quick. To avoid this sorry fate, you have to find a way to take some of the pain out of the practice of backing up. Fortunately, you can do two things to make backups more painless:

- ■ Use the Backup accessory that comes with Windows 95. This program has a few nice features that make it easy to select files for backup and to run backups regularly.

- ■ Practice what I call *real-world* backups. In short, these are backups that protect only your most crucial files.

The next few sections show you how to use Backup and explain real-world backups in more detail.

Starting Backup

Assuming that you've installed the Backup accessory, select Start | Programs | Accessories | System Tools | Backup to get the show on the road. The first time you start Backup, you'll see the dialog box shown in Figure 15.2. It gives you an overview of the backup process and summarizes everything into three general steps. Unfortunately, this dialog box doesn't give you the full story. Backing up your data often takes as many as five steps:

1. Select the files you want to back up.
2. Select the type of backup (full or incremental).
3. Select the drive you want to use for the backup.
4. Save your backup set.
5. Start the backup.

I'll explain each step in detail in a moment. For now, activate the `Don't show this again` check box (unless, of course, you do want to see this dialog box every time you start Backup), and click OK.

FIGURE 15.2.

This dialog box appears the first time you start Backup.

Backup takes a few moments to root around in your system, and then it displays the dialog box shown in Figure 15.3. In Backup lingo, a *backup set* is a file that defines your backup. It includes three things:

- A list of the files you want to include in your backup.
- Backup options you selected, including the type of backup you want to use (which I'll explain later).
- The destination drive and folder for the backed-up files.

This dialog box tells you that Backup has created a backup set named Full System Backup that includes all the files on your system, including the Registry files (SYSTEM.DAT and USER.DAT). Again, activate the Don't show this again check box and click OK.

FIGURE 15.3.

This dialog box lets you know that Backup has created a backup set that will archive your entire system.

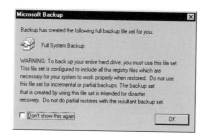

If you don't have a tape drive on your system, yet another dialog box will appear to let you know that Backup didn't detect a tape drive. Click OK. At long last, you'll see the Microsoft Backup window, shown in Figure 15.4.

FIGURE 15.4.

The Microsoft Backup window.

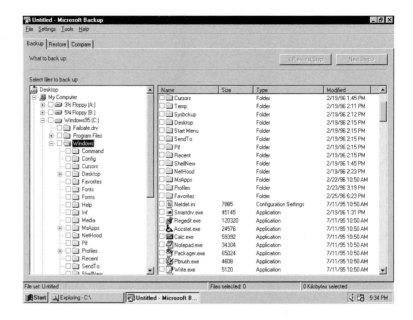

Selecting the Files to Back Up

The Backup window is reminiscent of the Explorer window, with one important difference: In the Backup window, all the disk drives, folders, and files have a check box next to them. The basic idea is that you activate the appropriate check box for each drive, folder, and file that you want to include in the backup. Here are a few notes to keep in mind while choosing your backup set:

- If a drive's tree is collapsed, activating the drive's check box selects every file and folder within the drive. Deactivating the drive's check box deselects every file and folder within the drive.

- If a drive's tree is expanded, activating the drive's check box selects only the files in the drive's root directory. Deactivating the drive's check box deselects only the files in the drive's root directory.

- If a folder's tree is collapsed, activating the folder's check box selects all of its files and subfolders. Deactivating the folder's check box deselects all of its files and subfolders.

- If a folder's tree is expanded, activating the folder's check box selects only its files and not its subfolders. Deactivating the folder's check box deselects only its files.

- If a drive or folder's check box has a gray background, only some of the objects in the drive or folder are included in the backup set.

- The status bar shows you the number of files selected and the total number of kilobytes.

Some Thoughts on Real-World Backups

Before getting down to business, you need to ask yourself which files you want to include in the backup. Your first inclination might be to use the Full Backup Set that the Backup program mentioned earlier just to be safe. This is fine if you have lots of room on your destination drive, whether it's a tape drive, another hard drive, or a network drive.

But what if you're backing up to a location with limited free space or even to floppy disks? Although Backup can compress your backed-up files so that they consume only about half their normal volume, that can still add up to hundreds of megabytes on a big system. And even a small hard disk contains enough data to fill a couple dozen floppy disks. Shuffling that many disks in and out of your machine every time you do a backup will get old in a hurry. For these limited situations, you need to take a real-world approach to backups:

- The problem with a full backup is that it includes all your program files. Presumably, however, you have these files on disk somewhere, so why include them in a backup? If necessary, you can always reinstall your programs (and even Windows 95 itself).

- If you're going to leave out your program files, however, you should seriously consider making backup copies of your program disks. You have to do it only once, and you probably can do it only for your most important programs. (I showed you how to copy disks in Chapter 14.)

- All the energy you put into backing up should go toward protecting your documents because, unlike your programs, these are usually irreplaceable. To make life easier, you should create separate folders to hold only your documents. That way, adding these documents to the backup set is an easy matter of activating the folder's check box in the Backup window.

- Take advantage of Backup's two different backup types: full and incremental. *Full* backs up all the files you select; *incremental* backs up only those files that have changed since the last full backup.

Your overall backup strategy might look something like this:

1. Perform a full backup of all your documents once a month or so.

2. If you do most of your work in one or two programs, do a full backup of these programs' documents every week or two.

3. Do an incremental backup of modified files every couple of days (although you might consider backing up really important documents every day).

Filtering Files

Besides letting you select individual drives, folders, and files, Backup also has a File Filtering feature that lets you exclude files based on the date they were last modified or the file type. Select Settings | File Filtering to display the File Filtering dialog box, shown in Figure 15.5.

FIGURE 15.5.

Use this dialog box to exclude files based on date and file type.

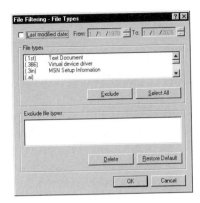

To exclude files from the backup set based on the date they were created or last modified, activate the Last modified date check box, and use the From and To spinners to enter your dates. Any files that have dates that fall within (or on) these dates will be removed from the Backup window.

To exclude files by type, use the File types list to highlight the types you want to avoid, and click Exclude. Backup adds the selected types to the Exclude file types list. If you change your mind, you can return a file type to the backup set by highlighting it in the Exclude file types list and clicking Delete.

Selecting Backup Options

Backup has various options you can work with, and the options you choose are stored with each backup set. To view the options, select Settings | Options to display the Settings - Options dialog box, shown in Figure 15.6. The General tab displays two check boxes:

Turn on audible prompts: If you activate this check box, Backup beeps your computer's speaker at certain steps during the backup process (such as when you need to insert another floppy disk).

Overwrite old status log files: If you activate this check box, Backup creates a new status log each time you perform a backup. The status log is a text file that records the date and time the backup was started, whether or not any errors occurred during the backup, and the date and time the backup was completed. (The file is named ERROR.LOG, and you'll find it in the \Program Files\Accessories\Log folder.) If you deactivate this check box, Backup appends the data to the end of the existing status log.

FIGURE 15.6.

*Selecting Settings |
Options displays this
dialog box.*

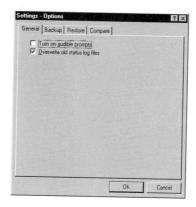

The Backup tab, shown in Figure 15.7, contains a few more options:

Quit Backup after operation is finished: If you activate this check box, Backup shuts itself down after it has completed the backup.

Full: This option backs up all the files in the current backup set.

Incremental: This option backs up only those files in the current backup set that have changed since the last full backup.

Verify backup data by automatically comparing files after backup is finished: If you activate this check box, Backup checks each backed-up file against its original to make sure that the backup archived the file without any errors. Note that activating this option effectively doubles the backup time.

Use data compression: If you activate this check box, Backup compresses the backed-up files. The backed-up files will take up approximately half the space of the originals.

Format when needed on tape backups: If you're using a tape backup system, activating this option tells Backup to format any unformatted tapes it encounters during the backup. If you deactivate this check box, you can use only formatted tapes with Backup.

Always erase on tape backups: If you activate this check box, Backup erases any data on the tapes you use for the backup. If you leave this check box deactivated, Backup appends the current backup set to the tape.

Always erase on floppy disk backups: If you activate this check box, Backup erases any data on the floppy disks you use for the backup. If you leave this check box deactivated, Backup appends the current backup set to the floppy disks.

15

FIGURE 15.7.

Use the Backup tab to set various Backup options.

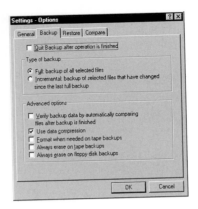

When you've chosen your options, click OK.

Working with Backup's Drag-and-Drop Settings

As you'll see later, if you create a shortcut for Backup on the desktop, you can drag a saved backup set and drop it on the Backup shortcut, and Windows 95 performs the backup automatically. Backup gives you a few settings that control the behavior of this drag-and-drop technique. To check them out, select Settings | Drag and Drop to display the dialog box shown in Figure 15.8. Here's a summary of the controls in this dialog box:

Run Backup minimized: If you leave this check box activated, the Backup progress window (shown later in Figure 15.11) doesn't appear on-screen. Instead, you see just the Backup icon on the taskbar.

Confirm operation before beginning: If you leave this check box activated, Backup displays a dialog box asking you to confirm that you want to back up your files. Deactivate this check box to avoid this dialog box.

Quit Backup after operation is finished: If you leave this check box activated, Backup shuts itself down after the backup is complete. If you deactivate this check box, the Backup dialog box remains open so that you can see the total number of files and kilobytes backed up and the total elapsed time.

After you've made your selections, click OK to return to the Backup window.

FIGURE 15.8.

Use this dialog box to set Backup's drag-and-drop options.

Selecting the Backup Destination

After you've selected all the documents you want to back up, click the Next Step > button. You use the revised window that appears to highlight the drive or folder where you want the backup copies of your documents to reside. (Note that the < Previous Step button is active in this window. This means you can always go back to adjust your file selections.) When you highlight a drive or folder in the Select a destination for the backup list, the destination's path appears in the Selected device or location box, and the Start Backup button is activated, as you can see in Figure 15.9.

FIGURE 15.9.

Use this version of the Backup tab to select your backup destination.

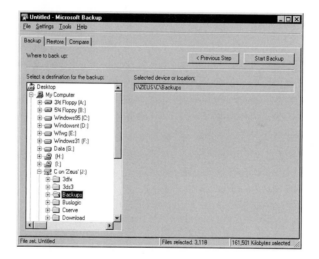

CAUTION: WATCH FOR DESTINATIONS THAT CAN'T HANDLE LONG FILENAMES

If you'll be backing up to a network drive, make sure that the drive can handle long filenames. If it can't, you need to use LFNBK (as described earlier) to back up and remove your long filenames before performing the backup. When you restore files from this drive, you can use LFNBK with the /r switch to restore the files' long names.

Saving Your Backup Set

The files, options, and destination you've selected together make up your *backup set*. Because this is a combination you'll likely use quite often, it's a good idea to preserve your selections by saving your backup set.

To do that, select File | Save or press Ctrl-S. In the Save As dialog box that appears, enter a name for the backup set, and click OK.

Performing the Backup

You're now ready to back up your files. Here are the steps to follow:

1. If necessary, insert a floppy disk in the drive you selected or a tape in the tape drive.
2. Click the Start Backup button. Backup displays the Backup Set Label dialog box, shown in Figure 15.10.

FIGURE 15.10.

Use this dialog box to enter a name for the backup file.

3. Your files aren't backed up individually. Instead, they're combined into a single file (of QIC type), and that file is what gets backed up. Use the Backup Set Label dialog box to enter a name for this file. (If you want to assign a password to this file, click Password Protect, enter the password twice in the dialog box that appears, and click OK.) When you're ready to go, click OK.
4. If the disk or tape you're using is full, Backup asks whether you want to erase the data. If that's not what you want, remove the disk and insert another one. Click Yes when you're ready to go. The Backup dialog box appears to keep you posted on the progress of the backup, as shown in Figure 15.11.

FIGURE 15.11.

This dialog box shows you the number of files and kilobytes that have been backed up as well as the elapsed time.

5. Depending on the number and size of the files you selected, and the destination folder, Backup might occasionally prompt you to enter more disks. If so, insert the new disk and then click OK. When you're done with a disk, you should label it for future reference (for example, Backup Disk #1).

6. Backup displays a dialog box to let you know when it's finished. Click OK to return to the Backup dialog box, and then click OK again to return to the Backup window.

Working with a Backup Set

If you saved your backup set to a SET file, you can reuse this backup set to perform another backup of the same files. (Actually, if you selected an entire drive or folder in the Backup window, any new files you added to this drive or folder are included in the new backup automatically.)

One way to do this is to rerun Backup, select File | Open File Set, and use the Open dialog box that appears to open your backup set. In this case, though, the backup set's files and folders are selected, but not the Backup options or the destination. This method is best if you want to make changes to the backup set.

If you don't want to make changes to the backup set, however, you can perform the backup without opening the Backup window. Here are the methods you can use:

- In Explorer, double-click the SET file, or highlight it and select File | Open, or right-click it and select Open from the context menu.

- Create a shortcut for Backup (you'll find BACKUP.EXE in the \Program Files\Accessories folder) on the desktop, drag the SET file from Explorer, and drop it on the Backup shortcut.

- Create a shortcut for the SET file on the desktop, and double-click it.

In each case, Windows 95 takes you right into the backup without bothering with the Backup window. Note that the backup file that's created uses the same name as the SET file, except with a QIC extension. (If you perform several backups to the same folder, subsequent files have numbers appended to their primary names to differentiate them.)

NOTE: USING OLDER BACKUP UTILITIES

The Windows 95 Backup program is decent, but it lacks many of the features found in high-end backup utilities. If you have a pre–Windows 95 version of a backup program that you don't want to give up, you can still use it. You must, however, go through the LFNBK rigmarole that I outlined earlier in this chapter.

Restoring Backed-Up Data

If some unforeseen disaster should occur, you'll need to restore your data from the backups. The next few sections take you through the process.

Selecting the Backup Set

The first thing you need to do is choose the backup set that contains the files you want to restore. Here are the steps to follow:

1. Start Backup, as described earlier.

2. In the Backup window, select the Restore tab.

3. If necessary, insert the tape or the first floppy disk from the backup set.

4. Use the Restore from list to highlight the drive or folder that contains the backup set. The name of the backup set should appear in the box on the right side of the window.

5. If there are multiple backup sets, highlight the one you want to use, as shown in Figure 15.12.

FIGURE 15.12.

Use the Restore tab to select the backup set that contains the files you want to restore.

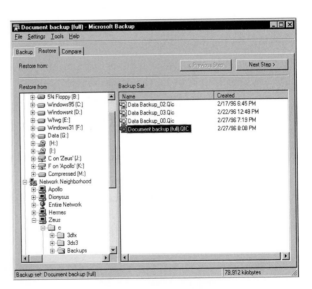

Setting Restore Options

Before proceeding with the restore, you might want to modify a few options. To view them, select Settings | Options to display the Settings - Options dialog box, and then select the Restore tab, as shown in Figure 15.13. Here's a rundown of the controls on this tab:

Quit Backup after operation is finished: If you leave this check box activated, Backup shuts itself down after the restore is complete.

Restore backed up files to: The option buttons in this group determine where Backup restores the files. If you select `Original locations`, Backup restores the files to the same drive and folder from which they were backed up. If you select `Alternate location`, you can restore the files to a drive or folder other than the one from which they were backed up. If you select `Alternate location, single directory`, you can restore the files to a specific folder other than the one from which they were backed up.

Verify restored data by automatically comparing files after the restore has finished: If you activate this check box, Backup checks each restored file with the backed-up version to make sure that the file was restored without any errors. Note that activating this option effectively doubles the restore time.

Never overwrite files: If you activate this option, Backup won't replace any files on the destination drive or folder with backed-up files that have the same name.

Overwrite older files only: If you activate this option, Backup replaces files on the destination drive or folder only with backed-up files of the same name that have a later date.

Overwrite files: If you activate this option, Backup replaces any files on the destination drive or folder with backed-up files that have the same name. To have Backup prompt you before overwriting these files, activate the `Prompt before overwriting files` check box.

When you're done, click OK to return to the Restore window.

FIGURE 15.13.

Use the Restore tab to set various options for your restore operation.

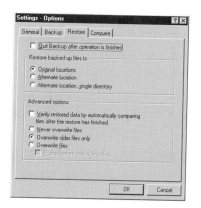

Selecting the Files to Restore

Now you need to choose which files you want to restore. In the Restore tab, click the Next Step > button. The window changes to show the folders and files in the selected backup set. Selecting the files to restore is basically the same as selecting the backup set: You activate the check boxes for the appropriate drives, folders, and files, as shown in Figure 15.14.

Figure 15.14.

Use this version of the Restore tab to select the files you want to restore.

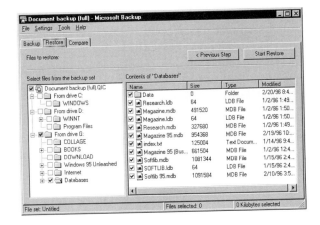

Restoring the Files

After you've made your selections, click the Start Restore button. If you chose to restore the files to a different location, you'll see the Browse for Folder dialog box, shown in Figure 15.15. Click OK to start the restore.

Figure 15.15.

Use this dialog box to select an alternative location for the restored files.

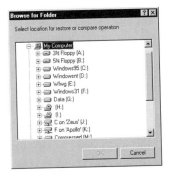

TIP: RESTORING OLD MICROSOFT BACKUP FILES

Unfortunately, Windows 95's Backup program isn't compatible with older versions of Microsoft Backup that came with DOS 6.x. If you backed up files with this older version, are they lost for good? Not if you have the Windows 95 CD-ROM. You'll find the old version of Microsoft Backup in the \Other\Oldmsdos\Msbackup\ folder.

Before using this program, however, you should use LFNBK to back up and remove your long filenames, as described earlier.

Backing Up the Registry

As you learned in Chapter 11, "Introducing the Windows 95 Registry," and Chapter 12, "Hacking the Registry," the Registry is Windows 95's most critical component. Need more proof? How about the fact that Windows 95 boasts no fewer than six ways to make backup copies of the Registry:

- Each time you make a change to the Registry, Windows 95 copies the original SYSTEM.DAT to SYSTEM.DA0 and USER.DAT to USER.DA0.

- You can copy SYSTEM.DAT and USER.DAT to a floppy disk or network drive. The next section shows you a batch file that will back up these files for you automatically.

- You can use the Registry Editor's Export Registry File command to copy some or all of the Registry to a REG (text) file.

- You can use the Backup program's Full System Backup SET file. (Note, however, that you can't include SYSTEM.DAT and USER.DAT in any other backup set.)

- You can use the Emergency Recovery Utility from the Windows 95 CD-ROM. See the section titled "Using the Emergency Recovery Utility" later in this chapter.

- You can use the Configuration Backup utility from the Windows 95 CD-ROM. I'll show you how this program works a little later.

A Batch File to Automate Registry Backups

Since backing up the Registry really only involves making copies of SYSTEM.DAT and USER.DAT, and since file copying can be done via DOS commands, it makes sense to create a batch file that will automate this procedure. Listing 15.1 provides an example of such a batch file.

Listing 15.1. REGSAVER.BAT: a batch file that backs up the Registry files.

```
@ECHO OFF
REM Change these lines to point to your main Win95 folder:
C:
CD\WINDOWS
IF NOT "%1"=="" GOTO EXTENSION
REM Copy the files as is:
XCOPY SYSTEM.DAT C:\ /H /K /R /Y
XCOPY USER.DAT C:\ /H /K /R /Y
GOTO END
:EXTENSION
REM Copy the files using the specified extension:
ECHO Backing up SYSTEM.DAT to SYSTEM.%1...
ECHO F ¦ XCOPY SYSTEM.DAT C:\SYSTEM.%1 /H /K /R /Y > NUL
ECHO Backing up USER.DAT to USER.%1...
ECHO F ¦ XCOPY USER.DAT C:\USER.%1 /H /K /R /Y > NUL
:END
```

You can use `REGSAVER.BAT` in one of two ways:

- You can run it without a parameter. In this case, `REGSAVER.BAT` copies `SYSTEM.DAT` and `USER.DAT` to `C:\SYSTEM.DAT` and `C:\USER.DAT`, respectively.

- You run it with a file extension parameter. In this case, `REGSAVER.BAT` copies `SYSTEM.DAT` and `USER.DAT` to the root folder but replaces the .DAT extensions with the extension you specified. For example, if you run the batch file with 1 as the parameter (that is, you enter the command `regsaver 1`), `SYSTEM.DAT` and `USER.DAT` are copied to `C:\SYSTEM.1` and `C:\USER.1`, respectively.

Let's see how `REGSAVER.BAT` works. After turning `ECHO` off, the batch begins by switching to the C drive and changing the directory to `C:\WINDOWS`. Note that you'll need to modify these lines to point to your main Windows 95 folder.

Then an `IF` test checks to see whether a parameter (`%1`) was included on the command line. If not, `XCOPY` is used to copy `SYSTEM.DAT` and `USER.DAT` to `C:\SYSTEM.DAT` and `C:\USER.DAT`. Here's a summary of the switches used in the `XCOPY` commands:

`XCOPY` *source destination* `/H /K /R /Y`

source	The file to be copied (`SYSTEM.DAT` or `USER.DAT`).
destination	The location of the file copies (`C:\` in this case).
/H	Copies hidden and system files (this saves you from having to adjust the files' attributes before copying).
/K	Copies the files' existing attributes. This means the backups will have the same attributes as the originals.
/R	Overwrites read-only files. This is required just in case the new backups have the same names as existing backups.
/Y	Overwrites existing files without prompting.

If there *was* a parameter on the command line, the `IF` test passes control down to the `EXTENSION` label. From here, a special version of the `XCOPY` command is run to copy the Registry files to files that have the specified extension. For example, here's the command that's used to make a backup of `SYSTEM.DAT`:

`ECHO F ¦ XCOPY SYSTEM.DAT C:\SYSTEM.%1 /H /K /R /Y > NUL`

Here's what's happening in this command:

- The `XCOPY` command can't be certain whether you're copying to a file or a directory. To force its hand, this command uses `ECHO F ¦ XCOPY` to send an F (for file) to the command.

■ The *destination* parameter is SYSTEM.%1. Here, %1 is the extension parameter that you specified on the REGSAVER command line. For example, if you used REGSAVER 970823, %1 equals 970823, so SYSTEM.DAT will be backed up to SYSTEM.970823.

■ The > NUL part prevents the XCOPY messages from appearing on-screen.

TIP: PROMPT FOR PARAMETERS

You might want to create a shortcut for REGSAVER.BAT on your desktop. If you do, there's a method you can use to have Windows 95 prompt you for the REGSAVER parameter:

1. Right-click the shortcut and then choose Properties from the context menu.
2. In the properties sheet that appears, activate the Program tab.
3. In the Cmd line text box, add a space and a question mark (?) after REGSAVER.BAT. In other words, your command line should now look something like this:

   C:\REGSAVER.BAT ?

4. Click OK.

When you launch the shortcut, a dialog box will appear in which you can enter your extension parameter if desired.

NOTE: BATCH FILE BASICS

If you'd like to learn more about batch files, check out Appendix F, "A Batch File Primer."

Using the Configuration Backup Utility

The Configuration Backup utility is a small program named CFGBACK.EXE. You'll find it—as well as a Help file named CFGBACK.HLP—in the \Other\Misc\Cfgback\ folder on your Windows 95 CD-ROM.

CAUTION: CONFIGURATION BACKUP DOESN'T WORK!

Since Windows 95 was released, Microsoft has acknowledged that version 4.0 of Configuration Backup (the version on the Windows 95 CD-ROM) contains bugs that prevent it from restoring all of the Registry's settings correctly. Therefore, I strongly urge you *not* to use this version of the utility.

At the time this chapter was written, however, Microsoft had not made an updated version available. I included the following instructions on the chance that a new version of this utility will be forthcoming. Otherwise, you should look at alternative Registry backup strategies for now.

Copy both files to your main Windows 95 folder. (If you don't have the Windows 95 CD-ROM, you can get Configuration Backup from one of Microsoft's online sites. Look for a compressed file named CFGBK.EXE.) Configuration Backup works by compressing the contents of SYSTEM.DAT and USER.DAT into a single file in your main Windows 95 folder. The resulting file is significantly smaller than the uncompressed files (on average, about one-fifth the size), so you could even include it on your Windows 95 Startup disk.

Configuration Backup can create up to nine different Registry backups, and each file uses the name REGBAKn.RBK, in which n is a number from 1 to 9. The basic idea is that before you make a major change to your system (such as adding a new hardware device or installing a large software program), you use Configuration Backup to save your existing Registry. That way, should anything go wrong after you've made your changes to the system, you can always restore your old Registry.

Creating a Registry Backup

Here are the steps to follow to make a backup copy of your Registry files with Configuration Backup:

1. Run CFGBACK.EXE. You'll see the Microsoft Configuration Backup dialog box, shown in Figure 15.16.

FIGURE 15.16.

This dialog box appears when you start Configuration Backup.

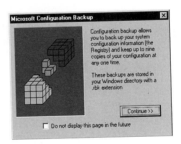

2. The first three dialog boxes describe Configuration Backup and tell you how it works. To avoid these explanations in the future, for each dialog box, activate the Do not display this page in the future check box, and then click Continue >>. You'll eventually see the Configuration Backup dialog box, shown in Figure 15.17.

FIGURE 15.17.

You'll use this dialog box to perform your Registry backups.

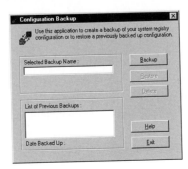

3. Use the `Selected Backup Name` text box to enter a descriptive name for the backup (such as `Before installing SCSI card - 3/15/96`).

4. Click Backup. Configuration Backup asks you to confirm that you want to back up your current configuration.

5. Click Yes. A dialog box appears when Configuration Backup has completed its labors.

6. Click OK.

7. Click Exit.

Restoring a Registry Backup

Configuration Backup can also restore any backed-up versions of your Registry. If you stored the RBK file in a different location, be sure to copy it back to your main Windows 95 folder. Here are the steps to follow to restore an old version of your Registry:

1. Run `CFGBACK.EXE` and, if necessary, run through the introductory dialog boxes until you get to the Configuration Backup dialog box.

2. Use the `List of Previous Backups` box to highlight the backup you want to restore, as shown in Figure 15.18.

FIGURE 15.18.

The Configuration Backup dialog box lists your previous Registry backups.

3. Click Restore. Configuration Backup asks you to confirm that you want to restore the selected backup.

4. Click Yes. Yet another dialog box asks for confirmation.

5. Click Yes one more time. Configuration Backup restores `SYSTEM.DAT` and `USER.DAT` and then displays a dialog box when it's finished restoring.

6. Click OK.

7. Click Exit and then restart your computer.

Using the Emergency Recovery Utility

Configuration Backup saves only your Registry, but you might need to restore a few other configuration files in case a major problem smites your system. These files include IO.SYS, MSDOS.SYS, COMMAND.COM, and, if you're still using 16-bit programs or real-mode drivers, WIN.INI, SYSTEM.INI, PROTOCOL.INI, CONFIG.SYS, and AUTOEXEC.BAT.

To make it easy to not only save these files (as well as SYSTEM.DAT and USER.DAT), but also restore them in case of a problem, the Windows 95 CD-ROM contains a program called the Emergency Recovery Utility (ERU). You'll find the ERU files in the folder \Other\Misc\Eru\.

There are four files in all:

ERU.EXE: The ERU executable file.

ERU.TXT: A text file that explains ERU.

ERU.INF: A setup file used by ERU.EXE.

ERD.E_E: A file used by ERU.EXE to create ERD.EXE, the executable file that restores the configuration files.

You'll need to copy these files to your main Windows 95 folder.

Saving Your Configuration Files

Here are the steps to follow to run the Emergency Recovery Utility:

1. Run ERU.EXE. You'll see the Emergency Recovery Utility dialog box.
2. Click Next >>. The ERU prompts you to select a location for the backed-up files, as shown in Figure 15.19.

FIGURE 15.19.

The Emergency Recovery Utility prompts you for a location.

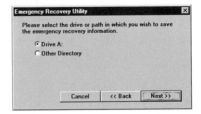

3. If you want to use drive A, click Next >>, insert a bootable disk in drive A, and click OK. Otherwise, activate the Other Directory option, click Next >>, enter the folder you want to use, and click Next >>.

TROUBLESHOOTING: ERU SHUTS DOWN

If the Emergency Recovery Utility shuts down at this point without displaying the list of files to be saved, one or more of the configuration files are missing. For example, if you don't have CONFIG.SYS or AUTOEXEC.BAT on your system, ERU just bails out without any kind of warning.

To fix this problem, find ERU.INF in your main Windows 95 folder, and display its properties sheet. Deactivate the Read-Only check box and click OK. Double-click ERU.INF to open it in Notepad. For each file that you're missing, insert a semicolon (;) to the left of the filename. This semicolon tells ERU not to look for the file on your system. Save and exit; then try running ERU again.

4. A dialog box shows you a list of the files that will be saved. If you want to change this list, click Custom to display the dialog box shown in Figure 15.20.

FIGURE 15.20.

Use this dialog box to select the files you want to save.

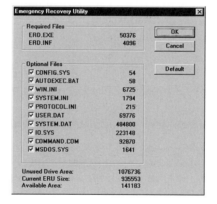

5. Deactivate the check boxes for the files you don't want to save, and then click OK.
6. Click Next >>. The Emergency Recovery Utility begins saving the configuration files to your selected location.
7. When the Emergency Recovery Utility is done, click OK.

Restoring Your Configuration Files

If a system emergency requires you to restore your configuration files, you can use the real-mode ERD.EXE program that the Emergency Recovery Utility copied along with the saved configuration. You start ERD in one of the following ways:

■ If you saved your configuration to a bootable floppy, insert the disk in drive A and reboot. ERD starts automatically.

- If you saved your configuration to a folder on your hard disk, boot Windows 95 with the `Safe mode command prompt only` option, change to the drive and folder where the configuration was saved, type `erd`, and press Enter.

The Microsoft Emergency Recovery screen that appears lists the configuration files you saved. For each file you want to restore, use the arrow keys to highlight the file, and then press the Spacebar. When you're done, highlight the `Start Recovery` option and press Enter.

Preventing and Repairing Hard Disk Errors with ScanDisk

An old ad for Steve Gibson's SpinRite hard disk utilities said it all: "Hard disks die." That's a stark message but, let's face it, an honest one. Just consider everything that a modern hard disk has to put up with:

General wear and tear: If your computer is running right now, its hard disk is spinning away at (probably) 3,600 revolutions per minute. That's right, even though you're not doing anything, the hard disk is hard at work. Because of this constant activity, most hard disks simply wear out after a few years.

The old bump-and-grind: Your hard disk includes "read/write heads" that are used to read data from and write data to the disk. These heads float on a cushion of air just above the spinning hard disk platters. A bump or jolt of sufficient intensity can send them crashing onto the surface of the disk, which could easily result in trashed data. If the heads happen to hit a particularly sensitive area, the entire hard disk could crash.

Power surges: The current that is supplied to your PC is, under normal conditions, fairly constant. It's possible, however, for your computer to be assailed by massive power surges (for example, during a lightning storm). These surges can wreak havoc on a carefully arranged hard disk.

Power outages: If a power outage shuts down your system while you're working in Windows, you'll almost certainly lose some data, and you might (in extremely rare cases) lose access to your hard disk as well.

Viruses: Unfortunately, computer viruses are all too common nowadays. Although some of these viruses are benign—they display cute messages or cause characters to "fall off" the screen—most are downright vicious and exist only to trash your valuable data (more on this topic later).

Bad programming: Some not-ready-for-prime-time software programs can end up running amok and destroying large chunks of your hard disk in the process. Luckily, these rogues are fairly rare these days.

So what can you do about it? Well, backing up your files regularly and keeping a bootable emergency disk nearby are good places to start. But Windows 95 also comes with a program called ScanDisk that can check your hard disk for problems and repair them automatically. It might not be able to recover a totally trashed hard disk, but it can at least let you know when a hard disk might be heading for trouble.

ScanDisk performs a battery of tests on a hard disk, including looking for invalid filenames, invalid file dates and times, bad sectors, and invalid compression structures. In the hard disk's file system, ScanDisk also looks for the following errors:

- Lost clusters
- Invalid clusters
- Cross-linked clusters

Understanding Lost Clusters

A *lost cluster* (also sometimes called an *orphaned cluster*) is a cluster that, according to the FAT, is associated with a file, but that has no link to any entry in the file directory. Lost clusters are typically caused by program crashes, power surges, or power outages.

If ScanDisk comes across lost clusters, it offers to delete them or convert them to files in the drive's root folder with names like `FILE0000.CHK` and `FILE0001.CHK`. You can take a look at these files to see whether they contain any useful data and then try to salvage the data. Usually, however, these files are unusable, and most people just delete them to save the disk space.

Understanding Invalid Clusters

An *invalid cluster* is one that falls under one of the following three categories:

- A FAT entry that refers to cluster 1. This is illegal because a disk's cluster numbers start at 2.
- A FAT entry that refers to a cluster number larger than the total number of clusters on the disk.
- A FAT entry of 0 (which normally denotes an unused cluster) that is part of a cluster chain.

In this case, ScanDisk asks whether you want to convert these "lost file fragments" to files. If you say yes, ScanDisk truncates the file by replacing the invalid cluster with an EOF marker and then converts the lost file fragments to files. These are probably the truncated portion of the file, so you can examine them and try to piece everything back together. More likely, however, you'll just have to trash these files.

Understanding Cross-Linked Clusters

A cross-linked cluster is a cluster that has somehow been assigned to two different files (or twice in the same file). Figure 15.21 shows a diagram of a FAT with a couple of cross-linked files. In this case, both BADFILE.DBF and NOGOOD.DOC contain FAT entries that refer to cluster 101, so they're cross-linked. BADFILE.DBF also has two FAT entries that refer to the same cluster (103), which is also a cross-link error.

FIGURE 15.21.

Files with cross-linked clusters.

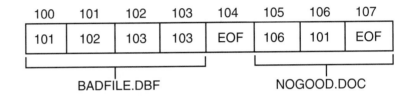

Getting ScanDisk Ready

To get ScanDisk up and running, select Start | Programs | Accessories | System Tools | ScanDisk. You'll see the ScanDisk window shown in Figure 15.22.

FIGURE 15.22.

The main ScanDisk window.

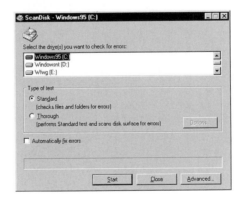

Use the Select the drive(s) you want to check for errors list to highlight the drive or drives you want ScanDisk to check. If you select a floppy drive, be sure to insert a disk in the drive before proceeding.

The Type of test group contains two options that determine how ScanDisk checks the disks:

Standard: This test checks for FAT problems, invalid filenames, invalid file dates and times, and compression errors. On most drives, this test should take only a few seconds.

Thorough: This test runs the Standard test and then checks the surface of the disk for bad sectors. Depending on the size of the disk, this test can take an hour or two.

Setting Surface Scan Options

If you select the Thorough test, ScanDisk enables the Options button. Clicking this command button displays the Surface Scan Options dialog box, shown in Figure 15.23. Here's a summary of the controls in this dialog box:

Areas of the disk to scan: The option buttons in this group determine which parts of the physical disk will be checked. The *system area* is where the master boot record and other system structures are stored. Although ScanDisk won't be able to fix errors in this area, an indication that errors exist might be a sign that your hard disk is about to fail. The *data area* is the area where your files and folders are stored on the disk. If ScanDisk finds a bad sector here, it can relocate the data to a safe part of the disk and mark the sector as bad so that no programs will use it in the future.

Do not perform write-testing: ScanDisk normally checks for bad sectors by reading each sector and then writing the data back to the disk. If this read/write cycle is performed successfully, the sector is good. To speed up the surface scan, you can activate this check box. This tells ScanDisk not to write the data back to the disk.

Do not repair bad sectors in hidden and system files: Some programs expect certain hidden and system files to be stored in specific clusters. If any part of these files are moved, the program might no longer function properly. If you activate this check box, ScanDisk won't move any bad sectors it finds in hidden and system files. (Of course, if a hidden or system file contains a bad sector, the program that needs the file might not work anyway, so you should probably just leave this option deactivated.)

FIGURE 15.23.

Use this dialog box to set options for Scan-Disk's Thorough test.

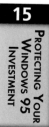

15

PROTECTING YOUR
WINDOWS 95
INVESTMENT

Click OK when you're done to return to the ScanDisk window.

Setting Advanced Options

ScanDisk has a few advanced options that determine its default behavior. To view these options, click the Advanced button in the ScanDisk main window to display the ScanDisk Advanced Options dialog box, shown in Figure 15.24.

FIGURE 15.24.

Use this dialog box to modify ScanDisk's default behavior.

Here's a rundown of the various settings you can work with in this dialog box:

Display summary: The options in this group determine whether ScanDisk Always or Never displays a summary at the end of the check. This summary shows the total disk space, the number of bytes used, the size of each cluster (or *allocation unit,* as Scan-Disk calls a cluster), the number of bad sectors, and the repairs that were made, if any. If you want to see this summary only if ScanDisk finds a problem, activate the Only if errors found option.

Log file: ScanDisk normally creates a file named SCANDISK.LOG in the drive's root folder. This file contains a log of the scan, including errors that were found and the steps that were taken to repair them. If you choose Replace log, ScanDisk creates a new SCANDISK.LOG file each time you check the drive; if you choose Append to log, ScanDisk adds the data from the current check to the end of the existing SCANDISK.LOG file; if you choose No log, ScanDisk doesn't log the progress of the check.

Cross-linked files: The options in this group determine how ScanDisk handles cross-linked files, as described earlier.

Lost file fragments: The options in this group determine how ScanDisk handles lost and invalid clusters, as described earlier.

Check files for: If you activate the Invalid file names check box, ScanDisk tests the name of each file for validity. If a name is invalid (if, for example, it contains an illegal character), ScanDisk attempts to fix the name. If you activate the Invalid dates and times check box, ScanDisk tests the date and time stamp of each file and attempts to fix any invalid entries it finds.

Check host drive first: Compressed drive errors are usually caused by problems on the host drive. So if you're checking a compressed drive, activate this check box to force ScanDisk to check the compressed drive's host drive first.

When you've made your selections, click OK to return to the ScanDisk window.

Starting the Test

Your final chore before letting ScanDisk do its thing is to decide how you want the program to handle any errors it finds. If you'd prefer to be informed of the error so that you can decide what to do about it, leave the Automatically fix errors check box deactivated. If, instead, you want ScanDisk to handle everything, activate the Automatically fix errors check box. This tells ScanDisk to use the settings in the Advanced Options dialog box to handle disk errors.

To get the ScanDisk show on the road, click the Start button. ScanDisk starts checking the disk, and the progress meter at the bottom of the window lets you know how it's doing. If ScanDisk comes across an error (and if you didn't activate the Automatically fix errors check box), you'll see a dialog box similar to the one shown in Figure 15.25. Choose the option you prefer and click OK. (If you need more data before making your decision, click the More Info button.)

FIGURE 15.25.

If ScanDisk trips over a disk error, it displays a dialog box like this one.

NOTE: USING AN OLDER DISK REPAIR UTILITY

I recommend that you not continue to use older, pre-Windows 95 disk utilities. If you prefer to stick with a favorite program, however, remember to back up your long filenames with LFNBK, as explained earlier in this chapter.

Running ScanDisk at Startup

Unrepaired disk problems can cause no end of headaches on your system, so it's a good idea to run ScanDisk regularly. The easiest way to do this is to create a ScanDisk shortcut in the StartUp folder. The ScanDisk executable file is SCANDSKW.EXE, and you'll find it in your main Windows 95 folder. To make ScanDisk easier to use, SCANDSKW.EXE can take a few command-line parameters:

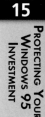

15

PROTECTING YOUR
WINDOWS 95
INVESTMENT

```
scandskw drive: [/a] [/n] [/p]
```

`drive:`	Specifies the drive or drives you want to check.
`/a`	Checks all your local, nonremovable hard disks.
`/n`	Starts and shuts down ScanDisk automatically.
`/p`	Prevents ScanDisk from correcting any errors it finds.

Enter these parameters in the shortcut's properties sheet by selecting the Shortcut tab and using the Target text box. For example, if you want ScanDisk to check drives C and D and shut down automatically, you'd use the following command line in the Target text box:

```
c:\windows\scandskw.exe c: d: /n
```

OSR2

NOTE: AUTOMATIC SCANS IN OSR2

There is a new feature in OSR2 that runs ScanDisk automatically after a bad shutdown (for example, if the system power is switched off before you exit Windows 95) or if Windows 95 detects one or more bad sectors on your hard disk. In this case, you'll see a message similar to the following at startup:

```
Windows was not properly shut down. One or more of your disk drives
may have errors on it. Press any key to run ScanDisk on these drives...
```

When you press a key, Windows 95 runs the real-mode version of ScanDisk. (Note, too, that you can modify MSDOS.SYS to change the behavior of the automatic scan. See Chapter 4, "Start It Your Way: Understanding Windows 95 Startup," for details.)

TIP: YOU CAN USE WINDOWS 95'S SCANDISK WITH DOS 6.X

If you've dual-booted to DOS 6.x and you need to check a disk for errors, you can run the real-mode version of Windows 95's ScanDisk. The executable file is SCANDISK.EXE, and you'll find it in Windows 95's COMMAND subfolder.

Using the Microsoft Diagnostics Utility

As you learned in Chapter 10, "How Windows 95 Handles Hardware," the Device Manager is a great tool for viewing your system's devices and working with the resources they use. If you can't get into Windows 95, however, the Device Manager won't do you much good. If you have the Windows 95 CD-ROM, however, you have the next best thing: the Microsoft Diagnostics (MSD) utility. You'll find this program in the \Other\Msd\ folder on the CD-ROM.

Copy MSD.EXE to your main Windows 95 folder. To start it from the DOS prompt, just type msd and press Enter; you'll see the screen shown in Figure 15.26.

FIGURE 15.26.

The main screen of the Microsoft Diagnostics utility.

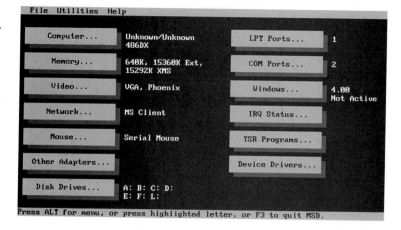

Each button in the MSD screen gives you some inside information about certain aspects of your system. Here's a quick rundown of what you'll find:

Computer: Gives you general information about your system: the manufacturer, BIOS data, the bus type, and so on.

Memory: Displays a map of the upper memory area. This map is useful for determining which blocks are being used in case you want to include more blocks using EMM386.

Video: Gives you general information about your video card and the current video mode.

Network: Displays information about your network configuration.

Mouse: Gives you mouse information, including the real-mode driver version, the IRQ it uses, and its current settings.

Other Adapters: Shows the status of any games cards installed on your system.

Disk Drives: Tells you the size and bytes free on your system's disk drives.

LPT Ports: Shows the I/O address and status of each parallel port on your system.

COM Ports: Shows the I/O address and current communications parameters assigned to your system's serial ports.

Windows: Displays information about the Windows version, mode, and location, and lists any drivers that are active.

IRQ Status: Displays the deployment of your system's hardware IRQs.

TSR Programs: Lists the name and memory address of any installed real-mode TSRs.

Device Drivers: Lists the names of the installed real-mode device drivers.

MSD's menus also have several commands that might be of interest. The Utilities menu has the following commands:

Memory Block Display: Displays a memory map that shows where each resident program sits in RAM.

Memory Browser: Lets you view a memory map by area (for example, ROM BIOS or Video ROM BIOS).

Insert Command: Displays a list of common commands you can insert into `CONFIG.SYS` or `AUTOEXEC.BAT`.

Test Printer: Sends a test page to your printer.

Black & White: Toggles the screen between color and black-and-white. You can also select this command by pressing F5.

To locate a file on your system, select File | Find File and use the dialog box that appears to perform the search.

If you want a report of these system settings, select File | Print Report. In the dialog box that appears, select which elements to include in the report and where you want it printed (LPT1, a file, or wherever).

Finally, the File menu also includes commands for several of your configuration files (`AUTOEXEC.BAT`, `CONFIG.SYS`, and so on). Selecting one of these commands displays the contents of the file.

When you're done, select File | Exit or press F3.

Scheduling Maintenance Tasks with System Agent

The key to keeping your system in fine fettle is to run your maintenance programs—Backup, ScanDisk, or whatever—regularly. Placing shortcuts for these programs in your Windows 95 Startup folder is one way to ensure regularity. Performing a large backup or a Thorough ScanDisk check, however, might not be the most productive way to start your day.

Ideally, it would be nice to be able to set up a schedule so that these chores not only run at regular intervals, but also run in the evening or overnight when you won't be using your machine. Well, I'm happy to report that Microsoft Plus! comes with a great little program called System Agent that will do exactly that.

Starting System Agent

When you install System Agent, Microsoft Plus! adds a `SystemAgent` setting to the following Registry key:

```
HKEY_LOCAL_MACHINE\SOFTWARE\Microsoft\Windows\CurrentVersion\Run
```

The value of the SystemAgent setting is the full pathname of the System Agent executable file (for example, C:\WINDOWS\SYSTEM\SAGE.EXE). Its presence in the Run key means that this command line gets executed whenever you start Windows 95. The result is the display of the System Agent icon in the taskbar's system tray, which tells you that System Agent is on the job.

To see what System Agent is all about, display its window by using either of the following techniques:

- Double-click the System Agent icon in the taskbar.
- Select Start | Programs | Accessories | System Tools | System Agent.

The window that appears, shown in Figure 15.27, lists the tasks that System Agent currently has scheduled. The five columns give you a description of the scheduled program, the time it's scheduled to run, the last time it started and ended, and the last result. By default, you should see four or five tasks:

Low disk space notification: Runs the Disk Alarm utility (DISKALM.EXE) that warns you if the free disk space on a drive drops below a certain threshold. This check is run hourly at a quarter past the hour.

ScanDisk for Windows (Standard test): Runs ScanDisk's Standard test each weekday at 5:00 PM (as long as you haven't used your computer for 10 minutes).

Disk Defragmenter: Runs Disk Defragmenter daily, Tuesday through Friday, at midnight (as long as you haven't used your computer for 10 minutes).

ScanDisk for Windows (Thorough test): Runs ScanDisk's Thorough test on the first day of the month at 9:00 PM (as long as you haven't used your computer for 60 minutes).

Compression Agent: Runs DriveSpace 3's Compression Agent every Monday at 7:00 PM (as long as you haven't used your computer for 30 minutes). You'll see this task scheduled only if you've compressed a drive with DriveSpace 3.

FIGURE 15.27.

The System Agent window shows a list of the currently scheduled tasks.

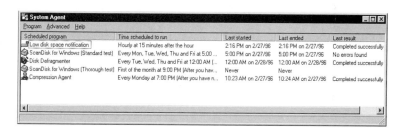

15

Here are a few techniques you can use to work with the scheduled programs:

- If you'd prefer to run the scheduled task right away, either highlight the program and select Program | Run Now, or right-click it and select Run Now from the context menu.

- To disable a program, either highlight it and select Program | Disable, or right-click it and select Disable from the context menu. Repeat either procedure to reenable the program.

- To remove a program, either highlight it and select Program | Remove, or right-click it and select Remove from the context menu. When System Agent asks you to confirm, click Yes.

- To suspend all the scheduled programs, select Advanced | Suspend System Agent. To enable System Agent, deactivate this command.

- If you no longer want to use System Agent at all, select Advanced | Stop Using System Agent. When the confirmation dialog box appears, click Yes.

Changing a Program's Schedule

The default times for the scheduled programs are reasonable, but they might not suit the way you work. For example, the ScanDisk Standard test runs at 5:00 every weekday afternoon. If you regularly work after 5:00, the test might begin at an inconvenient moment. Similarly, you might want to run Disk Defragmenter or the ScanDisk Thorough test more often. System Agent is happy to respond to all these requests and, in fact, gives you an impressive array of options for scheduling you programs.

To reschedule a program, either highlight it in the System Agent window and select Program | Change Schedule, or right-click the program's description and select Change Schedule from the context menu. Figure 15.28 shows an example of the Change schedule dialog box that appears.

Figure 15.28.

Use the Change schedule dialog box to reschedule a program.

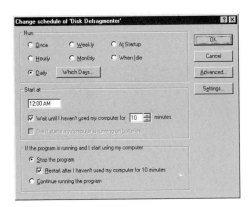

This dialog box lets you modify not only the time the program runs, but also the frequency at which it runs. Here's a quick look at the various scheduling options you can manipulate:

Run: The options in this group determine how often the program runs (Once, Weekly, At Startup, and so on). If you choose Daily, click the Which Days button to choose the days of the week you want the program to run; if you choose When Idle, the program runs after you haven't used the computer for the amount of time specified in the Start at group.

Start at: Use this group's text box to enter the start time for the program. To avoid having the program run while you're working, activate the Wait until I haven't used my computer for check box, and enter an interval in the spinner. If you're using System Agent on a notebook computer, you can also activate the Don't start if my computer is running on batteries check box to save battery power.

If the program is running and I start using my computer: The options in this group tell System Agent what to do if you start using your computer while the scheduled operation is still in progress. Select either Stop the program or Continue running the program. If you choose the former option, you can ensure that the program resumes if you activate the Restart after I haven't used my computer for *x* minutes check box.

Settings: This button displays a dialog box that lets you set various settings specific to the program. For example, clicking Settings for Disk Defragmenter lets you choose which drive you want to defragment and which defragmentation method to use.

Advanced Scheduling Options

The Change schedule dialog box also has an Advanced button that displays the Advanced Options dialog box, shown in Figure 15.29. You use the Deadline group to handle situations when the program can't run at the scheduled time. System Agent keeps trying to run the program until whatever time you specify in the text box. You can also work with two other options:

If the program is still running, stop it at this time: If the program is still running by the time the deadline rolls around, it might be that the program is hung or stuck. To allow for this possibility, you should leave this check box activated so that System Agent shuts down the program if it's still running at the specified time.

Notify me if the program never started: If you activate this check box, System Agent displays a dialog box to let you know that the program never got off the ground.

FIGURE 15.29.
*The System Agent's
Advanced Options
dialog box.*

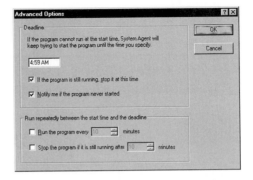

If the intervals in the Run group aren't exactly what you need, System Agent lets you specify a custom interval. For example, if you want to run the program at 20-minute intervals, activate the Run the program every check box and enter 20 into the spinner. The program then runs every 20 minutes between the start time and the deadline.

Some programs might not shut down automatically after they complete their mission. Rather than leave these programs running, you can ensure that they shut down by activating the Stop the program if it is still running after check box. Use the spinner to enter the number of minutes after the program starts that you want System Agent to shut it down.

Modifying a Scheduled Program's Properties

Each scheduled program has various properties that control the program's executable file, how it runs, which folder it runs in, and more. To view and modify these properties, either highlight a scheduled program in the System Agent window and select Program | Properties, or right-click the program's description and select Properties from the context menu. Figure 15.30 shows an example of the properties sheet that appears.

FIGURE 15.30.
*The properties sheet for
the scheduled Disk
Defragmenter program.*

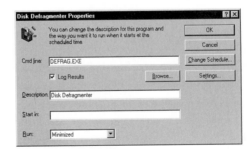

Here are the properties you get to play with:

Cmd line: This is the name of the executable file that starts the program. If the program isn't in the main Windows 95 folder (or its COMMAND subfolder), you need to use the full pathname of the executable file.

Log Results: If you activate this check box, System Agent keeps a log of the progress and results of each scheduled program (the log is written to SAGELOG.TXT in the \Program Files\Plus!\ folder). To view the log, select Advanced | View Log.

Description: This is the text that appears in the System Agent window in the Scheduled program column.

Start in: This specifies the drive and folder that the program should use as its default.

Run: This specifies whether you want the program to run minimized, maximized, or in a normal window.

You can also use this dialog box to change the program's schedule (click the Change Schedule button) or its settings (click the Settings button). When you're done, click OK.

Adding a New Scheduled Program

Although certain programs are built to work directly with System Agent (such as Disk Defragmenter and ScanDisk), you're free to schedule any Windows 95 application, macros, DOS programs, or even batch files.

To try this, select File | Schedule a New Program to display the Schedule a New Program dialog box, which uses many of the same controls as the dialog box shown in Figure 15.30. Enter the program's command line (and any extra parameters or switches you want to use) in the Program text box, enter a Description, and so on. In Figure 15.31, for example, I'm scheduling a backup set. (For best operation, you should make sure that the backup set runs and shuts down automatically, as described earlier in this chapter.) To set up the schedule, click the When To Run button.

FIGURE 15.31.

You can set up System Agent to run backup sets and most other applications.

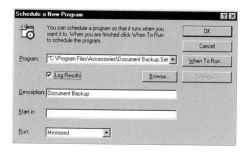

15

PROTECTING YOUR
WINDOWS 95
INVESTMENT

Guarding Against Viruses

Viruses are nasty little programs that live for the sheer thrill of trashing your valuable data. They're crafted in dank basements by pale, Jolt cola–fueled miscreants—programming wizards who've succumbed to the dark side of The Force. These amoral hackers like to muddy the waters by describing their wicked offspring as "self-propagating, autonomous computer programs" and giving them innocent-sounding names such as Michelangelo and Christmas. But don't be fooled: These small slices of evil can do irreparable harm to your files. (Just so you know, many viruses have names that more directly reflect their intentions. These include Armageddon, Beast, Black Monday, Dark Avenger, and Darth Vader.)

Viruses comes in three basic flavors:

- *File infectors,* which attach themselves to executable files and spread among other files when you run the program.
- *Boot sector* viruses, which replace the hard disk's master boot record (or the boot sector on a floppy disk) with their own twisted version of the bootstrap code. This lets them load themselves into memory whenever you boot your system (the famous "Michelangelo" virus is one of these boot sector beasts).
- *Trojan horse* viruses, which appear to be legitimate programs at first glance but, when loaded, proceed to viciously maul your data.

Viruses are, by now, an unpleasant fact of computing life, and you just have to learn to live with the threat. That makes it all the more puzzling why Microsoft didn't include an anti-virus utility in Windows 95. Not to worry, though, quite a few Windows 95–specific anti-virus programs are on the market that will help you sleep better at night.

Boza: A Virus That Windows 95 Can Call Its Own

In early 1996, it was announced that the first virus program designed specifically for Windows 95 had been let loose upon the world. Dubbed the *Boza* virus (after a Bulgarian liquor "so powerful that just looking at it will give you a headache"; it's also known as the *Bizatch* virus), this program infects 32-bit executable files that are in Microsoft's Portable Executable (PE) format. It uses direct calls to the Windows 95 operating system.

Boza is a simple file infector virus. If you execute a Boza-infected program, the Boza code proceeds to infect up to three other programs in the same folder. It does this by adding an extra code section to these files and then manipulating the file header so that program execution begins with the viral code. After the virus has done its dirty work, it hands control back to the original program entry point, which means that infected files appear to work as usual. Note that Boza doesn't set itself up in memory.

By itself, Boza is more annoying than destructive. (On the 30th of the month, it displays a dialog box that says "The taste of fame just got tastier! VLAD Australia does it again with the world's first Win95 virus." VLAD is an Australian virus-creation cabal.) According to virus experts, however, the Boza code is sloppily written and buggy, so it can accidentally destroy the files it infects.

Within days of the discovery of this virus, all major anti-virus firms had "Boza detectors" ready for public consumption.

Windows 95 Anti-Virus Programs

When Microsoft announced that there would be no virus protection program included with Windows 95, plenty of utilities vendors sniffed opportunity in the air. As a result, there's no lack of anti-virus programs designed specifically for Windows 95. Here are three I recommend:

Norton AntiVirus for Windows 95: This is a powerful program capable of recognizing and nuking thousands of viruses (including Boza). Norton AntiVirus comes with its own scheduler and has many customization options. Regular updates are available. This program sells for $79.95. For an evaluation copy, check out the Symantec Web site at http://www.symantec.com.

ThunderBYTE for Windows 95: ThunderBYTE's anti-virus utilities are justly renowned for their speed and sophistication. For example, ThunderBYTE has a "heuristic viral analysis" technique that can recognize even unknown viruses. Version 7.0 recognizes and eradicates the Boza virus. ThunderBYTE sells for $149.95. You can get an evaluation copy at http://thunderbyte.com.

VirusScan for Windows 95: This one is an excellent utility (although a touch on the slow side) from McAfee Associates, one of the veterans of the anti-virus wars. VirusScan is loaded with options, integrates seamlessly with System Agent, and can eradicate the Boza virus. A monthly update program is available. VirusScan sells for $65. You can get more information and a free evaluation copy at http://www.mcafee.com/.

More Virus Tips

Here are a few other tips to help keep your system virus free:

- If your computer has a BIOS setting that disables boot-sector writes, be sure to activate this setting.

- Most viruses are transmitted from machine to machine via floppy disks, so you should always be careful about which used disks you trust in your computer. If you've inherited some old disks, you can make sure that no viruses are lurking in the weeds by formatting each disk before you use it.

■ Trust no one when it comes to loading programs on your machine. Whether they come from family, friends, a BBS, or the Internet, use an anti-virus program to scan downloaded files before running anything.

■ Keep your virus utility's virus library up-to-date. By some accounts, more than 100 new virus strains are released each month, and they just get nastier and nastier. Regular updates will help you keep up-to-date.

Summary

This chapter showed you a few preventive measures that can help keep your Windows 95 system trouble free. I showed you how to create an emergency boot disk (just in case); how to use Windows 95's Backup, ScanDisk, and System Agent accessories; and how to use four utilities from the Windows 95 CD-ROM: Long Filename Backup, Configuration Backup, Emergency Recovery Utility, and the Microsoft Diagnostics program.

Here's a list of chapters where you'll find related information:

■ For more background on the Windows 95 boot process, see Chapter 4, "Start It Your Way: Understanding Windows 95 Startup."

■ To get the details on clusters and hard disk performance tuning, turn to Chapter 9, "Windows 95 Performance Tuning and Optimization."

■ I told you how the Registry works in Chapter 11, "Introducing the Windows 95 Registry."

■ You'll find an explanation of the FAT in Chapter 14, "Disk Driving: Dealing with Disks."

■ I explain a little more about using System Agent with batch files in Chapter 21, "DOS Isn't Dead: Optimizing DOS Applications Under Windows 95."

■ You can also use passwords to add an extra level of protection to your system. I cover how Windows 95 works with passwords in Chapter 31, "Windows 95 Networking."

IV

PART

Unleashing Day-to-Day Windows 95

Installing and Uninstalling Applications

CHAPTER 16

We do not quite say that the new is more valuable because it fits in; but its fitting in is a test of its value.

—*T.S. Eliot*

For your consideration, I submit the following examples of hardware longevity: The computer I use to test software and run beta copies of programs is a trusty old 486 that has served me faithfully for nearly four years; I recently purchased a new laser printer, but the old LaserJet I had before it was four-and-a-half years young; my first notebook computer is still going strong after five years (albeit in the company of my goddaughter, to whom I donated it last year); and my fax machine will celebrate its sixth birthday later this year.

Why the litany of Methuselan machines? Because I want to compare these old hardware codgers with the software I use. To wit, of all the programs and utilities I crank up regularly, the *oldest*—an accounting package I use to track my finances—has been out of its shrink wrap for a little less than a year!

Hardware, then, is a typical high-end commodity—we buy it and then tend to hang on to it until it wears out. Software, on the other hand, is a new kind of consumer product, one that reinvents itself constantly. Thanks to cheap, frequent upgrades and an unending stream of new, innovative products, it's tough to resist the siren song of the latest and greatest.

The upshot is that we spend a not insignificant chunk of our computing lives installing software. The designers of Windows 95, bless their fully-vested hearts, understood this all too well, so they included some features in Windows 95 that make it easier to install applications. And, even better, there's also support for *uninstalling* programs, just in case the two of you don't get along very well. This chapter shows you how to use Windows 95's built-in install/uninstall features, and it also shows you how to add and remove older Windows applications and DOS programs.

Practicing Safe Setups

For those who enjoy working with computers, few things are as tempting as a new software package. The tendency is to just rip into the box, liberate the source disks, and crank up the installation program without further ado. This approach usually loses its luster when, after a willy-nilly installation, your system starts to behave erratically. That's usually because the application's setup program has made adjustments to one or more important configuration files and given your system a case of indigestion in the process. That's the hard way to learn the hazards of a haphazard installation.

To avoid such a fate, you should always look before you leap. That is, you should follow a few simple safety measures before double-clicking that SETUP.EXE file. The next few sections give you some precautionary tales.

Check the New Program for Viruses

If the application you're installing is from a well-known developer, if you purchased it from a reputable dealer, and if the box is unopened, you almost certainly don't have to think twice about viruses. Yes, there have been documented cases of viral code infecting a disk or two in brand-name programs, but these are *extremely* rare, to the point where worrying about it verges on the paranoiac.

However, there are other situations in which it pays to be paranoid. You should check for viruses before installing if

- you ordered the program directly from an unknown developer
- the package was already open when you purchased it from a dealer (buying opened software packages is never a good idea)
- a friend or colleague gave you the program on a floppy disk (most viruses are transmitted via floppies, but CD-ROMs can catch these bugs as well)
- you downloaded the program from the Internet or a BBS

Ideally, your virus checker should be able to hunt down viruses even in ZIP files and other compressed archives. All of the anti-virus programs I mentioned in Chapter 15, "Protecting Your Windows 95 Investment," can do this.

Make Sure You Have a Bootable Disk

It's a rare (and poorly constructed) installation program that will bring an entire system to its knees, but it can happen. An amateurish Windows 95 installer could rip apart the Registry, for example, or a dumb DOS setup program could write to a verboten memory address. Although having a bootable disk within reach is *always* a good idea, make sure you have one handy before installing any new software. To learn how to create a bootable disk and stock it with utilities and files that will let you recover gracefully, see Chapter 15 (in the "Creating an Emergency Boot Disk" section).

Understand the Effect on Your Data Files

Few software developers want to alienate their installed user base, so they usually emphasize upward-compatibility in their upgrades. That is, the new version of the software will almost always be able to read and work with documents created with an older version. However, in the interest of progress, you'll often find that the data file format used by the latest incarnation of a program is different from its predecessors, and this new format is rarely *downward-*compatible. That is, an older version of the software will usually gag on a data file that was created by the new version.

So you'll often be faced with the following choices:

- Continue to work with your existing documents in the old format, thus possibly foregoing any benefits that come with the new format.

    or

■ Update your files and thus risk making them incompatible with the old version of the program, should you decide to uninstall the upgrade.

One possible solution to this dilemma is to make backup copies of all your data files before installing the upgrade. That way, you can always restore the good copies of your documents if the upgrade causes problems or destroys some of your data. If you've already used the upgrade to make changes to some documents, but you want to uninstall the upgrade, most programs have a Save As command that lets you save these documents in their old format.

Back Up the Registry

If you're installing a Windows 95 application, it will write the bulk of its configuration data to the Registry. Most of these changes will be application-specific, but some installation programs also make changes to more global settings. For example, installing Microsoft Plus! changes the file that supplies the Windows 95 system icons from SHELL32.DLL to COOL.DLL. That's no big deal, but it's possible that other changes might not be so benign. You could end up with a system that behaves strangely or, in the worst case, doesn't behave at all!

Fortunately, as you'll see later, true Windows 95 applications have an uninstall feature that not only removes the program's files, but also purges any traces of the program from the Registry. However, programs designed for Windows 3.1 and Windows for Workgroups might also change some Registry settings in the HKEY_CLASSES_ROOT key.

So, just to be safe, you should make a backup copy of the Registry before installing any application that might fiddle with the Registry. You should do two things:

■ Use the Registry Editor's Registry | Export Registry File command to export the entire Registry to a REG (text) file (I showed you how to do this in Chapter 11, "Introducing the Windows 95 Registry"). As you'll see a bit later, you can use this file to compare the Registry before and after the installation, and possibly make adjustments.

■ Save the Registry data files (SYSTEM.DAT and USER.DAT) using any of the techniques I showed you in Chapter 15 (see the section titled "Backing Up the Registry").

In Fact, Back Up *All* Your Configuration Files

While you're in a backing-up frame of mind, you can add an extra level of protection to your installations by backing up all your configuration files: the Registry, CONFIG.SYS, AUTOEXEC.BAT, WIN.INI, SYSTEM.INI, and so on. This is particularly important before installing 16-bit or DOS applications that routinely make changes to these files.

The best way to back up all these configuration files in one fell swoop is to use the Emergency Recovery Utility found on the Windows 95 CD-ROM. This handy program can save some or all of your system's configuration files to a bootable floppy disk or to your hard drive. It even comes with a recovery program that will restore everything for you automatically. Once again, you'll find the details in Chapter 15 (in the "Using the Emergency Recovery Utility" section).

Save Directory Listings for Important Folders

When I discuss uninstalling applications later in this chapter, you'll see that one of the biggest problems you'll face is figuring out which files the program used outside of its home folder. Many 16-bit Windows applications like to add files to both the main Windows folder and the SYSTEM subfolder. Unfortunately, there's no easy method of determining which files an application inserts into these two folders. (However, as I explain later, Windows 95's Quick View accessory can help ferret out which DLLs a program uses.)

The only way to be sure is to take a "snapshot" of the current state of the main Windows 95 folder and the SYSTEM subfolder both before and after you install the software. To do this, head to the DOS prompt and run the following two commands before you install:

```
dir c:\windows /a-d /on > dirwin1.txt
dir c:\windows\system /a-d /on > sysdir1.txt
```

The first line runs the DIR command on C:\WINDOWS (which you should change to the path of your main Windows 95 folder) and saves it in a file named DIRWIN1.TXT. (The /A-D switch tells DIR not to display folders, and the /ON switch sorts the files alphabetically by name.) The second line saves a file listing of the SYSTEM subfolder in the file SYSDIR.TXT1.

When the installation is complete, go back to the prompt and enter the following commands:

```
dir c:\windows /a-d /on > dirwin2.txt
dir c:\windows\system /a-d /on > sysdir2.txt
```

You can then compare DIRWIN1.TXT to DIRWIN2.TXT, and SYSDIR1.TXT to SYSDIR2.TXT, to see which files the setup program foisted upon your system.

One way to do this would be to open two copies of Notepad and load the contrasting files into each window. In the post-installation versions, if you delete the lines corresponding to the files that haven't changed, you'll end up with a list of the new files. You could then keep this list in a safe location in case you need it later while uninstalling.

Another way to compare these files is to use the DOS FC (file compare) command. I'll explain how this command works later in this chapter (see "The FC Command").

Read README Files and Other Documentation

If you do nothing else to prepare for a software installation, you should read whatever documentation the program provides that pertains to the setup. This includes the appropriate installation material in the manual, README files found on the disk, and whatever else looks promising. By spending a few minutes perusing these resources, you can glean the following information:

■ Any advance preparation you need to perform on your system

■ What to expect during the installation

■ Information you need to have on hand in order to complete the setup (such as a product's serial number)

- Changes the install program will make to your system
- Changes to the program and/or the documentation that were put into effect after the manual was printed
- Whether or not the installation will make changes to configuration files, program-specific INI files, or your data files

Many programs nowadays offer to display their README files when the installation is complete, but that might be too late. On more than one occasion, I have installed a program, viewed the README file, and then groaned when I read some crucial tidbit that I should have known before the setup procedure began. (You should always assume that setup programs were coded in haste at the end of the development cycle and therefore tend to be somewhat poorly designed.)

Take Control of the Installation

Some setup programs give new meaning to the term "brain-dead." You slip in the source disk, run SETUP.EXE (or whatever), and the program proceeds to impose itself upon your hard disk without so much as a how-do-you-do. Thankfully, most installation programs are a bit more thoughtful than that. They usually give you some advance warning about what's to come, and they prompt you for information as they go along. You can use this newfound thoughtfulness to assume a certain level of control over the installation. (The Windows 95 Setup program is a perfect example of a polite installer that gives you as much or as little control over the installation process as you'd like.) Here are a few things to watch for:

Choose your folder wisely: Most installation programs offer to install their files in a default folder. Rather than just accepting this without question, think about where you want the program to reside. Personally, I prefer to use the Program Files folder to house all my applications. If you have multiple hard disks or partitions, you might prefer to use the one with the largest amount of free space. If the setup program lets you select data directories, you might want to use a separate folder that makes it easy to back up the data.

Use the custom install option: Like Windows 95 Setup, the best programs offer you a choice of installation options. Whenever possible, choose the "Custom" option, if one is available. This will give you maximum control over the components that are installed, including where they're installed and how they're installed.

Perform your own configuration file modifications: If an installation program is truly polite, it will let you know that it needs to modify one or more of your configuration files. Hopefully, you'll also be able to choose between letting the program make the modifications automatically or making the modifications yourself. If so, you should always opt for the latter so that you can change the files in a way that won't harm your system.

Comparing Files Before and After

I've mentioned three separate examples of files that you might need to compare before and after an installation:

- Registry files exported to REG text files
- Other configuration files (CONFIG.SYS, AUTOEXEC.BAT, and so on)
- Redirected file listings of your main Windows 95 folder and its SYSTEM subfolder

In each case, you compare the pre-installation version with its post-installation counterpart to see what changes were made (if any). You can use three basic methods to make these comparisons: brute force, the DOS FC command, and your word processor's compare feature.

The Brute Force Method

The most straightforward method is to load the before and after files into separate Notepad (or WordPad) windows and compare them line-by-line. This is fine for small files (such as CONFIG.SYS) or ordered files (such as the results of the DIR command I showed you earlier), but it's next to useless for a large file such as the exported Registry.

The FC Command

DOS has an FC (file compare) command that will compare two files and report on their differences. Here are the two syntaxes you can use with this command:

```
FC [/A] [/C] [/L] [/LBn] [/N] [/T] [/W] [/n] filename1 filename2

FC /B filename1 filename2
```

/A	Displays only first and last lines for each set of differences.
/B	Performs a binary comparison.
/C	Disregards the case of letters.
/L	Compares files as ASCII text.
/LBn	Sets the maximum consecutive mismatches to the specified number of lines.
/N	Displays the line numbers on an ASCII comparison.
/T	Does not expand tabs to spaces.
/W	Compresses white space (tabs and spaces) for comparison.
/n	Specifies the number of consecutive lines that must match after a mismatch.
filename1	The first file you want to compare.
filename2	The second file you want to compare.

For example, to compare the SYSTEM folder file listings I mentioned earlier, you'd use the following command (assuming that the files are in the root folder of drive C):

```
fc /l c:\sysdir1.txt c:\sysdir2.txt > fc.txt
```

In this case, I've redirected the output of the FC command into a file named FC.TXT. Figure 16.1 shows part of this output. Each time FC finds a difference, it displays the lines that are changed, as well as the lines before and after that are still the same. For example, FC shows the following output for SYSDIR1.TXT:

```
OLE2      DLL       39,744   07-11-95   9:50a OLE2.DLL
OLE2CONV DLL       57,328   07-11-95   9:50a OLE2CONV.DLL
```

This is followed by the output for SYSDIR2.TXT:

```
OLE2      DLL       39,744   07-11-95   9:50a OLE2.DLL
OLE2      REG       23,330   09-24-93  12:00a OLE2.REG
OLE2AUTO REG        2,699   08-27-93  12:00a OLE2AUTO.REG
OLE2CONV DLL       57,328   07-11-95   9:50a OLE2CONV.DLL
```

As you can see, two files have been added between OLE2.DLL and OLE2CONV.DLL—namely, OLE2.REG and OLE2AUTO.REG.

FIGURE 16.1.

The output of an FC *command.*

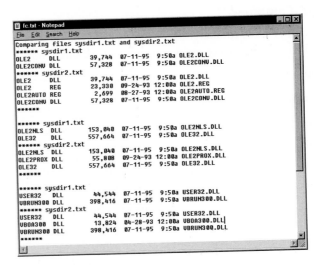

Your Word Processor's Compare Feature

Most high-end word processors have a feature that lets you compare two files. In Word for Windows, for example, open the post-install file, select Tools | Revisions, click the Compare Versions button, and then use the Open dialog box to open the pre-install file. Click Review to run through the changes.

Working with the Add/Remove Programs Wizard

You've seen throughout this book that Windows 95 has a Wizard for almost every occasion. Installing applications is another one of those occasions. The Add/Remove Programs Wizard is a simple series of dialog boxes that help you find and run an application's setup program. This might sound like something that's useful only for novices, but there are good reasons to use this Wizard to launch all your installation programs. The biggest reason is that it warns Windows 95 that you're about to install an application, so the operating system can set itself up accordingly. Also, for Windows 95 applications, it ensures that the appropriate data is stored in the Registry (the program's installed components, the parameters needed to run the program successfully, the information needed to uninstall the program, and so on).

Here are the steps to follow to run the Add/Remove Program Wizard:

1. In Control Panel, open the Add/Remove Programs icon to display the Add/Remove Program Properties dialog box.
2. Click the Install button. The first of the Wizard's dialog boxes appears, as shown in Figure 16.2.

FIGURE 16.2.

The first Wizard dialog box just prompts you to enter the appropriate source disk.

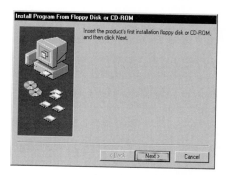

3. Insert the floppy disk or the CD-ROM that contains the installation program.
4. Click Next >. The Wizard scours your floppy disk drives and CD-ROM drives for a file named SETUP or INSTALL (with an extension of EXE, COM, or BAT) and then displays the dialog box shown in Figure 16.3. If it found an installation program, it displays the file's pathname in the Command line for installation program text box; otherwise, it leaves the text box blank.

FIGURE 16.3.

If the Wizard finds an installation program, it displays its pathname.

5. Edit the command line as necessary. If you're not sure, or if the program uses an installation program with a different name, you can click the Browse button, choose the install program from the Browse dialog box, and then click Open.

6. Click Finish. The Wizard launches the installation program.

7. Complete the installation normally.

If the installation program tells you to restart your computer, try to avoid letting the program do it for you. It's safer to just exit the installation program, close your running applications, and then restart the system manually.

Installing Applications

Let's now turn our attention to the three main types of applications you might need to install: 32-bit applications, 16-bit applications, and DOS applications. The next few sections discuss the installation issues involved with each type of application, as well as approaches that work best with each type.

Installing 32-Bit Applications

There are plenty of reasons to use 32-bit applications under Windows 95, including long filename support, preemptive multitasking, and protected memory space. Here are two more to add to the list: a standard installation procedure that's easy to use, and the ability to uninstall applications.

Before proceeding, I should clarify that when I talk about "32-bit" applications, I'm referring specifically to applications that qualify for the Windows 95 logo. In other words, I'm not talking about applications written specifically for computers running Win32s (a subset of the Win32 API) or Windows NT. To qualify for the Windows 95 logo, an application must meet the following guidelines:

■ It must use the Win32 application programming interface (API) and must be compiled using a 32-bit compiler that generates an executable file of the Portable Executable (PE) format.

■ It must support the Windows 95 user interface as published in *The Windows Interface Guidelines for Software Design*. This includes using the system-defined dialog boxes and controls, registering both 16×16-pixel and 32×32-pixel icons for each file type and the application, using the system metrics for setting the size of elements within the application, using the system-defined colors, and using the right mouse button for context menus (and not for any other purpose).

■ It must support long filenames and use them to display all document and data filenames in the shell, in title bars, in dialog boxes and controls, and with icons. In addition, an application should hide the extensions of filenames that are displayed within the application itself.

■ It must be aware of Plug and Play events. For example, it must react to system messages that occur when a new device is attached or removed.

■ It must run on Windows NT 3.5 or later. If the application uses features that are available only in Windows 95, the features must degrade gracefully in Windows NT. Conversely, if it uses features available only in Windows NT, the features must degrade gracefully in Windows 95. The application must run successfully with both Windows 95 and Windows NT, unless architectural differences between the two operating systems prevent it.

■ It must support Universal Naming Conventions (UNC) names for paths.

■ It must support OLE containers or objects, or both. It must also support the OLE style of drag-and-drop. An application should also support OLE automation and compound files (with document summary information included). (See Chapter 17, "Sharing Data in Windows 95: The Clipboard and OLE," for more information about OLE.)

■ It must support simple mail enabling using the Messaging Application Programming Interface (MAPI) or the Common Messaging Call (CMC) API. In other words, it must include some kind of "Send Mail" command that lets the user send the current document via e-mail.

■ It must follow the Windows 95 application installation guidelines to make the application properly visible in the shell.

Installation Guidelines for 32-Bit Applications

32-bit applications that qualify for the coveted Windows 95 logo have strict guidelines they must follow during installation. These guidelines are designed to make the installation easier for the user and to make sure that the application fits into the Windows 95 way of doing things (what Microsoft calls, somewhat chillingly, being a "good Windows 95 citizen"). These guidelines include the following points:

■ The user should have a choice of installations, such as Typical, Compact, and Custom.

■ Each step of the installation should have default choices so that the user, if he wants to, can work through the entire process by pressing the Enter key.

■ Each floppy disk should be needed only once during the installation, and the computer should beep whenever a new disk is required.

■ There should be a progress meter so that the user knows how far into the installation he is.

■ The user should be able to cancel the installation at any time. The install program should keep track of the files copied so that it can reverse any changes made to the system in the event of a cancellation.

■ The installation program should determine the user's hardware and software configuration before starting to copy files. This means determining whether the user's system has all the resources needed to run the program successfully and has enough disk space (the program should always display how much disk space it requires). The program also should check to see if any files needed by the application (especially shared DLLs) already exist on the system. For the latter, the install program should check the version number of existing files to make sure a newer version of the file doesn't get overwritten by an older version.

■ The program should not use `WIN.INI`, `SYSTEM.INI`, `CONFIG.SYS`, or `AUTOEXEC.BAT` to store configuration information.

■ The program must use the Registry to store configuration options as well as the information required to uninstall the product.

What Happens to the Registry

The Registry is crucial because it identifies the application to Windows 95 and sets up functionality such as file types, default document actions, OLE information, application-specific paths, uninstall data, and more. The next few sections run through some of the changes that a typical installation program might make to the Registry.

Version-Specific Settings

Most programs add a new subkey to `HKEY_LOCAL_MACHINE\SOFTWARE` that uses the following general format:

`HKEY_LOCAL_MACHINE\SOFTWARE\CompanyName\ProductName\Version`

`CompanyName` is the name of the vendor, `ProductName` is the name of the software package, and `Version` is the version number of the application. This key stores general information pertaining to this copy of the application.

User-Specific Settings

Most programs also add the following key:

`HKEY_CURRENT_USER\Software\CompanyName\ProductName`

Installing and Uninstalling Applications

CHAPTER 16

531

16

INSTALLING AND
UNINSTALLING
APPLICATIONS

This key stores user-specific preferences and generally has a number of subkeys. For example, Figure 16.4 shows the various subkeys added by Netscape Navigator. Applications used to store this data in WIN.INI.

FIGURE 16.4.

Applications use HKEY_CURRENT_USER\Software *to store their user-specific options and preferences.*

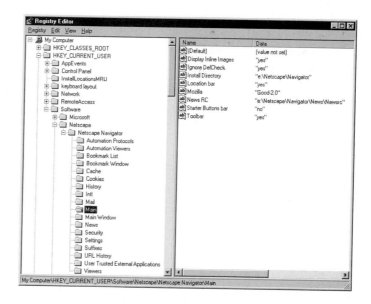

Application-Specific Paths

As explained in Chapter 12, "Hacking the Registry," Windows 95 uses application-specific paths instead of a general PATH statement. When you enter just the primary name of an application's executable file, Windows 95 will launch the program successfully.

To set up this feature, the installation program must add a new subkey to the following key:

HKEY_LOCAL_MACHINE\SOFTWARE\Microsoft\Windows\CurrentVersion\AppPaths

This new subkey will have the same name as the application's executable file, and its Default setting will contain the full pathname to the executable. The install program might also create a Path setting that specifies a default folder (or folders) for the application. Netscape, for example, adds a NETSCAPE.EXE subkey with the following settings:

```
Default    C:\Program Files\Netscape\Navigator\Program\Netscape.exe
Path       C:\Program Files\Netscape\Navigator\Program;e:\Program Files\Netscape
           ➥\Navigator\System
```

Extensions and Actions

If the program creates data files with a unique extension, the installation procedure will register a new file type with Windows 95. This involves adding an extension subkey to HKEY_CLASSES_ROOT (the alias of HKEY_LOCAL_MACHINE\SOFTWARE\Classes), as well as a corresponding file type subkey. The latter will define the default icon for the file type, actions available for the file type, and a few other things. For OLE applications, a unique CLSID subkey will be added to HKEY_CLASSES_ROOT\CLSID (you'll learn more about this in Chapter 17).

Shared DLLs

As you'll see later when we talk about uninstalling, one of Windows 95's nicest features is that it keeps track of shared DLLs—DLL files that are used (or can be used) by multiple applications. A common example is the VBRUN300.DLL file that's used by most programs created with Visual Basic version 3.

It's up to the installation program to check the user's system for any shared DLLs (and other components) that are required by the application. If it finds any, the installation program should increment the Registry's *usage counter* for each DLL. You'll find these usage counters in the following key:

HKEY_LOCAL_MACHINE\SOFTWARE\Microsoft\Windows\CurrentVersion\SharedDLLs

Figure 16.5 shows some sample entries in this key. Each setting uses a DWORD value that tells you how many applications use each DLL. For example, Figure 16.5 tells you that four applications use the file MFC30.DLL.

Figure 16.5.

Windows 95 uses the SharedDLLs *key to keep track of the number of 32-bit applications using a particular DLL file.*

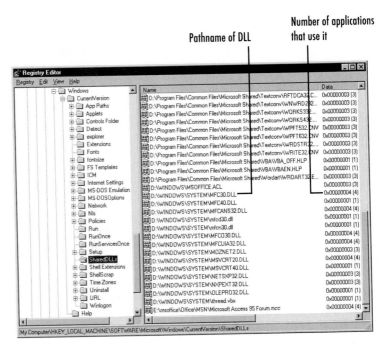

Uninstall Data

To facilitate easy removal of an application, the setup program stores uninstall information in the following Registry key:

```
HKEY_LOCAL_MACHINE\SOFTWARE\Microsoft\Windows\CurrentVersion\Uninstall
```

I'll talk more about this feature later in this chapter in the section called "Uninstalling 32-Bit Applications."

The 32-Bit Installation Procedure

Installing 32-bit applications is easy. Use the Add/Remove Programs Wizard to launch the setup program, and the installation proceeds with (generally speaking) little in the way of user input. (This depends on the complexity of the application, of course.) Many Windows 95 developers use the InstallShield SE Toolkit that's included in the Win32 Software Development Kit (SDK) to develop their installation programs. This means that most of your 32-bit programs will have a similar look and feel during installation. You'll know that a program is using the InstallShield Wizard if you see the dialog box shown in Figure 16.6.

FIGURE 16.6.

If you see this dialog box, you know that the setup program was developed using the InstallShield SE Toolkit.

From here, the InstallShield Wizard takes you through a series of dialog boxes like the ones shown in Figures 16.7 and 16.8. Unlike with Windows 3.x, in the vast majority of cases you won't have to reboot after installing your 32-bit application. Because all the configuration information is stored in the Registry, Windows 95 can handle the newcomer dynamically. (The exceptions to this rule are applications that require device drivers to be loaded at startup.)

FIGURE 16.7.

The first of the InstallShield Wizard's dialog boxes.

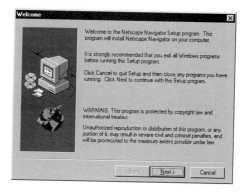

FIGURE 16.8.

This InstallShield Wizard dialog box prompts you for a file location.

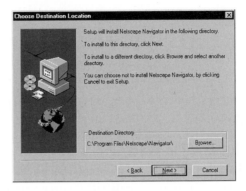

Installing 16-Bit Applications

16-bit Windows 3.x applications are, by definition, ineligible for the Windows 95 logo, so their installation programs don't have all the fancy features that 32-bit applications have. In particular, 16-bit install programs don't know about the Registry—or, more accurately, they only know, at best, about a small part of the Registry: HKEY_CLASSES_ROOT. Therefore, they don't support new features such as application-specific paths, shared DLLs, and uninstall data.

Microsoft, of course, was well aware of this, so they made sure that any 16-bit application would install in Windows 95 exactly as it would install in Windows 3.x. To accomplish this, Microsoft made the following design decisions in Windows 95:

Support for older configuration files: Most 16-bit applications store their configuration data in WIN.INI and SYSTEM.INI, and they read data from these files as well. Therefore, Windows 95 still maintains these files so as not to break 16-bit installation programs. 16-bit install programs are also free to add or edit lines in CONFIG.SYS and AUTOEXEC.BAT, and Windows 95 will honor these changes.

Built-in 32-bit functionality to replace 16-bit components: Most drivers and TSRs that used to get loaded in CONFIG.SYS and AUTOEXEC.BAT are now part of the Windows 95 operating system in 32-bit versions. 16-bit applications don't know this, however, so they'll often look to CONFIG.SYS and AUTOEXEC.BAT for the appropriate files. The polite ones will let you know that you're "missing" a particular component and offer to add it for you, as shown in Figure 16.9. Other, ruder install programs will just go ahead and add lines to your startup files.

> **NOTE: CHECK YOUR STARTUP FILES AFTER INSTALLING**
>
> After installing any 16-bit application, check your CONFIG.SYS and AUTOEXEC.BAT files to see if any extraneous lines have been added, and delete them if necessary.

FIGURE 16.9.
Here, VISIO's setup program wants to add the SHARE *command to* AUTOEXEC.BAT. SHARE *is now implemented as the VSHARE VxD, so you could ignore this request.*

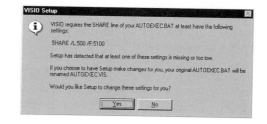

A SYSTEM **subfolder:** Microsoft now encourages developers to store DLLs and other behind-the-scenes components in their program's main folder. However, most 16-bit applications are set up to just toss all their DLLs, font files, and whatever else into the SYSTEM subfolder of the main Windows folder. Since these install programs can't update the SharedDLLs usage counters, it's a good idea to save a DIR file listing for the SYSTEM subfolder before and after installing 16-bit applications.

Windows 95 watches the SYSTEM subfolder: Microsoft wanted to avoid letting bull-in-a-china-shop install programs overwrite newer DLLs or add useless DLLs to the SYSTEM subfolder. Therefore, while you're installing, Windows 95 keeps an eye on activity in this folder and prevents install programs from messing with any of the existing files. This is another good reason to use the Add/Remove Programs Wizard to install 16-bit applications, because it alerts Windows 95 that an installation is underway.

NOTE: DO YOU HAVE TO REINSTALL YOUR 16-BIT APPS?

If you chose to install Windows 95 in a folder separate from Windows 3.x, you might think that you have to reinstall all your 16-bit applications to get them to work from Windows 95. Actually, in many cases you won't have to. As long as you add the main Windows 3.x folder and its SYSTEM subfolder to your Windows 95 PATH, many of your 16-bit applications will run just fine. To do this, add the following line to your AUTOEXEC.BAT file:

PATH %PATH%;C:\WIN31;C:\WIN31\SYSTEM

Be sure to substitute your main Windows 3.x folder for C:\WIN31. Note that, in some cases, you might also need to add the application's folder to the PATH as well.

Installing DOS Programs

Since DOS programs (for the most part) don't bother with any Windows-related procedures, they're the simplest of all programs to install. Just crank up the Add/Remove Programs Wizard, find the installation program, and proceed from there. As usual, it's best to use this procedure and not simply install the program from Explorer or the DOS prompt. That way, Windows 95 can monitor the progress of the installation and make sure nothing untoward goes on. Also, this ensures that Windows 95 checks APPS.INF for program-specific configuration information. (I'll explain APPS.INF in Chapter 21, "DOS Isn't Dead: Optimizing DOS Applications Under Windows 95.")

You may occasionally find that a DOS-based setup program won't run under Windows 95. If this happens, you have no choice but to abandon Windows 95 and install the program using MS-DOS mode. (For details on MS-DOS mode, see Chapter 21.)

As with 16-bit applications, you need to watch out for unnecessary changes to CONFIG.SYS and AUTOEXEC.BAT. If the program adds drivers or TSRs that have been replaced by protected-mode components in Windows 95, you'll need to remove the offending lines from the startup files. However, if the program will run only in MS-DOS mode, you have two choices:

- Leave the lines in CONFIG.SYS and AUTOEXEC.BAT so that they'll be loaded automatically each time you reboot.

- Create "custom" CONFIG.SYS and AUTOEXEC.BAT files for the application. These files are loaded only when you run the program in MS-DOS mode. Again, see Chapter 21 to learn how to create custom startup files for a DOS program.

Installing Applications from a Network Server

If you're a system administrator and you often install software on multiple machines on your network, Windows 95 gives you a handy method for allowing users to install these applications themselves. Setting this up requires three steps:

1. On your server, create a folder for each application you want to make available. Each folder should contain the setup program and source files for the application.

2. Create an APPS.INI file that specifies where on the server each application's setup program can be found.

3. Modify the user's Registry to point to the APPS.INI file.

The next two sections expand on steps 2 and 3.

Creating an APPS.INI File

APPS.INI is an initialization file that specifies both the name of each application and the location on the server of the application's setup program. Create APPS.INI as a plain text file in a read-only folder on the server. Then open APPS.INI and enter the following section title:

```
[AppInstallList]
```

Below this heading, enter the specifics for each application using the following general format:

Application Name=[*]UNC-Path

Installing and Uninstalling Applications

CHAPTER 16

537

16

INSTALLING AND
UNINSTALLING
APPLICATIONS

`Application Name` is any descriptive name you give to the application (this is the name the user will see when he goes to install the application). `UNC-Path` is the UNC path to the application's setup program. Here's an example:

```
Internet Explorer for Win95=\\ZEUS\C\Applications\IE95\msie301.exe
```

If the application's setup program doesn't support UNC paths, append an asterisk (*) to the front of the UNC path. This tells the server to temporarily map a drive letter for the application's folder.

Modifying the User's Registry

To enable the network install feature on a user's machine, you need to modify the user's Registry. Specifically, you need to launch the Registry Editor and travel to the following key:

```
HKEY_LOCAL_MACHINE\SOFTWARE\Microsoft\Windows\CurrentVersion
```

From here, select Edit | New | String Value, and then name the new setting `AppInstallPath`. Open this new setting and, in the Edit String dialog box that appears, enter a UNC path that points to the `APPS.INI` file on the server. Figure 16.10 shows an example.

FIGURE 16.10.

You need to add an `AppInstallPath` *setting to each user's Registry.*

This new setting goes into effect as soon as you exit the Edit String dialog box. The result is a new Network Install tab in the Add/Remove Programs Properties sheet, as shown in Figure 16.11. This tab contains a list of all the applications you entered into your `APPS.INI` file. To install the application from the server, highlight it and click Install.

FIGURE 16.11.

With the `AppInstallPath` *setting in effect, the Add/Remove Programs Properties dialog box sprouts a new Network Install tab.*

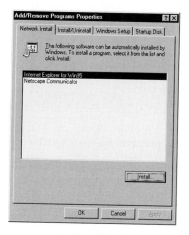

Uninstalling Applications

Applications, like the people we meet, fall into three categories: friends for life, acquaintances we deal with occasionally, and those we hope never to speak to again. Avoiding people we dislike is usually just a matter of avoiding contact with them—they'll get the hint after a while. Unlikable applications, however, just don't seem to get it. They keep hanging around like party guests who won't leave. If you have an application that's worn out its welcome, this section shows you the proper way to uninstall it so that it's out of your life forever.

Uninstalling 32-Bit Applications

One of the truly useful features you get with 32-bit Windows 95 logo-compliant applications is the ability to uninstall these programs easily. When you install one of these programs, it adds a new subkey to the following Registry key:

`\HKEY_LOCAL_MACHINE\SOFTWARE\Microsoft\Windows\CurrentVersion\Uninstall`

As you can see from Figure 16.12, this subkey contains two settings:

DisplayName: This setting is usually the name of the program, and it's what appears in the list of programs to uninstall that you see in the Add/Remove Programs Properties dialog box (discussed later).

UninstallString: This is the command line for the program that performs the removal. Note that it's not Windows 95 that's doing the removing. Instead, it's a program provided by the developer of the application (a sort of "anti-install" program, if you will).

FIGURE 16.12.

32-bit applications store uninstall data in the Registry.

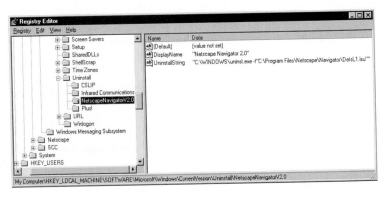

When removing an application from your system, the uninstall program does the following:

■ If the application used any shared DLLs, the uninstall program decrements the appropriate usage counter in the Registry. If the usage counter for a particular file is 0, the program usually asks if you want to delete the DLL. Because a 16-bit program might need the DLL, you should leave the file alone. However, if you're using only 32-bit applications, you can delete the file safely.

- Delete all program files related to the application. Data files will remain in place.
- Delete Start menu folders and shortcuts.
- Remove empty directories left by the application.
- Remove from the Registry all information used by the application.

To uninstall an application, open Control Panel's Add/Remove Program icon. The box in the bottom half of the Install/Uninstall tab lists the applications that you can uninstall, as shown in Figure 16.13. To remove an application, highlight it and click the Add/Remove button. A dialog box will appear, asking you to confirm the deletion. Click Yes to continue. If the program finds a shared DLL that isn't used by another program (that is, a DLL with a usage counter at 0), you'll see a Remove Shared File? dialog box similar to the one shown in Figure 16.14. Click Yes or No as appropriate. You might need to repeat this process a few times.

FIGURE 16.13.

The Add/Remove Programs Properties dialog box lists the applications you can uninstall.

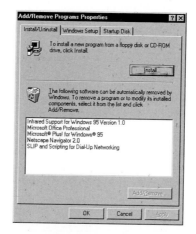

FIGURE 16.14.

You'll see this dialog box for shared DLLs with a usage counter that's now down to 0.

Uninstalling 16-Bit Applications

Unfortunately, removing a 16-bit application from your system is much less straightforward. Unless the program comes with its own uninstall feature (and some do), you have to employ a bit of guesswork to eradicate these older programs.

The real problem with 16-bit applications is that they tend to litter the main Windows 95 folder and the SYSTEM subfolder with all kinds of extraneous files. Determining which files can be deleted is often a tricky business. Here are some ideas:

- If you used the before and after DIR snapshots that I suggested earlier, you'll know exactly which files the program added.

- Look for filenames that match the program. For example, many WordPerfect DLLs begin with WP.

- Check out the application's program files to see if they have a common date and time stamp. If they do, you can check other folders for files that use the same date and time.

- Open WIN.INI and SYSTEM.INI and look for lines that refer to specific DLLs.

- Use Windows 95's Quick View accessory to get a list of the DLLs that the program uses. To do this, either highlight the executable file and select File | Quick View or right-click the executable and select Quick View from the context menu. In the window that appears, scroll down until you find a section called either Imported-Name Table or Import Table. You'll see a list of the DLLs that the program uses. Figure 16.15 shows the DLLs used by WPWIN60.EXE.

FIGURE 16.15.

The Quick View accessory can tell you which DLLs an executable file uses.

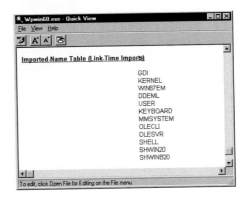

You can delete some of these files without a second thought. A private INI file is a good example. However, it's dangerous to delete DLLs and other SYSTEM folder files, because other applications might need them. There are a couple of ways to check, however.

For example, you could examine the SharedDLLs key in the Registry to see if any 32-bit applications are using the DLLs. You could also use the Find feature (Start | Find | Files or Folders) to look for mentions of the DLL in other files. You probably just need to search the main Windows 95 folder and all its subfolders. (For example, if the DLL is named OLDAPP.DLL, search for oldapp.) You'll need to select the Advanced tab and enter the primary name of the DLL in the Containing text box. If Find locates any executable files or other DLLs that mention the DLL in question, you can assume it's being used by another application.

If, in the end, you're still not sure about a particular DLL, just move it to another folder. Then, down the road, if a program complains that the file is missing, you can always restore it.

When all that's done, you can get rid of the rest of the program by following these steps:

1. If you want to save your data files, move them to a safe location if necessary.
2. Delete the program's main folder and all its subfolders.
3. Display Windows 95's `Start Menu` subfolder and delete any folders and shortcuts used by the program.
4. Scour `WIN.INI` and `SYSTEM.INI` and remove any traces of the program that you find.
5. Check the `CONFIG.SYS` and `AUTOEXEC.BAT` files for evidence of the program (such as a folder added to the `PATH` statement).
6. Check `HKEY_LOCAL_MACHINE\SOFTWARE\Classes` and delete any keys and settings related to the program (such as extension keys, file type keys, `CLSID` keys, and so on).

Uninstalling DOS Programs

Uninstalling DOS programs is usually more straightforward, because they tend to store all their files in one folder. This means you can remove most DOS programs with a simple four-step procedure:

1. If you have data files you want to preserve for posterity, move them to a different location if necessary.
2. Delete the program's main folder and all its subfolders.
3. Delete any shortcuts (PIFs) you might have created for the program.
4. Remove any traces of the program from `CONFIG.SYS` and `AUTOEXEC.BAT`.

Troubleshooting Install and Uninstall Problems

Other than program incompatibilities, there's not a whole lot that can go wrong while you're installing or uninstalling applications. However, these aren't foolproof operations. Here are a few common problems you might run into, along with their solutions.

When you remove a program using the Add/Remove Programs tool in Control Panel, you receive the following error message:

```
An error occurred while trying to remove <Program Name>.
Uninstallation has been canceled
```

This error occurs if a program that's listed in the Install/Uninstall tab has already been deleted manually. To remove a program from the list in the Install/Uninstall tab, delete the appropriate subkey under the following Registry key:

```
HKEY_LOCAL_MACHINE\SOFTWARE\Microsoft\Windows\CurrentVersion\Uninstall
```

When you try to reinstall Microsoft Plus!, you receive the following error message:

```
Microsoft Windows 95 Plus! setup was not completed successfully.
```

You'll see this error if one or more of the Microsoft Plus! files are corrupted. To solve this problem, you have to uninstall Microsoft Plus! by hand. Here are the steps to follow:

1. Delete the `\~Mssetup.t` folder.

2. Delete the `Program Files\Plus!` folder.

3. Start the Registry Editor and delete the following key:

   `HKEY_LOCAL_MACHINE\SOFTWARE\Microsoft\Plus!`

4. Highlight the following key:

   `HKEY_LOCAL_MACHINE\SOFTWARE\Microsoft\MS Setup(ACME)\Table Files`

5. Delete the setting that begins with `PLUS!DLL@`—for example:

   `PLUS!DLL@v4.40.310(1033))`

6. Delete the following key:

   `HKEY_LOCAL_MACHINE\SOFTWARE\Microsoft\Windows\CurrentVersion\Uninstall\Plus!`

7. Exit the Registry Editor.

You'll now be able to reinstall Microsoft Plus!. (Note that, despite these changes, the Microsoft Plus! logo will still appear on the Windows 95 startup bitmap. This is normal.)

The Microsoft Plus! Setup program was interrupted while it was uninstalling the Plus! components. When you restart your computer, you receive the following error message:

```
Cannot find a device file that may be needed to run Windows or a
Windows application.  The Windows registry or SYSTEM.INI file refers
to this device file, but the device file no longer exists.  If you
deleted this file on purpose, try uninstalling the associated
application using its uninstall or setup program.  If you still want
to use the application associated with this device file, try
reinstalling that application to replace the missing file. SAGE.VXD.
Press any key to continue.
```

Interrupting Microsoft Plus! while it's uninstalling could prevent the Plus! Registry entries from being deleted. You'll need to delete these entries by hand, as described in the preceding section.

An install program displays incorrect values for Space required and Space available on disk, and these values aren't updated when you select components to add or remove.

This is a Windows 95 bug that surfaces occasionally. You can use Explorer to check out the free disk space on a drive before you start to install, but other than that, there's not much you can do. Unless you know you're tight on disk space, go ahead and install the application. Even if you run into a problem, Windows 95 should be able to recover gracefully.

Summary

This chapter showed you how to install and uninstall applications in Windows 95. I began by showing you a few tips and techniques for practicing "safe" setups. These included checking for viruses, having a bootable disk nearby, backing up configuration files, reading the documentation, and taking control of the installation. I then showed you how to wield the Add/Remove Programs Wizard. The rest of the chapter showed you how to install and uninstall 32-bit applications, 16-bit applications, and DOS programs.

Here's a list of chapters where you'll find related information:

- I covered Windows 95 installation, as well as how to add and remove Windows 95 components, in Chapter 2, "Running the Windows 95 Setup."

- For a Registry refresher course, turn to Chapter 11, "Introducing the Windows 95 Registry."

- Backup, Configuration Backup, and the Emergency Recovery Utility are all covered in Chapter 15, "Protecting Your Windows 95 Investment."

- For information on how best to run DOS programs, including the full scoop on PIF shortcuts, MS-DOS mode, custom configuration files, and APPS.INF, check out Chapter 21, "DOS Isn't Dead: Optimizing DOS Applications Under Windows 95."

Sharing Data in Windows 95: The Clipboard and OLE

CHAPTER 17

Father (eating chocolate bar): What did you learn in school today?

Daughter (eyeing chocolate bar): Sha-a-a-a-ring.

Chocolate bar commercial from the '70s

It used to be that applications operated in splendid isolation. For example, if you needed to write a memo, you'd fire up your word processor program and start hunting and pecking. If you then realized you needed a spreadsheet to complement the text, you'd shut down the word processor, crank up your spreadsheet program, and start crunching numbers. The only tools you had at hand to connect these two documents were a paper clip and a "See attached" message.

Now, thanks to Windows wonders such as multitasking, the Clipboard, and OLE, applications have gone from isolation to collaboration. Not only can you have your word processor and spreadsheet applications running at the same time, but you can easily share data between them, to the point where you can actually place, for example, an entire spreadsheet inside a word processing document.

This willingness to share data between applications is one of Windows 95's best features, and it's the subject of this chapter. I'll show you the full gamut of data sharing tools, from simple cut-and-paste Clipboard techniques to sophisticated linking and embedding operations involving OLE.

How the Clipboard Works

The Clipboard is used in all kinds of data sharing operations, from the humblest cut-and-paste to full-blown OLE transfers, so it's important to understand how it works. In this section, I'll examine the Clipboard from two equally instructive perspectives: the user and the programmer.

How the User Sees the Clipboard

From the user's perspective, the Clipboard is a temporary storage location for data that has been cut or copied from an application. In this sense, the Clipboard is another Windows 95 object: Its properties are the data that was cut or copied and the format of that data, and its actions are the Cut and Copy commands that send data to the Clipboard and the Paste command that grabs data from the Clipboard. (As you'll see a bit later, the Clipboard Viewer accessory provides a few more Clipboard actions.)

How the Programmer Sees the Clipboard

From the programmer's perspective, the Clipboard is both a memory location that's used as a buffer to store data, and a set of API functions (part of Windows 95's USER component) that manage this memory area. Here's the basic procedure that a program follows when you cut or copy data in an application:

1. Open the Clipboard by calling the `OpenClipboard` API function.

2. Empty the Clipboard by calling the `EmptyClipboard` function. This clears the existing Clipboard contents, frees resources associated with the old Clipboard data, and assigns Clipboard ownership to the window that has the Clipboard open.

3. Send the selected data to the Clipboard by calling the `SetClipboardData` function. (This command may be repeated multiple times if the data can be viewed in multiple formats. More on these formats later.)

4. Close the Clipboard by calling the `CloseClipboard` function.

Even though developers can control the Clipboard directly, programming "etiquette" dictates that changes to the Clipboard should be user-driven. In other words, a program should never use the Clipboard to transfer data without the user's knowledge. The reason for this is found in step 2 of the preceding list. Here you see that a program must delete the current contents of the Clipboard before it can insert any new data. If a user has cut data from a document for later pasting, it would be the height of rudeness (not to mention irresponsibility) for a program to destroy this Clipboard data before the user gets a chance to paste it.

Understanding Clipboard Formats

Since the Clipboard is really just a memory location, it can handle any kind of data you care to toss its way: text, bitmaps, even entire files. However, each type of data can be represented in many different ways. Text copied from WordPad, for example, can be represented as plain text or as "rich" text (text that includes formatting information, such as bolding and fonts), to name just two. Each of these different types is represented by a specific *Clipboard format*.

When an application adds data to the Clipboard, it also sends information about each format that the data can use (hence the multiple calls to the `SetClipboardData` function in step 3). When you're pasting the data, the destination application can use these formats to give you a choice of pasting options. Table 17.1 presents a few Clipboard formats that are commonly used by applications. (I'll run through a few more Clipboard formats when I discuss OLE later in this chapter.)

Table 17.1. Common Clipboard formats.

Format	Type	Description
BIFF	Spreadsheet	Microsoft's Binary File Format.
Bitmap	Graphics	A bitmap image, where a *bitmap* is an array of bits (pixels) that contains data that describes the colors found in an image.
CSV	Spreadsheet	Comma-Separated Value format. Separates data values with commas.
DIB bitmap	Graphics	Device-Independent Bitmap format.

continues

Table 17.1. continued

Format	Type	Description
DIF	Spreadsheet	Data Interchange format.
OEM text	Text	A text format containing characters in the OEM character set.
Palette	Graphics	The color palette associated with the image that's currently stored on the Clipboard.
Picture	Graphics	A *metafile* image. Metafiles are collections of drawing commands from Windows 95's GDI component. These commands create the basic primitives (lines, circles, and so on) that make up the image.
Rich text format	Text	Text with formatting information, including font, style, typeface, and type size.
SYLK	Spreadsheet	Microsoft's Symbolic Link format.
Text	Text	Unformatted characters from the ANSI character set.
WaveAudio	Sound	The standard Windows 95 waveform audio format.
WK1	Spreadsheet	Lotus 1-2-3 release 2 format.

Cut-and-Paste Clipboard Techniques

At its most basic level, the Clipboard is a "don't-reinvent-the-wheel" device. In other words, if you've created something that works—whether it's a bit of polished prose, an attractive graphic, or a complex spreadsheet formula—and you'd like to reuse it, don't waste time re-creating the data from scratch. Instead, you can send the existing data to the Clipboard and then insert a copy of it in a different document or even in a different application altogether.

The Clipboard is the best thing to happen to document editing since the invention of White-Out. If you need to restructure a letter or a spreadsheet model, the best way to do so is to move the text or cells from their current position to some other part of the document. The Clipboard makes this easy, because you can cut the data out of the document, store it on the Clipboard, and then paste it into a different location.

The next couple of sections review the specifics of cutting and copying data via the Clipboard.

Working with Data and Files

Before you can send anything to the Clipboard, you have to select the data you want to work with. How you do this depends on the application you're using. In Paint, for example, you use the Select and Free-Form Select tools to select part of the current image (or you can choose Edit | Select All to select the entire image). In Windows 95, you can also use the Clipboard to cut or copy files and folders in Explorer. I described several techniques of selecting multiple objects in Explorer in Chapter 5, "Windows 95: The 50¢ Tour."

Since you'll often use the Clipboard for copying and moving text, Windows 95 has a few generic techniques for selecting chunks of text:

- Drag the mouse over the text you want to select.
- Click at the beginning of the text, hold down the Shift key, and then click at the end of the text.
- To select a word, double-click it.
- In WordPad, you can use the following techniques:

    You can select an entire paragraph by triple-clicking it.

    You can select an entire line by clicking in the left margin beside the line.

    You can select the entire document by holding down Ctrl and clicking anywhere in the left margin.

- In WordPad and Notepad (and many other Windows applications), choose Edit | Select All to select the entire document. (In WordPad, you can also press Ctrl-A to select the entire document.)
- Place the insertion point cursor at the beginning of the text, hold down the Shift key, and use the application's navigation keys (the arrow keys, Page Up, Page Down, and so on) to select the text.

As soon as the data is selected, you then cut or copy it (as appropriate) to the Clipboard, head for the destination (which could be a different part of the same document, a different document, or a document in another application), and paste the data from the Clipboard. Table 17.2 lists the Edit menu commands, shortcut keys, and toolbar buttons that are usually associated with these Clipboard operations.

Table 17.2. Commands and shortcuts for managing the Clipboard.

Command	Keyboard Shortcut	Toolbar Button	Description
Edit	Cut	Ctrl-X	✄	Removes the selected data from the document and stores it on the Clipboard.
Edit	Copy	Ctrl-C	📋	Makes a copy of the selected data and stores it on the Clipboard.
Edit	Paste	Ctrl-V	📋	Inserts the Clipboard's contents at the current position of the insertion point cursor.

TIP: DON'T FORGET THE CONTEXT MENU

Many applications also display the Cut, Copy, and Paste commands on the context menu if you right-click the selected data.

CAUTION: PASTE YOUR CUT DATA AS SOON AS POSSIBLE

Remember that each time you cut or copy a selection, the application deletes the current contents of the Clipboard. To avoid losing data after a cut, you should perform the paste operation as soon as you can.

Pasting Data in a Different Format

Clipboard data usually has a default format that's used when you select the Paste command. For example, if you send a piece of a Paint image to the Clipboard and then paste it into WordPad, the image is inserted using the bitmap format. However, as you saw earlier, there are often multiple formats for a given data type. Images, for example, can be bitmaps, pictures (metafiles), or DIBs.

If you'd like to use a different format when you paste data, most applications have a Paste Special command on their Edit menu. Selecting this command displays a dialog box similar to the one shown in Figure 17.1. Here, the As box lists the various formats that are available. You simply highlight the one you want and click OK. (However, you need to be careful that you don't *embed* the data. In many cases, the first item shown in the As list is an *object* format. If you select this item, Windows 95 pastes the data as an embedded object. I'll discuss this in more detail when I talk about Object Linking and Embedding later in this chapter.)

FIGURE 17.1.

The Paste Special command gives you access to the other formats available with the data you're pasting from the Clipboard.

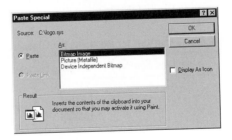

Sending Screen Shots to the Clipboard

A number of programs on the market will capture a snapshot of your screen and save it to a graphics file. (I used a program called Collage Capture to take all the screen shots in this book.) These screen captures are useful in manuals and training documentation, or just as a starting point for an image you want to create.

If you don't have a screen capture program, you can still take screen shots. Windows 95 gives you two techniques:

- Press your keyboard's Print Screen key. This captures an image of the entire screen and sends it to the Clipboard.
- Press Alt-Print Screen. This captures only an image of the current application window and sends it to the Clipboard.

Once you've captured the screen or window, you can open a graphics program (such as Paint) and paste the screen shot.

Sharing Data Between DOS and Windows Applications

DOS programs don't know about the Clipboard, so they don't support the standard cut, copy, and paste techniques. However, there *are* methods you can use to share data between DOS and Windows applications. I'll spell them out in the next few sections.

Copying Text from a DOS Application

The best way to copy text from a DOS application is to place the program in a window and highlight the text you want. The following procedure takes you through the required steps:

1. Switch to the DOS application and place it in a window (if it isn't already) by pressing Alt-Enter.

NOTE: SWITCH TO TEXT MODE

If the DOS application has a graphics mode, copying a section of the screen will copy a graphic image of the text, not the text itself. If you want text only, make sure the program is running in character mode before you continue.

2. Make sure the text you want to copy is visible on-screen.
3. Use any of the following techniques to put the window into *select* mode:
    - Pull down the window's control menu and select Edit | Mark.
    - Right-click the title bar and select Edit | Mark from the context menu.
    - Click the Mark button on the toolbar.
4. Use the mouse or keyboard to select the data you want to copy, as shown in Figure 17.2.

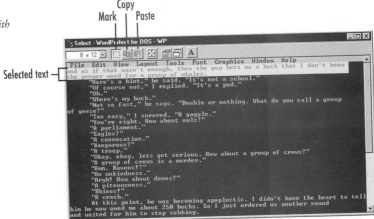

FIGURE 17.2.

A DOS program with selected text.

5. Use any of the following techniques to copy the selected data to the Clipboard:

- Pull down the window's control menu and select Edit | Copy.
- Right-click the title bar and select Edit | Copy from the context menu.
- Press Enter.
- Click the Copy button on the toolbar.

6. Switch to the Windows application you want to use as the destination, and position the insertion point where you want the copied data to appear.

7. Select Edit | Paste.

TIP: USING QUICKEDIT

If you have a lot of text to copy, you might find it easier to activate Windows 95's QuickEdit option. QuickEdit leaves the DOS window in select mode permanently so that you can select text anytime you like. (The downside, however, is that you can no longer use the mouse to manipulate the DOS program itself.) To enable QuickEdit, open the properties sheet for the DOS program, display the Misc tab, and activate the QuickEdit check box.

TIP: COPYING TEXT FULL-SCREEN

If the DOS program is running full-screen instead of in a window, you can still copy text. Pressing the Print Screen key will send all the window text—menu names, status bar text, and all—to the Clipboard.

Pasting Text to a DOS Application

If you've sent some text to the Clipboard from a Windows application (or even from another DOS application, for that matter), it's possible to copy the text into a DOS program. Make sure you've positioned the DOS program's cursor appropriately, and then use any of the following techniques:

■ Pull down the window's control menu and select Edit | Paste.

■ Right-click the title bar and select Edit | Paste from the context menu.

■ Click the Paste button on the toolbar.

TROUBLESHOOTING: YOU HAVE PROBLEMS PASTING TEXT TO DOS

You might encounter problems pasting text from the Clipboard to your DOS program. For example, you might see garbage characters, or some characters might be missing. This probably means that Windows 95 is sending the characters too fast, and the DOS program can't handle the onslaught. To solve this problem, open the DOS program's properties sheet, select the Misc tab, and deactivate the Fast pasting check box. This tells Windows 95 to hold its horses and send the characters at a slower rate.

Sharing Graphics Between DOS and Windows

Unlike with Windows-to-Windows transfers, there's no clean way to transfer graphics between Windows and DOS.

If you have a DOS graphic you'd like to place on the Clipboard, display the program in a window, adjust the window so that the image is visible, and then press Alt-Print Screen. Windows 95 will copy an image of the entire window to the Clipboard. You could then paste this image into a graphics program and remove the extraneous data.

Unfortunately, the Clipboard can't handle graphics transfers from a Windows application to a DOS program. Your only choice here is to save the image in a graphics format that the DOS program understands and then open this file in the DOS program.

Using the Clipboard Viewer

Windows 95 ships with a Clipboard Viewer utility that you can use to display and work with the current contents of the Clipboard. Assuming that Clipboard Viewer is installed, you can launch it by selecting Start | Programs | Accessories | Clipboard Viewer. The Clipboard Viewer window that appears displays the last piece of data you cut or copied to the Clipboard. In Figure 17.3, for example, I copied an address from the WordPad window, and it now appears in the Clipboard Viewer.

FIGURE 17.3.

The Clipboard Viewer shows you the last hunk of data that you cut or copied.

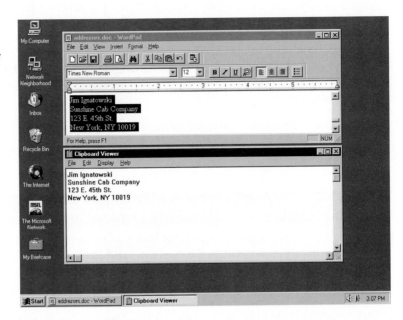

To see the formats that the current data supports, pull down the Display menu. You can select one of the commands to display the data in a different format. (You might see lots of dimmed commands on this menu. The data supports these formats; they just can't be displayed in the Clipboard Viewer window.)

Saving the Clipboard's Contents

What do you do if you cut some data to the Clipboard and then realize you have to work with other data in the meantime? You could paste the current Clipboard contents into a different document, but that might not be convenient. Instead, you can use the Clipboard Viewer to store the current Clipboard contents in a separate Clipboard (CLP) file. You can then open this file later when you need it. Here's how it's done:

1. Select the data you want to save, and cut or copy it to the Clipboard if you haven't done so already.
2. Open the Clipboard Viewer.
3. Select File | Save As to display the Save As dialog box.
4. Select a location and enter a name for the file. Use a short name (eight characters or less), and don't add an extension.
5. Click OK.

To use the saved data down the road, first make sure you've pasted any existing Clipboard data. Then open the Clipboard Viewer, select File | Open, and choose the file you need in the Open dialog box that appears. When the Clipboard Viewer asks if you want to clear the contents of the Clipboard, click Yes.

Deleting the Clipboard's Contents

As I mentioned earlier, the Clipboard is a memory buffer. So, of course, anything that's sitting on the Clipboard uses up some of your system's memory. If you've cut or copied a large graphic image or file, the Clipboard will be correspondingly large. If your system doesn't have much physical RAM to begin with, a massive Clipboard can slow down your system. To solve this problem, you can reduce the size of the Clipboard by using either of the following methods:

- Copy a smaller piece of data to the Clipboard (such as a single character).
- In the Clipboard Viewer, select Edit | Delete or press Delete. When the Clipboard Viewer asks if you want to clear the contents of the Clipboard, click Yes.

Understanding OLE

The Clipboard-based methods we've looked at are certainly simple ways to work, but they suffer from three major drawbacks. First, if the data gets changed in the original application, the document containing the copy will become out-of-date. This has two consequences:

- If you know that the data needs to be updated, you have to repeat the whole copy-and-paste procedure to get the latest version of the data.
- If you don't know that the data needs to be updated (for example, if someone else changes the original data without telling you), you'll be stuck with an old version of the info.

Second, what if you want to make changes to the copied data? You might be able to edit the data directly (if it's just text, for example), but more often than not you'll need to crank up the original application, change the data there, and then copy the data via the Clipboard again. However, problems can arise if you're not sure which application to use, or if you're not sure which file contains the original data.

Third, copying data between documents is often wasteful since you end up with multiple copies of the same data. You could cut the data from the original application and then paste it, but then there would be no easy way to edit the data using the original application.

It would be nice if you didn't have to worry about the updating of your shared data. It would be nice if there were a system that would accomplish three goals:

- If the data changes in the original application, update the copied data automatically.
- If you want to edit the copied data, make it easy to find both the original application and the original data file.
- Let you store nonnative data inside a document without having to maintain separate documents for the original data.

17

THE CLIPBOARD
AND OLE

Happily, OLE—Object Linking and Embedding—meets all three goals and adds a few extra conveniences to the mix for good measure. OLE is one of Microsoft's most important technologies. It can be described without hyperbole as the foundation of all Microsoft's future development efforts in operating systems, applications, and the Internet. Understanding how OLE operates, then, is crucial to understanding not only Windows 95 (which, as you'll soon see, makes extensive use of OLE internally) but also Windows 95 applications, which must support OLE in order to qualify for the Windows 95 logo.

OLE wasn't always such a big deal. Microsoft originally hoped that Dynamic Data Exchange (DDE) would carry the data-sharing torch into the future. DDE works by establishing a communications "channel" between two applications along which data can be transferred. Unfortunately, DDE failed miserably. It was slow, flaky, and inflexible, and it was a programmer's solution to what is, really, an end-user's problem.

OLE leaped into the breach by making it easy for users to share data between applications, keep shared data updated automatically, and mix multiple data types in a single document without wasting disk space. The problem, however, was that OLE was implemented only sporadically. Because Microsoft relied on individual applications to execute OLE functionality, users could never be sure of what they were getting and whether or not two applications could work together. That all changed with the release of Windows 95, however, because now OLE is built right into the operating system. For example, you're working with OLE when you create a shortcut to a program or document. Not only that, but all Windows 95 applications that deal with documents are guaranteed to be OLE-compliant, so you always know what you're getting.

First, Some Fundamentals

You'll spend the rest of this section exploring some important OLE underpinnings. Before diving into these theoretical waters, however, you should know about three crucial OLE concepts: *objects, servers,* and *containers:*

Object: In the OLE world, an object is not only data—a slice of text, a graphic, a sound, a chunk of a spreadsheet, or whatever—but also one or more functions for creating, accessing, and using that data.

Server application: The application that you use to create and edit an object. Also known as the *source application.*

Container application: The application that you use to store a linked or embedded object created with a server application. Also known as the *client application.*

With these simple fundamentals in hand, you can now take a closer look at OLE architecture. However, OLE is a large, complicated standard, and it's hideously complex to program. Lucky for you, though, unleashing OLE in Windows 95 in no way requires you to delve too deeply into this complexity. Instead, I'll restrict your look at OLE's plumbing to just the following five topics:

- Compound documents
- The Component Object Model
- OLE drag-and-drop
- OLE automation
- ActiveX controls (formerly OLE controls)

Compound Documents

A *compound document* is a document that contains, along with its native data, one or more objects that were created using other applications. The key point is that the compound document's native data and its objects can have entirely different data formats. For example, a word processing document can include a spreadsheet range object or a sound clip object. The container application doesn't need to know a thing about these alien data formats, either. All it has to know is the name of the server application that created the data and how to display the data. All this information (and more) is included free of charge as part of the object, so it's readily available to the container application.

As the name Object Linking and Embedding implies, you create a compound document by either linking objects to the document or embedding objects in the document. The next three sections explain linking and embedding in more depth, and then I'll examine four more issues related to linking and embedding: visual editing, OLE-related Clipboard formats, nested objects, and object conversion.

Understanding Linking

Linking is one of the OLE methods you can use to insert an object into a file from a container application and thus create a compound document. In this case, the object includes only the following information:

- The Registry key needed to invoke the object's server application (see "OLE and the Registry" later in this chapter for details).
- A metafile that contains GDI instructions on how to display the object. These instructions simply generate the primitives (lines, circles, arcs, and so on) that create an image of the object. These primitives are the heart of the GDI, and they form the basis of any image you see on-screen. So the container application doesn't have to know a thing about the object itself; it just follows the metafile's instructions blindly, and a perfect replica of the object's image appears.
- A pointer to the server application file (the *source document*) that contains the original data.

Linking brings many advantages to the table, but three are most relevant to our purposes. First, the link lets the container application check the source document for changes. If it finds that the data has been modified, OLE can use the link to update the object automatically. For example, suppose you insert a linked spreadsheet object into a word processor document. If you revise some of the numbers in the spreadsheet sometime down the road, the object inside the document is automatically updated to reflect the new numbers. However, this updating is automatic only under certain conditions:

- If the container application is running and has the compound document open, the update is automatic.
- If the compound document isn't open when the data is changed, the object gets updated automatically the next time you open the compound document.
- Most OLE applications let you disable automatic updating either for individual documents or for the application as a whole. In this case, you need to perform the updates manually. (I'll show you how this is done later in this chapter.)

Second, since the object "knows" where to find both the server application and the source document, you can edit the object from within the container application. In most cases, double-clicking the object invokes the server and loads the appropriate source file. You can then edit the original data and exit the server application, and your object is, once again, updated automatically.

Third, since the source data exists in a separate file, you can easily reuse the data in other compound documents, and you can edit the data directly from within the server application.

Understanding Embedding

One of the problems associated with linking is that if you distribute the compound document, you also have to distribute the source document. Similarly, if you move the source document to a different location on your system, the link breaks. (However, you can edit the link to reflect the new location.)

NOTE: LINK TRACKING

Microsoft promises that future versions of Windows will support *link tracking*. This means that the operating system will monitor links and update them automatically if you move a source file to a new location.

Embedding solves these problems by inserting an object not only with the server's Registry information and the metafile for displaying the object, but also with the object's *data*. This way, everything you need to display and work with the object exists within the object itself. There's no need for a separate source file, so you can distribute the compound document knowing that the recipient will receive the data intact.

In fact, embedding lets you *create* server objects from within the container application. If you're working with Word for Windows, for example, you can insert a new spreadsheet object right from Word. OLE will start Excel so that you can create the new object, but when you exit Excel, the object will exist only within the Word compound document. There will be no separate Excel file.

Note that many applications can operate only as OLE servers. This means that they aren't standalone applications and therefore have no way to create files on their own. They exist only to create OLE objects for compound documents. Microsoft Office ships with several examples of these applications, including WordArt and Microsoft Graph.

Should You Link or Embed?

Perhaps the most confusing aspect of OLE is determining whether you should link your objects or embed them. As you've seen, the only major difference between linking and embedding is that a linked object stores only a pointer to its data, while an embedded object stores its own data internally.

With this in mind, you should link your objects if any of the following situations apply:

■ You want to keep your compound documents small. The information stored in a linked object—the pointers to the server and source document, and the metafile—consume only about 1.5 KB, so very little overhead is associated with linking. (If you're using WordPad as the container, you can check this out for yourself. Click the object and select Edit | Object Properties, or right-click the object and select Object Properties from the context menu. The properties sheet that appears shows you the size of the object, as shown in Figure 17.4.)

FIGURE 17.4.

The WordPad properties sheet for a linked object. Notice that the linked object takes up only 1.5 KB.

■ You're sure the source document won't be moved or deleted. To maintain the link, OLE requires that the source file remain in the same place. If the document gets moved or deleted, the link is broken. (Although, as I've said, most OLE applications let you reestablish the link by modifying the path to the source document.)

■ You need to keep the source file as a separate document in case you want to make changes to it later, or in case you need it for other compound documents. You're free to link an object to as many container files as you like. If you think you'll be using the source data in different places, you should link it to maintain a separate file.

■ You won't be sending the compound document via e-mail or floppy disk. Again, OLE expects the linked source data to appear in a specific place. If you send the compound document to someone else, he might not have the proper source file to maintain the link.

Similarly, you should embed your objects if any of the following situations apply:

■ You don't care how big your compound documents get. Embedding works best in situations in which you have lots of hard disk space and lots of memory. For example, Figure 17.5 shows the WordPad properties sheet for an embedded object. This is the same Excel worksheet that was linked in Figure 17.4, but you can see that the embedded object is much larger.

FIGURE 17.5.

The WordPad properties sheet for an embedded object. Because embedded objects store their own data, they're much larger than linked objects.

■ You don't need to keep the source file as a separate document. If you need to use the source data only once, embedding it means you can get rid of the source file (or never have to create one in the first place) and reduce the clutter on your hard disk.

■ You'll be sending the compound documents and you want to make sure the object arrives intact. If you send a file containing an embedded object, the other person will see the data complete and unaltered. If he wants to edit the object, however, he'll need to have the server application installed.

NOTE: OLE NEEDS MEMORY

Whether you link or embed, OLE will still put a strain on your system's memory resources. Although Microsoft has made some strides in improving the efficiency of the OLE standard, the memory cost is still high. You'll need a minimum of 12 MB of physical RAM to achieve anything approaching reasonable performance out of OLE.

Linking and Embedding via the Clipboard

As you'll learn later in this chapter (see "Working with OLE"), you can paste data from the Clipboard to a container document as either a linked or embedded object. The secret to this is that when you cut or copy an OLE object to the Clipboard, the server application also throws in a few extra formats that the container application can use to link or embed the object. Table 17.3 lists a few of these OLE-related formats.

Table 17.3. OLE-related Clipboard formats.

Format	Description
Embed Source	A copy of the server object to be used for embedding.
Filename	The name of a file that was sent to the Clipboard.
Link Source	The link to the server.
Link Source Descriptor	A description of the link.
Native	The format that the source application uses to store the data internally.
Object Descriptor	Describes the object, including its class ID and size.

Visual Editing

In the original incarnation of OLE, double-clicking an object opened a new window for the server application and loaded the source document (if the object was linked) or loaded the object's data (if the object was embedded). This process is called *open editing*.

When OLE 2.0 debuted a couple of years ago, it introduced the idea of *visual editing* (also known as *in-place editing*). When you double-click an embedded object, instead of your seeing the server application in a separate window, certain features of the container application's window are temporarily hidden in favor of the server application's features. (Linked objects still use open editing.) Here's a summary of the changes that occur in the container application:

- The document window's title bar changes to tell you what kind of object you're now working with. (Not all applications do this.)
- The menu bar (with the exception of the File and Window menus) is replaced by the server application's menu bar.
- The toolbars are replaced by the server application's toolbars.

Essentially, the container application "becomes" the server application while still maintaining the object's context in the compound document. Let's look at an example. First, Figure 17.6 shows the normal Microsoft Excel window.

FIGURE 17.6.

The Microsoft Excel window before you insert an object.

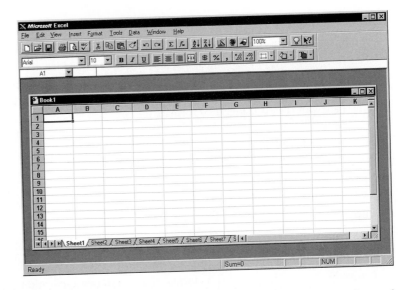

If you now insert a Microsoft Word document into Excel, OLE changes the menu bar and toolbars from Excel's to Word's, as you can see in Figure 17.7. However, the rest of the Excel interface—including the row and column headers, the underlying worksheet cells, and the sheet tabs—remain visible to give context to the embedded object. (To exit visual editing, click outside the object.)

FIGURE 17.7.

During visual editing, the Excel window assumes many features of the Word window.

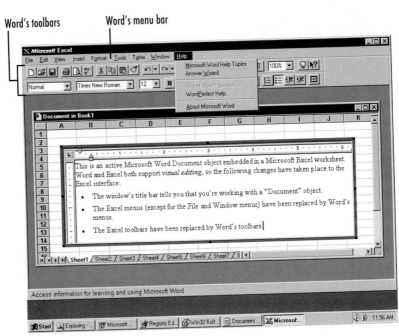

Nested Objects

Once you've opened the server application to create or edit an object, most of the server's features become available. (During visual editing, you can't access server features that relate to files and windows; that's why the container application's File and Window menus don't change.) In particular, if the server application can also double as a container application, you have access to the server features that let you insert linked or embedded objects. In other words, you can double-click an object to activate the server application, and you can then insert a linked or embedded object inside the existing object. This is called *nesting objects*. OLE has no limit on the number of nesting levels you can use.

For example, Figure 17.8 shows a WordArt object nested inside the Word Document object that's embedded in an Excel worksheet.

FIGURE 17.8.

OLE lets you nest objects within objects.

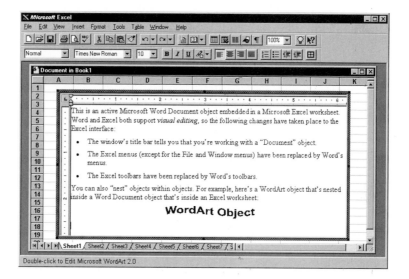

Object Conversion

I mentioned earlier that if you send a compound document to another person, he won't be able to edit the linked or embedded objects unless he has the appropriate server application. However, that's not true in all cases. OLE has a feature called *object conversion* that lets OLE servers convert objects into formats they can work with.

For example, suppose you embed an Excel worksheet into a Word document. If you then send the resulting compound document to a colleague, she'll be able to read the document as long as she has Word. If she wants to edit the embedded worksheet, however, she might not need Excel. All she needs is a spreadsheet program that's capable of converting Excel worksheet objects into the program's native object format.

Note as well that object conversion can also be used by the server application to convert its own objects, as follows:

- To convert an existing object to a related format. In Excel, for example, you can convert a Worksheet object to a Chart object, and vice versa.

- To upgrade older objects to a new format. If a server enhances its objects with extra functionality, for example, it can use object conversion to upgrade existing objects so that they too have access to the same functions.

The Component Object Model

The Component Object Model (COM) is the heart and soul of OLE. It defines not only the standards that server applications use to create objects, but also the mechanisms by which server and container applications interact when dealing with objects.

These features are implemented as *interfaces,* which are collections of related functions. A server application makes an OLE component (that is, an object) available by implementing an interface for the component. When a container application needs to work with a server's OLE components, it just uses the appropriate interface. The container application doesn't have to know anything about the underlying structure of the component. It just works with the interface functions and the linking or embedding (or whatever) happens in a consistent manner.

This is analogous to the way Windows 95 itself operates. To make an operating system component available to the user, Windows 95 implements an interface. For example, to give you access to the file system, Windows 95 offers the Explorer (or My Computer) interface. You don't have to know anything about how Explorer was programmed or what internal data structures it uses; you just have to manipulate the interface.

One of the chief features of COM is that the interfaces it supports are extensible. In other words, when a vendor upgrades its components, it doesn't change the existing behavior of the interface; it just adds new functionality. (This is done either by extending an existing interface or by creating new interfaces; container applications can query the server to find out what's new.) This way, container applications know they can work with a server reliably and that an interface function used today will work exactly the same 10 years from now. The *OLE Programmer's Reference* says that, metaphorically, an object's interface acts like a "contract" that guarantees its behavior for prospective container applications.

(This explains why Microsoft has dropped version numbering from OLE. A new version number for a software product implies that the underlying functionality of the product has changed. However, thanks to its extensibility, that will never happen with OLE because existing functions will always work the same. So, in a sense, you'll never get a "new" version of OLE, just a better implementation of the existing version.)

The starting point for COM is the *class factory*. This is an object in the server application that creates instances of OLE components. When you tell your container application that you want to insert a particular object, the container notifies the appropriate server's class factory that an instance of the object is required. The class factory then creates the object and informs the container application of the appropriate interface to use in order to access the new object.

After the class factory has done its work, the server and container communicate (with COM as the intermediary) through various interfaces. These interfaces control a number of OLE features, including compound documents, visual editing, how data is transferred between server and container, how an object is stored in the container, how the server notifies the container of changes, and many more.

OLE Drag-and-Drop

You can use the Clipboard to do the OLE thing, but in keeping with Windows 95's drag-and-drop nature, the latest OLE applications also let you use drag-and-drop to insert linked or embedded objects. This lets you perform OLE chores without having to resort to the Cut, Copy, and Paste commands and without using the Clipboard. Windows 95 supports three kinds of OLE drag-and-drop:

Inter-window: You drag a selected object from the server application's window and drop it on the container application's window.

Inter-object: You drag a selected object and drop it on another object to produce a nested object. Or you can "un-nest" an object by dragging it out of an object.

Icons: You drag a selected object and drop it on a desktop icon, such as a printer or a disk drive.

OLE Automation

The beauty of OLE is not only how easy it is to insert objects in a container application (especially via drag-and-drop), but the access you have to the object's original tools. With a simple double-click, you can edit the object with the full power of the server's menus and commands.

But, until recently, the one thing that was missing was the ability to control the server via macros. If you program in, say, VBA (Visual Basic for Applications), it would be nice to be able to create new objects using VBA procedures. This is especially true if you're developing corporate applications for end-users. Editing or creating an object, whether you use visual editing or open editing, has meant that you must at least be familiar with the server application. And although *you* might be willing to spend time and effort learning a new program, the users of your VBA applications might not be.

This has all changed with the advent of OLE automation. Applications that support OLE automation "expose" their objects to VBA (and any other applications and development tools that support the OLE automation standard). So just as VBA can recognize and manipulate, say, an Excel worksheet range (a Range object), it can also recognize and manipulate objects from other OLE automation applications. VISIO, for example, exposes a number of objects to VBA, including its documents, pages, shapes, and windows. Access 7.0 exposes dozens of objects, including its forms and reports. Also, the Binder application that ships with Office 95 supports OLE automation and exposes its sections as objects.

Each of these objects has its own collection of properties and actions (or *methods,* as they're called among OLE automationists) that can be read or altered. For example, you can use OLE automation to create a new PowerPoint presentation object and then use the Add method of the Slides object to add a slide object to the presentation.

OLE automation has really caught fire in the last year or two, to the point where it's now *the* standard for application interoperability. And with Microsoft now licensing VBA to all-comers, these other VBA-enabled applications will be OLE-automated (this includes Microsoft's own Office 97, which now has VBA at the core of its Big Four applications: Word, Excel, PowerPoint, and Access).

ActiveX Controls

If you're using Microsoft Office 95, you've probably gasped at the disk real estate that these applications gobble up. Consider just the executable files: MSACCESS.EXE, 2.7 MB; EXCEL.EXE, 4.6 MB; POWERPNT.EXE, 4.16 MB; WINWORD.EXE, 3.66 MB. These behemoth files are indicative of the biggest disease facing software today: code bloat. Each new iteration of an application (and I don't mean to pick on Office; *every* application suffers from this) crams in more bells, more whistles, and more gee-aren't-our-programmers-clever features. If you can use these new baubles, the toll on your hard disk free space is probably worth it. More likely, however, you might use one or two of the new features, and the rest you couldn't care less about. In the end, most software programs follow the old 80-20 rule: you spend 80 percent of your time using 20 percent of the features.

In response to user complaints, the software industry is finally doing something about this problem. Someday soon you'll be able to install only the features you'll actually use and consign the rest to the obscurity they deserve. The engine behind this change is *component-based software.* These are small software modules that perform specific tasks. For example, a spell-checking component would do nothing but check an application's spelling. By combining such modules, you can create a customized version of a software package that's tailored to your needs.

The current standard for these software components is the ActiveX control (formerly known as the OLE control). These are prebuilt OLE objects that developers can plug into existing applications. These objects expose various properties and actions, so the developer can manipulate how the program appears and works with the user. This functionality will eventually come to the end-user as well, allowing you to mix and match components to create a package that contains only the features you need.

The first place you'll see ActiveX controls in action is on the Internet. In version 3 of Microsoft's Internet Explorer World Wide Web browser, when developers insert ActiveX controls into Web pages, Internet Explorer downloads them to the user's computer and executes them. This technique is used mostly to spice up Web pages with dynamic content, such as an animation or an order form that includes running totals. (I'll show you an example of ActiveX controls running in Internet Explorer 3 in Chapter 38, "Exploring the Web with Internet Explorer.")

OLE and the Registry

You saw back in Chapter 11, "Introducing the Windows 95 Registry," that Windows 95 makes extensive use of the Registry to store all kinds of information about your system. So it will come as no surprise that the Registry plays a big part in OLE as well.

Programmatic Identifier Keys

Most OLE-related Registry data can be found in the HKEY_CLASSES_ROOT key (an alias, you'll recall, of HKEY_LOCAL_MACHINE\SOFTWARE\Classes). HKEY_CLASSES_ROOT consists of a long list of extensions, followed by an equally long list of file types, which are known, officially, as *programmatic identifiers*. For example, Figure 17.9 shows the key for the programmatic ID for an Excel worksheet.

FIGURE 17.9.

The programmatic ID keys contain lots of useful OLE info.

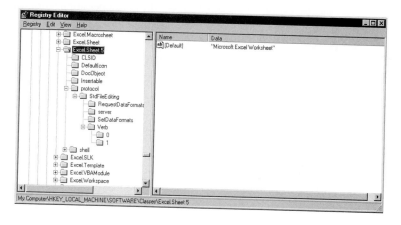

The key's default value is the name of the file type that the programmatic ID represents (Microsoft Excel Worksheet in Figure 17.9). Here's a rundown of the OLE-related subkeys that you'll find in the programmatic ID key:

CLSID: This is the object's *class ID,* a 16-byte (32 hexadecimal digit) value that's also known as the object's Globally Unique Identifier (GUID). As the latter name implies, CLSIDs are values that uniquely identify an object. The value of the CLSID key points to a subkey of the HKEY_CLASSES_ROOT\CLSID key (discussed in a moment).

NOTE: HOW CLSID VALUES ARE GENERATED

CLSIDs are either assigned by Microsoft or generated by a program that comes in the Microsoft Software Development Kit. How can a vendor be sure that its object's CLSID is unique? Well, if you get the value from Microsoft, Microsoft can check its database to ensure uniqueness. All Microsoft-generated CLSID values use the following format (where *xxxxxxxx* is a unique sequence of eight hexadecimal digits):

`{xxxxxxxx-0000-0000-C000-000000000046}`

If you use the program, consider how each value is generated. The first eight digits are random, the next four digits are generated by the current date and time, and the last 20 digits are generated based on the hardware details of the developer's computer. That combination is about as unique as it gets!

Insertable: This key is a flag that tells COM that this type of object can be inserted into a container document. When you select Insert | Object, COM gathers all the objects that have the Insertable key and displays them in the Object dialog box.

DefaultIcon: If you elect to insert an object as an icon, OLE uses the data in this key to determine which icon to display.

StdExecute\server: This subkey gives the container application the pathname of the server application to be used to execute the object.

StdFileEditing\server: This subkey gives the container application the pathname of the server application to be used to edit the object.

Verb: This subkey lists the actions you can take with a linked or embedded object. Most objects have two verbs: Edit (which activates visual editing) and Open (which activates open editing). Others—such as AVIFile (video files) and SoundRec (audio files)—also have a Play verb that plays the object.

CLSID Keys

As I said, the CLSID subkey contains a setting that points to a subkey of HKEY_CLASSES_ROOT\CLSID. For example, the Excel worksheet object's CLSID subkey points to the following key, as shown in Figure 17.10:

`HKEY_CLASSES_ROOT\CLSID\{00020810-0000-0000-C000-000000000046}`

FIGURE 17.10.

Each OLE object has a subkey in the HKEY_CLASSES_ROOT\CLSID *key.*

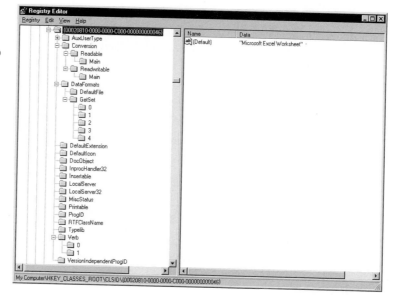

The default value of this key is the name of the object. The subkeys contain lots of OLE-related data. Here's a summary of a few of these keys:

AuxUserType: Alternative (shorter) names for the object type.

Conversion: Information used during object conversion. Items in the Readable subkey are formats that the server application can convert into the object's format; items in the Readwritable subkey are file formats that the server can convert the object into.

DataFormats: The data formats supported by the server application. Most of the formats are listed as integer values that correspond to default formats defined by Windows 95.

DefaultExtension: The default extension for this type of object. If you leave off the extension when you enter a filename in the Insert Object dialog box (described later), OLE tacks on the extension specified in this subkey.

DefaultIcon: If you elect to insert an object as an icon, OLE uses the data in this key to determine which icon to display. (This is the same as DefaultIcon in the programmatic ID subkey, discussed earlier.)

InProcHandler and InProcHandler32: In-process handlers (DLL files) used to help the server and container applications communicate. InProcHandler is for 16-bit server applications; InProcHandler32 is for 32-bit applications.

InProcServer and InProcServer32: In-process servers (DLL files) that a container application can call instead of a full-blown server application.

Insertable: This key is a flag that tells COM that this type of object can be inserted into a container document. When you select Insert | Object, COM gathers all the objects that have the `Insertable` key and displays them in the Object dialog box. (This is the same as `Insertable` in the programmatic ID subkey, discussed earlier.)

LocalServer and LocalServer32: The full pathname of the server application. 32-bit applications need only the `LocalServer32` subkey, but the `LocalServer` subkey is also added for backwards compatibility with 16-bit container applications.

ProgID: A pointer to the object's programmatic ID.

Verb: This subkey lists the actions you can take with a linked or embedded object. (This is the same as `Verb` in the programmatic ID subkey, discussed earlier.)

OLE and the Windows 95 Shell

Windows 95 not only implements OLE, it also *uses* it. The next three sections give you a taste of the OLE features implemented directly in the Windows 95 shell.

Quick View

The Quick View accessory lets you view many different Windows 95 file types. When you invoke Quick View, Windows 95 checks the Registry's `HKEY_CLASSES_ROOT\QuickView` key to make sure that the object is registered with Quick View. This key contains various extension subkeys that point to a `CLSID`. For example, if you open `HKEY_CLASSES_ROOT\QuickView\.BMP`, you'll see the following subkey:

```
{F0F08735-0C36-101B-B086-0020AF07D0F4}
```

(For objects that don't have an extension—such as drives and folders—there's a generic * subkey.) In turn, this `CLSID` has a corresponding subkey in `HKEY_CLASSES_ROOT\CLSID`. This subkey defines an in-process server (for Quick View, it's `SCCVIEW.DLL`) that uses OLE to pass the name of the file and the file's contents and display the file.

Shortcuts

Shortcuts are OLE objects. In this case, the container application is the shell, and the shortcut is a linked object that points to the original file. If you check out the `HKEY_CLASSES_ROOT\lnkfile` Registry key, you'll find a `CLSID` subkey that points to an in-process server (`SHELL32.DLL`) that handles the OLE details.

Similarly, shell scraps (bits of data dragged from a server application and dropped on the desktop) are objects that are embedded in the shell.

Shell Extensions

Windows 95 supports *shell extensions* as a method of extending the interface. For example, when you install Microsoft Plus!, it extends the shell by adding a Compression tab to the properties sheet for each disk drive. These shell extensions are OLE in-process servers that are defined by `shellex` Registry keys. For the Compression tab, you'd look in the following key:

```
HKEY_CLASSES_ROOT\Drive\shellex\PropertySheetHandlers\Compression
```

The default setting is a `CLSID` that points to the in-process server (`COMPEXT.DLL`) that uses OLE to extend the disk drive properties sheet.

Windows 95 uses a similar OLE mechanism to extend other aspects of the shell, including context menus, special-drag menus, icons, and more.

Working with OLE

After all that OLE theory, you're due for some hands-on techniques. To that end, I'll spend the rest of this chapter showing you how to put OLE to work creating compound documents. I'll run through several methods of both linking and embedding objects, I'll talk about editing those objects, and I'll show you how to maintain links.

Linking an Object

If you have data you'd like to share between applications, and you feel that linking is the best way to go, Windows 95 gives you two methods: linking via the Clipboard, and inserting a linked file. The next two sections discuss each method. Then I'll show you how to work with and maintain your links.

Linking via the Clipboard

You saw earlier in this chapter how to use the Clipboard's cut, copy, and paste methodology to transfer static data between applications. However, the Clipboard is no slouch when it comes to OLE data transfers. If the original application is an OLE server, a cut or copy operation passes not only the selected data to the Clipboard, but also formats such as Object Descriptor, Link Source, and Link Source Descriptor (see Table 17.3). A container application can use these formats to determine whether the object on the Clipboard can be linked, and to perform the actual linking.

Once you've placed the data on the Clipboard, switch to the container application and position the cursor where you want the data to be pasted. Now select the Edit | Paste Special command to display the Paste Special dialog box, shown in Figure 17.11.

FIGURE 17.11.

Use the Paste Special dialog box to paste Clipboard data as a linked object.

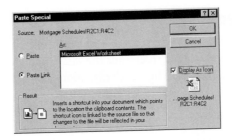

The As box lists the various formats available for the data, but you can ignore most of them. To establish a link between the container and the server, activate the Paste Link option. Usually, most of the formats will disappear, and you'll be left with only the object format. If you'd like the data to appear as an icon in the container document, activate the Display As Icon check box. When you're ready, click OK to paste the linked object into the container, as shown in Figure 17.12.

FIGURE 17.12.

A linked object displayed as an icon.

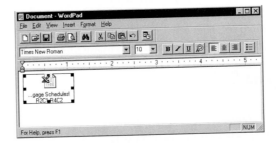

NOTE: LINKING VIA DRAG-AND-DROP

You'll see later that some OLE applications let you embed objects by dragging them from a server and dropping them on a container. In theory, you can use this method to create a linked object as well by holding down Ctrl-Shift as you drop the object. However, few applications currently support this feature.

Inserting a File as a Linked Object

Instead of pasting part of a document as a linked object, you might prefer to insert an entire file as a linked object. For example, if you insert a linked Excel worksheet into a Word document, the container object will reflect *any* changes made to the original worksheet, including data added or removed, global formatting adjustments, and so on.

Also, there are situations in which you have no choice but to insert a file. For example, you can't insert part of a bitmap as a linked object; instead, you have to insert the entire file.

Here are the basic steps to follow to insert a file as a linked object:

1. In the container application, position the cursor where you want the file inserted.

2. Depending on the application, select either Insert | Object or Edit | Insert Object.

3. Select `Create from File`. How you do this depends on the application. In the Microsoft Office 95 applications, for example, you select the Create from File tab, as shown in Figure 17.13. In WordPad, on the other hand, you activate the `Create from File` option button.

FIGURE 17.13.

The Object dialog box from Excel for Windows 95. You use the Create from File tab to insert a file object in the container.

4. Enter the filename of the file you want to link. You can also click the Browse button to choose the file from a dialog box.

5. Activate the `Link to File` check box. (In some dialog boxes, this option is named `Link`.)

6. If you want the linked file to appear as an icon, activate the `Display as Icon` check box.

7. Click OK to insert the linked file object.

Managing Links

All container applications that support object linking also give you some kind of method to manage document links. This involves updating a link so that the container displays the most recent changes, changing a link's source, determining how links are updated in the container, and breaking links you no longer need to maintain.

In most container applications, you manage links by selecting Edit | Links. You'll see a Links dialog box similar to the one shown in Figure 17.14 (this is the Links dialog box from WordPad). Here's a rundown of the basic link management chores you can perform:

Changing the link update method: By default, links are updated automatically. In other words, if both the source and the container are open, whenever the source data changes, the data in the container also changes. If you would prefer to update the container document by hand, highlight the link and activate the `Manual` option.

Updating the link: If you've set a link to Manual, or if the server document isn't open, you can make sure a link contains the latest and greatest information by highlighting it and clicking the Update Now button.

Changing the link source: If you move the source document, you'll need to modify the link so that it points to the new location. You can do this by highlighting the appropriate link and clicking the Change Source button.

Breaking a link: If you no longer want to maintain a link between the source and the container, you can break the link. This will leave the data intact, but changes made to the original data will no longer be reflected in the container. To break a link, highlight it and click the Break Link button.

FIGURE 17.14.

Container applications that support object linking have a Links dialog box that you can use to maintain the links.

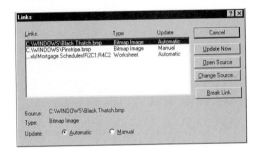

Embedding an Object

If you prefer to embed an object instead of linking it, Windows 95 gives you three or four methods to choose from (depending on the server application): the Clipboard, drag-and-drop, inserting a new embedded object, and inserting an embedded file.

Embedding Via the Clipboard

Assuming that the original application is an OLE server, a cut or copied object in the Clipboard includes not only link-related formats, but also a few formats that let a container application embed the data (such as the Embed Source format). Again, the container application can use these formats to perform the embedding.

To embed data that's been placed on the Clipboard, switch to the container application, position the cursor where you want the data to be pasted, and select Edit | Paste Special. In the Paste Special dialog box that appears, select the object format from the As list (this format should be highlighted by default) and make sure that the Paste option is activated. Also, if you'd like the data to appear as an icon in the container document, activate the Display As Icon check box. When you're ready, click OK to paste the embedded object into the container.

Embedding Via Drag-and-Drop

Server and container applications that support OLE 2 also support drag-and-drop embedding. This means you can select some data in the server document, drag the data with the mouse, and then drop it inside the container window. Most applications move the data from the source to the container, but this isn't universally true. To be sure that you're moving the data, hold down the Shift key while you drag-and-drop. If you'd prefer to copy the data, hold down Ctrl during the drag-and-drop.

TIP: DROPPING AN OBJECT ON A MINIMIZED WINDOW

Remember that you can't drop an object on a window that's been minimized. However, if you drag the object over the minimized window's taskbar button and then wait a second or two, the window will be restored automatically, and you can then drop the data inside the window.

Inserting a New Embedded Object

If the object you want to embed doesn't exist, and you don't need to create a separate file, OLE lets you insert the new object directly into the container application. Here's how it works:

1. In the container application, move the cursor to where you want the new object to appear.

2. Depending on the application, select either Insert | Object or Edit | Insert Object. In either case, you'll see a dialog box similar to the one shown in Figure 17.15.

FIGURE 17.15.

Use this dialog box to select the type of embedded object you want to create.

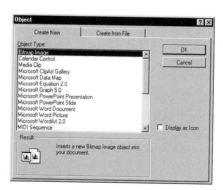

3. The Object Type list displays all the available objects on your system. (Recall that Windows 95 generates this list by looking for all the Registry entries in HKEY_CLASSES_ROOT that have an Insertable subkey.) Highlight the type of object you want to create.

4. Click OK. Windows 95 starts the server application for the object type you selected. The server will either appear in-place or in a separate window.

5. Create the object you want to embed.

6. Exit the server application. If you were working with the server using visual editing, click outside the object. Otherwise, select File | Exit & Return to *document,* where *document* is the name of the active document in the container application.

Inserting an Embedded File

You can insert an entire existing file (as opposed to an object within a file) as an embedded object. This is useful if you want to make changes to the file from within the container without disturbing the original. Follow these steps:

1. In the container document, position the cursor where you want to embed the object.

2. Depending on the application, select either Insert | Object or Edit | Insert Object.

3. Select `Create from File`. How you do this depends on the application. In the Microsoft Office 95 applications, for example, you select the Create from File tab. In WordPad, on the other hand, you activate the `Create from File` option button.

4. Enter the filename of the file you want to embed. You can also click the Browse button to choose the file from a dialog box.

5. If you want the linked file to appear as an icon, activate the `Display as Icon` check box.

6. Click OK to insert the linked file object.

Editing a Linked or Embedded Object

If you need to make some changes to a linked or embedded object, you can use the container application to launch the server application and load the object automatically. (Remember, too, that for a linked object you can always run the server application and work with the object directly.) How you do this depends on the application, but here are a few methods that work for most OLE containers:

■ Double-click the object.

■ Select the object, pull down the Edit menu, and then select either Linked *ObjectType* Object (for a linked object) or *ObjectType* Object (for an embedded object). In both cases, *ObjectType* is the type of object you selected (for example, Bitmap Image or Worksheet). From the cascade menu that appears, select Edit. If the server application supports visual editing, this will launch the object in-place.

■ Select the object, pull down the Edit menu, and then select either the Linked *ObjectType* Object command (for a linked object) or the *ObjectType* Object command (for an embedded object). In the cascade menu that appears, select Open. For servers that support the `Open` verb, this will launch the object in a separate window.

■ Right-click the object, select either Linked *ObjectType* Object or *ObjectType* Object, and select either Edit or Open.

NOTE: EDIT ISN'T ALWAYS THE DEFAULT VERB

Sometimes, when you double-click an object (such as a sound file or a video file), Windows 95 will play the object instead of editing it. In this case, you can edit the object only by using the appropriate Edit command.

Summary

This chapter showed you how to share data in Windows 95. We began with the Clipboard. I showed you how the Clipboard works; how to cut, copy, and paste data between Windows applications; and how to share data between DOS and Windows programs. I also gave you a quick tour of the Clipboard Viewer. We then turned our attention to OLE. I gave you an extensive look at OLE theory—including compound documents, objects, linking, embedding, and the Component Object Model—and then I showed you how to put OLE to good use in your applications.

Here's a list of chapters where you'll find related information:

- ■ You're using OLE when you cut, copy, and paste files, and when you create shortcuts. I showed you how to do all these things in Chapter 5, "Windows 95: The 50¢ Tour," and Chapter 13, "Working with Files and Folders."

- ■ To refresh your memory on some Registry basics, head for Chapter 11, "Introducing the Windows 95 Registry."

- ■ I showed you how to work with the DOS window in Chapter 21, "DOS Isn't Dead: Optimizing DOS Applications Under Windows 95."

- ■ Microsoft Exchange is an OLE container application, which means that you can add all kinds of goodies to your e-mail messages. I'll show you how in Chapter 28, "Exchanging E-Mail with Microsoft Exchange."

17

THE CLIPBOARD
AND OLE

Using Fonts in Windows 95

IN THIS CHAPTER

Letterforms conceal arbitrarily deep mysteries.

—*Douglas Hofstadter*

Windows has turned many otherwise-ordinary citizens into avid amateur typographers. People at cocktail parties the world over are debating the relative merits of serif versus sans serif fonts, expounding the virtues of typefaces with names like Desdemona and Braggadocio, and generally just byte-bonding over this whole font foofaraw.

OK, so most of us don't take fonts to that extreme. However, we certainly appreciate what they do to jazz up our reports, spreadsheets, and graphics. There's nothing like a well-chosen font to add just the right tone to a document and to make our work stand out from the herd.

This chapter shows you how Windows 95 and fonts work together. You'll learn just what fonts are and how Windows 95 sees them, and then you'll learn a few techniques for dealing with the fonts on your system.

Fontamentals, Part I: The Architecture of Characters

Back in the days when DOS dinosaurs dominated the PC landscape, people rarely had to pay much attention to the characters that made up correspondence and memos. Outside of a measly few effects (such as making words bold), there wasn't a whole lot you could do with individual letters and symbols, so they became mere foot soldiers in any given war of words.

The advent of the graphical interface changed all that, however. With Windows, it suddenly became a snap to alter the size and shape of letters and numbers and therefore impart an entirely different atmosphere to writings. The engine behind this newfound typographical prowess was, of course, the *font*.

I always like to describe fonts as the "architecture" of characters. When you examine a building, certain features and patterns help you identify the building's architectural style. A flying buttress, for example, is usually a telltale sign of a Gothic structure. Fonts, too, are distinguished by a unique set of characteristics. Specifically, four items define the architecture of any character: the typeface, the type size, the type style, and the character spacing.

Typeface

A *typeface* is a distinctive design that is common to any related set of letters, numbers, and symbols. This design gives each character a particular shape and thickness (or *weight*, as it's called in type circles) that is unique to the typeface and difficult to classify. However, three main categories serve to distinguish all typefaces: serif, sans serif, and decorative.

A *serif* typeface contains fine cross strokes (called *feet*) at the extremities of each character. These subtle appendages give the typeface a traditional, classy look that's most often used for long stretches of text. In Windows 95, Times New Roman is an example of a serif typeface.

A *sans serif* typeface doesn't contain these cross strokes. As a result, sans serif typefaces usually have a cleaner, more modern look that works best for headings and titles. Arial is an example of a sans serif font that comes with Windows 95.

Decorative typefaces are usually special designs that are supposed to convey a particular effect. So, for example, if your document needs a fancy, handwritten effect, something like Brush Script would be perfect. (Unfortunately, the Brush Script typeface doesn't come with Windows 95. However, lots of companies sell font collections that include all kinds of strange and useful fonts. Expect to pay about a dollar a font.)

Figure 18.1 shows examples of a few typefaces. As you can see, they can produce wildly different effects.

FIGURE 18.1.

Some sample typefaces in WordPad.

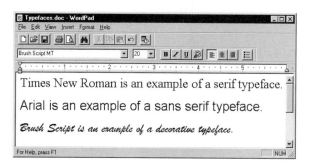

18

USING FONTS IN WINDOWS 95

Type Size

The *type size* measures how tall a font is. The standard unit of measurement is the *point;* there are 72 points in an inch. So, for example, the letters in a 24-point font would be twice as tall as those in a 12-point font. Technically, type size is measured from the highest point of a tall letter, such as "f," to the lowest point of an underhanging letter, such as "g." (In case you're wondering, this book is laid out in a 10.5-point AGaramond font.)

Type Style

The *type style* of a font refers to extra attributes added to the typeface, such as **bold** and *italic*. Other type styles (often called type *effects*) include underlining and ~~strikeout~~ (sometimes called *strikethrough*). These styles are normally used to highlight or add emphasis to sections of your documents.

Character Spacing

The *character spacing* of a font can take two forms: *monospaced* or *proportional*. Monospaced fonts reserve the same amount of space for each character. For example, look at the Courier New font shown in Figure 18.2. Notice how skinny letters such as "i" and "l" take up as much space as wider letters such as "m" and "w." While this is admirably egalitarian, these fonts tend to look like they were produced with a typewriter (in other words, they're *ugly*).

FIGURE 18.2.

Monospaced versus proportional.

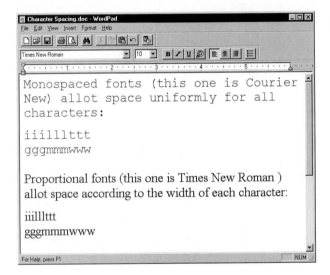

By contrast, in a proportional font, such as the Times New Roman font shown in Figure 18.2, the space allotted to each letter varies according to the width of the letter. This gives the text a more natural feel.

Fontamentals, Part II: Screen Fonts Versus Printer Fonts

Windows 95 also characterizes fonts by their intended output device: the screen or the printer:

- *Screen fonts* are designed to represent characters on a display screen only.
- *Printer fonts* are used by the printer to generate the characters that will appear on the printed page. Windows 95 can work with three kinds of printer fonts:

  Device fonts, which are generated by the printer hardware

  Downloadable soft fonts, which are sent to the printer during a print job

  Printable screen fonts, which can be rendered both on-screen and on the printer

With some applications, the Font dialog box identifies printer fonts by putting a printer icon beside the name, as shown in Figure 18.3. Fonts shown with the "double-T" symbol are TrueType fonts, which are printable screen fonts. I'll discuss TrueType fonts in depth later in this chapter.

FIGURE 18.3.

Printer fonts are often shown with a printer icon. TrueType fonts are printable screen fonts.

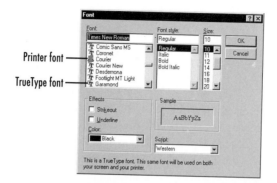

Printer font ———

TrueType font ———

NOTE: FONT VERSUS TYPEFACE

In Windows 95, the words *typeface* and *font* are often used interchangeably. In the Font dialog box shown in Figure 18.3, for example, the Font list should really be called the Typeface list.

Fontamentals, Part III: The Font-Rendering Mechanism

Windows 95 also categorizes fonts according to how they're rendered on-screen or on the printer. Windows 95 can work with three different font-rendering mechanisms: raster, vector, and TrueType.

Raster Fonts

With *raster fonts*, each character is represented by a bitmap pattern, something like the one shown in Figure 18.4. These simple patterns are easy to manipulate, so Windows 95 can display and print raster fonts quickly. Windows ships with five raster fonts: Courier, MS Sans Serif, MS Serif, Small Fonts, and Symbol. You can also get raster fonts by purchasing third-party products such as Adobe Type Manager, Bitstream FaceLift, and Hewlett-Packard Type Director.

Raster fonts are stored in files as graphic images (or *bitmaps,* which is why they're are also called *bitmapped fonts*). These files contain everything the system needs to know about the font (what styles it can display, what sizes are available, and so on). However, to show even a single character from the font, Windows 95 must load the entire file into memory.

The available representations of a given raster font are set in stone according to what's in the font file. You get only a fixed number of font sizes (for example, 8-, 10-, 12-, and 14-point) for each output device (display or printer). You can try a different size, but it must be a multiple of one of the supplied sizes (for example, 16-, 20-, or 24-point), and the resulting text usually suffers from excessive jagged lines (or "jaggies").

For each raster font, Windows 95 provides two display varieties: VGA and 8514. Each variety is identified by a letter appended to the font's filename. The VGA raster fonts have an E tacked on, so their filenames are COURE.FON, SSERIFE.FON, SERIFE.FON, SMALLE.FON, and SYMBOLE.FON. For 8514 raster fonts, the filenames have an F: COURF.FON, SSERIFF.FON, SERIFF.FON, SMALLF.FON, and SYMBOLF.FON. (You'll find these files in the Fonts subfolder of your main Windows 95 folder.)

Vector Fonts

Vector fonts are created from GDI (Graphical Device Interface) functions that define an outline for each character (which is then filled in with whatever the current text color is). The big advantage of vector fonts is that they can be scaled at will to different sizes, because all Windows has to do is adjust the GDI parameters. (So these are also called *scalable* fonts.) This also saves memory, because you don't have to keep the full font family loaded. Vector fonts do have their downside, though:

- The complexity of the GDI calls tends to slow things down a tad.
- You need separate fonts for your screen and printer.
- The character outlines tend to break down at smaller font sizes (anything smaller than 14 points or so) and thus become virtually unreadable.

Windows 95 dropped a couple of vector fonts from Windows 3.x and thus comes with just one example of the species: Modern.

TrueType Fonts

TrueType fonts use a newer, more sophisticated outline technology. Instead of a few hard-wired equations, TrueType fonts are displayed using a full-fledged *font management program* (called TrueType, which is where the fonts get their name). This program can produce great-looking characters at any size. For example, check out the differences between the three font types shown in Figure 18.5. The raster font (Courier) looks good in 10-point type, but it's downright hideous at 72 points. The vector font (Modern) is barely legible at the smaller size, but it looks okay scaled up to 72 points. The TrueType font (Times New Roman) passes with flying colors by looking good at both sizes.

FIGURE 18.5.

Raster, vector, and TrueType fonts compared at 10-point and 72-point sizes.

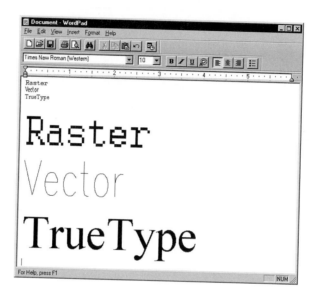

The reason TrueType fonts look good at all type sizes (even rotated) is that they're shapes that are described by their outlines. Instead of being composed of bitmaps (like raster fonts) or lines (like vector fonts), TrueType fonts consist of a series of contours.

But truly scalable characters are by no means the only advantage TrueType brings to the table:

- ■ TrueType uses the same fonts for both the screen and the printer. This makes your characters truly WYSIWYG (What You See Is What You Get).

- ■ TrueType fonts use less disk space because, for each font, you need only a single TTF file for every size, resolution, and output device.

- ■ TrueType fonts will print on any printer—laser or dot-matrix—that Windows supports. Other fonts are often printer-specific, so if you switch printers, you have to switch fonts.

- ■ Many companies have put together collections of TrueType fonts that can be had for just a few cents a font.

- ■ TrueType doesn't cost a dime, because everything you need is built right into Windows 95.

18

USING FONTS IN WINDOWS 95

Windows comes with five TrueType font families: Arial, Courier New, Symbol, Times New Roman, and Wingding. Table 18.1 lists the filenames you'll find in each font family.

Table 18.1. Windows 95's TrueType font families.

Font Name	Normal	Bold	Bold/Italic	Italic
Arial	ARIAL.TTF	ARIALBD.TTF	ARIALBI.TTF	ARIALI.TTF
Courier New	COUR.TTF	COURBD.TTF	COURBI.TTF	COURI.TTF
Symbol	SYMBOL.TTF	N/A	N/A	N/A
Times New Roman	TIMES.TTF	TIMESBD.TTF	TIMESBI.TTF	TIMESI.TTF
Wingding	WINGDING.TTF	N/A	N/A	N/A

For comparison, Table 18.2 shows you which types of fonts can be used with the four main varieties of printers.

Table 18.2. Font types that can be used with different printers.

Type of Printer	Raster Fonts	Vector Fonts	TrueType Fonts
Dot matrix	Yes	No	Yes
Hewlett-Packard laser	No	Yes	Yes
PostScript	No	Yes	Yes
Plotter	No	Yes	No

Other Windows 95 Fonts

The Windows 95 user interface is mostly based on TrueType fonts, but four other fonts enter into the mix: System, Fixed, OEM (or Terminal), and DOS:

■ *System* is a proportional font used by default to draw menus, dialog box controls, and other text in Windows 95. Its font files are VGASYS.FON and 8514SYS.FON.

■ *Fixed* is a fixed-width font used in Windows 2.x and earlier versions as the system font (for menus and dialog boxes). Its font files are VGAFIX.FON and 8514FIX.FON.

■ *OEM font* (which is also known as the *Terminal font*) is a fixed-width font used in various applications (such as the Clipboard). The OEM font also provides an OEM character set used by some Windows applications. Its font files are VGAOEM.FON and 8514.FON.

■ *DOS fonts* are used for displaying DOS programs. Their font files are CGA40WOA.FON, CGA80WOA.FON, and DOSAPP.FON.

Working with Fonts

Windows 95 makes it easy to work with the fonts on your system. Using a special `Fonts` folder, you can view individual fonts, add new fonts, and remove fonts. Windows 95 gives you two main methods of getting to the `Fonts` folder:

■ In Explorer, highlight the `Fonts` subfolder of your main Windows 95 folder, as shown in Figure 18.6.

FIGURE 18.6.

You can work with the Fonts *folder either from Explorer...*

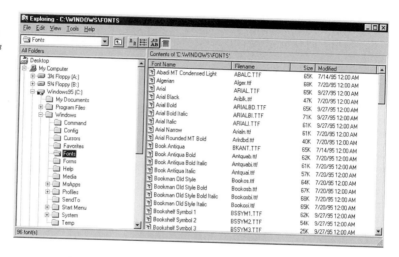

■ In Control Panel, open the Fonts icon to display the folder window shown in Figure 18.7.

FIGURE 18.7.

...or by opening Control Panel's Fonts icon.

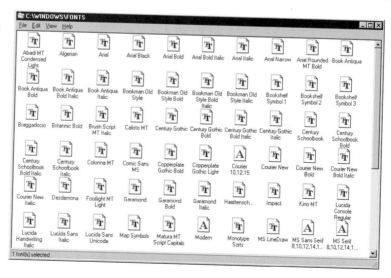

18

USING FONTS IN WINDOWS 95

Opening a Font

The Font dialog box in most applications gives you a sneak preview of what a particular combination of typeface, type style, and type size will look like. However, it's not particularly convenient to continually select all these options, and the little preview screens show you only a few characters. A much easier way to see how a particular font looks is to open a font file directly from the Fonts folder. You can use any of the following methods:

- Double-click a font file.
- Highlight a font file and select File | Open.
- Right-click a font file and select Open from the context menu.

Whichever method you use, the Font Viewer application (FONTVIEW.EXE) runs and loads the font, as shown in Figure 18.8. The window displays a few font facts (such as the file size and version), shows you how each letter, each number, and a few symbols are represented in the font, and displays the font at various type sizes. If you'd like a printout of the window, click the Print button. When you're finished, click Done to return to the Fonts folder.

FIGURE 18.8.

When you open a font, the Font Viewer displays various bits of font info and a few font examples at different type sizes.

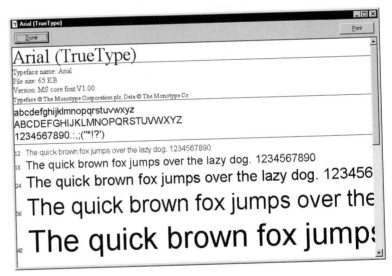

Changing the Fonts Folder View

If you have lots of fonts installed on your system, the Fonts folder will be jammed with tons of TTF and FON files. To help you manage this mess, Windows 95 offers two useful methods to filter the Fonts folder:

View | List Fonts By Similarity: This command displays the fonts according to how similar they are to a specified font. When you select this command (or click the Similarity button on the toolbar), the window changes as shown in Figure 18.9. Use the List fonts by similarity to drop-down list to select the comparison font. The Similarity to column tells you whether the other fonts are Very similar, Fairly similar, or Not similar.

FIGURE 18.9.

You can use the Fonts *folder to list the fonts according to how similar they are to a given font.*

Similarity

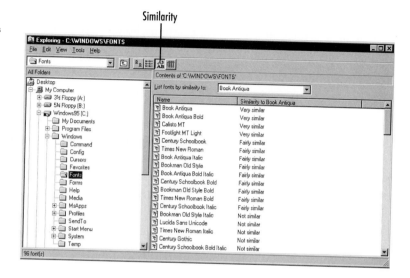

View | Hide Variations: If you select this command, Windows 95 shows only the main font file. The variations (bold, italic, bold italic, and so on) are removed from the view to simplify things, as shown in Figure 18.10.

FIGURE 18.10.

Select View | Hide Variations to simplify the Fonts *folder by removing the font variations.*

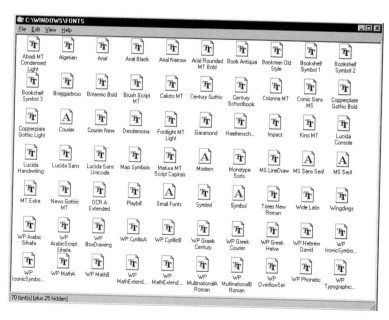

Adding New Fonts to Windows 95

As I mentioned earlier, there are all kinds of TrueType font collections on the market nowadays. If you're feeling cramped by the paltry selection that comes with Windows 95, perhaps one of these packages can provide just the right typeface to give your documents that certain *je ne sais quoi*. Before you can use your new fonts, however, you need to add them to Windows 95. The following steps show you how it's done:

1. Display the Fonts folder.
2. Select File | Install New Font. The Add Fonts dialog box, shown in Figure 18.11, appears.

FIGURE 18.11.

Use the Add Fonts dialog box to select the new fonts you want to add to your system.

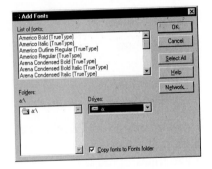

3. Insert the disk containing the font files, and then select the appropriate disk drive from the Drives list. (If the font files are in a different folder, use the Folders list to select the appropriate location.) Windows reads the font names from the disk and displays them in the List of fonts box.

4. Use the List of fonts box to highlight the fonts you want to install. Alternatively, you can install all the fonts on the disk by clicking the Select All button.

5. Windows 95 normally likes to see the font files copied to the Fonts folder. So, in most cases, you should make sure the Copy fonts to Fonts folder check box is activated. There are three exceptions to this rule:

   - If hard disk space is at a premium and the font files already exist elsewhere on the hard disk. In this case, there isn't much point in creating an extra copy of each file.
   - If you're loading the font files from a network drive.
   - If you're loading the font files from a CD-ROM drive. CD-ROMs can have tens (if not hundreds) of megabytes of fonts, so it's usually impractical to load all this chaff onto your hard disk.

6. Click OK. Windows 95 installs the fonts. If you elected not to copy the fonts to the Fonts folder, Windows 95 creates shortcuts to the original files instead.

NOTE: EMBEDDING FONTS

You might have problems sending files that use third-party fonts to other people because they won't have the proper font files on their system. The result is usually a mess as Windows tries to convert the fonts into something like Courier. To avoid this, you either need to stick with the standard fonts that come with Windows 95 or send the font files with your document (along with a note telling the recipient that he needs to install the fonts; he'll be very pleased, I'm sure).

Some applications (such as Microsoft PowerPoint and Microsoft Word for Windows) let you *embed* fonts in your documents. Embedded fonts let the other person view the file properly without having to clutter his hard drive with your fancy fonts. Over the next year or so, you'll likely see this feature included in most mainstream Windows applications.

Deleting Old Fonts

Although TrueType fonts take up considerably less disk space than the other font types, you're still looking at anywhere from 30 KB to 80 KB per font file. If you have hundreds of fonts, the numbers can add up to a big chunk of hard disk acreage in a hurry. Also, all your installed fonts take up memory, whether you use them or not.

To keep a lid on both hard disk and memory usage, you should periodically clean out those font files you never use. To do this, just delete the appropriate font files from the Fonts folder.

TIP: DISABLING OLD FONTS

If you'd like to keep your old fonts around but not have them load when you start Windows 95, just move them to another folder. Windows 95 will remove the fonts from the Registry, so they won't load in the future.

Font Tips

Windows makes it easy to add unique and eye-catching fonts to all your documents. However, some restraint is called for here. Nothing looks worse than—or is as confusing as—a document with too many fonts crammed together on one page. This is known in the trade as the *ransom note look*.

Here are a few things to keep in mind when performing your font formatting chores:

- Try to restrict your fonts to no more than a couple per document. If you need various looks, use larger sizes or different styles of the same fonts.

- A good font combination is a sans serif font for titles and headings and a serif font for the document's main body text (which, you'll notice, is the combination used in this book).

- If you need to emphasize something, bold or italicize it in the *same* typeface as the surrounding text. Avoid using underlining for emphasis.

- Use larger sizes only for titles and headings. Also, avoid using anything smaller than 10 points; text that small is just too difficult to make out.

- Avoid using decorative or excessively narrow fonts for large sections of text. They're almost always hard on the eyes after a half dozen words or so.

Using Character Map for Extra Symbols and Characters

A given typeface covers not only the letters, numbers, and symbols you can see on your keyboard, but dozens of others as well. For example, were you stumped the last time you wanted to write "Dag Hammarskjöld" because you didn't know how to get an ö character? I thought so. Well, Windows 95 gives you an easy way to get not only an ö, but a whole universe of interesting symbols.

It all begins with one of the accessories that comes with Windows 95: Character Map. To check it out, select Start | Programs | Accessories | Character Map. You'll see the Character Map window, shown in Figure 18.12.

FIGURE 18.12.

The Character Map window gives you access to the full spectrum of Windows 95 characters.

The layout is pretty simple: the squares show you all the symbols available for whatever typeface is displayed in the Font drop-down list. If you select a different typeface, a whole new set of symbols is displayed. (Wingdings, in particular, has many interesting symbols, including astrological signs, currency symbols, and even clock faces.)

To use a symbol from Character Map in an application, you first select the symbol you want by using either of the following methods:

■ Double-click the symbol.

■ Highlight the symbol and click Select or press Enter.

The symbol will appear in the Characters to copy box. Feel free to select multiple characters if you like.

When you're ready, click the Copy button to copy the character (or characters) to the Clipboard. Finally, return to your application, position the cursor where you want the character to appear, and select Edit | Paste.

NOTE: MULTILINGUAL FONTS

Don't forget that you can access a number of language fonts (such as Cyrillic) by installing Windows 95's Multilanguage Support. I showed you how to do this in Chapter 7, "Customizing Windows 95."

Font Limitations

When you install a font, Windows 95 adds that font to the GDI and to the following Registry key:

```
HKEY_LOCAL_MACHINE\SOFTWARE\Microsoft\Windows\CurrentVersion\Fonts
```

Unfortunately, this puts certain restrictions on how many fonts you can install:

■ The GDI reserves about 10 KB for font filenames. This means that if font filenames average about 10 characters (including the period and extension), you won't be able to add any more than about 1,000 fonts to the GDI.

■ The Fonts subkey in the Registry stores both the font name and the font filename. Unfortunately, Registry keys are limited to 64 KB. This means that if your fonts average 40 or 45 characters for their names and 10 characters for their filenames, you won't be able to cram much more than about 1,000 fonts into the key.

So, all in all, your system is restricted to about 1,000 total fonts.

Troubleshooting Fonts

Fonts, especially TrueType fonts, are a proven technology, so their implementation is fairly straightforward. However, a few things can go wrong. This section discusses a few of the most common problems and offers some solutions.

Your Font dialog boxes show only TrueType fonts, despite the fact that you have other kinds of fonts installed on your system.

If you don't see any other kinds of fonts in your Font dialog boxes, this means that Windows 95 has been set up to show only TrueType fonts. To remedy this, display the Fonts folder, select View | Options, and head for the TrueType tab, shown in Figure 18.13. Deactivate the Show only TrueType fonts in the programs on my computer check box, and then click OK. When Windows 95 asks if you want to restart your computer, click Yes.

FIGURE 18.13.

The TrueType tab determines whether or not your Font dialogs show only TrueType fonts.

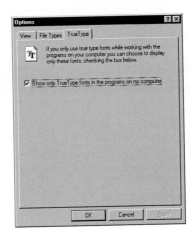

You don't see any information on your PostScript fonts in the Registry.

PostScript fonts are installed by Setup programs just as they were in earlier versions of Windows. Therefore, you'll still find data on PostScript fonts in WIN.INI.

After you upgrade to Windows 95, the TrueType fonts you installed in Windows 3.x don't appear in the Fonts folder. Alternatively, if you try to add a TrueType font, the font seems to be installed correctly but doesn't appear in the Fonts folder. Or, you receive the following error message:

```
The fontname TrueType font is already installed. To install a new version, first
remove the old version.
```

This behavior can occur if the Registry's Fonts key is missing or damaged. To resolve this problem, either delete the existing Fonts key and then add it back in, or add the Fonts key if it doesn't already exist. Restart your computer. Windows 95 will rebuild the font list based on the font files that exist in the Fonts folder.

After you upgrade, only Windows 95's default fonts are shown in the Fonts folder, despite the fact that you installed many extra fonts under Windows 3.x.

If you upgrade a version of Windows that has more than 1,000 TrueType fonts installed, only the default fonts are displayed in the Fonts folder. Use the procedure just mentioned to delete and reinstate the Fonts key in the Registry.

The Fonts folder is missing several menu commands, including File I Open, File I Print, File I Install New Font, View I List Fonts By Similarity, and View I Hide Variations.

This problem likely means that the Fonts folder's System attribute has been turned off. To reinstate this attribute, open a DOS window, make sure you're in your main Windows 95 folder, and then enter the following command:

```
attrib +s fonts
```

Close the DOS window and restart your computer.

You can can't change the font in a DOS window while running a DOS program.

This problem is probably caused by the DOS program. If the program is running in graphics mode, you won't be able to change the DOS window's font because the program manages the font directly. If you really need to change the font, switch the DOS program to text mode if possible.

When you attempt to add a TrueType font, you receive the following error message:

```
Unable to install the fontname (TrueType) font. The font file may be damaged.
```

This error means that one of two things has happened:

- The font file you're trying to install is corrupted. In this case, you'll need to contact the vendor for a replacement.
- Windows 95 has reached its font limit, as described earlier. In this case, you'll need to delete some existing fonts before you can add more.

After installing Adobe Type Manager (ATM) to the Fonts folder, you receive the following error message when you start the ATM Control Panel:

```
Invalid Fonts Directory
```

As you've seen, the Fonts folder, with its extra commands and views, isn't your average folder. In particular, Fonts has its System attribute set, which means that although ATM can install into Fonts, it doesn't function correctly from this folder.

The solution is to use either of the following methods:

- Create a new folder for the ATM fonts and then move the ATM fonts from the Fonts folder to the new folder. Be sure to edit the ATM.INI file in your main Windows 95 folder and change the path for the ATM fonts to reflect the new folder.
- Remove the ATM fonts from the Fonts folder, remove the ATM.INI file from your main Windows 95 folder, and then reinstall ATM. This time, however, choose a folder other than the Fonts folder for the installation.

Summary

This chapter looked at how Windows 95 works with fonts. You began by learning some font fundamentals, including the three main classification schemes for fonts: "architectural" (typeface, type size, type style, and character spacing), output device (screen or printer), and font-rendering mechanism (raster, vector, or TrueType.) I then showed you how to view and open font files, install new fonts, delete old fonts, and troubleshoot some font woes. I even threw in some info about the Character Map accessory for good measure. For more font-related information, check out the following chapters:

- I showed you how to work with keyboard layouts and Windows 95's Multilanguage support in Chapter 7, "Customizing Windows 95."

- Chapter 7 is also the place to learn how to change the system fonts—the fonts used in the Windows 95 interface.

- If you need some background on the Registry, try Chapter 11, "Introducing the Windows 95 Registry."

- Fonts and printing are closely related. I'll discuss printing in Chapter 19, "Prescriptions for Perfect Printing."

- You learned how to adjust the DOS window font in Chapter 21, "DOS Isn't Dead: Optimizing DOS Applications Under Windows 95."

CHAPTER 19

Prescriptions for Perfect Printing

IN THIS CHAPTER

The moment a man sets his thoughts down on paper, however secretly, he is in a sense writing for publication.

—*Raymond Chandler*

Remember when all this high-falutin' computer technology was supposed to result in the proverbial "paperless office" of tomorrow? Clearly, tomorrow never came. If anything, we're awash in more paper than ever since computers took over. It's just like all the other pipe dreams from those "here's-what-the-future-will-bring" flicks from the '50s. By the time the '90s roll around, they assured us, we'll all have endless leisure hours to spend rocketing around in flying cars. As someone once said, we always overestimate change in the long term and underestimate it in the short term.

I suspect one of the reasons for this plenitude of paper is that we all have a real need for hard copy. For one thing, it just feels good to create something tangible, something we can literally get our hands on. For another, I don't think we trust our computers fully. Electronic files, with their unfortunate tendency to get wiped out by the merest power surge or an accidental press of a Delete key, seem so fragile. Printouts, on the other hand, seem heartier and, well, *safer*.

So I say if we're going to be printing fools, we might as well be wise printing fools. Happily, as this chapter will show you, such wisdom is fairly easy to come by thanks to Windows 95's easy and consistent approach to printing. You'll begin with some printing basics, and then you'll graduate to some intermediate and advanced techniques that will help you unleash Windows 95 printing.

Understanding the Windows 95 Printing Subsystem

The Windows 95 Graphical Device Interface (GDI) includes a 32-bit printing subsystem. This subsystem is completely revamped from Windows 3.x to add new features and improve performance, through both smoother background printing and faster return-to-application time. The next few sections run through these new printing subsystem features.

Spooling Enhanced Metafiles

Printing is a notoriously slow business. It's not that unusual for even small documents to take a few minutes to wend their way through your printer. And large documents with lots of graphics can seem to take forever. To prevent users from wearing out their thumbs from excess twiddling while documents print, Windows 95 performs a nifty trick. When you print a document, the printing subsystem first makes a temporary copy of the file (this is called *spooling* the file) and then hands control back to the application. This lets you keep working while Windows 95 prints the copy in the background.

Windows 3.x also spooled print jobs, but the copy it created contained raw printer data. Windows 95 spools to files that use the *enhanced metafile* (EMF) format. These files are generated by the GDI and include instructions about how the document should be printed. After the EMF file is created, the printing subsystem hands control back to the application. The GDI can create these EMF files quickly, so your return-to-application time is much faster than it was in Windows 3.x. (Depending on the file, it could be as much as twice as fast.)

While you continue working, the spooler starts feeding the data to the printer driver. This processing should in no way affect the performance of your applications, because the printing subsystem uses a 32-bit background thread. In Windows 3.x, in contrast, you had to make a trade-off between printing speed and application performance.

Printer Drivers

When I gave you an overview of Windows 95's hardware features in Chapter 10, "How Windows 95 Handles Hardware," I told you about the universal driver/mini-driver model for device support. In this model, Windows 95 supplies a "universal driver" that incorporates the code necessary for the devices in a particular hardware class to work with the appropriate operating system component. This universal driver is then augmented with smaller, simpler *mini-drivers* that provide the commands and routines necessary to operate a specific device.

This universal driver/mini-driver model originated in Windows 3.x's printing system, so it should come as no surprise that Windows 95 printing also uses this model. The universal driver (UNIDRV.DLL) provides the basic support for the printing subsystem, so all each printer manufacturer needs to do is create a mini-driver that implements the printer-specific functionality. This mini-driver acts as a go-between for the printer and the Windows 95 printing subsystem.

NOTE: MAKE SURE YOU HAVE THE LATEST DRIVER

To get the most out of printing, make sure you have Windows 95-specific drivers for your printer. Windows 95 supports hundreds of printers, so it should have a driver that meets your needs. If not, be sure to contact the manufacturer and ask for an updated driver.

Deferred Printing

The new Windows 95 printing subsystem also supports *deferred printing*. This means that you can run a print job even if your printer isn't available. This is handy, for example, if you normally print to a network printer that isn't available, or if you have an undocked notebook computer that prints from a docking station.

With deferred printing, you print your document normally. Windows 95 will spool the file, place each print job in a queue, and take no further action. Then, when your network printer becomes available or you dock your notebook, the print jobs waiting in the queue can be sent to the printer without your opening the original application. I'll show you how to set up deferred printing later in this chapter.

Support for the Extended Capabilities Port

An Extended Capabilities Port (ECP) is, essentially, a parallel port on steroids. Supported by Windows 95 and now included in many new systems, an ECP provides support for high-speed printing; new devices that use parallel ports, such as CD-ROMs and modems; and *bidirectional printing*.

Bidirectional printing means that not only can Windows 95 send data to the printer, but the printer can send data to Windows 95. So, for example, the printer could let Windows 95 know its configuration (say, how much memory it has installed), and it could keep the operating system informed of the current printer status (for example, out of paper). In order for you to use bidirectional printing, your printer must be attached to your computer (it won't work over a network), both your printer and your cable must support the bidirectional standard (IEEE 1284), and you must have a bidirectional printer driver. Here's a list of the Windows 95 printer drivers that support bidirectional printing:

Apple LaserWriter Pro 810

Apple LaserWriter Pro 810 with fax card

Digital DEClaser 5100

HP DesignJet 650C

HP DeskJet 1200C/PS

HP LaserJet 4

HP LaserJet 4 Plus

HP LaserJet 4L

HP LaserJet 4M

HP LaserJet 4M Plus

HP LaserJet 4ML

HP LaserJet 4MP

HP LaserJet 4MV

HP LaserJet 4P

HP LaserJet 4Si

HP LaserJet 4Si MX

HP LaserJet 4Si/4SiMX PS 300dpi

HP LaserJet 4Si/4SiMX PS 600dpi

HP LaserJet 4V

HP LaserJet 5MP

HP LaserJet 5P

HP PaintJet XL300

IBM 4039 LaserPrinter Plus

TI MicroLaser Pro 600 2013 PS23

TI MicroLaser Pro 600 2013 PS65

Improved DOS Printing

The Windows 95 printing subsystem can also work with DOS programs. Specifically, Windows 95 will spool print jobs that originate from any DOS program (although it won't spool these print jobs to EMF files). This improves the speed of DOS printing (since these print jobs spool in the background) and ensures that you won't run into conflicts if you try to print from a DOS application and a Windows application at the same time.

Most DOS programs should have no problem printing under Windows 95. However, if you do run into difficulties, you can always turn off spooling for DOS print jobs (as explained in the section "Troubleshooting Windows 95 Printing" near the end of this chapter).

Point and Print

The Windows 95 printing subsystem supports *Point and Print*. This feature lets you install printer drivers automatically simply by browsing a network printer. In this case, the printing subsystem uses the configuration that exists on the network computer to configure the printer on your machine. All the necessary files are copied from the network resource, so you don't even need your Windows 95 source disks. This feature is supported by networked Windows 95 clients and Windows NT or NetWare servers. I'll explain Point and Print in more detail in Chapter 31, "Windows 95 Networking."

Installing a Printer with the Add Printer Wizard

Windows 95 is the control freak of the computer world. It has to know absolutely *everything* about your machine and whatever peripherals—especially printers—are along for the ride. This isn't a bad thing, though, because it actually makes your life easier. How? Well, for example, in the anarchic world of DOS, every program has its own particular printing agenda. Although there's nothing wrong with such digital individualism, the downside is that you have to perform the rigmarole of setting up your printer for every DOS program.

Windows 95, though, is different, because it performs the printing drudgery itself. As a result, you only have to tell Windows what kind of printer you have, and then you're in business. Windows applications handle print jobs by simply passing the buck to the printing subsystem, so there's no need to perform separate printer setups for all your programs.

As with any device, you need to install a driver in order to get Windows 95 to print properly. If you didn't do this during the Windows 95 installation, or if you have a new printer to set up, you can use the `Printers` folder to do it from the desktop. Here are the steps you need to follow:

1. Select Start | Settings | Printers to open the Printers folder. (You can also open the Printers folder by double-clicking the Printers icon in Control Panel.)

2. Open the Add Printer icon to start the Add Printer Wizard.

3. Click Next >.

4. If your computer is on a network, the Wizard will ask if you want to set up a local printer or a network printer. Choose the appropriate option and click Next >.

5. If you chose the Network printer option, the Wizard will prompt you to enter a network path. Enter the appropriate UNC path, or use the Browse button to choose the printer from a dialog box. The Wizard also wants to know if you print from DOS programs. Select Yes or No as appropriate and click Next >.

6. The next Wizard dialog box, shown in Figure 19.1, lists the manufacturers and printers that Windows 95 supports. Use these lists to track down your printer, and then highlight it. If your printer isn't in the list, you have two choices:

   ■ Check your printer manual to see if the printer works like (*emulates*) another printer. If it does, see if you can find the emulated printer in the list.

   ■ If your printer comes with a disk, click Have Disk and follow the on-screen prompts.

FIGURE 19.1.

Use this Wizard dialog box to highlight your printer.

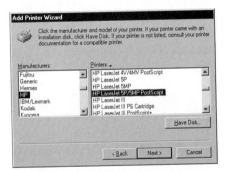

7. Click Next >.

8. In the next Wizard dialog box, shown in Figure 19.2, use the Available ports list to select your printer port, and then click Next >. If you've installed the Windows 95 infrared driver (as explained in Chapter 20), make sure you select the infrared printing port.

FIGURE 19.2.

Use this Wizard dialog box to select the port your printer is attached to.

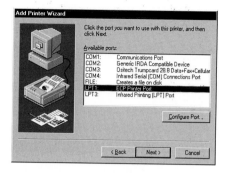

9. The next Add Printer Wizard dialog box that appears is shown in Figure 19.3. Use the `Printer name` text box to enter a descriptive name for the printer. If you've installed other printers, the Wizard will ask if you want this printer to be the default for all your Windows applications. If so, activate the Yes option. Click Next > to continue.

FIGURE 19.3.

Use this dialog box to name your printer and, optionally, set it as the default printer.

10. Finally, the Wizard asks if you'd like to print a text page. This is a good idea, so select Yes and then click Finish.

11. Follow the on-screen prompts to insert your Windows 95 source disks.

12. After the Wizard installs the drivers, it sends the test page to the printer, and a dialog box asks if the page printed properly. If it did, click Yes. If it didn't, select No. In this case, Windows 95 runs the Print Troubleshooter. I'll show how this works in the section "Troubleshooting Windows 95 Printing" near the end of this chapter.

When all is said and done, you'll be dropped off at the `Printers` folder. Your new printer will have its own icon, as shown in Figure 19.4.

19

PRESCRIPTIONS FOR PERFECT PRINTING

Figure 19.4.

For each printer you install, an icon appears in the Printers *folder.*

NOTE: PLUG AND PLAY PRINTERS

If you have a printer that is Plug and Play–compliant, installation is easy. Just connect the printer to your computer, turn the printer on, and restart your computer. When Windows 95 starts, it will detect the printer, query it for its device ID, and prompt you for your Windows 95 source disks.

TIP: USING MULTIPLE SETTINGS? INSTALL MULTIPLE PRINTERS

Windows 95 is happy to install as many printers as you like, even multiple copies of the same printer. Why would you want to do that? One good reason is that you can use each copy to create printers that use different settings. For example, many printers let you choose between printing on letter-size and legal-size paper. Rather than constantly changing these settings for a particular printer, you can install the printer twice and set up each one to use a different paper size. I'll show you how to work with these and other printer settings later in this chapter (see "Working with Printer Properties").

Removing a Printer

If you've upgraded to a new printer, you should remove your old printer to reduce clutter in the Printers folder and free up some disk space. To remove a printer, highlight it in the Printers folder and then either select File | Delete, press the Delete key, or right-click the printer and select Delete from the context menu. When Windows 95 asks if you're sure you want to delete the printer, click Yes. If no other printer is using some or all of the printer's files, another dialog box asks if you want to delete these files. (You won't see this dialog box if all the printer's files are being used by another printer.) They're useless, so you might as well click Yes to get rid of them. If the printer you deleted was your default printer, another dialog box shows up to let you know. Click OK to end the process.

Printing Documents in Windows 95

One of Windows 95's principle missions in life is to give all the applications you use a reasonably consistent look and feel. This means that the vast majority of Windows applications use, say, the same dialog box controls, the same method of selecting text, the same command for saving a file, and so on. Printing is a good example of this consistency. In most applications, with some relatively minor exceptions, you select File | Print (or, in many programs, press Ctrl-P), fill out the Print dialog box that appears (see Figure 19.5), and click OK. The options in this dialog box vary between applications, but you'll usually see the following controls:

Name: This drop-down list tells you the name of the currently selected printer. When you first open the Print dialog box, the Name list displays the default Windows 95 printer. If you'd prefer to use a different printer (assuming you've installed more than one), select it from the list. The other fields in the Printer group give you information about the printer, such as its status and port.

Properties: This button displays a dialog box with a few options that are specific to the current printer. These options let you choose from various printer settings (such as selecting a paper tray).

Print to file: If you activate this check box, the document will be saved to a printer (PRN) file instead of going to the printer. When you click OK, the Print to File dialog box will appear so that you can enter the filename and select a location. See "Getting a 'Soft' Copy: Printing to a File" later in this chapter for more information on printing to a file.

Print range: Most applications let you print some or all of a document. In a word processor, for example, you can usually print the entire document, a range of pages, or the current selection.

Copies: You'll usually see a text box or spinner control for entering the number of copies you want. In some cases, you can also choose whether or not you want multiple copies *collated*. For example, suppose you want two copies of a three-page document. If you collate the print job, you'll get one copy of all three pages, followed by the second copy. If you don't collate, you'll get two copies of page 1, then two copies of page 2, and then two copies of page 3.

FIGURE 19.5.

Select File | Print in most applications to display the Print dialog box. The one shown here is from WordPad.

Using Drag-and-Drop to Print Files

As you've seen throughout this book, Windows 95's drag-and-drop capabilities can be extremely useful. But, to my mind, one of the best uses of drag-and-drop is to print a file without having to open the source application and load the document.

All you have to do is drag the document from Explorer or My Computer and drop it on a printer icon in the Printers folder. Alternatively, you can create a shortcut for a printer (by dragging its icon from the Printers folder to the desktop) and then drop your documents on this shortcut.

With either method, the source application loads just long enough to send the document to the printer, and then it shuts down automatically.

Other Printing Methods

You've seen how Windows 95 delights in offering users a veritable cornucopia of methods to perform just about any task. Printing is no exception. Besides the two methods you've seen already, there are a few other methods you can use. Here's a rundown:

- Many applications have a Print button on their toolbar.
- In Explorer or My Computer, you can print a file by highlighting it and selecting File | Print or by right-clicking the file and selecting Print from the context menu.
- If you've defined a new, printable file type, you can add the Print action to the file type's definition. (I showed you how to work with file types in Chapter 13, "Working with Files and Folders.") In most cases, you define the Print action by entering the application's executable path, followed by the /P switch, as in the following example:

  ```
  C:\WINDOWS\NOTEPAD.EXE /P
  ```

- You can create a shortcut for a printer in the Send To folder. If you then right-click a file, select Send To from the context menu, and select the printer, Windows 95 will print the document.

Note that all these methods bypass the Print dialog box and send the document to the printer immediately.

Deferring Print Jobs

Taking advantage of Windows 95's new deferred printing feature is easy. In the Printers folder, highlight your printer and select File | Work Offline, or right-click the printer icon and select Work Offline from the context menu. Windows 95 indicates that the printer is offline by dimming the printer's icon.

You can still "print" your documents the way you normally would. Windows 95 spools the files and then stores each print job in a queue. Later, when the printer is available, just deactivate the Work Offline command, and Windows 95 will start printing the documents right away.

NOTE: YOU CAN ALSO DEFER PRINTING BY PAUSING

If you're using a local printer, you might not see the Work Offline command on the File menu. If you still would like to defer your print jobs, you can pause the printer. See "Managing Print Jobs" later in this chapter for details.

Getting a "Soft" Copy: Printing to a File

What do you do if you don't have a printer? Or what if you only have a dot matrix printer and you want to print your résumé on a laser printer? If you know someone who has the printer you need, Windows 95 lets you print your document to a file. You can then transport the file to the other computer and print it from there. The other computer doesn't even have to have the source application.

You saw earlier that you can print to a file by activating the Print to file check box in the Print dialog box. If you'd prefer a more permanent solution, you can tell Windows 95 to print to a port named FILE instead of, say, LPT1. To do this, use either of the following methods:

■ If you haven't installed the printer (that is, the type of printer you'll eventually use to print the file), run the Add Printer Wizard as described earlier. When the Wizard asks you to specify a port, select FILE.

■ For an installed printer, open the Printers folder and display the properties sheet for the printer you want to use (by highlighting the printer icon and selecting File | Properties or by right-clicking the icon and selecting Properties). Select the Details tab, and then use the Print to the following port list to select the FILE port. Click OK to put the new setting into effect.

When that's done, use any of the methods outlined earlier to print a document. When you do, you'll see the Print To File dialog box, shown in Figure 19.6. Enter the filename, choose a location, and click OK.

19

PRESCRIPTIONS
FOR PERFECT
PRINTING

FIGURE 19.6.

Use the Print To File dialog box to enter the name of the file you want to print to.

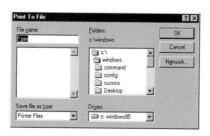

Once the document has been "printed" to the file, what happens next? Now you copy the file to a floppy disk, head to where the printer is located, and copy the file to the other computer. To print the file, start up a DOS session and enter the following generic command:

```
COPY /B filename port
```

The /B switch tells DOS to print a binary file, filename is the name of your file, and port is the port the printer is attached to. For example, if your file is named PRINT.PRN, and the printer is attached to LPT1, you would enter the following:

```
COPY /B print.prn lpt1
```

I'm assuming that the file is in the current folder. If it isn't, you'll need to include the drive and folder with the filename.

Managing Print Jobs

The printing subsystem is one of those unassuming components that does its job quietly and without a lot of fanfare. In most cases, you can just let it go about its business, safe in the knowledge that your printing chores are in the hands of a competent professional. But what if you need to cancel a print job in progress or pause the printing while you insert some paper? For these situations, Windows 95 lets you interrupt the printing subsystem's peace and quiet so that you can manipulate various aspects of the print job.

In Windows 3.x, you used Print Manager to mess around with your print jobs. In Windows 95, however, each printer is given its own status window. To open this window, use any of the following techniques:

- In the Printers folder, double-click the printer's icon, select File | Open, or right-click the icon and select Open.

- Double-click the Printer icon in the taskbar's system tray. This icon appears while the printing subsystem is spooling the file, so you'll have only a few seconds (depending on the size of the job) in which to do this.

Figure 19.7 shows an example of a printer window. It lists each pending print job and tells you the name of the document, its current status, the document's owner, the progress of the print job, and the date and time it began.

FIGURE 19.7.

Each printer window shows the current print jobs for the printer.

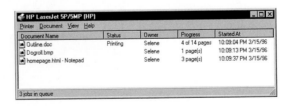

Pausing a Print Job

If you need to add paper to your printer or change the ribbon or toner cartridge, you can tell the printing subsystem to hold its horses. Just select Printer | Pause Printing. When you're ready to roll again, deactivate Printer | Pause Printing to resume the print jobs. (The Pause Printing command is also available in the `Printers` folder.)

You can also pause individual documents. Highlight the document you want to delay and either choose Document | Pause Printing or right-click the document and choose Pause Printing from the context menu. Select one of these commands again to deactivate it and resume the print job.

Canceling a Print Job

If you accidentally print the wrong file, or if you simply change your mind, you can delete a file from the queue. Highlight the appropriate document in the printer window and then select Document | Cancel Printing, press Delete, or right-click the document and select Cancel Printing from the context menu.

If you want to get rid of all the pending print jobs, select Printer | Purge Print Jobs. (The Purge Print Jobs command is also available in the `Printers` folder.)

TIP: SEND PRINT JOBS TO THE RECYCLE BIN

Another way to delete print jobs is to drag them from the printer window and drop them on the desktop's Recycle Bin icon.

Changing the Order of Print Jobs

The printing subsystem prints documents in the order it receives them. If you'd like to change this order, all you have to do is drag a print job up or down in the queue. Note, however, that you can't drag a print job higher than the currently printing document.

Working with Printer Properties

Each printer you install becomes an object in the Windows 95 shell. These printer objects have just one action—printing—but they have a boatload of properties, some of which vary from printer to printer. To view the properties sheet for an installed printer, try out either of the following methods:

- In the `Printers` folder, highlight a printer icon and select File | Properties, or right-click an icon and select Properties from the context menu.
- In a printer's window, select Printer | Properties.

The dialog box that appears depends on the printer, but it will look something like the one shown in Figure 19.8. Here's a summary of the various tabs you might see in your printer's properties sheet:

General: Contains a few miscellaneous controls that don't fit anywhere else. See the next section, "General Properties."

Details: Lets you set various options for the printer port, printer driver, and spooler. See "The Details Tab" later in this chapter.

Sharing: Sets up the printer as a shared network resource. See Chapter 31 for details.

Paper: Contains a number of controls that let you manipulate paper-related properties (such as the paper size used in the printer). I cover this tab in the "Paper Properties" section later in this chapter.

Graphics: Determines how the printer handles graphics. The options you see depend on your printer, so I won't cover them here. Check your printer manual and the What's This? Help system for details on the available controls.

Fonts: Determines how your printer works with TrueType fonts. See "Fonts Properties" later in this chapter for details.

Device Options: Contains printer-specific options such as memory settings. Since the controls you see depend on the printer, I won't cover them here. Check your printer manual and the What's This? Help system for details.

PostScript: Sets various properties for PostScript printers. I discuss these options later in this chapter, in the "PostScript Properties" section.

FIGURE 19.8.

The properties sheet for a printer.

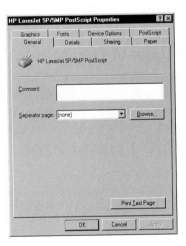

General Properties

When you first open a printer's properties sheet, you'll see the General tab, as shown in Figure 19.8. This tab contains the following controls:

Comment: Use this text box to add a short description of the printer. This comment appears in the Print dialog box, and it's transferred to network users who install your printer on their systems. You can use the `Comment` box to describe unique features of the printer (such as the paper size it's designed to handle), hours it can be accessed, and so on.

Separator page: A *separator page* is a sheet that prints in advance of each document you send to the printer. The idea is that this extra sheet marks the beginning of each print job, thus separating multiple printed documents. The `Separator page` drop-down list gives you three choices:

(none)	No separator page
Full	A graphical separator page that includes the document name, the name of the person who submitted the print job, and the date and time of the print job
Simple	A text-only separator page that gives the same information as the Full page

If you prefer, you can specify your own separator page by clicking the Browse button and choosing a WMF file from the dialog box that appears. (If you have Microsoft Office 95 installed, you'll find a large collection of WMF files in the \MSOffice\ ClipArt folder.)

NOTE: SEPARATOR PAGES ARE LOCAL PHENOMENA

You can only assign a separator page to a local printer (that is, a printer that's attached directly to your computer).

Print Test Page: If you've made changes to your printer's properties, you can click this button to test the new configuration by sending a page to the printer. After the test page has been sent, Windows 95 displays a dialog box that asks if the page printed correctly. If the page showed up without any mistakes, click Yes; otherwise, click No to start the Print Troubleshooter (explained later in this chapter).

Details Properties

The Details tab, shown in Figure 19.9, is a busy screen that contains all kinds of controls. These options let you modify various aspects of the printer port, the printer driver, and the spooler.

FIGURE 19.9.

Use the Details tab to set various port and driver options.

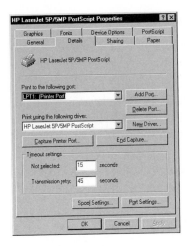

Here's the rundown of what's available in this tab:

Print to the following port: Use this drop-down list to select the port you want to use for printing. This is useful if you need to print only to files (the FILE "port," as described earlier) or if you have an infrared port and want to switch between a cable connection and the infrared connection.

Add Port: This button displays the Add Port dialog box, shown in Figure 19.10, which lets you specify a new printer port (activate the Other option and highlight the port in the list) or a path to a network printer (activate the Network option and either enter the UNC path to the shared printer or click Browse and choose the printer from the dialog box that appears).

FIGURE 19.10.

Use the Add Port dialog box to specify a new printer port.

Delete Port: Click this button if you want to remove a port from the Print to the following port list. First, make sure that no printers are using the port. Then, in the Delete Port dialog box that appears, highlight the port and click OK.

Print using the following driver: This drop-down list contains all the printer drivers that are installed on your system. If you want to use a different driver (as long as it can work with the current printer), select it from the list. If you'd prefer to add a new driver, click the New Driver button and follow the dialog boxes that appear.

Capture Printer Port: In the same way that you can map a shared network drive or folder and have it appear as though it were a physical drive on your system, so too can you map a shared network printer and have it appear as though it were a physical printer port on your system. This is called *capturing* a printer port. To try this out, click the Capture Printer Port button. In the Capture Printer Port dialog box, shown in Figure 19.11, use the Device list to select a logical printer port (such as LPT2), and use the Path combo box to enter the network path to the shared printer.

FIGURE 19.11.

Use the Capture Printer Port dialog box to map a shared network printer to a logical printer port on your system.

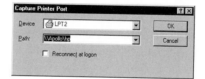

End Capture: Click this button when you no longer want to capture a network printer as a logical port on your system. In the End Capture dialog box that appears, highlight the printer and click OK.

Not selected: This value (which is available for local printers only) determines how long Windows 95 waits before the printer signals that it's online. The default is 15 seconds. So, for example, if you submit a print job while the printer is turned off, you have 15 seconds to get the printer online before Windows 95 generates an error. If your printer takes longer than that to warm up, you might consider increasing this value.

Transmission retry: This value (which is available for local printers only) determines how long Windows 95 attempts to resend data to the printer before declaring an error. There are many reasons why Windows 95 might not be able to send data to the printer successfully: The printer's buffer might be full, there might be a paper jam or some other printer problem, or the printer might be taking a long time to process graphics or some other large chunk of data. For the latter, you might want to bump up the Transmission retry value if your print jobs are usually large, or if you're using a PostScript printer (which requires extra overhead for processing fonts and other goodies).

Spool Settings: This button displays the Spool Settings dialog box, shown in Figure 19.12, which controls various aspects of the printing subsystem's spooler:

Spool print jobs so program finishes printing faster: Activate this option to enable spooling. For the fastest return-to-application time, activate `Start printing after last page is spooled`. In this case, Windows 95 spools the entire print job before sending anything to the printer. This is the quickest method, but it uses more disk space. For a slower method that uses less disk space, try the `Start printing after first page is spooled` option.

Print directly to the printer: Activate this option to bypass the spooler and send your print jobs right to the printer.

Spool data format: This drop-down list determines the type of format Windows 95 uses to spool the data: EMF or RAW. You read earlier in this chapter that EMF files are faster to spool, so they get you back to your application quicker. The RAW format is printer-specific, so it takes longer to spool. Choose RAW only if you're having trouble printing with the EMF format.

Enable bi-directional support for this printer: Activate this option to tell Windows 95 to use your printer's bidirectional capabilities. To bypass this feature, activate `Disable bi-directional support for this printer` instead.

FIGURE 19.12.

Use this dialog box to control how Windows 95 spools your print jobs.

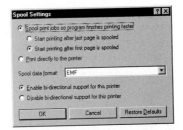

NOTE: DIRECT PRINTING

If you activate the `Print directly to the printer` option, you won't be able to pause your print jobs or work offline. Also note that if you've shared your printer on a network, this option will be disabled.

Port Settings: Clicking this button displays the Configure LPT Port dialog box. The `Spool MS-DOS print jobs` check box toggles spooling for DOS programs on and off. The `Check port state before printing` check box determines whether or not Windows 95 checks the current status of the port before starting a print job.

Paper Properties

The layout of the Paper tab depends on the printer driver you're working with. Figure 19.13 shows how the Printer tab looks for the LaserJet 5P/5MP driver. Here are a few options that are common to most Paper tabs:

Paper size: This is a list of the paper sizes and envelope sizes that the printer supports. You can either highlight the material your printer uses or select one of the custom icons at the end of the list. If you see an icon covered by the international "not" symbol, it means you can't use that particular size until you select another option (such as a paper tray).

Orientation: These options specify the layout of the data on the page. With Portrait, the page is oriented so that the height of the page is greater than the width. This is the more common orientation. With Landscape, the page is oriented so that the width of the page is greater than the height.

NOTE: DISPLAYING THE PAGE DIMENSIONS

To see the page's dimensions (the height and width, and where the top, bottom, left, and right margins are), move your mouse pointer over the page icon in the Orientation group and hold down the left mouse button.

Paper source: This drop-down list determines what part of the printer the paper is fed from (for example, a paper tray, envelope feeder, or manual feed). The AutoSelect Tray choice tells Windows 95 to determine the tray based on the selected paper size.

Copies: The default number of copies to use with this printer.

Unprintable Area: This button displays the Unprintable Area dialog box, shown in Figure 19.14. You use the spinners in this dialog box to set the default margins for the printer. (If you intend to reduce one or more of these values, first check your printer manual to find out the minimum values allowed. If you enter any values below these numbers, you could end up truncating text in your printouts.)

FIGURE 19.13.

Use the Paper tab to specify various paper options for your printer.

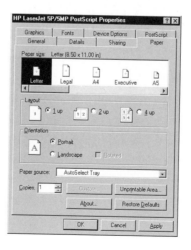

FIGURE 19.14.

The Unprintable Area dialog box determines the default page margins.

Fonts Properties

The Fonts tab, shown in Figure 19.15, contains three options that determine how your printer works with Windows 95's TrueType fonts:

> **Send TrueType fonts to printer according to the font Substitution Table:** If you activate this option, Windows 95 doesn't download all of a document's TrueType fonts to the printer. Instead, it substitutes a built-in printer font for some of the TrueType fonts to speed up printing. These substitutions are controlled by the Font Substitution Table. If you like, you can make changes to these substitutions by clicking the Edit the Table button. In the dialog box that appears (see Figure 19.16), highlight a font and use the `Printer font for` drop-down to select a substitute. (Or you can select `Send As Outlines` to send the TrueType font without substitution.)

> **Always use built-in printer fonts instead of TrueType fonts:** If you activate this option, Windows 95 won't download any TrueType fonts to the printer. Instead, it will select substitute fonts from the printer's built-in fonts. Note, however, that, since your screen shows TrueType fonts, your printed document might look different.

> **Always use TrueType fonts:** Activate this option to always download TrueType fonts to the printer. This might slow down the print job (but not by much), but your printouts will look exactly as they did on-screen.

> **Send Fonts As:** This button displays the Send Fonts As dialog box. The controls in this dialog box let you determine how Windows 95 sends fonts to the printer.

FIGURE 19.15.

The Fonts tab determines how your printer works with TrueType fonts.

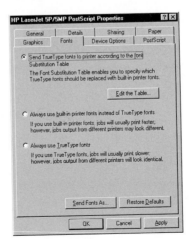

FIGURE 19.16.
Use this dialog box to make changes to the Font Substitution Table.

PostScript Properties

If you're using a PostScript printer, the properties sheet will have a PostScript tab, as shown in Figure 19.17. Here's a review of the available controls:

PostScript output format: This drop-down control contains a list of the various PostScript formats you can use. You'll probably want to use the PostScript (optimize for speed) choice most of the time. However, if you need to use Adobe Document Structuring Conventions (ADSC) or Encapsulated PostScript (EPS) format, select the appropriate choice.

PostScript header: PostScript printers use header information to set up the printer's page layout and other options before processing the print job. If you're sure the header information won't change from job to job, you can activate the Assume header is downloaded and retained option. (If you select this option, you can send new header information at any time by clicking the Send Header Now button.) For most print jobs, however, you'll want to activate the Download header with each print job option.

Print PostScript error information: If you're having trouble printing to a PostScript printer, make sure this check box is activated. This will force the printer to report any PostScript errors that occur (errors that Windows 95 might miss).

PostScript timeout values: These spinners determine how patient Windows 95 is with PostScript jobs. The Job timeout value specifies how long Windows 95 will wait for a print job to get to the printer before signaling an error. A value of 0 means Windows 95 will wait indefinitely. The Wait timeout value specifies how long the printer should wait for Windows 95 to send more data before terminating the print job and printing an error report.

Advanced: This button displays a dialog box filled with advanced PostScript settings. These settings include the PostScript language level, compression for bitmaps, the format used for the data, and when Ctrl-D is sent to indicate that the print job is complete.

FIGURE 19.17.

*Use the PostScript tab
to set various options for
your PostScript printer.*

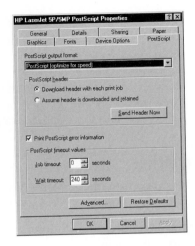

Tips for Saving Paper

As you've seen in this chapter, Windows 95 and its printing subsystem make printing so easy that you now have yet another reason to print too many documents. So, to keep your paper costs down and save a tree or two, here are some tips that will help you cut down on the amount of paper you use:

- Print a document only when you have to. Too many people print intermediate drafts or whenever they make the slightest change. With Windows' WYSIWYG (What You See Is What You Get) display, you shouldn't need a hard copy until the document is finished.

- Take advantage of the Print Preview feature. Many Windows applications have a Print Preview command that lets you see exactly what your document will look like (including things such as headers and footers, page numbers, and footnotes) when it's printed. A sneak peek at the document will save you many a reprint.

- Proofread your documents carefully before printing them. You usually need to reprint because of spelling and grammatical errors that you didn't catch until you read the printout. You can avoid this by giving a document the once-over before printing it. And, by all means, use your application's built-in spell checker and grammar checker.

- Try to maximize the print area on each page. You can do this by reducing the margins and by using smaller type sizes. Many word processors also have a feature that suppresses *widows:* single lines that appear by themselves at the top of the last page.

- Print only what you need. Most applications let you print a selection of text, a single page, or a range of pages. There's no point in printing the entire document if you need only a small chunk of it.

- If you print a document and then discover a small mistake (such as a spelling gaffe) on one page, just reprint the offending page.

- Distribute your documents electronically if you can. Rather than sending a printout to someone, you can send the file over a network, as an e-mail attachment, or even via floppy disk.

- Reuse printouts you no longer need. If you're printing an unimportant document that only you will see, turn some used pages around and print on the other side.

Troubleshooting Windows 95 Printing

When you need hard copy, the last thing you need is for your printer to play hard-to-get. If your printer does mess up, however, Windows 95 offers a couple of troubleshooting features that might help. I discuss these features, as well as solutions to specific printer woes, in the next few sections.

Using the Print Troubleshooter

If your printer won't print anything, or if your printouts contain garbage characters or only partial data, or if printing seems to take forever, you'll need to do some troubleshooting. For these kinds of problems, the Windows 95 Help system has a Print Troubleshooter that can help you narrow down the cause.

To try it out, select Start | Help and choose the Contents tab in the Windows Help dialog box that appears. Open the Troubleshooting book and display the If you have trouble printing topic. This loads the Print Troubleshooter, shown in Figure 19.18. As with Windows 95's other Troubleshooters, the Print Troubleshooter operates by asking you a series of questions. You simply click the appropriate hyperlinks to gradually narrow down the problem and (hopefully) reach a solution.

FIGURE 19.18.

The Print Trouble-shooter asks a series of questions to help you narrow down the printing problem.

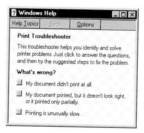

19

PRESCRIPTIONS FOR PERFECT PRINTING

Using the Enhanced Print Troubleshooter

If you have the Windows 95 CD-ROM, you'll find an application called the Enhanced Print Troubleshooter (EPTS) in the Other\Misc\Epts folder. This tool, developed by Microsoft's research arm, uses probabilities and costs associated with various problems to generate recommended actions. If the regular Print Troubleshooter won't solve your problem, perhaps the EPTS will.

If you'd like to try it out, copy the Epts folder from the CD to your hard drive. You can start the Troubleshooter either by running the EPTS.EXE file or by using the Run dialog box or a shortcut with a command line that uses the following syntax:

drive:*folder*\EPTS.EXE [/SY¦/SN¦/SA][/RY¦/RN] [*datafile*]

drive	The letter of the disk drive where EPTS is installed.
folder	The folder where EPTS is installed.
/SY	Sense Yes: Detect the default printer configuration (the default).
/SN	Sense No: Don't detect the default printer configuration.
/SA	Sense Ask: Ask the user at startup.
/RY	Recommendations Yes: Display a ranked list of recommended steps in the status window.
/RN	Recommendations No: Don't show recommendations (the default).
datafile	Contains probability and cost information. The default is PTS.BIN, which is included in the Epts folder.

The EPTS works the same way as the regular Print Troubleshooter. That is, a Help window appears, you're asked a series of questions, and you click hyperlinks to proceed through the session. However, the EPTS is much more sophisticated and can provide many more possible solutions. Figure 19.19 shows the EPTS after a few hyperlinks. Notice that the EPTS uses two windows. The Enhanced Print Troubleshooter window is the Help window that poses questions and recommended actions. The first six sections of the EPTS Status window show you the information that the EPTS gleaned from your system. This window also has two other sections:

User Observations: This section shows you the results you entered for previous EPTS recommendations.

Recommended Actions: This section shows you the list of recommendations that the EPTS will run through. Note that you'll see this list only if you started the EPTS with the /RY switch.

FIGURE 19.19.

The Enhanced Print Troubleshooter uses a sophisticated algorithm for tracking down printer problems.

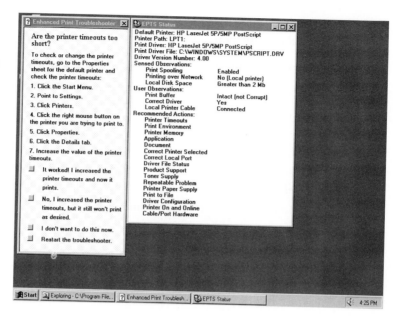

FIGURE 19.19.

The Enhanced Print Troubleshooter uses a sophisticated algorithm for tracking down printer problems.

Miscellaneous Printing Perplexities

This section presents some miscellaneous printing problems (and, of course, their appropriate solutions) that might come your way.

Your printer won't print.

If your printer refuses to print, there are a number of possible reasons. Here are a few things to check out:

- Make sure that the printer is powered up and online and that the cable connections are secure.
- Make sure that the printer has paper and that there is no paper jam.
- Clear the printer's buffer by turning off the power, waiting for a few seconds, and then turning the power back on again.
- If your printer can switch between PostScript and normal operation, make sure the driver you're using matches the printer's current configuration.
- Try sending your print job directly to the printer. If this works, Windows 95 is having a problem spooling the document. You should run ScanDisk to check the integrity of the disk and file system. If Windows 95 still won't spool, you probably need to turn off spooling permanently.
- Delete the printer icon from the Printers folder and then reinstall it. This will fix any problems related to a corrupt driver or a corrupt Registry setting.

19

PRESCRIPTIONS FOR PERFECT PRINTING

■ Try printing to a file. If this works, head for the DOS prompt and try copying the PRN file to the printer port.

Your printer takes a long time to print.

If your printing seems to be taking longer than normal, here are some possible solutions:

■ Make sure that that spooling is enabled and that Windows 95 is spooling to EMF files.

■ Make sure the drive where Windows 95 is installed isn't running low on disk space. The printing subsystem needs hard disk space to create the temporary EMF files.

■ Use Disk Defragmenter to defragment the hard disk where Windows 95 is installed.

■ Make sure your system resources aren't running low.

■ Reinstall the printer driver, or upgrade to the latest printer driver from the manufacturer.

■ Make sure Windows 95 is sending TrueType fonts as outlines and not bitmaps. In the Fonts tab of your printer's properties sheet, click Send Fonts As and make sure the `Send TrueType fonts as` list shows `Outlines`.

Your printouts contain garbage characters or are missing data.

Here are a few things to look for if your printouts are faulty:

■ Your printer might not have enough memory. Try printing at a lower resolution.

■ Try printing directly to the printer, or try spooling using the RAW format instead of the EMF format.

■ If possible, try printing the document using a PostScript driver. If the document prints OK, the Windows 95 universal printer driver might be corrupted. Try extracting the file `UNIDRV.DLL` from `WIN95_09.CAB` on your Windows 95 source disks.

■ Try printing just one job at a time to avoid conflicts.

■ Make sure the printable region isn't larger than what is supported by the printer.

You can't print a document because the File | Print command is dimmed.

If you can't select File | Print, you haven't yet installed a printer in Windows 95. See the earlier section "Installing a Printer with the Add Printer Wizard."

Your computer has an Extended Capabilities Port, but it doesn't show up in Device Manager.

The Windows 95 Setup program should recognize your ECP port automatically. If it doesn't, this probably means one of two things:

■ Your computer's BIOS isn't set up to use the ECP.

■ Windows 95 failed to recognize the ECP.

Either way, you'll need to run your computer's BIOS setup program (how you do this depends on the machine). Once you're inside the program, find the setting that controls the parallel port and change it to ECP mode (if necessary). Make a note of the memory address, IRQ, and DMA channel used by the ECP. Exit the BIOS program and restart Windows 95.

You'll now need to run the Add New Hardware Wizard (see Chapter 10) to set up the ECP. However, you should bypass the automatic search for hardware and opt to specify the new device by hand. When the Wizard displays the list of hardware types, select `Ports (COM & LPT)`. In the next dialog box, select `Standard port types` and highlight the `ECP Printer Port` "model" (as shown in Figure 19.20). Run through the remaining dialog boxes, but don't restart the computer when you're done. You now need to use Device Manager to set up the ECP resources.

Figure 19.20.

Use the Add New Hardware Wizard to specify the ECP by hand.

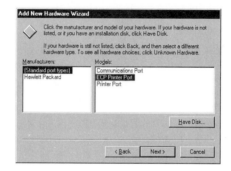

Open the System Properties dialog box and select the Device Manager tab. In the hardware tree, open `Ports (COM and LPT)`, highlight `ECP Printer Port (LPT1)`, and select `Properties`. In the Resources tab, shown in Figure 19.21, make sure the values in the `Resource settings` box match those used in the BIOS. If they don't, either select a different configuration or edit the individual resources by hand. (I showed you how to do this in Chapter 10.) When you're done, exit Device Manager and restart your system.

Figure 19.21.

Use the Resources tab to make sure that the ECP resource settings match those assigned to the ECP in the BIOS.

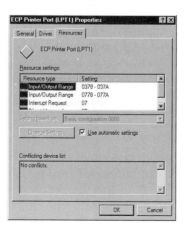

19

PRESCRIPTIONS
FOR PERFECT
PRINTING

You're having trouble printing from a DOS program.

Most DOS programs should print properly using Windows 95's new spooling feature for DOS. However, if you do have problems, here are the steps required to turn off the spooling of DOS print jobs:

1. Open the `Printers` folder.

2. Open the properties sheet for the printer you're using.

3. Activate the Details tab.

4. Click the Port Settings button.

5. In the Configure LPT Port dialog box, shown in Figure 19.22, deactivate the `Spool MS-DOS print jobs` check box and click OK.

Figure 19.22.

If you're having trouble printing from DOS, deactivate the `Spool MS-DOS print jobs` *option.*

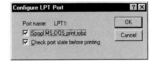

6. Click OK to return to the `Printers` folder.

Summary

This chapter took you on a tour of Windows 95 printing facilities. I began with a behind-the-scenes look at the revamped printing subsystem, with its support for EMF spooling, the 32-bit universal driver/mini-driver model, deferred printing, and ECP. You then learned how to install a printer driver, remove a printer, manage print jobs, and work with printer properties. I closed with a look at some printer troubleshooting issues. You'll find related information in the following chapters:

■ To learn more about the GDI and how it fits into the Windows 95 architecture, see Chapter 9, "Windows 95 Performance Tuning and Optimization."

■ For more information on drivers, including the universal driver/mini-driver model, see Chapter 10, "How Windows 95 Handles Hardware."

■ In case you have a printer that has an infrared port, I showed you how to install Windows 95's new infrared driver in Chapter 20, "Windows 95 on the Road: Notebook Computers and the Briefcase."

■ Windows 95 sets up Microsoft Fax as a printer driver. To find out how this works, see Chapter 29, "Using Microsoft Fax to Send and Receive Faxes."

■ Network printing issues are covered in Chapter 31, "Windows 95 Networking."

CHAPTER 20

Windows 95 on the Road: Notebook Computers and the Briefcase

IN THIS CHAPTER

A man must carry knowledge with him, if he would bring home knowledge.

—Samuel Johnson

It used to be that notebook computers occupied very specific and unalterable niches in the computing ecology. Sales professionals didn't leave home without them, executives on business trips routinely packed their portables, and corporate employees without a personal machine would lug a laptop home to do some extra work. In each case, though, the notebook computer—with its cramped keyboard, hard-to-read LCD display, and minuscule hard disk—was always considered a poor substitute for a desktop machine.

For many years it seemed that notebooks were doomed to remain among the lower castes in the social hierarchy of personal computers. But recent developments have caused notebooks to shed their inferiority complex. Today's luggables have impressive 800×600 displays, gigabyte-sized hard disks, and built-in sound and CD-ROMs. There's even one—the IBM ThinkPad 701C—with a keyboard that expands when you flip the cover! Add a couple of PC card slots, connectors for full-sized keyboards and monitors, maybe even a docking station, and suddenly your desktop system doesn't look so superior.

The notebook community's bid for respectability wasn't lost on the designers of Windows 95. They incorporated many notebook-specific features into the operating system, including support for power management and PC card devices, and applets that let you exchange data between your portable and a desktop or network. I cover many of these features in this chapter.

Windows 95's Advanced Power Management Features

A certain level of anxiety is always involved with running your notebook on its batteries, especially if no AC is in sight. You know that you have only a limited amount of time to get your work done (or play your games, or check your e-mail, or whatever), so the pressure's on. To help change road worriers back into road warriors, most notebooks support some kind of power management. This means that the system conserves battery life by shutting down system components after the computer has been idle for a specified interval. Depending on the system, the power management BIOS might do the following:

- Reduce the brightness of the display or turn it off.
- Stop the hard drive from spinning.
- Slow down the processor and/or put it into "sleep" mode.
- For Pentium machines, shut off the CPU cooling fan.

On most machines, the power management feature and the specified idle time are controlled through the BIOS setup program. Your system might also have a utility program for controlling these settings, as shown in Figure 20.1.

FIGURE 20.1.

Many notebooks come with utilities for controlling power management features.

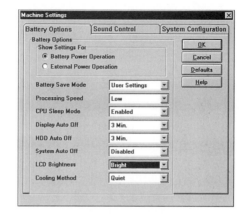

Understanding Advanced Power Management

Advanced Power Management (APM) is a specification developed by Microsoft and Intel that lets the operating system, the applications, the BIOS, and the system hardware work cooperatively to manage power and extend battery life. For example, APM lets notebooks go into *suspend mode,* which shuts off the machine but preserves the operating system's current state. When you turn the machine back on, your programs and documents appear immediately, exactly as they were when you initiated suspend mode.

Windows 95 has built-in support for APM-enabled computers, and it can work with either the APM 1.0 or the APM 1.1 specification. What's the difference? APM 1.1 gives Windows 95 more control over the machine's power management services:

- With an APM 1.1 machine, Windows 95 can force the APM BIOS to wait indefinitely until Windows has prepared the running programs and drivers for suspend mode. With APM 1.0, the BIOS just waits for a predetermined time after it has received the suspend request and then shuts down, regardless of the operating system's current state.

- Windows 95 can reject requests for suspend mode on APM 1.1 systems.

- APM 1.1 provides Windows 95 with more accurate reports on the remaining battery life.

20

NOTEBOOK COMPUTERS AND THE BRIEFCASE

OSR2

NOTE: OSR2 SUPPORTS APM 1.2

Windows 95 OSR2 supports APM 1.2, which includes the wake-on-ring feature for modems and the ability to handle multiple batteries. OSR2 also supports the powering down of inactive PC Card modems and hard disk spin-down. (The latter feature puts the hard disk into low-power mode after it has been idle for a specified amount of time. You can control this interval by opening the Power icon in Control Panel.)

Enabling Advanced Power Management Support

The Windows 95 Setup program should recognize APM-compliant notebooks. If so, it installs the APM driver (VPOWERD.VXD) and enables Windows 95's APM support. If Setup somehow misses the fact that your system is APM-compliant, or if you disabled APM support during the installation, you can activate it from within Windows 95. How do you know whether APM support is enabled? You can find out in various ways, but the most straightforward method is to open the Control Panel folder. If you don't see a Power icon, APM isn't enabled.

If you don't see this icon in the Control Panel folder, APM is disabled.

To enable APM, display the Device Manager, open the System devices class, highlight the Advanced Power Management support device, and click Properties. In the dialog box that appears, select the Settings tab, shown in Figure 20.2. Activate the Enable power management support check box.

FIGURE 20.2.

Use the Settings tab to enable APM support.

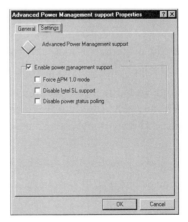

NOTE: NO APM SUPPORT DEVICE?

If you don't see the Advanced Power Management support device, your notebook doesn't support APM.

Other APM Settings

After you've enabled APM support, the other options in the APM support properties sheet become available. Here's a rundown of these extra options:

Force APM 1.0 mode: Activate this check box if you're having trouble initiating suspend mode or using any of the APM features. The BIOS in some laptops doesn't support APM 1.1 correctly, so moving Windows 95 down to APM 1.0 might solve your problem.

Disable Intel SL support: Activate this check box to turn off Windows 95's support for Intel's SL Enhanced processor features (these are power management features that do things such as control the CPU clock speed to save battery life). If your notebook doesn't return from suspend mode, or if it hangs for no reason, activating this check box might help.

Disable power status polling: Activate this command to tell Windows 95 to stop querying the APM BIOS about the current state of the battery. You should need to do this only if the keyboard or mouse stops responding while you're working in a DOS session. Activating this check box removes the Battery Meter (or the AC Power icon) from the system tray.

If you change any of these settings, you need to restart your computer.

Monitoring Battery Life

When power management is enabled, Windows 95 displays a Battery Meter icon in the taskbar's system tray, as shown in Figure 20.3. (This is assuming, of course, that your notebook is operating on battery power.)

FIGURE 20.3.

When your notebook is running on batteries, Windows 95 displays a Battery Meter icon in the taskbar.

Battery Meter icon

20

NOTEBOOK COMPUTERS AND THE BRIEFCASE

When the notebook battery is fully charged, the Battery Meter is completely blue. As battery power is used up, the Battery Meter's "level" decreases. For example, if the battery power is down to half, the Battery Meter displays as half blue, half gray.

When the battery life starts to get low, Windows 95 adds an exclamation point to the Battery Meter, as shown in Figure 20.4. When only 20 minutes of battery power are left, Windows 95 places a red X over the Battery Meter and displays the warning dialog box shown in Figure 20.5.

Battery power is getting low

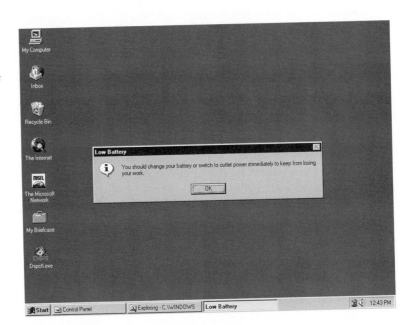

At this point, you should consider either swapping in a fresh battery or connecting your notebook to an AC outlet. If you choose to connect to an outlet, Windows 95 changes the Battery Meter to the AC Power icon shown in Figure 20.6.

AC Power icon

You can also get an exact value for the number of minutes remaining on your battery by using either of the following methods:

■ Move the mouse pointer over the Battery Meter. After a second or two, a banner appears that tells you the number of minutes remaining.

■ Double-click the Battery Meter to display the dialog box shown in Figure 20.7. Make sure that the `Enable low battery warning` check box is activated.

FIGURE 20.7.

Double-clicking the Battery Meter displays this dialog box.

Working with Power Management Properties

Windows 95 has a few power management properties you can manipulate. To check them out, run the Control Panel and open the Power icon to display the Power Properties dialog box, shown in Figure 20.8. Here's a summary of the controls on this properties sheet:

Power management: This drop-down list controls the power management features that Windows 95 uses. If you select `Advanced`, the power management features provided by both the BIOS and Windows 95 are used; if you select `Standard`, Windows 95 uses only the power management features provided by the BIOS; if you select `Off`, Windows 95 disables power management.

Power status: This group tells you whether the computer is on AC power or battery and how much battery life is left.

Enable battery meter on taskbar: This check box toggles the taskbar's Battery Meter icon on and off.

Show Suspend command on Start menu: This group determines when the Suspend command (see the next section) appears on the Start menu. If you select `Only when undocked`, Windows 95 displays the Suspend command only when the notebook isn't attached to a docking station. (This option is available only if your notebook is dockable.)

Click OK to put your new settings into effect.

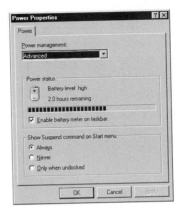

FIGURE 20.8.

Use this dialog box to set various power management options.

Entering Suspend Mode

I mentioned earlier that APM can place your notebook into suspend mode. This effectively shuts down the machine, but it preserves the current state of your programs. When you bring the computer out of suspend mode, your applications and documents appear exactly as they were before, and you can continue working immediately.

To activate suspend mode in Windows 95, select Start | Suspend. When you're ready to resume, turn your notebook's power back on. (How you do this might vary from system to system; check your documentation to be sure.)

CAUTION: SUSPEND MODE CAVEATS

Here are a few things to watch out for when using suspend mode:

- Some notebooks have a suspend button that you can press to initiate suspend mode. Unfortunately, if you have an APM 1.0 BIOS, these hardware suspends tend to shut down the machine faster than Windows 95 can save its current state. In this case, you should always use the Suspend command.

- If you suspend the system while a DOS session is active, full functionality might not be restored when you resume. Again, this is an APM 1.0 problem.

- Some systems might not restore network connections when they come out of suspend mode, so you should save your work in advance.

Synchronizing Laptop and Desktop with Briefcase

Previous versions of Windows refused to admit the existence of notebook computers. They simply assumed that a computer was a computer, and it really didn't matter whether *your* computer could be slung over your shoulder and lugged home at night.

Windows 95, however, not only knows about notebooks, but it also recognizes an important fact of portable computing life: Your notebook machine often has to use documents from your desktop machine, and vice versa. For example, if you're traveling to a client's offices to make a presentation, you'll probably use your desktop computer to build the presentation, copy the files to your notebook, and take the notebook on the road. If you make any changes to these files while you're away (such as adding some annotations), you'll need to copy the updated files back to your desktop computer.

This apparently simple procedure is fraught with all kinds of unforeseen complications and perils:

■ If you modify only some of the documents when you're working on the notebook, how can you be sure which ones to copy to the desktop?

■ What if you create a *new* document on the notebook?

■ What if the floppy disk you're using to move the files back and forth contains other files?

■ What if you make changes to the same document on both the desktop and the notebook?

These are thorny issues that until now required patience, careful planning, and often some knowledge of DOS batch files to overcome. Now, however, these problems are a thing of the past because Windows 95 includes a feature that solves them all in one shot: Briefcase.

Briefcase works with special folders on your computer that you can use to hold the documents you transfer between your desktop and notebook computers. Instead of always copying individual documents back and forth, you usually just work with the Briefcase folder. Briefcase really shines, however, in that it synchronizes the documents on both machines automatically. If you work on a few documents on your notebook, for example, Windows 95 can figure out which ones are different, and then it lets you update the desktop by running a simple command. There's no guesswork involved and no chance of copying a file to the wrong folder.

Here are the basic Briefcase steps you follow to keep notebook and desktop files in sync:

1. After you've finished working with the files on the desktop machine, copy them to a Briefcase folder, and then copy the Briefcase folder to a floppy disk.

2. Insert the floppy disk into the notebook, and copy the Briefcase files to the notebook's hard drive.

3. Use your notebook to work on the files. When you're done, open the floppy disk Briefcase folder, and run the Update command. This action updates the floppy disk files with the changes you made on the notebook.

4. Insert the floppy disk into the desktop, open its Briefcase folder, and run the Update command. This action updates the hard disk files with the changed files in the floppy disk Briefcase.

The next few sections take you through each of these steps in detail.

20

NOTEBOOK
COMPUTERS AND
THE BRIEFCASE

Step 1: Copy the Files to the Briefcase Folder

When you install Briefcase, Windows 95 adds a My Briefcase icon to the desktop. This is a special kind of folder that supports the Briefcase features and that can be used to keep files synchronized. You can use this folder if you like, but you can also create new Briefcase folders by using either of the following techniques:

- In Explorer, highlight the folder you want to contain the Briefcase, and then select New | Briefcase.

- Right-click either in Explorer's Contents pane or on the desktop, and select Briefcase from the context menu.

TROUBLESHOOTING: MY BRIEFCASE IS A REGULAR FOLDER

When you activate user profiles in Windows 95, the My Briefcase folder turns into a regular folder. This is a bug in Windows 95, and you can work around it either by turning off user profiles or by deleting the My Briefcase icon and creating a new Briefcase object.

After you've completed your desktop work and decided which documents you want to work with on your notebook, you need to copy those documents to My Briefcase (or whichever Briefcase folder you want to use). Because My Briefcase has an icon on the desktop, it's easiest just to drag the files from Explorer and drop them on the My Briefcase icon. Alternatively, you can right-click each file and select Send To | My Briefcase.

The first time you copy a file to My Briefcase (or attempt to open the My Briefcase folder), you'll see the dialog box shown in Figure 20.9. This dialog box just gives you an overview of the Briefcase process, so you can click Finish to remove it.

FIGURE 20.9.

This dialog box appears the first time you copy a file to My Briefcase.

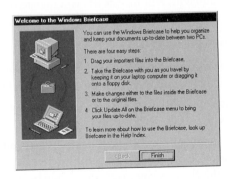

The file you copy to a Briefcase folder is called a *sync copy* because Briefcase attempts to synchronize this file with the original. It does this by using a database to keep track of where the original file is located, as well its date and time stamp, size, and file type. If any of these attributes changes, Briefcase knows that the files are out of sync.

To see how the Briefcase folders work, use Explorer to display the contents of My Briefcase. As you can see in Figure 20.10, the Contents pane for a Briefcase folder is a bit different from the one you see with a regular folder. (Make sure that you have Explorer's Details view turned on.) Besides the usual Name, Size, Type, and Modified columns, Briefcase folders also show two extra columns:

Sync Copy In: This column shows the drive and folder where the original document resides.

Status: This column tells you the current state of each document. At first, the status is Up-to-date because you haven't done anything to the files. The status will change after you've made modifications to a file (as you'll see later).

FIGURE 20.10.

The Contents pane for a Briefcase *folder has a few extra columns.*

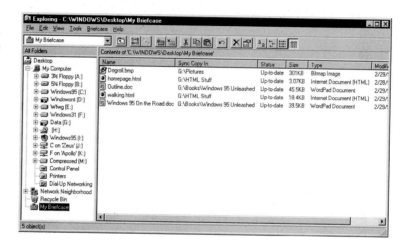

What happens if, after copying the files to My Briefcase, you make a change to one of the originals? No problem. You can either copy the modified document into My Briefcase or use Briefcase itself to update the document automatically. For example, if I make a change to the original of the file named homepage.html and then display My Briefcase again, the Status column will tell me that the file Needs updating, as shown in Figure 20.11.

To update the file, use any of the following techniques:

- Highlight the file and select File | Update.
- Right-click the file and click Update.
- Highlight the file and click the Update Selection button in the toolbar.
- For multiple files, either highlight them all and use the preceding techniques, or click the Update All toolbar button.

20

NOTEBOOK COMPUTERS AND THE BRIEFCASE

FIGURE 20.11.

If you change an original document, Briefcase lets you know that the sync copy needs to be updated.

Update All
Update Selection

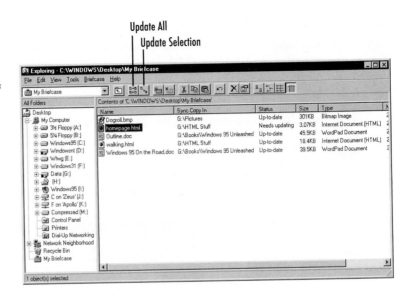

In each case, you'll see an Update dialog box similar to the one shown in Figure 20.12. The arrow shows you the direction of the update. In this case, the modified version of homepage.html in the G:\HTML Stuff folder will replace the unmodified file in the Briefcase. If this is what you want, click Update. If, for some reason, you want to reverse the replacement, right-click either file and select the opposite arrow from the context menu that appears.

FIGURE 20.12.

When you run the Update command, Briefcase displays a list of the files that need updating.

After you've copied all your documents to the Briefcase, insert a disk into one the desktop's floppy disk drives, and then copy the Briefcase folder to the floppy disk. If you've used this disk to copy the Briefcase before, Windows 95 asks whether you want to replace any files in the folder that have the same name. In this case, you want to click Yes to replace the files.

CAUTION: THE SEND TO COMMAND MOVES THE FOLDER

When putting the Briefcase on the floppy disk, you might be tempted to use the Send To command. Be warned, however: Send To *moves* the Briefcase folder to the floppy. To make Send To copy the folder, hold down the Ctrl key.

NOTE: NEED A BIGGER BRIEFCASE?

I'm discussing the "sneakernet" Briefcase method in this chapter—that is, using a floppy disk to transfer files between desktop and notebook. The disadvantage of this method is that the size of your Briefcase is limited to the capacity of the floppy disk. If the files you need to transfer won't fit on a floppy, you have two choices: Hook up your notebook to your network or use Windows 95's Direct Cable Connection accessory. I discuss the second option in Chapter 34, "From Laptop to Desktop and Back: Direct Cable Connection."

Step 2: Copy the Files to the Notebook

Your next task is to get the files from the floppy disk Briefcase onto the notebook computer. Insert the disk into the notebook, and then open the Briefcase folder. As you can see in Figure 20.13, the floppy version of the Briefcase folder has two changes:

- The paths in the Sync Copy In column include the name of the computer where the original files reside (Hermes, in this case).

- The Status column shows Unchanged in Briefcase for each file.

FIGURE 20.13.

The floppy copy of the Briefcase *folder.*

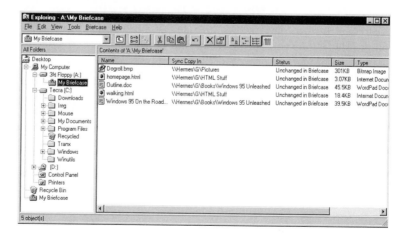

Now copy the files to whatever destination you like on the notebook's hard disk. Whatever you do, don't *move* the files to the notebook, and don't move or copy the `Briefcase` folder from the floppy disk. If you do, you'll break the link between the Briefcase files and the original files.

When you copy the files to the notebook, you're creating another sync copy, so Briefcase sets up a link between the floppy Briefcase files and the notebook files. For example, suppose that I copy all the files in my floppy `Briefcase` folder to the `C:\My Documents` folder on the notebook. The floppy Briefcase now appears as shown in Figure 20.14. As you can see, Briefcase has set up a link to the sync copies in `C:\My Documents`. The Briefcase database is still keeping track of the original files, however.

FIGURE 20.14.

When you copy the files from the floppy Briefcase to the notebook, Briefcase maintains a link between them.

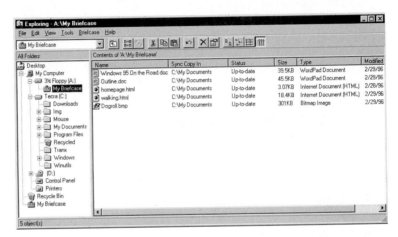

Step 3: Work on the Files and Then Update the Floppy Briefcase

With the documents now safely stowed in the notebook's Briefcase, you can go ahead and work on the files. When you've completed your notebook labors, the documents you worked with are out of sync with the documents in the floppy disk Briefcase. So your next chore is to update the Briefcase on the floppy disk.

Once again, display the floppy `Briefcase` folder. The Status column tells you which files need updating, as shown in Figure 20.15.

Use the techniques I outlined earlier to run the Update command and display an Update dialog box similar to the one shown in Figure 20.16. Change the replacement arrows if necessary, and then click Update. Briefcase updates the files in the floppy Briefcase with the modified files on the notebook.

FIGURE 20.15.

If you modified files on the notebook, the floppy Briefcase keeps track and tells you which files need updating.

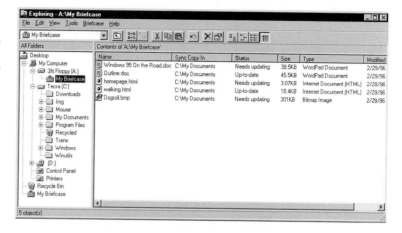

FIGURE 20.16.

Run the Update command to display this dialog box, which summarizes the files that need to be updated.

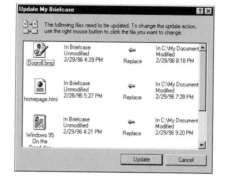

Step 4: Update the Briefcase on the Desktop

When you get back to the office, slip the floppy disk into your desktop, and open the disk's My Briefcase folder. This time, Briefcase checks the floppy Briefcase files with the originals and lets you know whether any files need updating, as shown in Figure 20.17. If they do, run the Update command again.

If one of the original files was also modified, Briefcase offers to skip the update for that file, as shown in Figure 20.18. If you still want to go ahead with the update (that is, if you don't want to keep the changes made to one of the files), right-click the file and select the appropriate replacement direction. Otherwise, you need to skip the update, open both files in the application, and incorporate the changes by hand.

FIGURE 20.17.

*When the floppy
Briefcase is inserted into
the desktop machine,
Briefcase compares the
floppy files to the
originals.*

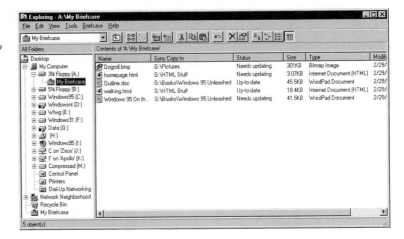

FIGURE 20.18.

*If both the original file
and the file in the
floppy Briefcase have
changed, Briefcase offers
to skip the update for
the file.*

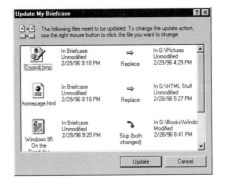

Some Windows 95 applications (such as Access for Windows 95) are programmed with
reconcilers that let you *merge* two modified files. In this case, the default Update action is Merge,
as shown in Figure 20.19. When you update, the application attempts to incorporate changes
from both files into the original file.

FIGURE 20.19.

*Some Windows 95
applications let you
merge two modified
files.*

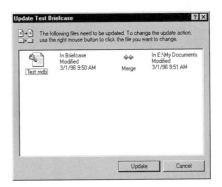

Working with PC Card (PCMCIA) Devices

Another problem that caused notebooks to be relegated to a lower status on the PC totem pole was their lack of expandability. Desktop systems had all kinds of bus slots and drive bays that intrepid hobbyists and power users could use to augment the capabilities of their systems. Notebook configurations, however, were generally set in stone; what you bought was what you got.

That all changed with the advent of the Personal Computer Memory Card International Association (PCMCIA) and the standards it developed for notebook expansion boards. These standards let notebook manufacturers add small slots (called *sockets*) to their machines that would hold credit card–sized expansion modules for memory cards, hard disks, CD-ROMs, modems, network adapters, SCSI controllers, tape backups, and more. PCMCIA cards are also part of the Plug and Play standard, which means you can insert and remove cards while your computer is running (this is called *hot-swapping*).

PCMCIA cards are now known as PC cards, and I'll use both terms interchangeably in this section.

Windows 95 and PC Cards

Windows 95 supports the PC card standards, so Setup should detect your notebook's PC card socket automatically and install the appropriate protected-mode device drivers. Windows 95 also supports real-mode and protected-mode PC card drivers from third-party vendors, but you'll lose some of the Plug and Play capabilities (such as hot-swapping).

Besides the PC card socket, Windows 95 also needs drivers for the individual PC card devices inserted into the slots. A PC card device driver can be implemented in three ways:

■ For PC cards that don't require device-specific functionality, Windows 95 uses a universal Plug and Play PC card device driver. This driver can handle hot-swapping and dynamic configuration, and it can receive configuration information from Windows 95 without knowing what kind of card is in the PC card socket.

■ For devices such as modems and hard disks, Windows 95 can use generic device drivers for the particular hardware class.

■ To implement device-specific functionality (such as memory-mapped I/O for network adapters or SCSI controllers), vendors can provide mini-drivers to supplement the standard universal PC card driver.

Enabling PC Card Socket Support in Windows 95

Before you use a PC card device, you need to enable Windows 95 support for the socket (and install the 32-bit PC card drivers) by running the PC Card Wizard.

To start this Wizard, display the Control Panel and open the PC Card (PCMCIA) icon. You'll see the Welcome to the PC Card (PCMCIA) Wizard dialog box, shown in Figure 20.20. Run through the Wizard's dialog boxes, answering the questions appropriately for your system. When you're done, Windows 95 prompts you to shut down your computer. Click Yes to shut down the system, and then turn it back on to enable the PC card socket. If you were using any real-mode PC card drivers, the Wizard comments them out from CONFIG.SYS so that they won't load when you reboot.

FIGURE 20.20.

Use this Wizard to enable Windows 95 support for your notebook's PC card socket.

Inserting a PC Card Device

Because PC card devices are hot-swappable, inserting them is a no-brainer: With Windows 95 still running, just slide the card into one of your notebook's PC card slots. If you've used and configured the card before, Windows 95 beeps the speaker, and the card is available for use immediately. You'll see the PC Card (PCMCIA) Status icon appear in the taskbar's system tray, as shown in Figure 20.21.

FIGURE 20.21.

When you insert a PC card device, the PC Card (PCMCIA) Status icon appears in the system tray.

PC Card (PCMCIA) Status icon

If this is the first time you've inserted the card, Windows 95 gets right to work loading and configuring the appropriate drivers, as shown in Figure 20.22. Depending on the device, you might need to fill in a dialog box or two. If Windows 95 doesn't have a driver for the device, it prompts you for an installation disk from the manufacturer.

FIGURE 20.22.

When you insert a PC card for the first time, Windows 95 loads and configures the appropriate driver automatically.

Removing a PC Card Device

Although PC card devices are hot-swappable, you shouldn't just yank a device out of its slot. For example, if your device is a network adapter, pulling the card out without warning could cut off another user while they're using one of your files. Also, Windows 95 might not be able to reallocate the card's resources correctly. If you do happen to pull a card out of its slot prematurely, Windows 95 displays the warning dialog box shown in Figure 20.23.

FIGURE 20.23.

Windows 95 displays this dialog box if you remove a PC card device without warning.

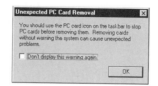

Before removing any PC card device, you should tell Windows 95 to stop the device. The easiest way to do this is to click the PC Card (PCMCIA) Status icon in the system tray. Windows 95 then displays a menu of commands that stop each of the PC card devices installed on your system, as shown in Figure 20.24. Click the command that corresponds to the device you want to stop. After a few seconds, Windows 95 displays a dialog box to let you know that it's safe to remove the device.

FIGURE 20.24.

If you click the PC Card (PCMCIA) Status icon, Windows 95 displays a menu of commands that stop each device.

Alternatively, you can stop PC card devices via the PC card properties sheet. To display this dialog box, use either of the following methods:

■ Double-click the taskbar's PC Card (PCMCIA) Status icon.

■ In Control Panel, open the PC Card (PCMCIA) icon.

Figure 20.25 shows the PC Card (PCMCIA) Properties dialog box that appears. To stop a device, highlight it and click the Stop button. Again, Windows 95 displays a dialog box to let you know that it's safe to remove the device.

Figure 20.25.

You can also stop a PC card device by using this dialog box.

Setting PC Card Properties

The PC Card (PCMCIA) Properties dialog box has a few other settings you can work with. In particular, the Socket Status tab, shown in Figure 20.25, has two check boxes:

> **Show control on taskbar:** If you deactivate this check box, Windows 95 removes the PC Card (PCMCIA) Status icon from the system tray.

> **Display warning if card is removed before it is stopped:** If you deactivate this check box, Windows 95 won't display the warning dialog box shown in Figure 20.23 when you remove a PC card device.

In the Global Settings tab, you can use the Card services shared memory to determine the memory range used by your PC card devices. The Windows 95 card services (device drivers) use a common pool of memory. Normally, this memory window is managed automatically by Windows 95. If, however, you have a device that doesn't work—despite having the correct drivers loaded and support for the PC card socket enabled—the notebook is probably using the wrong memory window.

To change this, deactivate the Automatic selection check box, and then use the Start, End, and Length text boxes to define the new memory window. Microsoft recommends a Start value of 100,000 or higher.

TROUBLESHOOTING: PC CARD DEVICE DOESN'T WORK

If you've adjusted the memory range in the Global Settings tab and your device still doesn't work, a conflicting IRQ might be the problem. Open Device Manager, display the properties sheet for the device, and change its IRQ value.

The Global Settings tab also has a Disable PC card sound effects check box. If you activate this control, Windows 95 won't beep the speaker each time you insert a PC card device.

Notes About Hot-Docking and Hardware Profiles

PC card devices are an innovative solution to the problem of notebook expandability, but they're not a total solution. For one thing, most notebooks have only a small number of PC card sockets (usually one or two), so the number of devices you can have plugged in at any one time is limited. For another thing, many devices still are available only as cards designed for bus slots (such as video capture cards).

If you need multiple devices attached to your notebook, or if you need a device that's not available in the PC card format, an excellent compromise is the *docking station*. These are platforms into which you can slide your notebook and thus create a full-fledged desktop machine. The notebook provides the guts—the CPU, the memory, the hard drive—and the docking provides everything else—drive bays; bus slots; and ports for an external monitor, keyboard, mouse, printer, modem, and so on.

If your notebook has a Plug and Play BIOS, Windows 95 supports *hot-docking:* inserting your notebook into, and removing it from, the docking station while Windows 95 is still running.

The first time you try this, the Plug and Play BIOS alerts Windows 95 of the hardware change. The Configuration Manager takes over, examines the new hardware configuration, and installs the appropriate drivers. When that's done, Windows 95 establishes a new hardware profile (usually called *Dock 1*) for the docked computer. You can then enable and disable devices in each profile.

On my notebook, for example, I have two profiles: Docked and Undocked. When the machine is docked, I use (among other things) an external mouse; when the machine is undocked, I use the notebook's built-in mouse. Each mouse, however, uses a different device driver: Standard Serial Mouse for the external mouse, and Standard PS/2 Port Mouse for the built-in mouse. To tell Windows 95 which driver to use in which profile, I use each device's properties sheet to disable the appropriate profile. For the built-in mouse, for example, I deactivate the Docked profile and activate the Undocked profile, as shown in Figure 20.26. (I showed you how to work with hardware profiles in Chapter 10, "How Windows 95 Handles Hardware.")

Another advantage you get with a Plug and Play notebook BIOS is the Eject PC command. You can find this command on the Start menu while your notebook is docked, as shown in Figure 20.27. Selecting the command tells Windows 95 to unload the drivers used in the docked profile. When that's done, Windows 95 either prompts you to undock your notebook or does it for you (if your docking station has an automatic undocking feature).

FIGURE 20.26.

If you have profiles for docked and undocked states, be sure to deactivate the appropriate profiles for your drivers.

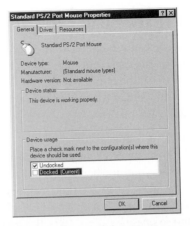

FIGURE 20.27.

Run the Eject PC command when you're ready to remove the notebook from the docking station.

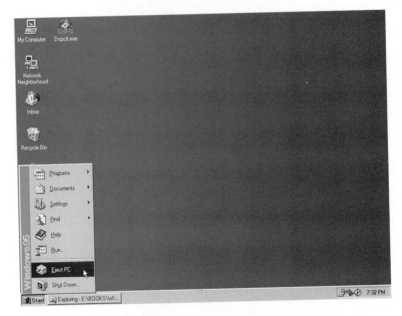

Setting Up Your Notebook's Infrared Port

Many of the latest notebook computers—such as the Toshiba Tecra and the Micron Millennia TransPort—come with a built-in infrared (IR) port. This port acts like both a serial port and a parallel port, and you can use it to transfer files and send print jobs. (For sending print jobs, you'll need a printer—such as the HP LaserJet 5MP—with an IR port. You can find more on this topic in Chapter 19, "Prescriptions for Perfect Printing.")

Although Windows 95 doesn't ship with IrDA (Infrared Data Association) drivers for these ports, it does recognize them and can work with third-party drivers. Microsoft did, however, release an IrDA driver in late 1995. You can either download it from an online Microsoft site (the filename is W95IR.EXE) or get it from the Windows 95 Service Pack.

Installing the Windows 95 IrDA Driver

When you install the Windows 95 Service Pack, the IrDA driver isn't loaded onto your system, so you need to install it by hand. Whether you're using the Service Pack or you've downloaded W95IR.EXE, the following steps tell you what's involved in installing the driver on your notebook.

> **CAUTION: REMOVE THE EXISTING DRIVER**
>
> If you've already installed the IrDA driver and want to change the device, you must first uninstall the existing driver. Use the Add/Remove Programs icon in Control Panel to do this.

1. If you downloaded the IrDA driver, run W95IR.EXE to decompress the files it contains.

2. One of the decompressed files is named SETUP.EXE. Run this file to start the installation process. If you have the Service Pack, you need to run the SETUP.EXE file in the *drive*:\ADMIN\COMPONTS\INFRARED folder, where *drive* is the drive letter of your CD-ROM. Either way, you'll eventually see the Add Infrared Device Wizard dialog box, shown in Figure 20.28.

FIGURE 20.28.

You'll use the Add Infrared Device Wizard to set up your notebook's IR port.

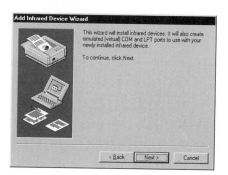

3. Click Next >. The Wizard displays a list of infrared manufacturers and models, as shown in Figure 20.29.

FIGURE 20.29.

Use this dialog box to select your IR device.

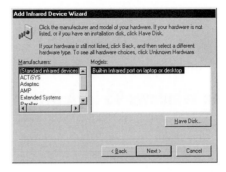

4. Because you're dealing with your notebook's internal IR port, select the Built-in Infrared port on laptop or desktop model, and then click Next >. The Wizard prompts you for your infrared port.

5. Highlight the appropriate port (for your notebook, this should be Generic IRDA Compatible Device) and click Next >. The next dialog box, shown in Figure 20.30, prompts you to specify simulated ports for the infrared serial and printer ports.

FIGURE 20.30.

Use this dialog box to specify the simulated ports to use with infrared operations.

6. If the default ports don't conflict with any devices on your system, click Next >. Otherwise, activate the Change ports option, use the text boxes to specify new ports, and click Next >. Windows 95 loads the IrDA drivers, sets up the simulated IR serial and parallel ports, and displays the last of the Add Infrared Device Wizard dialog boxes.

7. Click Finish.

Your IR port is now ready to go. Windows 95 adds an infrared icon to the system tray; the icon you see depends on whether the driver has another IR port in its sights. If no other port is in range, you see the icon shown in Figure 20.31. If the port finds another IR device, the icon changes to the one shown in Figure 20.32.

FIGURE 20.31.

The infrared icon when no other IR device is within range.

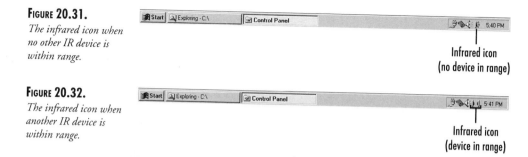

Infrared icon
(no device in range)

FIGURE 20.32.

The infrared icon when another IR device is within range.

Infrared icon
(device in range)

NOTE: INFRARED RANGE

For IR devices to recognize each other, their ports must be facing each other, and they should be no closer than 6 inches and no farther than 3 feet to 9 feet (depending on the device).

NOTE: YOU NEED TO REINITIALIZE THE PORT WHEN YOU RESTART

The IR port isn't initialized automatically each time you restart Windows 95. To crank it up again, you need to open the Control Panel's Infrared icon, as described in the next section. To save this step each time you restart Windows 95, add a shortcut for the Infrared icon to your StartUp folder (see Chapter 13, "Working with Files and Folders," for details).

Adjusting the IrDA Driver's Properties

The IrDA driver has a properties sheet called the Infrared Monitor that you can use to modify the behavior of the driver. To display the Infrared Monitor, use either of the following methods:

- Double-click the infrared icon in the taskbar.

- Display the Control Panel and open the Infrared icon.

Either way, the Infrared Monitor dialog box, shown in Figure 20.33, appears. The Status tab tells you how many devices are within the port's range and the names of those devices.

20

FIGURE 20.33.

Use the Infrared Monitor to adjust the properties for the IrDA driver.

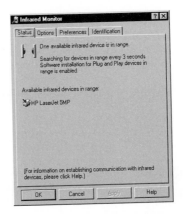

The Options tab, shown in Figure 20.34, gives you the following settings:

Enable infrared communication on: Activate this check box to enable the IrDA driver. Use the drop-down list to select the physical port used by the IR device.

Search for and provide status for devices in range: When this check box is activated, the IrDA driver checks for IR ports within its range. Use the Search every spinner to determine the interval between checks.

Enable software install for Plug and Play devices in range: When this option is activated, Windows 95 automatically installs the appropriate drivers for any Plug and Play devices that fall within the IrDA driver's range.

Limit connection speed to: The IrDA driver defaults to its maximum communications speed of 115.2 Kbps (kilobits per second). If you find that your communications are unreliable at this speed, activate this check box and select a lower speed from the drop-down list.

If you want to return these settings to their default values, click the Restore Defaults button.

FIGURE 20.34.

Use the Options tab to set various options for the IrDA driver.

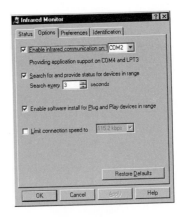

The Preferences tab, shown in Figure 20.35, contains various settings related to Infrared Monitor. You have the following choices:

Display the infrared icon in the taskbar: This check box toggles the taskbar's infrared icon on and off.

Open Infrared Monitor for interrupted communication: If you keep this check box activated, the infrared Monitor appears automatically if any IR communications are interrupted. You can then use Infrared Monitor to change settings and (hopefully) get the communication reestablished.

Play sounds for devices in range and interrupted communication: When this check box is activated, Infrared Monitor plays a sound when a device comes into range or moves out of range, or if communications are interrupted.

FIGURE 20.35.

The Preferences tab controls various Infrared Monitor settings.

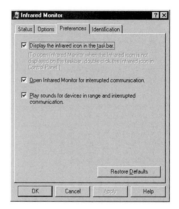

Finally, the Identification tab lets you enter a name and a short description for the computer. If you've already set up networking on the computer, these fields are filled in for you already.

Summary

This chapter explained the various Windows 95 features related to notebook computers. I showed you how to use Windows 95's support for Advanced Power Management to monitor and extend battery life, you learned how to use Briefcase to keep notebook and desktop files synchronized, and then I went through a few notebook hardware issues: PC cards, hot-docking, and infrared ports.

Windows 95 has a few more notebook tricks up its electronic sleeve, and I talk about them in the following chapters:

■ Windows 95 supports *deferred printing*. This means that if you print a document on your notebook, Windows 95 holds the print job in a queue and then prints it later when you get back to the office (or to a site with a printer). I demonstrate how this works in Chapter 19, "Prescriptions for Perfect Printing."

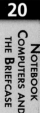

- I also talk about infrared printing in Chapter 19.

- Transferring files between two machines is easier if you do it over a cable rather than by floppy disk. I explain how to do this in Windows 95 in Chapter 34, "From Laptop to Desktop and Back: Direct Cable Connection."

- To learn how to use your notebook to dial in to a network, see Chapter 35, "Remote Computing with Dial-Up Networking."

DOS Isn't Dead: Optimizing DOS Applications Under Windows 95

IN THIS CHAPTER

There's many a good tune played on an old fiddle.

English proverb

The dogs bark, but the caravan moves on.

Arab proverb

As DOS enters the autumn of its life, the news is not good:

- Windows is now the Big Thing and has become practically synonymous with the PC.
- The fortunes of DOS and Windows have been on opposite tracks for several years, with the sales of Windows applications in full "boom" mode and DOS sales in the doldrums.
- Few (if any) companies are upgrading their DOS programs or creating new ones.
- It's rare to see DOS defended in the popular press nowadays. Most DOS diehards, it seems, can't be bothered to rage against the dying of the light.
- Even games, that once unassailable bastion of DOS supremacy, are going GUI thanks to Microsoft's aggressive push of its speedy graphics APIs.
- And, as a final insult, DOS isn't even an operating system any more. It's just another Windows 95 accessory or, at best, a Windows 95 "mode."

However, DOS does have one (not insignificant) thing going for it: Untold tens of millions of legacy applications are still sitting on computers around the world. Even if those computers are running Windows, there are plenty of users who still like to sneak out to the DOS prompt to run these old programs. And why not? After all, these programs are familiar, fast, and paid for!

If you're still running an old DOS app or two, this chapter shows you how to squeeze the best and most reliable performance out of them under Windows 95.

The Windows 95 DOS Shell

cruft together *v* To throw together something ugly but temporarily workable.

MS-DOS *n* A clone of CP/M for the 8088 crufted together in six weeks by hacker Tim Paterson, who is said to have regretted it ever since.

from *The New Hacker's Dictionary*

In Internet circles, a *holy war* is a never-ending debate on the merits of one thing versus another, in which people use the same arguments over and over, and nobody's opinion budges even the slightest bit one way or the other. Common holy war topics include liberalism versus conservatism, pro-choice versus pro-life, and neatness versus sloppiness.

Operating systems cause frequent holy war skirmishes, with most battles pitting Macintosh against Windows, and UNIX against NT. Until recently, the mother of all operating system holy wars was DOS versus Windows, with correspondents devoting obscene amounts of time and energy extolling the virtues of one system and detailing the shortcomings of the other. But with Windows's decisive victory over DOS both technologically and in the marketplace, the DOS devoted are heard from only rarely nowadays.

That isn't to say that DOS is dead. Far from it. DOS is alive and well and adjusting nicely to its new role as just another Windows 95 accessory. With DOS no longer the boss, it's entirely possible that you might go your entire Windows 95 career without having to crank up a DOS session. But if you *do* need DOS, you need to know a few things in order to get the most out of your command-line sessions. This first half of this chapter introduces you to the Windows 95 DOS prompt and shows you how to unleash the full potential of the new DOS.

What's New

Members of the Windows 95 design team directed their energies into the Windows 95 interface and core components and spent relatively little time tweaking DOS. The new DOS is not, however, the same as the old DOS. Here's a partial list of improvements:

- You can start Windows programs from the DOS prompt and even from within batch files.
- The new DOS includes support for long filenames.
- Reduced reliance on real-mode drivers means that more conventional memory is available for DOS programs.
- Each DOS program can have its own settings and environment (CONFIG.SYS and AUTOEXEC.BAT). These are controlled via properties sheets, so there's no need to create program information files (PIFs) from scratch for each program.
- You can run DOS programs in MS-DOS mode if they need full access to the computer's resources.
- The DOS session window has a toolbar for easy access to common features.
- You can access shared network folders via the command prompt.
- Most DOS commands are now native Windows 95 commands.

DOS Commands in Windows 95

Windows 95 is, for the most part, *the* operating system on your machine. Yes, it comes with some real-mode components (such as IO.SYS) that are DOS-like, but they really just handle a few chores until Windows 95 can get itself into protected mode. After Windows 95 is running, however, "DOS" is just two things:

- COMMAND.COM, which provides the DOS prompt and a collection of internal DOS commands (such as COPY and DIR).
- A few external DOS commands, such as FORMAT.COM and XCOPY.EXE.

For Windows 95, Microsoft enhanced some of these commands, dropped other commands, and made a few of the dropped commands available on the CD-ROM.

Table 21.1 lists the internal DOS commands available within the Windows 95 version of COMMAND.COM.

Table 21.1. The Windows 95 internal DOS commands.

Command	Description
BREAK	Sets or clears extended Ctrl-C checking.
CD	Changes to a different directory or, if run without parameters, displays the name of the current directory.
CHCP	Displays the number of the active character set (code page). You can also use this command to change the active character set for all devices that support character-set switching.
CHDIR	Takes the same action as the CD command.
CLS	Clears the screen.
COPY	Copies one or more files to the location you specify.
CTTY	Changes the terminal device used to control the computer.
DATE	Displays or sets the current date.
DEL	Deletes the files you specify.
DIR	Displays a list of the files and subfolders that exist in the current or specified folder.
ERASE	Deletes the files you specify.
EXIT	Quits COMMAND.COM and returns to the program that started the command interpreter, if one exists.
LH	Loads a program into upper memory.
LOADHIGH	Takes the same action as the LH command.
LOCK	Enables direct disk access.
MD	Creates a folder or subfolder.
MKDIR	Takes the same action as the MD command.
PATH	Specifies which folders Windows 95 should search for executable files.
PROMPT	Changes the appearance of the command prompt.
RD	Deletes a folder.
REN	Changes the name of the specified file or files.
RENAME	Takes the same action as the REN command.
RMDIR	Takes the same action as the RD command.

Command	*Description*
SET	Displays, sets, or removes environment variables.
TIME	Displays or sets the current time.
TYPE	Displays the contents of the specified text file.
UNLOCK	Disables direct disk access.
VER	Displays the operating system version number.
VERIFY	Directs the operating system to verify that files are written correctly to a disk, and displays the status of verification.
VOL	Displays the volume label and serial number for a disk.

The DOS external commands are located in the COMMAND subfolder of the main Windows 95 folder. Table 21.2 lists the external DOS commands that ship with Windows 95.

Table 21.2. The Windows 95 external DOS commands.

Command	*Description*
ATTRIB.EXE	Displays or changes the attributes of the specified files.
CHKDSK.EXE	Checks a disk for (and optionally repairs) lost and cross-linked clusters. ScanDisk does a better job at finding and repairing these errors.
CHOICE.COM	Used in batch files to present the user with a list of options.
COMMAND.COM	Starts a new instance of the command interpreter. This file is usually found in the root directory of the boot drive.
DEBUG.EXE	Tests and edits executable files.
DELTREE.EXE	Deletes a folder and all its files and subfolders.
DISKCOPY.COM	Makes an exact copy of a floppy disk.
DOSKEY.COM	A memory-resident program that recalls commands, edits previous command lines, and runs macros.
EDIT.COM	Starts a text editor you can use to create and edit ASCII text files.
EXTRACT.EXE	Extracts files from a compressed cabinet (CAB) file.
FC.EXE	Compares two files and displays the differences between them.
FDISK.EXE	Starts the FDISK utility.
FIND.EXE	Searches files for a specified text string.
FORMAT.COM	Formats a disk.
KEYB.COM	Configures a keyboard for a specific language.

continues

Table 21.2. continued

Command	Description
LABEL.EXE	Creates or modifies the volume label of a disk.
MEM.EXE	Displays the amount of used and free memory on the computer.
MODE.COM	Configures a printer, serial port, or display adapter; sets the keyboard repeat rate; redirects printer output from a parallel port to a serial port; prepares, selects, refreshes, or displays the numbers of the character sets (code pages) for parallel printers or the keyboard and screen; and displays the status of all the devices installed on the computer.
MORE.COM	Pauses command output to display one screen at a time.
MOVE.EXE	Moves files and renames folders.
MSCDEX.EXE	Loads the real-mode CD-ROM driver.
NLSFUNC.EXE	Loads country-specific information for national language support.
SCANDISK.EXE	The real-mode version of ScanDisk.
SETVER	Reports a DOS version number to programs or device drivers designed for earlier versions of MS-DOS.
SMARTDRV	Loads the SMARTDrive disk cache. No longer needed in AUTOEXEC.BAT.
SHARE.EXE	Sets up file locking.
SORT.EXE	Reads input, sorts data, and writes the results to the screen, a file, or another device.
START.EXE	Lets you set various parameters for running Windows programs from the DOS prompt.
SUBST.EXE	Substitutes a drive letter for a pathname.
SYS.COM	Creates a bootable disk by copying Windows 95's system files and COMMAND.COM to the disk.
XCOPY.EXE	The extended copy command.
XCOPY32.EXE	The 32-bit version of XCOPY.

Microsoft also deleted quite a few DOS commands when it put together the Windows 95 package. Most of these commands were either obsolete (such as EGA.SYS) or dangerous (such as RECOVER). A few of these commands can, however, be found on the Windows 95 CD-ROM in the \OTHER\OLDMSDOS\ folder. These are all DOS 6.22 commands that haven't been updated for Windows 95. I've summarized them in Table 21.3.

DOS Isn't Dead: Optimizing DOS Applications Under Windows 95

CHAPTER 21

659

21

OPTIMIZING
DOS
APPLICATIONS

Table 21.3. Old DOS commands available on the Windows 95 CD-ROM.

Command	Description
APPEND.EXE	Lets applications work with data files in a specified folder as though they were in the current folder.
CHKSTATE.SYS	Used by MEMMAKER.EXE during memory optimization.
EXPAND.EXE	Decompresses a compressed file from the DOS 6.x or Windows 3.x source disks.
GRAPHICS.COM	A memory-resident program that lets you print screen shots.
HELP.COM	Displays descriptions, syntax, and examples for all DOS commands.
INTERLNK.EXE	Connects two computers (one client and one server) via a null-modem cable attached to their serial or parallel ports.
INTERSVR.EXE	Initializes a computer as a server for INTERLNK.
LOADFIX.COM	Loads a program above the first 64 KB of conventional memory.
MEMMAKER.EXE	Optimizes conventional memory by moving device drivers and TSRs into the upper memory area.
MSBACKUP.EXE	Backs up and restores files. This file (and its support files) can be found in the \OTHER\OLDMSDOS\MSBACKUP folder.
PRINT.EXE	Prints a text file in the background.
QBASIC.EXE	The programming environment for creating QBASIC applications.
REPLACE.EXE	Replaces files in a destination folder with files from a source folder that have the same name.
RESTORE.EXE	Restores files that were backed up using the DOS BACKUP program (versions 2.0 through 5.0; for version 6.0, see MSBACKUP.EXE).
SIZER.EXE	Used by MEMMAKER.EXE during memory optimization.
TREE.COM	Displays the structure of the specified folder using a tree-like display.
UNDELETE.EXE	Restores files that were deleted using either DEL or ERASE.

Here's a list of DOS commands that are gone for good in Windows 95:

ASSIGN	BACKUP	COMP
DOSSHELL	EDLIN	FASTHELP
FASTOPEN	GRAFTABL	JOIN
MEMCARD	MIRROR	MSAV
POWER	RECOVER	SMARTMON
UNFORMAT	VSAFE	

Getting to DOS

Okay, so Windows 95 comes with DOS, and DOS comes with all kinds of internal and external commands. The next question is, how do you get to DOS so that you can work with these commands? The next few sections explain everything you need to know.

Starting a DOS Session

As you'll see in just a bit, Windows 95 offers various methods of running DOS commands. One of these methods is the most obvious one: Start a DOS session and run your commands from the DOS prompt. If this is your preferred method, you'll find that Windows 95 (as usual) offers umpteen different ways to get to the DOS prompt.

Starting DOS Without Exiting the Windows 95 GUI

If you want to start a DOS session without exiting the Windows 95 GUI, use any of the following methods:

- Select Start | Programs | MS-DOS Prompt.
- Double-click COMMAND.COM in the root folder of your computer's boot drive.
- Create a shortcut for COMMAND.COM on your desktop, and then double-click the shortcut.
- Select Start | Run, enter command in the Run dialog box, and click OK.

TIP: STARTING YOUR DOS SESSION IN A SPECIFIC FOLDER

If you highlight a folder in Explorer before starting COMMAND.COM via Start | Run, the DOS window that appears will open in the highlighted folder.

For the last two methods, you can specify extra parameters and switches after the COMMAND.COM filename. Here's the syntax used by COMMAND.COM:

```
COMMAND [[drive:]path] [device] [/E:x] [/L:y] [/U:z] [/P] [/MSG] [/LOW]
➡[/Y [/[C¦K] command]]
```

[drive:]path	Specifies the drive and folder containing COMMAND.COM.
device	Specifies the device to use for command input and output.
/E:x	Sets x as the initial environment size (in bytes), in which x is between 256 and 32768.
/L:y	Sets y as the size of each internal buffer (requires /P), in which y is between 128 and 1024).

/U:z	Sets *z* as the size of the input buffer (requires /P), in which *z* is between 128 and 255. Set this to a higher value (the default is 127) if you plan on entering long filenames at the prompt.
/P	Makes COMMAND.COM permanent (that is, you can't quit with the EXIT command).
/MSG	Stores all error messages in memory (requires /P).
/LOW	Forces COMMAND.COM to keep its resident data in low (conventional) memory.
/Y	Steps through the batch program specified by /C or /K.
/C command	Executes the specified *command* and returns.
/K command	Executes the specified *command* and continues running.

An Easier Method of Opening a DOS Session in the Current Folder

I mentioned in the preceding tip that if you start COMMAND.COM from the Run dialog box, Windows 95 opens the DOS window in whichever folder is currently highlighted in Explorer. This capability is very handy, but having to open the Run dialog box and enter the command is a pain. You can, however, do this another way, and after you've set it up, it takes only a couple of mouse clicks.

The secret is that a folder is a file type in Windows 95. All you need to do is create a new action for the folder file type that runs COMMAND.COM and automatically displays the correct folder. Here are the steps to follow:

1. In Explorer, select View | Options, and in the Options dialog box that appears, display the File Types tab.

2. Highlight Folder in the Registered file types list, and then click Edit. The Edit File Type dialog box appears.

3. Click the New button. The New Action dialog box, shown in Figure 21.1, appears.

FIGURE 21.1.

Fill in the New Action dialog box to create a new action for the Folder file type.

4. In the Action text box, type Open in DOS &Window (or whatever you want to name the command), and in the Application used to perform action text box, type command.com /k cd %1. The cd %1 part runs the CD (change directory) command on the current folder.

5. Click OK to return to the Edit File Type dialog box.

6. Click Close to return to the Options, and then click Close again to return to Explorer.

Now when you right-click a folder in Explorer, the context menu has an Open in DOS Window command, as shown in Figure 21.2. Clicking this command starts a DOS session in the folder.

FIGURE 21.2.

The new Open in DOS Window command starts COMMAND.COM *in the current folder.*

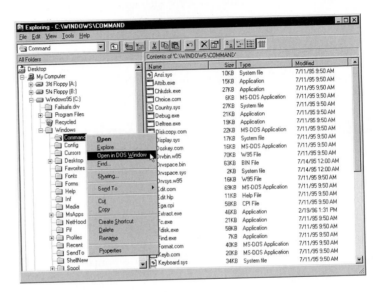

Starting a DOS Session in MS-DOS Mode

If you want to exit the Windows 95 GUI and then start your DOS session, use any of these techniques:

■ Select Start | Shut Down, activate the `Restart the computer in MS-DOS mode?` option, and click Yes.

TIP: A FASTER WAY TO GET TO MS-DOS MODE

Windows 95 has a shortcut that gives you quicker access to MS-DOS mode. It's called `Exit to DOS.PIF`, and you'll find it in your main Windows 95 folder. Running this file takes you directly to the MS-DOS mode prompt, without your having to deal with the Shut Down dialog box. For even easier access, you might want to copy this shortcut to the desktop.

■ Reboot the computer, invoke the Windows 95 Startup menu, and select `Command prompt only`.

■ In MSDOS.SYS, add the line BootGUI=0 in the [Options] section (or edit the line if it already exists). Each time you restart your computer, Windows 95 will boot to the DOS prompt.

These methods not only shut down the Windows 95 GUI, but also take Windows 95 out of protected mode and change to MS-DOS mode (which I'll explain in more detail in a moment). To get back to the safety of the Windows 95 GUI and protected mode, type win (or exit) and press Enter at the DOS prompt.

TIP: GETTING TO DOS AFTER A SHUTDOWN

If you shut down Windows 95 and then decide you want to go to the DOS prompt, there's an easy way to get there, provided that you started the Windows 95 GUI from the command line (by typing win and pressing Enter). When you see the It's now safe to turn off your computer bitmap, type mode co80 and press Enter. This changes the screen from the current graphics mode to the regular 80-column text mode used by DOS. To avoid this step and exit to the DOS prompt automatically (just as in Windows 3.x), rename LOGOS.SYS—the bitmap that displays the It's now safe to turn off your computer message—to, say, LOGOS.SAV.

One caveat, though: Microsoft claims that Windows 95 is in an unstable state after the It's now safe... message appears, and that switching to MS-DOS mode at this point could cause your system to crash (if not right away, then after running a few commands). I haven't been able to verify this weakness (this method works perfectly on my machines), but you might want to exercise caution the first few times you try it.

What Happens When You Start a DOS Session?

When you create a new DOS session, whether you're running an instance of COMMAND.COM, a DOS command, or a DOS program, the Virtual Machine Manager kicks in and sets up a new virtual machine for the DOS session.

First, it carves out 1 MB of virtual memory that the DOS session can call its own. To the DOS session, this megabyte of virtual memory will look just like 640 KB of conventional memory and 384 KB of upper memory.

Next, the Virtual Machine Manager creates the DOS environment in which the session will operate. This environment is determined at startup and is based on the default settings and drivers used by IO.SYS. An "invisible" DOS machine is set up as though it were booted using the following CONFIG.SYS and AUTOEXEC.BAT files (assuming that Windows 95 is installed in C:\WINDOWS):

CONFIG.SYS:

```
DEVICE=C:\WINDOWS\HIMEM.SYS
DEVICE=C:\WINDOWS\IFSHLP.SYS
```

```
DEVICE=C:\WINDOWS\SETVER.EXE
DOS=HIGH
FILES=30
BUFFERS=30
STACKS=9,256
FCBS=4
LASTRIVE=Z
```

AUTOEXEC.BAT:

```
PROMPT=$P$G
PATH=C:\WINDOWS;C:\WINDOWS\COMMAND
SET TMP=C:\WINDOWS\TEMP
SET TEMP=C:\WINDOWS\TEMP
SET COMSPEC=C:\WINDOWS\COMMAND.COM
SET windir=C:\WINDOWS
SET winbootdir=C:\WINDOWS
```

Entries in your real CONFIG.SYS or AUTOEXEC.BAT are also taken into account, in the following ways:

- If you have an entry that duplicates one of the IO.SYS settings, your entry takes precedence. For example, if your CONFIG.SYS has a FILES=60 line, the invisible DOS machine is set up with FILES equal to 60.

- If you have any other lines in your CONFIG.SYS and AUTOEXEC.BAT files, they're incorporated into the DOS machine's environment.

The environment of this invisible DOS virtual machine acts as a kind of template on which the real DOS sessions are based. This is equivalent to "booting" each virtual machine with the preceding CONFIG.SYS and AUTOEXEC.BAT files.

Note, too, that many of the goodies available to Windows 95 applications are also available at the DOS prompt: 32-bit disk caching and file access, protected-mode drivers for the mouse, CD-ROM and other devices, multitasking, and so on.

> **NOTE: A STARTUP BATCH FILE FOR DOS SESSIONS**
>
> Besides editing your real CONFIG.SYS and AUTOEXEC.BAT files, another way to customize each DOS session is to tell Windows 95 to run a batch file each time you start the session. I'll show you how this is done later.

What Happens When You Switch to MS-DOS Mode?

By their very nature, DOS programs like to monopolize a computer's resources. That's contrary to Windows 95's nature, of course, so the Virtual Machine Manager's job is to make DOS programs think they have total control over the computer. Few DOS programs see through this ruse, so they run happily ever after.

However, some DOS programs—especially DOS games—insist on full control over the computer's resources, and they won't be hoodwinked into thinking they've got it when they really don't. For these control freaks, Windows 95 can run in *MS-DOS mode*, which gives the program exclusive access to the computer.

When you switch to MS-DOS mode, the Virtual Machine Manager shuts down all running applications, unloads all protected-mode drivers, exits Windows 95, and "reboots" the system into a pure real-mode DOS environment. (Well, if you exit to MS-DOS mode from within Windows 95, it's not quite pure: A 3 KB remnant of Windows 95 remains in memory.) As before, the settings created for the invisible DOS virtual machine are used to boot the new DOS session. (I tell how to customize this environment for individual DOS programs later in this chapter—see the section titled "Creating a Program-Specific Startup Configuration.") The Virtual Machine Manager also runs the DOSSTART.BAT batch file, which contains the lines (if any) that Setup commented out from AUTOEXEC.BAT during installation. If it exists, you'll find DOSSTART.BAT in your main Windows 95 folder.

While you're in MS-DOS mode, you can't multitask applications, work with long filenames, or access protected-mode drivers.

Running DOS Commands

Although many of the Windows 95 accessories provide more-powerful and easier-to-use replacements for nearly all DOS commands, a few commands still have no Windows 95 peer. These include MEM, FDISK, and REN, as well as the many DOS prompt–specific commands, such as CLS, DOSKEY, and PROMPT.

How you run a command depends on whether it's an internal or external command, and on what you want Windows 95 to do after the command is finished.

For an internal command, you have two choices: You can either enter the command at the DOS prompt or include it as a parameter with COMMAND.COM. As you saw earlier, you can run internal commands with COMMAND.COM by specifying either the /C switch or the /K switch. If you use /C, the command executes and then the DOS sessions shut down. This is fine if you're running a command for which you don't need to see the results. For example, if you want to redirect the contents of drive C's root folder in the text file ROOT.TXT, entering the following command in the Run dialog box (for example) will do the job:

```
command.com /c dir c:\ > root.txt
```

On the other hand, you might want to examine the output of a command before the DOS window closes. In this case, you need to use the /K switch. The following command runs DIR on drive C's root folder and then drops you off at the DOS prompt:

```
command.com /k dir c:\
```

For an external command, you have three choices: Enter the command at the DOS prompt, enter the command by itself from within Windows 95, or include it as a parameter with COMMAND.COM.

NOTE: A FULL PATHNAME ISN'T REQUIRED FOR DOS COMMANDS

When you use the DOS prompt or the Run dialog box to start an external DOS command, you don't need to use the command's full pathname. For example, the full pathname for MEM.EXE is C:\WINDOWS\COMMAND\MEM.EXE (assuming that the main Windows 95 folder is C:\WINDOWS), but to run this command, you need only enter mem. The reason is that the COMMAND subfolder is part of the PATH statement for each virtual DOS machine.

Entering the command by itself from within Windows 95 means double-clicking the command in Explorer, entering the command in the Run dialog box, or creating a shortcut for the command. For the latter two methods, you can embellish the command by adding parameters and switches. Whichever command you run in this manner, Windows 95 adds Finished to the DOS window's title bar and leaves the window open so that you can examine the results, as shown in Figure 21.3. To close the window, press Alt-F4 or click the window's Close button.

FIGURE 21.3.

When you run an external DOS command, Windows 95 leaves the window open after the command has finished.

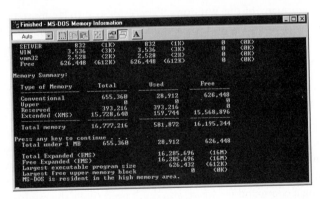

To change this behavior, you can run the command as a parameter with COMMAND.COM, as explained here:

- If you use COMMAND.COM with the /C switch (for example, command.com /c mem.exe), Windows 95 shuts down the DOS window when the external command has completed its labors.

- If you use COMMAND.COM with the /K switch (for example, command.com /k mem.exe), Windows 95 leaves the DOS window open *and* returns you to the command prompt when the external command is complete.

DOS Isn't Dead: Optimizing DOS Applications Under Windows 95

CHAPTER 21

667

21

OPTIMIZING
DOS
APPLICATIONS

Adding Parameters and Switches to a DOS Command

If you use the DOS prompt or the Run dialog box to enter your DOS commands, you can easily tack on any extra parameters or switches you want to use to modify the command. If, however, you start an external command from Explorer, the command runs without any options. To modify how an external command operates, you can add parameters and switches by following these steps:

1. In Explorer, display the properties sheet for the external DOS command.

2. Select the Program tab.

3. In the Cmd line text box, add a space after the command line, and then add your parameters and switches. Figure 21.4 shows an example.

FIGURE 21.4.

Use the Cmd line *text box to append extra parameters to an external DOS command.*

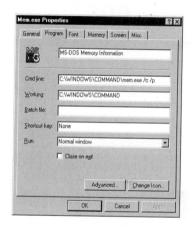

4. Click OK.

NOTE: WINDOWS 95 CREATES A PIF FOR THE COMMAND

After you've modified a DOS command's properties sheet, Windows 95 creates a PIF—a program information file—for the command. This is a separate file that has the same name as the command, but with a PIF extension. Unfortunately, Explorer always hides the PIF extension. You can recognize the PIF, however, if you display Explorer in Details view: The PIF says Shortcut to MS-DOS Program in the Type column. I give you complete PIF details later in this chapter (see "Understanding PIFs").

If you want to vary the parameters each time you run the command, add a space and a question mark (?) to the end of the command line, like so:

```
C:\WINDOWS\COMMAND\mem.exe ?
```

Each time you run the command (whether from Explorer or from the Run dialog box), Windows 95 displays a dialog box similar to the one shown in Figure 21.5. Use the Parameters text box to enter your switches and options, and then click OK.

FIGURE 21.5.

If you add a question mark (?) to the end of the command line, Windows 95 displays a dialog box similar to this one each time you run the command.

Working at the DOS Prompt

After you have your DOS session up and running, you can work with it more or less as you've always worked with DOS. You can run commands and DOS programs, create and launch batch files, perform file maintenance, and so on. The Windows 95 DOS, however, brings a few extra goodies to the command prompt. The next few sections highlight some of the more useful ones.

CAUTION: DOS DELETIONS ARE DELETED!

When you're working at the DOS prompt, be warned that any files you delete aren't sent to the Recycle Bin, but are purged from your system. However, if you accidentally delete a file at the DOS prompt, you might still be able to recover it. Before performing any other operations, see the section titled "Undeleting Files" later in this chapter.

Working with Long Filenames

If you've started your DOS session within Windows 95 (that is, you're not running in MS-DOS mode), the VFAT file system is still available. This means that you can work with long filenames with a DOS session.

For example, if you run the DIR command to get a listing of files in a folder, you'll see not only the usual data—the file's 8.3 filename, size, and date and time stamp—but also the file's long filename. Figure 21.6 shows an example.

DOS Isn't Dead: Optimizing DOS Applications Under Windows 95

CHAPTER **21**

669

21

OPTIMIZING
DOS
APPLICATIONS

FIGURE 21.6.

The new DIR *command shows each file's long filename.*

NOTE: THE WINDOWS 95 WILDCARDS ARE DIFFERENT

In earlier versions of DOS, the question mark (?) wildcard character represented a single character or no character. For example, the command DIR MEMO??.DOC would display MEMO23.DOC, MEMORY.DOC, MEMOS.DOC, and MEMO.DOC. In Windows 95, however, the question mark represents only a single character. Therefore, DIR MEMO??.DOC will display only filenames with a six-character primary name that begins with MEMO, such as MEMO23.DOC and MEMORY.DOC.

Entering Long Filenames

If you want to use long filenames in a command, however, you need to be careful. If the long filename contains a space or any other character that's illegal in an 8.3 filename, you need to surround the long name with quotation marks. For example, the following command will generate a Too many parameters error:

```
copy black thatch.bmp booby hatch.bmp
```

Instead, you need to enter this command as follows:

```
copy "black thatch.bmp" "booby hatch.bmp"
```

Note that if you use the CD command to change to a folder that has a long name, Windows 95 shows the full name in the command prompt. For example, if you change to Windows 95's Start Menu subfolder, you'll see the following prompt:

```
C:\WINDOWS\Start Menu>
```

Don't forget, as well, that if you need to work with commands that are longer than 127 characters, you have to adjust the input buffer length of COMMAND.COM. Recall from the COMMAND.COM syntax shown earlier that you do this by specifying the /U:*z* switch, where *z* is a number between 128 and 255 that represents the new buffer length. For example, to set the buffer to 255 characters for all DOS sessions, you'd add the following SHELL command to your CONFIG.SYS file (assuming that C:\Windows is your main Windows 95 folder):

```
shell=c:\windows\command.com /u:255 /p
```

Easier Ways to Work with Long Filenames

Long filenames are, of course, long, so they tend to be a pain to type at the command line. You can always use the 8.3 short names, but Windows 95 offers a few other methods for knocking long names down to size:

- In Explorer, drag a folder or file and drop it inside the DOS window. Windows 95 pastes the name of the folder or file to the end of the command line.

- Create application-specific and document-specific paths, as described in Chapter 12, "Hacking the Registry."

- If you're trying to run a DOS application that resides in a folder with a long name, add the folder to the PATH. This technique lets you run programs from the folder without having to specify the full pathname. (I talk about this in more detail in the next section.)

- Use the SUBST command to substitute a virtual drive letter for a long pathname. For example, the following command substitutes drive E for the path C:\Windows\Start Menu\Programs\Accessories:

  ```
  subst e: "C:\Windows\Start Menu\Programs\Accessories"
  ```

Changing Folders Faster

You probably know by now that you use the CD (change directory) command to change to a different folder on the current drive. However, DOS has always had a couple of short forms you can use to save time, and Windows 95 has added a few more.

Both DOS and Windows 95 use the dot symbol (.) to represent the current folder, and the double-dot symbol (..) to represent its parent folder. Windows 95 adds even more symbols: The triple-dot (...) represents the grandparent folder (two levels up), the quadruple-dot (....) represents the great-grandparent folder (three levels up), and so on.

Let's try to make this more concrete. Suppose that the current folder is C:\ANIMAL\MAMMAL\DOLPHIN. You can combine the CD command and the dot notation to jump immediately to any of this folder's parent folders, as shown in Table 21.4.

Table 21.4. Combining the CD command with dot notation.

Current Folder	Command	New Folder
C:\ANIMAL\MAMMAL\DOLPHIN	CD..	C:\ANIMAL\MAMMAL
C:\ANIMAL\MAMMAL\DOLPHIN	CD...	C:\ANIMAL
C:\ANIMAL\MAMMAL\DOLPHIN	CD....	C:\
C:\ANIMAL\MAMMAL\DOLPHIN	CD..\BABOON	C:\ANIMAL\MAMMAL\BABOON

Starting Applications from the DOS Prompt

The DOS prompt isn't just for running DOS commands. You can also use it to start applications, as described in the next two sections.

Starting DOS Applications

For DOS applications, you need to either change to the drive and folder where the program resides and enter the executable file's primary name from there, or enter the executable file's full pathname from the current folder. There are two situations in which you don't have to change folders or use the full pathname:

■ If the program's executable file is in the current folder.

■ If the folder in which the program's executable file resides is part of the PATH statement.

If you enter only the primary name of an executable file, DOS first searches the current folder for a file that combines your primary name with an extension of either COM, EXE, or BAT. If it doesn't find such a file, it searches the folders listed in the PATH statement. Recall that the PATH statement is a series of folder names separated by semicolons (;). The default PATH for a virtual DOS machine is this:

```
C:\WINDOWS;C:\WINDOWS\COMMAND
```

This is stored in an environment variable called PATH, so you can easily add new folders to the PATH right from the command prompt. For example, suppose you have a DOS program that resides in the C:\Program Files\Dosapp folder. To start the program without having to change folders or specify the pathname, use the following command to add this folder to the PATH statement (%path% represents the PATH environment variable):

```
set path=%path%;"c:\program files\dosapp"
```

Starting Windows Applications

The big news about starting programs from the DOS prompt is that you can also start Windows applications, launch documents, and even open folder windows. As with DOS programs, you start a Windows application by entering the name of its executable file.

This works fine if the executable file resides in the main Windows 95 folder, because that folder is part of the PATH. But most Windows 95 applications (and even some Windows 95 accessories) store their files in a separate folder and don't modify the PATH to point to these folders. Instead, as you learned in Chapter 12, the Registry has an AppPaths key that tells Windows 95 where to find an application's files. The DOS virtual machine can't use the Registry-based application paths directly, but there's a new Windows 95 DOS command that can. This command is called START, and it uses the following syntax:

```
start [/m ¦ /max ¦ /r] [/w] filename parameters
```

/m	Starts the application minimized.
/max	Starts the application maximized.
/r	Starts the application in its restored window (this is the default).
/w	Waits until the program has finished before returning to DOS.
filename	Specifies the name of the executable file or document. If you enter a document name, be sure to include the extension so that Windows 95 can figure out the file type.
parameters	Specifies options or switches that modify the operation of the program.

When you use START to launch a program, Windows 95 checks not only the current folder and the PATH, but also the Registry. For the Registry, Windows 95 looks for an AppPaths setting or a file type (if you entered the name of a document). For example, if you type wordpad and press Enter at the DOS prompt, you get a Bad command or file name error (unless you happen to be in the \Program Files\Accessories folder). If, however, you enter start wordpad, WordPad launches successfully.

The START command is also useful for opening folder windows. For example, you can open a window for the current folder by entering the following command (recall that the dot symbol represents the current folder):

```
start .
```

Similarly, the following command opens a window for the C:\Windows\Start Menu folder:

```
start "c:\windows\start menu"
```

NOTE: USE THE /W SWITCH TO PAUSE BATCH FILES

The START command's /W switch is useful in batch files. If you launch a program from within a batch file by using START /W, the batch file pauses while the program runs. This lets you, for example, test for some condition (such as an ERRORLEVEL code) after the program has completed its work.

Undeleting Files

When you delete a file from the Recycle Bin or hold down Shift while you delete a file from any other folder, Windows 95 purges the file from the system. In other words, it deletes the file in the old-fashioned way:

- The file's FAT entries are set to 0 to indicate that these clusters can now be used by another file.

- The first letter of the file's name is changed to the Greek sigma character to indicate that the file has been deleted.

Note that the file's clusters remain untouched. That means it's still possible to recover the file, as long as you do it before another file comes along and overwrites one or more of the deleted file's clusters.

To recover the file, you need to use the DOS 6.x UNDELETE command. If you upgraded over DOS 6.x, you'll find UNDELETE.EXE in your original DOS directory; otherwise, you'll find UNDELETE.EXE in the \OTHER\OLDMSDOS folder of the Windows 95 CD-ROM. In either case, you should copy UNDELETE.EXE to the COMMAND subfolder of your main Windows 95 folder. When that's done, follow these steps to undelete a file:

1. Restart Windows 95 in MS-DOS mode, as described earlier.

2. Change to the drive and folder where the deleted file used to reside.

3. Type lock and press Enter to enable direct disk access for the UNDELETE command. (If you don't do this, Windows 95 won't let the UNDELETE command modify the FAT.) When Windows 95 asks whether you're sure, press Y and Enter.

4. Type undelete *filename*, in which *filename* is the 8.3 name of the file you want to recover. UNDELETE displays a message similar to this:

```
UNDELETE - A delete protection facility
Copyright (C) 1987-1993 Central Point Software, Inc.
All rights reserved.
Directory C:\
File Specification: SAVEME.TXT
    Delete Sentry control file not found.
    Deletion-tracking file not found.
    MS-DOS directory contains   1 deleted files.
    Of those,    1 files may be recovered.
Using the MS-DOS directory method.
        ?AVEME   TXT    41894   2-29-96  5:47p  ...A  Undelete (Y/N)?
```

5. Press Y. UNDELETE displays the following prompt:

```
Please type the first character for ?AVEME  .TXT:
```

6. Press the appropriate character. UNDELETE recovers the file.

7. Type unlock and press Enter to disable direct disk access.

8. Restart Windows 95.

Customizing the DOS Window

If you figure you'll be spending a reasonable amount of time lounging around the DOS prompt, you'll want to configure the DOS window so that you're comfortable with how it works and how it's displayed. The next few sections take you through the various options available for giving DOS a makeover. Note that although I'll be using COMMAND.COM and its MS-DOS Prompt window as an example, each technique I'll be discussing is available for any DOS program.

DOS Properties

A DOS program, like any Windows 95 object, has various properties you can manipulate to fine-tune how the program works. To display the properties sheet for a DOS program, you have two choices:

- In Explorer, highlight the program's executable file and select File | Properties, or right-click the file and select Properties.

- While the program's DOS window is open, click the Properties button in the toolbar (see Figure 21.7) or right-click the title bar and select Properties. (If you can't see the toolbar, right-click the title bar and activate the Toolbar command.)

FIGURE 21.7.

In Windows 95, the DOS windows have a toolbar for easy access to settings and properties.

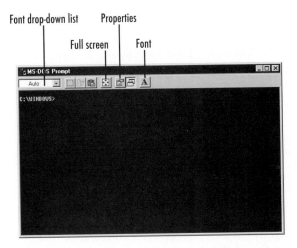

Font drop-down list   Properties

Full screen   Font

- If the program's DOS window is open, you can get to the properties sheet from the keyboard by pressing Alt-Spacebar and selecting Properties from the control menu that appears.

NOTE: TOGGLING BETWEEN FULL SCREEN AND A WINDOW

Most of the properties I'll be talking about affect the DOS program only while it's running in a window. If your program is running full-screen, press Alt-Enter to place it in a window. To change back to full-screen mode, press Alt-Enter again or click the Full Screen button in the toolbar.

Setting Program Properties

The Program tab, shown in Figure 21.8, contains various settings that control the startup and shutdown of the DOS program. The untitled text box at the top of the dialog box specifies the text that appears in the DOS window's title bar.

FIGURE 21.8.

Use the Program tab to set various properties for the DOS program's startup.

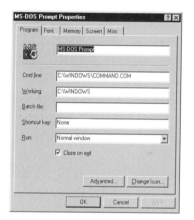

Here's a rundown of the rest of the options:

Cmd line: This text box specifies the pathname of the program's executable file. As you saw earlier, you can use this text box to add parameters and switches to modify how the program starts.

Working: Use this text box to set the application's default folder.

Batch file: This text box specifies a batch file or command to run before starting the program. This is useful for copying files, setting environment variables, changing the PATH, or loading memory-resident programs.

> **TIP: LOAD DOSKEY FOR THE MS-DOS PROMPT**
>
> The DOSKEY command lets you recall previous commands, edit the current command line, and create macros (multiple commands that run with a single command). To make this highly useful command available all the time in your MS-DOS prompt sessions, include the DOSKEY command in the Batch file text box of the COMMAND.COM properties sheet.

Shortcut key: Use this text box to assign a key combination to the DOS program. For launching the program, this key combination seems to work only if you create a shortcut for the program on the desktop. When the program is running, however, you can use the key combination to switch to the program quickly.

The default key combo is Ctrl-Alt-*character*, in which *character* is any keyboard character you press while this text box has the focus. If you prefer a key combination that begins with Ctrl-Shift, hold down both Ctrl and Shift and then press a character; for a Ctrl-Alt-Shift combination, hold down all three keys and press a character.

Run: If the shortcut starts an application, this drop-down list determines how the application window appears. Select Normal window, Minimized, or Maximized.

Close on exit: When you activate this check box, the DOS window closes when the program is complete. This is useful for batch files and other programs that leave the DOS window on-screen when they're done.

Advanced: This button displays a dialog box that controls various MS-DOS mode settings. I discuss these options later in this chapter (see "Running a Program in MS-DOS Mode").

Change Icon: Use this command button to assign a different icon to the program's PIF. Clicking this button displays the Change Icon dialog box.

Changing the DOS Window's Font Size

The font size Windows 95 uses to display text in a DOS window isn't set in stone. You're free to make the font size larger or smaller, depending on your tastes. You can adjust the size of the DOS text font in three ways:

- Select a font size from the toolbar's Font drop-down list.
- Set the font to Auto and resize the window.
- Use the program's properties sheet.

Selecting a Font Size

The easiest way to select a different font size is to use the Font drop-down list in the DOS window's toolbar. This list contains more than a dozen possible sizes, from 4×6 to 12×22. (The numbers represent the size of each character in the font, in pixels. The first number is the

DOS Isn't Dead: Optimizing DOS Applications Under Windows 95

CHAPTER 21

677

21

OPTIMIZING
DOS
APPLICATIONS

width and the second number is the height.) Windows 95 adjusts the size of the window to compensate for the new font size. For example, Figure 21.9 shows a DOS window that's using the 12 × 22 font. Notice that, in this case, there isn't enough room in the window to display the entire DOS screen, so the window sprouts scrollbars on the right and bottom.

FIGURE 21.9.

A DOS window using the 12 × 22 font size.

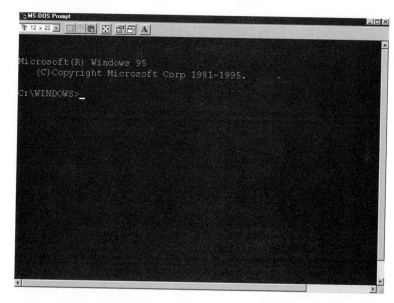

Adjusting the Size of the DOS Window

As you saw in the preceding section, Windows 95 adjusts the size of the DOS window to suit the size of the selected font. DOS windows are also sizable by hand (unlike in previous versions of Windows). You can use the mouse to drag a border to a different location and thus resize the window.

If you select Auto from the Font drop-down list, Windows 95 compensates for the new window size by scaling the DOS text font accordingly: If you make the window smaller, the font shrinks; if you make the window larger, the font increases to compensate.

Don't expect to be able to size DOS windows as smoothly as regular windows, however. Because Windows 95 must constantly recalculate font sizes, your border dragging will occur in fits and starts. In fact, Windows 95 will often get "stuck" on a window size, and no amount of border dragging will adjust the window size. In these situations, you'll usually find that the lower-right corner still works, so you can use it to readjust the window and get Windows "unstuck." Also note that you won't be able to size a DOS window if it's maximized.

Setting Font Properties

Another way to select a specific font size is to use the Font tab on the DOS program's properties sheet, shown in Figure 21.10. Use the Font size list to select the font you want to use (or Auto). The Window preview area shows you how the new DOS window will appear, and the Font preview area shows you the font size you'll get.

FIGURE 21.10.

Use the Font tab to select the font size to use in the DOS window.

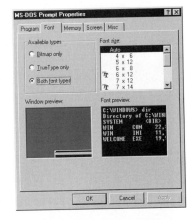

To narrow down the list of fonts, you can use the options in the Available types group:

Bitmap only: Activate this option to display only the bitmap fonts in the Font size list. These are Terminal fonts, and they're the ones that don't have any symbol to the left of the font size (for example, 4 × 6).

TrueType only: Activate this option to display only the TrueType fonts in the Font size list. These are Courier New fonts, and they're the ones that have the double-T symbol to the left of the font size (for example, 6 × 12).

Both font types: Activate this option to show both the bitmap and the TrueType fonts in the Font size list.

NOTE: MICROSOFT PLUS! CHANGES THE DOS FONT

If you've installed Microsoft Plus!, it changes the fonts used by DOS. Specifically, it replaces the Courier New font and some of the Terminal fonts with a TrueType font named Lucida Console, and it adds a few more sizes.

NOTE: MORE FONT INFO

For more information on bitmap and TrueType fonts, see Chapter 18, "Using Fonts in Windows 95."

Setting Screen Properties

The properties sheet for a DOS program also includes a Screen tab, shown in Figure 21.11, that controls various aspects of the program's display. Here are your options (I discuss the controls in the Performance group when I talk about optimizing DOS programs later in this chapter; see "Setting Performance Properties"):

Usage: The Full-screen and Window options determine whether the DOS program starts full-screen or in a window. The Initial size drop-down list determines the number of screen lines that appear (23, 43, or 50). This setting doesn't take effect until you restart the program.

Window: Activate the Display toolbar check box to display the DOS window toolbar automatically. If you activate the Restore settings on startup check box, Windows 95 remembers the last window position and size and restores them the next time you run the program. If you deactivate this check box, Windows 95 just uses the original settings the next time you start the program; any adjustments you make in the current session are ignored.

FIGURE 21.11.

Use the Screen tab to control the appearance of the DOS program.

Some Miscellaneous Properties

To complete our look at DOS customization, let's turn our attention to the Misc tab of the DOS program properties sheet, shown in Figure 21.12. This tab contains a grab bag of options that cover a whole host of otherwise unrelated properties.

Here's a summary of what each control contribute0s to the DOS program:

Allow screen saver: When this check box is turned on, Windows 95 allows your Windows screen saver to kick in while you're using the DOS program (that is, when the DOS program is in the *foreground*). This is probably safe for most DOS programs, but if you find that the screen saver is causing your program to hang or is causing the program's graphics to go batty, you should deactivate this check box. You should definitely clear this check box if you're using a terminal emulation program or a communications program.

FIGURE 21.12.

The Misc tab contains an assortment of controls for customizing a DOS program.

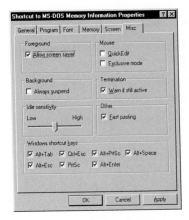

QuickEdit: When this check box is active, you can select DOS text with the mouse. I explain how this works in Chapter 17, "Sharing Data in Windows 95: The Clipboard and OLE."

Exclusive mode: If you check this option, Windows 95 offers the DOS program exclusive use of the mouse. This means that the mouse will work only while you use the DOS program; it won't be available in Windows 95. You should need to activate this check box only if the mouse otherwise won't work in the DOS program.

Always suspend: When you activate this check box, Windows 95 doesn't supply any CPU time to a running DOS program that doesn't have the focus. (Such a program is said to be in the *background*.) If your DOS program doesn't do any background processing when you switch to another window, you should activate this check box. Doing so improves the performance of your other applications. This is also a good idea if a background DOS program interferes with your foreground applications. (For example, some DOS games can mess up the sound in your foreground window.) If, however, you're using the DOS program to download files, print documents, or perform other background chores, you should leave Always suspend unchecked.

Warn if still active: For safest operation, and to make sure that you don't lose unsaved data, you should always exit your DOS program completely before trying to close the DOS window. If you leave the Warn if still active box checked, Windows 95 displays the warning dialog box shown in Figure 21.13 if you attempt to shut down the program prematurely. You can force Windows 95 to close the program (if it has hung, for example) by clicking Yes.

FIGURE 21.13.

If the Warn if still active *check box is activated, Windows 95 displays this warning if you try to close a DOS window before exiting the program.*

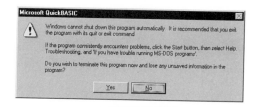

Idle sensitivity: This slider determines how much CPU time Windows 95 devotes to the DOS program when the program is idle. I discuss this option in more detail later in this chapter (see "Setting the Idle Sensitivity").

Fast pasting: This check box controls the speed at which Windows 95 pastes information from the Clipboard to the DOS program. I discuss pasting data to DOS windows in Chapter 17.

Windows shortcut keys: These check boxes represent various Windows 95 shortcut keys. For example, pressing Alt-Tab while working in a DOS program takes you to another open application. Your DOS program, however, might use one or more of these key combinations for its own purposes. To allow the program use of any of the shortcuts, deactivate the appropriate check boxes. Just so you know what you're giving up, here's a review of what each key combination does in Windows 95:

Alt-Tab	Cycles through the icons of the open applications.
Ctrl-Esc	Opens the Start menu.
Alt-Print Screen	Takes a screen shot of the active window and copies it to the Clipboard.
Alt-Space	Pulls down the control menu for the active window.
Alt-Esc	Cycles through the open applications, showing the entire window for each program.
Print Screen	Takes a screen shot of the entire desktop and copies it to the Clipboard.
Alt-Enter	Toggles a DOS program between a window and full-screen.

Understanding PIFs

If you ran DOS programs under Windows 3.x, you probably became familiar with Program Information Files (PIFs) and the PIF Editor. A PIF is a file that's associated with a specific DOS program. Windows 3.x used PIFs to store various settings and options that controlled how DOS programs operated. For example, you'd use a PIF to tell Windows how much memory to allocate to a program.

PIFs are still alive and well in Windows 95, but their role has been expanded significantly. A particular PIF now contains settings for all the DOS program properties you learned about earlier in this chapter (screen options, fonts, and so on), as well as properties related to memory, environment, MS-DOS mode, and many more. (I'll talk about most of these other properties throughout the rest of this chapter.)

NOTE: OBSOLETE PIF SETTINGS

Some of the settings that were available in Windows 3.x PIFs are gone from Windows 95 PIFs because Windows handles them automatically. These settings include video memory usage, video port monitoring, exclusive priority, and background and foreground priorities.

The PIF Editor is history. Instead, each DOS program has its own properties sheet with various tabs that contain the settings and options you can manipulate for the program. A separate DLL (PIFMGR.DLL) handles these properties and stores them in the program's PIF.

If the DOS program comes with its own PIF, Windows 95 uses the settings in this file to run the program. If you upgraded over Windows 3.x, any existing PIFs in your main Windows folder are upgraded to the Windows 95 format.

If no PIF exists for a DOS program, Windows 95 creates a PIF the first time you run the program, the first time you make a change to the executable file's properties, or if you create a shortcut for the program (the shortcut file is the PIF). If there's no existing PIF for the program, Windows 95 uses three methods to determine the contents of a program's initial PIF:

- If you upgraded over Windows 3.x, you'll still have a file named _DEFAULT.PIF (upgraded to the new format) in your main Windows folder. Windows 95 uses the contents of this file to create the new PIF.

- If you don't have _DEFAULT.PIF, Windows 95 copies the settings from DOSPRMPT.PIF (which you'll find in your main Windows 95 folder).

- Windows 95 also checks the APPS.INF file for program-specific settings. See the section "Understanding the Role of APPS.INF" later in this chapter for more information.

The PIF is (usually) stored in the same folder as the program's executable, and it uses the same primary name as the executable, but with a PIF extension. (The only time Windows 95 doesn't create the PIF in the same folder as the executable is when you run the DOS program from a CD-ROM. Since Windows 95 can't create new files on a CD-ROM, it creates the PIF in its PIF subfolder—for example, C:\WINDOWS\PIF.)

NOTE: ALWAYS USE PIFS TO START PROGRAMS

As soon as you have a shortcut PIF in place for a DOS program, always use the shortcut to start the program. That way, you ensure that Windows 95 uses the appropriate settings for the application (and not just its defaults).

As you learned earlier in this chapter, you can modify a DOS program's settings (and hence its PIF) by using any of the following methods:

■ Highlight the executable file and select File | Properties, or right-click on the executable file and select Properties.

■ Highlight the PIF and select File | Properties, or right-click on the PIF and select Properties.

■ When the program is running in a DOS window, click the Properties toolbar button or right-click the window title bar and select Properties. From the keyboard, press Alt-Spacebar and select Properties from the control menu.

NOTE: CHOOSING PIFS

Explorer displays PIFs without an extension, even if you have the Hide MS-DOS file extension for file types that are registered check box turned off (select View | Options to see this check box). You can recognize PIFs as follows:

■ Look for the MS-DOS icon with the shortcut arrow. (This is assuming that you didn't change the icon in the DOS program's properties sheet.)

■ If you're in Details view, look in the Type column for Shortcut to MS-DOS Program.

Running a Program in MS-DOS Mode

If you have a DOS program that resolutely refuses to run under Windows 95 (even full-screen), you may have no choice but to run the program in MS-DOS mode. One way to do this would be to reboot Windows 95 into MS-DOS mode (as described earlier in this chapter) and then run the program from the DOS prompt. In other cases, Windows 95 itself will start the program in MS-DOS mode if it determines that the program won't run in a DOS window. Alternatively, you can adjust the program's properties so that it runs in MS-DOS mode automatically. The next section shows you how to set this up.

Modifying a Program to Run in MS-DOS Mode

To make sure a program runs in MS-DOS mode, you need to configure its PIF. Here are the steps to follow:

1. In the program's properties sheet, select the Program tab.

2. Click the Advanced button. Windows 95 displays the Advanced Program Settings dialog box, shown in Figure 21.14.

FIGURE 21.14.

Use this dialog box to tell Windows 95 to start a DOS program in MS-DOS mode.

3. Activate the MS-DOS mode check box.

4. If you activate the Warn before entering MS-DOS mode check box, Windows 95 displays the warning dialog box shown in Figure 21.15 each time you start the program.

FIGURE 21.15.

When you start the DOS program, you can have Windows 95 warn you that the system is about to switch to MS-DOS mode.

5. If you want Windows 95 to boot the DOS virtual machine using its default settings, keep the Use current MS-DOS configuration option activated. If you'd prefer to use a different environment for this program, activate the Specify a new MS-DOS configuration option. I'll explain how to specify the new configuration later in this chapter (see "Creating a Program-Specific Startup Configuration").

6. Click OK to return to the properties sheet.

7. Click OK.

> **NOTE: MS-DOS MODE DISABLES MOST PROGRAM OPTIONS**
>
> Once you activate the MS-DOS mode check box, all the options on the Font, Memory, Screen, and Misc tabs become unavailable. Windows 95 doesn't use any of these settings in MS-DOS mode. However, a few of the options on the Program tab remain enabled (the program title, the Cmd line text box, and the Close on exit check box).

Modifying DOSSTART.BAT

Earlier in this chapter, I showed you how to specify a batch file that would run each time you launched a DOS program. Unfortunately, when you activate the MS-DOS mode option, the Batch file text box becomes disabled. All is not lost, however: you can still run a batch file when Windows 95 reboots to MS-DOS mode. The secret is that, when Windows 95 switches to MS-DOS mode, it always looks for a batch file named DOSSTART.BAT in your main Windows 95 folder. If it finds this file, Windows 95 processes the batch commands before running the DOS program.

DOSSTART.BAT is created by the Windows 95 Setup program during installation. DOSSTART.BAT stores any lines that Setup comments out of AUTOEXEC.BAT (such as the line that loads MSCDEX.EXE, the real-mode CD-ROM driver). However, you're free to add any extra commands you like, such as DOSKEY, real-mode device drivers (such as a mouse driver), a PATH statement, or a different PROMPT. If you'd like to run program-specific batch files, use the CALL command to run them from DOSSTART.BAT. For example, to run a batch file named DOSPROG.BAT, you would add the following command to DOSSTART.BAT:

```
CALL DOSPROG.BAT
```

Troubleshooting MS-DOS Mode

MS-DOS mode is Windows 95 at its simplest, so not a whole lot can go wrong. Most of the problems you might encounter are related to the DOS program's not liking something about the default environment that Windows 95 uses for MS-DOS mode. You can usually fix these kinds of difficulties by specifying custom startup files for the program, as explained in the next section. However, a few other things can go haywire in MS-DOS mode. This section tells you about these problems and shows you how to solve them.

Windows 95 doesn't restart after you quit the DOS program.

Windows 95 should restart automatically after you've finished the MS-DOS mode program. If it doesn't, type win and press Enter to restart Windows 95 by hand.

When you choose the `Restart the computer in MS-DOS mode` option in the Shut Down Windows dialog box and click OK, you receive the following error message:

```
Invalid COMMAND.COM
```

This error usually implies that the command line in the Exit To Dos PIF is pointing to a different version of COMMAND.COM from the one loaded in RAM (or it might be pointing to a nonexistent version of COMMAND.COM).

To solve this problem, open the properties sheet for the Exit To Dos PIF and make sure that the `Cmd line` text box points to the version of COMMAND.COM that exists in your main Windows 95 folder (for example, `C:\WINDOWS\COMMAND.COM`).

When you restart Windows 95 in MS-DOS mode, or when a program runs in MS-DOS mode with the `Use Current Configuration` option activated, SET statements in the `DOSSTART.BAT` file are ignored.

Because of the way COMMAND.COM is run when you switch to MS-DOS mode, any SET statements added to DOSSTART.BAT are ignored. If you need to run SET statements for your file, you have two choices:

- Include them in AUTOEXEC.BAT. This will make them available at startup, and Windows 95 will include them as part of its default DOS environment.

- If you want the SET statements to apply only to a specific program, you need to create a custom AUTOEXEC.BAT file for that program (as explained in the next section) and include the SET statements in this custom AUTOEXEC.BAT.

There is no `DOSSTART.BAT` file in your main Windows 95 folder.

If you installed Windows 95 on a clean system, you might not have had an AUTOEXEC.BAT file. In this case, you might not find DOSSTART.BAT in your main Windows 95 folder. That's okay, though: You can always use Notepad to create it from scratch.

Creating a Program-Specific Startup Configuration

DOS was never a one-size-fits-all operating system. Every program had its own unique combination of device drivers, memory requirements, environment variables, and settings. Trying to satisfy all your programs' needs was time-consuming, frustrating, and, sad to say, only rarely successful. Things improved a little when DOS 6 introduced the Startup menu, which let you execute lines in CONFIG.SYS and AUTOEXEC.BAT conditionally (that is, based on the menu item you selected at startup). Unfortunately, the resulting configuration files were usually hideously complex and could be irreparably damaged by brain-dead installation programs that couldn't figure out the new structure.

Happily, Windows 95 does away with all that poppycock. You can now create custom CONFIG.SYS and AUTOEXEC.BAT files for each of the programs that you want to run in MS-DOS mode. This lets you specify only those drivers and settings that are needed by the program, thus immeasurably simplifying the configuration process (and improving the chances that your program will run successfully and reliably).

Specifying Custom CONFIG.SYS and AUTOEXEC.BAT Files

To set up your custom CONFIG.SYS and AUTOEXEC.BAT files, display the properties sheet for the program, select the Program tab, and click the Advanced button. In the Advanced Program Settings dialog box, shown in Figure 21.16, activate the Specify a new MS-DOS configuration option. The two boxes below this option become enabled:

CONFIG.SYS for MS-DOS mode: This box shows the default commands used in the custom CONFIG.SYS file.

AUTOEXEC.BAT for MS-DOS mode: This box shows the default commands used in the custom AUTOEXEC.BAT file.

FIGURE 21.16.

You can create custom
CONFIG.SYS *and*
AUTOEXEC.BAT *files*
for each of your MS-
DOS–mode DOS
programs.

NOTE: CUSTOM COMMAND PROMPT CONFIGURATION

If you want to create custom CONFIG.SYS and AUTOEXEC.BAT files for the Restart the computer in MS-DOS mode? option (found in the Shut Down Windows dialog box), modify the properties for the Exit To Dos PIF.

Feel free to modify these lines and add new lines as needed. Before you do, however, you might want to try the Configuration button. It displays the Select MS-DOS Configuration Options dialog box, shown in Figure 21.17. (If you've already made changes to the CONFIG.SYS and AUTOEXEC.BAT files, Windows 95 will display a warning dialog box to tell you that your changes will be overwritten. If you still want to proceed, click Yes.)

FIGURE 21.17.

Use this dialog box to choose the CONFIG.SYS *and* AUTOEXEC.BAT *settings you want to include in your custom configuration.*

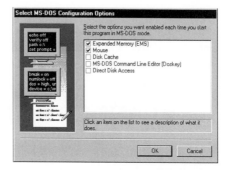

This dialog presents a list of common items that appear in CONFIG.SYS and AUTOEXEC.BAT. The items you see depend on your system and on the DOS program, but the ones listed next are the most common (I'm assuming that the default Windows 95 folder is C:\WINDOWS):

Expanded Memory (EMS): The DOS memory manager (EMM386), which provides access to upper memory blocks (UMBs) as well as expanded memory. Activating this check box adds the following line to CONFIG.SYS:

```
DEVICEHIGH=C:\WINDOWS\EMM386.EXE
```

Mouse: A real-mode mouse driver that supplies mouse support to DOS programs. Activating this check box adds the following line to AUTOEXEC.BAT:

```
LOADHIGH C:\MOUSE\SYSTEM\MOUSE.EXE
```

Disk Cache: The real-mode SMARTDrive disk cache. If your DOS program can take advantage of a disk cache, activating this check box is a must if you want top performance. (I explained how disk caches work in Chapter 9, "Windows 95 Performance Tuning and Optimization.") Activating this check box adds the following line to AUTOEXEC.BAT:

```
LOADHIGH C:\WINDOWS\SMARTDRV
```

MS-DOS Command Line Editor (Doskey): The DOSKEY command-line editor. Activating this check box adds the following line to AUTOEXEC.BAT:

```
LOADHIGH C:\WINDOWS\COMMAND\DOSKEY
```

Direct Disk Access: The LOCK command, which lets programs work with disk data structures directly. Activating this check box adds the following line to AUTOEXEC.BAT:

```
LOCK
```

CAUTION: USE LOCK ONLY WHEN NECESSARY

Add the LOCK command only if you're sure the program requires direct access to the disk. Many DOS programs might get confused by the extra directory entries that Windows 95 uses to track long filenames, and, given direct disk access, they might end up destroying some of your long names. Most DOS programs don't require direct disk access, so you can usually leave this option unchecked.

Note that for the mouse, SMARTDrive, and DOSKEY, the LOADHIGH command is added to the line only if you also included EMM386 in CONFIG.SYS. (I'll talk more about EMM386, LOADHIGH, upper memory blocks, and other memory optimization techniques later in this chapter.)

Activate the check boxes for the settings you want and then click OK to return to the Advanced Program Settings dialog box. You can now make any extra adjustments you need to the new settings. For example, if you know your DOS program doesn't use expanded memory, you can save an extra 64 KB in the upper memory area by adding the NOEMS parameter to EMM386, like so:

```
DEVICEHIGH=C:\WINDOWS\EMM386.EXE NOEMS
```

When you're done, click OK to return to the properties sheet.

TIP: ADDING A STARTUP BATCH FILE

When you specify custom CONFIG.SYS and AUTOEXEC.BAT files, the Batch file text box on the Program tab becomes available. If you enter the pathname of a batch file in this text box, Windows 95 runs the file after it has processed the custom CONFIG.SYS and AUTOEXEC.BAT files.

NOTE: ACCESSING YOUR CD-ROM DRIVE IN MS-DOS MODE

If you want to have access to your CD-ROM drive while in MS-DOS mode, make sure you add your CD-ROM's real-mode drivers to CONFIG.SYS and MSCDEX.EXE to AUTOEXEC.BAT.

What Happens When You Run the Program

Once you've configured a DOS program to use custom CONFIG.SYS and AUTOEXEC.BAT files, Windows 95 goes through a much more elaborate process to run the program in MS-DOS mode.

When you start the program, Windows 95 first goes through the usual MS-DOS mode routine: shutting down programs, unloading device drivers, and so on. It then renames the current CONFIG.SYS and AUTOEXEC.BAT files to CONFIG.WOS and AUTOEXEC.WOS (the WOS extension stands for, presumably, Windows Operating System). Then Windows 95 creates the new CONFIG.SYS and AUTOEXEC.BAT files for the DOS program.

For CONFIG.SYS, it takes the lines you specified in the Advanced Program Settings dialog box and tacks on one more line at the beginning:

```
DOS=SINGLE
```

This is the signal for your computer to reboot in MS-DOS mode. For AUTOEXEC.BAT, Windows 95 uses the lines you specified in the Advanced Program Settings dialog box and appends the following lines to the end:

```
REM
REM The following lines have been created by Windows. Do not modify them.
REM
drive:
CD \folder
CALL program
C:\WINDOWS\WIN.COM [/W ¦ /WX]
```

drive, folder, and *program* are the drive letter, folder name, and filename, respectively, of the DOS program's executable file. I'll explain the WIN.COM switches in a moment.

Windows 95 then performs a cold reboot of your system. After the computer's power-on self test (POST) is complete, instead of seeing the usual Starting Windows 95... message, you see the following:

```
Windows 95 is now starting your MS-DOS-based program.
Press Esc now to cancel MS-DOS mode and restart Windows 95...
```

If you change your mind about running the program, you have a couple of seconds in which to press Esc. If you do, Windows 95 will load normally. Otherwise, your system processes the new CONFIG.SYS and AUTOEXEC.BAT files. In particular, the AUTOEXEC.BAT file changes to the drive and folder where the executable file resides, and then it uses the CALL command to run the file.

When you're done with the program, the last line of AUTOEXEC.BAT is executed. This line runs WIN.COM with either the /W switch or the /WX switch. Both switches tell Windows 95 to restore CONFIG.SYS from CONFIG.WOS and AUTOEXEC.BAT from AUTOEXEC.WOS. The difference is in how Windows 95 restarts.

Windows 95 uses the /W switch if the Close on exit check box (found on the Program tab of the DOS program's properties sheet) is deactivated. In this case, Windows 95 displays the following prompt:

```
Press any key to continue...
```

When you press a key, Windows 95 restarts.

Windows 95 uses the /WX switch if the Close on exit check box is activated. In this case, Windows 95 restarts immediately.

TIP: USE MS-DOS MODE TO DUAL-BOOT WITH WINDOWS 3.X

If you upgraded from Windows 3.x but installed Windows 95 in a separate folder, you can dual-boot between the two systems. Instead of booting to Windows 3.x via the Startup menu, however, you can do it directly from Windows 95. Just create a new shortcut PIF for the Windows 3.x version of WIN.COM and set it to run in MS-DOS mode. For best performance, you'll probably want to create custom CONFIG.SYS and AUTOEXEC.BAT files. In AUTOEXEC.BAT, you'll want to make the following adjustments:

- Include the SMARTDrive disk cache.

- Adjust the PATH statement to include the Windows 3.x folder.

- Add the command NET START if you'll be starting Windows for Workgroups in a networked environment.

Optimizing Memory for DOS Applications

If you run only Windows applications, especially 32-bit applications, you may never have to worry about memory. More accurately, you might worry about the total amount of memory in your system (the more, the merrier), but you never have to worry about how that memory is managed. Windows 95's Virtual Memory Manager takes care of all the dirty work of memory paging, disk caching, and so on. (I described how this works in Chapter 9.)

This is also true for DOS programs, although to a lesser extent. As long as you run the DOS program under Windows 95 (either in a window or full-screen), the Virtual Memory Manager will still take care of the virtual memory supplied to the DOS virtual machine. No matter what kind of memory the program needs—conventional, extended, expanded, or whatever—the VMM can dish it out. However, there are two ways you can manipulate memory for DOS programs run under Windows 95:

- You can adjust the program's memory properties.

- You can maximize the amount of conventional memory available in the DOS virtual machine.

These methods are discussed in the next two sections. When that's done, I'll talk about optimizing memory for programs that run in MS-DOS mode.

Adjusting Memory Properties

For DOS programs that don't run in MS-DOS mode, the properties sheet has a Memory tab that lets you manipulate various memory-related settings used by the Virtual Memory Manager, as shown in Figure 21.18.

Here's a rundown of the available controls:

Conventional memory: The Total drop-down list specifies the amount of conventional memory (in kilobytes) supplied to the DOS program's virtual machine. (Recall that conventional memory is defined as the first 640 KB of memory.) If you leave this value at Auto, the VMM handles the memory requirements automatically. However, it doesn't always do a good job. For example, if you run a DOS command, the VMM carves out a full 640 KB of memory for the DOS virtual machine. Since most DOS commands run happily in much less, you're either wasting precious physical memory or unnecessarily paging to the swap file. You can specify a smaller value (say, 160 KB) and save memory resources. Before changing this value, check the documentation for your DOS program to find its minimum memory requirement.

FIGURE 21.18.

Use the Memory tab to customize the memory usage for a DOS program.

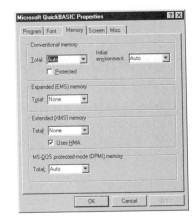

Initial environment: This drop-down list specifies the size (in bytes) of the DOS environment. The *environment* is a small memory buffer that holds the DOS *environment variables,* which are settings used to control certain aspects of DOS and DOS programs. For example, the PATH, the PROMPT, and the values of all SET statements are part of the environment. If you're using the Batch file text box to run SET statements or add folders to the PATH, you might want to increase the size of the environment. You shouldn't need a value any larger than 1,024 bytes.

TIP: DISPLAYING THE ENVIRONMENT

To see the contents of the environment while you're in a DOS session, type set and press Enter.

Protected: While your DOS program is running, small chunks of Windows 95 come along for the ride in the system memory area. These include IFSHLP.SYS (the real-mode file system helper) and part of VMM32 (the Virtual Memory Manager). If the DOS program is ill-behaved, it might accidentally overwrite part of the system area and cause Windows 95 to crash. To prevent this, activate the Protected check box to write-protect the system memory area.

Expanded (EMS) memory: The Total drop-down list specifies the amount of expanded memory (in kilobytes) supplied to the program. If you know your program doesn't use expanded memory, you can set this value to None. If you set this value to Auto, Windows 95 will supply the program with whatever it needs. If you'd prefer to set a limit on the amount of expanded memory the program uses, select a specific value (1,024 KB should be plenty for most programs).

TROUBLESHOOTING: EXPANDED MEMORY SETTING IS UNAVAILABLE

If there is no Total drop-down list in the Expanded (EMS) memory group, your system isn't set up to use expanded memory. In other words, you're loading EMM386 in CONFIG.SYS with the NOEMS parameter, like so:

```
C:\WINDOWS\EMM386.EXE NOEMS
```

If you need expanded memory, you either have to delete the NOEMS parameter from CONFIG.SYS or create a custom CONFIG.SYS that doesn't include the NOEMS parameter.

Extended (XMS) memory: If your DOS program can make use of extended memory, use the Total drop-down list to specify the amount of extended memory (in kilobytes) that the VMM allocates to the program. Again, use Auto to allow the VMM to allocate extended memory automatically. However, virtual memory is mapped by the VMM as extended memory, so your programs might end up grabbing *all* the available virtual memory for themselves! Setting a limit of, say, 1,024 KB will prevent this from happening.

Uses HMA: This check box determines whether or not the DOS program has access to the high memory area (HMA). The HMA is the first 64 KB of extended memory. Programs can use it to load device drivers. By default, Windows 95 uses the HMA for DOS, so it's unavailable to your programs. However, you can free up the HMA by making sure your CONFIG.SYS file includes the following three lines at the top:

```
C:\WINDOWS\HIMEM.SYS
C:\WINDOWS\EMM386.EXE
DOS=UMB
```

(I'm assuming here that C:\WINDOWS is your main Windows 95 folder.) Also, feel free to add the NOEMS parameter to EMM386 if your DOS programs don't need expanded memory.

MS-DOS protected-mode (DPMI) memory: This Total drop-down list specifies the amount of DOS protected-mode memory (in kilobytes) that is supplied to the program. Use Auto to let the VMM configure this type of memory automatically.

Optimizing Conventional Memory

By itself, Windows 95 does a pretty good job of clearing out the conventional memory area. This is thanks to its protected-mode device drivers, which operate in extended memory.

However, if you use any real-mode drivers or TSRs, these will reside in conventional memory. And since most DOS programs like to use conventional memory to do their thing, you'll have less room for these programs to operate. If things are really bad, the programs might refuse to run at all.

Upper Memory Blocks

To make sure that your DOS programs have enough memory to operate correctly, you need to optimize conventional memory by moving device drivers and other RAM interlopers into the upper memory area (the area between 640 KB and 1 MB). The UMA is normally the province of the BIOS and video buffers. However, it's never completely filled in. There are always gaps—called upper memory blocks (UMBs)—that aren't used by the system. You can take advantage of this fact to move device drivers out of conventional memory and into the UMBs.

A Benchmark: The MEM Command

To measure your progress, you need to have some way of determining how much memory you have available at any time. Happily, DOS provides just the tool: the MEM command. For a quick and dirty listing, just run MEM without any parameters. For something more detailed, use the /C switch, like so (the /P switch just pauses the output):

```
mem /c /p
```

You'll see a report that looks something like this:

```
Modules using memory below 1 MB:
  Name        Total            Conventional        Upper Memory
  --------    -------------    ----------------     ----------------
  MSDOS       17,840  (17K)    17,840   (17K)          0   (0K)
  ASPI2DOS     9,680   (9K)     9,680    (9K)          0   (0K)
  ASPICD      11,648  (11K)    11,648   (11K)          0   (0K)
  HIMEM        1,168   (1K)     1,168    (1K)          0   (0K)
  ASPI2HLP       592   (1K)       592    (1K)          0   (0K)
  IFSHLP       2,864   (3K)     2,864    (3K)          0   (0K)
  SETVER         832   (1K)       832    (1K)          0   (0K)
  WIN          3,568   (3K)     3,568    (3K)          0   (0K)
  vmm32        1,008   (1K)     1,008    (1K)          0   (0K)
  MSCDEX      41,008  (40K)    41,008   (40K)          0   (0K)
  COMMAND      7,408   (7K)     7,408    (7K)          0   (0K)
  DOSKEY       4,688   (5K)     4,688    (5K)          0   (0K)
  Free       552,896 (540K)   552,896  (540K)          0   (0K)
Memory Summary:
  Type of Memory       Total          Used          Free
  ---------------     ----------    ----------    ----------
  Conventional          655,360       102,464       552,896
  Upper                       0             0             0
  Reserved              393,216       393,216             0
  Extended (XMS)     15,728,640       229,376    15,499,264
  ---------------     ----------    ----------    ----------
  Total memory       16,777,216       725,056    16,052,160
  Total under 1 MB      655,360       102,464       552,896
  Total Expanded (EMS)              16,220,160       (15M)
  Free Expanded (EMS)               16,220,160       (15M)
```

```
Largest executable program size        552,880    (540K)
Largest free upper memory block              0     (0K)
MS-DOS is resident in the high memory area.
```

The report from the MEM command contains lots of information, but you can break it down into five areas:

Modules using memory below 1 MB: This is a listing of programs (modules) currently in memory—including both conventional memory and upper memory. The last line (Free) tells you how much free memory you have in both areas. Your goal is to maximize these values.

Memory Summary: This is a summary of the total memory (used plus free) for each of the five major memory areas: conventional, upper, reserved (adapter RAM/ROM), extended, and expanded.

Largest executable program size: This value tells you the largest DOS program you can run in the current setup. Increasing this number means you can load larger programs and more data.

Largest free upper memory block: To get this number, MEM scans upper memory and looks for the largest gap. This is important, because you can't load a TSR or device driver into upper memory if there is no block large enough to accommodate it.

NOTE: YOU NEED A MEMORY MANAGER FOR UMBS

MEM reports a value of 0 for the largest UMB if no memory manager is loaded.

MS-DOS is resident in the high memory area: By default, Windows 95 loads DOS into the HMA and leaves only a 17 KB MS-DOS stub behind. This saves about 60 KB.

Loading Modules into Upper Memory Blocks

As you saw in the sample MEM listing just shown, a few real-mode drivers (such as ASPI2DOS.SYS, ASPICD.SYS, and MSCDEX.EXE) are usurping space in conventional memory, as well as some Windows 95 objects (such as IFSHLP.SYS and SETVER.EXE). This brings the total free space down to 540 KB, which isn't enough for many DOS programs (which often require 600 KB or more). To increase this number, you need to load as many device drivers as you can into UMBs.

To accomplish this, you first need to add the following lines to the top of your CONFIG.SYS file:

```
DEVICE=C:\WINDOWS\HIMEM.SYS
DEVICE=C:\WINDOWS\EMM386.EXE NOEMS
DOS=HIGH,UMB
```

> ### NOTE: USE THE RAM PARAMETER FOR EXPANDED MEMORY
>
> If your DOS programs need expanded memory, substitute the RAM parameter for the NOEMS parameter in the EMM386.EXE line. Note, however, that this will reduce the amount of free upper memory by 64 KB. This 64 KB chunk is the page frame that EMM386 uses to swap data to and from expanded memory.

HIMEM.SYS is the DOS extended memory manager. EMM386.EXE is the DOS device driver that manages the upper memory area. The command DOS=HIGH,UMB loads DOS into the high memory area and tells EMM386 to make upper memory blocks available for storing device drivers and TSRs. (Why do you have to load DOS into the HMA if Windows 95 already does so? Because if you only used the command DOS=UMB, this would nullify the DOS=HIGH command that IO.SYS uses to load DOS high.)

The next step is to modify CONFIG.SYS so that, for each of your device drivers (except HIMEM.SYS and EMM386.EXE), you change the word DEVICE to DEVICEHIGH. For example, my CONFIG.SYS file used to look like this:

```
DEVICE=ASPI2DOS.SYS /D /Z
DEVICE=ASPICD.SYS /D:ASPICD0
```

Now it looks like this:

```
DEVICE=C:\WINDOWS\HIMEM.SYS
DEVICE=C:\WINDOWS\EMM386.EXE NOEMS
DOS=HIGH,UMB
DEVICEHIGH=ASPI2DOS.SYS /D /Z
DEVICEHIGH=ASPICD.SYS /D:ASPICD0
```

Finally, edit AUTOEXEC.BAT to include the word LOADHIGH (or just LH) at the beginning of each line that runs a memory-resident program:

```
LOADHIGH C:\WINDOWS\COMMAND\DOSKEY.COM
LOADHIGH C:\WINDOWS\COMMAND\MSCDEX.EXE /D:ASPICD0 /L:H /M:12 /S
```

When you've completed these steps, reboot your computer to put the changes into effect and run MEM again. Here's my new listing:

```
Modules using memory below 1 MB:
  Name         Total          Conventional      Upper Memory
  --------   -------------    ---------------   ----------------
  SYSTEM     17,872  (17K)     9,984  (10K)       7,888   (8K)
  HIMEM       1,168   (1K)     1,168   (1K)           0   (0K)
  EMM386      4,320   (4K)     4,320   (4K)           0   (0K)
  WIN         3,568   (3K)     3,568   (3K)           0   (0K)
  vmm32      80,640  (79K)     1,472   (1K)      79,168  (77K)
  COMMAND     7,408   (7K)     7,408   (7K)           0   (0K)
  ASPI2DOS    9,680   (9K)         0   (0K)       9,680   (9K)
  ASPICD     11,648  (11K)         0   (0K)      11,648  (11K)
  ASPI2HLP      592   (1K)         0   (0K)         592   (1K)
  IFSHLP      2,864   (3K)         0   (0K)       2,864   (3K)
  SETVER        832   (1K)         0   (0K)         832   (1K)
  MSCDEX     41,008  (40K)         0   (0K)      41,008  (40K)
```

```
DOSKEY      4,688    (5K)        0   (0K)       4,688    (5K)
Free      627,200  (613K)  627,200 (613K)          0    (0K)
Memory Summary:
 Type of Memory       Total           Used         Free
 ---------------   -----------     ----------   ----------
 Conventional          655,360         28,160      627,200
 Upper                 158,368        158,368            0
 Reserved              393,216        393,216            0
 Extended (XMS)     15,570,272        140,640   15,429,632
 ---------------   -----------     ----------   ----------
 Total memory       16,777,216        720,384   16,056,832
 Total under 1 MB      813,728        186,528      627,200
 Largest executable program size      627,184      (612K)
 Largest free upper memory block            0       (0K)
 MS-DOS is resident in the high memory area.
```

EMM386 has moved the device drivers and TSRs into upper memory, and there is now 613 KB free, which is more than respectable. Notice, however, that there is no room left in upper memory. That's because VMM32 (literally) grabs whatever is left of free upper memory for its own devices. However, as you add or remove drivers in CONFIG.SYS and AUTOEXEC.BAT, VMM32 adjusts its upper memory footprint accordingly. Note, though, that you won't be able to load TSRs into upper memory from the DOS prompt.

Optimizing MS-DOS–Mode Memory

To optimize memory for MS-DOS–mode programs, you follow basically the same procedure I showed you in the last section. In this case, however, you can either edit the real CONFIG.SYS and AUTOEXEC.BAT files (to optimize the default MS-DOS–mode environment) or your custom CONFIG.SYS and AUTOEXEC.BAT files (to optimize the environment for specific DOS programs).

Setting Performance Properties

In the DOS program's properties sheet, select the Screen tab, shown in Figure 21.19. Here, the Performance group contains two optimization controls: Fast ROM emulation and Dynamic memory allocation.

FIGURE 21.19.

The Screen tab's Fast ROM emulation *and* Dynamic memory allocation *check boxes can affect the performance of your DOS program.*

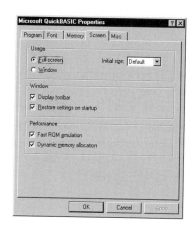

When the Fast ROM emulation check box is activated, Windows 95 uses the video display VxDs to reproduce (or *emulate*) the video services (that is, writing text to the screen) that are normally the province of the ROM BIOS functions. These RAM-based VxDs are faster, so the overall performance of the DOS program's display is improved. However, if the program expects to use nonstandard ROM calls, you might see garbage characters on-screen. If so, deactivate this check box.

Some DOS programs (such as WordPerfect) can operate in both text and graphics modes; the latter requires more memory. When the Dynamic memory allocation check box is activated, the Virtual Memory Manager supplies memory to the program as required by the program's current mode. If you run the program in graphics mode, the VMM allocates more memory to the virtual DOS machine; if you switch the program to text mode, the VMM reduces the memory allocated to the DOS machine, which makes more memory available to other applications. If you find that your program hangs when you switch to graphics mode, it could be that the VMM can't allocate enough memory to handle the new mode. In this case, you should deactivate the Dynamic memory allocation check box to force the VMM to always supply the program with enough memory to run in graphics mode.

Setting the Idle Sensitivity

When it's multitasking applications, Windows 95 doles out to each running process fixed-sized chunks of processor cycles called *time slices*. Ideally, active applications get more time slices, and idle applications get fewer. How does Windows 95 know if an application is idle? Windows applications send a message to the scheduler that specifies their current state. For example, an application might tell the scheduler that it's just waiting for user input (a keystroke or mouse click). In this case, Windows 95 will reduce the number of time slices for the application and redistribute them to other processes running in the background.

DOS programs are a different kettle of time slice fish. In most cases, Windows 95 has no way of knowing the current state of a DOS program. (However, some newer DOS applications are Windows-aware and can send messages to the scheduler.) In the absence of keyboard input, Windows 95 just assumes that a DOS program is in an idle state after a predetermined amount of inactivity, and it then redirects time slices to other processes. The amount of time that Windows 95 waits before declaring a DOS program idle is called the *idle sensitivity*.

You can control the idle sensitivity for a DOS program by using the Idle sensitivity slider on the Misc tab of the program's properties sheet, shown in Figure 21.20. As you can see, the slider has a range between Low and High. Here's how to work with this slider:

Low Idle sensitivity: Windows 95 waits longer before declaring the DOS program idle. Use a Low setting to improve performance for DOS programs that perform background tasks. This ensures that, despite the lack of keyboard input, these tasks still get the time slices they need.

High Idle sensitivity: Windows 95 takes less time to declare a DOS application idle. If you know your DOS program does nothing in the background, using the High setting will improve the performance of your other running applications, because the scheduler will reallocate its time slices sooner.

FIGURE 21.20.

Use the Idle *sensitivity slider to set the idle sensitivity for your DOS program.*

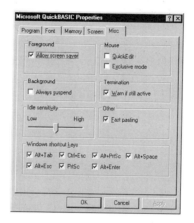

Understanding the Role of APPS.INF

As I mentioned earlier, when you launch a DOS program for the first time, Windows 95 scouts around for an existing PIF for the program. (Windows 95 checks the executable's folder, the INF folder, and the folders listed in the PATH statement.) If it can't find a PIF, it then checks out a file called APPS.INF. This file contains listings for hundreds of DOS programs and specifies the PIF parameters that are known to work best with the program. Before running a DOS program for the first time under Windows 95, you might want to see if it's listed in APPS.INF before creating a PIF shortcut on your own. Even if you've already done so, you should probably examine APPS.INF anyway to see if you need to make any changes to the PIF.

You'll find APPS.INF in the INF subfolder of your main Windows 95 folder (for example, \WINDOWS\INF). This is a hidden folder, so you'll need to activate Explorer's Show all files option. APPS.INF is a large file (61 KB), so you'll need to open it in WordPad or a text editor that's more powerful than Notepad. (If you just double-click APPS.INF, Windows 95 will ask if you want to open the file in WordPad.)

APPS.INF is divided into three areas: the [PIF95] section, the PIF settings for each program, and the [Strings] section. The next few sections give you the lowdown on each of these areas.

The [PIF95] Section

The first 400 or so lines in APPS.INF constitute the [PIF95] section. Figure 21.21 shows the first few lines of [PIF95] as they appear in WordPad.

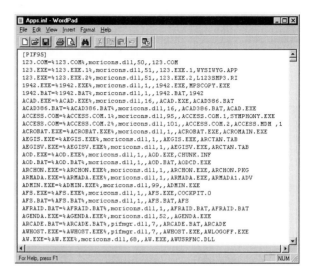

Each of these lines represents a specific DOS program with the following general syntax:

```
Exec=%Title%,IconFile,Icon#,SetWorkingFolder,Section,KeyFile,PIFFlag
```

`Exec`	The name of the program's executable file.
`%Title%`	A pointer to an entry in the `[Strings]` section that specifies the text that should appear in the title bar when you run the program in a DOS window.
`IconFile`	The name of the file that contains the icon used by the program.
`Icon#`	The number of the icon to use from `IconFile` (the first icon is 0).
`SetWorkingFolder`	A flag that determines whether Windows 95 can set the program's working folder. If this value is 0 (or absent), Windows 95 sets the working folder to be the same folder that contains the executable file. If this value is 1, Windows 95 can't set the working folder.
`Section`	The name of the section in `APPS.INF` that contains the program's PIF settings (see the next section).
`KeyFile`	The name of the file that uniquely identifies the contents of the program's folder. For example, there are two entries for `123.EXE`—one for Lotus 1-2-3 version 2.3 (WYSIWYG) and one for Lotus 1-2-3 version 3, respectively. If Windows 95 finds an executable file named `123.EXE`, how does it know which is which? According to the `KeyFile` settings, if it finds a

file named WYSIWYG.APP, it knows that 123.EXE refers to Lotus 1-2-3 version 2.3 (WYSIWYG); if it finds a file named L123SMP3.RI, it knows that 123.EXE refers to Lotus 1-2-3 version 3.

PIFFlag   A flag that determines whether Windows 95 can create a PIF for the DOS program. If it's 0 (or absent), Windows 95 can create a PIF; if it's 1, Windows 95 can't create a PIF.

The PIF Settings

After the [PIF95] section, APPS.INF has a section for each of the applications listed in [PIF95]. As you can see in Figure 21.22, the name of each section is the same as the *Section* parameter for the corresponding [PIF95] setting. For example, here's a setting from [PIF95]:

```
123.EXE=%123.EXE.1%,moricons.dll,51,,123.EXE.1,WYSIWYG.APP
```

Here, the *Section* parameter is 123.EXE.1, which corresponds to the following section in APPS.INF:

```
[123.EXE.1]
LowMem=350
XMSMem=None
Disable=win,bgd,hma
```

FIGURE 21.22.

There's a section of PIF settings for each application listed in [PIF95].

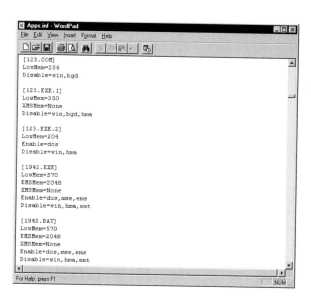

The lines beneath each section name are the PIF settings that work best with the program. These lines use the following syntax:

Setting=Value

Setting can be any one of the following values: AppHack, BatchFile, Disable, DPMIMem, EMSMem, Enable, LowMem, Params, or XMSMem.

The AppHack Setting

AppHack is a hexadecimal flag that changes the behavior of Windows 95 to work around problems with the DOS program. You'll see this flag for a DOS application that worked fine in earlier versions of Windows but that has problems with certain aspects of Windows 95. The AppHack (application hack) flag tells Windows 95 to bypass the problem area and use different code to service the application. For obvious reasons, this setting shouldn't be changed.

The BatchFile Setting

The BatchFile setting specifies the name of a batch file or DOS command to run prior to the executable file. This setting normally is used to change the PATH or some other DOS environment setting, or to load TSRs that the program might need.

The BatchFile setting's value corresponds to the Batch file text box in the Program tab of the DOS program properties sheet.

The Disable Setting

The Disable setting is used to turn off certain PIF options that are usually activated by default. This setting refers to these options using the three-letter entries listed in Table 21.5. This table also shows you the corresponding properties sheet tabs and controls for each entry.

Table 21.5. Three-letter entries used by the Disable setting.

Entry	Tab	Control
aen	Misc	Alt+Enter
aes	Misc	Alt+Esc
afp	Misc	Fast pasting
aps	Misc	Alt+PrtSc
asp	Misc	Alt+Space
ata	Misc	Alt+Tab
bgd	Misc	Always suspend
ces	Misc	Ctrl+Esc
dit	Misc	Idle sensitivity
emt	Screen	Fast ROM emulation
hma	Memory	Uses HMA
psc	Misc	PrtSc
rvm	Screen	Dynamic memory allocation

DOS Isn't Dead: Optimizing DOS Applications Under Windows 95

CHAPTER 21

703

21

OPTIMIZING
DOS
APPLICATIONS

Entry	*Tab*	*Control*
sav	Misc	Allow screen saver
win	Screen	Window/Full-screen

For example, consider the following setting:

```
Disable=win,bgd,hma
```

This tells Windows 95 to deactivate the Window option (that is, activate the Full-screen option), the Always suspend check box, and the Uses HMA check box.

The DPMIMem Setting

The DPMIMem setting specifies the amount of protected-mode DOS memory that should be allocated to the program. The DPMIMem setting's value corresponds to the MS-DOS protected-mode (DPMI) memory drop-down list in the Memory tab of the DOS program properties sheet. If DPMIMem is absent or –1, Windows 95 uses the Auto setting.

The EMSMem Setting

The EMSMem setting specifies the amount of expanded memory that should be allocated to the program. The EMSMem setting's value corresponds to the Expanded (EMS) memory drop-down list in the Memory tab of the DOS program properties sheet. If EMSMem is absent or –1, Windows 95 uses the Auto setting.

The Enable Setting

The Enable setting is used to activate PIF options that are usually turned off by default. As with the Disable setting, Enable refers to these options using three-letter entries. The entries that Enable uses are listed in Table 21.6, along with their corresponding properties sheet tabs and controls. (You'll notice, however, that some of these entries have no corresponding control in the properties sheet.)

Table 21.6. Three-letter entries used by the Enable setting.

Entry	*Tab*	*Control/Description*
cfg	Program | Advanced	Specify a new MS-DOS configuration
cwe	Program	Close on exit
dos	Program | Advanced	MS-DOS mode
eml	None	Lock EMS memory
exc	Misc	Exclusive mode

continues

Table 21.6. continued

Entry	Tab	Control/Description
gmp	None	Enable global memory protection
lie	Program | Advanced	Prevent MS-DOS-based programs from detecting Windows
lml	Memory	Protected
uus	None	Run program in a separate session
xml	None	Lock XMS memory

NOTE: THE cfg ENTRY IS AN MS-DOS–MODE SETTING

The cfg setting can be used only in conjunction with the dos (MS-DOS mode) setting.

If an Enable setting includes the dos entry, the entries listed in Table 21.7 can also be used. These entries control which options appear in the Select MS-DOS Configuration Options dialog box. (You'll recall that these are the drivers and TSRs that you can add to your custom CONFIG.SYS and AUTOEXEC.BAT files.)

Table 21.7. Three-letter entries used by the Enable setting to specify the available options for custom configuration files.

Entry	Option
cdr	CD-ROM
dsk	Direct Disk Access
ems	Expanded Memory (EMS)
mse	Mouse
net	Network
vsa	VESA Display Driver

The LowMem Setting

The LowMem setting specifies the amount of conventional memory that should be allocated to the program. (Conventional memory is also sometimes called *low memory*.) The LowMem setting's value corresponds to the Conventional memory drop-down list in the Memory tab of the DOS program properties sheet. If LowMem is absent or –1, Windows 95 uses the Auto setting.

DOS Isn't Dead: Optimizing DOS Applications Under Windows 95

CHAPTER 21

705

21

OPTIMIZING
DOS
APPLICATIONS

The Params Setting

The Params setting specifies extra parameters and switches that should be added to the program's command line. The Params setting's value is added to the Cmd line text box in the Program tab of the DOS program properties sheet.

The XMSMem Setting

The XMSMem setting specifies the amount of extended memory that should be allocated to the program. The XMSMem setting's value corresponds to the Extended (XMS) memory drop-down list in the Memory tab of the DOS program properties sheet. If XMSMem is absent or –1, Windows 95 uses the Auto setting.

The [Strings] Section

The [Strings] section, shown in Figure 21.23, is the last part of APPS.INF. There's a setting for each application listed in [PIF95]. These strings tell Windows 95 which text to display in the program's title bar (when you run the program in a DOS window, that is). Windows 95 finds the correct string by using the *Title* parameter from the program's setting in [PIF95]. For example, consider the following setting from [PIF95]:

```
123.EXE=%123.EXE.1%,moricons.dll,51,,123.EXE.1,WYSIWYG.APP
```

Here, the *Title* parameter is 123.EXE.1, which corresponds to the following setting in [Strings]:

```
123.EXE.1="Lotus 1-2-3   2.3 WYSIWYG"
```

This means that, when you run this version of 123.EXE, Windows 95 will display Lotus 1-2-3 2.3 WYSIWYG in the title bar.

FIGURE 21.23.

The [Strings] section specifies the text that will appear in the DOS program's title bar.

Troubleshooting DOS Difficulties

This section runs through a few problems you might encounter when running DOS commands or DOS programs.

When you double-click a shortcut for an MS-DOS–based program, you receive the following error message:

```
Cannot find the file 'Path.' Make sure that the file
exists on your system and that the path and filename
are correct.
```

Shortcuts for DOS programs are stored in PIFs rather than LNK files, and the maximum length for a command line in a PIF is 62 characters. Therefore, you'll receive the preceding error message if the program's command line is longer than 62 characters.

You can work around this problem in several ways:

- Add the program's folder to the PATH so that you have to enter only the executable filename in the command line.

- Use SUBST to create a virtual drive that points to the program's folder. You can then use this virtual drive in place of the folder's path in the command line.

- Create a batch file that launches the program, and then create a shortcut for the batch file.

- Reinstall the program to a folder with a shorter path, and then create a shortcut to the new location.

While working at the DOS prompt, you can't create files with names longer than 127 characters.

By default, the DOS command line is limited to 127 characters, so you won't be able to create filenames any longer than that. (In fact, your filenames will be less than that because the total length of the command line also includes whatever command you're using.)

To increase the command-line character limit, use the /U switch with COMMAND.COM. For example, the following line increases the maximum number of characters in a command line to 250:

```
c:\windows\command.com /u:250
```

You can use this switch while you're opening a DOS session or while you're running a command. To make this change available to all DOS virtual machines, enter the following line in CONFIG.SYS:

```
shell=c:\windows\command.com /u:250
```

When you restart your computer, you receive the following error message:

```
Bad or missing Command Interpreter
Enter name of Command Interpreter (for example, C:\Windows\Command.com)
```

This error message indicates that COMMAND.COM is missing or has become corrupted. If you've moved COMMAND.COM from the main Windows 95 folder, you'll need to restore it. Otherwise, reboot your system with the Windows 95 Startup disk in drive A. When you get to the A:\ prompt, enter the following command:

```
sys c:
```

If drive C is compressed, however, you must use the SYS command on the host drive. For example, if the host drive is drive H, use the following command instead:

```
sys h:
```

When that's done, remove the Startup disk and reboot the computer.

While using the standard VGA driver, your computer hangs when you start a DOS session.

This problem indicates that the video adapter in your system requires special support to run an MS-DOS command-prompt session reliably. Some video adapters require special support in Windows 95 to run DOS sessions without hanging. This support is installed when you use the correct driver for the display adapter. If you use the standard VGA video driver, however, Windows 95 doesn't install any adapter-specific support.

If you want to run a standard display type (640×480 or 800×600 resolution with 16 colors), you should select the proper video driver for the video adapter installed in your computer rather than the standard VGA driver.

The COPY command incorrectly copies files with plus signs (+) in their names.

The COPY command has a little-known property called concatenation that lets you combine two or more files into a third file. For example, suppose that you have three files named JAN.TXT, FEB.TXT, and MAR.TXT. You can combine all three files into a single file named 1STQTR.TXT by using the following command:

```
copy jan.txt+feb.txt+mar.txt 1stqtr.txt
```

When COMMAND.COM sees a plus sign in a COPY command, it concatenates the files. If you have a plus sign in a filename, therefore, COMMAND.COM assumes that you're trying to concatenate. For example, consider the following command:

```
copy black+white.txt gray.txt
```

Here, you're trying to copy the file named BLACK+WHITE.TXT to the file GRAY.TXT. But COMMAND.COM thinks you're trying to concatenate two files—BLACK and WHITE.TXT—into GRAY.TXT. To make your intentions clear, enclose the file with the plus sign in quotation marks, like so:

```
copy "black+white.txt" gray.txt
```

Files with long names aren't copied when you use the XCOPY command.

First, make sure that you're not in MS-DOS mode. If you're not, display the properties sheet for the DOS prompt, activate the Program tab, and click the Advanced button to display the Advanced Program Settings dialog box. Deactivate the Prevent MS-DOS-based programs from detecting Windows check box, and click OK.

I talked about the other options in the Advanced Program Settings dialog box in the section "Running a Program in MS-DOS Mode."

When you use the COPY command on a source or destination file with a long filename that begins with a period (.), you receive the following error message:

```
Path not found
```

This error occurs only if you include a path to the source or destination file, like so:

```
copy c:\folder\subfolder\.source destination
```

Or like this:

```
copy source c:\folder\subfolder\.destination
```

This problem occurs because COMMAND.COM assumes that any filename beginning with a period is a directory name, even though long filenames can begin with a period.

To work around this problem, either use the file's 8.3 name or use Explorer to copy the file.

When you use the MORE command with a document that has a long filename, you receive the following error message:

```
Invalid file name in command line
```

Unfortunately, the MORE command doesn't support long filenames. If you need to use MORE, either specify the 8.3 alias for the file or use a redirection symbol to display the file. For example, to display the file named Long Filename.txt and pause the output after each screenful, use the following command:

```
more < "long filename.txt"
```

When you run a graphics mode DOS program in a DOS window, its colors aren't displayed correctly.

Some graphics mode DOS programs that change their color tables will display incorrectly in a DOS window. (Some programs that exhibit this behavior are B-Wing, Dragon Lore, and Sierra Online Game Pak, for example.) This is a bug in Windows 95. To work around it, run the DOS program full-screen rather than in a window.

If you have to display the program in a window (for example, if you need to send something to the Clipboard), minimize the window and then restore it. This action might cause the colors to be redrawn correctly.

You can't move or resize a DOS window with the mouse.

If you can't use the mouse to drag a DOS window's title bar or borders, the DOS application likely is using the mouse in exclusive mode. As you learned earlier, this means that only the DOS program can use the mouse. Because the title bar and borders are part of Windows 95, they're off-limits.

To turn off exclusive mode, press Alt-Spacebar to pull down the DOS window's control menu, and select the Properties command. When the program's properties sheet appears, you'll have your mouse pointer back. Head for the Misc tab, and deactivate the Exclusive mode check box in the Mouse group. The mouse is now available to Windows 95. Click OK and then move or resize the window.

Summary

This chapter showed you a few techniques for working with the DOS shell. You saw what's new for DOS in Windows 95, I listed all the DOS commands (including those that are no longer part of Windows 95), and you learned various methods for starting DOS sessions and running commands. At the DOS prompt, I showed you how to work with long filenames, start programs (including Windows applications), undelete files, and customize the DOS screen.

I also showed you how to optimize DOS applications under Windows 95. After some introductory remarks about PIFs, I showed you how to set up a DOS program to run in MS-DOS mode. Then you learned how to really leverage MS-DOS mode by creating custom CONFIG.SYS and AUTOEXEC.BAT files for each program. I then took you through a conventional memory optimization session and showed you how to set some performance properties and idle sensitivity. I closed this chapter by taking a detailed look at the APPS.INF file and a few DOS troubleshooting issues.

Here are a few places to go in this book for more DOS data:

- I showed you how to install and uninstall DOS programs in Chapter 16, "Installing and Uninstalling Applications."

- Cutting and pasting data to and from the DOS window were covered in Chapter 17, "Sharing Data in Windows 95: The Clipboard and OLE."

- Windows 95 boasts a number of network-related DOS commands. I'll tell you about them in Chapter 31, "Windows 95 Networking."

- Windows 95 also has a few Internet-related DOS commands. I'll cover these in Chapter 37, "Windows 95 and the Internet."

- To learn a few batch file basics, head for Appendix F, "A Batch File Primer."

V

Part

Unleashing Multimedia: The Sights and Sounds of Windows 95

CHAPTER 22

Miscellaneous Multimedia: Graphics, CD-ROMs, and More

IN THIS CHAPTER

> *The essential is to excite the spectators. If that means playing Hamlet on a flying trapeze or in an aquarium, you do it.*
>
> —*Orson Welles*

The English language is a veritable factory of new words and phrases. Inventive wordsmiths in all fields are constantly forging new additions to the lexicon by blending words, attaching morphemic tidbits to existing words, and creating neologisms out of thin air. Some of these new words strike a chord in popular culture and go through what I call the "cachet-to-cliché" syndrome. In other words, the word is suddenly on the lips of cocktail party participants and water-cooler conversationalists everywhere, and on the fingertips of countless columnists and editorialists. As soon as the word takes root, however, the backlash begins. Rants of the if-I-hear-the-word-*x*-one-more-time-I'll-scream variety start to appear, the Unicorn Society includes the word in its annual list of phrases that should be stricken from the language, and so on.

The word *multimedia* went through this riches-to-rags scenario a couple of years ago. Buoyed by the promise of media-rich interactive applications and games, techies and non-techies alike quickly made *multimedia* their favorite buzzword. It didn't take long, however, for the bloom to come off the multimedia rose.

Part of the problem was that when multimedia first became a big deal in the early '90s, the average computer just wasn't powerful enough to handle the extra demands made on the system. Not only that, but Windows' support for multimedia was sporadic and half-hearted. That's all changed now, however. The typical PC sold today has more than enough horsepower to handle basic multimedia, and Windows 95 has a number of slick new features that let developers and end-users alike incorporate multimedia seamlessly into their work. So now, instead of railing uselessly against overuse of the word *multimedia,* people can get down to the more practical matter of creating exciting multimedia-based documents.

This chapter kicks off your look at Windows 95 multimedia by examining some multimedia background and architecture and looking at two important multimedia components: graphics and CD-ROMs. I'll focus on video in Chapter 23, "Windows 95 Video: The Big Picture," and audio in Chapter 24, "Getting the Most Out of Windows 95 Sound."

Some Multimedia Background

In its most basic guise, multimedia is a simple concept: the computer-based presentation of data using multiple modes of communication. These modes, or *media,* usually include two or more of the following: text, graphics, sound effects, music, animation, or video. The main idea, of course, is to make your point more effectively. Descriptive prose is an art form, but it's best left to professional novelists. In a business presentation or application, a well-placed image or sound snippet can convey your meaning unambiguously and with greater depth. In this sense, multimedia is the modern equivalent of the old a-picture-is-worth-a-thousand-words axiom. In Figure 22.1, for example, how much better it is to be able to hear a passage from Bach's famous *Toccata and Fugue in D Minor* than to have it merely described to you.

FIGURE 22.1.
*Multimedia applica-
tions are a rich source
of information and
entertainment.*

Multimedia also is a useful tool to have in this era of shrinking attention spans and increased desire for stimuli. One of the easiest ways to make the eyes of your audience glaze over is to throw up a slide that contains nothing but a forbidding wall of text. Thanks to heavy doses of fast-paced TV shows and movies, as well as untold numbers of slick magazines, fancy Web sites, and other eye (and ear) candy, information consumers require what people in marketing circles call JPMs: Jolts Per Minute. Today's multimedia technologies can provide jolts by the bushel.

A History of Windows Multimedia

It wasn't always this way. Computers used to be taciturn beasts that would sit quietly and passively, letting out only an occasional beep to let you know someone was home. The path to today's garrulous machines was long and not altogether smooth. The next few sections review the history of multimedia and Windows.

Windows 3.0 with Multimedia Extensions 1.0

Multimedia extensions are additions to an operating system that let developers work with multimedia devices—such as sound cards and CD-ROM drives—directly. They're implemented as a series of application programming interface (API) functions that programs can call. This saves programmers from having to code these calls themselves. It also imposes standards where none previously existed. This means that developers don't have to build support for multiple devices into their programs. A call to a particular API function works the same way with all devices in a particular hardware class.

The first such API—Multimedia Extensions 1.0—was released by Microsoft in 1991 and was designed to bring a multimedia subsystem to Windows 3.0. This API included support for the following:

> **Waveform audio:** A process that re-creates an audio waveform by using digital samples of the waveform. This is the standard Windows sound format.

MIDI: Musical Instrument Digital Interface. This is a communications protocol that standardizes the exchange of data between a computer and a musical synthesizer.

CD audio: Lets CD-ROM drives play audio compact discs.

Joystick services: Calibration for joystick devices.

Windows 3.1

Windows 3.1, released in 1992, incorporated the Multimedia Extensions and so became the first version of Windows to include a multimedia subsystem as part of the base operating system. Windows 3.1 included support for waveform audio, MIDI, and CD audio. It also included the Media Player applet for playing media files and the Sound Recorder applet for playing and recording waveform audio (WAV) files.

Video for Windows

Released later in 1992, Video for Windows was Microsoft's first attempt at a system that could play and record digitized video files. This initial release of Video for Windows was limited to playing AVI (Audio Video Interleave) files in a small 160×120-pixel window (a mere 1/16th of the standard 640×480 screen). Video for Windows also introduced a compression/decompression (*codec*) algorithm for video files.

Microsoft Multimedia Pack 1.0

This CD-ROM product was released in 1993 and was made available exclusively through multimedia hardware OEMs (original equipment manufacturers). It added the following features to the multimedia subsystem:

Media Browser: An application for browsing the system for multimedia data files (AVI, MID, RMI, WAV, and so on).

Minesweeper (multimedia version): Included waveform audio support.

Music Box: A CD audio playback application.

Sound Recorder: Beefed up with support for multiple sampling rates and compressed audio files.

Video for Windows 1.1: Increased the playback window to 320×240 pixels (one-fourth of a 640×480 screen) and included the Audio Compression Manager (ACM).

Windows 95 and Multimedia

These advances in multimedia software technology coincided with advances in multimedia hardware technology. Graphics accelerator boards, 16-bit audio cards, increasingly fast CD-ROM drives, video capture cards, and local bus technologies all served to make the PC an attractive multimedia platform.

However, Windows-based multimedia suffered from two glaring problems:

■ All this new hardware was still difficult to set up thanks to the rigors of setting IRQs and other configuration parameters.

■ Except for the basic multimedia subsystem included in Windows 3.1, Microsoft relied on third-party developers, OEMs, and end-users to implement, distribute, and install new features.

Windows 95 solves these problems by making it easier to install and upgrade hardware and by incorporating all key multimedia technologies in the base operating system. Here's a summary of the Windows 95 features that make it an ideal multimedia platform:

Plug and Play: Multimedia has always depended on hardware of one form or another. Now, with Windows 95's Plug and Play support, installing, adjusting, and removing all multimedia devices—from CD-ROMs to sound cards to graphics adapters—gets a lot easier.

CD-ROM support: CDFS, Windows 95's installable CD-ROM file system, brings 32-bit support to CD-ROM drives, and the separate CD-ROM cache ensures the best performance for your discs. Also, the new AutoPlay features make using your CD-ROMs easier than ever.

Built-in digital video support: Windows 95 comes with the latest version of Video for Windows (VfW) built right into the operating system. This means that you'll see more applications incorporating AVI files since developers know that users have the VfW runtime engine. The new VfW uses a 32-bit engine to deliver 640×480 playback.

32-bit codecs for audio and video: New and improved drivers for audio and video compression and decompression ensure faster and better multimedia support.

Full support for General MIDI: General MIDI is a standard that specifies which instruments are supported on different MIDI channels. Windows 95 now supports the full 16 General MIDI channels.

Preemptive multitasking and multithreading: Multimedia applications tend to demand a lot of CPU time and are sensitive to interruptions from outside sources. Now, however, 32-bit multimedia applications can take advantage of Windows 95's preemptive multitasking to ensure uninterrupted play. And the support for multithreading is a real boon to multimedia titles, which can use multiple threads to load data or play music in the background.

The Windows 95 multimedia subsystem supports the following types of multimedia devices and drivers:

Waveform input devices: Convert analog audio signals into digital audio data.

Waveform output devices: Convert digital audio data into analog audio signals.

MIDI input ports: Receive MIDI data from external MIDI devices such as keyboards and drum machines.

MIDI output ports: Send MIDI data to external MIDI devices.

Internal MIDI synthesizers: Synthesize music from MIDI data sent by applications.

Mixer devices: Control volume and balance for multiple audio lines.

Auxiliary audio devices: Support audio data that's a mixture of waveform audio and MIDI.

Video-capture devices: Digitize still images and motion video images. Some video-capture devices can also overlay and play video images.

Audio compression and decompression drivers: Support a variety of audio data formats and files for playback and recording.

Video compression and decompression drivers: Support a variety of video formats and files for playback and recording.

Windows 95's multimedia subsystem controls these devices using the following five components:

- The Media Control Interface
- The Display Control Interface
- The Audio Compression Manager
- The Video Compression Manager
- Multimedia Applets

The Media Control Interface

The Media Control Interface (MCI) gives applications a device-independent interface that lets them control multimedia devices and files. For example, without knowing the specifics of a multimedia device or file, an application can send a "Play" command to the MCI. The MCI will then work with the appropriate device driver to enable playback of the file or whatever media is in the device (such as an audio CD in a CD-ROM drive). Windows 95's Media Player applet (discussed later in this chapter) is an example of an application that uses the MCI to control multimedia devices.

Windows 95 defines a number of *device types,* which are classes of multimedia devices that respond to generic MCI commands (such as Play, Stop, and Rewind). Table 22.1 lists the currently defined MCI device types.

Table 22.1. The MCI device types.

Device Type	Description
animation	Animation playback device.
avivideo	AVI digital video player.
cdaudio	Compact disc audio player.
dat	Digital audio tape player.
digitalvideo	Digital video in a window (not GDI-based).
MPEGVideo	ActiveMovie digital video player (OSR2).
other	Undefined MCI device.
overlay	Overlay device (analog video in a window).
scanner	Image scanner.
sequencer	MIDI sequencer.
vcr	Videocassette recorder or player (VISCA).
videodisc	Videodisc player.
waveaudio	Audio device that plays waveform audio files.

OSR2

22

GRAPHICS,
CD-ROMS,
AND MORE

NOTE: INSTALLING MCI DRIVERS

Which MCI drivers Windows 95 Setup installs on your system depends on the hardware you have. For example, if you have a CD-ROM drive, Setup will install the driver for CD audio. If you later add a device (such as a laserdisc player or a VISCA-compatible VCR), you'll need to run the Add New Hardware Wizard to install the appropriate MCI drivers. When the Wizard asks if you want your hardware detected automatically, choose No. In the list of hardware classes, select Other Devices and then select Microsoft MCI. The Models list contains the MCI devices supported by Windows 95.

The Display Control Interface

Developed jointly by Microsoft and Intel, the Display Control Interface (DCI) is a new interface for display drivers. Drivers that support the DCI specifications can access the video frame buffer directly. However, as you'll see later, DCI has been supplanted by Microsoft's new DirectX family of multimedia APIs (see the section "DirectX: The Future of Windows Multimedia").

The Audio Compression Manager

The Audio Compression Manager (ACM) is a 32-bit API (there's also a 16-bit version) that acts as an intermediary between an application and an audio device driver. Called a *mapper,* the ACM attempts to match audio data with the appropriate driver by taking into account any compression or decompression required, the format of the audio data, and whether any filtering is required. The ACM implements system-level support for the following audio services:

> **Audio compression and decompression:** The ACM's main task is to manage the various audio compressor/decompressor (codec) drivers. Depending on the format, uncompressed audio data can consume large amounts of disc space, so most audio is distributed in compressed form. During playback, the compressed data needs to be decompressed; during recording, the uncompressed data needs to be compressed. A codec driver handles both of these tasks. Windows 95 supports several different audio codecs (see Chapter 24), so the ACM determines the appropriate driver to use.

> **Audio data format conversion:** The audio data format specifies various characteristics of the sound, including its sampling frequency, its sample depth, and whether it's mono or stereo. If you want to change the format of a WAV file (which I'll show you how to do in Chapter 24), the ACM calls a *format converter driver* to handle the specifics.

> **Audio data filtering:** Audio data filters are effects, such as an echo, added to an audio file. The ACM handles audio data that needs to be filtered by calling a *filter driver.*

The Video Compression Manager

The Video Compression Manager (VCM) works with Windows 95's installable video codecs to provide compression and decompression of video streams for applications. Compression of video data is even more important than for audio data because of the massive amounts of information involved. For example, suppose you have an AVI file that contains 640×480 video at 256 colors. It takes 8 bits (that is, 1 byte) to represent the 256 possible colors in each pixel, and each image has 307,200 pixels. That's 300 KB of data in each frame, and there could be as many as 30 frames per second! So a minute of uncompressed video will consume about half a gigabyte of hard disc storage without breaking a sweat! The math gets even uglier if the video uses TrueColor (24 bits per pixel). Codecs help reduce the load on your system by shrinking video files to more manageable sizes. I'll discuss video compression in more depth in Chapter 23.

Windows 95's Multimedia Applets

The final pieces of the Windows 95 multimedia puzzle are the various applets that come with the operating system. Here's a summary:

OSR2

> **ActiveMovie Control (OSR2):** Lets you play MPEG video files as well as AVI files and all audio file types supported by Windows 95. (ActiveMovie is also a component of Internet Explorer 3.02.)

CD Player: Lets you play audio CDs in a CD-ROM drive. I'll show you how CD Player works later in this chapter.

Media Player: Lets you select and then work with an MCI device. I also talk about Media Player later in this chapter.

Sound Recorder: Lets you play, edit, and record waveform audio files. I cover this program in Chapter 24.

Volume Control: Lets you control the sound levels of various audio inputs. This is a vendor-independent implementation that works with all Windows 95 sound card drivers. Again, see Chapter 24 for details.

Multimedia Hardware: The Evolving MPC Standard

Most computer manufacturers trumpet their systems, especially those directed at home users, as being "multimedia-ready." In some cases, this just means that the machine has been outfitted with a cheap sound card and a low-end CD-ROM drive. How are you supposed to know if the system you're buying is truly capable of handling the demands that modern multimedia titles will place on it?

In an effort to solve this conundrum, the Multimedia PC Marketing Council created a standard for computers to meet in order to be able to call themselves multimedia-ready. These so-called Multimedia PC (MPC) specifications define a minimum hardware configuration that's capable of running mainstream multimedia titles. In turn, multimedia developers are supposed to place the MPC logo on their products so that you'll know instantly whether or not you have the horsepower to install and operate a certain program. So far, there have been three iterations of the MPC standard: Level 1, Level 2, and Level 3.

The Level 1 MPC

The Level 1 MPC standard was released in 1990. Even then, this standard took a lot of flak from critics who thought the requirements were too low-end, so you can imagine how it fares in today's environment. Sure enough, as you can see from Table 22.2, the Level 1 specifications are woefully inadequate for today's demanding multimedia programs. (In fact, the Level 1 MPC wouldn't even be able to run a bare-bones Windows 95 configuration.)

Table 22.2. The Level 1 MPC specification.

Component	Minimum Requirements
RAM	2 MB
Processor	16 MHz 386SX
Hard drive	30 MB
CD-ROM	150 KB/sec sustained data transfer rate, one-second maximum average seek time, XA-ready, multisession-capable

continues

Table 22.2. continued

Component	Minimum Requirements
Sound	8-bit digital sound, 8-note synthesizer, MIDI playback, microphone input, 22.5 and 11.025 KHz sample rate, 8-bit digital-to-analog converter (DAC), 8-bit analog-to-digital converter (ADC)
Video display	640×480, 16 colors
User input	101-key keyboard, two-button mouse
I/O	Serial port, parallel port, MIDI I/O port, joystick port
System software	Windows 3.0 with Multimedia Extensions

The Level 2 MPC

The MPC standard became a little more realistic in 1993 when the Level 2 (MPC2) specification was released. Still, as you can see from Table 22.3, a Level 2 MPC is no high-end, mortgage-the-house barn burner.

Table 22.3. The Level 2 MPC specification.

Component	Minimum Requirements
RAM	4 MB
Processor	25 MHz 486SX
Hard drive	160 MB
CD-ROM	Double-speed, 300K/sec sustained data transfer rate, 400ms maximum average seek time, XA-ready, multisession-capable
Sound	16-bit digital sound, eight-note synthesizer, MIDI playback, microphone input, 44.1 KHz sample rate, 16-bit digital-to-analog converter (DAC), 16-bit analog-to-digital converter (ADC)
Video display	640×480, 65,536 colors
User input	101-key keyboard, two-button mouse
I/O	Serial port, parallel port, MIDI I/O port, joystick port
System software	Windows 3.1

The Level 3 MPC

My sister and her family have a machine that more or less meets the MPC2 standard. However, I've found that trying to buy them any kind of reasonably interesting multimedia titles is just about impossible. That's because today's mainstream multimedia apps have minimum requirements that go well beyond the MPC2 specs.

Input device querying: DirectInput can query a joystick or other device to determine its capabilities. Also, programs can process a joystick's position and button information by querying the joystick.

Support for multiple devices: DirectInput can simultaneously monitor either two analog joysticks that track up to four axes of movement and use up to four buttons, or four analog joysticks that track two axes of movement and use up to four buttons. For digital joysticks, DirectInput can support up to 16 devices, each with up to six axes of movement and up to 32 buttons.

DirectPlay

The DirectPlay API is an OLE interface that simplifies connectivity between applications over communications links. Designed specifically for multiplayer games, DirectPlay gives developers an easy way to connect players either over a network or via modem. Specifically, DirectPlay lets applications connect in a way that's independent of the underlying transport hardware, network protocol, or online service. It does this by implementing a simple send/receive communications model that has been optimized for game play.

Getting Great Graphics

Your computer's display is what you look at all day long, so you need to be comfortable with what you see. This is especially important for multimedia applications. To get the most out these titles, you'll need graphics hardware that can handle the blizzard of data produced by the bitmaps, videos, and animations that are *de rigueur* in modern multimedia. Mainstream business applications also can benefit from a strong graphics system. After all, Windows 95 *is* a graphical operating system, so even day-to-day chores can create quite a graphics workload.

Fortunately, simply upgrading to Windows 95 can give your graphics a speed boost. Microsoft revamped the graphics subsystem to provide greater performance as well as enhanced reliability. For one thing, some of the data structures used by the graphics device interface (GDI) were converted to 32-bit, thus making better use of system resources. Also, the GDI gained a new engine for controlling output to the screen. It's called the Device Independent Bitmap (DIB) engine, and it includes 32-bit code that takes advantage of features found in 386 and higher processors to generate highly optimized generic drawing routines for everything from lowly 4-bit graphics devices to 24-bit powerhouses. Microsoft claims that this new engine can almost double the performance of even unaccelerated graphics adapters.

Windows 95's display driver architecture was upgraded as well. In Windows 3.x, manufacturers had to write monolithic drivers that included not only the specific implementations of their hardware, but also the basic instructions for drawing to the screen. Now, however, the graphics subsystem uses the universal driver/mini-driver model found in the rest of Windows 95's hardware architecture. The universal driver supplied by Microsoft handles the basic interaction with the GDI and the DIB engine, while mini-drivers handle the device-specific functionality.

Beyond these internals, the attractiveness and performance of your computer's display is a function of two components: the graphics adapter and the monitor. I'll examine both of these components in the next few sections.

Understanding Graphics Adapters

The *graphics adapter* (also known as the *video adapter, graphics card,* or *video card*) is the internal component in your system that generates the output you see on your monitor.

Accelerated Graphics Adapters

It used to be that graphics adapters relied on the CPU to handle most of the dirty work of graphics processing. However, most graphics adapters sold today are *accelerated.* This means that they come with a graphics coprocessor that assumes most of the graphics duties from the CPU, including time-consuming tasks such as drawing lines and circles. The coprocessor is specially designed to handle these sorts of tasks, so not only do screens update faster, but the CPU is relieved of a massive processing burden. For the most part, as far as graphics are concerned, all that remains for the CPU is to send the basic instructions to the graphics card about what to draw and where.

Local Bus Adapters

Most graphics adapters are designed to work with *local bus* systems—usually the VL-Bus for 486 systems and the PCI bus for Pentiums. A local bus is a high-speed data pathway that provides a direct link between the CPU and the adapter's video circuitry. This way, the CPU can send its graphics instructions directly to the adapter without having to go through the slower expansion bus. Local bus systems make a huge difference in graphics performance. There are two reasons for this:

■ A local bus is designed to work at higher speeds. Whereas an ISA bus is designed for 8.33 MHz operation, the VL-Bus and PCI bus typically operate at 25 MHz or 33 MHz.

■ Both the VL-Bus and PCI bus have 32-bit data paths, compared to the 16-bit data path of the ISA bus.

Data Width

Once the graphics adapter gets some data, it usually shuffles it around between various components on the board. To speed up this part of the process, adapter manufacturers have been increasing the width of the data path (which generally refers to the path between the adapter's processor and its frame buffer—the on-board graphics memory). Although you still see 32-bit adapters on the market, the new standard is a 64-bit data width, so that's the minimum you should look for in an adapter. Some manufacturers are even shipping 128-bit adapters, but they show a speed boost only at higher color depths (at least 16-bit).

Display Resolution

Resolution is a measure of the sharpness of an on-screen image. Resolution is expressed as the number of pixels displayed horizontally by the number of pixels displayed vertically. For example, 640×480 resolution means that there are 640 pixels across the image and 480 pixels down the image. Because most screen objects have a fixed size in pixels, the resolution determines how large or small an object appears, and therefore how much apparent room you have on-screen.

For example, suppose that you have a dialog box on-screen that is 160 pixels wide and 120 pixels tall. In a 640×480 resolution, this dialog box would take up 1/16th of the desktop area. If you switched to 800×600 resolution, however, the dialog box's dimensions would remain the same, so the dialog box would end up usurping only 1/25th of the desktop. At 1,024×768, the same dialog box would fit into a mere 1/40th of the screen. To make this concrete, Figure 22.2 shows a dialog box displayed at 640×480, and Figure 22.3 shows the same dialog box displayed at 1,024×768.

FIGURE 22.2.

A dialog box displayed at 640×480.

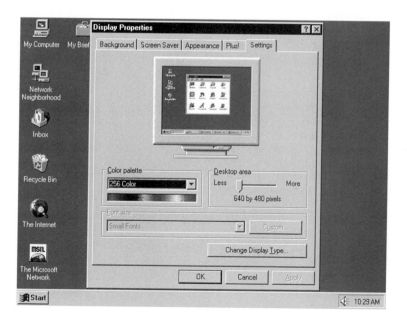

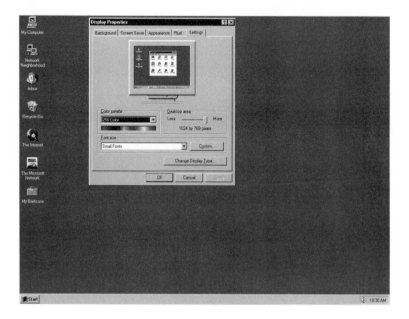

You can use the various resolutions supported by your graphics adapter to enlarge or shrink the desktop. If you move to a higher resolution, objects appear smaller, so, in a virtual sense, you end up with more room. In turn, this lets you either display more windows or make your existing windows larger. Before adjusting the resolution, however, you should keep the following points in mind:

The higher the resolution, the smaller your text will appear. You'll need to trade extra screen real estate for text readability. (Many applications also let you "zoom" their window contents larger or smaller. In addition, don't forget that you can scale Windows 95's system fonts. See Chapter 7, "Customizing Windows 95," for details.)

In most cases, you'll also need to trade color depth for resolution. Unless you have lots of video memory on your graphics adapter, the higher the resolution, the fewer colors you'll be able to display (more on this in the next section).

You need to match the resolution produced by the graphics adapter to that supported by your monitor. For one thing, monitors have a maximum supported resolution, so you won't be able to exceed that. For another, the size of the monitor determines the maximum comfortable resolution: The smaller the monitor, the smaller the resolution you should use. Here are my maximum resolution suggestions for various monitor sizes:

Monitor Size	*Suggested Maximum Resolution*
13 inches	640×480
14 inches	800×600

Monitor Size	Suggested Maximum Resolution
15 inches	800×600
17 inches	1,024×768
21 inches	1,600×1,200

Recall from Chapter 7 that you control the resolution via the Settings tab in the Display Properties dialog box. Use the Desktop area slider to adjust the dimensions. In most cases, you should be able to set the new resolution on-the-fly (that is, without having to restart Windows 95).

Color Depth

Color depth determines the number of colors (that is, the *color palette*) available to your applications and graphics. Color depth is expressed either in bits or total colors. The bits value specifies the number of bits each pixel can use to display a color. In the simplest case—a 1-bit display— each pixel could use only two colors: If the bit were 0, the pixel would show black; if the bit were 1, the pixel would show white.

The higher the number of bits, the more combinations a pixel can assume, and the more colors you have available. The minimum realistic color depth is 4-bit, which produces 16 colors in each pixel (since 2 to the power of 4 equals 16). Table 22.5 lists the fundamental color depths.

Table 22.5. Fundamental color depths.

Bits	Colors
4	16
8	256
15	32,268
16	65,536 (High Color)
24	16,777,216 (True Color)

If you're just working with mainstream business applications, 256 colors is plenty. In multimedia applications, however, you might need to jump up to 16-bit to get the best-looking output. (If you're working with photographic-quality images, you'll need to use 24-bit for faithful reproduction.)

To adjust the color depth, open the Display Properties sheet, select the Settings tab, and use the Color palette drop-down list to select the depth you want. You'll need to restart Windows 95 to put the new setting into effect.

OSR2

TIP: COLOR DEPTH CHANGES ON-THE-FLY

The retail version of Windows 95 doesn't support on-the-fly color depth changes. However, this capability is part of OSR2. Microsoft also has a QuickRes utility that does the job. This utility is one of the Power Toys, and you'll find it at the following URL:

`http://www.microsoft.com/windows/download/quik_res.exe`

After you've downloaded this file, double-click it to extract two files—QUICKRES.EXE and QUICKRES.INF—which you'll need to copy to your main Windows 95 folder.

When you run QUICKRES.EXE (and in OSR2 by default), a new icon appears in the system tray. Clicking this icon displays the available color depths for each resolution supported by your adapter. To select a new color depth and resolution, just click the appropriate item.

Video Memory

The resolution you can display and the number of colors available at that resolution are both a function of the amount of video memory that's installed on your graphics adapter. (Unlike system RAM, video RAM has nothing to do with performance.) To understand why, consider that the current state of each pixel on your screen has to be stored somewhere in memory. A screen displayed at 640×480 will have 307,200 pixels and therefore will need 307,200 memory locations. However, each pixel also requires a particular number of bits, depending on the color depth. At a 4-bit depth, those 307,200 pixels use 1,228,800 bits, or 153,600 bytes (150 KB).

In general, you use the following formula to calculate the amount of video memory required by a particular resolution and color depth:

Horizontal * *Vertical* * *Bits* / 8

Here, *Horizontal* is the horizontal resolution, *Vertical* is the vertical resolution, and *Bits* is the number of bits in the color depth. Table 22.6 lists various resolutions and color depths and shows the memory required to support each combination. (The Adapter Memory column tells you the amount of memory that needs to be installed in the graphics adapter.)

Table 22.6. Adapter video memory requirements for various resolutions and color depths.

Resolution	Color Depth	Actual Memory in Bytes	Adapter Memory
640×480	4-bit	153,600	256 KB
640×480	8-bit	307,200	512 KB
640×480	16-bit	614,400	1 MB
640×480	24-bit	921,600	1 MB

Resolution	Color Depth	Actual Memory in Bytes	Adapter Memory
800×600	4-bit	240,000	256 KB
800×600	8-bit	480,000	512 KB
800×600	16-bit	960,000	1 MB
800×600	24-bit	1,440,000	2 MB
1,024×768	4-bit	393,216	512 KB
1,024×768	8-bit	786,432	1 MB
1,024×768	16-bit	1,572,864	2 MB
1,024×768	24-bit	2,359,296	4 MB
1,280×1,024	4-bit	655,360	1 MB
1,280×1,024	8-bit	1,310,720	2 MB
1,280×1,024	16-bit	2,621,440	4 MB
1,280×1,024	24-bit	3,932,160	4 MB
1,600×1,200	4-bit	960,000	1 MB
1,600×1,200	8-bit	1,920,000	2 MB
1,600×1,200	16-bit	3,840,000	4 MB
1,600×1,200	24-bit	7,680,000	8 MB

22

GRAPHICS, CD-ROMs, AND MORE

Besides the amount of RAM installed on the graphics adapter, the *type* of RAM can also affect performance. Four types are available:

DRAM (Dynamic RAM): This type of RAM is cheap, so it's used on most low-end graphics adapters. However, it's slow (since the information within the RAM must be constantly updated), and it can't be read from and written to at the same time.

VRAM (Video RAM): As its name implies, this type of RAM is optimized for graphics operations and is much faster than DRAM. (Unlike DRAM, the adapter can read and write to VRAM simultaneously.) However, adapters that utilize VRAM chips tend to be expensive.

EDO (Extended Data Out) DRAM: This type of RAM is slightly faster than conventional DRAM, so it's slowly becoming the standard on low-end adapters.

WRAM (Window RAM): This type of RAM, although still relatively rare, offers many advantages over VRAM. For one thing, it incorporates special graphics features that let the adapter process graphics faster. For another, because it uses fewer components, it will be cheaper than VRAM (at least in the long run).

Installing a Graphics Adapter Driver

Windows 95 shipped with mini-drivers for many of the most popular graphics adapters, and the Setup program should install the appropriate driver for you. Even if your adapter doesn't come with a Microsoft driver, it's likely that the manufacturer has released its own mini-driver designed to work with Windows 95. (Check the vendor's Internet site or BBS to find out.) So although your old adapter drivers will probably work under Windows 95, you should take advantage of the newer drivers if they're available. Here are four good reasons to upgrade from your current Windows 3.x driver to a Windows 95 driver:

- Windows 95's 32-bit drivers are faster and more reliable than the older drivers.
- Windows 3.1 drivers don't support on-the-fly resolution changes.
- Windows 3.1 drivers don't support animated cursors.
- Windows 3.1 drivers don't support Energy Star power-saving features.

CAUTION: INSTALL A NEW ADAPTER IN VGA MODE

If you're installing a new graphics adapter, you should always place Windows 95 in VGA mode before doing so. All graphics adapters can handle plain-vanilla VGA, so you're less likely to run into problems. First, follow the steps listed next to change the driver to Standard VGA. Instead of rebooting, however, shut down your system and install the new graphics adapter. Then restart Windows 95 and follow the steps listed next once again to install the correct driver for the new adapter.

Here are the steps to follow to install an adapter driver:

1. Open the Display Properties dialog box, select the Settings tab, and click the Change Display Type button. The Change Display Type dialog box appears, as shown in Figure 22.4.

FIGURE 22.4.

The Change Display Type dialog box shows the current settings for your adapter driver and monitor.

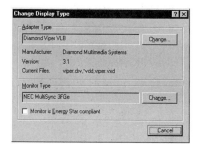

2. In the Adapter Type group, click the Change button.

3. If you have a disc from the manufacturer, insert it and click the Have Disk button. In the Install from Disk dialog box, enter the appropriate drive and folder in the Copy manufacturer's files from box and click OK. Windows 95 displays a list of possible device drivers in the Select Device dialog box.

   Otherwise, activate the Show all devices option to display a list of the adapter manufacturers and models supported by Windows 95 (see Figure 22.5).

FIGURE 22.5.

Choose the appropriate manufacturer and model from this dialog box.

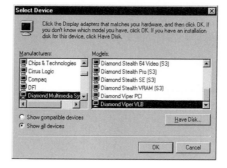

4. Highlight the driver you want to install.

TROUBLESHOOTING: WHAT TO DO IF YOUR ADAPTER ISN'T LISTED

If you don't see your graphics adapter listed, and you don't have a disc from the manufacturer, select Standard Display Types at the top of the Manufacturers list. The Models box lists a couple of generic adapters, one of which should work with your adapter.

5. Click OK.

6. Follow the on-screen prompts if Windows 95 asks for your source discs.

7. When you're back at the Change Display Type dialog box, click Close to return to the properties sheet.

8. Click Close. Windows 95 asks if you want to restart your computer.

9. Click Yes to reboot and put the new driver into effect.

TROUBLESHOOTING: IF YOUR VIDEO DISPLAY IS GARBLED

You might find that your display is a mess once you reboot after installing a new video driver. This probably means one of three things:

- You installed the wrong driver
- The driver you're using is corrupt
- The display resolution or color depth is beyond the capacity of the driver

If this happens, you need to shut down your computer and restart in safe mode (as described in Chapter 4, "Start It Your Way: Understanding Windows 95 Startup"). How do you shut down if you can't see anything on-screen? Here are the keyboard techniques to use:

- If the logon dialog box is displayed, press Ctrl-Alt-Delete and then press Alt-S to select the Shut Down command.
- If you're in Windows 95, press Ctrl-Esc, then press U, then Enter.

Once Windows 95 restarts, you can troubleshoot the problem (by, say, selecting a different video driver).

If the disc that came with your graphics adapter has extra utilities, be sure to install them. The drivers created by Microsoft offer good performance, but they lack any extra bells and whistles. However, adapter vendors often create utilities that offer features such as on-the-fly color depth changes, virtual desktops, and more. Some even integrate these features right into the Windows 95 shell. For example, Figure 22.6 shows the Display Properties dialog box with an extra MGA Settings tab. This tab is added when you install the Matrox MGA Millennium adapter.

FIGURE 22.6.

Some graphics adapters add their own extensions to the Windows 95 shell.

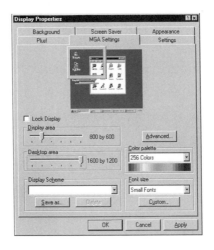

What to Look for in a Monitor

Your monitor shows the end result of all the pixel pushing done by the graphics adapter. You can have the best adapter on the market, but if your monitor is cheap, you'll end up with a display that's uncomfortable and hard on the eyes. If you're shopping around for a monitor, here are a few things to look for:

- Make sure that your monitor and graphics adapter can work together. For example, if you've purchased a graphics adapter that operates at 1,280×1,024 resolution, make sure that your monitor can handle that many pixels as well.

- Make sure that the monitor's refresh rate (also known as its vertical frequency) is at least 72 Hz. This is a measure of the number of times the screen is refreshed per second. The higher the refresh rate, the easier the display will be on your eyes.

- You need to make sure that the refresh rate generated by your graphics adapter matches the refresh rate supported by your monitor. One easy way to ensure refresh rate compatibility is to purchase a *multisync* monitor. These monitors can adjust themselves to the frequencies generated by the graphics adapter.

- Some monitors use *interlacing* to display higher resolutions. Interlacing means that the electron beam that generates the screen images doesn't paint the entire screen with each pass. (The frequency of these passes is determined by the monitor's refresh rate.) Instead, one pass will paint the odd lines, and the next pass will paint the even lines. This can cause a noticeable flicker on the screen, which will become annoying and hard on your eyes after a short period. You should always buy noninterlaced monitors, which paint the entire screen with each pass.

- The electron beam that paints the screen does so by using electrons to activate phosphors in the back of the monitor. The distance between each of these phosphors is called the *dot pitch;* it's a measure of the clarity of a monitor's image. The smaller the dot pitch, the sharper the image. Look for a monitor with a dot pitch of .28 mm or less.

- Many of the latest monitors are Plug and Play–compliant. This means that you just need to attach the monitor's cable, and Windows 95 will recognize the new monitor automatically.

- To save money and energy, look for monitors that meet the Energy Star requirements. These monitors have power-saving features that can switch the monitor to a low-power standby mode after a specified number of minutes. In some cases, the monitor can even completely shut down automatically. Windows 95 supports these Energy Star features (I talked about them in Chapter 7).

Changing the Monitor Type

If you change your monitor, and it's not Plug and Play–compliant, here's how to let Windows 95 know about it:

1. In the Display Properties dialog box, select the Settings tab.
2. In the Monitor Type group, click the Change button.
3. If you have a disc from the manufacturer, insert it and click the Have Disk button. In the Install from Disk dialog box, enter the appropriate drive and folder in the Copy manufacturer's files from box and click OK. Windows 95 displays a list of monitors in the Select Device dialog box.

   Otherwise, activate the Show all devices option to display a list of the monitor manufacturers and models supported by Windows 95 (see Figure 22.7).

FIGURE 22.7.

Choose the appropriate manufacturer and model for your monitor from this dialog box.

4. Use the Manufacturers and Models lists to track down and highlight your monitor.

TROUBLESHOOTING: WHAT TO DO IF YOUR MONITOR ISN'T LISTED

If you don't see your monitor listed, and you don't have a disc from the manufacturer, select Standard Monitor Types at the top of the Manufacturers list. The Models box lists various generic monitors, one of which should work with your monitor.

5. Click OK to return to the Change Display Type dialog box.
6. If your monitor meets the Energy Star requirements, activate the Monitor is Energy Star compliant check box (if Windows 95 hasn't done so already).
7. Click Close to return to the properties sheet.
8. Click OK.

Multimedia and the CD-ROM Craze

CD-ROM drives are a big part of the multimedia revolution. Now that 5¼-inch floppy drives have been relegated to the dustbin of computer history, CD-ROM drives have moved in and taken their place. In fact, the vast majority of new systems sold today come with a CD-ROM drive. This critical mass of drives convinced multimedia developers to release their new titles on CD-ROM and, with now hundreds of megabytes to play with, many of these titles are truly spectacular. (Games such as Myst and encyclopedias such as Encarta come to mind.) The quality of these applications, the reduced price, and a constant increase in performance (double-speed drives begat quad-speed, quad-speed begat six-speed, and now six-speed has begat eight-speed) convinced even more people to add CD-ROM drives to their systems.

CD-ROM Drive Specifications

If you're looking to purchase a CD-ROM drive for multimedia applications, what should you look for? There are many drives on the market, and they all have different features and different specifications. To help you make your decision, the following sections discuss a few essentials to keep in mind.

Sustained Data Transfer Rate

The sustained data transfer rate is a measure of how much data the CD-ROM drive can read from the disc and transfer to the computer. It's a "sustained" rate because it measures how quickly *sequential* data is transferred. For example, if a drive has a transfer rate of 150 KB per second and it must read 300 consecutive kilobytes, the transfer will take two seconds. The original single-speed drives had a data transfer rate of 150K/sec, and all subsequent drives use a multiple of that rate. So, for example, a quad-speed drive transfers data at 600K/sec. Since multimedia titles often work with large files (such as video clips), a high data transfer rate is crucial for top multimedia performance.

NOTE: VIDEO PERFORMANCE IS OFTEN FIXED

Unfortunately, buying an eight-speed CD-ROM drive won't necessarily double the video performance of a quad-speed drive. The reason is that the transfer rate for video clips is usually set in advance by the developer. For example, if a clip is set to play at quad-speed, you'll need at least a quad-speed drive to play it, but having an eight-speed drive won't make any difference. Still, it's best to get the highest data transfer rate you can afford so that you'll be able to run the next generation of multimedia titles.

Average Access Time

As with a hard drive, the access time for a CD-ROM drive is a measure of the delay between the drive's receiving a "read" command and actually reading the first chunk of data. These days, average access times for CD-ROM drives range from 90 ms to 300 ms. (This is still quite slow compared to the typical access times for hard drives, which are down around 10 ms.) The lower the access time the better, of course, but this value isn't as crucial for multimedia applications, which tend to work with a few large files and sequential data.

On-Board Cache

Most drives now come with a small cache of on-board memory. These buffers let the drive store bits of data temporarily while the drive seeks other chunks of a file or related data. It can then send the data together, thus maintaining a constant rate. You should look for a minimum on-board cache of 256 KB.

Drive/Computer Interface

The interface is the drive's physical connection to the computer's bus. The two most common are SCSI and EIDE. There's little difference between them as far as performance goes (although EIDE drives do tend to place a little more of a load on the system's CPU). Probably the biggest determining factor is the existing interface on your system. If you already have a SCSI card installed, purchasing a SCSI CD-ROM is a natural.

Internal Versus External

Whether you opt for an internal or external CD-ROM drive depends on a number of factors:

> **Internal drive:** Internal drives cost less, don't use up space on your desk, don't require a separate power source, and usually have audio cables that connect directly to your sound card. However, installing these drives is usually more difficult, because it requires opening up your PC. Also, with today's "mini-tower" and small-footprint systems, drive bays are often hard to come by.

> **External drive:** The biggest advantages of external drives are that they're a breeze to install—usually, you just plug in the cable and power cord—and they're portable. However, they cost more than comparable internal drives, and they tend to be on the big side, so they'll usurp some of your desk space.

Loading Mechanism

Today's CD-ROMs come with one of the following types of loading mechanisms: tray, caddy, or roller:

> **Tray:** This mechanism operates just like the loading mechanism on most audio CD players: A plastic tray slides out, you place the disc in a round depression, and you close the tray. Drives that use this mechanism are cheap, but they have a few disadvantages. The disc often just sits in the tray without being held securely in place; you need

to handle the disc directly, thus increasing the chances of scratching it or getting fingerprints on its surface, and the loaded disc has no protection from dust or other stray particles.

Caddy: This mechanism is a plastic container with a hinged lid that resembles the jewel boxes that most CDs are shipped in. Caddies are a bit more expensive, but they hold the disc securely and provide excellent protection. For convenient loading and unloading, you should buy a caddy for each CD-ROM you use regularly. This way, you have to handle the disc only once—when you first load it into its caddy.

Roller: Still relatively rare, a roller mechanism operates like the CD players in car audio systems. You insert the disc into a slot in the front of the drive, and the drive itself takes care of loading the disc into place.

NOTE: DVD: WELCOME TO THE NEXT LEVEL

Although CD-ROMs will be around for a long time, the writing is on the wall, and its says "DVD." DVD stands for *Digital Versatile Disc*, and it's the end result of a long battle to settle on the new standard for digital media. Supported by all the major players in the electronics industry, DVD promises previously unheard-of levels of performance, storage, and compatibility. The first units began shipping in the spring of 1997. They play not only the new consumer video titles in DVD format (hundreds of movies will be released throughout 1997), but also today's audio CDs, CD-ROMs, laserdiscs, and the new DVD-ROM format (which supports MPEG-2 digital video). The latter promises up to 4.7 GB (yes, *gigabytes*) of the same kind of data that we see on regular CD-ROMs, with the performance of an eight-speed CD-ROM drive. This technology also supports "double-layered" discs that can pack a walloping 8.5 GB, which is the equivalent of about 13 of today's CD-ROMs. When the DVD format hits its full stride in 1998, discs will be able to store 17 GB and will be writable *and* erasable.

Windows 95 and CD-ROMs

Windows 95 supports CD-ROM drives with a 32-bit protected-mode driver named VCDFSD.VXD (the CDFS stands for CD-ROM File System). This driver replaces MSCDEX.EXE, the real-mode driver used in previous versions of DOS and Windows. If a line loading MSCDEX.EXE already existed in AUTOEXEC.BAT when you installed Windows 95, the Setup program comments out the line and adds VCDFSD.VXD to its list of protected-mode drivers to load at startup. If you've added a CD-ROM drive since installing Windows 95, you'll need to run the Add New Hardware Wizard (in automatic mode) to detect the drive and load VCDFSD.VXD. (The exception to this is if your CD-ROM drive is attached to a SCSI controller. In this case, Windows 95 will detect the drive automatically at startup.)

With CDFS, you should notice improved performance from your CD-ROM drive. Not only is CDFS faster than the old real-mode driver, but it also boasts improved multitasking abilities and works with VCACHE (the protected-mode cache driver) to create a separate (and dynamic) pool of cache memory to help optimize CD-ROM performance. I showed you how to make adjustments to the CD-ROM cache in Chapter 9, "Windows 95 Performance Tuning and Optimization."

The AutoPlay Feature

Windows 95 continually performs a number of chores in the background. One of these chores is to use the CDVSD.VXD driver to constantly poll your CD-ROM drive to see if a new disc has been inserted. If it finds a new disc, it alerts Explorer to update the Folders pane, and then it looks for a file named AUTORUN.INF. This file gives Windows 95 instructions on what to do with the CD-ROM. For example, here's the AUTORUN.INF file from the Windows 95 CD-ROM:

```
[autorun]
OPEN=AUTORUN\AUTORUN.EXE
ICON=AUTORUN\WIN95CD.ICO
```

The OPEN line tells Windows 95 the name and location of an executable file. When Windows 95 detects this line, it runs the file automatically. In most cases, the executable either loads a Setup program or starts the applications.

TIP: CHANGING DISK DRIVE ICONS

Although AutoPlay was designed for CD-ROMs, it works on other types of disc drives, too. This isn't all that useful for running programs, but it does give you an easy way to change the drive icons that are displayed in Explorer or My Computer. All you have to do is create a new AUTORUN.INF in the root folder of a disc drive and then enter the following lines in this file:

```
[autorun]
ICON=IconFile,IconNumber
```

IconFile is the name of an icon file, and *IconNumber* is the position of the icon within the file. (Chapter 13, "Working with Files and Folders," lists a few files that contain icons.) Once you've saved the file, refresh the display (by pressing F5) to put the new setting into effect.

If the disc is an audio CD, Windows 95 starts playing it automatically. ("Play" is the default action for the AudioCD file type.)

If you'd prefer that Windows 95 not run the AutoPlay executable when you load a disc, just hold down the Shift key. Windows 95 will still update Explorer, but it will ignore the OPEN line in AUTORUN.INF.

For a more permanent solution, follow these steps:

1. Open the System Properties dialog box and display the Device Manager tab.

2. Open the CD-ROM hardware class.

3. Highlight your CD-ROM and click Properties.

4. Display the Settings tab, as shown in Figure 22.8.

FIGURE 22.8.

Use the Settings tab to disable AutoPlay for a CD-ROM drive.

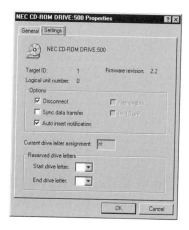

5. Deactivate the Auto insert notification check box.

6. Click OK to return to the System Properties dialog box.

7. Click OK. When Windows 95 asks if you want to restart your computer, click Yes.

Playing Audio CDs

One of the advantages you get if you have a sound card lurking inside your system is that you can use it to play audio CDs through your CD-ROM drive. That's right: Whether you're into opera or alternative, classical or country, rock or rap, your favorite tunes are now only a few mouse clicks away.

The Windows 95 program that makes this possible is called CD Player. Before we take a look at it, take a moment to pop an audio CD into your CD-ROM drive. After a few seconds, Windows 95 will launch the CD Player, shown in Figure 22.9, and start playing the disc. (If you don't see the toolbar in your window, select View | Toolbar.) If the CD Player doesn't appear automatically, you can run it manually by selecting Start | Programs | Accessories | Multimedia | CD Player.

FIGURE 22.9.

Use the CD Player window to play your favorite tunes through your CD-ROM drive.

If you'd prefer that audio CDs not start automatically, you can either follow the steps from the preceding section to deactivate the `Auto insert notification` check box, or you can follow this audio CD–only procedure:

1. In Explorer, select View | Options to display the Options dialog box.
2. In the File Types tab, use the `Registered file types` list to highlight the AudioCD file type.
3. Click the Edit button to display the Edit File Type dialog box.
4. Click Set Default. The Play action should no longer be shown in bold text. (In other words, it is no longer the default action for audio CDs.)
5. Click Close to return to the File Types tab, and click Close again to return to Explorer.

Specifying a Different Audio CD Application

What do you do if you want to use a different application to run your audio CDs? One solution would be to hold down the Shift key when you insert the CD to prevent CD Player from starting. You could then launch your player of choice. Alternatively, you can tell Windows 95 to always use a different program to play audio CDs. Here are the steps to follow:

1. In Explorer, select View | Options to display the Options dialog box.
2. In the File Types tab, use the `Registered file types` list to highlight the AudioCD file type.
3. Click the Edit button to display the Edit File Type dialog box.
4. In the `Actions` list, highlight Play and then click Edit. The Editing Action dialog box appears.
5. In the `Application used to perform action` text box, enter the full pathname of the application you want to use to play audio CDs.
6. Click OK to return to the Edit File Type dialog box.
7. Click Close to return to the File Types tab, and click Close again to return to Explorer.

TROUBLESHOOTING: AUTOPLAY FOR AUDIO DISCS DOESN'T WORK

If you insert an audio CD and it doesn't start playing automatically, make sure that the `Auto insert notification` check box isn't deactivated, as explained in the preceding section.

Also, if you installed the FlexiCD Power Toy (described in Chapter 7) and then uninstalled it, AutoPlay will be disabled for audio CDs. To reinstate this feature, follow the steps just outlined for editing the AudioCD file type. When you get to the Editing Action dialog box, enter the following in the `Application used to perform action` text box (assuming that `C:\Windows` is your main Windows 95 folder):

```
c:\windows\cdplayer.exe /play
```

Operating the CD Player

The CD Player is set up to look more or less like a real CD player. The large black box shows the current track number in square brackets (for example, [01]) and (once the disc starts playing) the elapsed time for the track. Beside the box are the controls you use to operate the CD. Table 22.7 summarizes each button.

Table 22.7. CD Player controls for operating a disc.

Button to Click	Action
▶	Starts playing the disc.
❚❚	Pauses the disc.
■	Stops playing the disc.
◀◀▏	Skips back to the previous track (or the beginning of the current track).
◀◀	Rewinds.
▶▶	Fast forwards.
▶▶▏	Skips ahead to the next track.
⏏	Ejects the disc (this doesn't work for some CD-ROM drives).

NOTE: CD PLAYER NEEDS A SOUND CARD CONNECTION

If you can't hear your audio CD, make sure there is a connection between the Line Out jack (or jacks) of your CD-ROM drive and the Line In jack (or jacks) of your sound card.

CD Player also gives you a few more playing options, some of which you'd normally find only on mid- to high-end CD players:

■ If you want to play a specific track, select it from the Track drop-down list.

■ To show the time remaining for the current track, click the toolbar's Track Time Remaining button or select View | Track Time Remaining.

■ To show the time remaining for the entire disc, click the Disc Time Remaining button or select View | Disc Time Remaining.

■ To play the tracks in random order, click the toolbar's Random Track Order button or select Options | Random Order.

■ If you have more than one CD-ROM drive, you can play tracks from multiple discs by clicking the Multidisc Play button or by selecting Options | Multidisc Play.

■ To play the disc continuously (that is, when the last track is done, the disc starts over again), click the Continuous Play button or select Options | Continuous Play.

■ To hear just the first 10 seconds of each track, click the Intro Play button on the toolbar or select Options | Intro Play.

Setting CD Player Preferences

If you select Options | Preferences, CD Player displays the Preferences dialog box, shown in Figure 22.10. Here's a rundown of the options in this dialog box:

Stop CD playing on exit: When this check box is activated, the disc stops playing if you exit CD Player. If you deactivate this check box, the disc keeps playing even if you exit CD Player.

Save settings on exit: When this check box is activated, CD Player saves its current settings each time you exit the program.

Show tool tips: When this check box is activated, CD Player shows tool tips over the toolbar buttons and disc controls when the mouse pointer lingers over each button.

Intro play length (seconds): This spinner controls the number of seconds that CD Player plays each track when you use the Intro Play feature.

Display font: These options determine the size of the track numbers and the time remaining numbers.

FIGURE 22.10.

Use this dialog box to set various CD Player preferences.

Creating a Play List

When you first slip in an audio CD, CD Player displays New Artist in the Artist box and New Title in the Title box. Since it's unlikely that these are the actual names of the artist and disc, you might want to fill in the correct info yourself. You also can enter a title for each track on the CD, and you can create a *play list*—a list of the tracks you want to hear in the order you want to hear them. Conveniently, CD Player stores this info in a database and loads it automatically the next time you insert the same CD into your CD-ROM. (Every CD has a unique ID that CD Player uses to tell one disc from another.)

To try this out, click the Edit Play List toolbar button or select Disc | Edit Play List. CD Player displays the Disc Settings dialog box, shown in Figure 22.11.

FIGURE 22.11.

Use the Disc Settings dialog box to tell CD Player about the disc and to set up a play list.

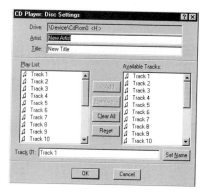

You can use the Artist text box to fill in the name of the group or artist, and you can enter the disc's title in the Title text box. To enter track titles, follow these steps:

1. Select a track in the Available Tracks list.

2. Use the Track text box to enter the title.

3. Click the Set Name button.

4. Repeat steps 1 through 3 for the other tracks.

The Play List box shows the current tracks in the disc's play list (which will be every track at first). To modify the play list, use the following techniques:

■ To remove a track from the play list, select it in the `Play List` and click Remove.

■ To add a track to the play list, select it in the `Available Tracks` list and click Add.

■ To clear everything from the `Play List`, click Clear All.

■ To revert to the original play list (all tracks, in disc order), click Reset.

When you're done (Figure 22.12 shows an example of a completed dialog box), click OK to put your play list into effect.

FIGURE 22.12.

A sample CD Player play list.

Disabling Automatic Playing of Audio CDs

By default, Windows 95 starts playing an audio CD as soon as you insert it into the CD-ROM drive. This is convenient, but it might not be the behavior you want. For example, if you're using a notebook computer in public, you might not want the CD to start playing until you've put on your headphones. To prevent Windows 95 from playing an audio CD automatically, follow these steps:

1. In Explorer, select View | Options to display the Options dialog box.
2. Select the File Types tab.
3. In the `Registered file types` list, highlight `AudioCD` and click Edit.
4. In the Edit File Type dialog box, highlight `Play` in the `Actions` list.
5. Click the Set Default button. The Play action changes from bold to regular text.
6. Click Close to return to the Options dialog box.
7. Click Close.

TIP: SPECIFYING YOUR OWN CD SOFTWARE

You can specify a different audio CD utility if you have your own audio CD software that you'd prefer to use instead of CD Player. In the Edit File Type dialog box, highlight the `Play` action, click Edit, and enter the path and name of the appropriate executable file.

Playing with the Media Player

I mentioned earlier that applications can use the Media Control Interface (MCI) to play multimedia files and control multimedia devices. Windows 95 comes with just such an application. It's called Media Player, and you can crank it up by selecting Start | Programs | Accessories | Multimedia | Media Player. Figure 22.13 shows the initial window you see at startup.

FIGURE 22.13.

Media Player is an MCI application that can play various multimedia files and devices.

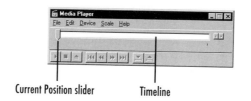

Current Position slider   Timeline

For every MCI driver installed on your system, Media Player places a command on the Device menu. The drivers that Windows 95 Setup installs depends on the hardware you have in your system, but there will probably be at least four MCI drivers installed, so you should see the following four commands:

Video for Windows: Select this command to open a video clip (AVI) file.

Sound: Select this command to open a waveform audio (WAV) file.

MIDI Sequencer: Select this command to open a MIDI (MID or RMI) file.

CD Audio: Select this command to play an audio CD.

Note, as well, that for file-based media you can also select File | Open and use the Open dialog box that appears to select any type of multimedia file. (Provided, that is, your system has an MCI driver for the media.)

For other types of media, you'll need to prepare the device for playing. For example, if you'll be playing an audio CD, you'll need to insert the disc in the CD-ROM drive.

Once you've selected your media, a scale appears underneath the timeline. You'll see seconds for a sound or MIDI file, tracks for an audio CD, and frames for a video clip. To use a different scale, select Scale | Time, Scale | Frames, or Scale | Tracks. (The available commands depend on the current media.)

Now click the Play button to start playing. You can also adjust Media Player's current playback position by dragging the Current Position slider bar left or right along the timeline. Table 22.8 presents a summary of Media Player's buttons.

22

GRAPHICS,
CD-ROMS,
AND MORE

Table 22.8. Media Player's buttons.

Button to Click	Action
▶	Play the media.
❚❚	Pause the media (available only while playing; you can click either Pause or Play to resume).
■	Stop the media (click Play to resume).
▲	Eject the media (this feature is only supported by some devices).
◀◀	Rewind the media.
▶▶	Fast-forward the media.
▼	Mark the current spot as the playback beginning.
▲	Mark the current spot as the playback ending.
|◀◀	Go back to the previous mark.
▶▶|	Jump ahead to the next mark.
◀	Scroll backward.
▶	Scroll forward.

TIP: MEDIA PLAYER PLAYBACK OPTIONS

Media Player has a couple of options that control the playback. You can check them out by selecting Edit | Options or by pressing Ctrl-O. In the Options dialog box, activate the Auto Rewind check box to rewind the media to the beginning when it finishes. Activate the Auto Repeat check box to play the media continuously. (I'll talk about the other options in this dialog box later.)

TIP: A SIMPLER MEDIA PLAYER

You can view a simpler version of Media Player by double-clicking its title bar. This reduces the window to the just the Play (or Pause when the media is playing) and Stop buttons and the timeline.

Media Player and OLE

The Media Player can act as an OLE server application for Media Clip objects. You can use two methods to get a Media Clip object into a container document:

- Use Media Player to copy a selected object to the Clipboard.
- Insert a Media Clip object from within the container application.

Copying a Media Clip Object to the Clipboard

With this method, the idea is that you load whatever media you want to work with, select the media clip, and copy it to the Clipboard. Once you've opened the appropriate file, you need to select the Media Clip object you want to work with. In a sound file, for example, you might want to use only the first couple of seconds as the object. You can select the object by using either of the following techniques:

- Move the slider to the start of the object and click the Start Selection button. Now move the slider to the end of the object and click the End Selection button.
- Choose Edit | Selection to display the Set Selection dialog box, shown in Figure 22.14. Activate the From option and use the From and To spinners to set the object's start and end points. (Note that the values used in these spinners reflect the currently selected scale. If you'd prefer to use a different scale, you need to exit the dialog box and choose the scale you want from the Scale menu.)

FIGURE 22.14.

Use the Set Selection dialog box to set the start and end points of the object you want to work with.

Media Player displays the currently selected object as a blue bar in the timeline. To send the object to the Clipboard, select Edit | Copy Object or press Ctrl-C.

Media Player also has a few options that control how it behaves as an OLE object server. Select Edit | Options (or press Ctrl-O) to display the Options dialog box, shown in Figure 22.15. Here's a summary of the OLE-related options in this dialog box:

FIGURE 22.15.

Use this dialog box to set various options related to Media Player's OLE object server capabilities.

Control Bar On Playback: When this option is activated, the object is inserted with a control bar underneath it. When the user double-clicks the object, he can use the control bar to manipulate the playback. (The control bar includes Play and Stop buttons as well as the timeline.)

Caption: If you activate the Control Bar On Playback check box, the text in the Caption text box appears underneath the inserted media.

Border around object: This option determines whether the inserted object is displayed with a border in the container document.

Play in client document: Determines whether double-clicking the object plays the media.

Dither picture to VGA colors: If you activate this check box, Windows 95 adjusts the colors of the video or animation file using the standard VGA palette. Otherwise, Windows 95 uses the color palette of the current file. However, if your system doesn't support the number of colors in this palette, the playback might appear distorted.

Inserting a Media Clip

The second way to get a Media Clip object into a container document is to insert the object from the container application. To try this, open the container application and select Insert | Object. In the dialog box that appears, highlight Media Clip in the Object Type list and click OK. Windows 95 will add an icon for the new Media Clip to the container document.

If the container doesn't support visual editing, Media Player appears so that you can load the appropriate object. Otherwise, the container window will assume the characters of the Media Player window, as shown in Figure 22.16. In this case, use the Insert Clip menu to open the media you want to work with, and then use the selection techniques outlined in the preceding section to choose the object. When you click outside the icon, Windows 95 inserts the selected object.

FIGURE 22.16.

When you insert a Media Clip object, the container window assumes the characteristics of the Media Player window.

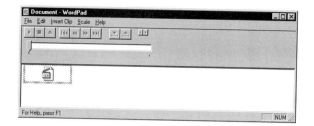

Setting the Default Audio CD Drive

If you have more than one CD-ROM drive, Media Player always defaults to the first CD-ROM (according to the letters assigned to the CD-ROM drives) when you select the CD Audio device.

To change this, display Control Panel and open the Multimedia icon. In the Multimedia Properties dialog box that appears, select the CD Music tab, as shown in Figure 22.17. Use the CD-ROM drive drop-down list to select the letter of the CD-ROM drive you want to use as the default for audio CDs.

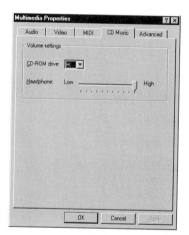

FIGURE 22.17.

Use the CD Music tab to set the default CD-ROM drive for audio CDs.

22

GRAPHICS, CD-ROMs, AND MORE

NOTE: DON'T WORRY ABOUT THE DEFAULT DRIVE FOR CD PLAYER

You don't have to worry about a default audio CD-ROM drive if you use the CD Player accessory to play your audio CDs. In the CD Player window, you can use the Artist drop-down list to select a different drive (as shown in Figure 22.9).

Summary

This chapter introduced you to the world of Windows 95 multimedia. After a brief history of Windows multimedia, I showed you the various multimedia features found in Windows 95, including the Media Control Interface and the Display Control Interface. I then showed you the various levels of MPC hardware, and we looked at DirectX, the future of Windows multimedia. In a more practical light, I showed you how to work with graphics adapters and monitors, CD-ROMs (including playing audio CDs in your CD-ROM drive), and the Media Player applet.

For more information on multimedia, check out the following chapters:

- Video and animation clips are the subject of Chapter 23, "Windows 95 Video: The Big Picture."
- To get the full scoop on sound and MIDI, see Chapter 24, "Getting the Most Out of Windows 95 Sound."
- Web-based multimedia is the current craze, and I'll talk about it in Chapter 37, "Windows 95 and the Internet."

Windows 95 Video: The Big Picture

CHAPTER 23

IN THIS CHAPTER

Pictures are for entertainment. Messages should be delivered by Western Union.

—Samuel Goldwyn

One of the hottest areas in all of multimedia these days is digital video. Games are using video sequences to add an extra level of realism to shoot-'em-ups and whodunits. CD-ROM encyclopedias and other reference aids are incorporating videos and animations to demonstrate concepts and engineering marvels. Videographers are using digital video applications to capture and edit video footage right on their PCs. Jazzing up World Wide Web sites by streaming video clips and animations to browsers is the latest in a long series of Internet crazes.

Whether you just want to get the best performance out of your video-enabled multimedia applications, or you want to create video-based content, you need to know how Windows 95 and video work together. That's my goal in this chapter as I focus on the nuts and bolts of video and take you through the specifics of Windows 95's video features.

Windows and the Evolution of Digital Video

Video used to be a strictly analog affair. After all, for most of its existence, video has been rendered on videotape, which, because it represents a continuous stream of data, is a relentlessly analog medium. The analog, of course, is anathema to computers, which prefer that data be broken into discrete (digital) chunks, so something had to be done to get video into the digital domain. To help you understand how Windows has achieved this, let's take a quick look back at the history of video's analog-to-digital journey and how Windows contributed to the transformation.

The First Step: Computer-Controlled VCRs

For a while, the closest anyone came to marrying the digital nature of computers with the analog nature of video was through special VCRs that could be controlled electronically. Using cables attached to RS-232 ports on both the computer and the VCR, the software could send signals that manipulated the VCR's transport mechanism. Using these signals, the video editor would mark the beginning and ending points of the video sequences he wanted to keep. He would then use this "edit decision list" to transfer the good video to a second VCR that was connected to the first by the standard analog cables.

NOTE: THE VISCA VISTA

The ability to control VCRs via software is still a viable technology today. Most of the decks that support this feature are compatible with Sony's VISCA standard for computer-controlled tape decks. In fact, Windows 95 ships with an MCI driver that supports VISCA-compatible VCRs.

The Dawn of Windows Digital Video: Video for Windows 1.0

Controlling video decks via software was an interesting idea, and it was a real boon to video editors who used to spend long hours performing manual edits between two decks. However, it was obvious to those who were into computers that this approach just didn't cut the digital mustard. It would be like editing a manuscript by using software to control two typewriters.

The obstacle here is the linearity of tape. Like a typewriter that can only add or delete letters in order, videotape can only be edited linearly: You either append footage to existing scenes, or you overwrite existing scenes. The word processor solved the linearity problem for text by making it a breeze to shuffle words or paragraphs around, insert new text anywhere, and delete text at will. In other words, text became nonlinear when it became digital.

To get the same nonlinear benefits for video, someone had to find a way to digitize videotape. Other computer platforms (notably the Macintosh) solved this problem earlier, but for the Windows crowd, the big moment came in 1992 with the release of Video for Windows (VfW) 1.0. As long as you installed a *video capture card* in your machine, you could hook up a camcorder or VCR to your computer. VfW came with a utility called VidCap that would take the incoming video, digitize it, and save the result to a file on your hard disk. You could then use VfW's VidEdit program to manipulate the digitized video frame-by-frame, just like your word processor manipulates text word-by-word.

Even if you weren't into editing video, VfW was a milestone, because it came with a runtime module and driver that let anyone view digital movies created in the VfW format (AVI).

This isn't to say that VfW was a complete success, however. Hardware limitations and the sheer newness of the technology placed major limitations on the VfW file format. For one thing, the video window was restricted to a puny 160×120 pixels, making it a mere 1/16th of a basic VGA (640×480) screen (see Figure 23.1). This led critics to dub VfW files "dancing postage stamps."

Another problem was that VfW playback limped along at 15 frames per second (fps), which, compared to the "full motion" rate of 30 fps used by videotape, made some digital videos look jerky.

And, finally, compression technology was still in its infancy, so VfW files took up huge amounts of hard disk space. Even VfW's tiny window and low frame rate still usurped almost 17 MB per minute! And that figure doesn't include the audio soundtrack that was part of each VfW file, which could easily add megabytes per minute to the total.

FIGURE 23.1.

Playback in Video for Windows 1.0 was restricted to 160×120 windows.

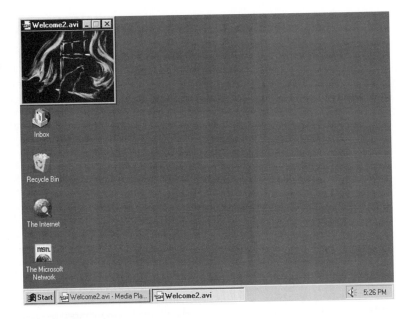

Things Get Better: Video for Windows 1.1

VfW 1.0 was far from perfect, but most people in the industry quickly realized the massive potential for this technology. As a result, there was a flurry of activity from vendors involved in all aspects of the digital video revolution: Capture cards were beefed up with features, improved compression technology allowed more data to fit into less space, new and improved sound cards made it easier to capture the audio portion of a video, and local bus graphics let PCs keep up with the demands made on them by massive video files.

And, of course, Microsoft kept improving Video for Windows itself. In 1993, VfW 1.1 was released to great fanfare. The "dancing postage stamp" was gone, replaced by a more substantial 320×240 window (see Figure 23.2) operating at a more-than-respectable frame rate of 24 fps. (However, proving that you can't please all of the people all of the time, some killjoys were still unimpressed with VfW 1.1's achievements. They called the new quarter-screen window a "dancing credit card.")

FIGURE 23.2.

In VfW 1.1, playback improved to 320×240.

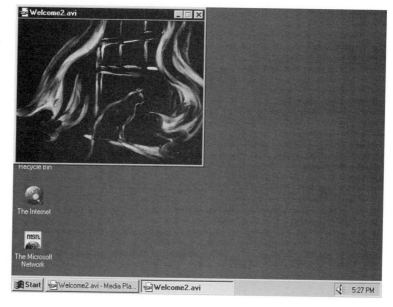

Video in Windows 95

VfW reaches yet another milestone in Windows 95. Not only is VfW now built right into the operating system, but its 32-bit architecture and the inclusion of some of the best compressor/decompressor drivers in the business bring playback up to full screen (640×480) and full motion (30 fps). Best of all, you don't need extra hardware or some high-end graphics behemoth of a computer to get all this. Windows 95 provides excellent video quality on mainstream desktop machines (486 and higher).

This isn't to say you'll see this high-quality video all the time. Full-screen, full-motion video clips still use up lots of hard disk space, so it's more likely that the video clips you'll see will compromise window size, frame rate, color depth, or all three.

Understanding Digital Video

The advances in the digital video industry over the past four years have been nothing short of remarkable. Considering the transition from an analog to a digital format, the massive amounts of data involved, the need to synchronize video and sound, and all the other seemingly insurmountable hurdles that have been cleared, the current state of the art is truly impressive.

Although much about digital video technology is hopelessly complex and arcane, there are a few "plumbing" issues you should know about in order to get the most out of Windows 95 video. The next few sections will do just that as I give you a behind-the-screens look at digital video in the Windows 95 world.

How Windows 95 Plays a Video Clip

When you launch a video clip from a CD-ROM or the Media Player, Windows 95 goes through quite an elaborate process to get the results to your screen and sound card. To give you some idea of the overall progression of a video clip through the system, the following steps take you through the process (see Figure 23.3):

1. When you play a video clip (an AVI file), Windows 95 first sends the data to the Video for Windows driver (MSVFW32.DLL).

NOTE: FOR OPTIMAL PLAYBACK, VFW CHECKS YOUR SYSTEM

If this is the first time you've played a video clip at the current screen resolution, VfW will run a series of tests on your display to choose the optimal playback settings. (You'll know this is happening if you see a Profiling Display window on-screen.) VfW also takes into account your CPU and clock speed. Since video puts such a strain on your system, you need a fast processor to handle the flood of data. The faster and more muscular your CPU, the more data it can handle. For example, if you have a slow 486, VfW might drop a 30 fps video down to 15 fps.

---

2. VfW reads the data and then splits it into two streams: video and audio.
3. The video data is in a compressed format, so VfW sends it to the Video Compression Manager (VCM) for processing.
4. The VCM checks the data to see which compressor/decompressor (codec) was used to compress the file.
5. The VCM then calls the appropriate video codec driver to decompress the video and return it to VfW.
6. The audio stream goes through a similar process: VfW sends the compressed audio to the Audio Compression Manager (ACM), the ACM checks the compression format and calls the appropriate audio codec driver, and the uncompressed audio is sent back to VfW.
7. VfW synchronizes the video and audio signals and sends the video stream to the graphics adapter and the audio stream to the sound card.
8. The video appears on-screen, and the sound is played through your speakers.

FIGURE 23.3.

How Windows 95 plays an AVI file.

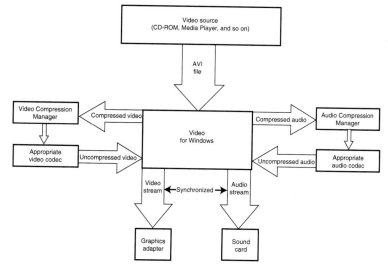

The Various Video Formats

Video clips come in many different formats, but only a few are of any interest to Windows 95 users. Here's a summary of the video formats you're likely to come across in your video travels:

ActiveMovie (ASF): ActiveMovie is Microsoft's next-generation digital video technology. Appearing now as part of Internet Explorer 3.0 and OSR2, and slated to replace Video for Windows in future Windows releases, Active-Movie is a cross-platform strategy that will support multiple formats, including AVI, QuickTime, and MPEG (described later). It's an OLE interface, so developers can easily add ActiveMovie functionality to applications and even Web sites, and it uses DirectX technology (described in the preceding chapter), so it offers high-performance playback. The new format is called ActiveMovie Streaming Format (ASF), and it allows multiple objects (such as audio objects, video objects, bitmaps, URLs, HTML pages, and programs) to be combined and stored in a single synchronized multimedia stream.

Video for Windows (AVI): This is the standard VfW format supported by Windows 95, and it has become the standard format for Windows digital video in general. (AVI, in case you're wondering, stands for Audio Video Interleave.) You'll find several examples of AVI files on the Windows 95 CD-ROM in the \Funstuff\Videos folder. See Figure 23.4 for an example.

OSR2

23

WINDOWS 95 VIDEO: THE BIG PICTURE

FIGURE 23.4.

One of the AVI files that comes on the Windows 95 CD-ROM.

QuickTime for Windows (MOV): QuickTime is the digital video format developed by Apple. It's the standard format for Macintosh users, but it's only recently made inroads on the Windows side of things with the release of QuickTime for Windows. The big advantage of QuickTime's MOV files is that they can be used on both Mac and Windows machines without alteration. Therefore, since so many video production houses are Mac shops, there are lots of MOV files out there. If you need to play a MOV file, you'll need to get QuickTime for Windows 95 from Apple, shown in Figure 23.5. If you have Web access, try the following site:

```
http://quicktime.apple.com/qt/sw/sw.html
```

FIGURE 23.5.

You'll need a copy of QuickTime for Windows to view QuickTime video clips.

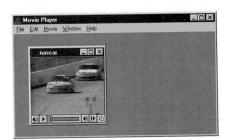

Animation Formats (FLC or FLI): Some video clips aren't digitized video at all, but instead are animations. The animation standard is the FLC (or sometimes FLI) format developed by AutoDesk. To view FLC files, you'll need a third-party player. AutoDesk has a Windows version of its AAPlay viewer (AAWIN.EXE, shown in Figure 23.6) that's available directly from AutoDesk or in many locations on the Internet.

FIGURE 23.6.

For industry-standard FLC animation files, use AAPlay, the animation viewer from AutoDesk.

NOTE: A QUICKTIME UPDATE ON THE WINDOWS 95 CD-ROM

If you're using an older QuickTime for Windows player, you might find that the performance of your QuickTime movies is slower under Windows 95. If so, there's relief in sight—provided that you have the Windows 95 CD-ROM. Look in the \Drivers\Other\Qtwfix folder. The file MSVHDW95.QTC contains a QuickTime for Windows upgrade that should improve performance. To install this upgrade, either highlight OPTIMIZE.INF and select File | Install or right-click OPTIMIZE.INF and select Install from the context menu. (If you have problems with this upgrade, you can remove it by running the Install command on the UN_OPT.INF file.)

Video Compression Schemes

If there were no limit to hard disk capacity, all digital video clips would be captured as raw footage and, provided you had a fast enough processor and a reasonable graphics adapter, there would be no concerns about video quality and tiny window sizes. Hard disks, however, are decidedly *not* infinite, so video files have to be literally cut down to size. Four factors determine the overall size of a video file:

The color depth of the images: Everything else being equal, 8-bit images take up only a third as much space as 24-bit images.

The size of the video playback window: A clip designed for a 320×240 window will be one-fourth the size of a clip that is designed to run full-screen (640×480).

The frame rate: Full-motion videos (30 fps) pack twice as much information into a given amount of time than do videos playing at 15 fps.

The quality of the sound: A video file incorporates synchronized audio as well as video. And, as with video, the higher the quality of the audio, the bigger the audio stream.

Quality-conscious video producers typically try to maximize as many of these variables as they can, so they capture their footage with as much data as possible. They then use some kind of compression technology to put the squeeze on the massive video files before distributing them. As I mentioned earlier, when you play a video clip, the VCM checks the compression used in the file and then calls the appropriate driver to handle the decompression.

Video compression is one of the most crucial components of digital video because it can have a huge impact on the quality of the resulting file. In general, compression involves trade-offs between file size and image quality. That's because most compression schemes are *lossy,* which means that some redundant information is discarded during the compression process. The higher the compression ratio, the more data that gets lost, and the more the image degrades. On the other hand, lower compression ratios improve quality, but at the cost of larger files that might require a fast CPU to decompress.

However, the compression ratio isn't the only characteristic that a video producer must be concerned with. The compression scheme itself is an important consideration as well. If an AVI file is compressed with a codec that the VCM doesn't recognize, you won't be able to play that video. Happily, Windows 95 ships with drivers for many of the most popular codecs in use today, so this is less of a concern for producers. The four Windows 95 codecs are Cinepak (`ICCVID.DLL`), Indeo (`IR32_32.DLL`), RLE (`MSRLE32.DLL`), and Microsoft Video 1 (`MSVIDC32.DLL`).

Unfortunately, Windows 95 doesn't support what is undoubtedly the best codec available today: MPEG (Motion Picture Experts Group). MPEG achieves extremely high compression ratios (up to 200-to-1) with excellent playback quality. Achieving this playback, however, requires either an MPEG hardware-based decoder or an MPEG software codec running on a machine with an extremely fast CPU (at least a 90 MHz Pentium). If your machine is fast enough, you'll need to look for a third-party MPEG player in order to play MPEG files in Windows 95.

Unleashing Video in Windows 95

Now that you understand a bit about digital video, we can turn to more practical matters. The next three sections talk about playing video files, checking out AVI file properties, and setting up your system for maximizing video performance.

Playing Video Clips

Playing videos in Windows 95 is usually straightforward. In most cases, you'll use one of the following methods:

■ Many CD-ROM applications have their own video players built in, so you can play video clips right from the application. For example, Figure 23.7 shows the built-in player that comes with Microsoft Bookshelf '95.

FIGURE 23.7.

Microsoft Bookshelf, like many multimedia applications, comes with its own player for viewing videos and animations.

■ As mentioned earlier, to view video clips not supported by Windows 95 (such as QuickTime or MPEG files), you'll need to install a third-party player.

■ For AVI files, you can either double-click the file in Explorer or open the Media Player and select Device | Video for Windows. As shown in Figure 23.8, the video clip appears in a separate window.

TIP: DRAG-AND-DROP VIDEO PLAYING

If the Media Player is open, you can also play a video clip by dragging the AVI file from Explorer and dropping it on the Media Player window.

FIGURE 23.8.

When you play an AVI file in the Media Player, the video appears in a separate window.

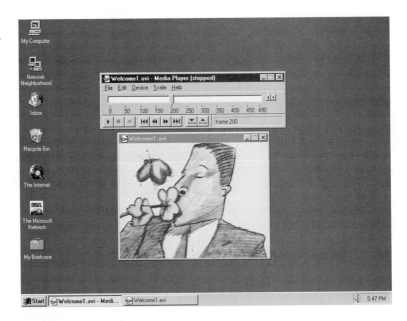

AVI File Properties

Like any Windows 95 file object, AVI files have their own properties. To check them out, either highlight an AVI file in Explorer and select File | Properties or right-click an AVI file and select Properties from the context menu. The properties sheet that appears comes with three tabs:

General: This tab gives you basic information, such as the size of the file, its DOS (8.3) name, its date stamp, its time stamp, and its attributes.

Details: This tab, shown in Figure 23.9, spells out a few video-specific properties. Media length tells you how long the clip runs. Audio format tells you the audio compression, frequency, and other data (I'll explain these values in the next chapter). Video format tells you the window size, color depth, total number of frames, frame rate (in frames per second), playback rate (in kilobytes per second), and codec. The list in the Other information group offers various tidbits about the file.

Preview: This tab, shown in Figure 23.10, lets you view the video clip. It comes with a single control that either starts or pauses the clip.

FIGURE 23.9.

The Details tab fills you in on some of the video properties of the clip.

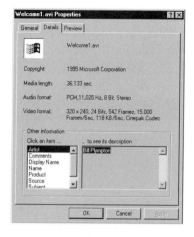

FIGURE 23.10.

The Preview tab lets you view the clip.

AVI Playback Properties

By default, an AVI file will play back in the window size specified in the file's properties. If you'd prefer a larger or smaller window, or if you want to run your videos full-screen, you can specify a new default size.

To do this, go to Control Panel and open the Multimedia icon. In the Multimedia Properties dialog box, select the Video tab, as shown in Figure 23.11. You have two options:

Window: The drop-down list beside this option gives you various relative window sizes. Original size is the default size specified in the file's properties. Your other options are Double original size, various screen fractions (1/16, 1/4, and 1/2), or Maximized. Note, however, that if you increase the original window size, the quality of the video might degrade considerably.

Full screen: If you activate this option, Windows 95 uses the entire screen to display the video (not even the taskbar will appear). To stop a clip that's playing full-screen, click the mouse or press any key.

Figure 23.11.

Use the Video tab to control the default window size for your AVI files.

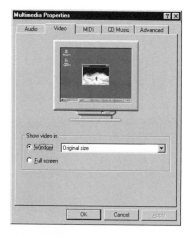

NOTE: ADJUSTING THE PLAYBACK WINDOW FROM MEDIA PLAYER

Once you've loaded an AVI file into the Media Player, you can adjust the size of the playback window by selecting Device | Properties. Note, however, that your changes will apply only to the current file.

Inserting a Video Clip Object

If you like, you can embed an OLE Video Clip object in a container document. There are two ways you can go about this:

- Follow the instructions in the preceding chapter for inserting a Media Clip object. In this case, of course, the object you'll select will be part of a video clip.

- To insert a Video Clip object directly from the container application, select Insert | Object and, in the dialog box that appears, highlight Video Clip in the Object Type list and click OK. Windows 95 will add an icon for the new Video Clip to the container document, and you can use the Media Player commands and controls to select the object.

Tips for Top Video Performance

Of all the mainstream applications you use, digital video probably puts the most strain on your system's resources. The constant stream of pixels and sounds, and the need to decompress both types of media simultaneously and on-the-fly, can bring even the most powerful system to its knees. To help out, here are a few tips that will let your machine achieve peak video performance:

- Except for MPEG, the codecs used by most video clips don't require a killer machine. However, most codecs do have a minimum system requirement, usually a 33 MHz 486. Obviously, anything over and above this minimum system will improve playback quality.

- Local bus graphics make a huge difference when displaying individual bitmaps, so you can imagine that they're a must for video clips that in effect display anywhere from 15 to 30 bitmaps a second.

- Memory is like manna from heaven for any application, but it's crucial for video. The more memory you have, the greater the portion of a huge video file that can be loaded into RAM. Consider 16 MB the absolute minimum for any kind of serious video work.

- Speaking of memory, you should, if possible, max out your graphics adapter's on-board memory. An adapter with 4 MB or even 8 MB of video memory will sail through a typical video clip.

- Adjust your display settings so that you're using 24-bit color depth. And, to reduce the burden on the graphics adapter, drop the resolution down to 640×480. This will not only speed things up, but it will also make videos that run in smaller windows (320×240, for example) appear larger.

- Videos place an enormous burden on your CPU at the best of times, so you can imagine that they don't react well to sharing the CPU with other applications. Your clips will play at their best rate if no other applications are running.

- Keep your hard disk defragmented. Video files run fastest when they're stored (and therefore accessed) contiguously.

- Keep the drivers for your graphics adapter and codecs up-to-date. The latest drivers are usually the fastest ones, so you'll get an easy speed boost this way.

- If you'll be working with a lot of video clips, consider investing in a video accelerator card. These cards have special video circuitry that will let you view your clips at larger sizes and greater color depths.

23

WINDOWS 95
VIDEO: THE BIG
PICTURE

Troubleshooting Video Woes

I'll finish this chapter by examining some video problems, troubleshooting techniques, and solutions to specific problems.

Reinstalling a Video Codec

If you have trouble with a specific codec, removing the codec and then reinstalling it will often solve the problem. Here are the steps to follow to remove a video codec:

1. In Control Panel, open the Multimedia icon and select the Advanced tab, as shown in Figure 23.12.

FIGURE 23.12.

In the Advanced tab of the Multimedia Properties dialog box, highlight the codec you want to remove.

2. Open the Video Compression Codecs tree and highlight the codec you want to remove.
3. Click the Properties button.
4. In the codec properties sheet that appears, click Remove.
5. When Windows 95 asks if you're sure, click Yes and then click OK in the next two dialog boxes. (Windows 95 will tell you to restart the system. You can ignore this.)
6. Close the Multimedia Properties dialog box to return to Control Panel.

To reinstall the codec, follow these steps:

1. In Control Panel, open the Add New Hardware icon.
2. Click Next >.
3. When the Wizard asks if you want Windows to search for your hardware, activate No and then click Next >.
4. In the Hardware types list, highlight the Sound, video, and game controllers item and click Next >.

5. In the Manufacturers list, highlight the appropriate item (see Figure 23.13):

   ■ For Cinepak, highlight SuperMatch.

   ■ For Indeo, highlight Intel.

   ■ For RLE or Video 1, select Microsoft Video Codecs.

FIGURE 23.13.

Highlight the codec manufacturer and model.

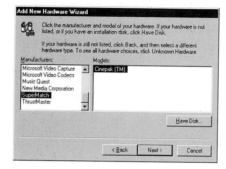

6. In the Models list, highlight the codec you want to install and click Next >.

7. Click Finish and follow the on-screen prompts for inserting your Windows 95 source disks.

8. When Windows 95 asks if you want to restart your system, click Yes.

Miscellaneous Video Ills

This section takes you through a few specific problems related to Windows 95 video and AVI files.

You have trouble playing an AVI file using a third-party program.

If a third-party program won't play an AVI file, there are a few things you can try.

First, see if you can play the file either by double-clicking it in Explorer or by using Media Player. If the file plays, the problem lies with the third-party program. You'll need to contact the vendor's tech support department.

If you can't play the file from Explorer or Media Player, the file might be corrupted. Try playing another AVI file that uses the same codec. If the second AVI file won't play, there's probably a problem with the codec driver, so you should try removing and then reinstalling the codec. If the second file does play, the original file is probably damaged. Either reinstall it or contact the vendor for a replacement.

If you can't play any AVI file, the MCI video device might be disabled. To enable this device, follow these steps:

1. Open Control Panel's Multimedia icon and select the Advanced tab.

2. Open the Media Control Devices tree.

3. Highlight Motion Video Device and select Properties.

4. In the properties sheet that appears (see Figure 23.14), activate the Use this Media Control device option and then click OK.

FIGURE 23.14.

Make sure the Use this Media Control device *option is activated.*

5. Click OK and then restart Windows 95 to put the change into effect.

An AVI file plays poorly (that is, the motion is jerky or the sound is intermittent).

These kinds of playback problems are usually related to window size. As described earlier in this chapter, adjust the playback window to the original size for the clip. If you still have a problem, try using a window that's smaller than the original.

Another reason that an AVI file might play poorly is if you run it over a network. You'll get much better performance if you copy the file to your local hard drive.

An AVI file plays poorly from a CD-ROM drive.

If video clip playbacks are jerky or have breaks in the sound when you run them from a CD-ROM drive, the AVI file's playback rate probably is greater than the throughput of the CD-ROM drive. For example, if the AVI file is designed to be played at 200K/sec and your CD-ROM is only rated at 150K/sec (single-speed), you won't be able to improve the playback. In this case, you'll need to copy the AVI file to your hard drive and run it from there.

If your CD-ROM drive's throughput should be greater than the file's playback rate (for example, if you have a 300K/sec drive and a 200K/sec file), you might need to perform some CD-ROM optimization to improve the throughput. See Chapter 9, "Windows 95 Performance Tuning and Optimization," for details.

The colors in a video clip appear washed out or blocky.

A video file's colors won't display properly if the current color depth is less than the color depth of the video file. Check the video file's properties to see the inherent color depth of the file.

Then adjust the color depth of your graphics adapter to match or exceed this value. For example, if the file uses 256 colors, set your graphics adapter to 256 colors or more.

If the colors still don't look right, try removing and reinstalling the graphics adapter driver, or even upgrading the driver to the latest version available from the manufacturer.

When you attempt to play an AVI file in Windows 95, you receive an error message similar to the following:

```
Video not available, cannot find x decompressor.
```

If *x* is one of the codecs that comes with Windows 95, this error means that Windows 95's video compression isn't installed. Here are the steps to follow to install video compression:

1. In Control Panel, open the Add/Remove Programs icon.
2. Select the Windows Setup tab.
3. In the `Components` list, highlight Multimedia and select `Details`.
4. Activate the `Video Compression` check box and click OK.
5. Click OK and then follow the on-screen prompts to insert your Windows 95 source disks.

If the decompressor that Windows 95 can't find is part of a third-party codec, you'll need to contact the manufacturer to get a copy of the appropriate codec and then install it. Here are the steps to follow to install a third-party codec:

1. In Control Panel, open the Add New Hardware icon.
2. Click Next >.
3. When the Wizard asks if you want Windows to search for your hardware, activate `No` and click Next >.
4. In the `Hardware types` list, highlight the `Sound, video, and game controllers` item and click Next >.
5. Insert the disk containing the codec.
6. Click the Have Disk button and follow the on-screen prompts.

Summary

This chapter looked at Windows 95 video. I began by running through the evolution of Windows-based digital video, from computer-controlled VCRs through the various iterations of Video for Windows. I then showed you how Windows 95 plays video clips, examined various video formats, and explained video compression schemes. In a more practical vein, I showed you how to play video clips in Windows 95, examine video clip and playback properties, and improve video performance. I closed with a look at some video troubleshooting issues.

Here's a list of chapters where you'll find related information:

■ Many of the factors that affect video performance also affect system performance as a whole. I talked about this in Chapter 9, "Windows 95 Performance Tuning and Optimization."

■ For information on graphics adapters, CD-ROM drives, and general multimedia, see Chapter 22, "Miscellaneous Multimedia: Graphics, CD-ROMs, and More."

■ Sound is a big part of AVI files, and I'll tell you all about how Windows 95 works with sound in Chapter 24, "Getting the Most Out of Windows 95 Sound."

■ The Internet Explorer World Wide Web browser can display AVI files in HTML documents. I'll show you how to work with Internet Explorer in Chapter 38, "Exploring the Web with Internet Explorer."

Getting the Most Out of Windows 95 Sound

CHAPTER 24

IN THIS CHAPTER

Most people have ears, but few have judgment; tickle those ears, and depend upon it you
will catch their judgments, such as they are.

—Lord Chesterfield

When I put together multimedia presentations, videos, and animations, the graphics are what make the audience "ooh" and "aah" during the playback. However, I've often found that what most people comment on *after* the show is, surprisingly, the soundtrack: the music and sound effects that accompany the visuals. It seems that adding bells and whistles (literally) to multimedia makes a big impact on people.

I'm not certain why this happens, but I'm sure that part of the reason has to do with our ears. The ear is a fine and sensitive instrument, attuned to nuance on the one hand, but shamelessly craving novelty on the other. How else do you explain, in a society supposedly in love with the visual image, the relentless popularity of radio after all these years?

I'm guessing that another reason why audio is such an important part of multimedia is that most people are used to their computers being, if not voiceless, at least monotonic. Most mainstream applications are content to utter simple beeps and boops to alert you to an error or otherwise get your attention. Multimedia, however, with its music and unusual sound bites, can provide quite a jolt to people who aren't used to such things.

In other words, there's no reason to think of sound as the poor cousin of flashy videos and graphics. To help you get the biggest bang for your sound buck, this chapter examines audio fundamentals, Windows 95's sound features, and a few troubleshooting procedures just in case you're hearing the sound of silence.

Understanding Audio

We'll begin our look at audio with a primer of digital audio concepts, formats, properties, and hardware. This will help you understand exactly what you're dealing with when you work with digital audio files later.

Analog-to-Digital Sound Conversion

Sound cards work by converting analog sound waves into digital signals that can be sent to your computer's speakers. To help you evaluate sound cards and choose the appropriate properties for your digital recordings, you should know a bit about how the analog-to-digital conversion takes place.

The Nature of Sound

When an object such as a violin string or a speaker diaphragm vibrates or moves back and forth, it alternately compresses and decompresses the air molecules around it. This alternating compression and decompression set up a vibration in the air molecules that propagates outward from the source as a wave. This is called a *sound wave.* When the sound wave reaches your ear, it sets up a corresponding vibration in your eardrum, and you hear the sound created by the object.

Each sound wave has two basic properties:

Frequency: This determines the pitch of the sound. It's a measure of the rate at which the sound wave's vibrations are produced. The higher the frequency, the higher the pitch. Frequency is measured in cycles per second, or *hertz* (Hz), where one cycle is a vibration back and forth.

Intensity: This is a measure of the loudness of the sound (that is, the strength of the vibration). It's determined by the *amplitude* of the sound wave. The greater the amplitude, the greater the motion of the sound wave's molecules, and the greater the impact on your eardrum. Amplitude is measured in *decibels* (dB).

Figure 24.1 shows part of a waveform for a typical sound. The amplitude is found by taking the midpoint of the wave (which is set to 0) and measuring the distance to a positive or negative peak. Since the period from one peak to the next is defined as a *cycle,* the frequency is given by the number of peaks that occur per second.

FIGURE 24.1.

An analog waveform for a sound.

Amplitude —

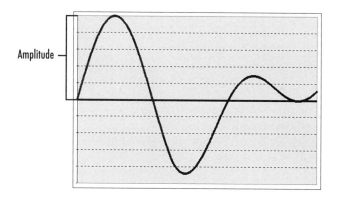

How an Analog Sound Wave Gets Digitized

Sound waves are inherently analog, so if you want to work with them on a computer, you must convert them to a digital audio format. A sound card has a small chip called an *analog-to-digital converter* (ADC), whose sole purpose is to convert analog sound waves into the digital ones and zeros that computers know and love. (Sound cards also have a *digital-to-analog converter* (DAC) chip that performs the reverse process: converting digitized audio back into an analog wave so that you can hear it.) This is done through a technique called *Pulse Code Modulation* (PCM): taking "snapshots" of the analog wave at discrete intervals and noting the wave's amplitude. These amplitude values form the basis of the digital representation of the wave. Since each snapshot is really a sample of the current state of the wave, this process is called *sampling.*

24

WINDOWS 95
SOUND

Digital Audio Quality I: The Sampling Frequency

One of the major determinants of digital audio quality is the rate at which the sound card samples the analog data. The more samples taken per second—that is, the higher the *sampling frequency*—the more accurately the digitized data will represent the original sound waveform.

To see how this works, consider the chart shown in Figure 24.2. This is a graph of digitized data sampled from the analog waveform shown in Figure 24.1. Each column represents an amplitude value sampled from the analog wave at a given moment. In this case, the sampling frequency is very low, so the "shape" of the digitized waveform only approximates the analog wave, and much data is lost.

FIGURE 24.2.

A digitized waveform generated by a low sampling frequency.

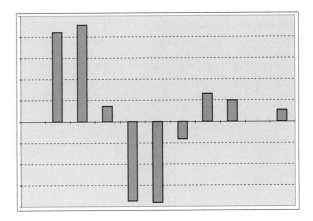

To improve the quality and fidelity of the digitized waveform, you need to use a higher sampling frequency. For example, the chart shown in Figure 24.3 shows the resulting digital waveform with a sampling frequency four times greater than the one shown in Figure 24.2. As you can see, the waveform is a much more accurate representation of the original analog wave.

FIGURE 24.3.

To improve the sound quality of the digitized waveform, you need to increase the sampling frequency.

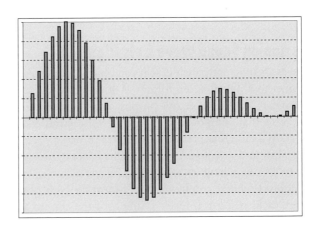

So what sampling frequency is best? Well, as you'll see later, disk space considerations come into play, because higher sampling rates create correspondingly bigger files. However, the general rule of thumb is that, for the most faithful reproduction of analog sound, your sampling frequency should be roughly twice the highest sound frequency you want to reproduce (plus another 10 percent for good measure).

Human hearing ranges from a low of 20 Hz to a high of about 20 KHz (20,000 Hz). So, for accurate reproduction of anything within the human audible range, you'd sample at a frequency of about 44 KHz (two times 20 KHz plus 10 percent). As you'll see a bit later, CD-quality digital audio—the highest quality supported by today's sound hardware—samples at 44.1 KHz.

Digital Audio Quality II: 8-Bit Versus 16-Bit

Another major determinant of digital audio quality is the number of bits used to digitize each sample. This is sometimes called the *sample depth*. To see why sample depth makes a difference, consider a simplified example. Suppose you're sampling a wave with amplitudes between 0 and 100 dB. If you had only a 2-bit sample depth, you'd have only four discrete levels with which to assign amplitudes. If you used, say, 25, 50, 75, and 100 dB, all the sampled values would have to be adjusted (by rounding up, for example) to one of these values. Figure 24.4 shows the result. The smooth line shows the original amplitudes, and the columns show the assigned sample values given a 2-bit sample depth. As you can see, much data is lost by having to adjust to the discrete levels.

FIGURE 24.4.

The lower the sample depth, the more information that gets lost during sampling.

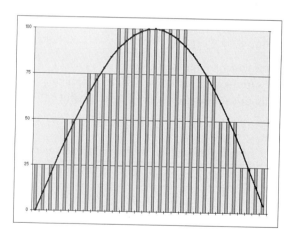

Fortunately, there is no such thing as 2-bit sampling. Instead, sound cards support two levels of sample depth: 8-bit and 16-bit. The 8-bit sample depth might sound like a lot more, but it means that the digitized amplitude values must be shoehorned into just 256 possible levels, which is a far cry from the infinite number of levels in the original analog waveform. With 16-bit sampling, 65,536 discrete levels are available, which makes a big difference in sound quality.

NOTE: SAMPLE DEPTH: THE RULER ANALOGY

Another way to look at sample depth is to consider a ruler. The accuracy with which you can measure something with a ruler depends on the number of divisions. A ruler with only quarter-inch divisions won't provide as exact a measurement as a ruler with sixteenth-inch divisions. In audio, an 8-bit sample depth is like a ruler with 256 divisions per sample, while a 16-bit sample depth is like a ruler with 65,536 divisions per sample.

Digital Audio Quality III: Mono Versus Stereo

The final consideration for digital audio quality is the number of channels you want to store. In other words, do you want your audio to be mono (one channel) or stereo (two channels)? The latter provides a richer sound, but only for sound cards that support two channels, and only for systems with two speakers attached to the card.

Quality Levels and Disk Space Considerations

As you might imagine, the various levels of digital sound quality also affect the size of the resulting audio file. A stereo capture with a 44.1 KHz sample rate and a 16-bit sample depth will use up approximately 22 times more hard disk area than a mono capture with an 8 KHz sampling rate and an 8-bit sample depth. Obviously, you need to think carefully about which options to use when capturing or recording audio. The quality level depends on the amount of disk space you have, your audience, and your need for fidelity. Music files, for example, almost certainly require a higher-quality file than does the spoken word.

To assign some concrete numbers to all this, Table 24.1 lists the number of kilobytes per second used for various combinations of sample frequency, sample depth, and channels. Later, I'll tell you about some audio codecs that can reduce the disk space requirements for audio files.

Table 24.1. Disk space requirements for various digital audio quality combinations.

Sample Frequency	Sample Depth	Channels	Disk Space
8 KHz	8-bit	Mono	8K/sec
8 KHz	8-bit	Stereo	16K/sec
8 KHz	16-bit	Mono	16K/sec
8 KHz	16-bit	Stereo	32K/sec
11.025 KHz	8-bit	Mono	11K/sec
11.025 KHz	8-bit	Stereo	22K/sec
11.025 KHz	16-bit	Mono	22K/sec
11.025 KHz	16-bit	Stereo	44K/sec

Sample Frequency	Sample Depth	Channels	Disk Space
22.05 KHz	8-bit	Mono	22K/sec
22.05 KHz	8-bit	Stereo	44K/sec
22.05 KHz	16-bit	Mono	22K/sec
22.05 KHz	16-bit	Stereo	88K/sec
44.1 KHz	8-bit	Mono	44K/sec
44.1 KHz	8-bit	Stereo	88K/sec
44.1 KHz	16-bit	Mono	88K/sec
44.1 KHz	16-bit	Stereo	176K/sec

NOTE: STANDARD DIGITAL AUDIO COMBINATIONS

Three of the combinations in Table 24.1 are standards in the digital audio realm:

Telephone: 11.025 KHz sample frequency, 8-bit sample depth, mono.

Radio: 22.05 KHz sample frequency, 8-bit sample depth, mono.

CD: 44.1 KHz sample frequency, 16-bit sample depth, stereo.

Audio File Formats

Just as video clips come in different file flavors (see the preceding chapter for details), so too are there various formats for audio clips. Windows 95 and its audio applets support only two sound file formats:

Waveform audio (WAV): This is the standard Windows digital audio format created via the PCM technique. All Windows-based sound applications can play WAV files, and each WAV file will sound the same no matter which sound application you use to play it.

Musical Instrument Digital Interface (MID or RMI): These are nonwaveform files that store musical instructions instead of waveform amplitudes. Sound cards that support MIDI have various synthesized instruments built into their chips. A MIDI file's instructions specify which instrument to play, which note to play, how long the note should be held, and so on.

There are dozens of other audio formats kicking around the PC world. AU, AIFF, SND, and VOC are some of the more popular ones. To play these files, you need a third-party application. For a list of audio players and other sound utilities, check out the following page on the World Wide Web:

```
http://www.windows95.com/apps/sound.html
```

24

**WINDOWS 95
SOUND**

Audio Codecs

You saw earlier that, as their quality increases, sound files take up a progressively bigger chunk of your hard disk. To help reduce the load, codecs are used to compress digitized audio and then decompress it for playing. Windows 95 comes with the following 32-bit codecs:

Adaptive Delta Pulse Code Modulation (ADPCM): This codec works by storing the differences between consecutive PCM samples. This allows ADPCM to store audio data in just 4 bits, which is a 4:1 compression ratio over 16-bit audio. This codec reproduces low frequencies well but tends to distort high frequencies. However, these distortions are barely noticeable at higher sampling frequencies.

Consultative Committee for International Telephone and Telegraph (CCITT) G.711 A-Law and μ-Law: Provided for compatibility with current Telephony Application Programming Interface (TAPI) standards. These codecs are supported by many hardware configurations but offer only a 2:1 compression ratio (from 16 bits to 8 bits per sample).

DSP Group TrueSpeech Software: This codec offers high compression rates for voice-oriented sound, which makes it a good codec to use when recording voice notes.

Groupe Special Mobile (GSM) 6.10: This codec offers real-time compression, which makes it a good choice for recording voice snippets with Sound Recorder. GSM gives you only a 2:1 compression ratio, but it lets you select from a relatively large range of sampling frequencies.

Interactive Multimedia Association (IMA) ADPCM: This is similar to ADPCM in that it will give you a 4:1 compression ratio over 16-bit audio. The advantage of IMA ADPCM is that it takes a little less time to compress files.

PCM Converter: This codec is included for use with older Sound Blaster and other 8-bit sound cards. It lets these cards play 16-bit audio clips. This codec also can convert the sampling frequency to a different rate for cards that don't support the original rate used to digitize a sound wave.

NOTE: THE INSTALLED CODECS DEPEND ON THE SOUND CARD

Since not all sound cards support all these codecs, the number of codecs that Setup foists upon your system will depend on the sound card you have installed.

Audio File Properties

WAV and MIDI files, like all Windows 95 file objects, have their own properties. To view these properties, either highlight a WAV, MID, or RMI file in Explorer and select File | Properties, or right-click an audio file and select Properties from the context menu. The properties sheet that appears comes with three tabs:

General: This tab gives you basic information, such as the size of the file, its DOS (8.3) name, its date stamp, its time stamp, and its attributes.

Details: The layout of this tab depends on the type of audio file you're dealing with. For a WAV file (see Figure 24.5), you'll see just the copyright information (if any), the length of the sound clip, and the audio format. For the audio format, you get the codec, the sampling frequency (in Hz), the sample depth, and whether the clip is mono or stereo. For a MIDI file (see Figure 24.6), you also get the sequence name and a few other details about the file in the `Other information` group.

FIGURE 24.5.

The Details tab for a WAV file.

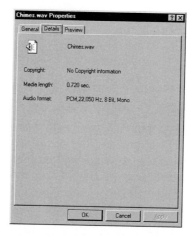

FIGURE 24.6.

The Details tab for a MIDI file.

24

WINDOWS 95 SOUND

Preview: This tab lets you play the audio clip. It comes with a single control that either starts or pauses the clip, as shown in Figure 24.7.

Figure 24.7.

The Preview tab lets you play the sound clip.

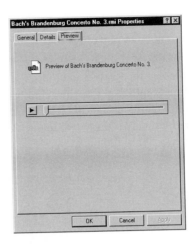

Audio Hardware: What to Look for in a Sound Card

Technically, it isn't necessary to have a sound card installed on your system if all you want to do is play WAV files. (See "Installing the PC Speaker Driver" later in this chapter to learn how to set up your computer to play sounds without a sound card.) However, you'll definitely want to invest in some audio hardware if you need or want any of the following: high-quality audio, external speakers connected to your system, the ability to record sounds, audio compression, or MIDI support.

If you're in the market for a sound card, here are a few options and features to look for:

Compatibility: One of the most important considerations when buying a sound card is whether your applications will be able to recognize and work with the card. Unfortunately, there are no universal standards for sound cards to ensure compatibility. However, there *is* a de facto standard: the Sound Blaster, made by Creative Labs. This was the first sound card to ship in mass-market quantities, so almost every application that uses sound will work with any card that bills itself as "Sound Blaster-compatible."

Playback features: To play sounds on your system, check out the card's digital-to-analog converter (DAC). It should support at least the highest levels of digitized sound that you plan on using. For example, if you have applications that use CD-quality audio, the card's DAC should support sampling frequencies up to 44.1 KHz, 16-bit sample depth, and stereo.

Sampling features: If you plan on recording audio, check the features supported by the card's analog-to-digital converter (ADC). The ADC features you get will depend on the level of recording quality that suits your needs. If all you want to do is voice annotations, a cheap 11 KHz, 8-bit, mono ADC is all you need. For music and other sounds, it doesn't cost a whole lot more to move up to a 44.1 KHz, 16-bit, stereo ADC.

Compression: Most cards support some kind of built-in audio compression. The codec used depends on the sound card, but the vast majority of cards support at least one of the codecs recognized by Windows 95. This is especially true if the card is Sound Blaster-compatible. If you're using some other card, you should check the codecs it uses to make sure they're among the set supported by Windows 95.

Device drivers: Make sure the card comes with drivers for Windows 95. Although the Add New Hardware Wizard offers dozens of sound card drivers, you're usually better off with the latest drivers from the manufacturer.

CD-ROM interface: Many stereo sound cards also operate your CD-ROM drive. You need to be careful, though: Some sound cards support only CD-ROM drives that use a proprietary controller, such as the Mitsumi interface or the Sony interface. If your CD-ROM doesn't work with these controllers, the sound card won't be able to operate the drive. It's best to look for sound cards that have a generic interface, such as a SCSI port or an IDE port.

FM synthesis versus wavetable synthesis: *FM synthesis* cards imitate musical instruments by using a mathematical approximation of the instrument's sound. For better instrumental imitations, buy a card that uses *wavetable synthesis.* These cards have ROM chips that contain digital recordings (samples) of real instruments.

Digital signal processor: Many of the latest sound cards come with a digital signal processor (DSP) chip. This chip augments the card's basic features by adding extra goodies such as on-the-fly audio compression, voice mail, "surround sound" audio, and more.

Cable connectors: Besides the CD-ROM interface discussed earlier, all sound cards have several mini-plug connectors for various types of cables:

- *Line Out* connector: For cable connections from the sound card to an external device, such as a pair of speakers, a headphone set, or a stereo receiver. Some cards provide two RCA-style connectors for connecting to the left and right channels of a stereo system.

- *Speaker/Headphone Out* connector: For amplified cable connections from the sound card to a pair of speakers or a headphone set. In this case, you don't need an AC power source for the speakers because the sound card connector provides up to 4 watts of power.

- *Line In* connector: For cable connections from an external sound source to the sound card. External sound sources include stereo system components, CD-ROM drives, synthesizers, and microphones. This lets you record audio from the external source.

- *Microphone* connector: For cable connections from an external microphone to the sound card. As opposed to the Line In connector, these connectors typically record in mono, which is fine for voice recordings.

■ *Joystick/MIDI Adapter* connector: For cable connections from the sound card to a joystick or a MIDI adapter. The latter is used to control a MIDI device, such as a MIDI-compliant keyboard.

■ *Internal CD-ROM sound* connector: For cable connections from an internal CD-ROM drive to the sound card. This lets you hear audio from your internal CD-ROM drive.

MIDI support: Besides the MIDI connector mentioned earlier, you'll need a few other features if you plan on working with MIDI files. These features include General MIDI support, polyphony, MIDI streams, and wavetable synthesis.

Plug and Play: Many of the latest sound cards are compliant with the Plug and Play standard, meaning that after you install them, Windows 95 will recognize and configure the card automatically. This is a huge benefit, because sound cards have always been notoriously difficult to install due to the fact that they usually require specific IRQ, DMA, and memory addresses.

External accessories: To get the most for your audio dollar, look for cards that come bundled with extras such as a microphone and headphones. Most sound cards also come with audio clips and programs for playing sounds, recording and editing digital audio, composing MIDI music, converting text to speech, and more. The latest-and-greatest sound card accessory is telephony software that lets your computer act as a sophisticated telephone, with answering machine capabilities, voice mailboxes, speed dial, and much more. Some even come with Internet-based phone software.

NOTE: INSTALLING SOUND CARDS

Many sound cards aren't Plug and Play-compliant, so Windows 95 won't be able to assign interrupts and DMA channels automatically. Ideally, you should install these cards before you install Windows 95. If you're installing the card with Windows 95 already on your machine, use the card's software to assign the appropriate resources. This software usually sets up a line or two in CONFIG.SYS or AUTOEXEC.BAT that specifies these resources, so you should leave these lines in place.

Installing the PC Speaker Driver

If you're just looking for basic sound capabilities (that is, the ability to play WAV files), you don't need to shell out a couple hundred bucks on a fancy sound card. Instead, Microsoft has a PC Speaker driver that lets WAV files be played, with adequate fidelity, through your computer's built-in speaker. This section tells you how to obtain and install the PC Speaker driver.

Getting Your Hands on the PC Speaker Driver

The PC Speaker driver comes in a self-extracting archive file named SPEAK.EXE. You'll find SPEAK.EXE on various Internet sites, as well as on the following Microsoft sites:

The Microsoft Network: Select Edit | Go To | Other Location, type mssupport, and click OK. Now open the following icons: MS Software Library, Microsoft Windows Software Library, Microsoft Windows 3.x and Windows for Workgroups Software Library, and Miscellaneous Files. Download the file Win 3.1 WDL: Audio - PC Speaker.

CompuServe: GO MSL and then select Access the Software Library. Perform a filename search for SPEAK.EXE, and then download the file.

Microsoft Download Service (MSDL): Dial (206) 936-6735 to connect to MSDL, search for SPEAK.EXE, and then download it.

FTP: Connect to ftp.microsoft.com, change to the Softlib/Mslfiles directory, and then get SPEAK.EXE.

Once you've got the file, double-click it to extract its contents (AUDIO.TXT, LICENSE.TXT, OEMSETUP.INF, SPEAKER.DRV, and SPEAKER.TXT). When the utility asks if you want to extract the files, press Y.

Installing the PC Speaker Driver

Here are the steps to follow to install the PC Speaker driver:

1. In Control Panel, open the Add New Hardware icon.
2. Click Next >. In the Wizard dialog box that appears, activate the No option and click Next >.
3. In the Hardware types list, highlight Sound, video, And game controllers and click Next >.
4. Click the Have Disk button.
5. In the Install From Disk dialog box that appears, type the pathname of the folder containing the extracted PC Speaker files and click OK.
6. The Select Device dialog box that appears should display Sound Driver for PC-Speaker in the Models list, as shown in Figure 24.8. Click OK.

24

WINDOWS 95
SOUND

FIGURE 24.8.

This dialog box appears after you've selected the folder that contains the PC Speaker files.

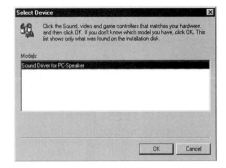

7. Click Finish. The PC-Speaker Setup dialog box, shown in Figure 24.9, appears.

FIGURE 24.9.

Use this dialog box to configure the PC Speaker driver.

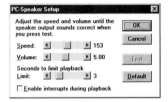

8. Adjust the settings and click Test to make sure the driver is working properly.

9. When Windows 95 asks if you want to restart your system, click Yes.

NOTE: ACCESSING THE PC SPEAKER DRIVER'S SETTINGS

To access the PC-Speaker Setup dialog box later, open Control Panel's Multimedia icon and select the Advanced tab. Open the Audio Devices tree, highlight Audio for Sound Driver for PC-Speaker, and click Properties. In the properties sheet that appears, click Settings.

NOTE: MEDIA PLAYER DOESN'T WORK WITH THE PC SPEAKER DRIVER

You can't use Media Player to play sounds using the PC Speaker driver. You have to use the Sound Recorder accessory.

Sounding Off: Playing Sounds in Windows 95

You'll find that playing sounds in Windows 95 is straightforward. In most cases, you'll use one of the following methods:

- Many CD-ROM applications have their own audio players built in, so you can play audio clips right from the application.

- As I've said, to play sound clips not supported by Windows 95, you'll need to install a third-party player.

- For WAV files, you can use either the Media Player (select Device | Sound) or the Sound Recorder. For the latter, select Start | Programs | Accessories | Multimedia | Sound Recorder. In the Sound Recorder window that appears, select File | Open to open the WAV file you want to hear. Now click the Play button (see Figure 24.10).

FIGURE 24.10.

You can use the Sound Recorder accessory to play WAV files.

Seek to Start — — Record

Seek to End   Play Stop

- For MIDI files, open the Media Player and select Device | MIDI Sequencer.

TIP: DRAG-AND-DROP AUDIO PLAYING

If the Media Player or Sound Recorder is open, you can also play an audio clip by dragging the sound file from Explorer and dropping it on the Media Player or Sound Recorder window.

NOTE: DEALING WITH MULTIPLE AUDIO DEVICES

Windows 95 is happy to let you have more than one audio playback device installed on your system. However, you might want to set up one of these devices as the default. To do this, first open Control Panel's Multimedia icon. In the Audio tab of the Multimedia Properties dialog box, use the Preferred device list in the Playback group to choose the playback device you want to use as the default.

24

WINDOWS 95
SOUND

Turning It Up (or Down): The Volume Control

Controlling the volume of your audio is crucial. During playback, you might want to turn the volume down if you're in a public place where you don't want to disturb others nearby. If you have no such worries, you might want to crank up a particularly good audio CD. During recording, setting the right input levels can make the difference between recording high-quality audio and distorted noise.

Windows 95's Volume Control lets you set not only overall volume for all audio, but also specific volume settings for individual audio sources. To display the Volume Control, use any of the following techniques:

- Double-click the Volume icon in the taskbar's system tray.
- In the Media Player, select Device | Volume Control.
- Select Start | Programs | Accessories | Multimedia | Volume Control.

Adjusting Audio Sources

Whichever method you use, you'll see the Volume Control window, shown in Figure 24.11. The Volume Control box on the left is a master control for all audio sources. The other boxes control individual audio sources. In each case, you can make the following adjustments:

- To adjust the volume, drag the appropriate Volume slider up or down.
- To turn the sound off, activate the appropriate Mute button (or, in the case of the master Volume Control, activate the Mute all button).
- To adjust the balance between the left and right speakers, drag the Balance slider right or left.

FIGURE 24.11.

Use the Volume Control accessory to adjust the volume levels of your audio playback and recording.

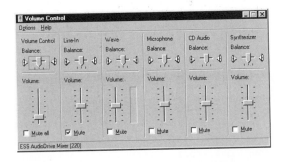

TIP: A FASTER MASTER VOLUME CONTROL

If you want to adjust the volume for, or mute, all audio sources, here's a quick way to do so: Click the Volume icon in the taskbar's system tray. A small window appears with a Volume slider and a Mute button.

Determining the Sources That Appear in Volume Control

When you open the Volume Control, you might not see all the audio sources displayed in Figure 24.11. To control the sources that Volume Control displays, select Options | Properties to open the Properties dialog box, shown in Figure 24.12. In the Adjust volume for group, select the type of sources you want to see: Playback, Recording, or Other. In the Show the following volume controls list, activate the check boxes for the sources you want to display. When you're done, click OK.

FIGURE 24.12.

Use this dialog box to customize the sources that are displayed in the Volume Control window.

NOTE: ADVANCED VOLUME CONTROL SETTINGS

If you select either Recording or Other in the Properties dialog box, a new Volume Control command becomes available: Options | Advanced Controls. Activating this command adds an Advanced button to the Volume Control window. Clicking this button lets you set, among other things, the bass and treble levels for recordings (assuming that your sound card supports these settings).

Giving Windows 95 a Voice: Assigning Sounds to Events

As you work with Windows 95, you'll hear various sounds emanating from your speakers. These sounds always correspond to particular events. There's that relaxing, New Age-like music when you start Windows 95, there's the short, sharp shock of a sound when a warning dialog box pops up, and there's a nice little chime when you exit Windows 95.

If you're getting tired of the same old sounds, however, Windows 95 lets you customize what you hear by assigning different WAV files to these events. There also are a couple dozen other events to which you can assign sounds. This section shows you how it's done.

Working with Sound Schemes

The sounds assigned to various Windows 95 events comprise a *sound scheme.* To view the current scheme, go to Control Panel and open the Sounds icon. You'll see the Sounds Properties dialog box, shown in Figure 24.13.

Figure 24.13.

*Use the Sounds
Properties dialog box to
change the current
Windows 95 sound
scheme.*

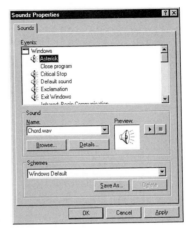

Here's a rundown of the various controls in the properties sheet:

Events: This list displays a number of Windows 95 events, including four that apply to the various types of dialog boxes displayed by Windows 95 and Windows applications: Asterisk, Critical Stop, Exclamation, and Question. If an event has a sound icon beside it, this means a WAV file is currently assigned to that event.

Name: This drop-down list shows you the name of the WAV file that's assigned to the currently highlighted event. You can use the Browse button to select a different WAV file (or just use the Name drop-down list to select a WAV file from Windows 95's Media subfolder), and you can use the Details button to view the properties sheet for the current WAV file.

Preview: Click the Play button to hear how the WAV file shown in the Name box will sound.

Schemes: This drop-down list displays the currently selected sound scheme.

You can use three methods to work with sound schemes:

■ To change the current sound scheme, highlight items in the Events list and change the associated WAV file.

■ To use a different sound scheme, select it from the Schemes drop-down list.

■ To create your own sound scheme, first associate WAV files with the various system events you want to hear. Then click Save As, enter a name for the new scheme, and click OK.

NOTE: SOUND SCHEMES ON THE WINDOWS 95 CD-ROM

The Windows 95 CD-ROM ships with a few predefined sound schemes (such as Jungle, Musica, and Robotz). If you don't see these schemes in the Schemes box, you need to install them.

Adding New Sound Events via the Registry

You might have noticed that the Events list includes entries for opening and closing both Sound Recorder and Media Player. If you'd like to assign sounds to the opening and closing of other applications, you can do so by editing the Registry. You also can assign application-specific sounds to other items shown in the Events list. For example, if you assign a WAV file to the Minimize event, Windows 95 plays that sound every time you minimize a window (which means that you'll get thoroughly sick of the sound in about an hour). Using the Registry, on the other hand, you can assign a different sound to the Minimize event for different applications.

Here are the steps to follow to use the Registry to assign sounds to application-specific events:

1. Start the Registry Editor and open the following key:

   HKEY_CURRENT_USER\AppEvents\Schemes\Apps

2. Highlight the Apps key and select Edit | New | Key to create a new subkey.

3. Type the name of the executable file (no extension) for the application you want to work with and press Enter. For example, if you want to work with Paint, type MSPaint and press Enter.

4. For the new key, double-click the Default setting, enter the name of the application, and click OK. (The name you enter is the name that appears in the Events list in the Sounds Properties dialog box.)

5. Now you need to add subkeys to the key you just created. These subkeys determine the events that will appear for this application in the Events list. Here are your choices:

   Close: Lets you assign a sound to closing the application.

   Maximize: Lets you assign a sound to maximizing the application.

   MenuCommand: Lets you assign a sound to selecting a menu command in the application.

   MenuPopup: Lets you assign a sound to pulling down a menu in the application.

   Minimize: Lets you assign a sound to minimizing the application.

   Open: Lets you assign a sound to opening the application.

   RestoreDown: Lets you assign a sound to clicking the Restore button after maximizing the application.

`RestoreUp`: Lets you assign a sound to clicking the application's taskbar button after minimizing the application.

6. When you've finished adding subkeys (see Figure 24.14 for an example), exit the Registry Editor.

FIGURE 24.14.

I've added a new application key to Apps, *along with several event subkeys.*

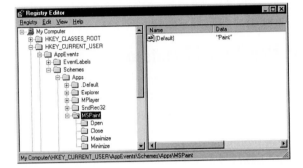

Now, when you open the Sounds Properties dialog box, your application and its events appear at the bottom of the Events list, as shown in Figure 24.15. Go ahead and assign sounds to these events.

FIGURE 24.15.

Once you've set things up in the Registry, the new events appear in the Sounds Properties dialog box.

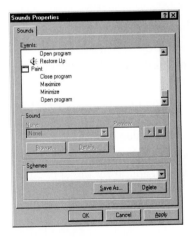

Recording and Editing Sounds with the Sound Recorder

If you have a sound card capable of recording sounds (and you have a microphone attached to the sound card), you can have hours of fun creating your own WAV files. Preserving silly sounds for posterity is the most fun, of course, but you can also create serious messages and embed them in business documents (I'll show you how in the next section).

To get started, open the Sound Recorder as described earlier. If the Sound Recorder already has a WAV file opened, and you want to start a new file, select File | New. If you'd prefer to add sounds to an existing file, open it and find the position in the sound file where you want your recording to start. (You do this by dragging the Sound Recorder's slider.)

Setting Audio Properties

Before you start recording, you need to specify the properties you want to use for the new WAV file. These properties include the codec to use, the sampling frequency, the sample depth, and whether the new file is stereo or mono.

To set these properties, select Edit | Audio Properties to display the dialog box shown in Figure 24.16. Here's a rundown of the options it provides:

> **Volume:** Use this slider to set the input volume level.
>
> **Preferred device:** If you have multiple recording devices, use this drop-down list to select the device you want to use.
>
> **Preferred quality:** Use this drop-down list to select the audio quality standard (as described earlier in this chapter) that you want to use: CD Quality, Radio Quality, or Telephone Quality.
>
> **Customize:** Use this button to set specific recording quality options. In the dialog box that appears, shown in Figure 24.17, use the Format drop-down list to select a codec, and use the Attributes drop-down list to select the sampling frequency, the sample depth, and mono or stereo. (If you'd like to preserve this combination, click the Save As button and enter a name in the dialog box.)

FIGURE 24.16.

Use this dialog box to set various recording options.

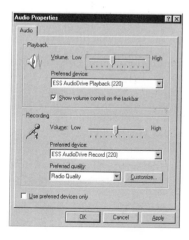

Figure 24.17.

Use this dialog box to specify the recording options you want to use.

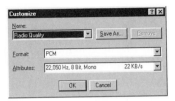

Recording a WAV File

When you're ready to start recording, here are the steps to follow:

1. With your microphone in hand, click the Record button.

2. Speak (yell, sing, whatever) into the microphone. Sound Recorder shows you the length of the file as you record. Note that you have a maximum of 60 seconds to do your thing.

3. When you're done, click the Stop button.

4. Check your recording by clicking the Seek to Start button and then the Play button.

5. If you don't like how your recording sounds, you can start over by clicking the Seek to Start button. (If you want to replace only part of the recording, drag the slider to the point where you want the replacement recording to start.) Then repeat steps 1 through 4.

6. If you're happy with your recording, select File | Save, enter a name and location for the file in the Save As dialog box, and click OK.

Editing a WAV File

Besides letting you record your own sounds, Sound Recorder comes with a host of interesting options for creating some really wild effects. Here's a summary:

Inserting an audio file: If you'd like to include another WAV file in your recording, position the slider where you want the other file to start. Then select Edit | Insert File, highlight the file in the Insert File dialog box, and click Open.

Mixing audio files: You can mix two or more WAV files so that they play at the same time. For example, you could combine one WAV file that contains narration with another that has soothing music. To try this, open one of the WAV files and move to where you want the second file to start. Select Edit | Mix with File, highlight the other WAV file in the Mix With File dialog box, and click Open.

NOTE: PASTING THE CURRENT AUDIO FILE

If you want to insert or mix the current audio file with another file, select Edit | Copy to send the current file to the Clipboard. Open the other file, position the slider appropriately, and select either Edit | Paste Insert or Edit | Paste Mix. (Note that, if you prefer to keep the current file open, you can always start up a second copy of Sound Recorder.)

Deleting chunks of audio: If there are sections of an audio file you no longer need, Sound Recorder lets you make deletions. To delete from the beginning of the file to a specific point, position the slider appropriately and select Edit | Delete Before Current Position. To delete from a specific point to the end of the file, position the slider appropriately and select Edit | Delete After Current Position. In either case, Sound Recorder will ask you to confirm the deletion. Click OK to proceed.

Changing the volume: If you've made your WAV file too loud or too soft, select either Effects | Increase Volume (to make the sound louder by 25 percent) or Effects | Decrease Volume (to make the sound quieter by 25 percent).

Altering the playback speed: You can make your voice recordings sound like either Alvin and the Chipmunks or Darth Vader by adjusting the speed of the playback. Choose either Effects | Increase Speed (to double the speed) or Effects | Decrease Speed (to cut the speed in half).

Adding an echo...echo...echo: If you select Effects | Add Echo, Sound Recorder creates a neat echo effect that makes your WAV files sound like they're being played in some cavernous location.

Reversing a sound: Playing a sound file backwards can produce some real mind-blowing effects. To check this out, choose Effects | Reverse.

TIP: REVERSING YOUR CHANGES

If you make a mess of your WAV file, you can get back to square one by selecting File | Revert. When Sound Recorder asks for confirmation, click Yes. This returns the file to the state it was in when you last saved it.

Inserting an Audio Object

If you want to, you can embed either a MIDI Sequence or Wave Sound object in a container document. There are two ways you can go about this:

- Follow the instructions from Chapter 22, "Miscellaneous Multimedia: Graphics, CD-ROMs, and More," for inserting a Media Clip object. In this case, of course, the object you'll select will be part of either a MIDI file or a WAV file.

- To insert a WAV file object directly from the container application, select Insert | Object. In the dialog box that appears, highlight Wave Sound in the Object Type list and click OK. Windows 95 will add an icon for the Wave Sound object to the container document and display the Sound Recorder so that you can create the new WAV file.

- To insert a MIDI file object directly from the container application, select Insert | Object. In the dialog box that appears, highlight MIDI Sequence in the Object Type list and click OK. Windows 95 will add an icon for the MIDI Sequence object to the

24

WINDOWS 95
SOUND

container document and display the Media Player commands and controls so that you can insert the MIDI object.

Troubleshooting Windows 95 Audio

To round out our look at Windows 95 audio, this section examines some audio troubleshooting techniques and solutions to specific problems.

Reinstalling an Audio Codec

If you have trouble with a specific audio codec, removing the codec and then reinstalling it will often solve the problem. Here are the steps to follow to remove an audio codec:

1. In Control Panel, open the Multimedia icon and select the Advanced tab, shown in Figure 24.18.

Figure 24.18.

In the Advanced tab of the Multimedia Properties dialog box, highlight the audio codec you want to remove.

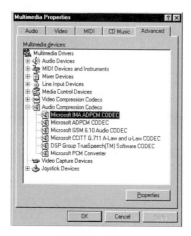

2. Open the Audio Compression Codecs tree and highlight the codec you want to remove.

3. Click the Properties button. In the codec properties sheet that appears, click Remove.

4. When Windows 95 asks if you're sure, click Yes and then click OK in the next two dialog boxes. (Windows 95 will tell you to restart the system. You can ignore this.)

5. Close the Multimedia Properties dialog box to return to Control Panel.

To reinstall the codec, follow these steps:

1. In Control Panel, open the Add New Hardware icon.

2. Click Next >.

3. When the Wizard asks if you want Windows to search for your hardware, activate No and click Next >.

4. In the Hardware types list, highlight Sound, video, and game controllers and click Next >.

5. In the Manufacturers list, highlight the appropriate item:

   ■ For IMA ADPCM, highlight Microsoft Audio Codecs.

   ■ For TrueSpeech, highlight DSP Group.

6. In the Models list, highlight the codec you want to install and click Next >.

7. Click Finish and follow the on-screen prompts for inserting your Windows 95 source disks.

8. When Windows 95 asks if you want to restart your system, click Yes.

Troubleshooting WAV Audio Problems

If you find that your WAV audio files won't play at all, or the sound is broken or noisy, any number of things might be wrong. Here's a checklist of things to look for:

■ If a third-party program won't play a WAV file, you can try a few things. First, see if you can play the file by double-clicking it in Explorer, by using Media Player, or by using Sound Recorder. If the file plays now, the problem lies with the third-party program. You'll need to contact the vendor's tech support department.

■ If you can't play the file from Explorer, Media Player, or Sound Recorder, the file might be corrupted. Try playing another WAV file that uses the same codec. If the second WAV file won't play, there is probably a problem with the codec driver, so you should try removing and then reinstalling the codec. If the second file plays, the original file is probably damaged. Either reinstall it or contact the vendor for a replacement. If you can't play any WAV file, the MCI video device might be disabled. To enable this device, follow these steps:

   1. Open Control Panel's Multimedia icon and select the Advanced tab.

   2. Open the Media Control Devices tree.

   3. Highlight Wave Audio Device and click Properties.

   4. In the properties sheet that appears, activate the Use this Media Control device option and click OK.

   5. Click OK and then restart Windows 95 to put the change into effect.

■ Open Control Panel's Multimedia icon and, in the Audio tab, make sure that the Volume level is set where you want and that the appropriate playback device is selected in the Preferred device list.

■ Open the Volume Control applet and make sure that the volume settings are appropriate for the playback device.

■ Your sound card might not be configured properly. Open the Device Manager and see if there are any conflicts between the sound card and another device. See Chapter 10,

24

WINDOWS 95
SOUND

"How Windows 95 Handles Hardware," for information on resolving hardware conflicts.

■ Check your sound card's documentation to make sure it's compatible with the WAV file's attributes. For example, your sound card might not support the WAV file's sampling frequency.

■ If you're trying to play the file from a CD-ROM drive, make sure that the CD-ROM's audio cables are connected to the sound card.

■ Make sure that your speakers are properly connected to the sound card. If the speakers have a volume control, make sure that the control is set appropriately.

Summary

This chapter closed out our look at Windows 95 multimedia by looking at various audio features. I began by showing you how analog sound waves are converted to digital audio files. In particular, you learned how the crucial concepts of sampling frequency and sample depth can affect audio quality. You also learned about the various audio formats and codecs that Windows 95 supports. I then showed you how to install the PC Speaker driver, play audio files, adjust the volume, assign sounds to events, and record new audio files.

Here's a list of chapters where you'll find related information:

■ For a more general look at hardware and device drivers, see Chapter 10, "How Windows 95 Handles Hardware."

■ I introduced you to the Registry and the Registry Editor in Chapter 11, "Introducing the Windows 95 Registry."

■ I covered OLE objects in Chapter 17, "Sharing Data in Windows 95: The Clipboard and OLE."

■ For a look at some larger multimedia issues, as well as how to play audio CDs in Windows 95, see Chapter 22, "Miscellaneous Multimedia: Graphics, CD-ROMs, and More."

■ Audio plays a big part in video clips. I told you all about Windows 95 video in Chapter 23, "Windows 95 Video: The Big Picture."

VI
PART

Unleashing Windows 95 Communications

Maximizing Modem Communications

CHAPTER

25

There is no pleasure to me without communication: there is not so much as a sprightly thought comes into my mind that it does not grieve me to have produced alone, and that I have no one to tell it to.

—Michel de Montaigne

Over the years, desktop PCs have stoutly resisted any and all attempts to gussy them up. Outside of the occasional design flourish and a few doomed-from-the-start efforts at hipness (such as the sleek NeXT computer), today's monitors and cases still look basically the same as they did 15 years ago: squat, rectangular, and unremittingly beige.

To inject their machines with some individuality, people have had to resort to accessorizing: plugging in peripherals and attaching add-ons. The popularity of some of these electronic adjuncts has waxed and waned in accordance with the trends of the day as dictated by the digerati (digital literati). The ubiquitous mouse, for example, was once a fashion statement that declared a person as "non-DOS." Other recent PC fashion accessories have included ergonomic keyboards (especially the curvaceous Microsoft Natural Keyboard with its Daliesque design) and CD-ROM drives.

These days, however, the de rigueur accessory for PC fashion plates is the modem. *Everyone,* it seems, is flocking online like so many swallows to Capistrano. The Internet, of course, is the Big Thing, but folks are connecting to commercial services, bulletin boards, and other online locales in record numbers. And we're not talking only about the extroverts of the world, like Montaigne, who just wanted to reach out and modem someone, *anyone.* No, people of all walks of life, temperaments, and levels of expertise are surfing like there's no tomorrow.

Windows 95 has jumped on this modem bandwagon in a big way with a totally revamped communications subsystem, easier modem setup, and some decent communications applets. This chapter gives you some background in modem communications, shows you how to get your modem's mojo working, and shows you how to work a couple of Windows 95 applets: Phone Dialer and HyperTerminal.

A Modem Communications Primer

Computers are, essentially, solitary beasts that prefer to keep their own company. However, that's not to say that PCs don't have a social side as well; you just have to work a bit to dig it out. In all, there are three ways to go about this:

- Add network interface cards to the computers, and then sling some cable around to set up a local area network (LAN). You'll learn how this is done in Chapter 30, "A Networking Primer," and Chapter 31, "Windows 95 Networking."

■ Use a special cable (or infrared) to connect the serial ports of two computers, and then use Direct Cable Connection to exchange files between them. I demonstrate how to do this in Chapter 34, "From Laptop to Desktop and Back: Direct Cable Connection."

■ Attach a modem to your computer, and use it to connect to remote systems.

The third method is the focus of this chapter. As an appetizer, this section presents a bit of background info that serves to get you comfortable with the underlying principles of modem communications. This knowledge will make it much easier for you to set up and work with your modem, and it will be invaluable when you need to troubleshoot the inevitable communications problems.

Modems: The Inside Story

Modems are, by now, a ubiquitous feature of the PC terrain, but they remain more mysterious than the other peripherals. Perhaps it's the alphabet soup of modem standards, or the inherent complexities of modem-to-modem communications, or just all those strange sounds modems make when they converse with one another. To help you penetrate the mysteries of the modem, this section examines the inner workings of these electronic marvels.

The Modulation/Demodulation Thing

In Chapter 24, "Getting the Most Out of Windows 95 Sound," I explained a bit about how sound waves are created. When you speak into a telephone, a diaphragm inside the mouthpiece vibrates. This vibration is converted into an electromagnetic wave that mirrors the amplitude and frequency of the original analog wave created by your voice. This wave travels along the telephone lines, and at the destination, electromagnets in the receiver vibrate another diaphragm that reproduces your voice.

Note that this process is entirely analog, from the original sound wave of your voice, to the electromagnetic wave that traverses the phone system, to the reconstituted sound wave created by the receiver. Computers, of course, are resolutely digital, so this analog state of affairs just won't do. For a computer to send data along a telephone line, the individual bits that make up the data must be converted into some kind of analog wave.

This digital-to-analog process is called *modulation*. In essence, the 1s and 0s that compose digital data are converted into signals (or *symbols*) that can be represented as tones that fall within the frequency range of the human voice (between 300 and 3,000 Hz). These tones can then be sent along regular telephone lines, where they're converted back into their original digital format. This reconversion process is called *demodulation*. The device that modulates the data, sends the resulting tones, and demodulates the tones on the receiving end is our friend the modem (the word *modem* is a blend of *modulator* and *demodulator*). Now you know why modems make such a racket while they're communicating with each other: it's all those tones exchanged back and forth.

> **NOTE: DIGITAL TELEPHONE LINES**
>
> Although most telephone systems are analog, digital phone lines are cropping up with increasing frequency. These lines work by sampling the voice, much like the way a sound card samples analog audio. The samples are then sent across the lines as bits without the need of modulation or demodulation, and so without the need of a modem.

The Difference Between Baud and Bits Per Second

The speed at which modems transmit data is called the *data transfer rate,* and it's measured in bits per second (bps). The current standards for the data transfer rate are 14,400 bps on the low end and 28,800 bps on the high end. (56,000 bps modems are now available, but at the time I wrote this, no standards had yet been set.) Another measure of transmission speed does, however, exist—the *baud rate*—and the two terms are often confused.

The baud rate defines the number of symbols (which might be variations in, say, voltage or frequency, depending on the modulation standard being used) per second that can be exchanged between two modems. Each of these symbols, however, can incorporate multiple bits of data. For example, a 2,400 baud modem might be able to cram 6 bits of data into a symbol, thus resulting in a data transfer rate of 14,400 bps.

In the old days, modems incorporated only a single bit per baud, so the bps and baud rates were synonymous. Now, however, almost all modems support multibit baud rates, so the only true measure of a modem's transmission speed is bps.

Understanding Modem Standards

For modems to communicate with each other successfully, they must speak the same language, "language" in this sense meaning, among other things, the type of modulation used, the data transfer rate, how errors are handled, and whether or not any data compression is used.

At one time, there were almost as many modem languages as there were modem manufacturers, resulting in what I call the "Tower of Babel" problem in communications. In other words, you could never be sure that the modem you were trying to connect with would have the faintest idea what your modem was saying. To solve this problem, the major players in the data communications game put together a series of modem standards to help ensure compatibility between devices from different manufacturers. These standards cover three aspects of modem communications: modulation, error correction, and data compression.

NOTE: THE "HAYES-COMPATIBLE" STANDARD

You might still see some modems described as "Hayes-compatible." This is a holdover from the days when Hayes modems were the market leader, so other modems had to fall in line with the Hayes standard to gain consumer acceptance. In this case, however, the standard had nothing to do with modem communications. Instead, it defined a command set used by applications to control the modem. For example, the command ATDT (Attention Dial Tone) tells the modem to get a dial tone. By now, however, *every* modem supports this command set (which is usually just called the *AT command set*, because most of the commands begin with "AT"), so being Hayes-compatible is no longer a big deal.

Modulation Standards

When a modem modulates digital data into a carrier wave, the receiving modem must understand how this modulation was performed in order to reverse the procedure during demodulation. This is, for obvious reasons, the most crucial aspect of modem compatibility, so having *modulation standards* is critical. These standards are set by a United Nations umbrella group called the International Telecommunication Union-Telecommunications Standardization Section (ITU-TSS; it was formerly another mouthful: the Consultative Committee on International Telephone and Telegraph, or CCITT). The ITU-TSS consists of representatives from modem manufacturers, telephone companies, and government agencies.

As modem technology improved, new standards had to be hammered out, so numerous modulation standards have been implemented over the years. Here's a review of the most common ones:

V.22: This is a 1,200 bps standard that was used mostly outside of the United States and Canada. (The corresponding standard used in the United States and Canada was called Bell 212A, which was a standard implemented by Bell Labs.)

V.22bis: This is a 2,400 bps standard, and the first of the international standards. (The "bis" part is French for *again* or *encore*.)

V.29: This is the standard for half-duplex (that is, one-way) communication at 9,600 bps. It's used for Group III fax transmissions and so is the standard facsimile implementation in fax/modems.

V.32: This is the standard for full-duplex (that is, two-way) communications at 9,600 bps. This standard incorporates a technique called *trellis coding* that enables on-the-fly error checking and reduces the effect of line noise.

V.32bis: This standard defines full-duplex transmission at 14,400 bps. It's basically the same as V.32, except that the number of bits per signal change was upped from 4 in V.32 to 6 in V.32bis (both standards operate at 2,400 baud).

V.32fast of V.FC: These standards upped the V.32 and V.32bis transmissions to 28,800 bps, but they've been replaced by V.34.

V.34: This is the standard for full-duplex transmission at 28,000 bps. V.34 represents the current state of the art for modem communications. Despite their latest-and-greatest status, V.34 modems are relatively inexpensive, so you should shoot for V.34 if you're in the market for a modem.

Most experts believe that V.34 represents the ceiling for analog transmission speed. Getting true V.34 speeds is problematic because of the poor quality of public telephone lines. Undaunted, modem companies continue to push the transmission rate envelope. U.S. Robotics, for example, recently introduced "x2" technology, which allegedly allows for 56 Kbps rates over standard phone lines. However, it's likely that you'll need an absolutely pristine connection (as well as an x2 modem on the other end) to achieve anything near this rate. It's more likely that reliable increases in data transmission speed will come only from digital lines, such as ISDN.

Error Correction Standards

One of the problems with analog telephone lines is that they suffer from line noise and other factors that can wreak havoc on the carefully crafted symbols sent by modems. To ensure that data arrives intact, the ITU-TSS has set up *error correction standards*. These standards let the receiving modem check the integrity of incoming symbols and, if it finds a problem, ask the originating modem to resend the data.

The current standard for error correction is V.42, which incorporates two protocols: Link Access Procedure for Modems (LAPM) and Microcom Networking Protocol (MNP) 4. Both protocols correct errors by asking that corrupted data be retransmitted. The default protocol is LAPM because it's a bit faster than MNP 4.

Compression Standards

You saw in Chapter 14, "Disk Driving: Dealing with Disks," that Windows 95's DriveSpace utility can compress files by replacing redundant character strings with tokens. Many modern modems can perform the same process on your outgoing data. In other words, the modem first uses a compression technique to reduce the size of the data and then converts the compressed data into symbols. This means that less data is sent, thus reducing upload times.

Of course, the receiving modem must be able to decompress the data, so the ITU-TSS has implemented compression standards. The current standard is V.42bis, which uses a variation of the classic Lempel-Ziv compression scheme (see Chapter 14). V.42bis can compress data up to 4:1, thus providing an effective data transfer rate of 57,600 bps for a 14,400 bps modem, or 115,200 bps for a 28,800 bps modem. (Most modems also support another compression scheme called MNP 5. This scheme, however, provides a maximum compression ratio of only 2:1.)

CAUTION: COMPRESSION CAN SLOW SOME FILE TRANSFERS

Data compression sounds great, but it only really works on text transfers. Because binary files contain few redundant character strings, they can't be compressed all that much, so you won't see a significant increase in throughput. In fact, if you're dealing with files that have already been compressed (such as ZIP files), data compression might lead to *slower* download times because compressing an already-compressed file generally *increases* the size of the file.

A Review of Modem Types

Modems come in various shapes and sizes, and most brand-name models provide similar features. If you're looking to purchase a modem, your main criterion should be that the modem supports the ITU-TSS standards, especially one of the modulation standards (such as V.32bis or V.34). Also, many modems come with built-in fax capabilities (these are required if you want to use Microsoft Fax, as described in Chapter 29, "Using Microsoft Fax to Send and Receive Faxes"), so look for V.29 compatibility as well.

After standards compliance, your next criterion will be the type of modem (or fax/modem) you need. Here's a summary of the four main types:

External: These modems are standalone boxes you connect to a serial port with a special cable. Although external modems require a separate power source and tend to be more expensive than an equivalent internal modem, they have several advantages. For one, they can be transported between machines fairly easily. For another, most external modems have a series of LED indicators on their front panel that tell you the current state of the modem. These lights can be invaluable during troubleshooting. Here's a summary of the LEDs that appear on most external modems and what each light represents:

LED	Description
AA	Auto Answer: When lit, indicates that the modem will answer incoming calls automatically.
CD	Carrier Detect: Lights up when the modem receives a valid data signal from a remote modem. This indicates that data transmission is possible, and the light remains on during the entire connection.
CS	Clear to Send: Lights up when the modem has determined that it's OK for an application to start sending data. (See the discussion of flow control in the later section "Modem-to-Modem Communications.")

continues

25

MAXIMIZING MODEM COMMUNICATIONS

LED	Description
MR	Modem Ready: Lights up when the modem's power is turned on.
OH	Off Hook: Lights up when the modem takes control of the phone line (which is the modem equivalent of taking the telephone receiver off the hook).
RD	Receive Data: Lights up when the modem receives data.
RS	Request to Send: Lights up when your computer has asked the modem whether it's OK to start sending data.
SD	Send Data: Lights up when the modem sends data.
TR	Terminal Ready: Lights up when the modem receives a DTR (data terminal ready) signal from the computer. This means that the current communications program is ready to start sending data.

Internal: These modems are cards you insert into a slot on your computer's expansion bus. This type of modem is convenient because no external power source is required, it's one less device taking up valuable desk space, and no external serial port is used up. Most modem jockeys, however, dislike internal modems because of the lack of LED indicators for troubleshooting. (As you'll see later, though, Windows 95 does provide an icon during modem connections that shows you the state of the RD and SD signals.)

Pocket: These are miniature, pocket-sized versions of external modems that plug directly into a computer's serial port. They're normally used with notebook computers.

PC Card: These are modems that use the credit-card-size, PC Card (PCMCIA) format and plug directly into a PC Card slot. If possible, look for PC Card modems that accept an RJ-11 jack directly, because these kinds are more reliable than the "dongles" used by most PC Card modems.

Serial Ports: Communicating One Bit at a Time

The link between your computer and your modem is the *serial port* (also known as a *COM port* or *RS-232 port*). For an external modem, this link usually comes in the form of a serial cable that runs from the port to an interface in the back of the modem. The exception is the pocket modem, which usually plugs into the serial port directly. For internal and PC Card modems, the serial port is built right into the modem's circuitry.

They're called "serial" ports because they transmit and receive data one bit at a time, in a series. (This is opposed to working with data in "parallel," in which multiple bits are transmitted simultaneously.) As such, serial ports can be used by many kinds of devices that require two-way communication, such as mice, infrared adapters, bar code scanners, and, of course, modems.

Serial Port Pin Configurations

Like most computer interfaces, serial ports send and receive data and signals via wires that correspond to single bits. For a serial port, these wires are metal pins that come in two configurations: 9-pin and 25-pin, as illustrated in Figure 25.1. From the context of modem communications, there is no essential difference between the 9-pin and 25-pin connectors, other than their layout. Table 25.1 shows the pin assignments for the 9-pin connector, and Table 25.2 shows the partial pin assignments for the 25-pin connector (the other pins can be safely ignored).

FIGURE 25.1.

The 9-pin and 25-pin serial port connectors.

9-pin serial port

25-pin serial port

Table 25.1. Pin assignments for a 9-pin serial port connector.

Pin Number	Signal
1	Carrier Detect (CD)
2	Receive Data (RD)
3	Transmit Data (TD)
4	Data Terminal Ready (DTR)
5	Signal Ground
6	Data Set Ready (DSR)
7	Request To Send (RTS)
8	Clear To Send (CTS)
9	Ring Indicator

25

MAXIMIZING MODEM COMMUNICATIONS

Table 25.2. Partial pin assignments for a 25-pin serial port connector.

Pin Number	Signal
2	Transmit Data (TD)
3	Receive Data (RD)
4	Request To Send (RTS)
5	Clear To Send (CTS)
6	Data Set Ready (DSR)
7	Signal Ground
8	Carrier Detect (CD)
20	Data Terminal Ready (DTR)
22	Ring Indicator

The key pins in both layouts are Transmit Data (TD) and Receive Data (RD). The computer uses the TD pin to send the individual bits of outgoing serial data to the modem. For incoming data, the modem uses the RD pin to get the bits into the computer. See "Modem-to-Modem Communications" later in this chapter to learn the functions of some of the other wires.

The UART: The Heart of the Serial Port

You might be wondering how the computer's processor and the serial port can possibly get along with each other. After all, the CPU deals with data in parallel: the 8 bits (1 byte) that are required to represent a single character of information. I've just told you, however, that serial ports are one-bit wonders. How do you reconcile these seemingly incompatible ways of looking at data?

The answer is a special chip that resides inside every serial port (or sometimes on the computer's motherboard): the *Universal Asynchronous Receiver/Transmitter* (UART). (For an internal or PC Card modem, the UART chip sits on the card itself.) It's the UART's job, among other things, to take the computer's native parallel data and convert it into a series of bits that can be spit out of the serial port's TD line. On the other end, individual bits streaming into the destination serial port's RD line are reassembled by the UART into the parallel format that the processor prefers.

It's clear, then, that the role of the UART in data communications is crucial. In fact, the UART is often the source of transmission bottlenecks that can hold up the entire process. To see why, consider what happens when serial data arrives via the modem. The UART assembles the incoming bits until it has a full byte, and it stores this byte in a special memory buffer. It then notifies the CPU—by generating an interrupt request—that data is waiting. Under ideal conditions, the CPU grabs the data from the buffer immediately, the UART processes the next byte, and the cycle repeats. However, what if the CPU is busy with some other task when it receives the interrupt request? Well, the UART continues processing the incoming bits, and if the processor can't get to the buffered data in time, the UART simply overwrites the existing buffer with the new data. This means, at best, that the lost byte must be retransmitted, and the overall performance of the download suffers as a result. (At worst, you might lose the character altogether!)

This isn't usually a problem at relatively slow data transfer rates (say, up to 9,600 bps), but it can cause all kinds of problems with modern high-speed modems. To prevent these overruns, you need a UART that can keep up with the deluge. Here's a summary of the various UART types and their suitability for fast data transfer rates:

8250: This was the chip used in the original IBM PC XT. Its design calls for a 1-byte data buffer, so it isn't suitable for high-speed transfers.

16450: This was the chip used in the IBM PC AT and compatible machines. Although it sported some improvements over 8250 (essentially the capability to work with computers that have higher internal clock speeds), it still used the 1-byte data buffer, so it too is limited to 9,600 bps.

16550: This chip represented a huge improvement over its predecessors. The major innovation was a 16-byte FIFO (first in, first out) buffer that let the UART handle high-speed data transfers, while reducing retransmissions and dropped characters. Also, the 16550 had a variable interrupt trigger that the user could configure to send an interrupt to the CPU when the buffer reached a certain number of bytes. (You'll see later that Windows 95 lets you configure this trigger.) The 16550, however, had a defective FIFO buffer that often caused data loss.

16550A: This is a replacement chip that fixes the bugs in the 16550 but is otherwise identical. The 16550A (or the updated 16550AF or 16550AFN) is the chip of choice for modems that support data transfer rates of 14,400 bps and up.

How can you tell what kind of UART your system has? Until you install your modem in Windows 95, the only way to tell is to use the Microsoft Diagnostics (MSD) utility that came with Windows 3.1. (It's also on the Windows 95 CD-ROM in the \OTHER\MSD folder. Copy the file MSD.EXE to your main Windows 95 folder.) Type msd at the DOS prompt and press Enter. In the MSD screen that appears, click the COM Ports button. You'll see a COM Ports dialog box like the one shown in Figure 25.2. The bottom line of each column tells you which UART chip is used by each serial port.

25

MAXIMIZING MODEM COMMUNICATIONS

FIGURE 25.2.

Use the Microsoft Diagnostics utility to find out the UART chips used by your serial ports.

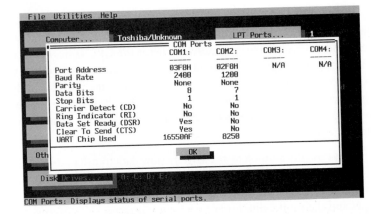

What do you do if MSD tells you that your UART doesn't cut the high-speed mustard? That depends on how the UART is installed on your system. In some cases, the chip sits in a socket and can be removed easily. In this case, you just need to buy a replacement chip and fit it into the socket. If the chip is soldered onto your system's I/O adapter, you'll have to replace the entire adapter.

Modem-to-Modem Communications

Modem communications is one of those ideas that, after you learn a bit of background, you wonder how on earth your system actually pulls it off. I mean, you're talking about tens of thousands of bits per second busily bustling between two computers, all the while negotiating compression routines, FIFO buffers, parallel-to-serial UART conversions, modulations, and who knows what else. To combine all of these complex technologies *and* achieve a remarkably high level of accuracy is an amazing achievement. To help you appreciate some of the hoops your computer, serial port, and modem have to jump through to accomplish this wizardry, this section takes a closer look at just how two modems communicate with each other.

Flow Control: The Communications Traffic Cop

Modem downloads come in fast and furious, so what's your computer supposed to do if it isn't ready to receive any data? Conversely, what if you're sending data and the remote system indicates that it can't receive any more data just now? How does your modem tell the CPU to stop processing data temporarily?

These kinds of situations fall under the rubric of *flow control*, which defines how the computer and the modem communicate with each other to coordinate data exchanges and prevent overruns when one device isn't ready to receive information from the other. There are two types of flow control: software and hardware.

Software Flow Control (XON/XOFF)

With *software flow control,* the computer and modem send signals to each other that indicate whether they're ready to receive data. For example, suppose that you're downloading a file and the computer needs to pause the download briefly while it attends to some other chores. To do this, it sends to the remote system's modem a special "hold your horses" signal called *XOFF.* (In data communications circles, "X" stands for transfer, so "XOFF" means "transfer off.") XOFF is an ASCII control code character (ASCII 19 or Ctrl-S) that gets shipped out to the remote system just like any other character. When the computer decides it's OK to resume the download, it notifies the remote system by sending a signal called *XON* (which is another control code character: ASCII 17 or Ctrl-Q). Because of these two signals, software flow control is also known as *XON/XOFF flow control.*

TROUBLESHOOTING: PRESS CTRL-Q TO RESUME DATA TRANSFERS

If you find that a data transfer has halted, it might be because your system has inadvertently sent an XOFF flow control signal. Try pressing Ctrl-Q to send an XON signal. If the remote system supports software flow control, this might be enough to get the transfer going again.

Hardware Flow Control (RTS/CTS)

Because of the high overhead associated with software flow control, it becomes inefficient at data transfer rates higher than 2,400 bps. For higher speeds, *hardware flow control* is a much better option. That's because instead of firing an entire character out to the remote device, hardware flow control just uses individual serial port lines to send signals. Earlier I showed you the various pin assignments associated with RS-232 serial ports. Hardware flow control uses two of these lines: RTS and CTS (which is why this method is also called *RTS/CTS flow control*).

For example, suppose that your modem wants to stop the computer from sending any more data (because, for example, it has lost its Carrier Detect signal and so doesn't have a connection with the remote system). To do that, all it does is turn off its CTS (Clear To Send) signal. The computer reads that the serial port's CTS wire is off, so it stops processing data for the modem.

Similarly, the processor's willingness to accept more data from the modem is controlled by the RTS (Request To Send) wire. If the processor turns off RTS, the modem reads that the serial port's RTS wire is off, so it pauses the data transfer.

Data Bits: The Crux of the Matter

As I mentioned earlier, the role of the UART is to convert the eight parallel bits that PCs use to represent data into a series of eight consecutive bits suitable for squeezing through the serial port's TD wire.

The problem, though, is that not all computer systems use 8 bits to represent their characters. All PCs do, because they need the 8 bits to represent all 256 characters in the ASCII character set (because each bit can use one of two states—on or off, 1 or 0—and 2 to the power of 8 is 256). Most mainframe systems, however, use only 7 bits to represent characters because they recognize only the first 128 ASCII characters (2 to the power of 7 is 128). The number of bits used to represent a character is called the *data bits* setting, or the *character length.*

So one of the most important parameters when a remote system is involved is the number of data bits it uses. Problems can arise, for example, if you send 8-bit bytes to a system that knows how to deal with only 7 of them. In PC systems, fortunately, the first 128 ASCII characters have a 0 as their eighth bit, so it can be safely discarded during communication with 7-bit systems.

Start and Stop Bits: Bookends for Your Data

The data coursing through your computer is transferred from place to place at extremely high speeds by using exquisitely timed procedures to coordinate the transfers. This type of communications is called *synchronous* because it depends on timing signals.

The vagaries of modem communications, however, prevent such precise timing, so modems use *asynchronous* communications. In asynchronous communications, as long as the remote system is willing and able to receive data, the data is just sent out whenever it's ready to go.

But with no timing involved, knowing where one character ends and the next begins becomes a problem. You might think that you could just use the number of data bits. For example, if your system and the remote system both use 8-bit bytes, you could simply define every eighth bit as the starting point for each character. Unfortunately, that approach would work only in a perfect world that boasted noiseless telephone lines and error-free data transfers. In the real world, in the journey between here and there, legitimate bits can go missing, and extraneous "bits" (that is, line noises) can get tossed into the mix.

To help the receiving end delimit incoming characters, the sending system's UART tacks on extra bits on both sides of the data. At the front of the data, the UART adds a *start bit* that defines the beginning of each character. This is followed by the data bits, and then the UART appends a *stop bit* to mark the end of the character.

The start bit is always the same, but different systems require different length stop bits. Most systems use a single stop bit, but a few rare cases insist on two stop bits. (You'll also read about systems that require 1½ stop bits. *Half* a bit? It doesn't make sense until you remember that these "bits" I'm talking are really electromagnetic pulses traveling along an analog carrier wave. Each pulse consumes a predefined amount of time—say, 1/14,400th of a second—so 1½ bits is really just 1½ pulses.)

At the receiving end, the UART busies itself by stripping off the start and stop bits before recombining the data bits into a full byte.

Parity: A Crude Error Check

The start and stop bits can tell the receiving modem it has received corrupted data. For example, if the modem is expecting 8 data bits but gets 7 or 9, it knows that something has gone haywire, and it can ask that the bit be retransmitted.

What if, however, a voltage spike or some line noise doesn't add or subtract bits from a character, but instead *changes* one of the existing bits? The receiving modem still gets the appropriate number of data bits, so it won't know that anything has gone awry. To cover this kind of trouble, many systems that use 7-bit characters also use *parity checking*. In this technique, an extra bit—called the *parity bit*—is added to the data bits (but before the stop bit). The parity bit is set to either 1 or 0, depending on the type of parity checking used:

Even parity: In this method, you first sum all the 1s in the data bits and see whether you end up with an odd or even number. Your goal is to send out an *even* number of 1s, so you use (or, technically, the UART uses) the extra parity bit to ensure this. For example, suppose that the data bits are 0000111. The sum of the 1s here is 3, which is odd, so the parity bit must be set to 1 to give you an even number of 1s. So the UART sends out 10000111. Similarly, suppose that your data bits are 1000001. The sum of the 1s is 2, which is even, so the parity bit can be set to 0, like so: 01000001.

Odd parity: This is the opposite of even parity. Again, you first sum all the 1s in the data bits and see whether you end up with an odd or even number. In this case, however, your goal is to send out an *odd* number of 1s, and you manipulate the parity bit accordingly.

Most systems use even parity. (Two other kinds of parity—mark and space—also exist, but these are virtually obsolete.)

How does this help the receiving system check the data? Well, if it's using even parity, the receiving system's UART checks the incoming bits and adds up all the 1s. If it finds an odd number of 1s, it knows that a bit was changed en route, so it can ask for a retransmit. Of course, if a voltage spike changes several bits, the number of 1s might remain even, so the receiving UART wouldn't detect an error. Therefore, parity is only a crude error-checking mechanism.

NOTE: COMMON CONNECTION SETTINGS

When setting up a connection to a remote system, you need to make sure that the three settings I've just talked about—data bits, stop bits, and parity—match the parameters expected by the remote computer. If you're not sure which settings to use, note that two combinations are the most common: 7 data bits, even parity, 1 stop bit (usually written as 7-E-1); and 8 data bits, no parity, 1 stop bit (8-N-1). The former combination is often used to connect to large online services that use mainframes (such as CompuServe); the latter works for most bulletin board systems and PC-to-PC connections.

Terminal Emulation: Fitting in with the Online World

When you use your modem to connect to a remote computer, you are, essentially, operating that computer from your keyboard and seeing the results on-screen. In other words, your computer has become a *terminal* attached to the remote machine.

It's likely, however, that the remote computer is completely different from the one you're using. It could be a mainframe or a minicomputer, for example. In that case, it isn't likely that the codes produced by your keystrokes will correspond exactly with the codes used by the remote computer. Similarly, some of the return codes won't make sense to your machine. So for your computer to act like a true terminal, some kind of translation is needed between the two systems. This translation is called *terminal emulation,* because it forces your system to emulate the kind of terminal that the remote computer normally deals with.

Most communications programs give you a choice of terminal emulation methods, such as ANSI for other DOS/Windows computers, TTY for teletype terminals, or specific terminal types, such as the DEC VT100 and VT52.

File Transfers: A Matter of Protocol

Although much of your online time will be spent grazing data marketplaces and chatting with others, the most common online activity involves transferring files back and forth. When you receive a file from a remote computer, it's called *downloading;* when you send a file to a remote computer, it's called *uploading.*

For your downloads and uploads to succeed, your system and the remote system must agree on which *file transfer protocol* to use. The protocol governs various aspects of the file transfer ritual, including starting and stopping, the size of the data packets being sent (in general, the larger the packet, the faster the transfer), how errors are handled, and so on. Many different file transfer protocols are available, but as you'll see later, Windows 95 supports the following six:

> **Xmodem:** Designed in 1977, this was the first protocol for PCs. Because it uses only a simple error-checking routine and sends data in small, 128-byte packets, Xmodem should be used only as a last resort.
>
> **1K Xmodem:** This is an updated version of Xmodem that uses 1,024-byte data packets and an improved 16-bit cyclic redundancy check (CRC) error-checking protocol. This makes 1K Xmodem more reliable than plain Xmodem and, as long as the telephone lines are relatively noise free, much faster as well.
>
> **Ymodem:** This protocol provides all the benefits of 1K Xmodem (including 1,024-byte packets and CRC error control) but also implements multiple-file transfers and the exchange of file data, including the name and size of each file.
>
> **Ymodem-G:** This protocol is the same as Ymodem, except that it performs no error checking. Instead, it relies on the built-in error checking of modern modems (such as V.42 and MNP 4).

Zmodem: This is the fastest of the file transfer protocols and the most reliable. Zmodem doesn't use a fixed packet size. Instead, it adjusts the size of each packet based on the line conditions. For error checking, Zmodem uses a 32-bit CRC for enhanced reliability. It also offers crash protection: If the file transfer bails out before completing, you can restart and the Zmodem protocol resumes where it left off. Zmodem is, by far, *the* choice among online aficionados.

Kermit: This is a flexible protocol that can handle the 7-bit bytes used by mainframes and minicomputers. It's very slow, however, and you should avoid it if the remote machine supports any other protocol.

Configuring Serial Ports

As you've seen so far, serial ports play a vital role in modem communications. To make sure that your serial ports are ready to do their duty, you might want to set a few properties. Here's how it's done:

1. Open the Control Panel's System icon, and in the System Properties dialog box that appears, select the Device Manager tab.

2. Open the Ports (COM and LPT) branch, highlight the COM port you want to work with, and click Properties.

3. Display the Port Settings tab, shown in Figure 25.3. These drop-down lists set up default communications settings for the port. You don't need to adjust these values for your modem's port, however, because the settings you specify for the modem will override the ones you see here. You need to change these values only if you'll be attaching some other kind of device to the port.

FIGURE 25.3.

The Port Settings tab controls various communications parameters.

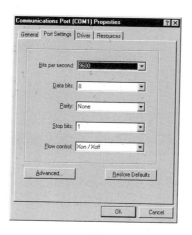

4. COM ports use interrupts to communicate with the processor. (For example, the UART uses an interrupt to let the processor know that the buffer contains incoming data.) If you have an IRQ conflict, use the Resources tab to make changes. (See Chapter 10, "How Windows 95 Handles Hardware," for the details.)

5. Click OK and, if necessary, restart your computer.

Installing and Configuring a Modem

Before you can use Phone Dialer, HyperTerminal, or any other communications software, you need to tell Windows 95 what kind of modem you have. After that's done, you need to configure the modem to suit the types of online sessions you plan to run. To that end, the next few sections take you through the rigmarole of installing and configuring your modem.

Installing Your First Modem

The route you take to install a modem differs slightly depending on whether you've already installed a modem in Windows 95. Here are the steps to follow to install your first modem:

1. Open the Control Panel's Modems icon. The Install New Modem Wizard, shown in Figure 25.4, appears.

Figure 25.4.

The Install New Modem Wizard takes you through your first modem installation.

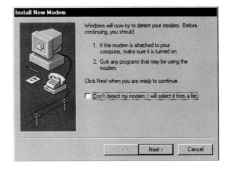

2. If the modem isn't attached to your machine yet, activate the Don't detect my modem; I will select it from a list check box, and click Next >. Otherwise, leave this check box deactivated, and click Next >.

3. If you have Windows 95 detect the modem, it queries your system's serial ports to see whether a modem is attached. When it's done, it displays the name of the modem it found. If this information is incorrect, click Change. Otherwise, click Next > and skip to step 6.

4. If you're selecting the modem by hand, you'll see the dialog box shown in Figure 25.5. Use the Manufacturers and Models lists to highlight your modem, and then click Next >. If your modem isn't in the list, you have two choices: Select Standard Modem Types in the Manufacturers list and choose a generic model; or, if you have a disk from the manufacturer, click the Have Disk button and follow the on-screen prompts.

FIGURE 25.5.

If you elect to specify your modem yourself, you'll use this dialog box to do it.

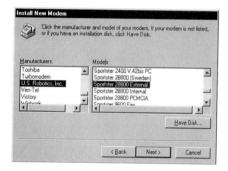

5. The next Wizard dialog box asks you to select a serial port. Highlight the appropriate port and click Next >.

6. The next Wizard dialog box asks for information that will help Windows 95 dial the modem, as shown in Figure 25.6. Select your country, enter your area code and the number to dial to access an outside line (if any), and choose either Tone dialing or Pulse dialing. When you're done, click Next >.

FIGURE 25.6.

This dialog box contains information related to dialing your modem.

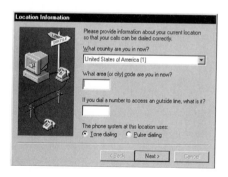

7. Click Finish.

Installing Another Modem

After you've installed your first modem, Windows 95 displays the Modems Properties dialog box, shown in Figure 25.7. (You can also display this properties sheet by opening the Modems icon in Control Panel.) To install a modem from here, click the Add button and follow the steps outlined in the preceding section. (You won't have to bother with step 6, however, because Windows 95 just uses the same values that you entered for your first modem.)

FIGURE 25.7.

The Modems Properties dialog box lists your currently installed modems.

Modifying the Modem's Dialing Properties

As you saw when you were setting up your modem, Windows 95 keeps track of various dialing properties for each modem. These properties determine how Windows 95 dials the modem. For example, the Country setting determines the country code used for long-distance calls (this is 1 in the United States and Canada), and the Area Code setting lets Windows 95 determine whether the outgoing call is long distance.

You can change these and other dialing parameters by clicking the Dialing Properties button in the Modems Properties dialog box. Figure 25.8 shows the dialog box that appears.

FIGURE 25.8.

Use this dialog box to adjust the settings that Windows 95 uses to dial your modem.

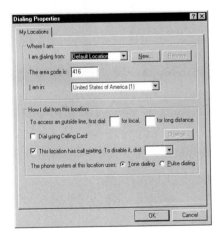

The controls in the Where I am group tell Windows 95 about your current location, and the How I dial from this location group specifies a few extra dialing parameters, such as accessing an outside line, using a calling card, and disabling call waiting.

CAUTION: ALWAYS DISABLE CALL WAITING

The extra beeps that call waiting uses to indicate an incoming call can wreak havoc on modem communications, so you should always disable call waiting before initiating a data call. The sequences *70, 70#, or 1170 usually disable call waiting, but you should check with your local phone company to make sure.

Specifying a Calling Card or Long-Distance Carrier

Although most of your phone calls are likely to be free, at times this might not be the case, and you'll want to make some other arrangements for charging the call. Two situations, in particular, might crop up from time to time:

- You're dialing from a hotel and want to charge the call to your calling card.

- You need to make a long-distance connection, in which case you might want to first dial the number of a long-distance carrier.

Windows 95 can handle both situations. To specify either a calling card number or a long-distance carrier phone number, activate the Dial using Calling Card check box. Windows 95 displays the Change Calling Card dialog box, shown in Figure 25.9. (If you've activated the Dial using Calling Card check box before, you can display the Change Calling Card dialog box by clicking the Change button instead.) Use the Calling Card to use list to choose the type of calling card you have, and then enter the number in the Calling Card number text box. For a long-distance carrier, select an item from the Calling Card to use list that has "Direct Dial" in the name.

FIGURE 25.9.

Use the Change Calling Card dialog box to enter a calling card number or select a long-distance carrier.

25

MAXIMIZING MODEM COMMUNICATIONS

If your calling card or long-distance carrier doesn't appear in the list, follow these steps to add it:

1. Click the New button to display the Create New Calling Card dialog box.

2. Enter a descriptive name for the calling card or carrier, and then click OK.

3. Click the Advanced button. The Dialing Rules dialog box, shown in Figure 25.10, is displayed. The dialing rules are codes that tell Windows 95 how to dial the phone to complete a calling card or long-distance carrier connection.

FIGURE 25.10.

Use the Dialing Rules dialog box to specify how Windows 95 dials a number with your new calling card or long-distance carrier.

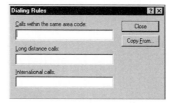

4. Fill in the three text boxes to define the rules Windows 95 should use for local calls, long-distance calls, and international calls. Table 25.3 lists the various symbols you can use to construct these rules.

TIP: COPY SIMILAR DIALING RULES

If you want to use dialing rules that are the same as or similar to one of the existing calling card entries, click the Copy From button, use the Copy Dialing Rules dialog box to highlight the calling card entry you want to use, and click OK.

---

5. Click OK to return to the Change Calling Card dialog box.

6. If you used the H (calling card number) symbol, the Calling Card number text box is enabled. Enter your calling card number in this box.

7. Click OK.

Table 25.3. Symbols to use when constructing dialing rules.

Symbol	Description
E	Dials the country code.
F	Dials the area code.
G	Dials the local number.
H	Dials the calling card number.
P	Switches to pulse dialing.

Symbol	Description
T	Switches to tone dialing.
W	Waits for a second dial tone.
0 through 9	Dials the digits as entered.
,	Pauses for two seconds.
!	Hook flash (½ second on-hook, ½ second off-hook).
@	Waits for a ringing tone followed by five seconds of silence.
$	Waits for a calling card prompt tone.
?	Displays an on-screen prompt so that you can continue dialing manually.

For example, consider the rule 8,0FG$TH. This rule dials 8 for an outside line, pauses for two seconds (,), dials 0 followed by the area code (F) and local number (G), waits for the calling card tone ($), switches to tone dialing (T), and sends your calling card number (H).

NOTE: DIALING RULES ARE A VERSATILE TOOL

Dialing rules are a great way to relieve the tedium of entering endless numbers when using a calling card or long-distance carrier. You don't need to restrict your use of dialing rules to just these contexts, however. Feel free to set up dialing rules for any special dialing situation you might need. For example, later in this chapter I'll show you how to use dialing rules to get the Phone Dialer accessory to successfully dial 10-digit phone numbers (see "Dialing 10-Digit Numbers" later in this chapter).

Working with Different Dialing Locations

If you have a notebook computer, you can set up multiple dialing locations. For example, you could have one location for dialing from the office that uses extra digits to access an outside line and uses your corporate calling card. You could then have a second location for home that doesn't require anything extra to access an outside line and disables your call waiting service.

CAUTION: WATCH FOR DIGITAL PHONE JACKS

If you travel with your notebook and use a modem to connect to the office or the Internet, watch out for the digital phone systems that are used by many hotels. Analog modems aren't compatible with digital systems, so you'll end up frying your modem if you attempt to connect over a digital line. Unfortunately, digital phone jacks look identical to regular analog jacks, so you'll need to ask the hotel staff what kind of phone jacks they use.

The location information you entered while installing your modem is stored in a location called Default Location. To set up another location, click New, enter a name in the Create New Location dialog box and click OK, and enter your dialing properties for the new location.

To choose a different location, use the I am dialing from drop-down list.

Modifying the Modem's General Properties

Your modem has all kinds of properties you can play with to alter how the device works and to troubleshoot problematic connections. To see these properties, highlight the modem in the Modem Properties dialog box, and then click the Properties button. Figure 25.11 shows the properties sheet that appears. The General tab offers the following controls:

Port: Use this drop-down list to specify the serial port you're using for the modem.

Speaker volume: This slider determines how loud your modem sounds (although not all modems support this feature). Because modems can make quite a racket, you might consider setting the volume low or even off while using it in public or in a quiet office. If adjusting this slider to its lowest setting still doesn't turn off your modem's sounds, check out the section "The Advanced Button" later in this chapter. The Advanced Connection Settings dialog box has an Extra settings text box in which you can enter the ATM0 command, which mutes the modem.

Maximum speed: This setting determines the maximum throughput (in bps) that the modem can handle. This speed depends on the modulation protocol, data compression used, and a few other factors. Later, I'll show you a test you can run to determine the maximum speed for your modem (see "Testing the Modem" later in this chapter). Your modem won't necessarily use this speed. Instead, it will determine the optimum speed based on the remote system and the line conditions. If, however, you prefer that your modem connect only at this speed, activate the Only connect at this speed check box (this feature isn't supported by all modems).

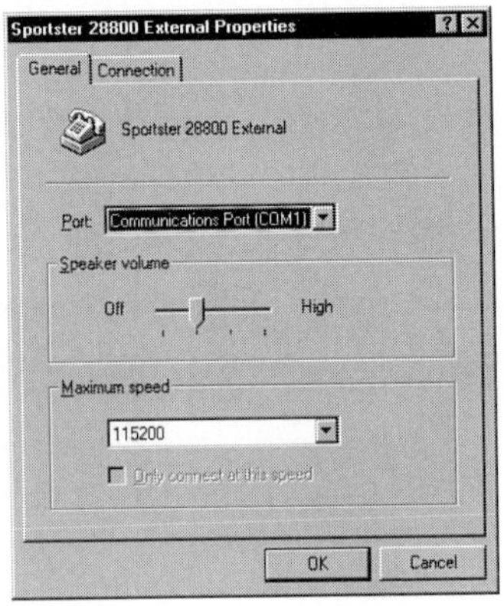

Figure 25.11.

Use the General tab to control the modem's port, speaker volume, and maximum speed.

TROUBLESHOOTING: ADJUST THE SPEED TO YOUR UART

If you're having trouble connecting and the serial port doesn't use a 16550 UART, be sure to set the `Maximum speed` value to no more than 9600.

Modifying the Modem's Connection Settings

The Connection tab, shown in Figure 25.12, contains several controls that determine the modem's default behavior for connecting to remote systems. Here's a rundown of the various options:

Connection preferences: These drop-down lists determine the default values you want to use for `Data bits`, `Parity`, and `Stop bits`. Note that these settings override any values you entered for the modem's serial port.

Wait for dial tone before dialing: When this check box is activated, the modem won't dial unless it can detect a dial tone, which is usually what you want. If, however, your modem doesn't seem to recognize the dial tone in your current location (if you're in a different country, for example), or if you need to dial manually, deactivate this check box.

Cancel the call if not connected within x secs: When this option is activated, it determines how long Windows 95 waits for a connection between your modem and a remote system to be established. If no connection is made within the allotted time, Windows 95 cancels the call.

Disconnect a call if idle for more than x mins: This option, when activated, determines how long Windows 95 waits for the modem to be idle before it disconnects the call. If you regularly go long intervals without modem activity, you can ignore this option. This option is invaluable, however, if you forget that you're connected or if you want to run a long file download unattended.

The next two sections explain the Port Settings and Advanced buttons.

FIGURE 25.12.

Use the Connection tab to set up the modem's default settings for connecting to remote computers.

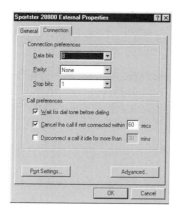

The Port Settings Button

Clicking the Port Settings button displays the Advanced Port Settings dialog box, shown in Figure 25.13. The options in this dialog box control the FIFO buffers in the serial port's UART chip (described earlier in this chapter). The two sliders determine the level at which the UART generates interrupts for the receive and transmit buffers.

Figure 25.13.

The Advanced Port Settings dialog box lets you customize the FIFO buffers for a 16550 UART.

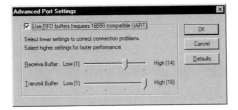

Fewer interrupts means better performance overall. For example, if you move the Transmit Buffer slider to High (16) (that is, all the way to the right), the UART won't generate an interrupt until all 16 buffers are full. Conversely, if you set the slider to Low (1), the UART generates an interrupt each time a buffer is filled. If you're having communications problems (such as dropped characters), however, a lack of interrupts might be the problem. In this case, you should move the sliders to the left to generate more interrupts.

The Advanced Button

Clicking the Advanced button displays the Advanced Connection Settings dialog box, shown in Figure 25.14. This dialog box sets up the various modem protocols, including error correction, compression, flow control, and modulation. Here's the summary:

Use error control: Activate this check box to enable the modem's built-in error-checking protocol (such as V.42 or MNP 4). Note that you must activate this option to use the three other check boxes in this group.

Required to connect: If you activate this check box, the modem uses its error-checking routine to establish a connection. If a reliable connection can't be established, the connection attempt is terminated.

Compress data: Activate this option to enable the modem's built-in data compression protocol (such as V.42bis or MNP 5). As explained earlier, you can use compression for text and binary files, but you should disable it for compressed file transfers.

Use cellular protocol: Activate this option to enable the cellular error-correction protocol. This is a feature in high-speed PC Card modems that you should use if you plan to initiate a connection via a cellular phone. This protocol helps reduce errors as the connection is transferred between cells.

Use flow control: Activate this check box to enable flow control. Select either Hardware (RTS/CTS) or Software (XON/OFF).

Modulation type: This drop-down list determines the type of modulation to use with the modem. The Standard option means the modem uses its default ITU-TSS modulation protocol. The Non-standard option usually implements whatever proprietary modulation is supported by the modem.

Extra settings: Use this text box to enter extra dialing strings to customize the modem's setup. See your modem's manual to determine the string formats to use.

Record a log file: If you activate this check box, Windows 95 creates a file named MODEMLOG.TXT in your main Windows 95 folder. The system monitors the call and uses the log to keep track of connection events, status messages, and other items that might be useful during troubleshooting.

TIP: MODEM ACTIVITY IN SYSTEM MONITOR

Enabling the Record a log file check box also gives you a bonus benefit: the ability to track modem data via the System Monitor. With the check box activated, start any 32-bit communications program (such as Windows 95's HyperTerminal) and establish a connection. Now select Start | Programs | Accessories | System Tools | System Monitor. When you select System Monitor's Edit | Add Item command, you'll notice a new category for your modem. This category contains two items: Bytes received/sec and Bytes sent/sec.

FIGURE 25.14.

The Advanced Connection Settings dialog box lets you specify error control, flow control, modulation, and other connection-related options.

TROUBLESHOOTING: THE U.S. ROBOTICS MODEM HANGS

If you have a U.S. Robotics Sportster modem (or a model based on the Sportster, such as the Gateway TelePath), you might have experienced frequent problems with the modem's hanging during a connection. If so, you probably can fix this problem by adding the string S12=0 to the Extra settings text box.

25

MAXIMIZING MODEM COMMUNICATIONS

Testing the Modem

After you've configured your modem, you'll want to test it to make sure that things are working correctly. To do this, return to the Modems Properties dialog box, and then select the Diagnostics tab. Highlight the port where your modem is attached, make sure that the modem is powered up, and click the More Info button.

If there's a problem with your modem, a dialog box lets you know. Otherwise, after a minute or two, you'll see a dialog box similar to the one shown in Figure 25.15. This dialog box tells you, among other things, the maximum speed for your modem, the UART (this saves you from using MSD to check out your serial ports), and numerous internal settings.

FIGURE 25.15.

The More Info button displays a heaping helping of modem info.

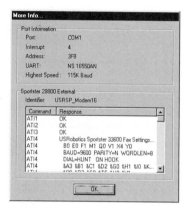

Getting Your Modem to Dial Voice Calls for You

If you don't have a speed-dial phone on your desk, Windows 95 can provide you with the next best thing: Phone Dialer. This is a simple telephony application that accepts a phone number and then uses your modem to dial the number for you automatically.

To take advantage of Phone Dialer, you need to make the following arrangements with your phone cables:

- Run one phone cable from your phone to the "Phone" jack on your modem.
- Run a second phone cable from your modem's "Line" jack to the phone jack on your wall.

When that's done, you can get into Phone Dialer by selecting Start | Programs | Accessories | Phone Dialer. You'll see the Phone Dialer window, shown in Figure 25.16.

FIGURE 25.16.

Phone Dialer is only too happy to use your modem to dial voice calls for you.

As you can see, Phone Dialer is set up to look more or less like a telephone keypad. To dial a number, you type it in the `Number to dial` text box (you can also use the mouse to click the appropriate numbers in the keypad) and then click the Dial button. After a couple of seconds, you'll hear the number being dialed through your modem's speaker. Pick up the receiver and, after the modem has completed dialing, click the Talk button in the dialog box that appears. If you want Windows 95 to keep a log of the call (who you called and for how long), type the person's name in the dialog box that remains on-screen. When the call is done, click the Hang Up button.

TIP: CHANGE DIALING PROPERTIES ON-THE-FLY

The Phone Dialer uses the dialing properties you established earlier for your modem. If you want to change the properties (to use a calling card, for example), you can access the Dialing Properties dialog box from within Phone Dialer (see "Phone Dialer's Dialing Properties" later in this chapter). You can also change properties in "mid-dial," so to speak. When you click the Dial button, a Dialing dialog box appears for a couple of seconds before the dialing begins. If you click the Change Options button, Phone Dialer displays the Change Options and Redial dialog box. From there, you can click the Dialing Properties button to change the properties and then click Redial to continue with the call.

NOTE: DISPLAYING THE CALL LOG

If you enter the call into the log, you can view the log later by selecting Phone Dialer's Tools | Show Log command. If you want to redial a number that's listed in the log, just double-click it.

If you want to dial the same number again later, just open the drop-down list next to the Number to dial box, and select the number. No retyping is needed.

Phone Dialer's Connection Properties

Phone Dialer has a few options you can use to configure your phone dialing. For example, if you have multiple modems or multiple lines on your phone, you can tell Phone Dialer which ones to use.

To work with these options, select Tools | Connect Using to display the Connect Using dialog box, shown in Figure 25.17. Here are your options:

Line: Use this drop-down list to select the modem you want Phone Dialer to use. If you need to make changes to the modem setup, click the Line Properties button to display the modem's properties sheet.

Address: Use this drop-down list to select the phone line you want Phone Dialer to use.

Use Phone Dialer to handle voice call requests from other programs: If you activate this check box, other programs that initiate voice calls (such as the Schedule+ program that comes with Microsoft Office 95) will use Phone Dialer.

FIGURE 25.17.

Use this dialog box to select the modem or phone line to use with Phone Dialer.

Phone Dialer's Dialing Properties

Phone Dialer also works with the dialing properties I showed you earlier in this chapter. This is convenient because it lets you specify calling card numbers, long-distance carrier numbers, and other dialing options, which saves you from having to enter the information manually for each voice call. If you need to make changes to the dialing properties, you can do it right from Phone Dialer by selecting Tools | Dialing Properties.

Dialing 10-Digit Numbers

In some larger cities, the phone company has run out of phone numbers in the main area code. To overcome this problem, the phone company usually splits off part of the existing customers into a new area code and requires that calls between the two areas be prefaced with the appropriate area code. These aren't long-distance calls, however, so no country code is required.

For example, suppose that a city uses the area code 123 and has some customers split off into a 456 area code. To call from the 123 area code to the number 555-1212 in the 456 area code, you would dial the following number:

456-555-1212

Phone Dialer, however, has a problem with these 10-digit phone numbers: It assumes that a 10-digit number is meant for a long-distance call, so it automatically appends the country code to the beginning of the number. Entering the preceding number into Phone Dialer normally causes it to dial this number:

1-456-555-1212

This situation is demonstrated in Figure 25.18. Notice that Phone Dialer shows the 10-digit number in the Number to dial text box, but the Dialing Properties dialog box shows the 11-digit long-distance number in the Number to be dialed area at the bottom of the dialog box.

FIGURE 25.18.

Phone Dialer automatically appends the country code to 10-digit numbers.

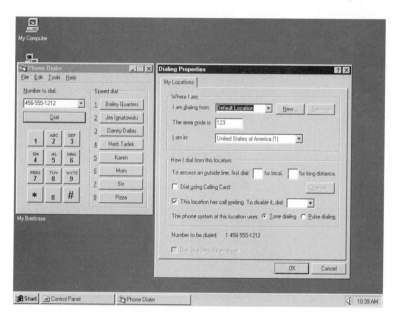

The call won't go through properly. To prevent this problem, you need to set up dialing rules that tell Phone Dialer to leave off the country code. Here are the steps to follow:

1. Select Tools | Dialing Properties to display the Dialing Properties dialog box.

2. Click New, enter a name for the new dialing location (such as To 456 Area Code), and click OK. (Technically, you're not really creating a new location per se. Instead, you're setting up a new "destination," but it works just the same.)

3. Activate the `Dial using Calling Card` check box (or click Change) to display the Change Calling Card dialog box.

4. Click New, enter a name (such as `456 Area Code`), and click OK.

5. Click Advanced and enter the following dialing rules (feel free to embellish these rules with other options, if needed):

Calls within the same area code	`G`
Long-distance calls	`FG`
International calls	`011EFG`

6. Click Close to return to the Change Calling Card dialog box.

7. Click OK.

The key here is that you specified the code `FG` for the long-distance dialing rule. This tells Phone Dialer to use only the area code (`F`) and the local number (`G`) when using this dialing location. As you can see in Figure 25.19, Phone Dialer leaves off the country code, so your 10-digit calls will go through properly.

FIGURE 25.19.

With the new long-distance dialing rule in effect, Phone Dialer leaves off the country code for 10-digit numbers.

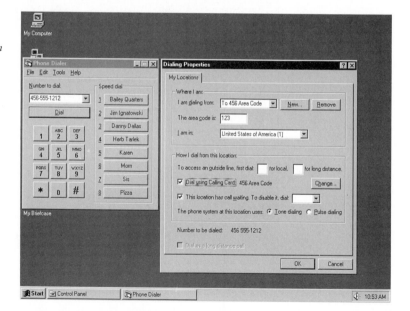

Quick Connections with Speed Dial

Phone Dialer is certainly handy, but it becomes downright useful when you take advantage of the speed dialing feature. The eight buttons arranged down the right side in the `Speed dial` group can all be programmed with frequently called numbers. You just click a programmed button, and Phone Dialer dials the number for you automatically.

Programming a Speed Dial Button

To program a speed dial button, click it to display the Program Speed Dial dialog box, shown in Figure 25.20. Use the Name text box to enter the name you want associated with the number, and use the Number to dial text box to enter the number itself. Then click the Save button to save the info, or click Save and Dial to save it and dial the number right away.

FIGURE 25.20.

Use this dialog box to program the selected speed dial button.

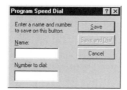

Editing Speed Dial Entries

If you want to change the name or number associated with one of the speed dial buttons, you can't just click it, because that action dials the number. Instead, select Edit | Speed Dial. In the Edit Speed Dial dialog box, shown in Figure 25.21, click the button you want to change, and then use the Name and Number to dial text boxes to edit the information. Click Save when you're done.

FIGURE 25.21.

Use the Edit Speed Dial dialog box to modify your programmed speed dial entries.

Using HyperTerminal for Modem-to-Modem Connections

The Phone Dialer is a handy tool, but it's almost certainly not why you bought your modem. Instead, your modem's true *raison dêtre* is to connect to other modems and thus propel you into the world of online services and bulletin board systems (BBSs). To do this, you need a communications program (or *terminal* program) that can operate your modem and handle the behind-the-scenes dirty work of dialing, connecting, downloading, and uploading.

In Windows 3.x, modem communications were handled by the Terminal accessory, a homely, Spartan program that proved to be merely adequate in everything it did. Few people liked Terminal, and even fewer actually used it, but the Windows 95 replacement—a program called HyperTerminal—should please all but the most discriminating modem jockeys. HyperTerminal is a slick, 32-bit application that integrates seamlessly with Windows 95's communications subsystem. It offers numerous improvements over Terminal, including an attractive interface, greater terminal emulation options, and support for most popular file transfer protocols, such as 1K Xmodem and Zmodem. The next few sections show you how to use HyperTerminal to set up, dial, and work with online connections.

NOTE: HYPERTERMINAL AND THE INTERNET

Although I'm assuming here that you'll be using HyperTerminal to connect to big online services such as CompuServe and America Online, or to BBSs, you can also use it to connect to your Internet service provider if you have a dial-up account. If you have a PPP or SLIP account, however, you'll need to use Windows 95's Dial-Up Networking accessory, which I discuss in Chapter 35, "Remote Computing with Dial-Up Networking."

Opening the `HyperTerminal` Folder

To get HyperTerminal happening, first select Start | Programs | Accessories | HyperTerminal. The HyperTerminal window, shown in Figure 25.22, appears. Note that this isn't the HyperTerminal program, but just the `HyperTerminal` folder, which is a subfolder of `\Program Files\Accessories`. This folder contains at least four icons. (You might see more icons if you have the `Show all files` option activated. To deactivate this option, select View | Options and select the View tab in the Options dialog box.) The Hypertrm icon leads you to the HyperTerminal program; the other icons represent predefined connections for AT&T Mail, CompuServe, and MCI Mail. In HyperTerminal, a *connection* is a file that defines how to connect to a remote system: the phone number, the communications settings to use, and so on. Other connections that you create will also appear as icons in this folder.

FIGURE 25.22.

Selecting the HyperTerminal command displays the `HyperTerminal` *folder.*

Creating a New HyperTerminal Connection

To create a new connection, you first need to start HyperTerminal. Then you set up the connection in three stages: defining the basic connection options, defining the connection's settings, and specifying the connection's modem properties.

Phase I: Defining the Basic Connection Options

Here are the steps to follow to get the basic connection options in place:

1. In the `HyperTerminal` folder, open the Hypertrm icon. HyperTerminal displays the Connection Description dialog box, shown in Figure 25.23.

FIGURE 25.23.

Use this dialog box to name your new connection and choose an icon.

2. Use the `Name` text box to enter a descriptive name for the connection. Note that this entry will also serve as the primary name of the new HyperTerminal file (with an HT extension), so you should follow Windows 95's rules for long filenames.

3. Use the `Icon` list to highlight an icon for the connection, and then click OK. The Phone Number dialog box, shown in Figure 25.24, appears.

FIGURE 25.24.

Use the Phone Number dialog box to supply HyperTerminal with the dialing details for your connection.

4. Fill in the Country code, Area code, and Phone number for the remote system.

TIP: EASIER 10-DIGIT PHONE NUMBERS

Earlier in this chapter, I showed you how to use dialing rules to force Phone Dialer to dial a 10-digit phone number without the country code. You can use the same technique with HyperTerminal, but an easier way is also available: Leave the Area code field blank (or just enter your own area code) and enter the entire 10-digit number in the Phone number field.

---

5. In the Connect using drop-down list, choose the modem you want to use for the connection. Alternatively, you can use HyperTerminal to connect to a PC via a serial cable that runs between the two machines' serial ports. In this case, choose the appropriate serial port (for example, Direct to Com 1).

6. Click OK. HyperTerminal displays the Connect dialog box, shown in Figure 25.25.

FIGURE 25.25.

You can use this dialog box to establish the connection or modify the dialing properties.

At this point, the connection is set up to use the default settings you defined for your modem. If you want to use those settings, you can either click Dial to connect to the remote system or click Cancel to get to the main HyperTerminal window. I suggest clicking Cancel, because then you can save the connection (by selecting File | Save). See "Connecting to a Remote System" later in this chapter to learn how to connect from the HyperTerminal window.

Phase II: Defining the Connection's Modem Properties

If you don't want to use the default modem settings, HyperTerminal lets you define alternative settings for the connection.

If you want to change the dialing properties for the connection, click the Dialing Properties button in the Connect dialog box. (If you canceled the Connect dialog box earlier, you can display it again by selecting Call | Connect.)

To change other settings (such as the connect speed and the terminal emulation), first display the properties sheet for the connection by using either of the following methods:

- In the HyperTerminal window, select File | Properties.
- In the Connect dialog box, click Modify.

Figure 25.26 shows the properties sheet that appears. The Phone Number tab lets you change the basic options (icon, country code, area code, and so on). For modem-related settings, click the Configure button to display the modem's properties sheet. This dialog box offers the same settings you saw earlier in this chapter, except that a new tab named Options has been added, as shown in Figure 25.27. Here's the skinny on the controls that populate this tab:

Bring up terminal window before dialing: When this check box is activated, each time you connect to the remote system, HyperTerminal displays the Pre-Dial Terminal Screen before it dials the modem. You can use this screen to enter modem commands (see your modem manual for a list of applicable commands). You enter your commands and then click the window's Continue button.

Bring up terminal window after dialing: When this check box is activated, Hyper-Terminal displays the Post-Dial Terminal Screen after it connects to the remote system. Again, you can use this screen to enter modem commands.

Operator assisted or manual dial: When this option is activated, each time you connect to the remote system, HyperTerminal displays a dialog box to prompt you to dial the phone number manually. This option is useful in hotels or in other situations when you might need to speak to an operator before you can dial. When you hear the remote modem, click the Connect button in the dialog box, and then hang up the receiver.

Wait for credit card tone x seconds: This spinner specifies how many seconds HyperTerminal should wait for a credit card tone before it continues dialing.

Display modem status: When this check box is activated, HyperTerminal displays a modem icon in the taskbar's system tray (more on this later).

FIGURE 25.26.

The properties sheet for a connection.

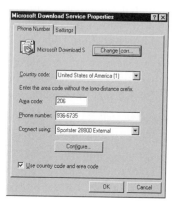

Figure 25.27.

For a connection, the modem properties sheet sprouts a new Options tab.

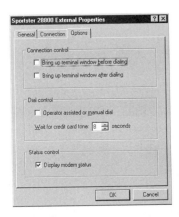

Phase III: Defining the Connection's Settings

To finish defining the connection, HyperTerminal has a few other options up its electronic sleeve. To view these options, display the connection's properties sheet, and select the Settings tab, shown in Figure 25.28. Here's the rundown:

Function, arrow, and ctrl keys act as: These options determine how HyperTerminal reacts when you press any of the function keys, arrow keys, or Ctrl key combinations. If you activate the Terminal keys option, HyperTerminal sends the keystrokes to the remote modem; if you activate Windows keys, HyperTerminal applies the keystrokes to the Windows 95 interface.

Emulation: Use this drop-down list to choose the terminal emulation you want to use with the remote system. The Auto detect option tells HyperTerminal to attempt to determine the remote terminal type automatically. If you choose one of the specific terminal emulations, you can also click the Terminal Setup button to configure various aspects of the emulation. (The available options depend on the emulation.)

Backscroll buffer lines: This setting determines the number of lines displayed by the remote system that HyperTerminal stores in its buffer. You can scroll up or down through this buffer by using the scrollbars or the Page Up and Page Down keys.

Beep three times when connecting or disconnecting: This check box determines whether HyperTerminal beeps the speaker whenever it connects and disconnects.

ASCII Setup: Clicking this button displays the ASCII Setup dialog box, shown in Figure 25.29. These controls set various options for ASCII text you send to the remote system, as well as ASCII text you receive.

FIGURE 25.28.

Use the Settings tab to define terminal emulation and a few other options for the connection.

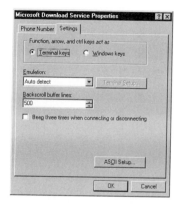

FIGURE 25.29.

Use this dialog box to set various options for incoming and outgoing ASCII text.

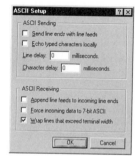

Connecting to a Remote System

After you have your connection set up to your liking, you're ready to dial in. HyperTerminal gives you a couple of methods of establishing a connection with the remote system:

- In the HyperTerminal folder, highlight the icon and select File | Connect, double-click the icon, or right-click the icon and select Connect from the context menu.

- In the HyperTerminal program, select File | Open and use the dialog box that appears to open the connection; then either select Call | Connect or click the Connect toolbar button, shown in Figure 25.30.

In either case, you then click the Dial button in the Connect dialog box that appears. HyperTerminal dials the modem and connects with the remote system. Text from the remote computer appears in the HyperTerminal window, as shown in Figure 25.30. The status bar tells you the length of time you've been connected, as well as indicating various connection settings. Note too that Windows 95 displays a modem icon in the taskbar's system tray after you're connected. Double-clicking this icon displays a dialog box like the one shown in Figure 25.31.

FIGURE 25.30.

*HyperTerminal
connected to a remote
system.*

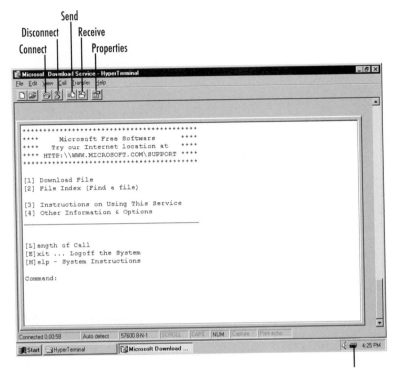

This icon appears
while you're connected

FIGURE 25.31.

*Double-clicking the
modem icon in the
taskbar displays this
dialog box.*

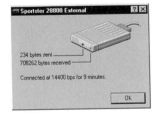

Performing File Transfers

If the remote system has a file you want to download, HyperTerminal makes it easy. After you've told the online service the name of the file you want to receive or send and the protocol to use, the service says something like `Ready to send/receive file. Please initiate file transfer.` At this point, you tell HyperTerminal that a file transfer is about to take place by using one of the following techniques:

- For a download, either select Transfer | Receive File or click the Receive button in the toolbar.

- For an upload, either select Transfer | Send File or click the Send button in the toolbar.

- For a text file upload, select Transfer | Send Text File.

(Note that, in some cases, HyperTerminal selects the appropriate command for you automatically.)

If you're downloading, the Receive File dialog box, shown in Figure 25.32, appears. In the `Place received file in the following folder` text box, enter the name of the folder in which you want to store the file. If you're not sure of the folder's name, click the Browse button, choose a folder in the Select a Folder dialog box that appears, and click OK to return to the Receive File dialog box. To select a protocol, drop down the `Use receiving protocol` list, and choose the same protocol you selected in the remote system. When you're ready, click the Receive button to proceed with the transfer.

FIGURE 25.32.

Use the Receive File dialog box to select a folder in which to store the file and a protocol.

If you're uploading, either the Send File dialog box or the Send Text File dialog box appears. Select the file to send, use the `Protocol` drop-down list to choose the same protocol you selected in the remote system, and click Send to make it so.

Whether you're sending or receiving, HyperTerminal displays the progress of the transfer in a dialog box similar to the one shown in Figure 25.33. If, for any reason, you need to abort the transfer before it's complete, you can click the Cancel button. You can also select `Skip file` to bypass the current file in a multifile transfer. (The `cps/bps` button toggles the value in the `Throughput` box between characters per second and bits per second.)

FIGURE 25.33.

After you start a file transfer, HyperTerminal displays a dialog box like this one to let you know how the transfer is proceeding.

When the transfer is complete, HyperTerminal returns control to the service, and you can continue with other service options or log off.

Disconnecting from the Remote System

When you've finished working with the remote system, disconnecting is as easy as selecting Call | Disconnect or clicking the toolbar's Disconnect button.

Connecting to Another Computer

Besides the usual online services and BBS computers, you can also use HyperTerminal to connect to another PC and then chat with the remote user or send files back and forth. All that's required is that both computers be running HyperTerminal or some other terminal program, and that one of the modems be set up to answer incoming calls.

To set up HyperTerminal for a PC-to-PC connection, follow these steps:

1. Create a new HyperTerminal connection, following these instructions:

   ■ If your computer is doing the dialing, enter the phone number of the remote PC.

   ■ If your computer is doing the answering, the phone number doesn't matter, but because HyperTerminal requires one anyway, you can just enter a bogus number.

   ■ Make sure that both computers are set up with the same connection settings (speed, data bits, emulation, and so on).

   ■ When HyperTerminal prompts you to dial, click Cancel.

2. Select File | Properties to display the properties sheet for the connection, and select the Settings tab.

3. Click the ASCII Setup button to display the ASCII Setup dialog box.

4. Activate the following check boxes:

   `Send line ends with line feeds`

   `Echo typed characters locally`

   `Append line feeds to incoming line ends`

   `Wrap lines that exceed terminal width`

5. Click OK to return to the properties sheet.

6. Click OK.

To make the connection, one computer dials and the other waits for the incoming call. When you see the ring indicator on the modem or hear the phone ring, type your modem's answer command and press Enter. You'll need to check your modem manual for the correct command, but on most modems you use either ATA or just A. (You can avoid this step if your modem supports automatic answering. If it does, check your manual to see how to set it up.)

After the connection has been established, you can send messages back and forth by typing on-screen and pressing Enter after each line. File transfers work just as I described earlier.

Entering AT Commands in HyperTerminal

If you're familiar with the AT command set, you might need to send a command or two to your modem. If so, here are the steps to follow to send commands via HyperTerminal:

1. Start HyperTerminal.

2. Enter a name for the connection (for example, AT Commands), select an icon, and click OK.

3. In the Phone Number dialog box, use the Connect using drop-down list to choose Direct to Com x, where x is the port number to which your modem is attached, and then click OK.

4. When the port properties sheet appears, click OK. The HyperTerminal window appears.

5. Select File | Properties, activate the Settings tab, and click ASCII Setup.

6. In the ASCII Setup dialog box, activate both the Send line ends with line feeds check box and the Echo typed characters locally check box, and click OK.

7. Click OK to return to HyperTerminal.

You can now enter AT commands in the terminal window. Don't forget to save your connection so that you can reuse it at any time.

Summary

This chapter showed you how to maximize modem communications in Windows 95. I began with an in-depth look at how modems do their thing, from modulation and demodulation through serial ports and modem-to-modem communications. I then showed you how to install and configure a modem in Windows 95. With all that out of the way, you then learned how to use two of Windows 95's communications programs: Phone Dialer and HyperTerminal.

This chapter represents only the beginning of our look at Windows 95 communications. Here's what's in store in chapters to come:

■ Looking for a place to point your modem? How about The Microsoft Network? I'll show you how to sign up, dial in, and look around in Chapter 26, "Getting Online with The Microsoft Network."

■ If you want to use Windows 95 to exchange e-mail between friends and colleagues, Microsoft Exchange is where you ought to be. I demonstrate how to configure it in

25

MAXIMIZING MODEM COMMUNICATIONS

Chapter 27, "Setting Up Microsoft Exchange," and I explain how to make good use of it in Chapter 28, "Exchanging E-Mail with Microsoft Exchange."

■ If you have a fax/modem, Microsoft Exchange is also useful for sending and receiving faxes. You'll see you how it's done in Chapter 29, "Using Microsoft Fax to Send and Receive Faxes."

■ If you're on the road, Windows 95's Dial-Up Networking feature lets you connect to your network. I provide all the particulars in Chapter 35, "Remote Computing with Dial-Up Networking."

■ These days, the Internet is where the action is in communications. If you want to see what all the fuss is about, head for Chapter 37, "Windows 95 and the Internet."

CHAPTER 26

Getting Online with The Microsoft Network

IN THIS CHAPTER

August 1, 1995—Is MSN really an awesome dreadnought from the Redmond Machine aimed at sinking all the other on-line services?

From a pre-launch review of MSN

February 6, 1996—America Online, Inc. announced today that it has passed the 5 million member mark, representing a tenfold increase in just two years.

America Online press release

When Microsoft first announced that it would be bundling the software for a new online service with Windows 95, and even placing an icon for it right on the desktop, howls of outrage could be heard from coast to coast. Pundits, politicians, and proprietors of existing online services spelled out one doomsday scenario after another to anyone who would listen. The Microsoft Network, they said, had an unfair advantage that would spell the death of competition in the online world, put long-established services such as CompuServe and America Online out to pasture, and generally undermine the well-being of Western civilization.

That's not exactly what happened. America Online has been struggling lately, but it has nothing to do with the Microsoft Network. Instead, AOL is a victim of its own success. It just grew too quickly and tried to offer its subscribers more than the AOL system could handle. CompuServe also is having troubles, but again, the culprit isn't MSN. In CompuServe's case, many long-time subscribers flocked to the more interesting and varied subject matter found on the Internet. CompuServe didn't adapt quickly enough (the way MSN did when the Internet's success became inevitable), and currently things don't look good for CIS.

In any case, you can't argue with the Microsoft Network's impressive debut: It passed the one million subscriber mark in a little over six months and continues to grow. This chapter shows you what all the fuss is about. You'll find out what The Microsoft Network (MSN) has to offer, how much this privilege will set you back, and how to sign up. I'll then show you how to connect to the service, navigate its interface, and explore its numerous nooks and crannies.

Getting Started with MSN

Before getting down to the brass tacks of signing up and connecting to MSN, let's begin by checking out what the service has to offer and what kind of dent it will make in your pocketbook.

What Does MSN Offer?

One of the early criticisms of MSN was that it lacked content compared to CompuServe and America Online. That was certainly true at the beginning because, after all, MSN was a new service. As I write this, 18 months after MSN's official launch, things have improved considerably, but MSN still isn't in the same content league as, say, America Online.

This isn't to say that MSN is a barren wasteland—far from it. You can find plenty of things to see and do, and with more than a million members now on board, there's no shortage of activity. Just so you know what to expect, here's a summary of a few of the treasures you'll find in MSN's coffers:

Channels: Version 1.3 has a new On Stage area that presents "channels" of information and entertainment.

E-mail: Using Windows 95's Microsoft Exchange program, you can exchange e-mail notes with fellow MSN members or Internet subscribers.

Bulletin boards: These are public message areas where you can read notes other people have posted, and even add your own two cents worth to the discussion. They're similar to the Internet's Usenet newsgroups.

File libraries: Here you can select files (such as games, utilities, and updates of software you own) to download to your PC.

Chat rooms: The garrulous and the gossipy will love chat rooms because you can meet and talk live with other MSN types who have an interest in the topic at hand.

Auditoriums: These are giant chat rooms where you can go to "hear" a lecture from some famous or important person, who might accept typed questions from the "audience."

Online reference materials and tech support: MSN has a wide variety of info you can read, and many hardware and software companies provide technical support for their users.

Classified ads: Many areas maintain their own classifieds, where you can buy or sell anything related to the topic.

Internet access: With version 1.3 now available, MSN is more of an Internet site than an online service. Its content is now entirely Web-based, and it has links to Usenet newsgroups and other World Wide Web sites scattered throughout all of its areas.

Signing Up with MSN

If you think you want to give MSN a whirl, you can perform the entire sign-up procedure right from the Windows 95 desktop. To get started, either double-click the desktop's The Microsoft Network icon, or select Start | Programs | The Microsoft Network.

How you proceed from here depends on which version of the MSN client you have. The next section runs through the sign-up procedure for the original MSN client (the one found in the original version of Windows 95). If you have OSR2, see "The Sign-Up Procedure for the OSR2 MSN Client" later in this chapter.

The Sign-Up Procedure for the Original MSN Client

The first dialog box that appears, shown in Figure 26.1, contains introductory information about MSN. If you're already a member of MSN (for example, if you've set up Windows 95 on a different machine), be sure to activate the `Click here if you're already a member...` check box. This tells MSN to bypass the usual sign-up routine. When you're ready, click OK to continue.

FIGURE 26.1.

This dialog box appears the first time you run The Microsoft Network in Windows 95.

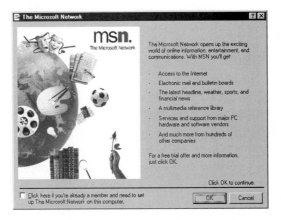

The next dialog box that appears, shown in Figure 26.2, asks for your area code and the first three digits of your phone number. MSN uses these values to determine the local access number closest to your location. Plug in the appropriate values, and click OK to continue.

FIGURE 26.2.

To figure out your local access number, MSN needs to know your area code and the first three digits of your phone number.

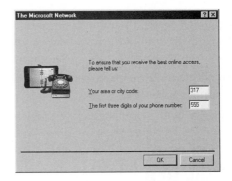

The Calling dialog box that shows up next lists a toll-free number that MSN will call to download the latest list of local access numbers. Make sure that your modem is attached and powered up. If you need to change any modem options, click the Settings button and make your selections from the Connection Settings dialog box. When you're ready to roll, click the Connect button. MSN dials your modem and connects to its central computer. The update takes a couple of minutes.

NOTE: THE 800 NUMBER IS FOR THE UNITED STATES ONLY

The 800 number that MSN uses for the initial connection is valid only in the United States. If you're connecting from Canada or any other non-U.S. country, here's how you choose a local access number manually:

1. In the Calling dialog box, click Settings.

2. In the Connection Settings dialog box, click Access Numbers.

3. Click the Change button beside the `Primary` text box.

4. Use the `Countries` list to highlight your country and the `State/region` list to highlight your state or province.

5. In the `Access numbers` list, highlight the number closest to your location, and then click OK.

6. Click OK until you're back to the Connect dialog box.

NOTE: LAN ACCESS TO MSN

The latest version of the MSN software lets you connect to MSN via TCP/IP and your local area network. You must, however, use your modem for the initial sign-up procedure.

When MSN has finished updating your system, you'll see the dialog box shown in Figure 26.3. This dialog box contains three icons you must select before you can join MSN.

Figure 26.3.

You must jump through three hoops before you can join MSN.

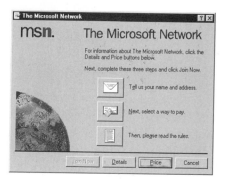

Here's a summary of what each step entails:

Tell us your name and address: Clicking this button displays the dialog box shown in Figure 26.4. Using the appropriate fields, enter your name, address, phone number, and so on. When you're done, click OK.

Next, select a way to pay: MSN, as I've said, isn't free, so you'll need to provide a credit card number so that you can be billed for the charges you accrue. Clicking this button displays the dialog box shown in Figure 26.5. Select the type of credit card you want to use, and then fill in the particulars (card number, expiration date, and so on) in the text boxes provided. Click OK to continue.

Then, please read the rules: Clicking this button displays a dialog box that spells out the Microsoft Network Membership Agreement. Read as much of the legalese as you can stomach, and then click the I Agree button.

FIGURE 26.4.

Use this dialog box to enter your personal information.

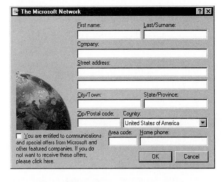

FIGURE 26.5.

Use this dialog box to enter your credit card info.

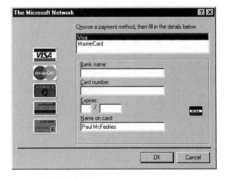

After you've completed these three steps, you'll see a check mark beside each of the options, and the Join Now button will become enabled. If you want to know more about what you're getting yourself into before going further, click the Details button or the Price button. In each case, read the data that's displayed, and click the Close button.

NOTE: THE LATEST AND GREATEST ABOUT MSN

The Details button gives you the latest information about The Microsoft Network. It also spells out whatever free offer MSN is providing for new members, so you should probably check it out to see what you're getting.

When you're finally ready to take the plunge, click Join Now. The dialog box that appears confirms the phone numbers MSN has selected for you. Click OK to move on. In the Calling dialog box that appears, click Connect to send your account information to MSN's central computer. After the connection is established, you'll see the dialog box shown in Figure 26.6.

You have to fill in two text boxes:

Member ID: This is the name that will identify you to others online, so you'll want to make up an ID that suits your style. Lots of people use their real names and/or initials, such as LBMelman, Larry_Bud_Melman, or LarryBudMelman. Other people go with something a little more daring, such as RebelYell, FemmeFatale, or ToGeekOrNotToGeek. You can't use spaces, but you can use any number or letter, a dash, or an underscore (_), up to a maximum of 64 characters. MSN lets you know if you choose a name that's already taken or one that contains illegal characters. Note that your member ID also forms the first part of your MSN e-mail address. For example, if your member ID is Biff, your e-mail address will be biff@msn.com.

Password: For a password, choose any combination of numbers or letters between 8 and 16 characters long. Note that the Password text box doesn't mask your password with asterisks, which is what any reasonable program should do. So bear in mind that any passersby will be able to read your password on-screen.

FIGURE 26.6.

Use this dialog box to specify a member ID and password.

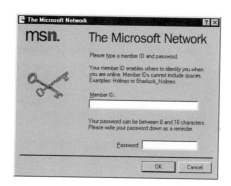

After you've entered your ID and password, click OK to complete the sign-up process. You might see a dialog box asking whether you want MSN with full Internet access—which includes Internet e-mail, Usenet newsgroups, the World Wide Web, FTP, Gopher, and more—or only the basic Internet services—e-mail and newsgroups. One last dialog box appears to let you know you're now a full-fledged member of MSN. Click Finish and Windows 95 takes you to the Sign In dialog box. This Sign In dialog box is what you'll see from now on when you start MSN.

NOTE: SIGNING UP A SECOND ACCOUNT

If you want to repeat the sign-up process to establish another account, you can do it by running the SIGNUP.EXE program. You'll find it in the \Program Files\The Microsoft Network folder.

NOTE: THE LATEST MSN SOFTWARE IS ON THE WAY

After you sign up with MSN, you'll receive a CD-ROM in the mail within 45 days. This disc contains the latest MSN software (version 1.3 as of this writing), which will give you access to all of MSN's new content.

The Sign-Up Procedure for the OSR2 MSN Client

OSR2

Windows 95 OSR2 comes with an updated version of MSN (version 1.3). This section takes you through the revised sign-up procedure that comes with this version of the MSN client.

When you launch MSN for the first time, you'll see the dialog box shown in Figure 26.7. You're given three choices:

Sign me up for MSN and a new Internet Connection: Choose this option if you want to create both an MSN account and an Internet connection. In this case, Windows 95 will first launch the Internet Connection Wizard. Using this Wizard to create a new Internet connection is described in Chapter 37, "Windows 95 and the Internet."

Sign me up for MSN but use my existing Internet Connection: Choose this option to create an MSN account and bypass the creation of an Internet connection.

I already have an MSN account: Choose this option to use your existing MSN account.

Click Next > after you've made your selection.

FIGURE 26.7.

The initial dialog box for the OSR2 MSN signup.

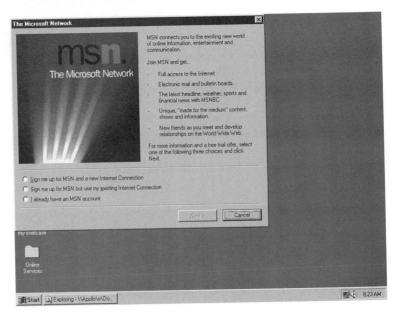

Once you're ready to create your MSN account, you'll see a dialog box with a Signup for MSN button. Click this button to launch Internet Explorer and display the MSN Signup Web page, shown in Figure 26.8. This Web page is part of the MSN Signup Wizard, which will take you through the process of creating an MSN account.

FIGURE 26.8.

MSN's Signup Web page.

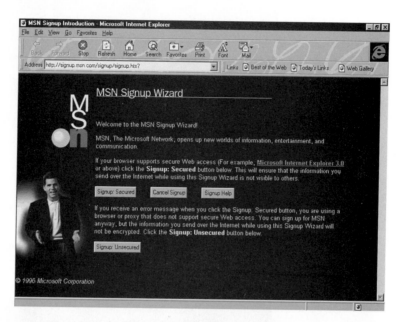

TIP: DIRECT ACCESS TO THE SIGNUP PAGE

You can head directly to the MSN Signup page by dialing the following address into your browser:

```
http://signup.msn.com/
```

From here, click the Signup: Secured button. (I'm assuming that you're using at least Internet Explorer 3.0; if not, click the Signup: Unsecured button instead.) The MSN Signup Wizard then asks which country you're in, as shown in Figure 26.9. Choose your country and then click Next.

U.S. users will then see the Price Plan Selector page, shown in Figure 26.10. Here, you must choose whether you want to use MSN to access the Internet (see Chapter 37), use your existing Internet access provider, or use an ISDN adapter. Make your choice and click Next.

FIGURE 26.9.

The MSN Signup Wizard needs to know what country you hail from.

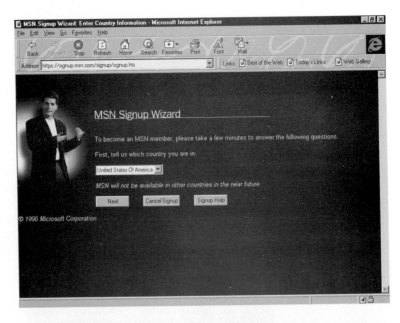

FIGURE 26.9.

The MSN Signup Wizard needs to know what country you hail from.

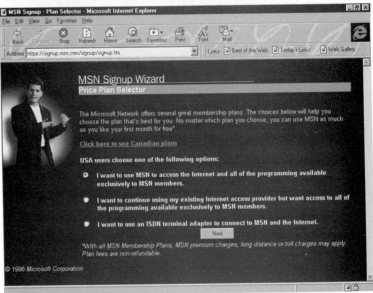

FIGURE 26.10.

U.S. users see the Price Plan Selector page.

If you chose to use your existing Internet service provider, the Wizard will then ask whether you want a monthly plan or an annual plan, as shown in Figure 26.11. Once again, make your choice and click Next.

FIGURE 26.11.

You can pay monthly or annually for your MSN account.

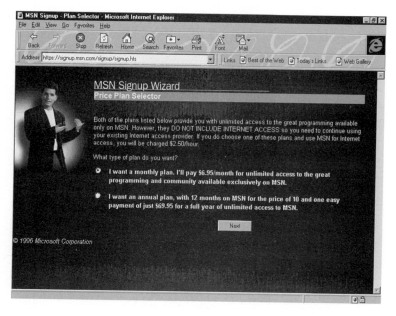

The MSN Signup Wizard then takes you on a five-step procedure for creating your account:

Step 1: In the first step, the Wizard asks for some basic personal information, as shown in Figure 26.12. Fill in all the fields and click Next.

Step 2: The next Web page presents you with a list of all the MSN membership plans. Make sure the plan you want is selected, and then click Next.

Step 3: In this step, the Wizard asks for your payment information, so enter your credit card data and click Next.

Step 4: Here the Wizard presents the membership rules. Click the MSN Membership Rules button to display the fine print, activate the I Agree option (assuming that you do), and click Next.

Step 5: Finally, you're asked to enter a Member ID and a password (twice), as shown in Figure 26.13. When you've done that, click Sign Me Up!.

Now the MSN Signup Wizard needs to change a few things on your computer. Here are the steps to plow through to (finally) finish the sign-up procedure:

1. Click Continue, and the Wizard will send a file to your computer.

2. In the dialog box that appears, make sure the Open it option is activated, and click OK.

3. Click Yes in the Authenticode dialog box that appears once the file transfer is complete.

4. After a few more files are transferred, a dialog box will prompt you to insert your Windows 95 CD-ROM. After you've done so, click OK.

5. When the update is done, click OK in the dialog box that appears.

FIGURE 26.12.

*Enter your personal
data in this Web page.*

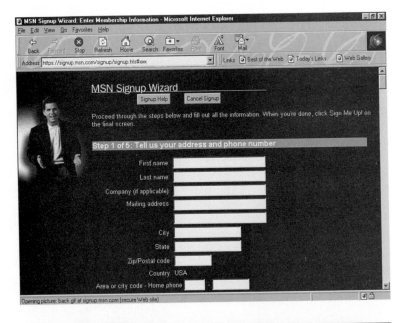

FIGURE 26.13.

*Use this page to enter a
Member ID and
password.*

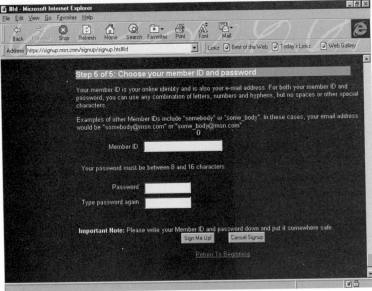

Signing in to MSN

If you've just completed the MSN sign-up process, you should see the Sign In dialog box, shown
in Figure 26.14. If you don't see it, or if you're already a member, here are the various methods
you can use to display the Sign In dialog box:

Getting Online with The Microsoft Network

CHAPTER 26

859

26

THE
MICROSOFT
NETWORK

■ Double-click the desktop's The Microsoft Network icon.

■ Select Start | Programs | The Microsoft Network.

■ Right-click The Microsoft Network icon, and click either Open or Explorer (see the later section "Navigating MSN" to learn the difference).

■ Select Start | Find | On the Microsoft Network or, from Explorer, select Tools | Find | On The Microsoft Network, enter your search criteria, and click Find Now. I'll explain this search procedure in more detail later in this chapter (see "Searching MSN").

■ Create shortcuts for MSN sites, and then launch them.

■ On the World Wide Web, head for the MSN site and select an MSN location. Here's the address of MSN on the Web:

```
http://www.msn.com/
```

FIGURE 26.14.
The Sign In dialog box is your launch point for MSN.

Use the Member ID text box to enter your member ID (MSN will fill in this field for you automatically with each subsequent sign in), and use the Password dialog box to enter your password. If you want MSN to fill in the Password field for you automatically each time you sign in, activate the Remember my password check box. If you need to make changes to your dialing properties or modem settings before connecting, click the Settings button and make your adjustments by using the Connection Settings dialog box that appears. When you're ready to take the plunge, click the Connect button.

The MSN Upgrade

MSN is, like most online sites, a work in progress. This means that the services offered by MSN are constantly changing either to provide new features or to improve existing features. To keep up with these changes, the MSN software that runs on your computer must be updated occasionally as well.

Late in 1996, Microsoft released MSN 1.3, an upgrade to the MSN software that shipped with Windows 95. Version 1.3 offers, among other things, lots of new content, faster downloads, ISDN access, and the capability to connect to MSN either via your local area network's Internet connection or via a third-party service provider.

When you sign in to MSN for the first time, the system checks the version of your MSN software (as specified in the Registry). If you still have the original version, the dialog box shown in Figure 26.15 appears to ask whether you want to upgrade. If you do (and I recommend it), click Yes and MSN will copy the new software to your machine. When the download is complete (it could take a half hour or more, depending on the speed of your connection), Windows 95 lets you know that your computer needs to be restarted. Click OK and then restart your computer to put into effect the changes made by the upgrade.

FIGURE 26.15.

When you first connect to MSN, you'll see this dialog box if the system detects that you're using an older version of the MSN software.

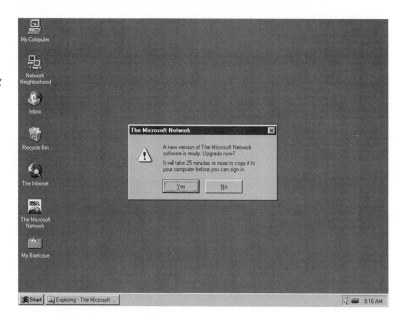

New Settings Available with the MSN Upgrade

After upgrading, you might want to change a few settings before connecting to MSN again. To see these settings, use either of the following techniques:

- Start MSN and click the Settings button in the Sign In dialog box.
- Right-click The Microsoft Network icon, select Connection Settings from the context menu, and then select Connection Settings in the properties sheet that appears.

Figure 26.16 shows the new Connection Settings dialog box that comes with the MSN upgrade. You now have three connection options:

> **MSN is my dial-up Internet access provider:** This group provides the standard MSN connection options. The only change is that you can choose from three types of MSN connection: The Microsoft Network, Internet and The Microsoft Network, and ISDN access to the Internet and MSN. To change this setting, click the Access Numbers button, and then use the Service type drop-down list to make your choice. See Chapter 37 to learn how to set up Internet access via MSN.

Connect using another dial-up Internet access provider: Select this option if you already have an Internet service provider. This means that the connection to MSN will be established via your Internet hookup, so you'll need to log on to your service provider before you can sign in to MSN.

Connect using my local area network: Select this option either to use your local area network's Internet connection to sign in to MSN, or to use a dedicated MSN access server on your LAN. For the second of these situations, click the Properties button and then activate the Use MSN access server check box.

FIGURE 26.16.
The upgraded Connection Settings dialog box.

A Tour of MSN Central

After you're inside the MSN system, you'll probably see one or more of the following windows:

MSN Today: This window tells you about a few things going on in the MSN world on that day. For now, you can close this window; I'll show you how to redisplay it later.

Welcome to MSN: This is a message of welcome from Bill Gates, and it appears only when you sign in for the first time. After you've read the message, close the window.

MSN Central: This window, shown in Figure 26.17, is the subject of the rest of this section.

MSN Central is your home base for The Microsoft Network. Each icon gives you access to a different area of MSN. Here's a rundown of what's available:

MSN Today: This item takes you to a daily online "newspaper" that alerts you to what's going on around MSN. See "MSN Today: The Daily MSN News" later in this chapter.

E-Mail: This item takes you to your Microsoft Exchange Inbox, where you can read and write e-mail messages. Refer to Chapter 27, "Setting Up Microsoft Exchange," and Chapter 28, "Exchanging E-Mail with Microsoft Exchange," for the gory e-mail details.

Favorite Places: Selecting this item doesn't do much now; it just opens an empty window. But after you've set up your Favorite Places list (as explained later in this chapter; see "Adding Favorite Places"), selecting it opens a folder full of your favorite MSN areas for easy access.

Member Assistance: This option takes you to an online area where you can get answers to questions, help with technical problems, billing information, and other administrative help.

Categories: Categories are the heart of MSN. Select this item to begin your journey through a maze of folders that takes you to the category that interests you. (You'll read more about this shortly. See "Categories: MSN's Meat and Potatoes.")

FIGURE 26.17.

MSN Central is your MSN starting point.

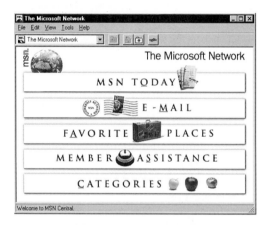

NOTE: MSN CENTRAL IS NOW MSN CLASSIC

MSN Central is the home base for MSN versions 1.2 and earlier, while MSN 1.3 sports a completely revamped interface. The next few sections discuss the MSN Central interface (which is now known as "MSN Classic"). I'll hold off discussing MSN 1.3 until later in this chapter (see "Working with MSN 1.3").

Navigating MSN

Unlike with other online services, almost no learning curve is involved in figuring how to get around in MSN. That's because MSN uses the same treelike, folder-within-a-folder metaphor as Windows 95. And in the same way that you negotiate your computer's folders until you get to the document or program you want to work with, you also negotiate MSN's folders until you get to the feature you need (whether it's a BBS, a chat room, or a file you want to download). MSN even offers you two Windows 95–like interfaces: one that resembles My Computer, and one that resembles Explorer.

MSN's My Computer Interface

MSN's My Computer interface is the default window you see when you launch MSN (or if you right-click the desktop's The Microsoft Network icon and select Open). This window resembles My Computer because you see only the contents of each window as you move through the various levels. And, as with My Computer, you can browse MSN by using either a new window for each level or a single window. (To set this up, select View | Options, display the Folder tab, and choose the option you want.)

MSN's Explorer Interface

To see MSN's Explorer interface, right-click the desktop's The Microsoft Network icon, and select Explorer from the context menu. (Note that you can run this command without exiting MSN. If you'd prefer not to have two MSN windows open, first close the existing window, and then, when MSN asks whether you want to disconnect, click No.) Figure 26.18 shows the window that appears. As you can see, this interface boasts a Folders pane on the left and a Contents pane on the right, just like Explorer.

FIGURE 26.18.

*The Microsoft
Network's Explorer
interface.*

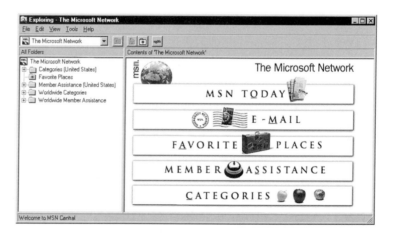

MSN Navigation Techniques

When you're inside the network, you can usually select an item by double-clicking it, or by highlighting it and pressing Enter. If you're using the My Computer interface, you can return to the preceding window by either selecting File | Up One Level or pressing Backspace. In some cases (such as when you're reading BBS messages), MSN always opens a separate window. You can navigate these windows in the usual way.

You can also use MSN's toolbar to leap around. To display it, pull down the View menu and activate the Toolbar command. Table 26.1 summarizes some of the toolbar's buttons. (Some of these buttons don't appear at first, and you'll see others as you move through MSN.)

Table 26.1. Some of The Microsoft Network's toolbar buttons.

Button	Name	Description
	Up One Level	Returns you to the previous window.
	Go to MSN Central	Takes you back to MSN Central.
	Go to Favorite Places	Takes you directly to your Favorite Places list (described later).
	Sign Out	Ends your MSN session.
	Properties	Displays the properties sheet for the current item.
	Add to Favorite Places	Adds the current item to your Favorite Places list.
	Large Icons	Displays the MSN window in Large Icons view.
	Small Icons	Displays the MSN window in Small Icons view.
	List	Displays the MSN window in List view.
	Details	Displays the MSN window in Details view.

TIP: GETTING BACK TO MSN CENTRAL

As you can see from Table 26.1, MSN's toolbar has a button that takes you back to MSN Central. Another way to get there is to right-click the MSN icon in the system tray and, from the context menu that appears, select Go to MSN Central.

Using GO Words to Navigate MSN

Most MSN services have a label that describes the service uniquely in the MSN environment. These labels, called GO *words,* let you jump to a service quickly without having to negotiate MSN's menus and folders. For example, MSN has a collection of BBSs that cover movies and cinema called The Movie Forum BBS. You normally have to drill down a half dozen folders to get there, but you can arrive at this site in no time flat by using its GO word: MoviesBBS.

To do this, use either of the following techniques:

- ■ Select Edit | Go to | Other Location.
- ■ Right-click the MSN icon in the taskbar's system tray, and then select Go to from the context menu.

In either case, the Go To Service dialog box, shown in Figure 26.19, appears. Enter the GO word in the text box, and then click OK.

FIGURE 26.19.

To jump to a service quickly, use its GO word.

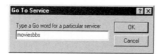

How do you find out the GO word for a service? One method is to drill down through MSN's folders until you see the icon for the service, right-click the icon, and click Properties. The properties sheet that appears tells you the service's GO word. Another method is to use the MSN Directory service. I'll show you how this works later in this chapter.

Navigating with Shortcuts

In Chapter 13, "Working with Files and Folders," I showed you how to create shortcuts on the Windows 95 desktop (and elsewhere). You saw that shortcuts were real time savers because they gave you quick access to documents or programs that were otherwise buried under a bunch of folders. You can get the same level of convenience in MSN by creating shortcuts to services. You can use several methods:

- ■ Highlight an icon and select File | Create Shortcut.
- ■ Right-click an icon and select Create Shortcut from the context menu.
- ■ Drag an icon from the MSN window, and drop it on the location you want to use for the shortcut.

Note that the first two techniques create desktop shortcuts. You'll also see a dialog box confirming that the shortcut was created. (If you don't want to see this dialog box each time you create a shortcut, deactivate the Show this confirmation next time check box.)

MSN Today: The Daily MSN News

MSN is a large service, and lots of things are always going on. To help keep you abreast of the latest news, events, and features, the MSN proprietors publish a daily electronic newspaper called MSN Today, shown in Figure 26.20. You usually see MSN Today by default each time you sign in to MSN, but you can view it at any time by selecting the MSN Today icon in MSN Central.

FIGURE 26.20.

MSN Today is a daily electronic newspaper that gives you the latest news and events in the MSN world.

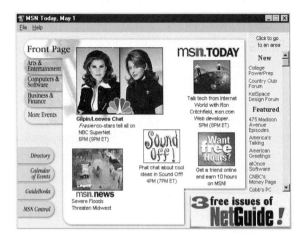

In most cases, you click an icon in the MSN Today window to head automatically to an MSN site that either explains the icon in more detail or launches a service. Any words or phrases that appear in a different color are also "live," in that clicking the text takes you to another MSN nook.

NOTE: MSN TODAY IS A "TITLE"

MSN Today is an example of what The Microsoft Network calls a *title*. These are interactive, multimedia mini-applications created with Internet Studio (formerly code-named Blackbird). Like World Wide Web pages, titles display a combination of text, graphics, and hypertext links that lead you to other parts of the application or to other MSN services.

TIP: TURN OFF MSN TODAY

MSN Today is usually loaded with graphics, so it takes quite a while to download. If you'd prefer not to see MSN Today each time you sign in, you can tell MSN to bypass it. Select View | Options, display the General tab, and deactivate the Show MSN Today title at startup check box.

Getting Online with The Microsoft Network

CHAPTER 26

867

26

THE
MICROSOFT
NETWORK

Categories: MSN's Meat and Potatoes

The heart of MSN is its collection of categories, which are subject areas that cover a general topic, such as Arts & Entertainment or Public Affairs. Whatever interests you have, MSN likely has a topic you'll want to investigate.

To get started, click the Categories icon in MSN Central. The window that appears, shown in Figure 26.21, shows you the available categories. Each of these icons leads you to specific topics within the category. These topics could be chat rooms, file libraries, bulletin boards, titles, kiosks, newsgroups, Web sites, documents, or subfolders that take you to more specific topics.

FIGURE 26.21.

Clicking the Categories icon in MSN Central displays this window.

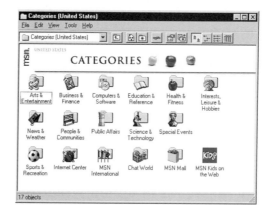

As a guideline to the various items you'll see in your travels, MSN uses specific icons to represent the different item types. Table 26.2 displays a few of the icons you'll see. (Note, however, that these icons aren't always used consistently throughout the service. Also, many topics customize the standard icon by superimposing an extra graphics image.)

Table 26.2. Standard icons used in MSN.

Icon	Description
ⓘ	Indicates a *kiosk*—a file that gives you information about a category or topic. Double-clicking a kiosk downloads the file to your computer and then displays the file in a window.
	Indicates a BBS or Usenet newsgroup (see the next section).
	Indicates a chat room. See "Real-Time Conversations in the Chat Rooms" later in this chapter.

continues

Table 26.2. continued

Icon	*Description*
	Indicates a document or file. Double-clicking the icon downloads the file to your computer.
	Indicates a folder. Double-clicking this icon opens the folder.
	Indicates a World Wide Web site. Double-clicking this icon starts your default Web browser (usually Internet Explorer) and loads the Web site.

TIP: USE PROPERTIES TO FIND OUT MORE ABOUT AN ICON

Depending on the speed of your connection, it can take quite a while for MSN to send all the contents associated with a particular icon. Before committing to the download, you can see a blurb that describes the icon by opening the icon's properties sheet.

Exchanging Messages in Bulletin Boards and Newsgroups

In MSN, a bulletin board service (BBS) and a Usenet newsgroup perform the same function: They provide a central storage location for MSN members to read and post messages on a particular topic. The only difference is that a BBS is an MSN-only phenomenon, whereas Usenet newsgroups are part of the Internet. (Usenet newsgroups are instantly recognizable because they use dots in their name—for example, rec.pets.dogs.)

NOTE: THE COMPLETE NEWSGROUPS

If it's Usenet newsgroups you're after, the Internet Newsgroups forum is the place to be. To get there, either enter the GO word newsgroups or select Categories | Internet Center | Internet Newsgroups.

If you've never used a BBS or newsgroup, the basic idea is simple: Someone sends a message to the BBS; then the other people on the BBS can read it and, if they feel so inclined, respond to it. This response also appears on the BBS, and people can then respond to the response, and so on. The original message and all its rebuttals are called a *conversation* or a *thread*.

Getting Online with The Microsoft Network

Chapter 26

869

26

THE
MICROSOFT
NETWORK

Figure 26.22 shows a typical BBS window with the following columns:

Subject: This column shows the subject line of each message. In the default view, messages are organized by conversation. If you see a plus sign (+) beside a message, there are replies to the original message. Clicking the plus sign displays the responses.

Author: This is the name of the person who sent the message.

Size: This is the size of the message.

Date: This column shows the date and time the message was posted.

FIGURE 26.22.

A BBS window lists the subjects and authors of the available conversations.

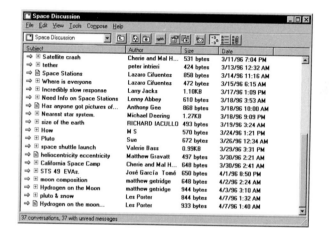

Reading Messages

Your first order of business will be to read any messages that sound interesting. To read a message, just double-click it (or highlight it with the arrow keys and press Enter). MSN displays the message in a separate window, as shown in Figure 26.23.

FIGURE 26.23.

When you open a message, MSN displays it in a separate window.

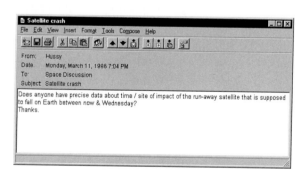

The gray area below the toolbar tells you four things: the member ID of the person who sent the message (the From line), the date and time that person sent it (Date), the name of the BBS (To), and the subject of the message (Subject). The rest of the window shows the content of the message.

NOTE: WINGDINGS OFTEN CAMOUFLAGE MESSAGES

You'll notice that some BBS messages have text that appears only as symbols, like so:

✳︎〰︎〉◆ 〉◆ 〉■ ✿〉■〼︎☊〉■〼︎◆ ⤢▢■◆

Officially, these symbols form part of the Wingdings font. This is common on MSN, and it's a way of camouflaging the answers to jokes or riddles or the endings of movies and books. To "decode" the symbols, highlight them, select Format | Font, and choose a regular font such as MS Sans Serif (which is the one used for most MSN messages) or Arial. When you click OK, the symbols transform themselves into regular letters for easy reading.

NOTE: ROT 13: MORE CAMOUFLAGE

Usenet newsgroups are text-only, so they can't use Wingdings to camouflage text. Instead, they use an encoding scheme called *ROT 13*. This scheme encodes messages by shifting their letters by 13 positions, so A becomes M, B becomes N, and so on. Letters after M are wrapped around to the beginning, so N becomes A, O becomes B, and so on.

Fortunately, you don't have to decipher ROT 13 by hand. MSN is happy to do it for you if you select Tools | ROT 13 Encode/Decode.

When you've finished reading a message, various options are available through the window's menus or toolbar. Table 26.3 summarizes your options.

Table 26.3. Commands available in a BBS message window.

Command	Toolbar Button	Keyboard Shortcut	Description
Compose	New Message		Ctrl-N	Composes a new message (see the next section).

Command	Toolbar Button	Keyboard Shortcut	Description
Compose | Reply to BBS		Ctrl-A	Replies to the message. (A window opens in which you type the reply, and then your response is sent to the BBS.)
Compose | Reply by E-mail		Ctrl-R	Replies to the message via e-mail only. (The reply goes only to the person who sent the original message.)
Compose | Forward by E-mail		Ctrl-F	Forwards the message to someone else.
View | Previous Message		Shift-F5	Reads the previous message.
View | Next Message		F5	Reads the next message.
View | Next Unread Message		F6	Reads the next unread message.
View | Previous Conversation		Shift-F7	Reads the previous conversation.
View | Next Conversation		F7	Reads the next conversation.
View | Next Unread Conversation		F8	Reads the next unread conversation.
Tools | File Transfer Status Status window.			Displays the File Transfer

Posting Your Own Messages

To send your own messages to the BBS or newsgroup (this is called *posting* a message), you have two options:

■ If you want to start a new conversation, select Compose | New Message.

■ To respond to an existing message, first open the message. Then select Compose |
Reply to BBS (to send the response to the BBS), Compose | Reply by E-mail (to send
your rebuttal directly to the author of the message), or Compose | Forward by E-mail
(to send the message to another person and, optionally, insert some text of your own).

In either case, a window appears into which you can type your message. For starters, use the
Subject field to enter a short description of your message. This description is what appears in
the BBS window, so make sure that it tells people what your message is about. Then click inside the large box below the Subject field (or press Tab), and type your message.

If you're posting your message to an MSN BBS, you can take advantage of the Rich Text format used with all MSN messages. This means you can format the message text, insert OLE
objects, and attach files. Here are the details:

Formatting message text: If you want to format your message, you can use Format |
Font or Format | Paragraph, or you can click the buttons in the Formatting toolbar.
Most of the formatting options are similar to those found in WordPad. (If you don't
see the Formatting toolbar, activate View | Formatting Toolbar.)

Inserting an OLE object: The MSN software can act as an OLE container, so you
can insert an OLE object in your message. To try it, select Insert | Object and then use
the Insert Object dialog box to either insert an existing object or create a new object.
(See Chapter 17, "Sharing Data in Windows 95: The Clipboard and OLE," to get the
details on working with OLE objects.)

Attaching a file: To attach a file to the message, select Insert | File (or click the Insert
File button on the toolbar). In the Insert File dialog box that appears, find the file you
want to use, and then highlight it. If you just want to copy the text from the file to
your message, activate the Text only option; for a true file attachment, highlight the An
attachment option. When you click OK, MSN inserts the file as an icon, as shown in
Figure 26.24.

FIGURE 26.24.

*Use this window to
compose your own
messages.*

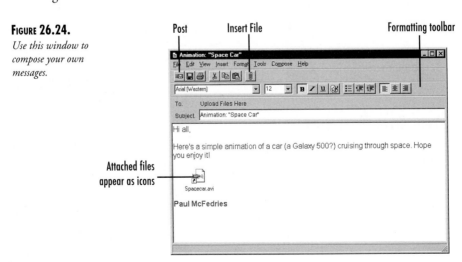

Post   Insert File   Formatting toolbar

Attached files
appear as icons

NOTE: FILE ATTACHMENTS NEED APPROVAL

All MSN BBS areas have *managers* who keep everyone up-to-date on what's happening and answer questions. These managers also need to approve your file attachment before posting it to the BBS. In many forums, a separate BBS is used for uploading files (this is the case in Figure 26.24).

When your message is complete, you can send it by selecting File | Post Message, by clicking the Post button on the toolbar, or by pressing Ctrl-Enter.

Downloading a File

As I mentioned earlier, most files can be found in MSN's file libraries. So, just as you did in the BBS, you'll need to select a category and then wade through the various levels of folders until you find the file you want. As you can see in Figure 26.25, file library windows are BBS windows, where the files are stored in individual messages as attachments. (A paper clip icon beside the subject line tells you which messages have file attachments.)

FIGURE 26.25.

MSN's file libraries are BBS windows where the messages have file attachments.

The paper clip icon indicates a file attachment

When you open a message, you'll see an icon representing the file that's available for downloading, as shown in Figure 26.26. To tell MSN you want to download the file, use any of these methods:

- Double-click the icon and select Download File from the dialog box that appears.
- Click the icon and select Edit | File Object | Download.
- Right-click the icon and select File Object | Download from the context menu.

The File Transfer Status Window

When the file transfer begins, the File Transfer Status window, shown in Figure 26.27, appears. (If you don't see the File Transfer Status window, either select Tools | File Transfer Status from the message window or click the toolbar's File Transfer Status button.) For each file you're downloading, the columns in the File Transfer Status window show you the filename, the file size, the estimated download time, the current status of the file, and the folder where the file will be stored on your hard disk. In addition, the status bar shows you the progress of the current download.

FIGURE 26.26.

*File attachments appear
as icons.*

File Transfer Status

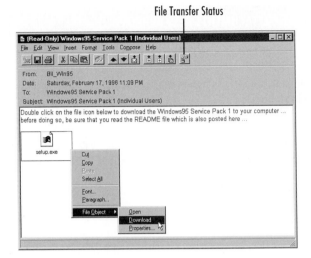

FIGURE 26.27.

*The File Transfer
Status window lets you
know how the down-
load is progressing.*

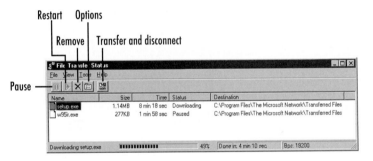

File Transfer Options

MSN offers a few options for controlling your downloads. Here's a summary:

■ If you change your mind about downloading a file, highlight the file in the File
Transfer Status window, and then select File | Remove. (You can also press Delete
or click the Remove button on the toolbar.)

■ If you want to sign off MSN after the file transfer is complete, MSN will do it for
you automatically if you activate File | Transfer and Disconnect, or if you press the
Transfer and Disconnect toolbar button.

■ The rest of the options can be found in the Options dialog box, shown in Figure
26.28. To display this dialog box, select Tools | Options (or press Ctrl-O or click the
Options button on the toolbar). Here's a rundown of the controls:

Pause files as they are queued: If you activate this check box, MSN places
each file in the File Transfer Status window but doesn't start the download
right away. To initiate the file transfer, highlight the file and select File | Restart
(or press Ctrl-S or click the Restart toolbar button).

Delete compressed file after decompressing: If you activate this check box, MSN deletes downloaded ZIP files automatically after it has decompressed them. (Note that this option applies only if you activate the `Automatically decompress files` check box.)

Automatically decompress files: If you activate this check box, MSN decompresses downloaded ZIP files for you automatically. It does this by creating a new folder (usually the name of the file with a 000 extension) and unzipping the files into this new folder.

Default download folder: Use this text box to specify the folder to use for your downloaded files.

FIGURE 26.28.

Use this dialog box to set various options for the file downloads.

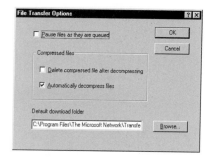

Real-Time Conversations in the Chat Rooms

The message exchanges in a BBS are called "conversations," but they aren't like a real conversation at all. The problem is that it usually takes a few hours for a message to wend its way through the MSN system before it shows up in the BBS, and it might take hours or even days before someone reads your message and responds to it.

If you prefer the give-and-take and immediacy of a real one-on-one conversation, you should try one of MSN's *chat rooms*. These are meeting places where any number of people can join and converse with each other in real time by typing messages. It's a bit chaotic, but it can be a lot of fun if you get in with a good crowd.

There are chat rooms all over MSN, so you won't have any trouble finding one. A good place to start, though, is with the Chat World category, shown in Figure 26.29 (from MSN Central, select Categories | Chat World).

When you open a chat room, you'll see a window similar to the one shown in Figure 26.30. This window is divided into three areas. On the left is the conversation that's taking place, on the right are the people participating (the *spectators*), and at the bottom is the area where you type your two cents worth. Press Enter or click Send to send your message into the fray.

Figure 26.29.

*Chat World boasts all
kinds of chat rooms
where you can find
people willing to
engage in real-time
conversations.*

Figure 26.30.

A typical chat room.

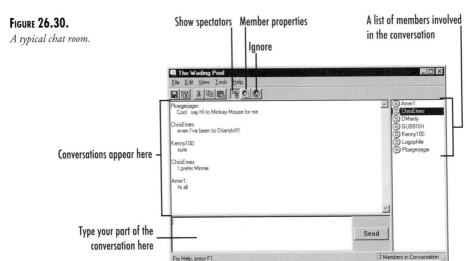

Here are a few techniques you can use to manipulate chat rooms:

■ If you want to know more about a participating member, highlight his member ID
and select View | Member Properties. (You can also click the Member Properties
toolbar button, or right-click the member ID and select Properties from the context
menu). In the properties sheet that appears, use the General, Personal, and Professional tabs to read about the member (not all members fill in these tabs, however).

NOTE: FILLING IN YOUR MEMBER PROPERTIES

Your member properties sheet shows only the information you entered when you signed up
for MSN. If you feel like filling in the other tabs, you need to do it from the Address Book in
Microsoft Exchange. I explain how it's done in Chapter 28.

- You can toggle the list of participating members on and off by selecting View | Show Spectators (or by clicking the Show Spectators button).

- If, for some reason, you don't want to see any comments from a member, highlight his member ID (you can highlight multiple members, if need be), and select View | Ignore Members. In the dialog box that appears, activate the Ignore messages from selected members check box, and click OK. (Alternatively, you can highlight the members and click the Ignore button, or right-click the members and select Ignore from the context menu.)

- To set some chat options, select Tools | Options. The dialog box that appears lets you choose whether you're notified of a member's joining or leaving the chat, and a few other options.

A recent innovation in the chat universe is *V-Chat*. This is like a regular chat, except that instead of showing just the text messages, you also see a 3-D world in which you and the other members can move around and "gesture" to each other. Figure 26.31 shows an example of a V-Chat *environment* (as they're called). To try V-Chat, you need to download the V-Chat software. You'll find it, as well as several V-Chat environments, in the V-Chat Forum (look for the icon in Chat World).

FIGURE 26.31.

V-Chat: another dimension in chat technology.

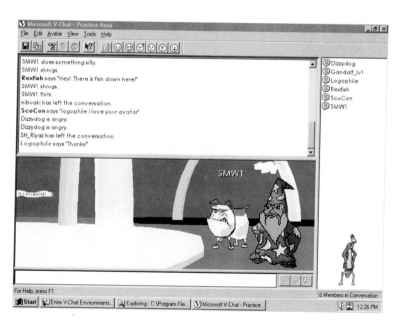

Adding Favorite Places

One of the problems with MSN is that it can take quite a while to navigate from place to place. The more folders you have to drill down into, the more icons MSN has to load, so the longer the whole process takes. (MSN does save some icons in its cache, which makes it easy to navigate the places you've already visited.)

If you have a BBS or a chat area or some other MSN locale that you think you'll be visiting often, there's an easier way to get there from here: Add it to your Favorite Places list. All you have to do is navigate to the appropriate spot and then select File | Add to Favorite Places. (There's also an Add to Favorite Places toolbar button you can click, or you can right-click an icon and select Add to Favorite Places.)

After you've saved a spot in the Favorite Places list, you can navigate to the spot by double-clicking its icon in the Favorite Places folder, shown in Figure 26.32. To display this folder, use any of the following techniques:

- Click the Favorite Places icon in MSN Central.
- Select Edit | Go to | Favorite Places.
- Click the Go to Favorite Places button on the toolbar.
- Right-click the MSN icon in the taskbar, and select Go to Favorite Places from the context menu.

Figure 26.32.

The Favorite Places folder gives you easy access to the MSN sites you visit most often.

Searching MSN

MSN is a huge service, with hundreds of areas to choose from. If you have time to kill, it's fascinating to just surf around and see what you trip over in your travels. If you're looking for something specific, however, MSN's sometimes helter-skelter organization can be frustrating. To help out, you can use a couple of tools to search MSN and find the info or service you need.

Getting Online with The Microsoft Network

CHAPTER 26

879

26

THE
MICROSOFT
NETWORK

Using the Find Feature

Using the Find feature with MSN is similar to using it with Explorer (as described in Chapter 13). To get started, use either of the following techniques:

- In Windows 95, select Start | Find | On The Microsoft Network.
- In an MSN window, select Tools | Find | On The Microsoft Network.

Either way, you'll see the Find window, shown in Figure 26.33. To set up your search, use the following controls:

Containing: Use this text box to enter your search text. You can use the Boolean operators AND and OR to refine your search. For example, the entry South and Carolina finds services that contain both South and Carolina (the searches aren't case-sensitive). Similarly, South or Carolina finds services that contain either South or Carolina. For exact phrase matches, enclose the phrase in quotation marks (for example, "South Carolina"). You can also use the standard wildcard characters (* for multiple characters and ? for individual characters).

In: Use these check boxes to specify where you want Find to look for the search text.

Of type: Use this drop-down list to specify the type of service you want to find (for example, chat rooms or bulletin boards).

Place: Use this field to enter geographical criteria, such as a city, state, or country. You can use Boolean operators and wildcard characters to refine your criteria.

FIGURE 26.33.

Use the Find window to search for MSN services that meet certain criteria.

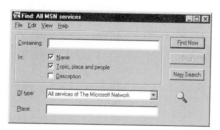

Click the Find Now button to start your search. As usual, Find displays the results at the bottom of the window. To display a service, highlight it and select File | Open.

Using the MSN Directory

If you're looking for forums or folders in a category, the MSN Directory is an easy way to find what you want. To get there, use either of the following techniques:

- From MSN Central, select Member Assistance | Maps & Information | MSN Directory.
- Use the GO word MSNDirect.

In the title that appears, you can display the forums by category; by topic, as shown in Figure 26.34; or alphabetically. Click the red page icon to the left of each forum name to get a description of the forum (including its GO word). To open the forum, click the blue hypertext.

FIGURE 26.34.

Use the MSN Directory title to find forums.

MSN Administrative Chores

While you're online, MSN offers a few methods of performing basic administrative chores. These include changing your password, modifying your billing information, and checking out your current charges. Here's a quick run-through for each task:

>   **Changing your MSN password:** It's a good idea to change your password regularly, just in case someone steals it. To do this, select Tools | Password. In the Change Your Password dialog box, shown in Figure 26.35, enter your old password, enter your new password twice, and click OK.

FIGURE 26.35.

Use this dialog box to set up a new MSN password.

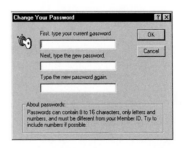

>   **Changing your billing information:** To change your billing address or credit card data, select Tools | Billing | Payment Method. In the next dialog box, shown in Figure 26.36, use the Name and address button to change your address, and use the Payment method button to change your credit card information.

Getting Online with The Microsoft Network

CHAPTER 26

881

26

THE
MICROSOFT
NETWORK

FIGURE 26.36.

Use this dialog box to make changes to your address or credit card particulars.

Displaying a summary of charges: To see how much damage your MSN rambling will do to your bank balance, select Tools | Billing | Summary of Charges. In the Online Statement dialog box, click Get Details and then choose the period you want to see.

Viewing your current subscriptions: While you're in the Online Statement dialog box, select the Subscriptions tab to review your current subscription. If you want to change your plan, click the Change button. If you want MSN to notify you when your bill hits a certain threshold, enter the value in the `Notify me when any one charge would exceed` text box.

Canceling your account: If you decide MSN isn't worth it (or if you love it so much that your monthly bills are putting you in the poorhouse), you can cancel your membership at any time. To do so, go to MSN Central and select Member Assistance | Member Support | Cancel My Account (you can also use the `GO` word `cancelmsn`). Fill out the MSN Cancellation dialog box that appears, and then click Finish.

Signing Out from MSN

When you've had your fill of MSN, you should sign out to avoid running up your online time. You can go about this in four ways:

- Select File | Sign Out.
- Click the Sign Out button on the toolbar.
- Close all MSN windows. When MSN asks whether you want to disconnect, click Yes.
- Double-click the MSN icon in the system tray. When MSN asks whether you want to disconnect, click Yes.

As a safeguard, you can tell MSN to sign you out automatically after a certain number of minutes of inactivity. To set this up, select View | Options, and in the Options dialog box that appears, select the General tab, shown in Figure 26.37. Use the `Disconnect after x minutes of inactivity` spinner to set the level you want (between 1 and 59).

FIGURE 26.37.

Use the General tab to set the number of minutes of inactivity MSN requires before signing you out automatically.

Working with MSN 1.3

Version 1.3 marks MSN's transition to an entirely Web-based service with a completely re-vamped interface and lots of new content. To access this new version of the service, you have two choices:

- Install the version 1.3 CD-ROM that MSN sends you once you've signed up. Figure 26.38 shows the MSN Program Viewer that's used to access MSN content in version 1.3. You'll need to use this viewer to access MSN-specific content such as forums and chat rooms.

FIGURE 26.38.

MSN 1.3 uses the MSN Program Viewer to display content.

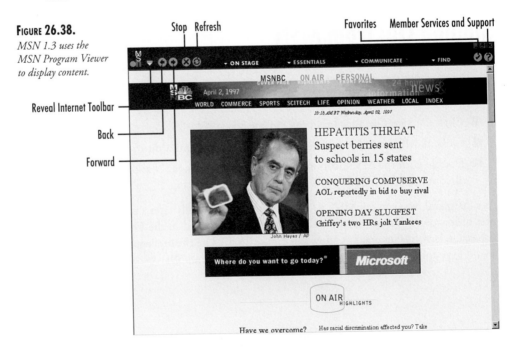

■ Use a Web browser to access MSN directly on the Web at the following address:

```
http://www.msn.com/
```

Once inside MSN (you might have to download a few extra components before getting there), you'll see a screen similar to the one shown in Figure 26.38.

Here's a rundown of the various controls that run across the top of the Program Viewer window:

Reveal Internet Toolbar: Click this button to display an extra toolbar in the Program Viewer. This toolbar shows you the Web address of the current MSN page.

Back: Click this button to go back to the previous document (you can also press Alt-left arrow).

Forward: After you've gone back to a previous document, you can move ahead to the next document by clicking the Forward button (or by pressing Alt-right arrow).

Stop: If you select a link and then change your mind (or if a link is busy loading large graphics or animation files and you don't want to wait), you can stop the download by clicking the Stop button (or by pressing Esc).

Refresh: If you select a link and some of the objects don't load properly, you can reload the page by clicking the Refresh button (you can also press F5).

On Stage: Hover the mouse pointer over this button to display a list of MSN's "channels." Most of these choices have cascade menus that let you select individual programs. For example, to display the *Slate* online magazine, select On Stage | Channel 3 | Slate.

Essentials: Hovering the mouse pointer over this button displays a list of MSN's Essential Services. Again, you use cascade menus to choose specific services.

Communicate: This button presents a list of MSN's communications services, including e-mail, chat, forums, bulletin boards, and more.

Find: This button displays a list of search features that covers both MSN and the Internet.

Favorites: Click this button to display a menu of commands related to the Favorites folder. Click Add To Favorites to add the current page to your favorites list; click Organize Favorites to edit, move, rename, and delete favorites. (See Chapter 38, "Exploring the Web with Internet Explorer," for details on the Favorites folder.)

Member Services & Support: Click this button to see a list of commands related to Member Services and technical support.

I won't go into the specifics of using the new MSN services and channels. However, most of them use the same techniques that you would use in a typical Web browser (see Chapter 38). Also, many of the services that were carried over from the original MSN work more or less as I described them earlier in this chapter.

Summary

This chapter put your modem to good use by showing you how to sign up and sign in to The Microsoft Network. I also showed you how to navigate MSN, exchange messages in BBS windows, converse in real time in chat rooms, search MSN, perform some administrative tasks, and sign out. You also learned a bit about the new Web-based MSN version 1.3.

Here's a list of chapters where you'll find related information:

- If you need to get a modem installed and configured in Windows 95, head for Chapter 25, "Maximizing Modem Communications."

- MSN e-mail is handled by Microsoft Exchange. I demonstrate how to configure Exchange in Chapter 27, "Setting Up Microsoft Exchange," and I show you how it works in Chapter 28, "Exchanging E-Mail with Microsoft Exchange."

- You can use MSN as your Internet service provider. To do so, however, you need to install and set up TCP/IP on your system. You'll see how it's done in Chapter 36, "Implementing TCP/IP for Internet and Network Connections."

- You'll get the full scoop on setting up the Internet within MSN in Chapter 37, "Windows 95 and the Internet."

- When you're surfing the Internet via MSN, you can access Web sites from within MSN services. You'll likely use Internet Explorer to view these sites, so check out Chapter 38, "Exploring the Web with Internet Explorer," to see how this works.

Setting Up Microsoft Exchange

CHAPTER 27

> *This is the kind of innovation that makes old people slap their brows and wish they had waited another 40 years to be born.*
>
> *—Robert Fulford on e-mail*

It wasn't all that long ago that the people were mourning the demise of letter writing. The evil twin influences of reduced leisure time and overexposure to television were usually cited as the reasons for the passing of a once-popular pastime. Now, however, letter writing is making a big comeback. That's not to say that you'll see mail carriers' mailbags groaning under the weight of epistles, postcards, and *billets-doux* as folks try to catch up on their correspondence. No, the real force behind this resurgence of the written word is *e-mail.* In corporations and colleges, at home and on the road, people who would never even consider putting pen to paper are exchanging electronic missives and messages in staggering numbers.

Windows 95 users can get in on this e-mail frenzy as well. Windows 95 comes with an e-mail client called Microsoft Exchange that lets you swap messages with others on your network, or with users on remote systems such as The Microsoft Network, the Internet, and CompuServe. This chapter gets you up to speed with Exchange by showing you how to install it and configure the services you need to work with. I explain how to use Exchange for reading and writing e-mail messages in Chapter 28, "Exchanging E-Mail with Microsoft Exchange." If it's fax capabilities you're after, you'll want to read Chapter 29, "Using Microsoft Fax to Send and Receive Faxes."

OSR2

NOTE: NAME CHANGE IN OSR2

In OSR2, Microsoft Exchange is now called Windows Messaging. However, I'll still refer to this program as "Microsoft Exchange" throughout this chapter.

NOTE: NETWORK KNOWLEDGE

This chapter presumes a certain level of knowledge about the ins and outs of networking. If you need to brush up on your networking, head for Chapter 30, "A Networking Primer," and Chapter 31, "Windows 95 Networking."

An Introduction to Exchange

Microsoft Exchange is an e-mail client application that lets you read and compose messages from within the Windows 95 environment. You can use Exchange for e-mail in three ways:

■ If your company already has an existing e-mail system based on Microsoft Mail or the Microsoft Exchange Server, you can use the Exchange client to plug into that system and swap messages with other network users.

- If you're setting up a small peer-to-peer network, you can establish a central *postoffice* for the workgroup and use the Exchange client to send messages to and retrieve messages from this postoffice.

- If you have an e-mail account on The Microsoft Network, CompuServe, or the Internet, you can use Exchange to manage this account from within Windows 95. (Note, however, that you'll get CompuServe mail access only if you have the Windows 95 CD-ROM, and you'll get Internet mail access only if you have the Microsoft Plus! add-on.)

For incoming missives, Exchange provides a common inbox for messages from different e-mail systems, including faxes. You can also use Exchange to create messages and then send them to the service of your choice. This "one-stop shopping" approach is handy because it means you can reduce the number of separate applications you must use to handle your various messaging needs. (Microsoft calls Exchange a "universal" inbox, but that's hardly the case because it supports only a few e-mail services. The ones that it does support, however, are among the most popular in the PC world, so it's a good start.)

27

SETTING UP MICROSOFT EXCHANGE

NOTE: EXCHANGE SERVICE PROVIDERS

The connections between Exchange and the various messaging services (such as a Microsoft Mail server, The Microsoft Network, or CompuServe) are handled by intermediaries called *service providers*. These are Messaging Application Programming Interface (MAPI) drivers that take instructions from the Exchange client and pass them along—in the correct format—to the appropriate messaging service. Don't confuse these service providers with *Internet* service providers, which provide Internet access to individuals and businesses.

Exchange brings many other advantages to the e-mail table. Here's a summary of just a few of them:

- You can compose messages in Rich Text format, which means you can use fonts and other formatting options to spruce up your messages. Exchange uses MIME or Uuencode to send the formatting to remote sites (as long as they support these protocols).

- Exchange is an OLE container application, so you can embed objects within your messages. Exchange supports OLE 2, which lets you use visual editing to work with an embedded object.

- Exchange's Remote Mail feature lets you create messages offline and connect only when you need to send them.

- Exchange offers techniques for organizing messages, including the capability to sort messages in various ways and the capability to create separate folders for storing related messages. (Unfortunately, Exchange doesn't support some crucial message organization techniques, such as filtering.)

- Exchange integrates with other Windows 95 applications, giving you the capability to send e-mail directly from an application.

- You can set up *profiles* that define the services you want to use and their configuration.

- You get an address book to store e-mail addresses and fax numbers, and you can configure it for separate mail services. Other applications can share this address book.

- Exchange can use any spell checker that is installed as part of a 32-bit application (such as Microsoft Office 95). Exchange doesn't, however, come with its own spell checker.

Overall, Exchange is a reasonable e-mail client with many attractive features. It does have its drawbacks, however: It has no message filtering, no support for automatic signatures, and no support for shared network folders. In other words, like most of the other applications that ship with Windows 95, Exchange isn't perfect. It will, however, do the job for all but the most demanding users.

Installing Exchange

Getting Exchange up and running on your system isn't all that hard, thanks to Wizards that ease some chores and thanks to a common interface for the various service providers. Here's an overview of the entire Exchange installation and configuration process:

1. Install the Microsoft Exchange client and any service providers you need, such as Microsoft Fax or Microsoft Mail.

2. If you're using Microsoft Mail and establishing a mail system on your peer-to-peer network, create a postoffice.

3. Add the service providers you want to use to your Exchange profile.

4. Configure each service provider as needed.

5. Configure Exchange as needed.

The rest of this chapter expands on each step.

Installing the Exchange Client and Service Providers

You can install the Exchange client and the service providers you need either during the Windows 95 installation or from the Control Panel. From the Control Panel, open the Add/Remove Programs icon, and in the properties sheet that appears, select the Windows Setup tab. Either way, after you have the list of Windows 95 components in front of you, follow these steps to install Exchange and the service providers:

1. In the list of Windows 95 components, highlight Microsoft Exchange and click Details.

2. The Microsoft Exchange dialog box that appears, shown in Figure 27.1, lists two components: Microsoft Exchange and Microsoft Mail Services. Activate the check boxes for the components you want to install (if you activate Microsoft Mail Services, you must also install Microsoft Exchange), and click OK.

FIGURE 27.1.

Use this dialog box to activate the Microsoft Exchange component. You can also install Microsoft Mail Services, if you need them.

27

SETTING UP MICROSOFT EXCHANGE

3. Activate the check boxes for any other service provider you want to install (such as Microsoft Fax and, if necessary, The Microsoft Network).

4. Click OK.

5. Follow the on-screen prompts to insert your Windows 95 source disks.

At this point, the Inbox Setup Wizard dialog box shown in Figure 27.2 appears. If you'll be using Microsoft Mail and you haven't yet created a postoffice, click Cancel and read the next section. (When Windows 95 asks whether you're sure you want to cancel, click Yes.) Otherwise, click Next > and skip to the section titled "Setting Up Your Default Exchange Profile."

FIGURE 27.2.

When you install Exchange, this dialog box appears so that you can set up the Exchange client.

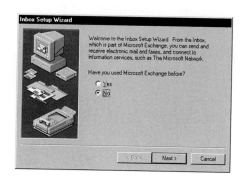

Setting Up a Microsoft Mail Postoffice

If you need to establish an e-mail system in a small office (or even at home), you don't need to set up a full-fledged mail server (such as Microsoft Mail Server or Microsoft Exchange Server). Instead, the Windows 95 Exchange client comes with a complete *workgroup postoffice* you can use as a central storage area for your network's e-mail messages. Users who have accounts on the postoffice can send mail back and forth by using any MAPI-compliant e-mail client (such as Exchange or Microsoft Mail 3.x).

If you installed the Microsoft Mail service provider, the Inbox Setup Wizard asks you to enter a path to your postoffice. You won't be able to supply a path if the postoffice doesn't exist yet, so that's why I had you cancel the Inbox Setup Wizard.

Here are a few notes that should help you better understand how postoffices work:

- The postoffice is really a shared folder on one of the network computers. The postoffice is used to store user account data and messages that are waiting to be delivered to a user.

- You can't exchange mail between users on different postoffices, so you should create only a single postoffice for your network.

- A message sent to another user is first stored in the postoffice. When the user retrieves the message, it's moved from the postoffice to the user's *personal message store,* which is a PST file that resides, usually, in the user's local Exchange folder.

- The message store contains all the user's messages, as well as any folders the user creates within Exchange to organize those messages.

- The version of Exchange that ships with Windows 95 doesn't support shared folders (that is, folders created in Exchange that can be accessed by other users). An update to Exchange in the Windows 95 Service Pack does, however, support shared folders. (You can also get this update from any Microsoft online file library. Look for a file named EXCHUPD.EXE.)

NOTE: CONSIDER A SERVER FOR LARGE NETWORKS

If you have a large network (say, more than 100 users), or if you have multiple workgroups and you need the capability to exchange messages between them, a simple Windows 95 postoffice won't cut the e-mail mustard. Instead, you need to upgrade to an e-mail server that can handle many users and multiple workgroups. Microsoft Mail Server and Microsoft Exchange Server are two such products that will satisfy your needs.

CAUTION: BACK UP EXISTING MMF FILES

If you're upgrading an existing version of Microsoft Mail, Windows 95 will work with your account without alteration. However, it will convert your MMF file into a personal message store (PST) file. Unfortunately, there's no way to convert a PST file back to MMF format, so you should probably make a backup copy of your existing MMF file before continuing.

Creating a Postoffice

Windows 95 includes a Microsoft Workgroup Postoffice Admin utility you can use to create and manage a postoffice. Here are the steps to follow to create a postoffice in Windows 95 using this utility:

1. In Control Panel, open the Microsoft Mail Postoffice icon. The Microsoft Workgroup Postoffice Admin dialog box appears.

TIP: REFRESH CONTROL PANEL

If you've just finished setting up the Microsoft Mail service provider, you might not see the Microsoft Mail Postoffice icon in Control Panel. If so, select View | Refresh or press F5 to update the Control Panel display.

---

2. Activate the Create a New Workgroup Postoffice option, and click Next >.

3. The next dialog box, shown in Figure 27.3, prompts you to enter a location for the postoffice. Use the Postoffice Location text box to enter the drive and folder where you want the postoffice to reside. You can enter either a local path or a UNC path to a network folder. Either way, Windows 95 will create a new subfolder called WGP00000 that will contain the postoffice.

FIGURE 27.3.

Use this dialog box to enter a location for the postoffice.

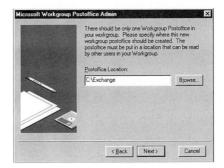

27

SETTING UP
MICROSOFT
EXCHANGE

4. Click Next > when you're ready to continue, and when Windows 95 shows you the location of the postoffice, click Next > again. The Enter Your Administrator Account Details dialog box, shown in Figure 27.4, appears.

FIGURE 27.4.

Use this dialog box to enter your name, account name, password, and other administrator account details.

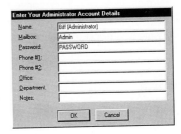

5. Fill in the details for your administrator account, including a password. If you don't want to use your personal account to administer the postoffice, create a new account (such as Admin). Click OK.

6. Windows 95 creates the postoffice and then displays a dialog box to let you know. This dialog box also reminds you to share the postoffice folder so that it's accessible to others on the network. Be sure to share the folder with full access. Click OK when you're done.

NOTE: CREATING POSTOFFICES ON OTHER SYSTEMS

You don't need to create your postoffice on a Windows 95 machine. You're free to install it on a Windows NT or NetWare system, if you prefer. This is a better arrangement, actually, because you can customize the access rights to the postoffice folder. (Granting full access privileges in Windows 95 means that users can delete the postoffice!)

To create a postoffice on a Windows NT system, open the Main program group and start Mail. In the Welcome to Mail dialog box, activate the Create a new Workgroup Postoffice, click OK, and follow the on-screen prompts. When you're done, share the folder with Change access rights.

For a NetWare machine, first create a folder to hold the postoffice and grant full trustee rights to this folder. Then follow the instructions in this section to create the postoffice folder in the NetWare folder.

Creating Accounts in the Postoffice

Before other users can install and configure Microsoft Mail, you need to create accounts for them in the postoffice. Here are the steps to follow:

1. Open Control Panel's Microsoft Mail Postoffice icon.

2. Make sure that the Administer an existing Workgroup Postoffice option is activated, and click Next >.

3. The next dialog box prompts you for the location of the postoffice. You should see the name of your postoffice displayed, so click Next >.

4. Enter your administrator mailbox name and password, and then click Next >. The Postoffice Manager dialog box, shown in Figure 27.5, appears.

FIGURE 27.5.

Use the Postoffice Manager to add and remove user accounts in your postoffice.

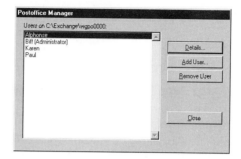

27

5. To create a user account, click Add User; fill in the user's name, mailbox, password, and other data in the Add User dialog box; and then click OK.

6. If you want to edit a user account, highlight the user's name in the Postoffice Manager, click Details, make your adjustments, and click OK.

7. If you want to remove a user account, highlight the user's name in the Postoffice Manager and click Remove User. When the Postoffice Manager asks whether you're sure, click Yes.

8. When you're done, click Close.

Setting Up Your Default Exchange Profile

To complete the installation of Microsoft Exchange, you must set up the default *profile*. This profile specifies the service providers you want to use as well as the configuration of those services. Later in this chapter, I'll show you how to create new profiles that use different services and configurations.

If you're continuing the installation of Microsoft Exchange, you should see the Inbox Setup Wizard dialog box shown in Figure 27.6. If you don't see this dialog box, either double-click the desktop's Inbox icon or select Start | Programs | Microsoft Exchange.

Make sure that the Use the following information services option is activated so that the Inbox Setup Wizard will guide you through the installation of whichever services have their check boxes activated. I won't discuss the various options for each service in detail (see Chapter 29 for the Microsoft Fax options), but here's a rundown of what you can expect:

Microsoft Fax: You'll be asked to specify the fax/modem you want to use, whether you want incoming calls answered automatically, and your fax number.

FIGURE 27.6.
Use this dialog box to select the services you want to use.

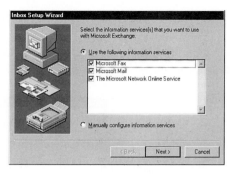

Microsoft Mail: The Inbox Setup Wizard will ask you to specify the location of the workgroup postoffice (enter a UNC path to the postoffice), your postoffice name (the Wizard displays a list of the users who have accounts on the postoffice, as shown in Figure 27.7), and your password. Other dialog boxes will ask you to enter a path to your Personal Address Book and Personal Folders (your personal message store). In both cases, you can just go with the default values (MAILBOX.PAB and MAILBOX.PST).

FIGURE 27.7.
Use this dialog box to select your postoffice name.

The Microsoft Network: The dialog box that appears for MSN just gives you an overview of the service.

You'll also see a dialog box asking whether you want to run Exchange automatically at startup (by inserting a shortcut into the Startup group). Make your choice and follow the rest of the prompts until Exchange is configured.

Adding Services After Exchange Is Installed

If you didn't include all the available services when you configured your Exchange profile, you can easily add them by hand later. To get started, use either of the following techniques:

■ Open Control Panel's Mail and Fax icon (or the Mail icon, depending on your system). This action displays the MS Exchange Settings Properties dialog box, shown in Figure 27.8.

FIGURE 27.8.

Use the Services tab to add new services to your profile.

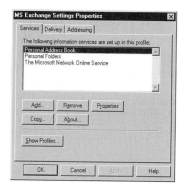

- Start Exchange (either by double-clicking the desktop's Inbox icon or by selecting Start | Programs | Microsoft Exchange), and select Tools | Services. In this case, you see a dialog box named Services that includes the Services tab shown in Figure 27.8.

To add a service, click the Add button, highlight the service in the Add Service to Profile dialog box, shown in Figure 27.9, and click OK. Exchange then asks you to configure the service. See the next few sections to learn about the various configuration options available for each type of service.

FIGURE 27.9.

Use this dialog box to highlight the service you want to add.

Configuring Exchange Services

The next few sections tell you how to configure each Exchange service (except Microsoft Fax; I'll leave that until Chapter 29). The properties you work with depend on the service, but you'll generally have to configure options such as how you connect to the service, what to do with incoming mail, and how to deliver outgoing mail.

Here are the techniques to use to display the properties sheet for a service:

- Open Control Panel's Mail and Fax icon to display the MS Exchange Settings Properties dialog box, highlight the service in the Services tab, and click Properties.
- Start Exchange, select Tools | Services to display the Services dialog box, highlight the service, and click Properties.
- Start Exchange, select Tools | Options to display the Options dialog box, select the Services tab, highlight the service, and click Properties.

Setting Up Microsoft Mail

The Microsoft Mail properties sheet, shown in Figure 27.10, contains eight tabs for your configuration pleasure (if that's the right word). The next few sections explain the various options. Note that, depending on the options you work with, your changes might not go into effect until the next time you start Exchange.

FIGURE 27.10.

The Microsoft Mail properties sheet is loaded with configuration options.

Connection Properties

The options in the Connection tab determine how you connect to the workgroup postoffice.

The `Enter the path to your postoffice` text box should show the UNC path for your postoffice (or a local path if the postoffice is on your machine). If the path isn't correct, type the correct value, or click the Browse button and highlight the path in the Browse for Postoffice dialog box.

The other options determine how Microsoft Mail connects to the postoffice when you start Exchange. You have four choices:

Automatically sense LAN or Remote: You can use Microsoft Mail either over your local area network (LAN) or remotely by using a modem and Windows 95's Dial-Up Networking utility. If you activate this options, Exchange will attempt to determine the type of connection automatically.

Local area network (LAN): Activate this option if you're accessing your postoffice over a LAN.

Remote using a modem and Dial-Up Networking: Activate this option if you're accessing the postoffice remotely. (Note that you need to have Dial-Up Networking installed on your computer to access your postoffice remotely. See Chapter 35, "Remote Computing with Dial-Up Networking.")

Offline: If you select this option, Exchange doesn't connect to the postoffice. This is useful if you're traveling and don't have remote access to the postoffice. You can compose messages and "send" them, and Exchange stores them until you can connect to the postoffice.

Logon Properties

The Logon tab, shown in Figure 27.11, displays the name of your postoffice mailbox and your password (or, at least, asterisks that represent your password).

Figure 27.11.

Use the Logon tab to configure various properties related to logging on to the postoffice.

If you want Exchange to enter your password for you automatically when you log on to the postoffice, activate the When logging on, automatically enter password check box. You might want to think twice before activating this option because it means that anyone with access to your computer can also log on to your account.

If you want to change your password, click the Change Mailbox Password button, and in the Change Mailbox Password dialog box that appears, enter your old password followed by your new one (twice).

TIP: ANOTHER WAY TO CHANGE YOUR PASSWORD

You can also access the Change Mailbox Password by selecting Tools | Microsoft Mail Tools | Change Mailbox Password in the Exchange window.

Delivery Properties

The Delivery tab, shown in Figure 27.12, contains various options for configuring how Microsoft Mail deals with sent and received messages:

Enable incoming mail delivery: This check box determines whether Exchange transfers messages from the postoffice to your inbox. If you don't want to receive any messages temporarily (because your disk space is running low, for example), deactivate this option.

Enable outgoing mail delivery: This check box determines whether Exchange transfers messages from your inbox to the postoffice. If you deactivate this option, Exchange stores your "sent" messages in your outbox.

Enable delivery to: Click the Address Types button to specify which types of e-mail addresses you want Exchange to send to the postoffice. The Address Types dialog box contains check boxes for the various types of mail. If you deactivate any of these check boxes, Exchange suspends mail service for that type.

Check for new mail every x minute(s): This value determines how often Exchange checks the postoffice for incoming mail.

Immediate notification: If you activate this check box, Exchange notifies you immediately if mail arrives for you in the postoffice. Note that the computers involved must support the NetBIOS protocol.

Display Global Address List only: If you activate this option, Exchange displays only the addresses from the postoffice (the Global Address List). Otherwise, Exchange also displays the addresses from your Personal Address Book.

FIGURE 27.12.

The properties in the Delivery tab control the delivery and receipt of mail messages.

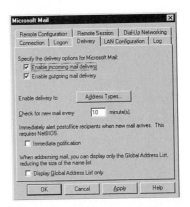

LAN Configuration Properties

When you're running Microsoft Mail over a local area network, you can use the LAN Configuration tab, shown in Figure 27.13, to set various LAN-related properties:

Use Remote Mail: Exchange normally delivers your incoming mail automatically at intervals determined by the Check for new mail every x minute(s) property you saw in the Delivery tab. If you activate the Use Remote Mail check box, however, Exchange doesn't download your mail automatically. Instead, you connect to the postoffice manually (by using the Tools | Remote Mail command), display the headers for the messages that are waiting for you, and download only the messages you want to read. (This procedure is explained in more detail in the next chapter.)

Use local copy: This check box determines whether Exchange uses the list of addresses stored in the postoffice. If you activate this check box, Exchange creates a copy of the postoffice address list, stores the copy on your computer, and then uses this list when you're composing messages. This is useful if your network is experiencing delays or poor performance. (To update the list, select Exchange's Tools | Microsoft Mail Tools | Download Address Lists command.)

Use external delivery agent: If you activate this check box, Exchange delivers your messages by using the EXTERNAL.EXE program, which can speed up delivery times on a slow LAN. EXTERNAL.EXE is available as part of the Microsoft Mail Post Office Upgrade, available from Microsoft. (This upgrade converts your Windows 95 postoffice into a full-fledged Microsoft Mail Server postoffice.)

FIGURE 27.13.

Use the LAN Configuration tab to configure Microsoft Mail on a local area network.

Log Properties

If you're having problems with Microsoft Mail, you can tell Exchange to monitor various mail events and record them in a log file. You use the Log tab, shown in Figure 27.14, to set this up:

Maintain a log of session events: Activate this check box to force Exchange to keep a log of each mail session.

Specify the location of the session log: Use this text box to specify the text file that Exchange uses to record the log.

The log includes a record of your logging in and out, messages sent and received, and any errors that occur. Here are a few lines from a typical session log:

```
4/10/96 - 6:39PM - Connection type selected: 'Automatically sense LAN or Remote'
4/10/96 - 6:39PM - You are using the connection type 'Local Area Network',
➥connected at a speed of 38400 Bytes/second.
4/10/96 - 6:39PM - Logged on to mailbox: 'Paul'.
4/10/96 - 6:39PM - Postoffice server: '\\Hermes\wgpo0000\'.
4/10/96 - 6:39PM - Checking for mail. 0 item(s) to download.
4/10/96 - 7:07PM - The Microsoft Mail Service has been disconnected from the
➥network due to a network failure.
```

```
4/10/96 - 7:08PM - You are using the connection type 'Local Area Network',
➡connected at a speed of 200000 Bytes/second.
4/10/96 - 7:08PM - The connection to the network has been restored.
4/10/96 - 7:17PM - Sent mail 'The network is up and running again'. [ID:00001231]
4/10/96 - 7:17PM - Checking for mail. 0 item(s) to download.
```

FIGURE 27.14.

Use the Log tab to set up a log file to monitor Microsoft Mail events.

Remote Properties

You use the properties in the Remote Configuration, Remote Session, and Dial-Up Networking tabs to set up Microsoft Mail for remote operation. I won't discuss the options in these tabs here. Instead, I'll wait until we look at Dial-Up Networking in Chapter 35.

Setting Up Microsoft Network Mail

Compared to Microsoft Mail's properties sheet, the properties sheet for The Microsoft Network's mail service is a walk in the park, as you can see in Figure 27.15. The Transport tab contains just three options:

Download mail when e-mail starts up from MSN: When this check box is activated, if you start Exchange while you're connected to MSN, Exchange automatically downloads any waiting MSN e-mail messages.

Disconnect after Updating Headers from Remote Mail: The Microsoft Network version of Exchange's Remote Mail feature lets you connect to MSN, download the headers of any waiting messages, and transfer to your inbox only the messages you select. If you activate this check box, Exchange disconnects you from MSN after it has obtained the message headers. This is useful for saving connect time because you can examine the headers offline.

Disconnect after Transferring Mail from Remote Mail: If you activate this check box, Exchange disconnects you from MSN automatically after it has transferred the messages you selected in Remote Mail.

FIGURE 27.15.

*The properties sheet for
The Microsoft Network
mail service.*

The Address Book tab contains a single check box: Connect to MSN to check names. If you leave this option deactivated, Exchange accepts any MSN addresses you use as is. If you activate this check box, however, Exchange connects to MSN to verify the addresses you select.

Installing and Setting Up CompuServe Mail

If you have a CompuServe account, you probably use a front-end client such as WinCIM to negotiate forums, file libraries, and other CompuServe connections. You can also use WinCIM to send and receive CompuServe e-mail. The Windows 95 CD-ROM, however, comes with an extra CompuServe service provider that lets Exchange work with the CompuServe mail system. This section shows you how to install and configure the CompuServe Mail for Microsoft Exchange service provider.

NOTE: OBTAINING THE COMPUSERVE MAIL SERVICE PROVIDER

If you don't have the Windows 95 CD-ROM, you can get the CompuServe Mail service provider for Exchange from any Microsoft online site. You can also obtain CompuServe Mail for Microsoft Exchange from CompuServe at GO CSMAIL. Note that a new version of CompuServe Mail (as of this writing, version 1.1) was released in late 1995. The new version fixes a few bugs and reflects CompuServe's new mail pricing policies (such as not applying surcharges to Internet mail messages).

Installing CompuServe Mail

You can find the files you need for CompuServe Mail for Microsoft Exchange on the Windows 95 CD-ROM in the \DRIVERS\OTHER\EXCHANGE\COMPUSRV folder.

Here are the steps to follow to install CompuServe Mail for Microsoft Exchange:

1. If Exchange is running, select File | Exit and Log Off to close the program and log off all messaging applications.
2. Display the preceding folder and run the SETUP.EXE program.

3. The Setup program copies a few files to your system (if you have the more recent version of CompuServe Mail, you're prompted for a destination folder) and then asks whether you want to include CompuServe Mail in your default Exchange profile. Click Yes.

4. The Inbox Setup Wizard starts and asks for a common CompuServe path. If the path shown in the Current Location box is incorrect, click the Browse button, highlight your CompuServe folder in the Browse for Folder dialog box, click OK, and click Next >.

5. The Inbox Setup Wizard prompts you for your name, CompuServe user ID, password, and access phone number, as shown in Figure 27.16. Fill in the blanks and click Next >.

FIGURE 27.16.

Use this dialog box to fill in your CompuServe account information.

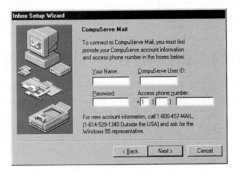

6. The next Wizard dialog box, shown in Figure 27.17, contains three check boxes:

Create Session Activity: When this check box is activated, Exchange creates a log file each time you connect to CompuServe. This log file is handy for troubleshooting problems and for monitoring activity if you set up CompuServe for unattended mail delivery (as explained in the next section).

Delete Retrieved messages: When this check box is activated, after Exchange has retrieved your messages, it deletes them from your CompuServe mailbox. This prevents your CompuServe mailbox from becoming overrun with old messages, so you should leave this check box activated.

Accept Postage Due messages: CompuServe no longer charges extra for items such as Internet messages and file attachments, so you won't ever receive any postage due messages. You can therefore ignore this check box. (It doesn't appear in the version 1.1 setup.)

7. Click Next >. The Wizard asks whether you want to include the Exchange Inbox in your Startup group.

8. Choose the option you want, and then click Next >. The Wizard adds CompuServe Mail to your Exchange profile.

FIGURE 27.17.

This dialog box sets a few CompuServe Mail options.

Setting CompuServe Mail Options

The CompuServe Mail properties sheet, shown in Figure 27.18, contains four tabs that let you configure how Exchange works with your CompuServe account. The next few sections discuss the controls available on each tab.

FIGURE 27.18.

In the CompuServe Mail Settings dialog box, the General tab displays your account info.

General Properties

The General tab contains your basic CompuServe account information: your Name, your CompuServe Id, and your Password. Note that if you leave the Password field filled in, Exchange connects to CompuServe automatically, which means anyone can work with your CompuServe mail. For greater security, leave the Password field blank so that Exchange prompts you to enter the password each time you connect.

Connection Properties

The Connection tab, shown in Figure 27.19, contains various settings that determine how Exchange connects to CompuServe to send and retrieve your mail. If you had an existing CompuServe setup when you installed CompuServe Mail, all this information should be filled in for you, and you shouldn't have to make any changes. Here's a quick rundown, however, just in case you change anything down the line:

Phone Number: This is the phone number of your local CompuServe access point.

Preferred tapi line: This is the modem you want to use for the connection.

Network: This is the type of network connection you use to access CompuServe.

FIGURE 27.19.

Use the Connection tab to specify how you want Exchange to connect to CompuServe.

NOTE: VERSION 1.1 SUPPORTS WINSOCK CONNECTIONS

If you have version 1.1 of CompuServe Mail, the Connection tab includes a Winsock Connection option. Activating this option tells Exchange to log on to CompuServe via your Internet connection. (Be sure to also select Internet in the Network list.) Alternatively, you can select Windows Modem Settings to use your modem for the connection, or you can choose Direct Connection if your machine is attached via a serial cable to another computer that provides your CompuServe connection.

Default Send Options Properties

The Default Send Options tab, shown in Figure 27.20, sets a few options for messages you send via CompuServe:

Send using Microsoft Exchange rich-text format: If you activate this check box, Exchange includes rich text formatting (fonts, colors, and so on) with any messages you send. Note that the recipient must be using a system that supports rich text messages. For CompuServe users, they must be using CompuServe Mail for Microsoft Exchange to view messages in rich text format.

Release Date: If you enter a date in this text box (using the MM/DD/YY date format), any CompuServe messages you send are held in the Exchange Outbox until that date, and only then are they shipped to the recipients. If you don't include a date, Exchange sends CompuServe messages immediately.

Expiration Date: If you enter a date in this check box (again, in MM/DD/YY format), Exchange checks your recipients' CompuServe mailboxes on that date. If your messages haven't been retrieved, Exchange deletes them.

FIGURE 27.20.

Use the Default Send Options tab to set some properties for outgoing CompuServe mail.

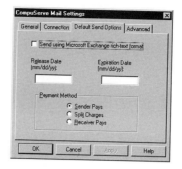

As I said, CompuServe no longer applies surcharges for sending and receiving mail, so you can ignore the options in the `Payment Method` group. (These options don't appear in version 1.1.)

Advanced Properties

One of CompuServe Mail's handiest features is the capability to schedule connections to CompuServe either at regular intervals or at specific times. The various options in the Advanced tab, shown in Figure 27.21, control how this works, as well as a few other properties. (Note, however, that none of the options in this tab applies when you're using Exchange's Remote Mail feature to download messages.) Here are the controls you can work with:

Create Event log: This check box determines whether Exchange records your CompuServe sessions in a log file. If you activate this check box, a "Log File" message appears in your inbox after each session.

Delete Retrieved messages: This check box determines whether Exchange deletes the messages you retrieve to your inbox from your CompuServe mailbox.

Accept Surcharges: This option no longer applies and doesn't appear in the version 1.1 dialog box.

Change CompuServe Dir: Click this button to change your common `CompuServe` folder.

Schedule Connect Times: This button lets you set up Exchange to connect to CompuServe automatically. If you click this button, the Connection Times dialog box, shown in Figure 27.22, appears. Choose `Startup of Mail` to establish a connection to CompuServe each time you launch Exchange; to set up connections at regular intervals, activate the `Every` check box and use the spinners to define the interval in hours and minutes; to set up a connection at a specific time each day, activate the `Scheduled at` check box and use the spinner to choose a time.

27

SETTING UP MICROSOFT EXCHANGE

FIGURE 27.21.

The Advanced tab controls various properties related to unattended CompuServe e-mail connections.

FIGURE 27.22.

Use the Connection Times dialog box to schedule Exchange connections to CompuServe.

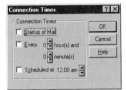

Installing and Setting Up Internet Mail

If you have an e-mail account with an Internet service provider, you can set up Exchange to send and retrieve messages via this account. To get the Internet Mail service provider, however, you must have the Microsoft Plus! add-on package. This section shows you how to Install and configure Internet Mail.

Installing Internet Mail

As I've said, the Internet Mail service comes as part of the Microsoft Plus! add-on. To get the service on your system, you must install Microsoft Plus! and include the Internet Jumpstart Kit option as part of the installation.

After that's done, follow the steps I outlined earlier in this chapter for adding new services to your Exchange profile (see "Adding Services After Exchange Is Installed"). After you've added the service, you'll see the Internet Mail properties sheet shown in Figure 27.23. I'll show you how to fill in this dialog box in the next section.

Configuring Internet Mail

Before you can use Exchange for your Internet mail missions, you need to configure your e-mail address, mail server, password, and more. You use the Internet Mail dialog box to do this.

NOTE: THE MICROSOFT INTERNET MAIL CLIENT

OSR2 comes with an Internet Mail program (which is also available on Microsoft's Web site). For e-mail, this client is designed to handle the Internet's SMTP/POP3 and MIME standards, and it offers a few features that Exchange doesn't (such as the capability to add signatures to your messages automatically). I'll take a closer look at this program in Chapter 40, "Internet Mail: Messaging Made Easy."

FIGURE 27.23.

Use the Internet Mail dialog box to configure your Internet e-mail account.

General Properties

The General properties tab covers the basic data for your account, such as your address, server, and password. Here are the fields to fill in:

Full name: Enter your name here (if it isn't filled in already).

E-mail address: Use this field to enter your Internet e-mail address.

Internet Mail server: This is the domain name of your service provider's mail server. If your service provider uses separate machines for Post Office Protocol (POP3) and Simple Mail Transport Protocol (SMTP), enter the POP3 machine in this field (and see the information on the Advanced button, at the end of this list).

Account name: This is the name of your POP3 account on the mail server.

Password: This is the password for your POP3 account.

Message Format: If you click this button, the Message Format dialog box, shown in Figure 27.24, appears. These options determine how Exchange sends rich text messages. If you activate the Use MIME when sending messages check box, Exchange uses the MIME (Multipurpose Internet Mail Extensions) format for sending messages; if you deactivate this check box, Exchange uses Uuencode instead (this applies to both incoming and outgoing messages). You can also use the Character Set button to specify the character set to be used when you're sending messages that include extended characters (you'll usually choose either ISO 8859-1 or US ASCII).

FIGURE 27.24.

Use this dialog box to specify the format and character set to use for your Internet e-mail messages.

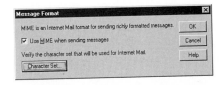

TROUBLESHOOTING: EXCHANGE ADDS EXTRA CHARACTERS

If your recipients complain that your messages contain extra characters, such as equals signs (=) at the end of every line, MIME is the likely culprit. If you activate the Use MIME when sending messages option, some gateways won't correctly interpret all the characters in your message. For example, soft returns often end up with an extraneous equals sign. To fix this problem, turn off the Use MIME when sending messages option.

Advanced Options: Clicking this button displays the Advanced Options dialog box. You use the text box to specify an alternative mail server to use for outgoing mail. You need to fill this in only if your mail server doesn't process outgoing mail. For example, some Internet systems use separate computers for POP3 (incoming mail) and SMTP (outgoing mail). In this case, use the Advanced Options dialog box to enter the domain name of the SMTP machine.

Connection Properties

The Connection tab, shown in Figure 27.25, controls how Exchange connects to your Internet mail server. Here are your choices:

Connect using the network: Activate this option if you connect to the Internet via your local area network.

Connect using the modem: Activate this option if you connect to the Internet via your modem. In the Dial using the following connection drop-down list, select the Dial-Up Networking connection you want to use. If you haven't yet set up a connection, you can learn how it's done in Chapter 35. (Note that you can create a new connection right from the Connection tab by clicking the Add Entry button. In addition, the Edit Entry button lets you modify an existing entry, and the Login As button lets you change the name and password for your account.)

Work off-line and use Remote Mail: When this check box is deactivated, Exchange downloads all waiting messages from your Internet mailbox. If you prefer to view your headers and then selectively download messages, activate this check box to use Exchange's Remote Mail feature.

Schedule: If you aren't using Remote Mail, click the Schedule button to set the interval at which Exchange will check for new mail. In the Schedule dialog box that appears, use the Check for new messages every *x* minute(s) spinner to set the interval you prefer.

Log File: This button lets you specify options that Exchange will use to keep a log of your Internet Mail sessions. In the Log File dialog box, use the `Specify the level of logging you want` list to choose `No Logging`, `Basic` (logs only logon and logoff times and error messages), or `Troubleshooting` (logs the complete transaction record between the client and server; use this option only if you're having problems, because the log file can get huge). Also, use the `Specify a location for the log file` text box to specify the log file to use (the default is `IMAIL.LOG` in your main Windows 95 folder).

FIGURE 27.25.

Use the Connection tab to determine how Exchange connects to your Internet mail server.

Customizing Exchange

Now that you have Exchange installed, your services added, and everything configured, you're ready to start sending e-mail with Exchange. Before you take the plunge, however, you might want to play around with a few customization options that apply to Exchange as a whole. I'll finish off this chapter by taking you through these options. (You need to open your Exchange Inbox to work with these settings.)

Setting Exchange Options

Exchange is loaded with extra options you can use to fine-tune the program. To work with these settings, select View | Options. You'll see the Options dialog box, shown in Figure 27.26. The next few sections run through most of the tabs in this dialog box. (I'll hold off on the Read and Send tabs until I talk about reading and sending e-mail in the next chapter.)

General Options

The General tab presents a mixed bag of settings that control everything from what Exchange does when new mail shows up to whether the Exchange toolbar shows ToolTips. Here's the rundown:

When new mail arrives: These check boxes determine what Exchange does to let you know that a new message has arrived in your inbox. These options are useful if Exchange is checking for new mail automatically. If you activate the Play a sound check box, Exchange beeps your speaker; if you activate Briefly change the pointer, the mouse pointer changes to an envelope icon for a split second (when they say briefly, they *mean* briefly); if you activate Display a notification message, you see the dialog box shown in Figure 27.27. If you click Yes, Exchange opens the first of your new messages.

FIGURE 27.26.

Use the Options dialog box to change a few global Exchange settings.

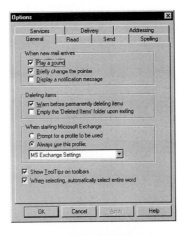

FIGURE 27.27.

If you activate the Display a notification message *check box, you'll see this dialog box whenever a new message arrives in your inbox.*

NOTE: EXCHANGE ALWAYS INDICATES NEW MAIL IN THE TASKBAR

No matter which options you activate in the When new mail arrives group, Exchange always indicates that you have new mail by displaying an envelope icon in the taskbar's system tray.

Deleting items: These check boxes control how Exchange reacts to message or folder deletions. As you'll see in the next chapter, deleting an item only sends it to a special folder called Deleted Items. You permanently delete items only when you remove them from this folder. If you activate the `Warn before permanently deleting items` check box, Exchange asks whether you're sure you want to remove an item from the `Deleted Items` folder. If you activate the `Empty the 'Deleted Items' folder upon exiting` check box, Exchange cleans out the `Deleted Items` folder each time you exit the program.

When starting Microsoft Exchange: These options control your Exchange profiles. Later in this chapter, I'll show you how to create new profiles (see "Creating New Exchange Profiles"). After you have multiple profiles in place, activate the `Prompt for a profile to be used` option so that Exchange will ask you which profile you want to use at startup. If you want to use a particular profile full-time, activate the `Always use this profile` option, and then select the profile you want from the drop-down list provided.

NOTE: CREATING MULTIPLE PROFILES

Before you can create multiple profiles, you must activate the `Prompt for a profile to be used` option, and then restart Microsoft Exchange.

Show ToolTips on toolbars: When this check box is activated, Exchange displays a short description (a *ToolTip)* of a toolbar button whenever you hover the mouse pointer over the button for a second or two.

When selecting, automatically select entire word: When this check box is activated, Exchange selects entire words as you drag the mouse over text. In other words, even if you drag the mouse over only part of the word, Exchange still selects the entire word. If you need the capability to select text letter by letter, deactivate this option.

Spelling Options

You'll see the Spelling tab, shown in Figure 27.28, only if you've installed a 32-bit application that comes with a spell-checking engine. (Microsoft Word for Windows 95 is one example.) In this case, the application "lends" the spell checker to Exchange. Most of the options are common to all spell checkers, but two are specific to Exchange:

Always check spelling before sending: If you activate this check box, Exchange runs your message through the spell checker before sending it. This feature is handy in case you forget to check for spelling blunders yourself.

The original text in a reply or forward: As you'll see in the next chapter, when you reply to or forward a message, Exchange can include the original message text as part of the new missive. If you activate this check box, Exchange won't bother checking the spelling in the original text, which can save some time.

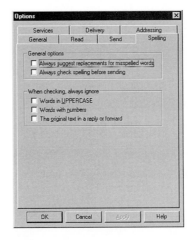

Delivery Options

The options in the Delivery tab, shown in Figure 27.29, modify a couple of settings that Exchange uses with incoming and outgoing messages:

Deliver new mail to the following location: This drop-down list determines which message store (PST file) is used to hold incoming messages. I demonstrate how to create new message stores in the next chapter. If you have multiple message stores defined, you can also use the **Secondary location** list to specify a backup store in case the main store is out of commission.

Recipient addresses are processed by these information services in the following order: This list determines the order in which outgoing messages are delivered. The service at the top of the list has its messages sent first, then the next service, and so on. To change the order, highlight a service and use the Move Up and Move Down arrow buttons provided.

FIGURE 27.29.

The Delivery tab's options control what Exchange does with incoming and outgoing messages.

Addressing Options

The Addressing tab, shown in Figure 27.30, contains a few options that control how Exchange works with the various address lists in your Personal Address Book (which I discuss in more detail in Chapter 28):

Show this address list first: This drop-down list determines the default address list that Exchange displays whenever you open the address book.

Keep personal addresses in: This drop-down list specifies the address book you want to use to store any addresses you create by hand.

When sending mail, check names using these address lists in the following order: Exchange can verify mail addresses before you send messages. This list determines the order Exchange uses when going through its checks. To change the order, highlight a list and use the Move Up and Move Down arrow buttons provided. To reduce the number of address lists you have to deal with, highlight a list and click Remove. If you later decide you need that list again, click Add to display the Add Address List dialog box, highlight the list, and click the Add button.

27

SETTING UP
MICROSOFT
EXCHANGE

FIGURE 27.30.

Use the Addressing tab to control how Exchange works with your address lists.

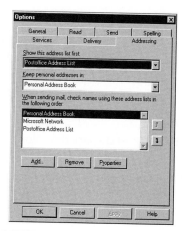

Creating New Exchange Profiles

If you use only one or two messaging services and you're the only person who uses your computer for e-mail, Exchange's default profile will be all you need. Having multiple profiles, however, does prove useful in plenty of situations:

■ If you do most of your e-mailing using a single service (Internet Mail, for example), you could speed up Exchange and simplify its operation by creating a profile that uses only that service. You could then create a second profile that includes your other services, and you could load that profile only when you need it.

- Remember that profiles store not only the services you use, but also the configurations of these services. Therefore, you could create different profiles for different configurations. For example, you could set up one profile to use Remote Mail while you're sitting at your computer. If you're going out, you could switch to a second profile that's configured to check your mail unattended.

- If you have multiple e-mail accounts in the same service, Exchange doesn't let you add the service twice in a single profile. Instead, you need to create a new profile, add the service, and then configure it for the other account.

- If you share your computer with other people, you can set up a profile for each person to use.

To create a new profile, follow these steps:

1. Make sure that you've activated the `Prompt for a profile to be used` option in the Options dialog box, as described earlier, and then select File | Exit and Log Off to quit all messaging applications.

2. Restart Exchange. You'll eventually see the Choose Profile dialog box, shown in Figure 27.31.

FIGURE 27.31.

Use this dialog box to create new profiles and select the profile you want to use.

3. Later, you'll use the `Profile Name` drop-down list to select the profile you want to work with. For now, though, click New. The Inbox Setup Wizard appears.

4. Run through the steps I outlined earlier for setting up a profile. (Be sure, of course, to specify a different name for this profile.) When you're done, you're returned to the Choose Profile dialog box, and your new profile is selected in the `Profile Name` list.

TIP: HOW TO AVOID RECONFIGURING EXISTING SERVICES

One of the problems with creating a new profile is that Exchange makes you reconfigure all of your services. You can, however, avoid this drudgery. When you're creating your new profile, be sure to select the `Manually configure information services` option in the first Inbox Setup Wizard dialog box. When the Wizard prompts you to add services, just click OK. Proceed normally, but when you get back to the Choose Profile dialog box, load one of your other profiles (specifically, the profile that contains the services you want to use for this new profile). Then, when you're in Exchange later, select Tools | Services to display the Services dialog box. Highlight one of the services you want to use in your new profile, and then click Copy. In the Copy Information Service dialog box that appears, highlight the name of your new profile, and click OK. Exchange copies the service and its configuration to the new profile.

5. If you want this profile to be your default (this means it will be selected automatically in the `Profile Name` list each time you start Exchange), click the Options>> button, and activate the `Set as default profile` check box in the expanded dialog box, shown in Figure 27.32.

FIGURE 27.32.

Here's the expanded dialog box you see when you click the Options>> button.

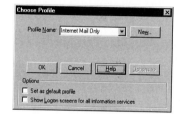

6. If you want to run through the logon screens and options for each service at startup, activate the `Show Logon screens for all information services` check box.

7. Click OK. Exchange loads the profile.

Customizing the Exchange Toolbar

One of Exchange's most useful customization tricks is the capability to set up the toolbar the way you want. This feature just cries out to be implemented in all the other Windows 95 accessories, but somehow only the Microsoft Exchange design team was able to get it done. Here are the steps to follow to customize the toolbar:

1. Select Tools | Customize Toolbar. Exchange displays the Customize Toolbar dialog box, shown in Figure 27.33.

FIGURE 27.33.

Use this dialog box to remake the Exchange toolbar in your own image.

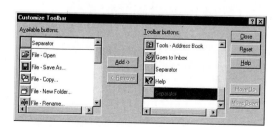

2. To add a button to the toolbar, highlight it in the `Available buttons` list, and click Add->. (Add the Separator button to generate a space between buttons.)

3. To remove a button from the toolbar, highlight it in the `Toolbar buttons` list and click <-Remove.

4. To change the order of the toolbar buttons, highlight a button in the `Toolbar buttons` list, and then use Move Up and Move Down to position the button where you want it.

5. When you're done, click Close.

Making Exchange Secure

Right out of the box, Exchange isn't very secure. If you're already logged on to Windows 95, anyone can start Exchange and view your mail with impunity. Even if Windows 95 isn't started, a new user can still log on under a new user name and view your mail! If you have sensitive information, you'll need to take further steps to keep prying eyes away from your messages.

Fortunately, securing your copy of Exchange is easy. Here are the steps to follow:

1. Select Tools | Services to display the Services dialog box.

2. In the list of services, highlight `Personal Folders` (this is your message store), and click Properties. This action displays the Personal Folders properties sheet, shown in Figure 27.34.

FIGURE 27.34.

Use this dialog box to set a password for your message store.

3. Click the Change Password button.

4. In the dialog box that appears, enter your new password in the two text boxes provided (you don't have to worry about entering an old password because, presumably, you don't have one), and click OK.

5. Click OK until you're back in the Exchange window.

6. Select File | Exit and Log Off.

When you start Exchange now, you'll see the dialog box shown in Figure 27.35. You (or anyone else) won't get access to your message store until the correct password is entered. Note too that after you're in Exchange, no one can change the properties of the message store without again entering the password.

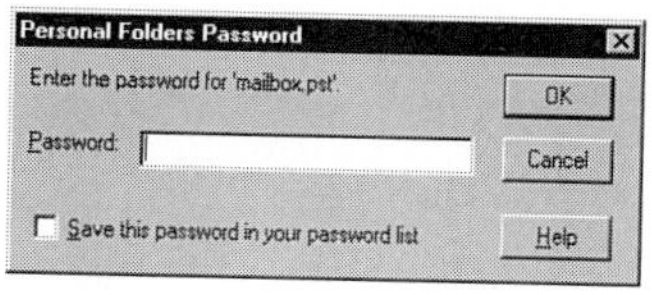

FIGURE 27.35.

After you've defined a password, Windows 95 won't load Exchange until you enter the magic word.

Summary

This chapter introduced you to Microsoft Exchange, Windows 95's e-mail and fax client. My goal was to help you get Exchange up and running on your system. To that end, I showed you how to install the client and services, establish a Microsoft Mail postoffice, and set up your default profile. From there, you learned how to configure four mail services: Microsoft Mail, The Microsoft Network Mail, CompuServe Mail, and Internet Mail. Finally, I showed you how to set various Exchange customization settings, including the Options dialog box, new profiles, the toolbar, and security.

I explain how to use Exchange to send and read e-mail in the next chapter, but here are a few more book nooks to check out for related Exchange information:

■ If you'll be using a modem to connect to your mailbox, see Chapter 25, "Maximizing Modem Communications," to learn how to set it up in Windows 95.

■ If you want to use The Microsoft Network to exchange e-mail, you'll find all the setup and configuration procedures in Chapter 26, "Getting Online with The Microsoft Network."

■ If it's faxing capabilities you're after, you'll find everything you need to know in Chapter 29, "Using Microsoft Fax to Send and Receive Faxes."

■ You can work with Exchange remotely via modem. To find out how this works, see Chapter 35, "Remote Computing with Dial-Up Networking."

■ You won't be able to use Internet Mail with Exchange until your system is set up for general Internet use. I show you how to do that in Chapter 37, "Windows 95 and the Internet."

■ If you're looking for coverage of Microsoft's new Internet Mail client, head for Chapter 40, "Internet Mail: Messaging Made Easy."

CHAPTER 28

Exchanging E-Mail with Microsoft Exchange

IN THIS CHAPTER

> *There's a kind of nakedness, and like real nakedness, it can lead to anything from embarrassment to intimacy.*
>
> —*Jack Mingo on e-mail*

At this point, you should have Microsoft Exchange installed, configured, and ready for action. You're now free to start firing off missives, notes, memos, tirades, harangues, and any other kind of digital correspondence (or *bit-spit,* as some wags like to call electronic text) that strikes your fancy. And, of course, you'll also want to read any incoming messages that others have sent your way.

This chapter shows you how to use Exchange to perform these kinds of e-mail chores. You'll learn how to compose messages, check for new mail, read received messages, reply to these messages, work with the Exchange Address Book, and do lots more.

A Tour of the Exchange Window

Just to review, you start Exchange either by double-clicking the desktop's Inbox icon or by selecting Start | Programs | Microsoft Exchange. After negotiating one or two dialog boxes (such as a Microsoft Mail logon dialog box or a Choose Profile dialog box), you'll eventually see a window similar to the one shown in Figure 28.1. As you can see, the Exchange window is divided into two areas: the *folders list* and the *message list.*

FIGURE 28.1.

The Microsoft Exchange window.

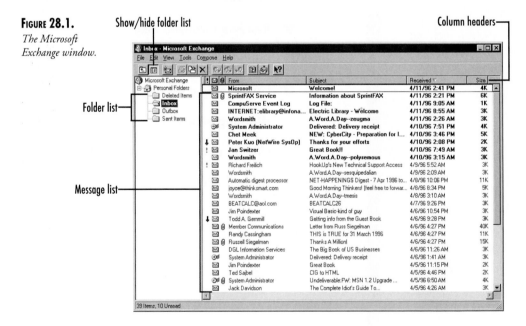

Show/hide folder list

Column headers

Folder list

Message list

The folders list is the box on the left side of the window. (If you don't see this list, either activate View | Folders or click the Show/Hide Folder List button on the toolbar.) These folders comprise your personal message store, and they serve as storage areas for different types of messages. I'll show you how to create folders and move messages between them later in this chapter, but for now, here's a rundown on Exchange's default folders:

Deleted Items: This folder holds the items (messages and other folders) you delete.

Inbox: This folder holds all of your incoming messages. When you first start Exchange, it displays the contents of the Inbox folder by default.

Outbox: This folder holds messages you've composed but haven't sent yet.

Sent Items: This folder holds a copy of each message you send.

The message list shows you the messages that reside in the currently selected folder. I'll show you how to customize the columns in the next section, but here's a review of the default columns:

This column tells you the priority level assigned to the message. A red exclamation mark indicates a high priority, and a blue down arrow indicates a low priority. If you don't see a symbol in this column, either the message has medium priority or no priority was assigned.

This column tells you the message type. E-mail and editable fax messages display an envelope; non-editable fax messages display a fax icon; system messages (such as errors and delivery notifications) use a postmark icon (see Figure 28.1 for some examples).

A paper clip icon in this column tells you that the message contains an attachment (that is, an OLE object embedded in the message).

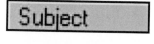

This column tells you the name or address of the person or system that sent you the message.

This column shows you the Subject line of the message.

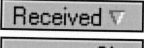

This column tells you the date and time the message was received.

This column tells you the size of the message.

28

MICROSOFT EXCHANGE

Customizing the Message Columns

The default columns in Exchange tell you the basic information you need for any message. Much more information is available, however. For example, you might want to know the date and time the message was sent, the number of lines in the message, and the first few words of the message. All of these items and many more can be displayed as columns in the message list. Here are the steps to follow to customize Exchange's columns:

1. Select View | Columns. Exchange displays the Columns dialog box, shown in Figure 28.2.

FIGURE 28.2.

Use the Columns dialog box to customize the columns displayed in the message list.

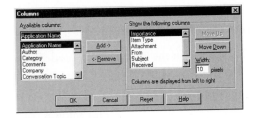

2. To add a column, highlight it in the Available columns list and click Add->.

3. To remove a column, highlight it in the Show the following columns list and click <-Remove.

4. To change the order of the columns, highlight a column in the Show the following columns list, and then use the Move Up and Move Down buttons to position the column where you want it. (Columns listed at the top are displayed on the left of the message list.)

5. To adjust the width of a column, highlight it and enter a value (in pixels) in the Width text box.

6. When you're done, click OK.

TIP: EASIER COLUMN SIZING

Entering pixel values is the hard way to size a message list column. The easy way is to use the mouse to drag the right edge of the column's header to the left or right.

Sorting the Messages

By default, Exchange sorts the messages in descending order according to the values in the Received column. But you're free to sort the messages based on any displayed column. Here are the techniques you can use:

- Select View | Sort to display the Sort dialog box, shown in Figure 28.3. Use the Sort items by list to choose the column you want to use for the sort, select either Ascending or Descending, and click OK.

FIGURE 28.3.

Use this dialog box to sort your messages.

- Click the header for the column you want to use for the sort. An arrow appears beside the column name to tell you the direction of the sort (an up arrow for ascending and a down arrow for descending).
- Right-click the header of the column you want to use, and then select either Sort Ascending or Sort Descending from the context menu.

Working with the Exchange Address Book

As you'll see a bit later, when you compose a new message or reply to a received message, Exchange provides fields in which you can specify the address of the recipient. If you have correspondents with whom you swap notes frequently, typing their e-mail addresses each time can be a pain. (This is especially true for some Internet e-mail addresses, which can be absurdly lengthy.)

Instead of typing your recipients' addresses by hand each time you compose a message, you can use Exchange's *Address Book* to store these frequently used addresses for easy recall. Here are the methods you can use to display the Address Book:

- Select Tools | Address Book.
- Press Ctrl-Shift-B.
- In the message composition window, click either the To or the Cc button.

- Click the Address Book button on the toolbar.

Figure 28.4 shows the Address Book window that Exchange displays. (If you're in the middle of composing a message, you'll see a slightly different version of this window.) The bulk of the window is taken up by a list of names, and these are determined by the currently selected item in the Show names from the box. This box contains the various address lists you have to work with. Depending on the services you installed, you should see one or more of the following lists:

Microsoft Network: Selecting this item displays the complete list of members of The Microsoft Network. To download this list, Exchange will connect you to MSN if you're not already online.

Postoffice Address List: This is the list of users in your Microsoft Mail postoffice.

CompuServe Address Book: This is the address information picked up from your existing CompuServe installation when you installed CompuServe Mail.

28

MICROSOFT EXCHANGE

Personal Address Book: You can use this list either to add new addresses or to add existing names from any of the other lists. I'll show you how this works later in this section.

FIGURE 28.4.

Use the Address Book to store your frequently used e-mail addresses.

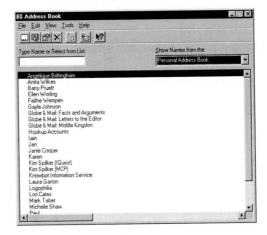

When you select an address list, the Address Book displays the names contained in the list. If you scroll to the right, you'll see two more columns: one that tells you the type of address (such as MS for a Microsoft Mail address or SMTP for an Internet address), and another that specifies the e-mail address.

To find a specific name in the address list, use any of the following techniques:

- Move into the list and scroll through it using the scrollbars or the navigation keys (up arrow, down arrow, Page Up, and Page Down).
- In the Type Name or Select from List text box, type the first few letters of the name you want.
- Select Tools | Find (or press Ctrl-Shift-F), enter the name in the Find dialog box, and click OK.

NOTE: SEARCHING FOR MSN MEMBERS

You can perform more specific searches if you're working with the list of addresses from The Microsoft Network. In this case, the Find dialog box includes fields for the member ID, first name, last name, address, company name, and even sex and marital status. (However, as I mentioned in Chapter 26, "Getting Online with The Microsoft Network," few MSN members provide such personal details.)

The Address Book Toolbar

Before getting into the various techniques you can use to work with the Address Book, let's take a second to examine the buttons available on the Address Book toolbar. Table 28.1 spells them out.

Table 28.1. Address Book toolbar buttons.

Button	Name	Description
	New Entry	Adds a new address to the Personal Address Book.
	Find	Displays the Find dialog box.
	Properties	Displays the properties sheet for the selected address.
	Delete	Deletes the selected address.
	Add to Personal Address Book	Adds the selected address to the Personal Address Book.
	New Message	Starts a new e-mail message.
	Help	Invokes What's This? Help. After clicking this button, click a control in the Address Book window to display a Help topic related to that control.

Adding Addresses to Your Personal Address Book

Your Personal Address Book is a PAB file that resides on your hard disk (usually in the Exchange folder under the filename MAILBOX.PAB). You use the Personal Address Book in either of two ways: to store addresses from the other address lists, or to store new addresses.

Adding Addresses from Other Address Lists

You can use the PAB to cull addresses from one of the other address lists. For example, if you have friends on The Microsoft Network, you might want to pull their addresses out of the MSN list and store them in your PAB. This way, you don't have to load the entire MSN address list every time you want to send them a message.

To move an address from another address list into your PAB, display the appropriate list, high-light the name, and then use any of the following techniques:

- Select File | Add to Personal Address Book.
- Click the Add to Personal Address Book button on the toolbar.
- Select File | Properties (or click the toolbar's Properties button), and in the properties sheet that appears, select `Personal Address Book`.
- Right-click the name and select Add to Personal Address Book from the context menu.

Adding New Addresses

To store new addresses that don't exist in the other address lists, follow these steps:

1. Select File | New Entry or click the New Entry toolbar button. Exchange displays the New Entry dialog box, shown in Figure 28.5.

FIGURE 28.5.

Use this dialog box to select the type of address you want to create.

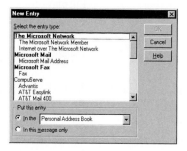

2. In the `Select the entry type` list, highlight the type of address you want to create, and then click OK. The dialog box that appears depends on the type of address you selected. For example, Figure 28.6 shows the properties sheet for an Internet Mail address.

FIGURE 28.6.

The properties sheet that Exchange displays depends on the address type you selected. This dialog box is for an Internet e-mail address.

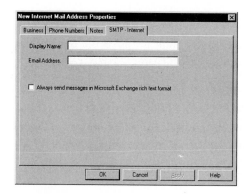

3. Fill in the address particulars. In most cases, the properties sheet also has Business, Phone Numbers, and Notes tabs you can fill out as well.

4. When you're done, click OK.

Changing the Properties of the Personal Address Book

Exchange keeps track of a few properties related to the Personal Address Book. These include the name that appears in the address list, the filename, and how names are arranged. To view these properties, select Tools | Options to display the Addressing dialog box, highlight `Personal Address Book`, and click Properties. Figure 28.7 shows the properties sheet that Exchange displays. Here's a summary of the available controls:

Name: This is the name that appears in the list of address lists in the Address Book dialog box.

Path: This is the full pathname of the PAB file. If you've created other PAB files in other profiles, you can use this text box to specify a different file.

Show names by: These two options determine whether the Personal Address Book displays names by first name or last name.

FIGURE 28.7.

Use the properties sheet to adjust some Personal Address Book options.

Exchange also provides a Notes tab you can use to add a description of the PAB or some other annotation.

TIP: SHARING A PERSONAL ADDRESS BOOK

If you use Exchange on multiple machines (say, at home and at work, or on a desktop and a notebook machine), don't re-create the Personal Address Book from scratch on each machine. Instead, create the PAB on one machine, and then copy the PAB file to your other

continues

continued

machines. If you use a different name, be sure to adjust the Path field in the PAB's properties sheet accordingly. (In case you're wondering, Exchange lets you specify a network path to a remote PAB file, but it doesn't let two installations of Exchange work with the file at the same time.)

Creating a Personal Distribution List

You'll see that the Address Book makes it a snap to include addresses in your correspondence. Even the Address Book method of choosing names can get tedious, however, if you regularly send messages to many people. For example, you might broadcast a monthly bulletin to a few dozen recipients, or you might send notes to entire departments.

To make these kinds of mass mailings easier to manage, Exchange lets you create a *personal distribution list* (PDL). This is a collection of e-mail addresses grouped under a single name. To send a message to every member of the PDL, you simply specify the PDL as the "recipient" of the message. Here are the steps to follow to create a PDL:

1. In the Address Book window, display the New Entry dialog box as described earlier.

2. At the bottom of the Select the entry type list, highlight Personal Distribution List and click OK. Exchange displays the properties sheet shown in Figure 28.8.

FIGURE 28.8.

Use the dialog box to define a new PDL.

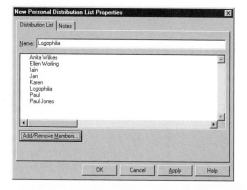

3. In the Name text box, enter the name you want to use for the PDL.

4. To include addresses (that is, *members*) in the PDL, click the Add/Remove Members button. Exchange displays the Edit Members dialog box, shown in Figure 28.9.

FIGURE 28.9.

Use the Edit Members dialog box to add PDL e-mail addresses.

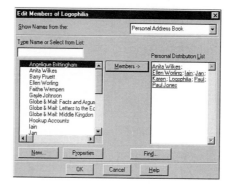

5. Use the Show Names from the box to select the address list you want to work with.

6. To add members, highlight the names and click Members->.

7. When you're done, click OK to return to the PDL properties sheet.

8. Click OK. Exchange adds the PDL to the Personal Address Book and identifies it as a PDL by placing a special icon beside the name.

Setting Your Member Properties for The Microsoft Network

In our discussion of The Microsoft Network in Chapter 26, I showed you how to view the properties sheet for each member. When you sign up with MSN, you provide some basic personal data, such as your name, company name, city, state, and country. If you're so inclined, however, you can add more details, such as your date of birth, sex, marital status, interests, job descriptions, and much more. Obviously, some of this information is highly personal, so you might not want the million-plus members of MSN to know so much about you. However, you're perfectly free to fill in whatever you like (or make it all up!). Here's how you go about it:

1. In the Address Book, select Microsoft Network in the Show names from the list.

2. Click Connect when Exchange prompts you to connect to MSN.

3. Find your name in the list of MSN members. This list is huge, so you'll probably want to type your name or use the Find feature.

4. Highlight your name and display its properties sheet (by selecting File | Properties or by clicking the Properties toolbar button). Figure 28.10 shows the properties sheet that appears.

5. Use the General, Personal, and Professional tabs to fill in your data.

6. Click OK. A dialog box appears to let you know that your info will be updated within 24 hours.

28

MICROSOFT
EXCHANGE

FIGURE 28.10.

Use your properties sheet to specify your MSN member properties.

Composing and Sending a New Message

It's time now to get down to the e-mail nitty-gritty. For starters, I'll show you how to use Exchange to compose and send a message. You'll also learn how to work with the Exchange address book, how to embed objects in your messages, and how to use WordMail, the Microsoft Word replacement for the default Exchange message editor.

Exchange's Send Options

Before we get started, let's examine the various options that Exchange provides for sending e-mail. Select Tools | Options and, in the Options dialog box that appears, select the Send tab. You'll see the controls shown in Figure 28.11. Here's a synopsis of the available options:

Use this font: Click the Font button to specify the default font to use in the message composition window.

Request that a receipt be sent back when: These check boxes determine the default level of notification you want for your messages. If you activate the item has been read, you'll receive a message (a *receipt*) telling you when the recipient read your message. If you activate the item has been delivered, you'll get a receipt when the message has been delivered to the recipient's mailbox.

Set sensitivity: This drop-down list assigns a default sensitivity level for your messages. Select Normal (no sensitivity), Personal (nonbusiness), Private (recipients can't modify your messages when replying), or Confidential (tells the recipient that the contents of your message should be forwarded with caution).

Set importance: These options determine the default importance level for your messages. Choose High, Normal, or Low.

Save a copy of the item in the 'Sent Items' folder: When this check box is activated, Exchange saves a copy of your message in the Sent Items folder. It's a good idea to leave this option checked because it gives you a record of the messages you send.

28

FIGURE 28.11.

Use the Send tab to configure Exchange's default settings for composing and sending messages.

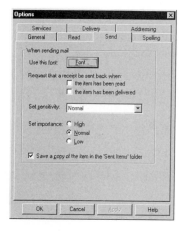

Here are some notes to bear in mind when setting these values:

- The notification, sensitivity, and importance options only set the default levels. You can always change the levels for individual messages.
- Not all remote systems will honor receipt requests or forward the assigned levels of sensitivity or importance.
- Your recipients will see the assigned importance and sensitivity levels only if they're displaying the Importance and Sensitivity columns in Exchange.

Composing a Message

Composing a message isn't all that much different from composing a letter or memo in WordPad. You just need to add a few extra bits of information, such as the e-mail address of your recipient and a description of your message.

To get started, use any of the following techniques:

- Select Compose | New Message.
- Press Ctrl-N.

- Click the New Message button on the toolbar.

Whichever method you choose, the New Message window, shown in Figure 28.12, appears. Here are the basic steps to follow to compose your message:

1. In the To field, enter the address of the recipient. If you want to send the message to multiple recipients, separate each address with a semicolon (;).

2. In the Cc field, enter the addresses of any recipients you want to receive copies of the message. Again, separate multiple addresses with semicolons.

3. In the Subject field, enter a brief description of the message. This description will appear in the Subject column of the recipient's mail client, so make sure that it accurately describes your message.

4. Use the box below the Subject field to enter your message. Feel free to use any of the formatting options found on the Format menu or the Formatting toolbar. Remember, however, that not all systems will transfer the rich text formatting.

5. To send your message, select File | Send, press Ctrl-Enter, or click the Send button on the toolbar.

Figure 28.12.

Use the New Message window to enter the e-mail addresses of your recipients, the Subject line, and the body of the message.

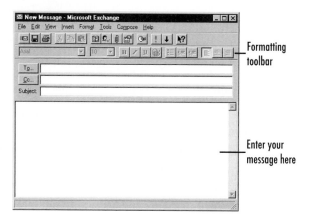

When you click Send, Exchange delivers the message to the recipient's mailbox or to the remote system (depending on the address). The exception to this rule is if you're using Exchange's Remote Mail feature (see "Retrieving Messages with Remote Mail" later in this chapter). In this case, Exchange doesn't deliver the message. Instead, it stores it in the Outbox folder. To deliver the message, you have two choices:

- Invoke Remote Mail and initiate the mail transfer.
- Select Tools | Deliver Now Using and, from the cascade menu that appears, select the appropriate service (such as Microsoft Mail or Internet Mail). If you have several messages destined for multiple services, select All Services (or press Ctrl-M) instead.

Using the Address Book to Specify Recipients

When you're composing a message, you can use the Address Book to add recipients without having to type their addresses. First, use the techniques described earlier to display the Address Book (remember that when you're in the composition window, you can click the To and Cc buttons to display the Address Book). Figure 28.13 shows the slightly different version of the Address Book that appears.

Use the Show names from the list to select the address list you want to work with. Highlight the recipient and then click either To-> (if you want the name to appear in the To field) or Cc-> (if you want the name to appear in the Cc field). When you've added all the recipients for your message, click OK.

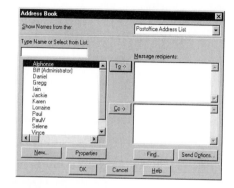

Inserting Objects in a Message

Exchange's OLE support means that you can insert objects into your messages. These objects are sent to the recipient using the Rich Text format, so as long as the recipient's system supports this format (specifically, the remote gateway must be able to handle MIME or Uuencode attachments, and the recipient's e-mail client must be MAPI-compliant), you can attach spreadsheets, word processing documents, graphics, files, and any other OLE object to your messages.

Depending on the type of object you want to work with, Exchange gives you three methods of inserting objects:

Inserting a file: To insert a file into the message, select Insert | File or click the toolbar's Insert File button. In the Insert File dialog box that appears, highlight the file you want to send. If you just want to include the file's text, activate the Text only option; to send the file as an attachment, activate the An attachment option. (For the second option, you can also link the embedded file by activating the Link attachment to original file check box.) When you click OK, Exchange embeds the file into the message as an icon.

TIP: TWO OTHER METHODS OF E-MAILING FILES

If you want to e-mail a file, Windows 95 offers a couple other methods that are easier to use:

- In Explorer, right-click the file you want to send, and then select Send To | Mail Recipient.

continues

continued

■ In a Windows 95 application that is "mail enabled" (such as WordPad or the Microsoft Office 95 programs), open the file you want to send, and select File | Send.

Either way, Exchange cranks out a new message and inserts the file automatically.

Inserting a message: If you want to insert another e-mail message, select Insert | Message. In the Insert Message dialog box, shown in Figure 28.14, highlight the message you want to use. Again, you can insert the message as text or as an attachment. Click OK when you're done.

FIGURE 28.14.

Use this dialog box to choose the message you want to insert.

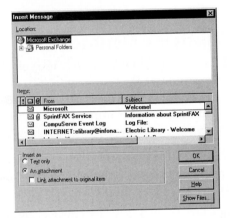

Inserting an OLE object: To insert an OLE object, select Insert | Object. In the Insert Object dialog box that appears, either select Create from new and choose the object type you want, or select Create from file and specify the filename. If you're creating a new object, Exchange invokes the appropriate application. If the application supports visual editing, the composition window assumes the characteristics (menus and toolbars) of the application. For example, Figure 28.15 shows the composition window displayed while you're creating a new Excel worksheet object.

Setting Message Properties

Before sending your message, you might want to specify a few extra options, such as asking for a delivery receipt or setting the importance and sensitivity levels. All of these items are part of the message's properties, and you can set them by selecting File | Properties. Figure 28.16 shows the properties sheet that appears. As you can see, the available controls more or less coincide with the default Send properties you saw earlier. The Internet tab lets you override the default options for the character set and message format, and the Send Options button displays controls for Microsoft Fax (covered in the next chapter) and CompuServe Mail (covered in the preceding chapter).

FIGURE 28.15.

When you insert a new object for an application that supports visual editing, the message window assumes the characteristics for the application (Excel, in this case).

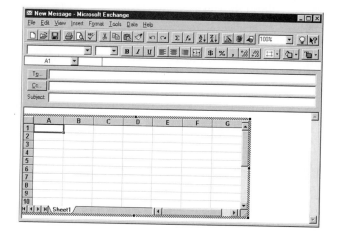

FIGURE 28.16.

Use this properties sheet to set various options for the message.

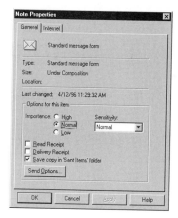

The composition window's toolbar also gives you a few buttons to make setting these properties easier. Table 28.2 presents a review of these buttons.

Table 28.2. Toolbar buttons in Exchange's composition window.

Button	Name	Description
	Properties	Displays the message's properties sheet.

continues

Table 28.2. continued

Button	Name	Description
![Read Receipt icon]	Read Receipt	Toggles the `Read Receipt` option on and off.
![Importance High icon]	Importance: High	Sets the Importance level to High.
![Importance Low icon]	Importance: Low	Sets the Importance level to Low.

Setting Up WordMail

If you have Microsoft Word for Windows 95, it comes with a component called *WordMail* that replaces the standard Exchange message editor with Microsoft Word. This is a great idea because it gives you access to some useful Word features, including on-the-fly spell checking, a grammar checker, a thesaurus, templates, AutoText, macros, and much more.

To tell Exchange that you prefer to use WordMail to compose your e-notes, select Compose | WordMail Options. In the WordMail options dialog box that appears, shown in Figure 28.17, activate the `Enable Word as Email Editor` check box.

FIGURE 28.17.

Use this dialog box to enable Word as your e-mail editor.

Word also comes with several e-mail templates: Email (`EMAIL.DOT`), Email Sample1 (`EMAIL1.DOT`), Email Sample2 (`EMAIL2.DOT`), and Email Sample3 (`EMAIL3.DOT`). Use the following techniques to work with these templates:

- Each new message you create is based on the default e-mail template. You can set one of the templates as the default by highlighting it and activating the `Set as Default Template` check box.

- To use a different template for an individual message, highlight the template and click the Compose button.

- To add a template to the list, click the Add button, highlight the template in the Add dialog box, and click Add.

- To make changes to a template, highlight it and click Edit. Exchange starts Word and loads the template.

Figure 28.18 shows the new message composition window you'll see when you use Word as your e-mail editor.

FIGURE 28.18.

With WordMail enabled, you have most of Word's commands and features at your disposal.

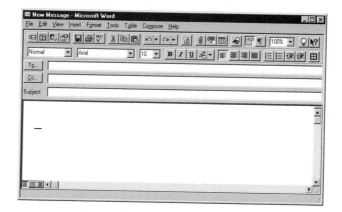

TIP: CREATING A SIGNATURE WITH WORDMAIL

In e-mail circles, a *signature* is a few lines of text at the end of a message that identifies the sender and includes their contact information (such as their company name, e-mail address, and fax number). Some people also include snappy quotations and other tidbits.

Most e-mail programs give you a method of appending a signature to your outgoing messages automatically. Unfortunately, Exchange does not. It's easy, however, if you use WordMail. Just edit the e-mail template you use for your messages, and add your signature to the template. Now, each time you compose a new message, your signature will show up automatically.

Reading Incoming Mail

Of course, you won't be spending all your time firing off notes and missives to friends and colleagues. Those people will eventually start sending messages back to you, and you might start getting regular correspondence from mailing lists, administrators, and other members of the e-mail community. This section shows you how to retrieve messages, read them, and then deal with them appropriately.

Retrieving Messages

As you saw in the preceding chapter, you can set up most of the mail services (with the exception of The Microsoft Network) to look automatically for messages that are waiting in your mailbox and, if any are found, to retrieve them to your Exchange Inbox folder. Also, Exchange checks for waiting messages each time you send a message to a particular service.

However, one of Exchange's little quirks (it has a few of them!) is that it doesn't have any kind of "Retrieve" command for downloading messages ad hoc. Instead, even if you don't have any messages to send, you get Exchange to check for incoming messages by selecting Tools | Deliver Now Using. As before, you then select the appropriate service from the cascade menu that appears. For example, if you select CompuServe Mail, Exchange connects to CompuServe, checks for waiting messages, and retrieves any it finds. (And, of course, it also sends any CompuServe messages you've composed and stored in your Outbox folder.)

This method isn't very intuitive, and it begins to make sense only when you realize that Exchange is using the verb "to deliver" in its most general sense—that is, to deliver messages *to* a service and to deliver messages *from* a service.

Retrieving Messages with Remote Mail

With each of the preceding methods, Exchange grabs any and all messages that are waiting for you and dumps them in your Inbox folder. You might not want to do this, however. For example, you might have dozens of messages waiting and you might need only one or two of them for now. Or you might have some messages that contain huge file attachments, and you might prefer to leave them on the server and then set up an unattended download overnight or while you're at lunch.

For this kind of control over your incoming messages, you have to use Exchange's Remote Mail feature. When you set up a service to use Remote Mail, Exchange doesn't retrieve your messages automatically. Instead, you must connect to the service manually. After you do, however, you can ask Remote Mail to download the headers for the waiting messages. You can then select the messages you want to retrieve and transfer only those to your inbox; the rest stay on the server.

CAUTION: REMOTE MAIL DOESN'T SEND, EITHER

As I mentioned in the preceding section, Exchange always performs sending and retrieving at the same time. This means that when you're using Remote Mail, Exchange doesn't send the messages you compose. Instead, it stores them in the Outbox folder until such time as you connect to the service via Remote Mail. The problem is that Exchange often gives you no indication that the message only went to the Outbox folder. So if you forget that you're using Remote Mail, you'll think that your message is winging its way to the recipient when, all along, it hasn't gone anywhere. (I'd be embarrassed to tell you how many times I've done this.)

Starting Remote Mail

I showed you in the preceding chapter how to set up the various mail services to use Remote Mail. (Note that The Microsoft Network always uses Remote Mail.) When you've done that, you can start Remote Mail by selecting Tools | Remote Mail and then, from the cascade menu that appears, selecting the mail service you want to use for the connection. (If you have just one service using Remote Mail, you need to select only Tools | Remote Mail.)

Remote Mail often connects to the mail server automatically at this point, so in the Remote Mail window that appears, your first task is to determine whether you're connected. You can check in several ways, but the easiest way is to examine the connection icon on the right side of the status bar. If the cable icon includes the international symbol for "not," as shown in Figure 28.19, you're not connected. In this case, select Tools | Connect.

FIGURE 28.19.

The connection icon with the "not" symbol indicates that you're not connected to the mail server.

| Last update: 4/8/96 7:51:16 PM | | 0 Items | |

This icon tells you that you're not connected

To make your life easier in the Remote Mail window, the toolbar offers one-click access to the most common features. Table 28.3 summarizes the available buttons.

Table 28.3. Remote Mail toolbar buttons.

Button	Name	Description
	Connect	Connects to the mail server.
	Disconnect	Disconnects from the mail server.
	Update Headers	Downloads the headers of the waiting messages.
	Transfer Mail	Transfers the marked messages to your Inbox (and sends any messages waiting in your Outbox).
	Mark to Retrieve	Marks the current message for retrieval.

continues

Table 28.3. continued

Button	Name	Description
	Mark to Retrieve a Copy	Marks the current message for retrieving only a copy.
	Mark to Delete	Marks the current message for deletion.
	Unmark All	Removes marks from all messages.

Downloading Message Headers

The next item on the agenda is to download the headers of the waiting messages. (Message headers include information such as the author's name and e-mail address, the Subject line of the message, the date and time the server received the message, and the size of the message.) To do this, select Tools | Update Headers. (Note too that if you're not yet connected, you can combine these two operations into one by selecting Tools | Connect and Update Headers.) After a few seconds (or minutes, depending on how many messages you have), the Remote Mail window displays the headers of the waiting messages, as shown in Figure 28.20.

FIGURE 28.20.

When you run the Update Headers command, Remote Mail grabs the message headers and displays them in the window.

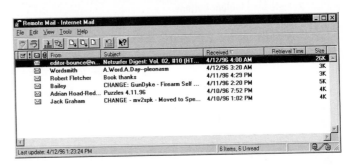

Marking and Retrieving Messages

From here, you need to decide which messages you want to retrieve. Here are the techniques to use:

- To mark a message for retrieval, highlight it and select Edit | Mark to Retrieve, or right-click it and select Mark to Retrieve from the context menu.
- To retrieve only a copy of a message (the original stays on the server), highlight it and select Edit | Mark to Retrieve a Copy, or right-click the message and select Mark to Retrieve a Copy from the context menu.

- To delete a message, highlight it and select Edit | Mark to Delete, or right-click the message and select Mark to Delete from the context menu.

- To start over, select Edit | Unmark All.

When that's taken care of, you can transfer the marked messages by selecting Tools | Transfer Mail. A dialog box similar to the one shown in Figure 28.21 appears. This dialog box lets you know how many items will be retrieved (and the size of these items) and how many will be deleted. It also reminds you that any items waiting in your Outbox folder will be submitted as well. Click OK to perform the transfer. When you're back in the Remote Mail window, select Tools | Disconnect to sever the connection to the server, and then exit.

FIGURE 28.21.

This dialog box gives you a summary of the items that will be transferred.

Exchange's Read Options

Before you start perusing your correspondence, you might want to check out Exchange's read-related properties. To view them, select Tools | Options and, in the Options dialog box, select the Read tab, shown in Figure 28.22. Here's a review of the available controls:

After moving or deleting an open item: Later in this section, I'll show you how to move messages to different folders and delete messages. These options determine what Exchange does when you move or delete the message you're reading. You can choose Open the item above it (above it in the list of messages, that is), Open the item below it, or Return to Microsoft Exchange.

Include the original text when replying: When this check box is activated, Exchange copies the text of the current message and includes it when you reply to or forward the message. (See "Replying to a Message" and "Forwarding a Message" later in this chapter.)

Indent the original text when replying: When this check box is activated, Exchange not only includes the original text in the reply, but also indents it from the left margin. This makes it easier for the recipient to differentiate between the original text and the text you add to the reply.

Close the original item: When this check box is activated, Exchange closes the original message when you reply to it or forward it.

Use this font for the reply text: Click the Font button to choose the font you want to use for the text you add to your reply or forward. (The default is a blue Arial font.)

28

MICROSOFT
EXCHANGE

FIGURE 28.22.

Use the Read tab to set various properties related to reading messages.

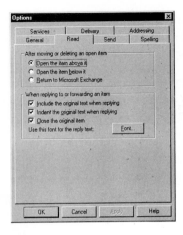

Opening a Message

At long last, you're ready to start reading your messages. In the message list, highlight the message you want to read, and then use any of the following techniques to open it:

- Select File | Open.
- Press Enter.
- Double-click the message.
- Right-click the message and select Open from the context menu.

Exchange displays that message in the window shown in Figure 28.23.

FIGURE 28.23.

Exchange uses this window to display your messages.

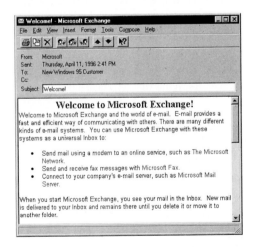

NOTE: MESSAGES THAT YOU'VE READ ARE NO LONGER BOLD

Unread messages appear in the message list in boldface type. After you've read a message, Exchange displays it in regular type so that you know right away whether you've read it. You can toggle boldfacing on and off by selecting Edit | Mark as Read or Edit | Mark as Unread.

TIP: A QUICK WAY TO ADD SENDERS TO YOUR PAB

If you want to add the sender of the message to your Personal Address Book, an easy way to do so is to right-click the sender's name in the From line in the header. From the context menu that appears, select Add to Personal Address Book.

Working with Your Messages

When you have a message open, you can do plenty of things with it (besides reading it, of course). You can print it, save it to a file, move it to another folder, delete it, and more. Most of these operations are straightforward, so I'll just summarize the basic techniques here:

Reading other messages: If you have several messages you want to read, you don't have to return to the message list to navigate your messages. If you want to move on to the next message (the one below the current message in the message list), select View | Next, or press Ctrl->, or click the Next toolbar button. If you prefer to move back to the preceding message (the one above the current message in the message list), select View | Previous, or press Ctrl-<, or click the Previous toolbar button.

  The Next button.

  The Previous button.

Dealing with attachments: If a message has an attachment, it will appear either as an icon or as an object embedded in the message. You can use the usual OLE methods of viewing the object (assuming that you have the correct server application; see Chapter 17, "Sharing Data in Windows 95: The Clipboard and OLE," for more about OLE).

Moving a message to a different folder: Later in this chapter, I'll show you how to create new folders you can use for storing related messages. To move a message to another folder, either select File | Move or click the Move Item toolbar button. In the Move dialog box that appears, highlight the folder you want to use, and then click OK.

28

MICROSOFT EXCHANGE

Saving a message: Instead of storing the message in a folder, you might prefer to save it to a file. To do this, select File | Save As. In the Save As dialog box, select a location, enter a filename, and select a format (`Text Only`, `Rich Text Format`, or `Message Format`). If the message has a file attachment (not an OLE object attachment), you can also choose `Save the Message(s) Only` or `Save these Attachments only` (for the second option, you also get a list of file attachments). When you're ready, click OK.

Printing a message: To print a copy of the message, select File | Print to display the Print dialog box. Enter your print options (including whether you want to print any attachments), and then click OK.

Deleting a message: If you want to get rid of the message you're reading, select File | Delete or press Ctrl-D. You can also click the toolbar's Delete button. Note that Exchange doesn't really delete the message. Instead, it just moves it to the `Deleted Items` folder. If you change your mind and decide to keep the message, just open the `Deleted Items` folder and move the message back. To permanently remove a message, open the `Deleted Items` folder and delete it from there.

TIP: DRAG-AND-DROP YOUR MESSAGES

The basic drag-and-drop technique comes in handy when you're dealing with Exchange messages. For example, with drag-and-drop you can carry out these actions:

- Move messages around by dragging them from the message list and dropping them on the folder where you want them moved

- Delete messages by dragging them from the message list and dropping them on the Deleted Items folder

- Save messages by dragging them from the message list and dropping them on the desktop or on a folder window

- Save file attachments by dragging them from the message and dropping them on the desktop or on a folder window

---

Replying to a Message

If you receive a message from someone who is looking for some information from you, or if you think of a witty retort to a friend's or colleague's message, you'll want to send a reply. Instead of requiring you to create a new message from scratch, however, Exchange (like all e-mail programs) has a "Reply" feature that saves you the following steps:

- Exchange starts a new message automatically.
- Exchange inserts the recipient automatically.

- Exchange inserts the original Subject line but adds "RE:" to the beginning of the text to identify this message as a reply.

- Exchange adds the header and the text of the original message into the body of the new message (unless, of course, you turned off this feature in the Read tab, as described earlier).

Exchange gives you two Reply options:

Reply to Sender: This option sends the reply only to the person who shipped out the original. Any names in the Cc line are ignored. To use this option, select Compose | Reply to Sender or press Ctrl-R. You can also click the Reply to Sender button on the toolbar.

Reply to All: This option sends the reply not only to the original author, but also to anyone else mentioned in the Cc line. To use this option, select Compose | Reply to All or press Ctrl-Shift-R. You can also click the Reply to All button on the toolbar.

Figure 28.24 gives you an idea of what the composition window looks like after you select (in this case) the Reply to Sender option.

FIGURE 28.24.

Using Exchange's "Reply to" commands saves you lots of time when you're composing responses to messages you've received.

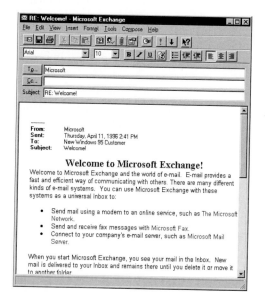

Forwarding a Message

Instead of replying to a message, you might prefer to forward it to another person. For example, you might receive a message in error, or you might think that a friend or colleague might receive some benefit from reading a message you received. Whatever the reason, you can forward a message to another address by using any of the following methods:

- Select Compose | Forward.
- Press Ctrl-F.

- Click the Forward button on the toolbar.

Exchange creates a new message, adds the original Subject line with FW: (to identify this as a forwarded message), and inserts the original text in the message body. If you like, you can add your own text as well.

Working with Folders

The four default folders that Exchange sets up are functional but not all that useful in the long term. At this early stage of your Exchange career, you might not have all that many messages in your Inbox folder, but it probably won't take long to fill up. Sure, you'll be deleting missives you don't want to bother with, but you'll still have plenty of messages you'll want to keep for posterity. So you'll still be faced with an unwieldy stack of messages before too long.

The problem here is that your messages aren't organized in any way. When you get paper memos and letters, you don't leave them cluttering your In basket, do you? No, you probably use file folders to store related correspondence. You can add the same level of organization to your e-mail correspondence by creating new folders in which to store related messages. So, for example, you could create a folder for each Internet mailing list you subscribe to, one for correspondence between you and your boss, another for your current project, one each for all your wired friends, and so on.

To create a new folder, first highlight the folder you want to use as the parent. If you want to add a folder to the main Personal Folders branch, for example, you first highlight Personal Folders. Then select File | New Folder. In the New Folder dialog box that appears, shown in Figure 28.25, enter a name for the folder, and then click OK. Figure 28.26 shows the Exchange window with a few new folders in place. (Notice how it's OK to set up folders within folders for even greater organizational depth.)

FIGURE 28.25.

Use this dialog box to enter a name for your new folder.

FIGURE 28.26.

The Exchange window with some new folders added.

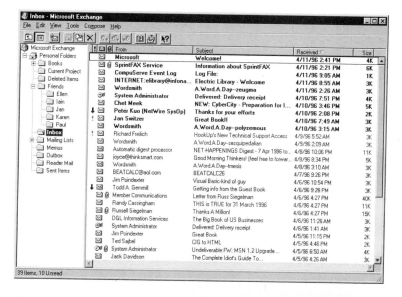

28

MICROSOFT
EXCHANGE

NOTE: CREATING NEW MESSAGE STORES

The `Personal Folders` branch is really your *message store*. Message stores are files (they use the PST extension) that can hold folders and messages. Although you probably won't ever need more than one message store, it *is* possible to add multiple message stores to a profile.

To do this, select Tools | Services, click Add, highlight `Personal Folders` in the Add Service to Profile dialog box, and click OK. Then enter a filename for the new message store, and click Open. The Create Microsoft Personal Folders dialog box appears. You use this dialog box to enter a name for the store (this is the name that appears in Exchange's folders list), the type of encryption you want, and an optional password.

Finding Data in Exchange

E-mail is one of those things that just snowballs after you begin using it. You might get only a few messages a week at first, but then you start getting a few messages a day; then, before you know it, a few *dozen* daily messages are streaming your way, and your folders are bursting at the seams. You'll probably find that you keep many of these messages because you never know when you'll need them again. But after you've accumulated many messages, finding the one you want down the road becomes a real challenge.

Fortunately, Exchange has a powerful Find command that makes the task easy. This command isn't like the Find command you saw in Chapter 13, "Working with Files and Folders," because it's geared toward searching through e-mail messages. To take a look, select Tools | Find or press Ctrl-Shift-F. Exchange displays the Find window, shown in Figure 28.27. Here's a summary of the various options you can use to define your search criteria:

Look in: This box tells you the folder Exchange will search (the default folder is the one that was highlighted when you ran the Tools | Find command). To specify a different folder, click the Folder button and highlight the folder in the Find Items in Folder dialog box. If you want Find to search all the folder's subfolders, make sure that the Include all subfolders check box is activated. Click OK to return to the Find window.

From: Use this text box to specify a sender as part of the search criteria. To choose from your address lists, click the From button.

Sent To: Use this text box to specify a recipient as part of the search criteria. Again, you can choose from your address lists by clicking the Sent To button.

Sent directly to me: Activate this check box to find messages in which your address is specified in the To line.

Copied (Cc) to me: Activate this check box to find messages in which your address is specified in the Cc line.

Subject: Use this field to search for text in the Subject line of the messages.

Message body: Use this field to search for text in the message bodies.

Advanced: If you click this button, you'll see the Advanced dialog box, shown in Figure 28.28. You can use this dialog box to narrow your search criteria to include message size, message date, importance and sensitivity levels, unread messages, and messages that have attachments.

FIGURE 28.27.

Exchange has a powerful Find command that can scour any part of your e-mail messages for text.

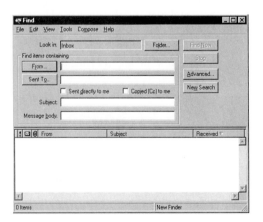

When you've specified your search criteria, click the Find Now button. Messages that match your criteria are displayed in the message list at the bottom of the window.

FIGURE 28.28.

Use this dialog box to specify advanced criteria for your search.

Using the Inbox Repair Tool

Windows 95 comes with a utility called the Inbox Repair Tool that you can use to overcome problems associated with your message store. Here are some of the problems you might encounter that can be fixed by the Inbox Repair Tool:

- You can't delete messages.
- You receive a message from Exchange stating that the PST file can't be mounted.
- You see invalid characters in messages or in the folder structure.
- You can't open attachments.
- The PST file isn't compressed automatically.
- The PST file was cross-linked, and you repaired it by using ScanDisk.

To run the Inbox Repair tool, follow these steps:

1. Exit Exchange.
2. Select Start | Programs | Accessories | System Tools | Inbox Repair Tool to display the dialog box shown in Figure 28.29.

FIGURE 28.29.

Use the Inbox Repair Tool to fix problems associated with your message store (PST file).

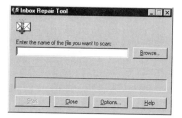

3. Enter the path and filename for the PST file you want to repair (or click Browse to use a dialog box to highlight the file).
4. Click Start to launch the scan.
5. If the Inbox Repair Tool finds any errors, follow the on-screen instructions for backing up the existing file and instituting the necessary repairs.
6. When the scan is complete, the Inbox Repair Tool displays a summary of the scan. Click OK.

28

MICROSOFT EXCHANGE

Note that the Inbox Repair Tool keeps a log of the scan. You'll find it in the same folder as the PST file. The log file has the same name as the PST file, but with a LOG extension.

Summary

This chapter took all of your Exchange installation and configuration efforts from the preceding chapter and put them to good use. Specifically, you learned how to work with the Address Book, compose and send messages, read and work with incoming mail, reply to and forward messages, create new folders, and use Exchange's Tools | Find command.

Here's a list of chapters where you'll find related information:

- If you use a modem to connect to your mailbox, see Chapter 25, "Maximizing Modem Communications," to learn how to set it up in Windows 95.

- For more information on signing up and using The Microsoft Network, give Chapter 26, "Getting Online with The Microsoft Network," a try.

- You can find faxing fun and foolishness in Chapter 29, "Using Microsoft Fax to Send and Receive Faxes."

- You can work with Exchange remotely via modem. To find out how it works, see Chapter 35, "Remote Computing with Dial-Up Networking."

- You won't be able to use Internet Mail with Exchange until your system is set up for general Internet use. I show you how to do that in Chapter 37, "Windows 95 and the Internet."

Using Microsoft Fax to Send and Receive Faxes

IN THIS CHAPTER

The fax machine is a serious blemish on the information landscape.

—Nicholas Negroponte

Remember when, a decade or so ago, the fax (or the facsimile, as it was called back then) was the hottest thing around, the new kid on the telecommunications block? How amazing it seemed that we could send a letter or memo or even a picture through the phone lines and have it emerge seconds later across town or even across the country. Sure, the fax that came slithering out the other end was a little fuzzier than the original, and certainly a lot slimier, but it sure beat using the post office.

Nowadays, though, faxing is just another humdrum part of the workaday world, and any business worth its salt has a fax machine on standby. Increasingly, however, dedicated fax machines are giving way to fax/modems—modems that have the capability to send and receive faxes in addition to their regular communications duties. Not only does this make faxing affordable for small businesses and individuals, but it also adds a new level of convenience to the whole fax experience:

■ You can send faxes right from your computer without having to print the document.

■ Because faxes sent via computer aren't scanned (as they are with a fax machine), the document that the recipient gets is sharper and easier to read.

■ You can store incoming faxes along with the rest of your e-mail.

■ You can use your printer to get a hard copy of a fax on regular paper, thus avoiding fax paper (which, besides being inherently slimy, has an annoying tendency to curl).

■ You can send binary files along with your faxes (provided that both the sending and the receiving fax/modems support this feature).

If you're looking to get into the fax fast lane, look no further than Exchange's Microsoft Fax service. This chapter shows you how to install and configure Microsoft Fax, and how to use it to send and receive faxes.

Configuring Microsoft Fax

Like all messaging services, Exchange gives you two ways to add Microsoft Fax to your profile and get it configured (I'm assuming that you've installed Windows 95's Microsoft Fax component):

■ Include Microsoft Fax while you're setting up Exchange, and then use the Inbox Setup Wizard to configure your faxing options.

■ Start Exchange, and then add and configure the Microsoft Fax service from within the Exchange environment.

Configuring Microsoft Fax Via the Inbox Setup Wizard

If you include the Microsoft Fax service while you're setting up Exchange initially, the Inbox Setup Wizard runs through a few dialog boxes that configure the basic faxing properties. Here's a summary of what to expect:

■ The Wizard first asks you to select the fax/modem you want to use with Microsoft Fax.

■ You then must decide whether you want Microsoft Fax to answer incoming calls, as shown in Figure 29.1. If you use the phone line for voice calls or if you use the modem with other communications programs, select No. Otherwise, select Yes and choose the number of rings after which Microsoft Fax should answer the phone.

FIGURE 29.1.

When you're installing Microsoft Fax, the Inbox Setup Wizard asks whether you want Microsoft Fax to take care of incoming calls.

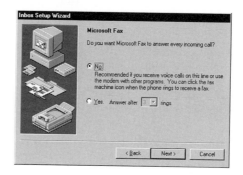

■ The Wizard asks you to enter your name, country, and fax phone number (the fax number is required).

Adding the Microsoft Fax Service Provider

If Exchange is already installed, you can add the Microsoft Fax service from within Exchange. Here are the steps to follow:

1. In Exchange, select Tools | Services to display the Services dialog box.

2. Click Add. Exchange displays the Add Services to Profile dialog box.

3. Highlight Microsoft Fax and click OK. Exchange displays a dialog box that gives you a summary of the steps you're about to follow to configure Microsoft Fax, and it asks whether you want to perform the configuration now.

4. Click Yes. Exchange displays the Microsoft Fax Properties sheet, shown in Figure 29.2.

5. I'll explain the controls in this dialog box in depth in the next section. For now, you need to fill in only the Fax number field.

6. Select the Modem tab.

Figure 29.2.

You use this properties sheet to configure Microsoft Fax. For now, you need enter only your fax number and the modem you want to use.

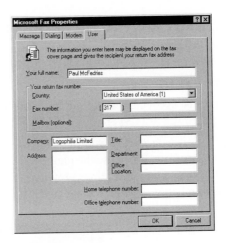

7. If you have more than one fax/modem, highlight it, select Set as Active Fax Modem, and click OK. (Again, I'll explain this tab in detail in the next section.) Exchange adds Microsoft Fax to your profile.

8. Click OK to return to Exchange, and then exit and restart Exchange.

Microsoft Fax Properties

You saw in the preceding section that Exchange requires you to specify a few properties before it will add Microsoft Fax to your profile. In this section, you'll return to the Microsoft Fax Properties sheet to examine the available options in more detail. To get the properties sheet back on your screen, use either of the following techniques:

- Select Tools | Services, highlight Microsoft Fax, and click the Properties button.
- Select Tools | Microsoft Fax Tools | Options.

When Exchange displays the properties sheet, you'll see the controls in the Message tab by default, as shown in Figure 29.3. The next few sections run through each of the tabs.

Message Properties

The Message tab contains a few properties that specify the default setup for the faxes you send. The Time to send group determines when Microsoft Fax sends your faxes. Here's a summary of what's available:

As soon as possible: Selecting this option (it's the default) means that your faxes get sent out right away (or as soon as the modem is free).

Discount rates: If you choose this option, Microsoft Fax sends a fax only if the current time falls within the time when your phone rates are discounted. To specify the start and end times for your discounted phone rates, click the Set button. In the Set Discount Rates dialog box, shown in Figure 29.4, enter the Start and End times, and click OK.

FIGURE 29.3.

You use the Message tab to set options for faxes you send.

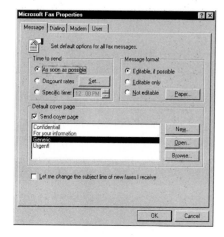

FIGURE 29.4.

Use this dialog box to specify the start and end times for your discounted phone rates.

Specific time: If you activate this option, you can use the spinner to specify a time for Microsoft Fax to send all of your pending faxes.

The options in the Message format group control the format that Microsoft Fax uses to send your faxes:

Editable if possible: When this option is activated, Microsoft Fax attempts to send faxes as editable, binary documents. When connecting with the remote system, Microsoft Fax queries the machine to see whether it supports this format. (The editable document format is supported by Microsoft Fax systems and Microsoft At Work–compliant systems.) If it doesn't, Microsoft Fax sends the fax as a noneditable image. Otherwise, Microsoft Fax sends the fax as an editable, binary message, which means that

■ If you send a text-only fax, the recipient can read and edit the fax just like a regular e-mail message.

■ If you include a file with the fax, the file is transferred in its native format, and it appears as an attachment when the recipient views the fax.

Editable only: If you activate this option, Microsoft Fax queries the remote system to see whether it supports the editable fax format. If it doesn't, the fax transmission is canceled.

Not editable: If you activate this option, Microsoft Fax sends all of your faxes in a noneditable format, as explained here:

- If the receiving system is a Group 3 fax machine, Microsoft Fax renders the fax as a bitmap image and sends it using whatever protocol is supported by the machine.

- If the receiving system is Microsoft Fax–compatible, the fax is sent using the Microsoft At Work rendered fax format.

For noneditable faxes, you can also click the Paper button to display the Message Format dialog box, shown in Figure 29.5. Use the options in this dialog box to specify the size, quality, and orientation of the image.

FIGURE 29.5.

Use this dialog box to specify the message format to use for noneditable faxes.

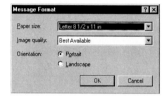

In the Default cover page group, activate the Send cover page check box to send a cover page with all of your faxes. The accompanying list gives you several cover pages to choose from. I'll discuss these cover pages in more detail, and show you how to modify them and create new ones later in this chapter (see "Working with Fax Cover Pages").

Finally, the Let me change the subject line of new faxes I receive check box determines how Microsoft Fax handles incoming noneditable faxes. The Subject line of a received noneditable fax always has the following form:

Fax from *FaxID*

Here, FaxID is either the phone number of the sending fax machine or the machine's internal fax identification string. (If Microsoft Fax can't determine either value, it displays just Fax in the Subject line.) The Let me change the subject line of new faxes I receive check box gives you the following choices:

- If this check box is deactivated, you can't change the Subject line of a noneditable fax. Moreover, opening a noneditable fax takes you directly to the Fax Viewer (see "Receiving Faxes" later in this chapter).

- If this check box is activated, you can change the Subject line of a noneditable fax. Microsoft Fax sets this up by inserting the noneditable fax as an attachment to an editable message. When you open the message, you can edit the Subject line, just as with any e-mail message, as shown in Figure 29.6.

FIGURE 29.6.

*You can set up
Microsoft Fax to enable
editing of the Subject
lines of your received
faxes.*

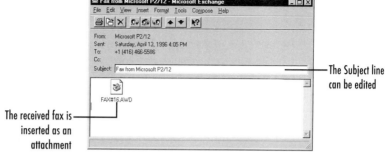

The Subject line
can be edited

The received fax is
inserted as an
attachment

Dialing Properties

You use the Dialing tab, shown in Figure 29.7, to determine how Microsoft Fax dials fax numbers. Here are your options:

Dialing Properties: Click this button to display the Dialing Properties dialog box. See Chapter 25, "Maximizing Modem Communications," for details on Windows 95's dialing properties.

Toll Prefixes: In some locations, you must dial certain numbers that are in your area code as long distance. In other words, even though the numbers share your area code, you must dial a 1 and the area code to connect. If you have a fax recipient with such a number, click the Toll Prefixes button. In the dialog box that appears, highlight the appropriate prefix and click Add->. This tells Microsoft Fax to append 1 and your area code to any numbers that use this prefix.

Number of retries: This value determines the number of times Microsoft Fax attempts to send a fax if it encounters a busy signal or some other error.

Time between retries: This value determines the number of minutes Microsoft Fax waits between retries.

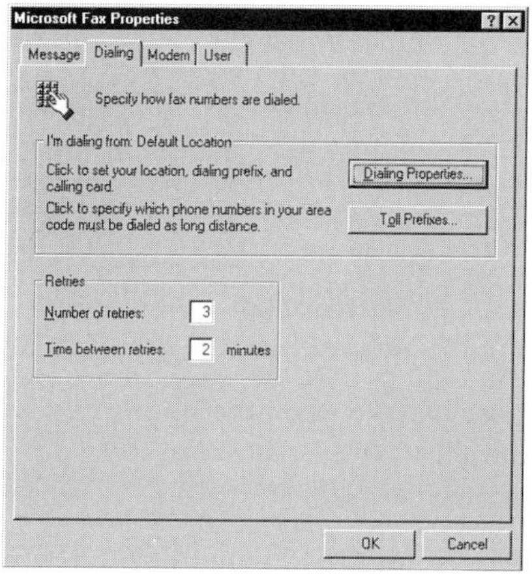

FIGURE 29.7.

*Use the Dialing tab to
specify how Microsoft
Fax dials fax numbers.*

29

USING
MICROSOFT
FAX

Modem Properties

The Modem tab, shown in Figure 29.8, controls how Microsoft Fax works with your fax/modem. The Available fax modems list displays the installed modems on your system. If you have more than one modem, you can designate one of them as the modem used by Microsoft Fax by highlighting it and clicking the Set as Active Fax Modem button. You can also use the Add button to install another modem, and the Remove button to delete a modem from the list.

FIGURE 29.8.

Use the Modem tab to tell Microsoft Fax which modem you want to use as the active fax/modem.

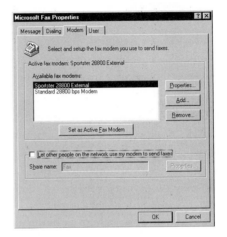

For each fax/modem, Microsoft Fax maintains several properties that determine how the program and the modem work together. To view these properties, highlight the fax/modem and then click the Properties button. Microsoft Fax displays the properties sheet shown in Figure 29.9.

FIGURE 29.9.

Use this dialog box to set various properties of the fax/modem.

Here's a rundown of the options this dialog box provides:

Answer after x rings: Activate this option to tell Microsoft Fax to answer incoming calls automatically. Use the spinner to specify the ring number on which Microsoft Fax should answer the call.

Manual: If you activate this option, Microsoft Fax displays a dialog box whenever it detects an incoming call. You can use this dialog box to have Microsoft Fax either answer the call or ignore it. Use this option if you also receive voice calls on the same line.

`Don't answer:` If you activate this option, Microsoft Fax ignores any incoming calls. Technically, this option means that Microsoft Fax won't monitor the serial port to which the modem is attached. This is useful if you're using 16-bit communications programs that need to use the port while Exchange is running. When Microsoft Fax is monitoring a serial port for incoming calls, only 32-bit TAPI (Telephony Application Programming Interface) programs can get access to the port.

`Speaker volume:` This slider determines the default volume level of the modem's speaker. Also, make sure that the `Turn off after connected` check box is activated to avoid listening to the squeaks and squawks the two machines make while they're transferring data.

`Call preferences:` See Chapter 25 for an explanation of the options in this group.

If you click the Advanced button, you'll see the Advanced dialog box, shown in Figure 29.10. You shouldn't need to change any of these settings, but just in case you're having trouble faxing, here's a summary of what each control represents:

`Disable high speed transmission:` This check box determines whether your modem transfers data at speeds any faster than 9,600 bps. If you're having trouble with your fax transmissions, try activating this check box to restrict data transfers to 9,600 bps or less.

`Disable error correction mode:` This check box determines whether Microsoft Fax uses the modem's built-in error correction protocol for transmitting noneditable faxes. If your fax transmissions are unreliable, the error correction protocol might be the culprit. Try activating this check box to turn off error correction.

`Enable MR compression:` MR compression is used by Group 3 fax machines for faster transfers. You can activate this check box when you have a large fax to send, but bear in mind that this compression scheme makes faxes more sensitive to phone-line noise.

`Use Class 2 if available:` If you activate this check box, Microsoft Fax operates your modem as a Class 2 device (even though your modem might support Class 1). This can overcome some transmission problems, but it disables the binary file transfer and security features of Microsoft Fax (because these aren't supported by Class 2 fax/modems).

`Reject pages received with errors:` If you activate this check box, Microsoft Fax rejects pages with errors that exceed the threshold specified in the Tolerance box. The lower the threshold, the fewer errors a page must have before it's accepted by Microsoft Fax.

The Modem tab also contains a `Let other people on the network use my modem to send faxes` check box. You can use this option to set up your modem as a fax server for your network. I'll explain how this works later in this chapter (see "Network Faxing").

29

USING
MICROSOFT FAX

Figure 29.10.
This dialog box controls various advanced modem properties.

User Properties

The final tab in the Microsoft Fax properties sheet is User, which you saw back in Figure 29.2. Microsoft Fax uses these properties to fill in various fields on your fax cover sheets. Also, the fields in the `Your return fax number` group tell the recipient the fax address to use when replying.

> **NOTE: ROUTING REPLIES TO YOUR MAILBOX**
>
> If you have a network fax server, use the Mailbox field to enter the name of your mailbox or account. That way, when your recipient replies, the incoming fax is routed to your mailbox automatically.

Sending a Fax

With Microsoft Fax installed, added to your profile, and configured to your liking, you can now start firing off fax missives to everyone you know. Microsoft Fax provides three ways to send a fax:

- You can create a message by using the e-mail techniques I showed you in the preceding chapter. In this case, though, the recipient's "address" is a fax phone number.
- You can use the Compose New Fax Wizard to lead you through the various faxing steps, from selecting a recipient to setting up your modem to entering your text.
- You can fax documents directly from applications.

Each of these methods requires that you specify a fax phone number as the message address, so let's first see how you add fax numbers to your Personal Address Book.

Creating Fax Addresses in Your Personal Address Book

You saw in Chapter 28, "Exchanging E-Mail with Microsoft Exchange," how you can use the Personal Address Book to store e-mail addresses from the other address lists (such as the list of

The Microsoft Network members) and for new recipients. You can also use the Personal Address Book to store fax numbers. Here are the steps to follow:

1. In Exchange, open the Address Book.

2. Select File | New Entry to display the New Entry dialog box.

3. In the Select the entry type list, highlight Fax and click OK. Exchange displays the New Fax Properties dialog box, shown in Figure 29.11.

FIGURE 29.11.

Use this properties sheet to fill in the particulars for the fax recipient.

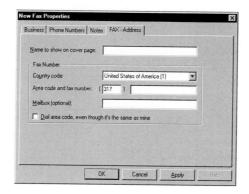

4. Fill in the following fields:

   Name to show on the cover page: Enter the name of the recipient. Microsoft Fax will place this entry in the To field on the fax cover sheet.

   Country code: Enter the recipient's country.

   Area code and fax number: Enter the area code and phone number of the recipient's fax machine.

   Mailbox (optional): If the recipient uses a fax server, enter his mailbox name or account number here. This information lets the server route the message appropriately.

   Dial area code, even though it's the same as mine: If the number uses the same area code but requires a long-distance dial, activate this check box.

5. The fax cover sheet will also include items such as the recipient's company name and business phone number, so you should also fill out the other tabs in the properties sheet.

6. When you're done, click OK.

Composing a Fax from Scratch

Microsoft Fax makes composing a new fax about as painless as any of this communications business gets. In fact, given what you learned about modems in Chapter 25, and what you learned about putting together an e-mail message in Chapter 28, you know practically everything you

29

USING MICROSOFT FAX

need to know to get the job done. The next two sections run through the two methods available for creating faxes from scratch: using the message composition window and using the Compose New Fax Wizard.

Using the Message Composition Window

You can create fax messages by using the same technique I showed you in the preceding chapter for creating an e-mail message. The only differences are that your recipient's address must be a fax address, and you can set some extra options for the fax message.

To compose the fax, select Compose | New Message, and in the New Message window that appears, fill in the fields as needed. When you're adding the recipient address, keep in mind that you can select names from your Personal Address Book, or you can enter a fax number ad hoc. For entering the fax number by hand, here's the general form of the address:

```
Name@+CountryCode (AreaCode) FaxNumber
```

Here, *Name* is the name of the recipient, and *CountryCode*, *AreaCode*, and *FaxNumber* are self-explanatory. For example, if you were sending a fax to Biff Pipeline at (234) 555-1212, you would make this entry in the To or Cc field (assuming that the country code is 1):

```
Biff Pipeline@+1 (234) 555-1212
```

Notice that you need to add the country code and area code even if it's a local call. In this case, Microsoft Fax ignores the country code and area code when making the call.

If you don't feel like memorizing the correct fax address syntax, Microsoft Fax has a Fax Addressing Wizard that makes it easy. To try it, select Tools | Fax Addressing Wizard to display the dialog box shown in Figure 29.12. Enter the recipient's name in the To text box, select the country code, enter the fax number, and click Add to List. The recipient appears in the Recipient list box. Keep adding recipients in this manner as needed, and then click Finish when you're done.

Figure 29.12.

Use the Fax Addressing Wizard to forge ad hoc fax addresses.

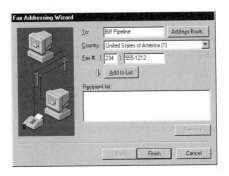

The only other difference between a fax and an e-mail message is that Microsoft Fax provides a few options you can set for each fax. To view these options, select File | Send Options to display the dialog box shown in Figure 29.13. As you can see, these options are similar to those found in the Message tab of the Microsoft Fax properties sheet, which was discussed earlier and shown in Figure 29.3. Note, too, that clicking the Dialing button displays properties similar to those you saw earlier in the Dialing tab, as shown in Figure 29.7.

FIGURE 29.13.

Use this dialog box to specify sending options for this fax message.

Other than these differences, you compose the message exactly the same as you do an e-mail note. You can even insert files to go along for the ride. When you're done, make sure that your modem is ready for action, and select File | Send.

NOTE: USE A LARGE FONT FOR NONEDITABLE FAXES

One of the advantages of working in the message composition window is that you can adjust the font size used in your message. This won't matter if you're sending an editable fax (because the reader will view the text in their regular e-mail font), but it can make a big difference for noneditable faxes sent to Group 3 fax machines. These machines typically have low resolution, so they reproduce small fonts poorly. To make sure that your faxes are readable, use a 12-point or even a 14-point sans serif font (such as Arial).

Using the Compose New Fax Wizard

As an alternative to the message composition window, Microsoft Fax offers the Compose New Fax Wizard that leads you step-by-step through the entire fax-creation process. This Wizard is geared more toward novice users, but even experienced types will find it handy for quick fax notes. Here's how it works:

1. To start the Wizard, use either of the following techniques:

   ■ Select Start | Programs | Accessories | Fax | Compose New Fax.

   ■ In Exchange, select Compose | New Fax.

2. The first Wizard dialog box asks you which dialing location you want to use (as explained in Chapter 25). You can click the Dialing Properties button to either select

29

USING
MICROSOFT FAX

a different location or adjust the properties of the current location. Otherwise, click
Next >.

3. The next Wizard dialog box is almost identical to the Fax Addressing Wizard you
   worked with earlier, as shown in Figure 29.12. Either enter a fax number or use the
   Address Book button to choose a fax recipient from your Personal Address Book, and
   then click Next >.

4. The next Wizard dialog box, shown in Figure 29.14, asks whether you want a cover
   page. Either click No, or click Yes and highlight the cover page you want to use. You
   can also click the Options button to display the Send Options dialog box you learned
   about earlier (see Figure 29.13). Click Next > to continue.

Figure 29.14.

*Select your cover page
and send options from
this Compose New Fax
Wizard dialog box.*

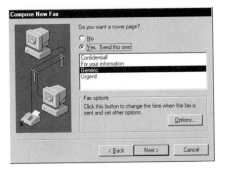

5. The Wizard now prompts you to enter the Subject and Note for the fax, as shown in
   Figure 29.15. If you're using a cover page, activating the Start note on cover page
   check box tells Microsoft Fax to begin your note on the cover page. If you deactivate
   this check box, the note begins on a fresh page. Click Next >.

Figure 29.15.

*Use this Wizard dialog
box to enter the Subject
and Note for the fax.*

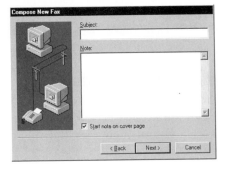

6. Your next chore is to specify any files you want to include with the fax transmission.
   Click the Add File button, highlight the file in the Open a File to Attach dialog box
   that appears, and click Open. Click Next > when you've added all the files you need.

7. In the last Wizard dialog box, click Finish to send your fax.

Faxing from an Application

The third method of sending a fax is to bypass Microsoft Exchange altogether and send a document directly from an application. You don't need applications with special features to do this, either. That's because when you install Microsoft Fax, it adds a new printer driver to Windows 95. This printer driver, however, doesn't send a document to the printer. Instead, it renders the document as a fax and sends it to your modem.

To try this, select File | Print in your application. When the Print dialog box appears, use the Name drop-down list to select the Microsoft Fax printer driver, as shown in Figure 29.16. When you click OK, the Compose New Fax Wizard starts so that you can specify a recipient, a cover page, and other fax options.

FIGURE 29.16.

To fax a document from an application, select File | Print and then choose the Microsoft Fax printer driver.

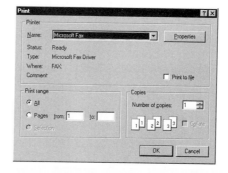

TIP: FAX DOCUMENTS VIA THE SEND TO COMMAND

If you have a particular document you want to fax, you don't have to open its application and print to the Microsoft Fax driver. Instead, just right-click the document and select Send To | Fax Recipient.

29

TROUBLESHOOTING: MICROSOFT FAX WON'T SEND A FAX

Here are a couple of solutions to try if Microsoft Fax won't send a fax.

You might receive an "Undeliverable" message that includes the following error:

```
The recipient's e-mail address is incorrect or does not exist. Be sure to
type the address correctly, and try sending the message again. If the message
cannot be sent, contact your administrator.
```

This error usually means that the Microsoft Fax service is listed behind the Microsoft Mail service in the delivery order. To fix this problem, select Tools | Options, select the Delivery tab, and move the Microsoft Fax Transport service above the Microsoft Mail service.

continues

continued

If you're using the Microsoft Fax printer driver, it could be that the driver is corrupt. To fix this problem, select Start | Run, type awadpr32.exe, and click OK. This command rebuilds the Microsoft Fax printer driver.

Working with Fax Cover Pages

I've mentioned fax cover pages a couple of times so far in this chapter, so it's time to take a closer look. In the fax world, a cover page performs the same function as an e-mail message header: It specifies who is supposed to receive the fax and who sent it. Unlike an e-mail message header, which is meant to be read and interpreted by a mail server or gateway, a fax cover sheet is meant for human consumption. In a company or department where several people share a fax machine, the cover page makes it clear which person is supposed to get the fax. And when that person does read the message, she can use the rest of the information to see who sent the fax.

Microsoft Fax comes with four pre-fab cover pages: Confidential!, For your information, Generic, and Urgent!. You can use these pages as circumstances dictate, you can modify them to suit your style, or you can create new pages from scratch.

NOTE: USE COVER PAGES ONLY FOR NONEDITABLE FAXES

You need to use a cover page only if you're sending a noneditable (bitmap) fax. If you send an editable fax, the receiving system converts it into a regular message (assuming, of course, that the system can deal with editable faxes), so the recipient never sees the cover page.

Starting the Fax Cover Page Editor

To edit and create fax cover pages, Microsoft Fax comes with the Fax Cover Page Editor application. To start this program, use either of the following techniques:

- Select Start | Programs | Accessories | Fax | Cover Page Editor.
- In Exchange, select Tools | Microsoft Fax Tools | Options to display the Options dialog box. In the Message tab, either select New in the Default cover page group, or highlight a cover page and click Open.

Figure 29.17 shows the window that appears. (If you don't see an open file, select File | Open and select one of the CPE files from your main Windows 95 folder.)

FIGURE 29.17.

Microsoft Fax provides the Fax Cover Page Editor so that you can edit and create cover pages to use with your faxes.

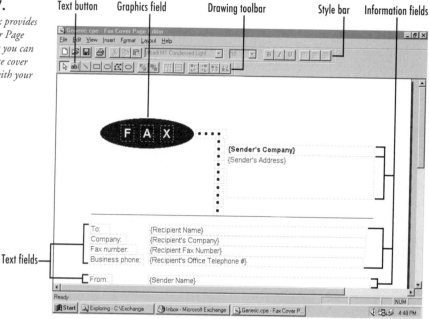

Editing a Cover Page

Keeping in mind that cover pages always get sent as bitmaps, the idea behind the Cover Page Editor is to create a template for the bitmap. So, as you might expect, the Cover Page Editor is really a graphics application that specializes in working with fax bitmaps. The templates you work with consist of three types of fields: information, text, and graphics.

Inserting Information Fields

Information fields are placeholders for data. For example, the {Sender's Company} field (information fields always appear surrounded by braces) tells Microsoft Fax to insert the name of the sender's company each time you use this cover page when you send a fax. With the Cover Page Editor, you can insert fields for recipient, sender, and message data:

■ For the recipient, you can insert fields for the person's name, fax number, company, address, and much more. This information is gleaned from the properties sheet for the recipient's address (assuming that you included the address in your Personal Address Book). Select Insert | Recipient to see a complete list of the available fields.

■ For the sender, you can insert fields for the name, fax number, company, address, telephone numbers, and more. Microsoft Fax gets this data from the User tab of the Microsoft Fax properties sheet. Select Insert | Sender to see the available fields.

■ For the message, the available fields include the note text, the Subject line, the time the fax was sent, the number of pages, and the number of attachments. Selecting Insert | Message displays a cascade menu that lists these fields.

Inserting Text Fields

Text fields are text boxes that either describe the contents of each information field or provide titles, subtitles, and headings. To insert a text field, click the Text button on the Drawing toolbar, drag the mouse inside the cover page to create a box for the field, and enter your text. To change the text in an existing field, double-click it. (Note, too, that you can format text fields by using the buttons on the Style toolbar or by selecting Format | Font or Format | Align Text.)

Inserting Graphics Fields

Graphics fields are bitmap objects you can use for logos or separators, or just to add some style to the cover page. The Cover Page Editor's Drawing toolbar lets you create many kinds of drawing objects, including lines, rectangles, circles, and polygons. Table 29.1 lists the buttons available on this toolbar.

Table 29.1. The Cover Page Editor's Drawing toolbar buttons.

Button	Name	Description
	Line	Creates a straight line.
	Rectangle	Creates a rectangle. (Hold down Shift while dragging to create a square.)
	Rounded Rectangle	Creates a rectangle with rounded corners.
	Polygon	Creates a polygon.
	Ellipse	Creates an ellipse. (Hold down Shift while dragging to create a circle.)
	Bring To Front	Moves the selected object in front of any objects that overlap it. You can also select Layout	Bring to Front, or press Ctrl-F.
	Send To Back	Moves the selected object behind any objects that overlap it. You can also select Layout	Send to Back, or press Ctrl-B.
	Space Across	Spaces the selected objects evenly across the page. You can also select Layout	Space Evenly	Across.

Button	Name	Description
	Space Down	Spaces the selected objects evenly down the page. You can also select Layout	Space Evenly	Down.
	Align Left	Aligns the selected objects along their left edges. You can also select Layout	Align Objects	Left.
	Align Right	Aligns the selected objects along their right edges. You can also select Layout	Align Objects	Right.
	Align Top	Aligns the selected objects along their top edges. You can also select Layout	Align Objects	Top.
	Align Bottom	Aligns the selected objects along their bottom edges. You can also select Layout	Align Objects	Bottom.

Receiving Faxes

You saw in the previous couple of chapters how Exchange hasn't quite yet achieved its goal of becoming a universal inbox, but its support for Microsoft Mail, The Microsoft Network Mail, CompuServe, and the Internet is a pretty good start.

If you use any of these e-mail systems, tossing Exchange's support for storing received faxes in the same Inbox into the mix makes Exchange an attractive messaging client. (Now, if we could just get it to field our voice mail, life would be perfect.) This section explains how Microsoft Fax handles incoming faxes and shows you how to view those faxes when they're sitting in your Inbox.

Answering Incoming Calls

How Microsoft Fax handles incoming calls from remote fax systems depends on how you set up your fax/modem. Recall that when you display the Fax Modem Properties dialog box (by clicking Properties in the Modem tab of the Microsoft Fax properties sheet), the Answer mode group boasts three options that determine how Microsoft Fax deals with incoming calls:

Answer after x rings: Tells Microsoft Fax to answer incoming calls automatically.

Manual: Lets you answer incoming calls manually.

Don't answer: Tells Microsoft Fax to ignore any incoming calls.

Answering Calls Automatically

Enabling the Answer after x rings option is the easiest way to handle incoming calls. In this mode, Microsoft Fax constantly polls the modem's serial port for calls. When it detects a call coming in, it waits for whatever number of rings you specified (which can be as few as two rings or as many as 10) and then leaps into action. Without any prodding from you, it answers the phone and immediately starts conversing with the remote fax machine. The Microsoft Fax Status window appears on-screen so that you can see the progress of the transfer, as shown in Figure 29.18.

FIGURE 29.18.

When Microsoft Fax answers an incoming fax call, this window keeps you abreast of the fax transfer.

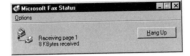

Answering Calls Manually

When you work with Microsoft Fax in manual mode, you'll see the Receive Fax Now? dialog box, shown in Figure 29.19, whenever the program detects an incoming call. To have Microsoft Fax field the call, click Yes. Otherwise, click No and answer the call yourself.

FIGURE 29.19.

In manual answer mode, Microsoft Fax displays this dialog box when it detects an incoming call.

This mode is ideal if you receive both voice calls and fax calls on the same phone line. Here's the basic procedure you need to follow for incoming calls:

1. When the phone rings, pick up the receiver.

2. If you hear a series of tones, you know that a fax is on its way. In this case, click the Yes button in the Receive Fax Now? dialog box. If it's a voice call, click No instead.

3. After you click Yes, Microsoft Fax initializes the modem to handle the call. Wait until Microsoft Fax reports `Answering call` in the Microsoft Fax Status window, and then hang up the receiver. (If you hang up before this, you'll disconnect the call.)

> **NOTE: IF YOU MISS THE RECEIVE FAX NOW? DIALOG BOX**
>
> The Receive Fax Now? dialog box stays on-screen for seven or eight seconds. If you miss it, you can still get Microsoft Fax to take the call by clicking the Answer Now button (or by selecting Options | Answer Now) in the Microsoft Fax Status window. Again, wait until Microsoft Fax reports `Answering call` before hanging up the receiver.

Working in Don't Answer Mode

If you select the Don't answer option, Microsoft Fax ignores any incoming calls. If you know you have a fax coming in (if, say, you pick up the receiver and hear the tones from the remote fax machine), click the Microsoft Fax icon in the toolbar's system tray. This opens the Microsoft Fax Status window. Now either select Options | Answer Now or click the Answer Now button.

Opening Received Faxes

Depending on the size of the fax transmission and whether it's an editable fax or a bitmap, Microsoft Fax takes anywhere from a few seconds to a few minutes to process the data. Eventually, though, your fax appears in the Inbox. (For noneditable faxes, Exchange displays a fax icon in the Item Type column; editable faxes get the usual envelope icon.)

How you view the message depends on whether the fax is editable and whether Microsoft Fax is set up to allow fax Subject lines to be edited:

■ If the fax is editable, it appears in the message list with the usual envelope icon in the Item Type column. To view the message, use the same techniques I outlined in the preceding chapter for e-mail messages.

■ For a noneditable fax, Exchange displays a fax icon in the Item Type column. When you open the message, Exchange displays the bitmap image of the fax in the Fax Viewer, as shown in Figure 29.20.

FIGURE 29.20.

When you open a noneditable fax, Exchange uses the Fax Viewer to display the bitmap.

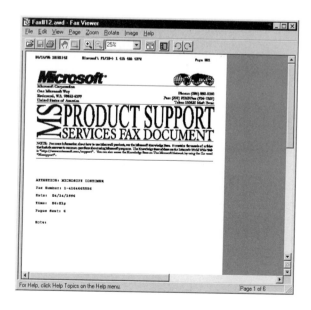

29

USING
MICROSOFT FAX

■ If you've enabled Subject line editing, opening the message displays an icon that represents the fax bitmap, as shown earlier in Figure 29.6. To get the fax into the Fax Viewer, double-click the icon.

TROUBLESHOOTING: A FAX ISN'T DELIVERED TO YOUR INBOX

If Microsoft Fax appeared to receive a document successfully, but the fax never showed up in your Inbox, the fax might have been too large (more than 1 MB), or there might have been errors during the transmission. You should first check to see whether the fax was received by heading for the \Spool\Fax folder in your main Windows 95 folder. Look for a file of the form RCVnnnnn.MG3 or RCVnnnnn.EFX. If you see one, your message was received. To get the file into your Inbox, exit Exchange, open the Registry Editor, and highlight the following key:

HKEY_LOCAL_MACHINE\SOFTWARE\Microsoft\At Work Fax\Local Modems\Received

Add two string settings named F00 and R00. (If settings with these names already exist, use the next available numbers, such as F01 and R01.) Set the value of F00 to the filename from the \Spool\Fax folder. Set the value of R00 to 001. For example, if the filename were RCV4BD10.EFX, you would end up with the following values for the settings:

F00=RCV4BD10.EFX
R00=001

Exit the Registry Editor and restart Exchange.

Using the Fax Viewer

The Fax Viewer is basically a graphics viewer with a few extra features that let you navigate multipage faxes. Here's a quick summary of the Fax Viewer techniques you can wield to examine your faxes:

Moving the fax image: To move the fax image inside the window, first make sure that the Edit | Drag command is activated or that the Drag button is pressed. Then use the mouse to drag the image around the window.

Zooming the image: The Zoom menu contains commands that let you zoom into (such as the Zoom In command) or out of (such as the Zoom Out command) the image. You can also choose specific magnifications: 25%, 50%, or 100%. To fit the image to the window, select Fit Width, Fit Height, or Fit Both. Some of these commands are also available as toolbar buttons:

The Zoom In button

The Zoom Out button

   The Predefined Zooms drop-down list

   The Fit Width button

Rotating the image: For faxes that come with the wrong orientation, the Rotate menu commands let you turn the image so that you can read the fax. Select either Right or Left to rotate the image 90 degrees, or select Flip Over to rotate the image 180 degrees.

   The Rotate Left button

   The Rotate Right button

Inverting the image: To reverse blacks and whites in the image, select Image | Invert.

Viewing thumbnails: To get the big picture in a multipage fax, activate View | Thumbnails (or press the Show Thumbnails button). As you can see in Figure 29.21, the Fax Viewer displays small versions of each page on the left side of the screen. Click a page's thumbnail to display that page.

FIGURE 29.21.

The Fax Viewer's thumbnails view.

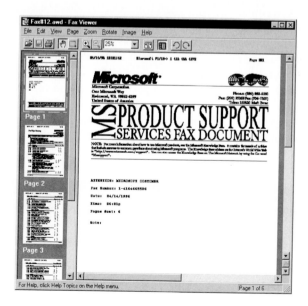

29

USING
MICROSOFT FAX

Navigating multiple pages: The Fax Viewer has a few more tricks up its sleeve for moving between pages. On the Page menu, select Next, Previous, First, and Last. You can also select the Go To command to head for a specific page number.

 Click this scrollbar button to move to the previous page.

 Click this scrollbar button to move to the next page.

Saving the fax to a file: Instead of working with a fax from Exchange, you might prefer to save it to a separate Fax Viewer file. This makes it easy to archive the fax or include it as a file attachment in a message. To save the fax, select File | Save Copy As, select a location and enter a filename in the Save Copy As dialog box, and click Save. Note that Fax Viewer files use the AWD extension.

 Copying data to the Clipboard: The fax is a bitmap, so you might want to copy some or all of a page to the Clipboard to use in other applications. First, make sure that the Edit | Select command is activated (or that the Select button is pressed). To copy the current page as a whole, select Edit | Copy Page. If you want just part of the page, use the mouse to drag a box around the area you want, and then select Edit | Copy.

TIP: SAVE YOUR SIGNATURE

One of the drawbacks with sending faxes via your computer is that you have no way to sign your documents. To get around this limitation, sign your name on a piece of paper, and then use a regular fax machine to send the signature to your computer. Display this document in the Fax Viewer, select your signature, and copy it to the Clipboard. Then open Paint and select Edit | Paste to paste the signature. Select Edit | Copy To, and save the signature to its own file. To add your signature to your faxes, select Insert | Object in the Cover Page Editor, and insert the signature's BMP file.

OSR2

NOTE: OSR2 USING WANG IMAGING FOR FAXES

In OSR2, the Fax Viewer is replaced by the Wang Imaging program. This program is similar to Fax Viewer, but it adds a number of options, including the following:

- An Annotation menu with commands that let you write notes on the fax.
- A View | Options command from which you can set preferences.
- The capability to receive documents from a scanner.

Accessing Fax-on-Demand Systems

Hundreds of businesses have implemented fax-on-demand systems. These are fax servers that contain dozens or even hundreds of documents that are available for downloading. You call the system, and after perhaps negotiating a few voice menus, you enter a document number and your fax number. A few minutes later, the server calls your fax number and sends you the document. (Most systems also have catalogs you can download to get the document numbers and titles.)

In some cases, the fax server supports the Group 3 poll-retrieve capability. This lets a program such as Microsoft Fax connect to the server and download the document you want automatically. This feature is called Request a Fax, and it works like this:

1. Select either Tools | Microsoft Fax Tools | Request a Fax or Start | Programs | Accessories | Fax | Request a Fax. The first Request a Fax Wizard dialog box shown in Figure 29.22 appears.

FIGURE 29.22.

The Request a Fax Wizard leads you step-by-step through a fax-on-demand session.

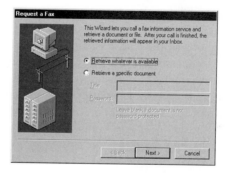

2. This dialog box gives you two options:

> `Retrieve whatever is available`: When you select this option, Microsoft Fax asks the server to send all the information it has on tap. This option is useful for fax-on-demand systems that cater to a single product.

NOTE: SPRINTFAX USES REQUEST A FAX

When you first install Microsoft Fax, a message from SprintFAX is placed in your Inbox. This message invites you to double-click an icon to get information about the SprintFAX broadcast fax service. This icon is an Object Packager package that runs the Request a Fax feature behind the scenes. This action is equivalent to selecting the Retrieve whatever is available option and calling 1-800-352-8575. If you like, you can use SprintFAX as an example to try out the Request a Fax service.

> `Retrieve a specific document`: Most fax-on-demand systems have multiple documents available, so you'll need to activate this option. Use the Title text box to enter the name or number of the document you want to retrieve, and use the Password text box to enter a password, if required. Click Next > when you're ready to continue.

3. Enter the name and number of the fax-on-demand system, and click Add. Alternatively, select Address Book and use your Personal Address Book to enter the number. Click Next > to move on to the next dialog box.

4. The Wizard next asks when you want to send the request. Select As soon as possible, When phone rates are discounted or A specific time. (For the last choice, use the spinner to enter the time you want Microsoft Fax to make the call.) Click Next >.

5. Click Finish to send the fax request.

Network Faxing

In the next chapter, I'll introduce you to networking. You'll see that one of the chief benefits of having networked computers is the capability to share peripherals—such as printers and CD-ROM drives—among all the machines. If you have a network and you have multiple users who need to fax documents, Microsoft Fax lets you share a single fax/modem on the network. The computer then becomes a fax server that lets any machine on the network send faxes. (Note, however, that all received faxes stay on the fax server until the administrator can route them manually. Microsoft Fax doesn't support routing of incoming faxes.)

Setting Up the Fax Server

To set up a computer to operate as a fax server, follow these steps:

1. Select Tools | Microsoft Fax Tools | Options to display the Microsoft Fax properties sheet, and then select the Modem tab.

2. Activate the `Let other people on the network use my modem to send faxes` check box.

3. If you have multiple disk drives, Microsoft Fax asks which drive you want to use for the network fax service. Use the drop-down list provided to select the drive, and then click OK to return to the Microsoft Fax properties sheet. Microsoft Fax creates a new folder called NetFax on the drive and shares this folder with the network.

4. To change the properties of the shared network fax folder, click the Properties button beside the Share name box.

5. The dialog box that appears, shown in Figure 29.23, lets you change the default values for the Share Name and Comment (which shouldn't be necessary), as well as set up security for the shared folder. Note that users need full access to the shared folder to send faxes via the fax server. See Chapter 31, "Windows 95 Networking," for a complete description of sharing network resources and implementing security.

FIGURE 29.23.

Use this dialog box to change the properties of the shared network fax folder.

6. Click OK to return to the properties sheet, and then click OK again to return to Exchange.

Specifying the Fax Server on a Client Machine

For network users to send faxes via the fax server, they must specify the fax server's network path rather than a fax/modem. Here are the steps each client has to follow:

1. On the client computer, start Exchange, select Tools | Microsoft Fax Tools | Options to display the Microsoft Fax properties sheet, and select the Modem tab.

2. Click the Add button. The Add a Fax Modem dialog box, shown in Figure 29.24, appears.

FIGURE 29.24.

This dialog box appears when you click the Add button.

3. Highlight Network fax server, and then click OK. Microsoft Fax displays the Connect To Network Fax Server dialog box, shown in Figure 29.25.

FIGURE 29.25.

Use this dialog box to enter the network path to the fax server.

4. Enter the network path for the fax server, and click OK. The network path always takes the form *ComputerName**FaxServer*, in which *ComputerName* is the network name of the fax server computer, and *FaxServer* is the share name of the network fax folder. In Figure 29.25, for example, the computer name is Hermes, and the share name of the fax folder is Fax.

29

USING
MICROSOFT FAX

5. In the Modem tab, highlight the network fax server, and select Set as Active Fax Modem.

6. Click OK.

Summary

This chapter closed out your look at Microsoft Exchange (and Windows 95 communications in general) by running through the features and capabilities of Microsoft Fax. I began by showing you how to add the Microsoft Fax service to your Exchange profile and then how to configure Microsoft Fax. You then learned the various methods available for sending faxes, including using the message composition window, the Compose New Fax Wizard, and the Microsoft Fax printer driver. I also showed you how to edit and create cover pages to include in your faxes. From there, you learned how to deal with incoming faxes, including the various phone-answering modes of Microsoft Fax, how to open a received fax, and how to use the Fax Viewer. I closed by covering Request a Fax and network faxing.

Here's a list of chapters where you'll find related information:

■ I showed you how get your modem set up and use it for data calls in Chapter 25, "Maximizing Modem Communications."

■ The general steps for adding and configuring services in Exchange are covered in Chapter 27, "Setting Up Microsoft Exchange."

■ To learn how to use Exchange for sending and retrieving e-mail, check out Chapter 28, "Exchanging E-Mail with Microsoft Exchange."

■ If some of this chapter's networking material has you scratching your head, don't worry. I'll explain everything in vivid detail in Chapter 30, "A Networking Primer," and Chapter 31, "Windows 95 Networking."

IN THIS PART

VII
PART

Unleashing Windows 95 Networking and Internet Connectivity

A Networking Primer

IN THIS CHAPTER

Transport of the mails, transport of the human voice, transport of flickering pictures—in this century as in others our highest accomplishments still have the single aim of bringing men together.

—*Antoine de Saint-Exupéry*

For many years, networking was the private playground of IT panjandrums. Its obscure lingo and arcane hardware were familiar to only this small coterie of computer cognoscenti. Workers who needed access to network resources had to pay obeisance to these powers-that-be, genuflecting in just the right way, tossing in the odd salaam or two.

Lately, however, we've seen a democratization of networking. Thanks to the trend away from mainframes and toward client/server setups, thanks to the migration from dumb terminals to smarter PCs, and thanks to the advent of easy peer-to-peer setups, networking is no longer the sole province of the elite. Getting connected to an existing network, or setting up your own network in a small office or home office, has never been easier.

In the next chapter, I cover how Windows 95 has helped take even more of the "work" out of networking. To truly unleash Windows 95's connectivity options, however, you need a bit of network know-how, and that's what this chapter is all about. You'll learn all the necessary network nomenclature (including the difference between *client/server* and *peer-to-peer*), hardware requirements, the ins and outs of cabling, protocol descriptions, and lots more. You can think of this chapter as your initiation into the black art of networking, except, as you'll see, things aren't as black as they used to be.

Some Networking Basics

If you just have a single computer in your office or at home, and if you're the only person who uses that computer, your setup will be inherently efficient. You can use the machine whenever you like, and everything you need—your applications, your printer, your CD-ROM drive, your modem, and so on—will be readily available.

Things will become noticeably less efficient if you have to share the computer with other people. Then you might have to wait for someone else to finish a task before you can get your own work done; you might need to have separate applications for each person's needs; and you might need to set up separate folders to hold each person's data. You learned in Chapter 7, "Customizing Windows 95," that you can improve the way in which a computer is shared among multiple users by setting up user profiles for each person who has access to the machine. However, although this solution might ease some of the burden, it won't eliminate it entirely. (For example, you might still have to twiddle a thumb or two while waiting for another person to complete her work.)

A better solution is to increase the number of computers available. Now that 166 MHz Pentium machines with 16 MB of RAM and 1 GB of hard disk acreage can be had for under $2,000, a multiple-machine setup is an affordable proposition for small offices. Even at home, the current trend is to buy a nice system for Mom and Dad to put in their office, while the kids inherit the old 386 for their games and homework assignments.

Multiple machines, however, bring with them new inefficiencies:

■ In many cases, it's just not economically feasible to supply each computer with its own complete set of peripherals. Printers, for example, are a crucial part of the computing equation—when you need them. If someone needs a printer only a couple of times a week, it's hard to justify shelling out hundreds of dollars so that he can have his own printer. The problem, then, is how to share a printer (or whatever) among several machines.

■ These days, few people work in splendid isolation. Rather, the norm is that colleagues and coworkers often have to share data and work together on the same files. If everyone uses a separate computer, how are they supposed to share files?

■ Most offices have standardized on particular software packages for word processing, spreadsheets, graphics, and other mainstream applications. Does this mean you have to purchase a copy of an expensive software program or suite for each machine? As with peripherals, what do you do about a person who uses a program only sporadically?

Yes, you can overcome these limitations. To share a printer, for example, you could simply lug it from machine to machine, as needed, or else get a 100-foot parallel cable that can be plugged into whichever computer needs access to the printer. This won't work if you need to share an internal CD-ROM drive, however. For data, there's always the old "sneaker net" solution: Plop the files on a floppy disk, and run them back and forth between computers. As for applications, you could install some programs on just a single machine and have users share, but that brings us back to the original problem of multiple people sharing a single machine.

There has to be a better way. For example, wouldn't it be better if you could simply attach a peripheral to a single machine and then have any other computer access that peripheral whenever needed? Wouldn't it be better if users could easily move documents back and forth between computers or had a common storage area for shared files? Wouldn't it be better if you had to install an application in only one location and everyone could run the program on his own machine at will?

Well, I'm happy to report that there *is* a better way, and it's called *networking*. The underlying idea of a network is simple: You connect multiple machines by running special cables from one computer to another. These cables plug into adapter cards (called *network interface cards;* I'll talk more about them later in this chapter) that are installed inside each computer. With this basic card/cable combination and a network-aware operating system (such as Windows 95), you can solve all the inefficiencies just described:

■ A printer (or just about any peripheral) that's attached to one machine can be used by any other machine on the network.

■ Files can be transferred along the cables from one computer to another.

■ Users can access disk drives and folders on network computers as though they were part of their own computer. In particular, you can set up a folder to store common data files, and each user will be able to access these files from the comfort of her own machine. (For security, you can restrict access to certain folders and drives.)

■ You can install an application on one machine and then set things up so that other machines can run the application without having to install the entire program on their local hard drive. (There's no such thing as a free lunch, however. You need to purchase a license to install the application on the other computers. However, depending on how many users you have, this is usually cheaper than buying a full-blown copy of the application.)

Not only that, but a whole new world of connected computing becomes available. You can establish an e-mail system, for example, so that users can send messages to each other via the network. You can set up a single Internet connection, and each user can access the Internet's resources via this connection. You can use *groupware* applications that let users collaborate on projects, schedules, and documents. As the administrator of the network, you can manage other computers remotely (such as installing new software or customizing the environment for each user).

It sounds great, but are there downsides to all of this? Yes. Unfortunately, as yet there is no such thing as a networking nirvana. In all, you have three main concerns: security, speed, and setup.

Security: This is a big issue, to be sure, because you're giving users access to resources outside of their own computers. You need to set things up so that people can't damage files or invade other peoples' privacy, intentionally or otherwise.

Speed: Network connections are fast, but they're not as fast as a local hard drive. So running networked applications or working with remote documents won't have quite the snap that users might prefer.

Setup: Networked computers are inherently harder to set up and maintain than standalone machines. Difficulties include the initial tribulations of installing and configuring networking cards and running cables, as well as the ongoing issues of sharing resources, setting up passwords, and so on.

The benefits of connectivity, however, greatly outweigh the disadvantages, so budding network administrators shouldn't be dissuaded by these few quibbles.

Now that I've got you convinced that a network is a good thing, let's turn our attention to the types of networks you can set up.

LANs, WANs, MANs, and More

Networks come in three basic flavors: *local area networks, internetworks,* and *wide area networks:*

Local area network (LAN): This is a network where all the computers occupy a relatively small geographical area, such as a department, office, home, or building. In a LAN, all the connections between computers are made via network cables.

Internetwork: This is a network that combines two or more LANs by means of a special device, such as a bridge or a router. (See "Hardware: NICs and Other Network Knicknacks" later in this chapter for explanations of these and other internetworking devices.) Internetworks are often called *internets* for short, but they shouldn't be confused with the Internet, the global collection of networks.

Wide area network (WAN): This is a network that consists of two or more LANs or internetworks spaced out over a relatively large geographical area, such as a state, a country, or the world. The networks in a WAN typically are connected via high-speed, fiber-optic phone lines, microwave dishes, or satellite links.

> ## NOTE: INTRANETS ARE THE LATEST NETWORKING CRAZE
>
> The current popularity of the Internet is spilling over into corporate networks. MIS types all over the world have seen how Internet technology can be both cost-effective and scaleable, so they've been wondering how to deliver the same benefits on the corporate level. The result is the *intranet:* the implementation of Internet technologies such as TCP/IP and World Wide Web servers for use within a corporate organization rather than for connection to the Internet as a whole.

> ## NETWORK NOMENCLATURE: LOCAL VERSUS REMOTE RESOURCES
>
> Network resources are usually divided into two categories: local and remote. Not to be confused with the "local" in "local area network," a *local resource* is any peripheral, file, folder, or application that either is attached directly to your computer or resides on your computer's hard disk. By contrast, a *remote resource* is any peripheral, file, folder, or application that exists somewhere on the network.

Other types of networks also exist. A *campus network* connects all the buildings in a school campus or an industrial park. They often span large geographical areas, like WANs, but use private cabling to connect their subnetworks. A *metropolitan area network* (MAN) connects computers in a city or county and is usually regulated by a municipal or state utility commission. Finally, an *enterprise network* connects all the computers within an organization, no matter how geographically diverse they might be, and no matter what kinds of operating systems and network protocols are used in individual segments.

Client/Server Versus Peer-to-Peer

It used to be that the dominant network model revolved around a single, monolithic computer with massive amounts of storage space and processing power. Attached to this behemoth were many "dumb" terminals—essentially just a keyboard and monitor—that contained no local storage and no processing power. Instead, the central mainframe or minicomputer was used for all data storage and to run all applications.

The advent of the PC, however, has more or less sounded the death knell for the dumb terminal. Not surprisingly, users prefer having local disks so that they can keep their data close at hand and run their own applications. (This is, after all, the *personal* computer we're talking about.) To accommodate the PC revolution, two new kinds of network models have become dominant: client/server and peer-to-peer.

Client/Server Networks

In general, the client/server model splits the computing workload into two separate, yet related, areas. On the one hand, you have users working at intelligent "front end" systems called *clients*. In turn, these client machines interact with powerful "back end" systems called *servers*. The basic idea is that the clients have enough processing power to perform tasks on their own, but they rely on the servers to provide them with specialized resources or services, or access to information that would be impractical to implement on a client (such as a large database).

This basic client/server relationship forms the basis of many network operating systems. In this case, a server computer provides various network-related services, such as access to resources (a network printer, for example), centralized file storage, password verification and other security measures, server-based application setup, e-mail, data backups, and access to external networks (such as the Internet).

The various client PCs, although they have their own storage and processing power, interact with the server whenever they need access to network-related resources or services, as illustrated in Figure 30.1. Client computers are also referred to as *nodes* or *workstations*.

Note that in most client/server networks, the server computer can perform only server duties. In other words, you can't use it as a client to run applications.

In this client/server networking model, two types of software are required:

> **Network operating system (NOS):** This software runs on the server and provides the various network services for the clients. The range of services available depends on the NOS. NetWare, for example, provides not only file and print services, but also e-mail, communications, and security services. Other network operating systems that use the client/server model are Windows NT Server, UNIX, Banyan VINES, and IBM LAN Server (now called Warp Server).

FIGURE 30.1.

In a client/server network, each client machine gets access to network services and resources via a server machine.

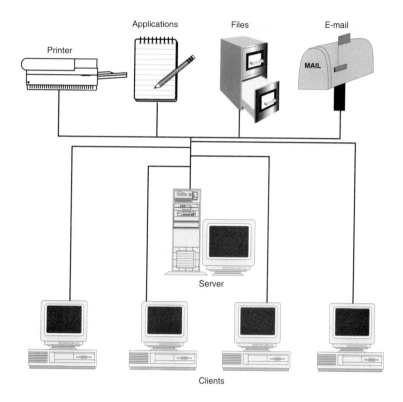

Printer Applications Files E-mail

MAIL

Server

Clients

Client software: This software provides applications that run on the client machine with a way to request services and resources from the server. If an application needs a local resource, the client software forwards the request to the local operating system; if an application needs a server resource, the client software redirects the request to the network operating system. Windows 95 provides various network client software, including clients for Microsoft networks and those for NetWare networks.

For small LANs, a single server is usually sufficient for handling all client requests. As the LAN grows, however, the load on the server increases, and network performance can suffer as a result. Nothing in the client/server model restricts a network to a single server, however. So to ease the server burden, most larger LANs utilize multiple servers. In these so-called *distributed networks,* administrators are free to organize the servers' duties in any way that maximizes network performance. For example, they can split clients into workgroups and assign each group to a specific server. Similarly, they can split up the duties performed by each server. For example, one server could handle file services, another could handle print services, and so on.

Peer-to-Peer Networks

In a *peer-to-peer* network, no one computer is singled out to provide special services. Instead, all the computers attached to the network have equal status (at least as far as the network is concerned), and all the computers can act as both servers and clients, as illustrated in Figure 30.2.

FIGURE 30.2.

In a peer-to-peer setup, every computer can act as both a client and a server, and no one machine has any special status in the network.

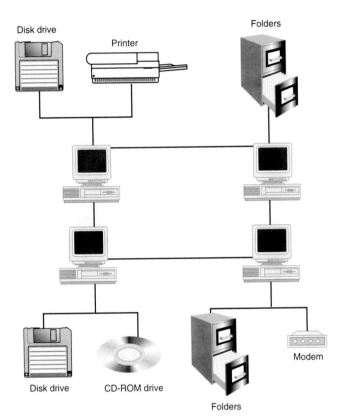

On the server side, each computer can share any of its resources with the network *and* control access to these shared resources. For example, if a user shares a folder with the network, she also can set up passwords to restrict access to that folder.

On the client side, each computer can work with the resources that have been shared by the other peers on the network (provided that they have permission to do so, that is).

Which One Should You Choose?

If you're thinking about networking a few computers, should you go with a client/server setup or a peer-to-peer model? That's a tough question to answer because it depends on so many factors: the number of computers you want to connect, the operating system (or systems) you're using, the services you need, the amount of money you have available to spend, and so on.

In general, though, the smaller the network, the more sense peer-to-peer makes. This is especially true if you're running Windows 95, because it's designed as a peer-to-peer NOS. After you've installed your network cards and run your cable, you're more or less ready to go. Windows 95's automatic hardware detection usually does a pretty good job of recognizing and configuring the network hardware, and the network client makes it easy to share and access network resources.

If, rather than just a few computers, you have a few dozen, you'll have to go the client/server route. Large peer-to-peer setups are just too unwieldy to maintain and administer, and performance quickly drops off as you add more nodes. A top-of-the-line client/server NOS (such as NetWare or Windows NT Server), on the other hand, comes with remote administration, scales nicely as you add more clients and servers, and is robust enough to handle large loads. The price you pay for all this power is, well, the price: These big-time operating systems are expensive and usually require an extra hardware investment beyond the standard card/cable combo. And with power, too, comes complexity: Unlike the relative simplicity of their peer-to-peer counterparts, administration of medium-to-large client/server networks isn't for the faint of heart, although the graphical interface you get with an NOS such as NT Server can help.

Hardware: NICs and Other Network Knickknacks

The client and operating system software is only part of the network picture. Whether you go with a client/server or a peer-to-peer setup, you need some kind of connection between machines. In other words, before the *metaphysical* network of file sharing and e-mail can become a reality, an underlying *physical* network must be in place. The next few sections introduce you to the various components that compose the nuts and bolts of this physical network.

The Network Interface Card

The network interface card (NIC) is an adapter that, usually, slips into an expansion bus slot inside a client or server computer. (External NICs that plug into parallel ports or PC Card slots are also on the market.) The NIC's main purpose in life is to serve as the connection point between the PC and the network. The NIC's backplate (that is, the portion of the NIC you can see after the card is installed) contains one or more ports into which you plug a network cable.

After the physical connection is established, the NIC works with a device driver to process incoming and outgoing network data. As such, the NIC is the focal point for the computer's network connection, so it plays a big part in the overall performance of that connection. In general, most NICs process data slower than either the network itself or the computer in which the NIC resides. So to avoid bottlenecks, you should get the fastest NICs you can afford. To that end, avoid 8-bit adapters and opt instead for 16-bit or even 32-bit cards. For servers, you should consider 32-bit PCI or EISA cards that offer *bus mastering,* a technique that lets the adapter transfer data between the card and RAM without interrupting the processor.

Each NIC is designed for a specific type of network architecture. The most common types are Ethernet, Token Ring, and ARCnet. These architectures differ in the *access method* used to prevent simultaneous access of the network cable.

Ethernet: This is, by far, the most popular type of network, and it provides 10 Mbps throughput. It uses a *Carrier Sense Multiple Access/Collision Detection* method. This means that Ethernet cards can sense a carrier signal on the network and so refrain from transmitting data. If no carrier signal is detected, the card sends data. However, if two or more cards attempt to send data simultaneously, a collision occurs. This is detected by the other cards on the network, and no data is sent until the collision has been resolved. (Specifically, the nodes involved in the collision resend their packets after waiting a random amount of time.)

Token Ring: This network type offers up to 16 Mbps throughput. For cable access, Token Ring networks use a *token-passing* method. In this method, cable access is determined by a *token* that is passed around the network. If a node wants to transmit data, it "captures" the token and then attaches the data to the token. When the transmission is complete, the node is stripped of the data and set free on the network. Other nodes must wait until the token has been freed before they can transmit their data. In this way, data collisions are avoided completely.

ARCnet: This network type offers 2.5 Mbps throughput. It also uses the token-passing method, but tokens are passed from node to node according to the numerical sequence of network addresses.

NETWORK NOMENCLATURE: PACKETS

To achieve efficient and reliable data transfers, any information sent over a network is broken down into smaller pieces called *packets.* (You can think of a packet as the network equivalent of a single unit of information.) Each packet contains not only data, but also a "header." This header contains information about which machine sent the data and which machine is supposed to receive the data. It also includes a few extra tidbits that let the network put all the original data together in the correct order and to check for errors that might have cropped up during the transmission. A typical packet size is 512 bytes.

NOTE: DEMAND PRIORITY ACCESS

The latest Ethernet iteration—Fast Ethernet—works at 100 Mbps. To support this high speed, Fast Ethernet uses a different cable access method called *Demand Priority Access.* With this method, a central hub (I explain hubs later in this chapter) handles access to the cable rather than the individual nodes. By assigning a priority level to data, this method makes sure that highest-priority data is sent along the cable first.

The Cable Connection

To set up a communications pathway between network computers, you need to install cables that connect the various network nodes together. (Although I discuss only cabling in this section, other types of "unguided" media exist. For example, some systems can transfer network packets by using infrared signals.)

The "starting point" (figuratively speaking) for any cable is the network adapter. As I mentioned in the preceding section, an NIC's backplate has one or more external ports into which you insert a network cable. The key point here is that the cable you use must match the configuration of one of the NIC ports. To understand why, consider the difference between telephone cables and the coaxial wiring used by cable TV. If you examine the wall jacks for each type of cable, you'll see that the ports into which you plug the cables are completely different. So there's no way, for example, to plug a coaxial cable into a telephone jack.

It's the same way with NIC ports: Each has a particular shape and pin arrangement that's designed for a specific type of cable. When buying network adapters, then, you need to either match the ports with the type of cabling you intend to use or, for greater flexibility, get adapter cards that carry multiple ports. If you decide to get adapter cards, look for a card that can automatically detect the type of cable that's inserted into it.

The network cables are of three main types: twisted-pair, coaxial, and fiber-optic. I discuss each type in the following text.

Twisted-Pair Cable

Twisted-pair is the most common type of network cable. It consists of a pair of copper wires that together form a circuit that can transmit data. The wires are twisted together to reduce interference. This is similar to the cable used in telephone wiring, but network cables are usually shielded by a braided metal insulation to further reduce interference problems. (You can use unshielded twisted-pair cabling, but the poorer line quality will restrict the distance between nodes and the total number of nodes.)

Twisted-pair cables use RJ-45 jacks to plug into corresponding RJ-45 connectors in an NIC or other type of network node, as shown in Figure 30.3. In Ethernet circles, twisted-pair cables are also often referred to as *10Base-T cables*, and RJ-45 ports are often called *10Base-T ports*.

FIGURE 30.3.

Twisted-pair cables use RJ-45 jacks to plug into the complementary RJ-45 connectors in network adapter cards.

RJ-45 jack   Twisted-pair cable

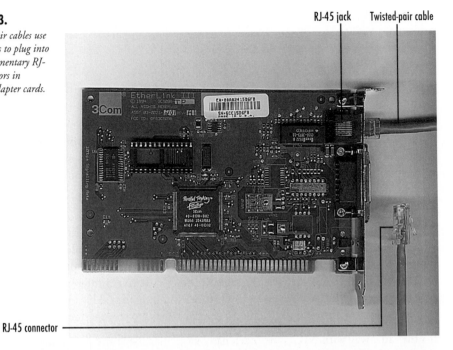

RJ-45 connector

NOTE: TWISTED-PAIR CABLE CATEGORIES

Twisted-pair cable is categorized according to the maximum transmission rates supported by various types of cable. For network data, for example, Category 3 cable supports the standard 10 Mbps transmission rates available in most network installations. These days, however, few people purchase anything but Category 5 cable, which is rated at 100 Mbps and can support higher-end network technologies such as Fast Ethernet.

Coaxial Cable

Coaxial cable consists of a copper wire core surrounded by an insulating layer of copper braid. Coaxial cable is available in two diameters: 0.4-inch (sometimes called *10Base-5* or *thicknet*) or 0.2-inch (sometimes called *10Base-2* or *thinnet*). Thinnet is used most often nowadays because it's cheaper and easier to manipulate.

For thin coaxial cable, you need a network adapter card with a BNC connector on the backplate, as shown in Figure 30.4. You then attach a T-connector to provide the NIC with cable in and cable out ports. Coaxial cables always have BNC cable connectors at the ends of each cable segment, so you attach these connectors to the T-connector. In this way, you can connect all your computers together. You might think that you could form a "circle" by connecting the last NIC in the segment with the first one, but that won't work. Instead, you must use a terminator on the first and last T-connectors, as shown in Figure 30.5. (Note too that if your cable isn't long enough to make it to the next card, you can string two cables together by using a *barrel connector*.)

FIGURE 30.4.

A network adapter with a BNC connector. You insert a T-connector into the port and then use BNC cable connectors to attach either a coaxial cable or a terminator to the T-connector.

Coaxial cable (thinnet)   BNC cable connector   T-connector   Terminator

BNC connector

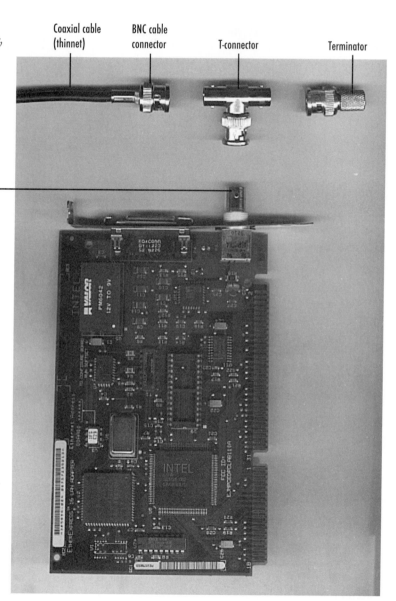

Figure 30.5.

With coaxial cable, you must terminate the first and last T-connectors.

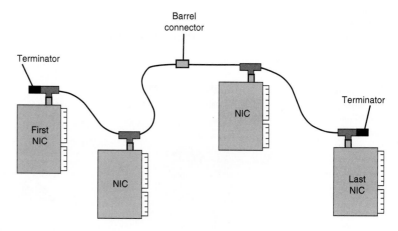

Fiber-Optic Cable

Instead of using the copper wire found in twisted-pair and coaxial cables, fiber-optic cables use glass fibers surrounded by Kevlar or some other strengthening material. Fiber-optic cables provide several advantages over copper wires:

- Digital signals are sent as photons, and the pure glass cable provides only negligible resistance. This lets fiber-optic achieve high transmission rates over extremely long distances without signal attenuation (that is, the loss of signal strength as distance increases).

- Fiber-optic cables don't suffer from *capacitance,* which is a major source of signal distortion in copper wire.

- Fiber-optic isn't subject to *crosstalk,* the leakage of signals from adjacent wires that often plagues copper.

- Fiber-optic cable isn't affected by surrounding electromagnetic interference. When you lay copper wires, you must make sure that they don't run next to electrical wires because the interference from these wires can cause problems.

- Fiber-optic lines are more secure than copper lines because they don't radiate energy that can be monitored by snoops. If someone attempts to read the photons by inserting a device into the cable to tap the signal, it's immediately detectable because the signal falls off or shuts down completely.

Fiber-optic cables, however, are much more expensive than their copper cousins (about a dollar a foot compared to about 9 cents a foot for the highest-grade twisted-pair cable). For this reason, many companies use fiber-optic cables only as a high-speed connection medium between LANs or buildings.

More Hardware Goodies

The network card/cable package is all each PC requires to broadcast and receive network packets, but they're by no means the only hardware you might need. Depending on the physical layout of your network, the types of services you need, and the type of card and cable you choose, you might have to spring for a few more trinkets. Just so you know what to expect, here's a list of some common network accessories:

Hub: A *hub* (also known as a *concentrator*) is a central connection point for network cables. Hubs range in size from small boxes with six or eight RJ-45 connectors to large cabinets with dozens of ports for various cable types. Note that a hub is a must if you use twisted-pair cable, because you can't connect two computers directly using this type of cable.

Repeater: I mentioned earlier that copper-based cables suffer from *attenuation:* The degradation of the electrical signal carried over the cable is proportional to the distance the signal must travel. A *repeater* is a device that boosts the cable's signal so that the length of the network can be extended. For example, if you're using thin coaxial cable, you'll need a repeater about every 600 feet. Some hubs also act as repeaters (in which case they're called *active* hubs).

Bridge: A *bridge* is a device that connects two LANs together, provided that the two LANs are using the same NOS. The bridge can be either a standalone device or implemented in a server by the addition of a second network card. One of the most common uses for a server bridge is to split an existing LAN into two segments. This distributes the network load between the server's two NICs and thus improves overall network performance.

Router: A *router* is a device that makes decisions about where to send the network packets it receives. Unlike a bridge, which merely passes along any data that comes its way, a router examines the address information in each packet and then determines the most efficient route the packet must take to reach its eventual destination. For example, if you'll be connecting your network to the Internet, you need a router to serve as the link between each node and the Internet's various sites. Routers are usually standalone devices, but some servers can be configured as routers with the addition of extra network cards. (This technique adds a significant chunk to the server's overall workload, however, so I don't recommend it.)

Gateway: A *gateway* is a computer or other device that acts as a middleman between two otherwise-incompatible systems. The gateway translates the incoming and outgoing packets so that each system can work the data. An e-mail gateway, for example, might be used to convert e-mail messages between an internal e-mail system and the e-mail protocols used on the Internet.

Topology: The Lay of the LAN

The next decision you need to make when putting together the specs for your network is the *topology* you want to use. The network topology describes how the various nodes that the network comprises—which include not only the computers, but also devices such as hubs and bridges—are connected. Three common topologies are used in LANs: star, bus, and ring.

The Star Topology

The *star* topology, as you can see in Figure 30.6, consists of multiple workstations connected to a hub (which is why this topology is also known as the *hub* topology). In the most common scenario, each computer has a network adapter with an RJ-45 connector running a twisted-pair cable to a port in the hub. The hub (usually) just passes along the signals, so each computer gains access to the other computers on the network.

Figure 30.6.

In the star topology, all the network computers are connected to a central hub.

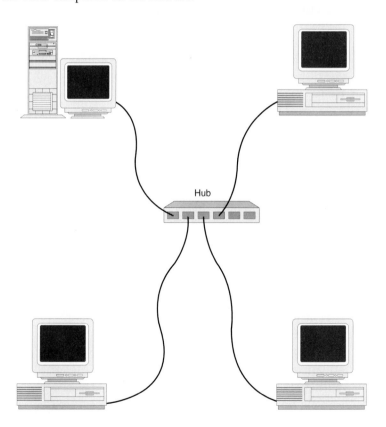

This is an excellent topology for peer-to-peer networks because it mirrors the no-machine-is-more-equal-than-any-other-machine philosophy of peer-to-peer. It's also easy to add machines to the network because it's a simple matter of running a new cable to the hub.

And if the hub's ports are used up, you can connect a second hub to the first one. Another advantage of the star topology is that if one machine goes down for the count, the network access of the other machines isn't affected. On the downside, star topology networks tend to need a lot of cable because you have to connect every node directly to the hub.

The Bus Topology

In a *bus* topology, shown in Figure 30.7, each node is attached to a single main cable called a *bus* or a *backbone.* For large networks, the backbone often extends throughout an entire building and is hidden behind the walls. For such lengthy cables, repeaters are often needed to boost the signal along various points of the backbone. Connections to the backbone are made via drop cables that run from network cards to wall jacks or some other junction box.

FIGURE 30.7.

In the bus topology, each computer is connected to a backbone cable.

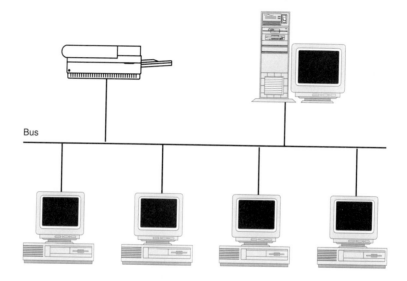

Bus

For smaller networks, the backbone usually consists of a connected series of coaxial cables, similar to the layout shown in Figure 30.5.

The big advantage of the bus topology is that it's relatively easy to set up, and its layout often mirrors the physical layout of an office or a building. The major drawback with bus topologies, however, is that a break in the backbone brings down the entire network.

The Ring Topology

At first glance, the *ring* topology sounds suspiciously like the star topology. Each network node is connected to a central device, which is a special kind of hub called a *multistation access unit* (MAU), as shown in Figure 30.8. The difference, though, lies in how the hub views the network. In the star topology, when the hub receives a packet, it checks the destination and then

30

A NETWORKING PRIMER

forwards the packet to the appropriate node without worrying about any other node on the network. In the ring topology, however, the circuitry of the MAU organizes the entire network as a ring, and each received packet is broadcast around the ring.

FIGURE 30.8.

In a ring topology, the central MAU organizes the network nodes in a ring.

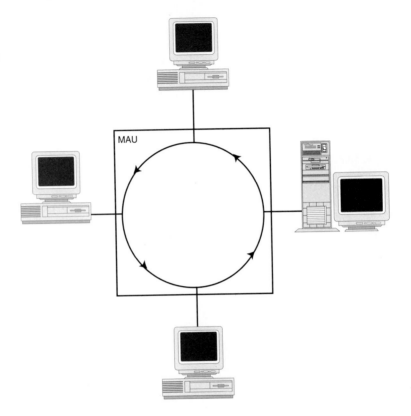

MAU

This is the topology used in Token Ring and ARCnet networks, described earlier. This makes sense because, you'll recall, these network architectures use a token-passing method to allocate cable access. The ring structure is a very efficient way to pass the token around to each node, so overall performance is improved.

Like star topologies, ring topologies are more stable than bus designs because one node going down doesn't affect the entire network. There is one exception, however. The ring topology requires that each node actively pass along each packet. If a node goes down before it has had a chance to pass along a packet, the entire network crashes. These situations, however, are relatively rare.

Talking the Talk: Networking Protocols

In diplomacy, *protocol* defines the rules and formalities that ensure smooth communications between nations and cultures. A *networking protocol* performs a similar function: It's a set of standards that defines how information is exchanged between two systems across a network connection.

For example, consider what appears at first blush to be a simple procedure: exchanging a file between two networked computers. I mentioned earlier that files and all other network transmissions are broken down into packets. Because a large file might consist of hundreds or even thousands of packets, there has to be some way of coordinating how all this information is sent and received. Here are just a few of the questions that need to be answered for even the simplest file transfer to succeed:

- Which computer is sending the packets?
- Where are the packets supposed to go?
- What is the structure of each packet? How big is the header? How big is each data field inside the header? What order are the data fields in? What kinds of addresses are being used? What kind of error checking mechanism is being used? Where does the data start?
- How many packets are in the transfer?
- In what order should the packets be reassembled?
- What happens if a packet arrives damaged?
- How long should the destination computer wait for a packet to arrive?
- What happens if a packet hasn't arrived after the allotted time?
- How does the source computer know that the destination computer has received a particular packet and, eventually, the entire file?

As you can see, it takes an incredible amount of give-and-take to coordinate any kind of network interaction. The inherent complexity of this process means that if the source and destination systems are even slightly out of sync, the file either will arrive corrupted or won't arrive at all. Network protocols are designed to ensure that this doesn't happen. The protocol specifies in no uncertain terms all the details of any kind of network transfer. Generally speaking, protocols fall into two categories: transport protocols and network protocols.

With a *transport* protocol (also called a *connection-oriented* protocol), a virtual communications channel is established between two nodes, and the protocol uses this channel to send packets between the nodes. Because the source and destination are defined in advance, the packets need not contain full address information. The constant link between the two nodes provides the protocol with an efficient path for exchanging messages, so this type of communications method is useful for applications that require a long-term connection (such as a network monitoring program). Some overhead, however, is involved in setting up the channel and closing it, so this method isn't suitable for short-lived communications.

With a *network* protocol (also called a *connectionless* protocol), no communications channel is established between nodes. Instead, the protocol builds each packet with all the information required for the network to deliver each packet and for the destination node to assemble everything together. These self-contained, independent packets are called *datagrams*. The protocol then starts shipping out the packets without notifying or negotiating with the destination node. All the network has to do is transmit the packets to the destination (or to some intermediate stop along the way). This method requires a bit more packet overhead, but it's efficient for short bursts because there's no need to set up (or shut down) a channel between nodes.

Many protocols are available, but three are most common (these are the standard protocols available with Windows 95):

IPX/SPX: *IPX/SPX* stands for Internet Packet eXchange/Sequenced Packet eXchange. IPX is a connectionless network layer protocol. As a network layer protocol, IPX addresses and routes packets from one network to another on an IPX internetwork. SPX, on the other hand, is an extension of IPX that provides for connection-oriented transport layer functions. SPX enhances the IPX protocol by providing reliable delivery. IPX/SPX is used by NetWare networks.

NetBEUI: This is the NetBIOS Extended User Interface protocol (NetBIOS is an API that lets network applications, such as redirectors, communicate with networking protocols.) It's a combined transport/network protocol developed by IBM and supported by all Microsoft networks. It's a simple, efficient protocol that works well in small LANs. However, it lacks the capability to route packets, so it isn't suitable for WANs.

TCP/IP: TCP/IP stands for Transmission Control Protocol/Internet Protocol; TCP is the transport protocol, and IP is the network protocol. TCP/IP is the *lingua franca* of most UNIX systems and the Internet as a whole. TCP/IP is also, however, an excellent choice for other types of networks because it's routable, robust, and reliable. And unlike previous versions of Windows, Windows 95 has built-in support for TCP/IP. I talk about this support in detail in Chapter 36, "Implementing TCP/IP for Internet and Network Connections."

When setting up your network, you don't have to commit to a single protocol. Windows 95 is happy to work with multiple protocols simultaneously, so you don't have to box yourself in. This is particularly handy in network environments that must access different types of machines. You can use IPX/SPX to access a NetWare server, NetBEUI to access Windows for Workgroups or Windows NT machines, and TCP/IP to access UNIX boxes, Windows NT systems, or the Internet.

An Introduction to Windows 95 Networking

You'll get down to the nuts and bolts of Windows 95 networking in the next chapter. For now, though, let's lay some groundwork by getting a bird's-eye view of how Windows 95 does the networking thing. In particular, I'll show you how Windows 95 provides networking support for Microsoft networks and NetWare networks.

Windows 95 and Microsoft Networks

Windows 95 happily interacts with Microsoft networks, which means networks that include computers running Windows NT Server, Windows NT Workstation, LAN Manager, Windows for Workgroups, and, of course, Windows 95. Connecting your Windows 95 machine to any of these networks gives you instant access to shared drives, folders, and printers and lets you share your resources with the network.

Architectural Overview

To give you an appreciation for how Windows 95 and Microsoft networks interact, Figure 30.9 lays out the architectural components used by Windows 95 to implement networking in such an environment.

FIGURE 30.9.

The architecture of Windows 95 networking on a Microsoft network.

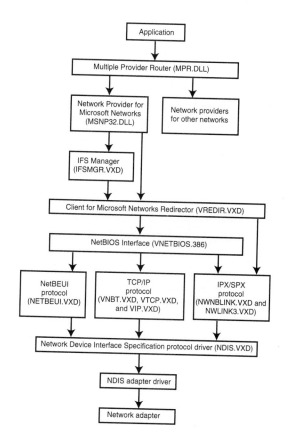

Here's a summary of the various layers used by Windows 95 to let an application communicate with a network adapter:

Multiple Provider Router: As I mentioned earlier, Windows 95 supports multiple network configurations. The service that lets Windows 95 support different networks concurrently is called the *Multiple Provider Router* (MPR.DLL). When an application needs a network resource, it calls the appropriate function in the WinNet32 API (or the WinNet16 API, if it's a 16-bit application). The MPR then routes the request to the appropriate *network provider,* which translates the request into a network-specific call.

Network Provider for Microsoft Networks: This is the network provider that is used to handle Microsoft networking requests. This provider supports operations such as browsing Microsoft networks, logging on and off Windows NT domains (including verifying passwords), and adding and removing mapped network connections.

Installable File System (IFS) Manager: If the network provider gets a request for a file system-related operation (such as mapping a network drive), it passes the request along to the IFS Manager. From here, the request is passed along to the redirector.

Client for Microsoft Networks Redirector: All other requests are sent directly to the Client for Microsoft Networks redirector (VREDIR.VXD). This is a 32-bit driver that provides all the mechanisms needed for an application to communicate with a remote device, including file reads and writes, print job submissions, and resource sharing. Packets are converted into the format specified by the Server Message Block (SMB) protocol used by Microsoft networks.

NETWORK NOMENCLATURE: SERVER MESSAGE BLOCK

A *server message block* is a packet of data that contains a request from a workstation to a server or that contains the response from the server to the workstation. SMBs are used for all communications that go through a Microsoft network, including file I/O, connecting and disconnecting remote connections, or performing any other network function the redirector needs to carry out.

NetBIOS Interface: This is the interface between the redirector and the network protocols. This interface is an API that gives the redirector a protocol-independent method of accessing the services provided by NetBEUI, TCP/IP, and other protocols.

Protocols: At this level, the request or data is converted into a packet that meets the specifications of whatever protocol the system is using (or that's required for the destination node). For example, if a message is being sent to a NetWare server, a driver converts the data into a packet suitable for transport via the IPX/SPX protocol.

Network Device Interface Specification (NDIS) protocol driver: This is a 32-bit protected-mode driver that lets the protocol driver interface with the network adapter driver.

NDIS adapter driver: This is the device driver that interacts directly with the network adapter. As with all of Windows 95 hardware drivers, the NIC hardware architecture uses a universal driver/mini-driver model.

This sequence of events (from the application contacting the Multiple Provider Router to the NDIS adapter driver passing the packets to the NIC) shows you what happens when a packet is sent by an application to the network. For incoming packets, this sequence is reversed.

Notes About Microsoft Networking

To enable support for Microsoft networks, you install Windows 95's Client for Microsoft Networks component (see Chapter 31, "Windows 95 Networking"). This client provides you with 32-bit protected-mode drivers for the redirector and protocol stacks, which means that this client uses no conventional memory. The Client for Microsoft Networks lets you access shared resources on other network nodes and lets you share local resources with the network. As well, all the Windows 95 networking goodies are available through this client: user profiles, system policies, share-level security, remote administration, Dial-Up Networking, automatic reconnection of mapped resources, unified logon, recognition of long filenames on NT machines, and more.

Here are a few notes to bear in mind before setting up Windows 95 to interact with a Microsoft network:

- For easier setups, keep in mind that you can install Windows 95 on remote machines via a computer running Windows NT Server.

- If you plan on taking advantage of user profiles or system policies, you must set up Windows 95 to use the Client for Microsoft Networks as the primary network logon client.

- You can share resources with other computers on a Microsoft network only if all the machines are using a common protocol.

- You can implement user-level security by adding an account to a Windows NT domain for each user on a Windows 95 system.

- Remember that Windows 95 clients can't view or access drives that use the Windows NT file system (NTFS).

Windows 95 and NetWare Networks

As I mentioned earlier, NetWare is a client/server–based network operating system. This means you need to load some client software on your Windows 95 workstation to gain access to a NetWare server. Windows 95 comes with Microsoft's 32-bit NetWare client, called *Client for*

NetWare Networks. You can get, at no charge, Novell's 32-bit NetWare client for Windows 95 (called *NetWare Client32 for Windows 95,* or more commonly known simply as *Client32*) from Novell; this client software isn't included in NetWare 3.12 or NetWare 4.1 because Windows 95 was released after these products started shipping.

Microsoft's NetWare client supports NetWare 3.1x, and it supports NetWare 4.1 if the server has bindery emulation enabled. If you need to access a NetWare 4 network using NetWare Directory Services (NDS), you need to use either Novell's Client32 or get a client update from Microsoft. (This update is available in the Windows 95 Service Pack. You can also get it from any of Microsoft's online sites; look for a file named MSNDS.EXE.)

If you're eager to try out your Windows 95 workstation and can't wait to get the 32-bit client from either Novell or Microsoft in order to access the NDS of your NetWare 4 network, you can install Novell's 16-bit VLM drivers to gain access to the NDS.

Client32 Overview

Novell's new 32-bit clients have an advanced architecture that is very different from the NetWare DOS Requester (the VLM-based client). The VLM drivers are a set of modules dynamically loaded into and unloaded from the workstation's memory by the VLM manager (VLM.EXE). In essence, they're a combination of terminate-and-stay-resident (TSR) modules and overlay programs. As a result, VLMs can be memory-hungry.

On the other hand, the new architecture used by the 32-bit clients lets the client software run in protected mode. This requires less than 4 KB of conventional memory while providing a larger cache.

Similar to the Microsoft 32-bit client, Client32 saves its configuration settings in the Registry, so you can manage Client32 parameters by using Windows 95's System Policies Editor. Client32 uses Microsoft's implementation of TCP/IP, NetBIOS, WinSock, and Named Pipes, which are all included as part of Windows 95. This means you can switch between Microsoft's and Novell's NetWare client without having to change anything else. Because Client32 uses the Microsoft protocol stack, it can coexist with the Microsoft Client for Microsoft Networks—a requirement if you have a mixture of NetWare and Microsoft networks in your networking environment.

Novell or Microsoft Client?

Both Novell's Client32 and Microsoft's NetWare Client perform equally well under most circumstances. But depending on your particular network requirements and environment, you might prefer to use Novell's Client32 over Microsoft's NetWare Client.

The two clients provide similar capabilities, but Novell's Client32 has the following features not found in Microsoft's:

- Support for multiple NDS tree access.
- Complete NetWare Directory Services access.

- ■ A graphical user interface login utility that lets the user execute a user or system login script, update search drives, and update environment variables. Bindery and NDS connections are supported.

- ■ Support for login script execution if logged in from Network Neighborhood, through the use of the GUI login utility—Microsoft client performs an "attach" rather than a login, so no login scripts are executed by the Microsoft client if you log in from Network Neighborhood.

- ■ Support for Novell's LANalyzer for Windows (a software-only protocol analyzer) product.

- ■ Support for industry standard SNMP (Simple Network Management Protocol).

- ■ Support for Novell's NetWare/IP environment.

You will also find that Client32, in general, has better integration with Windows 95's Explorer and Network Neighborhood utilities than Microsoft's NetWare Client.

You can find detailed information about the installation and use of Novell's Client32 and Microsoft's NetWare Client in Chapter 31.

Summary

This chapter introduced you to the world of networking. My goal was to show you the kinds of issues and decisions you face when implementing your own network. To that end, I began by telling you about the various network types (such as LANs and WANs) and contrasting client/server and peer-to-peer networks. From there, you learned about some networking hardware specifics, such as adapter cards, cables, hubs, and more. I then showed you various topological layouts for this hardware and told you about the various protocols available for co-ordinating the transport of packets around a network. I closed by giving you an introduction to Windows 95 networking and explaining how it relates to Microsoft networks and NetWare networks.

Plenty more networking know-how is to come, though. Here's a summary:

- ■ You'll learn various techniques for implementing and using networking under Windows 95 in Chapter 31, "Windows 95 Networking."

- ■ Administration and security are important networking issues, so I've devoted an entire chapter to them. See Chapter 32, "Network Administration and Security."

- ■ It sometimes seems that networks are accidents waiting to happen. I cover a variety of networking woes in Chapter 33, "Network Troubleshooting."

- ■ If you just have a couple of computers, you can bypass the expense of network adapter cards and cables by using Windows 95's Direct Cable Connection. You still have to set up a "network," however, and I demonstrate how it's done in Chapter 34, "From Laptop to Desktop and Back: Direct Cable Connection."

- To learn how to access a network remotely, check out Chapter 35, "Remote Computing with Dial-Up Networking."

- TCP/IP is quickly becoming the protocol of choice for both large and small networks. I show you how to work with TCP/IP in Chapter 36, "Implementing TCP/IP for Internet and Network Connections."

- The Internet, of course, is *the* network. I show you how Windows 95 connects to, and works with, Internet resources in Chapter 37, "Windows 95 and the Internet." For Web-based Internet sites, Internet Explorer offers easy access. I give you a complete primer in Chapter 38, "Exploring the Web with Internet Explorer."

Windows 95 Networking

CHAPTER 31

Let us work without theorizing; 'tis the only way to make life endurable.

—Voltaire

After all that theory and background in the preceding chapter, you're probably champing at the bit for some practical know-how. Well, now that you're comfortable with notions such as clients, servers, adapters, and protocols, you can finally get down to brass tacks and turn all these abstractions into something concrete. That's just what you'll do in this chapter as I concentrate on the nitty-gritty of networking. I'll show you how to jack into a network by installing and configuring a network interface card, a network client, and the network protocols you need. From there, I'll show you how to access network resources, share your computer's resources with others, and print over the network.

So whether you just need to get a single machine tied into an existing network, or whether you're setting up your own network at home or at the office, this chapter provides the essential information you need to know.

Network Installation and Configuration

When you're setting up a network, your first chore should be to install all the necessary hardware in each machine. That means adding the network adapters, running cables, and tying everything together with whatever other components you need (such as a hub if you're using a star topology).

After that's done, you need to set up Windows 95's networking components. How you do this depends on whether you're installing Windows 95 itself or adding networking to an existing Windows 95 installation:

■ If you're installing Windows 95, be sure to choose the Custom option. If you do, the Setup Wizard will eventually display the Network Configuration dialog box, shown in Figure 31.1.

FIGURE 31.1.

When you're installing Windows 95, the Custom setup option displays the Network Configuration dialog box.

■ If Windows 95 is already installed, you'll need to set up the network components from within Windows 95. In this case, you open the Control Panel's Network icon to display the Network dialog box, shown in Figure 31.2.

FIGURE 31.2.

Opening the Control Panel's Network icon displays this dialog box.

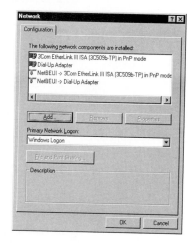

The next few sections show you how to use either dialog box to install and configure an adapter, a client, protocols, and network services. When you're done, click Next > or OK, as appropriate. (When you click OK, Windows 95 might ask you to insert one of your Windows 95 source disks. Follow the on-screen prompts, and when Windows 95 asks whether you want to restart your computer, click Yes.)

Installing and Configuring a Network Adapter

Windows 95 usually does a pretty good job of detecting your network hardware (particularly if your NIC is Plug and Play–compliant). If you're installing Windows 95, the Detection Manager should figure out your card and display it in the Network Configuration dialog box. If Windows 95 is already installed, the system should detect the new card the next time you restart.

In either case, Windows installs the appropriate device driver for the card (you might be asked to insert a Windows 95 source disk). Windows 95 comes with 32-bit protected-mode drivers for many adapter types, although you're free to use existing 16-bit drivers if Windows 95 doesn't support your card.

Adding an Adapter

If Windows 95 didn't detect your card, or if it detected the wrong type of card, you can easily change the adapter component. If the Network dialog box shows the wrong adapter, you should first remove it by highlighting the adapter's name and then clicking the Remove button. When that's done, follow these steps to install your adapter:

1. Click the Add button to display the Select Network Component Type dialog box, shown in Figure 31.3.

FIGURE 31.3.

Use this dialog box to choose the type of network component you want to add.

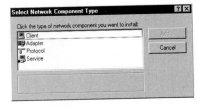

2. Highlight Adapter and then click Add. The Select Network adapters dialog box, shown in Figure 31.4, appears.

FIGURE 31.4.

Use this dialog box to choose the vendor and make of your network card.

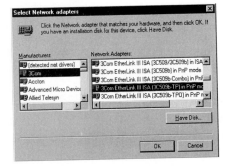

3. Use the Manufacturers list to highlight the vendor of your network card, and then use the Network Adapters list to highlight the specific card. If you don't see your NIC listed, and the card came with a disk of drivers, insert the disk, click the Have Disk button, and follow the on-screen prompts to choose the driver.

4. Click OK.

TIP: INSTALLING WITH THE ADD NEW HARDWARE WIZARD

If you're not sure which driver to install for your NIC, you can use the Add New Hardware Wizard to have Windows 95 detect your card automatically.

NOTE: USING MULTIPLE ADAPTERS

If you have the room and the available resources, you can add extra adapters to a computer. Note, however, that Windows 95 supports a maximum of "only" four network adapters in a single machine.

Installing a Client

The next step is to select the network client or clients you want to use. Windows 95 comes with several clients, but you can also add third-party clients (such as the 32-bit NetWare client from Novell called the NetWare Client32 for Windows 95, or more commonly called Client32). The next two sections show you how to install network clients for Microsoft networks and NetWare networks.

Installing a Client for Microsoft Networks

To install the Client for Microsoft Networks, follow these steps:

1. Click the Add button to display the Select Network Component Type dialog box.
2. Highlight Client and then click Add. The Select Network Client dialog box, shown in Figure 31.5, appears.

FIGURE 31.5.

Use this dialog box to highlight Client for Microsoft Networks.

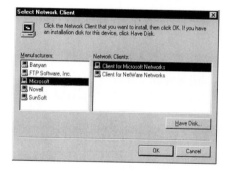

3. In the Manufacturers list, highlight Microsoft.
4. In the Network Clients list, highlight Client for Microsoft Networks.
5. Click OK. Windows 95 adds the client to the list of network components.

Installing a Client for NetWare Networks

As I mentioned in Chapter 30, "A Networking Primer," two NetWare clients are available. The Microsoft version (Client for NetWare Networks) comes with your Windows 95 package. If, however, you need to connect to a NetWare 4.1 network with NetWare Directory Services (NDS) connections, you need to get an update from Microsoft. The file is called MSNDS.EXE, and you'll find it on any Microsoft download site or in the Windows 95 Service Pack. (The NDS client is included in the OSR2 package.) The Novell implementation of the 32-bit NetWare client for Windows 95 is called NetWare Client32 for Windows 95. You can get it free from the regular Novell file update sources, such as CompuServe and the Novell FTP sites.

Installing Microsoft's NetWare Client

The steps for installing the Microsoft Client for NetWare are very similar to those for the Client for Microsoft Networks, as described in the preceding section. The only difference is that when you get to the Select Network Client dialog box, highlight `Microsoft` in the `Manufacturers` list, and in the `Network Clients` list, highlight `Client for NetWare Networks`.

Installing the Microsoft Service for NDS

If you want to install the Microsoft NetWare Client update to provide NDS support, it's installed as a service rather than as a client. Here are the steps to follow:

1. Open the Network icon from the Control Panel.
2. Click the Add button to display the Select Network Component Type dialog box.
3. Highlight `Service` and then click Add. The Select Network Client dialog box appears.
4. In the `Manufacturers` list, highlight `Microsoft`.
5. In the `Network Services` list, click the Have Disk button, and specify the path in which the update files are located. You might need to use the Browse button to navigate through the directory structure to locate the `NDSCLI.INF` file.
6. In the second Select Network Services dialog box, highlight `Service for NetWare Directory Services`.
7. Click OK. Windows 95 adds the client to the list of network components.

Installing the 32-Bit Novell Client

The installation procedure for Novell's client is slightly different. Use the steps given next.

TIP: USE THE SERVER INSTALLATION METHOD

You can obtain the NetWare client in two formats: one for floppy disk installation, and one for server (or hard disk) installation. Because of the size of the uncompressed files (almost 12 MB), using the server installation method is recommended. You can put the files on the local hard disk of your Windows 95 workstation and install from there.

1. Obtain the Client32 files from Novell, and create the installation disks according to its instructions.
2. Open the Network icon from the Control Panel.
3. Click the Add button to display the Select Network Component Type dialog box.
4. Highlight `Client` and then click Add. The Select Network Client dialog box appears.
5. In the `Manufacturers` list, highlight `Novell`.
6. In the `Network Clients` list, click the Have Disk button, and specify the path in which the Client32 files are located. You might need to use the Browse button to navigate through the directory structure to locate the `MSBATCH.INF` file—you should find it in the `\ADMIN\BATCH95\NLS\ENGLISH` directory.

7. In the second Select Network Client dialog box, highlight `Novell NetWare Client 32`, as shown in Figure 31.6.

FIGURE 31.6.

If all goes well, you should see Novell NetWare Client 32 *in the dialog box.*

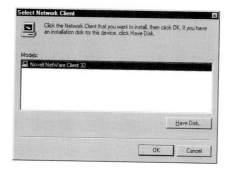

8. Click OK. Windows 95 adds the client to the list of network components, as shown in Figure 31.7.

FIGURE 31.7.

The Network properties sheet after Novell's Client32 has been installed.

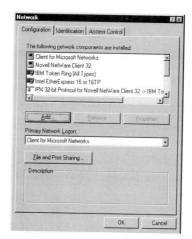

Note that the installation of Client32 also adds an entry to your Start menu: Start | Programs | Novell | NetWare Login.

Configuring Your NetWare Client

After you install the Novell Client32, a dialog box appears with a recommendation that you set some properties for the client. Click Yes to display the Novell NetWare Client 32 Properties dialog box, shown in Figure 31.8.

FIGURE 31.8.

This tab configures options for the general Client32 user login information.

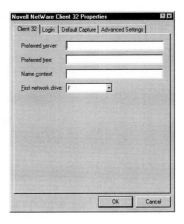

To configure your login, use the following tabs:

Client32: This is the tab where you specify your Preferred server (if NetWare 2.x/3.x), Preferred tree, and Name context (if NetWare 4). You also specify the DOS drive letter to be used for your First network drive; the default is F.

Login: From the Login tab, shown in Figure 31.9, you can select the type of connection (bindery or NDS) to be made by the client workstation to the NetWare server. You can also specify whether the login scripts are to be executed, whether alternative login scripts are to be used instead, and whether the results of the login scripts are to be displayed on-screen.

FIGURE 31.9.

The options in this tab cover the login connection and login script information.

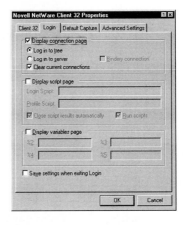

Default Capture: This tab, shown in Figure 31.10, sets up the print capture defaults for the workstation. For example, this is where you specify whether a banner page should be printed and whether a form feed should be sent at the end of each print job.

FIGURE 31.10.

This tab defines the printer capture information.

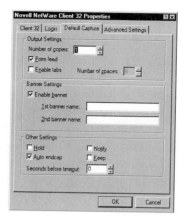

Advanced Settings: You can use this tab to change the various settings that might affect how Client32 functions. For example, from this sheet you can turn Packet Burst on or off. If you're accustomed to the VLM drivers and the NET.CFG file, you'll find that this sheet contains similar parameters.

You can access these sheets at any time through the Network icon in the Control Panel: Highlight Novell NetWare Client32 and click the Properties button.

The configuration for the Microsoft NetWare client is much simpler than that of Novell's because you have only two tabs to work through, as shown in Figure 31.11. From this properties sheet, you configure options such as the Preferred Server, the first network drive, whether you want the login script to be executed during login, and so on.

FIGURE 31.11.

The properties sheet for the Microsoft NetWare Client.

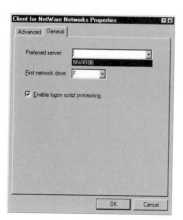

Installing and Configuring Protocols

Windows 95 will install some networking protocols automatically, depending on the client you installed. For example, if you added the Client for Microsoft Networks, Windows 95 adds the NetBEUI and IPX/SPX protocols. You can also, however, add, remove, and configure protocols by hand, as described in the next few sections.

NOTE: TCP/IP PROPERTIES

To learn how to configure the TCP/IP protocol, see Chapter 36, "Implementing TCP/IP for Internet and Network Connections."

Adding a Protocol

Here are the steps to follow to install another protocol:

1. From the Network properties sheet, click the Add button to display the Select Network Component Type dialog box.

2. Highlight `Protocol` and click Add. The Select Network Protocol dialog box, shown in Figure 31.12, appears.

FIGURE 31.12.

Use this dialog box to highlight the protocol you want to add.

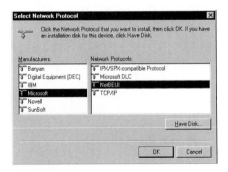

3. In the `Manufacturers` list, highlight the maker of the protocol you want to use.

4. In the `Network Protocols` list, highlight the protocol.

5. Click OK. Windows 95 adds the protocol to the list of network components.

If you want to get rid of a protocol you don't need, simply highlight it in the list of network components, and then click the Remove button.

NOTE: NOVELL ODI AND CLIENT32 ARE INCOMPATIBLE

You can't install the Novell ODI protocol and Novell's Client32 at the same time.

Binding Protocols

For Windows 95 networking to function properly, you must associate a network client with a protocol, and a protocol with a network adapter driver. These associations are called *bindings*. Windows 95 usually handles all of this for you automatically. (In other words, each installed client is bound to each installed protocol, and each installed protocol is bound to each installed adapter.) However, you might prefer to remove bindings for certain components to improve performance. For example, if you've installed clients for both Microsoft and NetWare networks, but only the NetWare network will use the IPX/SPX protocol, you should remove the Microsoft networking client binding from the IPX/SPX protocol.

To work with the client bindings for a protocol, highlight the protocol in the list of network components, and then click Properties. In the properties sheet that appears, select the Bindings tab, shown in Figure 31.13. This tab lists each installed client, and the clients that are bound to the protocol have their check boxes activated. To remove a client binding, deactivate its check box.

FIGURE 31.13.

You use the Bindings tab of a protocol's properties sheet to choose which clients are bound to the protocol.

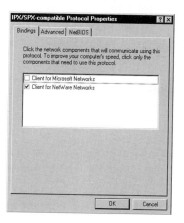

To work with the protocol bindings for a network adapter, highlight the adapter in the list of network components, and then click Properties. In the properties sheet that appears, select the Bindings tab, shown in Figure 31.14. This tab lists each installed protocol, and the protocols that are bound to the adapter have their check boxes activated. To remove a protocol binding, deactivate its check box.

FIGURE 31.14.

You use the Bindings tab of an adapter's properties sheet to choose which protocols are bound to the adapter.

NetBEUI Properties

The NetBEUI protocol's properties sheet has an Advanced tab that controls a couple of NetBEUI settings. When Windows 95 is running in protected mode, these values are managed automatically, so you don't need to worry about them. If, however, you start Windows 95 using the `Safe mode with network support` option, these settings come into play. Here's what they mean in case you need to make adjustments:

Maximum Sessions: This value determines the maximum number of connections to remote computers that the redirector will allow.

NCBS: These are Network Control Blocks, and the setting determines the maximum number of NetBIOS commands that can be used.

IPX/SPX Properties

The IPX/SPX-compatible protocol's properties sheet has an Advanced tab that controls various IPX/SPX settings. Six parameters are available under the Advanced tab setting:

Force Even Length Packets: Certain network card drivers want the IPX packet to have an even number of bytes. This setting forces an IPX packet to contain an even number of bytes by providing a padding byte, if necessary.

Frame Type: This specifies the frame type to which the IPX protocol is bound. By default, it's set to `AUTO`. If you use multiple frame types (such as Ethernet II and Ethernet 802.3) on your Windows 95 workstation, and you want to have IPX bound to a specific frame type—say, Ethernet 802.3 rather than "randomly"—use this option to specify the frame type setting.

Maximum Connections: This specifies the maximum number of concurrent IPX/SPX connections the Windows 95 workstation can have with other devices.

Maximum Sockets: This specifies the maximum number of sockets that the workstation can allocate for communications over IPX/SPX. Typically, an application uses at least one socket.

Network Address: This identifies the IPX network address. By default, the driver auto-detects the IPX number being used on the cable.

Source Routing: This parameter is useful only in a Token Ring network environment. It enables source routing capability if you have source route bridges on your network.

This properties sheet also has a NetBIOS tab, which specifies whether NetBIOS applications are to use IPX/SPX as the transport/network protocol.

Installing and Configuring Network Services

The clients you install should provide all or most of the network services you need (such as sharing files and printers, the capability to browse shared resources, and so on). Windows 95 does, however, support extra services that provide additional networking support. For example, the Windows 95 CD-ROM has a Remote Registry feature that lets you administer remote computers. (I'll talk about this topic in detail later in this chapter.) To set this up, you must install Remote Registry as a network service.

Adding a Service

Here are the steps to follow to install a network service:

1. In the Network properties sheet, click the Add button to display the Select Network Component Type dialog box.

2. Highlight Service and then click Add. The Select Network Service dialog box, shown in Figure 31.15, appears.

FIGURE 31.15.

Use this dialog box to choose the service you want to install.

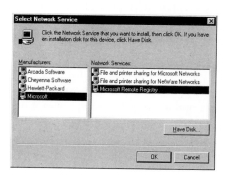

3. Use the Manufacturers list and the Network Services list to highlight the service you want to install. Alternatively, click the Have Disk button, and follow the on-screen prompts to choose the service.

4. Click OK.

Establishing Your Primary Network Logon

To complete the Configuration tab of the Network properties sheet (or the Network Configuration dialog box, if you're installing Windows 95), you must choose your primary network logon. This determines both the logon dialog box you'll see at startup and the procedure Windows 95 uses to log you on to your network. For example, you might need to have a Windows NT Server validate your password, or you might want to run a NetWare login script.

To make sure that all of this happens without incident, you need to choose an appropriate network logon. To do that, open the Primary Network Logon drop-down list, and select either Windows Logon (if you don't want to log on to the network or if you're logging on to a peer-to-peer network) or the appropriate network client. (For example, if you need to process a NetWare login script, select your installed NetWare client.)

Microsoft Networking Logon Options

If you choose Client for Microsoft Networks as your primary network logon, you have a few logon options to work with. To view these options, highlight Client for Microsoft Networks in the list of components, and then click Properties. The properties sheet that appears (see Figure 31.16) gives you the following controls:

Logon validation: If you're using a client/server setup, you can establish user accounts on a Windows NT server for each client. If so, you should activate the Log on to Windows NT domain check box to have the server verify each client logon. Use the Windows NT domain text box to enter the name of the domain to which your computer belongs.

Network logon options: You'll see later in this chapter that you can map a network drive so that it appears to be part of your own system. If you use lots of these connections, it can take a while for them to be reestablished each time you start Windows 95. To speed up your restarts, activate the Quick logon option. This logs you on to the network, but it doesn't reestablish the mapped network drive connections. If you use only a few mapped network drives, you can activate the Logon and restore network connections option instead. This option not only logs you on to the network, but also reestablishes all of your mapped network drive connections automatically.

Setting Up Server Accounts

After each machine is network-ready, you can get right down to business if you're setting up a peer-to-peer system. If you're going with the client/server model, however, you're not out of the woods yet. Besides setting up the server with the appropriate NOS (such as NT Server or NetWare), you need to tell the server about the client machines on the network. In other words, you need to set up accounts and passwords for each user, establish domains or workgroups, set

31

WINDOWS 95
NETWORKING

up common directories, and so on. (A *workgroup* is a related collection of computers on the network. For example, all the computers in the Marketing department might constitute one workgroup, and all the computers in Accounting might constitute another.) How you do all this depends on the network operating system.

FIGURE 31.16.

The properties sheet for the Client for Microsoft Networks lets you set various logon options.

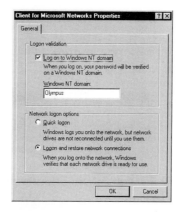

Identifying Your Computer

Your final network installation task is to set up your computer's network identity. If you're installing Windows 95, the Setup Wizard displays an Identification dialog box after you've clicked Next > in the Network Configuration dialog box. Otherwise, select the Identification tab in the Network properties sheet, shown in Figure 31.17.

FIGURE 31.17.

Use the Identification tab to establish your computer's network identity.

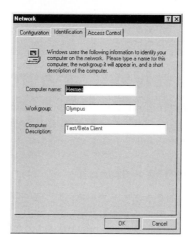

Either way, you must enter three pieces of ID:

Computer name: This is the name other people will see when they browse the network resources. It must be unique on the network and must be 15 or fewer characters. You can't use spaces in the name, but all alphanumeric characters are fair game, as are the following symbols:

`~ ! @ # $ % ^ & ( ) _ - { } ' .`

Workgroup: In a peer-to-peer network, you organize computers into workgroups simply by giving them the same name in their respective `Workgroup` text boxes. (If you need to log in to a specific Windows NT Server domain, enter the name of the domain in this space.) You use the same naming rules that I outlined for the computer name.

Computer Description: You use this text box to provide a more detailed description of your computer. The description can be up to 48 characters long and can include any character except commas.

TIP: A UTILITY FOR MULTIPLE NETWORK CONFIGURATIONS

What do you do if you have to set up your computer for connections to multiple networks? I'm sorry to say that you have to repeat all of the steps you just went through *each time* you need to connect to a different network!

If the thought of that kind of hassle scares the heck out of you, you'll almost certainly want to check out NetSwitcher, a utility that lets you set up multiple network configurations and switch between them easily. NetSwitcher was written by J.W. Hance and is available either via fax (1-317-575-9435) or via the Web at the following URL:

`http://www.bysnet.com/netsw.html`

Accessing Network Resources

If all has gone well to this point, you'll be just about ready for action. Your newfound network will be up and running, and your Windows 95 machines will be able to connect to the network. Now all that remains is to log on and start looking around your net.

Logging On to the Network

With networking enabled on a Windows 95 machine, you'll be faced with a logon prompt each time you restart the system. One of the innovations with Windows 95 is that you can use a single unified logon for all your networks (and Windows 95 itself). The first time you start Windows 95, however, you might have to negotiate multiple logon dialog boxes. The trick to establishing the unified logon is to assign the same password for each logon.

Windows 95 Logon

If you chose the `Windows Logon` option as your primary network logon, you'll see the dialog box shown in Figure 31.18. In this case, even though the user name and password are meaningful only in the context of user profiles (as explained in Chapter 7, "Customizing Windows 95"), you should still enter your network user name so that it will be visible automatically the next time you log on to the network. (Note that the first time you start Windows 95, you'll need to enter your password twice.)

FIGURE 31.18.

You'll see this dialog box if you're using the Windows Logon.

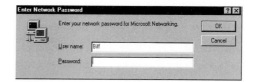

Client for Microsoft Networks Logon

If you set up the Client for Microsoft Networks to log on to a Windows NT domain, you'll see the dialog box shown in Figure 31.19. In this case, you need to enter the user name and password defined in your account on the NT machine, and you need to make sure that the `Domain` text box correctly identifies the domain you belong to. When you click OK, your password is verified by the NT machine.

FIGURE 31.19.

You'll see this dialog box if you're logging on to a Windows NT domain.

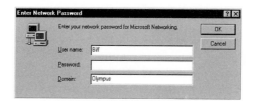

NetWare Client32 Logon

When Client32 is loaded on your Windows 95 workstation, you'll get the graphical Novell NetWare Login when you log in to Windows 95, as shown in Figure 31.20. Use the Login tab to enter your user name and password. The Connection tab is where you can specify the name of the NDS tree or the name of a NetWare server you want to log in to, and the name context if you're performing an NDS login. If you've configured this information under the Client32 properties sheets as described earlier, you won't need to access this tab at all while logging in, unless you want to change the defaults.

FIGURE 31.20.

*The GUI Login of
Novell Client32.*

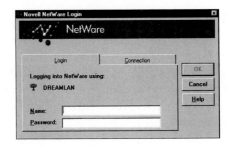

Client for NetWare Networks Logon

If you're using the Microsoft NetWare client, the login screen will look similar to the one shown in Figure 31.21. If you're logging in using a bindery connection, just enter your user name and password; if you're using an NDS connection, enter your user name using the "full path" if a name context isn't set.

FIGURE 31.21.

*The login screen of the
Microsoft NetWare
Client.*

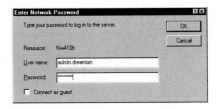

NetWare Login Scripts

When you log in to a NetWare server using either the Microsoft client or the Novell client, the various login scripts are executed. With the NetWare client, if the option is selected, you can see the result of the login script execution, as shown in Figure 31.22. Both Microsoft and Novell clients support drive mapping, including search drives, in the login script processing.

FIGURE 31.22.

*The login script result
screen of Client32.*

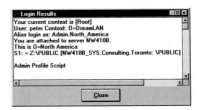

The Network Neighborhood

If you used Windows for Workgroups, you know that one of its biggest drawbacks was that it gave you no easy way of browsing the network and checking out which shared resources were available. Windows 95 rectifies that glaring omission with the Network Neighborhood. This is a special folder that appears as part of the Windows 95 desktop. To view the Network Neighborhood, use either of the following methods:

- Double-click the Network Neighborhood icon on the desktop.
- In Explorer, highlight Network Neighborhood in the Folders pane.

TIP: 32-BIT COMMON DIALOG BOXES ALSO DISPLAY THE 'HOOD

You can also access the Network Neighborhood via the Save As and Open dialog boxes in 32-bit applications. In any Save As dialog box, open the Save in drop-down list, and select Network Neighborhood; in any Open dialog box, use the Look in drop-down list instead.

The top level of the Network Neighborhood shows you the various computers that share your workgroup or domain (including your computer). As you can see in Figure 31.23, Explorer's Details view shows you not only the name of each computer, but also a descriptive Comment column (this is the text that was entered into the Computer description field in the Identification tab; refer to Figure 31.17).

FIGURE 31.23.

The Network Neighborhood as seen from Explorer.

The top level of the Network Neighborhood also has an item called Entire Network. As the name implies, this item displays all the available network resources. Specifically, it shows you the workgroups and domains that compose the network. In Figure 31.24, for example, there are two workgroups: Olympus and Valhalla. These groups act as folders, so you can open them to display each group's computers.

FIGURE 31.24.

The Entire Network item displays all the workgroups and domains.

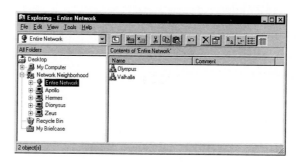

At the computer level, the Network Neighborhood shows you which resources each computer is sharing with the network. For example, Figure 31.25 shows you the resources shared by the Apollo computer, which include a printer, a floppy drive, a folder, and a CD-ROM drive.

FIGURE 31.25.

When you highlight a computer in the Network Neighborhood, Explorer displays the resources that the computer is sharing with the network.

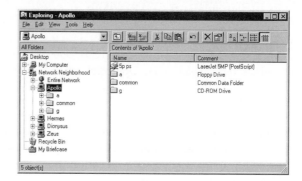

You can use any drives and folders shared by a network computer just as though they were part of your computer. If, however, the owner has assigned a password to a resource, you'll see a dialog box like the one shown in Figure 31.26 when you try to access the object. You won't be able to use the resource unless you know the correct password. Note, as well, that Windows 95 can create a *password list.* This list caches the passwords you enter for each resource, which saves you from typing the password the next time you access the resource. To cache a password, make sure that the Save this password in your password list check box is activated.

FIGURE 31.26.

If a resource is protected by a password, you'll see a dialog box like this one when you attempt to access the resource.

CAUTION: PASSWORD CACHE SECURITY LOOPHOLE

Windows 95's password caching is a major security loophole. Methods have been posted on the Internet and elsewhere that make it easy for any malicious person to crack the Windows 95 password encryption. If you're even remotely concerned about security on your network, don't use password caching. Note, however, that both the Windows 95 Service Pack and OSR2 include an update that fixes this security breach.

Universal Naming Convention

If you examine Figure 31.26 closely, you'll see that Windows 95 uses the name \\APOLLO\COMMON for the resource. This format, called the *universal naming convention* (UNC), uses the following syntax:

\\COMPUTER\SHARE

Here, COMPUTER is the name of the computer, and SHARE is the name given to the shared resource.

The UNC offers you several alternative methods of accessing shared network resources:

- In the Run dialog box, enter the UNC for a shared resource to open the resource in a folder window. You can also do this from the DOS prompt by preceding the resource name with the START command (for example, start \\apollo\common).

- In a 32-bit application's Open or Save As dialog box, you can use a UNC name in the File name text box.

- At the DOS prompt, you can use a UNC name as part of a DOS command. For example, to copy a file named DATA.DOC to \\APOLLO\COMMON, you use the following command:

  ```
  copy data.doc \\apollo\common
  ```

Mapping a Network Drive

UNC names are often convenient, but they can be a bit unwieldy because you'll usually have to return to the Network Neighborhood to check the correct computer and share names. To avoid this hassle, you can *map* a shared network drive or folder to your own computer. Mapping assigns a drive letter to the resource so that it appears to be just another disk drive on your machine.

Connecting a Resource

To map a shared drive or folder, first use any of the following methods:

- In Explorer, highlight the resource and select Tools | Map Network Drive, or click the Map Network Drive button on the toolbar.

- In the Network Neighborhood, highlight the resource and select File | Map Network Drive.

- In either Explorer or Network Neighborhood, right-click the resource and select Map Network Drive from the context menu.

Whichever method you choose, you'll see the Map Network Drive dialog box, shown in Figure 31.27. The Drive drop-down list displays the first available drive letter on your system, but you can pull down the list and select any available letter. If you want Windows 95 to map the resource each time you log on to the network, make sure that the Reconnect at logon check box is activated. When you click OK, Windows 95 adds the new drive letter to your system. (Note that you might have to enter a password at this point.)

FIGURE 31.27.

Use the Map Network Drive dialog box to assign a drive letter to a network resource.

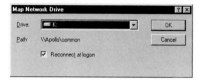

Disconnecting a Resource

If you no longer need to map a network resource, you should disconnect it. Here are the methods you can use:

- In Explorer or My Computer, right-click the mapped resource and select Disconnect from the context menu.
- In My Computer, highlight the mapped resource and select File | Disconnect.

- In Explorer, select Tools | Disconnect Network Drive, or click the Disconnect Net Drive toolbar button. In the Disconnect Network Drive dialog box, highlight the mapped resource and click OK.

CAUTION: DON'T DISCONNECT WITH OPEN FILES

If you're using files on the mapped drive, disconnecting causes you to lose the connection to these files, and you might lose your work. Fortunately, Windows 95 displays a warning if you try to disconnect a resource in which you're using files. In this case, you should cancel the disconnect, close the files, and try again.

Accessing Resources on NetWare Networks

Both the NetWare Client32 and the Microsoft NetWare Client are tightly integrated with My Computer, Explorer, and Network Neighborhood. However, Novell's Client32 adds some extensions, so in the following subsections and the rest of this chapter, the discussion is Client32-specific (unless otherwise noted). The overall concepts, however, apply to both Client32 and NetWare Client.

Browsing a NetWare Network

You can browse your NetWare network by using My Computer, Explorer, or Network Neighborhood. The easiest way is to use Network Neighborhood (bear in mind, as well, that Network Neighborhood will show NDS printers, whereas My Computer will not). Use the following steps to browse your Novell network:

1. Open Network Neighborhood to start browsing. If you're not already authenticated to the network, only the Entire Network icon is shown. If you're authenticated to the network, you'll see the Entire Network icon, a list of NDS trees, a list of NetWare servers, and an icon that represents your current name context, as shown in Figure 31.28.

Figure 31.28.

Network Neighborhood showing the Novell NetWare 4.1 network.

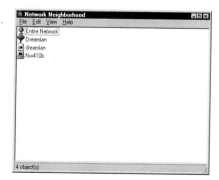

2. Double-click the Entire Network icon, and you're presented with two options: `NetWare Directory Services` and `NetWare Servers`.

3. Double-click `NetWare Directory Services`. You see a list of NDS tree names.

4. Double-click a tree name. If you're authenticated to that tree, you're presented with a list of containers starting at the `[Root]` level. As you walk the tree, you'll see file and print objects in a given context, as shown in Figure 31.29; you won't see other NDS objects.

Figure 31.29.

Print and file objects in an NDS context.

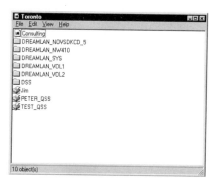

Another way to view and walk the tree is to right-click the tree and select Explore from the context menu to bring up the Explorer. Open the `NetWare Directory Services` branch to see a list of NDS tree names. Open the `NetWare Servers` branch to see a list of servers. From there, you can open a server to see a list of volume names, and you can open a volume name to see a list of directories and files, starting at the root, as shown in Figure 31.30. Note too that you can use the Windows Explorer to explore the network printers and logical drives (created by NetWare drive mappings) as though they were local devices.

FIGURE 31.30.

Exploring a NetWare volume.

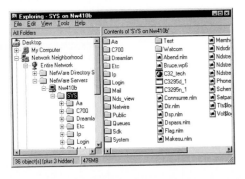

NOTE: GET THE SHELL UPDATE TO SEE NDS PRINTERS

If you want to see NDS printers in My Computer, Explorer, and the Add Printer Wizard, you need to get an update from Microsoft. The name of the patch is SHELLUPD.EXE, which has an updated SHELL32.DLL. (This patch is also available in the Windows 95 Service Pack.)

Connecting to a NetWare Server

We have already discussed how you can log in to a NetWare server using either Client32's GUI Login or the logon screen from NetWare Client. You can also log in to a NetWare server or a NetWare 4 NDS tree from either Explorer or Network Neighborhood, by using the following steps:

1. Use either Explorer or Network Neighborhood to bring up a list of NetWare servers or NDS trees.

2. If you're using Windows Explorer, right-click the server or tree name of interest to bring up an options list. If you left-click instead of right-clicking, it's assumed that you want to authenticate to the selected server or tree, and the login dialog box appears automatically.

   If you're using Network Neighborhood, highlight the server or tree name of interest first, and then right-click to bring up an options list.

3. Select either Authenticate or Login to NDS Tree. A login dialog box appears for you to enter a user name and password. The Authenticate option doesn't execute any login script commands, whereas the Login to NDS Tree selection does.

To disconnect from a server or NDS tree, select Options | Logout.

Mapping a Network Drive

You can map a network drive in two ways. One is the traditional NetWare way of using the MAP.EXE command from a DOS prompt. But because Windows 95 is GUI based, you can easily map a drive from within either Explorer or Network Neighborhood.

To try this, use either Explorer or Network Neighborhood to locate the directory you want to map. Right-click the directory and select Map Network Drive from the context menu to display the Map Network Drive dialog box, shown in Figure 31.31. Use the Drive drop-down list to select the drive letter you want to use. If you want the drive to be reconnected at logon, activate the Reconnect at logon check box. Click OK and the mapped drive shows up as a networked drive icon. (Note that all network drives connected using this method are automatically "map rooted.")

FIGURE 31.31.

*Use this dialog box
to map a NetWare
directory to a local
drive letter.*

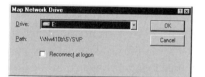

NetWare 3.x and Long Filenames

NetWare 4.x supports long filenames. However, NetWare 3.x only provides support for the long filenames used by Windows 95 through the use of name space. Specifically, you need to add the OS/2 name space to the volumes you want to support Windows 95 long filenames. You need to perform the following steps on your NetWare server console:

1. Enter the command LOAD OS2.NAM.

2. Add the name space to the volumes by entering the following command (in which *volumename* is the name of the volume you want to set up with long filename support):

   ADD NAME SPACE OS2 to *volumename*

3. Repeat step 2 for each volume you want to have long filename support.

4. Edit your STARTUP.NCF file and include the LOAD OS2.NAM command in the file.

You need to perform these tasks only once. The changes are made permanently to the volumes.

NOTE: REMOVING NAME SPACE SUPPORT

If for any reason you need to remove the name space support, use the VREPAIR.NLM that is shipped with NetWare to delete the name space.

Changing Your Password

If you ever want to change your password, you can't do it from the logon dialog box (which makes sense). Instead, you need to do it from within Windows 95. First, open the Control Panel's Passwords icon to display the Passwords Properties dialog box. The Change Passwords tab gives you two options:

Change Windows Password: Click this button to change your Windows 95 logon password. You'll also get a chance to change any of your networking passwords at the same time. This way you can keep all your passwords the same and maintain Windows 95's unified logon dialog box. In the dialog box that appears (see Figure 31.32), activate the check box beside each password you want to change, and then click OK.

FIGURE 31.32.

Use this dialog box to select the passwords you want to change in addition to your Windows 95 password.

Change Other Passwords: Click this button to change any of your other passwords (such as the password you use to log on to a Microsoft or NetWare network). In the list of passwords that appears, highlight the password you want to modify, and then click the Change button.

Whichever button you click, you'll eventually see the Change Windows Password dialog box, shown in Figure 31.33. Enter your existing password in the Old password text box, enter the new password you want to use in the New password text box, and then enter the new password again in the Confirm new password text box. (If you're changing multiple passwords, click the Details>> button to see a list.) When you're done, click OK.

FIGURE 31.33.

Use the Change Windows Password dialog box to enter your new password (twice).

31

WINDOWS 95
NETWORKING

Network Printing

As I mentioned in the preceding chapter, one of the benefits of setting up a network is that you can share peripherals among several machines. Printers are a good example of this. Any printer that's attached to a network computer can be shared with the network. This means that any user on the network can use that printer as though it were attached to her own machine. Windows 95 offers you several methods of accessing network printers; I describe them in the next three sections.

In each case, note that thanks to Windows 95's *Point and Print* feature, you won't need to insert any of your Windows 95 source disks. Instead, Point and Print grabs the printer driver and any other files it needs from the network computer where the printer is installed locally. As well, Point and Print borrows the remote printer's current settings (such as paper size and page orientation) and uses them to set up the local printer. Any changes you make, however, are retained on the local computer.

After you've installed a network printer, it appears in the Printers folder along with your other printers (if any). The only difference is that a cable appears underneath the printer icon to identify this as a network printer. As with folders, printers can also be password protected, so you might need to enter a password the first time you use the printer.

Installing a Shared Printer Via the Add Printer Wizard

In Chapter 19, "Prescriptions for Perfect Printing," I showed you how to use the Add Printer Wizard to install a printer in Windows 95. You can use the same method to install a network printer. Here are the steps to follow:

1. Select Start | Settings | Printers to open the Printers folder. (You can also open the Printers folder by double-clicking the Printers icon in the Control Panel.)
2. Open the Add Printer icon to start the Add Printer Wizard.
3. Click Next >.
4. Select the Network printer option and click Next >. The Wizard prompts you to enter a network path, as shown in Figure 31.34.

FIGURE 31.34.

Use the Add Printer Wizard dialog box to enter the UNC path for the network printer you want to install.

5. Use the `Network path or queue name` text box to enter the appropriate UNC path for the network printer you want to install. If you're not sure, use the Browse button to choose the printer from a dialog box, as shown in Figure 31.35.

FIGURE 31.35.

If you're not sure of the printer's correct UNC path, click Browse to choose the printer from this dialog box.

6. Continue with the installation in the usual manner.

Using Point and Print with a NetWare Server

Client32 from Novell supports "deviceless" printing. In other words, it's no longer necessary to use print captures and to associate a printer port with a specific printer, as was traditionally done on the DOS/Windows 3.x platform. Instead, when you set up a printer, Windows 95 writes all the printer configuration information to the Registry. To use the printer, simply click the printer's icon.

Use the following steps to configure your NetWare server to store Point and Print information:

1. Log in to the NetWare server as Supervisor or Supervisor Equivalent.

2. Right-click a server print queue, and click Properties.

3. In the properties sheet, select the Setup Point and Print tab, shown in Figure 31.36. (If you're not logged in with Supervisor rights, you won't see this tab.)

FIGURE 31.36.

*The Setup Point and
Print tab of a NetWare
print queue.*

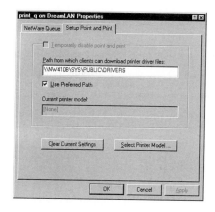

4. Ensure that the path listed under `Path from which clients can download printer driver files` is a valid UNC path. If it isn't correct, deactivate the `Use Preferred Path` check box, and enter the correct path.

5. Click the Select Printer Model button.

6. Select the `Manufacturer` and `Model` from the standard print setup selection boxes as appropriate for your printer.

7. Click OK to copy the printer driver files.

8. Make sure that the users will have at least Read and File Scan rights to the directory in which the printer driver files were copied.

To access this print queue, you now need to add the queue to the `Printers` folder by using the Add Printer Wizard. Follow these steps:

1. Use Network Neighborhood or Explorer to locate the print queue of interest.

2. Drag the print queue over to the `Printers` folder and drop it.

3. Follow the Add Printer Wizard as it prompts you to set up printing. When you're done, the `Printers` folder is updated to show the new printer.

Windows 95 automatically copies the printer driver files (.DRV, .DLL, .HLP, and so on) from the server to the Windows 95 `SYSTEM` directory.

Other Point and Print Methods

The Add Printer Wizard is only one of the methods available for installing a printer. The Point and Print feature also lets you install a remote printer by using the following techniques:

■ In Explorer or the Network Neighborhood, either highlight a shared printer and select File | Install, or right-click the printer and select Install from the context menu.

■ In Explorer or the Network Neighborhood, drag a shared printer and drop it inside the `Printers` folder.

■ Drag a document and drop it on the remote printer's icon in the Network Neighborhood. When Windows 95 asks whether you want to set up the printer, click Yes. After the printer is installed, the document you dropped will print.

■ In the Run dialog box, enter the UNC path to the shared printer, and click OK. When Windows 95 asks whether you want to set up the printer, click Yes.

In each case, a scaled-down version of the Add Printer Wizard appears. Follow the prompts to install the printer.

Capturing a Printer Port

In the same way that you can map a shared network drive or folder and have it appear as though it were a physical drive on your system, so too can you map a shared network printer and have it appear as though it were a physical printer port on your system. This is called *capturing* a printer port. To try this, use either of the following methods:

■ Open the properties sheet for any installed printer, display the Details tab, and click the Capture Printer Port button.

■ In Explorer or the Network Neighborhood, either highlight a shared printer and select File | Capture Printer Port, or right-click the printer and select Capture Printer Port from the context menu.

Then, in the Capture Printer Port dialog box, shown in Figure 31.37, use the Device list to select a logical printer port (Windows 95 automatically selects the next available port). If you're using the Details tab, you'll need to use the Path combo box to enter the network path to the shared printer. Click OK to map the printer.

FIGURE 31.37.

Use the Capture Printer Port dialog box to map a shared network printer to a logical printer port on your system.

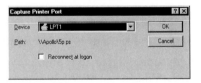

When you no longer want to capture a network printer as a logical port on your system, follow these steps:

1. Open the properties sheet for any installed printer.

2. Display the Details tab.

3. Click the End Capture button.

4. In the End Capture dialog box that appears, highlight the port you want to release.

5. Click OK.

Windows 95 as a Server: Sharing Your Resources

In Chapter 30, I told you that in a peer-to-peer network each computer can act as both a client and a server. So far you've seen how to use a Windows 95 machine as a client, so now let's turn our attention to setting up your system as a peer server. In Windows 95, that means enabling the file and print sharing service and then sharing individual drives, folders, and printers with the network.

File and Print Sharing for Microsoft Networks

If you're using the Client for Microsoft Networks, Windows 95 comes with a 32-bit server (VSERVER.VXD) you can use to share resources with other Windows 95 machines, as well as machines running Windows NT, Windows for Workgroups, LAN Manager, and any other networks that use the SMB (Server Message Block) file-sharing protocol.

Setting Up File and Print Sharing

To enable file and print sharing on your system, first display the Network properties sheet (by opening the Network icon in the Control Panel, or by right-clicking the Network Neighborhood icon and clicking Properties). Use one of the following methods to enable file and print sharing:

- ▪ If Client for Microsoft Networks is your primary logon, click the File and Print Sharing button.

- ▪ If Client for Microsoft Networks isn't your primary logon, click Add, highlight Service, and click Add again. In the Select Network Service dialog box, highlight Microsoft in the Manufacturers list, highlight File and printer sharing for Microsoft Networks, and click OK. When you're back in the Network properties sheet, click the File and Print Sharing button.

In the File and Print Sharing dialog box that appears, shown in Figure 31.38, you have two options:

> **I want to be able to give others access to my files:** Activate this check box to allow sharing of drives and folders.

> **I want to be able to allow others to print to my printer(s):** Activate this check box to allow print sharing.

FIGURE 31.38.

Use this dialog box to turn your Windows 95 client into a peer server.

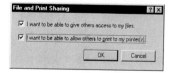

Click OK to return to the properties sheet, and then click OK to put the new setting into effect.

Sharing Drives and Folders

With file sharing activated, you can share any file-related devices that are attached to your computer: hard drives, CD-ROM drives, floppy drives, and folders. To set up any of these devices as a shared resource, use either of the following techniques:

- Right-click the device, and select Sharing from the context menu.
- Open the properties sheet for the device, and display the Sharing tab.

The Sharing tab, shown in Figure 31.39, contains the following options:

Shared As: Activate this option to share the selected device.

Share Name: Use this text box to enter a name for the shared resource. This text appears in the Name column when others browse your computer with Explorer, and it's also the text used as part of the shared resource's UNC path. The name can be up to 12 characters long. You can't use spaces in the name, but all alphanumeric characters are OK, as are the following symbols:

~ ! @ # $ % ^ & ( ) _ - { } ' .

Comment: Use this text box to enter a brief description of the shared resource. This text appears in the Comment column when others browse your computer with Explorer. The comment can be up to 48 characters in length.

Access Type: The options in this group determine the level of access granted to users who access the resource remotely.

Read-Only: This option only lets users view the contents of the resource; they can't modify the resource in any way. In a shared folder, for example, users can view the contained files, but they can't delete, edit, or rename existing files, and they can't add new files or subfolders. (They can, however, open a file in the shared folder and then save it to a local folder.)

Full: This option gives users complete access to all the contents within the shared resource.

Depends on Password: This option determines the level of access applied to a user based on the password he enters when attempting to work with the resource.

Passwords: Use the text boxes in this group to set up one or more passwords for the shared resource. The Read-Only Password text box sets the password for read-only access; the Full Access Password text box sets the password for users to get full access.

FIGURE 31.39.

Use the Sharing tab to set up a shared resource.

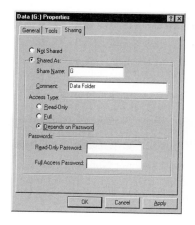

Click OK to put the settings into effect. If you entered any passwords, you're asked to confirm them. As you can see in Figure 31.40, Windows 95 appends a hand icon underneath the resource's existing icon to denote that the resource is shared.

FIGURE 31.40.

Windows 95 adds a hand icon to denote a shared resource.

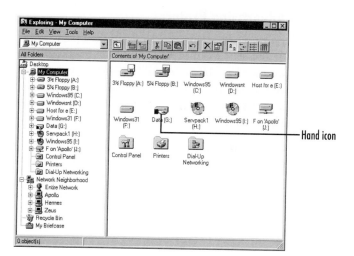

Sharing a Local Printer

To share a local printer, you use an almost identical process. First, you need to display the Sharing tab for a printer by using either of the following methods:

■ In the Printers folder, either highlight the printer and select File | Sharing, or right-click the printer and select Sharing from the context menu.

■ Open the properties sheet for the printer, and display the Sharing tab.

As before, you activate the Shared As option and then fill in the Share Name, Comment, and Password text boxes.

File and Print Sharing for NetWare Networks

Windows 95 supports two types of file and print sharing services. One type, as discussed earlier, is for Microsoft and IBM type networks. This uses the SMB protocol. The other type is for NetWare networks. It uses Novell's NCP (NetWare Core Protocol) and is supported using the NWSERVER.VXD driver.

NOTE: ONLY MICROSOFT'S CLIENT SUPPORTS SHARING

The file and printer sharing for NetWare service is available only with Microsoft's Client for NetWare Networks. Therefore, if you're using Novell's Client32, you cannot enable File and Printer Sharing for NetWare Networks service on Windows 95 workstations.

Before I show you how to enable the File and Printer sharing for NetWare Networks service, you should understand the possible implications of doing so. You need to first understand what NetWare Service Advertising Protocol (SAP) is.

Service Advertising Protocol

Every NetWare service, whether it's a server, a print server, or even your RCONSOLE access (REMOTE.NLM and RSPX.NLM), advertises itself on the network every 60 seconds. This is done by the broadcasting of a *SAP packet*. All NetWare servers and routers listen to these SAP broadcasts and accumulate them in their internal SAP tables. Because broadcast traffic is generally restricted to the segment it's broadcast on, the routers rebroadcast the packets to the other subnets they route between so that the whole network is aware of all the services available.

As a result, every service causes SAP packets to be sent across the *entire* IPX network. Also, each service must be remembered by every router and server on the network. This works well for a small number of services (up to perhaps 1,000), but as the number of services increases, the bandwidth utilization due to SAP packets and the resource requirements on the routers and servers get very large.

NetWare Services Client

On a large network on which there might be hundreds or even thousands of Windows 95 workstations, it isn't practical to use SAP advertising as the method of advertising services. Instead, Microsoft created a component called NetWare Services Client (NSCL) that's used to implement browsing for large NetWare networks.

Each Windows 95 workstation is assigned to a workgroup (set in the Identification tab in the Network properties sheet). As I've said, a workgroup is a collection of related computers, and they're grouped logically, not necessarily geographically. The important thing is that they're grouped.

When an NWSERVER starts up, it registers its name and workgroup with NSCL. NSCL examines the workgroup name and locates the "master" of the workgroup. If it can't locate a master, it elects itself to be the master. The master, known as the Browse Master, advertises itself by using SAP. Any subsequent servers in the workgroup register with the master.

This scheme reduces the number of SAP packets sent out by the Windows 95 workstations. Rather than one SAP packet per Windows 95 workstation, you now have one SAP packet *per workgroup.*

Enabling File and Print Sharing for NetWare

The procedure to enable file and print sharing for NetWare is the same as that described earlier for Microsoft networks:

- Make sure that the Microsoft Client for NetWare Networks is your primary logon, and click the File and Print Sharing button.

- If the File and Printer Sharing for NetWare service isn't already installed, it will be installed automatically.

In the File and Print Sharing dialog box that appears, you have two options:

> **I want to be able to give others access to my files:** Activate this check box to allow sharing of drives and folders.

> **I want to be able to allow others to print to my printer(s):** Activate this check box to allow print sharing.

Click OK to return to the properties sheet, and then click OK to put the new settings into effect.

Note that you need to configure your Access Control for user-level access control and specify a NetWare server name. Access Control is discussed in Chapter 32, "Network Administration and Security," in the section "Access Control: Share-Level Versus User-Level."

Sharing Files, Folders, and Printers

In order for other NetWare clients to be able to access your Windows 95 workstation's resources, you need to either turn on SAP or correctly configure the NSCL setup on the Windows 95 machine. To configure for SAP operation, use the following steps:

1. From the Network properties sheet, highlight File and Printer Sharing for NetWare Networks and click the Properties button.

2. In the dialog box that appears, highlight SAP Advertising in the Property list and select Enabled from the Value drop-down list.

3. Highlight Workgroup Advertising in the Property list and select Disabled from the Value drop-down list.

4. Click OK to return to the Network dialog box.

5. Click OK again to save the settings.

To use the NSCL setup, follow the preceding steps, but make sure that SAP Advertising is disabled. Then configure one Windows 95 workstation to be master, and the rest to use the `Enabled: may be master` option.

TIP: VERIFYING ADVERTISING

To verify that your Windows 95 workstation is advertising, head for the MS-DOS prompt, and enter either the `SLIST` or the `NLIST SERVER /B /A` command. If everything is working, you should see your computer name listed as a NetWare server. (Or you should see it listed in the Network Neighborhood.)

Accessing Files, Folders, and Printers

When the Windows 95 workstation is set up for file sharing using the SAP mode, a folder called NWSYSVOL is created in your main Windows folder and automatically shared. This folder has a subfolder named LOGIN that contains a special version of LOGIN.EXE from Microsoft. You can use this to log in to the preferred server of the Windows 95 workstation.

To access files and printers on the Windows 95 workstation, simply MAP or CAPTURE to it from your workstation as though it were a real NetWare server. The only difference is that any files you can have access to need to be placed in NWSYSVOL and any subfolders below it.

The Windows 95 workstation (actually, NWSERVER) uses the bindery of the preferred server (a real NetWare server) to look up user names and passwords for authentication purposes. Therefore, when you're asked for a user name and password, be aware of which NetWare server is the default server. If it's a NetWare 3.1x server, the bindery information is server-centric. On the other hand, if the preferred server is a NetWare 4 server, the NetWare 4 server must have Bindery Services enabled, and the user name you specify must be located in the bindery contexts of the server—NWSERVER isn't NDS-aware.

Summary

After the relentless (but, I hope, useful) theory in the preceding chapter, this chapter took a decidedly more practical approach to Windows 95 networking. In your tour around Windows 95's Network Neighborhood, you learned how to install networking, access network file and print resources, and share your resources with the network.

That's a lot of material, but we're not done yet; there's a lot more networking know-how to come. Here's what to expect:

■ To learn about administering and securing your network, see Chapter 32, "Network Administration and Security."

■ If you're having trouble with Windows 95 networking, you might find the solution in Chapter 33, "Network Troubleshooting."

■ If you have just a couple of computers, you can bypass the expense of network adapter cards and cables by using Windows 95's Direct Cable Connection. You still must set up a "network," however, and I explain how it's done in Chapter 34, "From Laptop to Desktop and Back: Direct Cable Connection."

■ To learn how to access a network via modem, check out Chapter 35, "Remote Computing with Dial-Up Networking."

■ TCP/IP is fast becoming the protocol of choice for both large and small networks. I demonstrate how to work with TCP/IP in Chapter 36, "Implementing TCP/IP for Internet and Network Connections."

■ The Internet, of course, is *the* network. I show you how Windows 95 connects to, and works with, Internet resources in Chapter 37, "Windows 95 and the Internet." For Web-based Internet sites, Internet Explorer offers easy access. I give you a complete primer in Chapter 38, "Exploring the Web with Internet Explorer."

31

WINDOWS 95 NETWORKING

Network Administration and Security

IN THIS CHAPTER

> *I always get back to the question, is it really necessary that men should consume so much of their bodily and mental energies in the machinery of civilized life?*
>
> —*William Allingham*

Whenever you string two or more computers together to form a network, security becomes an issue. On the user level, you want to make sure that others can access only those parts of your system you designate as fit for public consumption. No one, whether a colleague or an administrator, should be able to poke around in areas of your system that you deem private. On the network level, administrators need to make sure that servers are set up with appropriate access limitations and that access to the administrator account (usually the most powerful account on the system) is suitably restricted. The first half of this chapter runs through a few solutions for enhancing security for users and for the network as a whole.

And if you're the administrator of your network fiefdom, setting up the machines on the network is only half the battle. You'll still need to spend untold amounts of time tweaking these machines, adjusting their configurations, creating and managing users and passwords, and so on. To make these chores easier, Windows 95 boasts various tools that offer you *remote administration:* the capability to work with a network computer from the comfort of your own system. The second half of this chapter shows you how to implement these tools on your network.

Hiding Shared Resources

Hiding your valuables is a time-honored method of securing them from prying eyes and would-be thieves. When you share a resource on your network, however, you're displaying that resource for all to see. Sure, you can set up password protection for the resource, but others will still be able to see that the resource is shared.

To prevent this situation, it's possible to share a resource *and* hide it at the same time. It's also extremely easy to do. When you set up the shared resource, just add a dollar sign ($) to the end of the share name. For example, if you're setting up drive C for sharing, you could use C$ as the share name. This prevents the resource from appearing in either Explorer's or Network Neighborhood's browse lists.

In Figure 32.1, for example, you can see that the current computer (named Hermes) is sharing two disk drives: drive C and drive G. Highlighting Hermes in the Network Neighborhood, however, shows only drive G in the browse list. That's because drive C is shared with the name C$. (Of course, since snoops will probably know about the $ trick, you'll probably want to set up your hidden shares with less obvious names.)

FIGURE 32.1.

Hidden shared resources (such as drive C shown here) don't appear in the browse list.

The two drives are shared...

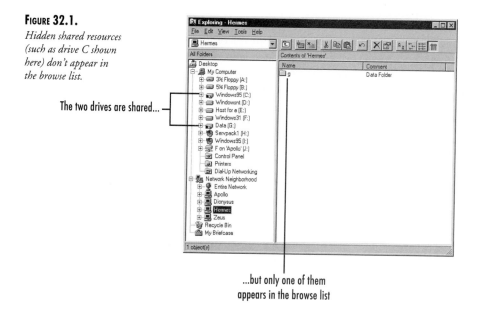

...but only one of them appears in the browse list

How do you connect to a hidden share? Well, you need to know the name of the shared resource, of course. After you know that, you can use any of the following techniques:

- In the Run dialog box, type the UNC path for the hidden resource. For example, to display the hidden C$ share on Hermes, you would enter this:

```
\\hermes\c$
```

- In Explorer, make sure that a shared resource isn't highlighted, and then either select File | Map Network Drive or click the Map Network Drive toolbar button. In the Map Network Drive dialog box, enter the UNC path for the hidden share in the Path text box.

- For a hidden shared printer, run the Add Hardware Wizard icon from Control Panel, and when you're prompted, enter the UNC path to the hidden printer.

Access Control: Share-Level Versus User-Level

You saw earlier that you can assign passwords to the resources you share. This is called *share-level* security because it sets up protection on a resource-by-resource basis, and any user with the correct password can access the share.

If, however, you have a Windows NT or NetWare server on your network, you can implement a more robust security system known as *user-level* or *pass-through* security. In this model, access to shared resources is controlled on a user-to-user basis. In other words, when you share a resource, you also specify the users (or groups of users) who are allowed access to the resource. This information is stored on a security server (an NT or NetWare machine). When someone tries to access one of your shared resources, Windows 95 asks the security server to validate the request. The server checks the person's user name and password and then checks to see whether the user is on your list of those allowed access. If she is, the server grants the request; otherwise, the user isn't allowed to access the resource.

Enabling User-Level Access Control for NT

If you're on an NT network and using the Client for Microsoft Networks, resources are secured using share-level access control by default. To switch to user-level access control, open the Network properties sheet and select the Access Control tab, shown in Figure 32.2. Activate the User-level access control option. Windows 95 should enter the name of your NT domain in the Obtain list of users and groups from text box. Windows 95 uses the server designated as the primary domain controller for your domain to get the user list. (If you like, you can enter the name of the backup domain controller instead.)

FIGURE 32.2.

Use the Access Control tab to enable user-level security on an NT network.

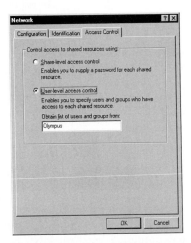

When you click OK, Windows 95 displays a message telling you that your existing shares will be removed. Click Yes to continue. When Windows 95 asks you to restart your system, click Yes.

Enabling User-Level Access Control for NetWare

You enable user-level access control for NetWare in exactly the same way as you would for NT as described in the preceding section. Open the Network properties sheet and select the Access Control tab. Activate the `User-level access control` option. Windows 95 should enter the name of your NetWare server in the `Obtain list of users and groups from` text box. Windows 95 uses the server's bindery to get the user list.

NOTE: ENABLE BINDERY SERVICES ON NETWARE 4 SERVERS

If you provided a NetWare 4 server's name in the `Obtain list of users and groups from` text box, make sure that the server has Bindery Services enabled. Any user names and group names you reference must exist in the bindery contexts of this server.

Sharing a Resource with User-Level Access

Now that your machine is set up to provide user-level access control, you'll need to reshare all of your previously shared resources. Let's see how user-level security affects the resource sharing procedure.

As before, open the properties sheet for the resource, and then select the Sharing tab. As you can see in Figure 32.3, the Sharing tab for user-level security is a bit different. You still enter the `Share Name` and a `Comment`, but the `Access Type` and `Passwords` groups are gone. In their place is a list box you'll use to add the groups and users to whom you want to give access to the resource.

FIGURE 32.3.

The Sharing tab sports a slightly different layout under user-level security.

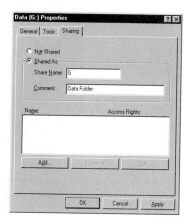

To specify which users and groups are allowed access to the resource, click the Add button to display the Add Users dialog box, shown in Figure 32.4. The Name list displays all the users and groups that are recognized as valid by the security server. This way, you're assured that the users and groups you designate for access are all legitimate and that no unauthorized user can work with the share.

FIGURE 32.4.

Use the Add Users dialog box to specify which users and groups should be allowed access to the resource.

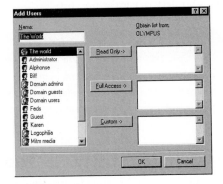

To set up the access, highlight a user or group in the Name list, and then click Read Only, Full Access, or Custom. (If you're setting up access for a printer, you get only the Full Access button.) When you're done, click OK. If you added any users or groups to the Custom list, you'll see the Change Access Rights dialog box, shown in Figure 32.5. Use this dialog box to set up specific access rights for the users. When you're done, click OK.

FIGURE 32.5.

Use this dialog box to add specific access rights for a user.

NOTE: CUSTOM ACCESS RIGHTS

To set specific access for rights for any user or group, highlight the appropriate name in the Sharing tab, click Edit, and activate the Custom Access Rights option in the Change Access Rights dialog box.

Tips for Choosing a Password

Whether you use share-level or user-level security, you'll be using some passwords to secure your system from intruders. Because the password is your first line of defense against snoops and other crackers (a *cracker* is someone who likes to break into computer systems), you should think carefully about the passwords you choose. Specifically, you need to choose a password that provides maximum protection without sacrificing convenience.

Keeping in mind that the whole point of a password is to select one that nobody can guess, here are some guidelines you can follow when choosing a password:

Don't be too obvious. Because forgetting a password is inconvenient, many people use meaningful words or numbers so that their password will be easier to remember. This means that they often use extremely obvious things such as their name, the name of a family member or colleague, their birth date or Social Security number, or even their system user name! Being this obvious is just asking for trouble.

Don't use single words. Many crackers break into accounts by using "dictionary programs" that just try every word in the dictionary. So, yes, *xiphoid* is an obscure word that no person would ever guess, but a good dictionary program will figure it out in seconds flat. Using two or more words in your password (or *pass phrase,* as multiword passwords are called) is still easy to remember, and would take much longer to crack by a brute force program.

Put lousy spelling to good use. If, like me, you know that your spelling leaves much to be desired, your password might be the one place where this shortcoming comes in handy. Misspelling a word or words in your password really throws those crackers a curve.

Use passwords that are at least eight characters long. Shorter passwords are susceptible to programs that just try every letter combination. You can combine the 26 letters of the alphabet into about 12 million different five-letter word combinations, which is no big deal for a fast program. If you bump things up to eight-letter passwords, however, the total number of combos rises to 200 *billion,* which would take even the fastest computer quite a while. If you use 12-letter passwords, as many experts recommend, the number of combinations goes beyond mind-boggling: 90 *quadrillion,* or 90,000 trillion!

Mix uppercase and lowercase letters. Almost all password systems are case-sensitive, which means that if your password is, say, YUMMY ZIMA, trying yummy zima won't work. So you can really throw snoops for a loop by mixing the case. Something like yuMmY zIMa would be almost impossible to figure out.

Add numbers to your password. You can throw a few more permutations and combinations into the mix by adding a few numbers to your password. In fact, some systems insist on passwords that include at least a couple of numbers.

Throw in a few punctuation marks and symbols. For extra variety, toss in one or more punctuation marks or special symbols, such as % or #.

Try using acronyms. One of the best ways to get a password that appears random but is easy to remember is to create an acronym out of a favorite quotation, saying, or book title. For example, if you've just read *The Seven Habits of Highly Effective People*, you could use the password *T7HoHEP*.

Don't write down your password. After going to all this trouble to create an indestructible password, don't blow it by writing it on a sticky note and then attaching it to your keyboard or monitor! Even writing it on a piece of paper and then throwing the paper away is dangerous. Determined crackers have been known to go through a company's trash looking for passwords (this is known in the trade as *Dumpster diving*).

Don't tell your password to anyone. If you've thought of a particularly clever password, don't suddenly become unclever and tell someone. Your password should be stored in your head alongside all those "wasted youth" things you don't want anyone to know about.

Change your password regularly. If you change your password often (say, once a month or so), even if some skulker does get access to your account, at least he'll have it for only a relatively short period.

OSR2 **Get the Enhanced Password Cache Security Update from Microsoft.** Windows 95 stores network and local logon passwords in a .PWL (password list) file that resides in your main Windows 95 folder. (The filename is *USER*.PWL, where *USER* is your user name.) This file is encrypted, but Microsoft only used 32-bit encryption, which can be (and has been) easily cracked. For a more robust cache, either upgrade to OSR2 or download the Enhanced Password Cache Security Update, which uses 128-bit encryption. Here's the URL:

```
http://www.microsoft.com/windows/software/passwd.htm
```

NetWare Security Issues

The security issues and recommendations for NetWare are pretty much the same as for any other operating systems. In short, NetWare uses four levels of security to control who can have access to the network, which resources users can access, and how they can utilize these resources. These are the four levels:

- Login/password security
- NDS security in NetWare 4
- File system security
- File server console security

Login/password security, the most common form of network security found in all networking operating systems, controls the initial access to the network. In a NetWare 4 environment, after initial access is obtained, NDS security controls which objects (such as users and groups) in the directory tree a logged-in user can see and access. File system security controls which files and directories users can access on network volumes. File system security also controls how a file and directory are to be accessed. For example, if a user doesn't have the Create right in a directory, no files or subfolders can be created. And, lastly, file server console security controls who can access the file server console.

A detailed discussion of these topics is beyond the scope of this book. I refer you to other Sams publications, such as *NetWare 4.1 Survival Guide,* for more information.

Setting Up Remote Administration

Windows 95's remote administration tools are powerful features that can make a harried network administrator's life immeasurably easier. Here's a summary of just a few of the benefits you'll realize from using remote administration:

- The capability to manage resource sharing on remote machines. You can also monitor remote resources to see which users are connected to a particular resource.
- The capability to customize desktop and system settings remotely. You can also set up a common configuration and apply that configuration to any remote machine.
- The capability to work directly with the Registry on any remote computer.
- The capability to set up enhanced security options (such as disabling password caching).
- The capability to monitor the performance of a remote system.

To unleash all of these benefits, however, you need to make sure that your network is set up properly. Specifically, you need to take the following actions:

1. Make sure that each computer on the network is set up for user-level access control.

2. Make sure that remote administration is enabled for each computer. To do this, open the Control Panel's Passwords icon, select the Remote Administration tab, shown in Figure 32.6, and activate the Enable Remote Administration of this server check box (if it isn't activated already). Use the Add button to add the names of the users or groups who can administer each machine.

3. If you want to configure settings for individual users on a machine, make sure that user profiles are enabled for the computer (see Chapter 7, "Customizing Windows 95"). Also, you need to make the following arrangements:

   - For a Microsoft network, make sure that Client for Microsoft Networking is the primary network logon. On a Windows NT server, set up a shared folder for each user as her home directory. Each user's profile (USER.DAT) will be stored in her home directory when she logs off.

   - For a NetWare network, make sure that Client for NetWare Networks is the primary network logon. On a NetWare server, set up a directory for each user in the MAIL directory. Each user's profile (USER.DAT) will be stored in this directory when she logs off.

FIGURE 32.6.

*Use the Remote
Administration tab to
enable remote
administration for each
computer.*

4. Install the Remote Registry network service on every computer. To do this, open the Network properties sheet, click Add, highlight `Service`, and click Add again. In the Select Network Service dialog box, click Have Disk, and then enter the following folder on the Windows 95 CD-ROM (where *drive* is the letter of your CD-ROM drive):

   drive`:\ADMIN\NETTOOLS\REMOTREG`

   Click OK until Windows 95 asks you to restart the computer, and then click Yes.

5. Make sure that all the machines on your network have at least one network protocol in common. It doesn't much matter whether the protocol is NetBEUI, TCP/IP, or IPX/SPX, just as long as at least one of them is installed on every machine.

NOTE: NO SERVER? NO PROBLEM

If you don't have a Windows NT or NetWare server (that is, you're running a peer-to-peer network), you can still use remote user profiles. Here are the steps you need to follow:

1. On one of the peers, create a home directory that can be accessed by all users (called, say, `HOMEDIR`).

2. Create a subdirectory for each user. For a user named Biff, for example, you would create a subdirectory named `\HOMEDIR\BIFF`.

3. In the `HOMEDIR` directory, create a text file named `PROFILES.INI` with a `[Profiles]` group and a line for each user that has the following form:

   UserName`=\\`*server*`\homedir\`*UserDir*

   Here, *UserName* is the name of the user, *server* is the name of the peer computer that contains `HOMEDIR`, and *UserDir* is the user's directory. Here's an example:

   ```
   [Profiles]
   Biff=\\Hermes\homedir\Biff
   Alphonse=\\Hermes\homedir\Alphonse
   Karen=\Hermes\homedir\Karen
   ```

> 4. For each computer, start the Registry Editor and highlight the following key:
>
>   `HKEY_LOCAL_MACHINE\Network\Logon`
>
> 5. Select Edit | New | String Value, enter `SharedProfileList`, and click OK.
>
> 6. Open the `SharedProfileList` setting, enter the UNC path and filename for the `PROFILES.INI` text file (for example, `\\Hermes\homedir\profile.ini`), and click OK.
>
> 7. Exit the Registry Editor.

Remote Administration Via the System Policy Editor

If you're an administrator setting up Windows 95 for another user, you can take advantage of any of the techniques from Chapter 7 to create a custom Windows 95 setup for that user. You might want to set things up according to your company's Windows 95 deployment guidelines, or you might want to make things easier for novice users, or perhaps you just want to establish a specific corporate look for all your users' desktops.

The problem, though, is that after the user takes over the machine, that user is free to do his own customizing, which might defeat the purpose of your original setup. Also, novice users with full access to the Windows 95 might take a few wrong turns and end up in places that could cause problems (or at least confusion).

The solution to these sorts of dilemmas is the System Policy Editor. Available on the Windows 95 CD-ROM, the System Policy Editor lets you control many aspects of the Windows 95 system, as well as restrict access to various Windows 95 components. With the System Policy Editor, you can take the following actions:

- Restrict access to any of the Control Panel icons
- Specify a desktop wallpaper and scheme
- Restrict access to specific folders (such as the `Programs` folder), programs (such as the Registry Editor), and objects (such as the Network Neighborhood)
- Control password-related settings (such as requiring alphanumeric passwords)

If the system is set up with different user profiles, you can use the System Policy Editor to establish specific restrictions for each user.

NOTE: DOWNLOADING THE SYSTEM POLICY EDITOR

No Windows 95 CD-ROM? Remember that you can get any of the CD-ROM extras from Microsoft's various online resources (see Chapter 2, "Running the Windows 95 Setup"). For the System Policy Editor, download the file `POLICY.EXE`.

Installing the System Policy Editor

Here are the steps to follow to install the System Policy Editor from the Windows 95 CD-ROM:

1. Insert the Windows 95 CD-ROM.

2. Select Start | Settings | Control Panel, and open the Add/Remove Programs icon in the `Control Panel` folder.

3. Select the Windows Setup tab.

4. Click the Have Disk button.

5. In the Install From Disk dialog box, either type the following path (where *drive* is the letter of your CD-ROM drive) or use the Browse button to select it:

    `drive:\ADMIN\APPTOOLS\POLEDIT\`

6. In the Have Disk dialog box, shown in Figure 32.7, activate the `System Policy Editor` check box.

FIGURE 32.7.

The Have Disk dialog box lists the System Policy Editor components.

7. Click Install. Windows 95 installs the System Policy Editor and returns you to the Add/Remove Programs Properties dialog box.

8. Click OK.

Setting Up Clients for Group Policies

If your network has a Windows NT or NetWare server, you can organize users into groups. This is handy for administering system policies because instead of setting policy entries for individual users, you can set them for an entire group of users at one fell swoop.

To enable group policies, you must install System Policy Editor's Group Policies component on each client computer. To do this, follow the installation steps outlined in the preceding section. When you get to the Have Disk dialog box, however, be sure to activate the `Group policies` check box. (Don't activate the `System Policy Editor` check box.)

Working with the System Policy Editor

After you've installed the System Policy Editor, you can start it by selecting Start | Programs | Accessories | System Tools | System Policy Editor. Three basic methods are available for using the System Policy Editor:

- Work with the local computer's Registry directly.
- Work with a remote computer's Registry directly.
- Create a network-wide policy file that contains settings for all users and computers on the network.

Working with a Local Registry

The most straightforward way to work with the System Policy Editor is to use it to customize the machine on which it is installed. In this sense, you're using the System Policy Editor as a front-end to the local computer's Registry. This isn't necessarily the best approach, however, because it means you must install the System Policy Editor on whichever machine you want to work with. This might be fine for a few machines, but it's a real time waster if you have to administer many different computers. It's much easier to use either of the next two methods (working with a remote Registry or creating a network-wide policy file).

To work with a local Registry, first log on as the user for whom you want to customize Windows 95. (I'm assuming here that the machine is set up for user profiles. If it's not, you don't have to worry about this step.) Then start the System Policy Editor, and select File | Open Registry. As you can see in Figure 32.8, the System Policy Editor displays Local Registry in the title bar, and it sprouts two icons:

Local User: This icon represents the current user. It's a front-end for settings that correspond to the HKEY_CURRENT_USER Registry key. See "Working with User Settings" later in this chapter for details.

Local Computer: This icon represents the local machine. It's a front-end for settings that correspond to the HKEY_LOCAL_MACHINE Registry key. See "Working with Computer Settings" later in this chapter for details.

FIGURE 32.8.

The System Policy Editor with a local Registry open.

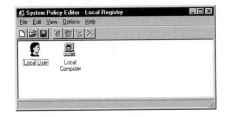

Working with a Remote Registry

Instead of going through the rigmarole of installing System Policy Editor on a local machine, changing the settings in the local Registry, and then uninstalling the program, it's much easier to install it on your own computer and then deal with other machines remotely.

To try this, in the System Policy Editor, select File | Connect. In the Connect dialog box that appears, shown in Figure 32.9, type the name of the remote computer you want to work with, and then click OK. You'll see the same Local User and Local Computer icons, but this time they're referring to the HKEY_CURRENT_USER and HKEY_LOCAL_MACHINE keys in the remote machine's Registry. The title bar tells you which Registry you're working with, as you can see in Figure 32.10. When you've completed your remote labors, select File | Disconnect.

FIGURE 32.9.

Use the Connect dialog box to enter the name of the remote computer.

FIGURE 32.10.

The System Policy Editor with a remote Registry open.

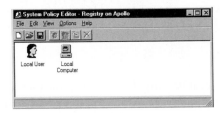

Creating a Network-Wide Policy File

The capability to connect to a remote Registry is certainly handy, but it's by no means the be-all and end-all of remote administration. One of the problems with this method is that you still must make sure that the appropriate user is logged on to the remote machine. (Again, this is meaningful only if the remote machine has multiple user profiles.) Another problem is that you're still customizing computers one by one. This is fine in some situations, but it's more likely that you'll want to implement certain settings network-wide. This ensures a consistent setup on all your machines, which makes them easier to configure and easier to support.

To set up network-wide policies, you have to work with *policy files*. These files (they have a POL extension) contain various system policy entries that correspond to settings in the Registry's HKEY_CURRENT_USER and HKEY_LOCAL_MACHINE keys. When you have a network-wide policy file, the settings from this file are read into the user's local Registry each time he logs on. This way, you need to maintain only a single set of system policies, and they'll be implemented across the network automatically. This method is the way system policies were designed to be used, and it's one of Windows 95's most powerful and useful remote administration features.

NOTE: SYSTEM POLICIES IN REAL-MODE NETWORKS

The automatic downloading of a network-wide system policy file works only if you're using a 32-bit protected-mode network client, such as Client for Microsoft Networks or Client for NetWare Networks. If you're using real-mode network clients (such as NetWare NETX or VLM), you must set up a "manual" download of a system policy file for each client.

To do this, first create a policy file (as described next), and store it on a mapped drive. Then you need to select File | Connect and work with the Registry for each client. When you're connected, open the Local Computer icon, open the Network tree, open Update, and highlight Remote Update. In the Update Mode drop-down list, select Manual. In the Path for manual update text box, enter the UNC path and filename for the policy file.

Here are the steps to follow to set up a network-wide policy file:

1. In the System Policy Editor, select File | New File.
2. Use the Default User and Default Computer icons, shown in Figure 32.11, to modify system policies that apply to the HKEY_CURRENT_USER and HKEY_LOCAL_MACHINE Registry keys for all users and computers.

FIGURE 32.11.

A new policy file contains Default User and Default Computer icons.

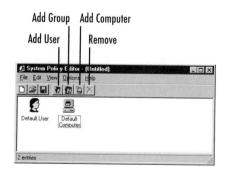

3. If you want to set up system policies for a specific user, select Edit | Add User (or click the Add User toolbar button), enter the name of the user in the Add User dialog box, and click OK. (Alternatively, you can click the Browse button and choose users from the list that appears.)

4. If you want to set up system policies for a specific computer, select Edit | Add Computer (or click the Add Computer toolbar button), enter the name of the computer in the Add Computer dialog box, and click OK. (Alternatively, you can click the Browse button and choose a computer from the list that appears.)

5. You can set up system policies for an entire group by selecting Edit | Add Group (or clicking the Add Group toolbar button), entering the name of the group in the Add Group dialog box, and clicking OK. (Or you can click the Browse button and choose a group from the list that appears.)

6. As you'll see later, Windows 95 loads group policy settings according to the priority assigned to each group, with the highest-priority group loaded last. To change the group priorities, select Options | Group Priority. In the Group Priority dialog box, shown in Figure 32.12, highlight groups in the Group Order list, and use the Move Up and Move Down buttons to arrange the groups (groups at the top of the list have the highest priority). Click OK when you're done.

FIGURE 32.12.

Use the Group Priority dialog box to arrange your groups in order of priority.

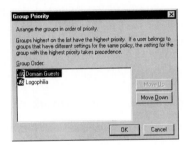

7. If you want to remove an icon from the policy file, highlight it and select Edit | Remove (or you can press Delete or click the Remove toolbar button). When the System Policy Editor asks whether you want to remove the icon, click Yes.

8. When you've finished setting up the system policies, select File | Save. In the Save As dialog box, enter config in the File name text box, and then save the policy file in one of the following locations:

   ■ If you're using the Client for Microsoft Networks, save the file in the NETLOGON share of the primary domain controller. (Note that you must have write access to this share.)

   ■ If you're using Client for NetWare Networks, save the file in the PUBLIC directory of the preferred NetWare server.

Figure 32.13 shows a saved CONFIG.POL file that includes several users, computers, and groups. To edit CONFIG.POL, either select File | Open File or select CONFIG.POL from the bottom of the File menu.

FIGURE 32.13.

A CONFIG.POL *file with various users, computers, and groups.*

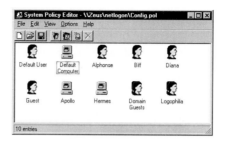

After CONFIG.POL is in place on the server, Windows 95 loads the system policy data from this file each time a client logs on to the network. During the logon, Windows 95 performs two tasks:

■ Downloads the user settings from CONFIG.POL into USER.DAT on the local machine (recall that USER.DAT holds the Registry settings for HKEY_CURRENT_USER).

■ Downloads the computer settings from CONFIG.POL into SYSTEM.DAT on the local machine (recall that SYSTEM.DAT holds the Registry settings for HKEY_LOCAL_MACHINE).

To get the user settings, Windows 95 runs through the following checks:

1. Are there specific settings for this user in CONFIG.POL? If so, these settings are downloaded.

2. If not, and if group policies are enabled on the client, are there settings for any groups that the user belongs to? If so, the group policies are downloaded in order of priority, with the highest-priority group downloaded last.

3. If no group settings apply to the user, the settings for the Default User are downloaded.

To get the computer settings, Windows 95 runs through the following checks:

1. Are there specific settings for this computer in CONFIG.POL? If so, these settings are downloaded.

2. If there are no computer-specific settings, the settings for the Default Computer are downloaded.

Working with User Settings

Whether you're dealing with the Local User or the Default User icon, or a specific user or group added to CONFIG.POL, you use the same techniques to work with the System Policy Editor's user settings. To display the available settings, highlight the appropriate icon and select Edit | Properties (you can also press Enter or double-click the icon).

The properties sheet that appears (see Figure 32.14) contains five headings—Control Panel, Desktop, Network, Shell, and System—arranged in a treelike hierarchy. Opening a branch (by clicking its plus sign, or by highlighting it and pressing + on the numeric keypad) displays its contents, which might be more branches or policy settings. The policy settings have a check box beside them. Each check box can have one of three states:

Checked: This means that the policy will be implemented the next time the user logs on to the network.

Unchecked: This means that the policy won't be implemented the next time the user logs on.

Grayed: This means that the policy will remain unchanged the next time the user logs on.

FIGURE 32.14.

The properties sheet for a user contains various policies that control settings in `HKEY_CURRENT_USER`.

CAUTION: CHECK THE STATE OF YOUR SETTING

You need to be a bit careful when you're working with these check boxes. If you activate a check box and then change your mind, don't clear the check box because this action wipes out the existing setting the next time the user logs on. Instead, make sure that the check box is grayed so that Windows 95 will ignore it during the next logon.

In some cases, you might also have to fill in a text box or some other control at the bottom of the properties sheet. In Figure 32.14, for example, activating the Wallpaper policy also requires you to fill in the `Wallpaper name` box and, optionally, activate the `Tile wallpaper` check box.

Most of the available policies are straightforward, so I won't go through all of them here. But just so you know where to look, here's a quick summary of what's in each branch:

Control Panel: Policies that customize five Control Panel components: Display, Network, Passwords, Printers, and System. In each case, you can disable the icon or remove specific tabs from the properties sheet associated with each icon.

Desktop: Policies that specify a wallpaper and color scheme. These are useful for supplying all of your clients with a consistent look (such as your corporate colors or logo).

Network: Policies that control whether the user can use file or print sharing.

Shell: Policies that customize the Windows 95 interface. There are two branches: Custom Folders and Restrictions. The Custom Folders branch lets you specify alternative locations for several folders, including Desktop, Startup, and Programs. The Restrictions branch, shown in Figure 32.15, toggles a number of user interface features—such as the Run command, the Settings menu items, and the Network Neighborhood—on and off.

FIGURE 32.15.

The policies on the Restrictions branch let you control numerous aspects of the Windows 95 user interface.

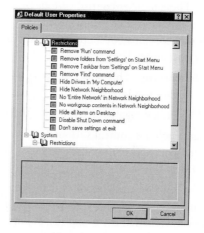

System: Policies that set restrictions for using the Registry Editor as well as several DOS-related settings (such as disabling the DOS prompt).

When you've completed your labors in this dialog box, click OK.

Working with Computer Settings

The Local Computer and Default Computer icons, as well as any specific computers you add to CONFIG.POL, all control the same set of system policies. As with the user policies, you display the available computer policies by highlighting the appropriate computer icon and selecting Edit | Properties (or pressing Enter or double-clicking the icon). The properties sheet that appears contains just two headings: Network and System.

The Network heading, shown in Figure 32.16, contains no fewer than 10 branches, and they all control various facets of how the client interacts with the network. Here's a quick summary of what you'll find in each branch:

Access Control: This policy toggles user-level access control on and off. If it's activated, you also must supply a server name and authenticator type.

Logon: These policies let you set a custom logon banner (a dialog box, actually) and to set whether an invalid logon gets access to the Windows 95 desktop.

Microsoft Client for NetWare Networks: These policies set the preferred NetWare server, specify whether NetWare supports long filenames, and more.

Microsoft Client for Windows Networks: These policies control various Microsoft networking settings, including whether the client logs on to an NT domain, the client's workgroup, and more.

File and printer sharing for NetWare Networks: This policy controls whether the Windows 95 workstation that is performing file and printer sharing should use the SAP to make its presence known to other servers and to the routers.

Passwords: These policies control various password-related settings. For added security, you should disable password caching, require alphanumeric passwords (passwords that contains both letters and numbers), and set a minimum password length of at least eight characters.

Dial-Up Networking: This policy controls whether Dial-Up Networking connections to the client are allowed.

Sharing: This policy toggles file and print sharing for the client on and off.

SNMP: These policies control various settings related to the Simple Network Management Protocol (SNMP) network service. (This service is available on the Windows 95 CD-ROM in the \ADMIN\NETTOOLS\SNMP folder.)

Update: The Remote Update policy determines whether the client downloads a policy file at startup. If it's activated, you can choose either an automatic update mode (policies are downloaded from CONFIG.POL) or a manual update mode (policies are downloaded from a specified policy file).

FIGURE 32.16.

The Network policies control tons of settings related to Windows 95 networking.

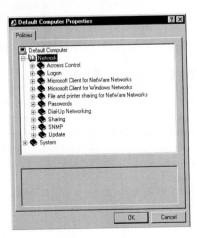

The System branch contains a mixed bag of policies that include toggling user profiles on and off, setting a network path for the Windows 95 source files, and specifying programs to run at startup. (Note that you use the Run Once policy to define one or more programs that will run only the next time the client is restarted. After that, the programs are removed.)

Connecting to a Remote Registry from the Registry Editor

I showed you earlier how you can use the System Policy Editor to connect to a remote Registry. The System Policy Editor, however, is a front-end for only a few Registry settings. If you need the whole Registry enchilada, there's a way to access an entire remote Registry (provided that you have the necessary access). Here are the steps to follow:

1. Open the Registry Editor.
2. Select Registry | Connect Network Registry.
3. In the Connect Network Registry dialog box, enter the name of the remote computer in the Computer name text box. (If you're not sure, click the Browse button, highlight the computer in the Browse for Computer dialog box, and click OK.)
4. Click OK.

The Registry Editor adds a new branch for the remote computer, as shown in Figure 32.17. You can use the keys in this new branch just like the keys on your local computer. When you're done, you can disconnect by selecting File | Disconnect Remote Registry, highlighting the computer in the dialog box that appears and clicking OK.

FIGURE 32.17.

You can work with a remote Registry from the comfort of your own computer.

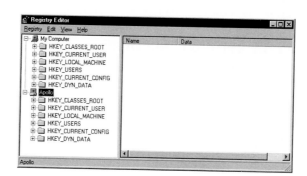

Watching the Network with Net Watcher

As the administrator of your network, you must know more than just the various folders and printers being shared by remote computers. To get a closer look at what's happening on your network, Windows 95 comes with a handy administrative tool called Net Watcher. This utility lets you carry out the following tasks:

■ For each shared folder on any remote computer, find out the users that are connected to the folder, how long they've been connected, and the files they have open.

■ Disconnect users from a shared folder or close files that have been opened on a shared folder.

■ Change the properties of a remote shared folder, including its share name and the access rights to the folder. You can even stop sharing a remote folder.

■ Set up a new shared folder on any remote machine.

These are powerful, not-to-be-wielded-lightly techniques. They're all described in the next few sections.

Connecting to a Remote Server

To get started with Net Watcher, select Start | Programs | Accessories | System Tools | Net Watcher. The Net Watcher window that appears shows you the connections to the local computer. If you prefer to work with a remote server (remember that in a peer-to-peer network, any computer that shares resources is a "server"), select Administer | Select Server (or you can click the Select Server button on the toolbar). In the Select Server dialog box, enter the name of the server you want to administer, and then click OK. (As usual, you can instead click the Browse button to choose the computer from a list.)

Viewing the Current Connections

The default Net Watcher view displays a list of the users connected to any shared folder on the server, as shown in Figure 32.18. (If Net Watcher isn't showing this view, you can select it by activating View | by Connections, or by clicking the Show Users toolbar button.) For each user, you get the following data:

User: The name of the user.

Computer: The name of the user's computer.

Shares: The number of shared folders.

Open Files: The number of open files in the shared folders.

Connected Time: The amount of time the user has been connected to the server.

Shared folders connected to and files opened: The shared folders and open files.

FIGURE 32.18.
Net Watcher's default view shows the users who are connected to the server.

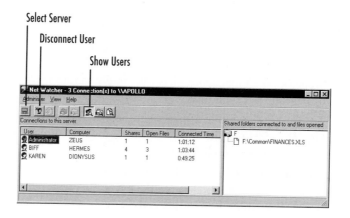

Although in the interest of network harmony you'll want to let users connect and disconnect as they please, at times you might need to boot someone off a server. For example, you might see that someone has gotten unauthorized access to a share. To disconnect that user, highlight her name in the list and select Administer | Disconnect User (or click the toolbar's Disconnect User button). When Net Watcher asks for confirmation, click Yes.

Working with Shared Folders

Net Watcher also lets you view the connections to a server by its shared folders. To get this display, select View | by Shared Folders (or click the Show Shared Folders button on the toolbar). As you can see in Figure 32.19, this view provides the following information:

Shared Folder: The drives and folders that the server is sharing.

Shared As: The share name.

Access Type: The access control method designated for each share.

Comment: The description of the share.

Connections to this share and files opened: The computers connected to the share and the files they have open.

FIGURE 32.19.
Net Watcher can display a server's connections by its shared folders.

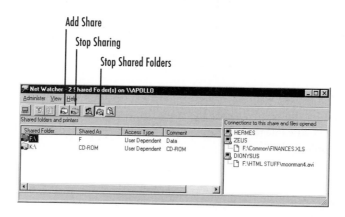

Here are the techniques you can use to work with the shared folders:

> **To change the properties of a shared folder:** Highlight the folder you want to work with, and then select Administer | Shared Folder Properties (or press Alt-Enter). The properties sheet that appears lets you modify various share options, including the name, comment, and users.

> **To stop sharing a folder:** Highlight the shared folder and select Administer | Stop Sharing Folder (or click the Stop Sharing toolbar button). When Net Watcher asks whether you're sure, click Yes.

> **To add a shared folder:** Select Administer | Add Shared Folder (or click the Add Share button on the toolbar). In the Enter Path dialog box that appears, type the path of the folder you want to share, and then click OK. (Alternatively, click Browse and choose the path from the Browse for Folder dialog box.)

Working with Open Files

Finally, Net Watcher can also display the server connection by the files that are open. To switch to this view, select View | by Open Files (or click the Show Files button on the toolbar). Figure 32.20 shows the result. Here's a summary of the columns in this view:

> **Open File:** The full pathname of the file.

> **Via Share:** The name of the share on which the file resides.

> **Accessed By:** The name of the computer that's using the file.

> **Open Mode:** The permissions the user has over the file.

FIGURE 32.20.

Net Watcher can also display a server's connections by its open files.

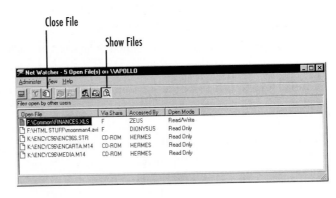

Again, you'll usually want to let users open and close files themselves so that they don't lose information. If you need to close a file, however, you can do so by highlighting it and selecting Administer | Close File (or by clicking the Close File toolbar button). When Net Watcher asks for confirmation, click Yes.

Using System Monitor on a Remote Computer

In Chapter 9, "Windows 95 Performance Tuning and Optimization," I showed you how to use System Monitor to keep an eye on the performance of your computer. If you're also interested in monitoring the health of the remote computers on your network, System Monitor is up to the task.

To connect to a remote computer from System Monitor, start the program and select File | Connect. In the Connect dialog box that appears, type the name of the remote computer, and then click OK. After the connection is established, you can add any System Monitor item to the window, and the program tracks that item for the remote machine, as shown in Figure 32.21. In particular, you might want to add some of System Monitor's network-related settings, such as those found in the Microsoft Network Client and Microsoft Network Server categories.

FIGURE 32.21.

System Monitor is only too happy to monitor remote systems as well as local ones.

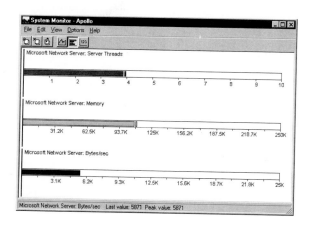

Remote Administration from the Network Neighborhood

When a client computer is set up for remote administration, you can perform many of the network administration chores we've looked at in this section right from the Network Neighborhood. For example, if you open the folder for a remote computer in the Network Neighborhood, you'll see not only the computer's shared resources, but *all* of its drives and folders. You can then set up (or modify or stop) sharing for any of these resources by either highlighting the resource and selecting File | Properties, or right-clicking the resource and selecting Sharing from the context menu.

Not only that, but Windows 95 also gives you quick access to some remote administration tools. Either highlight a remote computer name and select File | Properties, or right-click a computer name and select Properties from the context menu. In the properties sheet that appears, select the Tools tab. As you can see in Figure 32.22, this tab gives you the following choices:

Net Watcher: Click this button to start Net Watcher and connect to the remote computer automatically.

System Monitor: Click this button to start System Monitor and connect to the remote computer automatically.

Administer: Click this button to display a folder window containing all the remote computer's drives and folders. You can then use this window to set up sharing, map drives, and so on.

FIGURE 32.22.

The properties sheet for a remote computer gives you quick access to several administrative tools.

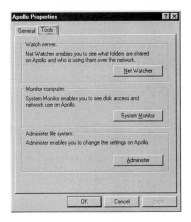

Summary

This chapter took you through a few network security and administration issues. Under the security banner, I showed you how to hide shared resources, set up user-level access control, and select a bullet-proof password. For administration, you learned how to set up remote administration, wield the System Policy Editor, work with remote Registries, and use the Net Watcher and System Monitor tools.

Here's a list of chapters where you'll find related information:

■ For some solutions to networking problems, try Chapter 33, "Network Trouble-shooting."

■ If you have just a couple of computers, you can bypass the expense of network adapter cards and cables by using Windows 95's Direct Cable Connection. You still must set up a "network," however, and I explain how it's done in Chapter 34, "From Laptop to Desktop and Back: Direct Cable Connection."

■ To learn how to access a network via modem, check out Chapter 35, "Remote Computing with Dial-Up Networking."

■ TCP/IP is fast becoming the protocol of choice for both large and small networks. I demonstrate how to work with TCP/IP in Chapter 36, "Implementing TCP/IP for Internet and Network Connections."

■ The Internet, of course, is *the* network. I show you how Windows 95 connects to, and works with, Internet resources in Chapter 37, "Windows 95 and the Internet." For Web-based Internet sites, Internet Explorer offers easy access. I give you a complete primer in Chapter 38, "Exploring the Web with Internet Explorer."

32

Network Administration and Security

Network
Troubleshooting

IN THIS CHAPTER

CHAPTER

33

The greater the difficulty, the greater the glory.

—*Cicero*

As you've seen in the last three chapters, networking is a complex, arcane topic that taxes the patience of all but the most dedicated wireheads (an affectionate pet name often applied to network hackers and gurus). There are so many hardware components to deal with (from the network adapter to the cable to the router to the hub) and so many layers of software (from the device drivers to the protocols to the redirectors to the network providers) that networks often seem like accidents looking for a place to happen.

If your network has become a "notwork" (some wags also refer to a downed network as a *nyetwork*), this chapter offers a few solutions that might help. I don't make any claim to completeness here, however. Most network ills are a combination of several factors and therefore are relatively obscure and difficult to reproduce. Instead, I'll just go through a few general strategies for tracking down problems as well as pose solutions for some of the most common network afflictions.

A Starting Point: Microsoft Network Diagnostics

If you suspect you're having network trouble—such as computers on the network not being able to see each other or file transfers or other network activity behaving erratically—but you aren't sure, one easy way to find out is to run the Microsoft Network Diagnostics (MND) utility. This is a real-mode connectivity troubleshooting tool that can help you isolate network problems.

To use MND, log on to another computer on your network and either start a DOS session or select Start | Run. Type the command net diag and press Enter. MND then checks your system to make sure that either a NetBIOS protocol (such as NetBEUI) or an IPX protocol is installed. If both are installed, you'll see the following lines:

```
IPX and NetBIOS have been detected.
Press I to use IPX for diagnostics, N to use NetBIOS, or E to exit this program.
```

Press I or N as necessary. MND then searches the network for a *diagnostics server,* which means a machine running MND. Assuming that no other machines are running MND, you'll see the following messages:

```
No diagnostics servers were detected on the network.
Is Microsoft Network Diagnostics currently running on any other computers
on the network ? (Y/N)
```

NOTE: NETWORKS RUNNING MULTIPLE DIAGNOSTICS SERVERS

If there *is* another machine operating as a diagnostics server, see the next section for instructions.

Press N. MND then sets up the computer for use as a diagnostics server. You'll see the following lines:

```
This computer will now begin acting as a diagnostics server.

Press any key to stop acting as a diagnostics server.
```

Now return to the computer on which you're having problems and run the net diag command. Select the protocol to use, if necessary. If all is well with the network connection, you'll see the following messages:

```
Searching for diagnostic server...
The diagnostic server has been located on the network.
Communicating with diagnostic server. This may take several seconds.
Validating reply from diagnostic server.
The diagnostic server's reply is correct.
This indicates that network information is being sent and received properly.

The command was completed successfully.
```

If instead you see the Is Microsoft Network Diagnostics currently running on any other computers on the network ? (Y/N) prompt, press Y. You'll know you have a connectivity problem if you then see the following message:

```
This computer is unable to communicate with the diagnostic server. This often
results from a problem with the network card, configuration, or cables.

The command was completed successfully.
```

TIP: FIND A COMPUTER TO TEST CONNECTIVITY

Another way to test basic network connectivity is to select Start | Find | Computer. In the Find: Computer dialog box that appears, enter the name of the computer and then click Find Now. If Windows 95 finds the computer, you know you have at least basic connectivity established.

Naming Your Diagnostics Server

What if there are other machines acting as diagnostic servers on the network? You have two choices: Use one of the other machines as the diagnostic server, or specify a name for your diagnostic server so that you can be sure that the other machines you test will be using your server.

To specify a diagnostic server name, run the NET DIAG command with the /NAMES switch, like so:

```
net diag /names
```

33
NETWORK
TROUBLESHOOTING

After the usual protocol selection, you'll see this message:

```
You have chosen to specify a custom name that will be used
during the diagnostic session.  You must enter the same custom
name on all workstations involved in the diagnostics, and this
name should not match any computer names that are currently on
the network.

Please type a name (up to 15 characters), and then press ENTER.
```

Enter a name for the server and press Enter. When testing another workstation, enter the net diag /names command and, when prompted, specify the same name that you assigned to the diagnostics server earlier.

Examining Adapter Status

NetBIOS has a network adapter status function that can supply you with general data about the current state of the adapter on your computer or on any computer on the network. To invoke the adapter status function (this is a NetBIOS-only call), run NET DIAG with the /STATUS switch, like this:

```
net diag /status
```

MND responds with the following prompt:

```
Please enter the remote computer's NetBIOS name, or press ENTER to examine
a local adapter's status.
```

Either enter the NetBIOS name for a remote machine and press Enter, or press Enter to examine the status of the adapter in your computer. MND then displays a report similar to the following:

```
Remote adapter status:

Permanent node name: 00A02415D6F8

Adapter operational for 23 minutes.
231 free NCBs out of 255 with 255 the maximum.
2 sessions in use
10 sessions allocated
762 packets transmitted 1002 packets received.
0 retransmissions 0 retries exhausted.
0 crc errors 0 alignment errors
0 collisions 0 interrupted transmissions.
name 2 SELENE          status 04
name 3 OLYMPUS         status 84
name 4 SELENE       ♥   status 04
name 5 SELENE          status 04
name 6 OLYMPUS      Δ   status 84
```

TIP: USE SYSTEM MONITOR TO TRACK NETWORK CLIENTS

Don't forget that you can set up Windows 95's System Monitor utility to watch a remote workstation's CPU activity, memory allocation, network traffic, and more. I described how to do this in Chapter 32, "Network Administration and Security."

Some System Policy "Problems"

If the administrator of your network has instituted system policies, and if she hasn't done a good job of explaining them, Windows 95 might seem to act strangely when it's really only honoring these policies. For example, Windows 95 might complain that a password is too short or doesn't contain a number. These are almost certainly policy "problems" and not Windows woes at all. A perusal of the various computer-related and user-related network settings available in the System Policy Editor will show you the kinds of things that can be affected (see Chapter 32 for details). Here's a summary:

You can't switch to share-level access control: The Network | Access Control | User-level Access Control policy has been activated.

At startup, an extra dialog box appears that says Do not attempt to log on unless you are an authorized user **(or some other nonstandard message):** The Network | Logon | Logon Banner policy is active.

You can't bypass the network logon. The system reports that You cannot use Windows unless your user name is validated by the network: The Network | Logon | Require Validation by Network for Windows Access policy is in force.

You can't share files or printers, and the File and Print Sharing button is missing from the Network properties sheet: One or both of the Network | Sharing | Disable file sharing and Network | Sharing | Disable print sharing policies are turned on. (Alternatively, these policies might be in force via the Local User properties sheet.)

Windows 95 doesn't remember your passwords: The Network | Passwords | Disable password caching policy is in effect.

Windows 95 tells you that Your password must contain a combination of letters and numbers: The Network | Passwords | Require alphanumeric Windows password policy has been activated.

Windows 95 complains that Your password must be x characters long: The Network | Passwords | Minimum Windows password length policy is in effect.

The Network properties sheet doesn't appear or is missing one or both of the Identification and Access Control tabs: The Control Panel | Network | Restrict Network Control Panel policy is active, and one or more of its settings are turned on. (Note that this is a user policy.)

The Passwords properties sheet doesn't appear or is missing one or more tabs: The Control Panel | Passwords | Restrict Passwords Control Panel policy is active, and one or more of its settings are turned on. (This is a user policy.)

There is no Network Neighborhood icon on your desktop or in Explorer: The Shell | Custom Folders | Restrictions | Hide Network Neighborhood policy is activated. (This is a user policy.)

The Entire Network icon is missing from the Network Neighborhood: The Shell | Custom Folders | Restrictions | No 'Entire Network' in Network Neighborhood policy is turned on. (This is a user policy.)

The machines in your workgroup or domain don't appear in the Network Neighborhood: The Shell | Custom Folders | Restrictions | No workgroup contents in Network Neighborhood policy is in effect. (This is a user policy.)

When All Else Fails, Reinstall Your Drivers

Whatever your network problem, if it still isn't fixed after you've tried the solutions found in the rest of this chapter (and you rule out hardware failure), you should try reinstalling the Windows 95 protected-mode network drivers. Here are the steps to follow:

1. Open the Network properties sheet.
2. For each component listed, highlight the component and then click Remove.
3. Follow the instructions in Chapter 31, "Windows 95 Networking," to reinstall all the components.

Troubleshooting General Network Nuisances

This section begins the troubleshooting portion of the show by looking at a few of the most common complaints that crop up with Windows 95 networking.

TIP: ACCESSING THE NETWORK PROPERTIES SHEET

Many of the solutions found in the rest of this chapter will require you to display the Network properties sheet. Here's a review of the various methods you can use to display this dialog box:

- In Control Panel, double-click the Network icon.
- Right-click the desktop's Network Neighborhood icon, and then choose Properties.
- Highlight Network Neighborhood in Explorer and then select File | Properties.

CAUTION: DON'T USE DEVICE MANAGER AT THE SAME TIME

Avoid having both the Network properties sheet and the properties sheet for your network adapter (which you access via Device Manager) open at the same time. Closing the Network properties sheet before you close the adapter properties sheet will cause a GPF in RUNDLL32.

You can't log on to your network, or you receive a logon error message such as `No domain server was available to validate your password`.

This is the most fundamental network problem, and it can be caused by a number of things. Here's a checklist:

- Make sure your user name and password are correct.

- In the Network properties sheet, check the `Primary Network Logon` list to ensure that your networking client, not Windows Logon, is selected.

- If you're using Microsoft Networking, open the Network properties sheet, double-click Client for Microsoft Networks, and make sure that the `Log on to Windows NT domain` check box is activated, as shown in Figure 33.1. Also, make sure that the name shown in the `Windows NT domain` text box is a valid domain name. If these settings are correct, check with the domain administrator to make sure that you have a valid account in that domain.

FIGURE 33.1.

Make sure you're logging on to the correct Windows NT domain.

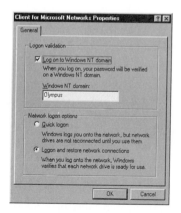

- If you receive a message telling you that `The computer name you specified is already in use on the network`, open the Network properties sheet, activate the Identification tab, and enter a new name in the `Computer name` text box.

33

NETWORK TROUBLESHOOTING

- For NetWare, double-click Client for NetWare Networks in the Network properties sheet and then, in the General tab, make sure that the `Preferred server` value is correct. (For the Novell Client32, use the Client 32 tab instead.) If it is, check with the server administrator to see if you have an account on that server.

- If the logon problem was caused by a NetWare logon script failing to run, activate the General tab in the Client for NetWare Networks properties sheet and make sure that the `Enable logon script processing` check box is checked.

- Make sure it's not a system policy problem (see the section "Some System Policy 'Problems'").

As a further troubleshooting aid to logon dilemmas, you can tell Windows 95 to display an extra logon message. This is a dialog box that provides the following potentially useful troubleshooting data:

- The domain you were logged on to
- The logon user name that was registered
- The UNC path of the validation server
- The privileges your account was assigned

You can set this up either by modifying the Registry or by using the System Policy Editor.

To do this via the Registry, open the Registry Editor (see Chapter 11, "Introducing the Windows 95 Registry") and then display the following key:

`HKEY_LOCAL_MACHINE\Network\Logon`

Now select Edit | New | DWORD Value, type `DomainLogonMessage`, and press Enter to write the new setting. Press Enter again to open the Edit DWORD Value dialog box, change the `Value data` text box to `1`, and click OK. Exit the Registry Editor. The new logon message will appear the next time you log on.

If you prefer to use the System Policy Editor, follow these steps:

1. Assuming that the System Policy Editor is installed (as described in Chapter 32), select Start | Programs | Accessories | System Tools | System Policy Editor.

2. Select File | Open Registry.

3. Double-click the Local Computer icon.

4. Open the Network | Microsoft Client for Windows Networks branch and highlight the `Log on to Windows NT` setting (which should have an activated check box).

5. Activate the `Display domain logon confirmation` check box, as shown in Figure 33.2, and click OK.

FIGURE 33.2.

Activate the Display
domain logon
confirmation
check box.

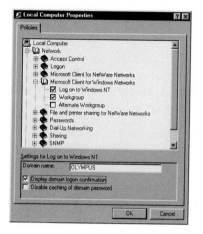

6. Select File | Exit.

7. When the System Policy Editor asks if you want to save changes, click Yes.

You can't share folders or printers.

If you are unable to use Windows 95's file and print sharing features, you either might be running on a network that doesn't support sharing, or your network administrator might have disabled sharing using the System Policy Editor (as described earlier). You might be able to tell if this is the case by opening the Network properties sheet. If you can't click the File and Print Sharing button, you know that sharing has been disabled.

Here are two other things to check:

■ Make sure that the appropriate file and printer sharing service is installed. For example, in Microsoft Networking, you must have the File and printer sharing for Microsoft Networks service installed (see Chapter 31).

■ If the service is installed, make sure you've activated the appropriate sharing check boxes. In the Network properties sheet, click File and Print Sharing and then activate the check boxes in the dialog box that appears, as shown in Figure 33.3.

FIGURE 33.3.

*Activate these check
boxes to enable file and
printer sharing.*

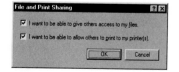

33

NETWORK
TROUBLESHOOTING

Other network users can't work with your shared folders or printers (or you can't work with resources shared by other users).

As long as the other users can see your shared resources, the most likely culprit here is that file and print sharing have been turned off. To turn them back on, display the Network properties sheet, click the File and Print Sharing button, and activate the check boxes in the dialog box (see Figure 33.2). Here are some other things to look for:

- If you're using share-level access control, make sure you've given each user the correct password for the type of access they're allowed (read-only or full).

- If you're using user-level access control, make sure you've given each user (or a group of which the user is a member) permission to work with the shared folder or printer. Also, check the type of permission you've granted each user (read-only, full, or custom).

- Make sure your shares aren't hidden. As explained in Chapter 32, you can hide a shared resource by tacking a dollar sign ($) to the end of its name.

- If the other users can't see your shared resources, open the Network properties sheet and check the network client you have installed. Make sure you're using the appropriate client for your network.

- While you're in the Network properties sheet, check the protocols that are installed. In order for any two machines to work together over a network, they must be running a common protocol. Compare protocols with the other nodes to ensure that a common protocol exists.

- If a common protocol is installed, make sure that it's bound to the File and print sharing service. In the Network properties sheet, double-click the common protocol that's bound to your network adapter. In the Bindings tab, make sure that the check box beside the File and print sharing service is activated, as shown in Figure 33.4.

FIGURE 33.4.

Make sure that your network's common protocol is bound to the File and print sharing service.

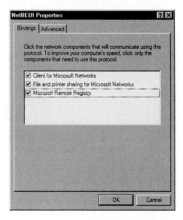

■ If someone on a Windows NT machine can't access one of your shared folders, the problem might be caused by the different password encryption schemes used by Windows 95 and Windows NT (this is a known Windows 95 bug). You can some-times resolve this problem by using either all uppercase or all lowercase letters in the shared folder's password. If that doesn't do the trick, you'll either have to remove the password or switch to user-level access control.

■ The user might be attempting to access a shared folder that you've deleted from your computer. If you delete a shared folder from the DOS prompt, Windows 95 doesn't update the Registry, so the folder still appears as a shared resource. (You should have turned off sharing before deleting the folder from DOS.) The solution is to create a new folder with the same name, turn off sharing for the folder, and then delete it from Explorer.

■ If you receive an error message such as `Invalid local device` when you try to access a mapped drive, check your `CONFIG.SYS` file's `LASTDRIVE` statement. You'll receive an error if this statement sets the last possible drive to a letter that's less than the one used for the mapped drive (for example, if `LASTDRIVE` is set to G and the drive was mapped to H). Either adjust the `LASTDRIVE` statement accordingly or, even better, remove the `LASTDRIVE` statement (it's not needed in Windows 95 if you're using protected-mode network drivers).

■ If a remote user has recently switched from using real-mode NetWare drivers to the protected-mode drivers in the Windows 95 NetWare client, drive mappings that were formerly made in `AUTOEXEC.BAT` won't appear. This happens because the real-mode drivers are no longer used, so the `MAP` commands in `AUTOEXEC.BAT` no longer work. The solution is to map the drives in Windows 95 (as described in Chapter 31) so that they can be handled by the protected-mode driver. (This applies to printers that were captured in `AUTOEXEC.BAT` as well.)

■ Windows 95 might report that the username or password for a shared resource isn't valid, even though you're sure that you entered the correct information. The likely problem here is that the security provider you specified is a Windows 95 machine set up to act as a NetWare server, which won't work. For proper validation, the security provider must be a true NetWare server. (This is a bug in Windows 95.)

■ Run MND with your computer as the diagnostics server (as described earlier) and check to see if the other machines can see the server.

No other computers appear in the Network Neighborhood.

The most obvious solution here is to make sure you have a networking client installed (and that it's the correct client for the type of network you're on). Also, make sure that you can log on to the network and, for Microsoft networks in particular, that you're logging on to the correct domain or workgroup (see the solutions earlier in this section).

If a client is installed and you can log on without mishap, here's a checklist to run through:

■ In the Network properties sheet, check the installed protocols to ensure that you're running a protocol that is common to the other network computers.

■ If a common protocol is installed, make sure that it's bound to your network adapter. In the Network properties sheet, double-click the network adapter, activate the Bindings tab, and ensure that the check box beside the common protocol is activated, as shown in Figure 33.5.

FIGURE 33.5.

The network's common protocol must be bound to your network adapter.

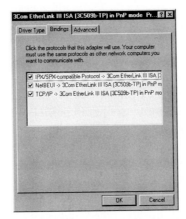

■ Open the Network properties sheet and check the network client you have installed. Make sure you're using the correct client for your network.

■ Check to see if the master browse server is operating properly. To do this, start a DOS session and enter the following command:

```
net view /workgroup:name
```

Here, *name* is the name of your workgroup or domain. (If the name contains spaces, enclose it in quotation marks.) You should then see a list of the servers available in the workgroup. If not, either you have a basic connectivity problem or the master browse server is down.

■ Make sure at least one computer in your workgroup is set up to be the browse master. If all the computers are Windows 95 machines, for example, they might all have the browse master property set to disabled. To make one machine the browse master, open the Network properties sheet and double-click File and printer sharing for Microsoft Networks. In the dialog box that appears, highlight Browse Master in the Property list and then select Enabled in the Value list.

■ If you've recently changed workgroups or domains, Windows 95 is sometimes a bit slow to broadcast the change, so the other workgroup machines won't show up right away. Reboot and check the Network Neighborhood again later. (You'll know this is the case if the Network Neighborhood shows your computer as the only machine in the workgroup.)

■ If you're either missing the Entire Network icon or no other machines from your workgroup or domain appear, this could be a system policy problem, as described earlier in this chapter.

■ If all you can see are NetWare servers in your workgroup, note that Windows 95 doesn't support browsing in a workgroup that doesn't have a server message block (SMB) server. To resolve this, open the Network properties sheet, activate the Identification tab, and then use the Workgroup text box to enter the name of a workgroup that contains an SMB server.

■ Run MND to ensure that a connection can be established between your computer and another computer on the network.

Windows 95 doesn't cache your Windows NT domain logon password.

By design, Windows 95 won't cache the logon password for your Windows NT domain. If security isn't an issue, there *is* a way to work around this:

1. Select Start | Settings | Control Panel | Passwords to display the Passwords Properties dialog box.
2. Click Change Windows Password. The Change Windows Password dialog box appears.
3. Clear the check boxes (especially Microsoft Networking) if necessary, and then click OK.
4. Use the Old password text box to enter your current Windows logon password. Leave the New password and Confirm old password text boxes blank, and then click OK.
5. When Windows 95 confirms that your password has been changed, click OK and then click Close to return to Control Panel.
6. Open Control Panel's Network icon to display the Network properties sheet.
7. Double-click the Client for Microsoft Networks component. Make sure that the Log on to Windows NT domain check box is activated and that the correct domain appears in the Windows NT domain text box, and then click OK.
8. In the Primary Network Logon list, select Windows Logon and click OK.
9. Follow the on-screen prompts until Windows 95 asks you to restart your computer, and then click Yes.
10. In the logon dialog box, use the Password text box to enter your NT domain password. Make sure that the Save this password in your password list check box is activated, and then click OK.

From here on out, you won't be prompted to enter a domain logon password when you start Windows 95.

33

NETWORK TROUBLESHOOTING

A password that you've cached in the password list has changed, but you can't update the cache because you don't recall the old password.

OSR2

In Windows 95, you can't make changes to a password unless you know the old password. As long as you're logged on with the correct user name and password, you can use the Password List Editor to remove the old password from the password list (.PWL) file. (Note, however, that the Password List Editor that comes on the original Windows 95 CD doesn't work with the enhanced password cache found in OSR2.)

To install the Password List Editor, follow these steps:

1. Select Start | Settings | Control Panel | Add/Remove Programs.
2. Select the Windows Setup tab, and then click Have Disk.
3. Insert your Windows 95 CD-ROM, enter the following path in the Install From Disk dialog box (where *drive* is the letter of your CD-ROM drive), and click OK:

   `drive:\admin\apptools\pwledit`
4. In the Have Disk dialog box, activate the check box beside Password List Editor, and then click Install.
5. Click OK to return to Control Panel.

To run the Password List Editor, select Start | Programs | Accessories | System Tools | Password List Editor. Figure 33.6 shows the Password List Editor window that appears. Highlight the password that's causing the problem, and click Remove.

FIGURE 33.6.

Use the Password List Editor to remove passwords from your password list file.

At startup, you're prompted for your networking password, and then you're prompted for your Windows password, but the latter fails despite the fact that you entered the correct password.

This behavior probably means that your password list (.PWL) file has become corrupted. As long as your networking password is valid, you should be able to press Esc at the Window password prompt and log on to Windows 95 successfully. From there, open Explorer, highlight your main Windows 95 folder, and find your password list file. The name of this file takes the form *User*.pwl, where *User* is your user name. Delete or rename this file, and then restart Windows 95. At the logon prompt, you will be able to reenter your Windows 95 password.

Cable Conundrums

If the software solutions discussed so far don't get you out of your networking quandary, the next logical suspect is the cabling that connects the workstations. This section discusses cabling, gives you a few pointers for preventing cable problems, and discusses some common cable kinks that can crop up.

Some Things to Bear in Mind When Running Cable

Although most large-scale cabling operations are performed by third-party cable installers, smaller setups are usually do-it-yourself jobs. You can prevent some cable problems and simplify your troubleshooting down the road by taking a few precautions and "ounce of prevention" measures in advance:

- First and foremost, always buy the highest-quality cable you can find (for example, Category 5 for twisted-pair cable). With network cabling, you get what you paid for.

> **NOTE: MORE CABLE DATA**
>
> I talk about the different types of network cable in Chapter 30, "A Networking Primer," in the section "The Cable Connection."

- Good-quality cable will be labeled (for example, RG-58/A-AU for coaxial). You should also add your own labels for things such as the source and destination of the cable.
- For complex installations, set up a complete wiring diagram that shows where the cables run and that indicates hubs, repeaters, wiring closets, and so on.
- To avoid electromagnetic interference, don't run cable near electronic devices, power lines, air conditioners, fluorescent lights, motors, and other electromagnetic sources.
- If you're running twisted-pair cable, try to avoid phone lines, because the ringer signal can disrupt network data.
- To avoid having the cable stepped on accidentally, don't run cable under carpet.
- If you plan on running cable outdoors, use conduit or some other casing material to prevent moisture damage.
- Don't use excessive force to pull or push a cable into place. Rough handling can cause pinching or even breakage.

Cable Limitations

Many cable problems are caused by exceeding the recommended limits on things such as cable length and trunk length. To help you avoid this, the following list summarizes the limitations inherent in some popular cable types:

10Base-T Limitations

The minimum cable length between computers is 8 feet.

Computers must be no more than 328 feet from the wiring closet.

One hub can connect up to 12 computers.

You can have up to 12 hubs to one central hub.

10Base-2 Limitations

The minimum cable length between computers is 20 inches.

The maximum length of a trunk segment is 607 feet.

You can connect up to 30 computers per trunk.

The maximum length of the total network trunk is 3,035 feet.

You can connect up to a maximum of 1,024 computers per network.

10Base-5 Limitations

The minimum cable length between taps is 8 feet.

The maximum length of a trunk segment is 1,640 feet.

The maximum length of the total network trunk is 8,200 feet.

Token Ring Limitations

The maximum distance between Multistation Access Units (MAUs) is 100 meters for Type 1 cable, 45 meters for Type 2 cable, and 4 kilometers for fiber optic cable.

You can connect a maximum of 260 computers on Type 1 cable and on fiber optic cable at 16 Mbps; you can have a maximum of 72 computers on Type 3 cable at 4 Mbps.

The maximum number of MAUs on each ring is 33.

ARCnet Limitations

The maximum distance between computers is 20,000 feet.

Computers can be no more than 600 feet from the active hub.

Passive hubs can be no more than 10 feet from the active hub.

You can connect a maximum of four computers to a passive hub, but none of these computers can be farther than 100 feet from the hub.

You can't connect one passive hub to another.

The maximum distance between two active hubs is 2,000 feet.

The maximum bus segment length for coaxial cable is 1,000 feet, with up to eight computers per segment.

The maximum bus segment length for twisted-pair cable is 400 feet with up to 10 computers per segment.

You can connect up to 255 computers per network.

Troubleshooting Cables

If you suspect cabling might be the cause of your network problems, here's a list of a few things to check:

Watch for electromagnetic interference: If you see garbage on a workstation screen, or if you experience random packet loss or temporarily missing nodes, the problem might be electromagnetic interference. Check your cables to make sure that they are at least 6 to 12 inches from any source of electromagnetic interference.

Check your connections: Loose connections are a common source of cabling woes. Be sure to check every cable connection associated with the workstation that's experiencing network difficulty, including connections to the network adapter, wall plate, barrel connector, hub, and so on. In particular, watch the BNC cable connectors associated with thin coaxial cable, because they can come loose quite easily, and it's not hard to connect them incorrectly in the first place.

For coaxial cable, check your terminators: If you use coaxial cable, you must terminate both ends of a network segment by installing BNC terminators. Make sure that terminators are installed at each end of the segment and that they are secured properly to the T-connector. Also, make sure that you use the proper terminator (for example, a 50-ohm impedance cable requires a 50-ohm terminator).

Isolate a thin coaxial cable problem by terminating the network adapter: If you're using thin coaxial cable, remove the T-connector from the network adapter of the problem workstation and replace it with a terminator. If the workstation now appears by itself in the Network Neighborhood, this probably means that you have a problem with either the cable or the connector used by the machine.

How's the lay of the line?: Loops of cable could be generating an electrical field that interferes with network communication. Try not to leave your excess cable lying around in coils or loops.

Inspect the cable for pinching or breaks: A badly pinched cable can cause a short in the wire, which would lead to intermittent connection problems. Make sure that no part of the cable is pinched, especially if the back of the computer is situated near a wall. A complete lack of connection with the network might mean that the cable's copper core has been severed completely and needs to be replaced.

Check your cable limitations: Double-check the limitations I outlined in the preceding section for cable length, maximum workstation numbers, and so on.

Check segment types: When you join two network segments, make sure that you're using the same type of cable for both segments.

Troubleshooting Adapter Afflictions

After cabling, network adapters are next on the list of common sources of networking headaches. Here's a list of items to check if you suspect that Windows 95 and your network adapter aren't getting along:

Make sure that Windows 95 installed the correct adapter: Windows 95 usually does a pretty good job of detecting the network card. However, a slight error (such as choosing the wrong transceiver type) can wreak havoc. Double-check that the network adapter listed in Device Manager is the same as the one installed in your computer. If it's not, click Remove to delete it, run the Add New Hardware Wizard, and choose your adapter manually.

Get the latest driver: Check with the manufacturer of the network adapter to see if they have newer Windows 95 drivers for the card. If so, download and install them.

Check the adapter settings: As with most hardware, conflicts at the adapter's IRQ, DMA, or I/O port address level can cause all kinds of problems. Use Device Manager to check the adapter's settings and to make sure no conflicts exist. Also, you can try restarting Windows 95, displaying the Startup menu, and choosing the Safe mode with network support option. If the network operates in this mode, there is a conflict with the driver.

Check your protocols: Some network adapters were designed to operate with only specific protocols, so make sure your adapter and your installed protocols are in sync.

Do a physical check of the adapter: Open the case and make sure that the adapter is properly seated in its slot. For a PC Card adapter, make sure that the card is inserted all the way into its slot, and check the external connection (these are notorious for breaking).

Try a new adapter: Try swapping out the adapter for one that you know works properly. If that fixes the problem, you'll need to replace the faulty adapter.

More Sophisticated Tools

If the solutions and workarounds presented in this chapter didn't solve your problem, you might need higher-end help. Specifically, many companies now offer sophisticated software and hardware tools for detecting, analyzing, and troubleshooting networks. This section lists (in no particular order) the best of these companies, the products they offer, and contact information.

Company: Novell
Product: LANalyzer for Windows
Phone: (800) 453-1267
World Wide Web: `http://www.novell.com/catalog/qr/sne54200.html`

Company: Triticom
Products: LANdecoder and LANVision
Phone: (612) 937-0772
World Wide Web: `http://www.triticom.com/`

Company: Hewlett-Packard
Products: NetMetrix and LanProbe
Phone: (800) 752-0900
World Wide Web: `http://www.tmo.hp.com/tmo/ntd/`

Company: Cinco Networks
Product: NetXRay
Phone: (800) 671-9272
World Wide Web: `http://www.cinco.com/`

Company: Network General
Product: Sniffer Network Analyzer
Phone: (800) 764-3337
World Wide Web: `http://www.ngc.com/product_info/sna/sna_dir.html`

Company: Fluke
Products: LANMeter, CableMeter, CableMapper, and more
Phone: (800) 443-5853
World Wide Web: `http://www.fluke.com/nettools/catalog.htm`

Company: Microtest
Products: COMPAS, LAN Assist
Phone: (800) 526-9675
World Wide Web: `http://www.microtest.com/html/network_diagnostics.html`

Company: Technically Elite
Products: EtherMeter, MeterWare, and more
Phone: (800) 474-7888
World Wide Web: `http://www.tecelite.com/products/default.htm`

Summary

This chapter took you through a few problems related to Windows 95 networking and proposed a few solutions and workarounds. I began by showing you how to wield the Microsoft Network Diagnostics tools to check network connections. From there, I told you about a few

33

NETWORK TROUBLESHOOTING

"problems" that are really system policies. I then took you through a list of general networking woes, followed by troubles related to cables and network adapters.

Here's a list of chapters where you'll find related information:

- For general network information, including cabling data, see Chapter 30, "A Networking Primer."

- To learn how to set up Windows 95 for networking, including installing components and sharing folders and printers, see Chapter 31, "Windows 95 Networking."

- Network security concerns and administration issues, including how to use the System Policy Editor, are the subject of Chapter 32, "Network Administration and Security."

- In case you'll be implementing TCP/IP on your network, I discuss a few troubleshooting issues in Chapter 36, "Implementing TCP/IP for Internet and Network Connections."

From Laptop to Desktop and Back: Direct Cable Connection

IN THIS CHAPTER

> *'Tis not in numbers but in unity that our great strength lies.*
>
> *— Thomas Paine*

You've seen in the last two chapters that Windows 95 (at least compared to Windows for Workgroups) is a powerful, feature-filled network client. And combining Windows 95 with a true network server operating system such as Windows NT or NetWare lets you fill in many of the gaping security holes that are part and parcel of the standard Windows 95 network package.

For many users, however, a full-blown network is overkill (and expensive overkill, to boot). For example, if you just want to share files or a printer between a desktop machine and a notebook, it makes no sense to install network interface cards and cables and run through the whole network configuration rigmarole. For these simpler situations, Windows 95 provides a simpler solution: Direct Cable Connection.

Direct Cable Connection is a network client that doesn't need the usual card/cable network hardware. Instead, as its name implies, Direct Cable Connection establishes a mini-network between two computers via a special cable that connects the computers' serial or parallel ports. (Direct Cable Connection can even work with connections established through infrared ports.) One computer is designated as the *host,* and it acts as a kind of server by sharing its resources. A second computer—called the *guest*—connects to the host and can access its shared resources. Moreover, if the host is attached to a network, the guest computer can access the Network Neighborhood and therefore work with any of the shared resources on the larger network.

This chapter shows you how to work with Direct Cable Connection. You'll learn what kind of cable you need, how to configure the host and guest, and how to establish the connection.

Port and Cable Considerations

As I said, the hardware requirements for Direct Cable Connection are modest, indeed:

- A free serial or parallel port on each computer (the computers must use the same type of port; you can't use, say, a parallel port on one machine and a serial port on the other). Alternatively, you can use infrared ports.
- A special cable running between the machines' ports. (Obviously, no cable is required for infrared connections.)

Before loading and configuring the Direct Cable Connection software, let's take a moment to examine these hardware requirements more closely.

Serial Ports and Null-Modem Cables

If you'll be using serial ports with Direct Cable Connection, you'll need to use a *null-modem cable* for the connection. Why not just use a regular serial cable? Well, recall from Chapter 25, "Maximizing Modem Communications," that serial ports use individual wires to transmit and receive data one bit at a time. In a 9-pin serial port, pin 3 is the Transmit Data wire, and pin 2 is the Receive Data wire. Because of these pin arrangements, you can't connect two serial ports with a garden-variety serial cable. Suppose you did, and then tried sending data from one machine to the other. The bits would go out through the Transmit Data wire, but because there is no modem in-between to route the signals appropriately, the other computer would receive them on *its* Transmit Data wire. Chaos would ensue.

To prevent this, use a null-modem cable instead. It uses a different pin arrangement than a regular serial cable, and therefore ensures that bits sent through the Transmit Data wire on one port head for the Receive Data wire of the other port. A null-modem cable also ensures that the correct wires are used on both ends for the Request To Send (RTS) and Clear To Send (CTS) signals, as well as the Data Set Ready (DSR) and Data Terminal Ready (DTR) signals. Table 34.1 specifies how a null-modem cable translates 9-pin serial port signals between a host computer and a guest computer.

Table 34.1. Wire translations for a 9-pin-to-9-pin null-modem cable.

Host Pin	Signal	Guest Pin	Signal
2	Receive Data	3	Transmit Data
3	Transmit Data	2	Receive Data
4	Data Terminal Ready	6	Data Set Ready
5	Signal Ground	5	Signal Ground
6	Data Set Ready	4	Data Terminal Ready
7	Request To Send	8	Clear To Send
8	Clear To Send	7	Request To Send

There are also null-modem cables that work with 25-pin serial ports. Table 34.2 spells out the wire translations for a host and guest.

Table 34.2. Wire translations for a 25-pin-to-25-pin null-modem cable.

Host Pin	Signal	Guest Pin	Signal
2	Transmit Data	3	Receive Data
3	Receive Data	2	Transmit Data
4	Request To Send	5	Clear To Send
5	Clear To Send	4	Request To Send
6	Data Set Ready	20	Data Terminal Ready
7	Signal Ground	7	Signal Ground
20	Data Terminal Ready	6	Data Set Ready

34

DIRECT CABLE CONNECTION

If you use a serial port connection, be aware that your data transfer speeds will be anything but snappy. If you have an older 8250 or 16450 UART, Direct Cable Connection's maximum theoretical throughput will be 57,600 bits per second (bps), or about 7 kilobytes per second (K/sec). If you have a 16650 UART, maximum throughput doubles to 115,200 bps, or about 14K/sec, which still isn't very fast compared to network cable.

Standard Parallel Ports and Cables

The main reason that serial ports are inherently slow is that they spit out data only one bit at a time. For faster data transfers with Direct Cable Connection, you should consider using a parallel port, which can handle 8 bits of data at a time. Again, you don't use the standard parallel (printer) cable, but a special cable designed for exchanging data between parallel ports. These are usually called *parallel LapLink cables* or *parallel InterLink cables*. (LapLink is a communications program that has been the standard for cable-based computer connections for many years. InterLink is the cable connection utility that comes with DOS 6.x.) Table 34.3 shows the wire translations that occur when you connect the parallel ports of a host and guest with one of these cables.

Table 34.3. Wire translations for a 25-pin-to-25-pin parallel cable.

Host Pin	Guest Pin
2	15
3	13
4	12
5	10
6	11
10	5
11	6
12	4
13	3
15	2
25 (Ground)	25 (Ground)

Standard parallel ports come in two varieties:

Unidirectional: This type of port is designed for one-way communication between a computer and a printer. It can be used for both output and input, but this will cost you some speed. Output uses the full 8 bits of the parallel port to transfer data, so it can reach throughput speeds of about 80 to 120K/sec. Input uses only 4 bits, so throughput is restricted to approximately 40 to 60K/sec.

Bidirectional: This type of port is designed for two-way communications between a computer and another device. Since the port can use all 8 bits for output or input, you'll usually achieve throughput speeds of 80 to 120K/sec for all data transfers. Note that bidirectional ports have been the standard for many years, so it's likely that your system will have this type of port (if not one of the advanced parallel ports discussed in the next two sections).

A standard bidirectional parallel port is six to eight times faster than even a serial port with a 16550 UART, so you should use parallel ports for Direct Cable Connection whenever possible.

Enhanced Parallel Ports and Cables

The Enhanced Parallel Port (EPP) specification was developed jointly by Intel, Zenith Data Systems, and Xircom. It's been around since 1991. Operating at high speeds compared to standard parallel ports, an EPP offers approximately 10 times the throughput (theoretically, up to 2 megabytes per second). For these ports, you use the same parallel LapLink cables I mentioned in the preceding section. Also note that both computers must have an EPP to achieve maximum throughput.

Extended Capabilities Ports and Cables

The Extended Capabilities Port (ECP) was developed by Microsoft and Hewlett-Packard in 1992. It includes the EPP specification but uses a DMA channel to ensure better multitasking. You'll need a cable that supports the ECP specification. ECP's performance is about equal to EPP's.

NOTE: USE A UCM CABLE FOR MAXIMUM THROUGHPUT

There are actually a couple of standards in existence for ECP, so you might have trouble getting the right cable or connecting two ECP-enabled machines. To prevent these problems, you should invest in a *Universal Cable Module* (UCM) cable. These cables can auto-detect the parallel port and adjust accordingly. Also, UCM cables include special hardware logic that can increase throughput. Therefore, you can achieve maximum possible data transfer speed by connecting ECPs with a UCM cable.

Parallel Technologies makes such a cable—it's called the DirectParallel Universal Cable. Here's the address of their Web site:

```
http://www.lpt.com/lpt/
```

Infrared Ports

Like serial ports, infrared ports should only be used as a last resort if no parallel port is available or if you don't have the necessary cables. The problem, again, is throughput: Current infrared

34

DIRECT CABLE
CONNECTION

port technology supports a maximum theoretical throughput of only 115,200 bps. This will change soon, however. Hewlett-Packard has demonstrated infrared devices that can achieve transfer rates of 4 Mbps (megabits per second), or about 35 times the speed of the current technology.

Configuring the Host Computer

To work with Direct Cable Connection, you must configure one computer as the *host* (this is usually the desktop machine) and the other computer as the *guest* (usually the notebook). Remember that the guest system gains access to the resources shared on the host, but not the other way around. In other words, the host computer can't work with the resources on the guest computer. Use this fact as a guide when determining which machines to use as host and guest.

You'll start this section of the chapter by learning how to configure the host machine, and then you'll move on to the guest configuration in the next section. Before performing either procedure, make sure you've connected the two machines with whatever ports and cable you've decided to use.

Step 1: Set Up Direct Cable Connection as a Host

To get started, select Start | Programs | Accessories | Direct Cable Connection. The first time you select this menu option, the Direct Cable Connection Wizard loads, and you'll see the dialog box shown in Figure 34.1. Make sure that the Host option is activated, and then click Next >.

FIGURE 34.1.

Select Host *in the initial Direct Cable Connection Wizard dialog box.*

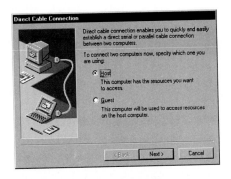

At this point, Direct Cable Connection might display the dialog box shown in Figure 34.2 to let you know that it needs to install the Microsoft Dial-Up Adapter. (You won't see this message if the Dial-Up Adapter is already installed.) When you click OK, Windows 95 shuts down the Direct Cable Connection Wizard and installs the Dial-Up Adapter. When this is complete, restart Direct Cable Connection, select Host, and click Next > to continue with the configuration.

FIGURE 34.2.

You'll see this dialog box if you don't have the Dial-Up Adapter installed.

The Direct Cable Connection Wizard checks the available ports on your system and displays a list of these ports, as shown in Figure 34.3. Highlight the port you want to use and click Next >.

FIGURE 34.3.

Use this Wizard dialog box to choose the port you want to use with Direct Cable Connection.

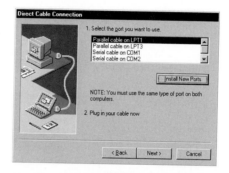

TIP: IF YOU ADD PORTS

If you add ports to your machine down the road, rerun the Direct Cable Connection Wizard. When you get to the dialog box shown in Figure 34.3, click the Install New Ports button to make the Wizard check for the new ports.

If the host computer isn't already on a network, you won't have file and print sharing set up. (File and print sharing lets you make resources such as folders, disk drives, and printers available to other computers on a network or, in this case, to the guest computer via Direct Cable Connection.) In this case, you'll see the dialog box shown in Figure 34.4.

FIGURE 34.4.

The Direct Cable Connection Wizard displays this dialog box if you haven't enabled file and print sharing on the host computer.

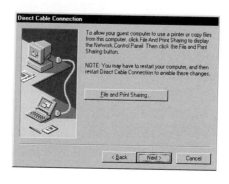

34

DIRECT CABLE
CONNECTION

Here are the steps to follow to enable file and print sharing:

1. Click the File and Print Sharing button to display the Network properties sheet, shown in Figure 34.5.

FIGURE 34.5.

Use the Network properties sheet to enable file and print sharing.

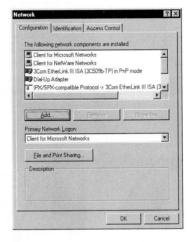

2. Click the File and Print Sharing button.
3. In the dialog box that appears, activate the two check boxes and then click OK.
4. Click OK. When Windows 95 asks if you want to restart your computer, click Yes.

When you're back in Windows 95, restart Direct Cable Connection and run through the Wizard's dialog boxes. You'll eventually see a dialog box asking if you want the guest computer to use a password to access the host, as shown in Figure 34.6. If you do, activate the Use password protection check box, click the Set Password button, enter your password (twice) in the Direct Cable Connection Password dialog box, and click OK. Click Finish to complete the host configuration. The Wizard will then wait for a connection from the guest. Click Close if you don't want to connect right away.

FIGURE 34.6.

Use this dialog box to set up a password for Direct Cable Connection.

Step 2: Share Folders, Drives, and Printers

The guest computer won't be able to do very much during a connection unless you share some resources on the host machine. If you've already shared some of the host's resources for a regular network connection, you might not need to do anything else (unless you want to give the guest machine access to different resources). Otherwise, follow the instructions for sharing resources that I outlined in Chapter 31, "Windows 95 Networking."

Configuring the Guest Computer

Configuring the guest computer is even easier than configuring the host. Again, there are two steps: configuring Direct Cable Connection for guest duty, and setting up some network properties.

Step 1: Set Up Direct Cable Connection as a Guest

You first need to move to your other computer and set it up as a Direct Cable Connection guest. Here are the steps:

1. Select Start | Programs | Accessories | Direct Cable Connection to get things off the ground.
2. In the first Direct Cable Connection Wizard dialog box, activate the Guest option and click Next >.
3. Highlight the port you want to use and click Next >.
4. Click Finish.

Step 2: Installing Network Protocols

The only other configuration chore you might have to perform on the guest computer is installing one or more network protocols, as follows:

- If you only want to share exchange data with the host computer, make sure that the two computers have at least one common protocol. If they don't use a common protocol, you won't be able to establish a connection between the two machines.

- If you want the guest computer to be able to access shared resources in the Network Neighborhood, make sure that the guest uses the common protocol used on the network.

See Chapter 31 for instructions on installing protocols.

NOTE: DON'T USE TCP/IP FOR NETWORK ACCESS

Direct Cable Connection can act as a gateway for networks running NetBEUI and IPX/SPX, but not TCP/IP.

34

DIRECT CABLE CONNECTION

Establishing the Connection

With Direct Cable Connection configured on the host and guest computers, and a cable running between their ports, you can now establish a connection between the two machines.

On the host computer, select Start | Programs | Accessories | Direct Cable Connection. You'll see the dialog box shown in Figure 34.7. When you click the Listen button, Direct Cable Connection initializes the port and then displays the dialog box shown in Figure 34.8.

FIGURE 34.7.

Click Listen to start the Direct Cable Connection host.

FIGURE 34.8.

Once Direct Cable Connection is started, the host computer waits for a connectin from the guest.

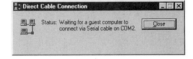

NOTE: CHANGING YOUR DIRECT CABLE CONNECTION SETUP

If you need to make changes to your Direct Cable Connection configuration—for example, to switch host and guest, to use a different port, or to add new ports—click the Change button and run through the Direct Cable Connection Wizard's dialog boxes again.

On the guest computer, you also select Start | Programs | Accessories | Direct Cable Connection. The dialog box that appears is similar to the one shown in Figure 34.7, except that you need to click the Connect button.

Now the two machines exchange pleasantries along the cable. Before the connection is established, you might be asked to enter more information:

■ If you're connecting to a larger network, you might be asked to enter a user name and password for verification from a server.

■ If the host computer is protected by a Direct Cable Connection password, you'll have to enter that password.

TROUBLESHOOTING: DCC AND DIAL-UP NETWORKING

When you try to connect to the host machine, you might receive the following error message:

```
Cannot connect to host computer. Make sure you have run Direct
Cable Connection on the host computer and you have connected
your cable to both computers.
```

Besides checking that the host is configured correctly and that the cables are connected securely, make sure that you don't have a Dial-Up Networking session running on a different port. Both Direct Cable Connection and Dial-Up Networking use the same network interface driver (PPPMAC.VXD), and only one instance of the driver can be loaded at a time. You won't be able to establish your connection to the host until you close the Dial-Up Networking session. (I discuss Dial-Up Networking in the next chapter.)

When the two machines finally see eye-to-eye, Direct Cable Connection opens a folder window on the guest computer that shows all the shared resources on the host, as shown in Figure 34.9. If the host is attached to a larger network, the guest computer can use this window (or the Network Neighborhood) to browse and work with the network's shared resources. As I've said, however, neither the host machine nor the other network computers can see the guest.

FIGURE 34.9.

When the Direct Cable Connection session is established, the guest computer sees a folder containing the host's shared resources.

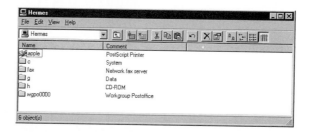

34

DIRECT CABLE CONNECTION

TROUBLESHOOTING: IF DCC FAILS

Direct Cable Connection might fail to establish a connection to the host. You won't receive any error messages, but the guest computer's Direct Cable Connection status window will tell you it was "Disconnected." The likely problem here is that the guest computer is also trying to log on to a network, but it has only the NetBEUI protocol installed. This confuses the NetBIOS, which in turn confuses the NetBEUI protocol, so the network logon fails. The solution is to install the IPX/SPX protocol as well.

Direct Cable Connection and Infrared Ports

If your host and guest computers have infrared ports, you can use these ports to establish a connection without having to bother with cables. When configuring the connection, note the following:

- When the Direct Cable Connection Wizard asks you to specify a port for the connection, select the virtual serial port used by your infrared adapter. Note that infrared ports aren't identified explicitly, but only by the virtual ports they use (such as COM 4, for example).

- Make sure you position the host and guest ports so that they're facing each other directly and are no closer together than six inches and no farther apart than three to nine feet.

- Since the infrared serial port isn't initialized at startup, you need to enable it before starting Direct Cable Connection. To do this, display Control Panel and open the Infrared icon to display the Infrared Monitor.

Once your connection is established, the Infrared Monitor will keep track of the connection by telling you the name of the computer that the guest is connected to and the current communication efficiency, as shown in Figure 34.10.

FIGURE 34.10.

During an infrared connection, the Infrared Monitor keeps tabs on the link's status.

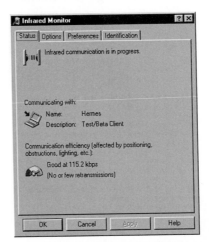

Direct Cable Connection and the Briefcase

I showed you how to use Windows 95's Briefcase feature in Chapter 20, "Windows 95 on the Road: Notebook Computers and the Briefcase." You saw how Briefcase took most of the guesswork out of synchronizing files between a desktop and notebook computer. However, you still had to face the drudgery of moving the Briefcase between machines via floppy disk.

To avoid this "sneakernet" situation, you can use Direct Cable Connection to transfer the Briefcase folder back and forth between the machines. Here's a rundown of the basic Briefcase procedure from a Direct Cable Connection point of view:

1. Once you've finished working with the files on the host machine, copy them to a Briefcase folder. Make sure that this folder is either shared directly or resides in a shared folder.

2. On the guest computer, access the shared folder and move the Briefcase folder to a location on the guest computer's hard drive (such as the desktop).

3. Use the guest computer to work on the files. You don't need to have the connection established at this point.

4. When you're done, reestablish the connection, if necessary, and then move the Briefcase folder back to the host.

5. On the host machine, open the Briefcase folder and select Briefcase | Update All. This updates the hard disk files with the changed files in the Briefcase.

Summary

This chapter showed you how to use Direct Cable Connection to set up a mini-network between two computers. The basic idea behind Direct Cable Connection is that by stringing a special cable between, say, a desktop and a notebook computer, you can share files, folders, disk drives, and printers between them. To that end, you learned about the various serial and parallel ports you can use with Direct Cable Connection, as well as the associated cables that are designed for these ports. I then showed you how to configure the host computer and the guest computer and establish a connection. I closed with a quick look at using Direct Cable Connection with infrared ports and Briefcase.

For related information, take a look at the following chapters:

- I showed you how to work with the Briefcase in Chapter 20, "Windows 95 on the Road: Notebook Computers and the Briefcase."

- Chapter 20 is also the place to go to learn how to install Microsoft's infrared driver.

- All the network basics you need for setting up Direct Cable Connection—including information on resource sharing and installing protocols—can be found in Chapter 31, "Windows 95 Networking."

- For remote connections between a notebook and a desktop, you'll need to use Dial-Up Networking. I'll show you how this works in Chapter 35, "Remote Computing with Dial-Up Networking."

34

DIRECT CABLE CONNECTION

Remote Computing with Dial-Up Networking

CHAPTER 35

IN THIS CHAPTER

Far folks fare well.

English proverb

The networking techniques you've seen so far have assumed some kind of physical connection between machines. For standard peer-to-peer and client/server networks, the computers use a network card/cable package to connect to each other either directly or indirectly via a hub or router. For a Direct Cable Connection mini-network, two computers are joined at the hip via a null-modem or LapLink-style cable attached to their serial or parallel ports (or possibly via an infrared hookup).

What do you do, however, when a physical connection just isn't possible? For example, suppose that you're on the road with your notebook computer and need to access a file on your network server. Or suppose that you're working at home and need to send a file to your office machine. Is there any way to access a network in the absence of a physical connection? The answer is that for these remote predicaments, you *can* connect to a network and use its resources just like you can with a physical connection (albeit more slowly). The solution is Windows 95's Dial-Up Networking client. With Dial-Up Networking, you can establish a connection and log on to a network over phone lines by using your modem. This chapter shows you how to configure and use Dial-Up Networking, how to use Microsoft Mail with a remote connection, how to create scripts for automatic logons, how to set up your Windows 95 machine to be a Dial-Up Networking server, and more. (Note that you also use Dial-Up Networking to establish a dial-up connection to an Internet Service Provider. I'll show you how this works in Chapter 37, "Windows 95 and the Internet.")

Dial-Up Networking Fundamentals

In Chapter 25, "Maximizing Modem Communications," I showed how your computer can exchange data with remote machines by attaching a modem to the serial port and by running a phone line to the modem. In Chapter 30, "A Networking Primer," I showed you how your computer can exchange data with machines on a network by inserting a network interface card (NIC) inside the computer and by running a network cable to the card.

Dial-Up Networking is an amalgam of these two technologies. It gives you access to a network, but a modem and phone line replace the NIC and cable. Your network access is identical to that of a machine attached directly to the network: You log on with your user name and password, you can browse and use shared resources, you can share your local resources, you can access the Internet if your network has the appropriate connection, you can retrieve mail, and so on. The main difference is that, because you're using a serial port and modem as the network connection point, data transfers are much slower.

Before examining the nuts and bolts of Dial-Up Networking connectivity, let's begin with a few fundamentals. This information will help you determine the best way to configure your remote access.

For starters, you should know that three methods are available for establishing a remote dial-up session:

- You can create a Dial-Up Networking connection and then initiate that connection manually.

- You can attempt to access a network resource that is normally available via a network card. If that card isn't present (say, if you're using an undocked notebook on the road), Windows 95 prompts you to make a dial-up connection.

- An application can use Dial-Up Networking to establish a remote session. Applications can use the Dial-Up Networking Session API to connect to a session with or without user intervention. For example, Microsoft Exchange uses these API functions to allow you to establish a remote Microsoft Mail session. (See "Configuring Microsoft Mail for Remote Sessions" later in this chapter.)

Dial-Up Networking Client Architecture

The architecture of the Dial-Up Networking client is similar to that of a regular networking client, such as the Client for Microsoft Networks or the Client for NetWare Networks. In both cases, the client packages network data into a form suitable for whatever network protocol is being used. The client then passes the data to the network adapter for transmission out to the network. In Dial-Up Networking, this process has three major architectural differences from regular networking:

Dial-Up Adapter: Instead of a physical network adapter card residing in a bus slot or PC Card slot, Dial-Up Networking uses Microsoft's *Dial-Up Adapter,* which you can think of as a "virtual" NIC. Or, more accurately, the Dial-Up Adapter turns your computer's serial port into a NIC. The driver (PPPMAC.VXD) is an NDIS 3.1 network driver to which you can bind whatever network protocols you need to use. I'll show you how to install and configure the Dial-Up Adapter later in this chapter.

Dial-Up Protocol: After the client has packaged its network requests appropriately for the underlying network protocol (which, for Dial-Up Networking, can be NetBEUI, IPX/SPX, or TCP/IP), the packets must be further modified for transmission through a serial port and along phone lines. The protocols that handle this conversion are called *dial-up protocols* (or sometimes *line protocols* or *connection protocols*).

Dial-Up Server: Instead of logging on to a network directly, Dial-Up Networking must first connect to a *dial-up server,* which then processes the network logon.

The next two sections look at dial-up protocols and dial-up servers in more detail.

Dial-Up Protocols

To ensure the safe and reliable transmission of data over phone lines between a dial-up server and a remote computer, both machines must use the same dial-up protocol. The protocol you use depends, in part, on the dial-up server. For example, you would use a different protocol to connect to a NetWare server than you would to connect to an Internet service provider. The Dial-Up Networking Client supports these dial-up protocols:

- Point-to-Point Protocol
- Remote Access Service
- NetWare Connect
- Serial Line Interface Protocol

The Point-to-Point Protocol

The Point-to-Point Protocol (PPP) is the standard dial-up protocol used by Windows 95's Dial-Up Networking, and it's rapidly becoming (if it isn't already) the standard for all types of remote access connections. For example, most Internet service providers offer PPP access to the Internet. Part of the PPP appeal is its flexibility: It defines a standard encapsulation protocol that lets different network protocols be transmitted across serial connections. As a result, PPP supports the three Windows 95 network protocols: NetBEUI, IPX/SPX, and TCP/IP. PPP also implements a few other useful features, such as link-quality testing, header compression, and error checking.

The Remote Access Service Protocol

The Remote Access Service (RAS) protocol is a variant of NetBEUI called *asynchronous NetBEUI* that is designed to work over slower serial links. It's used by various Microsoft operating systems, including Windows NT and LAN Manager. To use RAS, both the client and the server must be running the NetBEUI network protocol. (RAS doesn't support multiple network protocols the way PPP does.)

The NetWare Connect Protocol

NetWare servers use a proprietary dial-up protocol that's part of a product called NetWare Connect. This product adds the following features to the NetWare server:

- A proprietary Remote Access Service dial-up protocol
- Modem sharing and pooling
- Remote workstation control

NetWare Connect dial-up servers don't support software compression and can work with only the IPX/SPX network protocol.

NOTE: DIAL-UP NETWORKING USES ONLY NETWARE CONNECT RAS

The Dial-Up Networking client uses only NetWare Connect's Remote Access Services. To gain access to the other NetWare Connect features, you must use Novell's NetWare Connect client software.

The Serial Line Interface Protocol

The Serial Line Interface Protocol (SLIP) is a simple protocol designed to work with the TCP/IP network protocol. Until PPP came along, SLIP was the standard Internet dial-up protocol for many years. The popularity of SLIP has waned for a number of reasons, but these are the main ones:

SLIP doesn't implement error correction: Unlike PPP, SLIP performs no error checking. This keeps the packet overhead required by SLIP to a minimum (PPP, for example, includes extra packet data to handle the error checking), but it makes SLIP connections susceptible to errors on noisy phone lines. This disadvantage is mitigated somewhat by using a modem with a built-in error correction protocol.

SLIP can handle only one protocol at a time: The SLIP header doesn't include a field for specifying the network protocol, so you can't change protocol horses midstream. Whatever protocol you specify at the beginning of the connection is the one you must use throughout the session.

SLIP can't handle dynamic addressing: Under a SLIP connection, the server and client can't exchange address data, so the machines must determine each other's IP addresses in advance. This prevents you from using a feature like Dynamic Host Configuration Protocol (DHCP) with Dial-Up Networking. (I explain IP addresses and DHCP in Chapter 36, "Implementing TCP/IP for Internet and Network Connections.")

SLIP doesn't support compression: The basic SLIP protocol doesn't support compression of the entire data packet. However, a different SLIP specification—called *Compressed SLIP,* or *CSLIP*—enables compression of just the IP header portion of a TCP/IP data packet.

Because of these drawbacks, you should use SLIP only for those TCP/IP dial-ups that don't support PPP.

NOTE: INSTALLING SLIP

Before you can use SLIP, however, you need to install it from the Windows 95 CD-ROM. I'll run through the necessary steps later in this chapter when I discuss the scripting tool. See "Using the Dial-Up Scripting Tool."

35

DIAL-UP
NETWORKING

NOTE: DIAL-UP NETWORKING NEGOTIATES THE PROTOCOL

For the most part, you don't have to worry too much about the dial-up protocol because Dial-Up Networking usually negotiates behind the scenes with the server to determine the correct protocol. PPP is the default dial-up protocol, and if the server can't handle PPP, Dial-Up Networking tries to use RAS.

Note, however, that Dial-Up Networking will *not* attempt to negotiate the NetWare Connect, SLIP, and CSLIP protocols. If your dial-up server requires one of these protocols, you must configure it manually (as explained later in this chapter).

Dial-Up Servers

With Dial-Up Networking, you can't just dial into any old machine willy-nilly and expect to get a connection. Rather, the remote computer must be configured as a *dial-up server,* which means that it can accept incoming calls, validate network logons, provide access to the network, and handle the intricacies of network and dial-up protocols. Clearly, not every computer—or even every network server, for that matter—has what it takes to be a dial-up server. Here's a rundown of the various dial-up servers that are supported by Windows 95 Dial-Up Networking:

Windows NT 3.5x RAS server: Windows NT 3.5x (both the Server and the Workstation) can act as dial-up servers by running the *Remote Access Service* (RAS). RAS lets the server run NetBEUI (and, through a process called *tunneling,* IPX/SPX and TCP/IP as well) over phone lines. The available dial-up protocols are PPP and, of course, RAS. Windows NT 3.5x Workstation allows only a single RAS connection at a time, but Windows NT 3.5x Server allows up to 256 simultaneous connections.

Windows NT 3.1 and Windows for Workgroups 3.11 RAS server: Both Windows NT 3.1 and Windows for Workgroups 3.11 can use RAS to act as dial-up servers using the RAS dial-up protocol. Note that because these servers run NetBEUI only, they aren't suitable for Internet connections (which require TCP/IP). You're limited to a single connection, unless you're using NT Advanced Server, which can support up to 64 simultaneous connections.

NetWare server: You can connect to a NetWare server either directly, if the server is running NetWare Connect, or indirectly via a Windows NT 3.5x RAS server that uses IPX/SPX to route to the NetWare server.

Shiva NetModem or LANRover server modem: These are modems designed to act as RAS servers and route IPS/SPX, TCP/IP, and AppleTalk.

UNIX server: You can use Dial-Up Networking to connect to UNIX servers to establish a TCP/IP session using the PPP, SLIP, and CSLIP dial-up protocols. Dial-Up Networking is most often used in this fashion to connect to an Internet service provider. I discuss setting up an Internet connection from a Windows 95 client in greater depth in Chapter 37.

Windows 95 Dial-Up Networking server: If you have Microsoft Plus!, you can set up a Windows 95 machine to act as a dial-up server. As with Windows NT 3.5x RAS, you can establish a connection using PPP or RAS and then route NetBEUI, TCP/IP, and IPX/SPX over the connection. The Windows 95 Dial-Up Networking server supports only one connection at a time.

Setting Up Windows 95 for Dial-Up Networking

Assuming that you've installed the Dial-Up Networking component on your computer, configuring Windows 95 so that it can connect to a dial-up server involves four steps:

1. Install the Dial-Up Adapter, if necessary.
2. Configure the Dial-Up Adapter.
3. Create a new Dial-Up Networking connectoid for the server.
4. Configure the connection.

The next four sections take you through each step.

Step 1: Install the Dial-Up Adapter

Windows 95 installs the Dial-Up Adapter automatically when you install Dial-Up Networking. To check that the Dial-Up Adapter is installed, open the Network properties sheet (right-click the Network Neighborhood icon and select Properties, or open the Control Panel's Network icon). Check the list of installed network components, and see whether Dial-Up Adapter is among them. If, for some reason, the Dial-Up Adapter isn't installed (say, because you or someone else removed it), here are the steps to follow to install it:

1. In the Network properties sheet, click Add.
2. In the Select Network Component Type dialog box, highlight Adapter and click Add.
3. In the Select Network Adapter dialog box, highlight Microsoft in the Manufacturers list. You should see Dial-Up Adapter highlighted in the Network Adapters list.
4. Click OK to return to the Network properties sheet.

Step 2: Configure the Dial-Up Adapter

After the Dial-Up Adapter is installed, you need to configure it for use with the dial-up server (or servers) you plan to use. You need to perform three tasks:

■ Install the network protocols you plan on using during your dial-up sessions. I showed you how to install protocols in Chapter 31, "Windows 95 Networking."

35

DIAL-UP NETWORKING

- Set various properties of the Dial-Up Adapter.
- Configure the protocols you've bound to the Dial-Up Adapter.

Setting Dial-Up Adapter Properties

To change the Dial-Up Adapter's properties, highlight `Dial-Up Adapter` in the list of network components, and then click Properties. In the Dial-Up Adapter properties sheet that appears, select the Bindings tab, shown in Figure 35.1. (You can ignore the Driver Type tab because Windows 95 offers only a 32-bit driver for the Dial-Up Adapter.) The Bindings tab determines which network protocols the Dial-Up Adapter can use. Activate the check box beside each protocol that is required by the dial-up server.

FIGURE 35.1.

Use the Bindings tab to specify the network protocols to use with the Dial-Up Adapter.

In the Advanced tab, shown in Figure 35.2, the `Property` list has two entries:

Record a log file: If you select `Yes` in the `Value` list, Dial-Up Networking creates a text file named `PPPLOG.TXT` in your main Windows 95 folder and uses this file to maintain a record of each PPP session. Because maintaining the log degrades performance slightly, select `Yes` only if you're having trouble with your connection.

Use IPX header compression: You need to select `Yes` for this property only if you're connecting to a server that supports CSLIP.

After you've finished setting properties, click OK to return to the Network properties sheet.

FIGURE 35.2.

The Advanced tab controls a couple of advanced Dial-Up Adapter properties.

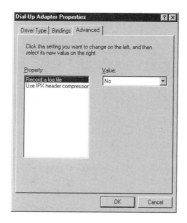

Setting Properties for Bound Protocols

Your final chore for configuring the Dial-Up Adapter is to modify, as needed, the properties for each protocol bound to the Dial-Up Adapter. How you do this depends on the network adapters you have installed:

■ If the Dial-Up Adapter is the only adapter installed, highlight a protocol and click the Properties button.

■ If you have multiple adapters installed, the Network dialog box indicates binding by using an arrow (->). For example, Figure 35.3 shows the Network dialog box with two adapters installed. Notice how the NetBEUI protocol indicates binding by using an arrow to point to each adapter. In this case, highlight a protocol bound to the Dial-Up Adapter, and then click Properties.

FIGURE 35.3.

If you have multiple adapters, arrows indicate the protocol/adapter bindings.

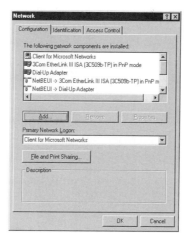

The properties you modify depend on the protocol. See Chapter 31 for more information.

NOTE: SETTING TCP/IP PROPERTIES

If you'll be setting up a Dial-Up Networking connection to either an Internet service provider or a TCP/IP network, you must specify some properties for the TCP/IP protocol that's bound to the Dial-Up Adapter. I'll give you the goods on these settings in Chapter 36.

When you're done, click OK, and when Windows 95 asks whether you want to restart your computer, click Yes.

NOTE: MORE NETWORK CONFIGURATION

If you'll be logging on to a Microsoft network or a NetWare network, and you've already set up a network connection using a regular network adapter, you'll be able to log on remotely without any trouble. That's because the Dial-Up Adapter will use your existing network settings (logon, computer identification, access control, and so on).

If, however, you've never established a regular network connection, you'll need to set up Windows 95 for networking. See Chapter 31 for all the gory details.

Step 3: Create a New Connection

You're now ready to start specifying the particulars of your Dial-Up Networking sessions. These are stored in the Dial-Up Networking folder as icons called *connections* (or sometimes *connectoids*). Each connection contains, among other things, the phone number to dial, the modem to use, and the dial-up server type.

To get started, select Start | Programs | Accessories | Dial-Up Networking. If this is your first connection, the Make New Connection Wizard appears. Otherwise, you get the Dial-Up Networking folder, shown in Figure 35.4. In this case, use either of the following techniques to launch the Wizard:

- Double-click the Make New Connection icon.
- Select Connections | Make New Connection.

In the initial Wizard dialog box, click Next > to continue. If you haven't yet installed a modem on your system, the Install New Modem Wizard steps in to take you through the procedure. I explained in Chapter 25 how this Wizard operates, so you might want to head back there for a description.

FIGURE 35.4.

After you've created your first connection, this folder window appears when you start Dial-Up Networking.

You'll eventually see the Make New Connection Wizard dialog box, shown in Figure 35.5. Enter a name for the connection, and choose the modem you want to use. If you want to adjust any modem settings, click the Configure button. When you're ready to move on, click Next >.

FIGURE 35.5.

Use this Wizard dialog box to name your connection and select a modem.

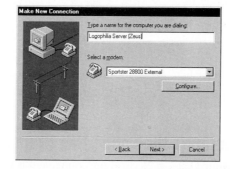

NOTE: ENTERING A USER NAME AND PASSWORD

Some Internet service providers (including The Microsoft Network) require you to enter your user name and password during logon. You might also have to run a command or select a menu item to choose between PPP and SLIP. To let you enter this kind of information, Dial-Up Networking can display a terminal window after the connection has been established. To set this up, click Configure in the dialog box shown in Figure 35.5. In the Modem properties sheet, select the Options tab, activate the `Bring up terminal window after dialing` check box, and click OK.

The Make New Connection Wizard then displays the dialog box shown in Figure 35.6. Enter the `Area code`, `Telephone number`, and `Country code` for the dial-up server, and then click Next >. In the final Wizard dialog box that appears, click Finish. (If you bypassed installing the Dial-Up Adapter earlier, Dial-Up Networking prompts you to do so now. Click OK to install the adapter.)

FIGURE 35.6.

Use this Wizard dialog box to enter the phone number of the dial-up server.

NOTE: TEN-DIGIT DIALING

In Chapter 25, I showed you how to use dialing rules to make Phone Dialer and Hyper-Terminal dial a 10-digit phone number. You can follow the same procedure for Dial-Up Networking. An easier way to do this, however, is to simply enter all 10 digits in the `Telephone` number field. (You should also enter your local area code in the `Area code` field so that Dial-Up Networking doesn't try to dial the number as long distance.)

Step 4: Configure the Connection Properties

OSR2

At this point, your Dial-Up Networking connection is set up with only the default properties (such as using the PPP dial-up protocol). To change these properties, highlight the connection's icon in the `Dial-Up Networking` folder, and then either select File | Properties or right-click the icon and select Properties from the context menu. You'll then see either the dialog box shown in Figure 35.7 or, if you're running OSR2, the dialog box shown in Figure 35.8.

FIGURE 35.7.

The properties sheet for a Dial-Up Networking connection.

FIGURE 35.8.

If you have OSR2 installed, you'll see a slightly revised version of the connection properties sheet.

NOTE: UPDATING DIAL-UP NETWORKING WITHOUT OSR2

The OSR2 Dial-Up Networking enhancements are also available to non-OSR2 users via Microsoft's ISDN Accelerator Pack 1.1. To download this software from the Web, check out the following page:

```
http://www.microsoft.com/windows/software/isdn.htm
```

Most of the properties you see are straightforward. To change how Dial-Up Networking works with the server, either click the Server Type button or, in OSR2, activate the Server Types tab to display the dialog box shown in Figure 35.9. Here's a rundown of the controls in this dialog box:

Type of Dial-Up Server: Use this drop-down list to specify the dial-up protocol you want to use with this dial-up server.

Log on to network: When this check box is activated, Dial-Up Networking attempts to log on to the dial-up server with the user name and password you use to log on to Windows 95.

Enable software compression: When this check box is activated, data transfers that are made between your computer and the server are compressed to save time. (Note, however, that if you'll be transferring mostly files that are already compressed, activating this option degrades the performance of the connection. That's because compressing already-compressed files actually *increases* the file size.)

Require encrypted password: When this check box is activated, Dial-Up Networking uses encryption to send your password to the server. This is a useful security precaution that you should enable as long as the server supports it.

Allowed network protocols: These check boxes let you define which network protocols to use with this connection. Note too that for TCP/IP connections, you can click the TCP/IP Settings button to define connection-specific TCP/IP properties (see Chapter 36 for details).

FIGURE 35.9.

Use the Server Types dialog box to configure how Dial-Up Networking works with the dial-up server.

Connecting to the Remote Network

You're now ready to connect to the dial-up server. Dial-Up Networking gives you various ways to proceed:

- Double-click the connection icon in the Dial-Up Networking folder.
- Highlight the icon and select either File | Connect or Connections | Connect.
- Right-click the icon and select Connect from the context menu.

NOTE: STARTING A CONNECTION FROM THE COMMAND LINE

You can start a Dial-Up Networking connection from the Run dialog box, the DOS command prompt, or a batch file by using the following command syntax:

```
rundll rnaui.dll,RnaDial connection
```

Here, *connection* is the name of the connection you want to run. For example, to start a connection named LAN Server, you would enter the following command:

```
rundll rnaui.dll,RnaDial LAN Server
```

Note that the RnaDial and *connection* parameters are case-sensitive.

Dial-Up Networking displays the Connect To dialog box, shown in Figure 35.10. Enter the User name and Password that are required for logging on to the dial-up server. If you want Windows 95 to save your password and display it automatically each time you start this connection, activate the Save password check box. You can also adjust the Phone number, if necessary, and specify a different dialing location or dialing properties (see Chapter 25 for details). When you're ready to make the connection, click the Connect button.

FIGURE 35.10.

Use this dialog box to specify any last-minute settings before making the connection.

Dial-Up Networking dials the modem and then negotiates your logon with the dial-up server. (Depending on the modem settings you're using, you might see a terminal window appear so that you can enter more information.) When you're safely connected, a dialog box appears to let you know and to track the duration of your session. Clicking the Details button in this dialog box shows you the server type and protocols being used, as shown in Figure 35.11. (In OSR2, the dialog box that appears is called Connection Established. In this case, you click the More Information button to get the server type and protocol data.)

OSR2

FIGURE 35.11.

Dial-Up Networking keeps track of the duration of the call.

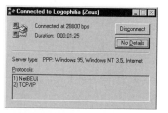

TIP: RETRYING THE CONNECTION

If the server is busy or down, your connection won't go through. Instead of retrying the connection manually, you can tell Dial-Up Networking to retry at regular intervals. To set this up, open the Dial-Up Networking folder, and select Connections | Settings. In the dialog box that appears, activate the Redial check box. Use the Before giving up retry spinner to specify the maximum number of redial attempts, and use the Between tries wait spinners to specify the number of minutes and seconds to pause between each retry.

35

DIAL-UP
NETWORKING

TROUBLESHOOTING: PROTOCOL PROBLEMS

When you attempt to connect to the dial-up server, a dialog box might appear with the following message:

```
Dial-Up Networking could not negotiate a compatible set of network protocols
you specified in the Server Type settings. Check your network configuration
in the Control Panel then try the connection again.
```

Check your network protocols to make sure that you have at least one protocol bound to the Dial-Up Adapter that matches a protocol used by the dial-up server. Also, make sure that the dial-up protocol you're using is supported by the server.

After you're connected, your computer becomes a full peer on the network. You can then access network resources and browse the Network Neighborhood, and others on the network can see your computer as well.

After you've finished your online work, click the Disconnect button to shut down the connection.

Dial-Up Networking Prompts

Another way to connect to the remote system via Dial-Up Networking is to have Windows 95 prompt you. For example, if you map a network drive during a Dial-Up Networking session and later attempt to access that drive while you're disconnected, Windows 95 displays the dialog box shown in Figure 35.12. Click Yes; then use the Dial-Up Networking dialog box that appears to select the Dial-Up Networking connection you want to use, and click OK.

FIGURE 35.12.

If you try to access a network resource when you're not connected, Windows 95 asks whether you want to connect via Dial-Up Networking.

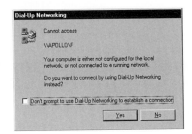

To make sure that Windows 95 prompts you to use Dial-Up Networking, you need to take the following actions:

■ In the Dial-Up Networking folder, select Connections | Settings to display the dialog box shown in Figure 35.13. Make sure that the Prompt to use Dial-Up Networking option is activated.

FIGURE 35.13.

Use this dialog box to determine whether Windows 95 prompts you to establish network connections via Dial-Up Networking.

- If you have a notebook computer that uses a regular NIC (say, a PC Card adapter or an adapter in a docking station) for a direct network connection, create a second hardware profile that doesn't use this NIC. Then, when you're on the road, boot Windows 95 with this new profile. If the NIC is part of a hardware profile—even if it's not attached to the computer—Windows 95 assumes that you want to use the NIC to establish your network connections. In this case, when you try to access a network resource, Windows 95 displays an error message instead of prompting you to use Dial-Up Networking. (See Chapter 10, "How Windows 95 Handles Hardware," to learn how to create hardware profiles.)

TROUBLESHOOTING: NO PROMPTING FOR DIAL-UP NETWORKING

After performing these steps, instead of prompting you to connect with Dial-Up Networking, Windows 95 might display an error when you attempt to access a network resource while disconnected. The problem might be that the regular NIC is still present in the list of installed components in the Network properties sheet. Try unbinding the network protocols from the NIC.

If you're running OSR2, you'll see the revised version of the Dial-Up Networking properties **OSR2** sheet, shown in Figure 35.14. This dialog box sports three new check boxes:

Show an icon on taskbar after connected: If you deactivate this check box, Dial-Up Networking doesn't display its icon in the system tray.

Prompt for information before dialing: If you deactivate this check box, Dial-Up Networking won't display the Connect To dialog box, shown earlier in Figure 35.10. If you never need to change the connection settings, deactivating this check box will give you one less dialog box to negotiate when connecting.

35

DIAL-UP NETWORKING

Show a confirmation dialog after connected: Deactivating this check box means that Dial-Up Networking won't show the "Connected to" dialog box (or the Connection Established dialog box in OSR2) after a connection to the remote server has been established.

FIGURE 35.14.

The Dial-Up Net-
working properties sheet
that comes with OSR2.

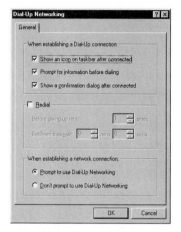

Configuring Microsoft Mail for Remote Sessions

In Chapter 27, "Setting Up Microsoft Exchange," I showed you how to configure Microsoft Mail to send and retrieve messages over a local area network. For those times when you want to perform e-mail chores while you're on the road, you can set up Microsoft Mail to use a re-mote Dial-Up Networking connection. This section shows you how it's done.

Creating a Remote Microsoft Mail Profile

Before proceeding, you should create a new Exchange profile for your remote Microsoft Mail sessions:

1. Follow the steps outlined in Chapter 27 for creating a new profile.
2. Log on to Exchange using your original profile. If you see the dialog box shown in Figure 35.15, activate the Offline option and click OK.

FIGURE 35.15.

Exchange displays this
dialog box if you start it
without your regular
LAN connection being
present.

3. Select Tools | Services to display the Services dialog box.

4. Highlight `Microsoft Mail` and click Copy.

5. In the Copy Information Service dialog box, highlight your remote Microsoft Mail profile and click OK.

6. Click OK to return to Exchange.

7. Select File | Exit and Log Off.

Setting Up Microsoft Mail's Remote Properties

With your new profile in place, restart Exchange and select the remote Microsoft Mail profile. You now need to configure a few properties for your remote connection.

The first step is to tell Exchange that this profile uses a Dial-Up Networking connection to retrieve mail. To do this, select Tools | Services to display the Services dialog box, highlight `Microsoft Mail`, and click Properties. Exchange displays the Microsoft Mail properties sheet. In the Connection tab, activate the `Remote using a modem and Dial-Up Networking` option, as shown in Figure 35.16.

FIGURE 35.16.

Use the Connection tab to specify that you want to use a Dial-Up Networking connection in this profile.

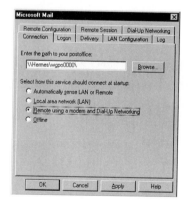

Next, select the Dial-Up Networking tab, shown in Figure 35.17. Here's a rundown of the available properties on this tab:

Use the following `Dial-Up Networking` connection: Use this drop-down list to choose the Dial-Up Networking connection you want to use for your remote Microsoft Mail sessions. Also note that you can use the Add Entry button to create a new Dial-Up Networking connection, and the Edit Entry button to make changes to a connection.

When `Dial-Up Networking` fails to connect: These text boxes tell Exchange what to do if the Dial-Up Networking connection fails. Enter the number of times to retry and the interval, in seconds, between retries.

Confirm the Dial-Up Networking connection before starting a session: These options determine whether Exchange prompts you to initiate the Dial-Up Networking connection. If you select `Never confirm`, Exchange establishes the connection automatically without prompting you for confirmation. If you select `Confirm on first session` and `after errors`, Exchange asks you to confirm that you want to establish the connection only for the initial session and each time an error occurs. If you select `Always confirm`, Exchange always prompts you to confirm the connections.

FIGURE 35.17.

Use the Dial-Up Networking tab to define how Microsoft Mail works with Dial-Up Networking.

NOTE: CONFIRMING THE CONNECTION GIVES YOU LOTS OF OPTIONS

As you'll see later, when Exchange asks you to confirm the connection, the dialog box that appears gives you lots of options for the remote session. These options are check boxes that determine whether Exchange sends mail, receives mail, updates your Microsoft Mail address list, and more. So even though it might seem like a hassle to always be asked to confirm the connection, there are advantages to doing so.

Next on the agenda is the Remote Session tab, shown in Figure 35.18. These check boxes determine when Exchange starts and ends the Dial-Up Networking session:

When this service is started: If you activate this check box, the Dial-Up Networking session is initiated as soon as you start Exchange.

After retrieving mail headers: If you're using Remote Mail, activating this check box tells Exchange to end the Dial-Up Networking session as soon as Remote Mail has retrieved the waiting message headers.

After sending and receiving mail: When this check box is activated, Exchange shuts down the Dial-Up Networking session as soon as it delivers (sends and receives) mail.

When you exit: When this check box is activated, your Dial-Up Networking session is closed when you exit Exchange.

Schedule Mail Delivery: Use this button to schedule your remote Microsoft Mail sessions at regular intervals. In the Remote Scheduled Sessions dialog box that appears, click Add to display the Add Scheduled Sessions dialog box, shown in Figure 35.19. In the Use drop-down list, select your Dial-Up Networking connection. In the When drop-down list, select Every, Weekly on, or Once at. In the hours : minutes spinner, enter a time. Click OK until you're back in the Microsoft Mail properties sheet.

FIGURE 35.18.

Use the Remote Session tab to specify events that start and end your remote Microsoft Mail sessions.

FIGURE 35.19.

The Add dialog box lets you schedule a remote session at regular intervals.

Finally, the Remote Configuration tab, shown in Figure 35.20, sets a few more options for your Microsoft Mail Dial-Up Networking session:

Use Remote Mail: Activate this check box to use Remote Mail during your Dial-Up Networking sessions.

Use local copy: If you activate this check box, Exchange creates a copy of the postoffice address list, stores the copy on your computer, and then uses this list when you're composing messages.

Use external delivery agent: If you activate this check box, Exchange delivers your messages using the EXTERNAL.EXE program, which can speed up delivery times on a slow link (see Chapter 27 for more information about this program).

35

DIAL-UP NETWORKING

FIGURE 35.20.

The Remote Configuration tab sets a few properties that control the behavior of Microsoft Mail during a connection to the remote server.

Using Microsoft Mail Remotely

As you saw in the preceding section, Microsoft Mail's Dial-Up Networking session properties give you no shortage of methods for retrieving and sending mail remotely. If you specified that Exchange should prompt you before establishing each connection, you'll see the Connect to Server dialog box, shown in Figure 35.21, whenever Exchange initiates the remote session. From here, you can select a different Dial-Up Networking connection and choose which actions you want Exchange to perform during the session.

FIGURE 35.21.

You'll see this dialog box if Exchange is set up to prompt you before establishing a remote Microsoft Mail session.

Using the Dial-Up Scripting Tool

For some dial-up servers, your logon to the remote network happens automatically. For example, if you connect to a Windows NT server on a Microsoft network, Dial-Up Networking logs you on with the user name and password you enter into the Connect To dialog box. However, plenty of Dial-Up Networking connections—especially online services and Internet service providers—require further input. In this case, you'll usually set up the connection to display a terminal window after the connection is made. In Figure 35.22, for example, you see a connection that requires entering a user name, a password, and a choice from a menu.

FIGURE 35.22.

For some Dial-Up Networking connections, you need to display a terminal window to enter logon data manually.

To avoid the hassle of constantly entering this extra data by hand, Microsoft has a Dial-Up Scripting Tool that lets you construct a *script* that enters your user name, password, and other data automatically. This section shows you how to install scripting support and create your own scripts.

Installing the Dial-Up Scripting Tool

You can get your hands on the Dial-Up Scripting Tool in the following ways:

- As part the Windows 95 Service Pack 1.
- As a standalone program from any Microsoft online site. Look for a file named SCRIPT.EXE.
- As part of the Windows 95 CD-ROM.
- Built in to Dial-Up Networking in OSR2.
- As part of the ISDN Accelerator Pack 1.1 (described in a note earlier in this chapter).

If you have the Windows 95 CD-ROM, here are the steps to follow to install scripting support (note that installing Dial-Up Scripting also installs support for the SLIP dial-up protocol):

1. In Control Panel, open the Add/Remove Programs icon, and in the dialog box that appears, select the Windows Setup tab.
2. Click the Have Disk button.
3. In the Install From Disk dialog box, enter the following path (in which *drive* is the letter of your CD-ROM drive):

   drive:\ADMIN\APPTOOLS\DSCRIPT

4. Activate the check box beside SLIP and Scripting for Dial-Up Networking, and then click Install. Windows 95 installs both the SLIP dial-up protocol and the Dial-Up Scripting tool.
5. Click OK.

35

DIAL-UP NETWORKING

Understanding Scripts

A script is a text file (using the SCP extension) that contains various commands for Dial-Up Networking to implement while making the connection. All scripts use the following structure:

```
proc main
    Enter your commands here
endproc
```

The commands you use can specify communications settings (such as the number of data bits you want Dial-Up Networking to use), control the flow of the script (such as looping through a set of commands to retry a logon), and interact with the remote system (such as waiting for a user name prompt and then sending the user name). You can use various commands, but four are the most common: `halt`, `delay`, `waitfor`, and `transmit`.

The halt Command

You use the `halt` command to shut down the script before the logon is complete. You might want to do this, for example, if the script encounters an unusual situation or if the remote server doesn't respond to the script's command. (I'll show you an example in a second.)

The delay Command

The `delay` command is useful for preventing Dial-Up Networking from continuing to log on while the remote server processes other data. Here's the syntax for the `delay` command:

```
delay seconds
```

    seconds   The number of seconds you want Dial-Up Networking to pause.

For example, to pause the logon for 3 seconds, use the following command:

```
delay 3
```

The waitfor Command

You use the `waitfor` command to tell Dial-Up Networking to wait until the remote system sends a particular prompt. For example, if the remote system prompts you to enter your user name by displaying a `User Name:` prompt, you can use the `waitfor` command to tell the script to look for the `"User Name:"` string. Here's the syntax for the `waitfor` command:

```
waitfor string [, matchcase] [then label] [until seconds]
```

string	The prompt you want the script to look for. You surround the prompt text with quotation marks (for example, `"User Name:"`).
matchcase	If you include this optional parameter, Dial-Up Networking looks for a prompt that exactly matches the case of *string*. For example, if *string* is `"User Name:"` and the system prompts with `User name:`, the command fails.

then *label*	If you include this optional parameter, when the *string* prompt is received, the script jumps to the line that begins with *label*.
until *seconds*	This optional parameter specifies the number of *seconds* that the script waits to receive the *string* prompt. If you leave out this parameter, the script waits indefinitely.

If the prompt is received, the script sets a system variable called $SUCCESS to TRUE; otherwise, $SUCCESS is set to FALSE. (Scripting supports an if...then...endif command you can use to test the value of $SUCCESS and have the script proceed accordingly.)

Here's a piece of a script that uses the waitfor command:

```
waitfor "User Name:" until 30 then Continue
halt
Continue:
waitfor "Password:"
...
```

The first waitfor command looks for the "User Name:" prompt and, when it arrives, jumps to the Continue label (the third line); then another waitfor command is executed. If the prompt doesn't come within 30 seconds, however, the halt command runs instead, to bail out of the script.

NOTE: MULTIPLE WAITFOR STRINGS

You don't have to use the waitfor command to look for just a single string. Instead, you can repeat any combination of the waitfor parameters to look for multiple strings. This capability is handy for writing generic scripts that can be used for multiple dial-up servers. For example, suppose that you have two Internet service providers: one that prompts for your user name with User Name:, and one that prompts with Login:. To handle both prompts with a single waitfor, you would use the following command:

```
waitfor "User Name" then DoThis, "Login:" then DoThat
```

Here, if the User Name: prompt is received, the script jumps to the DoThis label; alternatively, if the Login: prompt is received, the script branches to the DoThat label.

The transmit Command

You use this command to send text to the remote system. Here's the syntax:

```
transmit string [,raw]
```

string	This is the text you want to send, enclosed in quotation marks. Two system variables, however, don't require quotation marks:

$USERID, which sends the contents of the User name field from the Connect To dialog box, and $PASSWORD, which sends the contents of the Password field from the Connect To dialog box. You can also use several literal strings:

Literal	*What It Sends*
^char	Control characters. For example, "^M" sends Ctrl-M, the carriage return control character.
<cr>	Carriage return
<lf>	Line feed
\"	Quotation mark
\^	Caret
\<	Less-than sign
\\	Backslash
raw	If you include this optional parameter, the script sends carets and other control characters as literal values. So, for example, "^M" would be interpreted as "^M" and not as a carriage return.

A Sample Script

To make all of this information more concrete, let's run through an example. In particular, let's see how you would handle the prompts shown in the terminal window in Figure 35.22. Here's a simple script that does the job:

```
proc main
    ; Delay for 3 seconds to allow the remote system
    ; enough time to send the initial characters.
    delay 3
    ; Now wait for the remote system to prompt for
    ; the user name. When it does, send the $USERID
    ; followed by a carriage return.
    waitfor "login:"
    transmit $USERID
    transmit "^M"
    ; Now wait for the remote system to prompt for
    ; the password. When it does, send the $PASSWORD
    ; followed by a carriage return.
    waitfor "Password:"
    transmit $PASSWORD
    transmit "^M"
    ; Next, wait for menu prompt.
    ; When it arrives, enter 3 for PPP
    ; followed by a carriage return.
    waitfor "choice:"
    transmit "3^M"
endproc
```

The procedure starts with a couple of lines that begin with semicolons (;). These are *comments* you can insert to make your script more readable. They're used for information purposes only; Dial-Up Networking ignores any lines that begin with a semicolon.

The first real command is delay 3, which delays the script for three seconds to give the remote system time to display its welcome messages.

Then the script uses a waitfor command to look for the login: prompt. (Notice that although the exact prompt in Figure 35.22 is hookup login:, you need specify only the last part of the prompt.) When the prompt arrives, the script sends $USERID followed by a carriage return.

Next, the script uses waitfor to look for the Password: prompt, and then it sends $PASSWORD and a carriage return.

Finally, one last waitfor command looks for the choice: menu prompt and enters "3" and a carriage return to select the PPP menu option.

NOTE: MORE SCRIPTING INFORMATION

There are many other scripting commands that you can use. For a complete list, see the SCRIPT.DOC file that comes with the Dial-Up Scripting Tool. You also get several sample SCP files that you can customize to suit your needs.

Assigning a Script to a Connection

After you've created the script you want to use, you need to assign it to the appropriate Dial-Up Networking connection. Before doing that, you need to open the connection and modify the modem configuration so that it no longer brings up the terminal window (the Dial-Up Scripting Tool has its own terminal window). Once that's done, how you proceed depends on which version of the Scripting Tool you're using:

- If you're using the Service Pack 1/Windows 95 CD-ROM version, select Start | Programs | Accessories | Dial-Up Scripting Tool. In the Dial-Up Scripting Tool window that appears, use the Connections list to highlight the Dial-Up Networking connection you want to work with.

- If you're using the OSR2/ISDN Accelerator Pack 1.1 version, open the properties sheet for the connection, and then activate the Scripting tab.

OSR2

In the File name text box, enter the path and filename of the script (SCP) file you want to assign to the connection, as shown in Figure 35.23. You can also click the Browse button to choose the file from the Open dialog box.

35

DIAL-UP
NETWORKING

FIGURE 35.23.

Use the Dial-Up Scripting Tool to assign a script to a Dial-Up Networking connection.

You also have the following options:

Step through script: If you activate this check box, Dial-Up Networking executes the script one line at a time. This feature is useful if your script isn't working properly. By stepping through the script, you can watch for error messages and see exactly where the script goes wrong.

Start terminal screen minimized: If you activate this check box, Dial-Up Networking displays the terminal screen minimized.

OSR2 Click Apply if you want to leave the Dial-Up Scripting Tool window open, or click Close to shut the window. (In the OSR2/ISDN Accelerator Pack 1.1 version, click OK to close the properties sheet.)

Running the Connection with the Script

With the script assigned to the connection, everything operates more or less on autopilot from here. You just crank up the Dial-Up Networking connection, and the script takes care of everything for you. The script's terminal screen appears (unless you elected to run the script's terminal screen minimized), and you see the remote system's prompts and the script's responses. When the script has completed its labors, it shuts down the terminal screen, and your connection continues normally.

If you have problems, however, activate the Step through script option, as described in the preceding section. (You should also make sure that the Start terminal screen minimized check box is deactivated.) Then when you start the connection, you see not only the script's terminal screen, but also a window named Automated Script Test, shown in Figure 35.24. Each time you click the Step button, another line of the script is executed. By watching the terminal screen as each command runs, you can determine where the script is going wrong.

NOTE: CLOSE THE TERMINAL WINDOW MANUALLY

When you run your script in this manner, the terminal screen doesn't close automatically, so you'll have to do it yourself by clicking the Continue button. Don't worry if you see a bunch of garbage characters in the terminal screen. This is normal on some remote systems.

FIGURE 35.24.

Stepping through the script lets you watch for errors.

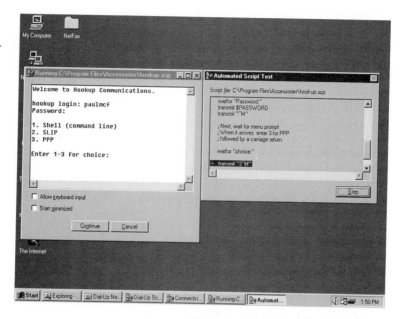

Using the Dial-Up Server from Microsoft Plus!

Although most people use Dial-Up Networking to connect to corporate networks, online services, and Internet service providers, your needs might not be so grandiose. You might just have a couple of Windows 95 machines—say, one at home and one at the office—and you need to connect from one to the other occasionally. Unfortunately, Windows 95 can't act as a dial-up server right out of the box. If you have the Microsoft Plus! add-on, however, you can install the Dial-Up Networking Server component. (This component is also available via the ISDN Accelerator Pack 1.1 update. Note, however, that you don't get the server in OSR2.) This component turns your Windows 95 machine into a dial-up server that supports the following features:

■ Remote machines running Windows 95 or Windows NT 3.5x can connect using the PPP dial-up protocol.

■ Remote machines running Windows NT 3.1 or Windows for Workgroups 3.11 can connect using the RAS dial-up protocol.

■ You can give remote callers access to the network via NetBEUI or IPX/SPX. Note that the Dial-Up Networking Server doesn't support TCP/IP connections, so you can't connect and get access to the Internet.

■ You can set up security to allow only authorized users to call in.

■ You can require an encrypted password for extra security.

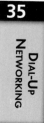

To use the Dial-Up Networking Server, you need to follow four steps:

1. Install Microsoft Plus!, being sure to include the Dial-Up Networking Server component.
2. Install and configure a modem.
3. Install and configure the Dial-Up Adapter.
4. Configure the dial-up server to allow callers, set security, and so on.

I'm going to assume that you've performed steps 1 through 3 already. The next section tells you how to configure the dial-up server.

Configuring the Dial-Up Server

To set up your Windows 95 machine for remote callers, you must set a few properties of the dial-up server. To view these properties, open the `Dial-Up Networking` folder and select Connections | Dial-Up Server. The dialog box that appears contains a tab for each installed modem, and the layout depends on whether your Windows 95 machine's access control is set to share-level or user-level.

Setting User-Level Caller Access

If you're set up for user-level access, you'll see the Dial-Up Server dialog box shown in Figure 35.25. In this case, you can specify the users who are allowed to dial in to the server. Here's how to do it:

1. Activate the `Allow caller access` option.
2. Click the Add button. The Add Users dialog box, shown in Figure 35.26, appears.
3. For each user you want to allow access to the server, highlight the name in the `Name` list and click Add->.
4. When you're done, click OK to return to the Dial-Up Server dialog box.

FIGURE 35.25.

You'll see this dialog box if your Windows 95 computer is set up for user-level access control.

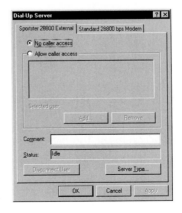

FIGURE 35.26.

Use this dialog box to select the users who are allowed access to the server.

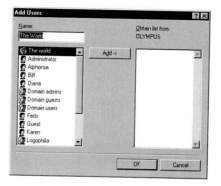

The users you selected will appear in the User name list. To prevent a user from connecting, highlight her name and click the Remove button.

Setting Share-Level Caller Access

If your Windows 95 machine is set up for share-level access, you'll see the Dial-Up Server dialog box shown in Figure 35.27. In this case, you set up a single password that all callers must enter to access the server. Here are the steps to follow:

1. Activate the Allow caller access option.

2. Click the Change Password button to display the Dial-Up Networking Password dialog box, shown in Figure 35.28.

3. If this is the first time you've run this command, your "old password" will be blank, so you can bypass the Old password text box. Otherwise, use this text box to enter your existing password.

4. Enter the password you want to assign to the server in both the New password and the Confirm new password text boxes.

5. When you're done, click OK to return to the Dial-Up Server dialog box.

FIGURE 35.27.

You'll see this dialog box if your machine is set up to use share-level access control.

FIGURE 35.28.

Use this dialog box to set a password for your dial-up server.

TROUBLESHOOTING: IF YOU FORGET YOUR PASSWORD

If you forget the password you've assigned to your dial-up server, you might think you can regain access to the server by uninstalling Microsoft Plus! and then reinstalling the server. Sounds reasonable, but it won't work. That's because when you uninstall Microsoft Plus!, it leaves the dial-up server's encrypted password file (RNA.PWL) intact. Instead, you must boot Windows 95 in MS-DOS mode and then delete RNA.PWL from your main Windows 95 folder.

Other Configuration Options

To complete the configuration of the dial-up server, you must set a few more properties. The Comment text box doesn't do all that much. It's just a field where you can enter descriptive information about the server, such as the access phone number.

If you click the Server Type button, you'll see the Server Types dialog box, shown in Figure 35.29. You have three options to work with:

Type of Dial-Up Server: Use this drop-down list to specify the type of server you want to run. If you select the Default option, the server first attempts to connect with the remote caller by using the PPP dial-up protocol. If that doesn't work, the server tries RAS (asynchronous NetBEUI). If, instead, you specify a server type, the server only tries to connect with the remote system using that protocol. If it can't negotiate the protocol, the server ends the connection.

Enable software compression: When this check box is activated, the server uses compression to send data to the remote system.

Require encrypted password: When this check box is activated, the server accepts only encrypted passwords during the logon. If the remote system sends a clear text (unencrypted) password, the server rejects the logon.

Click OK to return to the Dial-Up Server dialog box.

FIGURE 35.29.

Use this dialog box to configure your computer's server type.

Activating and Deactivating the Server

Your computer is now ready for duty as a dial-up server. To activate the server, click OK to close the Dial-Up Server dialog box. If you want to keep an eye on what's happening with the server, select Connections | Dial-Up Server again. This time, you'll notice that the Status box says Monitoring to indicate that it's monitoring the serial port for incoming calls. When a remote call comes in, this box displays status messages to keep you apprised of the connection, as shown in Figure 35.30.

FIGURE 35.30.

The Status box tells you the current state of the remote connection.

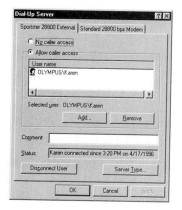

To shut down the server and prevent remote connections, activate the No caller access option and click OK.

NOTE: DISCONNECTING A USER

If you suspect that someone has gained unauthorized access to the server, or if a forgetful user has neglected to disconnect, you can shut him down by clicking the Disconnect User button.

Summary

This chapter showed you how to connect to remote networks by using Windows 95's Dial-Up Networking. To give you a solid background in the fundamentals, I first told you how Dial-Up Networking works and gave you some info on the Dial-Up Networking client architecture, including the dial-up protocols and dial-up servers supported by the Dial-Up Networking client. From there, I took you step-by-step through the Dial-Up Networking configuration process: installing and configuring the Dial-Up Adapter, creating a new Dial-Up Networking connection, and configuring the connection. I then showed you how to connect to a dial-up server.

You also learned plenty of related features: how to configure Microsoft Mail for remote sessions, how to create and use scripts to automate remote logons, and how to set up a Windows 95 machine as a dial-up server.

Here's a list of chapters where you'll find related information:

- A modem is a must for Dial-Up Networking, and I showed how to install and configure modems in Chapter 25, "Maximizing Modem Communications."

- To learn about the other configuration options available with Microsoft Mail and Exchange, see Chapter 27, "Setting Up Microsoft Exchange." To learn about Remote Mail and other Exchange features, see Chapter 28, "Exchanging E-Mail with Microsoft Exchange."

- Dial-Up Networking is a networking client, so understanding how networks do their thing is essential. You can get all the info you need to know in Chapter 30, "A Networking Primer," and Chapter 31, "Windows 95 Networking."

- If you want to use Dial-Up Networking to connect to your Internet service provider, you have to know how to configure the TCP/IP protocol. You can get the full scoop in Chapter 36, "Implementing TCP/IP for Internet and Network Connections."

- With your knowledge of Dial-Up Networking and TCP/IP in place, I'll put everything together and show you how to connect to the Internet from Windows 95 in Chapter 37, "Windows 95 and the Internet."

Implementing TCP/IP for Internet and Network Connections

CHAPTER 36

IN THIS CHAPTER

> *There is, however, one Rosetta stone of the computer world that can link a wide variety of mainframe, minicomputer, and PC systems. That common denominator is called TCP/IP.*
>
> —*Frank J. Derfler, Jr.*

One of the problems facing network administrators these days is the need to support multiple protocols. If the network includes Windows NT servers and Windows machines, NetBEUI is often the protocol of choice. Throw in some NetWare nodes, and you also need IPX/SPX. If any UNIX boxes are on the network, or if the network has an Internet gateway, TCP/IP must also be supported. Diverse networks might also need to support AppleTalk, Banyan VINES, and who knows what else.

Increasingly, administrators are throwing up their hands and saying, "Enough already!" Instead of putting up with the headache of supporting umpteen protocols, they're simplifying both their networks and their lives by implementing a single protocol on *all* their network machines. That protocol is TCP/IP, thanks to its near-universal support by networking vendors, its large packet size and speed, its robustness, and its unmatched scalability.

But TCP/IP isn't just for network honchos. The explosion of interest in the Internet has thrust TCP/IP into the spotlight. That's because TCP/IP is the *lingua franca* of Internet communication, and you can't get online without it. So even if you're using a standalone machine with no network in sight, you'll need to know how to implement TCP/IP in Windows 95 to take advantage of all the Net has to offer.

This chapter will help you do just that. Whether you work with one machine or one thousand machines, you'll find everything you need to know to install and configure TCP/IP in the Windows 95 environment.

Understanding TCP/IP

If there's a downside to TCP/IP, it's that compared to other protocols, TCP/IP is much more complex to implement and manage. However, we're still not talking about brain surgery here. With just a smattering of background info, the mysteries of TCP/IP will become clear, and your configuration chores will become downright comprehensible. That is my goal in this section: to give you enough knowledge about TCP/IP plumbing to stand you in good stead when you get down to the brass tacks of actually setting up, using, and, if necessary, troubleshooting TCP/IP.

What Is TCP/IP?

Although people often speak of TCP/IP as being *a* protocol, it is in fact a *suite* of protocols (more than 100 in all!) housed under one roof. Here's a summary of the most important of these protocols:

Internet Protocol (IP): This is a connectionless protocol that defines the Internet's basic packet structure and its addressing scheme, and that also handles routing of packets between hosts.

Transmission Control Protocol (TCP): This is a connection-oriented protocol that sets up a connection between two hosts and ensures that data is passed between them reliably. If packets are lost or damaged during transmission, TCP takes care of retransmitting the packets.

File Transfer Protocol (FTP): This protocol defines file transfers among computers on the Internet.

Simple Mail Transport Protocol (SMTP): This protocol describes the format of Internet e-mail messages and how messages get delivered.

Hypertext Transport Protocol (HTTP): This protocol defines the format of Uniform Resource Locator (URL) addresses and how World Wide Web data is transmitted between a server and a browser.

Network News Transport Protocol (NNTP): This protocol defines how Usenet newsgroups and postings are transmitted.

Of these, IP and TCP are the most important for our purposes, so the next two sections look at these protocols in greater detail.

NOTE: THE TCP/IP STACK

You'll often see references to the *TCP/IP stack*. Networks are always implemented in a layered model that begins with the *application* and *presentation* layers at the top (these layers determine how programs interact with the operating system and user, respectively) and the *data-link* and *physical* layers at the bottom (these layers govern the network drivers and network adapters, respectively). In between, you have a three-layer stack of protocols:

Session layer: These are protocols that let applications communicate across the network. This is where protocols such as FTP and SMTP reside.

Transport layer: These are connection-oriented protocols which ensure that data is transmitted correctly. This is where TCP resides.

Network layer: These are connectionless protocols that handle the creation and routing of packets. This is where IP resides.

Understanding IP

As the name *Internet Protocol* implies, the Internet, in a very basic sense, *is* IP. That's because IP has a hand in everything that goes on in the Internet:

■ The structure of all the data being transferred around the Internet is defined by IP.

■ The structure of the address assigned to every host computer and router on the Internet is defined by IP.

■ The process by which data gets from one address to another (this is called *routing*) is defined by IP.

Clearly, to understand the Internet (or, on a smaller scale, an internetwork), you must understand IP. In turn, this understanding will make your life a lot easier when it comes time to implement TCP/IP in Windows 95.

The Structure of an IP Datagram

As I mentioned in Chapter 30, "A Networking Primer," network data is broken down into small chunks called *packets*. These packets include not only the data (such as part of a file), but also *header information* that specifies items such as the destination address and the address of the sender. On the Internet, data is transmitted in a packet format defined by IP. These IP packets are known as *datagrams*.

The datagram header can be anywhere from 160 to 512 bits in length, and it includes information such as the address of the host that sent the datagram, and the address of the host that is supposed to receive the datagram. Although you don't need to know the exact format of a datagram header to implement TCP/IP, Table 36.1 spells it out in case you're interested.

Table 36.1. The structure of a datagram header.

Field	Bits	Description
Version	0 to 3	Specifies the format of the header.
Internet Header Length	4 to 7	The length of the header, in words (32 bits).
Type of Service	8 to 15	Specifies the quality of service desired (for example, this field can be used to set precedence levels for the datagram).
Total Length	16 to 31	The length of the datagram, including the header and data. Because this is a 16-bit value, datagrams can be as large as 65,536 bytes.
Identification	32 to 47	An identifying value that lets the destination reassemble a fragmented datagram. (Some systems can't handle packets larger than a particular size, so they'll fragment datagrams as needed. The header is copied to each fragment, and the next two fields are altered as necessary.)
Flags	48 to 50	One flag specifies whether a datagram can be fragmented. If it can't, and the host can't handle the datagram, it discards the datagram. If the datagram can be fragmented, another flag indicates whether this is the last fragment.

Field	Bits	Description
Fragment Offset	51 to 63	If the datagram is fragmented, this field specifies the position in the datagram of this fragment.
Time to Live	64 to 71	Specifies the maximum number of hosts through which the datagram can be routed. Each host decrements this value by 1, and if the value reaches 0 before arriving at its destination, the datagram is discarded. This prevents runaway datagrams from traversing the Internet endlessly.
Protocol	72 to 79	Represents the session layer protocol being used (such as FTP or SMTP).
Header Checksum	80 to 95	Used to check the integrity of the header (not the data).
Source Address	96 to 127	The IP address of the host that sent the datagram.
Destination Address	128 to 159	The IP address of the host that is supposed to receive the datagram.
Options	160 and over	This field can contain anywhere from 0 to 352 bits, and it specifies extra options such as security.

The rest of the datagram is taken up by the data that is to be transmitted to the destination host.

The Structure of an IP Address

You saw in the preceding section that the addresses of both the source and the destination hosts form an integral part of every IP datagram. This section looks at the structure of these so-called *IP addresses.* When setting up TCP/IP in Windows 95, you'll have to face the chore of entering the IP address of your computer (and, if you're an administrator, each computer on your network), as well as several other IP addresses. You therefore need to know how they work.

An IP address is a 32-bit value assigned to a computer by a network administrator or, if you've signed up for an Internet account, by your Internet service provider (ISP). As you'll see in a minute, these addresses are designed so that every host and router on the Internet or within a TCP/IP network has a unique address. That way, when an application needs to send data to a particular locale, it knows that the destination address it plops into the datagram header will make sure that everything ends up where it's supposed to.

Dotted-Decimal Notation

The problem with IP addresses is their "32-bitness." For example, here's the IP address of my Web server:

11001101110100000111000100000010

Not very inviting, is it? To make these numbers easier to work with, the TCP/IP powers-that-be came up with the *dotted-decimal notation* (also known in the trade as *dotted-quad notation*). This notation divides the 32 bits of an IP address into four groups of 8 bits each (each of these groups is called a *quad*), converts each group into its decimal equivalent, and then separates these numbers with dots.

Let's look at an example. Here's my Web server's IP address grouped into four 8-bit quads:

11001101 11010000 01110001 00000010

Now you convert each quad into its decimal equivalent. (Recall that you can do this easily by using the Calculator's Scientific view. Make sure that the Bin option is selected, enter the appropriate 1's and 0's, and select the Dec option.) When you do, you end up with this:

11001101 11010000 01110001 00000010
   205   208   113   2

Now you shoehorn dots between each decimal number to get the dotted-decimal form of the address:

205.208.113.2

IP Address Classes

So how is it possible, with millions of hosts on the Internet the world over, to ensure that each computer has a unique IP address? The secret is that each network that wants on the Internet must register with the Internet Network Information Center (called the InterNIC, for short). In turn, the InterNIC assigns that network a block of IP addresses that the administrator can then dole out to each computer (or, in the case of an ISP, to each customer). These blocks come in three classes: A, B, and C.

In a *class A* network, the InterNIC assigns the first (that is, the leftmost) 8 bits of the address: The first bit is 0, and the remaining 7 bits are an assigned number. Two to the power of 7 is 128, so 128 class A networks are possible. The dotted-decimal versions of these IP addresses begin with the numbers 0 (that is, 00000000) through 127 (that is, 01111111). However, 0 isn't used and 127 is used for other purposes, so there are really only 126 possibilities.

NOTE: NETWORK IDS AND HOST IDS

The numbers assigned by the InterNIC are called *network IDs,* and the numbers assigned by the network administrator are called *host IDs.* For example, consider the following address from a class A network: 115.123.234.1. The network ID is 115 (or it's sometimes written as 115.0.0.0), and the host ID is 123.234.1.

The number 126 might seem small, but consider that the remaining 24 address bits are available for the network to assign locally. In each quad, you have 254 possible numbers (0 and 255 aren't used), so you have 254×254×254 possible addresses to assign, which comes out to a little more than 16 million. In other words, you need to have a *large* system to rate a class A network. (If you do have such a system, don't bother petitioning the InterNIC for a block of IP addresses, because all the class A networks were snapped up long ago by behemoths such as IBM.) Figure 36.1 shows the layout of the IP addresses used by class A networks.

FIGURE 36.1.

The IP address structure for class A networks.

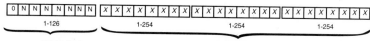

NOTE: REGISTERED IP ADDRESSES ARE FOR INTERNET USE ONLY

Bear in mind that you need to register your network with the InterNIC only if you require Internet access. If you're just creating an internal TCP/IP network, you can create your own block of IP addresses and assign them at will.

In a *class B* networks, the InterNIC assigns the first 16 bits of the address: The first two bits are 10, and the remaining 14 bits are an assigned number. This allows for a total of 16,384 (2 to the power of 14) class B networks, all of which have a first quad dotted-decimal value between 128 (that is, 10000000) and 191 (that is, 10111111). Note that, as with class A networks, all the possible class B numbers have been assigned.

Again, the network administrator can dole out the remaining 16 bits to the network hosts. Given 254 possible values in each of the two quads, that produces a total of 64,516 possible IP addresses. Figure 36.2 shows the layout of class B network IP addresses.

FIGURE 36.2.

The IP address structure for class B networks.

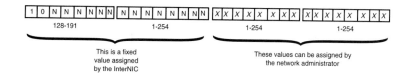

In a class C network, the InterNIC assigns the first 24 bits of the address: The first three bits are 110, and the remaining 21 bits are an assigned number. So the total number of class C networks available is 2,097,152 (2 to the power of 21), all of which have a first quad dotted-decimal value between 192 (that is, 11000000) and 223 (that is, 11011111).

This leaves only the remaining 8 bits in the fourth quad for network administrators to assign addresses to local computers. Again, 0 and 255 aren't used, so a class C network has a total of 254 possible IP addresses. The layout of class C network IP addresses is shown in Figure 36.3.

FIGURE 36.3.
The IP address structure for class C networks.

This is a fixed value assigned by the InterNIC

These values can be assigned by the network administrator

NOTE: WHAT HAPPENED TO THE REST OF THE ADDRESSES?

Because the first quad of an IP address is 8 bits, the range of possible values should be between 0 and 255, but class A, B, and C networks usurp only 0 through 223. What happened to 224 through 255? Well, the values between 224 and 239 are used for special multicast protocols (these are class D addresses), and the values between 240 and 255 are used for experimental purposes (these are class E addresses).

NOTE: CLASS C ADDRESS BLOCKS ARE GOING FAST!

I already mentioned that the address blocks for class A and class B networks are long gone, but with more than 2 million class C blocks available, there's plenty to go around, right? Wrong! These blocks are being gobbled up quickly, and it's predicted that the InterNIC will run out before too long. As you read this, the Internet Engineering Task Force and other industry mavens are busy hammering out an agreement for a 64-bit replacement to IP—usually known as IPng (next generation)—that will solve this crisis.

IP Routing

So far you've seen that IP datagrams include the source and destination IP addresses in their headers and that these addresses use the dotted-decimal notation. The next question is, How do the datagrams get from the source to the destination? The answer is that IP also defines how datagrams travel from host to host in a process called *routing*. (Each leap from one host to the next is called a *hop*.)

When IP is ready to send data, it compares the addresses in the datagram header to see whether the source and destination reside on the same network. If they do, IP just hands the packets over to the LAN for delivery, and the data is sent directly to the destination. If the addresses are on different networks, however, the packets must be routed outside of the network.

Subnet Masks

At first blush, deciding whether the source and destination hosts are on the same network sounds easy: Just compare the network IDs of the two addresses. For example, consider the following two addresses:

Source	200.100.55.101
Destination	200.100.66.72

These are class C networks, so the source address has a network ID of 200.100.55, and the destination has a network ID of 200.100.66. Therefore, they're on different networks. Or are they? One of the consequences of having no more class A and class B address blocks is that many large corporations can handle their addressing needs only by obtaining multiple blocks of class C addresses. So it's entirely possible that the 200.100.55 and 200.100.66 network IDs belong to the same company and could therefore be part of the same network! If so, IP should look at only the first two quads (200.100) to determine whether the addresses are on the same network.

So how does IP know to compare the first one, two, or three quads? By using a *subnet mask.* A subnet is a subsection of a network that uses related IP addresses. On a class C network, for example, you could define the first 127 addresses to be on one subnet and the second 127 addresses to be on another subnet. On a larger scale, from the point of view of the Internet—which you can think of as being *the* network—each class A, B, and C network is a subnet.

The subnet mask is a 32-bit value that is usually expressed in the same dotted-decimal notation used by IP addresses. The purpose of the subnet mask is to let IP separate the network ID (or, as you saw in the preceding example, part of the network ID) from the full IP address and thus determine whether the source and destination are on the same network. Table 36.2 spells out the default subnet masks used for each type of network class.

Table 36.2. Normal subnet masks used for each network class.

Network	Subnet Mask	Bit Values
Class A	255.0.0.0	11111111 00000000 00000000 00000000
Class B	255.255.0.0	11111111 11111111 00000000 00000000
Class C	255.255.255.0	11111111 11111111 11111111 00000000

When IP applies the subnet mask to an IP address, the part of the mask that is all 0's strips off the corresponding section of the address. Consider the following example:

	IP Address	*Mask*	*Result*
Source	205.208.113.2	255.255.255.0	205.208.113.0
Destination	205.208.113.50	255.255.255.0	205.208.113.0

The mask produces the same result, so these two addresses are on the same network. Now consider the example I used earlier. In this case, we need to use a nonstandard mask of 255.255.0.0:

	IP Address	*Mask*	*Result*
Source	200.100.55.101	255.255.0.0	200.100.0.0
Destination	200.100.66.72	255.255.0.0	200.100.0.0

NOTE: HOW THE SUBNET MASK WORKS

The operation of the subnet mask is a bit more complex than I've let on. It's actually a two-step process. In the first step, the IP addresses are both compared bit by bit with the subnet mask using a Boolean AND operation—if both bits are 1, a 1 is returned; otherwise, a 0 is returned:

Source:

205.208.113.2	11001101 11010000 01110001 00000010
255.255.255.0	11111111 11111111 11111111 00000000
Result of AND	11001101 11010000 01110001 00000000

Destination:

205.208.113.50	11001101 11010000 01110001 00110010
255.255.255.0	11111111 11111111 11111111 00000000
Result of AND	11001101 11010000 01110001 00000000

Now the two results are compared bit by bit using a Boolean *Exclusive Or* (XOR) operation—if both bits are 0 or both bits are 1, a 0 is returned; otherwise, a 1 is returned:

Source Result	11001101 11010000 01110001 00000000
Destination Result	11001101 11010000 01110001 00000000
Result of XOR	00000000 00000000 00000000 00000000

If the result of the XOR operation is all 0's, the source and destination are on the same network.

Routing and the Default Gateway

As I said, if IP determines that the source and destination exist on the same network, it hands the datagrams over to the LAN for immediate delivery. If the destination is outside the network, however, IP's routing capabilities come into play.

Routing is the process by which a datagram travels from the source host to a destination host on another network. The first part of the routing process involves defining a *default gateway*. This is the IP address of a computer or dedicated router on the same network as the source computer. When IP sees that the destination is on a different network, it sends the datagrams to the default gateway.

When the gateway gets the datagrams, it checks the IP header for the destination address and compares that address to its internal list of other gateways and network addresses on the Internet. In some cases, the gateway will be able to send the datagrams directly to the destination. More likely, though, the gateway will only be able to forward the packet to another system that's en route to the destination. This system repeats the procedure: It checks the destination and forwards the datagrams accordingly. Although many hops might be involved, the datagrams will eventually arrive at their destination.

NOTE: THE TIME TO LIVE

Actually, if the datagram has to perform too many hops, it might never reach its destination. That's because each datagram is supplied with a Time to Live (TTL) value in its header (as described earlier). If the TTL value is 64, for example, if the datagram has made 64 hops before getting to its destination, it's discarded without a second thought. The TTL is useful for preventing datagrams from running amok and wandering the Internet's highways and byways endlessly.

TIP: USE TRACERT TO MONITOR HOPS

If you're curious about how many hops it takes to get from here to there (wherever "there" might be), TCP/IP provides a way to find out. You use a utility called TRACERT. I'll show you how it works later in this chapter (see "Wielding the TCP/IP Utilities").

Dynamic IP Addressing

If your network just has a few computers and if the organization of the network is static (the computers attached to the network remain attached at all times), it's easiest to assign an IP address to every computer from the block of addresses supplied by the InterNIC.

Managing IP addresses, however, can get quite cumbersome if the network has many computers or if the network configuration changes constantly, thanks to users logging on to the network remotely (using, say, the Dial-Up Networking accessory you learned about in the preceding chapter) or computers being moved from one subnet to another. One way to solve this problem is to assign IP addresses to network computers *dynamically*. In other words, when a computer logs on to the network, it is assigned an IP address from a pool of available addresses. When the computer logs off, the address it was using is returned to the pool.

The system that manages this dynamic allocation of addresses is called *Dynamic Host Configuration Protocol* (DHCP), and the computers that implement DHCP are called *DHCP servers*. Windows 95 supports DHCP via either Windows NT DHCP servers on the network, or PPP dial-up routers.

Domain Name Resolution

Of course, when you're accessing a Web site or sending Internet e-mail, you don't use IP addresses. Instead, you use "friendlier" names such as `www.windows.com` and `president@whitehouse.gov`. That's because TCP/IP, bless its heart, lets us mere humans use English-language equivalents of IP addresses. So, in the same way that IP addresses can be seen as network IDs and host IDs, these English-language alternatives are broken down into *domain names* and *host names*.

When you register with the InterNIC, what you're really doing is registering a domain name that is associated with your network. In my case, I'm registered under the domain name `mcfedries.com`, which points to my network ID of 205.208.113. The computers—or *hosts*— on my network have their own host names. For example, I have one machine with the host name `hermes`, so its full Internet name is `hermes.mcfedries.com` (this machine's IP address is 205.208.113.4); similarly, my Web server's host name is `www`, so its full Internet name is `www.mcfedries.com` (its IP address is 205.208.113.2).

NOTE: COMPUTER NAMES AND HOST NAMES ARE NOT RELATED

You might recall from Chapter 31, "Windows 95 Networking," that I used the computer name Hermes as an example when I was going through the steps required for setting up a computer on a network. That is the same machine as `hermes.mcfedries.com`, but the computer name and host name are in no way related. I just happened to use the same name for both.

Even though domain names and host names look sort of like IP addresses (a bunch of characters separated by dots), there's no formula that translates one into the other. Instead, a process called *name resolution* is used to look up host names and domain names to find their underlying IP addresses (and vice versa). Three mechanisms are used to perform this task: the HOSTS file, the Domain Name System, and the Windows Internet Name System.

The HOSTS File

The simplest method of mapping a host name to an IP address is to use a HOSTS file. This is a simple text file that implements a two-column table with IP addresses in one column and their corresponding host names in the other, like so:

```
127.0.0.1 localhost
205.208.113.2 www.mcfedries.com
205.208.113.4 hermes.mcfedries.com
```

(The address 127.0.0.1 is a special IP address that refers to your computer. If you send a packet to 127.0.0.1, it comes back to your machine. For this reason, 127.0.0.1 is called a *loopback* address.) You just add an entry for every host on your network. In your main Windows 95 folder, you'll find a file named HOSTS.SAM that includes the loopback address. You can use this file as a start by copying it to a file named HOSTS (no extension). Note, however, that after you have the HOSTS file set up for your network, you must copy it to *every* machine on the network.

The Domain Name System

The HOSTS system is fine for resolving host names within a network, but with millions of hosts worldwide, it's obviously impractical for resolving the names of computers that reside outside of your subnet.

You might think that because the InterNIC handles all the registration duties for domains, your TCP/IP applications could just query some kind of central database at the InterNIC to resolve host names. There are two problems with this approach: The number of queries this database would have to handle would be astronomical (and thus extremely slow), and you'd have to contact the InterNIC every time you added a host to your network. Because it now takes a few weeks to get a domain registered, it's reasonable to assume that it would take at least as long to get your host onto the database, which is unacceptable.

Instead of one central database of host names and IP addresses, the Internet uses a distributed database system called the *Domain Name System* (DNS). The DNS databases use a hierarchical structure to organize domains. The top level of this hierarchy consists of seven categories, as described in Table 36.3.

Table 36.3. Top-level domains in the DNS.

Domain	What It Represents
com	Commercial businesses
edu	Educational institutions
gov	Governments
int	International organizations
mil	Military organizations
net	Networking organizations
org	Nonprofit organizations

Top-level domains also exist for various countries. Table 36.4 lists a few of these geographical domains.

Table 36.4. Some top-level geographical domains in the DNS.

Domain	The Country It Represents
at	Austria
au	Australia
ca	Canada
ch	Switzerland
cn	China
de	Germany
dk	Denmark
es	Spain
fi	Finland
fr	France
hk	Hong Kong
ie	Ireland
il	Israel
jp	Japan
mx	Mexico
nl	Netherlands
no	Norway
nz	New Zealand
ru	Russia
se	Sweden
uk	United Kingdom
us	United States

NOTE: NEW TOP-LEVEL DOMAINS PROPOSED

In February 1997, the International Ad Hoc Committee (IAHC) announced a plan to add seven new top-level domains to the DNS:

firm	Businesses or firms
store	Businesses offering goods to purchase

web	Organizations emphasizing activities related to the World Wide Web
arts	Organizations emphasizing cultural and entertainment activities
rec	For organizations emphasizing recreational activities
info	Organizations providing information services
nom	Individual or personal Internet sites (incomprehensibly, "nom" comes from the word *nomenclature*)

Below these top-level domains are the domain names, such as `whitehouse.gov` and `microsoft.com`. From there, you can have subdomains (subnetworks) and then host names at the bottom of the hierarchy. The database maintains a record of the corresponding IP address for each domain and host.

To handle name resolution, the DNS database is distributed around the Internet to various computers called *DNS servers,* or simply *name servers.* When you set up TCP/IP, you specify one of the DNS servers, and your TCP/IP software uses this server to resolve all host names into their appropriate IP addresses.

The Windows Internet Name Service

Earlier, I told you about how DHCP can be used to assign IP addresses to hosts dynamically. On a Microsoft TCP/IP network, how are these addresses coordinated with host names? By using a name resolution feature called the *Windows Internet Name Service* (WINS). WINS maps NetBIOS names (the names you assign to computers in the Identification tab of the Network properties sheet) to the IP addresses assigned via DHCP.

Understanding TCP

IP is a connectionless protocol, so it doesn't care whether datagrams ever reach their eventual destinations. It just routes the datagrams according to the destination address and then forgets about them. This is why IP is also called an *unreliable* protocol.

We know from experience, however, that the Internet *is* reliable (most of the time!). So where does this reliability come from if not from IP? It comes from the rest of the TCP/IP equation: TCP. You can think of TCP as IP's better half, because through TCP, applications can make sure that their data gets where it's supposed to go and that it arrives there intact.

To help you visualize the difference between IP and TCP, imagine IP as analogous to sending a letter through the mail. You put the letter in an envelope, address the envelope, and drop it in a mailbox. You don't know when the letter gets picked up, how it gets to its destination, or even *whether* it gets there.

Suppose, however, that after mailing the letter you were to call up the recipient and tell her that a letter was on its way. You could give the recipient your phone number and have her call you when she receives the letter. If the letter doesn't arrive after a preset length of time, the recipient could let you know so that you could resend it.

That phone link between you and the recipient is analogous to what TCP does for data transfers. TCP is a connection-oriented protocol that sets up a two-way communications channel between the source and the destination to monitor the IP routing.

TCP Sockets

In the TCP scheme of things, this communications channel is called a *socket,* and it has two components on each end:

IP address: You've already seen that each IP datagram header includes both the source and the destination IP address. For a TCP socket, these addresses are analogous to the sender and receiver having each other's phone number.

Port number: Having a phone number might not be enough to get in touch with someone. If the person works in an office, you might also have to specify his extension. Similarly, knowing the IP address of a host isn't enough information for TCP. It also must know which application sent the datagram. After all, in a multitasking environment like Windows 95, you could be running a Web browser, an e-mail client, and an FTP program all at the same time. To differentiate between programs, TCP uses a 16-bit number called a *port* that uniquely identifies each running process.

> ### NOTE: SOME PORT NUMBERS ARE FIXED
>
> On the source host, the port number usually specifies an application. On the destination host, the port can also specify an application, but it's more likely that the port is a fixed number that is used by an Internet service. For example, FTP uses port 21, Telnet uses port 23, and HTTP uses port 80.

The Structure of a TCP Segment

When a TCP/IP application sends data, it divides the data into a number of *TCP segments.* These segments include part of the data along with a header that defines various parameters used in the TCP communication between the source and the destination. These TCP segments are then encapsulated within the data portion of an IP datagram and sent on their way.

Wait a minute. If TCP segments are sent inside IP datagrams, and I just said that IP is unreliable, how can TCP possibly be reliable? The trick is that, unlike straight IP, TCP expects a *response* from its TCP counterpart on the receiving end. Think of it this way: Imagine mailing a letter to someone and including a Post-it Note on the letter that specifies your phone number and tells the recipient to call you when she receives the letter. If you don't hear from her, you know she didn't get the letter. To ensure reliable communications, TCP includes a "Post-it Note" in its header that does two things:

■ When the application requests that data be sent to a remote location, TCP constructs an initial segment that attempts to set up the socket interface between the two systems. No data is sent until TCP hears back from the receiving system that the sockets are in place and that it's ready to receive the data.

■ When the sockets are ready to go, TCP starts sending the data within its segments and always asks the receiving TCP to acknowledge that these data segments have arrived. If no acknowledgment is received, the sending TCP retransmits the segment.

As with IP, you don't need to know the exact format of a TCP header. In case you're curious, however, I've laid it all out in Table 36.5.

Table 36.5. The structure of a TCP segment header.

Field	Bits	Description
Source Port	0 to 15	The source port number.
Destination Port	16 to 31	The destination port number.
Sequence Number	32 to 63	In the overall sequence of bytes being sent, this field specifies the position in this sequence of the segment's first data byte.
Acknowledgment Number	64 to 95	If the ACK Control Bit is set (see the Control Bits entry), this field contains the value of the next sequence number the sender of the segment is expecting the receiver to acknowledge.
Data Offset	96 to 99	The length of the TCP segment header, in 32-bit words. This tells the receiving socket where the data starts.
Reserved	100 to 105	This field is reserved for future use.
Control Bits	106 to 111	These codes specify various aspects of the communication. When set to 1, each bit controls a particular code, as listed here:
	106	URG: Urgent Pointer field significant.
	107	ACK: Acknowledgment Number field is to be used.

continues

Table 36.5. continued

Field	Bits	Description
	108	PSH: Push function.
	109	RST: Reset the connection.
	110	SYN: Synchronize sequence numbers. This bit is set when the connection is opened.
	111	FIN: No more data from sender, so close the connection.
Window	112 to 127	The number of data bytes that the sender can currently accept. This *sliding window* lets the sender and receiver vary the number of bytes sent and thus increase efficiency.
Checksum	128 to 143	This value lets the receiver determine the integrity of the data.
Urgent Pointer	144 to 159	If the URG Control Bit is set, this field indicates the location in the data where urgent data resides.
Options	160 and over	This variable-length field specifies extra TCP options such as the maximum segment size.

TCP Features

To ensure that IP datagrams are transferred in an orderly, efficient, and reliable manner, TCP implements the following six features:

Connection opening: On the sending host, a process (such as a Web browser) issues a request to send data (such as a URL) to a destination host (such as a Web server). TCP creates an initial segment designed to open the connection between the sender and the receiver (the browser and server). In this initial contact, the two systems exchange IP addresses and port numbers (to create the socket interface) and set up the flow control and sequencing (discussed next).

Flow control: One of the parameters that the sending and receiving hosts exchange is the number of bytes each is willing to accept at one time. This way, one system doesn't end up sending more data than the other system can handle. This value can move up or down as circumstances change on each machine, so the systems exchange this information constantly to ensure efficient data transfers.

Sequencing: Every segment is assigned a sequence number (or, technically, the first data byte in every segment is assigned a sequence number). This technique lets the receiving host reassemble any segments that arrive out of order.

Acknowledgment: When TCP transmits a segment, it holds the segment in a queue until the receiving TCP issues an acknowledgment that it has received the segment. If the sending TCP doesn't receive this acknowledgment, it retransmits the segment.

Error detection: A checksum value in the header lets the receiver test the integrity of an incoming segment. If the segment is corrupted, the receiver fires back an error message to the sender, which then immediately retransmits the segment.

Connection closing: When the process on the sending host indicates that the connection should be terminated, the sending TCP sends a segment that tells the receiver that no more data will be sent and that the socket should be closed.

These features illustrate why Internet communications are generally reliable. They show that TCP acts as a sort of chaperone for the IP datagrams traveling from host to host.

Installing and Configuring TCP/IP

TCP/IP is a complex set of protocols (I've really only scratched the surface here), but the good news is that it's much easier to implement than it is to understand. With this chapter's background info in hand, after you've installed the protocol, configuring a computer to use TCP/IP becomes a simple matter of plugging in a few values. Here's what you need to know before getting started:

■ Whether your network or ISP uses dynamic IP addressing.

■ If dynamic addressing isn't used, the IP address that has been assigned to your computer and the appropriate subnet mask for your network.

■ The IP address of your network's default gateway.

■ The host name of your computer and the domain name of your network.

■ Whether your network uses DNS. If it does, you need to know the IP address of one or more DNS servers.

■ Whether your network uses WINS. If it does, you need to know the IP address of your WINS server.

■ Which network clients and services use TCP/IP. For each of these clients and services, you need to bind the TCP/IP protocol.

After you have all of this information in hand (which you can get from your network administrator or your ISP), you're ready to install TCP/IP on your computer.

Installing the TCP/IP Protocol

Unlike previous versions of Windows, Windows 95 comes with its own TCP/IP stack. Before installing this TCP/IP stack, you need to make sure that you've installed the necessary network adapters. If you're running TCP/IP on a network, you need to install the driver for your network interface card, as described in Chapter 31. If you're connecting to the Internet, you need to install the Dial-Up Adapter, as described in Chapter 35, "Remote Computing with Dial-Up Networking." After that's done, follow these steps to install the TCP/IP protocol:

1. Display the Network properties sheet either by opening Control Panel's Network icon or by right-clicking the Network Neighborhood and selecting Properties from the context menu.

2. Click the Add button to display the Select Network Component Type dialog box.

3. Highlight Protocol and click Add. The Select Network Protocol dialog box appears, as shown in Figure 36.4.

FIGURE 36.4.

Use this dialog box to highlight the TCP/IP protocol.

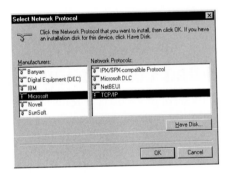

4. In the Manufacturers list, highlight Microsoft.

5. In the Network Protocols list, highlight TCP/IP.

6. Click OK and follow the prompts for inserting your Windows 95 source disks. Windows 95 then adds TCP/IP to the list of network components.

Windows 95 binds the TCP/IP protocol to the installed network adapters automatically. (To make sure, highlight the network adapter you'll be using with TCP/IP and click Properties. In the properties sheet that appears, select the Bindings tab and make sure that the check box beside the TCP/IP protocol is activated.)

NOTE: MULTIPLE TCP/IP CONFIGURATIONS

Windows 95 is quite flexible when it comes to having multiple TCP/IP configurations. For example, you might need to use TCP/IP on your LAN with one configuration and through your ISP with a different configuration. In this case, you can run through one configuration using the LAN adapter and through another using the Dial-Up Adapter. And what if you have multiple Internet accounts? No problem. Windows 95 lets you establish connection-specific TCP/IP configurations (as described later in this chapter).

Configuring the TCP/IP Protocol

With TCP/IP safely ensconced on your system, you now need to configure it to your liking. To do this, highlight the TCP/IP protocol in the list of network components, and then click Properties. (If TCP/IP is bound to multiple adapters, you'll have multiple entries for the TCP/IP protocol. In this case, highlight the appropriate binding and click Properties.) You'll see the TCP/IP Properties dialog box, which contains several tabs for configuring TCP/IP. The next few sections take you though each of these tabs.

IP Address Properties

You use the IP Address tab to tell Windows 95 about your computer's IP address. You have two options:

> **Obtain an IP address automatically:** Select this option if your network uses DHCP or if your ISP supplies you with an IP address on-the-fly whenever you log on.

> **Specify an IP address:** Select this option if your computer has been assigned a permanent IP address, which you'll then enter in dotted-decimal notation in the IP Address text box. Also, you'll need to enter the appropriate dotted-decimal subnet mask in the Subnet Mask text box, as shown in Figure 36.5.

FIGURE 36.5.

The IP Address tab with an IP address and a subnet mask filled in.

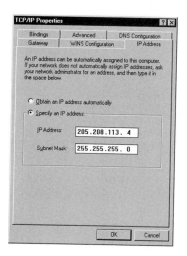

WINS Configuration Properties

If your network uses WINS for name resolution, select the WINS Configuration tab and activate the `Enable WINS Resolution` option, as shown in Figure 36.6. From here, you have two choices:

- If your network has a DHCP server, activate the `Use DHCP for WINS Resolution` option. This option tells Windows 95 to use the DHCP server to get all the WINS info it needs.

- If you aren't using DHCP, fill in the IP address of the `Primary WINS Server` and `Secondary WINS Server`, as well as the `Scope ID`. (Note that the last of these fields is usually left blank. If your network runs NetBIOS over TCP/IP, however, only computers with the same scope ID can talk to one another.)

FIGURE 36.6.

Use the WINS Configuration tab to enable WINS name resolution on your computer.

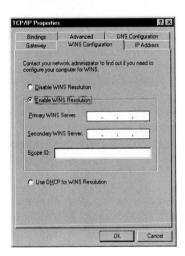

Gateway Properties

Your next chore is to tell Windows 95 the IP address of the machine to use as your gateway. This is the address either of a computer or router on your network, or of a computer on your ISP's system. In the Gateway tab, shown in Figure 36.7, enter the dotted-decimal IP address of the default gateway in the `New gateway` text box, and then click Add to place it on the `Installed gateways` list. Repeat this procedure if your network uses multiple gateways. (Note that the gateway at the top of the list is the one that Windows 95 tries first.)

FIGURE 36.7.

*You use the Gateway
tab to enter your
network's default
gateway.*

DNS Configuration Properties

The next item on the TCP/IP configuration agenda involves setting up DNS properties for
the host. If your network uses DNS, or if you're configuring the host for an Internet connection, select the DNS Configuration tab, shown in Figure 36.8, and then activate the Enable
DNS option. Then fill in the following properties:

Host: This is the host name for your computer.

Domain: This is the domain name of your network or your ISP. DNS combines the
host name and domain name to create the fully qualified domain name (FQDN) for
the computer. In Figure 36.8, for example, the Host is hermes and the Domain is
mcfedries.com, so this computer's FQDN is hermes.mcfedries.com. This is the name
Windows 95 sends to the DNS for resolution into an IP address.

DNS Server Search Order: Use this group to enter the IP addresses for one or more (up
to three) DNS servers either on your network or on your ISP's network. For each
server, enter the dotted-decimal IP address, and then click Add. Windows 95 queries
these servers in the order in which you enter them.

Domain Suffix Search Order: A host computer can belong to multiple domains. In my
case, I have two domains—mcfedries.com and logophilia.com—so the hermes host
has two FQDNs: hermes.mcfedries.com and hermes.logophilia.com. Just in case the
DNS has trouble with the main FQDN, you can use the Domain Suffix Search Order
group to specify other domains Windows 95 can use when building an FQDN. Enter
the domain name and click Add. You can specify as many domains as required.

FIGURE 36.8.

*If you're using DNS,
you need to fill in
various properties
in the DNS Con-
figuration tab.*

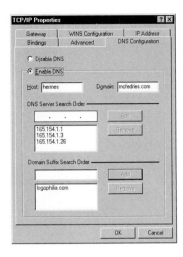

Bindings Properties

You next have to specify which clients and services should use the TCP/IP protocol. Select the
Bindings tab, shown in Figure 36.9, and, for each network component that should use TCP/
IP, activate the appropriate check box. If your network uses a different protocol for these components (such as NetBEUI or IPX/SPX), or if you're just using TCP/IP to connect to an ISP,
you can clear these check boxes.

FIGURE 36.9.

*Use the Bindings tab to
specify which network
components will use
TCP/IP.*

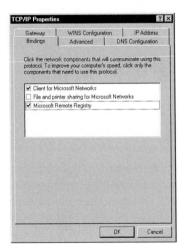

> **CAUTION: DON'T ENABLE SHARING FOR THE DIAL-UP ADAPTER**
>
> If you're configuring TCP/IP for the Dial-Up Adapter (for, say, an Internet connection), you'll create a huge security breach if you enable file and print sharing. I explain why in the next chapter, but for now, you should make sure that file and print sharing is disabled in the Bindings tab.

Advanced Properties

The Advanced properties tab, shown in Figure 36.10, is pretty stark compared to the other tabs. In this case, you have only one option: Set this protocol to be the default protocol. Again, you need to activate this option only if you're setting up this host on a local TCP/IP network. Leave this option deactivated if your network uses a different protocol or if you're using TCP/IP to connect to an ISP.

FIGURE 36.10.

You can use the Advanced tab to set TCP/IP as the default protocol.

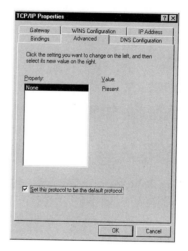

Finishing the Configuration

After you've filled in all the necessary options in the TCP/IP Properties dialog box, click OK to return to the Network properties sheet. Remember that if you want to use TCP/IP with multiple network adapters, you need to repeat the preceding configuration procedure for each adapter. When all that's done, click OK, and when Windows 95 asks whether you want to restart your computer, click Yes.

Connection-Specific TCP/IP Settings

You might be among the many people who have multiple Internet accounts. For example, you might have one account that you access for business and another that you access for personal use. You might also have to dial in to your company's TCP/IP network while you're on the road. What do you do if you often use the same computer for all of these scenarios (such as a notebook computer that you lug between the office and home and to remote locations)? The prospect of modifying all those TCP/IP properties each time you need to access a particular account is unattractive, to say the least. Luckily, however, you don't have to. Windows 95 lets you set up a different TCP/IP configuration for each Dial-Up Networking connection you use. When you establish the connection, Dial-Up Networking uses the correct TCP/IP configuration automatically.

To set this up, follow these steps:

1. In the Dial-Up Networking folder, highlight the connection you want to work with.
2. Either select File | Properties or right-click the icon and select Properties.
3. In the properties sheet that appears, select Server Type to display the Server Types dialog box.
4. In the Allowed network protocols group, make sure that the TCP/IP check box is activated, and then select TCP/IP Settings.
5. In the TCP/IP Settings dialog box, shown in Figure 36.11, configure the following options:

   Server assigned IP address: Activate this option if the dial-up server assigns an IP address automatically when you log on.

   Specify an IP address: Activate this option if you have a permanent IP address with this connection. Enter the dotted-decimal address in the IP address box.

   Server assigned name server addresses: Activate this option if the dial-up server assigns the addresses of DNS and WINS servers automatically.

   Specify name server addresses: Activate this option if this connection uses specific IP addresses for DNS and WINS servers. Use the text boxes provided to enter up to two dotted-decimal IP addresses for DNS and WINS servers.

   Use IP header compression: Activate this check box if the dial-up server supports IP header compression. If you have trouble using an Internet connection, one likely cause is that your ISP doesn't support IP compression, so you should deactivate this check box.

   Use default gateway on remote network: When this check box is activated, the dial-up server's default gateway is used. If you deactivate this check box, the default gateway defined in your TCP/IP properties is used.

FIGURE 36.11.

*Use the TCP/IP
Settings dialog box to
configure TCP/IP
properties specific to the
current Dial-Up
Networking connection.*

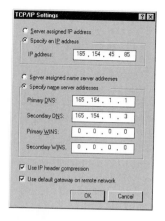

6. Click OK until you're back in the `Dial-Up Networking` folder.

Wielding the TCP/IP Utilities

Windows 95 TCP/IP comes with a few utilities you can use to review your TCP/IP settings and troubleshoot problems. Here's a list of the available utilities:

ARP: This DOS command displays (or modifies) the IP-to-Ethernet or IP-to-Token Ring address translation tables used by the Address Resolution Protocol (ARP) in TCP/IP. Enter the command `arp -?` for the syntax.

NBTSTAT: This DOS command displays the protocol statistics and the current TCP/IP connections using NBT (NetBIOS over TCP/IP). Enter `nbtstat -?` for the syntax.

NETSTAT: This DOS command displays the protocol statistics and current TCP/IP connections. The command `netstat -?` displays the syntax.

PING: This DOS command can check a network connection to a remote computer. This is one of the most commonly used TCP/IP diagnostic tools, so I describe it more detail in the next section.

ROUTE: This DOS command can be used to manipulate a network routing table (HOSTS). Enter `route -?` for the syntax.

TRACERT: This DOS command can check the route taken to a remote host. I'll explain this valuable diagnostic command in more detail later.

WINIPCFG: This Windows 95 utility displays the current TCP/IP network configuration. Select Start | Run, enter `winipcfg`, and click OK to display the IP Configuration window. For each installed network adapter, this window tells you the adapter's physical address, IP address, subnet mask, and default gateway. Click More Info>> to expand the window, as shown in Figure 36.12.

FIGURE 36.12.

The WINIPCFG utility displays information about the TCP/IP configuration associated with each network adapter.

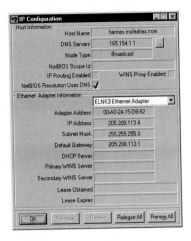

The PING Command

As you might know, a submarine can detect a nearby object by using sonar to send out a sound wave and then seeing whether the wave is reflected. This is called *pinging* an object.

TCP/IP has a PING command that performs a similar function. PING sends out a special type of IP packet—called an *Internet Control Message Protocol (ICMP) echo packet*—to a remote location. This packet requests that the remote location send back a response packet. PING then tells you whether the response was received. This way, you can check your TCP/IP configuration to see whether your host can connect with a remote host.

Here's the PING syntax:

```
ping [-t] [-a] [-n count] [-l length] [-f] [-i TTL] [-v TOS] [-r count]
     [-s count] [[-j route-list] ¦ [-k route-list]] [-w timeout] host
```

-t	Pings the specified *host* until you interrupt the command.
-a	Specifies not to resolve IP addresses to host names.
-n count	Sends the number of echo packets specified by *count*. The default is 4.
-l length	Sends echo packets containing the amount of data specified by *length*. The default is 32 bytes; the maximum is 8192.
-f	Sends a Do Not Fragment flag in the packet's header. The flag ensures that the packet won't be fragmented by gateways along the route.
-i TTL	Sets the Time To Live field to the value specified by *TTL* (the default is 32).
-v TOS	Sets the Type Of Service field to the value specified by *TOS*.

`-r count`	Records the route of the outgoing packet and the returning packet in the Record Route field. A minimum of 1 to a maximum of 9 hosts must be specified by `count`.
`-s count`	Specifies the time stamp for the number of hops specified by `count`.
`-j route-list`	Routes packets by means of the list of hosts specified by `host`. Consecutive hosts may be separated by intermediate gateways (loose source routed). The maximum number allowed by IP is 9.
`-k route-list`	Routes packets by means of the list of hosts specified by `host`. Consecutive hosts may not be separated by intermediate gateways (strict source routed). The maximum number allowed by IP is 9.
`-w timeout`	Specifies a time-out interval in milliseconds. The default is 1000 (1 second).
`host`	Specifies either the IP address or the host name (a fully qualified domain name) of the remote host you want to ping. (You can enter multiple hosts.)

Here's an example that uses PING on the Microsoft Web site (`www.microsoft.com`):

```
C:\>ping www.microsoft.com
Pinging www.microsoft.com [198.105.232.6] with 32 bytes of data:
Reply from 198.105.232.6: bytes=32 time=251ms TTL=19
Reply from 198.105.232.6: bytes=32 time=471ms TTL=19
Reply from 198.105.232.6: bytes=32 time=331ms TTL=19
Reply from 198.105.232.6: bytes=32 time=206ms TTL=19
C:\>
```

Here you see that each echo packet received a reply. If you can't connect to the remote host, PING returns a `Request timed out` message for each packet.

If you can't connect to a remote host, here are some notes on using PING to troubleshoot TCP/IP problems:

- First, check to see whether you can use PING successfully on the loopback address: `ping 127.0.0.1`. If you can't, make sure that you restarted Windows 95 after installing TCP/IP. If PING still doesn't work on the loopback address, you might need to remove TCP/IP and reinstall it.

- If your loopback test works properly, try using PING on your computer's IP address. (If you're using DHCP, run the IP Configuration utility to get your current IP address.) If you don't get a successful echo, it could be that you entered an invalid IP address or subnet mask.

- The next test you should run is on your default gateway. If you can't ping the gateway successfully, you won't be able to access remote Internet sites. In this case, check the IP address you entered for the gateway. Make sure that TCP/IP is bound to the network adapter you're using.

- If you get this far, now try using PING on the remote host you're trying to contact. If you're unsuccessful, check to make sure that you're using the correct IP address for the host and that the gateway (router) is set up to route IP packets.

- You can also try pinging the remote host by both its IP address and its host name. If you get a response with the IP address but not the host name, you likely have a name resolution problem.

The TRACERT Command

If you can't ping a remote host, it could be that your echo packets are getting held up along the way. To find out, you can use the TRACERT (trace route) command:

```
tracert [-d] [-h maximum_hops] [-j route-list] [-w timeout] host
```

-d	Specifies not to resolve IP addresses to host names.
-h *maximum_hops*	Specifies the maximum number of hops to search for the *host* (the default is 30).
-j *route-list*	Specifies loose source route along the *route-list*.
-w *timeout*	Waits the number of milliseconds specified by *timeout* for each reply.
host	Specifies the host name of the destination computer.

TRACERT operates by sending ICMP echo packets with varying TTL values. Recall that TTL places a limit on the number of hops a packet can take. Each host along the packet's route decrements the TTL value until, when the TTL value is 0, the packet is discarded (assuming that it hasn't reached its destination by then).

In TRACERT, the ICMP packets specify that whichever host decrements the echo packet to 0 should send back a response. So the first packet has a TTL value of 1, the second has a TTL value of 2, and so on. TRACERT keeps sending packets with incrementally higher TTL values until either a response is received from the remote host or a packet receives no response. Here's an example of a TRACERT command in action:

```
C:\>tracert www.microsoft.com
Tracing route to www.mcp.com [206.246.150.10]over a maximum of 30 hops:  1     5 ms
4 ms    4 ms  router.logophilia.com [205.208.113.1]    2    39 ms    39 ms    41 ms
max-hp-1.tor.hookup.net [165.154.1.31]   3    88 ms    44 ms    44 ms
router.tor.hookup.net [165.154.1.10]    4    64 ms    53 ms    52 ms
core-spc-tor-2-Serial5-7.Sprint-Canada.Net [207.107.244.73]    5    66 ms    48 ms
64 ms  core-spc-tor-1-fddi0/0.Sprint-Canada.Net [204.50.251.33]    6    79 ms
90 ms   90 ms  sl-pen-15-H11/0-T3.sprintlink.net [144.228.165.25]    7    68 ms
```

```
  62 ms    74 ms  sl-pen-17-F6/0/0.sprintlink.net [144.228.60.17]   8   150 ms       *
 294 ms  sl-chi-2-H1/0-T3.sprintlink.net [144.228.10.38]   9   164 ms    317 ms
 143 ms  sl-chi-19-F0/0.sprintlink.net [144.228.50.19]  10        *      294 ms       *
sl-napnet-2-s-T3.sprintlink.net [144.228.159.18]  11   140 ms    293 ms       *
iquest-fddi0.nap.net [206.54.225.250]  12   134 ms    391 ms   156 ms  204.180.50.9
 13       *       107 ms    145 ms  www.mcp.com [206.246.150.10]
Trace complete.
C:\>
```

The first column is the hop number (that is, the TTL value set in the packet). Notice that, in my case, it took 13 hops to get to www.mcp.com. The next three columns contain round-trip times for an attempt to reach the destination with that TTL value. (Asterisks indicate that the attempt timed out.) The last column contains the host name (if it was resolved) and the IP address of the responding system.

TROUBLESHOOTING: TTL TOO LOW

One of the reasons your packets might not be getting to their destination is that the default TTL value used by Windows 95 might be set too low. The default is 32, as compared to 64 in most UNIX systems. To increase this value, start the Registry Editor and highlight the following key:

`HKEY_LOCAL_MACHINE\System\CurrentControlSet\Services\VxD\MSTCP`

Select Edit | New | String Value, enter `DefaultTTL`, and press Enter. Change the value of this new setting to 64.

Summary

This chapter showed you how to implement Microsoft's TCP/IP stack in Windows 95. I spent a good chunk of this chapter taking you through various TCP/IP concepts that are crucial if you hope to understand what you're doing when you set up TCP/IP on a computer. To that end, I showed you the basics behind the two main protocols: IP (including the structure of IP datagrams and addresses, IP routing, and name resolution) and TCP (including TCP sockets, segments, and features). From there, you dove right into TCP/IP installation and configuration. I showed you how to configure TCP/IP for an adapter and for a specific Dial-Up Networking connection. To finish, I showed you how to use various TCP/IP tools, especially the PING and TRACERT commands.

Here's a list of chapters where you'll find related information:

- If you need to brush up on your networking background, make a beeline for Chapter 30, "A Networking Primer."

- For practical network knowledge—such as how to install adapters, clients, and services—check out Chapter 31, "Windows 95 Networking."

■ To get the scoop on Dial-Up Networking, Chapter 35, "Remote Computing with Dial-Up Networking," is the place to be.

■ You'll put all of this TCP/IP know-how to good use when I show you how to use Windows 95 to connect to the Internet in Chapter 37, "Windows 95 and the Internet."

Windows 95 and
the Internet

IN THIS CHAPTER

CHAPTER

37

> *A man may know the world without leaving his own home.*
>
> —*Lao-Tzu*

In Chapter 22, "Miscellaneous Multimedia: Graphics, CD-ROMs, and More," I introduced you to the "cachet to cliché" syndrome, whereby concepts that were once hip and fashionable suddenly become yesterday's news and the victims of a none-too-subtle backlash. This hasn't happened to the Internet just yet (unless you count the righteous backlash leveled against the "Information Superhighway" metaphors that have been done to death). In fact, by just about any measure—popularity, technological innovation, number of industry millionaires—the Internet is still growing by leaps and bounds.

There's no shortage, however, of neo-Luddites and other head-in-the-sand types willing to sound off on whatever soapbox they can find about what they perceive as the evils of all this technology. Even among industry pundits who should know better, it has become almost fashionable to predict an imminent Internet backlash. The rest of us who use the Internet in our daily lives and wonder how we ever got along without it just nod our heads at all this chin-wagging and get back to being productive.

If you're interested in getting on the Internet, this chapter shows you how to do it in Windows 95. I'll review the Internet-related concepts you've seen in previous chapters, and then I'll show you some alternative methods you can use to get connected. From there, you'll learn about Internet security, Windows 95's ftp and Telnet utilities, and other Windows 95 Internet programs.

NOTE: YOU CAN READ THIS CHAPTER ONLINE

Once you get yourself online and have a Web browser up and running, feel free to drop by my Web site and have a look around. Here's the address:

http://www.mcfedries.com/

One of the things you'll find is a hypertext version of this chapter that includes links to all the Internet resources mentioned later. To check it out, head for this book's home page and then click the Sample Chapter link:

http://www.mcfedries.com/Books/Win95Unleashed/

Setting Up Windows 95 to Connect to the Internet

If you've been following along here in Part VII, you already know everything you need to know in order to connect to the Internet in Windows 95. In fact, you're probably off investigating the Net's nooks and crannies right now. However, if you're just starting out at this chapter, this section will get your cyberjourney off the ground. You have four ways to proceed:

■ Review the relevant material from the past few chapters, especially the information about Dial-Up Networking and TCP/IP.

■ Use the Internet Setup Wizard (called the Internet Connect Wizard in OSR2) to take you step-by-step through the process of setting up your connection.

■ Access the Internet via The Microsoft Network either directly (by connecting to MSN) or indirectly (by using MSN as your Internet service provider).

■ Use Dial-Up Networking to access the Internet via CompuServe.

The next four sections take you through each method. Note that in each case, I'm assuming that you have an account with an Internet service provider (ISP).

What You've Learned So Far

Networking and the Internet are intimately related. After all, participating in the Internet is like logging on to a giant TCP/IP network, and networking a few computers is like creating your own mini-Internet (in fact, small networks are often called *internets*). That's why I named Part VI "Unleashing Windows 95 Networking and Internet Connectivity." I wanted to make it clear that the two concepts are inseparable.

If you've been following along, you've seen that many of the ideas we've looked at apply equally well to either setting up a network or setting up an Internet connection. These ideas are scattered among several chapters, however (mostly in Chapter 35, "Remote Computing with Dial-Up Networking," and Chapter 36, "Implementing TCP/IP for Internet and Network Connections"). So what I want to do now is review the relevant material and summarize everything in one nice, neat package. To that end, here's the general procedure you would follow if you were setting up an Internet connection in Windows 95 from scratch:

1. Make sure that your ISP has provided you with all the information required to create the connection (your IP address, subnet mask, default gateway, and so on). For a list of the TCP/IP settings you'll need, see the section "Installing and Configuring TCP/IP" in Chapter 36. You also need to find out the following information:

   ■ The phone number to dial, as well as your user name and password.

   ■ Whether your connection is PPP or SLIP. (I explain the difference in the section "Dial-Up Networking Fundamentals" in Chapter 35.) For PPP, you need to know whether the connection supports software compression or encrypted passwords; for SLIP, whether it supports CSLIP.

   ■ Your e-mail address; your POP account name and password; the domain name of the POP server; and the domain name of the SMTP server (if it's different from the POP server).

   ■ Whether the connection requires a specific modem setup (such as turning off compression).

2. Install your modem in Windows 95, and configure it to your liking. You'll find the relevant instructions in Chapter 25, "Maximizing Modem Communications," in the section titled "Installing and Configuring a Modem."

3. Install Dial-Up Networking and configure the Dial-Up Adapter. (In Chapter 35, see the section "Setting Up Windows 95 for Dial-Up Networking.")

4. Install TCP/IP and make sure that TCP/IP is bound to the Dial-Up Adapter. (In Chapter 36, see "Installing the TCP/IP Protocol.")

5. Configure the Dial-Up Adapter's TCP/IP stack (the instructions are in the section "Configuring the TCP/IP Protocol" in Chapter 36). Alternatively, configure TCP/IP for the Dial-Up Networking connection you'll create for your ISP (in Chapter 36, see "Connection-Specific TCP/IP Settings").

6. Create and configure a Dial-Up Networking connection for your ISP. In particular, you'll probably need to configure the connection to display a terminal window after the connection is made. You'll use this window to enter your user name, password, and possibly the connection type (PPP, SLIP, or dial-up). I showed you how to do all of this in the section "Setting Up Windows 95 for Dial-Up Networking" in Chapter 35.

7. If you want to use either SLIP or the Dial-Up Scripting Tool, install the Microsoft Plus! SLIP and Scripting for Dial-Up Networking component. Create the appropriate script for your logon, and assign it to your Dial-Up Networking connection. (I explain how to do all of this in Chapter 35, in the section "Using the Dial-Up Scripting Tool.")

8. Install the Internet Mail service from Microsoft Plus!, and configure it for your ISP e-mail account. You'll find the details in Chapter 27, "Setting Up Microsoft Exchange," in the "Installing and Setting Up Internet Mail" section.

That's it; you're ready for action on the Internet. From here, head to the section later in this chapter titled "Connecting to Your Service Provider" to run through the connection procedure.

A Note About `WINSOCK.DLL`

If you upgraded to Windows 95 over a previous version of Windows that had an Internet connection installed, you might find that that connection no longer works in Windows 95. Similarly, you might install an Internet access program under Windows 95, set it up so that it works perfectly, and then find that it no longer works once you reboot Windows 95.

Both problems are related to the file that provides access to the TCP/IP protocol stack for Windows-based Internet applications. For 16-bit applications, this *Windows socket* (*WinSock*) support is provided by a file named `WINSOCK.DLL`. The problem is actually threefold:

- When you install Dial-Up Networking, the TCP/IP protocol, or the IPX/SPX protocol, Windows 95 renames your existing `WINSOCK.DLL` file to `WINSOCK.OLD` and then copies its own version of `WINSOCK.DLL`.

- If you install an Internet access program under Windows 95, the program will probably install its own version of `WINSOCK.DLL`. When you reboot, Windows 95 compares its .DLL files with those in the `Sysbckup` subfolder (which you'll find in your main Windows 95 folder). If it finds a file that is different (such as `WINSOCK.DLL`), it "fixes the problem" by replacing the new file with the backup copy that exists in `Sysbckup`.

- Some 16-bit WinSock applications aren't compatible with this new `WINSOCK.DLL` (and its supporting WinSock interface files).

Here's a list of programs known to experience problems with the new `WINSOCK.DLL`:

Chameleon

CompuServe Internet Dialer or CompuServe Net Launcher

FTP Software

Internet In a Box

Internet Office

Mosaic In a Box

NetCom Net Cruiser

Pipeline

Spry Air Series

Trumpet

To resolve this problem, you have two choices:

- Connect to your ISP using Dial-Up Networking exclusively.

- Copy the `WINSOCK.OLD` file into the folder that contains the program you're having problems with. Rename this `WINSOCK.OLD` to `WINSOCK.DLL`.

Using Wizards to Set Up a Connection

If you don't feel like slogging through all the steps described earlier, Microsoft has a couple of Wizards that give you an easier way to get your Windows 95 machine connected to the Internet:

- If you have Microsoft Plus! and you've installed the Internet Jumpstart Kit, you can use the Internet Setup Wizard. See the next section.

- If you have OSR2 installed, you can use the Internet Connection Wizard. See "The Internet Connection Wizard" later in this chapter.

Either one will help you create the connection by leading you through all the necessary steps in typical Wizard fashion. Note that you'll still need to know the various TCP/IP settings assigned by your ISP as well as the other data mentioned earlier.

The Internet Setup Wizard

With all that information in hand, you have a choice of three ways to launch the Internet Setup Wizard:

■ After Microsoft Plus! has installed the appropriate Internet files, the Wizard will start automatically.

■ You can double-click the Internet icon on your Windows 95 desktop. (Note that this method works only once. After you've completed the Wizard, double-clicking the Internet icon runs Internet Explorer, Microsoft's World Wide Web browser.)

■ You can select Start | Programs | Accessories | Internet Tools | Internet Setup Wizard.

The initial Wizard dialog box just gives you some introductory information, so click Next > to continue. The dialog box shown in Figure 37.1 presents you with your first choice:

Use The Microsoft Network: Activate this option if you want to use The Microsoft Network as your ISP. Note that this doesn't mean connecting to MSN and accessing Internet resources from within the service. Instead, it means using MSN as an intermediary to establish a TCP/IP connection to the Internet. You can then use a Web browser and other Internet tools to access Net resources.

I already have an account with a different service provider: Activate this option if you have an account with a third-party ISP.

Figure 37.1.

For your ISP, you can use either MSN or a third party.

I'll talk about using MSN as your ISP in the next section, so the rest of this section assumes that you're using a third-party ISP. Make sure that the I already have an account with a different service provider option is activated, and click Next > to proceed with the setup.

The Wizard now asks whether you want to use Microsoft Exchange to work with your Internet e-mail, as shown in Figure 37.2. Activate the Yes option if you plan on using the Exchange Internet Mail service. If you'll be using a different e-mail client, activate No. Click Next >.

FIGURE 37.2.

For your Internet e-mail, you can use either Exchange or a third-party client.

The Wizard next installs a few files. You'll likely be prompted to enter your Windows 95 source CD-ROM or disks. When that's done, the Wizard prompts you to enter the name of your ISP, as shown in Figure 37.3. This will actually be the name of the Dial-Up Networking connection that the Wizard will create for your Internet access, so you can enter whatever you like. Click Next > when you're ready to move on.

FIGURE 37.3.

Enter the name of your ISP or a description of the connection.

The next Wizard dialog box, shown in Figure 37.4, asks for the Area code, Telephone number, and Country code of the ISP's dial-in phone number. In most cases, when connecting to the ISP, you'll need to enter your user name, your password, and other options (such as PPP or SLIP connection) by hand. To do this, activate the Bring up terminal window after dialing check box. When you're done, click Next >.

FIGURE 37.4.

Use this dialog box to enter your dial-in phone number.

37

WINDOWS 95 AND THE INTERNET

NOTE: YOU DON'T NEED THE TERMINAL WINDOW FOR SCRIPT LOGONS

If you'll be using the Dial-Up Scripting Tool to create a script to automate your logon, you can leave the `Bring up terminal window after dialing` check box deactivated.

The next item on the Internet Setup Wizard's to-do list is to enter your user name and password, as shown in Figure 37.5. Enter the appropriate values in the `User name` and `Password` fields, and then click Next >.

FIGURE 37.5.

Use this Wizard dialog box to spell out the user name and password supplied by your ISP.

The Wizard next asks about your IP address. You have two choices:

My Internet Service Provider automatically assigns me one: Activate this option if your ISP uses DHCP or some other method to dole out IP addresses on-the-fly.

Always use the following: Activate this option if your ISP has assigned you an IP address. Use the `IP Address` text box to enter the dotted-decimal IP address, and use the `Subnet Mask` text box to enter the dotted-decimal subnet mask, as shown in Figure 37.6.

Click Next > to proceed with the setup.

FIGURE 37.6.

Use this dialog box to either enter your IP address (and appropriate subnet mask) or tell the Wizard that your ISP assigns an address automatically.

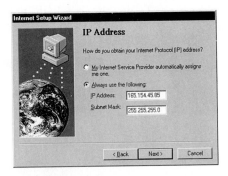

You're next asked to specify one or two DNS servers, as shown in Figure 37.7. Use the DNS Server text box to enter the dotted-decimal IP address of your ISP's DNS server. If the ISP also has a secondary DNS server, enter its dotted-decimal IP address in the Alternate DNS Server text box. Click Next >.

FIGURE 37.7.

Use this Wizard dialog box to specify the ISP's DNS server.

If you'll be using Exchange for your Internet e-mail, activate the Use Internet Mail check box in the next Wizard dialog box that appears, as shown in Figure 37.8. (Note that you'll see this dialog box only if you told the Wizard earlier that you'll be using Exchange to handle your Internet e-mail duties.) Enter your e-mail address in the Your Email address text box, and enter the host name of your ISP's mail server in the Internet mail server text box. Click Next > to continue.

FIGURE 37.8.

Use this dialog box to specify your Internet e-mail address and server.

The next task is to specify the Exchange profile you want to use for the Internet Mail service, as shown in Figure 37.9. (I explained Exchange profiles in Chapter 27.) You'll probably want to use the default profile (MS Exchange Settings), but feel free to either highlight a different profile or create another profile by clicking the New button. Click Next >.

37

WINDOWS 95 AND THE INTERNET

FIGURE 37.9.

Use this dialog box to choose the Exchange profile you want to use for Internet Mail.

In the final Internet Setup Wizard dialog box, click Finish. When the Wizard prompts you to restart your computer, click Yes. When you get back to Windows 95, you'll find a new connection in your Dial-Up Networking folder. To use this connection to establish an Internet session, see "Connecting to Your Service Provider" later in this chapter.

NOTE: USING THE WIZARD TO MAKE MULTIPLE CONNECTIONS

It's not unusual to need multiple Internet connections. For example, your provider might have separate lines for 14.4 Kbps and 28.8 Kbps access. Or you might want to set up separate connections for PPP and SLIP. Whatever the reason, you can create new connections by running through the Internet Setup Wizard again. Just be sure to enter a different name when the Wizard prompts you to enter the name of your service provider.

Note, however, that you must launch the Wizard by selecting Start | Programs | Accessories | Internet Tools | Internet Setup Wizard. Double-clicking the Internet icon on your Windows 95 desktop starts the Internet Explorer Web browser.

The Internet Connection Wizard

OSR2

OSR2 uses a slightly different Wizard to get your Internet connection established. To launch this Wizard, use either of the following methods:

- Double-click the Internet icon on your Windows 95 desktop. (Note that this method works only once. After you've completed the Wizard, double-clicking the Internet icon runs Internet Explorer, Microsoft's World Wide Web browser.)
- Select Start | Programs | Accessories | Internet Tools | Get on the Internet.

The initial Wizard dialog box just gives you some introductory information, so click Next > to continue. The dialog box shown in Figure 37.10 presents you with your first choice. Assuming that you don't already have an Internet connection set up, you have two choices here:

Automatic: This option gives you a choice of Internet Service Providers.

Manual: If you choose this option, Windows 95 runs the Internet Setup Wizard, which I described in the preceding section.

FIGURE 37.10.

*The Internet
Connection Wizard
takes you on a slightly
different path to the
Internet.*

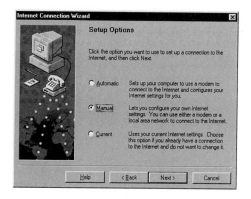

In this section, I'll take you through the dialog boxes that appear when you choose the Automatic option, so activate Automatic and then click Next >.

The dialog box that appears gives you an overview of the Automatic setup, so click Next > again, and then click OK in the Installing Files dialog box. If you're asked to insert your Windows 95 CD-ROM or floppy disks, follow the on-screen instructions. When prompted to restart your computer, click OK.

When your computer restarts, you might see the dialog box shown in Figure 37.11. In this message, Windows 95 is complaining that your system is configured for specific Domain Name Service servers and is asking if you want the existing servers removed. If you want the Wizard to choose your DNS server, click Yes; otherwise, click No.

FIGURE 37.11.

*You might see this
dialog box if you've
already set up a DNS
server on your system.*

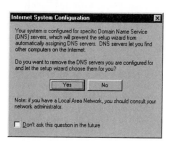

At this point the Wizard will kick in again, and you'll see the dialog box shown in Figure 37.12. Make sure your area code is correct, and then enter the first three digits of your phone number.

When you click Next >, the Wizard dials your modem and proceeds to grab a list of the Internet service providers in your area. When that's done, the Wizard displays a window similar to the one shown in Figure 37.13. This window lists a few providers and gives you a short description of each one. To get extra information, click the More Info icon beside the provider.

FIGURE 37.12.

The Wizard wants to know your area code and the first three digits of your phone number.

FIGURE 37.13.

The Wizard will eventually present you with a list of possible providers.

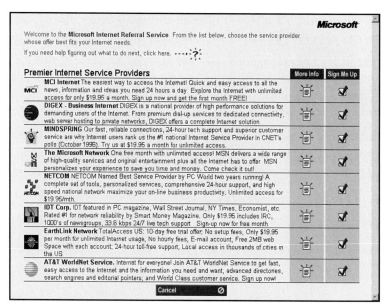

When you decide which one you want, click the Sign Me Up icon beside the provider. The Wizard then connects you with the provider so that you can complete the sign-up procedure. (This procedure varies from provider to provider.)

Internet Access Via The Microsoft Network

As you saw in Chapter 26, "Getting Online with The Microsoft Network," MSN has plenty of internal services and features to keep you entertained and informed. You can also, however, use The Microsoft Network as your ISP, giving you a TCP/IP link to the Internet whenever you connect to MSN. This lets you use Internet software (such as Web browsers and FTP clients) to access the full range of Internet services, all without ever seeing MSN Central (unless, of course, you want to).

How you set up MSN as your ISP depends on whether you have access to the Internet Setup Wizard. If you do (that is, if you've installed the Internet Jumpstart Kit in Microsoft Plus!), run the Wizard as described earlier. You'll come across two forks in the Wizard road that will affect the setup:

- When the Wizard asks how you want to connect to the Internet, activate the Use The Microsoft Network option.

- When the Wizard asks whether you're a member of MSN, either activate the No: sign me up option and the Wizard will lead you through the MSN sign-up procedure (see Chapter 26), or activate Yes to continue without the sign-up.

When you're done, you'll end up with two new icons in your Dial-Up Networking folder: The Microsoft Network and The Microsoft Network (Backup). As you'll see later, you can use these icons to connect to MSN and establish a PPP session without displaying MSN Central.

Alternatively, if you have OSR2 or the CD-ROM for MSN 1.3, start the signup procedure and be sure to select the Sign me up for MSN and a new Internet Connection option. This will run the Internet Connection Wizard as described earlier.

If you don't have Microsoft Plus!, OSR2, or MSN 1.3, you'll need to configure MSN for Internet access manually. (If you're not yet a member of MSN, you should first follow the procedure outlined in Chapter 26 for signing up with MSN.) Here are the steps to follow to change your MSN configuration to allow Internet access (these steps assume that you've upgraded to at least version 1.2 of the MSN software):

1. Double-click The Microsoft Network desktop icon and then click Settings, or right-click the icon and select Connection Settings from the context menu.

2. In the Connection Settings dialog box, activate the MSN is my dial-up Internet access provider option.

3. Click the Access Numbers button.

4. In the Service type drop-down list, select Internet and The Microsoft Network, and then click OK.

5. If you've already configured the Dial-Up Adapter's TCP/IP properties to use a specific DNS server, you'll see the dialog box shown in Figure 37.14. You have two choices:

   - If you'll be using MSN as your ISP exclusively, click Yes to remove the references to specific DNS servers in your TCP/IP properties. This lets MSN assign a DNS server automatically each time you connect.

   - If you'll be using MSN with a third-party ISP to access the Internet, click No to leave your DNS server settings as is.

FIGURE 37.14.

You'll see this dialog box if you've already configured the Dial-Up Adapter's TCP/IP properties with a specific DNS server.

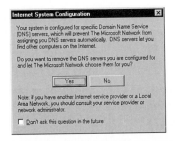

NOTE: A BETTER WAY TO HANDLE DNS

You actually have a third alternative that offers the best of both worlds. Click Yes to let MSN assign a DNS server automatically. Then create a connection-specific TCP/IP setup for your third-party ISP. In particular, be sure to specify the DNS server used by your ISP. (I showed you how to create connection-specific TCP/IP setups in the preceding chapter.)

---

6. When MSN prompts you to restart Windows 95, click OK.

To use MSN to establish an Internet session, see "Connecting to Your Service Provider" later in this chapter.

Internet Access Via CompuServe

If you have a CompuServe account with Internet access, you can create a Dial-Up Networking connection that logs on to CompuServe and establishes a PPP connection. This gives you a TCP/IP link to the Internet, and you can then use any Internet software package. Here are the steps to follow:

1. In the Dial-Up Networking folder, select Connections | Make New Connection.
2. In the first Make New Connection Wizard dialog box, type CompuServe as the name of the connection, select the modem you want to use, and click Next >.
3. Enter your local CompuServe access number, and click Next >.
4. Click Finish to create the connection.
5. In the Dial-Up Networking folder, highlight the CompuServe icon and select File | Properties.

6. Click Configure, display the Options tab, activate the `Bring up terminal window after dialing` check box, and click OK.

7. Click the Server Type button.

8. Set up the Server Types dialog box controls as shown here:

Type of Dial-Up Server	PPP: Windows 95, Windows NT 3.5, Internet
Log on to network	Deactivated
Enable software compression	Activated
Require encrypted password	Deactivated
NetBEUI	Deactivated
IPS/SPX Compatible	Deactivated
TCP/IP	Activated

9. Click the TCP/IP Settings button.

10. Set up the TCP/IP Settings dialog box controls as shown here:

Server assigned IP address	Activated
Specify name server addresses	Activated
Primary DNS	149.174.213.5
Secondary DNS	149.174.211.5
Use IP header compression	Activated
Use default gateway on remote network	Activated

11. Click OK to return to the connection's properties sheet.

12. Click OK to return to the `Dial-Up Networking` folder.

To use this connection to establish an Internet session, see "Connecting to Your Service Provider" later in this chapter.

Windows 95's Internet Properties

Before you establish a connection to your ISP, you should check out a few Internet properties. To view them, display the Control Panel and open the Internet icon. (Note that you'll see this icon only if you installed the Internet Jumpstart Kit from the Microsoft Plus! add-on.) Windows 95 displays the Internet Properties dialog box, shown in Figure 37.15. (Note that OSR2 offers the same features as the Internet Jumpstart Kit. In this case, though, you'll find the options—in a slightly revamped format—in the Connection tab of the Internet Properties dialog box.)

FIGURE 37.15.

Use this dialog box to set various properties that determine how Windows 95 establishes your Internet connection.

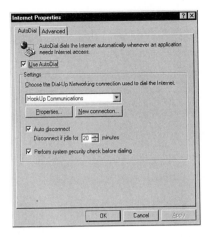

The AutoDial tab contains various properties that modify the Microsoft Plus! AutoDial feature. When this feature is activated, you'll be prompted to connect to your ISP whenever you launch an Internet application or whenever a program requires Internet access. Here's a rundown of the controls on the AutoDial tab:

Use AutoDial: Activate this check box to enable the AutoDial feature.

Choose the Dial-Up Networking connection used to dial the Internet: Use this dropdown list to select AutoDial's default Dial-Up Networking connection. You can use the Properties button to modify the connection, or you can use the New connection button to create a new Dial-Up Networking connection.

Auto disconnect: When this check box is activated, Windows 95 will shut down your Internet connection after a period of inactivity equal to the number of minutes specified in the `Disconnect if idle for x minutes` spinner.

Perform system security check before dialing: When this check box is activated, Windows 95 performs a security check before it makes an AutoDial connection. See "TCP/IP and Internet Security" later in this chapter for a detailed explanation of what Windows 95 checks and how you can safeguard your system.

TROUBLESHOOTING: AUTODIAL DOESN'T DIAL

If you activated the AutoDial feature, you might find that AutoDial doesn't work with some Internet applications. The problem is that 16-bit Internet applications don't support the 32-bit Windows sockets (WSOCK.VXD) used by Windows 95. You'll need to upgrade to a 32-bit version of the program that supports Windows 95's sockets.

If you're connecting to the Internet through a LAN, you can configure a *proxy server* for extra security. A proxy server is a computer that processes Internet packets: All data heading out to the Internet and all data coming in from the Internet goes through the proxy server. This lets the proxy server filter this data selectively and thus prevent unauthorized access to the LAN.

If your LAN has a proxy server, use the Advanced tab to specify the server, as shown in Figure 37.16. Activate the Use Proxy Server check box, and then enter the address and port number of the proxy server in the Proxy Server text box. If you want to access Internet resources (computers, domains, and port numbers) without going through the proxy server, enter the appropriate values in the Bypass proxy on text box, being sure to separate each value with a comma. For example, if you want to access msn.com and Web sites (port 80) without going through the proxy server, you enter msn.com, :80.

FIGURE 37.16.

Use the Advanced tab to specify a proxy server for Internet access.

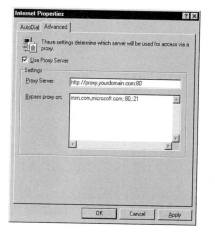

Connecting to Your Service Provider

With your Internet connection set up and ready for action, you can establish your Net session at any time. You have two ways to proceed:

- Open the appropriate Dial-Up Networking connection directly.

- Launch an Internet application and access a Net-based resource (such as a Web site or an FTP site). If you activated the AutoDial feature, Windows 95 prompts you to initiate your Internet connection.

The next three sections take you through some of the specifics for connections to your third-party ISP, The Microsoft Network, and CompuServe.

Connecting to a Third-Party ISP

When you're connecting to a third-party ISP, you'll see the Post-Dial Terminal window, shown in Figure 37.17. Here you can enter your logon options. Depending on the ISP (and whether you're using a script), you might have to enter some or all of the following information (if you just see a blank terminal window, try pressing Enter):

- Your user name.
- Your password.
- The connection type. In some cases, you'll enter a command (such as ppp); in other cases, you'll select the connection type from a menu of choices.

FIGURE 37.17.

Connecting to a third-party ISP usually requires entering a few parameters in the terminal window.

When you've entered all your options, click the terminal window's Continue button or press F7. If you're establishing a SLIP connection, you'll need to fill in the dialog box shown in Figure 37.18. Enter your dotted-decimal IP address (if the displayed address isn't correct for some reason), and then click OK.

FIGURE 37.18.

You'll have to enter an IP address if you're establishing a SLIP connection.

TROUBLESHOOTING: GARBAGE CHARACTERS IN THE TERMINAL SCREEN

When you connect to your ISP, you might see garbage characters in the Post-Dial Terminal Screen. If you see these characters after you've logged on, you can ignore them. Simply click Continue, and your connection will be established normally. If, however, you see garbage characters as soon as the Post-Dial Terminal Screen appears, your ISP might not support your modem's compression. Open the properties sheet for the Dial-Up Networking connection you're using, click Configure, click Advanced in the Connection tab, and deactivate the Compress data check box.

TROUBLESHOOTING: YOU CAN'T ESTABLISH A CONNECTION

If you can't get a connection to your ISP, here are a few things to check:

- If you have a PPP account, make sure that you're using the PPP server type.

- If you have a SLIP account, check with your provider to see whether it's a SLIP or CSLIP connection. Also, be sure to enter the correct IP address in the SLIP Connection IP Address dialog box (see Figure 37.14).

- Make sure that the Dial-Up Networking connection is using only the TCP/IP protocol. (In the properties sheet, select Server Type and then deactivate the NetBEUI and IPX/SPX Compatible check boxes.)

- In the Server Types dialog box, deactivate the Require encrypted password check box.

- Use the PING utility that I described in the preceding chapter to check your TCP/IP settings.

- Make sure that the modem's flow control matches what your ISP requires. For example, if the ISP requires hardware (RTS/CTS) flow control, make sure that your modem configuration doesn't specify software (XON/XOFF) flow control.

- Some ISPs require that your modem's DTR signal be disabled. Use your modem manual to find the command that disables DTR (on many modems it's &D0). Open the properties sheet for the connection, click Configure, click Advanced in the Connection tab, and enter the command in the Extra settings text box.

Connecting to MSN

If you're using MSN as your ISP, connecting is easy. For starters, you can simply connect to MSN in the usual manner: Double-click the desktop's The Microsoft Network icon, and then click Connect in the Sign In dialog box. The problem with this method is that it loads MSN Central (and probably MSN Today as well), which can really slow down the logon. If all you want is Internet access, use either of the following methods to bypass MSN Central:

- In the Dial-Up Networking folder, double-click the icon named The Microsoft Network. (If you've just set up The Microsoft Network as your ISP, you might not see these icons. Press F5 to refresh the folder.)

- Specify The Microsoft Network as the default connection for AutoDial (as described earlier). Then launch an Internet program and access a resource (such as a Web site).

In either case, click Connect in the Connect To dialog box that appears. You'll be logged on to MSN, but you won't see MSN Central. If you want to access a service on MSN later, double-click the desktop's The Microsoft Network icon to get MSN Central on-screen.

Connecting to CompuServe

If CompuServe is your ISP of choice, you have two methods available for establishing a PPP session and enabling access to the Internet:

- In the Dial-Up Networking folder, double-click your CompuServe icon.
- Specify the CompuServe connection as the default connection for AutoDial. Then fire up an Internet application, and load a resource (such as a Web site).

Click Connect in the Connect To dialog box, and the Post-Dial Terminal Screen appears. Follow these steps to initiate the PPP session:

1. Press Enter.
2. At the Host Name: prompt, type CIS and press Enter.

> **NOTE: YOUR PROMPTS MIGHT LOOK A BIT STRANGE**
>
> Instead of the usual CompuServe prompts, you might see what appears to be garbage characters. For example, instead of the Host Name prompt, you might see Hoót Naáe. These strange symbols appear because CompuServe uses 7-bit characters. Your logon isn't affected, however. Just enter your responses (which will also contain unusual characters), and everything will work normally.

3. At the User ID: prompt, enter your CompuServe user ID.
4. At the Password: prompt, enter your CompuServe password.
5. At the Enter choice ! prompt, type go ppconnect and press Enter.
6. Click the Continue button (or press F7).

TCP/IP and Internet Security

Earlier in this chapter, I showed you how to use the Internet properties sheet to tell Windows 95 to perform a security check before performing an AutoDial connection. If you activated that option and you've enabled file and print sharing for TCP/IP on the Dial-Up Adapter (or on your network adapter if you access the Internet via a LAN connection), you'll see the dialog box shown in Figure 37.19 each time Windows 95 uses AutoDial to establish a Net connection.

FIGURE 37.19.

If you've enabled security in the Internet properties sheet, you'll see this dialog box whenever you attempt to connect to the Internet.

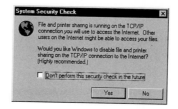

You have two choices here:

■ If you click Yes, Windows 95 disables file and print sharing for TCP/IP on the network adapter you're using to connect to the Internet. (In most cases, this will be the Dial-Up Adapter.) Specifically, it deactivates the file and printer sharing binding in the TCP/IP properties sheet, as shown in Figure 37.20. Note that you must restart Windows 95 to put this change into effect.

FIGURE 37.20.

If you click Yes in the dialog box shown in Figure 37.19, Windows 95 disables file and printer sharing for TCP/IP.

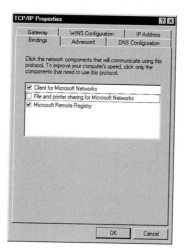

■ If you click No, Windows 95 carries on with the connection normally. If you don't want to be bothered with this dialog box again, activate the Don't perform this security check in the future check box.

Why is file and print sharing such a security risk? Because unless you're careful, folders and drives that you're sharing on your network can also be accessed by people on the Internet! In other words, if you bind file and print sharing to the TCP/IP protocol (specifically, the TCP/IP protocol associated with the Dial-Up Adapter), you extend your shared resources to the Internet as a whole. So it wouldn't be that hard for some total Net stranger to run amok in your files and folders.

Here's how someone on the Net could access your shared resources:

- They would need to be on a system running Microsoft networking.
- They would need to know the IP address and NetBIOS name of your computer.
- They would need to add an entry in their LMHOSTS file that includes your IP address and NetBIOS name, like so:

```
205.208.113.4 Hermes
```

NOTE: LMHOSTS IS SIMILAR TO HOSTS

LMHOSTS is similar to the HOSTS file I told you about in the preceding chapter. But whereas HOSTS mapped IP addresses to host names, LMHOSTS maps IP addresses to NetBIOS names. (This is the computer name you enter in the Identification tab in the Network properties sheet, as described in Chapter 31, "Windows 95 Networking.") You'll find a sample LMHOSTS file—named LMHOSTS.SAM—in your main Windows 95 folder.

Given these not-too-far-fetched conditions, the remote user could display a list of the resources being shared on your computer by entering the NET VIEW command at his DOS prompt:

```
NET VIEW \\NetBIOSName
```

Here, *NetBIOSName* is the NetBIOS name of your computer. This command displays a listing similar to this:

```
C:\>net view \\Hermes
Shared resources at \\HERMES
Sharename    Type      Comment
C            Disk      C'mon in and look around!
D            Disk      No password required!
H            Disk      CD-ROM (go ahead and start the program!)
The command was completed successfully.
C:\>
```

To map one of your resources to his computer, the person can use the NET USE command:

```
NET USE \\NetBIOSName\DriveLetter
```

Here, *DriveLetter* is the letter of the shared drive he wants to map.

NOTE: MICROSOFT'S NET COMMANDS

NET VIEW and NET USE are just two examples of the various "NET" commands available in Microsoft's network operating systems (including Windows 95). To see a complete list of these commands, enter net help at the DOS prompt.

To protect yourself, you should disable file and print sharing over the Dial-Up Adapter's TCP/IP protocol. If you use your LAN for Internet access, you need to disable file and print sharing for the network adapter's TCP/IP protocol. You can still use another protocol (such as NetBEUI) for sharing resources.

The only problem you might run into is if your network uses the TCP/IP protocol exclusively. In this case, it might be impractical to disable file and print sharing. Your alternative is to set up a reasonable level of security for the resources you share:

- If you use share-level security, assign passwords to each shared resource. A remote user trying to access a shared resource will have to enter the correct password.

- If you use user-level security, your server will prevent access from any unauthorized interlopers. You should, however, make sure that you don't have The World or Guest with full access privileges to your shared folders.

NOTE: A POOR MAN'S WAN

This apparent security breach I've just described can actually be a handy feature. By enabling TCP/IP over your Internet connection, you can set up a cheap wide area network (WAN) that gives remote users access to network resources. You just have to be sure to plan your security appropriately.

The Net Is Your Oyster

With your Internet connection up and running and the appropriate security measures in place, you're free to take full advantage of all the Net has to offer. To do that, you need the appropriate client applications, and the clients you use will depend on the Internet services you want to access. The various services—the World Wide Web, FTP, Telnet, Usenet, and so on—are separate pieces of the overall Internet puzzle, so they require separate applications. (Some applications, though—Web browsers, mostly—are making a bid for becoming the "Swiss army knife" of the Internet by offering access to several different services in one package.)

Many service providers supply their customers with collections of Internet programs. This is an easy way to get started because you can usually download everything you need from the ISP's site with a single command, and most of the programs will be preconfigured with the appropriate options for your ISP.

Unfortunately, Windows 95 ships with only a limited collection of Internet appliances. In fact, you get just two programs:

ftp: This is a command-line utility for transferring files from remote Internet sites (see the next section).

Telnet: This is a graphical terminal emulation client for connecting to remote Internet computers. See "Using Telnet for Remote Internet Sessions" later in this chapter.

Microsoft Plus! and the Windows 95 Service Pack also ship with Internet Explorer, Microsoft's Web browser. I explain the ins and outs of this browser in Chapter 38, "Exploring the Web with Internet Explorer."

If you want to work with any other clients or Internet services, you'll have to either purchase the appropriate applications or head out to the Internet and use the `ftp` utility to download the files you need. I'll tell you about a few programs designed for Windows 95 (and how to get your hands on them) later in this chapter, in the section titled "A Review of Windows 95 Internet Software."

Using FTP for Internet File Transfers

The File Transfer Protocol (FTP) sits just above TCP in the TCP/IP food chain. FTP's purpose in life is to coordinate file transfers to and from remote Internet sites. If you're just starting out on the Internet, for example, you can use FTP to download programs that let you access the services that interest you.

To initiate these transfers, you need an FTP client. This section shows you how to use the `ftp` command-line utility that ships with Windows 95. I won't explore this utility in any great depth because I'm assuming that you'll want to get a graphical FTP client at the earliest opportunity. The Internet has several free FTP clients designed for Windows 95, and I'll show you how to get them later in this chapter.

The idea behind the `ftp` utility (and, indeed, any FTP client) is that you connect to a remote host that's running an FTP server and then use various commands to change directories, display files, and transfer files. It's a lot like working with files in a DOS session (which is why you'll likely want to get a graphical FTP client!).

Here's the syntax for Windows 95's `ftp` utility:

```
ftp [-v] [-n] [-i] [-d] [-g] [host] [-s: filename]
```

`-v`	Suppresses the display of the remote server's responses.
`-n`	Turns off autologon on initial connection.
`-i`	Turns off interactive prompting during multiple-file transfers.
`-d`	Enables debugging, displaying all FTP commands passed between the client and the server.
`-g`	Disables filename "globbing," which permits the use of wildcard characters in local file and pathnames.
`host`	Specifies the host name or IP address of the remote host to which you want to connect.
`-s: filename`	Specifies a text file containing FTP commands that will run automatically after the `ftp` utility starts. You can use this switch to automate your FTP sessions.

For example, the following command starts the `ftp` utility and initiates a connection to Microsoft's FTP site (`ftp.microsoft.com`):

```
ftp ftp.microsoft.com
```

Note that all the parameters in the `ftp` command are optional. If you like, you can just enter the `ftp` command by itself to start a local FTP session. This replaces your usual DOS prompt with the FTP prompt: `ftp>`. From here, you can use the `open` command to start an FTP session with a remote server, like so:

```
open ftp.microsoft.com
```

After you're connected to the remote computer, you'll be asked for a user name and password. In most cases, you won't have an account on the remote machine, so you won't have a user name or a password. This doesn't mean you're out of luck, however. Most FTP servers are *anonymous FTP sites,* which means they offer public access to their files. With anonymous FTP access, you don't need a user name or password to access the remote computer. The remote machine accepts anonymous as your user name, and your e-mail address as the password. After that, you can access files on the remote machine, although your wanderings are usually restricted to one or more public directories.

A typical FTP session progresses in the following way:

1. Start FTP and connect to the host computer.
2. Change to the directory you want to work with.
3. Set some file transfer options.
4. Download (or upload) the file or files.
5. End the FTP session.

Table 37.1 summarizes the `ftp` commands you'll use most often during each step.

Table 37.1. A summary of frequently used `ftp` commands.

Command	*Description*
Working with Directories	
cd *remote_directory*	Changes the directory of the remote computer to *remote_directory.*
cd .. or cdup	Changes the directory of the remote computer to the parent of the current directory.
lcd *local_directory*	Changes the directory of the local computer to *local_directory.*
ls	Displays a short listing of the files in the current remote directory.

continues

Table 37.1. continued

Command	Description
	Working with Directories
`ls -l` or `dir`	Displays a long listing of the files in the current remote directory.
`mkdir new directory`	Creates the directory *new directory* on the remote computer.
`pwd`	Prints (displays) the name of the current working directory on the remote computer.
`rmdir remote directory`	Removes *remote directory* from the remote computer.
	Setting File Transfer Options
`ascii`	Sets FTP to ASCII mode for transferring text files.
`bell`	Toggles the bell setting on and off. When it's on, `ftp` beeps your computer's speaker after each file is transferred.
`binary`	Sets FTP to binary mode for transferring binary files.
`hash`	Toggles display of # symbols for each data block transferred.
`prompt`	Toggles confirmation prompt for multiple-file transfers. The default setting is on.
`status`	Displays the current option settings.
	Working with Files
`delete rfile`	Deletes *rfile* from the remote computer.
`get rfile [lfile]`	Downloads *rfile* to your local computer and stores it as *lfile*.
`mget rfile1 [rfile2...]`	Downloads the remote files *rfile1*, *rfile2*, and so on to your local computer.
`mput lfile1 [lfile2...]`	Uploads the local files *lfile1*, *lfile2*, and so on from your local computer to the remote machine.
`put lfile rfile`	Uploads *lfile* from your computer to the remote machine and stores it as *rfile*.
`rename rfile new name`	Renames *rfile* to *new name* on the remote computer.
	Ending the FTP Session
`bye` or `quit`	Quits the `ftp` program and returns you to the DOS prompt.
`close` or `disconnect`	Ends the FTP session with the remote computer and returns you to the `ftp>` prompt.

> **CAUTION: USE BINARY MODE FOR BINARY FILE TRANSFERS**
>
> Before downloading a binary file to your computer, be sure to run the `binary` command. Downloading a binary file while `ftp` is in ASCII mode will damage the file.

> **NOTE: TURN OFF PROMPTS WITH** `MGET`
>
> If you're using the `mget` command to retrieve multiple files, be sure to use the `prompt` command first to turn off prompting. This will save you from having to answer the confirmation prompt for each file.

Using Telnet for Remote Internet Sessions

The command-line nature of the `ftp` utility will probably doom that program to the dustbin of unused Windows 95 accessories. After all, why wrestle with cryptic commands when excellent graphical clients are available that do everything `ftp` does, and more besides?

By contrast, Windows 95's other Internet utility—the Telnet program—will likely find a permanent place in most people's Internet tool chest. Not that the Telnet program is all that spectacular—some third-party clients have more features—but it's certainly more than adequate for those few times you'll need to use the telnet protocol.

What is the telnet protocol? It's another member of the TCP/IP suite of protocols. In this case, telnet is a terminal emulation protocol that lets you log on to remote systems and use their services as though you were sitting at a local terminal. For example, you can use telnet to log on to a library's server and access its card catalog database.

Starting the Telnet Client

To run the Windows 95 Telnet client, either open the TELNET.EXE file in your main Windows 95 folder, or select Start | Run, enter `telnet`, and click OK. You'll see the Telnet window, shown in Figure 37.21. The next few sections show you how to set preferences, connect to a remote host, and log your sessions.

Setting Telnet Preferences

Before connecting to a remote host, the Telnet client offers a few preferences you can use to customize your sessions. Select Terminal | Preferences to display the Terminal Preferences dialog box, shown in Figure 37.22.

FIGURE 37.21.

You can use Windows 95's Telnet client to connect to remote hosts.

FIGURE 37.22.

Use this dialog box to customize your Telnet sessions.

Here's a rundown of the various options you can work with:

Local Echo: The remote system might not "echo" the characters you enter, so you won't see anything on-screen as you type. In this case, you should activate the Local Echo check box so that you can see your typing. If you see double characters while you're typing, you should deactivate this check box.

Blinking Cursor: If you activate this check box, the cursor that tells you where your next typed character will appear blinks on and off.

Block Cursor: This check box toggles the cursor between a block and a line.

VT100 Arrows: This option determines how Telnet handles your keyboard's arrow keys. When the VT100 Arrows check box is activated, Telnet sends arrow keystrokes to the remote host; when it's deactivated, Telnet doesn't send the keystrokes but instead uses them to navigate locally.

Buffer Size: This text box specifies the number of lines of text from the remote host that Telnet stores in its buffer. You can use the window scrollbar to see the lines stored in this buffer.

TIP: USE A LARGER BUFFER SIZE

Some remote hosts will send you a large chunk of text (say, an introductory message) in one shot. In some cases, this text might contain more than 25 lines, so the first part of the text won't be preserved in the Telnet client's buffer. To prevent this situation, use a larger buffer size. I'd suggest starting with 50 lines and moving up as you need to (buffers of 100 lines are quite common).

Emulation: These options determine the type of terminal emulation Telnet uses with the remote host. The setting you use depends on the host, but you'll find that VT100/ANSI should suffice for most hosts.

Fonts: Use this button to display the Font dialog box, from which you can choose the font you want the Telnet client to use when displaying text from the remote host.

Background Color: This button displays the Color dialog box, in which you can select the background color of the Telnet window. Note that if you select a darker color, you'll probably want to use the Fonts button to specify a lighter color for the text.

Click OK to put your new settings into effect.

Connecting to a Remote Host

When you're ready to initiate a telnet session, select Connect | Remote System. Telnet displays the Connect dialog box, shown in Figure 37.23. You need to specify three options for each connection:

Host Name: Use this combo box to specify the host to which you want to connect. You can enter a fully qualified domain name or an IP address. After you've connected to at least one host, your previous selections appear in the drop-down list.

Port: Use this combo box to choose the port to use for the connection. Most systems use the telnet port, but you can choose one of the other ports in the drop-down list or enter a specific port number.

TermType: If the remote host uses TermType sub-negotiation, use this drop-down list to specify the terminal type string you want Telnet to send to the host.

After you've entered your options, click Connect to initiate the telnet session.

FIGURE 37.23.

Use this dialog box to fill in your connection options.

TIP: COMMAND-LINE CONNECTIONS

If you have a telnet host that you use frequently, you can connect to the host directly by specifying the host name (and the port, if necessary) along with the TELNET command. Here's the syntax:

```
telnet host [port]
```

You might want to consider creating a shortcut for this remote host on the desktop or in one of the Start menus.

After Telnet makes the connection to the remote host, you'll likely have to log on. How you do this depends on the host. In Figure 37.24, for example, I logged on using www so that I could access a command-line World Wide Web browser (called Lynx) and the New Jersey Institute of Technology.

FIGURE 37.24.

After the connection is established, you'll probably have to log on to the remote telnet server.

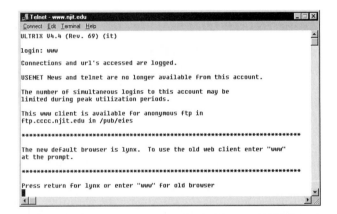

TIP: DELETING CHARACTERS

If you enter the wrong character while typing in the Telnet window, you might not be able to erase it with the Backspace key. In this case, try pressing Ctrl-H or Ctrl-Backspace to expunge the offending character.

Logging a Telnet Session

To save the text that is displayed in a telnet session, the Telnet client gives you two choices:

- For text that has already been displayed, drag the mouse over the text to highlight it, and then select Edit | Copy. Alternatively, you can choose Edit | Select All to highlight all the text in the window and then copy it to the Clipboard.

■ For text that hasn't been displayed yet, select Terminal | Start Logging, specify a name and location for the log file in the Open log file dialog box, and click Open. All text that appears in the Telnet window will also be saved to the log file. When you're done, select Terminal | Stop Logging to close the file. Use Notepad or some other text editor to view the log file.

Disconnecting from the Remote Host

When your session is complete, select Connect | Disconnect, and then click OK when Telnet reports that the connection was lost.

A Review of Windows 95 Internet Software

Windows 95 comes with only a measly collection of Internet clients, but don't let that hold you back. Hundreds of programs are available on the Net for accessing the World Wide Web, FTP, Usenet, and more. In this section, I'll present short descriptions of a few of my favorite Internet clients. All of these programs are available on the Internet (many of them free for the asking), and they're all designed to take advantage of Windows 95's interface and features.

Web Browsers

The way some folks carry on, you'd think the World Wide Web and the Internet were synonymous. Everywhere you turn, people are yakking about some cool Web site they visited or trading URLs (Uniform Resource Locators—the addresses of Net-based resources, especially Web pages) like there's no tomorrow.

If you want to get in on the Web action, you'll need a Web browser. And because most of the Web's appeal lies in its graphical nature, you'll want to get a graphical browser that shows Web pages in their best light. If you have Microsoft Plus! or the Windows 95 Service Pack, you already have Microsoft's first-class browser: Internet Explorer. I show you how this client works in the next chapter (and I also show you how to get it directly from the Internet). However, there are other browsers designed for Windows 95; I'll give you the rundown in this section.

Netscape Navigator

Company/Developer	Netscape Communications Corporation
Current version	3.01
Where to get it	`ftp://ftp20.netscape.com/pub/navigator/3.01/windows/`
Filename	`n32e301.exe` (varies with version number)
File size	3,548 KB
Price	Free for nonprofit use. A commercial version is available for $39.95.

continues

Netscape Navigator

For more info   http://home.netscape.com/

Comments   This is the de facto standard on the Web. (Figure 37.25 shows a Welcome screen for Netscape.) Although Internet Explorer is making inroads, most Web wanderers still use Netscape (despite many annoying bugs in recent versions). Netscape is fast and feature rich, and because many sites use Netscape's HTML extensions, you'll often need to view these pages with Netscape to get the best effect. This browser can handle most other Internet services, including FTP, Gopher, Usenet, and e-mail.

FIGURE 37.25.

Netscape Navigator: For now, it's the Web standard.

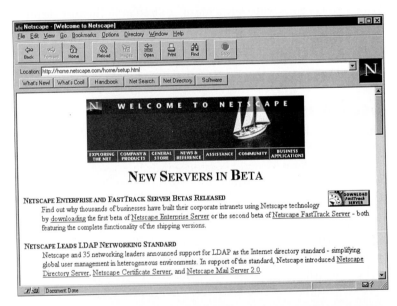

NOTE: NETSCAPE FTP ALTERNATIVES

Netscape Communications has various FTP servers you can use to download Navigator. If the ftp20.netscape.com server is busy, try ftp2.netscape.com through ftp12.netscape.com.

Netscape Navigator Gold

Company/Developer	Netscape Communications Corporation
Current version	3.01
Where to get it	`ftp://ftp20.netscape.com/pub/navigator/gold/3.01/windows/`
Filename	`g32e301.exe` (varies with version number)
File size	3,5882 KB
Price	Free for nonprofit use. A commercial version is available for $79.
For more info	`http://home.netscape.com/`
Comments	This is Netscape Navigator with a twist: You can edit HTML pages right from the browser. The Netscape Editor, shown in Figure 37.26, gives you a WYSIWYG interface that lets you avoid the intricacies of HTML tags and build Web pages like you'd build any graphical interface.

37

WINDOWS 95 AND THE INTERNET

FIGURE 37.26.

Navigator Gold gives you WYSIWYG Web page editing right from the browser.

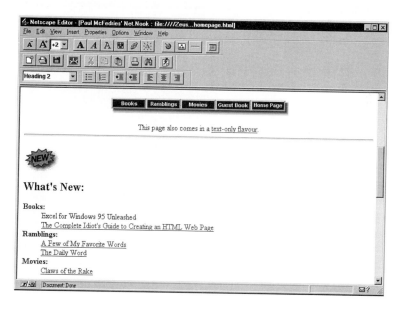

NCSA Mosaic

Company/Developer	National Center for Supercomputing Applications
Current version	3.0
Where to get it	`ftp://ftp.ncsa.uiuc.edu/Web/Mosaic/Windows/v3.0/`
Filename	`mos30.exe` (varies with version number)
File size	2,936 KB
Price	Free
For more info	`http://www.ncsa.uiuc.edu/SDG/Software/mosaic-w/`
Comments	Mosaic was the original graphical Web client, and it's still a formidable competitor to Netscape (see Figure 37.27). The latest version supports most advanced HTML tags and also includes a Usenet newsreader and the capability to send e-mail. (Note, however, that the NCSA has suspended development of Mosaic, and it appears that version 3.0 is the last update we'll see.)

FIGURE 37.27.

*The NCSA Mosaic
Web browser.*

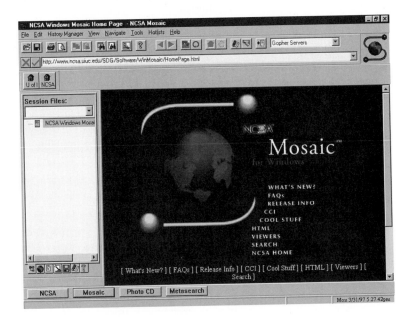

FTP Clients

As I've said, you'll almost certainly want to shelve Windows 95's `ftp` utility in favor of a graphical client. Not only will you trade the ugly `ftp` interface (such as it is!) for a handsome GUI-oriented style, but you'll also get easy access to commands, automated logons, the capability to save your favorite sites, and much more. It's the only way to download. This section presents the particulars of two made-for-Windows 95 FTP clients: WS_FTP and CuteFTP.

WS_FTP LE

Company/Developer	Freeware: John A. Junod; Commercial version: Ipswitch, Inc.
Current version	4.12
Where to get it	`ftp://ftp.ipswitch.com/pub/win32/`
Filename	`ws_ftp32.zip`
File size	566 KB
Price	Free for nonprofit use
For more info	`http://www.csra.net/junodj/ws_ftp32.htm`
Comments	This is an outstanding FTP client. As you can see in Figure 37.28, you get graphical, Explorer-like views of both the remote system and your local folders. You also get easy pushbutton access to common commands, tons of customization options, automated logons, and the capability to save "session profiles" for your favorite sites.

FIGURE 37.28.

WS_FTP: One of the best FTP clients (graphical or otherwise) on the Net.

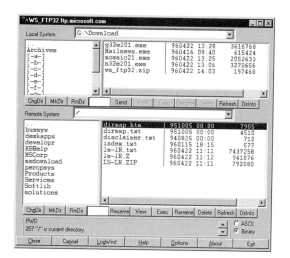

CuteFTP

Company/Developer	Alex Kunadze
Current version	1.8
Where to get it	`ftp://ftp.cuteftp.com/pub/cuteftp/winsock-1/Windows95/FTP/`

continues

CuteFTP

Filename	`32cftp18.exe` (varies with version number)
File size	484 KB
Price	Shareware: $30 registration fee
For more info	`http://www.cuteftp.com/`
Comments	This is a rich FTP client (see Figure 37.29) that is easily the equal of WS_FTP (in fact, it exceeds WS_FTP in many ways). Features include multiple file listing views, numerous session options, Site Manager (an excellent utility for organizing FTP sites), bookmarks, and custom commands.

FIGURE 37.29.

CuteFTP is the new kid on the graphical FTP client block but is rapidly becoming the fave rave of knowledgeable file fiends.

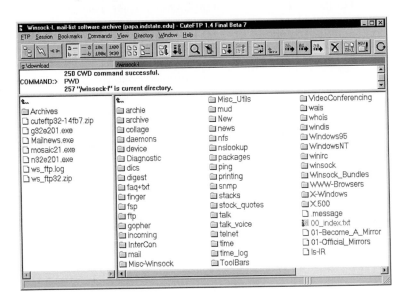

Usenet Newsreaders

If you feel like braving the muddy waters of Usenet newsgroups, you'll need a good Usenet client to help you through your travails. These clients are called *newsreaders*. The Net boasts a few good ones for Windows 95.

Free Agent

Company/Developer	Forte, Inc.
Current version	1.0
Where to get it	`ftp://ftp.forteinc.com/forte/agent/`
Filename	`fagent10.zip` (varies with version number)
File size	727 KB

Free Agent

Price	Free. (A commercial version—called Agent—also is available; it's $29 if you download it, $40 if you order it from Forte.)
For more info	`http://www.forteinc.com/agent/index.html`
Comments	Free Agent puts the lie to the old saw that you can't get something for nothing. Free Agent is just that—free. Yet you get a first-rate newsreader with far too many features to list here. As you can see from Figure 37.30, the Free Agent layout is clean and easy to navigate, and you have many options for managing newsgroups and messages. And Free Agent handles binaries as painlessly as any program I know.

FIGURE 37.30.

Free Agent is a top-notch newsreader.

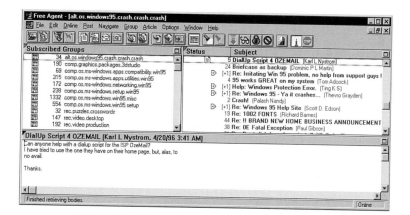

Microsoft Internet News

Company/Developer	Microsoft
Current version	1.0
Where to get it	`http://www.windows.com/ie/download/`
Filename	`Mailnews.exe`
File size	1,000 KB
Price	Free
For more info	`http://www.windows.com/ie/imn/`
Comments	Microsoft News is a simple newsreader that comes as part of the Microsoft Internet Mail and Newsreader package. It doesn't pack a lot of bells and whistles (although only a beta version was available when I tested it), but the interface is nice, as you can see from Figure 37.31, and it has all the basic features.

NOTE: MORE ON NEWS

For a complete look at Internet News, see Chapter 41, "Internet News: Usenet News and Views."

FIGURE 37.31.

Microsoft News is a simple, yet functional, newsreader.

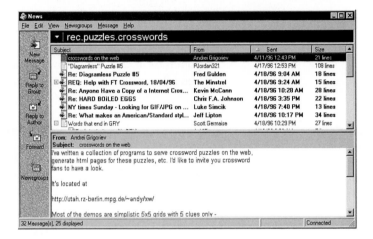

News Xpress for Windows 95

Company/Developer	W.L. Ken, Ng
Current version	2.01
Where to get it	`ftp://ftp.malch.com/`
Filename	`nx201.zip` (varies with version number)
File size	259 KB
Price	Free
For more info	`http://www.malch.com/nx2faq.html`
Comments	News Xpress is a competent newsreader (although the beta version I tested was a bit buggy). It has all the required features of a modern-day newsreader, but some users might not like the MDI interface that spawns a new window every time you open a newsgroup or message, as you can see in Figure 37.32.

FIGURE 37.32.

News Xpress is a decent newsreader, but all those windows might drive you crazy after a while!

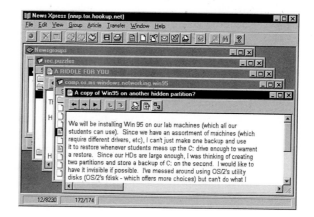

Miscellaneous Applications

This section presents a few more applications that should make your online life a bit easier.

LView Pro for Windows 95 (Graphics viewer and converter)

Company/Developer	Leonardo Loureiro
Current version	1.D2
Where to get it	`ftp://ftp.lview2.com/`
Filename	`lvsetup.exe`
File size	460 KB
Price	Shareware: $30
For more info	`http://world.std.com/~mmedia/lviewp.html`
Comments	If you do any work with graphics, whether it's adding them to a Web page or just viewing them, LView Pro makes the task a snap. Web authors will appreciate how LView Pro makes it easy to create transparent GIF images. And if you need to convert graphics from one format to another, LView Pro can handle the job.

NetTerm (Terminal emulation client)

Company/Developer	InterSoft International, Inc.
Current version	4.1.0
Where to get it	`ftp://www.neosoft.com/pub/users/z/zkrr01/`
Filename	`nt32410.exe` (varies with version number)
File size	794 KB
Price	Shareware: $20

continues

NetTerm (Terminal emulation client)

For more info	`http://starbase.neosoft.com/~zkrr01/netterm.html`
Comments	If the Windows 95 Telnet client doesn't turn your crank, the 32-bit version of NetTerm surely will. This program is loaded with everything you'll ever need for telnet sessions (and a few things you didn't know you needed). You can run multiple sessions, set up keystroke macros and scripts, save favorite terminal sites in a phone book, and even edit documents remotely. This is perfect for editing Web pages that are stored on your service provider's site.

Wingate (Internet gateway)

Company/Developer	Qbik Software
Current version	2.0 (Lite and Pro versions)
Where to get it	`http://www.deerfield.com/wingate/download.htm`
Filename	`wg1310.zip` (varies with version number)
File size	242 KB
Price	Varies according to the number of users: one user, free; two users, $60 (Lite version only); five users, $110 for Lite and $250 for Pro; 10 users, $215 for Lite and $450 for Pro; unlimited, $320 for Lite and $700 for Pro.
For more info	`http://www.deerfield.com/wingate/`
Comments	Wingate lets you establish an Internet connection on one Windows 95 machine and then have other networked Windows 95 machines access the Internet through that same connection. In other words, it lets you set up a Windows 95 client as an Internet gateway.

WinZip for Windows 95 (Compression program)

Company/Developer	Niko Mak Computing, Inc.
Current version	6.2
Where to get it	`ftp://ftp.winzip.com/`
Filename	`winzip95.exe`
File size	614 KB
Price	Shareware: $29
For more info	`http://www.winzip.com/`

WinZip for Windows 95 (Compression program)

| Comments | If you perform even a moderate amount of file downloading, you should place WinZip at the top of your shopping list. This insanely great little utility can handle just about any kind of compressed file you throw at it, including files in ZIP, LZH, ARJ, ARC, TAR, and GZIP formats. And it does all the work in a superb interface that makes both decompressing *and* compressing files a breeze (see Figure 37.33). A must. |

FIGURE 37.33.

WinZip is a must-have utility for handling compressed files in all flavors.

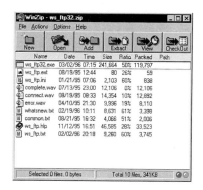

WPlany (Audio player)

Company/Developer	Bill Neisius
Current version	1.2a
Where to get it	`ftp://ftp.ncsa.uiuc.edu/Web/Mosaic/Windows/viewers/`
Filename	`wplny12a.zip` (varies with version number)
File size	35 KB
Price	Free
For more info	`http://www.ncsa.uiuc.edu/SDG/Software/WinMosaic/` `➡Viewers/wplany.htm`
Comments	Many Web sites include sounds in their pages. To make sure that you can play these sounds (they come in various formats), use WPlany (Windows Play ANY). Note that this is a Windows 3.x program. As of this writing, no Windows 95–specific sound clients exist.

Summary

This chapter showed how Windows 95 and the Internet get along. As you saw, they get along just fine, thank you. I began by summarizing what you've learned in previous chapters regarding modems, Dial-Up Networking, and TCP/IP, and then I distilled the info into a procedure for getting Internet access. I also showed you three other ways to get connected: via the Internet Setup Wizard, via The Microsoft Network, and via CompuServe. Other topics in this chapter included the relationship between TCP/IP and Internet security, how to use ftp and Telnet, and a review of some Windows 95 Internet software applications.

One more time, here's a list of chapters that contain all the information you need to get an Internet connection up and running in Windows 95:

- For modem setup and configuration, connect to Chapter 25, "Maximizing Modem Communications."

- For The Microsoft Network's complete sign-up and sign-in procedure, try Chapter 26, "Getting Online with The Microsoft Network," on for size.

- If you plan on using Exchange as your Internet e-mail client, I showed you how to set up the Internet Mail service in Chapter 27, "Setting Up Microsoft Exchange." For the mechanics of using Exchange to read and send messages, head for Chapter 28, "Exchanging E-Mail with Microsoft Exchange."

- If you have a TCP/IP network with an Internet connection, getting your computer hooked up to the network and installing TCP/IP are all that's required to access the Net from your PC. See Chapter 31, "Windows 95 Networking," to learn everything you need to know.

- For dial-up Internet connections, the key piece of Windows 95 technology is Dial-Up Networking. I gave you the full scoop in Chapter 35, "Remote Computing with Dial-Up Networking."

- Whichever kind of connection you use, you can surf the Internet without running a TCP/IP stack on your computer. I explained TCP/IP in glorious detail in Chapter 36, "Implementing TCP/IP for Internet and Network Connections."

- The next piece of the Windows 95 Internet puzzle is Internet Explorer, Microsoft's Web browser. You'll take it for a test drive in Chapter 38, "Exploring the Web with Internet Explorer."

- OSR2 users get a new Net utility called NetMeeting (which is also available on Microsoft's Web site). I'll show you how to use it in Chapter 39, "Remote Collaboration with Microsoft NetMeeting."

- See Chapter 40, "Internet Mail: Messaging Made Easy," and Chapter 41, "Internet News: Usenet News and Views," to learn about Microsoft's e-mail and Usenet clients.

■ If you'd like to use Windows 95 as a Web server, I'll show you how it's done in Chapter 42, "Setting Up a Windows 95 World Wide Web Server."

■ I've put together a large list of online sites that contain Windows 95 files and information in Appendix A, "Windows 95 Online Resources."

Exploring the Web with Internet Explorer

For my part, I travel not to go anywhere, but to go. I travel for travel's sake. The great affair is to move.

—*Robert Louis Stevenson*

For some people, *Wired* magazine is the unofficial arbiter of all that's too hip for words among the digerati. (The *digerati*—the digital literati—are the beautiful people of the online world—the Internet intelligentsia, if you will.) *Wired* has a section called "Net Surf" that lists various interesting Internet sites. I checked an early issue of *Wired* from a couple years ago, and Net Surf had 14 listings: four FTP sites, four Usenet newsgroups, one e-mail address, one mailing list, and four listings related to minor Internet services. The "Net Surf" section in the most recent issue of *Wired* also had 14 entries, *and every one of them was a World Wide Web site!*

What's the big deal? Well, how about this: In 1993, traffic on the World Wide Web increased by *443,931 percent!* Or this: Alta Vista, the world's largest Web index (`http://www.altavista.digital.com/`), monitors tens of millions of Web pages and indexes billions of words from these pages.

These mind-blowing numbers tell you that the World Wide Web is no ordinary phenomenon. Clearly, something big is happening. (Of course, nobody knows exactly *what's* happening, but whatever it is, it's *big*.) If you want to see what all the fuss is about, you'll need to get a Web browser to go along with your Internet connection so that you can surf for yourself.

I told you about a few third-party browsers in the preceding chapter, but if you've installed Microsoft Plus! or the Windows 95 Service Pack 1, or if you're running OSR2, you already have a browser at hand: Internet Explorer. This chapter shows you how to use Internet Explorer to traverse the highways and byways of the World Wide Web. I'll show you how to download the latest version, navigate links, deal with files and multimedia, and set up Internet Explorer to your liking.

First, a Few Words from the Web

Like all of the Internet's services, the Web has its own vernacular and acronyms. To make sure that we're reading from the same Web page, so to speak, here's a glossary of some common Web jargon:

arachnerd   A person who spends way too much time either surfing the Web or fussing with his home page.

Barney page   A page whose sole purpose is to capitalize on a trendy topic. The name comes from the spate of pages bashing poor Barney the Dinosaur that were all the rage a while back. Recent Barney pages have been dedicated to O.J. and the Heaven's Gate cult.

Century-21 site   A Web site that has moved to a new location and now contains only a link to the new address.

clickstream   The "path" a person takes as she navigates through the World Wide Web.

dirt road   A frustratingly slow connection to a Web site, as in, "Geez, that GIF still hasn't loaded yet? The *Web server* must be on a dirt road." See also *JPIG*.

flooded   Being unreadable because of a poorly chosen background image, as in "I had to bail out of that page because the background was flooded with some butt-ugly tartan." See also *wrackground image*.

form   A Web document used for gathering information from the reader. Most forms have at least one text field where you can enter text data (such as your name or the keywords for a search). More sophisticated forms also include check boxes, option buttons, and command buttons.

GIF   Graphics Interchange Format. The most commonly used graphics format on the Web.

hit   A single access of a Web page. A hit is recorded for a particular Web page each time a browser displays the page.

hit-and-run page   A Web page that gets a huge number of *hits* and then disappears a week later. Most hit-and-run pages contain pornographic material, and they get shut down when the Web site's system administrators figure out why their network has slowed to a crawl.

home page   The first hypertext document displayed when you follow a link to a Web server.

hot list   A collection of links to cool or interesting sites that you check out regularly.

HTML (Hypertext Markup Language)   The encoding scheme used to format a Web document. The various HTML *tags* define hypertext links, reference graphics files, and designate nontext items such as buttons and check boxes.

HTTP (Hypertext Transfer Protocol)   The protocol used by the Web to transfer hypertext documents and other Net resources.

hyperlink   Another name for a hypertext link.

image map   A "clickable" *inline image* that takes you to a different page, depending on which part of the image you click.

inline image   An image displayed within a Web page.

Java   A programming language designed to create software that runs inside a Web page.

JPEG   A common Web graphics format developed by the Joint Photographic Experts Group. See also *GIF*.

JPIG   A Web page that takes forever to load because either it's jammed to the hilt with graphics or it contains one or two large images. See also *dirt road*.

link   A word or phrase that, when selected, sends the reader to a different page or to a different location on the same page.

one-link wonder   A Web page that contains only a single useful link.

38

EXPLORING THE
WEB WITH
INTERNET EXPLORER

surf   To leap from one Web page to another by furiously clicking any link in sight; to travel through cyberspace.

ubiquilink   A link found on almost everyone's *hot list,* as in "Yahoo! must be on every hot list on the planet. It's a total ubiquilink."

URL (Uniform Resource Locator)   An Internet addressing scheme that spells out the exact location of a Net resource. Most URLs take the following form:

```
protocol://host.domain/directory/file.name
```

`protocol`	The TCP/IP protocol to use for retrieving the resource (such as http or ftp).
`host.domain`	The domain name of the host computer where the resource resides.
`directory`	The host directory that contains the resource.
`file.name`	The filename of the resource.

vanity plate   An annoyingly large Web page graphic that serves no useful purpose. See also *JPIG.*

vaporlink   A link that points to a nonexistent Web page.

VRML   Virtual Reality Modeling Language. Used to create Web sites that are 3-D "worlds" that you "enter" using a VRML-enhanced browser. You can then use the mouse to "move" around this world in any direction.

Web server   A program that responds to requests from Web browsers to retrieve resources. This term is also used to describe the computer that runs the server program.

wrackground image   A background image that ruins a page by making the text unreadable. See also *flooded.*

Getting Your Hands on Internet Explorer

As I mentioned earlier, Internet Explorer is one of the tidbits you get if you've installed either Microsoft Plus! (specifically, the Internet Jumpstart Kit) or the Windows 95 Service Pack 1. Note, however, that these products have Internet Explorer 2.0. At the time this chapter was written, the latest version was 3.02, so you'll want to upgrade. This also applies to OSR2 users, who have version 3.0. The 3.02 release fixes some important security bugs, so it's a must-have. If for some reason you don't have at least version 3.02, you can still obtain it from various online sites:

World Wide Web	`http://www.microsoft.com/ie/`
FTP	`ftp://ftp.microsoft.com/SOFTLIB/MSLFILES/msie302.exe`
MSN	Select Categories | Internet Center | Introducing Internet Explorer and then double-click one of the download icons.

The file you download is a self-extracting, self-installing file. Double-clicking it launches the InstallShield Wizard and installs Internet Explorer for you automatically.

Alternatively, you can get the latest version via the Internet Startup Kit at your local computer retailer.

Starting Internet Explorer

After Internet Explorer is installed on your system, you're ready to start your Web journeys. First, establish the connection to your Internet service provider. (This isn't necessary if you're using the AutoDial feature, which I explained in the preceding chapter.) Then use either of the following methods to start Internet Explorer:

- Double-click the desktop's The Internet icon.
- Select Start | Programs | Accessories | Internet Tools | Internet Explorer.

If you see a dialog box asking whether you'd like to make Internet Explorer your default browser, click either Yes or No. (The "default" browser is the one that Windows 95 loads when you launch a Web shortcut or enter a Web URL in the Run dialog box. More on this a bit later.)

A Tour of the Internet Explorer Screen

When you crank up Internet Explorer version 3.02 for the first time, you'll see the screen shown in Figure 38.1. This Web page is a sort of online Wizard that takes you through the steps of registering the browser, downloading other components, and so on. Click the Next > button to run through this process.

FIGURE 38.1.

You see this screen when you launch Internet Explorer for the first time.

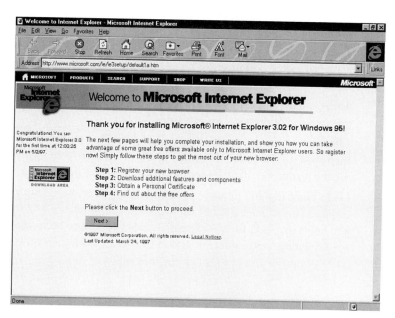

Each subsequent time you run Internet Explorer, you'll see the window shown in Figure 38.2.

FIGURE 38.2.

The Internet Explorer home page.

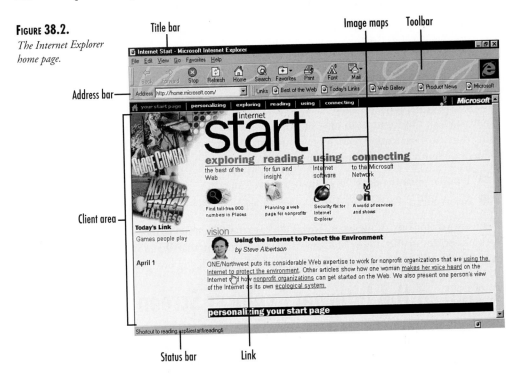

Title bar

Image maps   Toolbar

Address bar

Client area

Status bar   Link

Here's a summary of the main features of this screen:

Title bar: The top line of the screen shows you the title of the current Web page.

Toolbar: These buttons give you point-and-click access to some of Internet Explorer's main features. If you prefer to hide the toolbar (because, for example, you want more screen real estate), deactivate View | Toolbar.

Address bar: This area shows you the URL of the current page. You also can enter text into the Address bar (as explained later).

Client area: This is the area below the Address bar that takes up the bulk of the Internet Explorer screen. It's where the body of each Web page is displayed. You can use the vertical scrollbars to see more of the current document.

Link: Links to other documents (or to other places in the same document) are displayed underlined and in a different color. You select a link by clicking it. When you point to a link, Internet Explorer does two things: It changes the mouse pointer to a hand with a pointing finger, and in the Status bar it displays `Shortcut to` and the name of the document to which the link will take you.

Image map: Although most Web graphics are used just for show, some of them are links. These linked graphics are called *image maps*. Clicking different areas of the map takes you to different pages.

Status bar: This bar lets you know Internet Explorer's current status, displays a description of the links you point to, and tells you the progress of the current Internet Explorer operation (such as downloading a file).

Navigating with Internet Explorer

Now that you're familiar with the lay of the Internet Explorer land, you can start using it to navigate sites. The next few sections take you through the various ways you can use Internet Explorer to wend your way through the Web.

Following the Links

As I've said, Internet Explorer displays hypertext links in an underlined font that's a different color from the rest of the text. To follow one of these links, you have three choices:

- Click it with the mouse. (Image maps work the same way: Position the mouse pointer over the portion of the map you want to see, and then click.)
- Right-click the link and choose Open.
- Right-click the link and choose Open In New Window. This command spawns a new Internet Explorer window and opens the link URL in that window.

NOTE: A NEW WINDOW ON INTERNET EXPLORER

You can open another Internet Explorer window at any time by selecting File | New Window or by pressing Ctrl-N.

Here are a few notes about working with links in Internet Explorer:

- To find out the name of the document that will open when you click a link, place the mouse pointer over the link, and the name will appear in the Status bar.
- If you want to see the full address of the link's URL, right-click the link and select Properties from the context menu.
- To copy the link's URL (say, to reference the URL in an e-mail message), right-click the link and select Copy Shortcut from the context menu. This copies the URL to the Clipboard.

- If you select a link and then change your mind (or if a link is busy loading large graphics or animation files and you don't want to wait), you can stop the download by selecting View | Stop, by pressing Esc, or by clicking the Stop button on the toolbar.

- If you select a link and some of the objects don't load properly, you can reload the page by selecting View | Refresh, by pressing F5, or by clicking the toolbar's Refresh button.

- To e-mail a link shortcut to someone, click the link to open the page, and then select File | Send To | Mail Recipient. A new e-mail message window appears, and the message body contains a shortcut that points to the page's URL. (The messaging system used is the default for your system. You can specify the system in Internet Explorer's Options dialog box. See the section "Programs Options" later in this chapter.) Specify a recipient and then send the message (see Chapter 28, "Exchanging E-Mail with Microsoft Exchange," for details). When the recipient gets the message, she can double-click the shortcut to load the Web page.

Entering a URL

If you want to head to a particular Web site, you can specify a URL by using any of the following methods:

- Click inside the Address bar, delete the current URL, type the one you want, and press Enter.

- Select File | Open or press Ctrl-O. In the Open Internet Address dialog box that appears (see Figure 38.3), type your URL in the Address text box. If you want to display the URL in a new window, activate the Open in new window check box. Click OK when you're done.

FIGURE 38.3.

Use this dialog box to enter the URL you want to see.

- From Windows 95, select Start | Run. Enter the URL in the Run dialog box, and click OK.

- If you want to open an HTML file that resides on your hard disk or on your LAN, select File | Open, click the Browse button, highlight the file in the Open dialog box, and click Open.

TIP: SHORTER URLS

If the URL you want to see is a Web page, you can leave off the `http://` part. Internet Explorer assumes that an address that's missing the protocol is a Web page, so it appends `http://` automatically.

Retracing Your Steps

After you've started leaping through the Web's cyberspace, you'll often want to head back to a previous site, or even to your start page. (Microsoft's home site is the default start page, but I'll show you later how to designate any URL as your start page.) Here's a rundown of the various techniques you can use to move to and fro in Internet Explorer:

- To go back to the previous document, click the Back button on the toolbar, select Go | Back, or press Alt-left arrow.

- After you've gone back to a previous document, you can move ahead to the next document by clicking the Forward button on the toolbar, selecting Go | Forward, or pressing Alt-right arrow.

- To return to the start page, either click the Home toolbar button or select Go | Start Page.

- To return to a specific document you've visited, pull down the Go menu and select the document's title from the list near the bottom of the menu. If you need to see the document's URL or a larger list, select Go | Open History Folder. In the `\Plus!\Microsoft Internet\history` folder that appears, shown in Figure 38.4, double-click the document you want to open.

38

EXPLORING THE WEB WITH INTERNET EXPLORER

Creating a Shortcut to a URL

Another way to navigate Web sites via Internet Explorer is to create shortcuts that point to the appropriate URLs. You can use two methods to do this:

- Use Internet Explorer to view the URL, and then select File | Create Shortcut. When Windows 95 tells you that a shortcut will be placed on your desktop, click OK.

- Copy the URL to the Clipboard, create a new shortcut as described in Chapter 13, "Working with Files and Folders," and then paste the URL into the `Command line` text box.

After your shortcut is in place, you can launch the Web site by double-clicking the shortcut's icon.

FIGURE 38.4.

The history *folder contains a list of the places you've been.*

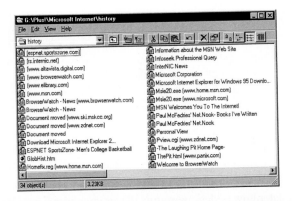

TIP: SHORTCUTS ARE TEXT FILES

Internet shortcuts are simple text files that use the URL extension. They contain only the address of the Internet site, as in the following example:

```
[Internet Shortcut]
http://www.microsoft.com/
```

If you need to make changes to that address, it's possible to edit the shortcut. First, create a new Edit action for the Internet Shortcut file type that uses Notepad to open the file (see Chapter 13 for the details). Then right-click the shortcut, choose Edit, and make your changes in Notepad.

Using the Search Page

The navigation approaches you've tried so far have encompassed the two extremes of Web surfing: clicking links randomly to see what happens, and entering URLs to display specific sites. However, what if you're looking for information on a particular topic, but you don't know any appropriate URLs and you don't want to waste time clicking aimlessly around the Web? In this case, you'll want to put the Web to work for you. In other words, you'll want to crank up one of the Web's search engines to try to track down sites that contain the data you're looking for.

Conveniently, Internet Explorer contains a link that gives you easy access to five of the Web's best search engines (you can search the Microsoft Web site as well). To view these links, select Go | Search the Internet, or click the toolbar's Search the Internet button. You'll see a page similar to the one shown in Figure 38.5. To try a search, enter your search text in one of the text boxes provided, and then click the Search button beside the text box. If you're not sure which search engine to try, select the choosing a search service link to see descriptions of each engine.

FIGURE 38.5.

Internet Explorer displays this page when you select Search the Internet.

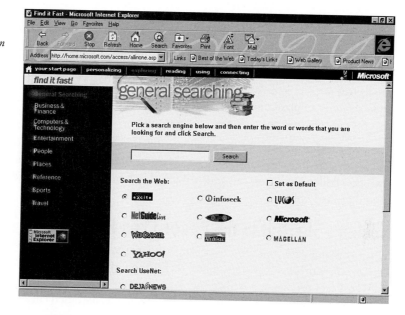

Dealing with Files

As you click your way around the Web, you'll find that some links don't take you to other pages but instead are tied directly to a file. In this case, you'll see the dialog box shown in Figure 38.6, which gives you two ways to proceed:

■ If you want to view the file (for example, if you want to open a text file in Notepad), select the Open it option and click OK.

■ If you prefer to download the file to disk, activate the Save it to disk option, and click OK. In the Save As dialog box that appears, choose a location for the file, and click Save.

FIGURE 38.6.

You'll see this dialog box if a link is tied to a file.

38

EXPLORING THE
WEB WITH
INTERNET EXPLORER

The Favorites Folder: Sites to Remember

The sad truth is that much of what you'll see on the Web will be utterly forgettable and not worth a second look. All kinds of gems, however, are out there waiting to be uncovered—sites you'll want to visit regularly. Instead of memorizing the appropriate URLs, jotting them down on sticky notes, or plastering your desktop with shortcuts, you can use Internet Explorer's handy Favorites feature to keep track of your choice sites.

The Favorites feature is really just a folder (you'll find it in your main Windows 95 folder) that you use to store Internet shortcuts. The advantage of using the Favorites folder as opposed to any other folder is that you can add, view, and link to the Favorites folder shortcuts directly from Internet Explorer.

Adding a Shortcut to the Favorites Folder

When you find a site you want to declare as a favorite, select Favorites | Add To Favorites, or click the Favorites toolbar button and then choose the Add To Favorites command. In the Add To Favorites dialog box that appears, shown in Figure 38.7, the title of the Web page appears in the Name text box. Edit the name, if you like, and then click OK.

FIGURE 38.7.

Use this dialog box to add a shortcut to the Favorites *folder.*

Viewing the Favorites Folder

If you want to work with the Favorites folder directly, use any of the following methods to display the folder:

- In Internet Explorer, Select Favorites | Open Favorites.
- Click the Favorites button on the Internet Explorer toolbar, and then choose Open Favorites.

Figure 38.8 shows the Favorites folder window that appears. From here, you can rename shortcuts, edit the contents of shortcuts (assuming that you created an Edit action for the URL file type, as described earlier), delete shortcuts, and create new subfolders to organize your shortcuts. Click Close when you're done.

FIGURE 38.8.

The Favorites *folder stores your Internet shortcuts.*

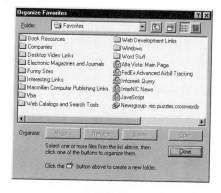

NOTE: EXPLORING THE FAVORITES FOLDER

You can also work with the Favorites folder in Explorer or My Computer. Just open your main Windows 95 folder and highlight the Favorites subfolder.

TIP: ADD URL SHORTCUTS TO THE START MENU

For even easier access to your favorite URLs, you can create shortcuts on your Start menu. You can either drag URLs from the Favorites folder and drop them on the Start button, or create a new Start menu folder (called, say, "Internet Sites") and then create URL shortcuts within that folder. (See Chapter 7, "Customizing Windows 95," for information on adding folders and shortcuts to the Start menu.)

Opening an Internet Shortcut from the Favorites Folder

The purpose of the Favorites folder, of course, is to give you quick access to the sites you visit regularly. To link to one of the shortcuts in your Favorites folder, you have two choices:

- In Internet Explorer, the Favorites menu contains the complete list of your Favorites folder shortcuts, as shown in Figure 38.9. To link to a shortcut, pull down this menu and select the shortcut you want. (Note that you can also display this list by clicking the Favorites button on the toolbar.)
- Open the Favorites folder and double-click a shortcut.

FIGURE 38.9.

*To open a shortcut,
select it from the
Favorites menu.*

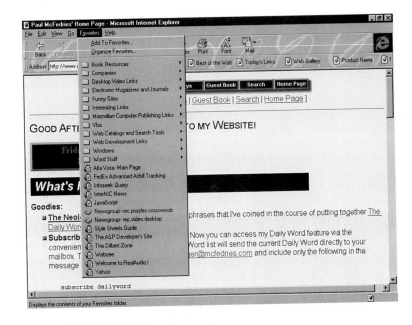

Setting Some Options

To get the most out of Internet Explorer, you should set up the program to suit your own personal style. This includes not only cosmetic options such as the fonts and colors used by the program, but also more important concerns, such as your Usenet news server and the level of security that Internet Explorer uses.

To display these options, select View | Options. You'll see the Options dialog box, shown in Figure 38.10. The next few sections discuss the details of most of the tabs in this dialog box.

FIGURE 38.10.

*Use the Options dialog
box to customize Inter-
net Explorer to suit the
way you work.*

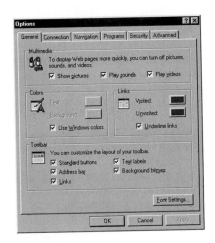

General Options

The controls in the General tab determine how Internet Explorer displays the Web pages you visit. Note that, in some cases, the designer of the Web page will have specified colors and fonts to use and that these settings will override the options you set in the Appearance tab. Here's a summary of the various properties you can work with:

Show pictures: When this check box is activated, Internet Explorer loads and displays whatever inline images are part of the Web page. If you're on a slow connection, you can speed up your Web work by turning off this option and thus preventing Web graphics from being displayed. Instead, you'll just see an icon that represents the image. If you then want to see a particular graphic, right-click the icon and select Show Picture from the context menu.

Play sounds: When this check box is activated, Internet Explorer plays any sounds embedded in a Web page. Again, it can take quite a while to download sound files on a slow link, so you can turn off this option for faster loading.

Play videos: Internet Explorer also supports inline AVI files that play animations. (For an example, check out the spinning moon on the home page of my Web site: http://www.mcfedries.com/.) Turning off this check box prevents Internet Explorer from downloading and playing these AVI files.

Use Windows colors: Deactivate this check box to set the default text and background colors used in the Internet Explorer window. (If you leave this check box activated, Internet Explorer uses the colors defined in the Display properties sheet; see Chapter 7.) Clicking the Text and Background buttons displays a Color dialog box from which you can select the color you want.

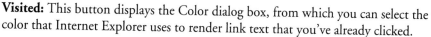

TIP: CHANGING FONT SIZES

To change the size of the fonts Internet Explorer uses, select View | Fonts, and then choose a relative font size from the cascade menu (for example, Large or Small). You can also click the Font toolbar button repeatedly to cycle through the font sizes.

Visited: This button displays the Color dialog box, from which you can select the color that Internet Explorer uses to render link text that you've already clicked.

Unvisited: This button displays the Color dialog box, from which you can select the color that Internet Explorer uses to render link text that you haven't yet clicked.

Underline links: When this check box is activated, Internet Explorer displays link text with an underline.

Standard buttons: This check box toggles the toolbar on and off.

Address bar: This check box toggles the address bar on and off.

Links: This check box toggles the Links toolbar on and off.

Text labels: This check box toggles toolbar text labels (that is, the text that appears below the toolbar buttons) on and off.

Background bitmap: This check box toggles the toolbar background image on and off.

Font Settings: Clicking this button displays the Fonts dialog box, which lets you determine how Web page fonts appear within Internet Explorer.

Connection Options

The Connection tab controls how your Internet connection is established. I discussed the options in this tab in Chapter 37, "Windows 95 and the Internet."

Navigation Options

The Navigation tab, shown in Figure 38.11, contains options that let you modify Internet Explorer's predefined pages—including the Start Page and the Search Page—as well as configure the History folder.

FIGURE 38.11.

Use this tab to modify Internet Explorer's default pages and to configure the History folder.

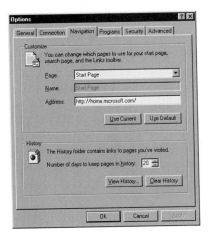

To change the Start Page, first navigate to the page you want to use. Then open the Options dialog box, select the Navigation tab, and make sure that Start Page is displayed in the Page drop-down list. Click the Use Current button to change the Start Page to the current page. To revert to Internet Explorer's default Start Page, click the Use Default button.

Changing the Search Page is similar. First, surf to the page you want to use, and then display the Navigation tab. Use the Page drop-down list to select Search Page, and then click the Use Current button. To revert to Internet Explorer's default Search Page, click the Use Default button.

It's also possible to customize the buttons that appear on Internet Explorer's Links toolbar. To do so, follow these steps:

1. Choose `Quick Link #n` from the Page list, where `n` is a number between 1 and 5 that represents the link you want to replace.
2. Use the `Name` text box to enter a name that will appear in the toolbar.
3. Use the `Address` text box to enter the page's URL. (You can also navigate to the page in Internet Explorer, display the Navigation tab, choose Quick Link, and click Use Current.)

The Navigation tab also has a History group that controls various options related to the History folder:

Number of days to keep pages in spinner: This spinner determines the maximum number of days that Internet Explorer will store a URL in its History list.

View History: Click this button to display the History folder.

Clear History: Click this button to remove all URLs from the History folder.

Programs Options

The controls in the Programs tab, shown in Figure 38.12, determine the applications used to read mail, view Usenet newsgroups, and handle other types of Internet files:

Mail: This drop-down list determines the mail system used from within Internet Explorer.

News: This drop-down list determines the Usenet newsreader to use while reading newsgroups from within Internet Explorer.

Viewers: Clicking the File Types button displays the File Types dialog box, which you then use to set up the applications you want to use to view particular file types. For a complete explanation of the controls in this dialog box, see Chapter 8.

Internet Explorer should check to see whether it is the default browser: When you activate this option, Internet Explorer checks the Registry to see which browser is specified in the Open action for the Internet Document (HTML) file type. If the default isn't Internet Explorer (it won't be if, say, you installed Netscape Navigator after installing Internet Explorer), you'll see a dialog box asking whether you want to set Internet Explorer as the default browser. Netscape Navigator does the same thing, so this seems to be a little game of one-upmanship on the part of Microsoft and Netscape. In the end, it's more annoying than anything else.

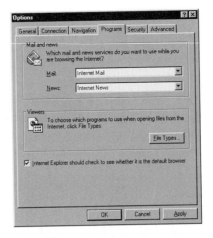

Security Options

A big push is on to turn the Web into a giant shopping mall where consumers can take conspicuous consumption (and their credit card balances) to new heights. This isn't surprising, because the Web's graphical nature makes it a natural venue for showing off products of all kinds and because it's easy to turn the Web's forms into full-fledged order forms.

The fly in this capitalistic ointment, however, is security. Those innocuous-looking order forms you fill out to buy your toys also contain sensitive data, such as your credit card number. You wouldn't leave credit card receipts lying in the street, but that's more or less what you're doing if you submit a normal Web form that has your Visa number on it.

Recognizing that most people are at least aware of the dangers involved in online commerce, would-be Web merchants realize that they won't break any sales records until the phrase "secure transaction" is no longer oxymoronic. So all kinds of programmers are working long hours to make the Web a safe place for consumers.

Internet Explorer supports many of the early security initiatives that have been developed. Moreover, the Internet Explorer window gives you visual cues that tell you whether a particular document is secure. For example, Figure 38.13 shows Internet Explorer displaying a secure Web page. Notice how a lock icon appears in the lower-right corner. Notice too that the URL of a secure page uses https rather than http. (HTTPS is a variation on regular HTTP that uses Netscape's Secure Sockets Layer to implement RSA encryption and other security features.)

NOTE: DISPLAYING SECURITY INFO

You can get some details about the current document's security level by selecting File | Properties and then displaying the Security tab in the properties sheet that appears.

FIGURE 38.13.

An example of a secure Web document.

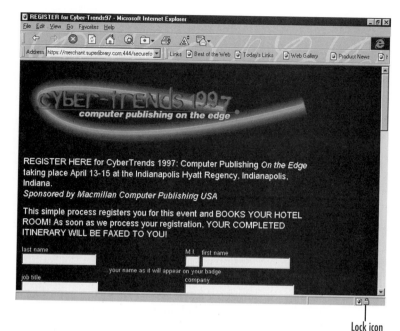

Lock icon

Internet Explorer also implements *security warnings.* These are dialog boxes that warn you about such concerns as submitting a form unsecurely, as shown in Figure 38.14, and entering or leaving a secure site.

FIGURE 38.14.

Internet Explorer warns you when you're about to send an unsecure form.

The Security tab in the Options dialog box, shown in Figure 38.15, lets you customize the level of security used by Internet Explorer.

The Content advisor group lets you control the type of content that appears in the browser:

Enable Ratings: Clicking this button displays the Create Supervisor Password dialog box, which you use to enter a password for the Content Advisor. Once you've done that, the name of this button changes to Disable Ratings. You can turn off the ratings by clicking this button and entering your password.

Settings: Clicking this button displays the Content Advisor, which you use to restrict sites.

FIGURE 38.15.

Use the Security tab to set the level of security you're comfortable with.

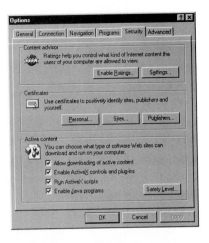

The `Certificates` group deals with site certificates that act as positive identifications on the Web. For example, when viewing a site that requires installing an ActiveX control, you'll see a dialog box like the one shown in Figure 38.16. This certificate tells you that the publisher of the control is legitimate. To install and run the control, click Yes. Also note that you can designate this publisher—or any publisher with these credentials—as "trustworthy" by activating one or both of the check boxes in the bottom-left corner of the dialog box.

FIGURE 38.16.

A certificate that tells you an ActiveX control is from a legitimate publisher.

Internet Explorer stores this and other certificate data in the `Certificates` group:

>   **Personal:** Lists your personal certificates (if any).

>   **Sites:** Certificates that have been issued by various Web sites.

>   **Publishers:** Web publishers and credentials agencies that you've deemed trustworthy.

The `Active content` group lets you set up safeguards for working with downloaded software:

Allow downloading of active content: Deactivating this check box prevents Internet Explorer from downloading all active contents, including ActiveX controls, audio files, and animations.

Enable ActiveX controls and plug-ins: Deactivating this check box tells Internet Explorer not to run downloaded ActiveX controls or Netscape plug-ins.

Run ActiveX scripts: Deactivating this check box prevents Internet Explorer from running ActiveX scripts embedded in Web pages.

Enable Java programs: Deactivating this check box prevents Internet Explorer from running Java programs.

Safety Level: This button displays the Safety Level dialog box, which controls the warning level used by Internet Explorer when dealing with sites that have active content.

Advanced Options

The Advanced tab controls, among other things, settings related to submitting forms and the disk cache, as shown in Figure 38.17.

FIGURE 38.17.

The Advanced tab controls settings related to submitting forms, the disk cache, and much more.

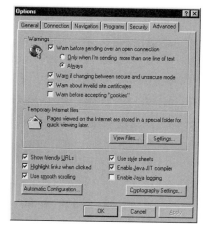

The `Warnings` group contains the following options:

Warn before sending over an open connection: Activate this check box to have Internet Explorer warn you before sending unsecure form data. If you select the `Only when I'm sending more than one line of text` option, Internet Explorer displays a security warning only if you submit an unsecure form that has multiple fields. If you activate the `Always` option, Internet Explorer displays a security warning for every unsecure form you submit.

Warn if changing between secure and unsecure mode: Activating this check box tells Internet Explorer to warn you when you switch between a secure document and an unsecure document.

Warn about invalid site certificates: When this option is turned on, Internet Explorer displays a warning if a site provides a certificate that appears to be invalid.

Warn before accepting cookies: With this option activated, Internet Explorer displays a warning whenever a Web page attempts to send you a cookie. (A cookie is a small text file that Web sites store on your computer to save information about you, such as selections you've made in a Web "shopping cart.")

The disk cache is a memory buffer that Internet Explorer uses to store data from pages you visited recently. This lets Internet Explorer redisplay a page quickly (even one that's heavy on graphics) if you return to that page. In the `Temporary Internet Files` group, you can click View Files to see what's in the cache. You can also click Settings to display the Settings dialog box, shown in Figure 38.18, which contains the following controls:

Check for newer versions of stored pages: These options determine what Internet Explorer does when you visit a site that's already in the cache. If you select the `Every visit to the page` option, Internet Explorer updates each page as you visit it. To update all pages in the cache, activate the `Every time you start Internet Explorer` option. To bypass these checks, activate the `Never` option.

Amount of disk space to use: This slider determines the maximum size of the cache as a percentage of the total disk space on the hard disk where the cache folder resides. If you have a lot of free space available, specifying a larger cache size speeds up your browsing.

Move Folder: Click this button to specify the pathname of the folder where Internet Explorer keeps the cache files.

View Files: Click this button to view the cache files.

Empty Folder: Click this button to wipe out the current cache and start again.

FIGURE 38.18.

The Settings dialog box lets you configure Internet Explorer's disk cache.

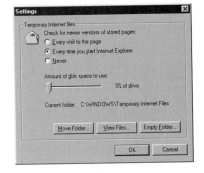

Here's a summary of the rest of the controls in the Advanced tab:

Show friendly URLs: When this check box is turned on, the URLs displayed in the status bar contain only the filename of the Web page. Deactivate this check box if you prefer to see the full URL.

Highlight links when clicked: Toggles whether or not Internet Explorer displays focus lines around a clicked link.

Use smooth scrolling: Toggles Internet Explorer's "smooth scrolling" feature.

Use style sheets: Toggles whether or not Internet Explorer uses Web page style sheets.

Automatic Configuration: Lets you specify a URL that contains Internet Explorer configuration data.

Enable Java JIT compiler: Toggles whether or not Internet Explorer uses its internal "just-in-time" Java compiler to compile and run Java applets.

Enable Java logging: Toggles whether or not Internet Explorer keeps a log of all Java applet activity on your system.

Cryptography Settings: Displays the Cryptography Protocols dialog box, which lets you specify which cryptography protocols are allowed.

Internet Explorer and VRML

A new technology is on the horizon that promises a radical change in the way people will approach the Web: VRML. VRML (pronounced "vermal") stands for Virtual Reality Modeling Language. Although this sounds like you'll be surfing the Web wearing funny gloves and ridiculous-looking headgear, that's not what VRML is all about. The *VR* in *VRML* indicates that VRML Web sites are 3-D "worlds" you "enter" by using a VRML-enhanced browser. You can then use the mouse to "move" around this world in any direction. For example, consider a Web-based shopping mall. With a page made up of standard HTML codes, you would probably see a few links that would take you to one store or another. With a shopping mall based on VRML, however, you could "walk" through the mall, examine the storefronts, and saunter through the door of a store that looks interesting.

This sounds miraculous, and when you first try it, you can't believe you're actually doing what you're doing. But the underlying principle of VRML is simple. Just as HTML is, in essence, a set of instructions that tell a browser how to display a document, VRML is a set of instructions that tell a browser how to create and navigate a three-dimensional world. These instructions are interpreted by a *renderer,* which either is a separate program or is incorporated into the browser. The renderer takes the VRML instructions, uses them to build the 3-D world, and lets you move anywhere—left and right, up and down, in and out—through this world.

Installing the Internet Explorer VRML Add-In

To try out VRML, you need to have the proper software that knows how to accept and render VRML worlds. Fortunately, just such a renderer exists for Internet Explorer: the VRML 1.0 ActiveX Control. To get it, head for the Internet Explorer for Windows 95 download area:

`http://www.microsoft.com/msdownload/ieplatform/iewin95.htm`

In the drop-down list, select VRML 1.0 ActiveX Control and then click Next to get a list of download sites. Click one of these links to get `VRMLOCX.EXE` sent to your computer. (This file weighs in at just under 2 MB, so this might be a good time to grab a cup of coffee.) When the file transfer is complete, double-click `VRMLOCX.EXE` to install the software.

Giving VRML a Whirl

Talking about VRML isn't nearly as much fun as trying it out. For some links to VRML worlds that will get you started, check out the following Microsoft site:

`http://www.microsoft.com/ie/addon/sites.htm`

Click a link that looks interesting. (Some of these worlds are huge, so you'll have to be patient.) Figure 38.19 shows the Ziff-Davis Terminal Reality world. To move around, hold down the left mouse button and drag the pointer. Dragging up moves you "into" the world; dragging down moves you "out" of the world; dragging left and right takes you to the left and right. To adjust how you move through the world, click Walk, Slide, Tilt, or Spin. In some cases, you can click a particular spot to jump into another part of the world.

FIGURE 38.19.

A VRML world: Ziff-Davis Terminal Reality.

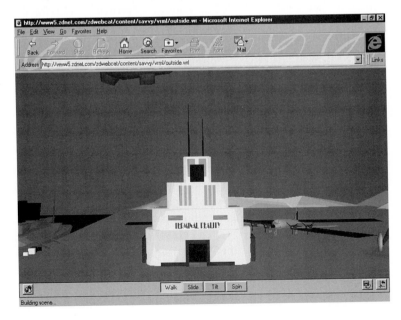

The number of VRML sites is growing rapidly, so you'll have no lack of worlds in which to fly around. Here are a few other general VRML sites you can check out for the latest and greatest:

The Web Gate to VR:

```
http://web.actwin.com/NewType/vr/vrml/index.htm
```

Protein Man's Top Ten VRML sites:

```
http://www.virtpark.com/theme/proteinman/
```

Yahoo's VRML Index:

```
http://www.yahoo.com/Computers_and_Internet/Internet/World_Wide_Web/
➡Virtual_Reality_Modeling_Language__VRML_/
```

Internet Explorer, ActiveX, and VBScript

Internet Explorer 3.0 boasts a whole host of new features, but two are most likely to set Web surfers' chins a-wagging: ActiveX support and Visual Basic scripting support.

ActiveX: Making Web Pages Sing and Dance

Many people, originally stunned and amazed at the sheer wealth and diversity of information on the Web, eventually find themselves asking "Is that all there is?" The problem is that after you've read all those marketing blurbs, lists of "hot links," and let-me-tell-you-about-myself home pages, you begin to yearn for something more substantial. Forms are a step in the right direction, because they at least let you interact with a page, but their usefulness is limited.

This year, 1997, will be the year that pages move away from the simple type-it-and-send-it world of forms and start performing the Web equivalent of singing and dancing. In other words, Web pages will no longer be restricted to static displays of text and graphics, but will instead become dynamic, kinetic, and truly *interactive* environments. Instead of being mere documents to read and look at, pages will become *programs* you can manipulate and play with.

One of the engines that's propelling this transformation is the ActiveX technology I mentioned in Chapter 17, "Sharing Data in Windows 95: The Clipboard and OLE." Web weavers can embed ActiveX controls right in their Web pages. These controls are miniprograms that can provide dynamic content that runs on the Web page. This content can be anything from games to stock market updates to OLE servers that let you view documents in their native format.

A good example is Microsoft's home page for Windows 95. As you can see in Figure 38.20, this page contains several ActiveX buttons that act as cascading menus.

For example, the Web page shown in Figure 38.20 looks like a typical form. However, it contains several ActiveX controls that make the page more dynamic than your average form. For example, when you select an option in the Pick A Style box, the Description box tells you a little about the item, and the Total box updates the dollar total of the items you've ordered.

FIGURE 38.20.

Internet Explorer showing a Web page with embedded ActiveX controls.

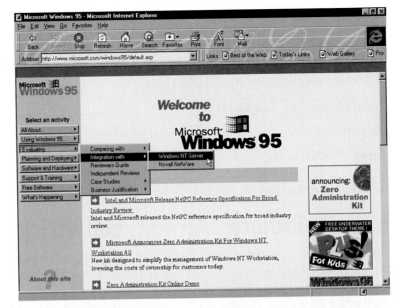

NOTE: THE JAVA JIVE

The other engine behind the trend toward interactive Web pages is the Java programming language. Developers can write Java programs and include them as part of a Web page. Java-enabled browsers then download these programs and run them in the page. Microsoft will support Java in Internet Explorer through the ActiveX technology.

Here are a few advantages that ActiveX controls have over traditional software:

- The controls are sent to your browser and are started "behind the scenes." You don't have to worry about installation, setup, or loading, because your browser takes care of all that dirty work for you.

- The controls are designed to be cross-platform. Whether you're running Windows, a Mac, or a UNIX box, the controls should (eventually) run without complaint.

- Because you're always sent the latest and greatest version of the control when you access a site, you don't need to worry about upgrades and new releases.

Currently, only Internet Explorer 3.0 supports embedded ActiveX controls. However, Microsoft has signed up a whole slew of other browser companies to license the ActiveX technology. Not only that, but a company called NCompass (www.ncompasslabs.com) has developed plug-in software that lets the Netscape Navigator browser support ActiveX controls. Combine this with the thousands of controls that already exist—and the fact that developers can create ActiveX controls without learning any new programming techniques and can create them using many different programming systems, from Visual C++ to Visual Basic—and you know that ActiveX will be ubiquitous on the Web before too long.

On a larger scale, Internet Explorer 3.0 is also the first application that supports Microsoft's new *Active Document* format. An Active Document is an OLE container that can hold any kind of ActiveX control. Internet Explorer 3.0, for example, is really just an empty container that can support various file types. If you load a Web page, Internet Explorer 3.0 loads its HTML parsing engine and displays the page appropriately. But it could just as easily operate as a spreadsheet engine or a word processing engine. In this case, Internet Explorer 3.0 would load the appropriate menus and toolbars for working with spreadsheet files or word processing documents.

For example, Figure 38.21 shows Internet Explorer 3.0 displaying an Excel 97 workbook. Notice that the screen includes the usual Excel interface: toolbars, row and column headers, and so on.

FIGURE 38.21.

Internet Explorer 3.0 displaying an Excel workbook.

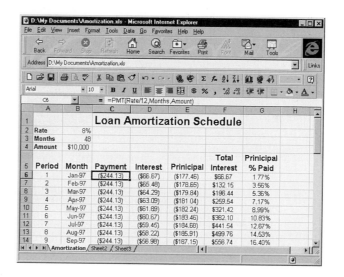

Visual Basic Scripting

ActiveX controls are a powerful way to create dynamic Web pages, but they still take a fairly high level of programming sophistication to create. For people with less programming time or inclination, Microsoft has created Visual Basic Scripting (VBScript). It provides support for this language in Internet Explorer 3.0.

VBScript is a subset of the Visual Basic programming language (in fact, it's a subset of Visual Basic for Applications). As such, it provides a simple way for developers of all skill levels to incorporate code into their Web pages. So, for example, you could run a program each time someone accesses a page, each time someone clicks a button, and so on. Developers can also use VBScript to access the properties and methods associated with ActiveX controls that are embedded in a Web page. And because Internet Explorer 3.0 is an ActiveX control itself, VBScript programs can control the browser's properties and methods.

You can try out a VBScript example on my Web site at the following address:

```
http://www.mcfedries.com/Toys/MortgageMinder.html
```

As you can see in Figure 38.22, this is a simple mortgage calculator. You enter the house price, down payment, interest rate, and term. When you click the Calculate button, VBScript enters the principal, number of payments, and monthly payment in the Results section.

FIGURE 38.22.

A simple VBScript application.

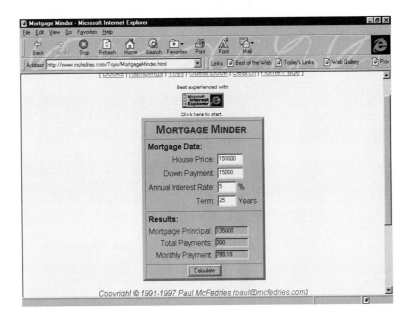

Summary

This chapter continued our look at Windows 95 and the Internet by showing you how to wield the Windows 95 Web browser of choice: Internet Explorer. After showing you how to get Internet Explorer, I took you on a tour of the screen. From there, you learned some basic browsing techniques, including how to create Internet shortcuts, how to use the Search page, and how to deal with files. Other topics included the Favorites folder, Internet Explorer options, working with Usenet newsgroups, and VRML. I closed with a look at Internet Explorer's support for VBScript and and ActiveX controls.

Here are some pointers to related chapters:

■ To learn how to install Microsoft Plus! and the Windows 95 Service Pack 1, see Chapter 2, "Running the Windows 95 Setup."

■ For more information on The Microsoft Network, see Chapter 26, "Getting Online with The Microsoft Network."

■ You can't explore the Web until you've set up Windows 95 to connect to the Internet. To find out how it's done, see Chapter 37, "Windows 95 and the Internet."

■ The full installation of Internet Explorer 3.x comes with a new Net utility called NetMeeting. I'll show you how to use it in Chapter 39, "Remote Collaboration with Microsoft NetMeeting."

■ See Chapter 40, "Internet Mail: Messaging Made Easy," and Chapter 41, "Internet News: Usenet News and Views," to learn about the e-mail and Usenet clients that come with the full installation of Internet Explorer 3.x.

■ I've put together a list of online sites that contain Windows 95 files and information; many of them are on the Web. See Appendix A, "Windows 95 Online Resources."

CHAPTER 39

Remote Collaboration with Microsoft NetMeeting

> *He sought to inject a few raisins of conversation into the tasteless dough of existence.*
>
> —*O. Henry*

As remote connection technologies improve, commuters find themselves morphing into telecommuters, and employees often end up with more freedom than ever to work where they want, when they want. In this new age of distance computing, the traditional definition of an office needs to be modified to include modern incarnations that are more "virtual" than physical.

Not only that, but the manner in which employees interact with each other also needs to be rethought. If members of, say, the editorial department are scattered all over the city, state, or even country, regular meetings just aren't possible. Sure, there is always e-mail or company Web pages (or even that almost-forgotten device, the telephone) to keep distance workers informed, but these methods lack the interaction of a true meeting.

If you have users or colleagues who must collaborate regularly but who are too far-flung to meet face-to-face, Microsoft NetMeeting might be the solution. NetMeeting is a communication and collaboration tool that allows users to establish "conferences" over an Internet, a network, or a modem connection. Within these conferences, remote users can interact in various ways:

- They can have voice conversations using sound card/microphone combinations.
- They can exchange files.
- They can "chat" by sending text messages in real time.
- They can use an electronic Whiteboard to collaborate on drawings.
- They can share applications and even work together on the same document.

This chapter shows you how to set up NetMeeting and then takes you through all of its collaboration features.

Configuring NetMeeting

OSR2 I'm going to assume that you have an Internet/network connection set up. I'll further assume that you've installed NetMeeting, either by installing the full version of Internet Explorer 3.0 (including the version that comes with OSR2) or by downloading NetMeeting from the NetMeeting home page:

```
http://www.microsoft.com/netmeeting/
```

TIP: EASY ACCESS TO THE NETMEETING HOME PAGE

After you've installed and started NetMeeting, you can load the NetMeeting home page either by selecting Help | NetMeeting Home Page or by clicking the NetMeeting Home Page button on the toolbar.

Given that, let's run through the steps necessary to configure the program. Begin by selecting Start | Programs | Microsoft NetMeeting. The first time you make this selection, Windows 95 launches the Microsoft NetMeeting Wizard, shown in Figure 39.1. This dialog box just gives you an overview of NetMeeting's capabilities, so click Next > to proceed.

FIGURE 39.1.

The first time you launch NetMeeting, this Wizard leads you through the configuration process.

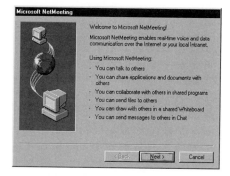

The next dialog box, shown in Figure 39.2, asks for a few particulars that help identify you in the NetMeeting user directory. At a minimum, you have to specify your first and last names and your e-mail address to coax NetMeeting into continuing. (Don't worry—you can tell NetMeeting not to publish this information if you'd prefer to be incognito.) When you're done, click Next >.

FIGURE 39.2.

Use this dialog box to enter your personal data.

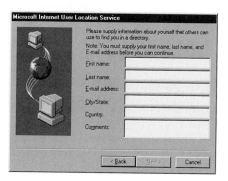

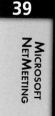
39
MICROSOFT
NETMEETING

In the next dialog box, shown in Figure 39.3, you can tell NetMeeting to publish your name on a User Location Server (select Yes) or to bypass this step (select No). You also can enter the domain name of a User Location Server in the text box provided. (You'll probably want to use the default uls.microsoft.com for now.) Click Next >.

NetMeeting now launches the Audio Tuning Wizard, which checks your sound card to see whether it supports full-duplex (two-way) or half-duplex (one-way) sound. Make sure that no other programs that use your sound card are running, and then click Next >.

Figure 39.3.

This dialog box sets up a couple of options for the User Location Service.

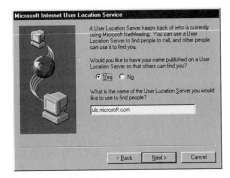

If your sound card can handle full-duplex audio, you'll see the dialog box shown in Figure 39.4. If these settings are correct (which they should be if you have no other audio input or output devices on your system), click Next > to continue.

Figure 39.4.

You'll see this dialog box if your sound card supports full-duplex audio.

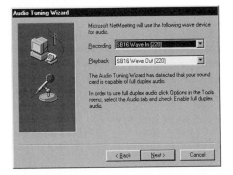

NOTE: YOU NEED TO ACTIVATE FULL-DUPLEX AUDIO

Even if the Audio Tuning Wizard detects that you have a sound card capable of supporting full-duplex audio, NetMeeting doesn't enable its full-duplex features automatically. To do this yourself, select Tools | Options when you get to the NetMeeting window, activate the Audio tab in the dialog box that appears, and then activate the Enable full duplex audio check box.

The next item on the Wizard's to-do list is selecting the speed of the connection you'll be using to make NetMeeting calls, as shown in Figure 39.5. Select the appropriate option and then click Next >.

The Audio Tuning Wizard now attempts to tune your audio settings automatically. First make sure that you have your sound card microphone plugged in and at the ready. In the dialog box that appears, as shown in Figure 39.6, click Start Recording and then speak into the microphone using your normal voice (the Wizard suggests that you read the couple of paragraphs under the Start Recording button).

FIGURE 39.5.

Specify the speed of your NetMeeting connection in this dialog box.

FIGURE 39.6.

Click Start Recording and then speak into the microphone using your normal voice.

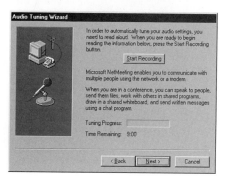

When the recording is complete, click Next > and then click Finish in the final Wizard dialog box to continue loading NetMeeting.

NOTE: NETMEETING AND FIREWALLS

If your network has a firewall separating it from the Internet, the firewall must be configured to allow Internet-based NetMeeting connections. Here are the ports NetMeeting uses for its connections:

Port	Purpose	Protocol
522	ULS server	TCP
1503	T.120	TCP
1731	Audio call control	TCP
Dynamic	Audio stream	RTP over UDP

In other words, the firewall must be configured to allow TCP connections on ports 522, 1503, and 1731, and secondary UDP connection on dynamically assigned ports.

39

MICROSOFT
NETMEETING

A Tour of the NetMeeting Window

After the Wizard has completed its labors (and each subsequent time you select Start | Programs | NetMeeting), the Microsoft NetMeeting window appears. Figure 39.7 shows how the window looks after you've set up a NetMeeting conference.

FIGURE 39.7.

The NetMeeting window with an active conference.

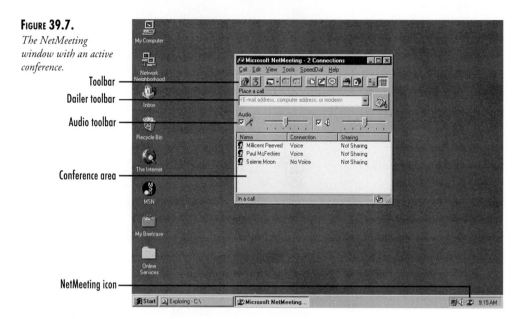

Toolbar

Dialer toolbar

Audio toolbar

Conference area

NetMeeting icon

Here's a quick review of the NetMeeting window's features:

Toolbar: This provides a few point-and-click shortcuts. You can hide the toolbar by deactivating the View | Toolbar command.

Dialer toolbar: You use this toolbar to specify who you want to call and to place the call. To hide this toolbar, deactivate the View | Dialer command.

Audio toolbar: This toolbar controls the NetMeeting volume. The slider on the left controls the volume of the microphone, and the slider on the right controls the volume of the speaker. You can mute either device by deactivating its check box. To hide the Audio toolbar, deactivate the View | Audio command.

Conference area: When you establish a conference, the participants appear in this area. In its default Details view, NetMeeting shows the name of each participant, the type of connection, and the status of shared applications. If you want to see only an icon for each person, as shown in Figure 39.8, select View | Large Icons. You can also switch between these views by using the following toolbar buttons:

 Large Icons

 Details

Note, too, that when NetMeeting is running it adds an icon to the system tray, as you saw in Figure 39.7. You can right-click this icon for access to certain commands.

FIGURE 39.8.

The NetMeeting window in Large Icons view.

Placing NetMeeting Calls

After NetMeeting is configured and you have the Internet or network connection established, you can get right down to business. In this section, I'll show you how to make calls in NetMeeting, use the Directory to find folks to talk with, place advanced and SpeedDial calls, and more.

Placing Simple Calls

If you know who you want to call, NetMeeting is simple to use. All you do is enter the name, e-mail address, computer name, or modem phone number of the person you want to call in the Place a call text box, and then click the Call button or press Enter. (Note, too, that you can use the Place a call drop-down list to select callers you've used previously.)

39

MICROSOFT
NETMEETING

NOTE: MODEM CALLS REQUIRING AN OUTSIDE LINE

If you want to call a remote modem and you need to get an outside line, preface the phone number with the characters -9, (that's a hyphen, followed by the number 9, followed by a comma). Here's an example:

-9,555-1212

TIP: TRY IP ADDRESSES

If you can't connect to a user by entering the user's network computer name, try entering his IP address.

NOTE: CALLING NETWARE USERS

If you want to call another user over a NetWare IPX network, the user's address must use the following format:

`network:node`

Here, *network* is the IPX network address, and *node* is the user's node address. Unfortunately, there is no built-in method for determining a user's network node address. However, Microsoft has created a tool that can sniff out network node addresses. The file is `IPXAddr.exe` and you can download it from the following page on Microsoft's Web site:

`http://www.microsoft.com/iesupport/netmeeting/content/node.htm`

After NetMeeting finds the user and places the call, the other person hears a ring and sees the dialog box shown in Figure 39.9. The remote user clicks Accept to "answer" the call, or clicks Ignore to reject the call. (NetMeeting rejects an incoming call automatically if it isn't answered after five rings.)

FIGURE 39.9.

This dialog box appears when there is an incoming NetMeeting call.

If the call went through, your name and the remote user's name are added to the conference area, and NetMeeting displays `In a call` in the status bar.

If NetMeeting can't locate the remote user, you see the dialog box shown in Figure 39.10. You can either click No and try again, or click Yes to use NetMeeting's advanced calling feature (see "Placing Advanced Calls" later in this chapter).

FIGURE 39.10.

NetMeeting displays this dialog box if it can't find the remote user.

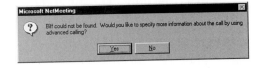

If the remote user is already involved in a conference, you see the dialog box shown in Figure 39.11. Click Yes to attempt to join the existing conference, or click No if you prefer to try again later.

FIGURE 39.11.

This dialog box shows up if the remote user is already in a conference.

Here are some notes to bear in mind when you're connected:

- To talk to the other person, just speak into your microphone. If the sound cards used by you and the remote user can handle full-duplex audio, both of you can speak at the same time. If the cards support only half-duplex audio, only one of you can speak at a time.

- If the remote user complains that your voice isn't loud enough, you can increase your microphone volume or they can increase their speaker volume.

- To find out the e-mail address and other particulars about the remote user (depending on what that person entered into her NetMeeting configuration), right-click the user and select Properties from the context menu.

- In a conference, only two people can communicate by voice at one time. If a third person joins the conference, that person can communicate only via Chat, Whiteboard, or some other NetMeeting feature. (For users who can't communicate by voice, NetMeeting displays No Voice in the Connection column.)

- Under ideal conditions, NetMeeting supports a maximum of 32 callers in a conference. In practice, the maximum number of participants might be less, depending on the available network bandwidth and the speed of the users' computers.

TROUBLESHOOTING: NO VOICE CONNECTION

If you can't seem to get a voice connection in NetMeeting (even when only two users are in the conference), make sure that you're connecting via the TCP/IP protocol. NetMeeting's voice features are enabled only on TCP/IP connections. To learn how to tell NetMeeting to use TCP/IP, see "Setting NetMeeting Properties" later in this chapter.

Hanging Up from a Call

When it's time to end a NetMeeting call, use any of the following techniques to hang up:

- Select Call | Hang Up.

- Click the Hang Up button on the toolbar.

- Select Call | Exit or close the NetMeeting window.

NetMeeting disconnects the call. If you began the conference and it includes three or more people, NetMeeting displays the warning dialog box shown in Figure 39.12. To disconnect everyone in the conference, click Yes.

FIGURE 39.12.

NetMeeting displays this dialog box when you attempt to hang up from a conference that contains three or more users.

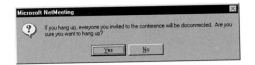

Using the Directory to Make a Call

When you launch NetMeeting, the program automatically logs you on to a User Location Service. This is a server that keeps track of the people who are currently running NetMeeting. If you're looking for someone to call, NetMeeting's Directory feature can provide you with a list of these users.

To open the Directory, use any of the following techniques:

- Select Call | Directory.
- Press Ctrl-D.

- Click the Directory button on the toolbar.

Figure 39.13 shows the Directory window that appears (note that it might take a minute or two to complete the download of users, depending on the speed of your connection).

The initial order of the users is random, but you can sort the entries by clicking the column headers. For example, click the Last Name header to sort the entries by last name in ascending order. Click the header again to switch to descending order. If you prefer to work with a different User Location Server, use the drop-down list at the top of the window to select the server you want.

FIGURE 39.13.

The Directory window shows you a list of all the people who are logged on to the displayed User Location Server.

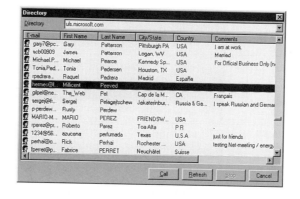

When you've found someone you want to connect with, highlight that Directory entry and then click the Call button.

NOTE: REMOVING YOUR NAME FROM THE SERVER

If you'd rather not have your name appear in the User Location Server (which is sort of like having an unlisted NetMeeting number), NetMeeting gives you two methods for leaving your name off the list:

■ Log off the server by selecting Call | Log Off from User Location Service. In the dialog box that appears, click OK. (Note that you'll still be able to use the service to find other people.)

■ Select Tools | Options, activate the My Information tab, and then deactivate the Publish this information in the User Location Service directory check box.

Accessing the Web Directory

Microsoft also maintains a Web-based Directory of NetMeeting users, shown in Figure 39.14. To display the Web Directory, use any of the following methods:

■ Select Call | Web Directory.

■ Click the Web Directory toolbar button.

■ Enter the server URL into a Web browser. The URL of the main server is `http://uls.microsoft.com/`. Other server URLs take the form `http://ulsx.microsoft.com/`, where *x* is a number (1 through 5 at the time of this writing).

The advantage of using the Web Directory is that after the page loads, you can use the browser's Find command to look for specific entries in the Directory. (If you're working in frames, you might need to click inside the list of users for the Find feature to operate properly.)

FIGURE 39.14.

NetMeeting's Web Directory page.

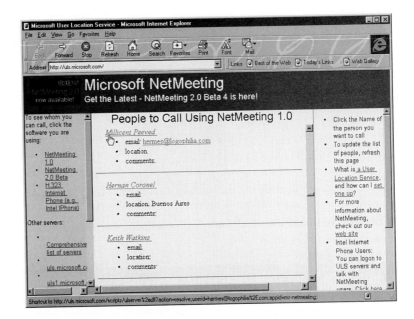

When you click a name, your browser might attempt to download a file and ask you whether you want to open the file or save it. There are two ways to fix this problem:

- In Internet Explorer, activate the Open it option, deactivate the Always ask before opening this type of file check box, and then click OK.

- In Windows Explorer, select View | Options, activate the File Types tab, and then highlight User Location Service in the Registered file types list. Click Edit, and then deactivate the Confirm open after download check box, as shown in Figure 39.15. Click OK and then click OK again to return to Explorer.

FIGURE 39.15.

If you'll be using the Web Directory, deactivate the Confirm open after download *check box.*

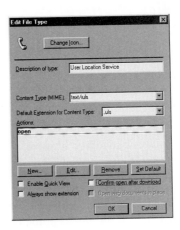

TIP: ADD NETMEETING LINKS TO YOUR WEB PAGE

Use the links on the Web Directory page as a general guide for creating NetMeeting links on your own Web pages. Here's the general format to use:

```
<A HREF="http://ULserver/scripts/ulserver.dll?action=resolve;
➥userid=EmailAddress;appid=ms-netmeeting">
```

Here, *ULserver* is the domain name of your User Location Server, and *EmailAddress* is the e-mail address you used when configuring NetMeeting. Here's a sample link (see Appendix E, "An HTML Primer," for information on the <A> tag):

```
<A HREF="http://uls.microsoft.com/scripts/ulserver.dll?action=resolve;
➥userid=paul@mcfedries.com;appid=ms-netmeeting">
Click here to talk to me live!
</A>
```

Placing Advanced Calls

Although the simple calling method I outlined should work for you most of the time, you might want to place calls using special criteria. For example, if you know a person's computer name or IP address, you might prefer to tell NetMeeting to call via TCP/IP instead of going through the User Location Service. Alternatively, you might want to establish audio-only or data-only calls.

You can accomplish all of this and more by using NetMeeting's Advanced Calling feature. To try this out, select Call | Place Advanced Call to display the Advanced Calling dialog box, shown in Figure 39.16.

FIGURE 39.16.

Use the Advanced Calling dialog box when you have more sophisticated calling needs.

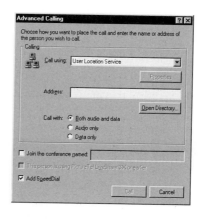

Here's a summary of the controls found in this dialog box:

Call using: Use this list to select a calling mechanism: User Location Service or TCP/IP.

Address: Enter the address of the person you want to call (or, if you selected `User Location Service` earlier, click Open Directory to get the address from the Directory).

Call with: These options determine the type of call to place: `Both audio and data`, `Audio only`, or `Data only`.

Join the conference named: If you're calling a conference service, use this text box to enter the name of the conference you want to join.

This person is using PictureTel LiveShare 3.X or earlier: If you've enabled the LiveShare video protocol (I'll show you how in the "Setting NetMeeting Properties" section later in this chapter), activate this check box if you know that the remote user also uses this protocol.

Add SpeedDial: When activated, this option tells NetMeeting to add the person you call to your SpeedDial folder (discussed in the next section).

When you're done, click Call to make the connection.

Using the SpeedDial Feature

If you call certain people frequently, you can use NetMeeting's SpeedDial feature to connect to these users with only a couple of mouse clicks or keystrokes.

You can use two methods to create a SpeedDial entry:

■   While you're connected to a user, either highlight his name and select SpeedDial | Add SpeedDial, or right-click his name and select Add SpeedDial from the context menu.

■   When placing a call with the Advanced Calling feature, make sure that the `Add SpeedDial` check box is activated.

After you've added someone to the SpeedDial, you can call the person by pulling down the SpeedDial menu and selecting her name from the list that appears at the bottom of the menu.

To remove someone from the SpeedDial menu, select SpeedDial | Open SpeedDial Folder, and then delete the corresponding file in the folder window that appears. (You can also work with this folder directly in Explorer. Look for the `\NetMeeting\SpeedDial` folder.)

TIP: CREATE A SPEEDDIAL FOR YOURSELF

If you want to give other people a SpeedDial file that connects to you, select Call | Create SpeedDial. In the dialog box that appears, select a calling method and enter your Net-Meeting address. You can then save the SpeedDial file on your desktop or opt to send it to an e-mail recipient.

Hanging Out a "Do Not Disturb" Sign

If you have NetMeeting running but you don't want to accept any new calls for a while, you can hang an electronic "Do Not Disturb" sign by activating the Call | Do Not Disturb command (click OK in the dialog box that appears). While this command is active, others attempting to call you will receive a message telling them The other party did not accept your call.

TIP: ACCEPTING CALLS WITHOUT AUDIO

Instead of cutting off calls altogether, you might prefer to avoid only voice calls. To do that, start a NetMeeting conference beforehand by selecting Call | Host a Conference (click OK in the dialog box that appears). With the conference started, all incoming calls will be "No Voice" connections. To return to regular operations, hang up the call.

Exchanging Files in NetMeeting

Assuming that you've established a data connection with one or more remote users, NetMeeting makes it easy to send files back and forth. To initiate a file transfer, use any of the following techniques:

- Select Tools | Send File.
- Press Ctrl-F.

- Click the Send File toolbar button.

- If you have multiple users in your conference, you can send the file to an individual by right-clicking the person's name in the conference area and then selecting Send File from the context menu.

NetMeeting then displays the Select a File to Send dialog box, as shown in Figure 39.17. Highlight the file you want to ship and then click Send. NetMeeting begins sending the file and displays the progress of the operation in the status bar. When the upload is complete, a dialog box lets you know.

39

MICROSOFT
NETMEETING

FIGURE 39.17.

Use this dialog box to choose the file you want to send to the remote user.

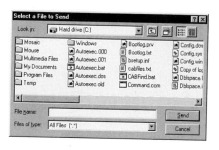

On the remote end, the user sees a dialog box similar to the one shown in Figure 39.18. There are three ways to proceed:

- To have NetMeeting store the file on your hard drive without further ado, click Accept. Alternatively, you can wait until the download is complete and then click Close.
- To cancel the file transfer (or to remove the file after the transfer is finished), click Delete.
- To work with the file after the transfer is done, click Open.

FIGURE 39.18.

This dialog box appears when a remote user attempts to send you a file.

NOTE: FILE TRANSFER OPTIONS

NetMeeting has a few options that allow you to prevent file downloads and specify the folder in which transferred files are stored (the default is `\NetMeeting\Received Files`). See "Setting NetMeeting Properties" later in this chapter for details.

Using the Chat Feature

If you have a "No Voice" connection in a conference, or if you don't have a microphone, NetMeeting's audio features won't do you much good. That doesn't mean you can't communicate with remote callers, however. For simple text communications in real time, NetMeeting's Chat feature is perfect.

To run Chat, use any of the following methods:

- Select Tools | Chat.
- Press Ctrl-T.

- Click the Chat toolbar button.

The Chat window that appears is shown in Figure 39.19.

FIGURE 39.19.

Use the Chat window to type messages to remote users in real time.

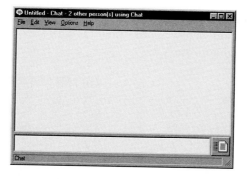

To use Chat, type your message in the text box at the bottom of the Chat window, and then press Enter. These messages appear in the upper text box, along with the name of each person who sent them. Figure 39.20 shows a sample Chat session.

FIGURE 39.20.

A Chat session in progress.

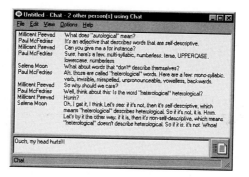

Chat also has a couple of customization features. For example, you can select Options | Font to choose the font that's displayed in the Chat window. Selecting Options | Chat Format displays the Chat Format dialog box shown in Figure 39.21. Here's a summary of the available options:

> **Information Display:** Use these check boxes to specify how much information Chat displays about each message. Besides the Person's name, you can also choose to display the Date and Time each message is sent.

> **Entire message is on one line:** If you activate this option, each Chat message is displayed on a single line across the window.

> **Wrap (message appears next to information display):** If you activate this option (this is the Chat default), the messages are wrapped within the Chat window, and they appear beside the person's name (or whatever is checked in the Information Display group).

39

MICROSOFT NETMEETING

Wrap (message appears below information display): If you activate this option, the messages again are wrapped within the Chat window, but they appear below the displayed information.

FIGURE 39.21.

Use this dialog box to customize the Chat window.

Using the Whiteboard

Whiteboards have become a standard feature in boardrooms and conference rooms across the land. Presenters, facilitators, and meeting leaders use them to record action points, highlight important information, and draw charts and diagrams.

If you're running a remote conference via NetMeeting, you can use its Whiteboard feature for the same purposes. The Whiteboard is basically a revamped version of the Paint window that allows you to enter text, highlight information, and draw lines and shapes. Everything you add to the Whiteboard is reflected on the other users' screens, so they see exactly what you're typing and drawing. You can create multiple Whiteboard "pages," and even save pages for later use.

To work with the Whiteboard, each user must display it by using any of the following techniques:

- Select Tools | Whiteboard.
- Press Ctrl-W.

- Click the Whiteboard toolbar button.

Figure 39.22 shows the Whiteboard window that appears.

For basic operations, you use Whiteboard just like you use Paint. That is, you select a tool to work with, select a line width (if applicable for the tool), select a color, and then draw your shape or type your text.

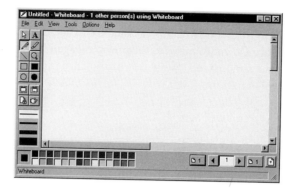

FIGURE 39.22.
Use the Whiteboard to draw text and pictures that can be seen by the other users in the conference.

However, Whiteboard has quite a few other techniques that aren't found in the Paint program. Here's a summary:

Locking the Whiteboard contents: To prevent the other users from changing the Whiteboard screen while you work, either select Tools | Lock Contents or click the Lock Contents tool.

Using the remote pointer: Whiteboard has a remote pointer that, when activated, appears on each user's Whiteboard. To activate it, either select Tools | Remote Pointer or click the Remote Pointer On tool. After the pointer appears, use the mouse to drag it around the screen.

Displaying the contents of another window in the Whiteboard: Whiteboard has a Select Window feature that allows you to display the contents of another open window inside the Whiteboard. To activate this feature, either select Tools | Select Window or click the Select Window tool. Click OK in the Whiteboard Select Window dialog box that appears, and then click the window you want to display.

Displaying part of the screen in the Whiteboard: Rather than an entire window, you might prefer to display only part of the screen in the Whiteboard. To do this, either select Tools | Select Area or click the Select Area tool. Click OK in the Whiteboard Select Area dialog box that appears, and then use the mouse to select the screen area you want to display.

Clearing the Whiteboard: If you want to start over, you can clear the contents of the Whiteboard either by selecting Edit | Clear Page or by pressing Ctrl-Delete.

Adding another page to the Whiteboard: The Whiteboard is capable of displaying multiple pages. To add a new page, either select Edit | Insert Page After or click the Insert New Page button. You can insert a new page before an existing page by selecting Edit | New Page Before.

39

MICROSOFT NETMEETING

Navigating Whiteboard pages: When you have multiple pages in the Whiteboard, you can navigate among them by pressing Ctrl-Page Up (to move to the next page) or Ctrl-Page Down (to move to the previous page). Note that as you move from page to page, the remote users' Whiteboards also change pages. You can also use the following navigation buttons:

 Previous Page

 Next Page

Sorting Whiteboard pages: To change the order in which the Whiteboard pages appear, select Edit | Page Sorter. In the Page Sorter dialog box, use the mouse to drag the pages into the order you prefer.

Deleting a Whiteboard page: To remove the current page from the Whiteboard, select Edit | Delete page.

Preventing remote users from seeing your changes: If you want to make some changes to a page without the other users seeing them, deactivate the Tools | Synchronize command, move to the page and make your changes, and then activate Tools | Synchronize again. The remote users will remain on the original page while you make your edits.

Saving the Whiteboard: If you think you'll need to use your Whiteboard again, select File | Save and then choose a location and name for the new file (Whiteboard files use the WHT extension). To reuse the Whiteboard, select File | Open and pick out the WHT file from the Open dialog box.

Sharing Programs

Chat and the Whiteboard are handy features, but their functionality is limited to text and simple drawings or screen shots. For truly collaborative computing, you need the ability to run a program on one computer and display what's happening on the remote machines. An even better scenario is one in which all the users can work with an application at the same time.

The good news is that NetMeeting can handle both situations, albeit with a few quirks and security concerns. The next two sections take you through NetMeeting's application sharing features.

Sharing an Application in Work Alone Mode

NetMeeting's default method for application sharing is called Work Alone mode. In this mode, you select one of your running programs to share, and the program's window appears on the other users' screens. However, only you can access the program's features and edit the program's documents. This is perfect if you just want to demonstrate a feature or display a document.

To share an application in this way, first run either of the following techniques:

- Select Tools | Share Application.

- Click the Share Application button on the toolbar.

As you can see in Figure 39.23, a list of your running applications appears. Now select the application you want to share, and in the NetMeeting dialog box that appears, click OK. A copy of the application's window is sent to each user, and any actions you perform within this window (including mouse movements) are mirrored on the remote screens. Note, too, that NetMeeting's conference area displays Not Sharing in the Sharing column of each user.

FIGURE 39.23.

The Share Application button (shown here) and menu contain a list of your running applications.

To end the sharing, either exit the program or select it again from the Share Application menu or button.

Sharing an Application in Collaborate Mode

Instead of merely demonstrating a program to the other users, you might prefer a more interactive approach that allows each user to work with the shared application. This is called Collaborate mode. After you've shared an application, you switch to this mode by using either of these methods:

- Activate the Tools | Collaborate command.

- Click the Collaborate toolbar button.

NetMeeting displays a dialog box warning you about possible security problems with Collaborate mode (which I'll discuss a bit later). Click OK to continue. Note that each person who wants to collaborate on this application will also have to switch to Collaborate mode.

Figure 39.24 demonstrates a few features that come with Collaborate mode, as described here:

The sharing status: In the conference area of the NetMeeting window, the Sharing column reports the sharing status of each user: In Control for the user who currently controls the shared application, Collaborating for users who are collaborating on the application but don't have control, and `Working Alone` for users who aren't collaborating.

The shared application window: Above the upper-right corner of the window, NetMeeting displays the name of the user who is running the application. (This banner appears only in nonmaximized windows.)

The mouse pointer: The mouse pointer shows the initials of the user who is currently in control of the application.

Taking control of the shared application: Only one person can work in a shared application window at one time. To take control of the application, just click the mouse anywhere within the application's window.

FIGURE 39.24.

A remote user's screen when in Collaborate mode.

The name of the user who is running the window

The initials of the user who has control

The current sharing status

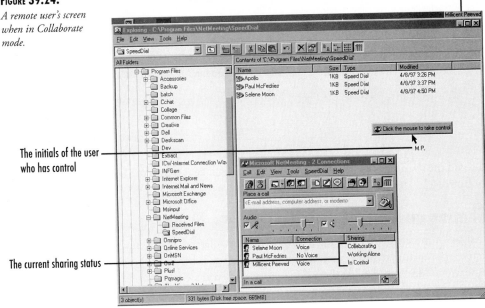

To end the collaboration, either exit the application or use one of the following techniques:

- Activate the Tools | Work Alone command.

- Click the Work Alone toolbar button.

Some Notes About Sharing Applications

NetMeeting's application sharing features are a real boon to collaborative computing, but they come with a few "gotchas" and limitations. Here are a few notes to keep in mind when sharing applications:

Graphics-intensive applications and DOS programs: NetMeeting doesn't do the greatest job sharing graphics-intensive applications (especially those that use the DirectX APIs) and DOS programs. Try to avoid sharing these types of applications.

Handling different screen resolutions: Application sharing works best when all users have their screens set to the same resolution. If a user running at high resolution (say 1,024×768) shares a maximized application with a user running at low resolution (say, 640×480), the user with the lower resolution sees only part of the shared application's window. However, that user can still see more of the window by moving the mouse pointer to the edge of the screen, which causes the window to scroll. (You have some control over this behavior; see the section "Setting NetMeeting Properties.")

Security concerns in Collaborate mode: When you share an application in Collaborate mode, remember that other people can assume control over that application and use it just as though they were sitting at your keyboard. Depending on the program, this might include the ability to open, save, and delete files, or even to launch programs.

Security bug with Explorer-based programs: A bug in NetMeeting 1.0 crops up when you share Windows Explorer, Control Panel, Briefcase, My Computer, or any other Explorer-based program. The problem is that sharing one of these applications automatically shares *all* Explorer-based programs. If you're sharing Explorer, for example, and then you open Control Panel on your system, the remote users will also see the Control Panel window. To work around this problem, either deactivate sharing for any unwanted applications or avoid sharing Explorer-based applications in NetMeeting 1.0.

Hiding part of a shared window: If you have data in an application window that you want to hide from others, use another open window to cover that portion of the shared window. The remote users will see a pattern over the obscured section of the window.

Setting NetMeeting Properties

To finish our look at NetMeeting 1.0, this section shows you how to customize the program using its extensive list of properties. To work with these options, select Tools | Options to display the NetMeeting Properties dialog box, shown in Figure 39.25. The next few sections run through the controls on each tab.

The General Tab

The options in the General tab control a mixed bag of NetMeeting settings. Here's a review:

Show Microsoft NetMeeting icon on the taskbar: This check box toggles the NetMeeting icon on and off in the system tray.

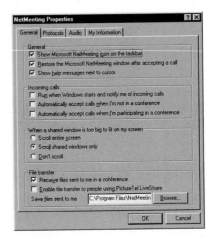

Restore the Microsoft NetMeeting window after accepting a call: When this check box is activated, a minimized NetMeeting window is restored whenever an incoming call is accepted.

Show help messages next to cursor: This check box toggles NetMeeting's ToolTips on and off.

Run when Windows starts and notify me of incoming calls: When this check box is activated, NetMeeting is launched automatically when you start Windows 95.

Automatically accept calls when I'm not in a conference: When this check box is activated, NetMeeting accepts all incoming calls, except when you're in a conference.

Automatically accept calls when I'm participating in a conference: When this check box is activated, NetMeeting accepts all incoming calls, even when you're in a conference.

When a shared window is too big to fit on my screen: These options control how NetMeeting handles shared application windows that extend beyond your screen. Activate Scroll entire screen to move the screen as a whole when you position the mouse at the edge of the screen. Activate Scroll shared windows only to scroll only those windows that are part of the shared application. Activate Don't scroll to turn off scrolling.

Receive files sent to me in a conference: When this check box is activated, NetMeeting accepts file transfers automatically. Deactivate this check box to prevent remote users from sending you any files.

Enable file transfer to people using PictureTel LiveShare: This check box toggles whether you can send files while using the LiveShare protocol.

Save files sent to me: Use this text box (or the Browse button) to specify the folder used to store incoming files.

The Protocols Tab

You use the Protocols tab, shown in Figure 39.26, to determine the networking protocols that are available to NetMeeting:

Modem: Use this protocol for modem-to-modem connections. You can set various properties for the Modem protocol by highlighting it and clicking Properties to display the dialog box shown in Figure 39.27.

Network (IPX): Activate this protocol for NetWare-based connections.

Network (TCP/IP): Activate this protocol to make TCP/IP-based connections over a network or the Internet.

FIGURE 39.26.

The Protocols tab determines the transport mechanisms available to NetMeeting.

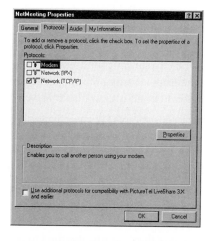

FIGURE 39.27.

Use this properties sheet to set some options for modem-to-modem connections.

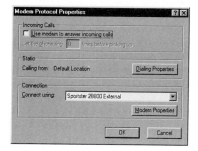

39

MICROSOFT
NETMEETING

If you activate the Use additional protocols for compatibility with PictureTel LiveShare 3.X and earlier check box, NetMeeting adds a few more LiveShare network protocol options to the list.

The Audio Tab

The Audio tab, shown in Figure 39.28, controls various settings related to the audio portion of the NetMeeting show. Here's a summary:

Enable full duplex audio: NetMeeting doesn't enable its full-duplex features even if the Audio Tuning Wizard detects that you have a sound card capable of supporting full-duplex audio. You need to activate this check box to work with full-duplex (two-way) audio.

Enable Auto-gain control: NetMeeting's automatic gain feature adjusts the microphone volume based on the volume of your voice. That is, if you speak quietly, NetMeeting increases the microphone volume to compensate; if you speak loudly, the value is decreased accordingly. If a noisy work environment causes the microphone level to fluctuate unpredictably, deactivate this check box to shut off automatic gain.

Audio Tuning Wizard: Click this button to run the Audio Tuning Wizard. This is a good idea if you change your sound card or the speed of your connection. (You can also launch the Audio Tuning Wizard by selecting Tools | Audio Tuning Wizard. Note that this command is unavailable while you're in an audio conference.)

Set compression automatically based upon the rate of your connection to the network: NetMeeting compresses the data to speed its passage along the connection, and the ratio of this compression is determined by the speed of the connection. To have NetMeeting determine this compression ratio automatically, leave this option button activated and choose the appropriate connection speed in the drop-down list.

Manually configure compression settings: If you prefer to configure your own audio codecs, activate this option and then click Advanced. In the Advanced Compression Settings dialog box that appears, use the Up and Down buttons to determine the codec order you want.

FIGURE 39.28.

Use the Audio tab to customize NetMeeting's sound capabilities.

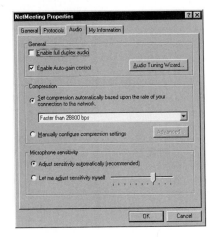

Microphone sensitivity: The sensitivity of your microphone is a measure of how it handles background noises. A high sensitivity setting means the microphone will pick up background noises. By default, NetMeeting adjusts this sensitivity automatically (that is, the `Adjust sensitivity automatically` option button is activated). If you prefer to make the adjustments yourself, activate the `Let me adjust sensitivity myself` option, and then use the slider to choose a setting (move the slider to the right for higher sensitivity; move it to the left for lower sensitivity).

The My Information Tab

The controls in the My Information tab, shown in Figure 39.29, let you set your personal NetMeeting data:

My information: These text boxes represent the data about you that is published on the User Location Service.

Publish this information in the User Location Service directory: Deactivate this check box if you prefer that your data not appear in the User Location Service directory.

User Location Service name: Use the text box to enter the name of the User Location Server on which you want your information published and on which you log each time you start NetMeeting. If you deactivate the check box, NetMeeting will not log you on to the server and won't use the server to look up NetMeeting addresses.

FIGURE 39.29.

Use the My Informa-tion tab to edit your published NetMeeting data.

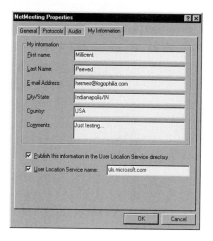

39

MICROSOFT
NETMEETING

What to Expect in NetMeeting 2.0

As I wrote this chapter, Microsoft was beta-testing NetMeeting 2.0. Although I won't cover the features of this new version (which should be released by the time you read this book), I'll summarize a few of the most interesting new features here:

Support for Windows NT: NetMeeting 1.0 runs only on Windows 95 machines, but version 2.0 has a build that runs on Windows NT 4.0.

Better standards support: One of the complaints many people have with NetMeeting 1.0 is its lack of support for audio and video conferencing standards. Version 2.0 supports the ITU H.323 standard, which allows it to work with compatible phone clients (such as the Intel Internet Video Phone).

Improved video conferencing: Besides support for H.323, NetMeeting 2.0 has greatly improved video conferencing capabilities, including support for standard video capture devices, high-quality video over low-bandwidth (28.8 Kbps) connections, the capability to receive video images without video hardware, and the capability to copy video frames to the Clipboard.

Internet Locator Service: This replacement for ULS gives NetMeeting a Lightweight Directory Access Protocol (LDAP) interface, which makes it easier to find other NetMeeting users.

NetMeeting as an answering machine: If you attempt to call someone and the person doesn't respond, version 2.0 allows you to send her an e-mail message.

Improved user interface: As you can see in Figure 39.30, NetMeeting 2.0 has a better interface that closely resembles the look and feel of Internet Explorer, Internet Mail, and Internet News.

FIGURE 39.30.

The improved user interface of Net-Meeting 2.0.

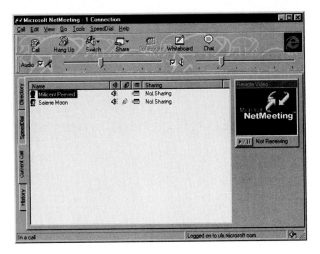

Summary

This chapter showed you how to work with Microsoft NetMeeting. After explaining how to configure the program, I gave you a tour of the NetMeeting window. From there, you learned various methods for placing calls within NetMeeting. I then showed you how to exchange files, how to use the Chat feature and the Whiteboard, and how to share applications. I finished by running through all of NetMeeting's customization options and by giving you a sneak peek at NetMeeting 2.0.

Here's a list of chapters where you'll find related information:

- To learn more about sound in Windows 95, see Chapter 24, "Getting the Most Out of Windows 95 Sound."

- If you'll be using a modem to make your NetMeeting calls, you'll want to read Chapter 25, "Maximizing Modem Communications."

- To set up a remote connection for use with NetMeeting, head for Chapter 35, "Remote Computing with Dial-Up Networking," and Chapter 37, "Windows 95 and the Internet."

39

Microsoft NetMeeting

Internet Mail: Messaging Made Easy

CHAPTER 40

And none will hear the postman's knock
Without a quickening of the heart.
For who can bear to feel himself forgotten?

—*W. H. Auden*

Back in Chapter 28, "Exchanging E-Mail with Microsoft Exchange," I showed you how to work with Exchange (or Windows Messaging, as OSR2 calls it) to send and receive e-mail messages. In that chapter, my focus was on the generic capabilities of Exchange, although I did give some specifics for different e-mail systems, including Microsoft Mail, CompuServe, and the Internet.

However, if all your online communicating involves sending only Internet missives, Exchange might feel like overkill. As an alternative, you might prefer to use Microsoft's Internet Mail program, which comes as part of the full install of Internet Explorer 3.x (and so is included in the OSR2 package). This chapter shows you how to use Internet Mail for exchanging notes with other Net denizens. You'll also learn a bit about how Internet e-mail works and will get some background information (etiquette, acronyms, and so on) that will stand you in good stead during your e-conversations.

How Does the Internet E-Mail System Work?

One of the nice things about the Internet e-mail system is that to use it, you don't have to know how its plumbing works. The missives you fire out, and the dispatches that come your way, are all routed automatically, without any help from the likes of you and me. However, one of the characteristics of the Internet is that its innards are never that far away. The programs we use to surf the Net are only a thin, shiny veneer covering the Net's insides.

So it pays, then, to know at least a little about the underlying mechanisms that make the Internet go. This information will come in handy, for example, when I tell you later in this chapter how to set up the Internet Mail program. It will also give you just enough background to let you pose intelligent questions to your system administrator, just in case something goes awry.

Internet E-Mail Addressing

I like to think of the Net as a giant city where the houses are computers. A neighborhood where the houses are connected with side streets is like an individual network connected via cables. In turn, each neighborhood is connected to other neighborhoods via larger roads and avenues or, for longer trips, by highways and expressways. The point is that in any city you can get from your house to any other house by traveling along a particular set of streets, roads, and highways. The Internet works the same way: You can "travel" to other computers on the Net by "following" the various communications lines that make up the Net's infrastructure.

This metaphor serves quite nicely to explain how electronic mail works. The first thing you need to know is that each user on the Internet has a unique *e-mail address*. Just like the full address of a house, your e-mail address tells everyone the exact location they can use to send messages to you. To help you understand the structure of these addresses, consider this generic e-mail address:

`user@provider.com`

This address has four parts:

> **user:** This is the recipient's user name. Most user names are a single word representing the person's first or last name, or a combination of the two names. Some companies insist that the user name be both the first name and last name separated by a period (for example, `paul.mcfedries`). Other e-mail systems will use different conventions. CompuServe, for example, uses two numbers separated by a period.
>
> **@:** This symbol (it's pronounced "at") separates the "who" part of the address (the part to the left of the @ sign) and the "where" part (the part to the right of the @ sign).
>
> **provider:** This is the Internet name (that is, *domain name*) of the user's access provider. It tells you where the user's mailbox is located.
>
> **com:** The last part tells you what type of organization you're dealing with. As you learned in Chapter 36, "Implementing TCP/IP for Internet and Network Connections," the Internet has several of these organization types, including com, edu, and org.

This type of e-mail address is a relatively straightforward affair. Here's one that's a bit more complex:

`biff@math.utoronto.ca`

Again, the address begins with a user name (`biff`, in this case) and the `@` sign. The `utoronto` part means this person is located at the University of Toronto. Why doesn't it have an `edu` at the end? Well, many newer e-mail addresses are forgoing the old "type" designations in favor of geographical designations (or *geographical domains,* as the pocket protector crowd calls them). In this case, the `ca` tells you that the University of Toronto is located in Canada. (Again, check out Chapter 36 to see a list of geographical domains.)

The `math` part of the address is called a *subdomain,* and it's used to narrow things down a bit. Universities and other large organizations usually have various networks. The University of Toronto, for example, probably has separate networks for the Mathematics department, the Physics department, the Chemistry department, and so on. The `math` subdomain tells you that this person is part of the Mathematics department's network.

When you know a person's (or a company's) e-mail address, you're in business. You just fire up your e-mail software, compose a message, tell the software the address to send the message to, and then fire it off. In the same way that the post office can use the address on an envelope or a package to track down the recipient, so too does the Internet e-mail system know how to locate the specified e-mail address. You just sit back and let the Net do all the dirty work.

40

INTERNET MAIL: MESSAGING MADE EASY

How Does My Mail Get There from Here?

When you dress up an e-mail message and send it out into the cold, cruel world of the Internet, it actually goes on quite a journey. The route it takes, the places it visits, and the sights it sees vary from message to message, but the basic itinerary is easy to spell out:

1. A special e-mail computer on your network (or on your access provider's network) wraps up the message in a electronic "envelope" (that has, like a regular envelope, the recipient's address and your return address, among other things) and sends it out. The Internet mechanism involved here is called SMTP (Simple Mail Transport Protocol), which is yet another member of the TCP/IP family. The provider's computer that handles outgoing mail is usually called an *SMTP server.*

2. Because there will only rarely be a direct connection between your network and the recipient's network, the mail will make a number of stops at intermediate networks along the way. At each stop, another e-mail computer temporarily stores the message while it figures out the best way to relay the message toward its ultimate destination. When that's done, the message is sent on its merry way, and the whole thing repeats at the next digital roadside rest stop.

3. Eventually, the message finds its way to the recipient's network, where an e-mail computer routes it to the person's mailbox. (If the recipient uses a networked e-mail program that doesn't understand Netspeak—such as Microsoft Mail or cc:Mail—the message will have to go through another computer called a *gateway* that converts the message into something the program can make sense of.)

This might sound like an awful lot of work just to send an e-mail note, but it's quite efficient for two reasons:

- The message is traveling at the speed of light, so even the longest hop between networks happens in less than the blink of an eye.
- Almost all the Net's e-mail computers use SMTP to transport the messages.

How Do I Get E-Mail If I'm Not on a Network?

If you use an access provider to do the Internet thing, there's no direct way to get an e-mail message onto your computer (because you're not jacked into a network full-time). You could use the Telnet service to log in to your access provider's network and read the mail directly from your mailbox, but most people prefer to store their private messages on their own hard disk.

To solve this problem, your access provider has probably set up a special account for you on one of its computers. This is called a *Post Office Protocol (POP) account*, and the computer it's set up on is called a *POP server.* POP essentially turns the server into the electronic equivalent of a post office. When people send messages to your e-mail address, the messages are stored in a special mailbox all your own. You can then use an e-mail program such as Internet Mail (or

Exchange) to log in to this account, grab the messages, store them on your computer, and then clean out the mailbox.

> **NOTE: MASSIVE MISSIVE MATH**
>
> Today, it's estimated that between 30 and 60 million people use e-mail and, on the Internet alone, send well over a *billion* messages a month. These messages range in length from a few dozen words to a few thousand, but let's take 500 words as the average. That means Net e-mail types send more than 500 billion words a month scurrying around the world. Too big a number to comprehend? OK, let's knock it down to size. 500 billion words a month is the equivalent of sending the manuscript of this book 2,000 times *every hour of every day.*

Message Anatomy

So that you can make heads or tails of the messages you read, let's inspect a typical specimen to see what's what. As you can see in the following example, a message has three main parts: the *header,* the *body,* and the *signature.*

```
Date: Sat, 1 Apr 95 13:45 GMT
To: htarlek@tweedledumb.com
From: vbassoon@buyordye.com (Vital Bassoon)
Subject: An incorrect shipment. AGAIN!
Cc: acarlson@tweedledumb.com
Herb,
Those Neanderthals in your Shipping department have done it again!
This time they sent me 5 skids of "Wavy Locks" perm lotion instead
of 5 boxes of "Wavy Lay's" potato chips! Either you hire people with
at least a double-digit IQ, or I'll find a new distributor!!!
Vital Bassoon
Buy or Dye Convenience Store and Hair Salon
Toad Suck, Arkansas
"At Intel, quality is job 0.9999992362"
```

The Header

The first few lines constitute the header, and they represent the message's vital statistics. Lots of obscure things can appear in a header (especially the headers of messages you receive), but only a few are truly useful items:

Date: This is the date and time the message was sent. The time given is usually Greenwich Mean Time (GMT), which is five hours earlier than Eastern Standard Time. (You'll also see GMT referred to as Universal Time, or UT.)

To: This is the e-mail address of the recipient.

From: This is the e-mail address and (usually) the real name of the person who sent the message.

Subject: This is a one-line description of what the message is about. This line is crucial because most Netizens with busy e-mail inboxes decide whether they'll read a message just by scanning the Subject line. To ensure that your missives get read, make the Subject line detailed enough that it accurately reflects what your message is about.

Cc: This is the "courtesy copy" line, and it shows the e-mail addresses of people who received copies of the message.

The Body

The body is the content of the message, and it's always separated from the header by a blank line. When composing the body, be sure to use only the so-called *printable ASCII characters*, which means just the letters, numbers, and symbols you can eyeball on your keyboard. (I'll have more to say about this topic later in this chapter.)

The Signature

The message's signature is an addendum that appears as the last few lines of the message. Its purpose is to let the folks out there reading your e-mail know a little more about the Renaissance man or woman who sent it. Although signatures are optional, many people use them because they can add a friendly touch to your correspondence. You can put anything you like in your signature, but most people just put their name, their company name and address, their other e-mail addresses, if they have multiples, and maybe a quote or two that fits in with their character.

Some signatures are absurdly elaborate; most Internet types get upset at any signature that extends for more than a half dozen lines or so. (This is called "wasting bandwidth," and I'll talk more about it when I talk about Netiquette later.)

Minding Your E-Mail Manners

One of the first things you notice when you're drifting around the Net is that it attracts more than its share of bohemians, nonconformists, and rugged individualists. And even though all of these people surf to the beat of a different drum, the Net resolutely refuses to degenerate into mere anarchy. Oh, sure, you get the odd every-nerd-for-himself hurly-burly, but civility reigns the vast majority of the time.

Usually, most Netizens are just too busy with their researching and rubbernecking to cause trouble, but there's another mechanism that helps keep everyone in line: *Netiquette* (a portmanteau of *network etiquette*). Netiquette is a collection of suggested behavioral norms designed to grease the wheels of Net social discourse. Scofflaws who defy the Netiquette rules can expect to see a few reprimands in their e-mail inbox. To help you stay on the good side of the Internet community, the next few sections tell you everything you need to know about the Netiquette involved in sending e-mail.

The Three B's of Composing E-Mail

Back in the long-gone days when I was a good corporate citizen, my boss used to call his secrets for successful presentations "the three B's": be good, be brief, be gone. These simple prescriptions also form a small chunk of the basic Netiquette landscape. Being good means writing in clear, understandable prose that isn't marred by sloppy spelling or flagrant grammar violations. Also, if you use some facts or statistics, cite the appropriate references to placate the Doubting Thomases who'll want to check things for themselves.

Being brief means getting right to the point without indulging in a rambling preamble. Always assume that your addressee is plowing through a stack of e-mail and so has no time or patience for verbosity. State your business and then practice the third "B": be gone!

DON'T SHOUT!

When writing with your high-end word processor, you probably use italics (or, more rarely, underlining) to emphasize important words or phrases. But because e-mail just uses plain vanilla text (that is, no fancy formatting options allowed), you might think that, in cyberspace, no one can hear you scream. That's not true, however. In fact, many e-mail scribes add emphasis to their epistles by using UPPERCASE LETTERS. This works, but please use uppercase sparingly. AN ENTIRE MESSAGE WRITTEN IN CAPITAL LETTERS FEELS LIKE YOU'RE SHOUTING, WHICH IS OK FOR USED-CAR SALESMEN ON LATE-NIGHT TV BUT IS INAPPROPRIATE IN THE MORE SEDATE WORLD OF E-MAIL CORRESPONDENCE.

> **NOTE: ADDING EMPHASIS**
>
> There are other ways to add emphasis to your e-mail prose. For example, you can *bracket* a word with asterisks. To find out more about these and other e-mail conventions, see "E-Mail Miscellanea," later in this chapter.

on the other hand, you occasionally see e-mail messages written entirely in lowercase letters from lazy susans, toms, dicks, and harrys who can't muster the energy to reach out for the shift key. this, too, is taboo because it makes the text quite difficult to read.

Just use the normal capitalization practices (uppercase for the beginning of sentences, proper names, and so on), and everyone will be happy.

Avoid Tabs and Other Unusual Characters

The Internet mail system works fine most of the time, but it's a temperamental, finicky beast. As long as things are just so, the mail should get through, and your recipient will be able to read your well-crafted thoughts. But if you throw any kind of monkey wrench into the works, well, who knows what can happen. One of these monkey wrenches involves using characters that aren't part of the alphanumeric array on your keyboard. (By that, I mean the letters and numbers, and symbols such as $, ?, and %.) Tossing in tabs or any of the so-called *control characters* (characters created by holding down the Ctrl key and pressing a letter or number) can throw your e-mail software for a loop.

Take Your Subject Lines Seriously

As I mentioned earlier, busy e-mail readers often use the contents of the Subject line to make a snap judgment about whether to bother reading a message. (This is especially true if the recipient doesn't know you from Adam.) Most mail mavens *hate* Subject lines that are either ridiculously vague (for example, "Info required" or "Please help!") or absurdly general (for example, "An e-mail message" or "Mail"), and they'll just click their mail software's "delete button" without giving the message a second thought. (In fact, there's a kind of illicit thrill involved in deleting an unread message, so don't give the person any excuse to exercise this indulgence.) Give your Subject line some thought, and make it descriptive enough that the reader can tell at a glance what your dispatch is about.

Experiment with Yourself

When you're just starting out with e-mail, you'll likely want to try a test drive or two to work out the kinks. Unless you can enlist a friend or colleague as a willing guinea pig, don't send out messages to just anybody, because, believe me, they've got better things to do than read a bunch of "Testing 1...2...3..." messages. The best way to perform e-mail shakedowns is just to send the tests to your own mail address.

More Snippets of Sending Sensitivity

Here, in no particular order, are a few more Netiquette gems that'll help ensure that you always put your best sending foot forward:

- If you receive private e-mail correspondence from someone, it's considered impolite to quote them in another message without their permission. (You're probably also violating copyright law, because the author of an e-mail message has a copyright on any and all messages he sends. There's even an acronym that covers this point with admirable succinctness: YOYOW—you own your own words; see "An Initial Look at Internet Acronyms," later in this chapter, for more acronym fun.)

- When replying to a message, include quotes from the original message for context. Few things are more frustrating in e-mail than to receive a reply that just says "Great idea; let's do it!" or "That's the dumbest thing I've ever heard." Which great idea or dumb thing are they talking about? To make sure that the other person knows what you're responding to, include the appropriate lines from the original message in your reply. You'll need to use some judgment here, though. Quoting the entire message is wasteful (especially if the message was a long one) and should be avoided. Just include enough of the original to put your response into context.

- As I mentioned earlier, keep your signatures down to a dull roar. Believe me, *nobody* is interested in seeing your resume or your *curriculum vitae* at the end of every message you send. The accepted maximum length for a signature is four to six lines.

- Forgive small mistakes. If you see a message with spelling mistakes, incorrect grammar, or minor factual blunders, resist the urge to "flame" the perpetrator. (In e-mail lingo, a *flame* is a nasty, caustic message designed to put Internet scofflaws in their place. I'll talk more about them later.) For one thing, the international flavor of e-mail just about guarantees a large percentage of participants for whom English isn't their primary language. For another, I hope you have better things to do than nitpick every little slip of the keyboard that comes your way.

Can I Get There from Here? Sending Mail Between Systems

Let's say you're schmoozing at some high-falutin' cocktail party and you meet someone who could send a lot of business your way. Dreams of new power boats dance in your head as the new acquaintance says, "Here's my card. E-mail me and we'll do lunch." You look at the card and—groan!—he's got an MCI Mail address! Now what? Or suppose you're a CompuServe user and your best buddy has just gotten an Internet e-mail account. How on earth are the two of you supposed to shoot the digital breeze?

These kinds of scenarios are increasingly common because although there are tens of millions of people exchanging electronic mail on the Net, there are tens of millions more who use other systems such as MCI Mail, AT&T Mail, CompuServe, and America Online.

Are all these systems just countries unto themselves where fraternization is strictly taboo? Well, they used to be, but things have changed. Now most e-mail systems have opened their borders (by installing things called, appropriately enough, *gateways*) to allow e-mail travelers safe passage. The next few sections show you how to exchange mail with the citizens of various other e-mail nations.

Exchanging Mail with America Online

America Online (AOL) is a commercial online service that boasts an increasing array of Internet services, including an e-mail gateway. Let's see how Internauts and America Onliners can exchange e-mail epistles.

Every AOL subscriber has a unique *screen name* that identifies that person to the AOL system. The e-mail address of an AOL subscriber takes the general form *screenname@aol.com*, where *screenname* is the user's screen name *in lowercase letters and without spaces*. For example, if you want to send e-mail from the Internet to an AOL user with a screen name of Will Tell, you'd use the following address:

```
willtell@aol.com
```

Sending mail from AOL to the Internet is the soul of simplicity. When composing a message, just enter the person's Internet e-mail address in the To box. For example, AOL types can send e-mail to me by entering the following address:

`paul@mcfedries.com`

Exchanging Mail with AT&T Mail

AT&T Mail is a commercial e-mail service that assigns each of its subscribers a unique *user name*. The e-mail address of an AT&T Mail subscriber uses the general format `username@attmail.com`, where *username* is the person's user name. For example, to send e-mail from the Internet to an AT&T Mail subscriber with the user name `jsprat`, you'd use this address:

`jsprat@attmail.com`

Sending messages from AT&T Mail to the Internet is a little more complicated. The general form is `internet!domain!user`, where *domain* is the domain name from the Internet address (that is, the part to the right of the @ sign) and *user* is the user name from the Internet address (the part to the left of the @ sign). For example, to send mail to my Internet address (`paul@mcfedries.com`), you'd use the following address:

`internet!mcfedries.com!paul`

Exchanging Mail with CompuServe

CompuServe is one of the largest and oldest of the big-time online services. It's slowly adding more and more Internet services, but it has had a gateway for Internet e-mail since 1989. Each CompuServe subscriber is assigned a unique user id number that's actually two numbers separated by a comma (for example, `12345,6789`).

The e-mail address of a CompuServe user takes the generic format `idnumber@compuserve.com`, where *idnumber* is the subscriber's user id number *with the comma replaced by a period*. For example, if the person's CompuServe user id is `12345,6789`, her e-mail address would look like this:

`12345.6789@compuserve.com`

Missives sent from CompuServe to the Internet use e-mail addresses that take the form `INTERNET:user@domain`, where *user@domain* is the person's regular Internet e-mail address. So any CompuServe user who wants to drop me a line would send a note to the following address:

`INTERNET:paul@mcfedries.com`

Exchanging Mail with MCI Mail

MCI Mail is another popular commercial e-mail service that has offered a gateway to the Internet for some years. When you sign up with MCI Mail, you get not one but *three* separate means of identification: an MCI ID number that looks like a seven-digit telephone number (for example, 123-4567); an MCI ID name (for example, `mpeeved`), and a full user name (for example, `Millicent Peeved`).

To send Internet mail to an MCI Mail user, you can address the message using any of these generic formats:

```
idnumber@mcimail.com
idname@mcimail.com
full_name@mcimail.com
```

Notice that the space in the user's full name gets replaced by an underscore (_). Also, if you're using the MCI ID number, you remove the dash. So, in the examples I used previously, you could use any of the following addresses:

```
1234567@mcimail.com
mpeeved@mcimail.com
Millicent_Peeved@mcimail.com
```

To send correspondence to an Internet e-mail address, MCI Mail users need to follow a three-step procedure:

1. Start a new message as you normally would (by typing `create` at the `Command:` prompt and pressing Enter), and then when MCI Mail displays the `To:` prompt, type the name of the person or company you're sending the message to, followed by `(EMS)`, followed by Enter. For example, if you're sending mail to me, you'd enter `Paul McFedries (EMS)` and press Enter.

2. At the `EMS:` prompt, type `Internet` and press Enter.

3. At the `MBX:` prompt, type the Internet e-mail address and press Enter. If you're sending mail to me, for example, you'd type `paul@mcfedries.com` and press Enter.

Exchanging Mail with Prodigy

Prodigy is another commercial online service that provides an Internet e-mail gateway. Note, however, that to exchange e-letters with the Net, you have to buy the Mail Manager program.

When sending mail to a Prodigy user from the Net, you use an address of the form `userid@prodigy.com`, where `userid` is the unique identification Prodigy assigns to its users. For example, if the Prodigy person you want to contact has the user id `abcd01a`, you'd mail your correspondence to the following address:

```
abcd01a@prodigy.com
```

Sending mail from Prodigy to the Internet is a breeze. When composing the message in Mail Manager, just use the person's Internet e-mail address. For example, Prodigy types can send e-mail to me by entering the following address:

```
paul@mcfedries.com
```

NOTE: THE "INTER-NETWORK MAIL GUIDE"

The systems we looked at in this section represent only the most popular of the dozens of e-mail systems available worldwide. If you want instructions about exchanging mail with a system I didn't cover, head for the "Inter-Network Mail Guide" at the following Web page:

```
http://www.nova.edu/Inter-Links/cgi-bin/inmgq.pl
```

Learning the Lingo: E-Mail Jargon and Acronyms

As you'd expect with anything that boasts millions of participants, the Internet is home to a wide variety of characters. In particular, the Net seems to attract more than its fair share of three kinds of folks: neologists, jargonauts, and nymrods.

Neologists are people who coin new words and phrases by making them up, by enlisting existing words to perform new duties, or by combining two or more words into a new creation (the offspring of these lexical unions are called *portmanteaus*—a meaning coined by the inveterate neologist Lewis Carroll).

Jargonauts are Net surfers who seek out new words and new phrases and who boldly try to get these coinages into general circulation by using them as often as possible.

Nymrods are Net types who, without even the slightest sting of conscience or pang of doubt, insist on turning every multiword computer term into an acronym.

As you interact with the Internet through your e-mail account, you're bound to run into many examples of each kind of Net word hound. This means you'll be exposed to all kinds of new jargon, acronyms, and symbols that could threaten to render your incoming missives unintelligible. To help you decipher these electronic Dead Sea Scrolls, this section presents translations of the most common e-mail neologisms and acronyms. (I also went through a list of more Web-related words back in Chapter 38, "Exploring the Web with Internet Explorer.")

Your Handy English-Internet Phrase Book

As I've said, learning the online vernacular is important if you hope to understand what the heck some Net denizens are talking about. At the same time, it'll also help if you can add to your e-mail messages a few choice morsels of Net patois (or *Netois*, as I guess you could put it). Experienced globetrotters maintain that you'll be greeted more warmly and treated more kindly by the locals if you learn a few key words and phrases in the language of the country you're visiting. This tip could easily be applied to the online world as well, so the jargon becomes a kind of *lingua franca* for the Net set. To get you on your way, here are some translations of a few common Internet idioms, with a special emphasis on e-mail-related terms:

attachment   A file linked to an e-mail message that hitches a ride to the recipient when the message is sent.

bandwidth   A measure of how much stuff can be crammed through a transmission medium such as a phone line or network cable. Or, to put it another way, bandwidth measures how much information can be sent between any two Internet sites. Because bandwidth is a finite commodity, many Net veterans are constantly cautioning profligate users against wasting bandwidth. In e-mail circles, this means keeping messages short and to the point, attaching large nontext files (especially graphics) only if you have to, quoting a minimal amount of the original article in a reply, and avoiding useless *flame wars* (I describe what these are later in this chapter).

blind courtesy copy (bcc)   A copy of an e-mail message that gets sent to a recipient without the knowledge of either the main recipient (the e-mail address in the To line) or the secondary recipients (the e-mail addresses in the Cc line).

bounce message   An error message returned by an e-mail system if a message can't be delivered (because, say, the address is wrong).

filter   A program or e-mail software command that scans incoming messages and automatically processes the messages based on the contents of, say, the From or Subject lines. For example, you can set up a filter to automatically delete messages sent from a particular e-mail address (this is known as a *bozo filter*).

flame   To post an insulting, emotional, caustic message. See the section "The Incendiary Internet: Playing the Flame Game," later in this chapter, for a complete look at Net flameology.

foo, bar, foobar   These words are used as placeholders in descriptions and instructions. For example, someone might say "To change to the /foo directory on a UNIX system, use the command cd/foo." Here, "foo" acts as a generic placeholder for a directory name. If two placeholders are needed, then both "foo" and "bar" are used, like so: "To FTP two files named foo and bar, use the mget command: mget foo bar." "Foobar" is often used as a single placeholder. It's derived from the military acronym FUBAR (bowdlerized version: Fouled Up Beyond All Recognition). Other, more rare placeholder words are baz and quux (don't ask).

forward   To pass along a received message to another e-mail address.

mail bombing   To send numerous (and, usually, long) e-mail messages to a person's e-mail address (this is also called e-mail terrorism).

mailbox   The file where your incoming messages are stored. As you'll see, Internet Mail lets you divide your mailbox into different *folders* (for example, one for business mail, one for personal mail, and so forth).

postmaster   The overworked, underpaid person in an e-mail system who has the responsibilities of making sure that the system runs smoothly and troubleshooting problems when it doesn't.

sig quote   A quotation added to a signature. Most people choose quotations that reflect their character or their politics.

spam   Unsolicited (and almost always unwanted) e-mail messages offering special deals or get-rich-quick schemes.

The Incendiary Internet: Playing the Flame Game

Everybody—even the calmest and most level-headed among us—has a particular bugaboo or bête noire that gets under their skin and makes their blood boil. In the real world, it could be people who drive too slow in the fast lane, discourteous types who butt in ahead of you in line, or those annoying late-night infomercials. In the online world, it could be a thoughtless remark, a misunderstood attempt at humor, or a vicious mail bomb.

Whatever the reason, the immediate reaction usually is to pull out the electronic version of your poison pen and compose an emotionally charged, scathing reply dripping with sarcasm and venomous abuse. Such messages are called *flames,* and they're an unfortunate fact of life on the Net. Firing off a particularly inventive flame might make *you* feel better, but its likely effect will be to make the recipient madder than a hoot owl. Your target will, almost certainly, flame your flame, and before you know it, a full-blown *flame war* will have broken out.

Flaming has become such an integral part of Internet culture that it has developed its own subgenre of colorful lingo and phrases. Here's a brief primer on flame jargon:

asbestos longjohns   What e-mailers put on (metaphorically speaking, of course) before sending a message that they expect will get flamed. Other popular flame-retardant garments are *asbestos overcoats* and *asbestos underwear.*

burble   Similar to a flame, except that the burbler is considered to be dumb, incompetent, or ignorant.

dictionary flame   A flame that criticizes someone for spelling or grammatical gaffes.

firefighters   People who attempt to put out flame wars before they get out of hand.

flamage   The content of a flame. This word seems to be a portmanteau of the words "flame" and "verbiage."

flame bait   Provocative material in a message that will likely elicit flames in response.

flame warrior   A person who surfs the Net looking for flame bait. Someone who tries to start flame wars intentionally.

flamer   A person who flames regularly.

rave   A particularly irritating type of flame in which the writer rambles on ad nauseam, even after a flame war has ended.

An Initial Look at Internet Acronyms

For many users, acronyms are the bugbears and hobgoblins of computer life. They imply a hidden world of meaning that only the cognoscenti and those "in the know" are privy to. The Internet, in particular, is a maddeningly rich source of TLAs (three-letter acronyms) and other ciphers. To help you survive the inevitable onslaught of Internet acronymy, here's a list of the most commonly used initials in Net discourse:

AAMOF	As a matter of fact.
AFAIK	As far as I know.
BTW	By the way.
CU	See you (as in "see you later").
DIIK	Damned if I know.
F2F	Face-to-face.
FAQ	Frequently Asked Questions. These are lists that appear in many Usenet newsgroups to provide answers to questions that newcomers ask over and over.
FAWOMPT	Frequently argued waste of my precious time.
FAWOMFT	Frequently argued waste of my foolish time (bowdlerized version).
FOAF	Friend of a friend. Used to imply that information was obtained third-hand, or worse.
FOTCL	Falling off the chair laughing.
FTF	Face-to-face.
FYA	For your amusement.
FYI	For your information.
HHOK	Ha ha only kidding.
HHOJ	Ha ha only joking.
HHOS	Ha ha only serious (used with ironic jokes and satire that contain some truth).
IANAL	I am not a lawyer.
IMCO	In my considered opinion.
IMHO	In my humble opinion. (In practice, however, opinions prefaced by IMHO are rarely humble. See IMNSHO.)
IMO	In my opinion.
IMNSHO	In my not-so-humble opinion. (This more accurately reflects most of the opinions one sees on the Internet!)
IOW	In other words.
IWBNI	It would be nice if.
IYFEG	Insert your favorite ethnic group. Used in off-color and offensive jokes and stories to avoid insulting any particular ethnic group, race, religion, or sex. You'll sometimes see *<ethnic>* instead.
KISS	Keep it simple, stupid.

LOL	Laughing out loud.
MEGO	My eyes glaze over.
MOTAS	Member of the appropriate sex.
MOTOS	Member of the opposite sex.
MOTSS	Member of the same sex.
MUD	Multiple User Dimension (or Multiple User Dungeon). A text-based, role-playing fantasy adventure game.
NRN	No response necessary.
OIC	Oh, I see.
OS	Operating system.
OTOH	On the other hand.
OTT	Over the top.
PD	Public domain.
PMJI	Pardon my jumping in.
PONA	Person of no account. Used disparagingly to describe someone who isn't part of the Internet set (that is, someone who doesn't have an Internet account).
ROTF	Rolling on the floor.
ROTFL	Rolling on the floor laughing.
ROTFLOL	Rolling on the floor laughing out loud.
RSN	Real soon now (read: never).
RTFF	Read the fine FAQ. (See RTFM.)
RTFM	Read the fabulous manual. (Another bowdlerized version.) This is an admonition to users that they should try to answer a question themselves before asking for help. This might seem harsh, but self-reliance is a fundamental characteristic of Internet life. Most Net types have figured things out for themselves, and they expect everyone else to do the same. This means reading hardware and software manuals and, in Usenet, checking out the FAQ lists newsgroups.
SO	Significant other.
TFS	Thanks for sharing.
TIA	Thanks in advance.
TIC	Tongue in cheek.
TPTB	The powers that be.
TTFN	Ta-ta for now.

TTYL	Talk to you later.
WOBTAM	Waste of both time and money.
WRT	With respect to.
YABA	Yet another bloody acronym.
YMMV	Your mileage may vary. This acronym means the advice/info/instructions just given might not work for you exactly as described.

NOTE: MORE ACRONYMS

If you come across an acronym that's not covered here, the Web's Acronym and Abbreviation Server lets you look up acronyms or find acronyms whose expansion contains a particular word. Surf to the following page to check it out:

`http://www.ucc.ie/info/net/acronyms/index.html`

Internet Hieroglyphics: Smileys

Flame wars ignite for various reasons: derogatory material, the skewering of one sacred cow or another, or just for the heck of it (see *flame warrior* in the list of flame phrases given earlier in this chapter). But one of the most common reasons for flame wars is that someone misinterprets a wryly humorous, sarcastic, or ironic remark as insulting or offensive. The problem is that the nuances and subtleties of wry humor and sarcasm are difficult to convey in print. *You* know your intent, but someone else (especially those for whom English isn't their first language) might see things completely differently.

To help prevent such misunderstandings, and to grease the wheels of Net social interaction, cute little symbols called *smileys* (or, more rarely, *emoticons*) have been developed. The name comes from the following combination of symbols: :-). If you rotate this page clockwise so the left edge is at the top, you'll see that this combination looks like a smiling face. You'd use it to indicate to your readers that the previous statement was intended to be humorous or, at least, not serious.

The basic smiley is the one you'll encounter most often, but there are all kinds of others to tilt your head over (some of which are useful, most of which are downright silly). Here's a sampling:

;-)	I'm winking
:-(	I'm sad
:->	I'm smug
:-t	I'm cross
:-\	I'm undecided
:-o	I'm shocked

:-&	I'm tongue-tied
¦-¦	I'm asleep (boredom)
:-c	I'm bummed out
:-#	My lips are sealed
8-¦	I'm in suspense
:-<	I'm sad
8-#	I'm dead
:-I	Hmmm
:-7	I'm being wry
:-p	I'm sticking my tongue out
:-9	I'm licking my lips
:-*	I just ate a sour pickle
:>)	I have a big nose
%-)	I'm cross-eyed
#-)	I partied all night
[:-)	I'm listening to headphones
(-:	I'm left-handed
:-	I'm male
:-Q	I smoke
:-?	I smoke a pipe
:-{	I have a mustache
:-%	I have a beard
(-)	I need a haircut
{:-)	I part my hair in the middle
{(:-)	I'm wearing a toupee
}(:-(	I'm wearing toupee in the wind
-:-)	I have a mohawk
(:)-)	I like to scuba dive
0-)	I wear a scuba mask
:-)X	I wear a bow tie
:-}	I wear lipstick
@:I	I wear a turban
8-)	I wear glasses

: : -)	I wear bifocals
B -)	I wear horn-rims
: -)8	I'm well-dressed
: - 0	I'm an orator
:<¦	I attend an Ivy League school
+: - ¦	I'm a priest
+ - (: -)	I'm the pope
[: ¦]	I'm a robot
* : o)	I'm a bozo
o -)	I'm a Cyclops
: >	I'm a midget
8 :]	I'm a gorilla
= : -)	I'm a punk rocker
% - ^	I'm Picasso
*<¦ : -)	I'm Santa Claus (Ho Ho Ho)

NOTE: DON'T OVERDO IT!

Smileys are an easy way to convey meaning in your online writings, but don't lean on them too heavily. Overusing smileys means that your writing isn't as clear as it could be, and it also can automatically brand you as a dreaded newbie or as terminally cute.

E-Mail Miscellanea

To round out our tour of the sights and sounds you'll come across in the e-mail world, let's look at a few miscellaneous conventions and symbols that you're sure to stumble upon in your travels:

Adding emphasis in your messages. Earlier, I told you that you can add emphasis to your messages by using UPPERCASE letters. However, many people interpret uppercase words as shouting, so other emphasis conventions are normally used. The most common is to bracket a word or phrase with asterisks, like *this*. You'll occasionally see other characters around a word such as the _underscore_, the exclamation !mark!, and the greater-than and less-than >signs<. To get degrees of emphasis, some people use multiple characters, like ****this**** or like >>>>>this<<<<<. Rarely, you'll also see words "underlined" with carets (^), as shown here:

```
Why does everyone hate poor Barney the Dinosaur?
              ^^^^^^^^
```

Conveying mood with non-smileys. As you saw in the preceding section, smileys are a handy way to make sure that your messages aren't misunderstood. However, many people find those little faces to be insufferably cute and so wouldn't be caught dead using them. Instead, they use the following "non-smileys":

Symbol	What It Means
<g>	Grinning, smiling
<vbg>	Very big grin
<eg>	Evil grin
<l>	Laughing
<lol>	Laughing out loud
<i>	Irony
<s>	Sighing
<jk>	Just kidding
<>	No comment

Simulating a backspace. In oral conversation, you can achieve an ironic effect by saying one thing, then saying, "Oops, I mean," and then saying something else. To simulate this effect in writing, you can use the ^H symbol. Let's look at an example:

```
"Please tell this bozo^H^H^H^Hperson that ads aren't allowed in this group!"
```

You'd read this as "Please tell this bozo—oops, I mean person—that ads aren't allowed in this group!" The idea is that you add as many ^Hs as there are letters in the word you're trying to "backspace" out. Why ^H? Well, the caret (^) stands for the Ctrl key on a keyboard, so ^H actually represents the key combination Ctrl-H. And, in some UNIX systems, you press Ctrl-H to delete the character to the left of the cursor.

A Note About E-Mail Security

If you made a list of the various tenets that constitute the Internet ethos, one of them would be that information should be free and easily accessible to all. This admirably egalitarian view is one of the reasons the Internet has been so successful. The composition of the Net's building blocks (the software that allows the various networks to communicate with each other and exchange data) is public knowledge, so it's relatively easy to write software that performs functions over the Net. In turn, the "information is free" ethic leads many of these software developers to make their creations free to all and sundry. So after you're wired, you can easily put together a suite of Internet applications, and your total cost would be precisely nothing. (Internet Explorer and its components—such as Internet Mail and Internet News—are a good example.)

The downside to all this openness (you knew there had to be a downside) is that it also makes it easy for the malicious and the malevolent to get into all kinds of mischief. By studying the published standards for how the Internet works, crackers (as hackers who've succumbed to the dark side of the Force are called) can apply their knowledge of programming and computer systems to compromise these systems and bypass the normal Internet operating procedures.

In the e-mail world, this situation leads to two major security issues: privacy and authenticity.

The Privacy Problem

Remember all the fuss a while back when some cellular snoop managed to listen in on a phone conversation between Princess Diana and "Squidgy," her alleged (and bizarrely nicknamed) lover? The problem with cellular phones, of course, is that their transmissions are just microwave radio signals that travel willy-nilly through the air just like any other radio signal. With a simple receiver, anyone can tour through the appropriate frequencies, intercept these transmissions, and listen in on what were supposed to be private conversations.

Internet e-mail suffers from a similar problem. When you send a message, it doesn't travel directly to the recipient; instead, it must first pass through a number of other systems (as described earlier in this chapter). Recall the analogy I used earlier in which I likened a message traveling through the Net to driving from one city neighborhood to another along a system of roads and highways. Well, on the Net, these roads and highways often have "checkpoints" that messages must pass through in their journey. These checkpoints are just computers on some other network, and at each stop there's always the possibility that someone with enough know-how could intercept your message, read it, and then send it on its way. Neither you nor your recipient would ever be the wiser. In this sense, using Internet e-mail is no different from sending snail-mail messages on the back of a postcard.

> **NOTE: PACKET SNIFFING**
>
> As you saw back in Chapter 36, all Internet communication—whether it's files, World Wide Web pages, or e-mail—is divided into small chunks called packets. These packets are sent individually and reassembled when they reach their destination. For this reason, the Net's electronic eavesdroppers are called *packet sniffers*.

The Authenticity Problem

You might recall a famous story from the '70s in which the sportscaster Howard Cosell was doing a Monday Night Football broadcast and received what he thought was a call from the boxer Muhammad Ali. At the time, Ali was in Zaire preparing to fight George Foreman, so this was a real coup for Cosell. In fact, he even did a brief interview with Ali right on the air to a nationwide TV audience. Much to Cosell's chagrin (not to mention his embarrassment), the call turned out to be a hoax (the caller was actually somewhere in the Midwest, I think).

This brings us to the second e-mail security problem: authentication. When you receive a message, the header's From line tells you the e-mail address of the person who sent the missive. Or does it? The Internet e-mail system is such an open book that it's ridiculously easy to forge other people's e-mail addresses! Now, obviously, if you get a message from president@whitehouse.gov or billg@microsoft.com, you can pretty well guess you're dealing with a forgery (depending on the social circles you run in). But if you get flamed by a total stranger, or if someone you know inexplicably asks for your credit card number, there's no way to tell whether the message is on the up-and-up.

Is This Mere Paranoia?

Well, perhaps we *should* keep some perspective here. Tens of millions of e-mail messages are sent every day, so what, really, are the chances of someone picking out *your* message to spy on? Besides, only criminals and other undesirables really need to keep their communications private, right?

Wrong! I mean, you "hide" most of your paper mail inside an envelope, don't you? Does that make you a criminal? Of course not. And what if your e-mail dispatches include sensitive material such as payroll data, credit-card or Social Security numbers, financial info, research results, or trade secrets? You'll probably want to protect these decidedly noncriminal messages, so you have every right to be at least a little paranoid. And you can forget that "safety in numbers" argument. Someone looking for your e-mail messages wouldn't have to sift through the millions of dispatches that are posted daily. It's possible to scan mail messages passing through a site and do "keyword searches" to intercept those that contain particular words, phrases, names, or even e-mail addresses.

As for e-forgeries, it's true that they're still quite rare, if only because the necessary know-how is well beyond the skills of most Netizens. But, still, they *do* happen. A couple of years ago, some prankster forged a Microsoft press release stating that the company had bought the Vatican! The very idea sounds preposterous, but Microsoft actually had to put out its own press release to confirm that the other was a fake!

In the end, it comes down to a matter of principle. With more and more people jumping on the Net bandwagon every day, with the possibility that all correspondence will be done via e-mail getting closer and closer to reality, and with the prospect of Net financial transactions looming large, e-mail security will have to become as much of a "right" as the privacy we enjoy in our own homes.

Configuring Microsoft Internet Mail

After that long introduction to the ins and outs of the Internet e-mail system, it's time to learn some specifics of the Microsoft Internet Mail program. Assuming that you've installed the program (either by installing Internet Explorer 3.x in OSR2 or by downloading the full install of IE from Microsoft's Web site: http://www.microsoft.com/ie/), let's run through the steps necessary to configure the program.

To get things off the ground, select Start | Programs | Internet Mail. The first time you do this, Windows 95 launches the Internet Mail Configuration Wizard, as shown in Figure 40.1. Click Next > to proceed.

FIGURE 40.1.

The Internet Mail Configuration Wizard leads you through the setup of Internet Mail.

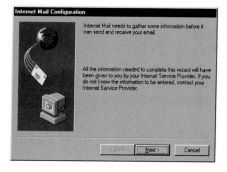

As shown in Figure 40.2, the Wizard then asks for your Name and your Email Address. Fill in these fields and then click Next >.

FIGURE 40.2.

Use this dialog box to enter your name and e-mail address.

The next item on the Wizard's agenda is the domain name of your provider's POP3 and SMTP servers, as shown in Figure 40.3. Fill in the domain names (they're the same computer on many systems), and then click Next >.

FIGURE 40.3.

Fill in the domain names of your provider's POP3 and SMTP servers.

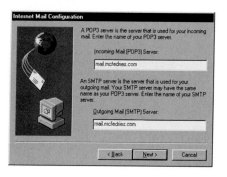

40

INTERNET MAIL:
MESSAGING
MADE EASY

The next dialog box that you see depends on the version of Internet Mail you're using. In the OSR2 version, you'll see the dialog box shown in Figure 40.4. Here, you fill in the name of your POP account and the password you use to access that account, and then click Next >.

FIGURE 40.4.

Internet Mail requires the name and password for your POP account.

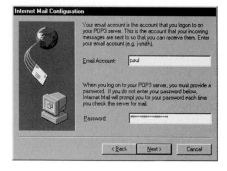

The latest version of Internet Mail supports Secure Password Authentication (SPA) and offers it as an option, as shown in Figure 40.5. Select the `Logon using secure password authentication` option only if you're sure your ISP supports it.

FIGURE 40.5.

The latest version of Internet Mail supports Secure Password Authentication.

From here, the Wizard next wonders about how you connect to the Internet, as shown in Figure 40.6. Activate the option that applies to how you'll be connecting to your e-mail servers. If you choose the `I use a modem to access my email` option, you'll also need to choose a Dial-Up Networking connection. When you're ready to continue, click Next > and then click Finish in the final dialog box.

FIGURE 40.6.

Use this Wizard dialog box to specify how you'll be connecting to your mail server.

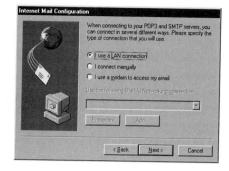

A Tour of the Internet Mail Window

With your configuration chores complete, the Wizard proceeds to load Internet Mail, and you see a window similar to the one shown in Figure 40.7.

FIGURE 40.7.

The Microsoft Internet Mail window.

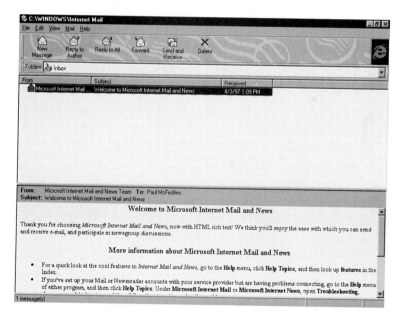

Besides the usual window elements (title bar, menu bar, toolbar, and status bar), the Internet Mail window also has a Folders drop-down list that you use to select the currently displayed folder. Below that, the window is divided into two areas: the *message list* and the *preview pane*.

The message list shows you the messages that reside in the currently selected folder. By default, the message list shows three columns: From (the name of the person who sent the message), Subject (the subject line of the message), and Received (the date and time the message was received).

Customizing the Message Columns

The default columns in Internet Mail tell you the basic information you need for any message. More information is available, however. For example, you might want to know the date and time the message was sent, the size of the message, and to whom the message was sent. All of these items can be displayed as columns in the message list. Here are the steps to follow to customize Internet Mail's columns:

1. Select View | Columns. Internet Mail displays the Columns dialog box, shown in Figure 40.8.

FIGURE 40.8.

Use the Columns dialog box to customize the columns displayed in the message list.

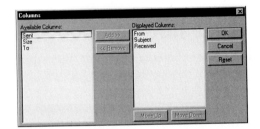

2. To add a column, highlight it in the Available Columns list and click Add>>.
3. To remove a column, highlight it in the Displayed Columns list and click <<Remove.
4. To change the order of the columns, highlight a column in the Displayed Columns list, and then use the Move Up and Move Down buttons to position the column where you want it. (Columns listed at the top are displayed on the left of the message list.)
5. When you're done, click OK.

TIP: SIZING COLUMNS

To change the width of a displayed column, use your mouse to drag the right edge of the column's header to the left or right.

Sorting the Messages

By default, Internet Mail sorts the messages in descending order according to the values in the Received column. But you're free to sort the messages based on any displayed column. Here are the techniques you can use:

- Select View | Sort By and then select the name of the column in the cascade menu that appears. Ascending is the default sort order, but you can change it to descending by selecting View | Sort By and then deactivating the Ascending command.

■ Click the header for the column you want to use for the sort. An arrow appears beside the column name to tell you the direction of the sort (an up arrow for ascending and a down arrow for descending).

■ Right-click the header of the column you want to use, and then select either Sort Ascending or Sort Descending from the context menu.

Working with the Internet Mail Address Book

As you'll see a bit later, when you compose a new message or reply to a received message, Internet Mail provides fields in which you can specify the address of the recipient. If you have correspondents with whom you swap notes frequently, typing their e-mail addresses each time can be a pain.

Instead of typing your recipients' addresses each time you compose a message, you can use Internet Mail's *Address Book* to store these frequently used addresses for easy recall.

To display the Address Book, select File | Address Book. Figure 40.9 shows the Address Book window that Internet Mail displays. The bulk of the window is taken up by a list of persons' names, their e-mail addresses, and their home and business numbers.

FIGURE 40.9.

Use the Address Book to store your frequently used e-mail addresses.

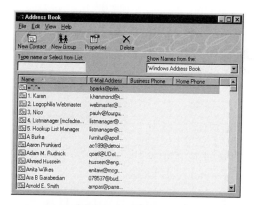

NOTE: IMPORTING ADDRESSES

If you have names in your Exchange Address Book, you can import them into Internet Mail by selecting (in the Internet Mail window) the File | Import | Address Book command. In the Import Tool window that appears, click Import, choose your Exchange profile, and then click OK.

To find a specific name in the address list, use any of the following techniques:

- Move into the list and scroll through it using the scrollbars or the navigation keys (up arrow, down arrow, Page Up, and Page Down).
- In the Type Name or Select from List text box, type the first few letters of the name you want.
- Select View | Sort by and then choose a sort order in the cascade menu that appears.

Adding New Addresses

To store a new address, follow these steps:

1. Select File | New Contact or click the New Contact toolbar button. Internet Mail displays the Properties dialog box shown in Figure 40.10.

FIGURE 40.10.

Use this dialog box to define the specifics of the new address.

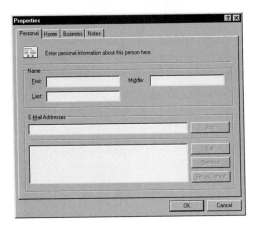

2. Fill in the address particulars.
3. When you're done, click OK.

Creating a Personal Distribution List

You'll see that the Address Book makes it a snap to include addresses in your correspondence. Even the Address Book method of choosing names can get tedious, however, if you regularly send messages to many people. For example, you might send a monthly bulletin to a few dozen recipients, or you might send notes to entire departments.

To make these kinds of mass mailings easier to manage, Internet Mail lets you group multiple e-mail addresses under a single name. To send a message to every member of the group, you simply specify the group as the "recipient" of the message. Here are the steps to follow to create a group:

1. In the Address Book window, either select File | New Group or click New Group in the toolbar. Internet Mail displays the Properties dialog box shown in Figure 40.11.

FIGURE 40.11.

Use this dialog box to define a new address group.

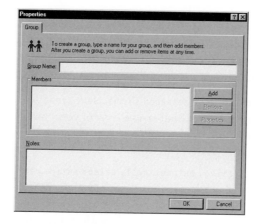

2. In the Group Name text box, enter the name you want to use for the group.

3. To include addresses (that is, *members*) in the group, click the Add button. Internet Mail displays the Select Group Members dialog box, shown in Figure 40.12.

FIGURE 40.12.

Use the Select Group Members dialog box to add e-mail addresses to the group.

4. To add members, highlight the names and click Add->.

5. When you're done, click OK to return to the group properties sheet.

6. Click OK. Internet Mail adds the PDL to the Address Book.

Composing and Sending a New Message

It's time now to get down to the e-mail nitty-gritty. For starters, I'll show you how to use Internet Mail to compose and send a message. You'll also learn how to work with the Internet Mail Address Book, how to embed objects in your messages, and more.

Internet Mail's Send Options

Before we get started, let's examine the various options that Internet Mail provides for sending e-mail. Select Mail | Options, and in the Options dialog box that appears, select the Send tab. You'll see the controls shown in Figure 40.13. Here's a synopsis of the available options:

Save copy of sent messages in the 'Sent Items' folder: When this check box is activated, Internet Mail saves a copy of your message in the Sent Items folder. It's a good idea to leave this option checked because it gives you a record of the messages you send.

When selecting, automatically select entire word: When this check box is activated, Internet Mail selects entire words as you drag the mouse over text. In other words, even if you drag the mouse over only part of the word, Exchange selects the entire word. If you need the capability to select text letter by letter, deactivate this option.

Include message in reply: If you activate this check box, Internet Mail includes the original message text as part of the new message when you reply to or forward a message.

Send messages immediately: This check box is deactivated by default, which means that all sent messages are stored in a special folder called Outbox. To actually send the messages, you have to run the Send and Receive command (explained in the next section). If you'd prefer that Internet Mail send your messages immediately, activate this check box.

Break apart messages larger than x KB: Some mail servers can't handle large messages (the usual limit in these cases is 64 KB). If you're working with such a server, activate this check box and specify a maximum message size in the spinner provided.

Make Microsoft Internet Mail your default e-mail program: If you activate this check box, Internet Mail will load whenever you click a "mailto" link in a Web page or run your Web browser's "mail" command.

HTML: Activate this option to have Internet Mail send your message in HTML format.

Plain Text: This is the default mail format; it sends your messages as simple text.

Indent the original text with x: If you choose the Plain Text option, this control determines how the original message in a reply is formatted. The greater-than sign (>) is regarded as the standard indicator.

Composing a Message

Composing a message isn't all that different from composing a letter or memo in WordPad. You just need to add a few extra bits of information, such as the e-mail address of your recipient and a description of your message.

FIGURE 40.13.

Internet Mail's options for sending e-mail.

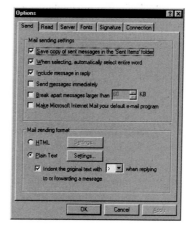

To get started, use any of the following techniques:

- Select Mail | New Message.
- Press Ctrl-N.
- Click the New Message button on the toolbar.

Whichever method you choose, the New Message window, shown in Figure 40.14, appears. Here are the basic steps to follow to compose your message:

1. In the To field, enter the address of the recipient. If you want to send the message to multiple recipients, separate each address with a semicolon (;).

2. In the Cc field, enter the addresses of any recipients you want to receive copies of the message. Again, separate multiple addresses with semicolons.

3. In the Subject field, enter a brief description of the message. This description will appear in the Subject column of the recipient's mail client, so make sure that it accurately describes your message.

4. Use the box below the Subject field to enter your message. Feel free to use any of the formatting options found on the Format menu or the Formatting toolbar. Remember, however, that not all systems will transfer the rich text formatting.

5. To send your message, select File | Send Message, press Alt-S, or click the Send button on the toolbar.

6. Internet Mail displays a dialog box telling you that your message is stored in the Outbox folder. Click OK.

When you click Send, Internet Mail stores the message in the Outbox folder. To deliver the message, you have three choices:

- Select Mail | Send and Receive.
- Press Ctrl-M.
- Click the Send and Receive toolbar button.

Using the Address Book to Specify Recipients

When you're composing a message, you can use the Address Book to add recipients without having to type their addresses. To display the Address Book from the New Message window, use any of the following techniques:

- Click the 3×5 card icon that appears to the left of either the To field or the Cc field.
- Select Mail | Choose Recipients.

- Click the toolbar's Pick Recipients button.

Figure 40.15 shows the slightly different version of the Address Book that appears.

Highlight the recipient and then click either To-> (if you want the name to appear in the To field) or CC-> (if you want the name to appear in the Cc field). When you've added all the recipients for your message, click OK.

FIGURE 40.15.

This dialog box appears when you invoke the Address Book from within the message composition window.

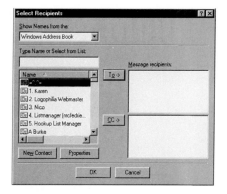

Inserting Objects in a Message

Internet Mail's OLE support means that you can insert objects into your messages. These objects are sent to the recipient using the rich text format, so as long as the recipient's system supports this format (specifically, the remote gateway must be able to handle MIME or Uuencode attachments, and the recipient's e-mail client must be MAPI-compliant), you can attach spreadsheets, word processing documents, graphics, files, and any other OLE object to your messages.

Depending on the type of object you want to work with, Internet Mail gives you two methods of inserting objects:

> **Inserting a text file:** If you have text in a separate file that you want to add to the message, select the Insert | Text File command. In the Inset Text File dialog box that appears, highlight the file and then click Open. Internet Mail adds the file's contents to the message.

> **Inserting a file:** To insert a file into the message, select Insert | File Attachment or click the toolbar's Insert File button. In the Insert Attachment dialog box that appears, highlight the file you want to send and then click Attach. Internet Mail embeds the file into the message as an icon.

Adding a Signature

Although Internet Mail isn't as full-featured as Exchange, it does come with a few options that are missing in its more powerful cousin. An example is Internet Mail's capability to add signatures to your messages automatically.

To do this, you must first follow these steps to define a signature:

1. In the main Internet Mail window, select View | Options.
2. Activate the Signature tab, shown in Figure 40.16.

FIGURE 40.16.

Use the Signature tab to define your signature.

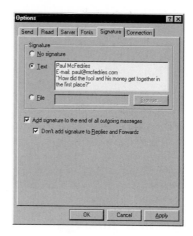

3. To define a text signature, activate the Text option and then enter your signature in the box provided.

4. If your signature text resides in a text file, activate the File option and then enter the full path to the file in the box provided. (Or click Browse to choose the file from a dialog box.)

5. If you want Internet Mail to add the signature to all of your messages, leave the Add signature to the end of all outgoing messages check box activated.

6. If you'd rather use the signature only on original messages, leave the Don't add signature to Replies and Forwards check box activated.

7. Click OK to put the signature options into effect.

If you choose not to have your signature added automatically, you can insert it manually by using either of the following techniques in the New Message window:

■ Select Insert | Signature.

■ Click the Insert Signature button on the toolbar.

Reading Incoming Mail

Of course, you won't be spending all your time firing off notes and missives to friends and colleagues. Those people will eventually start sending messages back to you, and you might start getting regular correspondence from mailing lists, administrators, and other members of the e-mail community. This section shows you how to retrieve messages, read them, and then deal with them appropriately.

Retrieving Messages

Internet Mail doesn't check for new messages on your server automatically. Instead, you use any of the following techniques:

- Select Mail | Send and Receive.
- Press Ctrl-M.
- Click the Send and Receive toolbar button.

Each new message that arrives is stored in the message list and appears in a bold font. To view the contents of any message, highlight it in the message list. Internet Mail then displays the message text in the preview pane.

NOTE: MESSAGES THAT YOU'VE READ ARE NO LONGER BOLD

After about five seconds, Internet Mail removes the bold from the message list item so that you know right away whether you've read the message. You can toggle boldfacing on and off by selecting Edit | Mark as Read (or press Ctrl-Enter) or Edit | Mark as Unread (or Ctrl-Shift-Enter).

NOTE: OPENING A MESSAGE IN ITS OWN WINDOW

If you find the preview pane too confining, you can open the highlighted message in its own window by selecting File | Open (or by pressing Ctrl-O).

Internet Mail's Read Options

To help you work with your correspondence, you might want to check out Internet Mail's read-related properties. To view them, select Mail | Options and select the Read tab in the Options dialog box, shown in Figure 40.17. Here's a review of the available controls:

`Play sound when new messages arrive:` When you activate this check box, Exchange beeps your speaker each time a new message is delivered.

`Mark message as read after previewed for x second(s):` Deactivate this check box to prevent Internet Mail from removing the bold while you're reading a message. Alternatively, you can use the spinner to adjust how long it takes Internet Mail to remove the bold.

`Check for new messages every x minute(s):` Activate this check box to have Internet Mail check for new messages automatically. Use the spinner to determine how frequently Internet Mail polls the server for new messages.

Empty messages from the 'Deleted Items' folder on exit: If you activate this check box, Internet Mail cleans out the Deleted Items folder each time you exit the program.

FIGURE 40.17.

Use the Read tab to set various properties related to reading messages.

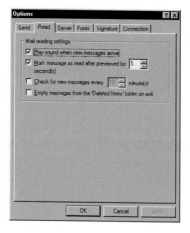

Working with Your Messages

When you have a message highlighted, you can do plenty of things with it (besides reading it, of course). You can print it, save it to a file, move it to another folder, delete it, and more. Most of these operations are straightforward, so I'll just summarize the basic techniques here:

Reading other messages: If you have several messages you want to read, you don't have to return to the message list to navigate your messages. If you want to move on to the next message (the one below the current message in the message list), select View | Next Message or press Ctrl->. If you prefer to move back to the preceding message (the one above the current message in the message list), select View | Previous Message or press Ctrl-<.

Dealing with attachments: If a message has an attachment, it appears either as an icon or as an object embedded in the message. You can use the usual OLE methods of viewing the object (assuming that you have the correct server application; see Chapter 17, "Sharing Data in Windows 95: The Clipboard and OLE," for more about OLE).

Moving a message to a different folder: Later in this chapter, I'll show you how to create new folders you can use for storing related messages. To move a message to another folder, select Mail | Move to and then choose the destination folder from the cascade menu that appears. (If you just want to make a copy of the message, use the Mail | Copy to command instead.)

Saving a message: Instead of storing the message in a folder, you might prefer to save it to a file. To do this, select File | Save As. In the Save As dialog box, select a location, enter a filename, select a file type, and then click Save.

Printing a message: To print a copy of the message, select File | Print to display the Print dialog box. Enter your print options (including whether you want to print any attachments), and then click OK.

Deleting a message: If you want to get rid of the message you're reading, select File | Delete or press Ctrl-D. You can also click the toolbar's Delete button. Note that Internet Mail doesn't really delete the message. Instead, it just moves it to the Deleted Items folder. If you change your mind and decide to keep the message, open the Deleted Items folder and move the message back. To permanently remove a message, open the Deleted Items folder and delete it from there.

Replying to a Message

If you receive a message from someone who is looking for some information from you, or if you think of a witty retort to a friend's or colleague's message, you'll want to send a reply. Instead of requiring you to create a new message from scratch, however, Internet Mail (like all e-mail programs) has a Reply feature that saves you the following steps:

- Internet Mail starts a new message automatically.
- Internet Mail inserts the recipient automatically.
- Internet Mail inserts the original Subject line but adds RE: to the beginning of the text to identify this message as a reply.
- Internet Mail adds the header and the text of the original message into the body of the new message (unless, of course, you turned off this feature in the Send tab, as described earlier).

Internet Mail gives you two Reply options:

Reply to Author: This option sends the reply only to the person who shipped out the original. Any names in the Cc line are ignored. To use this option, select Mail | Reply to Author or press Ctrl-R. You can also click the Reply to Author button on the toolbar.

Reply to All: This option sends the reply not only to the original author, but also to anyone else mentioned in the Cc line. To use this option, select Mail | Reply to All or press Ctrl-Shift-R. You can also click the Reply to All button on the toolbar.

Forwarding a Message

Instead of replying to a message, you might prefer to forward it to another person. For example, you might receive a message in error, or you might think that a friend or colleague might receive some benefit from reading a message you received. Whatever the reason, you can forward a message to another address by using either of the following methods:

- Select Mail | Forward, press Ctrl-F, or click the Forward toolbar button.

■ If you'd prefer to send the message as an attachment, select Mail | Forward as Attachment.

Internet Mail creates a new message, adds the original Subject line with FW: (to identify this as a forwarded message), and inserts the original text either in the message body or as an attachment. If you like, you can add your own text as well.

Working with Folders

The four default folders that Internet Mail sets up are functional but not all that useful in the long term. At this early stage of your Internet Mail career, you might not have all that many messages in your Inbox folder, but it probably won't take long to fill up. Sure, you'll be deleting missives you don't want to bother with, but you'll still have plenty of messages you'll want to keep for posterity. So you'll still be faced with an unwieldy stack of messages before too long.

The problem here is that your messages aren't organized in any way. When you get paper memos and letters, you don't leave them cluttering your In basket, do you? No, you probably use file folders to store related correspondence. You can add the same level of organization to your e-mail correspondence by creating new folders in which to store related messages. So, for example, you could create a folder for each Internet mailing list you subscribe to, one for correspondence between you and your boss, another for your current project, one each for all your wired friends, and so on.

To create a new folder, select the File | Folder | Create command. In the Create New Folder dialog box, shown in Figure 40.18, enter the name of the folder and then click OK.

FIGURE 40.18.

Use this dialog box to enter a name for your new folder.

NOTE: INTERNET MAIL FOLDERS AREN'T HIERARCHICAL

Unfortunately, Internet Mail's folders aren't hierarchical, which means you can't create subfolders. Keep this in mind when deciding which folders to create.

NOTE: DELETING FOLDERS

To delete a folder you've created, select File | Folder | Delete, and then choose the folder from the cascade menu that appears.

Finding Data in Internet Mail

E-mail is one of those things that just snowballs after you begin using it. You might get only a few messages a week at first, but then you start getting a few messages a day. Before you know it, a few *dozen* daily messages are streaming your way, and your folders are bursting at the seams. You'll probably find that you keep many of these messages because you never know when you'll need them again. But after you've accumulated many messages, finding the one you want down the road becomes a real challenge.

Fortunately, Internet Mail has a decent Find command that makes the task easy. This command isn't like the Find command you saw in Chapter 13, "Working with Files and Folders," because it's geared toward searching through e-mail messages. To take a look, first choose the folder in which you want to search, and then select Edit | Find Message. Internet Mail displays the Find Message dialog box, shown in Figure 40.19. Here's a summary of the various options you can use to define your search criteria:

From: Use this text box to specify a sender as part of the search criteria.

Recipients: Use this text box to specify a recipient as part of the search criteria.

Subject: Use this field to search for text in the Subject line of the messages.

Received After: Drop down this list to use the displayed calendar to pick the earliest received date for the message.

Received Before: Drop down this list to use the displayed calendar to pick the latest received date for the message.

FIGURE 40.19.

Internet Mail has a Find command that can scour parts of your e-mail messages for text.

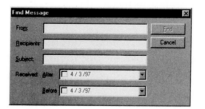

When you've specified your search criteria, click the Find button. Internet Mail then highlights the first message that matches your criteria. To continue searching, select Edit | Find Next, or press F3.

Using the Inbox Assistant to Filter Messages

As e-mail becomes a ubiquitous feature on the business (and even home) landscape, you'll find that e-mail chores take up more and more of your time. And I'm not just talking about the three R's of e-mail: reading, 'riting, and responding. Basic e-mail maintenance—moving, deleting, and so on—also takes up large chunks of otherwise-productive time.

To help ease the e-mail time crunch, Outlook lets you set up "rules" that allow Internet Mail to automatically move an incoming message to a specific folder if the message contains a particular keyword in the subject or body, or if it's from a particular person.

Internet Mail comes with an Inbox Assistant that makes it easy to set up and define these rules. To get started, select Mail | Inbox Assistant. In the Inbox Assistant dialog box that appears, click the Add button. You'll see the Properties dialog box shown in Figure 40.20.

FIGURE 40.20.

Use this dialog box to define a rule.

Your first step is to define the criteria that will cause Internet Mail to invoke this rule. That is, you specify what conditions an incoming message must meet for the rule to be applied to that message. That's the purpose of the controls in the When a message arrives that meets the following criteria group:

To: Use this text box to specify the addresses or names of the direct message recipients that will invoke the rule.

CC: Use this text box to specify the addresses or names of the CC message recipients that will invoke the rule.

From: Use this text box to specify one or more e-mail addresses or names. In this case, Internet Mail will invoke the rule for any message sent from one of these addresses.

Subject: Use this text box to enter a word or phrase that must appear in the Subject line to invoke the rule.

After you've determined *when* the rule will be invoked, you need to specify where Internet Mail will move any message that satisfies these criteria. You do that by selecting a folder from the Move To list.

When you're done, click OK to add the new rule to the Inbox Assistant, shown in Figure 40.21.

NOTE: RULE MAINTENANCE

You can use the Inbox Assistant dialog box to maintain your rules. For example, each rule you've defined has a checkbox beside it that toggles the rule on and off. You can change a rule by highlighting it and clicking Properties. To get rid of a rule, highlight it and click Remove.

FIGURE 40.21.

The rules you've defined appear in the Inbox Assistant dialog box.

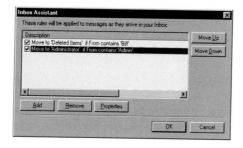

Summary

This chapter showed you how to use Microsoft's Internet Mail messaging client. I began by giving you quite a bit of Internet e-mail background information. You learned how the Internet e-mail system works, what the structure of a message looks like, how to follow Netiquette, and how to send mail between different systems. I also showed you some e-mail jargon, acronyms, and smileys.

From there, I turned your attention to the Internet Mail program. I showed you how to configure it, how to work with the Address Book, how to compose new messages, and how to read incoming messages. You also learned some useful techniques for replaying, forwarding, finding, and using rules to filter messages.

Here's a list of chapters where you'll find related information:

- To get the goods on TCP/IP and other Net plumbing, turn to Chapter 36, "Implementing TCP/IP for Internet and Network Connections."

- To learn how to get an Internet connection established, see Chapter 37, "Windows 95 and the Internet."

- I showed you how to work with Internet Explorer in Chapter 38, "Exploring the Web with Internet Explorer."

- To learn how to wield Internet News, the companion program to Internet Mail, see Chapter 41, "Internet News: Usenet News and Views."

CHAPTER 41

Internet News:
Usenet News
and Views

IN THIS CHAPTER

"The time has come," the Walrus said,
"To talk of many things:
Of shoes—and ships—and sealing wax—
Of cabbages—and kings—
And why the sea is boiling hot—
And whether pigs have wings."

—Lewis Carroll

The vast majority of the attention, buzz, and hype about the Internet is centered on the World Wide Web. That's not surprising because it's the easiest Net service for novices to use, and it's where all the cutting-edge development is taking place. The rest of the Internet services fall into two categories: those that have fallen more or less into disuse (Gopher, for example) and those that just keep on keeping on.

A good example of the latter type of service is Usenet. Usenet is, in essence, a collection of topics available for discussion. These discussion groups (or *newsgroups,* as they're normally called) are open to all and sundry, and they won't cost you a dime (aside from the usual connection charges, of course).

Will you find anything interesting in these discussion groups? Well, let's put it this with way: with more than 25,000 (that's right, twenty-five *thousand*) groups to choose from, if you can't find anything that strikes your fancy, you'd better check your pulse. (Not all service providers offer the complete menu of Usenet groups, so the number available to you might be considerably less than 25,000.)

In this chapter, I'll now turn your attention (if I may) to the Usenet service. I'll give you some background about Usenet, and then I'll show you how to wield Microsoft's Internet News newsreader.

NOTE: USENET HISTORY

Usenet began its life back in 1979 at Duke University. A couple of resident computer whizzes (James Elliot and Tom Truscott) needed a way to easily share research, knowledge, and smart-aleck opinions among Duke students and faculty. So, in true hacker fashion, they built a program that would do just that. Eventually, other universities joined in, and the thing just mushroomed. Today, it's estimated that more than 20 million people participate in Usenet, sending a whopping 150,000 messages a day.

Some Usenet Basics

To get your Usenet education off on the right foot, this section looks at a few crucial concepts that will serve as the base from which you can explore the rest of Usenet:

Internet News: Usenet News and Views

CHAPTER 41

1321

41

INTERNET NEWS:
USENET NEWS
AND VIEWS

article   An individual message in a newsgroup discussion.

follow up   To respond to an article.

hierarchy   Usenet divides its discussion groups into several classifications, or *hierarchies*. There are seven so-called *mainstream* hierarchies:

`comp`	Computer hardware and software
`misc`	Miscellaneous stuff that doesn't really fit anywhere else
`news`	Usenet-related topics
`rec`	Entertainment, hobbies, sports, and more
`sci`	Science and technology
`soc`	Sex, culture, religion, and politics
`talk`	Debates about controversial political and cultural topics

Most Usenet-equipped Internet service providers will give you access to all the mainstream hierarchies. There's also a huge `alt` (alternative) hierarchy that covers just about anything that either doesn't belong in a mainstream hierarchy or is too wacky to be included with the mainstream groups. There are also many smaller hierarchies designed for specific geographic areas. For example, the `ba` hierarchy includes discussion groups for the San Francisco Bay area, the `can` hierarchy is devoted to Canadian topics, and so on.

newsgroup   *Newsgroup* (or, often, simply *group*) is the official Usenet moniker for a discussion topic. Why are they called *news*groups? Well, the original Duke University system was designed to share announcements, research findings, and commentary. In other words, people would use this system if they had some "news" to share with their colleagues. The name stuck, and now you'll often hear Usenet referred to as *Netnews* or simply as *the news*.

newsreader   The software you use to read a newsgroup's articles and to post your own articles.

post   To send an article to a newsgroup.

subscribe   In a newsreader, to add a newsgroup to the list of groups you want to read. If you no longer want to read the group, you unsubscribe from the group.

thread   A series of articles related to the same `Subject` line. A thread always begins with an original article and then progresses through one or more follow-ups.

Figuring Out Newsgroup Names

Newsgroup names aren't too hard to understand, but we need to go through the drill to make sure that you're comfortable with them. In their basic guise, newsgroup names have three parts: the hierarchy to which they belong, followed by a dot, followed by the newsgroup's topic. For example, check out the following name:

`rec.boats`

Here, the hierarchy is `rec` (recreation), and the topic is `boats`. Sounds simple enough so far. But many newsgroups were too broad for some people, so they started breaking the newsgroups into subgroups. For example, the `rec.boats` people who were into canoeing got sick of speed-boat discussions, so they created their own "paddle" newsgroup. Here's how its official name looks:

`rec.boats.paddle`

You'll see lots of these subgroups in your Usenet travels. (For example, there are also newsgroups named `rec.boats.building` and `rec.boats.racing`.) Occasionally, you'll see sub-subgroups, such as `soc.culture.african.american`, but these are still rare in most hierarchies (the exception is the `comp` hierarchy, in which you'll find all kinds of these sub-subgroups). One variation on this theme is to tack on extra subgroup names for emphasis. For example, consider the following newsgroup:

`alt.tv.dinosaur.barney.die.die.die`

This newsgroup, of course, is designed for people who don't exactly like TV's Barney the Dinosaur (to put it mildly).

Understanding Articles and Threads

Articles, as you can imagine, are the lifeblood of Usenet. As I mentioned earlier, every day tens of thousands of articles are posted to the different newsgroups. Some newsgroups might get only one or two articles a day, but many get a dozen or two, on average. (And some very popular groups—`rec.humor` is a good example—can get a hundred or more postings in a day.)

Happily, Usenet places no restrictions on article content. (However, as you'll see shortly, a few newsgroups have *moderators* who decide whether an article is worth posting.) Unlike, say, the heavily censored America Online chat rooms, Usenet articles are the epitome of free speech. Articles can be as long or short as you like (although extremely long articles are frowned on because they take so long to retrieve), and they can contain whatever ideas, notions, and thoughts you feel like getting off your chest (within the confines of the newsgroup's subject matter). You're free to be inquiring, informative, interesting, infuriating, or even incompetent—it's entirely up to you. (Having said all that, however, I don't want you to get the impression that Usenet is total anarchy. If you want to get along with your fellow newshounds, you should follow a few guidelines. See the section "Some Netiquette Niceties for Usenet," later in the chapter, to get some pointers on minding your Usenet p's and q's.)

Earlier I told you that newsgroups were "discussion topics," but that doesn't mean they work like a real-world discussion, where you have immediate conversational give and take. Instead, newsgroup discussions lurch ahead in discrete chunks (articles) and unfold over a relatively long period (sometimes even weeks or months).

To get the flavor of a newsgroup discussion, think of the "Letters to the Editor" section of a newspaper. Someone writes an article in the paper, and later someone else sends in a letter commenting on the content of the article. A few days after that, more letters might come in, such as a rebuttal from the original author, or someone else weighing in with his two cents worth. Eventually, the "discussion" dies out either because the topic has been exhausted or because everyone loses interest.

Newsgroups work in just the same way. Someone posts an article, and then the other people who read the group can, if they like, respond to the article by posting a *follow-up* article. Others can then respond to the response, and so on down the line. This entire discussion—from the original article to the last response—is called a *thread*.

Some Useful Usenet Jargon

Usenet, as you'll soon find out, has lots of buzzwords and a wealth of colorful lingo and jargon. To help you decipher what some people are talking about, this section introduces you to the jargon you'll encounter most often in your Usenet voyages:

catch up   A newsreader command that marks all the articles in a newsgroup as having been read. You normally do this when you have scanned the Subject lines in a group, read the ones you found interesting, and decided to ignore the rest. This wipes the newsgroup's slate clean, so you'll see only new articles the next time you open the group.

cross-post   To post an article in multiple newsgroups.

expired article   An article that no longer appears in a newsgroup because it was deleted by your access provider's system administrator. The volume of Usenet news is so huge that the only way most access providers can keep their heads above water is to purge articles after a certain period (usually anywhere from two to seven days). The moral of the story is that you should check your favorite newsgroups as often as you can. Otherwise, an interesting article could come and go, and you'd never know it.

NOTE: EXPIRATION = CONFUSION!

Article expiration is the principal cause of one of the biggest frustrations for Usenet rookies: the feeling that you've stepped into the middle of a conversation. That's because many of the articles you see at first are either follow-ups to an expired article or original posts commenting on some previous state of affairs. The best thing you can do is muddle through and keep reading. After a while, you'll catch on to new threads, and you'll be an old hand before you know it.

holy war   A never-ending, unchanging (and very boring for the rest of us) argument in which the opinions of combatants on both sides of the issue never budge an inch. Common holy-war topics include religion, abortion, which operating system is superior, and the optimum way to dispense toilet paper.

lurk   To read articles without posting any of your own. This behavior is considered de rigueur for Usenet newcomers, but because Usenet thrives on participation, everyone is expected to post eventually.

moderator   Overworked, underpaid (read: volunteer) Usenet jockey who reads all submissions to a particular newsgroup and selects only the best (or most relevant) for posting.

Netnews   Another name for Usenet news.

ob-   This prefix means *obligatory*. For example, it's traditional that each post to `rec.humor` contains a joke. If someone writes in with some nonjoke material, they'll usually finish with an *objoke*, or *obligatory joke*.

ROT13   An encoding scheme in which each letter in an article gets replaced by the letter that is 13 positions away in the alphabet (*A* is replaced by *N*, for example). You mess up an article with ROT13 when your article contains offensive material or gives away a riddle answer or movie ending.

signal-to-noise ratio   This electronics term is used ironically to compare the amount of good, useful information ("signal") in a newsgroup with the amount of bad, useless dreck ("noise"). The best groups have a high signal-to-noise ratio, whereas groups that have lots of flame wars and spamming (see *spam*) rate low on the signal-to-noise ratio totem pole. For example, the group `rec.humor` has a low signal-to-noise ratio because most of the jokes are bad and many of the posts comment on how bad the jokes are. By contrast, the moderated newsgroup `rec.humor.funny` has a relatively high signal-to-noise ratio because only jokes that are at least mildly amusing make the moderator's cut and appear in the group.

spam   In general, irrelevant prattle that has nothing whatsoever to do with the current topic under discussion. In Usenet, this means to post an ad, chain letter, get-rich-quick scheme, or other superfluity to umpteen different newsgroups. A while back, a law firm posted an ad for its green-card service to hundreds of newsgroups. This created an unbelievable firestorm of controversy, and those poor lawyers are probably still trying to dig themselves out from the avalanche of nasty e-mail messages they received. That was a textbook example of a spam. This is a major Usenet no-no and usually elicits responses that are both ferocious and voluminous.

spewer   A person who specializes in spam, trolling, and flame bait.

spoiler   An article that gives away the ending to a movie or book, or contains the answer to a puzzle or riddle. Proper Netiquette requires that you put the word `spoiler` in the `Subject` line of such an article. (The next section gives you many more pointers on Usenet politeness.)

trolling To post a purposely facetious, flippant, or aggressively dumb article. Its purpose is to dupe the gullible or the self-important into responding with follow-ups that make them look foolish.

Some Netiquette Niceties for Usenet

Back in Chapter 40, "Internet Mail: Messaging Made Easy," I introduced you to Netiquette and showed you how it can grease the wheels of Net social discourse. These prescriptions for politeness are particularly useful in the potentially rough seas of Usenet, so you'll want to make sure that you have given the "Minding Your E-Mail Manners" section in Chapter 40 a thorough going-over before setting sail. To make your voyage an even smoother one, this section presents a few more Netiquette gems that relate specifically to Usenet.

General Usenet Netiquette

In Usenet lingo, a *newbie* is someone new to the Net. Although the term sounds sort of cute, it's actually an insult you'll want to avoid at all costs. How do you do that? Easy: just read this chapter and take its lessons to heart, and in everyone's eyes you'll appear to be a true Net veteran (which, of course, you will be before long). Most Netiquette applies to *all* Usenetters, but there are a few guidelines aimed specifically at newcomers. These are covered in the next few sections.

Lurk Before You Leap

You might sorely be tempted to dive right in to the Usenet deep end and start posting articles left, right, and center. However, you should first get the lay of the Netnews land by picking out a few interesting-sounding groups and limiting yourself to just reading articles posted by others. This gives you a chance to gauge the tone of the group, the intellectual level of the articles, and the interests of the various group members. Then, after you feel comfortable with the newsgroup (which could take as little as a few days or as long as a few weeks, depending on how often you're on the Net), you can start posting some original articles and following up on articles written by your group colleagues.

One caveat: Introverted types, or those uncomfortable with their writing skills, might decide to become full-time lurkers, never posting their own articles. That's their decision, of course, but it's considered bad form in Usenet circles. Why? Well, Usenet thrives on participation and the constant thrust and parry of post and follow-up. Mere rubbernecking adds no value whatsoever to a group, so everyone is expected to post sooner or later. If you're really reluctant, feel the fear and do it anyway (to borrow a book title). You'll be amazed at the pride and sense of accomplishment you'll feel when you see your first post appear in a newsgroup.

Check Out the Newcomer Newsgroups

The news hierarchy contains a couple of dozen newsgroups devoted exclusively to Usenet topics. There are, however, two groups you should read religiously when you're just starting out:

`news.announce.newusers`: This group posts regular articles (these are called *periodic postings*) that explain Usenet concepts to beginners. Some good articles to look for include "What Is Usenet?" "Hints on writing style for Usenet," and "A Primer on How to Work with the Usenet Community."

`news.newusers.questions`: This is the group in which Usenet rookies ask questions about Netiquette, newsreaders, groups, and lots more. In particular, be sure to read the article titled "Welcome to `news.newusers.questions`," which is posted weekly.

Read the Frequently Asked Questions Lists

In your travels through the `alt` hierarchy, you might come across, say, the newsgroup `alt.buddha.short.fat.guy` (really!). This group could be described as "Buddhism with an attitude," and it can be a lot of fun. So you check it out for a while, and when you decide to post, the first question that comes to mind is "Who the heck was the Buddha, anyway?" That's a good question, but the problem is that most of the other readers of this group probably asked the same question when they were newcomers. You can imagine how thrilled the group regulars are to answer this question for the thousandth time.

To avoid these kinds of annoyingly repetitive queries, many newsgroups have a Frequently Asked Questions list, or FAQ (which is pronounced *fack*). Before you even think about posting to a newsgroup for the first time, give the group's FAQ a thorough going over to see whether your question has come up in the past.

How do you get a FAQ for a group? There are lots of methods you can use, but the following four are the most common:

- Check out the newsgroup itself. Some newsgroups post their own FAQs regularly (usually monthly).

- Look in the answers group under each mainstream hierarchy (such as `rec.answers` or `comp.answers`). These groups are set up to hold nothing but FAQ lists for the various groups in the hierarchy. Alternatively, the `news.answers` group contains periodic FAQ postings from most groups that have them.

- Use anonymous FTP to log in to `rtfm.mit.edu` and head for the `/pub/usenet-by-group/news.answers` directory. This directory contains the archived FAQ for every group that has one.

By the way, Usenet has its own FAQ called "Answers to Frequently Asked Questions About Usenet." It's posted monthly in both `news.announce.newusers` and `news.answers`. If you can't find it there, FTP to `rtfm.mit.edu` and grab the file named `part1` in the `/pub/usenet-by-group/news.answers/usenet/faq` directory.

A Primer on Posting Politesse

OK, you've had a lengthy lurk in your favorite newsgroups, you've faithfully scoured `news.announce.newusers` and `news.newusers.questions`, and you've studied the appropriate FAQ

Internet News: Usenet News and Views
Chapter 41

1327

41

INTERNET NEWS:
USENET NEWS
AND VIEWS

files. Now you can just plow ahead and start posting willy-nilly, right? Wrong. There's a whole slew of Netiquette niceties related to posting, which isn't surprising because posting is the life-blood of the Usenet system. To get you prepared, the next few sections tell you everything you need to know.

Use Your Subject Line to Warn Others

Use the Subject line of your article to warn others of material that might be offensive. In brackets, write Offensive to x, where x is the group your article is slamming (such as computer book authors). Similarly, if your article gives away an ending to a movie, TV show, or book, or if it contains the answer to a riddle, include Spoiler in the Subject line so that everyone knows what's coming.

Pick Your Groups with Care

If you put together a list of the top Usenet pet peeves, "articles posted to inappropriate groups" would be a shoo-in to appear on the list. For whatever reasons, Usenet participants always seem to blow a gasket when they come across an article that doesn't fit into their group's theme. To keep the Net on your good side, think carefully about which newsgroup would welcome your article with open arms. Not only will you avoid some wrathful replies, but you'll be more likely to get a good response to your post.

Here are a few other points to bear in mind when selecting a newsgroup:

- Although cross-posting is occasionally useful, you should rarely need to do it. If you're debating sending an article to a couple of closely related groups, keep in mind that the same people probably read both groups, so your potential audience won't be any bigger. (And, believe me, nobody likes to read the same article twice!)

- If your article applies only to a specific geographic area (if you're selling a car, for example, or if you're discussing a local restaurant), be sure to post to the appropriate newsgroup in a hierarchy that covers your area. For example, Toronto Usenetters can post classifieds to the tor.forsale group or want ads to the tor.jobs group. If you don't have any local newsgroups, you can post to one of the main groups, but be sure to specify in the Subject line that your article applies only to a certain area. (An example is Cubic zirconia jewelry for sale: Hoboken, NJ in rec.collecting.)

- If you want to run a test to see whether your newsreader is posting articles properly, be sure to use one of the test newsgroups (such as misc.test). Do not—repeat, do not—use any of the regular newsgroups, unless you want your e-mail inbox stuffed with angry complaints. For faster feedback, use a test group in your area. (Many access providers have set up their own test groups, and you'll find that it's best to use them.)

TIP: HOW TO AVOID AUTOMATIC TEST REPLIES

Many Usenet sites have programs that will automatically fire off e-mail messages to you when they receive your test posts. If you'd prefer not to receive these messages, include the word `ignore` in the `Subject` line of your test article.

■ If you want to advertise a product on Usenet, you need to be *very* careful how you go about it. (Remember what happened to those green-card lawyers!) If you really want to advertise, use the groups in the `biz` hierarchy (for example, `biz.comp.software`).

Practice Posting Patience

If you post an article and it doesn't show up in the newsgroup five minutes later, don't resend the article. A posted article goes on quite a journey as it wends its way through the highways and byways of the Internet. As a result, it can often take a day or two before your article appears in the newsgroup. (This is why it's also considered bad Usenet form to post articles "announcing" some current news event. By the time the article appears, the event is likely to be old news to most readers, and you'll end up looking just plain silly. If you're aching to discuss it with someone, try the `misc.headlines` group.)

Avoiding Follow-up Faux Pas

One of the best ways to get your Usenet feet wet is to respond to an existing article with a follow-up message. You can answer questions, correct errors, or just weigh in with your own opinions on whatever the topic at hand happens to be. Following up has its own Netiquette rules, however, and I've summarized the most important ones here:

Read any existing follow-ups first. Before diving in, check to see whether the article already has any follow-ups. If so, read them to make sure that your own follow-up won't just repeat something that has already been said.

Use your newsreader's follow-up command. Don't respond to an article by posting another original article. Instead, use your newsreader's follow-up command to make sure that your article becomes part of the appropriate thread.

Quote the original article sparingly. To make sure that others know what you're responding to, include the appropriate lines from the original article in your follow-up. You'll need to use some judgment here, though. Quoting the entire article is wasteful (especially if the article was a long one) and should be avoided at all costs.

Reply by e-mail. If you think your follow-up will have interest only to the original author and not the group as a whole, send your response directly to the author's e-mail address.

Avoid "Me too" or "Thanks" replies. Few Usenet experiences are more frustrating than a follow-up that consists only of a brain-dead "Me too!" or "Thanks for the info" response (especially if the dope sending the follow-up has quoted the entire original article!). If you feel the need to send missives of this kind, do it via e-mail.

Use summaries to reduce group clutter. Some posts can elicit many different replies. For example, sending a request for "mother-in-law jokes" to rec.humor could get you all kinds of responses from disgruntled spouses. To avoid cluttering the group with all these follow-ups (especially if there's a chance the replies will have lots of repeats), tell the respondents to send their jokes (or whatever) to you via e-mail, and offer to summarize the results. Then, when all the follow-ups are in, post your own follow-up that includes a summary of the responses you received.

Configuring Microsoft Internet News

Now that you know a bit about Usenet, it's time to get down to more practical matters. Specifically, the rest of this chapter will show you how to use Microsoft Internet News to subscribe to, read, and post to newsgroups. Assuming that you have installed Internet News (either by installing Internet Explorer 3.0 in OSR2 or by downloading the full install of IE from Microsoft's Web site: http://www.microsoft.com/ie/), let's run through the program's configuration procedure.

To get going, select Start | Programs | Internet News. The first time you do this, Windows 95 launches the Internet News Configuration Wizard, shown in Figure 41.1. Click Next > to proceed.

NOTE: MSN NEWS SERVERS

If you've installed version 1.3 of the MSN client (as described in Chapter 26, "Getting Online with The Microsoft Network"), Internet News will already be configured to use the following MSN news servers:

msnnews.msn.com
netnews.msn.com

In this case, you'll likely be prompted to display a list of newsgroups so that you can do some subscribing. If you click Yes, Internet News connects to MSN and downloads the list of newsgroups on its servers.

If you prefer to use a different news server, select News | Options from Internet News, activate the Server tab, and click Add. Use the News Server Properties dialog box to enter the data for the server.

As you can see in Figure 41.2, the Wizard then asks for your Name and your Email Address. Fill in the appropriate data and click Next >.

FIGURE 41.1.

The Internet News Configuration Wizard leads you through the steps necessary to configure Internet News.

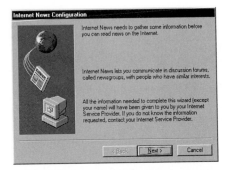

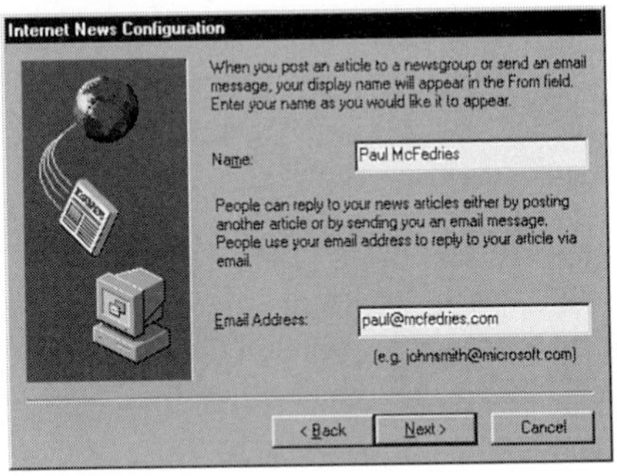

FIGURE 41.2.

Use this dialog box to enter your name and e-mail address.

Now the Wizard needs to know the domain name of your provider's news server (sometimes called an NNTP, or Network News Transport Protocol, server), as shown in Figure 41.3. Enter the domain name in the News Server text box.

FIGURE 41.3.

Enter the domain name of your news server and, optionally, the logon data for the server.

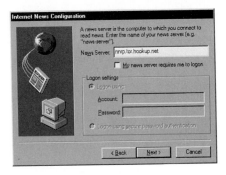

If you have to log on to the server, activate the My news server requires me to logon check box, and fill in the Account and Password text boxes. When you're done, click Next >.

The Wizard next needs to know how you connect to the Internet, as shown in Figure 41.4. Activate the option that applies to how you'll be connecting to your news server. If you choose the I use a modem to access my newsgroups option, you'll also need to choose a Dial-Up

Internet News: Usenet News and Views

CHAPTER 41

1331

41

INTERNET NEWS:
USENET NEWS
AND VIEWS

Networking connection. When you're ready to continue, click Next > and then click Finish in the final dialog box.

FIGURE 41.4.

Use this Wizard dialog box to specify how you'll be connecting to your news server.

With the configuration complete, Internet News connects to your news server and proceeds to download the list of newsgroups available on the server, as shown in Figure 41.5.

FIGURE 41.5.

After the configuration is complete, Internet News connects to your news server and downloads the list of available newsgroups.

When that's done (it might take quite a while depending on the speed of your connection), you'll see the Newsgroups dialog box. You use this dialog box to view and subscribe to newsgroups. I'll show you how it works a bit later, so for now you should click Cancel so that you can take a tour of the Internet News window.

Checking Out the Internet News Window

After you've subscribed to some newsgroups and downloaded some messages, your Internet News window will look something like the one shown in Figure 41.6.

Besides the usual window elements (title bar, menu bar, toolbar, and status bar), the Internet News window also has a Newsgroups drop-down list that you use to select the currently displayed newsgroup. Below that, the window is divided into two areas: the *message list* and the *preview pane*.

FIGURE **41.6.**

The Internet News window.

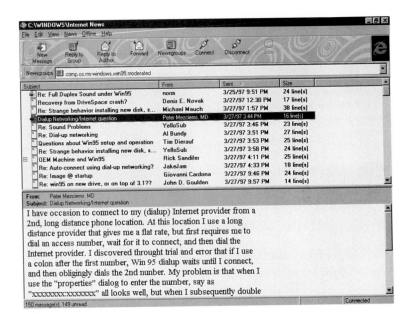

The message list shows you the messages that reside in the currently selected newsgroup. By default, the message list shows four columns: Subject (the subject line of the message), From (the name of the person who sent the message), Sent (the date and time the message was sent), and Size (the number of lines in the message). A plus sign (+) beside a messages tells you that the message is part of a thread. Click the plus sign to see the other messages in the thread.

Customizing the Message Columns

The default columns in Internet News show you all the information that's available for each message. If you don't need to see all this data (for example, you might not want to view the size of each message), it's easy enough to remove a column. Here are the steps to follow to customize Internet News's columns:

1. Select View | Columns. Internet News displays the Columns dialog box, shown in Figure 41.7.

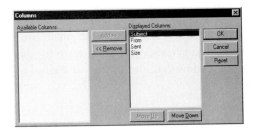

2. To remove a column, highlight it in the `Displayed Columns` list and click <<Remove.

3. To add a column, highlight it in the `Available Columns` list and click Add>>.

4. To change the order of the columns, highlight a column in the `Displayed Columns` list, and then use the Move Up and Move Down buttons to position the column where you want it. (Columns listed at the top are displayed on the left of the message list.)

5. When you're done, click OK.

TIP: SIZING COLUMNS

To change the width of a displayed column, use your mouse to drag the right edge of the column's header to the left or right.

Sorting the Messages

By default, Internet News sorts the messages in ascending order according to the values in the Sent column. But you're free to sort the messages based on any displayed column. Here are the techniques you can use:

- Select View | Sort By and then select the name of the column in the cascade menu that appears. Ascending is the default sort order, but you can change it to descending by selecting View | Sort By and then deactivating the Ascending command. Note, too, that you can sort the messages by thread by activating the Group Messages by Thread command (which is activated by default).

- Click the header for the column you want to use for the sort. An arrow appears beside the column name to tell you the direction of the sort (an up arrow for ascending and a down arrow for descending).

- Right-click the header of the column you want to use, and then select either Sort Ascending or Sort Descending from the context menu.

Working with Newsgroups

Newsgroups are at the heart of Usenet, so you'll need to become comfortable with basic newsgroup chores such as subscribing and unsubscribing. This section takes you through the basics.

For starters, you'll be doing most of your newsgroup work in the Newsgroups dialog box, shown in Figure 41.8. Use any of the following techniques to display this dialog box:

- Select News | Newsgroups.
- Press Ctrl-W.
- Click the Newsgroups toolbar button.

Note that you'll see the News servers list only if you've defined multiple servers (as described earlier).

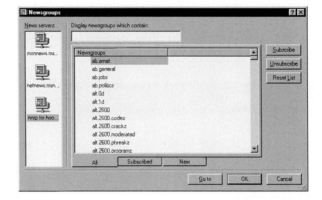

Subscribing to a Newsgroup

Before you can read or post articles, you need to display a newsgroup in the Newsgroups drop-down list. You have two ways of doing this: you can subscribe to a newsgroup or you can open a newsgroup without committing to a subscription.

Either way, you must first display the group you want in the Newsgroups list. Begin by selecting the news server you want to use (if you have multiple servers defined). Then you can either scroll through the groups or type all or part of the newsgroup name in the Display newsgroups which contain text box. Note that Internet News looks for group names that *contain* the text you type. If you type startrek, for example, Internet News will match alt.startrek, rec.arts.startrek.fandom, and so on. This example is shown in Figure 41.9.

After you've highlighted a newsgroup, use either of the following techniques:

■ If you just want to view the group without subscribing, click Go to. You'll be returned to the Internet News window with the newsgroup displayed. If you later want to subscribe to this group, select News | Subscribe to this Group. (Note, too, that if you don't subscribe and then you move to another newsgroup, Internet News asks whether you want to subscribe. In this case, click Yes to subscribe to the group; if you click No, Internet News removes the group from the list.)

■ If you want to subscribe to the group, click the Subscribe button. You can repeat this process for any other newsgroup subscriptions. In each case, Internet News adds the name of the group to the Subscribed tab. When you're done, click OK to return to the main Internet News window.

Unsubscribing from a Newsgroup

If you get tired of a newsgroup, you can unsubscribe at any time by using either of the following techniques:

■ In the Newsgroups window, select the Subscribed tab, highlight the newsgroup, and click Unsubscribe.

■ In the Internet News window, use the Newsgroups list to select the group, and then select News | Unsubscribe from the Group.

Downloading Messages

With some newsgroups selected, you're now ready to start grabbing messages to read. With Internet News, you have two ways to proceed:

Online: Working online means you're connected to the news server. You can download message headers at any time, and highlighting a message downloads the message text immediately.

Offline: Working offline means that you connect briefly to get the available headers in a group. Then, while you're not connected, you examine the message Subject lines and mark those that you want to retrieve. You then connect once again and tell Internet News to download the marked messages.

Connecting and Downloading Messages Online

In Internet News, you can connect to your news server at any time by selecting File | Connect, or by clicking the Connect button. Selecting any newsgroup also establishes a connection.

After you're connected, Internet News should download the group's message headers for you automatically. For busy groups, the default download limit of 300 might not grab every header. To get more headers, select News | Get Next 300 Headers. (As you'll see later, you can adjust this header limit to your liking.)

Each new message that arrives is stored in the message list and appears in a bold font. To view the contents of any message, highlight it in the message list. Internet News then downloads the message body and displays the message text in the preview pane.

> **NOTE: MESSAGES THAT YOU'VE READ ARE NO LONGER BOLD**
>
> After about five seconds, Internet News removes the bold from the message list item so that you know right away whether you've read the message. You can toggle boldfacing on and off by selecting Edit | Mark as Read (or press Ctrl-Enter) or Edit | Mark as Unread (or Ctrl-Shift-Enter).

Downloading Messages Offline

If you elect not to establish a connection when you start Internet News, or if you disconnect during a session (by selecting File | Disconnect or by clicking the toolbar's Disconnect button), you can then work offline. From here, you can either mark entire newsgroups to download or you can mark individual messages to download.

Downloading Headers for Entire Newsgroups

The easiest way to grab the headers for an entire newsgroup is to select the group and then connect to the news server. This action downloads the available headers for that group. Continue downloading headers, as needed, and then disconnect to scan the message subjects offline.

Alternatively, you can ask Internet News to download the headers for multiple newsgroups by following these steps:

1. Select Offline | mark Newsgroups. Internet News displays the Mark Newsgroups dialog box.

2. If you want to download the headers for all your subscribed groups, make sure that the All Subscribed Newsgroups option is activated.

3. If you prefer to specify the newsgroups you want to work with, activate the Selected Newsgroups option, open the appropriate news server branch, and activate the check boxes beside each newsgroup, as shown in Figure 41.10.

4. When activated, the Download headers only option tells Internet News to grab only the header data for each message. If you prefer to get the message bodies as well, activate the Download entire message option instead.

5. If you prefer to bypass older messages, activate the Don't download new messages posted more than x days ago check box, and enter the number of days in the spinner.

6. Click Download Now to perform the download.

Internet News: Usenet News and Views

CHAPTER 41

1337

41

INTERNET NEWS:
USENET NEWS
AND VIEWS

FIGURE 41.10.

Use this dialog box to choose the newsgroups you want to download.

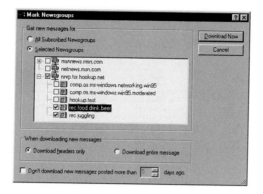

Downloading Individual Messages

After you've downloaded a group's message headers, you can peruse the `Subject` lines of the headers and mark those messages you want to retrieve. Here's a review of the techniques you can use:

- To download an individual message, highlight it in the message list and then connect to the server.

- To mark a message for later downloading, highlight it and then select Offline | Mark Message for Download. You can also right-click the message and then select Mark Message for Download from the context menu.

- To mark an entire thread for later downloading, highlight any message in the thread and then select Offline | Mark Thread for Download.

- To mark all the messages for later downloading, highlight any message and then select Offline | Mark Message for Download.

- If you change your mind, you can tell Internet News not to download a message by highlighting it and selecting Offline | Unmark for Download. (To start over again, choose Edit | Select All and then choose the Unmark for Download command.)

To retrieve the marked messages, select Offline | Post and Download. How do you know which messages are marked and which have already been downloaded? As you can see in Figure 41.11, Internet News adds a green arrow to marked messages and adds a push-pin to downloaded messages.

NOTE: WHAT ABOUT ROT13 MESSAGES?

If you come across a message that has been encoded using ROT13, you can use Internet News's built-in decoder. To use it, select Edit | Unscramble (ROT13).

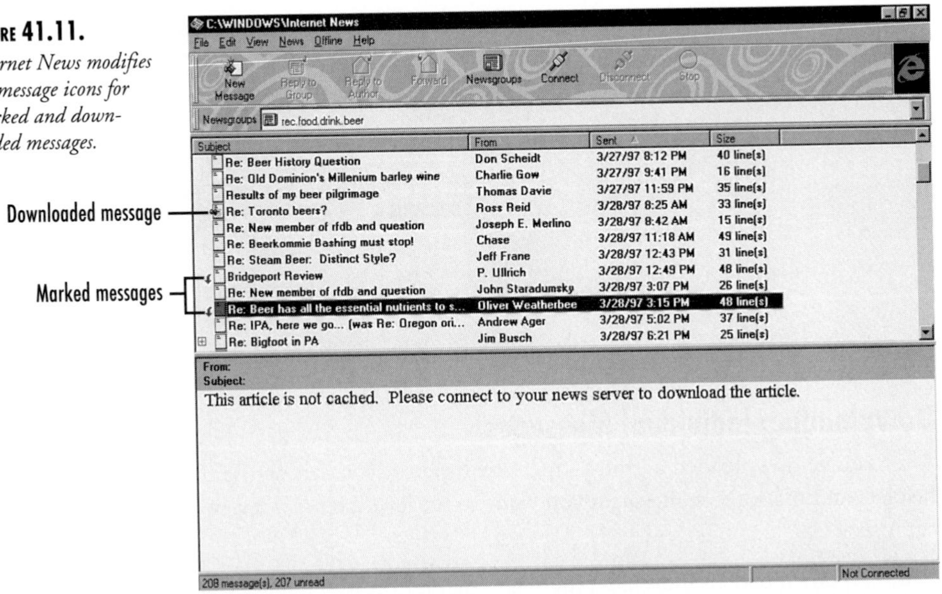

FIGURE 41.11.

Internet News modifies the message icons for marked and downloaded messages.

Downloaded message ———

Marked messages ———

NOTE: OPENING A MESSAGE IN ITS OWN WINDOW

If you find the preview pane too confining, you can open the highlighted message in its own window by selecting File | Open (or by pressing Ctrl-O).

Message Options in Internet News

To help you work with your messages, you might want to check out Internet News's read-related properties. To view them, select News | Options, and in the Options dialog box, select the Read tab, shown in Figure 41.12. Here's a review of the available controls:

Download x headers at a time: If you deactivate this check box, Internet News does not download headers automatically when you select a newsgroup. If you leave this option activated, use the spinner to determine the maximum number of headers downloaded at a time.

Auto expand conversation threads: Activating this check box tells Internet News to expand all downloaded threads.

Message is read after being previewed for x second(s): Deactivate this check box to prevent Internet News from removing the bold while you're reading a message. Alternatively, you can use the spinner to adjust how long it takes Internet News to remove the bold.

Check for new messages every *x* minute(s): Activate this check box to have Internet News check for new messages automatically. Use the spinner to determine how frequently Internet News polls the server for new messages.

Notify me if there are any new newsgroups: When this check box is activated, Internet News polls the server for the names of newsgroups added since you last connected. If there are any, Internet News displays a dialog box to let you know. (A list of the new groups appears in the New tab of the Newsgroups dialog box.)

Mark all messages as read when exiting a newsgroup: If you activate this check box, Internet News marks every group message as read whenever you move to a different newsgroup.

Make Microsoft Internet News your default news reader: If you activate this check box, Internet News loads whenever you run your Web browser's "news" command. (In Internet Explorer, for example, select Go | Read News.)

Always start me in this newsgroup: If you have a favorite newsgroup you like to read first, activate this check box and then select the group from the drop-down list.

FIGURE 41.12.

Use the Read tab to set various properties related to reading messages.

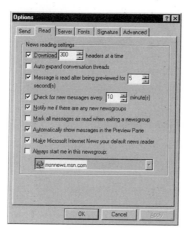

You'll find a few more message-related options in the Advanced tab, shown in Figure 41.13. All of these options affect the local storage that Internet News uses for downloaded messages. Here's a summary:

Delete messages *x* days after being downloaded: When this check box is activated, Internet News deletes any downloaded message a specified number of days after the download.

Don't keep read messages: When this option is activated, Internet News removes read messages from local storage after you exit the program.

Compact files when there is *x* percent wasted space: This spinner determines the threshold point at which Internet News cleans up its local storage to reduce disk space usage. (Messages removed from local storage don't reduce the size of the cache, but just leave gaps. These gaps must be compacted to retrieve the disk space.)

Clean Up Now: Click this button to force Internet News to compact its local storage space immediately.

FIGURE 41.13.

The Advanced tab contains various options related to the local storage of downloaded messages.

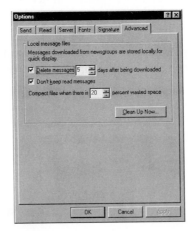

Writing a Rejoinder: Following Up a Message

Usenet is at its best when it's interactive: questions are asked and answered; the swords of conflicting opinions are crossed; debaters cut and parry to score points on contentious issues. The engine behind all this verbal jousting is, of course, the follow-up message. To post a follow-up with Internet News, follow these steps:

1. Highlight the original message in the message list.
2. Select News | Reply to Newsgroup. (You can also press Ctrl-G or click the Reply to Group toolbar button.) Internet News opens a message composition window and fills it with the text from the original article.
3. Cut out any unnecessary text from the original article.
4. Enter your own text in the article body.
5. Select File | Post Message. (Alternatives for faster service: Alt-S or click the Post Message button.) Internet News displays a dialog box telling you that your message will be stored in the Outbox folder.
6. Click OK.

After you've posted a few messages, you can send them to the newsgroups by selecting Offline | Post and Download.

NOTE: REPLYING VIA E-MAIL

Instead of posting a follow-up message, you might prefer to reply directly to the author via e-mail. To do this, highlight the message and select News | Reply to Author. (Or else press Ctrl-R or click the Reply to Author button.)

NOTE: INTERNET MAIL SIMILARITIES

Internet News has a few options related to sending messages. You'll find them by selecting News | Options and then activating the Send tab. Note that the controls in this tab are identical to those found in the Send tab of Internet Mail. I discussed all of them in depth in Chapter 40, so you should head there for explanations.

Chapter 40 is also the place to turn for information on creating and using signatures.

Composing a New Message

As I've said before, original messages are the lifeblood of Usenet because they get the discussions off the ground and give the rest of us something to read (as well as laugh at, sneer at, and hurl verbal abuse at). So if you're feeling creative, you can take advantage of this section, which shows you how to post a new message from Internet News.

To get started, select the newsgroup to which you want to post, and then use any of the following techniques:

- Select News | New Message to Newsgroup.
- Press Ctrl-N.
- Click the New Message button on the toolbar.

Whichever method you choose, the New Message window, shown in Figure 41.14, appears. Here are the basic steps to follow to compose your message:

1. The Newsgroups field should show the name of the current newsgroup. If you want to send the message to multiple newsgroups, separate each name with a comma (,). (Alternatively, click the newsgroup icon on the left side of the field and then choose a newsgroup from the dialog box that appears.)

2. In the Cc field, enter the e-mail addresses of any recipients you want to receive copies of the message.

3. In the Subject field, enter a brief description of the message. This description will appear in the Subject column of the recipient's mail client, so make sure that it accurately describes your message.

4. Use the box below the Subject field to enter your message.

5. To post your message, select File | Post Message (or press Alt-S, or click the Post Message button in the toolbar).

6. Internet News displays a dialog box telling you that your message is stored in the Outbox folder. Click OK.

FIGURE 41.14.

Use the New Message window to enter the newsgroups, the Subject *line, and the body of the message.*

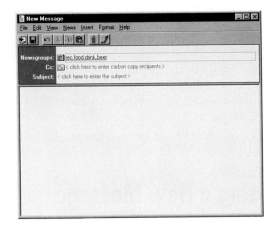

When you click Send, Internet News stores the message in the Outbox folder.

To deliver the message, you have two choices:

■ Select Offline | Post and Download.

■ Display the newsgroup and click Connect.

Working with Messages

When you have a message highlighted, you can do plenty of things with it (besides reading it, of course). You can print it, save it for posterity, cancel it, and more. Most of these operations are straightforward, so I'll just summarize the basic techniques here:

Reading other messages: If you have several messages you want to read, you don't have to return to the message list to navigate your messages. If you want to move on to the next message (the one below the current message in the message list), select View | Next Message (or press Ctrl->), View | Next Unread Message, or View | Next Unread Thread. If you prefer to move back to the preceding message (the one above the current message in the message list), select View | Previous Message (or press Ctrl-<).

Dealing with attachments: If a message has an attachment, you'll see a paper-clip icon in the upper-right corner of the preview pane. To view the attachment, click the paper clip and then click the name of the file.

Saving a message: Much of what you'll read on Usenet is complete and utter blarney—just a bunch of geeks blathering away to each other. But Usenet would not be nearly as popular as it is if there weren't at least some quality to be had. Once in a while, you'll even come across an article (such as a FAQ or joke collection) that's worth preserving. In Internet News, you can send an article to the Saved Items folder by selecting File | Save Message.

Printing a message: To print a copy of the message, select File | Print to display the Print dialog box. Enter your print options and then click OK.

Canceling one of your messages: If you post a message and then have second thoughts, you can remove it from the newsgroup by selecting File | Cancel.

Summary

This chapter showed you how to use Microsoft's Internet News program for reading Usenet news. I began by giving you quite a bit of Usenet background information. You learned how Usenet works and how to understand newsgroup names, and I ran through a few Usenet buzzwords and Netiquette items.

From there, you learned how to operate the Internet News program. I showed you how to configure it, how to work with newsgroups, how to download and read messages, how to post replies, and how to compose new messages.

Here's a list of chapters where you'll find related information:

- To get the goods on TCP/IP and other Net plumbing, turn to Chapter 36, "Implementing TCP/IP for Internet and Network Connections."

- To learn how to get an Internet connection established, see Chapter 37, "Windows 95 and the Internet."

- Chapter 38, "Exploring the Web with Internet Explorer," shows you how to work with Internet Explorer.

- To learn how to wield Internet Mail, the companion program to Internet News, see Chapter 40, "Internet Mail: Messaging Made Easy."

CHAPTER 42

Setting Up a Windows 95 World Wide Web Server

IN THIS CHAPTER

It is more blessed to give than to receive.

From the New Testament

It has always seemed that the lot in life for Microsoft's mainstream Windows products (3.x through 95) was to be left holding the client end of the client/server stick. That's not surprising, because Windows has always been designed as a standalone operating system. However, one of the benefits of a (mostly) 32-bit architecture and built-in multithreading is that Windows can at least aspire to higher ground. For example, in Chapter 35, "Remote Computing with Dial-Up Networking," you saw that running the Dial-Up Server component enabled a Windows 95 machine to act as a Dial-Up Networking host. In this chapter, you'll learn about a way to send Windows 95 even further into server territory. Specifically, I'll show you how to implement Personal Web Server to turn your Windows 95 client into a competent World Wide Web server.

Getting Personal Web Server

OSR2

Personal Web Server is available from various sources: in the Internet Explorer Starter Kit, as a component in the Microsoft FrontPage package, with OSR2, and at Microsoft's Web site as an Internet Explorer 3.0 (and higher) component:

```
http://www.microsoft.com/ie/download/
```

It's important to note, however, that Microsoft has released a version 1.0a for Personal Web Server that fixes a few problems in the 1.0 release. Before running Personal Web Server, be sure to download this latest version (there's also a patch available for 1.0 users).

> **NOTE: INSTALL TCP/IP NETWORKING**
>
> Personal Web Server runs both the HTTP and the FTP protocols. So before you can use Personal Web Server, you must install and configure TCP/IP on your computer. See Chapter 36, "Implementing TCP/IP for Internet and Network Connections," for details. Note, as well, that Personal Web Server's administration tool is browser-based, so you'll need a Web browser installed on your system.

Viewing the Personal Web Server Defaults

After you install Personal Web Server and restart your computer, you'll see a new Personal Web Server icon in the system tray, which tells you that the server's HTTP service has started. Before you start serving pages, though, you need to understand some of the defaults that are set for Personal Web Server. To do this, you need to display the Personal Web Server properties sheet by using either of the following methods:

- Double-click the Personal Web Server icon in the system tray.
- Select Start | Settings | Control Panel, and then launch the Personal Web Server icon from the Control Panel window.

Either way, you'll see the Personal Web Server Properties dialog box, shown in Figure 42.1.

FIGURE 42.1.

Use this properties sheet to configure Personal Web Server.

The General tab shows you the root address of your Web server. This address always takes the following form:

```
http://name.domain
```

The interpretation of this address depends on several factors. If you're on a TCP/IP network, for example, *name* is your computer's network name, and *domain* is the domain name of your TCP/IP network. In my example, the computer name is hermes and the domain name is logophilia.com, so the address of my server is http://hermes.logophilia.com. (If you'll be using Personal Web Server exclusively on an intranet, the root address uses the format http://name.)

NOTE: CHANGING THE COMPUTER NAME

If you don't like the name used by Personal Web Server, you can change it by right-clicking Network Neighborhood and selecting Properties. In the Network properties sheet that appears, click Identification and then use the Computer Name text box to change the name. Note, however, that changing this name might mess up either the DNS or the WINS resolution for your computer (this doesn't apply if you're using DHCP on an intranet).

NOTE: MY REAL WEB SERVER ADDRESS

The `http://hermes.logophilia.com` address is a temporary server setup for the purposes of this chapter. My full-time Web server can be found at the following URL:

`http://www.mcfedries.com/`

The `Default Home Page` group shows you the path and filename of the HTML file that will serve as the initial page that users see when they access your root address. There are two things to note here:

■ The path name of the default home page is mapped to the server's root directory. So the default path of `C:\WebShare\wwwroot\` corresponds to the root (/) of your Web site. In my example, the server's root directory is `http://hermes.logophilia.com/`, which is the same thing as `C:\WebShare\wwwroot\`.

■ All Web servers define a default document for every directory. If a user does not specify an HTML document in the URL, the server displays the default document. For Personal Web Server, the default document is named `default.htm`, so the following URLs will display the same document:

`http://hermes.logophilia.com/`
`http://hermes.logophilia.com/default.htm`

Note that you can click the Display Home Page and More Details buttons to load some pages into your browser. However, I'll hold off discussing the display of pages until later in this chapter (see "Testing the Web Server," a little later in the chapter).

Personal Web Server Startup

This section takes a look at the various startup options that are available with Personal Web Server. These options are divided into two categories: the Web server itself and the services it supports.

The Web Server Startup Options

As I mentioned earlier, the Web server is launched automatically each time you start Windows 95. The controls in the Startup tab of the Personal Web Server properties sheet, shown in Figure 42.2, determine several Personal Web Server startup options:

Web Server State: This group tells you whether the Web server is currently running. Click Stop to shut down the Web server; to restart the server, click Start.

Run the Web server automatically at startup: When this check box is activated, the Web server is launched each time you start Windows 95.

Show the Web server icon on the taskbar: This check box toggles the Personal Web Server icon in the system tray on and off.

FIGURE 42.2.

Personal Web Server's startup options are found in the Startup tab.

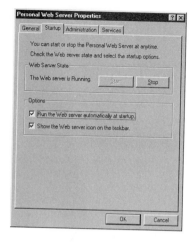

Service Startup Options

Personal Web Server supports both World Wide Web and File Transfer Protocol operations, and these are supported respectively by the HTTP and FTP protocols. Personal Web Server has a separate service to handle each protocol, and these services must be running for users to be able to access Web pages and FTP files.

The Services tab, shown in Figure 42.3, allows you to start and stop each service. To do so, highlight the service and then click either Start or Stop.

FIGURE 42.3.

You can start and stop both the FTP server and the Web (HTTP) server from the Services tab.

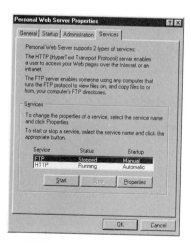

By default, the HTTP service launches automatically at startup, but the FTP service does not. To change these defaults, highlight a service, click Properties to display the service's properties sheet (Figure 42.4 shows the dialog box that appears for the HTTP service), and activate either Automatic or Manual.

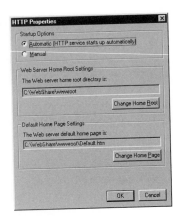

FIGURE 42.4.

Use this dialog box to determine whether the HTTP service launches automatically at startup. The properties sheet for the FTP service is similar.

Testing the Web Server

With both the Web server and the HTTP service started, you should now check to make sure that the server works properly before moving on to more serious administration issues. The next two sections show you how to test the server on both an intranet and an Internet connection.

Testing an Intranet Connection

If you'll be using Personal Web Server on an intranet, you need to do two things before trying out the Web server:

■ Establish a connection to the network.

■ Enable WINS resolution on the server computer. Recall from Chapter 37, "Windows 95 and the Internet," that WINS (Windows Internet Name Service) maps NetBIOS computer names to IP addresses. Enabling WINS allows other computers on the intranet to find your server.

To test the connection, start a Web browser and enter a URL of the following form:

```
http://name/
```

Here, *name* is the NetBIOS name of the computer running the Web server (for example, `http://hermes/`). You should see the default Personal Web Server home page, shown in Figure 42.5.

TROUBLESHOOTING: THE HOME PAGE DOES NOT APPEAR

If you don't see the home page, try entering a URL of the following format:

```
http://IPaddress/
```

Here, *IPaddress* is the IP address of the computer running the Web server (for example, `http://205.123.45.6/`).

If that doesn't work, try the `localhost` address:

`http://localhost/`

FIGURE 42.5.

The default Personal Web Server home page.

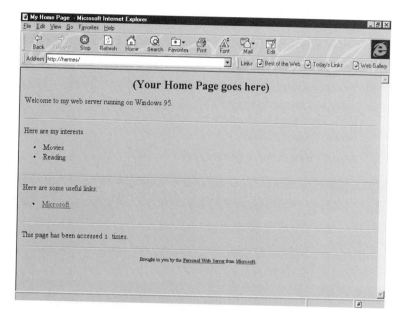

As you can see from this figure, the `default.htm` supplied with Personal Web Server isn't much to look at, so you'll need to make changes before inviting guests to your Web home.

NOTE: HTML KNOW-HOW

If you want to get up to speed on HTML, a good place to start is Appendix E, "An HTML Primer," which gives you information on all the basic HTML tags.

Testing an Internet Connection

If you want to use Personal Web Server to hand out Web pages to Internet-based surfers, note that you must have a static IP address. That way, the Domain Name System (DNS) can always find your computer (which isn't possible if you use DHCP or some other on-the-fly IP address assignment). If you don't have a static IP address assigned to your computer, an alternative is to set up a proxy server that uses "IP masquerading" to make it look as though your computer has a static IP address (see the WinGate software mentioned in Chapter 37).

Now establish a connection to your ISP (if necessary), load your Web browser, and enter the root address of your server. What is your root address? It's `http://` followed by the DNS name assigned to your computer. This name will take one of the following forms:

■ If you're on a TCP/IP network, the name is *name.domain*, where *name* is your computer's network name and *domain* is the domain name of your TCP/IP network. In the Personal Web Server example I'm using in this chapter, the computer's name is `hermes` and the domain is `logophilia.com`, so here's my root address:

`http://hermes.logophilia.com/`

■ If you connect to an ISP, the name is usually *user.domain*, where *user* is your user name and *domain* is the domain name of your ISP (or a domain suffix supplied by the ISP). For example, given a user name of `biff` and an ISP domain of `provider.com`, here's the root address:

`http://biff.provider.com/`

TROUBLESHOOTING: THE ROOT ADDRESS DOESN'T WORK

If the default Personal Web Server home page doesn't appear, there could be a DNS problem. As before, try connecting again using only your IP address.

NOTE: MORE TROUBLESHOOTING IDEAS

If you still can't connect to your home page, there might be a problem with either your TCP/IP settings or your Internet connection. Head back to Chapters 36 and 37 to verify that you installed and configured everything correctly, and check out the troubleshooting notes in those chapters.

Administering the Web Server

Assuming that Personal Web Server is serving up Web pages without a complaint, it's now time to get your site ready for external access. This task involves a number of administrative details, such as setting up security, establishing time-outs, mapping directories, and setting up Web site monitoring. The next few sections take you through all the Web server's administrative details.

Starting the Internet Services Administrator

Personal Web Server's Internet Services Administrator is a series of Web pages, forms, and scripts that allows you to perform all the required chores within the friendly confines of your favorite browser. To start the Administrator, use any of the following techniques:

■ In the Personal Web Server properties sheet, activate the Administration tab and then click Administration.

■ Right-click the Personal Web Server icon in the system tray and select Administer from the context menu.

■ In your browser, enter the following URL (where *server* is the address of your Web server):

```
http://server/htmla/htmla/htm
```

Figure 42.6 shows the Administrator page that appears.

FIGURE 42.6.

Use the browser-based Internet Services Administrator to set up your Web and FTP servers.

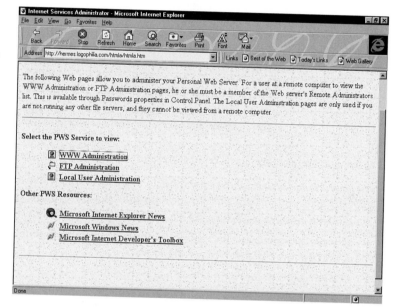

The Service Options

In the Main Administrator page, click the WWW Administration link to display the page shown in Figure 42.7. As you can see, this page has three "tabs" that represent the three aspects of Web server administration: Service, Directories, and Logging. I discuss the Service tab in this section and cover the other two tabs in the following sections. When you're done, click the OK button at the bottom of the page to put the new settings into effect.

FIGURE 42.7.

The Service "tab" for the WWW Administration page.

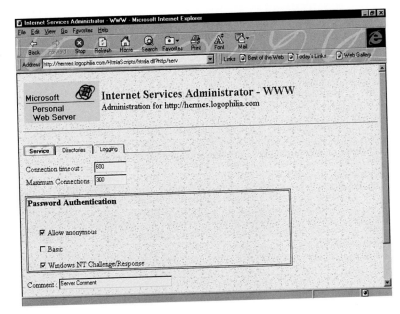

The Service tab contains several controls related to the HTTP service. Here's a summary:

Connection timeout: This is the time, in seconds, that the Web server will allow remote users to make a successful connection. If a connection can't be made within this time frame, the Web server sends a `Connection timed out` error message.

Maximum Connections: This value determines the maximum number of simultaneous connections the Web server will allow.

Allow anonymous: Leave this check box activated to enable anonymous logons. In other words, people who do not have an account on your network can still access your pages. If you want to restrict your pages to those with the correct user names and passwords, clear this check box.

Basic: If you have Web pages that require client authentication (user name and password), activating this check box tells the Web server to accept user names and passwords in unencrypted form. This is a dangerous practice, but few browsers support the Windows NT Challenge/Response, discussed next.

Windows NT Challenge/Response: This is a more robust form of client authentication that accepts only encrypted user names and passwords. As of this writing, the only browser that supports this method is Internet Explorer (version 2.0 and later).

NOTE: CHALLENGE/RESPONSE REQUIRES USER-LEVEL SECURITY

You can use Windows NT Challenge/Response password authentication only if the Web server computer is configured for user-level security with validation provided by a Windows NT domain. See Chapter 32, "Network Administration and Security," for details on setting up user-level security.

Configuring Web Folders

Personal Web Server handles folders in two different ways:

- If a folder is a subfolder of the root (`C:\WebShare\wwwroot`), browsers can access the folder directly. For example, if you add a home subfolder (`C:\WebShare\wwwroot\home`), users can access this folder by adding home/ to the root address:

  `http://server/home/`

- For all other folders, you must set up an *alias* that maps the folder path to a virtual server folder. For example, the HTML files for the Administrator are located in the `C:\Program Files\WebSvr\Htmla` folder, and Personal Web Server maps this folder path to the /Htmla alias. This means you access this folder in a Web browser like so:

  `http://server/htmla/`

These aliases are controlled by the Directories tab on the WWW Administrator page. As you can see in Figure 42.8, the Administrator displays a table showing the current aliases and their "real" folder paths.

FIGURE 42.8.

The Directories tab allows you to map aliases for the folders on your computer.

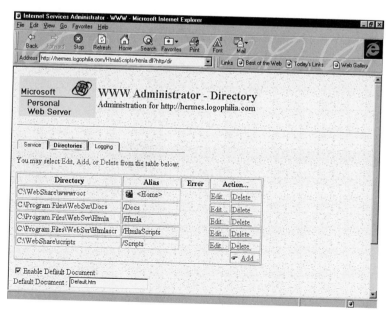

To add a new folder alias, follow these steps:

1. Click the Add link. The Administrator displays the form shown in Figure 42.9.

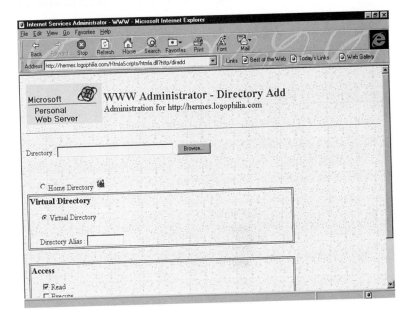

2. Use the Directory text box to enter the path of the folder you want to work with (or click Browse to use another form to choose the folder).

3. If you want this folder to be the home directory for your Web site, activate the Home Directory option button. Otherwise, activate the Virtual Directory option and use the Directory Alias text box to enter an alias for the folder.

4. Use the Access options to determine the type of access allowed in this folder: Read and/or Execute (you need only Execute access if you'll be placing scripts within the folder).

5. Click OK to add the alias and return to the Directories tab.

NOTE: WORKING WITH EXISTING ALIASES

To make changes to an existing alias, click the appropriate Edit link. The page that appears is similar to the one shown in Figure 42.9.

If you no longer need an alias, click its Delete link.

The Directories tab also includes a few other controls:

Enable Default Document: When this check box is activated, users who don't specify a document when entering a URL will be shown the default document (assuming that one exists in the folder).

Default Document: Use this text box to specify the name of the default document used in each folder. The most common names for default documents are default.htm, default.html, index.htm, and index.html.

Directory Browsing Allowed: When this check box is activated and no default document exists in a folder (or if you deactivate the Enable Default Document check box), the user sees a list of all the files in the folder.

Another Way to Set Up Web Folders

Instead of cranking up the WWW Administrator to set up Web folders, you can do it directly from Windows Explorer. Here are the steps to follow:

1. Right-click the folder you want to share and select Sharing.

2. In the dialog box that appears, activate the Shared As option and enter the alias name for the folder in the Share Name text box, as shown in Figure 42.10.

FIGURE 42.10.

You can set up Web folders directly from the folder's properties sheet.

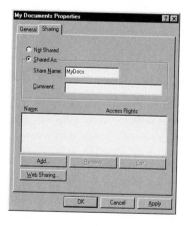

3. Click Web Sharing. Windows 95 displays the Web Sharing Folder Properties dialog box, shown in Figure 42.11.

4. Activate the Share folder for HTTP check box.

5. Activate either or both of the Read Only and Execute Scripts check boxes.

6. Click OK to return to the folder's properties sheet.

FIGURE 42.11.

Use this dialog box to specify that this folder is to be shared for the HTTP service.

7. Click Add to display the Add Users dialog box.

8. Highlight The world and then click Read Only.

9. Click OK to return to the folder's properties sheet.

10. Click OK to put the share into effect.

The Logging Options

After your Web server is chugging along and serving pages to all and sundry, you might start to wonder which pages are popular with surfers and which ones are languishing. You might also want to know if users are getting errors when they try to access your site.

You can tell all of this and more by working with Personal Web Server's logs. A log is a text file that records all the activity on your Web site, including the IP address and computer name (if applicable) of the surfer, the file that was served, the date and time the file was shipped to the browser, and the server return code (see the next Note box). For each server request, the log file writes a sequence of comma-separated values, which means it would be easy to import the file into a database or spreadsheet program for analysis.

To customize the Web server's logging, activate the Logging tab to display the form shown in Figure 42.12. Here's a review of the controls on this form:

Enable logging: The Web server maintains a log of server activity when this check box is activated.

Automatically open new log: When this check box is activated, the Web server starts a fresh log at the interval specified in the option buttons below it: Daily, Weekly, Monthly, or When the file size reaches *x* MB. If you deactivate this check box, the server uses a single log file to record all activity.

Log file directory: Use this text box to specify the folder in which the Web server will create the log files. Note that the name of each log file depends on the interval you choose for logging. If you choose monthly logging, for example, the log file for August 1997 would be In0897.log.

FIGURE 42.12.

Use the Logging tab to enable monitoring of Web server activity.

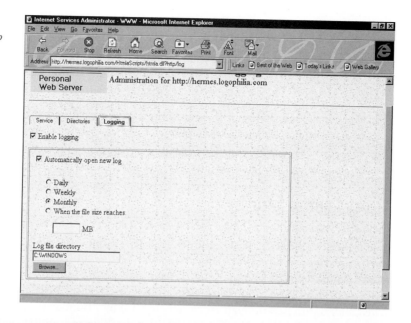

42

SETTING UP A
WORLD WIDE
WEB SERVER

NOTE: SERVER RETURN CODES

A server return code of 200 means the document was sent successfully to the browser. For unsuccessful operations, here's a summary of some of the return codes you'll find in the log:

Return Code	What It Means
204	File contains no content
301	File moved permanently
302	File moved temporarily
400	Bad request
401	Unauthorized access
403	Access forbidden
404	File not found
500	Internal server error
501	Service not implemented
502	Bad gateway
503	Service unavailable

Web Server Security

Depending on the type of Web site you're running and the information stored in your Web pages, you might want to invest a little or a lot of time and effort in securing your site against unauthorized access. There are two basic approaches to Personal Web Server security:

- You can use the same type of access control security that is used by the computer on which Personal Web Server is running.
- You can configure Personal Web Server to use local security, which is a list of users and groups of users given specific access rights within the Web server.

Access Control Security

The easiest (and most robust) form of Web server security is the access control that's built into Windows 95 networking. As you learned back in Chapter 32, you can configure your Windows 95 machine to use either share-level or user-level security. Specifically, if the "File and printer sharing for Microsoft Networks" service is installed, you can use either share-level security (passwords assigned to specific folders) or user-level security (users and groups assigned to shared folders with pass-through validation provided by a Windows NT server). Similar security levels are available on NetWare networks if the "File and printer sharing for NetWare Networks" service is installed. See Chapter 32 for more information on setting up access control security.

> **NOTE: RESHARE FOLDERS AFTER CHANGING ACCESS TYPE**
>
> As noted in Chapter 32, Windows 95 removes all folder shares after you change the access security type. This means that you'll need to reshare your aliased Web folders.

Local User Security

Local user security is a list of users (or groups of users) that are allowed access to your Web site. You use local security if your server is not on a network or if you want to keep server security separate from your computer's overall security. Personal Web Server uses local security only under either of the following conditions:

- If neither the "File and printer sharing for Microsoft Networks" service nor the "File and printer sharing for NetWare Networks" service is installed.
- If one of those services is installed, but you deactivate file and printer sharing. (To do this, right-click Network Neighborhood, select Properties, and click File and Print Sharing. In the dialog box that appears, deactivate both the I want to be able to give others access to my files check box and the I want to be able to allow others to print to my printer(s) check box.)

After local security is enabled, start the Internet Services Administrator and click the Local User Administration link. This action loads the Local User Administrator page, shown in Figure 42.13. The next couple of sections show you how to put this Administrator to work with local users and groups.

FIGURE 42.13.

Use the Local User Administrator to create lists of local users and groups for your Web site.

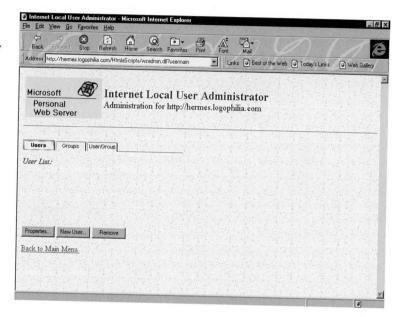

Adding a Local User

The local user list is empty initially, so you need to add users. Here are the steps to follow:

1. To get started, click the New User button. The Administrator displays the form shown in Figure 42.14.
2. Enter a unique name in the User Name field.
3. Enter the user's password in the User Password field. Note that Personal Web Server does not allow null passwords.
4. Enter the password again in the Confirm Password field.
5. Click Add to create the user and return to the Users tab.

To make changes to an existing user, highlight the user's name in the User List and then click Properties. You can delete the highlighted name from the user list by clicking Remove.

Creating a Group

Instead of working with individual users, you might prefer to work with multiple users at once by adding them to a local group. You can then specify access permissions for the group, and they'll apply to every member of the group.

FIGURE 42.14.

Use this form to add a user to the list of local users.

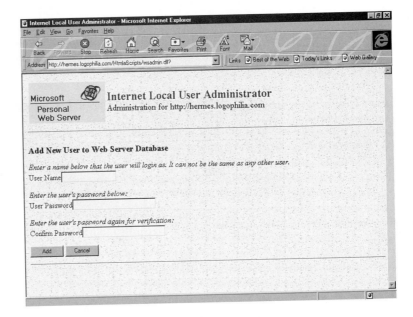

To create a new local group, follow these steps:

1. Click the Groups tab in the Local User Administrator page.

2. Click New Group to display the form shown in Figure 42.15.

FIGURE 42.15.

Use this form to create a new local group.

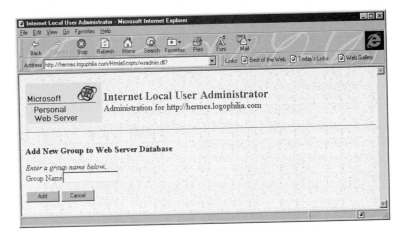

3. Enter a name for the new group in the Group Name text box.

4. Click Add to create the group and return to the Groups tab.

Now you need to populate the group with users. Here are the steps to follow:

1. Activate the User/Group tab in the Local User Administrator page. Figure 42.16 shows the form that appears.

FIGURE 42.16.

Use this form to assign users to groups.

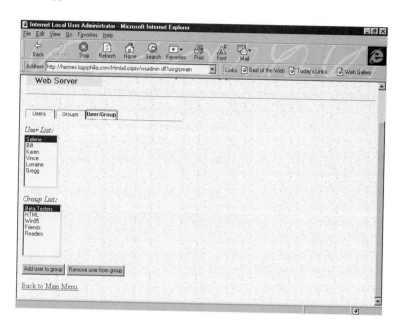

2. In the User List box, highlight the name of a user you want to add to the group.
3. In the Group List box, highlight the name of the group.
4. Click Add user to group.
5. Repeat steps 2 through 4 to add other users to the group.

Implementing Local Security

With your local users and groups set up the way you want, you now need to assign permissions for your Web folders. Here's how the job is done:

1. Right-click the folder you want to work with and select Sharing.
2. Click Add to display the Add Users dialog box.
3. Highlight the users or groups you want to give access to the folder, and then click Read Only.
4. Click OK to return to the folder's properties sheet.
5. Click OK to put the permissions into effect.

Administering the FTP Server

When the FTP service is started, remote users can download files from, and upload files to, your server. The root address of your FTP server takes the following form (where *server* is the network name or DNS name of the computer running Personal Web Server):

```
ftp://server/
```

Note that this root directory is an alias for `C:\WebShare\ftproot`.

Recall that Personal Web Server doesn't start the FTP service automatically. To get the service running, display the Personal Web Server properties sheet and activate the Services tab. Highlight the FTP service and then click Start.

With the service started, you can set some administrative options. To do so, launch the Internet Services Administrator and click the FTP Administration link. Figure 42.17 shows the form that appears.

FIGURE 42.17.

The FTP administration form.

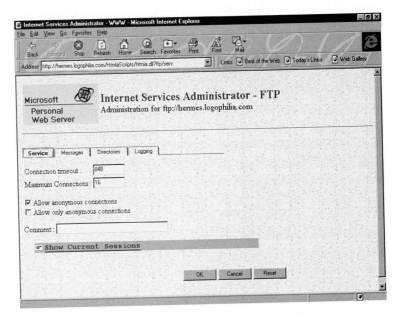

Many of the available administration options are identical to the ones you saw earlier for the Web server, so I'll just summarize the unique points about each tab:

Service: Activate the Allow anonymous connections check box to allow users to establish anonymous FTP sessions. (These are sessions in which the user logs on with the user name anonymous and the e-mail address as the password. If you want only anonymous users, activate the `Allow only anonymous connections` check box. Note, too, that you can view a list of the current FTP connections by clicking the `Show Current Sessions` link. Figure 42.18 shows the page that appears.

Messages: The controls in this tab specify messages that are sent to the user. The `Welcome message` appears when the user logs on, and the `Exit message` appears when the user ends the session. If the service reaches its connection limit (defined in the Service tab), Personal Web Server displays the message shown in the `Maximum connections message` text box.

Directories: As with the Web server, you can use the Directories tab to set up aliases for folders on your computer. You can also choose to display the FTP directory listings in either `Unix` or `MS-DOS` format.

Logging: This tab is identical to the Logging tab for the Web server. Note, however, that the default value for starting a new log is `Daily`.

FIGURE 42.18.

Personal Web Server can show you your current FTP connections.

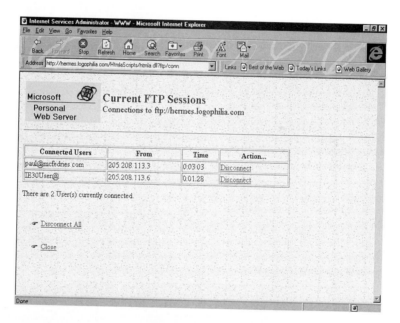

Remote Administration of Personal Web Server

Although you'll likely perform most of your Web and FTP server administration duties from the computer on which Personal Web Server was installed, at times you might need to make changes from another computer. You can configure Personal Web Server to allow administration either from another computer on your network or via the Internet. Here are the steps to follow:

1. If you've set up Personal Web Server to use local security, make sure that you add a user name (say, Administrator) and password to use for remote administration.

2. Select Start | Settings | Control Panel, and then launch the Passwords icon.

3. Display the Remote Administration tab, shown in Figure 42.19.

FIGURE 42.19.

Use the Remote Administration tab to activate remote administration and specify one or more administrators.

4. Make sure that the Enable Remote Administration of this server check box is activated.

5. Click Add to display the Choose Administrators dialog box.

6. Highlight your administration user (or another appropriate user name) and click Add->.

7. Click OK to return to the Remote Administration tab.

8. Click OK to put the new settings into effect.

To access the Internet Services Administrator page remotely, enter the following address into a Web browser (where, as usual, *server* is the network name or DNS name of the server):

```
http://server/htmla/htmla.htm
```

NOTE: YOU CAN'T MODIFY LOCAL USER LIST REMOTELY

If you're using local security, note that you can't modify the local user list when administering the server remotely.

> **NOTE: MORE POWERFUL SOLUTIONS**
>
> Personal Web Server is fine for small Web sites that don't get much traffic. If you're planning a large site, however, you might want to consider a more powerful solution. Here are a few Windows 95 Web servers to check out:
>
> | | |
> |---|---|
> | WebSite | `http://website.ora.com/` |
> | Alibaba | `http://alibaba.austria.eu.net/DOCS/index.htm` |
> | ZBServer Pro | `http://www.zbserver.com/` |

Summary

This chapter showed you how to set up a Web server on a Windows 95 machine. After examining the Personal Web Server defaults and startup options, I showed you how to test your server. From there, you learned how to administer the Web server, set up Web server security, and administer the FTP server. I also showed you how to enable remote administration of the server.

Here's a list of chapters where you'll find related information:

- For the complete story on setting up a Windows 95 computer on a network, see Chapter 31, "Windows 95 Networking."

- Access levels and other network security issues can be found in Chapter 32, "Network Administration and Security."

- See Chapter 36, "Implementing TCP/IP for Internet and Network Connections," for information on TCP/IP.

- To learn how to set up an Internet connection in Windows 95, head for Chapter 37, "Windows 95 and the Internet."

- For instructions on using Internet Explorer, see Chapter 38, "Exploring the Web with Internet Explorer."

PART

Appendixes

Windows 95 Online Resources

IN THIS APPENDIX

APPENDIX A

Although I've crammed as much useful Windows 95 information as I could into this book, there's just no way to cover absolutely everything. Besides, the Windows world is in a constant state of flux, so keeping up with what's new is a full-time job. To help you keep your head above the Windows waters, this appendix presents a list of some online sites that offer practical information, the latest news, and first-rate shareware and other files.

The World Wide Web

There's no shortage of Windows 95 pages on the Web (a search for "Windows 95" in the Alta Vista index produced over 200,000 matches!), but many of these pages are pure dreck. The following is a list of the Windows 95 Web pages I think you'll find useful.

> **NOTE: MORE WEB SITES**
>
> For a larger list of Windows 95 Web sites, head for this book's home page, located at
>
> `http://www.mcfedries.com/books/win95unleashed/`
>
> and click the `Windows 95 Web Sites` link.

Windows 95 Home Page

URL:	`http://www.microsoft.com/windows95/default.asp`
Content:	Files, how-to, news, shareware, troubleshooting
Comments:	This is the place to begin *all* your Windows 95 Web wandering (see Figure A.1). All the latest Windows 95 news from Microsoft, updates, new Windows 95 programs—it's all here.

Microsoft Knowledge Base

URL:	`http://www.microsoft.com/kb/`
Content:	How-to, troubleshooting
Comments:	If you're scratching your head over some weird Windows 95 behavior, chances are someone else has found the same thing and has asked Microsoft Tech Support about it, and the engineer has posted a solution in the Microsoft Knowledge Base (see Figure A.2). This Web site lets you search the Knowledge Base to track down a problem you might be having.

FIGURE A.1.

The Windows 95 Home Page.

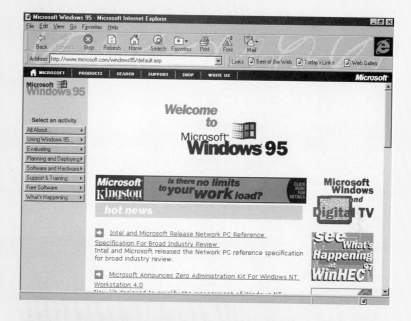

FIGURE A.2.

This Web page lets you search the Microsoft Knowledge Base for Windows 95 information.

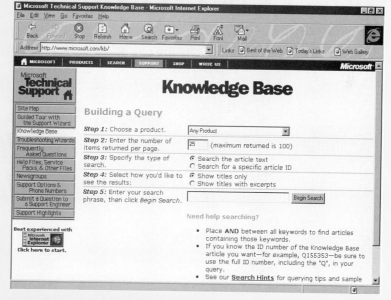

Windows 95 Software Library

URL: http://www.microsoft.com/windows/software.htm

Content: Files

Comments: This site contains miscellaneous Windows 95 files from Microsoft, including the CD-ROM Extras, Service Pack 1, the Power Toys, device drivers, and more.

Windows95.com

URL: `http://www.windows95.com/`

Content: Files, how-to, shareware

Comments: This site is annoying (it's laced with advertising graphics and has lame background music), but it's worth the effort. There are loads of useful links here, and the shareware collection is second to none. The site's clever layout is designed to resemble the Windows 95 interface (see Figure A.3).

FIGURE A.3.

Windows95.com contains lots of useful how-to links and a superb Windows 95 shareware collection.

Dylan Greene's Windows 95 Starting Page

URL: `http://www.dylan95.com/`

Content: Files, how-to, shareware, troubleshooting

Comments: This is one of the busiest Windows 95 sites on the Net, and no wonder: Besides a nice collection of shareware, how-to, and trouble-shooting links, you'll also find Java-based live chat, a message board, a search engine, and links to many Windows 95 sites around the world.

Randy's Windows 95 Resource Center

URL:	`http://pcwin.com/`
Content:	Files, how-to, news, shareware, troubleshooting
Comments:	A nice collection of Windows 95 software.

32BIT.com

URL:	`http://www.32bit.com/software/index.phtml`
Content:	Files, shareware
Comments:	Perhaps *the* place to find Windows 95 shareware.

Get Help with Windows Featuring Exchange

URL:	`http://ourworld.compuserve.com/homepages/G_Carter/`
Content:	Files, how-to, shareware, troubleshooting
Comments:	This huge and well-designed page (see Figure A.4) features numerous links to Windows 95 resources. Includes links to some interesting tools for Microsoft Exchange.

FIGURE A.4.

The Get Help With Windows Featuring Exchange Web site.

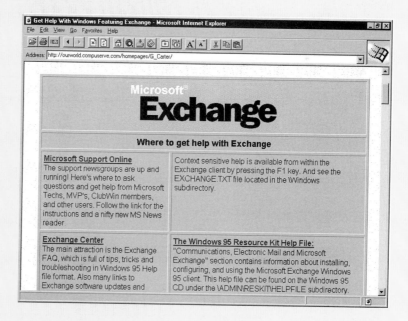

DOWNLOAD.COM

URL:	`http://www.download.com/PC/Win95/`
Content:	Files, how-to, news, shareware, troubleshooting
Comments:	This site has it all: files, tips, links. Unique features include the Win95 Help Desk and the Win95 Newswire.

PC World Magazine's Windows 95 Page

URL:	http://www.pcworld.com/workstyles/win95/index.html
Content:	How-to, news, troubleshooting
Comments:	A huge list of articles on Windows 95 from the pages of *PC World* magazine. Includes a search engine.

The Consummate Winsock Apps List

URL:	http://cws.iworld.com/
Content:	Files, shareware
Comments:	Not just your average list of Windows 95 shareware and files. This site sticks out from the crowd thanks to the in-depth reviews given to each program by the site's proprietor: Forrest Stroud.

Usenet Newsgroups

If you need help with a specific Windows 95 question, fumbling around various Web sites looking for the answer might not be the best way to go. In some cases, posting a question to the appropriate Usenet newsgroup is often a better approach. Table A.1 summarizes newsgroups that focus on Windows 95 that are available through regular channels.

Table A.1. Usenet's Windows 95-related newsgroups.

Newsgroup	Description
alt.os.windows95.crash.crash.crash	The name sounds like a joke, but this group has plenty of serious posts related to troubleshooting issues.
comp.os.ms-windows.apps.compatibility.win95	This is the place to look for help related to applications that won't run under Windows 95.
comp.os.ms-windows.apps.utilities.win95	This group deals with issues related to the Windows 95 accessories.
comp.os.ms-windows.networking.win95	Check out this group if you need help with networking, Internet access, or other connectivity issues.
comp.os.ms-windows.setup.win95	This group covers setup, configuration, and installation issues.
comp.os.ms-windows.win95.misc	This is a catchall group for other Windows 95 issues. A word of warning: This is a *very* busy group with hundreds of posts each day.

Newsgroup	Description
`comp.os.ms-windows.win95.moderated`	A high-signal, low-noise group that posts about one-tenth the number of messages that go through the `misc` group.
`comp.os.ms-windows.win95.setup`	Another group related to installation. No, I don't know why there are two of them.

Microsoft also runs its own newsgroups. To view them, set up your newsreader to use the server `msnews.microsoft.com`. Table A.2 lists the newsgroups that deal with Windows 95 topics.

Table A.2. Microsoft's Windows 95-related newsgroups.

Newsgroup	Description
`microsoft.public.win95.commtelephony`	Deals with issues related to modems, serial ports, HyperTerminal, Phone Dialer, and general telephony.
`microsoft.public.win95.dialupnetwork`	Covers installation, configuration, and use of Dial-Up Networking.
`microsoft.public.win95.exchangefax`	Discusses Exchange and Microsoft Fax.
`microsoft.public.win95.filediskmanage`	Primarily a forum for disk drive issues, especially questions related to ScanDisk, DriveSpace, and DoubleSpace.
`microsoft.public.win95.general.discussion`	Miscellaneous Windows 95 topics.
`microsoft.public.win95.msdosapps`	Covers all aspects of running DOS programs under Windows 95.
`microsoft.public.win95.multimedia`	Questions and answers related to audio, video, and other multimedia.
`microsoft.public.win95.networking`	Installation, configuration, and trouble-shooting of Microsoft and NetWare networks.
`microsoft.public.win95.printfontvideo`	Covers printing setup and problems, font issues, and display questions and answers.
`microsoft.public.win95.setup`	Covers issues related to Windows 95 installation.

A

WINDOWS 95
ONLINE
RESOURCES

continues

Table A.2. continued

Newsgroup	Description
microsoft.public.win95.shellui	Covers the Windows 95 shell and user interface.
microsoft.public.win95.win95applets	Covers Windows 95 applets that don't fit into any of the other groups.

The Microsoft Network

If you get a membership in The Microsoft Network, you'll find plenty of Windows 95-related forums, file libraries, and chat areas. If you're still using classic MSN, you'll find everything in the Windows 95 Forum, shown in Figure A.5, which you can get to as follows:

- Select Categories | Computers & Software | Computing Forums | Microsoft Windows 95 Forum.

- GO word: Windows

- From MSN 1.3, select Essentials | MSN Classic & Custom Page | Classic Categories. In the Categories window that appears, select Computers & Software | Computing Forums | Microsoft Windows 95 Forum.

FIGURE A.5.

The Windows 95 Forum on The Microsoft Network.

Table A.3 summarizes the icons you'll find there.

Table A.3. Icons you'll find in the Windows 95 Forum.

Service	GO *Word*	Description
Windows 95 News & Events	None	Contains late-breaking news and official Microsoft announcements. Also contains the WinNews electronic newsletter (GO word: WinNews).

Service	GO *Word*	*Description*
Windows 95 Chat Expo	ChatExpo	Contains a number of Windows 95 chat areas.
Windows 95 Free Software	Win95Free	A number of file libraries with Windows 95-related downloads, including drivers, the CD-ROM Extras, the Power Toys, and Service Pack 1.
Windows 95 Forum Update	Win95Update	Regular updates about what's happening in the Windows world.
Windows 95 Forum Guide	Win95Guide	A file containing hints and shortcuts about navigating the Windows 95 Forum.
Introducing Internet Explorer	None	Contains documents related to Internet Explorer, a BBS, and the VRML Add-In.

America Online

America Online members have access to an excellent Windows 95 resource called Inside Windows 95. To check it out, select Go To | Keyword and enter the keyword Win95 to display the window shown in Figure A.6. From here, you can access the latest Windows 95 news (the Win 95 News icon), a library of Windows 95 files (the Software Library icon), a message area (the Message Board icon), and a chat room (the Win 95 Live Chat icon).

FIGURE A.6.

Inside Windows 95 on America Online.

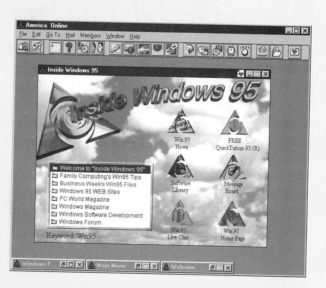

A

WINDOWS 95 ONLINE RESOURCES

CompuServe

CompuServe users have plenty of places to go for Windows 95 help, questions, and trouble-shooting. Table A.4 is a summary.

Table A.4. CompuServe's Windows 95-related areas.

Topic	GO *Word*	Description
Windows Forum	WUGNET	General Windows files and messages.
Microsoft Connection	MICROSOFT	The central CompuServe area for all things Microsoft (see Figure A.7).
Microsoft Knowledge Base	MSKB	Accesses the articles in the Microsoft Knowledge Base.
Microsoft Software Library	MSL	The complete listing of files in the Microsoft Software Library.
MS Windows News Forum	WINNEWS	Contains the latest issue and back issues of the WinNews electronic newsletter.
Microsoft Internet Explorer	INTEXPLORER	Discussions related to the Internet Explorer Web browser.
WinSupport 95	WIN95	A tech-support forum for Windows 95.

FIGURE A.7.

The Microsoft Connection on CompuServe.

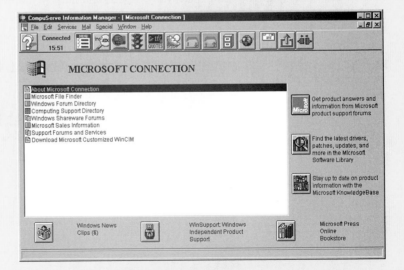

Glossary

accelerator key   The underlined letter in a menu name or menu command.

active partition   A disk drive's bootable partition. Its boot sector tells the ROM BIOS at startup that this partition contains the operating system's bootstrap code. The active partition is usually the same as the *primary partition.*

ADC   See *analog-to-digital converter.*

Advanced Power Management   A specification developed by Microsoft and Intel that lets the operating system, applications, BIOS, and system hardware work cooperatively to manage power and extend battery life.

allocation unit   See *cluster.*

amplitude   A measure of a sound's loudness (that is, the strength of the sound wave's vibration). The greater the amplitude, the greater the motion of the sound wave's molecules, and the greater the impact on your eardrum. Amplitude is measured in decibels. See also *frequency.*

analog-to-digital converter   A chip in a sound card that converts analog sound waves to the digital audio format. See also *digital-to-analog converter.*

APM   See *Advanced Power Management.*

backup set   A backup (SET) file that includes a list of files to back up, the type of backup to use (a *full backup* or an incremental backup), and the backup destination.

baud rate   The number of signal changes (which might be variations in voltage or frequency, depending on the *modulation* standard being used) per second that can be exchanged between two *modems.* In most cases, this isn't the same as *bps.*

bidirectional printing   Printing in which not only can Windows 95 send data to the printer, but the printer can send data to Windows 95. For example, the printer could let Windows 95 know its configuration (say, how much memory it has installed), and the printer could keep the operating system informed of the current printer status (for example, out of paper). See also *Extended Capabilities Port.*

bitmap   An array of bits (pixels) that contains data that describes the colors found in an image.

bit-spit   Any form of electronic text.

block I/O subsystem   The Windows 95 mechanism that talks directly to disk hardware.

BootKeys   Shortcut keys or key combinations that either invoke the Windows 95 Startup menu or select a Windows 95 Startup option (such as *Safe mode*).

bps   Bits per second. The rate at which a *modem* or other communications device transmits data.

bridge   A *network* device that connects two *LANs*, provided that the two LANs are using the same *NOS*. The bridge can either be a standalone device or can be implemented in a server with the addition of a second network card.

CDFS   An *installable file system* for CD-ROM drives. CDFS uses a 32-bit *protected-mode VxD* (VCDFSD.VXD) that replaces MSCDEX.EXE, the 16-bit *real-mode* driver used in previous versions of Windows. See also *VFAT*.

CD-ROM File System   See *CDFS*.

character spacing   The amount of space allotted to each character in a *font*. A font's character spacing can be either *monospaced* or *proportional*.

client   In a *client/server network*, a computer that uses the services and resources provided to the network by a *server*.

client application   See *container application*.

client/server network   A *network* model that splits the computing workload into two separate but related areas. On the one hand, you have users working at intelligent "front-end" systems called *clients*. In turn, these client machines interact with powerful "back-end" systems called *servers*. The basic idea is that the clients have enough processing power to perform tasks on their own, but they rely on the servers to provide them with specialized resources or services, or access to information that would be impractical to implement on a client (such as a large database). See also *peer-to-peer network*.

Clipboard   A memory location used to store data that has been cut or copied from an application.

cluster   The basic unit of storage on a hard disk or floppy disk.

cluster chain   The sequence of *clusters* that defines an entire file.

codec   A compressor/decompressor device driver. During playback of audio or video data, the codec decompresses the data before sending it to the appropriate multimedia device. During recording, the codec decompresses the raw data so that it takes up less disk space. Most codecs offer a variety of compression ratios.

color depth   Determines the number of colors (that is, the color palette) available to your applications and graphics. Color depth is expressed in either bits or total colors. See also *High Color* and *True Color*.

COM   See *Component Object Model*.

Component Object Model   The heart and soul of *OLE*. It defines not only the standards that server applications use to create objects, but also the mechanisms by which server and container applications interact when dealing with objects.

compound document   A *container* document that holds, along with its native data, one or more *objects* that were created using *server applications*.

compress   To reduce the size of a file by replacing redundant character strings with tokens. Windows 95 compresses data and manages the resulting *CVF* using the DriveSpace *device driver.*

compressed volume file   A hidden file on a *host drive* that contains the *compressed* files.

compression ratio   The ratio of the size of an uncompressed file to its compressed size. For example, a file that is 10,000 bytes uncompressed and 5,000 bytes compressed has a compression ratio of 2:1.

concentrator   See *hub*.

Configuration Manager   A Windows 95 component (CNFGMGR.VXD) that enumerates the various *Plug and Play* devices on your system, identifies the *resources* used by each device, resolves resource conflicts, monitors the system for hardware changes, and ensures that the proper *device drivers* are loaded.

connection-oriented protocol   See *transport layer protocol.*

connectionless protocol   See *network layer protocol.*

container application   The application that you use to store a *linked* or *embedded OLE object* created with a *server application.* Also known as the *client application.*

context menu   A menu that appears when you right-click an object. The context menu gives you access to the properties and actions associated with that object.

cooperative multitasking   The *multitasking* mode used by Windows 3.x and 16-bit applications. It's up to the individual applications to decide when they will relinquish control of the system. See also *preemptive multitasking.*

cross-linked cluster   A *cluster* that has somehow been assigned to two different files, or that has two *FAT* entries that refer to the same cluster.

CVF   See *compressed volume file.*

DAC   See *digital-to-analog converter.*

data bits   In *modem* data transfer, the number of bits used to represent a character.

datagram   An *IP packet.* The datagram header includes information such as the address of the *host* that sent the datagram and the address of the host that is supposed to receive the datagram.

deadly TSR   A *terminate-and-stay-resident* program that causes the Windows 95 Setup program to hang. If Setup detects a known deadly TSR in memory, it will warn you and prevent you from continuing the installation process. Many anti-virus utilities are known to be deadly TSRs (check out Appendix C for the complete list). See also *dirty TSR.*

decorative   A specially designed *typeface* that is supposed to convey a particular effect. See also *sans serif* and *serif.*

delay   When you press and hold down a key, the time interval between the appearance of the first character and the second character. See also *repeat rate.*

demand paging   An algorithm used by the *Memory Pager* for swapping program code and data between physical RAM and the *paging file.* Once physical RAM has been used up, the Memory Pager begins managing the paging file.

demodulation   The conversion into digital data of an analog wave (a series of tones) transmitted over a telephone line. This conversion is performed by a *modem.* See also *modulation.*

device driver   Small software programs that serve as intermediaries between hardware devices and the operating system. Device drivers encode software instructions into signals that the device understands, and, conversely, the drivers interpret device signals and report them to the operating system. See also *virtual device driver.*

Device Manager   A tab in the System properties sheet that provides a graphical outline of all the devices on your system. It can show you the current configuration of each device (including the *IRQ, I/O ports,* and *DMA channel* used by each device). It even lets you adjust a device's configuration (assuming that the device doesn't require you to make physical adjustments to, say, a DIP switch or jumper). The Device Manager actually gets its data from, and stores modified data in, the *Registry.*

DHCP   See *Dynamic Host Control Protocol.*

differential backup   Backs up only files in the current *backup set* that have changed since the last *full backup.*

digital-to-analog converter   A sound card chip that converts digitized audio back into an analog wave so that you can hear it. See also *analog-to-digital converter.*

directory entry   See *file directory.*

dirty TSR   A *terminate-and-stay-resident* program that might cause problems with the Windows 95 Setup program but that doesn't cause it to hang. If Setup detects a known dirty TSR, it will warn you but still let you proceed with the installation. Appendix C lists all the known dirty TSRs. See also *deadly TSR.*

Display Power Management Signaling   A specification that lets a *device driver* use the video adapter to send a signal to the monitor that can either blank the screen (standby mode) or turn off the monitor entirely.

DMA   Direct Memory Access. See also *DMA channel.*

DMA channel   A connection that lets a device transfer data to and from memory without going through the processor. The transfer is coordinated by a DMA controller chip.

B

GLOSSARY

DNS   See *Domain Name System.*

Domain Name System   On the Internet, a hierarchical distributed database system that converts *host names* into *IP addresses.*

dotted-decimal notation   A format used to represent *IP addresses.* The 32 bits of the address are divided into quads of 8 bits, which are then converted into their decimal equivalent and separated by dots (for example, 205.208.113.1).

dotted-quad notation   See *dotted-decimal notation.*

double-click speed   The time interval that Windows 95 uses to distinguish between two successive single clicks and a double-click. Anything faster is handled as a double-click; anything slower is handled as two single clicks.

DPMS   See *Display Power Management Signaling.*

dual-booting   Having the option, at startup, of running Windows 95 or some other operating system (such as Windows 3.x). See also *multi-booting.*

Dynamic Host Control Protocol   A system that manages the dynamic allocation of *IP addresses.*

ECP   See *Extended Capabilities Port.*

embedding   An *OLE* technique of inserting an *object* into a *container application's* document. An embedded object includes not only a pointer to the *server application,* but also the object's native data. See also *linking.*

environment   A small memory buffer that holds the DOS *environment variables.*

environment variables   Settings used to control certain aspects of DOS and DOS programs. For example, the PATH, the PROMPT, and the values of all SET statements are part of the environment.

Exchange profile   Specifies which Microsoft Exchange service providers you want to use, as well as the configuration of those services.

Extended Capabilities Port   A parallel port that provides support for high-speed printing; new devices that use parallel ports, such as CD-ROMs and modems; and *bi-directional printing.*

extended partition   The hard disk space that isn't allocated to the *primary partition.* For example, if you have a 1.2 GB disk and you allocate 300 MB to the primary partition, the extended partition will be 900 MB. You can then subdivide the extended partition into *logical DOS drives.*

extension   In a filename, the part to the right of the period. Windows 95 uses extensions to determine the file type of a file.

FAT   See *File Allocation Table.*

fax-on-demand system   Fax servers that contain dozens or even hundreds of documents that are available for downloading. You call the system and, after perhaps negotiating a few voice menus, you enter a document number and your fax number. A few minutes later, the server calls your fax number and sends you the document. See also *Request a Fax.*

FIFO buffer   A 16-byte memory buffer included with 16550 and later *UART* chips that lets a serial port handle high-speed data transfers while reducing retransmissions and dropped characters.

File Allocation Table   A built-in filing system that is created on every formatted disk. The FAT contains a 16-bit entry for every disk *cluster* that specifies whether the cluster is empty or bad, or else points to the next cluster number in the current file.

file directory   A table of contents for the files on a disk that is maintained by the *File Allocation Table.* The entries in the file directory specify each file's name, extension, size, attributes, and more.

file transfer protocol   In *modem* communications, this protocol governs various aspects of the file transfer ritual, including starting and stopping, the size of the data *packets* being sent, how errors are handled, and so on. (Don't confuse this with *File Transfer Protocol.*) Windows 95 supports six protocols: Xmodem, 1K Xmodem, Ymodem, Ymodem-G, Zmodem, and Kermit.

File Transfer Protocol (FTP)   An Internet protocol that defines file transfers between computers. Part of the *TCP/IP* suite of protocols.

font   A unique set of design characteristics that is common to a group of letters, numbers, and symbols. Four items define the font of any character: the *typeface,* the *type size,* the *type style,* and the *character spacing.*

frequency   Determines the pitch of a sound. This is a measure of the rate at which the sound wave's vibrations are produced. The higher the frequency, the higher the pitch. Frequency is measured in cycles per second, or hertz (Hz). See also *amplitude.*

FTP   See *File Transfer Protocol.*

full backup   Backs up all the files in the current *backup set.* See also *differential backup.*

gateway   A *network* computer or other device that acts as a middleman between two otherwise-incompatible systems. The gateway translates the incoming and outgoing *packets* so that each system can work the data.

GDI   See *Graphical Device Interface.*

Graphical Device Interface   A core Windows 95 component that manages the operating system's graphical interface. It contains routines that draw graphics primitives (such as lines and circles), manage colors, display fonts, manipulate bitmap images, and interact with graphics drivers. See also *kernel* and *User.*

graphics adapter The internal component in your system that generates the output you see on your monitor.

hardware flow control A system whereby the computer and *modem* use individual wires to send signals to each other that indicate whether they're ready to receive data. To stop outgoing data, the modem turns off its CTS (Clear To Send) line. To stop incoming data, the processor turns off its RTS (Request To Send) line. See also *software flow control.*

hardware profile Hardware configurations in which Windows 95 loads only specified *device drivers.*

High Color A *color depth* of 16 bits, or 65,536 colors.

host A computer on the Internet.

host drive The hidden drive that contains the *compressed volume file* after a disk has been *compressed.*

host name The unique name of an Internet *host* expressed as an English-language equivalent of an *IP address.*

HTTP See *Hypertext Transport Protocol.*

hub A central connection point for *network* cables. They range in size from small boxes with six or eight RJ-45 connectors to large cabinets with dozens of ports for various cable types.

hyperlink In the Windows 95 Help system, an underlined word or phrase that takes you to another topic or runs a program.

hypertext In a World Wide Web page, an underlined word or phrase that takes you to a different Web site.

Hypertext Transport Protocol An Internet *protocol* that defines the format of *Uniform Resource Locator* addresses and how World Wide Web data is transmitted between a server and a browser. Part of the *TCP/IP* suite of protocols.

idle sensitivity The amount of time that Windows 95 waits before declaring a DOS program idle. In the absence of keyboard input, Windows 95 just assumes that a DOS program is in an idle state after this predetermined amount of inactivity, and it then redirects to other running processes the *time slices* that it would otherwise devote to the DOS program.

IFSHLP.SYS A *real-mode* file that helps install the Windows 95 *installable file systems* (such as *VFAT* and *CDFS*).

in-place editing See *visual editing.*

installable file system A file system that can be loaded into the operating system dynamically. Examples in Windows 95 are *VFAT* and *CDFS*.

Installable File System Manager A 32-bit *protected-mode device driver* that's loaded at startup. The IFS Manager loads the *installable file systems* and arbitrates access to these systems. The IFS Manager automatically determines the format of a storage medium and then reads and writes files in the correct format.

Internet Protocol A network layer protocol that defines the Internet's basic *packet* structure and its addressing scheme, and also handles routing of packets between *hosts*. See also *TCP/IP* and *Transmission Control Protocol*.

internetwork A *network* that combines two or more *LANs* by means of a special device, such as a *bridge* or *router*. Internetworks are often called internets for short, but they shouldn't be confused with *the* Internet, the global collection of networks.

interrupt request An instruction to the CPU that halts processing temporarily so that another operation (such as handling input or output) can take place. Interrupts can be generated by either hardware or software.

intranet The implementation of Internet technologies such as *TCP/IP* and World Wide Web servers for use within a corporate organization rather than for connection to the Internet as a whole.

invalid cluster A *cluster* that falls under one of the following three categories:

- A *FAT* entry that refers to cluster 1. This is illegal, because a disk's cluster numbers start at 2.

- A FAT entry that refers to a cluster number larger than the total number of clusters on the disk.

- A FAT entry of 0 (which normally denotes an unused cluster) that is part of a *cluster chain*.

I/O port A memory address that the processor uses to communicate with a device directly. Once a device has used its *IRQ line* to catch the processor's attention, the actual exchange of data or commands takes place through the device's I/O port address.

I/O Supervisor Part of the *block I/O subsystem*, the I/O Supervisor acts as an intermediary between the disk drivers and the file systems. Besides loading the appropriate drivers for accessing disk controllers and disk drives, the I/O Supervisor arbitrates all I/O operations, including the queuing and routing of file service requests. It also uses the *Real Mode Mapper* to assume control of any *real-mode* drivers that have been loaded.

IO.SYS The *real-mode* portion of Windows 95. IO.SYS processes MSDOS.SYS, CONFIG.SYS, and AUTOEXEC.BAT, reads the Registry, switches the processor into *protected mode,* and then calls on VMM32.VXD to load the Windows 95 protected-mode drivers.

IP See *Internet Protocol*.

IP address   The unique address assigned to every *host* and *router* on the Internet. IP addresses are 32-bit values that are usually expressed in *dotted-decimal notation.* See also *host name.*

IPX/SPX   Internet Packet eXchange/ Sequenced Packet eXchange. IPX is a *network layer protocol* that addresses and routes *packets* from one *network* to another on an IPX *internetwork.* SPX, on the other hand, is a *transport layer protocol* that enhances the IPX protocol by providing reliable delivery. IPX/SPX is used by NetWare networks.

IRQ line   A hardware line over which peripherals and software can send *interrupt requests.*

Kbps   One thousand bits per second.

kernel   A core Windows 95 component that loads applications (including any DLLs needed by the program), handles all aspects of file I/O, allocates *virtual memory* and works with the *Memory Pager,* and schedules and runs *threads* started by applications. See also *Graphical Device Interface* and *User.*

LAN   See *local area network.*

linking   An *OLE* technique of inserting an *object* into a *container application's* document. A linked object doesn't include the object's native data; instead, it includes only pointers to both the *server application* and the original data file. If the original data changes, the linked object gets updated automatically. See also *embedding.*

local area network   A *network* in which all the computers occupy a relatively small geographical area, such as a department, office, home, or building. Most connections between computers are made via network cables, but wireless technology is gaining a toehold in some organizations.

local bus   A high-speed data pathway that provides a direct link between the CPU and a *graphics adapter's* video circuitry. This way, the CPU can send its graphics instructions directly to the adapter without having to go through the slower expansion bus. The local bus is usually a VL-Bus for 486 systems and a PCI bus for Pentiums.

local resource   Any peripheral, file, folder, or application that is either attached directly to your computer or resides on your computer's hard disk. See also *remote resource.*

logical DOS drive   A subset of an *extended partition.* For example, if the extended partition is 900 MB, you could create three logical DOS drives, each with 300 MB, and they would use drive letters D, E, and F. You can assign up to 23 logical DOS drives to an extended partition (letters D through Z).

lost cluster   A *cluster* that, according to the *FAT,* is associated with a file but has no link to any entry in the *file directory.* Lost clusters are typically caused by program crashes, power surges, or power outages.

master boot record The first 512-byte sector on your system's *active partition* (the partition your system boots from). Most of the MBR consists of a small program that locates and runs the core operating system files (*IO.SYS* and *MSDOS.SYS*).

Mbps One million bits per second.

MBR See *master boot record.*

MDI See *Multiple Document Interface.*

Memory Pager A component of the *Virtual Machine Manager* that moves data back and forth between the hard disk and the system's physical memory and allocates hard disk space as *virtual memory* addresses.

message store See *personal message store.*

metafile An image that consists of a collection of drawing commands from Windows 95's *GDI* component. These commands create the basic primitives (lines, circles, and so on) that make up the image.

MIDI See *Musical Instrument Digital Interface.*

mini-driver A small *device driver* that augments the functionality of a *universal driver* by providing the commands and routines necessary to operate a specific device.

miniport driver A *device driver* supplied by a SCSI controller manufacturer that provides support for device-specific I/O requests. See also *mini-driver* and *SCSI layer.*

modem A device used to transmit data between computers via telephone lines. See also *modulation* and *demodulation.*

modulation The conversion, performed by a *modem,* of digital data into an analog wave (a series of tones) that can be transmitted over a telephone line. See also *demodulation.*

monospaced A font that allots the same amount of space to each character. Skinny letters such as "i" and "l" take up as much space as wider letters, such as "m" and "w." See also *proportional.*

Moore's Law Processing power doubles every 18 months (from Gordon Moore, cofounder of Intel).

MSDOS.SYS A text file that controls certain Windows 95 startup parameters.

multi-booting Having the choice of three or more operating systems at startup. See also *dual-booting.*

multimedia The computer-based presentation of data using multiple modes of communication, including text, graphics, sound, animation, and video.

Multiple Document Interface   A Windows 95 programming interface that lets applications display several documents at once, each in its own window. These "child" windows can be displayed only within the application's "parent" window.

multitasking   See *cooperative multitasking* and *preemptive multitasking*.

multithreading   A multitasking model in which multiple *threads* run simultaneously.

Musical Instrument Digital Interface   A communications protocol that standardizes the exchange of data between a computer and a musical synthesizer.

name resolution   A process that converts a *host name* into an *IP address*. See *Domain Name System* and *Windows Internet Name Service*.

NetBEUI   The NetBIOS Extended User Interface *protocol*. (NetBIOS is an API that lets network applications—such as *redirectors*—communicate with *networking* protocols.) It's a combined *transport layer protocol* and *network layer protocol* developed by IBM and supported by all Microsoft networks. It's a simple, efficient protocol that works well in small *LANs*. However, it lacks the ability to route *packets,* so it isn't suitable for *WANs*.

network   A collection of computers connected via special cables or other network media (such as infrared) in order to share files, folders, disks, peripherals, and applications.

network adapter   See *network interface card*.

network interface card   An adapter that usually slips into an expansion bus slot inside a *client* or *server* computer. (There are also external *NICs* that plug into parallel ports or PC Card slots.) The NIC's main purpose is to serve as the connection point between the PC and the *network*. The NIC's backplate (the portion of the NIC that you can see once the card is installed) contains one or more ports into which you plug a network cable.

network layer protocol   A *protocol* in which no communications channel is established between nodes. Instead, the protocol builds each *packet* with all the information required in order for the network to deliver each packet and for the destination *node* to assemble everything. See also *transport layer protocol*.

Network News Transport Protocol   An Internet *protocol* that defines how Usenet newsgroups and postings are transmitted. Part of the *TCP/IP* suite of protocols.

network operating system   Operating system software that runs on a *network server* and provides the various network services for the network *clients*.

network redirector   A *virtual device driver* that lets applications find, open, read, write, and delete files on a remote drive.

NIC   See *network interface card*.

NNTP   See *Network News Transport Protocol*.

node   A computer on a *network*.

NOS   See *network operating system.*

object   A separate entity or component that is distinguished by its properties and actions. In the *OLE* world, an object is not only data—a slice of text, a graphic, a sound, a chunk of a spreadsheet, or whatever—but also one or more functions for creating, accessing, and using that data.

object linking and embedding   A technology that lets you share data between applications. Data can be transferred from a *server application* to a *container application* via either *linking* or *embedding.*

OLE   See *object linking and embedding.*

open editing   In *OLE*, when you open an object for editing in a separate window. See also *visual editing.*

packet   The data transfer unit used in *network* and *modem* communications. Each packet contains not only data, but also a "header" that contains information about which machine sent the data, which machine is supposed to receive the data, and a few extra tidbits that let the receiving computer put all the original data together in the correct order and check for errors that might have cropped up during the transmission.

paging file   A special file used by the *Memory Pager* to emulate physical memory. If you open enough programs or data files that physical memory becomes exhausted, the paging file is brought into play to augment memory storage. Also called a *swap file.*

parity bit   In *modem* data transfers that use 7 *data bits,* this is an extra bit that lets the receiving system check the integrity of each character.

Parkinson's Law of Data   Data expands to fill the space available for storage (from the original Parkinson's Law: Work expands to fill the time available).

PCM   See *Pulse Code Modulation.*

peer-to-peer network   A *network* in which no one computer is singled out to provide special services. Instead, all the computers attached to the network have equal status (at least as far as the network is concerned), and all the computers can act as both *servers* and *clients.* See also *client/server network.*

personal message store   A PST file that Microsoft Exchange uses to hold your e-mail messages and folders.

port driver   A 32-bit *protected-mode device driver* that provides complete functionality for working with devices such as hard disk controllers and floppy disk controllers.

port number   A 16-bit number that uniquely identifies each running process on a computer. See also *socket.*

POST   At system startup, the POST detects and tests memory, ports, and basic devices such as the video adapter, keyboard, and disk drives. If everything passes, your system emits a single beep.

Power-On Self Test   See *POST*.

preemptive multitasking   A multitasking model used by 32-bit applications in which the *Process Scheduler* uses a sophisticated algorithm to monitor all running processes, assign each one a priority level, and allocate CPU resources according to the relative priority of each process. See also *cooperative multitasking*.

primary name   In a filename, the part to the left of the period.

primary partition   The first partition (drive C) on a hard disk. See also *active partition* and *extended partition*.

Process Scheduler   The *Virtual Machine Manager* component that doles out resources to applications and operating system processes. In particular, the Process Scheduler organizes running applications so that they take advantage of *preemptive multitasking* and *multithreading*.

properties sheet   A dialog box with controls that let you manipulate various properties of the underlying *object*.

proportional   A *font* that varies the amount of space given to each character according to the actual width of the letter. See also *monospaced*.

protected mode   An operating mode introduced with the 80286 microprocessor. Unlike *real mode*, which can address only up to 640 KB of memory and gives a running program direct access to hardware, protected mode lets software use memory beyond 640 KB. It also sets up a protection scheme so that multiple programs can share the same computer resources without stepping on each other's toes (and, usually, crashing the system).

protocol   A set of standards that defines how information is exchanged between two systems across a *network* connection. See also *transport layer protocol* and *network layer protocol*.

Pulse Code Modulation   A technique that converts analog sound into digital format by taking "snapshots" of the analog wave at discrete intervals and noting the wave's *amplitude*. These amplitude values form the basis of the digital representation of the wave. Also called *sampling*.

real mode   The operating mode of early Intel microprocessors (the 8088 and 8086). It's a single-tasking mode in which the running program has full access to the computer's memory and peripherals. Except for the Windows 95 Setup program (which uses real mode at first if you start it from the DOS prompt), Windows 95 doesn't use real mode. Real mode is also called *MS-DOS mode*. See also *protected mode, standard mode,* and *386 enhanced mode*.

Real Mode Mapper (RMM)   A driver that lets *VFAT* work with *real-mode* disk drivers (such as DBLSPACE.BIN or a third-party disk not supported by Windows 95). The RMM makes the real-mode driver appear as though it's operating in *protected mode*.

redirector   A networking driver that provides all the mechanisms needed for an application to communicate with a remote device, including file reads and writes, print job submissions, and resource sharing.

Registry   A central repository that Windows 95 uses to store anything and everything that applies to your system's configuration. This includes hardware settings, object properties, operating system settings, and application options.

remote resource   Any peripheral, file, folder, or application that exists somewhere on the *network*. See also *local resource*.

repeat rate   When you press and hold down a key, the speed at which the characters appear. See also *delay*.

repeater   A device that boosts a *network* cable's signal so that the length of the network can be extended. Repeaters are needed because copper-based cables suffer from attenuation—a phenomenon in which the degradation of the electrical signal carried over the cable is proportional to the distance the signal has to travel.

Request a Fax   A feature of Microsoft Fax that lets it retrieve fax documents automatically from *fax-on-demand systems* that support the Group 3 poll-retrieve capability.

router   A device that makes decisions about where to send the *network packets* it receives. Unlike a *bridge*, which merely passes along any data that comes its way, a router examines the address information in each packet and then determines the most efficient route that the packet must take to reach its eventual destination.

routing   The process whereby *packets* travel from *host* to host until they eventually reach their destination.

RTS/CTS flow control   See *hardware flow control*.

Safe mode   A Windows 95 startup mode that loads a minimal system configuration. Safe mode is useful for troubleshooting problems caused by incorrect or corrupt device drivers.

sampling   See *Pulse Code Modulation* and *analog-to-digital converter*.

sans serif   A *typeface* that doesn't contain the cross strokes found in a *serif* typeface. See also *decorative*.

SCSI layer   A 32-bit *protected-mode* driver that provides the basic high-level functionality that is common to all SCSI devices. See also *miniport driver*.

SCSI Manager   Part of the *block I/O subsystem* that ensures compatibility between the *SCSI layer* and Windows NT *miniport drivers*.

separator page   A sheet that prints in advance of each document you send to the printer.

serif   A *typeface* that contains fine cross strokes (called "feet") at the extremities of each character. See also *sans serif* and *decorative*.

server   In a *client/server network,* a computer that provides and manages services (such as file and print sharing and security) for the users on the network.

server application   The application that you use to create and edit an *OLE object.* Also known as the *source application.*

shortcut   A pointer to an executable file or a document. Double-clicking the shortcut starts the program or loads the document.

signature   A few lines of text at the end of an e-mail message that identify the sender and include his contact information (such as his company name, e-mail address, and fax number). Some people also include snappy quotations or other tidbits. Microsoft Exchange doesn't provide any method of adding a signature automatically. However, if you have WordMail, you can customize one of the included e-mail templates with your signature.

Simple Mail Transport Protocol   An Internet protocol that describes the format of Internet e-mail messages and how messages get delivered. Part of the *TCP/IP* suite of protocols.

socket   In the *Transmission Control Protocol,* a communications channel between two *hosts* that consists of their *IP addresses* and *port numbers.*

software flow control   A system whereby the computer and *modem* send signals to each other that indicate whether they're ready to receive data. To stop the transfer, a device sends an XOFF signal (ASCII 19 or Ctrl-S). To restart the transfer, a device sends an XON signal (ASCII 17 or Ctrl-Q). See also *hardware flow control.*

source application   See *server application.*

special drag   Using the right mouse button to drag an object. When you drop the object, Explorer displays a *context menu* with various commands.

standard mode   A Windows 3.x operating mode that takes advantage of the extended memory available through 80286 and higher processors. Standard mode lets Windows programs multitask, but DOS applications take over the system. As with *real mode,* only the Windows 95 Setup program uses standard mode; Windows 95 itself runs exclusively in *386 enhanced mode.*

start bit   An extra bit added to the beginning of the *data bits* in a *modem* data transfer. This bit marks the beginning of each character. See also *stop bit.*

stop bit   An extra bit (or sometimes two) added to the end of the *data bits* in a *modem* data transfer. This bit marks the end of each character. See also *start bit.*

subnet mask   A 32-bit value, usually expressed in *dotted-decimal notation,* that lets *IP* separate a network ID from a full *IP address* and thus determine whether the source and destination hosts are on the same network.

swap file   See *paging file.*

system tray   The box on the right side of the taskbar that Windows 95 uses to display icons that tell you the current state of the system.

TCP   See *Transmission Control Protocol.*

TCP/IP   Transmission Control Protocol/Internet Protocol. TCP/IP is the lingua franca of most UNIX systems and the Internet as a whole. However, TCP/IP is also an excellent choice for other types of *networks* because it's routable, robust, and reliable.

terminate-and-stay-resident   See *TSR.*

thread   A small chunk of executable code with a very narrow focus. In a spreadsheet, for example, you might have one thread for recalculating, another for printing, and a third for accepting keyboard input. See also *multithreading.*

time slice   A fixed number of processor cycles. In a *multitasking* environment, the Windows 95 *Process Scheduler* doles out time slices to running processes.

topology   Describes how the various *nodes* that comprise a *network*—which include not only the computers, but also devices such as *hubs* and *bridges*—are connected.

Transmission Control Protocol   A *transport layer protocol* that sets up a connection between two *hosts* and ensures that data is passed between them reliably. If *packets* are lost or damaged during transmission, TCP takes care of retransmitting the packets. See also *Internet Protocol* and *TCP/IP.*

transport layer protocol   A *protocol* in which a virtual communications channel is established between two systems. The protocol uses this channel to send *packets* between *nodes.* See also *network layer protocol.*

True Color   A *color depth* of 24 bits, or 16,777,216 colors.

TSR   A terminate-and-stay-resident program. These programs load themselves into memory and remain there until a keystroke or some other prompt goads them into action. See also *deadly TSR, device driver,* and *dirty TSR.*

tunneling   A process that Windows 95 uses to preserve long filenames when files are used by 16-bit applications. When these programs write a file to disk (during, say, a save), they record only the file's 8.3 filename in the *file directory.* Windows 95 recognizes this and attaches the file's long filename to its directory entry.

type size   A measure of the height of a *font.* Type size is measured from the highest point of a tall letter, such as "f," to the lowest point of an underhanging letter, such as "g." The standard unit of measurement is the point. There are 72 points in an inch.

type style   Extra attributes added to a font's *typeface,* such as **bold** and *italic.* Other type styles (often called type effects) include underlining and ~~strikeout~~ (sometimes called "strikethrough").

B

GLOSSARY

typeface   A distinctive design that is common to any related set of letters, numbers, and other symbols. This design gives each character a particular shape and thickness that is unique to the typeface and difficult to categorize. However, three main typeface types serve to distinguish all typefaces: *serif, sans serif,* and *decorative.*

UART   Universal Asynchronous Receiver/Transmitter. A special chip that resides inside every serial port (or sometimes on the computer's motherboard). (For an internal or PC Card modem, the UART chip sits on the card itself.) It's the UART's job (among other things) to take the computer's native parallel data and convert it into a series of bits that can be spit out of the serial port's Transmit Data line. On the other end, individual bits streaming into the destination serial port's Receive Data line are reassembled by the UART into the parallel format that the processor prefers.

Uniform Resource Locator   An Internet addressing scheme that spells out the exact location of a Net resource. Most URLs take the following form:

`protocol://host.domain/directory/file.name`

`protocol`	The TCP/IP protocol to use for retrieving the resource (such as http or ftp).
`host.domain`	The domain name of the host computer where the resource resides.
`directory`	The host directory that contains the resource.
`file.name`	The filename of the resource.

universal driver   A *device driver* that incorporates the code necessary for the devices in a particular hardware class to work with the appropriate Windows 95 operating system component (such as the printing subsystem). See also *mini-driver.*

URL   See *Uniform Resource Locator.*

User   A core Windows 95 component that handles all user-related I/O tasks. On the input side, User manages incoming data from the keyboard, mouse, joystick, and any other input devices that are attached to your computer. For "output," User sends data to windows, icons, menus, and other components of the Windows 95 user interface. User also handles the sound driver, the system timer, and the communications ports. See also *Graphical Device Interface* and *kernel.*

user profiles   Separate sets of customization options for each person who uses a computer. Each profile includes most of Windows 95's customization options, including the colors, patterns, wallpapers, *shortcut* icons, screen saver, and programs that appear on the Start menu.

VFAT   An *installable file system* that works with the *block I/O subsystem* to access disk services. Because it's a 32-bit *protected-mode VxD* and is multithreaded, VFAT provides superior performance (especially compared to the 16-bit *real-mode* disk access found in Windows 3.1), enhanced reliability, and easier *multitasking.* In particular, VFAT avoids the slow processor mode switches between protected mode and real mode that plagued Windows 3.1. VFAT also supports many more drive and controller types than did Windows 3.x. However, it still uses the 16-bit *FAT* for physical storage of files and folders, so it inherits FAT's legendary fragility. See also *CDFS*.

virtual device driver   A 32-bit *protected-mode device driver.*

Virtual File Allocation Table   See *VFAT.*

virtual machine   A separate section of memory that simulates the operation of an entire computer. Virtual machines were born with the release of Intel's 80386 microprocessor. Thanks to *protected mode,* the 80386 circuitry could address up to 4 GB of memory. Using this potentially huge address space, the 80386 allowed software to carve out separate chunks of memory and use these areas to emulate the full operation of a computer. This emulation is so complete and so effective that a program running in a virtual machine thinks it's dealing with a real computer. Combined with the resource sharing features of *protected mode,* virtual machines can run their programs simultaneously without bumping into each other.

Virtual Machine Manager   A Windows 95 driver (VMM32.VXD) that allocates and manages the resources needed by your system's software—your applications and the various operating system processes. If a program or the operating system needs a resource—whether it's a chunk of memory or access to an I/O port—the Virtual Machine Manager handles the request and allocates the resource appropriately.

virtual memory   Memory created by allocating hard disk space and making it look to applications as though they are dealing with physical RAM.

visual editing   In *object linking and embedding,* when you double-click an embedded object, instead of the *server application's* being displayed in a separate window, certain features of the *container application's* window are temporarily hidden in favor of the server application's features. (Linked objects use *open editing.*) Here's a summary of the changes that occur in the container application:

- The document window's title bar changes to tell you what kind of object you're now working with. (Not all applications do this.)
- The menu bar (with the exception of the File and Window menus) is replaced by the server application's menu bar.
- The toolbars are replaced by the server application's toolbars.

VxD   See *virtual device driver.*

WAN   See *wide area network.*

waveform audio   A process that re-creates an audio waveform by using digital samples of the waveform. This is the standard Windows sound format.

wide area network   A *network* that consists of two or more *LANs* or *internetworks* that are spaced out over a relatively large geographical area, such as a state, country, or the entire world. The networks in a WAN typically are connected via high-speed fiber-optic phone lines, microwave dishes, or satellite links.

B

GLOSSARY

Windows Internet Name Service   A service that maps NetBIOS names (the names you assign to computers in the Identification tab of the Network properties sheet) to the *IP addresses* assigned via *DHCP*.

WINS   See *Windows Internet Name Service.*

XON/XOFF flow control   See *software flow control.*

A Setup Smorgasbord: Custom and Server-Based Setups

APPENDIX C

As you saw in Chapter 2, "Running the Windows 95 Setup," installing Windows 95 on a single machine doesn't require much in the way of brainpower, but it's still a bit of a chore because of all the options and prompts that come your way. Multiply that chore by a dozen or a hundred PCs, and Setup becomes a mind-numbing, time-consuming nightmare.

Fortunately, Microsoft realized this and came up with a few methods for automating Setup to reduce the burden on administrators and power users. This appendix tells you about two of these methods: custom setups and server-based setups.

Custom Setups with Batch Setup 2.0

Although the original Windows 95 CD-ROM came with a batch setup program, Microsoft has released a 32-bit update—Batch Setup 2.0—that makes it even easier to install Windows 95 clients from a server. It includes the following goodies:

- Support for NetWare Directory Services
- A network adapter resource conflict Wizard
- Improved setup options for networking and components
- The ability to propagate a machine's Registry settings across the network
- Uninstall support

The idea behind Batch Setup is to create a custom setup information file (an .INF file) that spells out all the Windows 95 Setup options that normally require user input (user name, company name, components, and so on). By letting Windows 95 Setup know that this .INF file exists, it can use the file to extract all the data it needs and operate virtually without user intervention. In fact, in most cases you can simply run Windows 95 Setup and then not touch the computer again until Windows 95 is completely installed!

Obtaining and Installing Batch Setup 2.0

Before installing Batch Setup, bear in mind that since this is a fully 32-bit program, it will run only on machines running Windows 95 or Windows NT 3.51 or higher. Note, too, that you'll achieve the greatest flexibility if you run Batch Setup on a Windows 95 computer. (For example, this lets you propagate a Windows 95 machine's Registry settings across other Windows 95 clients.)

You can get the Batch Setup 2.0 update either in Service Pack 1 (look in the \Admin\Tools\Batch folder) or on Microsoft's Web site at the following address:

http://www.microsoft.com/windows/software/servpak1/batch.htm

If you download the update, run the batch20.exe file to extract the files.

To install Batch Setup 2.0, close all running applications and then launch the setup.exe file. Follow the on-screen prompts until Batch Setup is installed.

From here, the server-based setup is a two-step procedure:

1. Run Batch Setup to create an .INF file that defines how you want Windows 95 installed on the network client.

2. Run Windows 95 Setup in batch mode on the client, and specify the .INF file created in step 1.

The next few sections supply the details.

Batch Setup Using a Common Registry

If you'll be setting up Windows 95 on a number of identically-configured computers, Batch Setup 2.0 includes an option for retrieving the Registry settings from one of the computers (that is, the one on which Batch Setup is running) and then using these same settings for the other computers. Here are the steps to follow:

1. Start Batch Setup by selecting Start | Programs | Windows Batch Setup. You'll see the Windows Batch Setup window, shown in Figure C.1.

Figure C.1.

The Batch Setup window.

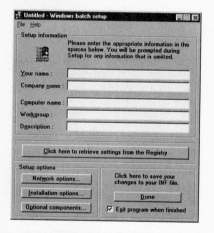

2. Click the button labeled "Click here to retrieve settings from the Registry." Batch Setup fills in the Setup information group and grabs other Setup-related data from the Registry.

3. Edit the Setup information fields as necessary. For example, you'll need to change the Computer name field to match the name you want to use for the network client (or the one that is currently being used by the network client).

4. Click Done. Batch Setup prompts you to save the .INF file.

5. Select a location for the file, edit the File name if necessary, and click Save.

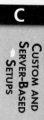

C

CUSTOM AND
SERVER-BASED
SETUPS

Specifying Setup Options

Most organizations include a variety of computers that have a variety of hardware configurations. So it's more likely that you'll need to create custom .INF files tailored to the specific configurations of these computers. Although this sounds like a lot of work, Batch Setup 2.0 includes a GUI interface that takes much of the tedium out of the process. This section takes you through the steps required to create a custom setup information file.

To get started, run Batch Setup by selecting Start | Programs | Windows Batch Setup to display the Batch Setup window. Use the `Setup information` group to fill in the particulars for the client. Note that during Setup, Windows 95 will prompt you for any data that you leave blank in this area.

Network Options

To specify how Windows 95 networking should be configured on the client, click the Network Options button to display the properties sheet, shown in Figure C.2.

FIGURE C.2.

Use this dialog box to specify how Windows 95 networking is to be installed on the client computer.

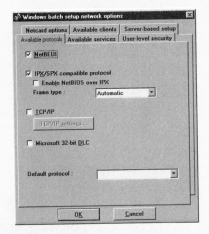

NOTE: NETWORKING INFORMATION SOURCES

You'll find information on most of the options in this dialog box in this book's networking chapters:

- Chapter 30, "A Networking Primer"
- Chapter 31, "Windows 95 Networking"
- Chapter 32, "Network Administration and Security"
- Chapter 36, "Implementing TCP/IP for Internet and Network Connections"

Here's a summary of the options controlled by each tab:

Available protocols: Use this tab to choose the networking protocols that will be installed and which of them should be the default protocol. If you activate the TCP/IP check box, click TCP/IP settings to enter the IP address, gateway address, DNS information, and so on.

Available services: This tab determines whether or not file and print sharing is enabled and controls the browse master setup for the client.

User-level security: Use this tab to activate user-level security.

Netcard options: The check boxes on this tab determine how Windows 95 Setup deals with network adapter cards. If you activate the Ignore detected net cards check box, Windows 95 Setup will bypass its detection of Network adapters. When the Display a wizard to resolve resource conflicts check box is activated, a Wizard will appear during Setup if a resource (for example, IRQ) conflict is detected.

Available clients: Use this tab to specify the networking client (or clients) to install.

Server-based setup: Use this tab to determine whether or not Windows 95 Setup uses a server-based setup, as well as how the system boots if it's using a shared Windows 95 installation. See "Server-Based Setups" later in this chapter for more information.

Installation Options

Next, you need to define some basic Windows 95 Setup options, including the installation folder, printers, time zone, and so on. To set these options, click the Installation Options button to display the dialog box shown in Figure C.3. Here's a summary of what to expect in each tab (see Chapter 2 for explanations of most of these settings):

Setup options: This tab contains a mixed bag of options that deal with Setup prompts (such as whether to create a startup disk). Most important are the Type of installation drop-down list and the installation directory text box.

Time zone: Use the lone control in this tab to choose the appropriate time zone for the client.

Monitor settings: Use this tab to specify default settings for the client's Color depth and Resolution.

Administrative options: This tab lets you specify points in the Windows 95 installation where Setup should stop and ask for user input. For example, if you'd like to give the user the opportunity to enter his name and organization, activate the Stop during setup at the following check box, and then activate the User settings only option button.

Uninstall options: These options determine whether or not Setup saves Windows 95 uninstall information.

Printers: Use this tab to specify one or more printers to install during Setup (or you can have Setup prompt the user for printer data).

File Locations: You can specify up to three Most Recently Used (MRU) paths. An MRU is a local or network path that should point to the possible location of the Windows 95 installation files. If Windows 95 Setup prompts the user to insert the Windows CD-ROM or disks in order to install a file, the MRU paths will appear in the list of possible locations.

FIGURE C.3.

Use this dialog box to specify some basic Windows 95 Setup options.

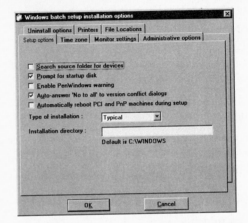

Specifying Windows 95 Components

If you chose the Custom setup in the Type of installation list (found in the Setup options tab, discussed in the preceding section), you can click the Optional Components button in the Batch Setup window to display the dialog box shown in Figure C.4. Use the Available Areas list to highlight a component category, and then use the Available Components list to activate the check box beside each component you want installed. Click OK when you're done.

FIGURE C.4.

Use this dialog box to choose which Windows 95 components to install on the client.

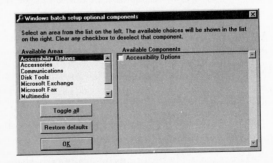

That's it for specifying custom setup options. From here, click Done, choose a location and a name for the .INF file, and click Save.

A Special Case: Static TCP/IP Configurations

Sites that use Dynamic Host Configuration Protocol (DHCP) to assign IP addresses to network clients on-the-fly are tailor-made for batch-mode setups. That's because you have to enable DHCP only when setting the network options for the .INF file. From there, the specific TCP/IP settings for each workstation are configured dynamically at logon.

However, what if you assign static IP addresses to each workstation? In this case, for each workstation you need to create a custom .INF file that includes the appropriate TCP/IP settings. This can mean a great deal of extra work in medium-to-large sites. To reduce some of the drudgery, Microsoft has an INF Generator tool that can take a list of individual clients' TCP/IP settings and incorporate that data into the .INF file you created with Batch Setup. The result is a no-fuss series of custom .INF files for each workstation.

As with Batch Setup 2.0, you can get the INF Generator either in Service Pack 1 (look in the \Admin\Tools\Batch folder) or on Microsoft's Web site at the following URL:

http://www.microsoft.com/windows/software/servpak1/inf.htm

If you'll be downloading INF Generator from Microsoft, save the ig.exe file to whichever folder you want to use to store the program, and then run ig.exe to extract the files.

Before running INF Generator, you need to create a CSV (comma-separated values) file that contains one line for each user and that specifies the following data on each line:

User name: The user name that the client uses to log on to Windows.

Computer name: The network name of the client computer.

Host name: The TCP/IP host name of the client.

IP address of the client: The IP address assigned to the client.

IP address of the gateway: The IP address of the network gateway.

Workgroup or domain: The name of the workgroup or domain that the client logs on to.

Here's an example of such a line:

Biff,Hermes,hermes,205.208.111.2,205.208.111.1,OLYMPUS

The easiest way to create such a file is to enter the data into a spreadsheet or database program and then use the program's export command to save the data in CSV format.

Once that's done, start INF Generator by running the infgen.exe file to display the INF Generator window, shown in Figure C.5. Click Next > to continue.

C

CUSTOM AND
SERVER-BASED
SETUPS

Figure C.5.
Use the INF Generator to create user-specific .INF setup files.

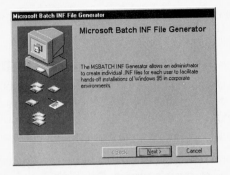

In the next dialog box, shown in Figure C.6, click Browse and then choose the .INF file you created earlier using Batch Setup. When that's done, click Next >.

Figure C.6.
Use this dialog box to find the .INF file created with Batch Setup.

The INF Generator dialog box that appears next (see Figure C.7) asks you for two things:

User specific settings: Click Browse to find the CSV file you created earlier.

Destination Folder: Use this group to choose a destination folder in which the custom .INF files will be created.

When you're done, click OK.

Figure C.7.
Use this dialog box to specify your CSV file and a destination for the new .INF files.

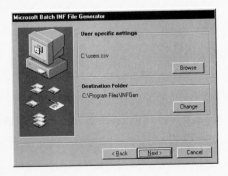

Now INF Generator presents you with a list of optional Windows 95 components, as shown in Figure C.8. Activate the check boxes beside the components you want to install, and then click Next >.

FIGURE C.8.

Use this dialog box to choose the optional components that will be installed on the client.

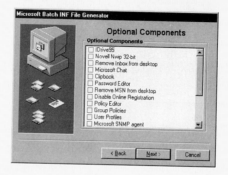

INF Generator then proceeds to incorporate the TCP/IP data into your Batch Setup .INF file and create custom .INF files for each user. When that's done, click Close to end the INF Generator session.

Setting Up Windows 95 on the Client

With your custom setup .INF file in place, applying the file to the Windows 95 Setup on the client is simplicity itself. All you have to do is launch Setup and specify the location of the .INF file as a parameter. For example, if the file is named `BSETUP.INF` and you copied it to the client root folder on drive C, you would run Setup as follows (assuming that the Windows 95 CD-ROM is in drive D):

`d:\win95\setup c:\bsetup.inf` *switches*

Note that UNC paths are OK as well:

`d:\win95\setup \\server\users\biff\bsetup.inf` *switches*

Either way, Windows 95 Setup runs in batch mode and uses the data in the .INF file. To ensure "hands-free" operation, you'll want to include some switches that tell Setup to bypass certain operations. Table C.1 summarizes these switches.

Table C.1. Command-line switches that bypass some Setup prompts.

Switch	Description
/id	Tells Setup not to check for the minimum disk space required to install Windows 95.
/it	Tells Setup not to check for the presence of dirty or deadly TSRs.

continues

Table C.1. continued

Switch	Description
/iq	Tells Setup not to check your drive for cross-linked files. This switch is valid only if you use the /is switch to bypass ScanDisk or if ScanDisk fails.
/is	Tells Setup not to run ScanDisk.
/IW	Tells Setup not to display the Windows 95 license agreement (you must use uppercase letters for this switch).

Assuming that there are no prompts along the way, you won't have to touch the computer again until Setup finishes and leaves you at the DOS prompt. From there, type win and press Enter to run Windows 95.

Server-Based Setups

The .INF files generated by Batch Setup can be a lifesaver for a busy administrator. However, what do you do if you find yourself dealing with a workstation that doesn't have a CD-ROM drive or that doesn't have local storage? For these situations, a server-based setup is the way to go, because it lets these clients install Windows 95 using files found on a server.

Configuring a server-based setup usually involves one or more of the following steps:

1. Copy the Windows 95 source files to a server.
2. (Optional) If you want to use a shared Windows 95 installation, create a machine directory for each client that uses either a floppy boot or a remote boot server.
3. (Optional) Create custom setup .INF files as described in the first half of this appendix.

The next couple of sections describe steps 1 and 2 in more detail.

Copying Windows 95 Source Files to a Server

As the name implies, a server-based setup is one in which the Windows 95 source files are located on a server. Not only is this handy for diskless workstations, but it can even be a good idea on regular workstations as a way of saving valuable hard disk real estate.

Whatever your reasons, your first chore is to get the Windows 95 source files from the CD-ROM to the server. Here are the steps to follow:

1. On a Windows 95 workstation (this procedure runs only under Windows 95), log on to the network and insert the Windows 95 CD-ROM (hold down the Shift key to prevent the Autorun.inf file from executing).

2. Launch `Netsetup.exe`, which you'll find in the CD's `\Admin\Nettools\Netsetup\` folder. You'll see the Server Based Setup dialog box, shown in Figure C.9.

FIGURE C.9.

This dialog box appears when you run
`Netsetup.exe`*.*

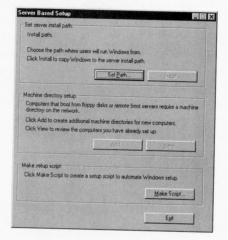

3. Click Set Path to display the Server Path dialog box, shown in Figure C.10.

FIGURE C.10.

Use this dialog box to enter the UNC path for the server folder that will contain the Windows 95 source files.

4. In the `Server path` text box, enter a UNC path that points to the server folder in which you want the Windows 95 source files to be stored. (This path doesn't have to exist, because Server-Based Setup will create it for you. Note, however, that you must have create privileges on the server.)

5. Click OK. If the program asks if you want to create the destination directory, click Yes.

6. In the Server Based Setup dialog box, click Install. The Source Path dialog box appears, as shown in Figure C.11.

7. Use the options in the `Install policy` group to determine where the Windows 95 files will be installed when you run a server-based setup. Choose `Server` to leave the files on the server. Choose `Local hard drive` to have the Windows 95 files installed on the client's disk. Choose `User's choice` to give each user a choice of locations.

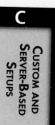

C

CUSTOM AND SERVER-BASED SETUPS

FIGURE C.11.

This dialog box determines where the source files are located and how the copied source files will be installed on each client.

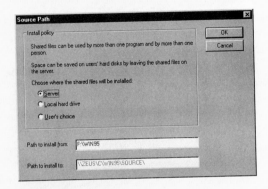

8. Make sure that the `Path to install from` text box contains the correct path to the source files on the Windows 95 CD-ROM.

9. Click OK. Server-Based Setup next asks if you want to create default setup batch scripts, as shown in Figure C.12. I'm assuming here that you want to create (or already have created) custom .INF files, so click Don't Create Default.

FIGURE C.12.

Server-Based Setup offers to create default setup batch scripts.

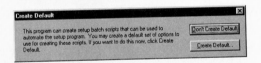

10. When the program asks for your Windows 95 Product Identification Number, enter it (it's on the back of the CD case). This is optional because this step is required only with the default script. Click OK to begin copying the source files to the server.

11. When the copying is complete, click OK to return to the Server Based Setup dialog box.

Setting Up Machine Directories

For users who don't have local storage (or who don't have enough local storage to install Windows 95), you can set up a *shared installation,* which lets these users share a single installation of Windows 95 on a server. In order for this to work properly, each user must have his own *machine directory,* which is a server-based folder that contains, among other things, the user's Registry files, other initialization files (such as `WIN.INI`), user-specific files for desktop settings and Start menu shortcuts, the swap file, and the `TEMP` folder that holds Windows 95's .TMP files.

If you want to configure such a shared installation, you can use Server-Based Setup to create the machine directory for an individual client by following these steps:

1. Specify a server installation path as described in the preceding section.

2. In the `Machine directory setup` group, click Add to display the Set Up Machine dialog box, shown in Figure C.13.

FIGURE C.13.

Use this dialog box to set up a machine directory for a shared installation.

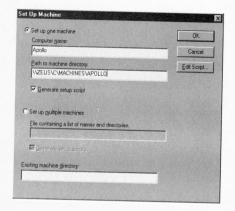

3. Make sure that the Set up one machine option is activated.

4. Enter the computer's network name in the Computer name text box.

5. Enter a UNC server path for the machine directory in the Path to machine directory text box.

6. If you already have a setup .INF file prepared, deactivate the Generate setup script check box.

TIP: UPDATING YOUR SCRIPT FOR A SHARED INSTALLATION

To modify your .INF file for a shared installation, run Batch Setup, click Installation Options, and enter the path to the machine directory in the Installation directory text box.

---

7. If an existing machine directory has a configuration you want to use, enter a path to the directory in the Existing machine directory text box.

8. Click OK.

Rather than creating a single machine directory at a time, Server-Based Setup gives you a shortcut method for creating several machine directories at once. To do this, first create a text file that contains a separate line for each machine directory you want to create. Each line should use the following format:

```
ComputerName, \\UNCPathToMachineDirectory
```

Here, ComputerName is the network name of each computer, and UNCPathToMachineDirectory is the UNC path to each machine directory.

Now run Server-Based Setup, set the install path, and click Add. In the Set Up Machine dialog box, activate the Set up multiple machines option, and then use the File containing a list of names and directories text box to enter the full path name for the text file you created.

Running the Server-Based Setup

To run the server-based setup, log on to the client and then run Setup from the server by entering a command that uses the following format:

```
\\SetupPath\setup \\ScriptPath\filename.inf switches
```

Here, *SetupPath* is the UNC path that points to the shared installation on the server, *ScriptPath* is the path to the .INF batch setup file for this client, and *switches* is any of the switches defined in Table C.1.

APPENDIX D

The Windows ANSI Character Set

This appendix presents the Windows ANSI character set. Table D.1 lists the ANSI numbers from 32 to 255. The first 32 numbers—0 to 31—are reserved for control characters such as ANSI 13, the carriage return. There are three columns for each number:

Column	Description
Text	The ANSI characters that correspond to normal text fonts such as Arial (Excel's default font), Courier New, and Times New Roman.
Symbol	The ANSI characters for the Symbol font.
Wingdings	The ANSI characters for the Wingdings font.

To enter these characters into your worksheets, you can use any of the following four methods:

- For the ANSI numbers 32 through 127, you can either type the character directly using the keyboard, or hold down the Alt key and type the ANSI number using the keyboard's numeric keypad.

- For the ANSI numbers 128 through 255, hold down the Alt key and use the keyboard's numeric keypad to enter the ANSI number, including the leading 0 shown in the table. For example, to enter the registered trademark symbol (ANSI 174), you would press Alt-0174.

- Use the CHAR(*number*) worksheet function, where *number* is the ANSI number for the character you want to display.

- In a Visual Basic procedure, use the Chr(*charcode*) function, where *charcode* is the ANSI number for the character.

Table D.1. The Windows ANSI character set.

ANSI	Text	Symbol	Wingdings
32			
33	!	!	✎
34	"	∀	✂
35	#	#	✁
36	$	∃	✆
37	%	%	✇
38	&	&	▥
39	'	∍	✌
40	(	(	☎
41	)	)	✆

ANSI	Text	Symbol	Wingdings
42	*	*	✉
43	+	+	✉
44	,	,	🖃
45	–	–	🖃
46	.	.	🖃
47	/	/	🖃
48	0	**0**	📁
49	1	1	📂
50	2	2	📄
51	3	3	📄
52	4	4	📄
53	5	5	🗄
54	6	6	⌛
55	7	7	⌨
56	8	8	🖱
57	9	9	🖱
58	:	:	🖥
59	;	;	▭
60	<	<	🖫
61	=	=	🖬
62	>	>	Ⓜ
63	?	?	✎
64	@	≅	✍
65	A	**A**	✌
66	B	**B**	✊
67	C	**X**	👌
68	D	**Δ**	👍
69	E	**E**	👎
70	F	**Φ**	☞
71	G	**Γ**	✋
72	H	**H**	✋
73	I	**I**	✋
74	J	**ϑ**	☺
75	K	**K**	😐
76	L	**Λ**	☹
77	M	**M**	💣
78	N	**N**	☠
79	O	**O**	🏳
80	P	**Π**	🏳
81	Q	**Θ**	✈

continues

Table D.1. continued

ANSI	Text	Symbol	Wingdings
82	R	P	☼
83	S	Σ	●
84	T	T	❈
85	U	Y	✝
86	V	ς	✞
87	W	Ω	◆
88	X	Ξ	✠
89	Y	Ψ	✡
90	Z	Z	☾
91	[	[	☯
92	\	∴	ॐ
93	]	]	✿
94	^	⊥	♈
95	_	—	♉
96	`	‾	♊
97	a	α	♋
98	b	β	♌
99	c	χ	♍
100	d	δ	♎
101	e	ε	♏
102	f	φ	♐
103	g	γ	♑
104	h	η	♒
105	i	ι	♓
106	j	φ	er
107	k	κ	&
108	l	λ	●
109	m	μ	○
110	n	ν	■
111	o	o	□
112	p	π	◻
113	q	θ	◻
114	r	ρ	◻
115	s	σ	◆
116	t	τ	◆
117	u	υ	◆
118	v	ϖ	❖
119	w	ω	◆
120	x	ξ	⊠
121	y	ψ	⊡
122	z	ζ	⌘

ANSI	Text	Symbol	Wingdings
123	{	{	✿
124	|	|	✹
125	}	}	"
126	~	~	"
127			▯
0128			⓪
0129			①
0130	,		②
0131	ƒ		③
0132	„		④
0133	…		⑤
0134	†		⑥
0135	‡		⑦
0136	ˆ		⑧
0137	‰		⑨
0138	Š		⑩
0139	‹		❶
0140	Œ		❷
0141			❸
0142			❹
0143			❺
0144			❻
0145	'		❼
0146	'		❽
0147	"		❾
0148	"		❿
0149	•		✇
0150	–		✇
0151	—		✇
0152	~		✇
0153	™		✇
0154	š		✇
0155	›		✇
0156	œ		✇
0157			✇
0158			·
0159	Ÿ		•
0160			
0161	¡	Υ	○
0162	¢	'	●
0163	£	≤	●
0164	¤	/	◉

continues

Table D.1. continued

ANSI	Text	Symbol	Wingdings
0165	¥	∞	◉
0166	¦	ƒ	○
0167	§	♣	▪
0168	¨	♦	□
0169	©	♥	▲
0170	ª	♠	✦
0171	«	↔	★
0172	¬	←	✶
0173		↑	✳
0174	®	→	✹
0175	¯	↓	✳
0176	°	°	⊕
0177	±	±	⊕
0178	²	″	✧
0179	³	≥	◻
0180	´	×	◈
0181	µ	∝	❂
0182	¶	∂	☆
0183	·	•	◷
0184	¸	÷	◷
0185	¹	≠	◷
0186	º	≡	◷
0187	»	≈	◷
0188	¼	…	◷
0189	½	⎮	◷
0190	¾	⎯	◷
0191	¿	↵	◷
0192	À	ℵ	◷
0193	Á	ℑ	◷
0194	Â	ℜ	◷
0195	Ã	℘	⤸
0196	Ä	⊗	⤷
0197	Å	⊕	⤴
0198	Æ	∅	⤵
0199	Ç	∩	⤶
0200	È	∪	⤹
0201	É	⊃	⤺
0202	Ê	⊇	⤻
0203	Ë	⊄	✖
0204	Ì	⊂	▦
0205	Í	⊆	✿
0206	Î	∈	✾

ANSI	*Text*	*Symbol*	*Wingdings*
0207	Ï	∉	
0208	Đ	∠	
0209	Ñ	∇	
0210	Ò	®	
0211	Ó	©	
0212	Ô	™	
0213	Õ	Π	
0214	Ö	√	
0215	×	·	
0216	Ø	¬	
0217	Ù	∧	
0218	Ú	∨	
0219	Û	⇔	
0220	Ü	⇐	
0221	Ý	⇑	
0222	Þ	⇒	
0223	ß	⇓	
0224	à	◊	
0225	á	⟨	
0226	â	®	
0227	ã	©	
0228	ä	™	
0229	å	∑	
0230	æ	⌠	
0231	ç			
0232	è	⌡	
0233	é	⌈	
0234	ê			
0235	ë	⌊	
0236	ì	⎧	
0237	í	⎨	
0238	î	⎩	
0239	ï			
0240	ð		
0241	ñ	⟩	
0242	ò	⌡	
0243	ó	⌠	
0244	ô			
0245	õ	⌡	
0246	ö	⎫	
0247	÷			
0248	ø	⎭	

continues

Table D.1. continued

ANSI	Text	Symbol	Wingdings
0249	ù	⌐	❑
0250	ú	|	❑
0251	û	⌡	✖
0252	ü	⌐	✔
0253	ý	}	☒
0254	þ	⌡	☑
0255	ÿ		▦

An HTML Primer

IN THIS APPENDIX

APPENDIX

I showed you how to turn a Windows 95 machine into a Web server in Chapter 42, "Setting Up a Windows 95 World Wide Web Server." Of course, there isn't much point in having a Web server if you don't have any Web pages to serve, and that's the point of this appendix.

If you've seen some World Wide Web pages in your Internet travels, you might think you need a high-end word processor or page layout application to achieve all those fancy effects. Well, although you *can* use a sophisticated software package, the truth is that any basic text editor (such as the Notepad accessory that comes with Windows) is all you need to create attractive Web pages. This appendix shows you how by giving you a primer on the basic elements that constitute HTML—Hypertext Markup Language.

Understanding HTML Tags

The Web's secret is that, underneath all the bells and whistles, pages are relatively simple affairs. You just type in your text and then insert markers—called *tags*—that dictate how you want things to look. For example, if you'd like a word on your page to appear in bold text, you surround that word with the appropriate tags for boldness.

In general, tags use the following format:

```
<TAG>The text to be affected</TAG>
```

The *TAG* part is a code (usually one or two letters) that specifies the type of effect you want. For example, the tag for bolding is <B>. So if you wanted the phrase ACME Coyote Supplies to appear in bold, you'd type the following into your document:

```
<B>ACME Coyote Supplies</B>
```

The first <B> tells the browser to display all the text that follows in a bold font. This continues until the </B> is reached. The slash (/) defines this as an *end tag*, which tells the browser to turn off the effect. As you'll see, there are tags for lots of other effects, including italics, paragraphs, headings, page titles, lists, and much more. HTML is just the sum total of all these tags.

These days you don't need to know HTML tags in order to create Web pages. For example, you can use Word 97's menus and toolbars to construct pages. However, you need to bear in mind that all the techniques you use in Word are, in the end, creating HTML tags (albeit behind the scenes). So knowing a bit about how HTML tags work will help you understand what's going on. And, if you're having trouble getting Word or some other WYSIWYG HTML editor to get your pages just right, you can always examine the HTML code and make some adjustments manually.

NOTE: HTML REFERENCES

This appendix presents only the briefest of introductions to HTML. Most of the tags I'll be talking about have a number of attributes that you can use to refine each tag's behavior. To learn more, you can find a number of HTML references on the Web. Yahoo! provides a list of these references at the following address:

```
http://www.yahoo.com/Computers_and_Internet/Information_and_Documentation/
➥Data_Formats/HTML/Reference/
```

Also, Microsoft maintains an excellent HTML reference (geared, of course, toward the abilities of Internet Explorer) at the following address:

```
http://www.microsoft.com/workshop/author/newhtml/default.htm
```

The Basic Structure of Web Pages

Web pages range from dull to dynamic, inane to indispensable, but they all have the same underlying structure. This consistent structure—which, as you'll see, is nothing more than a small collection of HTML tags—is the reason why almost all browser programs running on almost all types of computers can successfully display almost all Web pages.

HTML files always start with the <HTML> tag. This tag doesn't do much except tell any Web browser that tries to read the file that it's dealing with a file that contains HTML codes. Similarly, the last line in your document will always be the </HTML> tag, which you can think of as the HTML equivalent of "The End."

The next items in the HTML tag catalog serve to divide the document into two sections: the *head* and the *body*.

The head section is like an introduction to the page. Web browsers use the head to glean various types of information about the page. Although a number of items can appear in the head section, the most common is the title of the page, which I'll talk about shortly. To define the head, you add a <HEAD> tag and a </HEAD> tag immediately below the <HTML> tag.

The body section is where you enter both the text that will actually appear on the Web page, and the other tags that control the look of the page. To define the body, you place a <BODY> tag and a </BODY> tag after the head section (that is, below the </HEAD> tag).

These tags define the basic structure of every Web page:

```
<HTML>
<HEAD>
Header tags go here.
</HEAD>
<BODY>
The Web page text and tags go here.
</BODY>
</HTML>
```

Adding a Title

The next item you need to add is the title of the Web page. The page's title is just about what you might think it is: the overall name of the page (not to be confused with the name of the file you're creating). If someone views the page in a graphical browser (such as Netscape or Internet Explorer), the title appears in the title bar of the browser's window.

To define a title, you surround the text with the <TITLE> and </TITLE> tags. For example, if you want the title of your page to be *My Home Sweet Home Page,* you would enter it as follows:

```
<TITLE>My Home Sweet Home Page</TITLE>
```

Note that you always place the title inside the head section. Your basic HTML document will now look like this:

```
<HTML>
<HEAD>
<TITLE>My Home Sweet Home Page</TITLE>
</HEAD>
<BODY>
</BODY>
</HTML>
```

Text and Paragraphs

With your page title firmly in place, you can now think about the text you want to appear in the body of the page. For the most part, you can simply type the text between the <BODY> and </BODY> tags.

Things get a little tricky when you want to start a new paragraph. In most text editors and word processors, starting a new paragraph is a simple matter of pressing the Enter key to move to a new line. You can try doing that in your Web page, but the browsers that read your page will ignore this "white space." Instead, you have to use the <P> tag to tell the browser that you want to move to a new paragraph:

```
<HTML>
<HEAD>
<TITLE>My Home Sweet Home Page</TITLE>
</HEAD>
<BODY>
This text appears in the body of the Web page.
<P>
This text appears in a new paragraph.
</BODY>
</HTML>
```

Adding Formatting and Headings

HTML has lots of tags that will spruce up your page text. You saw earlier how a word or phrase surrounded by the <B> and </B> tags will appear in **bold** in a browser. You can also display text in *italics* by bracketing it with the <I> and </I> tags, and you can make your words appear in monospace by surrounding them with the <TT> and </TT> tags.

NOTE: MORE FONT FUN

Internet Explorer also supports the <FONT> tag:

<FONT SIZE=*n* FACE=*name* COLOR=*color*>

Here, the SIZE attribute specifies the text size, FACE specifies a font name, and COLOR specifies the text color. See an HTML reference for details on these attributes.

Like the chapters of a book, many Web pages have their contents divided into several sections. To help separate these sections and make life easier for the reader, you can use *headings*. Ideally, these headings act as mini-titles that convey some idea of what each section is all about. To make these titles stand out, HTML has a series of heading tags that display text in a larger, bold font. There are six heading tags in all, ranging from <H1>, which uses the largest font, down to <H6>, which uses the smallest font.

To illustrate these text formatting and heading tags, Figure E.1 shows how Internet Explorer displays the following text:

```
<HTML>
<HEAD>
<TITLE>My Home Sweet Home Page</TITLE>
</HEAD>
<BODY>
This text appears in the body of the Web page.
<P>
This text appears in a new paragraph.
<P>
You can create various text formatting effects,
including <B>bold text</B>, <I>italic text</I>,
and <TT>monospaced text</TT>.
<H1>An H1 Heading</H1>
<H2>An H2 Heading</H2>
<H3>An H3 Heading</H3>
<H4>An H4 Heading</H4>
<H5>An H5 Heading</H5>
<H6>An H6 Heading</H6>
</BODY>
</HTML>
```

NOTE: DOWNLOAD THE CODE

I've placed all the examples in this appendix on my *Windows 95 Unleashed* Web site:

http://www.mcfedries.com/books/win95unleashed/

So if you don't feel like typing in the examples, feel free to surf by and grab them with your browser. To get the proper filenames, look at the Address box in each figure. In Figure E.1, for example, the displayed file is named Formats.htm.

FIGURE E.1.

*Examples of text
formatting and
heading tags.*

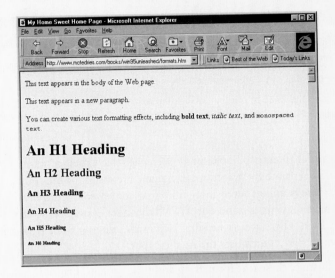

Setting Up Lists

HTML offers three different list styles: numbered lists, bulleted lists, and definition lists. This section takes you through the basics of each list type.

If you want to include a numbered list of items—a Top Ten list, bowling league standings, or any kind of ranking—you don't need to add the numbers yourself. Instead, you can use HTML *ordered lists* to make the Web browser generate the numbers for you.

Ordered lists use two types of tags:

■ The entire list is surrounded by the <OL> and </OL> tags.

■ Each item in the list is preceded by the <LI> (list item) tag.

The general setup looks like this:

```
<OL>
<LI>First item.
<LI>Second item.
<LI>Third item.
<LI>You get the idea.
</OL>
```

Of course, numbered lists aren't the only kinds of lists. If you want to list just a few points, a *bulleted list* might be more your style. They're called "bulleted" lists because a Web browser displays a small dot or square (depending on the browser) called a *bullet* to the left of each item.

The HTML tags for a bulleted list are pretty close to the ones you saw for a numbered list. As before, you precede each list item with the <LI> tag, but you enclose the entire list in the <UL>

and `</UL>` tags. Why `<UL>`? Well, what the rest of the world calls a bulleted list, the HTML powers-that-be call an *unordered list*. Here's how they work:

```
<UL>
<LI>First bullet point.
<LI>Second bullet point.
<LI>Third bullet point.
<LI>And so on
</UL>
```

The final type of list is called a *definition list*. It was originally used for dictionary-like lists in which each entry had two parts: a term and a definition. However, definition lists are useful for more than just definitions.

To define the two different parts of each entry in these lists, you need two different tags. The term is preceded by the `<DT>` tag, and the definition is preceded by the `<DD>` tag:

```
<DT>Term<DD>Definition
```

You then surround all your entries with the `<DL>` and `</DL>` tags to complete your definition list. Here's how the whole thing looks:

```
<DL>
<DT>A Term<DD>Its Definition
<DT>Another Term<DD>Another Definition
<DT>Yet Another Term<DD>Yet Another Definition
<DT>Etc.<DD>Abbreviation of a Latin phrase that means "and so forth."
</DL>
```

Figure E.2 shows how the various types of lists appear in Internet Explorer.

FIGURE E.2.

How HTML lists appear in a browser.

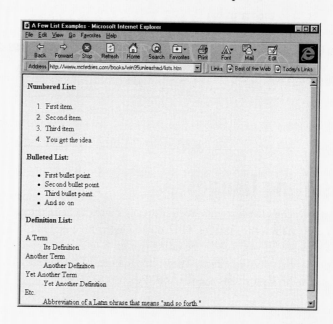

Working with Hyperlinks

The "H" in HTML stands for *hypertext*, which is dynamic text that defines a *link* to another document. The user clicks the hypertext, and the browser takes him to the linked document.

The HTML tags that set up links are `<A>` and `</A>`. The `<A>` tag is a little different from the other tags you've seen. Specifically, you don't use it by itself; instead, you add the address of the document to which you want to link. Here's how it works:

```
<A HREF="address">
```

Here, `HREF` stands for *hypertext reference*. Just replace `address` with the actual address of the Web page you want to use for the link (and, yes, you have to enclose the address in quotation marks). Here's an example:

```
<A HREF="http://www.mcp.com/sams/">
```

You're not done yet, though. Next, you have to give the reader some descriptive link text to click on. All you do is insert the text between the `<A>` and `</A>` tags, like so:

```
<A HREF="address">Link text goes here</A>
```

Here's an example:

```
Why not head to the <A HREF="http://www.mcp.com/sams">Sams home page</A>?
```

Figure E.3 shows how this looks in a Web browser. Notice how the browser highlights and underlines the link text. When you point the mouse cursor at the link, the address you specified appears in the status bar.

FIGURE E.3.

How Internet Explorer displays the hypertext link.

Inserting Images

If you're looking to make your Web site really stand out from the crowd, you need to go graphical with a few well-chosen images. How do you insert images if HTML files are text-only? As you'll see a bit later, all you'll really be doing (for each image you want to use) is adding a tag to the document that says, in effect, "Insert image here." This tag specifies the name of the graphics file, so the browser opens the file and displays the image.

Some computer wag once said that the nice thing about standards is that there are so many of them! Graphics files are no exception. It seems that every geek who ever gawked at graphics has invented his own format for storing them on disk. There are images in GIF, JPEG, BMP, PCX, TIFF, DIB, EPS, and TGA formats, and those are just the ones I can think of off the top of my head. How's a budding Web page architect supposed to make sense of all this?

The good news is that the vast majority of browsers can handle only two formats: GIF and JPEG. (And some older browsers can't even handle JPEG.) Internet Explorer, however, can also work with Windows' native BMP and DIB formats.

As I mentioned a moment ago, there's an HTML code that tells a browser to display an image: the `<IMG>` tag. Here's how it works:

```
<IMG SRC="filename">
```

Here, SRC is short for *source,* and `filename` is the name and path of the graphics file you want to display. For example, suppose you have an image named `logo.gif` and it's located in the Graphics folder. To add it to your page, you'd use the following line:

```
<IMG SRC="/Graphics/logo.gif">
```

> **NOTE: HANDLING NONGRAPHICAL BROWSERS**
>
> Some browsers can't handle images, and some surfers speed up their downloads by turning graphics off in their browser. In these situations, you should include a text description of the image by including the ALT attribute in the `<IMG>` tag:
>
> ```
> <IMG SRC="filename" ALT="Alternative text">
> ```

Setting Up Tables

An HTML table is a rectangular grid of rows and columns in a Web page. You can enter all kinds of information into a table, including text, numbers, links, and even images. Your tables will always begin with the following basic container:

```
<TABLE>
</TABLE>
```

All the other table tags fit between these two tags. There are two things you need to know about the `<TABLE>` tag:

- If you want your table to show a border, use the `<TABLE BORDER>` tag.
- If you don't want a border, just use `<TABLE>`.

Once that's done, most of your remaining table chores will involve the following four-step process:

1. Add a row.
2. Divide the row into the number of columns you want.
3. Insert data into each cell.
4. Repeat steps 1 through 3 until done.

To add a row, you toss a <TR> (table row) tag and a </TR> tag (its corresponding end tag) between <TABLE> and </TABLE>:

```
<TABLE BORDER>
<TR>
</TR>
</TABLE>
```

Now you divide that row into columns by placing the <TD> (table data) and </TD> tags between <TR> and </TR>. Each <TD>/</TD> combination represents one column (or, more specifically, an individual cell in the row). Therefore, if you want a three-column table, you'd do this:

```
<TABLE BORDER>
<TR>
<TD></TD>
<TD></TD>
<TD></TD>
</TR>
</TABLE>
```

Now you enter the row's cell data by typing text between each <TD> tag and its </TD> end tag:

```
<TABLE BORDER>
<TR>
<TD>Row 1, Column1</TD>
<TD>Row 1, Column2</TD>
<TD>Row 1, Column3</TD>
</TR>
</TABLE>
```

Remember that you can put any of the following within the <TD> and </TD> tags:

- Text
- HTML text-formatting tags (such as <B> and <I>)
- Links
- Lists
- Images

Once you've got your first row firmly in place, you simply repeat the procedure for the other rows in the table. For our sample table, here's the HTML that includes the data for all the rows:

```
<TABLE BORDER>
<TR>
<TD>Row 1,  Column1</TD>
```

```
<TD>Row 1, Column2</TD>
<TD>Row 1, Column3</TD>
</TR>
<TR>
<TD>Row 2,  Column1</TD>
<TD>Row 2, Column2</TD>
<TD>Row 2, Column3</TD>
</TR>
<TR>
<TD>Row 3,  Column1</TD>
<TD>Row 3, Column2</TD>
<TD>Row 3, Column3</TD>
</TR>
</TABLE>
```

Figure E.4 shows the result in Internet Explorer.

FIGURE E.4.

*An HTML table in
Internet Explorer.*

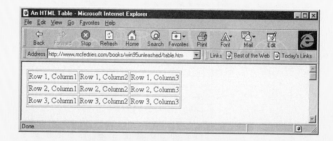

NOTE: TABLE HEADINGS

If you want to include headings at the top of each column, use <TH> (table heading) tags in the first row. Most browsers display text within a <TH>/</TH> combination in bold type. (Note, too, that you can just as easily use <TH> tags in the first column to create headers for each row.)

Working with HTML Forms

The Web pages we've talked about so far have been more or less static—just a collection of text and images that provide no user interaction. It's possible to provide a very basic level of interaction by including hyperlinks in your pages, as described earlier. Beyond this, however, there lies a whole genre of interactive Web pages called *forms*. The rest of this appendix introduces you to HTML forms.

To understand forms, think of the humble dialog box. Most modern applications display a dialog box whenever they need to extract information from you. For example, selecting a program's Print command will most likely result in some kind of Print dialog box showing up. The purpose of this dialog box is to pester you for information such as the number of copies you want, which pages you want to print, and so on.

A form is simply the Web page equivalent of a dialog box. It's a page that's populated with dialog box-like controls—such as text boxes, drop-down lists, and command buttons—that are used to obtain information from the reader. For example, Figure E.5 shows a form from my Web site. This is a "guest book" that people "sign" when they visit my Web abode. (At this point it's worth mentioning that although most new browsers can handle forms, some older browsers might choke on them.)

FIGURE E.5.

A form used as a guest book.

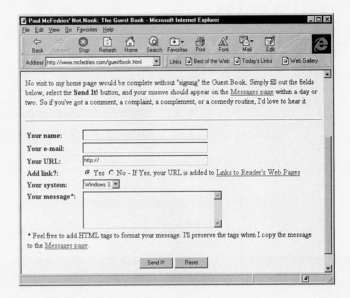

As you can imagine, guest books are only the beginning of what you can do with forms. If you publish a newsletter or magazine, you can use forms to gather information from subscribers. If your Web site includes pages with restricted access, you can use a form to get a person's user name and password for verification. If you have information in a database, you can use a form to construct a query.

It's one thing to build a form, but it's quite another to actually make it do something useful. In other words, having a form on your Web site doesn't do you much good unless you have some way to process whatever data the user enters into the form. There are a number of ways to go about this, but the most common is to create a "script" that runs on the Web server. This script reads the form data, performs some sort of operation on the data (such as adding it to a database), and then returns some kind of "results" page (which might only be a simple "Thanks!" message). These scripts must conform to the Common Gateway Interface (CGI) standard, which defines how the browser sends the form data to the server.

CGI is a complex topic that is beyond the scope of this book. If you'd like to learn more about it, I recommend the book *HTML & CGI Unleashed* (Sams Publishing, 1995). However, if you'll be using the form to work with an Access database on Microsoft's Internet Information Server

(IIS), you can also use Internet Database Connector (IDC) files and Active Server Pages to construct dynamic pages.

Defining the Form

In HTML, you define a form by entering the `<FORM>` and `</FORM>` tags within the body of the page. The `<FORM>` tag always includes a couple of extra attributes that tell the Web server how to process the form. Here's the general format:

```
<FORM ACTION="URL" METHOD=METHOD>
</FORM>
```

Here, the `ACTION` attribute tells the browser where to send the form's data. This will almost always be the script that you've set up to process the data. The *URL* part is the program's address.

The `METHOD` attribute tells the browser how to send the form's data to the URL specified by `ACTION`. You have two choices for `METHOD`:

> `GET`: The browser appends a question mark (?) and the data to the end of the `ACTION` attribute's URL and then requests this URL/data combination from the server.

> `POST`: The browser sends the data to the server in a separate message.

When deciding which method to use, bear in mind that each control on your form sends two things to the server: the name of the control and the data the user entered into the control. This means that a form could end up sending quite a bit of data to the server (especially if the form contains many controls or text boxes that could potentially hold long strings). However, some systems restrict the size of a URL sent to a Web server. This means that the `GET` method's URL/data combination might end up truncated. The `POST` method doesn't suffer from this problem, so you should always use it when large amounts of form data are involved. If you're not sure, use `POST`.

Let's look at an example. If you don't have a script for processing the form, you can still test the form by using one of the NCSA's public scripts. There's one for the `POST` method and one for the `GET` method. Here's how to use the `POST` method version:

```
<FORM ACTION="http://hoohoo.ncsa.uiuc.edu/htbin-post/post-query" METHOD=POST>
```

For the `GET` method, use the following:

```
<FORM ACTION="http://hoohoo.ncsa.uiuc.edu/htbin/query" METHOD=GET>
```

You can try this after you build a working form.

The Submit Button

Most dialog boxes, as I'm sure you know by now, have an OK button. Clicking this button says, in effect, "All right, I've made my choices. Now go put everything into effect." Forms also have command buttons that come in two flavors: submit and reset.

A submit button is the form equivalent of an OK dialog box button. When the reader clicks the submit button, the form data is shipped out to the program specified by the `<FORM>` tag's `ACTION` attribute. Here's the simplest format for the submit button:

```
<INPUT TYPE=SUBMIT>
```

As you'll see, most form elements use some variation of the `<INPUT>` tag. In this case, the `TYPE=SUBMIT` attribute tells the browser to display a command button labeled `Submit` (or, on some browsers, `Submit Query` or `Send`). Note that each form can have just one submit button.

If the standard `Submit` label is too prosaic for your needs, you can make up your own label, as follows:

```
<INPUT TYPE=SUBMIT VALUE="Label">
```

Here, `Label` is the label that will appear on the button.

Using a Submit Image

A variation on the submit button theme is the *submit image*. This is similar to a submit button, but the user clicks a picture instead. Here's the general tag syntax:

```
<INPUT TYPE=IMAGE SRC="Path">
```

Here, `Path` is the path and filename of the image file.

Starting Over: The Reset Button

If you plan on creating fairly large forms, you can do your readers a big favor by including a reset button somewhere on the form. A reset button clears all the data from the form's fields and reenters any default values that you specified in the fields. (I'll explain how to set up default values for each type of field as we go along.) Here's the tag to use to include a reset button:

```
<INPUT TYPE=RESET>
```

You can create a custom label by tossing the `VALUE` attribute into the `<INPUT>` tag, as in the following example:

```
<INPUT TYPE=RESET VALUE="Start From Scratch">
```

Using Text Boxes for Single-Line Text

For simple text entries, such as a person's name or address, use text boxes. Here's the basic format for a text box tag:

```
<INPUT TYPE=TEXT NAME="FieldName">
```

In this case, `FieldName` is a name you assign to the field that's unique among the other fields in the form. For example, to create a text box named FirstName, you'd enter the following:

```
<INPUT TYPE=TEXT NAME="FirstName">
```

Here's some HTML code that utilizes a few text boxes to gather some information from the user:

```
<HTML>
<HEAD>
<TITLE>Text Box Example</TITLE>
</HEAD>
<BODY>
<H3>Please tell me about yourself:</H3>
<FORM ACTION="http://hoohoo.ncsa.uiuc.edu/htbin-post/post-query" METHOD=POST>
First Name: <INPUT TYPE=TEXT NAME="First">
<P>
Last Name: <INPUT TYPE=TEXT NAME="Last">
<P>
Nickname: <INPUT TYPE=TEXT NAME="Nick">
<P>
Stage Name: <INPUT TYPE=TEXT NAME="Stage">
<P>
<INPUT TYPE=SUBMIT VALUE="Just Do It!">
<INPUT TYPE=RESET VALUE="Just Reset It!">
</FORM>
</BODY>
</HTML>
```

Figure E.6 shows how this code looks in Internet Explorer, and Figure E.7 shows the page that's returned by the NCSA server if you click the Just Do It! button. Notice how the page shows the names of the fields followed by the value the user entered.

FIGURE E.6.

A form with a few text boxes.

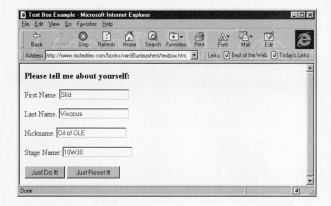

Text boxes also come with the following bells and whistles:

Setting the default value: If you'd like some text to appear in the field by default, include the VALUE attribute in the <INPUT> tag. For example, suppose you want to know the URL of the reader's home page. To include http:// in the field, you'd use the following tag:

```
<INPUT TYPE=TEXT NAME="URL" VALUE="http://">
```

FIGURE E.7.

An example of the page that's returned when you send the form data to the NCSA public server.

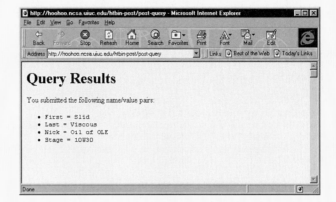

Setting the size of the box: To determine the length of the text box, use the SIZE attribute. (Note that this attribute affects only the size of the box, not the length of the entry; for the latter, use the MAXLENGTH attribute.) For example, the following tag displays a text box that is 40 characters long:

```
<INPUT TYPE=TEXT NAME="Address" SIZE=40>
```

Limiting the length of the text: In a standard text box, the reader can type away until his fingers are numb. If you'd prefer to restrict the length of the entry, use the MAXLENGTH attribute. For example, the following text box is used to enter a person's age; it restricts the length of the entry to three characters:

```
<INPUT TYPE=TEXT NAME="Age" MAXLENGTH=3>
```

NOTE: PASSWORD TEXT BOXES

A slight variation on the text box theme is the password box:

```
<INPUT TYPE=PASSWORD NAME="FieldName">
```

This is a text box that displays only asterisks as the user types.

Using Text Areas for Multiline Text

If you want to give your readers extra room to type their text, or if you need multiline entries (such as an address), you're better off using a *text area* than a text box. A text area is also a rectangle that accepts text input, but text areas can display two or more lines at once. Here's how they work:

```
<TEXTAREA NAME="FieldName" VALUE="Text" ROWS=TotalRows COLS=TotalCols WRAP>
</TEXTAREA>
```

Here, *FieldName* is a unique name for the field, *Text* is the initial text that appears in the field, *TotalRows* specifies the total number of lines displayed, and *TotalCols* specifies the total number of columns displayed. The WRAP attribute tells the browser to wrap the text onto the next line whenever the user's typing hits the right edge of the text area. (The WRAP attribute is supported by most browsers, but not all of them.) Note, too, that the <TEXTAREA> tag requires the </TEXTAREA> end tag. (If you want to include default values in the text area, just enter them—on separate lines, if necessary—between <TEXTAREA> and </TEXTAREA>.)

The following HTML tags show a text area in action, and Figure E.8 shows how it looks in a browser.

```
<HTML>
<HEAD>
<TITLE>Text Area Example</TITLE>
</HEAD>
<BODY>
<H3>Today's Burning Question</H3>
<HR>
<FORM ACTION="http://hoohoo.ncsa.uiuc.edu/htbin-post/post-query" METHOD=POST>
First Name: <INPUT TYPE=TEXT NAME="FirstName">
<P>
Last Name: <INPUT TYPE=TEXT NAME="LastName">
<P>
Today's <I>Burning Question</I>: <B>Why is Jerry Lewis so popular in France?</B>
<P>
Please enter your answer in the text area below:
<BR>
<TEXTAREA NAME="Answer" ROWS=10 COLS=60 WRAP>
</TEXTAREA>
<P>
<INPUT TYPE=SUBMIT VALUE="I Know!">
<INPUT TYPE=RESET>
</FORM>
</BODY>
</HTML>
```

FIGURE E.8.

An example of a text area.

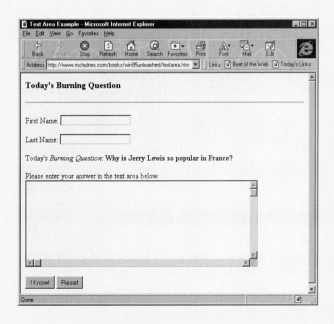

Toggling an Option On and Off with Check Boxes

If you want to elicit yes/no or true/false information from your readers, check boxes are a lot easier than having the user type in the required data. Here's the general format for an HTML check box:

```
<INPUT TYPE=CHECKBOX NAME="FieldName">
```

As usual, *FieldName* is a unique name for the field. You can also add the attribute CHECKED to the <INPUT> tag, which tells the browser to display the check box "pre-checked." Here's an example:

```
<INPUT TYPE=CHECKBOX NAME="Species" CHECKED>Human
```

Notice in this example that I placed some text beside the <INPUT> tag. This text is used as a label that tells the reader what the check box represents. Here's a longer example that uses a few check boxes. Figure E.9 shows how it looks.

```
<HTML>
<HEAD>
<TITLE>Check Box Example</TITLE>
</HEAD>
<BODY>
<H3>Welcome to Hooked On Phobics!</H3>
<HR>
<FORM ACTION="http://hoohoo.ncsa.uiuc.edu/htbin-post/post-query" METHOD=POST>
What's <I>your</I> phobia? (Please check all that apply):
<P>
<INPUT TYPE=CHECKBOX NAME="Ants">Myrmecophobia (Fear of ants)<BR>
<INPUT TYPE=CHECKBOX NAME="Bald">Peladophobia (Fear of becoming bald)<BR>
<INPUT TYPE=CHECKBOX NAME="Beards">Pogonophobia (Fear of beards)<BR>
<INPUT TYPE=CHECKBOX NAME="Bed">Clinophobia (Fear of going to bed)<BR>
<INPUT TYPE=CHECKBOX NAME="Chins">Geniophobia (Fear of chins)<BR>
<INPUT TYPE=CHECKBOX NAME="Flowers">Anthophobia (Fear of flowers)<BR>
<INPUT TYPE=CHECKBOX NAME="Flying">Aviatophobia (Fear of flying)<BR>
<INPUT TYPE=CHECKBOX NAME="Purple">Porphyrophobia (Fear of the color purple)<BR>
<INPUT TYPE=CHECKBOX NAME="Teeth">Odontophobia (Fear of teeth)<BR>
<INPUT TYPE=CHECKBOX NAME="Thinking">Phronemophobia (Fear of thinking)<BR>
<INPUT TYPE=CHECKBOX NAME="Vegetables">Lachanophobia (Fear of vegetables)<BR>
<INPUT TYPE=CHECKBOX NAME="Fear">Phobophobia (Fear of fear)<BR>
<INPUT TYPE=CHECKBOX NAME="Everything">Pantophobia (Fear of everything)<BR>
<P>
<INPUT TYPE=SUBMIT VALUE="Submit">
<INPUT TYPE=RESET>
</FORM>
</BODY>
</HTML>
```

Multiple Choice: Option Buttons

Instead of yes/no choices, you might want your readers to have a choice of three or four options. In this case, option buttons are your best bet. With option buttons, the user gets two or more choices, but he can choose only one. Here's the general format:

```
<INPUT TYPE=RADIO NAME="FieldName" VALUE="Value">
```

Figure E.9.

Some check box examples.

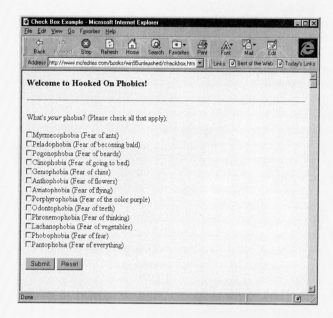

FieldName is the usual field name, but in this case you supply the same name to *all* the option buttons. That way, the browser knows which buttons are grouped. *Value* is a unique text string that specifies the value of the option when it's selected. In addition, you can also add CHECKED to one of the buttons to have the browser activate the option by default.

The following HTML document puts a few option buttons through their paces, as shown in Figure E.10.

```
<HTML>
<HEAD>
<TITLE>Radio Button Example</TITLE>
</HEAD>
<BODY>
<H3>Survey</H3>
<HR>
<FORM ACTION="http://hoohoo.ncsa.uiuc.edu/htbin-post/post-query" METHOD=POST>
Which of the following best describes your current salary level:
<UL>
<INPUT TYPE=RADIO NAME="Salary" VALUE="Salary1" CHECKED>Below the poverty line<BR>
<INPUT TYPE=RADIO NAME="Salary" VALUE="Salary2">Living wage<BR>
<INPUT TYPE=RADIO NAME="Salary" VALUE="Salary3">Comfy<BR>
<INPUT TYPE=RADIO NAME="Salary" VALUE="Salary4">DINK (Double Income, No Kids)<BR>
<INPUT TYPE=RADIO NAME="Salary" VALUE="Salary5">Rockefellerish<BR>
</UL>
Which of the following best describes your political leanings:
<UL>
<INPUT TYPE=RADIO NAME="Politics" VALUE="Politics1" CHECKED>So far left,
➥I'm right<BR>
<INPUT TYPE=RADIO NAME="Politics" VALUE="Politics2">Yellow Dog Democrat<BR>
<INPUT TYPE=RADIO NAME="Politics" VALUE="Politics3">Right down the middle<BR>
```

E

An HTML Primer

```
<INPUT TYPE=RADIO NAME="Politics" VALUE="Politics4">Country Club Republican<BR>
<INPUT TYPE=RADIO NAME="Politics" VALUE="Politics5">So far right, I'm left<BR>
</UL>
<P>
<INPUT TYPE=SUBMIT VALUE="Submit">
<INPUT TYPE=RESET>
</FORM>
</BODY>
</HTML>
```

Figure E.10.

A form that uses radio buttons for multiple-choice input.

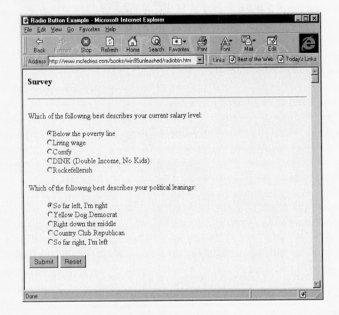

Selecting from Lists

Option buttons are a great way to give your readers multiple choices, but they get unwieldy if you have more than about five or six options. For longer sets of options, you're better off using lists. Setting up a list requires a bit more work than the other form tags. Here's the general format:

```
<SELECT NAME="FieldName" SIZE=Items>
<OPTION>First item text</OPTION>
<OPTION>Second item text</OPTION>
<OPTION>And so on...</OPTION>
</SELECT>
```

For the SIZE attribute, *Items* is the number of items you want the browser to display. If you omit SIZE, the list becomes a drop-down list. If SIZE is 2 or more, the list becomes a rectangle with scrollbars for navigating the choices. Also, you can insert the MULTIPLE attribute into the <SELECT> tag. This tells the browser to allow the user to select multiple items from the list.

Between the `<SELECT>` and `</SELECT>` tags are the `<OPTION>` and `</OPTION>` tags; these define the list items. If you add the `SELECTED` attribute to one of the items, the browser selects that item by default.

To show you some examples, the following document defines no less than three selection lists. Figure E.11 shows what the Internet Explorer browser does with them.

```
<HTML>
<HEAD>
<TITLE>Selection List Example</TITLE>
</HEAD>
<BODY>
<H3>Putting On Hairs: Reader Survey</H3>
<HR>
<FORM ACTION="http://hoohoo.ncsa.uiuc.edu/htbin-post/post-query" METHOD=POST>
Select your hair color:<BR>
<SELECT NAME="Color">
<OPTION>Black</OPTION>
<OPTION>Blonde</OPTION>
<OPTION SELECTED>Brunette</OPTION>
<OPTION>Red</OPTION>
<OPTION>Something neon</OPTION>
<OPTION>None</OPTION>
</SELECT>
<P>
Select your hair style:<BR>
<SELECT NAME="Style" SIZE=7>
<OPTION>Bouffant</OPTION>
<OPTION>Mohawk</OPTION>
<OPTION>Page Boy</OPTION>
<OPTION>Permed</OPTION>
<OPTION>Shag</OPTION>
<OPTION SELECTED>Straight</OPTION>
<OPTION>Style? What style?</OPTION>
</SELECT>
<P>
Hair products used in the last year:<BR>
<SELECT NAME="Products" SIZE=5 MULTIPLE>
<OPTION>Gel</OPTION>
<OPTION>Grecian Formula</OPTION>
<OPTION>Mousse</OPTION>
<OPTION>Peroxide</OPTION>
<OPTION>Shoe black</OPTION>
</SELECT>
<P>
<INPUT TYPE=SUBMIT VALUE="Hair Mail It!">
<INPUT TYPE=RESET>
</FORM>
</BODY>
</HTML>
```

FIGURE E.11.

A form with a few selection list examples.

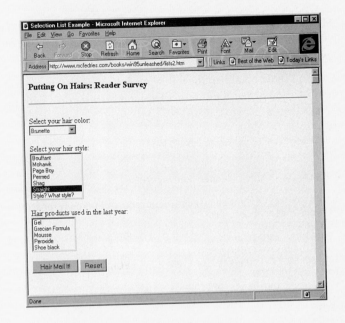

Hidden Controls

If you put together a lot of forms, you might find that some of them use similar layouts and controls. For forms that are only slightly dissimilar, it might not make sense to write separate scripts to handle the data. It would be nice if you could use a single script and have it branch depending on which form was being used.

An easy way to accomplish this is to include a "hidden" control in each form:

```
<INPUT TYPE=HIDDEN NAME="FieldName" VALUE="Value">
```

As the HIDDEN type implies, these controls aren't visible to the user. However, their NAME and VALUE attributes get sent to the script along with the rest of the form data. Consider the following example:

```
<INPUT TYPE=HIDDEN NAME="FormName" VALUE="Form A">
```

A script could test the FormName variable. If its value were Form A, it could process one set of instructions. If it were Form B, it could process a different set of instructions.

A Batch File Primer

IN THIS APPENDIX

As you saw back in Chapter 21, "DOS Isn't Dead: Optimizing DOS Applications Under Windows 95," DOS is still an indispensable part of computing life, and most power users will find themselves doing at least a little work at the command prompt. Part of that work might involve writing short batch file programs to automate routine chores, so that's where this appendix comes in. You'll learn what batch files are, how they work, and what commands are available.

Batch Files: Some Background

As you learned in Chapter 21, DOS uses a program called COMMAND.COM to handle anything you type at the prompt. COMMAND.COM has some DOS commands—such as COPY, DIR, and DEL—built right in (these are called *internal* commands).

For most anything else, including your software applications and the *external* DOS commands such as FORMAT, UNDELETE, and BACKUP, COMMAND.COM calls a separate program. DOS executes the command or program and returns to the prompt to wait for further orders.

If you tell COMMAND.COM to execute a batch file, however, things are a little different. COMMAND.COM goes into *batch mode,* where it takes all its input from the individual lines of a batch file. These lines are just commands that (in most cases) you otherwise have to type in yourself. COMMAND.COM repeats the following four-step procedure until it has processed each line in the batch file:

1. It reads a line from the batch file.
2. It closes the batch file.
3. It executes the command.
4. It reopens the batch file and reads the next line.

The main advantage of batch mode is that you can lump several commands together in a single batch file and tell DOS to execute them all simply by typing the name of the batch file. This is great for automating routine tasks such as backing up the Registry files or deleting leftover .TMP files at startup. And if you throw in any of the eight DOS commands that enhance batch files, you can do many other interesting and useful things.

Creating Batch Files

Before getting started with some concrete batch file examples, you need to know how to create them. Here are a few things to bear in mind:

- Batch files are simple text files, so Notepad is probably your best choice.
- If you decide to use WordPad or another word processor, make sure that the file you create is a text-only file.
- Save your batch files using the .BAT extension.

■ When naming your batch files, don't use the same name as a DOS command. For example, if you create a batch file that deletes some files, don't name it `DEL.BAT`. If you do, the batch file will never run! Here's why: When you enter something at the prompt, `COMMAND.COM` first checks to see if the command is an internal DOS command. If it's not, `COMMAND.COM` then checks for (in order) a .COM, .EXE, or .BAT file with a matching name. Because all external DOS commands use a .COM or .EXE extension, `COMMAND.COM` never bothers to check if your batch file even exists!

Once you've created the batch file, the rest is easy. Just enter any DOS commands exactly as you would at the DOS prompt (with a couple of exceptions, as you'll see later), and include whatever batch instructions you need.

A Home for Your Batch Files

Once you start using batch files regularly, you'll probably wonder how you got along without them. In fact, many people find that once they get the hang of batch files (which is usually pretty quickly), they seem to multiply when you're not looking.

Things can get pretty confusing if you have .BAT files scattered all over your hard disk. To remedy this, it makes sense to create a new folder to hold all your batch files.

To make this strategy effective, however, you have to tell DOS to look in the batch file folder to find these files. You do this with the PATH command, which has the following general form:

`PATH dir1;dir2;...`

Here, `dir1`, `dir2`, and so on are the names of folders. What this command effectively tells DOS is, "Whenever I run a command, if you can't find the appropriate file in the current folder, look for it in any of the folders listed in the PATH statement." In this case, you should enter at least the following (assuming that Windows 95 is installed in `C:\Windows` and that your batch file folder is `C:\Batch`):

`path c:\windows;c:\windows\command;c:\batch`

It's a good idea to put this command in your `AUTOEXEC.BAT` file so that it runs at startup each time and will be available in all your DOS sessions.

Using Batch Files to Start Programs

The most straightforward type of batch file is one that runs command-line programs. This usually involves changing to the program's folder and entering the command to start the program (including any switches or parameters required by the program). For example, here's a short batch file that changes to the Windows 95 folder and executes ScanDisk in automatic mode (assuming that Windows 95 is installed in `C:\Windows`):

```
C:
CD\WINDOWS
SCANDISK /N
```

The first two lines log on to drive C and change the folder to Windows. The third line starts ScanDisk with the /N switch (which tells ScanDisk to start and stop the check automatically).

Note that in this case it isn't really necessary to change to the Windows 95 folder, because that folder is in the default DOS PATH. I included the first two lines here to illustrate the basic procedure.

TIP: WAITING FOR THE PROGRAM TO FINISH

Batch files run asynchronously, which means that once the batch file executes the command to load the program, it continues processing the rest of its commands. If you'd prefer that the batch file suspend execution until the launched program is finished, use the START command with the /W parameter:

```
start /w program
```

Here, *program* is the executable file that launches the application.

REM: The Simplest Batch File Command

The first of the batch-file-specific DOS commands is REM (which stands for "remark"). This simple command tells DOS to ignore everything else on the current line. It's used by batch file mavens almost exclusively to add short comments to their files:

```
REM This batch file changes to the Windows 95
REM folder and starts ScanDisk in automatic mode.
C:
CD\WINDOWS
SCANDISK /N
```

Why would anyone want to do this? Well, it's probably not all that necessary with short, easy-to-understand batch files, but some of the more complex programs you'll be seeing later in this appendix can appear incomprehensible at first glance. A few pithy REM statements can help clear things up (not only for other people, but even for you if you haven't looked at the file in a couple of months).

CAUTION: DON'T OVERDO IT

It's best not to go overboard with REM statements. Having too many slows a batch file to a crawl. You really need only a few REM statements at the beginning to outline the purpose of the file and one or two to explain each of your more cryptic commands.

ECHO: A Voice for Your Batch Files

When it's processing a batch file, DOS normally lets you know what's going on by displaying each command before executing it. This is fine, but it's often better to include more expansive descriptions, especially if other people will be using your batch files. The ECHO batch file command lets you do just that.

For example, here's a simple batch file that deletes all the text files in the C:\Windows\Cookies folder and all the shortcut files in the C:\Windows\Recent folder and courteously tells the user what's about to happen:

```
ECHO This batch file will now delete all cookie text files
DEL C:\WINDOWS\COOKIES\*.TXT
ECHO This batch file will now delete the Documents list
DEL C:\WINDOWS\RECENT\*.LNK
```

The idea here is that when DOS stumbles upon the ECHO command, it simply displays the rest of the line on-screen. Sounds pretty simple, right? Well, here's what the output looks like when you run the batch file:

```
C:\>ECHO This batch file will now delete all cookie text files
This batch file will now delete all cookie text files
C:\>DEL C:\WINDOWS\COOKIES\*.TXT
C:\>ECHO This batch file will now delete the Documents list
This batch file will now delete the Documents list
C:\>DEL C:\WINDOWS\RECENT\*.LNK
```

What a mess! The problem is that DOS is displaying the command and ECHOing the line. Fortunately, DOS provides two solutions:

- To prevent DOS from displaying a command as it executes it, precede the command with the @ symbol:

  ```
  @ECHO To let you get a good night's sleep, this batch
  ```

- To prevent DOS from displaying any commands, place the following at the beginning of the batch file:

  ```
  ECHO OFF
  ```

This tells DOS not to display anything unless you explicitly invoke the ECHO command.

TIP: HIDING ECHO OFF

In the second solution, DOS still displays the ECHO OFF command. To prevent this, add an @ symbol so that the command becomes @ECHO OFF. Most batch file creators use this command instead of individual @ symbols.

Here's what the output looks like with the commands hidden:

```
This batch file will now delete all cookie text files
This batch file will now delete the Documents list
```

> **NOTE: ECHOING A BLANK LINE**
>
> You might think that you can display a blank line simply by using ECHO by itself. That would be nice, but it doesn't work (DOS just tells you the current state of ECHO—on or off). Instead, use ECHO. (that's ECHO followed by a dot).

The PAUSE Command

Sometimes you want to see something a batch file displays (such as a folder listing produced by the DIR command) before continuing. Or, you might want to alert users that something important is about to happen so that they can consider the possible ramifications (and bail out if they get cold feet). In both cases, you can use the PAUSE command to temporarily halt the execution of a batch file.

For example, the DOS FORMAT command has an undocumented /AUTOTEST switch that formats a floppy without prompting you for the disk or volume label or asking if you want to format another. This is pretty handy, but if you happen to forget to insert a disk, the entire format is abruptly aborted. Here's a batch file that formats a disk in drive A: with the /AUTOTEST switch but uses PAUSE to make sure you've inserted the disk:

```
REM This batch file formats a disk in drive A using
REM the /AUTOTEST switch. PAUSE is used to prompt the
REM user to insert a disk.
@ECHO OFF
CLS
ECHO About to run FORMAT on drive A . . .
ECHO To cancel, press Ctrl+C or Ctrl+Break.
ECHO Otherwise, place a floppy disk in drive A and then
PAUSE
FORMAT A: /AUTOTEST
```

When you run this batch file, the following output is produced:

```
About to run FORMAT on drive A . . .
To cancel, press Ctrl+C or Ctrl+Break.
Otherwise, place a floppy disk in drive A and then
Press any key to continue . . .
```

Notice that the PAUSE command displays the following:

```
Press any key to continue . . .
```

To continue processing the rest of the batch file, all you do is press any key. If you don't want to continue, you can cancel simply by pressing Ctrl-C or Ctrl-Break. DOS asks you to confirm:

```
Terminate batch job (Y/N)?
```

Either press Y to return to the prompt or N to continue the batch file.

> **NOTE: CANCELING BATCH FILES**
>
> Pressing Ctrl-C or Ctrl-Break (they're the same thing) cancels any batch file.

Using Variables for Batch File Flexibility

Most DOS commands require extra information such as a filename (for example, when you use COPY or DEL) or a folder path (such as when you use CD or MD). These extra pieces of information—they're called *variables* or, to use the guru term, *parameters*—give you the flexibility to specify exactly how you want a command to work. You can add the same level of flexibility to your batch files; this section will show you how.

How Variables Help

To see how variables work in a batch file, look at the following example:

```
@ECHO OFF
ECHO.
ECHO The first parameter is %1
ECHO The second parameter is %2
ECHO The third parameter is %3
```

As you can see, this batch file doesn't do much except ECHO four lines to the screen (the first of which is just a blank line). Curiously, however, each ECHO command ends with a percent sign (%) and a number. Type in and save this batch file as PARAMETERS.BAT. Then, to see what these unusual symbols mean, enter the following command at the DOS prompt:

```
parameters Tinkers Evers Chance
```

This produces the following output:

```
C:\BATCH>parameters Tinkers Evers Chance
The first parameter is Tinkers
The second parameter is Evers
The third parameter is Chance
```

The first line in the output is produced by the following ECHO command in PARAMETERS.BAT:

```
ECHO The first parameter is %1
```

F

A BATCH FILE
PRIMER

When DOS sees the %1 symbol in a batch file, it examines the original command and looks for the first word after the batch filename and then replaces %1 with that word. In the example, the first word after parameters is Tinkers, so DOS uses that to replace %1. (This is why batch file programmers often call %1 a *replaceable parameter*.) Only when it has done this does it proceed to ECHO the line to the screen.

The replaceable parameter %2 is similar, except that, in this case, DOS looks for the second word after the batch filename (Evers in this example).

NOTE: EXTRA PARAMETERS ARE IGNORED

If your batch file command has more parameters than the batch file is looking for, the extras are ignored. For example, adding a fourth parameter to the PARAMETERS command line has no effect on the file's operation.

Let's look at a real-world example. Consider the following slightly useful but highly inflexible batch file, called NEWFOLDER.BAT:

```
@ECHO OFF
CLS
MD \GALLERIA
CD \GALLERIA
```

This batch file simply creates a new folder called GALLERIA and then changes to it. You'll be surprised how often you need to do something like this, so it makes sense to try to automate the whole procedure.

Unfortunately, this isn't the best way to go about it. You could set up a batch file each time you needed to create and move to a folder, but I assume that you want to spend your remaining years in a more fruitful enterprise. Instead, you can use replaceable parameters to add instant flexibility to NEWFOLDER.BAT:

```
@ECHO OFF
CLS
MD %1
CD %1
```

Now, if you want to create and move to a new GALLERIA folder, enter the following command:

```
newfolder \galleria
```

DOS replaces each %1 in NEWFOLDER.BAT with \galleria (the first word after newfolder), so the batch file works as it did before. The difference, of course, is that you can now use it for other folders as well. For example, to create a new MALL folder and move to it, use the following command:

```
newfolder \mall
```

> **NOTE: REPLACEABLE PARAMETER LIMITATION**
>
> You can't use more than nine replaceable parameters in a batch file (%1 through %9). Note, however, that there is a tenth replaceable parameter (%0). It holds the name of the batch file itself.

Improving on DOS

Because a batch file's replaceable parameters work just like the parameters used in DOS commands, it's not hard to create batch files that mimic—and even improve upon—the standard DOS fare.

Making DEL Safer

Probably 99.9 percent of all accidental command-line deletions occur when you use wildcard characters to delete multiple files. A question mark in the wrong place, or a *.* in the wrong folder, can lead to disaster.

It would help if you could see a list of all the files you were about to delete and then have the option of canceling the deletion if things weren't right. The easiest way to do this, of course, is to run a DIR command using the same file specification you would use with DEL. But it's usually a pain typing two commands and making sure that you get the ?s and *s in the right place each time. This situation cries out for a batch file, and here it is (it's called SAFEDELETE.BAT):

```
@ECHO OFF
CLS
ECHO %0 %1
ECHO.
ECHO Here's a list of the files that will be deleted:
REM Display a wide DIR list in alphabetical order
DIR %1 /ON /W
ECHO.
ECHO To cancel the deletion, press Ctrl+C. Otherwise use the following:
PAUSE
DEL %1
```

You use SAFEDELETE.BAT just like the DEL command. For example, to delete all the .BAK files in the current folder, enter the following:

```
safedel *.bak
```

The following list is a quick summary of what happens:

- The command ECHO %0 %1 simply redisplays the batch file name (%0) and the file specification (%1) for reference.

- The DIR %1 /ON /W command is used to get an alphabetical listing (in wide format so that you can see more files) of everything that's about to be deleted.

■ The batch file then runs PAUSE so that you can examine the files.

■ If you decide to continue, the DEL %1 command takes care of the job.

CAUTION: WATCH PERCENT SIGNS IN FILENAMES

The percent sign (%) is a perfectly good character to use in a filename, but if you try to reference a file named, for example, PERCNT%.XLS, you'll run into problems. The reason is that when DOS processes batch files, it mindlessly deletes any single occurrences of % as part of its parameter replacement chores. So PERCNT%.XLS becomes PERCNT.XLS, and things go haywire. To fix this, use double percent signs when referring to the file in a batch command (for example, PERCNT%%.XLS).

Changing Folders and Drives in One Step

The CD command falls down on the job if you need to change to a folder on a different drive. You have to change to the drive first and then run CD. Use CDD.BAT to do this all in one command:

```
@ECHO OFF
%1:
CD \%2
```

For example, to change to the A: drive's BACKUP folder, simply use the following command:

```
cdd a backup
```

If you hate typing backslashes, you can avoid them altogether by adding a couple extra CD commands:

```
@ECHO OFF
%1:
CD \%2
CD %3
CD %4
```

Now, to change to the \BACKUP\123\DATA folder on drive A:, enter the following:

```
cdd a backup 123 data
```

Excluding Files from a Copy Command

The wildcard characters are used to include multiple files in a single DOS command. But what if you want to exclude certain files? For example, suppose you have a WP\DOCS folder that has files with various extensions—.DOC, .TXT, .WP, and so on. What do you do if you want to copy all the files to drive A: except those with a .TXT extension? One solution is to use separate XCOPY commands for each extension you do need, but that's too much work (and besides, you might miss some). Instead, try this batch file (it's called DONTCOPY.BAT):

```
@ECHO OFF
CLS
ATTRIB +H %1
ECHO.
ECHO Copying all files to %2 except %1:
ECHO.
XCOPY32 *.* %2
ATTRIB -H %1
```

To use this batch file to copy all the files in the current folder to drive A:, except, for example, those with the extension .TXT, use the following command:

```
dontcopy *.txt a:
```

The secret here is that DOS won't copy hidden files. So DONTCOPY.BAT uses the ATTRIB command to hide the files that you want to ignore. The first command, ATTRIB +H %1, does just that. So now all that's needed is an XCOPY32 command that copies everything that's not hidden (use *.* to do this) to the target (%2). When that's done, DONTCOPY.BAT uses another ATTRIB command to show the files.

CAUTION: CHECK FOR THE DESTINATION

To be safe, DONTCOPY.BAT should check to make sure that a destination parameter (%2) was entered. This can be done, but you need to use the batch file commands IF and GOTO, which are discussed later in this appendix.

NOTE: YOU CAN APPLY THIS TRICK TO OTHER COMMANDS

You can use the same idea to exclude files with other DOS commands. For example, DOS won't delete or rename hidden files, so it wouldn't be hard to create the appropriate DONTDELETE.BAT and DONTRENAME.BAT batch files.

F

A BATCH FILE PRIMER

SHIFT: A Different Approach to Parameters

Although you won't be using it until later in this appendix, you should know that there's another way to handle parameters inside batch files—the SHIFT command. To see how it works, rewrite the PARAMETERS.BAT file to get PARAMETERS2.BAT:

```
@ECHO OFF
ECHO.
ECHO The first parameter is %1
SHIFT
ECHO The second parameter is %1
SHIFT
ECHO The third parameter is %1
```

If you enter the command parameters2 Tinkers Evers Chance, you get the same output as before:

```
C:\BATCH>parameters2 Tinkers Evers Chance
The first parameter is Tinkers
The second parameter is Evers
The third parameter is Chance
```

How does this work? Well, each SHIFT command shuffles the parameters down one position. In particular, %2 goes to %1, so the following command really does display the second parameter:

```
ECHO The second parameter is %1
```

All the other parameters change as well, of course: %3 goes to %2, %1 goes to %0, and %0 heads off into oblivion.

This sort of behavior is handy for two types of situations:

- Batch files that require more than 10 parameters. There aren't a lot of times when you'll need this many variables, but at least you know you can handle it when the need arises.

- Batch files that use a varying number of parameters. This is a much more common scenario; you'll see a couple of examples a bit later.

> **NOTE: SHIFT NEEDS IF**
>
> Just so you know, I'm passing the buck on the SHIFT examples, because to use it properly you need an IF command to test whether there are any more parameters left to shift. I'll discuss the IF command later in this appendix.

Looping with the FOR Command

Pound for pound, the FOR command is easily the most underutilized and misunderstood of all DOS commands. This is bad news, because FOR is an extremely powerful weapon that shouldn't be left out of any DOS guru's arsenal. The problem, I think, is that FOR has a somewhat bizarre syntax that makes it wildly unappealing at first glance. So before we look at it, I'll give you some background.

Looping: The Basics

If you wanted to instruct someone on how to dress each day, you might begin with a simple step-by-step approach:

1. Step 1: Put on underwear.
2. Step 2: Put on socks.

3. Step 3: Put on pants.

4. Step 4: Put on shirt.

This is fine, but you can make things simpler by creating a list—underwear, socks, pants, shirt—and telling the person to put on everything in this list in the order they appear. Now, instead of a linear approach, you've got a primitive "loop": The person looks at the list, puts on the first item, looks at the list again, puts on the second item, and so on.

Now you can formalize the instructions into a single, pithy statement: for each item *X* in the following set (underwear, socks, pants, shirt), put on *X*.

Programmers often use loops like this to add generality to programs. Instead of writing a dozen different instructions, they can often write a single, generic instruction (something like put on *X*) and loop through it a dozen times, each time supplying it with a different input (underwear, socks, and so on).

Finally, the FOR Command

The FOR command is a batch file's way of looping through an instruction:

```
FOR %%variable IN (set) DO command
```

Looks like bad news, doesn't it? Well, see how it looks if you plug in the dressing instructions:

```
FOR %%X IN (underwear, socks, pants, shirt) DO put on %%X
```

That's a little more comprehensible, so let's break down the FOR command for a closer look:

`%%variable`	This is the variable that changes each time through the loop (`%%X` in the example). You can use any single character after the two `%` signs (except 0 through 9). There are two `%` signs because, as I explained earlier, DOS deletes single ones as it processes the batch file.
`IN (set)`	This is the list (it's called the *set* officially) of choices for `%%X` (in the example, underwear, socks, and so on). You can use spaces, commas, or semicolons to separate the items in the set, and you must enclose them in parentheses.
`DO command`	For each item in the set, the batch file performs whatever instruction is given by *command* (such as put on `%%X`). The variable `%%X` is normally found somewhere in *command*.

A Simple Batch File Example

Here's an example of the FOR command in a simple batch file that might help clear things up:

```
@ECHO OFF
FOR %%B IN (Tinkers Evers Chance) DO ECHO %%B
```

This batch file (call it PARAMETERS3.BAT) produces the following output:

```
C:\BATCH>parameters3
Tinkers
Evers
Chance
```

All this does is loop through the three items in the set (Tinkers, Evers, and Chance) and substitute each one for %%B in the command ECHO %%B. In other words, this FOR loop is equivalent to the following three ECHO commands:

```
ECHO Tinkers
ECHO Evers
ECHO Chance
```

Different Sets for Different Folks

The set in a FOR command can hold more than simple strings such as Tinkers and Evers. The real power of FOR becomes evident when you use file specifications, DOS command names, and even replaceable parameters as part of a set.

For example, have you ever copied a bunch of files into the wrong folder? This happens occasionally, and it's usually a mess to clean up because these files get all mixed up with whatever was already in the folder. Before smashing your monitor, check out the following batch file (called CLEANUP.BAT):

```
@ECHO OFF
FOR %%F IN (*.*) DO DEL C:\WRONGDIR\%%F
```

This batch file assumes that you copied all the files from the current folder into the WRONGDIR folder. In this case, the set is given by the *.* file specification. FOR ends up looping through every file in the current folder and, for each one, deleting it in the WRONGDIR folder.

To see how to use DOS command names in a set, you can redo the NEWFOLDER.BAT batch file created earlier. Here's NEWFOLDER2.BAT:

```
@ECHO OFF
CLS
FOR %%C IN (MD CD) DO %%C %1
```

As you can see, the set consists of the two DOS commands MD and CD. These are substituted for %%C each time through the loop, so this single FOR command is equivalent to the two commands in NEWFOLDER.BAT:

```
MD %1
CD %1
```

The FOR command is very powerful if you use replaceable parameters inside the set. The most common use of this potent combination is to create your own versions of DOS commands that accept multiple parameters. For example, here's a batch file (called SUPERDELETE.BAT) that deletes up to nine file specifications at once:

```
@ECHO OFF
ECHO.
```

```
ECHO About to delete the following files:
ECHO %1 %2 %3 %4 %5 %6 %7 %8 %9
ECHO.
ECHO Press Ctrl+C to cancel. Otherwise,
PAUSE
FOR %%F IN (%1 %2 %3 %4 %5 %6 %7 %8 %9) DO DEL %%F
```

To use this file to delete, for example, all files in the current folder that have the extensions .BAK, .TMP, and .$$$, use the following command:

```
superdelete *.bak *.tmp *.$$$
```

DOS must do two things to process the FOR command in SUPERDEL.BAT. First, it replaces the parameters inside the set so that the command looks like this:

```
FOR %%F IN (*.bak *.tmp *.$$$) DO DEL %%F
```

Then it loops through the set to delete each file specification. In the end, this is equivalent to the following three DEL commands:

```
DEL *.bak
DEL *.tmp
DEL *.$$$
```

Making Smart Batch Files

The things you learned about in the last few sections—replaceable parameters and the SHIFT and FOR commands—are great for creating limber batch programs that can handle different inputs. But as far as the batch files we've seen—well, let's be honest: They haven't been terribly bright. What you need now is to learn how to construct batch files that can make decisions and alter their behavior based on those decisions. That's what the next few sections are about.

Tell Your Batch Files Where to Go

Your basic batch file lives a simple, linear existence. The first command gets processed, then the second, the third, and so on to the end of the file. It's pretty boring, but that's all you need most of the time.

However, there are situations in which this linear approach breaks down. For example, depending on a parameter or the result of a previous command, you might need to skip over a line or two. How do you do this? With the GOTO batch command:

```
...
... (the first batch commands)
...
GOTO NEXT
...
... (the batch commands that get skipped)
...
:NEXT
...
... (the rest of the batch commands)
...
```

F

A BATCH FILE
PRIMER

Here, the GOTO command is telling the batch file to look for a line that begins with a colon and the word NEXT (this is called a *label*) and to ignore any commands in between.

Let's look at an example. Suppose your computer has two high-density disk drives and that drive A: accepts 3½-inch disks and drive B: accepts 5¼-inch disks. If you regularly format double-density disks in these drives, it can be a pain to remember the correct switches for each one. (I realize this is an unlikely scenario in this day and age, but it illustrates my point.)

One solution would be to set up two batch files that use the appropriate FORMAT command to format double-density disks in each drive. A much more elegant solution (and one that would allow me, finally, to get to the point) would be a single batch file (I'll call it DDFORMAT.BAT) that would accept the drive letter as a parameter. So the command ddformat a would automatically format a double-density disk in drive A:, and ddformat b would do the same for drive B:.

The tricky part is how to handle two different FORMAT statements in a single batch file. The old linear approach just won't cut it, but GOTO makes it easy:

```
REM A batch file to handle formatting double-density
REM disks in both a 3.5-inch high-density drive
REM (drive A) or a 5.25-inch high-density drive
REM (drive B).
@ECHO OFF
CLS
GOTO %1
:A
FORMAT A: /F:720
GOTO END
:B
FORMAT B: /F:360
:END
```

The command GOTO %1 becomes GOTO A or GOTO B, depending on the parameter you use in the command. If it's A, the batch file skips down to the :A label, formats the disk accordingly, and then skips to :END to avoid the second FORMAT statement. With the B parameter, the program skips past the first FORMAT to the :B label and then formats the disk in drive B:.

Another handy use of the GOTO command is for those times when you need to add copious comments to a batch file. As you know, you normally use REM to add batch file remarks. DOS doesn't try to execute these lines, but it still has to read them, and this can really slow things down. Here's a way to use GOTO to get around this (literally!):

```
@ECHO OFF
GOTO START
You place your batch file comments here. Notice how
I'm not using the REM command at all. This not only
saves typing (a constant goal for some of us) but it
certainly looks a lot nicer, don't you think?
:START
...
... (Batch file commands)
...
```

As you can see, GOTO just leaps over the comments to end up at the :START label. DOS doesn't even know that the comments exist.

Handling Forks in a Batch File's Road

We make decisions all the time. Some are complex and require intricate levels of logic to answer (Should I get married? Should I start a chinchilla farm?). Others are simpler and depend only on existing conditions (the proverbial fork in the road):

- If it's raining, I'll stay home and work. Otherwise, I'll go to the beach.
- If this milk smells OK, I'll drink some. Otherwise, I'll throw it out.

No batch file (indeed, no software program yet developed) is sophisticated enough to tackle life's complex questions, but the simpler condition-based decisions are no problem. Here are a few examples of what a batch file might have to decide:

- If the %2 equals /Q, jump to the Quick Format section. Otherwise, do a regular format.
- If the user forgets to enter a parameter, cancel the program. Otherwise, continue processing the batch file.
- If the file that the user wants to move already exists in the new folder, display a warning. Otherwise, proceed with the move.
- If the last command failed, display an error message and cancel the program. Otherwise, continue.

Using IF for Batch File Decision-Making

For these types of decisions, you need to use the IF batch command. IF has the following general form:

```
IF condition command
```

The *condition* is a test that evaluates to a yes or no answer ("Is it raining?" "Did the user forget a parameter?"). The *command* is what gets executed if the test produces a positive response ("Go to the beach," "Cancel the batch file"). The next few sections discuss the various ways you can use IF in your batch files.

Testing Parameters with IF

One of the most common uses of the IF command is to check the parameters that the user entered and proceed accordingly. For example, in the DDFORMAT.BAT batch file you saw earlier, the program formatted drive A: if %1 was A, and it formatted drive B: if %1 was B. You can use IF to rewrite the batch file:

```
@ECHO OFF
CLS
IF "%1"=="A" FORMAT A: /F:360
IF "%1"=="B" FORMAT B: /F:720
```

F

A BATCH FILE
PRIMER

In both `IF` statements, the command part is easy to spot—it's just the two `FORMAT` statements. The condition is a little trickier. Let's look at the first one: `"%1"=="A"`. Remember that the condition is always a question with a yes or no answer. In this case, the question boils down to the following:

```
Is the first parameter (%1) equal to A?
```

(The double equal sign (==) looks weird, but that's just how you compare two strings of characters in a batch file.) If the answer is yes, the format proceeds. If it's no, the batch file moves on to the next `IF`, which checks to see if the parameter was `"B"`.

NOTE: USE QUOTATION MARKS

Strictly speaking, you don't need to include the quotation marks ("). Using %1==A accomplishes the same thing. However, I prefer to use them for two reasons: First, it makes it clearer that the `IF` condition is comparing strings; second, as you'll see in the next section, the quotation marks let you check whether the user forgot to enter a parameter at all.

NOTE: A FLAW IN THE BATCH FILE

This batch file has a serious flaw that will prevent it from working under certain conditions. Specifically, if you use the lowercase "a" or "b" as a parameter, nothing happens because, to the `IF` command, "a" is different from "A". The solution is to add extra `IF` commands to handle this:

```
IF "%1"=="a" FORMAT A: /F:360
```

Checking for Missing Parameters

Proper batch file techniques require you to not only check to see what a parameter is, but also whether or not one exists at all! This can be vital, because a missing parameter can cause a batch file to crash and burn. For example, earlier I showed you a batch file called `DONTCOPY.BAT` designed to copy all files in the current folder to a new destination (given by the second parameter) except those you specified (given by the first parameter). Here's the listing to refresh your memory:

```
@ECHO OFF
CLS
ATTRIB +H %1
ECHO.
ECHO Copying all files to %2 except %1:
ECHO.
XCOPY32 *.* %2
ATTRIB -H %1
```

What happens if the user forgets to add the destination parameter (%2)? Well, the XCOPY32 command becomes XCOPY32 *.*, which terminates the batch file with the following error:

```
File cannot be copied onto itself
```

The solution is to add an IF command that checks to see whether %2 exists:

```
@ECHO OFF
CLS
IF "%2"=="" GOTO ERROR
ATTRIB +H %1
ECHO.
ECHO Copying all files to %2 except %1:
ECHO.
XCOPY32 *.* %2
ATTRIB -H %1
GOTO END
:ERROR
ECHO You didn't enter a destination!
ECHO Please try again...
:END
```

The condition "%2"=="" is literally comparing %2 to nothing (""). If this proves to be true, the program jumps (using GOTO) to the :ERROR label, and some sort of message is displayed to admonish the user. Notice, too, that if everything is okay (that is, the user entered a second parameter), the batch file executes normally and jumps to the :END label to avoid displaying the error message.

The SHIFT Command Redux

Now that you know a little about how IF works, I can show you how to use the SHIFT command introduced earlier. Recall that SHIFT operates by shuffling the batch file parameters down one position, so that %1 becomes %0, %2 becomes %1, and so on. The most common use of this apparently strange behavior is to process batch files with an unknown number of parameters. As an example, redo the SUPERDELETE.BAT batch file so that it can delete any number of file specifications:

```
@ECHO OFF
IF "%1"=="" GOTO NO_FILES
:START
ECHO Now deleting %1 . . .
DEL %1
SHIFT
IF "%1"=="" GOTO DONE
GOTO START
:NO_FILES
ECHO You didn't enter a file spec!
:DONE
```

The first IF is familiar—it just looks for a missing parameter and, if that proves to be the case, leaps to :NO_FILES and displays a message. Otherwise, the program deletes the first file specification and then SHIFTs everything down. What was %2 is now %1, so you need the second IF to check the new %1. If it's blank, this means that the user didn't enter any more file specs, and the program jumps to :DONE. Otherwise, you loop back to :START and do it all again.

> ## CAUTION: WATCH FOR ENDLESS GOTO LOOPS
>
> As you can see from the preceding example, it's OK to use GOTO to jump backward in a file and create a loop. This is often better than a FOR loop, because instead of a single command, you can process any number of commands. However, you need to be careful, or you might end up in the never-never land of an endless loop. Always include an IF command that will take you out of the loop once some condition has been met (such as running out of parameters).

Using IF to Check Whether or Not a File Exists

Another variation of IF is the IF EXIST command, which checks for the existence of a file. This is handy, for example, when you're using COPY or MOVE. You can check, first of all, whether or not the file you want to copy or move exists. Second, you can check to see if a file with the same name already exists in the target folder. (As you probably know, a file that has been copied over by another of the same name is downright impossible to recover.) Here's a batch file called SAFEMOVE.BAT, which uses the MOVE command to move a file but first checks the file and then the target folder:

```
@ECHO OFF
CLS
IF EXIST %1 GOTO SO_FAR_SO_GOOD
ECHO The file %1, like, doesn't exist!
GOTO END
:SO_FAR_SO_GOOD
IF NOT EXIST %2 GOTO MOVE_IT
ECHO The file %1 exists on the target folder!
ECHO Press Ctrl+C to bail out or, to keep going,
PAUSE
:MOVE_IT
MOVE %1 %2
:END
```

To explain what's happening, I'll use a sample command:

```
safemove moveme.txt c:\docs\moveme.txt
```

The first IF tests for the existence of %1 (MOVEME.TXT in the example). If there is such a file, the program skips to the :SO_FAR_SO_GOOD label. Otherwise, it tells the user that the file doesn't exist, and then jumps down to :END.

The second IF is slightly different. In this case, I want to continue only if MOVEME.TXT doesn't exist in the \DOCS folder, so I add NOT to the condition. (You can include NOT in any IF condition.) If this proves true (that is, the file given by %2 doesn't exist), the file skips to :MOVE_IT and performs the move. Otherwise, the user is warned and given an opportunity to cancel.

> ### TIP: CHECKING FOR AN EXISTING FOLDER
>
> Some batch files need to know if a folder exists (especially those such as NEWFOLDER.BAT, discussed earlier, which creates new folders). Trying to plug a folder name into an IF EXIST condition won't work, but there's a trick that will. If you want to see if, say, the A:\BACKUP folder exists, use the following condition:
>
> ```
> IF EXIST A:\BACKUP\NUL
> ```
>
> It's a quirk of DOS that the NUL device "exists" in every folder and that DOS treats it as a file. So this condition will be true only if there's a folder called A:\BACKUP.

Checking for Command Errors

Good batch files (especially those that other people will be using) always assume that if anything bad can happen, it will. So far you've seen how IF can handle missing parameters and file problems, but there's much more that can go haywire. For example, what if a batch file tries to use XCOPY32, but there's not enough memory? Or what if the user presses Ctrl-C during a format or copy? It might seem impossible to check for these kinds of errors, but not only is it possible, it's really quite easy.

When certain DOS commands finish, they always file a "report" on the progress of the operation. This report, or *exit code,* is really just a number that tells DOS how things went. For example, Table F.1 lists the exit codes used by the XCOPY32 command.

Table F.1. XCOPY32 exit codes.

Exit Code	What It Means
0	Everything's OK; the files were copied.
1	Nothing happened because no files were found to copy.
2	The user pressed Ctrl-C to abort the copy.
4	The command failed because there wasn't enough memory or disk space, or because there was something wrong with the command's syntax.
5	The command failed because of a disk error.

What does all this mean for your batch files? Well, you can use yet another variation of the IF command—IF ERRORLEVEL—to test for these exit codes. For example, here's a batch file called CHECKCOPY.BAT, which uses some of the XCOPY32 exit codes to check for errors:

```
@ECHO OFF
XCOPY %1 %2
IF ERRORLEVEL 4 GOTO ERROR
IF ERRORLEVEL 2 GOTO CTRL-C
```

F

A BATCH FILE
PRIMER

```
IF ERRORLEVEL 1 GOTO NO_FILES
GOTO DONE
:ERROR
ECHO Bad news! The copy failed because there wasn't
ECHO enough memory or disk space or because there was
ECHO something wrong with your file specs . . .
GOTO DONE
:CTRL-C
ECHO Hey, what gives? You pressed Ctrl+C to abort . . .
GOTO DONE
:NO_FILES
ECHO Bad news! No files were found to copy . . .
:DONE
```

As you can see, the ERRORLEVEL conditions simply check for the individual exit codes and then use GOTO to jump to the appropriate label.

NOTE: DOS STORES THE EXIT CODE

How does a batch file know what a command's exit code was? Well, when DOS gets an exit code from a command, it stores it in a special data area set aside for exit code information. When DOS sees the IF ERRORLEVEL command in a batch file, it retrieves the exit code from the data area so that it can be compared to whatever is in the IF condition.

NOTE: SCANDISK EXIT CODES

Here's a list of exit codes generated by ScanDisk:

Exit Code	What It Means
0x00	The drive was checked, and no errors were found.
0x01	Errors were found, and all were fixed.
0xFA	The check couldn't start because ScanDisk couldn't load or find DSKMAINT.DLL.
0xFB	The check couldn't start due to insufficient memory.
0xFC	Errors were found, but at least some weren't fixed.
0xFD	At least one of the specified drives couldn't be checked.
0xFE	The user canceled the check.
0xFF	The check was terminated because of an error.

One of the most important things to know about the IF ERRORLEVEL test is how DOS interprets it. For example, consider the following IF command:

```
IF ERRORLEVEL 2 GOTO CTRL-C
```

DOS interprets this command as "If the exit code from the last command is equal to or greater than 2, jump to the :CTRL-C label." This has two important consequences for your batch files:

■ The test IF ERRORLEVEL 0 doesn't tell you much because it's always true. If you simply want to find out if the command failed, use the test IF NOT ERRORLEVEL 0.

■ To get the correct results, always test the highest ERRORLEVEL first and then work your way down.

Do You Need to Get Input from the User [Y,N]?

One of the nicest batch-file features is the ability to ask the user questions and perform different actions based on the answer. This neat trick is handled by the CHOICE command. In its simplest form, you use CHOICE like this:

```
CHOICE Are you sure
```

When DOS processes this line, you see the following query:

```
Are you sure[Y,N]?
```

DOS then waits for the user to press either Y or N and then continues. The user's selection is stored in the ERRORLEVEL. The first choice (Y) would be ERRORLEVEL 1, and the second choice (N) would be ERRORLEVEL 2. So all you need is one or more IF ERRORLEVEL tests to find out what the user selected.

Check out an example. Have you ever tried to change to a folder, only to have DOS give you an Invalid directory message because the folder doesn't exist? Here's a batch file that checks to see if the folder exists and asks if you want to create it if it doesn't:

```
@ECHO OFF
IF EXIST %1\NUL GOTO OK
ECHO The folder %1 doesn't exist.
CHOICE Do you want to create it
IF ERRORLEVEL 2 GOTO EXIT
MD %1
:OK
CD %1
:EXIT
```

If the folder exists, the program jumps to :OK and runs the CD command. Otherwise, the user is asked if he wants to create it. If he presses N (ERRORLEVEL 2), the batch files skips to :EXIT, and nothing is done. Otherwise, the folder is created with MD.

These simple yes/no questions are helpful, but that's not all CHOICE can do. For example, you can use the /C switch to specify the allowable keys in the prompt. Consider the following command:

```
CHOICE Red, Green, or Blue /C:RGB
```

This produces the following prompt:

```
Red, Green, or Blue [R,G,B]?
```

Pressing R, G, or B produces, in this case, an ERRORLEVEL code of 1, 2, or 3, respectively. There are endless uses for this, but one of the most obvious is a simple menu system:

```
@ECHO OFF
CLS
ECHO 1. WordPerfect
ECHO 2. Lotus 1-2-3
ECHO.
CHOICE Which program do you want to run /C:12
IF ERRORLEVEL 2 GOTO LOTUS
CD\WP51
WP
GOTO END
:LOTUS
CD\123
123
:END
```

When you run this batch file, you see the following:

```
1. WordPerfect
2. Lotus 1-2-3
Which program do you want to run [1,2]?
```

TIP: HIDING CHOICE CHOICES

Use the /N switch with the CHOICE command whenever you don't want the choices and question mark to appear at the end of the prompt. This is useful for prompts that are instructions instead of questions (for example, "Make your selection" or "Pick a number, any number").

Redirecting DOS

DOS is always directing things here and there. This generally falls into two categories:

- Directing data into its commands from a device called *standard input*
- Directing data out of its commands to a device called *standard output*

Standard input and standard output are normally handled by a device called CON (console), your keyboard and monitor. DOS assumes that all command input comes from the keyboard and that all command output (such as a DIR listing or a system message) goes to the screen. *Redirection* is just a way of specifying different input and output devices.

NOTE: HOW DOS HANDLES STANDARD INPUT AND OUTPUT

Standard input and standard output are actually mapped to files in DOS's internal file table. DOS assigns the first file handle in the table (handle 0) to standard input and the second handle (handle 1) to standard output. Redirection actually remaps these file handles so that the input or output goes elsewhere.

Redirecting Command Output

To send command output to somewhere other than the screen, you use the *output redirection operator* (>). One of the most common uses for output redirection is to capture the results of a command in a text file. For example, you might want to use the report produced by the MEM command as part of a word processing document. You could use the following command to first capture the report as the file MEM.TXT:

```
mem /c > mem.txt
```

When you run this command, don't be alarmed when the usual MEM data doesn't appear on-screen. Remember, it has been directed away from the screen and into the MEM.TXT file.

You can use this technique to capture DIR listings, CHKDSK reports, and more. One caveat: If the file you specify as the output destination already exists, DOS overwrites it without any warning. To be safe, you can use the double output redirection symbol (>>). This tells DOS to *append* the output to the file if it exists. For example, if you want to add the results of the CHKDSK command to MEM.TXT, use the following command:

```
chkdsk >> mem.txt
```

You can also redirect output to different devices. Table F.2 lists the various devices that Windows 95 installs each time you start your system.

Table F.2. Devices installed by Windows 95 when you start your system.

Device Name	Device
AUX	Auxiliary device (usually COM1)
CLOCK$	Real-time clock
COM*n*	Serial port (COM1, COM2, COM3, or COM4)
CON	Console (keyboard and screen)
LPT*n*	Parallel port (LPT1, LPT2, or LPT3)
NUL	NUL device (nothing)
PRN	Printer (usually LPT1)

F

A BATCH FILE
PRIMER

For example, you can send a DIR listing to the printer with the following command (of course, you need to be sure that your printer is on before doing this):

```
dir > prn
```

The *NUL device* usually throws people for a loop when they first see it. This device (affectionately known as the "bit bucket") is, literally, nothing. It's normally used in batch files to suppress the usual messages DOS displays when it completes a command. For example, DOS normally says 1 file(s) copied when you copy a file. However, the following command sends that message to NUL, so you wouldn't see it on-screen:

```
copy somefile.doc a:\ > nul
```

Redirecting Input

Getting input to a DOS command from somewhere other than the keyboard is handled by the *input redirection operator* (<). Input redirection is almost always used to send the contents of a text file to a DOS command. The most common example is the MORE command, which displays one screen of information at a time. If you have a large text file that scrolls off the screen when you use TYPE, the following command, which sends the contents of BIGFILE.TXT to the MORE command, solves the problem:

```
more < bigfile.txt
```

When you run this command, the first screenful of text appears, and the following line shows up at the bottom of the screen:

```
-- More --
```

Just press any key, and MORE displays the next screenful. (Whatever you do, don't mix up < and > when using MORE. The command more > bigfile.txt erases BIGFILE.TXT!) MORE is an example of a *filter* command. Filters process whatever text is sent through them. The other DOS filters are SORT and FIND, discussed in a moment.

Another handy use for input redirection is to send keystrokes to DOS commands. For example, create a text file called ENTER.TXT that consists of a single press of the Enter key, and then try this command:

```
date < enter.txt
```

DOS displays the current date, and instead of waiting for you to either type in a new date or press Enter, it just reads ENTER.TXT and uses its single carriage return as input. (For an even easier way to input the Enter key to a command, check out the next section.)

TIP: SENDING MULTIPLE KEYSTROKES

You can send keystrokes to any DOS command that waits for input. You can even send multiple keystrokes. For example, a typical FORMAT command has three prompts: one to insert a disk, one for the volume label, and one to format another disk. If your normal responses to these prompts are Enter, Enter, N, and Enter, include these in a text file called, say, INFORMAT.TXT, and run FORMAT with the following command:

```
format a: < informat.txt
```

One common recipient of redirected input is the SORT command. SORT, as you might guess from its name, sorts the data sent to it and displays the results on-screen. So, for example, here's how you would sort a file called JUMBLED.TXT:

```
sort < jumbled.txt
```

Instead of merely displaying the results of the sort on-screen, you can use > to redirect them to another file.

NOTE: SORT SWITCHES

SORT normally starts with the first column and works across. To start with any other column, use the /+n switch, where n is the number of the column you want to use. To sort a file in reverse order, use the /R switch.

Piping Commands

Piping is a technique that combines both input and output redirection. Using the *pipe operator* (¦), the output of one command is captured and sent as input to another command. For example, using MEM with the /C or /D switch usually results in more than a screenful of data. MEM has a /P switch to pause the output, but you can also pipe it to the MORE command:

```
mem /c ¦ more
```

The pipe operator captures the MEM output and sends it as input to MORE, which then displays everything one screen at a time.

NOTE: HOW PIPING WORKS

Piping works by first redirecting the output of a command to a temporary file. It then takes this temporary file and redirects it as input to the second command. A command such as MEM /C ¦ MORE is approximately equivalent to the following two commands:

```
MEM /C > tempfile
tempfile < MORE
```

I showed you in the preceding section how to use input redirection to send keystrokes to a DOS command. But if you have to send only a single key, piping offers a much nicer solution.

The secret is to use the ECHO command to echo the character you need and then pipe it to the DOS command.

For example, if you use the command DEL *.*, DOS always asks whether you're sure you want to delete all the files in the current directory. This is a sensible precaution, but you can override it if you do things this way:

```
echo y ¦ del *.*
```

Here, the y that would normally be echoed to the screen is sent to DEL instead, which interprets it as a response to its prompt. This is a handy technique in batch files in which you want to reduce or even eliminate user interaction.

TIP: PIPING THE ENTER KEY

You can even use this technique to send an Enter to a command. The command ECHO. (that's ECHO followed by a period) is equivalent to pressing Enter. So, for example, you could use the following command in a batch file to display the time without user input:

```
ECHO. ¦ TIME
```

A command that's commonly used in pipe operations is the FIND filter. FIND searches its input for a specified string and, if it finds a match, it displays the line that contains the string. For example, the last line of a DIR listing tells you the number of bytes free on the current drive. Rather than wade through the entire DIR output just to get this information, use this command instead:

```
dir ¦ find "free"
```

You'll see something like the following:

```
90333184 bytes free
```

FIND scours the DIR listing that was piped to it and looks for the word free. You can use this technique to display specific lines from a MEM report (for example, you could search for the word largest to display the largest executable program size) or CHKDSK (searching for user finds the number of bytes used on the disk).

CAUTION: DON'T REDIRECT IN REM STATEMENTS

Don't use any of the redirection operators (<, >, and ¦) on a REM line in a batch file. Bizarrely, DOS attempts the redirection *before* it realizes that the line is a REM and should be ignored. If you want to comment out a bunch of lines that use these symbols, use GOTO to leap over them (as explained earlier).

Known Dirty and Deadly TSRs and Device Drivers

As explained in Chapter 1, "Understanding the Windows 95 Installation," some terminate-and-stay-resident (TSR) programs and device drivers can cause problems with Windows 95 Setup. So-called *dirty* TSRs are programs and drivers that can give Setup indigestion but that don't necessarily cause it to hang. You can usually get through Setup without disabling these TSRs, but they should be your first suspects if something goes wrong. *Deadly* TSRs and device drivers are known to cause Setup to hang. You should definitely unload these before installing Windows 95. (In fact, if Setup detects one of these TSRs, it will halt the installation.)

Tables G.1 and G.2 list the known dirty and deadly TSRs and device drivers that the Setup program detects.

Table G.1. Dirty TSRs and device drivers.

Filename	*Description*
Allemm4.sys	All Charge 386
Anarkey.com	Anarkey
Append.com	MS-DOS APPEND utility
Asplogin.exe	ASP Integrity Toolkit
Assign.com	MS-DOS ASSIGN utility
Cache.exe	Disk cache utility
Ced.com	CED command-line editor
Ced.exe	PCED command-line editor
Cmdedit.com	Command-line editor
Cubitr.exe	Cubit
Datamon.exe	PC Tools Datamon
Desktop.exe	PC Tools Desktop TSR
Diskmon.exe	Norton disk monitoring TSR
Doscue.com	DOSCUE command-line editor
Dubldisk.sys	Double Disk data compression utility
Ecyddx.sys	IBM PC support
Eimpcs.sys	IBM PC support
Ems386.sys	Memory Manager
Ep.exe	Norton Desktop/Windows Erase Protect TSR
Flash.exe	Flash disk cache utility
Graphics.com	MS-DOS GRAPHICS utility
Hpemm386.sys	HP Expanded Memory Manager
Hpemm486.sys	HP Expanded Memory Manager

Filename	Description
Hpmm.sys	HP Memory Manager
Hyper286.exe	Hyper disk cache utility
Hyper386.exe	Hyper disk cache utility
Hyperdkc.exe	Hyper disk cache utility
Hyperdke.exe	Hyper disk cache utility
Hyperdkx.exe	Hyper disk cache utility
Iemm.sys	Memory Manager
Ilim386.sys	Intel Expanded Memory Emulator
Join.exe	MS-DOS JOIN utility
Kbflow.exe	Artisoft KBFlow TSR
Lansel.exe	Lansight network utilities TSR
Le.com	Le Menu menuing package
Lsallow.exe	Lansight network utilities TSR
Melemm.386	Memory Manager
Ncache.exe	Norton disk cache utility
Ncache2.exe	Norton Utilities NCache
Ndosedit.com	Command-line editor
Newres.exe	Newspace disk compression utility
Newspace.exe	Newspace disk compression utility
Pa.exe	Printer Assist
Pc-cache.com	PC Tools disk cache utility
Pc-kwik.exe	PC-Kwik disk cache utility
Pcpanel.exe	LaserTools Printer Control Panel
Pcsxmaem.sys	PCSXMAEM utility
Print.exe	MS-DOS PRINT utility
Pyro.exe	Pyro! screen saver
Qcache.exe	386 Max disk cache utility
Qmaps.sys	QMAPS memory manager
Ramtype.sys	RamType utility
Rm386.sys	NetRoom memory manager
S-ice.exe	SoftIce
Sk.com	Sidekick version 1.0

G

TSRs AND DEVICE DRIVERS

continues

Table G.1. continued

Filename	Description
Sk2.exe	Sidekick version 2.0
Skplus.exe	Sidekick Plus
Smartcan.exe	Norton Utilities SmartCan
Speedrv.exe	Norton Speed Drive
Speeddrv.exe	Norton Speed Drive
Speedfxr.com	SpeedFXR
Subst.exe	MS-DOS SUBST utility
Tscsi.sys	Trantor T100 SCSI driver
Umbpro.sys	UMB Pro memory manager
Undelete.exe	MS-DOS UNDELETE Utility
Vaccine.exe	Vaccine anti-virus program
Vdefend.com	PC Tools VDefend
Vdefend.sys	PC Tools VDefend
Vdisk.sys	IBM RAM disk utility
Vems.drv	Memory manager
Viralert.sys	Data Physician Plus TSR
Vmm386.exe	Memory Manager
Vmm386.sys	Memory Manager
Xgaaidos.sys	8514 emulation driver
Xtradrv.sys	IIT XtraDrive software
Xmaem.sys	XMAEM utility

Table G.2. Deadly TSRs and device drivers.

Filename	Description
Cdremap.exe	CD-ROM drive remapper utility
Ic.sys	Ironclad Software
Iddrv.sys	INFINITE disk software
Idres.exe	INFINITE disk software
Nav.drv	Norton anti-virus software
Nav.sys	Norton anti-virus software
Navtsr.exe	Norton anti-virus software

Filename	Description
Pc-cache.com	PC Tools disk cache utility
Super.exe	PC-Kwik disk cache utility
Superpck.exe	Super PC-Kwik disk cache utility
Tspdrv.sys	Symantec Disklock utility
Virstop.exe	F-Prot anti-virus
Vsafe.com	Central Point anti-virus TSR
Vsafe.sys	Central Point anti-virus
Vwatch.exe	C-Tools anti-virus software

What's on the CD-ROM

IN THIS APPENDIX

- About Shareware *1488*

The CD-ROM contains nearly 100 32-bit Windows 95 utilities, including fully functional evaluation software from InstallShield Corporation, Imagination Software, Seagate Software, and Frontier Technologies Corporation.

Product Name:	InstallShield Express 2
Company Name:	InstallShield Corporation
Location on the CD-ROM:	`\instlers\inshield`

With the full evaluation version of InstallShield Express 2, you can create professional software setups for use in Windows 95 or Windows NT without having to write a single line of code. All you do is point and click!

Product Name:	IMAGinE Viewer
Company Name:	Imagination Software
Location on the CD-ROM:	`\imagview`

The full commercial version of IMAGinE Viewer is the first commercial imaging viewer that is built on top of a custom control. It supports view, print, scan (TWAIN), and annotations. IMAGinE Viewer can be upgraded to support board-level scanning and printing, image cleanup, barcode recognition, OCR, ICR (handwriting recognition), mark sense, forms processing, forms overlay, zone definition, and workflow batch processing.

Product Name:	Crystal Reports
Company Name:	Seagate Software
Location on the CD-ROM:	`\crystal`

The full 60-day evaluation version of Crystal Reports combines the ease-of-use of a leading Windows-based application with report design and data analysis features that make reporting tasks highly efficient. You can sort and subtotal in just one step, sort on groups, export reports to many file formats, distribute reports via integrated e-mail, and much more!

Product Name:	SuperTCP Suite
Company Name:	Frontier Technologies Corporation
Location on the CD-ROM:	`\com\frontier`

SuperTCP Suite is an integrated solution that turns PCs into full members of the corporate network, utilizing the TCP/IP multiplatform communications protocol. Users can access and share information anywhere on their internal network and the Internet using the products for dozens of applications that support intranetwork and internetwork communications, Internet information management, mainframe and minicomputer host access, and network administration.

Table H.1 lists all the products on this CD-ROM. You'll see the product name, the company or author, and the directory location on the CD-ROM. Most of the companies have provided readme files that include information on licensing, ordering, and installation, troubleshooting questions and answers, and URLs for downloading the latest version of the demo or evaluation software.

Table H.1. The products included on the CD-ROM.

Product Name	Company/Author	Location on the CD
ACDSee	ACD Systems Ltd.	\graphics\acdsee
Adobe Acrobat Viewer	Adobe Systems, Inc.	\misc\acrobat
Alarm	Jeff Parker	\schedule\alarm32
Analyst/Probe	Network Instruments, LLC	\netutils\an_probe
Atismail for Windows	A.T.I.S.	\com\atismail
Barry Press Utilities	Barry Press	\sysutils\bputil
Bog 2	Personal MicroCosms	\games\bog2
CaLANdar and Web Scheduler	Microsystems Software, Inc.	\schedule\calandar
Casino Verite Blackjack	QFIT	\games\casino
CDQuick	Circuit Systems	\misc\cdquick
CGI Perform	Real Time Internet Services	\webutils\realtime
CleanSweep	Quarterdeck Systems	\sysutils\csweep
ClockMan95	Graphical Dynamics, Inc.	\schedule\clockman
CommNet for Windows	Radient Software	\com\commnet
Complete Program Deleter	Leithauser Research	\sysutils\comdel
DemoShield	DemoShield Corporation	\instlers\demo
DumpReg	SomarSoft	\sysutils\somrsoft\dumpreg
e-Mail Notify	Ludovic Dubost	\netutils\email95
Emergency Recovery System	Theodore Fattaleh	\sysutils\ers32
EMWAC Freeware HTTP Server	Edinburgh University Computing Service	\netutils\emwac
Eudora Lite	Qualcomm	\com\eudora lite
EZ-Install	The Software Factory, Inc.	\instlers\ezinstal
Finger32	Laurence G. Kahn	\com\finger32
FixIt	Quarterdeck Systems	\sysutils\fixit
Forehelp	Forefront, Inc.	\misc\forehelp
Galt Utilities	Galt Technologies	\misc\galt

continues

H

Table H.1. continued

Product Name	Company/Author	Location on the CD
Goldwave	Chris Craig	\misc\goldwave
Hangman 2	Personal MicroCosms	\games\hang2
Hedit32	Yuri Software	\editors\he32
HelpBreeze	SolutionSoft	\misc\helpbrz
HelpTrac	Monarch Bay Software,Inc.	\netutils\helptrac
HotMetal Pro	SoftQuad, Inc.	\webutils\hotmetal
HTML Handler	JonCo Software	\webutils\handler
HTMLnote	Cranial Software	\webutils\htmlnote
HyperSnap	Hyperionics	\graphics\hypersnap
ImgLib	SimSoft	\controls\imglib
Internet Control Center	UsefulWare, Inc.	\netutils\internet control
Internet Utilities 97	Starfish Software	\netutils\inet
LifeSaver	JB Systems	\sysutils\lifesaver
Live Markup	MediaTech, Inc.	\webutils\lvmarkup
Mapedit	Thomas Boutell	\netutils\mapedit
MapThis	Todd C. Wilson	\webutils\mapthis
Milestones, Etc. Trial Version	KIDASA Software, Inc.	\schedule\milesetc
More Properties	Imaginary Software	\sysutils\more
Observer	Network Instruments, LLC	\netutils\observr
Paintshop Pro	JASC, Inc.	\graphics\psp
Post.Office	Software.com, Inc.	\webutils\post.ofc
PowerTCP Demo Toolkit	Dart Communications	\com\dart
PowerTools	Opposite	\webutils\powertools
PowWow for Windows	Tribal Voice	\com\powwow
Pping	Intellisoft, Inc.	\com\pping
Pronto/IP	CommTouch Software, Inc.	\com\prontoip
Puzzle-8 2	Personal MicroCosms	\games\pz18
QuickColor	EnTech	\graphics\qcolor
QWS3270	Jolly Giant Software, Inc.	\com\qws3270

Product Name	Company/Author	Location on the CD
R&R Report Writer	Concentric Data Systems, Inc.	`\misc\rrwriter`
RegFind	Intellisoft, Inc.	`\sysutils\regfind`
Registry Search & Replace	Steven J. Hoek	`\sysutils\regsrch`
RemoveIt	Quarterdeck Systems	`\sysutils\removeit`
RipSpace	Jonathan Carroll	`\sysutils\ripspace`
RocketShop GIFs	RocketShop	`\graphics\rocket`
Sax Setup Wizard	Sax Software	`\instlers\saxdemo`
SlipKnot	MicroMind, Inc.	`\com\slipknot`
SnagIt/32	Techsmith Corporation	`\graphics\snagit`
SomarSoft ACTS	SomarSoft	`\sysutils\somrsoft\acts`
SpartaCom Asynchronous Port Shaking	TSP Companies	`\misc\tsp\`
Stereograms 2	Personal MicroCosms	`\games\st_grams`
Sticktest	Brian Feldman	`\misc\stiktest`
Tapedisk	Tapedisk Corporation	`\misc\tapedisk`
Teach Yourself Office 97 in 24 Hours	Sams Publishing	`\ebooks\tyoffice97`
Teach Yourself Outlook 97 in 24 Hours	Sams Publishing	`\ebooks\tyoutlook97`
TechFacts95	Dean Software Design	`\sysutils\techfact`
TextPad	Helios Software Solutions	`\editors\tpad32`
Thumbs Plus	Cerious Software	`\graphics\thmpls`
Time & Chaos Professional	Isbister International, Inc.	`\schedule\timchaos`
Toggle Mouse	Toggle Software	`\misc\togglem`
TRACK for Windows	Soffront Software, Inc.	`\sysutils\track`
TrackIt	Dietmar Bos	`\sysutils\trackit`
Tropic TCP/IP	Tropic Software	`\com\tropic`
UltraEdit	Ian D. Mead	`\editors\uedit32`
UpTime	Creative Element	`\netutils\uptime30`

continues

Table H.1. continued

Product Name	Company/Author	Location on the CD
VidCall	MRA Associates, Inc.	\com\vidcall
Visual Basic Runtime	Microsoft	\misc\vbrun
Visual Speller	Visual Components	\controls\vspell
Visual Voice	Stylus Innovation, Inc.	\misc\visvoice
WebEdit Pro	Nesbitt Software	\webutils\weditpro
WinBatch 96	Wilson WindowWare, Inc.	\sysutils\wbatch32
Windows Enforcer	Posum Software	\sysutils\wenforce
WinEdit 96	Wilson WindowWare, Inc.	\editors\winedit
WinQVT/NET	QPC Software	\com\qvtnet
WinTalk	ELF Communications	\com\wintalk
WinWhois	Laurence G. Kahn	\com\whois32
Winzip	Nico Mak Computing, Inc.	\compress\winzip95
Winzip Self-Extractor	Nico Mak Computing, Inc.	\compress\winzipse
WSIRC	Caesar M. Samsi	\com\wsirc20
Zetafax	TSP Companies	\misc\tsp

About Shareware

We'd like to take a moment to tell you how software worth hundreds of dollars can be included with a book costing $59.99. This wouldn't be possible if it weren't for the wonderful concept of shareware.

Anyone who has ever tried to write a computer program knows it's a complex undertaking. This is especially true when you consider all the features that modern software must have before many users will even consider trying it. And as if the development process isn't tough enough, packaging, marketing, and distributing the program becomes another roadblock to the success of the software venture.

When you stop and think about it, it's pretty amazing that the shareware concept solves all these problems. Shareware is a win-win deal for both the developer and the user. Developers can concentrate on writing new code (which is what they usually do best) without having to worry about software packaging and distribution issues, and users can try the software for free before they decide if it fits their needs. That's not something you can easily do with shrink-wrap software.

But don't be fooled. Shareware isn't free! First of all, if a package is free, it's clearly labeled as *freeware,* not shareware. Second, if the shareware author has taken the time to develop a program, with the hope that others will find it useful, he will have no incentive to enhance the program if nobody agrees to pay the registration fee. In other words, the user will lose a lot more than a few dollars, because the program will age and cease to be compatible with other new technologies that will inevitably come along.

Shareware registration fees are trivial—frequently between $10 and $60 (much less than commercial software, and often of equal or greater quality). If you decide that a shareware program is convenient, you're expected to follow the registration instructions that come with the package. You will get several benefits in return, depending on what the author states in the license.txt file. It usually includes a printed copy of the user's guide and a new version of the program that doesn't constantly prompt you with a reminder to register.

Unlike many software developers, shareware authors like to hear from their customers directly. You can usually reach them by e-mail, on the Web, or on a relevant listserver or newsgroup. Keep in mind, however, that they like to hear from paying customers the most.

I

INDEX

X-Z

MACMILLAN COMPUTER PUBLISHING USA

A VIACOM COMPANY

Technical ---- Support:

If you need assistance with the information in this book or with a CD/Disk accompanying the book, please access the Knowledge Base on our Web site at **http://www.superlibrary.com/general/support**. Our most Frequently Asked Questions are answered there. If you do not find the answer to your questions on our Web site, you may contact Macmillan Technical Support **(317) 581-3833** or e-mail us at **support@mcp.com**.

Troubleshooting and Configuring the Windows NT/95 Registry

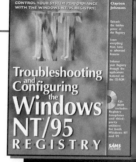

Clayton Johnson

Written for systems administrators who run networks with Windows NT Server, NT Workstation, and Windows 95, this book is a complete reference. It includes detailed coverage of Registry entries for both systems, noting instances where the entries differ. It also offers complete troubleshooting sections that outline known problems and detail their solutions. The CD-ROM contains Registry entries and third-party utilities relating to the Registry for both Windows 95 and NT.

$49.99 USA/$70.95 CAN　　*0-672-31066-X*　　　　　　*648 pages*
Operating Systems　　　　　　*Intermediate - Expert*　　*Sams*

Peter Norton's Complete Guide to Windows 95, Second Edition

Peter Norton and John Mueller

This complete reference gives readers in-depth, detailed insights into Windows 95. You will master all the tricks of the trade, as well as learn how to create a Web page. This book covers the new Internet Explorer interface, DSD, OEM Service Pack 2.1 enhancements, and more. It provides advanced tips, optimization techniques, and detailed architectural information. In addition, this book has extensive coverage of the Microsoft Plus! Pack, and it features a tear-our survival guide.

$35.00 USA/$49.95 CDN　　*0-672-31040-6*　　　　　*1,224 pages*
Operating Systems　　　　　　*Accomplished - Expert*　　*Sams*

Teach Yourself Windows CE in 24 Hours

David Hayden

Analysts predict that 250,000 Windows CE handheld PCs will be sold in 1997, with sales growing exponentially in the future. *Teach Yourself Windows CE in 24 Hours* focuses on using Windows CE with Windows 95 or NT and how to share information among the operating systems. It covers the CE environment and how to use it for scheduling, tasks, and other time-management applications. You'll see how to use Windows CE as a remote computer, including faxing, Web surfing, sending and receiving e-mail, and synchronizing with the desktop computer.

$19.99 USA/$28.95 CAN　　*0-672-31065-1*　　　　　*256 pages*
Operating Systems　　　　　　*New - Casual - Accomplished*　　*Sams*

Teach Yourself Microsoft Office 97 in 24 Hours

Greg Perry

An estimated 22 million people use Microsoft Office, and with the new features of Office 97, much of that market will want the upgrade. To address this market, Sams has published a mass-market version of its best-selling *Teach Yourself* series. This book shows you how to use the most widely requested Office features. It includes many illustrations, screen shots, and a step-by-step plan for learning Office 97. You'll see how to use each Office application, as well as how to use them together. You'll also create documents in Word that include hypertext links to files created with one of the other Office applications.

$19.99 USA/$28.95 CDN　　*0-672-31009-0*　　　　　*450 pages*
Integrated Software/Suites　　*New - Casual - Accomplished*　　*Sams*

Microsoft Office 97 Unleashed, Second Edition

Paul McFedries

Microsoft has brought the Web to its Office suite of products. Hyperlinking, Office Assistants, and Active Document Support let you publish documents to the Web or an intranet site. They also completely integrate with Microsoft FrontPage, making it possible to point-and-click a Web page into existence. This book details each of the Office applications—Excel, Access, PowerPoint, Word, and Outlook—and shows you how to create presentations and Web documents. You'll see how to extend Office to work on a network, and you'll learn about the various Office Solution Kits and how to use them.

$39.99 USA/$56.95 CDN *0-672-31010-4* *1,316 pages*
Integrated Software/Suites *Accomplished - Expert* *Sams*

Windows NT 4 and Web Site Resource Library

Sams Development Group

This comprehensive library is the most complete reference available for Windows NT and Web administrators and developers. The six volumes and more than 3,500 pages offer key information about the Windows NT Registry, Web site administration and development, networking, BackOffice integration, and much more. The three CD-ROMs include networking utilities, third-party tools, support utilities, Web site development tools, HTML templates, CGI scripts, and more.

$149.99 USA/$209.95 CDN *0-672-30995-5* *3,500 pages*
Internet/WWW Applications *Accomplished - Expert* *Sams*

Robert Cowart's Windows NT 4 Unleashed, Professional Reference Edition

Robert Cowart

This is the only book Windows NT administrators need in order to learn how to configure their NT systems for maximum performance, security, and reliability. This comprehensive reference explains how to install, maintain, and configure an individual workstation, as well as how to connect computers to peer-to-peer networking. It includes comprehensive advice for setting up and administering an NT server network, and it focuses on the new and improved administration and connectivity features of version 4.0.

$59.99 USA/$84.95 CDN *0-672-31001-5* *1,400 pages*
Operating Systems *Intermediate - Expert* *Sams*

Developing Personal Oracle7 for Windows 95 Applications, Second Edition

David Lockman

An update to the successful first edition, this comprehensive reference takes you through the process of developing powerful applications while teaching you how to effectively use Personal Oracle7. The CD-ROM includes current versions of Personal Oracle7 for Windows 3.1 and Windows 95.

$49.99 USA/$70.95 CDN *0-672-31025-2* *800 pages*
Databases *New - Casual* *Sams*

Add to Your Sams Library Today with the Best Books for Programming, Operating Systems, and New Technologies

The easiest way to order is to pick up the phone and call

1-800-428-5331

between 9:00 a.m. and 5:00 p.m. EST.
For faster service please have your credit card available.

ISBN	Quantity	Description of Item	Unit Cost	Total Cost
0-672-31066-X		Troubleshooting and Configuring the Windows NT/95 Registry (book/CD-ROM)	$49.99	
0-672-31040-6		Peter Norton's Complete Guide to Windows 95, Second Edition	$35.00	
0-672-31065-1		Teach Yourself Windows CE in 24 Hours	$19.99	
0-672-31009-0		Teach Yourself Microsoft Office 97 in 24 Hours	$19.99	
0-672-31010-4		Microsoft Office 97 Unleashed, Second Edition (book/CD-ROM)	$39.99	
0-672-30995-5		Windows NT 4 and Web Site Resource Library (6 books/3 CD-ROMs)	$149.99	
0-672-31001-5		Robert Cowart's Windows NT 4 Unleashed, Professional Reference Edition (book/CD-ROM)	$59.99	
0-672-31025-2		Developing Personal Oracle7 for Windows 95 Applications, Second Edition (book/CD-ROM)	$49.99	
❏ 3 ½" Disk		Shipping and Handling: See information below.		
❏ 5 ¼" Disk		TOTAL		

Shipping and Handling: $4.00 for the first book, and $1.75 for each additional book. Floppy disk: add $1.75 for shipping and handling. If you need to have it now, we can ship product to you in 24 hours for an additional charge of approximately $18.00, and you will receive your item overnight or in two days. Overseas shipping and handling adds $2.00 per book and $8.00 for up to three disks. Prices subject to change. Call for availability and pricing information on latest editions.

201 W. 103rd Street, Indianapolis, Indiana 46290

1-800-428-5331 — Orders   1-800-835-3202 — Fax   1-800-858-7674 — Customer Service

Book ISBN 0-672-31039-2

What's on the CD-ROM

The companion CD-ROM contains an assortment of third-party tools and product demos. The disc creates a new program group for this book and utilizes the Windows 95 Explorer. Using the icons in the program group and Windows Explorer, you can view information concerning products and companies and install programs with just a few clicks of the mouse.

To create the program group for this book, follow these steps:

Windows 95 Installation Instructions

1. Insert the disc into your CD-ROM drive.
2. If Windows 95 is installed on your computer and the AutoPlay feature is enabled, a Program Group for this book is automatically created whenever you insert the disc into your CD-ROM drive. Follow the directions provided in the installation program.

   If AutoPlay is not enabled, using Windows Explorer, choose Setup.exe from the root level of the CD-ROM to create the Program Group for this book.
3. Double-click the Browse the CD-ROM icon in the newly created Program Group to access the installation programs of the software or reference material included on this CD-ROM.
4. To review the latest information about this CD-ROM, double-click the About this CD-ROM icon.

NOTE

For best results, set your monitor to display between 256 and 64,000 colors. A screen resolution of 640×480 pixels is also recommended. If necessary, adjust your monitor settings before using the CD-ROM.

Technical Support

If you need assistance with the information in this book or with the CD-ROM that accompanies this book, please access the Knowledge Base on our Web site at

http://www.superlibrary.com/general/support

Our most Frequently Asked Questions are answered there. If you do not find the answer to your questions on our Web site, you may contact Macmillan Technical Support at (317) 581-3833 or e-mail us at support@mcp.com.